# Current Law

## Case Citator

2014

# Current Law

## Case Citator

2014

*SWEET & MAXWELL*



SWEET & MAXWELL

THOMSON REUTERS

Published in 2015 by Thomson Reuters (Professional) UK Limited, trading as Sweet & Maxwell, Friars House, 160 Blackfriars Road, London, SE1 8EZ (Registered in England & Wales, Company No.1679046. Registered Office and address for service: 2nd floor, 1 Mark Square, Leonard Street, London, EC2A 4EG).

For further information on our products and services, visit
*http://www.sweetandmaxwell.co.uk.*

Computerset by Sweet & Maxwell
Printed and bound by CPI Group (UK) Ltd, Croydon, CR0 4YY.

A CIP catalogue record for this book is available from the British Library.

Orders to: Sweet & Maxwell, PO Box 1000, Andover, SP10 9AF. Tel: 0845 600 9355. Email: TRLUKI.orders@thomsonreuters.com.

No natural forests were destroyed to make this product: only farmed timber was used and replanted.



ISBN: 978-0-414-03602-4

# CONTENTS

# PREFACE

## The Sweet & Maxwell Current Law Service

The Current Law Service began in 1947 and provides a comprehensive guide to developments in case law, primary legislation and secondary legislation in the United Kingdom and mainland Europe. The Current Law Service presently consists of the Monthly Digests, the Year Book, Current Law Statutes Annotated, the Legislation Citator, the Case Citator, Current Law Weekly and European Current Law.

## The Case Citators

The Current Law Case Citators comprise four cumulative volumes covering the years 1947-1976, 1977-1997, 1998-2001, and 2002-2004. Single volumes have been produced since 2005. Together they provide a comprehensive reference guide to case law after 1946.

### *How to use the Citators*

When searching for a case, users should consult the most recent citator volume first, since it provides the most comprehensive and authoritative information. The current volume contains a guide to the complete history of cases digested or judicially considered in 2014. For earlier case law not considered since 2014, users should consult previous citator volumes.

The material in this volume is arranged in alphabetical order in three sections:

*English Citator*
*Scottish Citator*
*Ships' Names Index*

The details in each entry can be used on a number of different levels, including identifying law report series in which a full report of a case can be found, the judicial history of a case and the location of an abstract of a case within a Current Law Yearbook. The following information is provided:

*(a) The full name of any case reported between 1947 and 2014*
Cases are listed alphabetically by the first party's name, giving the most recent Current Law Year Book paragraph reference to the appropriate digest. Most references have a year before the paragraph number, e.g. 14/**239** alludes to the 2014 Year Book, paragraph 239. If no year is given, the case is contained in the Current Law Consolidation 1947-1951. (For Scotland see the Scottish Year Books 1948-1951.)

*(b) An extensive list of references to the law reports and journals reporting each case*
Each entry gives details about one case, beginning with the case name and any joined cases or other names by which the case might be known, followed by the reports in descending order of authority and the court in which the case was heard. Where cases go on to an appellate court, the entry states whether the higher court affirmed or reversed the decision of the lower court.

*(c) The judicial history of a case*
If a case has been applied, considered, approved, distinguished, overruled, etc., since it was decided, Current Law Year Book references to digests of cases in which the judicial consideration took place are provided. These references are in normal type while the paragraph number of the actual digest of each case is given in bold.

*(d) Details of Scottish cases*
Part II of the Citator contains details of cases decided or judicially considered in the Scottish Courts. References to English cases judicially considered in Scotland are also included in this part, so subscribers wishing to follow the full history of an English case should consult both parts of the Citator. Scottish cases published in English Law Reports are included in both the Scottish and English sections.

*(e) Ships' Names Index*
This is an alphabetical listing of all ships' names and their law report citations to assist where only the ship's name is known by the user. The official party names for these cases will be located in the main body of the Citator.

Whilst every effort has been made to ensure that details of cases in this citator are correct, there may be occasions when a citation is wrong. The editor would be grateful for notification of any errors to enable them to be rectified on the database from which this volume was derived.

*Case Citator Editor*
*Sweet & Maxwell*
*The Hatchery*
*Hall Bank Lane*
*Mytholmroyd, Hebden Bridge*
*West Yorkshire*
*HX7 5HQ*

# TABLE OF ABBREVIATIONS

## Court Abbreviations

AAT = Administrative Appeals Tribunal (Australia)
AD = Anotato Dikastirio (Cyprus)
Afr Comm HPR = African Commission on Human and Peoples Rights
AG = Amtsgericht (Germany)
AGO = Advocate Generals Opinion
AIT = Asylum and Immigration Tribunal
APDPK = Arkhe Prostasias Dedomenon Prosopikou Kharaktera (Greece)
App (B) = Cour d'Appel (Belgium)
App (I) = Corte di Appello (Italy)
App Person = Trade Marks Registry (Appointed Person)
Ar Pag = Areios Pagos (Greece)
ArbG = Arbeitsgericht (Germany)
ARRS = Afdeling Rechtspraak van de Raad van State (NL)
As Huk Mah = Asliye Hukuk Mahkemesi (Turkey)
As Tic Mah = Asliye Ticaret Mahkemesi (Turkey)
AT = Augstakas Tiesas (Latvia)
ATMC = Administrative Trade Mark Committee (Greece)
Aud = Audiencia Provincial (Spain)
BAG = Bundesarbeitsgericht (Germany)
Bar Standards Bd = Bar Standards Board Review Panel
Bd of Trade = Board of Trade
BezG = Bezirksgericht (Switzerland)
BFH = Bundesfinanzhof (Germany)
BG = Bundesgericht (Switzerland)
BGH = Bundesgerichtshof (Germany)
BKA = Bundeskartellamt (Germany)
BOIP = Benelux Office for Intellectual Property
BPG = Bundespatentgericht (Germany)
BRB = Burgerlijke Rechtbank (Belgium)
BsozG = Bundessozialgericht (Germany)
BverfG = Bundesverfassungsgericht (Germany)
BverwG = Bundesverwaltungsgericht (Germany)
C Adm A = Cour Administrative d'Appel (Belgium/France)
C Concurrence = Conseil de la Concurrence (Belgium/France)
C Cost = Corte Costituzionale (Italy)
C d'A = Cour d'Appel (France/Luxembourg)
CA = Court of Appeal
CA (Civ Div) = Court of Appeal (Civil Division)
CA (Crim Div) = Court of Appeal (Criminal Division)
CAC = Central Arbitration Committee
CAEW = Central Authority for England and Wales
Care Standards Tr = Care Standards Tribunal
Cass = Cour de Cassation (Belgium/France/Luxembourg)
CAT = Competition Appeal Tribunal
CC = County Court
CCA = Court of Criminal Appeal
CCAT = Competition Commission Appeal Tribunal
CCP = Court of Common Pleas
CE = Conseil d'Etat (Belgium/France)
CEC = Commission of the European Communities
Cent Crim Ct = Central Criminal Court (Ireland)
Central Crim Ct = Central Criminal Court
CFA (HK) = Court of Final Appeal (Hong Kong)
CFI = Court of First Instance
CFI (HK) = Court of First Instance of the High Court (Hong Kong Special Administrative Region)
CFI (Phl) = Court of First Instance (Philippines)
Charity Comm = Charity Commissioners
Ch D = Chancery Division
Ch D (Bankruptcy Ct) = Chancery Division (Bankruptcy Court)
Ch D (Companies Ct) = Chancery Division (Companies Court)
Ch D (Irl) = Chancery Division (Ireland)
Ch D (NI) = Chancery Division (Northern Ireland)
Ch D (Patents Ct) = Chancery Division (Patents Court)
Ch D (RPC) = Chancery Division (Restrictive Practices Court)
CICA = Criminal Injuries Compensation Authority
CICAP = Criminal Injuries Compensation Appeals Panel
CICB = Criminal Injuries Compensation Board
Circ Ct = Circuit Court (Ireland)
Civil Ct = Civil Court (M)
CJ = Court of Justice
CJ (Gen Div) (Ont) = Ontario Court of Justice (General Division)
CMAC = Courts Martial Appeal Court
CollvB = College van Beroep voor het Bedrijfsleven (NL)
Comm Cartels = Commission des Cartels (Switzerland)
Comm Conc = Commission de la Concurrence (France)
Comm Ministers = Committee of Ministers
Commr Pat = Commissioner of Patents (Australia)
Comm Sec Cons (F) = Commission de la Securite des Consommateurs
Comm Tributaria PG = Commissione Tributaria di Primo Grado (Italy)
Comm Tributaria SG = Commissione Tributaria di Secondo Grado (Italy)
Comp Auth = Competition Authority (Ireland)
Company Names Tr = Company Names Tribunal
Cons Const = Conseil Constitutionnel (France)
Cons Ct = Consistory Court
Cons Stato = Consiglio di Stato (Italy)
Const Ct = Constitutional Court
Cour d'Arb = Cour d'Arbitrage (Belgium)
Cour Const = Cour Constitutionnelle (Belgium)
CP = Court of Protection
CPD = Common Pleas Division
CRC = Commission Federale de Recours en Matiere de Contributions (Switzerland)
Crim CA = Criminal Court of Appeal (Ireland)
CRvB = Centrale Raad van Beroep (Netherlands)
CS = Court of Session
CSJ = Cour Superieure de Justice (Luxembourg)
CST = Civil Service Tribunal
Ct Sup = Corte Suprema de Justicia (Argentina)
DC = Divisional Court
DR = District Registry
EAT = Employment Appeal Tribunal
EC Council = European Council
Eccl Ct = Court of Ecclesiastical Causes Reserved
ECHR = European Court of Human Rights
ECHR (Grand Chamber) = European Court of Human Rights (Grand Chamber)
ECJ = European Court of Justice
ECSR = European Committee of Social Rights

# TABLE OF ABBREVIATIONS

ED = Eparhiako Dikastrio (Cyprus)
EFTA = EFTA Court of Justice
Epit Antag = Epitropi Antagonismou (Greece)
EPO = European Patent Office
ERGI (Swi) = Eidgenossische Rekurskommission fur Geistiges Eigentum (Switzerland)
ES = Eidgenossisches Steuerrekurskommission (Switzerland)
ET = Employment Tribunal
Eur Comm HR = European Commission on Human Rights
Ex Chamber = Court of Exchequer Chamber
Ex Ct = Court of Exchequer
Ex Div = Extra Division
Fam Ct = Family Court
Fam Div = Family Division
FAS Mosk Okr (RF) = Federalnyi Arbitrazhnyi Sud Moskovskogo Okruga (Russian Federation)
Fed CA = Federal Court of Appeal
Fed Ct = Federal Court
Fed HC = Federal High Court
FG = Finanzgericht (Germany)
FET= Fair Employment Tribunal (Northern Ireland)
FSMT = Financial Services & Markets Tribunal
FTT = First-Tier Tribunal
GC = General Court
GC = Giudice Conciliatore (Italy)
HC = High Court
HCJ = High Court of Justiciary
HD = Hogsta Domstolen (Finland/Sweden)
HerrR = Herredsrett (Norway)
HFD = Hogsta forvaltningsdomstolen (Finland)
HL = House of Lords
HO = Hovioikeus/Hovratt (Finland)
Hof = Gerechtshof (Netherlands)
HR (DK) = Hojesteret (Denmark)
HR (N) = Hoyesterett (Norway)
HR (NL) = Hoge Raad (NL)
HR (Swe) = Hovratt (Sweden)
HR Ch = Human Rights Chamber for Bosnia and Herzegovina
HvB = Hof van Beroep (Belgium)
HvC = Hof van Cassatie (Belgium)
IA Comm HR = Inter American Commission on Human Rights
IACHR = Inter American Court of Human Rights
IAT = Immigration Appeal Tribunal
ICC = International Chamber of Commerce, Arbitration Tribunal
ICJ = International Court of Justice
ICTA Tr = Tribunal constituted under the Income and Corporation Taxes Act 1988 s.706
IH = Inner House
IH = Court of Session (Inner House)
IH (1 Div) = Court of Session (Inner House, First Division)
IH (2 Div) = Court of Session (Inner House, Second Division)
IH (Ex Div) = Court of Session (Inner House, Extra Division)
IPEC = Intellectual Property Enterprise Court
IPT = Investigatory Powers Tribunal
IT = Industrial Tribunal
ITAT (Ind) = Income Tax Appellate Tribunal (India)
It Cass = Corte di Cassazione (Italy)
J de Paix = Justices de la Paix (Luxembourg)
JP = Juge de Paix (Belgium)
JPI = Juzgado de Primera Instancia (Spain)
KBD = King's Bench Division
KBD (Comm) = King's Bench Division (Commercial Court)
KBD (Irl) = King's Bench Division (Ireland)
KBD (NI) = King's Bench Division (Northern Ireland)
KG (Ger) = Kammergericht (Germany)
KG (Swi) = Kassationsgericht (Switzerland)
KHO = Korkein Hallinto-Oikeus (Finland)
KKO = Korkein Oikeus (Finland)
KO = Kihlakunnanoikeus/Haradsratt (Finland)
Ktg = Kantongerecht (Netherlands)
Lab Ct = Labour Court (Ireland)
Land Ct (IoM) = Land Court (Isle of Man)
LArbG = Landesarbeitsgericht (Germany)
LCD = Lord Chancellors Department
Legf Bir = Legfelsobb Birosag (Hungary)
LG (A) = Landesgericht (Austria)
LG (Ger) = Landgericht (Germany)
LGO = Local Government Ombudsman
LJ in Lunacy = Lords Justices sitting in Lunacy
LR = Lagmannsrett (Norway)
LSozG = Landessozialgericht (Germany)
LVAC = Lands Valuation Appeal Court
LVT = Leasehold Valuation Tribunal
MC = Magistrates Court
MCLC = Mayor's and City of London Court
MD = Marknadsdomstolen (Sweden)
MMC = Monopolies and Mergers Commission
MR = Markedsradet (Norway)
Nat Ct = National Court
NI Comm = National Insurance Commissioner
NIRC = National Industrial Relations Court
NO = Naringsfrihetotombudsman (Swe)
NS CR = Nejvyssi soud Ceske republiky (Czech Republic)
NSA (PL) = Naczelny Sad Administracyjny (Poland)
ObG = Obergericht (Switzerland)
ODEI = Office of the Director of Equality Investigations (Ireland)
OGH = Oberster Gerichtshof (Austria)
OH = Outer House
OHIM = Office for Harmonization in the Internal Market
Okr Sod = Okrozno Sodisce (Slovenia)
OL = Ostre Landsret (Denmark)
OLG = Oberlandesgericht (Austria/Germany)
OPM = Oberster Patent- und Markensenat (Austria)
OR = Official Referee
OVG = Oberverwaltungsgericht (Germany)
Pat App Tr = Patents Appeal Tribunal
Pat Val Apel Pad = Patentu Valdes Apelacijas Padome (Latvia)
PC = Privy Council
PCA = Parliamentary Commissioner for Administration
PCC = Patents County Court
PDAD = Probate, Divorce & Admiralty Division
PO = Patent Office
Prer Ct = Prerogative Court
Pret = Pretura (Italy)
PVO = Plant Variety Office
PVST = Plant Varieties & Seeds Tribunal
QB = Court of Queen's Bench
QBD = Queen's Bench Division
QBD (Admin) = Queen's Bench Division (Administrative Court)
QBD (Admlty) = Queen's Bench Division (Admiralty Court)
QBD (Comm) = Queen's Bench Division (Commercial Court)
QBD (Merc) = Queen's Bench Division (Mercantile Court)
QBD (NI) = Queen's Bench Division (Northern Ireland)
QBD (OR) = Queen's Bench Division (Official Referee)

QBD (TCC) = Queen's Bench Division (Technology & Construction Court)
QBD (UK-Irl) = Queen's Bench Division (UK - Ireland)
R = Riigikohus (Estonia)
RB (B) = Tribunal de Premiere Instance (Belgium)
RB (NL) = Arrondissementsrechtbank (Netherlands)
RDAT = Registered Designs Appeal Tribunal
Refugees Status Apps = Refugees Status Appeals Authority (New Zealand)
Rel = Tribunal de Relacao (Portugal)
RP Comm = Restrictive Practices Commission (Ireland)
RPC = Restrictive Practices Court
RR = Regeringsratten (Sweden)
RvK = Rechtbank van Koophandel (Belgium)
Ry & Canal Comm = Railway and Canal Commission
Ry Rates Tr = Railway Rates Tribunal
Sad Apel = Sad Apelacyjny (Poland)
Sad Rej = Sad Rejonowy (Poland)
SC = Supreme Court
SCSL (UN) = Special Court for Sierra Leone (Appeals Chamber)
Sen Cts = Senior Courts
Sen Cts Costs Office = Senior Courts Costs Office
SENT = Special Educational Needs Tribunal
SH = So- og Handelsret (Denmark)
Sh Ct = Sheriff Court
Sh Pr = Sheriff Principal
Solicitors Disc Ctte (SC) = Solicitors Discipline (Scotland) Committee
Solicitors Disc Tr = Solicitors Disciplinary Tribunal
SozG = Sozialgericht (Germany)
Sp Comm = Special Commissioners
Sp Imm App Comm = Special Immigration Appeals Commission
Spec Crim Ct = Special Criminal Court (Ireland)
SS Comm = Social Security Commissioner
Star Chamber = Star Chamber
Sup Ct = Supreme Court
STJ = Superior Tribunal de Justica (Brazil)
Sup Trib = Supremo Tribunal de Justica (Portugal)
Sup Trib Admin = Supremo Tribunal Administrativo (Portugal)
Sym Ep = Symvoulio tis Epikrateias (Greece)
TAR = Tribunale Amministrativo (Italy)
TMR = Trade Marks Registry
Tr = Tribunal
TR = Tingsratt (Sweden)
Transport Arb Tr = Transport Arbitration Tribunal
Trib = Tribunale (Italy)
Trib Ad = Tribunal Administratif (France)
Trib Civil = Tribunal Civil (Belgium)
Trib Comm = Tribunal de Commerce (Belgium/France)
Trib Comp = Tribunal de Defensa de la Competencia (Spain)
Trib Const = Tribunal Constitucional (Spain)
Trib Corr = Tribunal Correctionnel (France)
Trib Correct = Tribunal Correctionnel (Belgium)
Trib d'Arr = Tribunal d'Arrondissement (Luxembourg)
Trib Fed = Tribunal Federal (Switzerland)
Trib Gde Inst = Tribunal de Grande Instance (Belgium/France)
Trib Police = Tribunal de Police (France)
Trib Prem Inst = Tribunal de Premiere Instance (Monaco)
Trib Reg Fed = Tribunal Regional Federal (Brazil)
Trib Sup = Tribunal Supremo (Spain)
Trib Travail = Tribunal du Travail (Belgium)
Tryb Konst = Trybunal Konstytucyjny (Poland)
UN CAT = UN Committee Against Torture
UN CEDW = UN Committee on the Elimination of Discrimination against Women
UN CERD = UN Committee on the Elimination of Racial Discrimination
UN CRPD - UN Committee on the Rights of Persons with Disabilities
UN HRC = UN Human Rights Committee
UN ICT = UN International Criminal Tribunal
Ur Last = Urad Republike Slovenije za Intelektualno Lastnino (Slovenia)
US CR = Ustavni Soud Ceske Republiky (Czech Republic)
US Ct = US Court
UT = Upper Tribunal
V&DTr = VAT and Duties Tribunal
VAC = Valuation Appeal Court
VfGH = Verfassungsgerichtshof (Austria)
VGH = Verwaltungsgericht (Germany/Switzerland)
Visje Sod = Visje Sodisce (Slovenia)
VKS = Vurhoven Kasatsionen Sud (Bulgaria)
VL = Vestre Landsret (Denmark)
VrS = Vrchni soud (Prague)
VT = Valuation Tribunal
VwGH = Verwaltungsgerichtshof (Austria)
Yrg = Yargitay (Turkey)

## Jurisdiction Abbreviations

A = Austria
Abu = Abu Dhabi (United Arab Emirates)
ACT = Australian Capital Territory
Afg = Afghanistan
AI = Ascension Island (St Helena)
AL = Albania
Ald = Alderney
Alg = Algeria
Alta = Alberta
And = Andorra
Ang = Anguilla
Ango = Angola
Ant = Antigua and Barbuda
Arg = Argentina
Arm = Armenia (CIS)
Aus = Australia
Aze = Azerbaijan (CIS)
B = Belgium
Bah = Bahamas
Bahr = Bahrain
Bang = Bangladesh
Bar = Barbados
BC = British Columbia
BEL = Belarus (CIS)
Ben = Benin
Ber = Bermuda
BF = Burkina Faso
BG = British Guiana
BH = British Honduras
Bhu = Bhutan
BIH = Bosnia Herzegovina
Bol = Bolivia
Bots = Botswana
Bru = Brunei
Bul = Bulgaria
Bur = Burundi
BVI = British Virgin Islands
Bze = Belize
Bzl = Brazil
Camb = Cambodia

# TABLE OF ABBREVIATIONS

Camn = Cameroon
Can = Canada
Canary I = Canary Islands (Spain)
Cape = Cape of Good Hope
CAR = Central African Republic
Cey = Ceylon
CI = Cayman Islands
CIS = Commonwealth of Independent States
Com = Comoros
Con = Congo
Cook I = Cook Islands
CR = Costa Rica
CV = Cape Verde
Cy = Cyprus
CZ = Czech Republic
Dji = Djibouti
DK = Denmark
Dom = Dominica
DomR = Dominican Republic
Dub = Dubai
EA = Eastern Africa
EC = European Communities
ECHR = European Commission on Human Rights
Ecu = Ecuador
Egy = Egypt
EIS = El Salvador
EPO = European Patent Office
EqG = Equatorial Guinea
Eri = Eritrea
Eth = Ethiopia
EU = European Union
EW = Estonia
F = France
FI = Falkland Islands
Fin = Finland
FL = Lichtenstein/Liechtenstein
FMS = Federated Malay States
FRY = Yugoslavia
Gab = Gabon
Gam = Gambia, The
GBi = Guinea Bissau
Geo = Georgia (CIS)
Ger = Germany
Gha = Ghana
Gib = Gibraltar
Gld = Greenland (Denmark)
GR = Greece
Gren = Grenada
Gua = Guatemala
Gue = Guernsey
Gui = Guinea
Guy = Guyana
H = Hungary
HK = Hong Kong
Hon = Honduras
HR = Croatia
I = Italy
Ind = India
Indo = Indonesia
IoM = Isle of Man
Iran = Iran
Iraq = Iraq
Irl = Ireland
IS = Iceland
Isr = Israel
Ivo = Ivory Coast
Jam = Jamaica
Jer = Jersey
Jor = Jordan
Jpn = Japan
Kaz = Kazakhstan (CIS)
Ken = Kenya
Kir = Kiribati
Kuw = Kuwait
Kyr = Kyrgyzstan (CIS)
L = Luxembourg
LA = Latvia
Leb = Lebanon
Les = Lesotho
Libe = Liberia
Libya = Libya
LT = Lithuania
M = Malta
Mace = Macedonia
Mad = Madagascar
Made = Madeira (Portugal)
Mal = Malaysia
Man = Manitoba
Mar = Martinique
Marshall I = Marshall Islands (Micronesia)
Mau = Mauritius
MC = Monaco
Mex = Mexico
Mic = Micronesia
Mnegro = Montenegro
Mnia = Mauritania
Mol = Moldova (CIS)
Mong = Mongolia
Mor = Morocco
Moz = Mozambique
Mrat = Montserrat
Mves = Maldives
Mwi = Malawi
Mya = Myanmar
N = Norway
Nam = Namibia
NAnt = Netherlands Antilles
Nau = Nauru
NB = New Brunswick
Nfld = Newfoundland
NI = Northern Ireland
Nic = Nicaragua
Nig = Nigeria
NK = North Korea
NL = Netherlands
NS = Nova Scotia
NSW = New South Wales
NT = Northern Territory
NWT = North West Territories
NZ = New Zealand
OAS = Organisation of American States
OECS = Organization of Eastern Caribbean States
OAU = Organisation of African Unity
Oman = Oman
Ont = Ontario
P = Portugal
Pak = Pakistan
Pal = Palestine
Pan = Panama
Par = Paraguay
PEI = Prince Edward Island
Phl = Philippines
PI = Pitcairn Islands (New Zealand)
PL = Poland
PNG = Papua New Guinea
Poly = Polynesia
PR = Puerto Rico
PRC = People's Republic of China
Qat = Qatar
Qld = Queensland
Que = Quebec
RF = Russian Federation
Rho = Rhodesia
RI = Rhode Island

RO = Romania
Rwa = Rwanda
SA = South Africa
Sask = Saskatchewan
Saudi = Saudi Arabia
SAus = South Australia
SC = Scotland
Sen = Senegal
Serb = Serbia
Sey = Seychelles
Sing = Singapore
SK = South Korea
SL = Sierra Leone
Slo = Slovakia
Slove = Slovenia
Smld = Somaliland
Sol = Solomon Islands
Som = Somalia
Sp = Spain
SrL = Sri Lanka
StC = Saint Christopher and Nevis
StH = St Helena
StL = Saint Lucia
StV = Saint Vincent and the Grenadines
Sud = Sudan
Sur = Surinam
Swa = Swaziland
Swe = Sweden
Swi = Switzerland
Syria = Syria
Tai = Taiwan
Taj = Tajikistan (CIS)
Tan = Tanzania
Tas = Tasmania
TCI = Turks and Caicos Islands
TDC = Tristan Da Cunha (St Helena)
Thai = Thailand
Tka = Tanganyika
Ton = Tonga
TR = Turkey
Trin = Trinidad and Tobago
Tun = Tunisia
Turkn = Turkmenistan (CIS)
Tuv = Tuvalu
UAE = United Arab Emirates
Ug = Uganda
UK = United Kingdom
UK-Irl = UK - Ireland (pre 1922)
UKEW = England and Wales
UKR = Ukraine (CIS)
UN = United Nations
UN ICT = United Nations International Criminal Tribunal
Uru = Uruguay
US = United States
Uzb = Uzbekistan (CIS)
Van = Vanuatu
Ven = Venezuela
VI = Virgin Islands
Vic = Victoria
Viet = Vietnam
WA = Western Australia
WI = West Indies
Wind = Windward Islands
WS = Western Samoa
WSah = Western Sahara
YT = Yukon Territory
Zai = Zaire
Zam = Zambia
Zim = Zimbabwe

## Law Reports/Journal Abbreviations

A.2d = Atlantic Reporter 2nd
A.B.C. = Australian Bankruptcy Cases
A.C. = Appeal Cases
A.C.D. = Administrative Court Digest
A.C.L.C. = Australian Company Law Cases
A.C.L.R. = Australian Company Law Reports
A.C.S.R. = Australian Companies and Securities Reports
A.C.T.R. = Australian Capital Territory Reports
A.D. = Appellate Division Reports (NY)
A.D.2d = Appellate Division Reports 2nd (NY)
A.F.T.R. = American Federal Tax Reports
A.I.R. All. = All India Reporter, Allahabad Series
A.I.R. Bom. = All India Reporter, Bombay Series
A.I.R. Delhi = All India Reporter, Delhi Series
A.I.R. Mad. = All India Reporter, Madras Series
A.I.R. P.C. = All India Reporter, Privy Council Series
A.I.R. S.C. = All India Reporter, Supreme Court Series
A.L.J. = Australian Law Journal
A.L.J.R. = Australian Law Journal Reports
A.L.M.D. = Australian Legal Monthly Digest
A.L.R. = Australian Law Reports
A.L.R. = American Law Reports (1919-48)
A.L.R. (C.N.) = Argus Law Reports, Current Notes (Australia)
A.L.R. Fed. = American Law Reports Federal
A.L.R. Int'l = American Law Reports International
A.L.R.2d = American Law Reports 2nd (1948-65)
A.L.R.3d = American Law Reports 3rd (1965-80)
A.M.C. = American Maritime Cases
A.R. = Alberta Reports (Canada)
A.T.C. = Annotated Tax Cases
A.T.R. = Australian Tax Reports
Act. = Acton's Prize Causes Reports
Ad. & El. = Adolphus & Ellis' Reports
Adam = Adam's Justiciary Reports (Scotland)
Add. = Addams' Ecclesiastical Reports
Admin. L.R. = Administrative Law Reports
Al. = Aleyn's Select Cases
All E.R. = All England Law Reports
All E.R. (Comm) = All England Law Reports (Commercial Cases)
All E.R. (EC) = All England Law Reports (European Cases)
All E.R. Rep. = All England Law Reports Reprints
All N.L.R. = All Nigeria Law Reports
Am.Dec. = American Decisions
Am.Rep. = American Reports
Am.St.Rep. = American State Reports
Amb. = Ambler's Chancery Reports
And. = Anderson's Common Pleas Reports
Andr. = Andrews' King's Bench Reports
Anst. = Anstruther's Exchequer Reports
Arb. L.R.= Arbitration Law Reports and Review
Ark. = Arkley's Justiciary Reports (Scotland)
Asp. = Aspinall's Maritime Cases (1870-1940)
Atk. = Atkyn's Chancery Reports
B. & Ad. = Barnewall and Adolphus's King's Bench Reports
B. & Ald. = Barnewall and Alderson's King's Bench Reports
B. & C. = Barnewall and Cresswell's King's Bench Reports
B. & C.R. = Reports of Bankruptcy and Companies (Winding up) Cases (1918-41)
B. & S. = Best and Smith's Queen's Bench Reports

# TABLE OF ABBREVIATIONS

B.C.C. = British Company Cases
BCCA = Court of Appeal of British Columbia (media neutral cite)
B.C.L.C. = Butterworths Company Law Cases
B.C.L.R. = British Columbia Law Reports (Canada)
BCSC = Supreme Court of British Columbia (media neutral cite)
B.H.R.C. = Butterworths Human Rights Cases
B.L.G.R. = Butterworths Local Government Reports
B.L.R. = Building Law Reports
B.M.L.R. = Butterworths Medico Legal Reports
B.N.C. = Brooke's New Cases
B.P.I.R. = Bankruptcy and Personal Insolvency Reports
B.R. = Bankruptcy Reporter
B.T.C. = British Tax Cases
B.T.L.C. = Butterworths Trading Law Cases Cases
B.V.C. = British VAT Cases
B.W.C.C. = Butterworths Workmen's Compensation Cases
Ball & B. = Ball and Beatty's Irish Chancery Reports
Bank. L.R. = Banking Law Reports
Bankr.Ct.Dec. = Bankruptcy Court Decisions (CRR)
Barn. Ch. = Barnardiston's Chancery Reports
Barn. K.B. = Barnardiston's King's Bench Reports
Barnes = Barnes' Notes of Cases in Common Pleas
Beat. = Beatty's Irish Chancery Reports
Beav. = Beavan's Rolls Court Reports
Bel. = Bellewe's Reports (Les Ans du Roy Richard le Second)
Bell C.C. = Bell's Crown Cases Reserved
Belt's Supp. = Belt's Supplement to Vesey Senior's Reports
Benl. = Benloe's Reports
Benl. & Dal. Benloe = Benloe & Dalison's Reports (Benloe)
Benl. & Dal. Dalison = Benloe & Dalison's Reports (Dalison)
Bing. = Bingham's Common Pleas Reports
Bing. N.C. = Bingham, New Cases, English Common Pleas
Binn. = Binney's Reports (U.S.A.)
Bli. = Bligh's House of Lords Reports
Bli. N.S. = Bligh's House of Lords Reports, New Series
Bos. & P. = Bosanquet and Puller's Common Pleas Reports
Bos. & P. N.R. = Bosanquet and Puller's New Reports, Common Pleas
Bott P.L. = Bott's Poor Law Cases
Br. & Col. Pri. Cas. = British and Colonial Prize Cases
Bro. C.C. = W. Brown's Chancery Reports
Bro. P.C. = J. Brown's Parliamentary Cases
Brod. & Bing. = Broderip and Bingham's Common Pleas Reports
Broun = Broun's Justiciary Reports (Scotland)
Brown. & Lush. = Browning and Lushington's Admiralty Reports
Brownl. = Brownlow and Goldesborough's Common Pleas Reports
Bull. N.P. = Buller's Nisi Prius Reports
Bulst. = Bulstrode's King's Bench Reports
Bunb. = Bunbury's Exchequer Reports
Burr. = Burrow's King's Bench Reports tempore Mansfield
Burrell = Burrell's Admiralty Reports
Bus. L.R. = Business Law Reports
Bus. L.R. D = Business Law Reports Digest Pages
C. Rob. = Christopher Robinson's Admiralty Reports
C.B. = Common Bench Reports (Manning)
C.B. N.S. = Common Bench Reports (Manning), New Series
C.C.C. = Canadian Criminal Cases
C.C.C. (2d) = Canadian Criminal Cases, 2nd Series
C.C.C. (3d) = Canadian Criminal Cases, 3rd Series
C.C.L. Rep. = Community Care Law Reports
C.C.L.R. = Consumer Credit Law Reports
C.C.L.T. = Canadian Cases on the Law of Torts
C.C.P.A. = Court of Customs & Patent Appeals Reports
C.E.C. = European Community Cases
C.I.L.L. = Construction Industry Law Letter
C.I.L.R. = Cayman Islands Law Reports
C.L.C. = Commercial Law Cases
C.L.R. = Commonwealth Law Reports
C.M.L. Rev. = Common Market Law Review
C.M.L.R. = Common Market Law Reports
C.M.L.R. D = Common Market Law Reports Restrictive Practices Supplement
C.M.L.R. M = Common Market Law Reports Merger Decisions
C.O.D. = Crown Office Digest
C.O.P.L.R. = Court of Protection Law Reports
C.P. Rep. = Civil Procedure Reports
C.P.C. (2d) = Carswell's Practice Cases, Second Series
C.P.C. (3d) = Carswell's Practice Cases, Third Series
C.P.L. = Current Property Law (1952-53)
C.P.L.R. = Civil Practice Law Reports
C.P.R. = Canadian Patent Reporter
C.P.R. (2d) = Canadian Patent Reporter, 2nd Series
C.P.R. (3d) = Canadian Patent Reporter, 3rd Series
C.P.R. (4th) = Canadian Patent Reporter, 4th Series
C.R. = Criminal Reports (Canada, 1946-67)
C.R. N.S. = Criminal Reports (New Series) (Canada, 1967-78)
C.R.R. = Canadian Rights Reporter
C.S. = Rapports Judiciaires de Quebec, Cour Superieure
CAT = Competition Commission Appeal Tribunal (media neutral cite)
CJ C.A.R. = Colorado Appellate Report
CSIH = Court of Session, Inner House (media neutral cite)
CSOH = Court of Session, Outer House (media neutral cite)
Cab. & Ell. = Cababe and Ellis' Queen's Bench Reports
Cal. = California Reports
Cal. Daily Op. Serv. = California Daily Opinion Service
Cal.3d = California Reports 3rd
Cal.4th = California Reports, 4th Series
Cal.Rptr.2d = California Reporter 2d (West's)
Cald. M.C. = Caldecott's Magistrates Cases
Calth. = Calthrop's City of London Special Cases
Camp. = Campbell's Nisi Prius Reports
Can. B.R. = Canadian Bar Review
Car. & K. = Carrington and Kirwan's Nisi Prius Reports
Car. & M. = Carrington and Marshman's Nisi Prius Reports
Car. & P. = Carrington and Payne's Nisi Prius Reports
CarswellFor = Carswell Foreign
Cart. = Carter's Common Pleas Reports
Carth. = Carthew's King's Bench Reports
Cary = Cary's Chancery Reports
Cas. t. Hard. = Lee's King's Bench Cases tempore Hardwicke
Cas. t. Talb. = Cases in Equity tempore Talbot
Ch. = Chancery Division
Ch. Cas. = Cases Argued and Decreed in Chancery (Select Cases in Chancery)
Ch. Cas. in Ch. = Choyce Cases in Chancery

## TABLE OF ABBREVIATIONS

Chit. = Chitty's King's Bench Practice and Pleading Reports
Cl. & F. = Clark and Finnelly's House of Lords Reports
Clark's Rep. = Clark's Reports (Jamaica)
Clay. = Clayton's Reports and Pleas of Assises at Yorke
Clunet = Journal du Droit International (France)
Co. Rep. = Coke's King's Bench Reports
Coll. = Collyer's Chancery Cases tempore Bruce
Colles = Colles' Parliament Reports
Com. = Comyns' King's Bench, Common Pleas and Exchequer Reports
Com. Cas. = Commercial Cases
Com. L.R. = Commercial Law Reports
Comb. = Comberbach's King's Bench Reports
Comp. A.R. = Competition Appeal Reports
Con. L.R. = Construction Law Reports
Const. L.J. = Construction Law Journal
C.T.L.C.= Consumer and Trading Law Cases
Cooke = Cooke's Common Pleas Reports
Coop. Pr. Cas. = Cooper's Practice Cases
Coop. t. Brough. = Cooper's Select Cases of Lord Brougham
Coop. t. Cott. = Cooper's Chancery Reports tempore Cottenham
Costs L.O. = Costs Law Reports Online
Costs L.R. = Costs Law Reports
Costs L.R. Online = Costs Law Reports Online
Costs L.R. (Core Vol.) = Costs Law Reports, Core Volume
Coup. = Couper's Justiciary Reports (Scotland)
Cowp. = Cowper's King's Bench Reports
Cox C.C. = Cox's Criminal Cases
Cox Eq. Cas. = Cox's Equity Cases
Cr. & J. = Crompton and Jervis' Exchequer Reports
Cr. & M. = Crompton and Meeson's Exchequer Reports
Cr. & Ph. = Craig and Phillip's Chancery Reports
Cr. App. R. = Criminal Appeal Reports
Cr. App. R. (S.) = Criminal Appeal Reports (Sentencing)
Cr. M. & R. = Crompton, Meeson and Roscoe's Exchequer Reports
Cr. S. & P. = Craigie, Stewart and Paton's Scottish Appeal Cases
Cranch = Cranch's United States Supreme Court Reports
Crim. L.R. = Criminal Law Review
Cro. Car. = Croke's King's Bench Reports tempore Charles
Cro. Eliz. = Croke's King's Bench Reports tempore Elizabeth
Cro. Jac. = Croke's King's Bench Reports tempore James
Cun. = Cunningham's King's Bench Reports
Curt. = Curteis' Ecclesiastical Reports
D. = Dunlop, Bell and Murray's Reports, Session Cases, 2nd series (Scotland)
D. & R. = Decisions and Reports of the European Commission of Human Rights
D. (H.L.) = Dunlop's Session Cases, 2nd Series (House of Lords cases, Scotland)
D.L.R. = Dominion Law Reports (Canada, 1912-55)
D.L.R. (2d) = Dominion Law Reports (2d) (Canada, 1956-68)
D.L.R. (3d) = Dominion Law Reports (3d) (Canada, 1969-84)
D.L.R. (4th) = Dominion Law Reports (4th) (Canada, 1985-94)
D.R.A. = De-rating Appeals
D.T.C. = Dominion Tax Cases
Daily Telegraph = Daily Telegraph
Dan. = Daniell's Exchequer Reports
Dav. = Davis' Irish Reports
De G. = De Gex's Bankruptcy Reports
De G. & J. = De Gex and Jones' Chancery Reports
De G. & Sm. = De Gex and Smale's Chancery Reports
De G.F. & J. = De Gex, Fisher and Jones' Chancery Reports
De G.J. & S. = De Gex, Jones and Smith's Chancery Reports
De G.M. & G. = De Gex, Macnaghten and Gordons' Chancery Reports
Dea. & Sw. = Deane and Swabey's Ecclesiastical Reports
Deac. & Ch. = Deacon and Chitty's Bankruptcy Reports
Dears. = Dearsley's Crown Cases Reserved
Dears. & B. = Dearsley and Bell's Crown Cases Reserved
Den. = Denison and Pearce's Crown Cases Reserved
Dick. = Dickens' Chancery Reports
Disc. L.R. = Discrimination Law Reports
Dods. = Dodson's Admiralty Reports
Donn. = Donnelly's Chancery Cases
Doug. K.B. = Douglas' King's Bench Reports
Dow = Dow's House of Lords Cases
Dow. & Cl. = Dow and Clark's House of Lords Reports
Dowl. & L. = Dowling and Lowndes' Bail Court Reports
Dowl. & Ry. K.B. = Dowling and Ryland's King's Bench Reports
Dowl. & Ry. N.P. = Dowling and Ryland's Nisi Prius Cases
Dowl. N.S. = Dowling's Bail Court Reports, New Series
Dowl. Pr. Cas. = Dowling's Bail Court Practice Cases
Dr. & War. = Drury and Warren's Irish Chancery Reports
Dr. t. Sug. = Drury's Irish Chancery Cases tempore Sugden
Drew. = Drewry's Chancery Reports tempore Kindersley
Drew. & Sm. = Drewry and Smales' Chancery Reports
Dyer = Dyer's King's Bench Reports
E.A. = East African Law Reports
E.A.C.A. = Law Reports of the Court of Appeals for Eastern Africa
E.A.T.C. = East African Tax Cases
E.B.L.R. = Electronic Business Law Reports
E.C.C. = European Commercial Cases
E.C.D.R. = European Copyright and Design Reports
E.C.D.R. CN = European Copyright and Design Reports Case Notes
E.C.R. = European Court Reports
E.C.R. IA = European Court Reports
E.G. = Estates Gazette
E.G.C.S. = Estates Gazette Case Summaries
E.G.D. = Estates Gazette Digest of Cases
E.G.L.R. = Estates Gazette Law Reports (Bound Volume)
E.H.L.R. = Environmental Health Law Reports
E.H.L.R. Dig. = Environmental Health Reports Digest Pages
E.H.R.R. = European Human Rights Reports
E.H.R.R. CD = European Human Rights Reports, Commission Decisions
E.H.R.R. SE = European Human Rights Reports, Summaries and Extracts
E.L.R. = Education Law Reports
E.M.L.R. = Entertainment and Media Law Reports
E.N.P.R. = European National Patent Reports
E.P.O.R. = European Patent Office Reports

# TABLE OF ABBREVIATIONS

E.P.O.R. A = European Patent Office Reports A (1979-85, J decisions)
E.P.O.R. B = European Patent Office Reports B (1979-85, T decisions)
E.P.O.R. C = European Patent Office Reports C (1979-85, T decisions)
E.R. = English Reports
E.T.M.R. = European Trade Mark Reports
E.T.M.R. CN = European Trade Mark Reports Case Notes
ERC = Environment Reporter Cases (BNA)
EWCA Civ = Court of Appeal (Civil)
EWCA Crim = Court of Appeal (Criminal)
EWCOP = Court of Protection
EWFC = Family Court
EWHC = High Court
EWHC Admin = High Court (Administrative Court)
EWPCC = Patents County Court
East = East's King's Bench Reports
East P.C. = East's Pleas of the Crown
Ed. C.R. = Education Case Reports
Ed. Law Rep. = Education Law Reporter
Eden = Eden's Chancery Reports
Edw. = Edward's Admiralty Reports
El. & Bl. = Ellis and Blackburn's Queen's Bench Reports
El. & El. = Ellis and Ellis' Queen's Bench Reports
El. Bl. & El. = Ellis, Blackburn and Ellis' Queen's Bench Reports
Emp. L.R. = Employment Law Reports
Employee Benefits Cas. = Employee Benefits Cases
Env. L.R. = Environmental Law Reports
Env. L.R. D = Environmental Law Reports Digest Pages
Envtl. L. Rep. = Environmental Law Reporter (ELR) (cases only)
Eq. Cas. Abr. = Abridgment of Cases in Equity
Eq. L.R. = Equality Law Reports
Eq. Rep. = Equity Reports
Esp. = Espinasse's Nisi Prius Reports
EU:C = European Case Law Identifier (European Court of Justice)
EU:F = European Case Law Identifier (Civil Service Tribunal)
EU:T = European Case Law Identifier (General Court)
Eu. L.R. = European Law Reports
Ex. = Exchequer Reports (Welsby, Hurlstone and Gordon)
Ex. C.R. = Canada Law Reports, Exchequer Court
Extradition L.R. = Extradition Law Reports
F. = Federal Reporter (U.S.A.)
F. = Fraser's Session Cases, 5th Series (Scotland)
F. & F. = Foster and Finlason's Nisi Prius Reports
F. (Ct. of Sess.) = Faculty Decisions, Court of Session (Scotland)
F. (H.L.) = Fraser's Session Cases, 5th Series (House of Lords, Scotland)
F. (J.) = Fraser's Session Cases, 5th Series (Justiciary cases, Scotland)
F.2d = Federal Reporter, 2nd Series (U.S.A.)
F.3d = Federal Reporter, 3rd Series (U.S.A.)
F.C. = Canada Law Reports, Federal Court
F.C.R. = Family Court Reporter
F.L.R. = Family Law Reports
F.R.D. = Federal Rules Decisions (U.S.A.)
F.S.R. = Fleet Street Reports
F.Supp. = Federal Supplement (U.S.A.)
F.Supp.2d = Federal Supplement, Second Series
F.T.L.R. = Financial Times Law Reports
F.T.R. = Federal Trial Reports
FCA = Federal Court of Australia (media neutral cite)
FCA = Federal Court of Appeal of Canada (media neutral cite)
FCAFC = Federal Court of Australia, Full Court (media neutral cite)
Fam. = Family Division
Fam. L.R. = Family Law Reports (Scotland)
Fam. Law = Family Law
FamCA = Family Court of Australia (media neutral cite)
Fed. L.R. = Federal Law Reports (Australia)
Fed. R. Evid. Serv. = Federal Rules of Evidence Service (Callaghan's)
Fed. Sec. L. Rep. P = Federal Securities Law Reports (CCH)
Fed.R.Serv.2d = Federal Rules Service 2nd (Callaghan's)
Fed.R.Serv.3d = Federal Rules Service 3rd (Callaghan's)
Fed.Sent.R. = Federal Sentencing Reporter (U.S.A.)
Fin. L.R. = Financial Law Reports
Financial Times = Financial Times
Fitzg. = Fitz-Gibbons' King's Bench Reports
Fla. L. Weekly Fed. S = Florida Law Weekly, United States Supreme Court
Forr. = Forrest's Exchequer Reports
Fort. = Fortescue's Courts of Westminster Hall Reports
Fost. = Foster's Crown Cases
Freem. Ch. = Freeman's Chancery Reports
Freem. K.B. = Freeman's King's Bench and Common Pleas Reports
G. Coop. = Cooper's Chancery Reports
G.W.D. = Green's Weekly Digest (Scotland)
GRUR = Gewerblicher Rechtsschutz und Urheberrecht
Ga. = Georgia Reports
Giff. = Giffard's Chancery Reports
Gilb. Ch. = Gilbert's Cases in Equity
Gilb. K.B. = Gilbert's King's Bench Cases
Gl. & J. = Glyn and Jameson's Bankruptcy Reports
Godb. = Godbolt's Courts of Record at Westminster Reports
Gould. = Gouldsborough's King's Bench Reports
Gow = Gow's Nisi Prius Reports
Guardian = Guardian
H. & Tw. = Hall and Twells' Chancery Reports
H. Bl. = H. Blackstone's Common Pleas Reports
H.B.R. = Hansell's Bankruptcy Reports (1915-17)
H.K. Cases = Hong Kong Cases
H.K.L.R. = Hong Kong Law Reports
H.K.L.R.D. = Hong Kong Law Reports and Digest
H.L. Cas. = Clark's House of Lords Cases
H.L.R. = Housing Law Reports
H.R.C.D. = Human Rights Case Digest
H.R.L.R. = Human Rights Law Reports - UK Cases
HCA = High Court of Australia (media neutral cite)
HCJAC = High Court of Justiciary, Appeal (media neutral cite)
HCJT = High Court of Justiciary, Trial (media neutral cite)
Hag. Adm. = Haggard's Admiralty Reports
Hag. Con. = Haggard's Consistorial Reports
Hag. Ecc. = Haggard's Ecclesiastical Reports
Har. & Woll. = Harrison and Wollaston's King's Bench and Bail Court Reports
Hardres = Hardres' Exchequer Reports
Hare = Hare's Chancery Reports
Hay & M. = Hay and Marriott's Admiralty Reports
Hayes = Hayes' Irish Exchequer Reports
Hayes & J. = Hayes and Jones' Irish Exchequer Reports
Hem. & M. = Hemming and Miller's Chancery Reports

# TABLE OF ABBREVIATIONS

Het. = Hetley's Reports
Hob. = Hobart's Reports (Common Pleas and King's Bench)
Hodg. = Hodges' Common Pleas Reports
Holt Eq. = Holt's Equity Reports
Holt K.B. = Holt's King's Bench Reports
Holt N.P. = Holt's Nisi Prius Reports
Hous. L.R. = Housing Law Reports (Scottish)
Hov. Supp. = Hovenden's Supplement to Vesey Junior's Reports
How. = Howard's United States Supreme Court Reports
Hume = Hume's Session Cases (Scotland)
Hurl. & C. = Hurlstone and Coltman's Exchequer Reports
Hurl. & N. = Hurlstone and Norman's Exchequer Reports
Hut. = Hutton's Reports
I.C.L.R. = Irish Common Law Reports, Second Series (1850-66)
I.C.R. = Industrial Cases Reports
I.C.R.D. = Industrial Cases Reports Digest Pages
I.H.R.R. = International Human Rights Reports
I.L.Pr. = International Litigation Procedure
I.L.R. = International Law Reports
I.L.R.M. = Irish Law Reports Monthly
I.L.T. = Irish Law Times
I.L.T.R. = Irish Law Times Reports
I.N.L.R. = Immigration and Nationality Law Reports
I.P.D. = Intellectual Property Decisions
I.P.L.R. = Industrial Property Law Reports (India)
I.P.R. = Intellectual Property Reports (Australia)
I.R. = Irish Reports
I.R. C.L. = Irish Reports, Common Law
I.R.L.R. = Industrial Relations Law Reports
I.T.C. = Srinivasan's Reports of Income Tax Cases (India)
I.T.C.L.R. = IT & Communications Law Reports
I.T.E.L.R. = International Trust and Estate Law Reports
I.T.L. Rep. = International Tax Law Reports
I.T.R. = Industrial Tribunal Reports
IEHC = High Court of Ireland (media neutral cite)
IESC = Supreme Court of Ireland (media neutral cite)
ITRD = International Trade Reporter Decisions (BNA)
Ill.2d = Illinois Reports, 2nd Series
Ill.Dec. = Illinois Decisions
Imm. A.R. = Immigration Appeal Reports
Ind. = Indiana Reports
Ind. Cas. = Indian Cases
Ind. L.R. = Indian Law Reports
Ind. L.R. All. = Indian Law Reports, Allahabad Series
Ind. L.R. Cal. = Indian Law Reports, Calcutta Series
Ind. L.R. Mad. = Indian Law Reports, Madras Series
Ind. L.R. Pat. = Indian Law Reports, Patna Series
Independent = Independent
Info. T.L.R. = Information Technology Law Reports
Inquest L.R. = Inquest Law Reports
Ir. Ch. R. = Irish Chancery Reports (1850-66)
Ir. Eq. = Irish Reports, Equity (1866-77)
Ir. Eq. R. = Irish Equity Reports, First Series (1838-50)
Ir. Jur. Rep. = Irish Jurist Reports
Ir. L.J. = Irish Law Journal
Ir. L.R. = Irish Law Reports
Irvine = Irvine's High Court and Circuit Courts of Justiciary Reports (Scotland)
J. & Lat. = Jones and La Touche's Irish Chancery Reports (1844-46)
J. Bridg. = Sir John Bridgman's Reports
J. Shaw. = Shaw's Justiciary Reports (Scotland)
J.C. = Justiciary Cases (Scotland)
J.J. = Jersey Judgments
J.L.R. = Jamaica Law Reports
J.P. = Justice of the Peace Reports
J.P. Rep. = Local Government Review Reports
J.P.I. Law = Journal of Personal Injury Law
J.P.I.L. = Journal of Personal Injury Litigation
J.P.L. = Journal of Planning & Environment Law
J.P.N. = Justice of the Peace Notes of Cases
Jac. = Jacob's Chancery Reports
Jac. & W. = Jacob and Walker's Chancery Reports
Jebb. & Sym. = Jebb and Syme's Queen's Bench Reports (Ireland, 1838-41)
Jenk. = Jenkins' Eight Centuries of Reports
Jer. L.R. = Jersey Law Reports
John. = Johnson's Chancery Reports
John. & H. = Johnson and Hemming's Chancery Reports
Jur. = Jurist
Jur. N.S. = Jurist, New Series
K.B. = King's Bench
K.I.R. = Knight's Industrial Law Reports
Kay = Kay's Chancery Reports
Kay & J. = Kay and Johnson's Chancery Reports
Keb. = Keble's King's Bench Reports
Keen = Keen's Rolls Court Reports
Keil. = Keilwey's Reports
Kel. = Kelyng's Divers Cases
Kel. W. = W Kelynge's King's Bench and Chancery Reports
Keny. = Kenyon's King's Bench Reports
Kn. = Knapp's Privy Council Appeal Cases
Ky. = Kentucky Reports
L. & T.R. = Landlord and Tenant Reports
L.D.B. = Legal Decisions Affecting Bankers
L.Ed. = Lawyers' Edition, United States Supreme Court Reporter
L.Ed.2d = Lawyers' Edition 2nd Series, United States Supreme Court Reporter
L.G. Rev. = Local Government Review
L.G.L.R. = Local Government Law Reports
L.G.R. = Local Government Reports
L.G.R.A. = Local Government Reports of Australia
L.J. = Law Journal (Newspaper)
L.J. Bcy. = Law Journal Reports, Bankruptcy (1832-80)
L.J. C.P. = Law Journal Reports, Common Pleas (1831-75)
L.J. Ch. = Law Journal Reports, Chancery (1831-1946)
L.J. Ex. = Law Journal Reports, Exchequer (1831-75)
L.J. K.B. = Law Journal Reports, King's Bench (1831-1946)
L.J. M.C. = Law Journal Reports, Magistrates Cases (1831-96)
L.J. N.C. = Law Journal, Notes of Cases
L.J. N.C.C.R. = Law Journal, County Court Reports (1934-47)
L.J. N.S. = Law Journal Reports, New Series (1832-1946)
L.J. O.S. = Law Journal Reports, Old Series (1822-31)
L.J. P. = Law Journal Reports, Probate, Divorce and Admiralty (1875-1946)
L.J. P. & M. = Law Journal Reports, Probate, Divorce and Matrimonial (1858-59, 1866-75)
L.J. P.C. = Law Journal Reports, Privy Council (1831-1946)
L.J. P.M. & A. = Law Journal Reports, Probate, Matrimonial and Admiralty (1860-65)
L.J. Q.B. = Law Journal Reports, Queen's Bench (1831-1946)
L.J.R. = Law Journal Reports (1947-49)
L.L.R. = Licensing Law Reports

# TABLE OF ABBREVIATIONS

L.M.C.L.Q. = Lloyd's Maritime and Commercial Law Quarterly
L.R. A. & E. = Admiralty and Ecclesiastical Cases (1865-75)
L.R. App. Cas. = Appeal Cases (1875-90)
L.R. C.C.R. = Crown Cases Reserved
L.R. C.P. = Common Pleas (1865-75)
L.R. C.P.D. = Common Pleas Division (1875-80)
L.R. Ch. App. = Chancery Appeals (1865-75)
L.R. Ch. D. = Chancery Division (1875-90)
L.R. Eq. = Equity Cases
L.R. Ex. = Exchequer (1865-75)
L.R. Ex. D. = Exchequer Division (1875-80)
L.R. H.L. = English and Irish Appeals (1866-75)
L.R. Ind. App. = Indian Appeals
L.R. Ir. = Ireland
L.R. P. & D. = Probate and Divorce (1865-75)
L.R. P.C. = Privy Council
L.R. P.D. = Probate Division (1875-90)
L.R. Q.B. = Queen's Bench (1865-75)
L.R. Q.B.D. = Queen's Bench Division (1875-90)
L.R. R.P. = Restrictive Practices (1958-72)
L.R. Sc. = Scotch and Divorce Appeals
L.R.B. = Law Reports of the Bahamas
L.R.C. = Law Reports of the Commonwealth
L.R.C. (Const) = Law Reports of the Commonwealth (Constitutional & Administrative Reports)
L.R.L.R. = Lloyd's Reinsurance Law Reports
L.R.R.M. (BNA) = Labor Relations Reference Manual (BNA)
L.S.G. = Law Society Gazette
L.T. = Law Times (1859-1965)
L.T. O.S. = Law Times (Old Series) (1843-59)
L.T.R. = Law Times Reports (1859-1947)
LS Law Medical = LS Law Medical
Lab.Cas. P = Labor Cases (CCH)
Lane = Lane's Exchequer Reports
Lat. = Latch's King's Bench Reports
Ld. Raym. = Lord Raymond's King's Bench Reports
Le. & Ca. = Leigh and Cave's Crown Cases Reserved
Leach = Leach's Cases in Crown Law
Lee = Lee's Ecclesiastical Reports
Leo. = Leonard's Reports of the Courts at Westminster
Lev. = Levinz's King's Bench and Common Pleas Reports
Lewin = Lewin's Crown Cases Reserved
Ley = Ley's Court of Wards Reports
Lil. = Lilly's Assise Cases
Litt. = Littleton's Common Bank and Exchequer Reports
Ll. & G. t Sug. = Lloyd and Goold's Reports of Chancery in Ireland tempore Sugden
Ll. L. Pr. Cas. = Lloyd's List Prize Cases (1914-24)
Ll. L. Pr. Cas. (N.S.) = Lloyd's List Prize Cases, Second Series (1939-53)
Ll. L. Rep. = Lloyd's List Law Reports (1919-50)
Lloyd's List = Lloyd's List
Lloyd's Rep. = Lloyd's Law Reports (1951-)
Lloyd's Rep. Bank. = Lloyd's Law Reports Banking
Lloyd's Rep. F.C. = Lloyd's Law Reports Financial Crime
Lloyd's Rep. I.R. = Lloyd's Law Reports, Insurance & Reinsurance
Lloyd's Rep. Med. = Lloyd's Law Reports Medical
Lloyd's Rep. P.N. = Lloyd's Law Reports Professional Negligence
Lofft = Lofft's King's Bench Reports
Lush. = Lushington's Admiralty Reports
Lut. = Lutwyche's Reports (Livre des Entries)
Lut. Reg. Cas. = Lutwyche's Entries and Reports, Common Pleas (Registration Cases)
M'Cle. = M'Cleland's Exchequer Reports
M'Cle. & Y. = M'Cleland and Younge's Exchequer Reports
M. = Macpherson's Session Cases, 3rd Series (Scotland)
M. & S. = Maule and Selwyn's King's Bench Reports
M. & W. = Meeson and Welsby's Exchequer Reports
M. (H.L.) = Macpherson's Session Cases, 3rd Series (House of Lords cases, Scotland)
M.C.C. = MacGillivray's Copyright Cases
M.H.L.R. = Mental Health Law Reports
M.L.J. = Malaysian Law Journal
M.P.L.R. = Municipal and Planning Law Reports (Canada)
M.P.R. = Maritime Provinces Reports (Canada)
M.R. = Mauritius Reports
Mac. & G. = Macnaghten and Gordon's Chancery Reports
Macl. & R. = Maclean and Robinson's House of Lords Cases
Macq. = Macqueen's Scottish Appeal Cases
Madd. = Maddock's Chancery Reports
Man. & G. = Manning and Granger's Common Pleas Reports
Man. & Ry. K.B. = Manning and Ryland's King's Bench Reports
Man. & Ry. M.C. = Manning and Ryland's Magistrates Cases Reports
Man. Law = Managerial Law
Mans. = Manson's Bankruptcy and Companies Winding up Cases (1894-1913)
Manx L.R. = Manx Law Reports
March N.C. = March's New Cases
Masons C.L.R. = Masons Computer Law Reports
Masons C.L.R. Rep. = Masons Computer Law Reports Reprints (Case Digests, 1994-97)
Mass. = Massachusetts Reports
Med. L.R. = Medical Law Reports
Media L. Rep. = Media Law Reporter (BNA)
Mer. = Merivale's Chancery Reports
Misc. = New York Miscellaneous Reports
Misc.2d = Miscellaneous Reports, 2nd Series (New York)
Mod. = Modern Reports
Mol. = Molloy's Chancery Reports (Ireland, 1927-31)
Mont. D. & De G. = Montagu, Deacon and De Gex's Bankruptcy Reports
Moo. Ind. App. = Moore's Appeals from the East Indies Reports
Moo. K.B. = Moore's King's Bench Reports
Moo. P.C. = Moore's Privy Council Cases
Moo. P.C. N.S. = Moore's Privy Council Cases, New Series
Mood. & M. = Moody and Malkin's Nisi Prius Reports
Mood. & R. = Moody and Robinson's Nisi Prius Reports
Mood. C.C. = Moody's Crown Cases Reserved
Mor. Dic. = Morison's Dictionary of Decisions (Scotland)
Morr. = Morrell's Bankruptcy Reports
Mos. = Moseley's Chancery Reports
My. & C. = Mylne and Craig's Chancery Reports
My. & K. = Mylne and Keen's Chancery Reports
N.B. Eq. = New Brunswick Equity Reports
N.B.R. = National Bankruptcy Register Reports
N.B.R. 2d = New Brunswick Reports, 2nd Series
N.C. = Notes of Cases, Ecclesiastical and Maritime (ed. Thornton)
N.E. = North Eastern Reporter (U.S.A.)
N.E.2d = North Eastern Reporter 2nd
N.H. = New Hampshire Reports
N.I. = Northern Ireland Law Reports

N.I.J.B. = Northern Ireland Judgment Bulletin
N.I.L.Q. = Northern Ireland Legal Quarterly
N.J. = New Jersey Reports
N.L.J. = New Law Journal
N.L.J. Rep. = New Law Journal Reports
N.L.R. = New Law Reports (Sri Lanka)
N.P.C. = New Property Cases
N.R. = National Reporter (Canada)
N.S.R. 2d = Nova Scotia Reports, 2nd Series
N.S.W.L.R. = New South Wales Law Reports
N.S.W.R. = New South Wales Reports (1960-70)
N.W. = North Western Reporter (U.S.A.)
N.W.2d = North Western Reporter, 2nd Series (U.S.A.)
N.Y. = New York Reports
N.Y.2d = New York Reports, 2nd Series
N.Y.S. = New York Supplement Reporter
N.Y.S.2d = New York Supplement Reporter, 2nd Series
N.Z.L.R. = New Zealand Law Reports
NDLR P = National Disability Law Reporter
NICA = Court of Appeal (Northern Ireland) (media neutral cite)
NICh = Chancery Division (Northern Ireland) (media neutral cite)
NIFam = Family Division (Northern Ireland) (media neutral cite)
NIQB = Queen's Bench Division (Northern Ireland) (media neutral cite)
NSWCA = Court of Appeal of New South Wales (media neutral cite)
NSWSC = Supreme Court of New South Wales (media neutral cite)
NZCA = Court of Appeal of New Zealand (media neutral cite)
NZSC = Supreme Court of New Zealand (media neutral cite)
Nels. = Nelson's Chancery Reports
Nev. & M. K.B. = Neville and Manning's King's Bench Reports
New Rep. = New Reports
Nfld. & P.E.I.R. = Newfoundland and Prince Edward Island Reports
Noy = Noy's Reports
O'M. & H. = O'Malley and Hardcastle's Election Cases
O. Bridg. = Sir Orlando Bridgman's Reports
O.F.L.R. = Offshore Financial Law Reports
O.J. E.P.O. = Official Journal of the European Patent Office
O.L.R. = Ontario Law Reports (1901-30)
O.P.L.R. = Occupational Pensions Law Reports
O.R. = Ontario Reports (1882-1900, 1931-)
O.R. (2d) = Ontario Reports, 2nd Series
O.R. (3d) = Ontario Reports, 3rd Series
Owen = Owen's King's Bench and Common Pleas Reports
P. = Pacific Reporter (U.S.A.)
P. = Probate
P. & C.R. = Property, Planning and Compensation Reports
P. & C.R. D = Property and Compensation Reports Digest Pages
P. & C.R. DG = Property, Planning and Compensation Reports Digest Pages
P. Wms. = Peere Williams' Chancery Reports
P.2d = Pacific Reporter, 2nd Series (U.S.A.)
P.A.D. = Planning Appeal Decisions
P.C.C. = Palmer's Company Cases
P.I.Q.R. P = Personal Injury and Quantum Reports
P.I.Q.R. Q = Personal Injury and Quantum Reports
P.L.C.R. = Planning Law Case Reports
P.L.R. = Planning Law Reports
P.N.G.L.R. = Papua New Guinea Law Reports
P.N.L.R. = Professional Negligence and Liability Reports
P.T.S.R. = Public and Third Sector Law Reports
P.T.S.R. (C.S.) = Public and Third Sector Law Reports (Case Summaries)
P.T.S.R D = Public and Third Sector Law Reports Digest Pages
Pal. L.R. = Palestine Law Reports
Palm. = Palmer's Reports
Park on Ins. = Park on Insurance, 8th ed.
Park. = Parker's Exchequer Reports
Pat. = Paton's Scottish Appeals, House of Lords
Peake = Peake's Nisi Prius Reports
Peake Add. Cas. = Peake's Additional Cases
Pens. App. R. = Pensions Appeal Reports
Pens. L.R. = Pensions Law Reports
Perry & K. = Perry and Knapp's Election Cases
Ph. = Phillips' Chancery Reports
Phil. Ecc. = Phillimore's Ecclesiastical Reports
Plow. = Plowden's Commentaries
Po. L.R. = Police Law Reports
Pollex. = Pollexfen's Special Cases
Pop. = Sir John Popham's Reports
Prec. Ch. = Precedents in Chancery
Price = Price's Exchequer Reports
Prison L.R. = Prison Law Reports
Q.B. = Queen's Bench
Q.B. = Queen's Bench Reports (1841-1856)
Q.J.P. = Queensland Justice of the Peace Reports
Q.L.J. = Queensland Law Journal Reports (1897-1901)
Q.R. = Quantum Reports (Kemp & Kemp)
Q.S.R. = Queensland State Reports (1902-57)
Q.W.N. = Queensland Law Reporter and Weekly Notes (1908-72)
QCA = Court of Appeal of Queensland (media neutral cite)
QSC = Supreme Court of Queensland (media neutral cite)
Qd. R. = Queensland State Reports (1958-)
R. = Retties Session Cases, 4th Series (Scotland)
R. & I.T. = Rating and Income Tax Reports
R. (H.L.) = Retties Session Cases, 4th Series (House of Lords cases, Scotland)
R. (J.) = Retties Session Cases, 4th Series (Justiciary cases, Scotland)
R.A. = Rating Appeals
R.C.N. = Rating Case Notes
R.F.L. = Reports of Family Law (Canada)
R.I.C.S. = Royal Institution of Chartered Surveyors, Scottish Lands Valuation Appeal Reports
R.J.Q. B.R. = Rapports Judiciares de Quebec, Cour du Banc du Roi (1875-91)
R.L.R. = Road Law Reports
R.P.C. = Reports of Patent Cases
R.P.R. = Real Property Reports (Canada)
R.R.C. = Ryde's Rating Cases
R.T.R. = Road Traffic Reports
R.V.R. = Rating and Valuation Reporter
RICO Bus.Disp.Guide = RICO Business Disputes Guide (CCH)
Ram. = Ramanathan's Reports, Sri Lanka
Re. L.R. = Reinsurance Law Reports
Recueil = Recueil de la Jurisprudence de la Cour (ECJ)
Rep. Ch. = Reports of Cases in Chancery
Rep. L.R. = Reparation Law Reports (Scottish)
Rep. L.R. (Quantum) = Reparation Law Reports, Quantum Cases (Scottish)
Rep. t. Finch = Reports in Chancery tempore Finch

# TABLE OF ABBREVIATIONS

Ridge. t. Hard. = Ridgeway's King's Bench and Chancery Reports tempore Hardwicke
Rob. = Robinson's Scottish Appeal Cases, House of Lords
Rob. Ecc. = Robertson's Ecclesiastical Reports
Roll. Abr. = Rolle's Abridgment des Plusieurs Cases
Rolle = Rolle's King's Bench Reports
Rose = Rose's Bankrupty Cases
Russ. = Russell's Chancery Reports
Russ. & M. = Russell and Mylne's Chancery Reports
Russ. & Ry. = Russell and Ryan's Crown Cases Reserved
Russ. Cr. = Russell on Crime
Ry. & M. = Ryan and Moody's Nisi Prius Reports
S. = Shaw's Session Cases, 1st Series (Scotland)
S. (H.L.) = Shaw's Session Cases, 1st Series (House of Lords cases, Scotland)
S.A. = South African Law Reports
S.A. (A.D.) = South African Law Reports (Appellate Division)
S.A. (T.P.D.) = South African Law Reports (Transvaal Provincial Division)
S.A.C.R. = South African Criminal Law Reports
S.A.L.J. = South African Law Journal
S.A.S.R. = South Australian State Reports
S.C. = Session Cases (Scotland)
S.C. (H.L.) = Session Cases (House of Lords cases, Scotland)
S.C. (J.) = Session Cases (Justiciary 1907-16, Scotland)
S.C. (P.C.) = Session Cases (Privy Council Cases, Scotland)
S.C. (S.A.) = Supreme Court Reports (South Africa)
S.C. (U.K.S.C.) = Session Cases (Supreme Court cases, Scotland)
S.C.C.R. = Scottish Criminal Case Reports
S.C.C.R. (Supp.) = Scottish Criminal Case Reports Supplement
S.C.L. = Scottish Criminal Law
S.C.L.R. = Scottish Civil Law Reports
S.C.R. = Canada Law Reports, Supreme Court
S.C.R. = Supreme Court Reports (India)
S.Ct. = Supreme Court Reporter
S.E. = South Eastern Reporter (U.S.A.)
S.E.2d = South Eastern Reporter, 2nd Series (U.S.A.)
S.F.T.D. = Simon's First-tier Tax Decisions
S.J. = Solicitors Journal (Old)
S.J.L.B. = Solicitors Journal Law Brief
S.L.C.R. = Scottish Land Court Reports
S.L.C.R. App. = Scottish Land Court Reports (Appendix)
S.L.L.P. = Scottish Licensing Law and Practice
S.L.R. = Scottish Law Reporter (1865-1924)
S.L.T. = Scots Law Times
S.L.T. (Land Ct) = Scots Law Times (Land Court Reports)
S.L.T. (Land Ct.) = Scots Law Times (Land Ct)
S.L.T. (Lands Tr) = Scots Law Times (Lands Tribunal Reports)
S.L.T. (Lands Tr.) = Scots Law Times (Lands Tr)
S.L.T. (Lyon Ct) = Scots Law Times (Lyon Court Reports)
S.L.T. (Lyon Ct.) = Scots Law Times (Lyon Ct)
S.L.T. (Notes) = Scots Law Times (Notes)
S.L.T. (P.L.) = Scots Law Times (Poor Law Reports)
S.L.T. (Sh Ct) = Scots Law Times (Sheriff Court Reports)
S.L.T. (Sh Ct.) = Scots Law Times (Sheriff Court)
S.L.T. (Sh. Ct.) = Scots Law Times (Sheriff Court)
S.N. = Session Notes
S.R. (N.S.W.) = New South Wales State Reports (1901-)
S.S.L.R. = Straits Settlements Law Reports (Malaysia)
S.T.C. = Simons Tax Cases
S.T.C. (S.C.D.) = Simons Tax Cases: Special Commissioners Decisions
S.T.I. = Simon's Tax Intelligence
S.W.2d = South Western Reporter, 2nd Series (U.S.A.)
SCC = Supreme Court of Canada (media neutral cite)
SGCA = Court of Appeal of Singapore (media neutral cite)
SGHC = High Court of Singapore (media neutral cite)
Salk. = Salkeld's King's Bench Reports
Sask. R. = Saskatchewan Reports
Saund. = Saunder's King's Bench Reports
Sav. = Savile's Common Bench Reports
Say. = Sayer's King's Bench Reports
Sc. Jur. = Scottish Jurist
Sch. & L. = Schoales and Lefroy's Irish Chancery Reports
Scotsman = Scotsman
Scott N.R. = Scott's New Common Pleas Reports
Sel. Cas. Ch. = Select Cases in Chancery tempore King
Sess. Cas. K.B. = Session Cases touching settlements (England, 1710-48)
Sh. App. = Shaw's Scottish Appeal Cases, House of Lords
Sh. Ct. Rep. = Scottish Law Review, Sheriff Court Reports (1885-1963)
Shaw = Shaw's Justiciary Cases (Scotland)
Ship. Gaz. = Shipping Gazette
Show. K.B. = Shower's King's Bench Reports
Show. Parl. Cas. = Shower's Cases in Parliament
Sid. = Siderfin's King's Bench Reports
Sim. = Simon's Vice Chancellors Reports
Sim. & St. = Simon and Stuart's Chancery Reports
Sim. N.S. = Simon's Vice Chancellors Reports, New Series
Skin. = Skinner's King's Bench Reports
Sm. & G. = Smales and Giffard's Chancery Reports
Smith & B. = Smith and Batty's King's Bench Reports (Ireland, 1824-25)
Smith L.C. = Smith's Leading Cases on Various Branches of the Law
Sneed (TN) = Sneed's Tennessee Reports
So.2d = Southern Reporter, 2nd Series (U.S.A.)
Sol. = The Solicitor
Sp. Ecc. & Ad. = Spinks' Ecclesiastical and Admiralty Reports
Sp. Pri. Cas. = Spinks' Admiralty Prize Court Reports
St. Tr. = Cobbett and Howell's State Trials
St. Tr. (N.S.) = MacDonnell's State Trials, New Series
Stark. = Starkie's Nisi Prius Reports
Str. = Strange's King's Bench Reports
Sty. = Style's Modern Reports
Sw. = Swabey's Admiralty Reports
Sw. & Tr. = Swabey and Tristram's Reports
Swans. = Swanston's Chancery Reports
Swin. = Swinton's Justiciary Reports (Scotland)
Syme = Syme's Justiciary Reports (Scotland)
T. Jones = Sir Thomas Jones' King's Bench Reports
T. Raym. = Sir Thomas Raymond's King's Bench Reports
T.C. = Tax Cases
T.C.L.R. = Technology and Construction Law Reports
T.L.R. = Times Law Reports
T.R. = Taxation Reports (1939-81)
T.S. = Transvaal Supreme Court Reports (South Africa)
TCC = Tax Court of Canada (media neutral cite)
Taml. = Tamlyn's Chancery Reports
Tang. L.R. (R.) = Tanganyika Law Reports

# TABLE OF ABBREVIATIONS

Tas. R. = Tasmanian Reports (1979-)
Tas. S.R. = Tasmanian State Reports (1941-98)
Taunt. = Taunton's Common Pleas Reports
Tenn. = Tennessee Reports
Term Rep. = Durnford and East's Term Reports
Times = Times
Toth. = Tothill's Chancery Transactions
Tr. Consist. J. = Tristram's Consistory Judgments
Tr. L. = Trading Law
Tr. L.R. = Trading Law Reports
Traff. Cas. = Traffic Cases
Trin. L.R. = Trinidad Law Reports
Turn. & R. = Turner and Russell's Chancery Reports
Tyr. = Tyrwhitt's Exchequer Reports
U.C.R. = Upper Canada Reports
U.K.C.L.R. = UK Competition Law Reports
U.K.H.R.R. = United Kingdom Human Rights Reports
U.K.T. = UK Transcripts
U.S. = United States Supreme Court Reports
U.S.App.D.C. = United States District Court for the District of Columbia
U.S.P.Q. = United States Patent Quarterly (BNA)
U.S.P.Q.2d = United States Patent Quarterly 2nd (BNA)
USTC P = United States Tax Cases
UCC Rep.Serv. = Uniform Commercial Code Reporting Service (Callaghan's)
UKAIT = Asylum and Immigration Tribunal (media neutral cite)
UKHL = House of Lords
UKIAT = Immigration Appeal Tribunal
UKPC = Privy Council
UKPC D = Privy Council (Devolution)
UKSC = Supreme Court
USLW = United States Law Week
V. & B. = Vesey and Beames' Chancery Reports
V. & D.R. = Value Added Tax and Duties Reports
V.A.T.T.R. = Value Added Tax Tribunal Reports
V.L.R. = Victorian Law Reports (1875-1956)
V.R. = Victorian Reports (1957 -)
VSC = Supreme Court of Victoria (media neutral cite)
VSCA = Court of Appeal of Victoria (media neutral cite)
Va. = Virginia Reports
Vaugh. = Vaughan's Common Pleas Reports
Vent. = Ventris' King's Bench Reports
Vern. = Vernon's Chancery Reports
Ves. Jr. = Vesey Junior's Chancery Reports
Ves. Sen. = Vesey Senior's Chancery Reports
W. & S. = Wilson and Shaw's Scottish Appeal Cases, House of Lords
W. Jones = Sir William Jones' Reports
W. Rob. = W. Robinson's Admiralty Reports
W.A.C.A. = West African Court of Appeal Reports
W.A.L.R. = Western Australian Law Reports (1875-1956)
W.A.R. = Western Australian Reports (1957-)
W.I.R. = West Indian Reports
W.L.R. = Weekly Law Reports
W.N. = Weekly Notes (1866-1952)
W.N. (N.S.W.) = Weekly Notes, New South Wales
W.P.A.R. = War Pensions Appeal Reports
W.P.C. = Webster's Patent Cases
W.R. = Weekly Reporter (1853-1906)
W.T.L.R. = Wills & Trusts Law Reports
W.W.R. = Western Weekly Law Reports (Canada)
Wall. = Wallace's United States Supreme Court Reports
West H.L. = West's House of Lords Cases
West t. Hard. = West's Chancery Reports tempore Hardwicke
Wheat. = Wheaton's Supreme Court Reports (U.S.A.)
White = White's Justiciary Reports (Scotland)
Wight. = Wightwick's Exchequer Reports
Will. Woll. & Dav. = Willmore, Wollaston and Davison's Queen's Bench Reports
Willes = Willes' Common Pleas Reports
Wilm. = Wilmot's Notes and Opinions, King's Bench
Wils. Ch. = Wilson's Chancery Reports
Wils. Ex. = Wilson's Exchequer in Equity Reports
Wils. K.B. = Wilson's King's Bench Reports
Winch = Winch's Reports
Wm. Bl. = W. Blackstone's King's Bench Reports
Y. = Younge's Exchequer in Equity Reports
Y. & C. Ch. = Younge and Collier's Chancery Cases
Y. & C. Ex. = Younge and Collier's Exchequer Reports
Y. & J. = Younge and Jervis' Exchequer Reports
Y.B. = Year Books
Y.B. (R.S.) = Year Books, Rolls Series
Y.B. (S.S.) = Year Books, Selden Society
Yel. = Yelverton's King's Bench Reports
Yer. = Yerger's Tennessee Reports
Z.L.R. = Zimbabwe Law Reports

CURRENT LAW
PART I

CASE CITATOR 2014 (ENGLAND)

**The Current Law Case Citator comprises in a single table:**
**(i) Full case name of cases reported in 2014**
**(ii) The judicial history of any case of whatever date which has been considered, applied, overruled, etc., in 2014**
**Note: Figures appearing in bold type indicate the paragraph in the Current Law Year Book at which the case is digested**

'Spotting the Ball' Partnership v Revenue and Customs Commissioners see Revenue and Customs Commissioners v IFX Investment Co Ltd

1 garantovana as v European Commission (C-90/13 P); *sub nom* Garantovana as v European Commission (C-90/13) [2014] 5 C.M.L.R. 2, ECJ (2nd Chamber)
1 garantovana as v European Commission (T-392/09); *sub nom* 1 garantovana as v European Commission (T-392/09) [2014] 5 C.M.L.R. 6, GC (3rd Chamber)
1 garantovana as v European Commission (T-392/09) see 1 garantovana as v European Commission (T-392/09)
1 garantovana as v European Commission (T-42/13) [2014] 4 C.M.L.R. 16, GC (8th Chamber)
1,3 and 5 Argall Avenue, Re; *sub nom* Long v Value Properties Ltd [2014] EWHC 2981 (Ch); [2014] 5 Costs L.R. 915, Ch D ........ *Digested,* 14/**330**
16 & 18 Alexandra Road, Mitcham, Surrey, CR4 3LT, Re see Colquhoun v Harris
180 Irregular Divorces, Re see Rapisarda v Colladon
180 Irregular Divorces, Re see Rapisarda v Colladon
1st Credit (Finance) Ltd v Carr [2013] EWHC 2318 (Ch); [2013] B.P.I.R. 1012, Ch D ... *Digested,* 14/**1777**

288 Group Ltd v Revenue and Customs Commissioners; *joined cases* Advanced Direct Mail v Revenue and Customs Commissioners; Global Mailing Ltd v Revenue and Customs Commissioners; Hayloft Plants Ltd v Revenue and Customs Commissioners; Hyundai Motor UK Ltd v Revenue and Customs Commissioners [2013] UKFTT 659 (TC); [2014] S.F.T.D. 592; [2014] S.T.I. 382, FTT (Tax) ........ *Digested,* 14/**3096**: *Considered* 14/3053

4finance UAB v Valstybine vartotoju teisiu apsaugos tarnyba (C-515/12) [2014] Bus. L.R. 574; [2014] 3 C.M.L.R. 33, ECJ (2nd Chamber)

7 Strathray Gardens Ltd v Pointstar Shipping & Finance Ltd; *sub nom* Pointstar Shipping & Finance Ltd v 7 Strathray Gardens Ltd [2004] EWCA Civ 1669; [2005] H.L.R. 20; [2005] L. & T.R. 16; [2005] 1 E.G.L.R. 53; [2005] 07 E.G. 144; [2005] 1 E.G. 95 (C.S.); (2005) 102(6) L.S.G. 32; (2005) 149 S.J.L.B. 58; [2005] 1 P. & C.R. DG23; Times, January 10, 2005; Independent, January 19, 2005, CA (Civ Div) ........ *Digested,* 05/**2652**: *Applied* 14/2011
7722656 Canada Inc (formerly Swift Trade Inc) v Financial Services Authority [2013] EWCA Civ 1662; [2014] Lloyd's Rep. F.C. 207, CA (Civ Div); affirming [2013] Lloyd's Rep. F.C. 381, UT (Tax) ........ *Digested,* 14/**1453**

889457 Alberta Inc v Katanga Mining Ltd [2008] EWHC 2679 (Comm); [2009] 1 B.C.L.C. 189; [2009] I.L.Pr. 14, QBD (Comm) ........ *Digested,* 09/**606**: *Considered* 11/325: *Doubted* 14/514

93 Feet East Ltd v Tower Hamlets LBC [2013] EWHC 2716 (Admin); [2014] L.L.R. 146, QBD (Admin)

A v A [2007] EWHC 99 (Fam); [2007] 2 F.L.R. 467; [2009] W.T.L.R. 1; [2007] Fam. Law 791, Fam Div ........ *Digested,* 08/**1433**: *Applied* 11/1314, 14/1373: *Considered* 09/360, 11/1315, 14/2494: *Followed* 12/1319

A v A (Abducted Children: Interim Care Order) [2013] EWHC 3554 (Fam); [2014] 2 F.L.R. 365; [2014] Fam. Law 285, Fam Div ........ *Digested,* 14/**1265**

A v A (Child Abduction) (Habitual Residence) [1993] 2 F.L.R. 225; [1993] 1 F.C.R. 829, Fam Div ........ *Digested,* 94/**3153**: *Applied* 14/1383

A v A (Children) (Habitual Residence); *sub nom* ZA v NA (Abduction: Habitual Residence); A (Children) (Jurisdiction: Return of Child), Re [2013] UKSC 60; [2014] A.C. 1; [2013] 3 W.L.R. 761; [2014] 1 All E.R. 827; [2014] 1 F.L.R. 111; [2013] 3 F.C.R. 559; [2013] Fam. Law 1528; (2013) 157(36) S.J.L.B. 37; Times, October 15, 2013, SC; reversing in part [2012] EWCA Civ 1396; [2013] Fam. 232; [2013] 2 W.L.R. 1061; [2013] 1 F.L.R. 1041; [2012] 3 F.C.R. 421; [2013] Fam. Law 380; (2013) 157(35) S.J.L.B. 41, CA (Civ Div) ........ *Digested,* 13/**1250**: *Applied* 13/1234, 14/2806: *Considered* 14/1381: *Followed* 14/1307, 14/1378, 14/2186

A v A (Maintenance Pending Suit: Provision for Legal Costs) see A v A (Maintenance Pending Suit: Provision for Legal Fees)

A v A (Maintenance Pending Suit: Provision for Legal Fees); *sub nom* A v A (Maintenance Pending Suit: Provision for Legal Costs) [2001] 1 W.L.R. 605; [2001] 1 F.L.R. 377; [2001] 1 F.C.R. 226; [2001] Fam. Law 96; (2000) 97(44) L.S.G. 45; (2000) 144 S.J.L.B. 273; Times, November 14, 2000; Independent, December 11, 2000, Fam Div ........ *Digested,* 00/**2528**: *Applied* 03/1586: *Considered* 14/1364

A v A (Return Order on the Basis of British Nationality) [2013] EWHC 3298 (Fam); [2014] 2 F.L.R. 244; [2014] Fam. Law 157, Fam Div ........ *Digested,* 14/**1307**

A v B [2010] I.C.R. 849; [2010] I.R.L.R. 844, EAT ........ *Digested,* 10/**1068**: *Applied* 12/1086, 14/1137

A v B (Contact: Alternative Families); *sub nom* A v B (Lesbian Co-Parents: Role of Father) [2012] EWCA Civ 285; [2012] 1 W.L.R. 3456; [2012] 2 F.L.R. 607; [2012] 1 F.C.R. 510; [2012] Fam. Law 644; Times, June 13, 2012, CA (Civ Div); reversing [2011] EWHC 2290 (Fam); [2013] 1 F.L.R. 149; [2012] Fam. Law 127, Fam Div ........ *Digested,* 12/**1405**: *Considered* 14/1422

A v B (Lesbian Co-Parents: Role of Father) see A v B (Contact: Alternative Families)

A v B (Unfair Dismissal) [2003] I.R.L.R. 405, EAT *Applied* 10/1143, 13/1065: *Considered* 14/1052

A v B see Leach v Office of Communications

A v BBC see BBC, Re

A v Commissioner of Police of the Metropolis see J v Commissioner of Police of the Metropolis

A v Confiance Ltd see Onorati Settlement, Re

A v D see A (Termination of Parental Responsibility), Re

A v HM Treasury; *sub nom* HM Treasury v Ahmed; *joined cases* R. (on the application of Youssef) v HM Treasury; HM Treasury v Al-Ghabra [2010] UKSC 2; [2010] 2 A.C. 534; [2010] 2 W.L.R. 378; [2010] 4 All E.R. 745; [2010] H.R.L.R. 15; [2010] U.K.H.R.R. 204; [2010] Lloyd's Rep. F.C. 217; (2010) 154(4) S.J.L.B. 28; Times, January 29, 2010, SC; reversing [2008] EWCA Civ 1187; [2009] 3 W.L.R. 25; [2009] 2 All E.R. 747; [2009] Lloyd's Rep. F.C. 14; [2009] A.C.D. 16; (2008) 105(43) L.S.G. 19; Times, November 12, 2008, CA (Civ Div); reversing in part [2008] EWHC 869 (Admin); [2008] 3 All E.R. 361; [2008] 2 C.M.L.R. 44; [2008] A.C.D. 66; Times, May 5, 2008, QBD (Admin) ........ *Digested,* 10/**2031**: *Considered* 11/480, 13/2779, 13/66, 14/55: *Distinguished* 10/2030: *Followed* 11/760

A v Hungary; *joined case* B v Hungary [2013] EWHC 3132 (Admin); [2014] A.C.D. 33, DC

A v Independent News and Media Ltd see Independent News and Media Ltd v A

A v M; *sub nom* YLA v PM [2013] EWHC 4020 (COP); [2014] C.O.P.L.R. 114, CP ...... *Digested,* 14/**1398**

A v N (Committal: Refusal of Contact); *sub nom* N (A Minor), Re [1997] 1 F.L.R. 533; [1997] 2 F.C.R. 475; [1997] Fam. Law 233; (1997) 161 J.P.N. 698, CA (Civ Div) ........ *Digested,* 97/**416**: *Applied* 98/2420, 14/1323

A v Netherlands (4900/06) (2014) 59 E.H.R.R. 33, ECHR

A v Netherlands (Admissibility) (60538/13) (2014) 58 E.H.R.R. SE8, ECHR

A v P Council see M (Notification of Step-parent Adoption), Re

A v SA see A (Parental Order: Domicile), Re

A v Secretary of State for the Home Department see BBC, Re

A v Secretary of State for the Home Department see IA (Iran) v Secretary of State for the Home Department

A v VW see Ward (A Child), Re

A (Children) (Abduction: Children's Objections: Domestic Violence), Re; *sub nom* A (Children) (Abduction: Objections: Non-Return), Re [2013] EWCA Civ 1256; [2014] 1 F.L.R. 1433; [2014] Fam. Law 143, CA (Civ Div) ........ *Digested,* 14/**1379**

A (Children) (Abduction: Objections: Non-Return), Re see A (Children) (Abduction: Children's Objections: Domestic Violence), Re

A (Children) (Fact-finding Appeal), Re see A (Children) (Fact-finding Hearing: Non-accidental Injuries), Re

A (Children) (Fact-finding Hearing: Non-accidental Injuries), Re; *sub nom* A (Children) (Fact-finding Appeal), Re [2013] EWCA Civ 1026; [2014] 1 F.C.R. 24; [2013] Fam. Law 1363, CA (Civ Div) ........ *Digested,* 14/**1404**: *Applied* 14/1283

A (Children) (Jurisdiction: Return of Child), Re see A v A (Children) (Habitual Residence)

A (Children), Re; *sub nom* EH v X LBC [2010] EWCA Civ 344; [2010] 2 F.L.R. 661; [2010] 2 F.C.R. 106; [2010] Fam. Law 577; (2010) 107(17) L.S.G. 15; [2010] P.T.S.R. (C.S.) 23, CA (Civ Div) ........ *Digested,* 10/**1425**: *Considered* 10/1309, 12/1327, 14/1232

A (Medical Treatment: Male Sterilisation), Re see A (Mental Patient: Sterilisation), Re

A (Mental Patient: Sterilisation), Re; *sub nom* RB (Male Patient: Sterilisation), Re; R-B (A Patient) v Official Solicitor; A (Medical Treatment: Male Sterilisation), Re [2000] 1 F.L.R. 549; [2000] 1 F.C.R. 193; [2000] Lloyd's Rep. Med. 87; (2000) 53 B.M.L.R. 66; [2000] Fam. Law 242; (2000) 97(2) L.S.G. 30; Times, March 15, 2000, CA (Civ Div) ........ *Digested,* 00/**2780**: *Applied* 04/3648, 05/1794, 05/1848, 08/1437, 11/2220, 12/2279, 12/2282, 14/2187: *Considered* 04/1690, 09/3727, 13/2069

A (One Parent Killed by the Other), Re see A and B (Children), Re

A (Parental Order: Domicile), Re; *sub nom* A v SA [2013] EWHC 426 (Fam); [2014] 1 F.L.R. 169; [2013] Fam. Law 675, Fam Div

A (Placement Order: Imposition of Conditions on Adoption), Re [2013] EWCA Civ 1611; [2014] 1 W.L.R. 2139; [2014] 2 F.L.R. 351; [2014] 2 F.C.R. 123; [2014] Fam. Law 279, CA (Civ Div) ........ *Digested,* 14/**1256**

A (Prohibited Steps Order), Re see R (A Child) (Prohibited Steps Order), Re

A (Reporting of Judgment), Re [2014] Fam. Law 163, Sup Ct (FI)

A (Termination of Parental Responsibility), Re; *sub nom* A v D [2013] EWHC 2963 (Fam); [2014] 1 F.L.R. 1305; [2014] Fam. Law 34, Fam Div ........ *Digested,* 14/**1425**

A (Wardship and Supervision Orders), Re [2014] Fam. Law 144, Sup Ct (FI)

A and B (Children), Re; *sub nom* A (One Parent Killed by the Other), Re [2010] EWHC 3824 (Fam); [2011] 1 F.L.R. 783; [2011] Fam. Law 21, Fam Div ........ *Digested,* 11/**1337**: *Considered* 14/1239

A County Council v M; *sub nom* B (Children) (Foreign Adoption: Refusal of Recognition), Re [2013] EWHC 1501 (Fam); [2014] 1 F.L.R. 881; [2013] Fam. Law 933, Fam Div ........ *Digested,* 14/**1242**

A County Council v MS (2014) 17 C.C.L. Rep. 229; [2014] W.T.L.R. 931, CP

A Karuse AS v Politsei- ja Piirivalveamet (C-222/12) [2014] R.T.R. 18, ECJ (6th Chamber)

A Local Authority v A Mother; *sub nom* J (Children) (Placement of Children outside Family), Re [2013] EWHC 1820 (Fam); [2014] Fam. Law 15, Fam Div

A Local Authority v A Mother see HA (Capacity to Change), Re

A Local Authority v A Mother see T (A Child) (Care Proceedings: Request to Assume Jurisdiction), Re

A Local Authority v A Mother see X (Children) (Disclosure of Judgment to Police), Re

A Local Authority v A see A (Capacity: Refusal of Contraception), Re

A Local Authority v B see D (A Child) (Fact-finding Hearing), Re

A Local Authority v C (Removal of Baby at Birth) [2013] EWHC 4036 (Fam); [2014] 2 F.L.R. 612; [2014] Fam. Law 453, Fam Div (Swansea)

A Local Authority v DG [2013] EWHC 734 (Fam); [2014] 1 F.L.R. 1216; [2013] Fam. Law 789, Fam Div

A Local Authority v DG (Concurrent Care and Criminal Proceedings) [2014] EWHC 63 (Fam); [2014] 2 F.L.R. 713; [2014] 2 F.C.R. 1; [2014] Fam. Law 432, Fam Div .. *Digested,* 14/**1330**

A Local Authority v DS [2012] EWHC 1442 (Fam); [2012] 1 W.L.R. 3098; [2013] 1 F.L.R. 1429; [2012] Fam. Law 1078, Fam Div ........ *Digested,* 13/**1225**: *Considered* 14/2041

A Local Authority v ED [2013] EWHC 3069 (COP); (2013) 16 C.C.L. Rep. 597, CP ...... *Digested,* 14/**2173**

A Local Authority v H [2012] EWHC 49 (COP); [2012] 1 F.C.R. 590; (2012) 124 B.M.L.R. 98, CP ........ *Digested,* 12/**2285**: *Applied* 14/2175

A Local Authority v K [2013] EWHC 242 (COP); [2014] 1 F.C.R. 209; (2013) 130 B.M.L.R. 195, CP ........ *Digested,* 13/**2075**: *Considered* 13/2069
A Local Authority v MM see Local Authority X v M
A Local Authority v NB see Hertfordshire CC v B
A Local Authority v O (A Child); *sub nom* A Local Authority v S [2011] EWHC 3764 (Fam); [2014] 1 F.L.R. 1313; [2013] Fam. Law 21, Fam Div
A Local Authority v P; *sub nom* X (Children) (Payments from Patient's Estate for Children's Maintenance), Re; *joined case* A Local Authority v SA [2014] EWHC 87 (COP); [2014] 2 F.L.R. 1051; [2014] C.O.P.L.R. 364; [2014] Fam. Law 811, CP ........ *Digested,* 14/**1267**
A Local Authority v PB [2011] EWHC 502 (Fam), CP
*Applied* 14/2182
A Local Authority v S see A Local Authority v O (A Child)
A Local Authority v SA see A Local Authority v P
A Local Authority v SY [2013] EWHC 3485 (COP); [2014] C.O.P.L.R. 1; (2013) 16 C.C.L. Rep. 571, CP ........ *Digested,* 14/**2190**
A Local Authority v Trimega Laboratories Ltd see X Local Authority v Trimega Laboratories Ltd
A Local Authority v TZ [2013] EWHC 2322 (COP), CP
*Applied* 14/2175
A Local Authority v TZ [2014] EWHC 973 (COP); [2014] C.O.P.L.R. 159, CP ........ *Digested,* 14/**2174**
A Local Authority v W see W (Children) (Identification: Restrictions on Publication), Re
A Local Authority v X [2013] EWHC 3274 (Fam); [2014] 2 F.L.R. 123; [2014] Fam. Law 293, Fam Div (Birmingham) ........ *Digested,* 14/**1392**
A London Borough v G [2014] EWHC 485 (COP); [2014] C.O.P.L.R. 292, CP ........ *Digested,* 14/**2176**
A Ltd v B Ltd [2014] EWHC 1870 (Comm); [2014] 2 Lloyd's Rep. 393; [2014] 1 C.L.C. 958, QBD (Comm) ........ *Digested,* 14/**414**
A NHS Foundation Trust v X [2014] EWCOP 35; (2014) 140 B.M.L.R. 41, CP
A Trust, Re 16 I.T.E.L.R. 195, Sup Ct (Ber)
A&E Television Networks LLC v Discovery Communications Europe Ltd [2013] EWHC 109 (Ch); [2013] E.T.M.R. 32, Ch D
*Applied* 14/1915
A&N Frozen Foods v Alexander (Valuation Officer) [2014] R.V.R. 326, VT
A, Re see An NHS Trust v A
A-C (A Child), Re see A (A Child) (Fact-finding: Possible Perpetrators), Re
A-M v A-M (Divorce: Jurisdiction: Validity of Marriage) see M v M (Divorce: Jurisdiction: Validity of Marriage)
A/Wear UK Ltd (In Administration), Re; *sub nom* Bristol Alliance Nominee (No.1) Ltd v Bennett; Bennett v Bristol Alliance Nominee (No.1) Ltd [2013] EWCA Civ 1626; [2014] 1 E.G.L.R. 9; [2014] 1 P. & C.R. DG15, CA (Civ Div); reversing [2012] EWHC 2050 (Ch), Ch D
A2Dominion Housing Group Ltd v Hammersmith and Fulham LBC; *joined cases* Notting Hill Housing Trust v Kensington and Chelsea RLBC; Notting Hill Housing Trust v Ealing LBC [2014] R.V.R. 268, VT
AA v TT (Recognition and Enforcement) [2014] EWHC 3488 (Fam); [2014] Fam. Law 1668, Fam Div
AA (Compulsorily Detained Patient: Elective Caesarean), Re; *sub nom* AA (Mental Capacity: Enforced Caesarean), Re [2012] EWHC 4378 (COP); [2014] 2 F.L.R. 237; [2014] 1 F.C.R. 630; (2014) 137 B.M.L.R. 123; [2014] Fam. Law 283, CP . *Digested,* 14/**2188**
AA (Mental Capacity: Enforced Caesarean), Re see AA (Compulsorily Detained Patient: Elective Caesarean), Re
AA (Nigeria) v Secretary of State for the Home Department [2010] EWCA Civ 773; [2011] 1 W.L.R. 564; [2010] Imm. A.R. 704; [2011] I.N.L.R. 1; Times, July 13, 2010, CA (Civ Div) ........ *Digested,* 10/**1805**: *Applied* 14/1716: *Followed* 11/1757, 11/1770
AA (Somalia) v Entry Clearance Officer, Addis Ababa [2013] UKSC 81; [2014] 1 W.L.R. 43; [2014] 1 All E.R. 774; [2014] 1 F.C.R. 548; [2014] Imm. A.R. 540; [2014] I.N.L.R. 273, SC; affirming [2012] EWCA Civ 563; [2013] 1 W.L.R. 268; [2012] 3 All E.R. 893; [2012] 3 F.C.R. 96; [2012] Imm. A.R. 858; [2013] I.N.L.R. 85, CA (Civ Div) ........ *Digested,* 14/**1684**
AA (Somalia) v Secretary of State for the Home Department; *joined case* AH (Iran) v Secretary of State for the Home Department [2007] EWCA Civ 1040; [2008] Imm. A.R. 241; [2008] I.N.L.R. 1, CA (Civ Div) ........ *Digested,* 08/**2025**: *Applied* 07/926: *Considered* 09/1095, 14/1665: *Followed* 11/1757
AA and Sons Ltd v Slough BC [2014] EWHC 1127 (Admin); [2014] R.T.R. 29, QBD (Admin) ........ *Digested,* 14/**2567**

AAN v Secretary of State for the Home Department see AAN (Veil: Afghanistan)
AAN (Veil: Afghanistan); *sub nom* AAN v Secretary of State for the Home Department [2014] UKUT 102 (IAC); [2014] Imm. A.R. 756, UT (IAC) ................................ *Digested,* 14/**1693**
AB v A Chief Constable [2014] EWHC 1965 (QB); [2014] I.R.L.R. 700, QBD ............... *Digested,* 14/**1062**
AB v Barristers Benevolent Association Ltd [2011] EWHC 3413 (QB), QBD *Applied* 14/496
AB v BB [2013] EWHC 227 (Fam); [2014] 1 F.L.R. 178; [2013] Fam. Law 531, Fam Div ........................................................................................................ *Digested,* 14/**1320**
AB v BC (Adoption Application: Gateway Requirements); *sub nom* X (Adoption Application: Gateway Requirements), Re [2013] EWHC 689 (Fam); [2014] 1 F.L.R. 1281; [2013] Fam. Law 1518, Fam Div
AB v CB (Divorce and Maintenance: Discretion to Stay); *sub nom* M v M; AB v CB (Divorce: Jurisdiction) [2013] EWCA Civ 1255; [2014] Fam. 102; [2014] 2 W.L.R. 1033; [2014] 1 F.L.R. 1514; [2014] 2 F.C.R. 208; [2014] Fam. Law 286, CA (Civ Div); affirming [2012] EWHC 3841 (Fam); [2013] 2 F.L.R. 29; [2013] Fam. Law 384, Fam Div ........................................................................ *Digested,* 14/**1326**
AB v CB (Divorce: Jurisdiction) see AB v CB (Divorce and Maintenance: Discretion to Stay)
AB v CB (Financial Remedies: Variation of Trust) [2014] EWHC 2998 (Fam); [2014] Fam. Law 1670, Fam Div
AB v CD; *sub nom* JK v KC [2011] EWHC 1284 (Fam); [2014] 1 F.L.R. 1439; [2011] Fam. Law 1204, Fam Div
AB v CD Ltd [2013] EWHC 1376 (TCC); [2013] B.L.R. 435, QBD (TCC) ...................... *Digested,* 14/**844**
AB v CD see B v D
AB v CD see E (Assisted Reproduction: Parent), Re
AB v DE see C (A Child) (Parental Order), Re
AB v Duke of York's Royal Military School; *sub nom* AB v DYRMS – An Academy with Military Traditions [2014] UKUT 403 (AAC); [2014] E.L.R. 443, UT (AAC)
AB v DYRMS – An Academy with Military Traditions see AB v Duke of York's Royal Military School
AB v Ministry of Defence see B v Ministry of Defence
AB v Secretary of State for the Home Department see AB (Ahmadiyya Association UK: Letters: Pakistan), Re
AB (A Child) (Abduction: Art.15: Procedure and Evidence), Re; *sub nom* DR v MB [2014] EWHC 276 (Fam); [2014] Fam. Law 941, Fam Div
AB (A Firm) v Revenue and Customs Commissioners [2007] S.T.C. (S.C.D.) 99; [2007] S.T.I. 157, Sp Comm ................................................................ *Digested,* 07/**4056**: *Considered* 12/3269: *Followed* 14/2979
AB (Ahmadiyya Association UK: Letters: Pakistan), Re; *sub nom* AB v Secretary of State for the Home Department [2013] UKUT 511 (IAC); [2014] Imm. A.R. 177, UT (IAC) ........................................................................................................ *Digested,* 14/**1677**
AB (Morocco) v Secretary of State for the Home Department see Harrison v Secretary of State for the Home Department
AB (Revocation of Enduring Power of Attorney), Re; *sub nom* Public Guardian v MD [2014] EWCOP 12; [2014] W.T.L.R. 1303, CP .................................................. *Digested,* 14/**2165**
AB (Somalia) v Secretary of State for the Home Department see VW (Uganda) v Secretary of State for the Home Department
AB, Re [2014] C.O.P.L.R. 381; [2014] W.T.L.R. 1117, CP
Abani Trading Pte Ltd v BNP Paribas [2014] SGHC 111; [2014] 2 Lloyd's Rep. 617, HC (Sing)
ABB AB/Surge arrester (T607/10) [2014] E.P.O.R. 40, EPO (Technical Bd App)
ABB Ltd v Bam Nuttall Ltd [2013] EWHC 1983 (TCC); [2013] B.L.R. 529; 149 Con. L.R. 172; [2013] C.I.L.L. 3401, QBD (TCC) ........................................................ *Digested,* 14/**584**
Abbey Forwarding Ltd (In Liquidation) v Hone see Hone v Abbey Forwarding Ltd (In Liquidation)
Abbey Investments Ltd v London Development Agency [2010] UKUT 325 (LC); [2011] R.V.R. 18; [2011] J.P.L. 76, UT (Lands) ................................................... *Digested,* 11/**2674**: *Considered* 14/2361
Abbey National Building Society v Cann [1991] 1 A.C. 56; [1990] 2 W.L.R. 832; [1990] 1 All E.R. 1085; [1990] 2 F.L.R. 122; (1990) 22 H.L.R. 360; (1990) 60 P. & C.R. 278; (1990) 87(17) L.S.G. 32; (1990) 140 N.L.J. 477; Times, March 30, 1990, HL; affirming [1989] 2 F.L.R. 265; (1989) 57 P. & C.R. 381; [1989] Fam. Law 314; [1989] E.G. 34 (C.S.); Times, March 15, 1989, CA (Civ Div) ...................... *Digested,* 90/**707**: *Applied* 94/4028, 96/4953, 01/4867, 09/3168, 12/2734, 14/2505: *Considered* 93/2538, 96/5031, 97/4258, 04/3248, 10/2724: *Distinguished* 09/2208: *Followed* 90/706

Abbey National Plc v Customs and Excise Commissioners (C-408/98) [2001] 1 W.L.R. 769; [2001] S.T.C. 297; [2001] E.C.R. I-1361; [2001] 2 C.M.L.R. 28; [2001] All E.R. (EC) 385; [2001] C.E.C. 80; [2001] B.T.C. 5481; [2001] B.V.C. 581; [2001] S.T.I. 244; Times, March 13, 2001, ECJ (5th Chamber) .................................... *Digested,* 01/**5586**: *Applied* 05/4380, 09/4052, 09/4058, 12/3396: *Considered* 01/5585, 03/4555, 14/3056: *Followed* 05/4363

Abbey National Plc v Lee see Lloyds TSB General Insurance Holdings Ltd v Lloyds Bank Group Insurance Co Ltd

Abbeyfield Newcastle Upon Tyne Society Ltd v Newcastle City Council [2014] EWHC 2437 (Ch); (2014) 17 C.C.L. Rep. 430, Ch D

Abbeyland Ltd v Revenue and Customs Commissioners [2013] UKFTT 287 (TC); [2013] S.F.T.D. 1212; [2013] S.T.I. 2474, FTT (Tax) .......................................... *Digested,* 14/**2868**

Abbycars (West Horndon) Ltd v Ford UKEAT/0472/07/DA, EAT *Applied* 14/3500

ABC Ltd v M (Inspector of Taxes) see Barclays Mercantile Business Finance Ltd v Mawson (Inspector of Taxes)

Abdalla v Transport for London [2013] EWHC 3916 (QB); [2014] L.L.R. 241, QBD

Abdi v Secretary of State for the Home Department see R. (on the application of Lumba) v Secretary of State for the Home Department

Abdirahman v Leicester City Council see Abdirahman v Secretary of State for Work and Pensions

Abdirahman v Secretary of State for Work and Pensions; *joined cases* Abdirahman v Leicester City Council; Ullusow v Secretary of State for Work and Pensions [2007] EWCA Civ 657; [2008] 1 W.L.R. 254; [2007] 4 All E.R. 882; [2007] 3 C.M.L.R. 37; [2007] Eu. L.R. 814, CA (Civ Div) .................................................. *Digested,* 07/**3824**: *Applied* 10/3128, 11/1652: *Considered* 09/1802: *Followed* 09/3622, 14/1739

Abdul v DPP [2011] EWHC 247 (Admin); (2011) 175 J.P. 190; [2011] H.R.L.R. 16; [2011] Crim. L.R. 553; [2011] A.C.D. 45, DC ...................................................... *Digested,* 11/**687**: *Considered* 14/673

Abdullah v Shropshire CC see R. v Barnet LBC Ex p. Shah

Abdullahi v Bundesasylamt (C-394/12) [2014] 1 W.L.R. 1895; [2014] Imm. A.R. 727; [2014] I.N.L.R. 411, ECJ (Grand Chamber)

Abela v Baadarani [2013] UKSC 44; [2013] 1 W.L.R. 2043; [2013] 4 All E.R. 119; [2013] 2 C.L.C. 92; [2013] I.L.Pr. 40; Times, August 7, 2013, SC; reversing [2011] EWCA Civ 1571; [2012] C.P. Rep. 11; [2012] 1 C.L.C. 66, CA (Civ Div); reversing [2011] EWHC 116 (Ch), Ch D ............................................................ *Digested,* 13/**425**: *Applied* 14/1139, 14/478: *Considered* 12/471: *Followed* 14/128

Abercrombie v Aga Rangemaster Ltd [2013] EWCA Civ 1148; [2014] 1 All E.R. 1101; [2014] I.C.R. 209; [2013] I.R.L.R. 953, CA (Civ Div); reversing [2013] I.C.R. 213; [2013] I.R.L.R. 13, EAT ................................................................................ *Digested,* 14/**1090**

Aberdeen Asset Management Plc v Revenue and Customs Commissioners [2012] UKUT 43 (TCC); [2012] S.T.C. 650; [2012] B.T.C. 1514; [2012] S.T.I. 1376, UT (Tax); affirming [2010] UKFTT 524 (TC), FTT (Tax) .......................................... *Digested,* 12/**3301**: *Applied* 13/3095: *Distinguished* 14/2921: *Followed* 14/2872: *Reversed in part* 14/3807

Aberdeen Asset Management Plc v Revenue and Customs Commissioners [2013] CSIH 84; [2014] S.T.C. 438; 2014 S.C. 271; 2014 S.L.T. 54; [2013] B.T.C. 726; 2013 G.W.D. 40-773, IH (1 Div) ............................................................................ *Digested,* 14/**3807**

Aberdeen City Council v McNeill; *sub nom* McNeill v Aberdeen City Council [2013] CSIH 102; 2014 S.C. 335; 2014 S.L.T. 312; [2014] I.R.L.R. 113; 2014 G.W.D. 1-15, IH (Ex Div); reversing [2010] I.R.L.R. 374, EAT (SC) ............................... *Digested,* 14/**3506**: *Followed* 14/1022

Aberdeen City Council v Morrison 2014 S.L.T. (Lands Tr) 113; [2014] R.V.R. 334; 2014 G.W.D. 25-502, Lands Tr (Scot)

Abernethy v Anderson see Abernethy v Mott

Abernethy v Hay see Abernethy v Mott

Abernethy v Mott; *joined cases* Abernethy v Anderson; Abernethy v Hay [1974] I.C.R. 323; [1974] I.R.L.R. 213; 16 K.I.R. 277; (1974) 118 S.J. 294, CA (Civ Div); affirming [1973] I.R.L.R. 123, NIRC ..................................................................... *Digested,* 74/**1285**: *Applied* 78/1174, 85/1271, 14/1140: *Approved* 78/1177: *Considered* 85/1262, 86/1280, 94/2028, 95/2106, 97/2288: *Distinguished* 97/2290

Abertawe Bro Morgannwg University Health Board v Ferguson [2013] I.C.R. 1108; [2014] I.R.L.R. 14, EAT ................................................................................... *Digested,* 13/**1025**

Ablack v Inner London Education Authority see R. v Barnet LBC Ex p. Shah

ABN Amro Commercial Finance Plc v McGinn [2014] EWHC 1674 (Comm); [2014] 2 Lloyd's Rep. 333, QBD (Comm) ..................................................................... *Digested,* 14/**256**

ABN Amro Group NV v European Commission (T-319/11) [2014] 3 C.M.L.R. 34, GC (3rd Chamber)

Abnett v British Airways Plc; *joined case* Sidhu v British Airways Plc [1997] A.C. 430; [1997] 2 W.L.R. 26; [1997] 1 All E.R. 193; [1997] 2 Lloyd's Rep. 76; 1997 S.C. (H.L.) 26; 1997 S.L.T. 492; 1997 S.C.L.R. 114; (1997) 94(2) L.S.G. 26; (1996) 146 N.L.J. 1851; (1997) 141 S.J.L.B. 26; Times, December 13, 1996; Independent, December 17, 1996, HL; affirming [1995] P.I.Q.R. P427, CA (Civ Div) ........ *Digested,* 97/**220**: *Applied* 97/879, 01/949, 07/297: *Considered* 00/5164, 02/243, 04/375, 14/165: *Followed* 11/168, 12/178, 14/161

Abramova v Oxford Institute of Legal Practice [2011] EWHC 613 (QB); [2011] E.L.R. 385, QBD ........ *Digested,* 11/**2245**: *Considered* 14/916

Abu-Qulbain v Secretary of State for the Home Department see Huang v Secretary of State for the Home Department

Abuja International Hotels Ltd v Meridien SAS [2012] EWHC 87 (Comm); [2012] 1 Lloyd's Rep. 461, QBD (Comm) ........ *Digested,* 12/**114**: *Applied* 14/118

Abusabib v Taddese [2013] I.C.R. 603, EAT ........ *Digested,* 13/**1019**: *Considered* 14/1056

AC v DC (Financial Remedy: Effect of s.37 Avoidance Orders) [2012] EWHC 2032 (Fam); [2013] 2 F.L.R. 1483; [2013] W.T.L.R. 745; 15 I.T.E.L.R. 811; [2013] Fam. Law 666, Fam Div ........ *Digested,* 13/**1305**: *Applied* 14/1372

AC v Devon CC; *sub nom* Devon CC v TR; AC v TR [2013] EWCA Civ 418; [2014] R.T.R. 1; [2013] P.I.Q.R. P19, CA (Civ Div); reversing in part [2012] EWHC 796 (QB); [2012] R.T.R. 32, QBD ........ *Digested,* 13/**2511**

AC v Partnerships in Care Ltd [2012] UKUT 450 (AAC); [2013] M.H.L.R. 52, UT (AAC) ........ *Digested,* 14/**2167**

AC v TR see AC v Devon CC

AC Ward & Sons Ltd v Catlin (Five) Ltd [2009] EWCA Civ 1098; [2010] Lloyd's Rep. I.R. 301, CA (Civ Div); affirming 2008 Folio 106, QBD (Comm) ........ *Digested,* 10/**1916**: *Applied* 14/138

AC Yule & Son Ltd v Speedwell Roofing & Cladding Ltd [2007] EWHC 1360 (TCC); [2007] B.L.R. 499; [2007] C.I.L.L. 2489, QBD (TCC) ........ *Digested,* 08/**589**: *Applied* 14/585

Accenture Services Ltd v Revenue and Customs Commissioners; *joined case* Barclays Bank Plc v Revenue and Customs Commissioners [2009] EWHC 857 (Admin); [2009] S.T.C. 1503; [2009] B.T.C. 5430; [2009] B.V.C. 429; [2009] S.T.I. 1601, QBD (Admin) ........ *Digested,* 09/**4110**: *Applied* 14/2971

ACCG v MN [2013] EWHC 3859 (COP); [2014] C.O.P.L.R. 11, CP ........ *Digested,* 14/**2182**

ACES System Development v Lily (t/a Access International Services) [2013] SGCA 53; 152 Con. L.R. 178, CA (Sing)

ACI Adam BV v Stichting de Thuiskopie (C-435/12) [2014] E.C.D.R. 13, ECJ (4th Chamber)

ACO Industries Tabor sro v Odvolaci financni reditelstvi (C-80/13) see Strojirny Prostejov as v Odvolaci financni reditelstvi (C-53/13)

Acons v City of Westminster Council [2014] P.A.D. 23, Planning Inspector

Acornwood LLP v Revenue and Customs Commissioners [2014] UKFTT 416 (TC); [2014] S.F.T.D. 694, FTT (Tax) ........ *Digested,* 14/**2975**

Acre 1127 Ltd (In Liquidation) (formerly Castle Galleries Ltd) v De Montfort Fine Art Ltd [2011] EWCA Civ 87, CA (Civ Div) ........ *Applied* 14/119

Actavis Group hf v Eli Lilly & Co; *joined case* Medis ehf v Eli Lilly & Co [2013] EWCA Civ 517; [2013] R.P.C. 37, CA (Civ Div); affirming [2012] EWHC 3316 (Pat), Ch D (Patents Ct) ........ *Digested,* 14/**474**

Actavis Group PTC EHF v Sanofi (C-443/12) [2014] R.P.C. 20, ECJ (3rd Chamber)

Actavis UK Ltd v Eli Lilly & Co [2014] EWHC 1511 (Pat); [2014] 4 All E.R. 331; [2014] 2 All E.R. (Comm) 669, Ch D (Patents Ct) ........ *Digested,* 14/**1894**

Active Commercial Interiors Ltd v Cluttons LLP see Harrison v Technical Sign Co Ltd

Acturus Properties Ltd v Attorney General (2000-01) 3 I.T.E.L.R. 360, Royal Ct (Jer) .. *Digested,* 01/**1047**: *Considered* 14/2893

Adam v Johnson (Listing Officer) [2014] EWHC 1110 (Admin); [2014] R.V.R. 229, QBD (Admin)

Adamally (Section 47 Removal Decisions: Tribunal Procedures), Re; *sub nom* Secretary of State for the Home Department v Adamally [2012] UKUT 414 (IAC); [2013] Imm. A.R. 306, UT (IAC) ........ *Digested,* 13/**1632**: *Approved* 14/1699

Adams v Al Malik; *sub nom* Adams v Al Malik Carpets PVT Ltd [2003] EWHC 3232 (QB); [2014] 6 Costs L.R. 985, QBD

Adams v Al Malik Carpets PVT Ltd see Adams v Al Malik

Adams v Bracknell Forest BC; *sub nom* Bracknell Forest BC v Adams [2004] UKHL 29; [2005] 1 A.C. 76; [2004] 3 W.L.R. 89; [2004] 3 All E.R. 897; [2004] E.L.R. 459; [2005] P.I.Q.R. P2; (2004) 101(26) L.S.G. 28; (2004) 148 S.J.L.B. 761; Times, June 24, 2004, HL; reversing [2003] EWCA Civ 706; [2003] E.L.R. 409; (2003) 100(26) L.S.G. 39; (2003) 147 S.J.L.B. 599; Times, May 14, 2003; Independent, May 15, 2003, CA (Civ Div) ........ *Digested,* 04/**372**: *Applied* 05/438, 07/473, 07/474, 07/483, 14/419: *Considered* 07/475, 10/374: *Distinguished* 08/385: *Explained* 13/2203

Adams v Cape Industries Plc [1990] Ch. 433; [1990] 2 W.L.R. 657; [1991] 1 All E.R. 929; [1990] B.C.C. 786; [1990] B.C.L.C. 479, CA (Civ Div); affirming Times, June 23, 1988; Independent, June 21, 1988, Ch D ........ *Digested,* 90/**3684**: *Applied* 98/2212, 01/705, 09/2317, 10/1943, 12/459, 14/474: *Considered* 97/880, 10/3362: *Distinguished* 95/4014: *Followed* 96/1666

Adams v Mason Bullock (A Firm) [2004] EWHC 2910 (Ch); [2005] B.P.I.R. 241; (2005) 102(4) L.S.G. 30; Times, January 6, 2005, Ch D ........ *Digested,* 05/**2279**: *Applied* 14/1787: *Considered* 06/2333

Adamson v Paddico (267) Ltd see Paddico (267) Ltd v Kirklees Metropolitan Council

Adcock v Wilson [1969] 2 A.C. 326; [1968] 2 W.L.R. 914; [1968] 1 All E.R. 929; (1968) 132 J.P. 234; (1968) 112 S.J. 213, HL; affirming [1967] 2 Q.B. 683; [1967] 2 W.L.R. 1189; [1967] 1 All E.R. 1028; (1967) 131 J.P. 292; (1967) 111 S.J. 294, DC ........ *Digested,* 68/**1712**: *Applied* 14/3048: *Followed* 14/3048

Addey and Stanhope School v Vakante see Vakante v Addey and Stanhope School Governing Body

Adegbulugbe v Nursing and Midwifery Council [2013] EWHC 3301 (Admin); (2014) 135 B.M.L.R. 171, QBD (Admin) ........ *Digested,* 14/**392**

Adelphoi Ltd v DC Comics; *sub nom* Adelphoi Ltd's Trade Mark Applications (Nos 2521514 and 2492278) [2014] E.C.C. 11, App Person ........ *Digested,* 14/**1918**

Adelphoi Ltd's Trade Mark Applications (Nos 2521514 and 2492278) see Adelphoi Ltd v DC Comics

Adenfirst Ltd v Newham LBC [2014] P.A.D. 18, Planning Inspector

Adese v Coral Racing Ltd UKEAT/0760/04/CK, EAT *Applied* 14/1083

Adesina v Nursing and Midwifery Council; *sub nom* R. (on the application of Adesina) v Nursing and Midwifery Council; *joined case* Baines v Nursing and Midwifery Council [2013] EWCA Civ 818; [2013] 1 W.L.R. 3156; (2013) 133 B.M.L.R. 196; Times, July 22, 2013, CA (Civ Div); affirming [2012] EWHC 2615 (Admin), QBD (Admin) ........ *Digested,* 13/**1490**: *Followed* 14/392

Adjo v Secretary of State for the Home Department see Anwar v Secretary of State for the Home Department

Adler v Crown Prosecution Service [2013] EWHC 1968 (Admin); (2013) 177 J.P. 558; [2014] Crim. L.R. 224; [2014] A.C.D. 4, QBD (Admin) ........ *Digested,* 13/**681**

Adlington v ELS International Lawyers LLP (In Administration) [2014] 1 Costs L.R. 105, QBD (Birmingham) ........ *Digested,* 14/**460**

Admiralty Commissioners v Owners of the SS Chekiang; *sub nom* Chekiang, The; Chekiang, The [1926] A.C. 637; (1926) 25 Ll. L. Rep. 173, HL; reversing [1925] P. 80; (1925) 21 Ll. L. Rep. 179, CA; reversing (1924) 20 Ll. L. Rep. 260, PDAD *Applied* 68/1010, 90/1522, 11/858: *Considered* 69/890, 14/826: *Distinguished* 47-51/9563

Admiralty Commissioners v Owners of the SS Susquehanna [1926] A.C. 655; (1926) 25 Ll. L. Rep. 205; 42 T.L.R. 639; [1926] W.N. 200; 95 L.J. P. 128; 135 L.T. 456, HL; affirming [1925] P. 196; (1925) 22 Ll. L. Rep. 466, CA; affirming (1925) 21 Ll. L. Rep. 126, PDAD *Applied* 61/8286, 68/1010, 69/2905, 11/858: *Approved* 66/3231: *Considered* 14/826

Advanced Direct Mail v Revenue and Customs Commissioners see 288 Group Ltd v Revenue and Customs Commissioners

Advanced Liquid Feeds LLP v Itochu Europe Plc see Transition Feeds LLP (formerly known as Advanced Liquid Feeds LLP) v Itochu Europe Plc

Advent Computer Training Ltd, Re see Gould v Advent Computer Training Ltd

Aeroflot - Russian Airlines v Berezovsky; *sub nom* Joint Stock Co Aeroflot Russian Airlines v Berezovsky [2013] EWCA Civ 784; [2013] 2 Lloyd's Rep. 242; [2013] 2 C.L.C. 206, CA (Civ Div); reversing in part [2012] EWHC 1610 (Ch); [2013] 1 Lloyd's Rep. 345; (2012) 109(27) L.S.G. 20, Ch D ........ *Digested,* 13/**509**: *Followed* 14/136

Aeroports de Paris v Commission of the European Communities (T-128/98) [2000] E.C.R. II-3929; [2001] 4 C.M.L.R. 38, CFI (3rd Chamber) ........ *Digested,* 01/**761**: *Affirmed* 03/550: *Applied* 14/528

Aerospace Publishing Ltd v Thames Water Utilities Ltd [2007] EWCA Civ 3; [2007] Bus. L.R. 726; 110 Con. L.R. 1; [2007] 3 Costs L.R. 389; (2009) 25 Const. L.J. 121; [2007] C.I.L.L. 2429; (2007) 104(4) L.S.G. 32; (2007) 151 S.J.L.B. 123; [2007] N.P.C. 5; Times, January 22, 2007, CA (Civ Div); reversing in part [2005] EWHC 2987 (QB), QBD ........ *Digested,* 07/**1059**: *Applied* 09/467, 14/2359: *Considered* 08/893, 11/531: *Distinguished* 14/1825: *Followed* 14/2989

Aerts v Belgium (2000) 29 E.H.R.R. 50; 5 B.H.R.C. 382; (2000) 53 B.M.L.R. 79; [1998] H.R.C.D. 749, ECHR ........ *Digested,* 99/**3094**: *Considered* 07/2232, 11/4477, 12/1712, 14/2181: *Distinguished* 03/2118

AES Ust-Kamenogorsk Hydropower Plant LLP v Ust-Kamenogorsk Hydropower Plant JSC; *sub nom* Ust-Kamenogorsk Hydropower Plant JSC v AES Ust-Kamenogorsk Hydropower Plant LLP [2013] UKSC 35; [2013] 1 W.L.R. 1889; [2014] 1 All E.R. 335; [2014] 1 All E.R. (Comm) 1; [2013] Bus. L.R. 1357; [2013] 2 Lloyd's Rep. 281; [2013] 1 C.L.C. 1069, SC; affirming [2011] EWCA Civ 647; [2012] 1 W.L.R. 920; [2012] 1 All E.R. (Comm) 845; [2012] Bus. L.R. 330; [2011] 2 Lloyd's Rep. 233; [2011] 2 C.L.C. 51; [2011] Arb. L.R. 15; (2011) 108(25) L.S.G. 18, CA (Civ Div); affirming [2010] EWHC 772 (Comm); [2010] 2 All E.R. (Comm) 1033; [2010] 2 Lloyd's Rep. 493; [2010] 1 C.L.C. 519; [2010] C.I.L.L. 2857, QBD (Comm) ........ *Digested,* 13/**97**: *Applied* 14/301: *Considered* 11/125: *Followed* 14/113

African Consolidated Resources Plc v Revenue and Customs Commissioners [2014] UKFTT 580 (TC); [2014] S.T.I. 2255, FTT (Tax)

AGA Medical Corp v Occlutech (UK) Ltd [2014] EWHC 2506 (Pat); (2014) 140 B.M.L.R. 81, Ch D (Patents Ct)

Agarwala v Agarwala [2013] EWCA Civ 1763; [2014] 2 F.L.R. 1069; [2014] W.T.L.R. 373; [2014] Fam. Law 815, CA (Civ Div) ........ *Digested,* 14/**2492**

Agbenowossi-Koffi v Donvand Ltd (t/a Gullivers Travel Associates) [2014] EWCA Civ 855; [2014] I.C.R. D27, CA (Civ Div); affirming UKEAT/0337/12/DM, EAT

Ageas (UK) Ltd v Kwik-Fit (GB) Ltd [2014] EWHC 2178 (QB); [2014] Bus. L.R. 1338, QBD

Aggeliki Charis Compania Maritima SA v Pagnan SpA (The Angelic Grace) [1995] 1 Lloyd's Rep. 87, CA (Civ Div); affirming [1994] 1 Lloyd's Rep. 168, QBD (Comm) ........ *Digested,* 94/**4066**: *Applied* 98/239, 05/2357, 05/599, 12/312, 13/96, 14/301: *Considered* 97/880, 99/4441, 99/733, 99/745, 01/950, 05/625, 09/172, 11/468

Agricultural Sector (Wales) Bill, Re see Attorney General for England and Wales v Counsel General for Wales

Aguilar Quila v Secretary of State for the Home Department see R. (on the application of Aguilar Quila) v Secretary of State for the Home Department

Agulian v Cyganik see Cyganik v Agulian

AH v PH (Scandinavian Marriage Settlement) [2013] EWHC 3873 (Fam); [2014] 2 F.L.R. 251; [2014] Fam. Law 441, Fam Div

AH (Iran) v Secretary of State for the Home Department see AA (Somalia) v Secretary of State for the Home Department

AH Field (Holdings) Ltd v Revenue and Customs Commissioners [2012] UKFTT 104 (TC); 81 T.C. 1; [2012] S.T.I. 1461, FTT (Tax) ........ *Digested,* 12/**3261**

AHK v Secretary of State for the Home Department [2013] EWHC 1426 (Admin); [2014] Imm. A.R. 32, QBD (Admin) ........ *Digested,* 14/**1724**

Ahmad v Secret Garden (Cheshire) Ltd [2013] EWCA Civ 1005; [2013] 3 E.G.L.R. 42; [2014] 1 P. & C.R. DG3, CA (Civ Div) ........ *Digested,* 14/**1991**

Ahmad v Secretary of State for the Home Department [2014] EWCA Civ 988; [2014] 3 C.M.L.R. 45, CA (Civ Div) ........ *Digested,* 14/**1739**

Ahmad Hamad Algosaibi & Bros Co v Saad Investments Co Ltd 17 I.T.E.L.R. 349, Grand Ct (CI)

Ahmadi v Secretary of State for the Home Department see Ahmadi (S.47 Decision: Validity: Sapkota: Afghanistan), Re

Ahmadi (S.47 Decision: Validity: Sapkota: Afghanistan), Re; *sub nom* Secretary of State for the Home Department v Ahmadi; Ahmadi v Secretary of State for the Home Department [2013] EWCA Civ 512; [2014] 1 W.L.R. 401; [2013] 4 All E.R. 442; [2013] Imm. A.R. 1081; [2014] I.N.L.R. 117, CA (Civ Div); reversing in part [2012] UKUT 147 (IAC); [2012] Imm. A.R. 875, UT (IAC) ........................ *Digested,* 13/**1588**: *Considered* 14/1699: *Followed* 13/1632

Ahmadi-Assalemi v NCR Ltd see Akanu-Otu v Secretary of State for Justice

Ahmadpour v Turkey (12717/08) (2014) 59 E.H.R.R. 27, ECHR

Ahmed v Barking and Dagenham LBC [2014] P.A.D. 8, Planning Inspector

Ahmed v HM Treasury see Guardian News and Media Ltd, Re

Ahmed v Leicester City Council [2007] EWCA Civ 843; [2008] H.L.R. 6, CA (Civ Div) .. *Digested,* 08/**1850**: *Considered* 10/1693, 14/1593

Ahmed v Mustafa [2014] EWCA Civ 277; [2014] Fam. Law 790, CA (Civ Div)

Ahmed v Secretary of State for Communities and Local Government [2014] EWCA Civ 566; [2014] 2 E.G.L.R. 197, CA (Civ Div); affirming [2013] EWHC 2084 (Admin); [2014] 2 P. & C.R. 11; [2014] J.P.L. 257, QBD (Admin) ........................ *Digested,* 14/**2423**

Ahmed v Secretary of State for the Home Department [2002] UKIAT 439; [2002] Imm. A.R. 318; [2002] I.N.L.R. 345, IAT ........................ *Digested,* 03/**2240**: *Followed* 14/1726

Ahmed v Secretary of State for the Home Department see Ahmed (PBS: Admissible Evidence)

Ahmed v Secretary of State for the Home Department see Liu v Secretary of State for the Home Department

Ahmed v Secretary of State for the Home Department see Secretary of State for the Home Department v Pankina

Ahmed (PBS: Admissible Evidence); *sub nom* Ahmed v Secretary of State for the Home Department [2014] UKUT 365 (IAC); [2014] Imm. A.R. 1304, UT (IAC)

AIB Group (UK) Plc v Mark Redler & Co Solicitors [2014] UKSC 58; [2014] 3 W.L.R. 1367; (2014) 158(43) S.J.L.B. 49, SC; affirming [2013] EWCA Civ 45; [2013] P.N.L.R. 19; [2013] W.T.L.R. 1303; [2013] 8 E.G. 106 (C.S.); (2013) 157(7) S.J.L.B. 31, CA (Civ Div); reversing in part [2012] EWHC 35 (Ch); [2012] P.N.L.R. 16, Ch D (Birmingham) ........................ *Digested,* 13/**227**: *Followed* 13/1951, 14/2055

AIMS Asset Management v Kazakhstan Investment Fund Ltd Ch/2002/APP/0198, Ch D *Disapproved* 14/433

Ainslie v Sun Life Assurance Co of Canada (UK) Ltd (t/a Sun Life Financial of Canada) [2014] EWHC 453 (Ch); [2014] Pens. L.R. 211, Ch D ........................ *Digested,* 14/**2290**

Ainsworth v Carmody (Unreported, April 22, 2014), CC (Stockport) [*Bernard Pressman, Barrister, Lamb Chambers, Temple, London*] ........................ *Digested,* 14/**2308**

Aintree University Hospitals NHS Foundation Trust v James; *sub nom* James v Aintree University Hospitals NHS Foundation Trust [2013] UKSC 67; [2014] A.C. 591; [2013] 3 W.L.R. 1299; [2014] 1 All E.R. 573; [2014] 1 F.C.R. 153; (2013) 16 C.C.L. Rep. 554; [2014] Med. L.R. 1; (2014) 135 B.M.L.R. 1; (2013) 163(7583) N.L.J. 16; (2013) 157(43) S.J.L.B. 53; Times, November 19, 2013, SC; affirming [2013] EWCA Civ 65; [2013] 4 All E.R. 67; [2013] Med. L.R. 110; (2013) 131 B.M.L.R. 124; (2013) 157(10) S.J.L.B. 31; [2013] P.T.S.R. D22, CA (Civ Div); reversing [2012] EWHC 3524 (COP), CP ........................ *Digested,* 14/**1526**: *Applied* 14/2182: *Followed* 14/1527

Air France v Saks 470 U.S. 392, US Court *Applied* 01/5385, 03/231, 06/252, 14/152

Air Liquide Italia SpA v Ministero delle Infrastrutture e dei Trasporti (C-186/13) see API - Anonima Petroli Italiana SpA v Ministero delle Infrastrutture e dei Trasporti (C-184/13)

Airtours Holiday Transport Ltd (formerly My Travel Group) v Revenue and Customs Commissioners; *sub nom* Revenue and Customs Commissioners v Airtours Holiday Transport Ltd [2014] EWCA Civ 1033; [2014] B.V.C. 32; [2014] S.T.I. 2521, CA (Civ Div); affirming [2010] UKUT 404 (TCC); [2011] S.T.C. 239; [2010] B.V.C. 1587; [2010] S.T.I. 3248, UT (Tax); reversing [2009] UKFTT 256 (TC); [2010] B.V.C. 2117; [2010] S.T.I. 1479, FTT (Tax) ........................ *Digested,* 14/**3061**

Airways Pension Scheme, Re see Stevens v Bell

Aitken v Granada Television Ltd see Aitken v Preston

Aitken v Preston; *joined case* Aitken v Granada Television Ltd [1997] E.M.L.R. 415; Times, May 21, 1997, CA (Civ Div) ........................ *Digested,* 97/**2030**: *Applied* 03/441: *Considered* 14/838: *Followed* 10/837

AJ v JJ see J (Abduction: Children's Objections), Re

AJ Building and Plastering Ltd v Dalling see AJ Building and Plastering Ltd v Turner

AJ Building and Plastering Ltd v Munday see AJ Building and Plastering Ltd v Turner

AJ Building and Plastering Ltd v Turner; *joined cases* AJ Building and Plastering Ltd v Munday; AJ Building and Plastering Ltd v Dalling [2013] EWHC 484 (QB); [2013] Lloyd's Rep. I.R. 629, QBD (Merc) (Cardiff) .......... *Digested,* 14/**635**

AJA v Commissioner of Police of the Metropolis; *joined case* AKJ v Commissioner of Police of the Metropolis [2013] EWCA Civ 1342; [2014] 1 W.L.R. 285; [2014] 1 All E.R. 882, CA (Civ Div) .......... *Digested,* 14/**36**

Ajilore v Hackney LBC [2014] EWCA Civ 1273; [2014] H.L.R. 46, CA (Civ Div)

AK (Afghanistan) v Secretary of State for the Home Department see KA (Afghanistan) v Secretary of State for the Home Department

AK (Gift Application), Re; *sub nom* Lomas v AK [2014] C.O.P.L.R. 180, CP .......... *Digested,* 14/**2183**

AK Investment CJSC v Kyrgyz Mobil Tel Ltd; *joined cases* Fellowes International Holdings Ltd v Kyrgyz Mobil Tel Ltd; CP-Credit Prive SA v Kyrgyz Mobil Tel Ltd; Altimo Holdings and Investment Ltd v Kyrgyz Mobil Tel Ltd [2011] UKPC 7; [2012] 1 W.L.R. 1804; [2011] 4 All E.R. 1027; [2012] 1 All E.R. (Comm) 319; [2011] 1 C.L.C. 205, PC (IoM)
*Considered* 11/139, 12/120, 12/472, 12/557: *Followed* 14/477

Akanu-Otu v Secretary of State for Justice; *joined case* Ahmadi-Assalemi v NCR Ltd [2014] I.C.R. D13, EAT

Akbarali v Brent LBC see R. v Barnet LBC Ex p. Shah

Akerman-Livingstone v Aster Communities Ltd (formerly Flourish Homes Ltd); *sub nom* Aster Communities Ltd (formerly Flourish Homes Ltd) v Akerman-Livingstone [2014] EWCA Civ 1081; [2014] 1 W.L.R. 3980; [2014] H.L.R. 44, CA (Civ Div) .......... *Digested,* 14/**1997**

Akers v Samba Financial Group [2014] EWCA Civ 1516, CA (Civ Div); reversing [2014] EWHC 540 (Ch); 16 I.T.E.L.R. 808, Ch D (Companies Ct) .......... *Digested,* 14/**566**

Akewushola v Immigration Officer (Heathrow) see Akewushola v Secretary of State for the Home Department

Akewushola v Secretary of State for the Home Department; *sub nom* Akewushola v Immigration Officer (Heathrow) [2000] 1 W.L.R. 2295; [2000] 2 All E.R. 148; [1999] Imm. A.R. 594; [1999] I.N.L.R. 433; Times, November 3, 1999, CA (Civ Div) .......... *Digested,* 99/**3210**:
*Applied* 01/3600, 01/3663: *Followed* 00/3382, 14/1493

Akhtar v Ayoub [2013] EWHC 3840 (Fam); [2014] 2 F.L.R. 619; [2014] Fam. Law 465, Fam Div .......... *Digested,* 14/**1437**

Akhtar v Birmingham City Council [2011] EWCA Civ 383; [2011] H.L.R. 28; Times, April 22, 2011, CA (Civ Div) .......... *Digested,* 11/**1663**:
*Followed* 14/1593

Akhtar v Boland (Costs) [2014] EWCA Civ 943; [2014] C.P. Rep. 41, CA (Civ Div) .......... *Digested,* 14/**342**

Akinosun v Certification Officer [2013] I.R.L.R. 937, EAT .......... *Digested,* 14/**1126**

AKJ v Commissioner of Police of the Metropolis see AJA v Commissioner of Police of the Metropolis

AKJ v Commissioner of Police of the Metropolis see J v Commissioner of Police of the Metropolis

Ako v Rothschild Asset Management Ltd; *sub nom* Rothschild Asset Management Ltd v Ako [2002] EWCA Civ 236; [2002] 2 All E.R. 693; [2002] I.C.R. 899; [2002] I.R.L.R. 348; (2002) 99(17) L.S.G. 36; Times, April 2, 2002; Independent, March 6, 2002, CA (Civ Div); affirming EAT/103/00, EAT .......... *Digested,* 02/**1309**:
*Applied* 06/1318, 06/1357, 14/1083: *Considered* 08/1154, 14/387:
*Followed* 13/1309, 13/266

Aktas v Adepta; *joined case* Dixie v British Polythene Industries Plc [2010] EWCA Civ 1170; [2011] Q.B. 894; [2011] 2 W.L.R. 945; [2011] 2 All E.R. 536; [2011] C.P. Rep. 9; [2011] P.I.Q.R. P4, CA (Civ Div) .......... *Digested,* 11/**354**:
*Applied* 11/385: *Considered* 12/315, 14/421

Aktas v Germany (Admissibility) (56102/12) (2014) 58 E.H.R.R. SE3, ECHR

Akwiwu v Onu see Onu v Akwiwu

Akzo Nobel NV v Competition Commission [2013] CAT 17; [2013] Comp. A.R. 386, CAT .......... *Digested,* 14/**546**

Akzo Nobel NV v Competition Commission [2014] EWCA Civ 482; [2014] Bus. L.R. 802; [2014] U.K.C.L.R. 1201, CA (Civ Div); affirming [2013] CAT 13; [2013] Comp. A.R. 326, CAT .......... *Digested,* 14/**540**:
*Considered* 14/551

AKZO NOBEL/Silica dispersion (T2532/11) [2014] E.P.O.R. 20, EPO (Technical Bd App)

Al Shamsi v Terna Bahrain Holding Co WLL see Terna Bahrain Holding Co WLL v Al Shamsi

Al Tabith and Alanfushi, The [1995] 2 Lloyd's Rep. 336, CA (Civ Div); affirming [1993] 2 Lloyd's Rep. 214, QBD (Admlty) .......... *Digested,* 94/**4044**:
*Applied* 95/593, 10/477: *Considered* 10/476, 14/2715: *Followed* 10/3006

Al-Adsani v United Kingdom (35763/97) (2002) 34 E.H.R.R. 11; 12 B.H.R.C. 88; Times, November 26, 2001, ECHR ........ *Digested,* 02/**2467**: *Applied* 06/2644: *Considered* 03/2109, 04/3849, 06/2642, 14/1632

Al-Almeri v Kensington and Chelsea RLBC see Al-Ameri v Kensington and Chelsea RLBC

Al-Ameri v Kensington and Chelsea RLBC; *sub nom* Al-Almeri v Kensington and Chelsea RLBC; *joined case* Osmani v Harrow LBC [2004] UKHL 4; [2004] 2 A.C. 159; [2004] 2 W.L.R. 354; [2004] 1 All E.R. 1104; [2004] H.L.R. 20; [2004] B.L.G.R. 161; (2004) 101(9) L.S.G. 31; (2004) 154 N.L.J. 225; (2004) 148 S.J.L.B. 182; [2004] N.P.C. 12; Times, February 6, 2004, HL; affirming [2003] EWCA Civ 235; [2003] 1 W.L.R. 1289; [2003] 2 All E.R. 1; [2003] H.L.R. 52; [2003] B.L.G.R. 501; (2003) 147 S.J.L.B. 296; Times, March 19, 2003, CA (Civ Div) ........ *Digested,* 04/**1885**: *Distinguished* 14/1613

Al-Dulimi v Switzerland (5809/08) 36 B.H.R.C. 58, ECHR

Al-Fayed v Commissioner of Police of the Metropolis (No.1) [2002] EWCA Civ 780; (2002) 99(30) L.S.G. 39; (2002) 146 S.J.L.B. 153; Times, June 17, 2002, CA (Civ Div); reversing [2002] EWHC 562 (QB), QBD ........ *Digested,* 02/**421**: *Applied* 04/872: *Not followed* 14/294

Al-Ghabra v HM Treasury see Guardian News and Media Ltd, Re

Al-Hilli (Reporting Restrictions), Re; *sub nom* Surrey CC v Al-Hilli [2013] EWHC 2190 (Fam); [2014] 1 F.L.R. 403; [2013] Fam. Law 1364, Fam Div ........ *Digested,* 14/**1279**

Al-Hilli (Summary of Final Judgment), Re; *sub nom* Surrey CC v Al-Hilli [2013] EWHC 2299 (Fam); [2014] 1 F.L.R. 428; [2013] Fam. Law 1366, Fam Div ........ *Digested,* 14/**1280**

Al-Jedda v Secretary of State for the Home Department; *sub nom* Secretary of State for the Home Department v Al-Jedda [2013] UKSC 62; [2014] A.C. 253; [2013] 3 W.L.R. 1006; [2014] 1 All E.R. 356; [2014] H.R.L.R. 2; [2014] Imm. A.R. 229; [2014] I.N.L.R. 131; (2013) 157(39) S.J.L.B. 37, SC; affirming [2012] EWCA Civ 358, CA (Civ Div) ........ *Digested,* 13/**1584**

Al-Khawaja v United Kingdom (26766/05); *joined case* Tahery v United Kingdom (22228/06) [2012] 2 Costs L.O. 139; (2012) 54 E.H.R.R. 23; 32 B.H.R.C. 1; [2012] Crim. L.R. 375; Times, December 22, 2011, ECHR (Grand Chamber) .... *Digested,* 12/**657**: *Applied* 12/653: *Considered* 13/600, 14/287

Al-Malki v Reyes; *sub nom* Reyes v Al-Malki [2014] I.C.R. 135; [2013] I.R.L.R. 929, EAT ........ *Digested,* 14/**1056**

Al-Rawi v Security Service [2011] UKSC 34; [2012] 1 A.C. 531; [2011] 3 W.L.R. 388; [2012] 1 All E.R. 1; [2011] U.K.H.R.R. 931; (2011) 108(30) L.S.G. 23; (2011) 155(28) S.J.L.B. 31; Times, July 15, 2011, SC; affirming [2010] EWCA Civ 482; [2010] 3 W.L.R. 1069; [2010] 4 All E.R. 559; [2010] C.P. Rep. 37; [2010] U.K.H.R.R. 728; (2010) 107(20) L.S.G. 19; [2010] N.P.C. 51; Times, May 7, 2010, CA (Civ Div); reversing [2009] EWHC 2959 (QB); (2009) 159 N.L.J. 1668; Times, November 24, 2009, QBD ........ *Digested,* 11/**261**: *Applied* 11/262, 13/247: *Cited* 14/1724: *Considered* 14/441, 14/48, 14/545: *Followed* 12/812, 14/1664

Al-Sabah v Grupo Torras SA see Grupo Torras SA v Al-Sabah (No.5)

Al-Sirri v Secretary of State for the Home Department; *joined case* DD (Afghanistan) v Secretary of State for the Home Department [2012] UKSC 54; [2013] 1 A.C. 745; [2012] 3 W.L.R. 1263; [2013] 1 All E.R. 1267; 34 B.H.R.C. 69; [2013] Imm. A.R. 330; [2013] I.N.L.R. 665; Times, December 19, 2012, SC; affirming [2009] EWCA Civ 222; [2009] Imm. A.R. 624; [2009] I.N.L.R. 586; 3 A.L.R. Int'l 829, CA (Civ Div) ........ *Digested,* 13/**1638**: *Considered* 14/700

Al-Skeini v United Kingdom (55721/07) (2011) 53 E.H.R.R. 18; 30 B.H.R.C. 561; [2011] Inquest L.R. 73; Times, July 13, 2011, ECHR (Grand Chamber) ........ *Digested,* 11/**1696**: *Applied* 13/121, 13/1551, 13/1929, 14/2044

Alacakanat v General Medical Council [2013] EWHC 1866 (Admin); [2014] 1 C.M.L.R. 5, QBD (Admin) ........ *Digested,* 14/**1498**

Aladeselu v Secretary of State for the Home Department; *sub nom* Secretary of State for the Home Department v Aladeselu; Aladeselu (2006 Regs: Reg 8: Nigeria), Re [2013] EWCA Civ 144; [2013] Imm. A.R. 780; [2014] I.N.L.R. 85, CA (Civ Div); affirming [2011] UKUT 253 (IAC); [2011] Imm. A.R. 765; [2012] I.N.L.R. 20, UT (IAC) ........ *Digested,* 14/**1740**: *Applied* 14/1732

Aladeselu (2006 Regs: Reg 8: Nigeria), Re see Aladeselu v Secretary of State for the Home Department

Alam v Secretary of State for the Home Department; *joined cases* Eghan v Secretary of State for the Home Department; Anwar v Secretary of State for the Home Department [2012] EWCA Civ 960; [2012] Imm. A.R. 974, CA (Civ Div) ............ *Digested,* 13/**1619**: *Affirmed* 14/1718: *Followed* 14/1711

Alam v Secretary of State for the Home Department see Patel v Secretary of State for the Home Department

Alarape v Secretary of State for the Home Department (C-529/11) [2013] 1 W.L.R. 2883; [2013] 3 C.M.L.R. 38; [2014] All E.R. (EC) 470; [2013] Imm. A.R. 752; [2013] I.N.L.R. 542, ECJ (2nd Chamber) ............ *Digested,* 14/**1736**

Albany Trustee Co Ltd v Jeandin 16 I.T.E.L.R. 28, Royal Ct (Gue) ............ *Digested,* 14/**374**

Albion Water Ltd v Dwr Cymru Cyfyngedig [2013] CAT 16; [2013] Comp. A.R. 377; [2013] 6 Costs L.O. 947, CAT ............ *Digested,* 14/**344**

Aldi GmbH & Co KG v Office for Harmonisation in the Internal Market (Trade Marks and Designs) (OHIM) (T-505/11) [2014] E.T.M.R. 8, GC (2nd Chamber)

Aldi Stores Ltd v WSP Group Plc [2007] EWCA Civ 1260; [2008] 1 W.L.R. 748; [2008] C.P. Rep. 10; [2008] B.L.R. 1; 115 Con. L.R. 49; [2008] P.N.L.R. 14; (2008) 24 Const. L.J. 334; [2008] C.I.L.L. 2549; (2007) 104(48) L.S.G. 24; [2007] N.P.C. 128; Times, December 4, 2007, CA (Civ Div); reversing [2007] EWHC 55 (TCC); [2007] B.L.R. 113, QBD (TCC) ............ *Digested,* 07/**346**: *Applied* 08/271, 14/2993: *Considered* 09/976

Aldone S v Royaume Uni (Unreported, December 14, 1948), Sad Najwyzszy (PL) *Considered* 14/1056

Aldrich v Cooper 32 E.R. 402; (1803) 8 Ves. Jr. 382, Ct of Chancery *Applied* 14/1205: *Explained* 11/1249

Aldridge v Wright [1929] 2 K.B. 117, CA; affirming [1929] 1 K.B. 381, KBD *Applied* 47-51/3227, 14/2509

Alekseev v Russia (1873/2009) 37 B.H.R.C. 275, UN HRC

Alemo-Herron v Parkwood Leisure Ltd (C-426/11) [2014] 1 C.M.L.R. 21; [2014] All E.R. (EC) 400; [2014] C.E.C. 575; [2013] I.C.R. 1116; [2013] I.R.L.R. 744; Times, October 2, 2013, ECJ (3rd Chamber) ............ *Digested,* 13/**1058**: *Considered* 14/1128

Alexander & Law Ltd v Coveside (21BPR) Ltd [2013] EWHC 3949 (TCC); 152 Con. L.R. 163, QBD (TCC) ............ *Digested,* 14/**581**

Alexandros T, The see Starlight Shipping Co v Allianz Marine & Aviation Versicherungs AG

Alford v West Bromwich Building Society see Investors Compensation Scheme Ltd v West Bromwich Building Society (No.1)

Alghussein Establishment v Eton College [1988] 1 W.L.R. 587; [1991] 1 All E.R. 267; [1988] E.G. 69 (C.S.); (1988) 132 S.J. 750, HL; affirming Times, February 16, 1987, CA (Civ Div); affirming (Unreported, July 9, 1986), HC ............ *Digested,* 91/**506**: *Applied* 92/2204, 93/552, 14/411: *Considered* 91/2226, 91/2635, 93/497, 03/2733, 09/1649: *Distinguished* 12/593: *Referred to* 90/1943

Ali v Ali [2013] EWHC 1233 (QB); [2013] 5 Costs L.O. 676; [2014] R.T.R. 6, QBD ....... *Digested,* 13/**306**

Ali v Birmingham City Council; *sub nom* Birmingham City Council v Ali; *joined cases* R. (on the application of Aweys) v Birmingham City Council; Moran v Manchester City Council; Ibrahim v Birmingham City Council; Tomlinson v Birmingham City Council [2010] UKSC 8; [2010] 2 A.C. 39; [2010] 2 W.L.R. 471; [2010] 2 All E.R. 175; [2010] P.T.S.R. 524; [2010] H.R.L.R. 18; [2010] U.K.H.R.R. 417; [2010] H.L.R. 22; [2010] B.L.G.R. 401; (2010) 154(7) S.J.L.B. 37; Times, February 19, 2010, SC; affirming [2008] EWCA Civ 1228; [2009] 2 All E.R. 501; [2009] U.K.H.R.R. 1; [2009] H.L.R. 23; [2009] B.L.G.R. 1; [2008] N.P.C. 119; [2009] P.T.S.R. (C.S.) 11, CA (Civ Div) ............ *Digested,* 10/**1694**: *Considered* 09/2652, 10/3180, 12/1625, 14/2181

Ali v Entry Clearance Officer see Mahad (Ethiopia) v Entry Clearance Officer

Ali v Newham LBC see Newham LBC v Ali

Ali v Secretary of State for the Home Department see Secretary of State for the Home Department v Pankina

Alk-Abello Ltd v Meridian Medical Technologies [2010] EWPCC 14; [2011] F.S.R. 13, PCC ............ *Digested,* 11/**399**: *Considered* 12/1957, 14/493

All Projects & Developments NV v Vlaamse Regering (C-203/11) see Libert v Gouvernement Flamand (C-197/11)

Allan v Wandsworth LBC [2014] Eq. L.R. 30, EAT ............ *Digested,* 14/**1042**

Allanz Marine and Aviation Vericherungs AG v Imperial Marine Co see Starlight Shipping Co v Allianz Marine & Aviation Versicherungs AG

Allbutt v Ministry of Defence see Smith v Ministry of Defence

Allcard v Skinner (1887) 36 Ch. D. 145, CA
*Applied* 52/1485, 70/1145, 70/1706, 73/419, 74/1691, 82/285, 85/396, 87/456, 01/4880, 02/4314, 05/3401, 08/3096, 14/1965: *Approved* 53/1532: *Considered* 60/1802, 85/1588, 89/1829, 05/4291, 10/2750: *Distinguished* 77/1207: *Followed* 97/4270: *Referred to* 75/112.u

Allen v Financial Services Authority FS/2012/0019, UT (Tax)
*Applied* 14/2247

Allen v Hounga; *joined case* Hounga v Allen [2014] UKSC 47; [2014] 1 W.L.R. 2889; [2014] 4 All E.R. 595; [2014] I.C.R. 847; [2014] I.R.L.R. 811; [2014] H.R.L.R. 23; [2014] Eq. L.R. 559; Times, August 6, 2014, SC; reversing [2012] EWCA Civ 609; [2012] I.R.L.R. 685; [2012] Eq. L.R. 679, CA (Civ Div); reversing [2011] Eq. L.R. 569, EAT ........ *Digested,* 14/**2994**: *Distinguished* 14/1119

Allen v Morrisons Facilities Services Ltd [2014] I.C.R. 792; [2014] I.R.L.R. 514, EAT ... *Digested,* 14/**1129**

Allen v Unigate Dairies Ltd see Ridehalgh v Horsefield

Allen v United Kingdom (25424/09) 36 B.H.R.C. 1; Times, July 30, 2013, ECHR (Grand Chamber) ........ *Digested,* 14/**1630**

Allen (Valuation Officer) v Bassetlaw DC see Allen (Valuation Officer) v Mansfield DC

Allen (Valuation Officer) v Mansfield DC; *joined case* Allen (Valuation Officer) v Bassetlaw DC [2008] R.A. 338, Lands Tr ........ *Digested,* 09/**2679**: *Considered* 14/2129

Alleyn Court RTM Co Ltd v Abou-Hamdan [2012] UKUT 74 (LC), UT (Lands)
*Applied* 14/2011

Alliance One International Inc. v European Commission (C-679/11); *sub nom* Spanish Raw Tabacco Cartel, Re [2014] 4 C.M.L.R. 8, ECJ (9th Chamber)

Allied Maples Group Ltd v Simmons & Simmons [1995] 1 W.L.R. 1602; [1995] 4 All E.R. 907; [1996] C.L.C. 153; 46 Con. L.R. 134; [1955-95] P.N.L.R. 701; (1995) 145 N.L.J. 1646; [1995] N.P.C. 83; (1995) 70 P. & C.R. D14, CA (Civ Div) ........ *Digested,* 96/**4489**: *Applied* 97/3832, 98/1447, 98/3604, 00/4266, 00/4276, 03/3015, 03/946, 05/2880, 05/3419, 06/1026, 07/1316, 10/2286, 10/461, 10/827, 11/2266, 13/487: *Considered* 96/4482, 96/4505, 97/3839, 97/3903, 00/4264, 02/1318, 06/2900, 08/3446, 09/430, 10/832, 13/2094: *Distinguished* 03/3121, 04/913: *Followed* 05/2877, 10/2291, 14/2214: *Not applied* 01/537: *Referred to* 97/3917

Allnutt v Allnutt see Allnutt v Wilding

Allnutt v Wilding; *sub nom* Allnutt v Allnutt; Strain (Deceased), Re [2007] EWCA Civ 412; [2007] B.T.C. 8003; [2007] W.T.L.R. 941; (2006-07) 9 I.T.E.L.R. 806, CA (Civ Div); affirming [2006] EWHC 1905 (Ch); [2006] B.T.C. 8040; [2006] W.T.L.R. 1317; (2006-07) 9 I.T.E.L.R. 381; (2006) 150 S.J.L.B. 1057, Ch D ...... *Digested,* 07/**4247**: *Applied* 11/3502: *Followed* 14/2831, 14/3029

Almer Beheer BV v Van den Dungen Vastgoed BV (C-441/12) [2014] Bus. L.R. 1276, ECJ (2nd Chamber)

Almos Agrarkulkereskedelmi Kft v Nemzeti Ado- es Vamhivatal Kozep-magyarorszagi Regionalis Ado Foigazgatosaga (C-337/13) [2014] B.V.C. 26; [2014] S.T.I. 1949, ECJ (7th Chamber)

Alokpa v Ministre du Travail, de l'Emploi et de l'Immigration (C-86/12) [2014] I.N.L.R. 145, ECJ (2nd Chamber)

Alpha Rocks Solicitors v Alade [2014] EWHC 3606 (Ch); [2014] 6 Costs L.R. 1039, Ch D

Alpha Sim Communications Ltd v Caz Distribution Services Ltd [2014] EWHC 207 (Ch); [2014] S.T.I. 743, Ch D

Alphasteel Ltd (In Liquidation) v Shirkhani [2013] EWCA Civ 1272; [2014] C.P. Rep. 1; [2014] C.I.L.L. 3433, CA (Civ Div) ........ *Digested,* 14/**381**

Alpstream AG v PK Airfinance Sarl [2013] EWHC 2370 (Comm); [2014] 1 All E.R. (Comm) 441, QBD (Comm) ........ *Digested,* 14/**278**

Alstom SA v European Commission (C-253/11 P) see Areva SA v European Commission (C-247/11 P)

Alstom Transport v Eurostar International Ltd [2010] EWHC 2747 (Ch); [2011] Eu. L.R. 229, Ch D (Companies Ct) ........ *Digested,* 11/**2638**: *Applied* 11/2629, 14/2477

Alstom Transport v Tilson [2010] EWCA Civ 1308; [2011] I.R.L.R. 169, CA (Civ Div); affirming UKEAT/0358/09/CEA, EAT ........ *Digested,* 11/**1073**: *Followed* 14/1064

Alternative A5 Alliance's Application for Judicial Review , Re [2013] NIQB 30; [2014] N.I. 96, QBD (NI)

Alternative Power Solution Ltd v Central Electricity Board [2014] UKPC 31; [2014] 4 All E.R. 882; [2014] 2 All E.R. (Comm) 1096, PC (Mau)

Altimo Holdings and Investment Ltd v Kyrgyz Mobil Tel Ltd see AK Investment CJSC v Kyrgyz Mobil Tel Ltd

Altomart Ltd v Salford Estates (No.2) Ltd [2014] EWCA Civ 1408; [2014] 6 Costs L.R. 1013; Times, December 9, 2014, CA (Civ Div)
Aluminium Industrie Vaassen BV v Romalpa Aluminium [1976] 1 W.L.R. 676; [1976] 2 All E.R. 552; [1976] 1 Lloyd's Rep. 443; (1976) 120 S.J. 95, CA (Civ Div); affirming (1975) 119 S.J. 318, Ch D ........ *Digested,* 76/**2474**: *Applied* 78/2639, 09/2187: *Considered* 83/3338, 84/3115, 14/2586: *Distinguished* 79/2389, 79/2390, 84/3113, 87/3325
Alvarez SA v European Commission (C-36/12 P) see Armando Alvarez SA v European Commission (C-36/12 P)
AM v Examining Magistrates Court No. 4 Murcia (Spain) see AM v Spain
AM v Spain; *sub nom* AM v Examining Magistrates Court No. 4 Murcia (Spain) [2014] EWHC 1113 (Admin); [2014] A.C.D. 111, QBD (Admin)
AM v SS (Legal Services Order) [2013] EWHC 4380 (Fam); [2014] Fam. Law 1242, Fam Div
AM (Ethiopia) v Entry Clearance Officer see Mahad (Ethiopia) v Entry Clearance Officer
AM (Pakistan) v Secretary of State for the Home Department see SA (Pakistan) v Secretary of State for the Home Department
Amadeus Trading Ltd, Re Times, April 1, 1997, Ch D ........ *Digested,* 97/**3100**: *Considered* 14/1788
Amalgamated Investment & Property Co Ltd, Re [1985] Ch. 349; [1984] 3 W.L.R. 1101; [1984] 3 All E.R. 272; (1984) 1 B.C.C. 99104; [1985] F.L.R. 11; (1985) 82 L.S.G. 276; (1984) 128 S.J. 798, Ch D ........ *Digested,* 84/**327**: *Considered* 14/1751
Amatori v Telecom Italia SpA (C-458/12) [2014] I.R.L.R. 400, ECJ
Amazon.com International Sales Inc v Austro-Mechana Gesellschaft zur Wahrnehmung mechanisch-musikalischer Urheberrechte Gesellschaft mbH (C-521/11) [2014] 1 C.M.L.R. 11; [2014] C.E.C. 18; [2013] E.C.D.R. 12, ECJ (2nd Chamber)
American Cyanamid Co v Ethicon Ltd (No.1) [1975] A.C. 396; [1975] 2 W.L.R. 316; [1975] 1 All E.R. 504; [1975] F.S.R. 101; [1975] R.P.C. 513; (1975) 119 S.J. 136, HL; reversing [1974] F.S.R. 312, CA (Civ Div) ........ *Digested,* 75/**2640**: *Applied* 75/2453, 75/445, 76/2155, 76/2156, 76/2157, 76/2806, 76/317, 77/1097, 77/2307, 77/2346, 77/375, 77/885, 78/239.u, 81/2164, 83/2987, 84/2644, 84/3529, 84/3553, 84/3554, 85/1791, 85/2054, 85/2058, 85/3478, 87/1296, 87/3023, 87/3037, 88/2656, 89/1729, 91/3463, 91/4030, 92/4143, 93/1734, 93/2356, 93/3264, 93/3285, 93/3799, 96/3816, 96/791, 97/4888, 98/3471, 98/3511, 99/686, 01/567, 10/1055, 10/3791, 10/488: *Considered* 76/276, 76/395u, 77/118.u, 77/413, 77/558u, 78/141, 78/238u, 78/861, 79/1656, 79/2201, 79/2716, 80/1354, 80/2152, 80/384.u, 81/1614, 81/30.u, 81/434u, 82/3280, 83/2969, 83/2973, 83/3605, 83/3796, 84/1903, 84/420, 85/1881, 86/2646, 87/2768, 87/3039, 88/1250, 88/2146, 88/2871, 89/1408, 89/1468, 89/3481, 89/3688, 90/3709, 91/2885, 91/4032, 92/2359, 92/4141, 92/4422, 93/3262, 93/391, 94/3046, 94/3702, 94/624, 96/2709, 96/3631, 96/4566, 97/4882, 97/631, 98/437, 99/5082, 01/2462, 01/570, 01/772, 09/2338: *Distinguished* 76/2160, 78/219, 87/3027, 91/2886, 93/2470, 03/2941: *Explained* 84/2656: *Followed* 91/2694, 92/4134, 97/3873, 97/868, 98/3445, 14/113, 14/2477: *Not followed* 77/2213: *Referred to* 75/323.u, 75/380.u, 75/381.u, 76/400.u, 76/402.u, 76/404.u, 93/2425
American Express Europe Ltd v Adamson see Olympia & York Canary Wharf Ltd (No.1), Re
American Express Marketing & Development Corp v Office for Harmonisation in the Internal Market (Trade Marks and Designs) (OHIM) (T-102/11) [2014] E.T.M.R. 33, GC (9th Chamber)
American Leisure Group Ltd v Garrard [2014] EWHC 2101 (Ch); [2014] 1 W.L.R. 4102, Ch D
American Overseas Marine Corp v Golar Commodities Ltd (The LNG Gemini) [2014] EWHC 1347 (Comm); [2014] 2 Lloyd's Rep. 113, QBD (Comm) ........ *Digested,* 14/**2712**
Americhem Europe Ltd v Rakem Ltd [2014] EWHC 1881 (TCC); 155 Con. L.R. 80; [2014] 4 Costs L.R. 682, QBD (TCC) ........ *Digested,* 14/**352**
Amey v Peter Symonds College [2013] EWHC 2788 (QB); [2014] I.R.L.R. 206, QBD .. *Digested,* 14/**1124**
AMF International v Magnet Bowling [1968] 1 W.L.R. 1028; [1968] 2 All E.R. 789; 66 L.G.R. 706; (1968) 112 S.J. 522, QBD ........ *Digested,* 68/**2647**: *Applied* 73/407, 14/599: *Considered* 82/501u
AMGEN INC/Apoptosis (T501/09) [2014] E.P.O.R. 24, EPO (Technical Bd App)
Amicus Horizon Ltd v Brand see Amicus Horizon Ltd v Mabbott's Estate
Amicus Horizon Ltd v Mabbott's Estate; *sub nom* Amicus Horizon Ltd v Brand [2012] EWCA Civ 895; [2013] 3 F.C.R. 47; [2012] H.L.R. 42, CA (Civ Div) ........ *Digested,* 13/**1868**: *Applied* 14/2822

Amlin Corporate Member Ltd v Oriental Assurance Corp [2014] EWCA Civ 1135; [2014] 2 Lloyd's Rep. 561; [2014] Lloyd's Rep. I.R. 645; (2014) 158(33) S.J.L.B. 41, CA (Civ Div); affirming [2013] EWHC 2380 (Comm); [2014] 1 All E.R. (Comm) 415; [2013] 2 Lloyd's Rep. 523; [2013] Lloyd's Rep. I.R. 644, QBD (Comm) ........ *Digested,* 14/**1858**

Amministrazione dell'Economia e delle Finanze v Fallimento Olimpiclub Srl (C-2/08) [2009] E.C.R. I-7501; [2010] B.V.C. 1019, ECJ (2nd Chamber) *Applied* 14/3057

AMN Group Ltd v Gilcomston North Ltd see ANM Group Ltd v Gilcomston North Ltd

AMOCO/Terephthalic acid (T971/92) [2014] E.P.O.R. 11, EPO (Technical Bd App)

Ampurius Nu Homes Holdings Ltd v Telford Homes (Creekside) Ltd; *sub nom* Telford Homes (Creekside) Ltd v Ampurius Nu Homes Holdings Ltd [2013] EWCA Civ 577; [2013] 4 All E.R. 377; [2013] B.L.R. 400; 148 Con. L.R. 1; [2013] 23 E.G. 76 (C.S.), CA (Civ Div); reversing [2012] EWHC 1820 (Ch); [2012] B.L.R. 387; 144 Con. L.R. 72, Ch D ........ *Digested,* 13/**533**: *Applied* 14/623: *Followed* 14/596

Amri v Revenue and Customs Commissioners [2014] UKFTT 317 (TC); [2014] S.T.I. 2117, FTT (Tax)

AMT Futures Ltd v Marzillier, Dr Meier & Dr Guntner Rechtsanwaltsgesellschaft mbH; *sub nom* Marzillier, Dr Meier & Dr Guntner Rechtsanwaltsgesellschaft mbH v AMT Futures Ltd [2014] EWHC 1085 (Comm); [2014] 2 Lloyd's Rep. 349; [2014] 1 C.L.C. 531; [2014] C.T.L.C. 190; (2014) 158(19) S.J.L.B. 37, QBD (Comm) ........ *Digested,* 14/**556**

An NHS Foundation Hospital v P see P (A Child), Re

An NHS Foundation Trust v A; *sub nom* A (A Child), Re [2014] EWHC 920 (Fam); (2014) 139 B.M.L.R. 165; [2014] Fam. Law 968, Fam Div

An NHS Foundation Trust v AB [2014] EWHC 1031 (Fam); [2014] Fam. Law 969, Fam Div

An NHS Foundation Trust v R [2013] EWHC 2340 (Fam); [2014] 2 F.L.R. 955; [2014] Fam. Law 294, Fam Div

An NHS Trust v A; *sub nom* A, Re [2013] EWHC 2442 (COP); [2014] Fam. 161; [2014] 2 W.L.R. 607; [2013] Med. L.R. 561; (2014) 136 B.M.L.R. 115, CP ........ *Digested,* 14/**2187**

An NHS Trust v A [2014] EWHC 1445 (Fam); [2014] Fam. Law 1229, Fam Div

An NHS Trust v L [2013] EWHC 4313 (Fam); (2014) 137 B.M.L.R. 141, Fam Div

Anakaa v Firstsource Solutions Ltd [2014] NICA 57; [2014] I.R.L.R. 941, CA (NI)

Anam v Secretary of State for the Home Department see R. (on the application of Anam) v Secretary of State for the Home Department

ANCC-Coop - Associazione Nazionale Cooperative di Consumatori v Ministero delle Infrastrutture e dei Trasporti (C-185/13) see API - Anonima Petroli Italiana SpA v Ministero delle Infrastrutture e dei Trasporti (C-184/13)

Anchor Brewhouse Developments v Jaggard see Marcel v Commissioner of Police of the Metropolis

Anderson v Jarvis Hotels Plc UKEATS/0062/05/RN, EAT (SC) *Applied* 14/1091, 14/1092: *Considered* 11/1100

Andreae v Selfridge & Co Ltd [1938] Ch. 1; [1937] 3 All E.R. 255, CA; reversing in part [1936] 2 All E.R. 1413, Ch D *Applied* 53/2812: *Considered* 62/2774, 00/4293, 14/2219: *Distinguished* 98/4041

Andreou v Lord Chancellor's Department [2002] EWCA Civ 1192; [2002] I.R.L.R. 728, CA (Civ Div); reversing EAT/36/01, EAT/37/01, EAT ........ *Digested,* 03/**1259**: *Considered* 12/1085, 14/1082: *Followed* 14/399

Andrew v Barclays Bank Plc; *joined case* Carroll v Egg Banking Plc [2012] C.T.L.C. 115, QBD (Manchester) ........ *Digested,* 13/**1364**: *Applied* 14/296

Andrews v SBJ Benefit Consultants Ltd [2010] EWHC 2875 (Ch); [2011] Bus. L.R. 1608; [2011] P.N.L.R. 29, Ch D ........ *Digested,* 11/**55**: *Approved* 14/1449: *Not followed* 13/2080

Angel v New Possibilities NHS Trust see Rhys-Harper v Relaxion Group Plc

Angiotech Pharmaceuticals Inc v Conor Medsystems Inc see Conor Medsystems Inc v Angiotech Pharmaceuticals Inc

Angiotech Pharmaceuticals Inc's Patent (No.706376) see Conor Medsystems Inc v Angiotech Pharmaceuticals Inc

Anglo Eastern Trust Ltd v Kermanshahchi (Costs) (No.1); *sub nom* Anglo Eastern Trust Ltd v Kermanshahgi (Security for Costs); Anglo Eastern Trust Ltd v Kermanshahghi [2002] EWHC 1702 (Ch), Ch D *Applied* 13/369: *Considered* 14/404

Anglo Eastern Trust Ltd v Kermanshahghi see Anglo Eastern Trust Ltd v Kermanshahchi (Costs) (No.1)

Anglo Eastern Trust Ltd v Kermanshahgi (Security for Costs) see Anglo Eastern Trust Ltd v Kermanshahchi (Costs) (No.1)

Angove Pty Ltd v Bailey see D&D Wines International Ltd (In Liquidation), Re

Animal Defenders International v United Kingdom (48876/08) [2013] E.M.L.R. 28; (2013) 57 E.H.R.R. 21; 34 B.H.R.C. 137; (2013) 163(7564) N.L.J. 20; Times, April 25, 2013, ECHR (Grand Chamber) ........ *Digested,* 14/**1628**: *Followed* 14/2152

ANM Group Ltd v Gilcomston North Ltd; *sub nom* AMN Group Ltd v Gilcomston North Ltd [2008] CSOH 90; 2008 S.L.T. 835; 2009 S.C.L.R. 1; [2008] B.L.R. 481; 2008 Rep. L.R. 130; 2008 G.W.D. 27-429, OH ........ *Digested,* 09/**5157**: *Doubted* 14/2470

Annova Ltd v Revenue and Customs Commissioners [2014] UKUT 28 (TCC); [2014] S.T.C. 1617; [2014] B.V.C. 505; [2014] S.T.I. 689, UT (Tax); affirming [2011] UKFTT 742 (TC), FTT (Tax) ........ *Digested,* 14/**3068**

Anoliefo v Secretary of State for the Home Department see Anoliefo (Permission to Appeal), Re

Anoliefo (Permission to Appeal), Re; *sub nom* Anoliefo v Secretary of State for the Home Department [2013] UKUT 345 (IAC); [2013] Imm. A.R. 1130, UT (IAC) ... *Digested,* 14/**1674**

Anonymi Viotechniki kai Emporiki Etairia Kataskevis Konservon - Palirria Souliotis AE v European Commission (T-380/11) [2014] All E.R. (EC) 708, GC (5th Chamber)

Ansari v Knowles [2013] EWCA Civ 1448; [2014] C.P. Rep. 9, CA (Civ Div); affirming [2012] EWHC 3137 (QB), QBD ........ *Digested,* 14/**835**

Anstruther Gough Calthorpe v McOscar; *sub nom* Calthorpe v Mcoscar [1924] 1 K.B. 716, CA; reversing [1923] 2 K.B. 573, KBD
*Applied* 47-51/5413, 57/1929, 64/2094, 05/5467, 14/1971: *Considered* 63/1958: *Followed* 13/1874

Ansul BV v Ajax Brandbeveiliging BV (C-40/01) [2005] Ch. 97; [2004] 3 W.L.R. 1048; [2003] E.C.R. I-2439; [2005] 2 C.M.L.R. 36; [2003] E.T.M.R. 85; [2003] R.P.C. 40; (2005) 28(4) I.P.D. 28022, ECJ ........ *Digested,* 04/**2386**: *Applied* 04/2416, 05/2540, 05/2582, 06/2553, 08/2388, 09/2428, 09/2447, 09/2448, 10/2013, 11/2005: *Considered* 03/2635: *Followed* 07/2676, 14/1930, 14/1931

Antonelli v Wade Gery Farr (A Firm) see Ridehalgh v Horsefield

Antonio Gramsci Shipping Corp v Lembergs see Antonio Gramsci Shipping Corp v Recoletos Ltd

Antonio Gramsci Shipping Corp v Recoletos Ltd; *sub nom* Antonio Gramsci Shipping Corp v Lembergs [2013] EWCA Civ 730; [2013] 4 All E.R. 157; [2013] 2 All E.R. (Comm) 781; [2014] Bus. L.R. 239; [2013] 2 Lloyd's Rep. 295; [2014] 1 B.C.L.C. 581; [2013] 2 C.L.C. 44; [2013] I.L.Pr. 36, CA (Civ Div); affirming [2012] EWHC 1887 (Comm); [2012] 2 Lloyd's Rep. 365; [2012] I.L.Pr. 36, QBD (Comm) ........ *Digested,* 13/**362**

Antonissen v Council of the European Union (C-393/96 P (R)) [1997] E.C.R. I-441; [1997] 1 C.M.L.R. 783, ECJ
*Considered* 14/1733

Anwar v Secretary of State for the Home Department; *joined case* Adjo v Secretary of State for the Home Department [2010] EWCA Civ 1275; [2011] 1 W.L.R. 2552; [2011] Imm. A.R. 314; [2011] I.N.L.R. 111; Times, November 25, 2010, CA (Civ Div) ........ *Digested,* 11/**1755**: *Considered* 13/1612, 14/1698

Anwar v Secretary of State for the Home Department see Alam v Secretary of State for the Home Department

Anwar v Secretary of State for the Home Department see Patel v Secretary of State for the Home Department

Aodhcon LLP v Bridgeco Ltd [2014] EWHC 535 (Ch); [2014] 2 All E.R. (Comm) 928; [2014] 2 B.C.L.C. 237, Ch D ........ *Digested,* 14/**277**

AOOT Kalmneft v Glencore International AG see Kalmneft v Glencore International AG

AP v First Tier Tribunal [2011] UKUT 368 (AAC), UT (AAC)
*Approved* 14/53

AP Racing Ltd v Alcon Components Ltd [2014] EWCA Civ 40; [2014] R.P.C. 27, CA (Civ Div); reversing [2013] EWPCC 3, PCC

Apcoa Parking (UK) Ltd, Re [2014] EWHC 997 (Ch); [2014] 4 All E.R. 150; [2014] 2 All E.R. (Comm) 1074; [2014] Bus. L.R. 1358; [2014] B.C.C. 538; [2014] 2 B.C.L.C. 285, Ch D ........ *Digested,* 14/**1820**

Apcoa Parking Holdings GmbH, Re [2014] EWHC 1867 (Ch); [2014] B.C.C. 538, Ch D

Apex Global Management Ltd v Fi Call Ltd; *sub nom* Prince Abdulaziz Bin Mishal Bin Abdulaziz Al Saud v Apex Global Management Ltd [2013] EWCA Civ 642; [2014] 1 W.L.R. 492; [2013] 4 All E.R. 216; [2014] 1 B.C.L.C. 523, CA (Civ Div); affirming [2013] EWHC 587 (Ch), Ch D ........ *Digested,* 13/**1858**

Apex Global Management Ltd v Fi Call Ltd [2013] EWHC 1652 (Ch); [2014] B.C.C. 286, Ch D ........ *Digested,* 14/**524**

Apex Global Management Ltd v Fi Call Ltd see Prince Abdulaziz v Apex Global Management Ltd

API - Anonima Petroli Italiana SpA v Ministero delle Infrastrutture e dei Trasporti (C-184/13); *joined cases* Confetra - Confederazione Generale Italiana dei Trasporti e della Logistica v Ministero delle Infrastrutture e dei Trasporti (C-187/13); Air Liquide Italia SpA v Ministero delle Infrastrutture e dei Trasporti (C-186/13); ANCC-Coop - Associazione Nazionale Cooperative di Consumatori v Ministero delle Infrastrutture e dei Trasporti (C-185/13) [2014] 5 C.M.L.R. 21, ECJ (5th Chamber)

APN Business Consultants Ltd v Revenue and Customs Commissioners [2014] UKFTT 905 (TC); [2014] S.T.I. 2983, FTT (Tax)

Apollo Engineering Ltd v James Scott Ltd [2013] UKSC 37; 2013 S.C. (U.K.S.C.) 286; 2014 S.L.T. 32; 2013 G.W.D. 21-409; Times, August 6, 2013, SC; no effect [2012] CSIH 88; 2012 G.W.D. 40-777, IH (Ex Div) ........ *Digested,* 13/**3540**

Apollo Fuels Ltd v Revenue and Customs Commissioners; *sub nom* Revenue and Customs Commissioners v Apollo Fuels Ltd [2014] UKUT 95 (TCC); [2014] B.T.C. 510; [2014] S.T.I. 875, UT (Tax); affirming [2013] UKFTT 350 (TC), FTT (Tax) ........ *Digested,* 14/**2911**

Apple and Pear Development Council v Customs and Excise Commissioners (102/86) [1988] 2 All E.R. 922; [1988] S.T.C. 221; [1988] E.C.R. 1443; [1988] 2 C.M.L.R. 394; Times, March 11, 1988, ECJ (6th Chamber) ........ *Digested,* 88/**1572**: *Applied* 90/4626, 91/3667, 91/5666, 92/4545, 92/4552, 93/4091, 93/4093, 94/4606, 00/5326, 08/4029, 08/4038, 11/3568, 12/3397, 12/3426, 14/3085: *Considered* 98/6219, 09/4075, 13/3226: *Distinguished* 89/3745, 97/5006: *Referred to* 95/5095

Apple Corps Ltd v Apple Computer Inc [2004] EWHC 768 (Ch); [2004] 2 C.L.C. 720; [2004] I.L.Pr. 34, Ch D ........ *Digested,* 04/**556**: *Applied* 14/477

Apple Inc v Crowther (B 2 063 322) [2014] E.T.M.R. 53, OHIM (Opposition Div)

Apple Inc v Deutsches Patent- und Markenamt (C-421/13) [2014] Bus. L.R. 962; [2014] E.T.M.R. 48, ECJ (3rd Chamber)

Apple Inc v HTC Corp see HTC Europe Co Ltd v Apple Inc

Appleby Corporate Services (BVI) Ltd v Citco Trustees (BVI) Ltd 17 I.T.E.L.R. 413, HC (BVI)

Application for Information about a Trust, Re 16 I.T.E.L.R. 955, CA (Ber); affirming 16 I.T.E.L.R. 85, Sup Ct (Ber)

Aprile Srl v Amministrazione delle Finanze dello Stato (C-228/96) [2000] 1 W.L.R. 126; [1998] E.C.R. I-7141, ECJ ........ *Digested,* 00/**2345**: *Applied* 00/2406: *Considered* 14/2885: *Distinguished* 11/3519

AQ (Pakistan) v Secretary of State for the Home Department [2011] EWCA Civ 833; [2011] Imm. A.R. 832; [2012] I.N.L.R. 33, CA (Civ Div) ........ *Digested,* 12/**1757**: *Considered* 12/1766, 14/1713

AR (Afghanistan) v Secretary of State for the Home Department see KA (Afghanistan) v Secretary of State for the Home Department

Arada v Windle see Windle v Secretary of State for Justice

Aramis, The [1989] 1 Lloyd's Rep. 213; Financial Times, November 22, 1988, CA (Civ Div); reversing [1987] 2 Lloyd's Rep. 58, QBD (Admlty) ........ *Digested,* 90/**4057**: *Applied* 06/1315, 07/1347, 11/1073: *Followed* 14/1064

ARB International Ltd v Baillie [2013] EWHC 2060 (Comm); [2013] 2 C.L.C. 255; [2014] Lloyd's Rep. I.R. 10, QBD (Comm) ........ *Digested,* 14/**1839**

Arbuckle Smith & Co Ltd v Greenock Corp; *sub nom* Greenock Corp v Arbuckle Smith & Co Ltd [1960] A.C. 813; [1960] 2 W.L.R. 435; [1960] 1 All E.R. 568; 1960 S.C. (H.L.) 49; 1960 S.L.T. 123; (1960) 124 J.P. 251; 58 L.G.R. 155; 6 R.R.C. 95; 53 R. & I.T. 182; (1960) 104 S.J. 207, HL; reversing 1958 S.C. 615; 1960 S.L.T. 49; 1959 S.L.T. (Notes) 56, IH (2 Div) ........ *Digested,* 60/**2677**: *Applied* 77/2468, 78/270, 08/2927, 14/2141: *Considered* 82/2655, 88/3030, 90/3917, 96/4905, 06/5657: *Distinguished* 85/2926

Arbuthnot Fund Managers Ltd v Rawlings; *sub nom* Arbuthnot Fund Managers Ltd v Rawlins [2003] EWCA Civ 518, CA (Civ Div); reversing in part [2002] EWHC 2823 (QB), QBD
*Considered* 06/1290, 14/1029

Arbuthnot Fund Managers Ltd v Rawlins see Arbuthnot Fund Managers Ltd v Rawlings

Arbuthnot Latham & Co Ltd v M3 Marine Ltd [2013] EWHC 1019 (Comm); [2014] 1 W.L.R. 190; [2013] 2 Lloyd's Rep. 307; [2013] I.L.Pr. 28, QBD (Comm) ............ *Digested,* 13/**255**

Arbuthnott v Fagan see Henderson v Merrett Syndicates Ltd (No.1)

Arcadia Group Ltd v Arcadia Group Pension Trust Ltd [2014] EWHC 2683 (Ch); [2014] B.T.C. 40; [2014] I.C.R. D35, Ch D ............ *Digested,* 14/**2283**

ARCELIK ANONIM SIRKETI/A cooling device (T390/11) [2014] E.P.O.R. 8, EPO (Technical Bd App)

Archer v Travis Perkins Plc [2014] EWHC 1362 (Ch); [2014] Pens. L.R. 311, Ch D ...... *Digested,* 14/**2271**

Archid Architecture and Interior Design v Dundee City Council [2013] CSOH 137; 2014 S.L.T. 81; [2014] J.P.L. 336; 2013 G.W.D. 28-569, OH ............ *Digested,* 14/**3736**

Ardagh Glass Ltd v Assesor for Ayrshire Valuation Joint Board 2014 S.L.T. (Lands Tr) 32; [2014] R.V.R. 103; 2014 G.W.D. 1-31, Lands Tr (Scot) ............ *Digested,* 14/**3669**

Ardagh Group SA v Pillar Property Group Ltd [2013] EWCA Civ 900; [2014] S.T.C. 26; [2013] S.T.I. 2564, CA (Civ Div); reversing [2012] EWHC 3649 (Ch), Ch D ........ *Digested,* 14/**644**

Ardingly College Ltd v Mid-Sussex DC [2014] P.A.D. 37, Planning Inspector

Ardmore Construction Ltd v Revenue and Customs Commissioners [2014] UKFTT 453 (TC); [2014] S.F.T.D. 1077; 16 I.T.L. Rep. 992; [2014] S.T.I. 2585, FTT (Tax)

Arduina Holdings BV v Celtic Resources Holdings Plc [2006] EWHC 3155 (Comm), QBD (Comm)
*Applied* 13/111: *Considered* 14/128

Arena Corp Ltd (In Provisional Liquidation) v Customs and Excise Commissioners see Customs and Excise Commissioners v Arena Corp Ltd (In Provisional Liquidation)

Arena Corp Ltd (In Provisional Liquidation) v Schroeder; *sub nom* Arena Corp Ltd (In Provisional Liquidation) v Shroeder [2003] EWHC 1089 (Ch), Ch D
*Applied* 11/1298, 14/496

Arena Corp Ltd (In Provisional Liquidation) v Schroeder see Customs and Excise Commissioners v Arena Corp Ltd (In Provisional Liquidation)

Arena Corp Ltd (In Provisional Liquidation) v Shroeder see Arena Corp Ltd (In Provisional Liquidation) v Schroeder

Arena Corp Ltd, Re see Customs and Excise Commissioners v Arena Corp Ltd (In Provisional Liquidation)

Areva SA v European Commission (C-247/11 P); *joined case* Alstom SA v European Commission (C-253/11 P) [2014] 4 C.M.L.R. 31, ECJ (4th Chamber)

Argenta Spaarbank NV v Belgium (C-350/11) [2013] S.T.C. 2097; [2014] 1 C.M.L.R. 9, ECJ (1st Chamber)

Arkeley Ltd v Revenue and Customs Commissioners; *sub nom* Revenue and Customs Commissioners v Arkeley Ltd [2013] UKUT 393 (TCC); [2014] S.T.C. 309; [2013] B.V.C. 1787; [2013] S.T.I. 2987, UT (Tax); affirming [2012] UKFTT 126 (TC), FTT (Tax) ............ *Digested,* 14/**3105**

Arkema France v European Commission (T-23/10); *joined case* CECA SA v European Commission (T-24/10) [2014] 4 C.M.L.R. 22, GC (3rd Chamber)

Arkhangelsky v Bank St Petersburg see Bank St Petersburg v Arkhangelsky

Arkin v Borchard Lines Ltd (Costs Order) [2005] EWCA Civ 655; [2005] 1 W.L.R. 3055; [2005] 3 All E.R. 613; [2005] 2 Lloyd's Rep. 187; [2005] C.P. Rep. 39; [2005] 4 Costs L.R. 643; (2005) 155 N.L.J. 902; Times, June 3, 2005; Independent, June 7, 2005, CA (Civ Div); reversing in part [2003] EWHC 2844 (Comm); [2004] 1 Lloyd's Rep. 88; [2004] 2 Costs L.R. 231; (2003) 153 N.L.J. 1903, QBD (Comm) ............ *Digested,* 05/**385**:
*Applied* 07/405: *Considered* 07/421, 14/1835

ARM Asset Backed Securities SA, Re [2014] EWHC 1097 (Ch); [2014] B.C.C. 260; [2014] 2 B.C.L.C. 364; [2014] I.L.Pr. 37, Ch D ............ *Digested,* 14/**1808**

ARM Asset Backed Securities SA, Re [2013] EWHC 3351 (Ch); [2014] B.C.C. 252, Ch D (Companies Ct) ............ *Digested,* 14/**1817**

Armando Alvarez SA v European Commission (C-36/12 P); *sub nom* Alvarez SA v European Commission (C-36/12 P) [2014] 5 C.M.L.R. 4, ECJ (6th Chamber)

Armitage v West Bromwich Building Society see Investors Compensation Scheme Ltd v West Bromwich Building Society (No.1)

Armstrong v DPP; *sub nom* DPP v Armstrong [1965] A.C. 1262; [1965] 3 W.L.R. 344; [1965] 2 All E.R. 745; (1965) 129 J.P. 493; (1965) 109 S.J. 534, HL; affirming [1965] 2 W.L.R. 765; [1965] 1 All E.R. 1012; (1965) 129 J.P. 266; (1965) 109 S.J. 192, QBD ............ *Digested,* 65/**1745**:
*Considered* 67/1760: *Followed* 14/3048

Arnold v Britton [2013] EWCA Civ 902; [2013] L. & T.R. 24; [2013] 3 E.G.L.R. 37; [2013] 31 E.G. 50 (C.S.), CA (Civ Div); affirming [2012] EWHC 3451 (Ch); [2013] L. & T.R. 13, Ch D (Cardiff) ........ *Digested,* 14/**1990**

Arnold v National Westminster Bank Plc (No.1) [1991] 2 A.C. 93; [1991] 2 W.L.R. 1177; [1991] 3 All E.R. 41; (1991) 62 P. & C.R. 490; [1991] 2 E.G.L.R. 109; [1991] 30 E.G. 57; [1991] E.G. 49 (C.S.); (1991) 135 S.J. 574; Times, April 26, 1991, HL; affirming [1990] Ch. 573; [1990] 2 W.L.R. 304; [1990] 1 All E.R. 529; (1990) 59 P. & C.R. 389; [1990] 01 E.G. 58; (1990) 87(7) L.S.G. 35; (1990) 134 S.J. 1010; Times, November 20, 1989; Independent, November 24, 1989, CA (Civ Div); affirming [1989] Ch. 63; [1988] 3 W.L.R. 1229; [1988] 3 All E.R. 977; (1989) 58 P. & C.R. 175; [1988] 45 E.G. 106; [1988] E.G. 101 (C.S.); (1988) 85(46) L.S.G. 41; (1988) 138 N.L.J. Rep. 218; (1988) 132 S.J. 1639; Times, July 11, 1988; Independent, July 7, 1988, Ch D ........ *Digested,* 91/**1736**: *Applied* 91/203, 95/3781, 97/487, 00/3772, 03/1579, 06/2591, 07/3225, 08/2278, 09/431, 10/3536: *Considered* 92/2742, 96/2578, 97/3886, 97/766: *Distinguished* 98/2162: *Followed* 99/370, 12/1178, 13/266, 14/1393: *Referred to* 94/2807

Arnold White Estates Ltd v National Grid Electricity Transmission Plc; *sub nom* National Grid Electricity Transmission Plc v Arnold White Estates Ltd; National Grid Electricity Transmission Plc v Anthony White Estates Ltd [2014] EWCA Civ 216; [2014] Ch. 385; [2014] 2 W.L.R. 1055; [2014] 3 All E.R. 626; [2014] R.V.R. 247, CA (Civ Div); affirming [2013] UKUT 5 (LC); [2013] R.V.R. 203, UT (Lands) ........ *Digested,* 14/**2527**

Arriva The Shires Ltd v London Luton Airport Operations Ltd [2014] EWHC 64 (Ch); [2014] U.K.C.L.R. 313, Ch D ........ *Digested,* 14/**528**

Arts & Antiques Ltd v Richards [2013] EWHC 3361 (Comm); [2014] Lloyd's Rep. I.R. 219; [2014] P.N.L.R. 10, QBD (Comm) ........ *Digested,* 14/**1842**

Arucana Ltd, Re [2009] EWHC 3838 (Ch), Ch D *Considered* 14/3194

AS (Afghanistan) v Secretary of State for the Home Department [2013] EWCA Civ 1469; [2014] Imm. A.R. 513, CA (Civ Div) ........ *Digested,* 14/**1700**

AS (Afghanistan) v Secretary of State for the Home Department; *joined case* NV (Sri Lanka) v Secretary of State for the Home Department [2009] EWCA Civ 1076; [2011] 1 W.L.R. 385; [2010] 2 All E.R. 21; [2010] Imm. A.R. 284; [2010] I.N.L.R. 111, CA (Civ Div) ........ *Digested,* 10/**1791**: *Approved* 14/1718: *Considered* 12/1757, 12/1759, 12/1760: *Followed* 12/1695, 12/1730: *Not applied* 13/1606

Asaad v Kurter [2013] EWHC 3852 (Fam); [2014] 2 F.L.R. 833; [2014] Fam. Law 459, Fam Div ........ *Digested,* 14/**1394**

Asbeek Brusse v Jahani BV (C-488/11) [2013] 3 C.M.L.R. 45; [2014] C.E.C. 3; [2013] H.L.R. 38, ECJ (1st Chamber)

Ascendi Beiras Litoral e Alta, Auto Estradas das Beiras Litoral e Alta SA v Autoridade Tributaria e Aduaneira (C-377/13) [2014] B.T.C. 30, ECJ (2nd Chamber)

Asda Stores Ltd v Revenue and Customs Commissioners; *sub nom* Revenue and Customs Commissioners v Asda Stores Ltd [2014] EWCA Civ 317; [2014] S.T.C. 1649, CA (Civ Div); affirming [2013] UKUT 223 (TCC); [2013] S.T.C. 2086, UT (Tax); reversing [2012] UKFTT 351 (TC), FTT (Tax) ........ *Digested,* 14/**816**

Ashan v Watt (formerly Carter) see Carter v Ahsan

Ashburton Trading Ltd v Secretary of State for Communities and Local Government see Islington LBC v Secretary of State for Communities and Local Government

Ashcroft v Cambro Waste Products [1981] 1 W.L.R. 1349; [1981] 3 All E.R. 699; 79 L.G.R. 612; [1982] J.P.L. 176; (1981) 125 S.J. 288, DC ........ *Digested,* 81/**2241**: *Considered* 14/684

Ashley v Cardiff CC [2014] P.A.D. 13, Planning Inspector

Ashori v Secretary of State for the Home Department see R. (on the application of Lumba) v Secretary of State for the Home Department

Ashraf v General Dental Council [2014] EWHC 2618 (Admin); [2014] I.C.R. 1244, DC

Ashworth v Royal National Theatre [2014] EWHC 1176 (QB); [2014] 4 All E.R. 238; [2014] I.R.L.R. 526; (2014) 164(7604) N.L.J. 19, QBD ........ *Digested,* 14/**1026**

Ashworth Frazer Ltd v Gloucester City Council (Rent Review) [1997] 1 E.G.L.R. 104; [1997] 26 E.G. 150; [1997] E.G. 7 (C.S.); [1997] N.P.C. 2, CA (Civ Div) ........ *Digested,* 97/**3321**: *Considered* 14/2004

Ashworth Hospital Authority v MGN Ltd; *sub nom* Ashworth Security Hospital v MGN Ltd [2002] UKHL 29; [2002] 1 W.L.R. 2033; [2002] 4 All E.R. 193; [2002] C.P.L.R. 712; [2002] E.M.L.R. 36; [2002] H.R.L.R. 41; [2002] U.K.H.R.R. 1263; 12 B.H.R.C. 443; [2003] F.S.R. 17; (2002) 67 B.M.L.R. 175; (2002) 99(30) L.S.G. 37; (2002) 146 S.J.L.B. 168; Times, July 1, 2002; Independent, July 3, 2002, HL; affirming [2001] 1 W.L.R. 515; [2001] 1 All E.R. 991; [2001] E.M.L.R. 11; [2001] F.S.R. 33; (2001) 61 B.M.L.R. 48; (2001) 98(6) L.S.G. 46; (2001) 145 S.J.L.B. 20; Times, January 10, 2001; Independent, January 18, 2001; Daily Telegraph, January 9, 2001, CA (Civ Div); affirming HQ 0000397, QBD ... *Digested,* 02/**3221**: *Applied* 06/990: *Considered* 02/415, 05/2064, 08/408, 13/397, 14/383: *Distinguished* 03/2922, 06/2096: *Followed* 07/486

Ashworth Security Hospital v MGN Ltd see Ashworth Hospital Authority v MGN Ltd

Asiansky Television Plc v Bayer-Rosin (A Firm) [2001] EWCA Civ 1792; [2002] C.P.L.R. 111, CA (Civ Div); reversing 1995-C-1189, QBD ................................ *Digested,* 02/**502**: *Applied* 04/479, 07/531, 14/487: *Considered* 02/302

Askarov v Turkey (46951/99) see Mamatkulov v Turkey (46827/99)

Aslam v Finn [2013] EWHC 3405 (Ch); [2014] B.P.I.R. 1, Ch D .................................. *Digested,* 14/**1832**

Asociacion de Consumidores Independientes de Castilla y Leon v Anuntis Segundamano Espana SL (C-413/12) [2014] 2 C.M.L.R. 24, ECJ (3rd Chamber)

Asos Plc v Office for Harmonisation in the Internal Market (Trade Marks and Designs) (OHIM) (T-647/11) [2014] E.T.M.R. 37, GC (7th Chamber)

Aspect Capital Ltd v Revenue and Customs Commissioners [2014] UKUT 81 (TCC); [2014] S.T.C. 1360; [2014] B.T.C. 508; [2014] S.T.I. 873, UT (Tax) .................. *Digested,* 14/**2873**

Aspect Capital Ltd v Revenue and Customs Commissioners [2012] UKFTT 430 (TC); [2012] S.F.T.D. 1208; [2012] S.T.I. 2888, FTT (Tax) ........................................ *Digested,* 13/**3033**: *Affirmed* 14/2873

Aspect Contracts (Asbestos) Ltd v Higgins Construction Plc [2013] EWCA Civ 1541; [2014] 1 W.L.R. 1220; [2014] Bus. L.R. 367; [2013] 2 C.L.C. 1019; [2014] B.L.R. 79; 151 Con. L.R. 72; [2014] 1 E.G.L.R. 5; [2014] C.I.L.L. 3449; [2013] 49 E.G. 77 (C.S.), CA (Civ Div); reversing [2013] EWHC 1322 (TCC); [2013] Bus. L.R. 1199; [2013] B.L.R. 417; [2013] C.I.L.L. 3369, QBD (TCC) ................ *Digested,* 14/**598**: *Considered* 14/358

Aspen Insurance UK Ltd v Adana Construction Ltd [2013] EWHC 1568 (Comm); [2013] Lloyd's Rep. I.R. 656, QBD (Comm) ........................................................ *Digested,* 14/**1845**

Aspinall v Secretary of State for Health [2014] EWHC 1217 (QB); (2014) 139 B.M.L.R. 151, QBD (Manchester)

Aspinalls Club Ltd v Revenue and Customs Commissioners [2013] EWCA Civ 1464; [2014] 2 W.L.R. 1574; [2014] S.T.C. 602; [2014] L.L.R. 255, CA (Civ Div); affirming [2012] UKUT 242 (TCC); [2012] S.T.C. 2124; [2013] L.L.R. 242, UT (Tax); affirming [2011] UKFTT 325 (TC); [2011] S.F.T.D. 849; [2012] L.L.R. 1; [2011] S.T.I. 2175, FTT (Tax) ........................................................................ *Digested,* 14/**2904**

Assange v Sweden; *sub nom* Assange v Swedish Prosecution Authority [2012] UKSC 22; [2012] 2 A.C. 471; [2012] 2 W.L.R. 1275; [2012] 4 All E.R. 1249; [2013] 1 C.M.L.R. 4; (2012) 109(24) L.S.G. 22; Times, June 19, 2012, SC; affirming [2011] EWHC 2849 (Admin); (2011) 108(44) L.S.G. 17, DC ........................... *Digested,* 12/**1284**: *Applied* 13/1307, 13/606, 14/1227: *Considered* 13/1179, 13/667, 14/1226: *Followed* 12/1286

Assange v Swedish Prosecution Authority see Assange v Sweden

Assaubayev v Michael Wilson and Partners Ltd [2014] EWCA Civ 1491; [2014] 6 Costs L.R. 1058, CA (Civ Div); affirming [2014] EWHC 821 (QB); [2014] 3 Costs L.O. 446, QBD ................................................................................ *Digested,* 14/**136**

Assessor for Dunbartonshire, Argyll and Bute v Akram; *sub nom* Dunbartonshire, Argyll and Bute Assessor v Akram [2011] CSIH 79; 2012 S.C. 235; [2012] R.A. 137; 2012 G.W.D. 1-6, LVAC ........................................................................ *Digested,* 12/**4241**: *Followed* 13/3943, 14/3678

Assessor for Lanarkshire Valuation Joint Board v Jane Norman Ltd; *sub nom* Lanarkshire Valuation Joint Board Assessor v Jane Norman Ltd [2012] CSIH 50; [2012] R.A. 387; 2012 G.W.D. 22-449, LVAC ............................................... *Digested,* 13/**3948**: *Considered* 14/3670

Assessor for Lothian Valuation Joint Board v Over The Counter Ltd; *sub nom* Lothian Valuation Joint Board Assessor v Over The Counter Ltd [2014] CSIH 28; [2014] R.V.R. 231; 2014 G.W.D. 12-223, LVAC ................................................................. *Digested,* 14/**3665**

Assessor for Tayside Valuation Joint Board v Hutchison 3G (UK) Ltd; *sub nom* Tayside Valuation Joint Board Assessor v Hutchison 3G (UK) Ltd [2014] CSIH 40; 2014 S.L.T. 699; [2014] R.A. 356; 2014 G.W.D. 16-302, LVAC .................. *Digested,* 14/**3664**

Asset Land Investment Plc v Financial Conduct Authority (formerly The Financial Services Authority) see Financial Services Authority v Asset LI Inc (t/a Asset Land Investment Inc)
Assica - Associazione Industriali delle Carni e dei Salumi v Associazione fra produttori per la tutela del 'Salame Felino' (C-35/13) [2014] E.T.M.R. 40, ECJ (9th Chamber)
Assicurazioni Generali SpA v Arab Insurance Group (BSC) [2002] EWCA Civ 1642; [2003] 1 W.L.R. 577; [2003] 1 All E.R. (Comm) 140; [2003] 2 C.L.C. 242; [2003] Lloyd's Rep. I.R. 131; (2003) 100(3) L.S.G. 34; Times, November 29, 2002, CA (Civ Div); affirming [2002] C.L.C. 164; [2002] Lloyd's Rep. I.R. 633, QBD (Comm) ........ *Digested,* 03/**2480**:
*Applied* 03/257, 05/10, 06/766, 07/3432, 09/731, 10/1929: *Considered* 03/2725, 07/4213, 09/2531, 11/539, 14/440: *Followed* 11/3484
Assicurazioni Generali SpA v CGU International Insurance Plc [2004] EWCA Civ 429; [2004] 2 All E.R. (Comm) 114; [2004] 2 C.L.C. 122; [2004] Lloyd's Rep. I.R. 457; (2004) 148 S.J.L.B. 475, CA (Civ Div); affirming [2003] EWHC 1073 (Comm); [2003] 2 All E.R. (Comm) 425; [2003] 2 C.L.C. 852; [2003] Lloyd's Rep. I.R. 725, QBD (Comm) ........ *Digested,* 04/**2242**:
*Applied* 07/2504: *Considered* 07/2505, 10/164: *Followed* 07/2507, 14/1844
Assisted Reproduction and Gynaecology Centre v Human Fertilisation and Embryology Authority see R. (on the application of Assisted Reproduction and Gynaecology Centre) v Human Fertilisation and Embryology Authority
Associated Electrical Industries Ltd v Alstom UK [2014] EWHC 430 (Comm); [2014] 3 Costs L.R. 415, QBD (Comm) ........ *Digested,* 14/**452**:
*Applied* 14/292
Associated Newspapers Ltd v Revenue and Customs Commissioners [2014] UKFTT 116 (TC); [2014] S.T.I. 948, FTT (Tax)
Associated Society of Locomotive Engineers and Firemen (ASLEF) v Brady [2006] I.R.L.R. 576, EAT ........ *Digested,* 06/**1392**:
*Applied* 14/3065
Association de mediation sociale v Union locale des syndicats CGT (C-176/12) [2014] 2 C.M.L.R. 41; [2014] All E.R. (EC) 501; [2014] I.C.R. 411; [2014] I.R.L.R. 310, ECJ (Grand Chamber)
Association Federale des Consommateurs de L'Isere v Foncia Alpes-Dauphine (Societe) [2014] E.C.C. 30, Cass (F)
Association Vent De Colere! Federation nationale v Ministre de l'Ecologie, du Developpement durable, des Transports et du Logement (C-262/12) [2014] 2 C.M.L.R. 35, ECJ (2nd Chamber)
Assuranceforeningen Gard Gjensidig v International Oil Pollution Compensation Fund 1971 [2014] EWHC 1394 (Comm); [2014] 2 Lloyd's Rep. 219; [2014] 1 C.L.C. 624, QBD (Comm) ........ *Digested,* 14/**1848**
Aster Communities Ltd (formerly Flourish Homes Ltd) v Akerman-Livingstone see Akerman-Livingstone v Aster Communities Ltd (formerly Flourish Homes Ltd)
Aster Healthcare Ltd v Shafi [2014] EWCA Civ 1350; [2014] P.T.S.R. 1507; (2014) 17 C.C.L. Rep. 419, CA (Civ Div); affirming [2014] EWHC 77 (QB); [2014] 3 All E.R. 283; [2014] P.T.S.R. 888; [2014] C.O.P.L.R. 397, QBD ........ *Digested,* 14/**2807**
Aston v Secretary of State for Communities and Local Government [2013] EWHC 1936 (Admin); [2014] 2 P. & C.R. 10, QBD (Admin)
Astrazeneca AB v Comptroller General of Patents, Designs and Trade Marks (C-617/12) [2014] R.P.C. 16, ECJ (8th Chamber)
Astrazeneca Insurance Co Ltd v XL Insurance (Bermuda) Ltd [2013] EWCA Civ 1660; [2014] 2 All E.R. (Comm) 55; [2013] 2 C.L.C. 1029; [2014] Lloyd's Rep. I.R. 509, CA (Civ Div); affirming [2013] EWHC 349 (Comm); [2013] 2 All E.R. (Comm) 97; [2013] 1 C.L.C. 478; [2013] Lloyd's Rep. I.R. 290, QBD (Comm) .... *Digested,* 14/**1849**
Aswat v United Kingdom (17299/12) (2014) 58 E.H.R.R. 1; 34 B.H.R.C. 656, ECHR ... *Digested,* 13/**1549**
ATEC Associates Ltd v Revenue and Customs Commissioners [2010] UKUT 176 (TCC); [2010] S.T.C. 1882; [2010] B.V.C. 1526; [2010] S.T.I. 1755, UT (Tax); reversing [2009] UKFTT 178 (TC); [2010] S.T.I. 1400, FTT (Tax) ........ *Digested,* 10/**3528**:
*Applied* 11/3577: *Considered* 14/304: *Doubted* 14/304
Atkinson v Community Gateway Association [2014] I.R.L.R. 834, EAT ........ *Digested,* 14/**1022**
Atkinson v Reynolds see Reynolds DIY Stores Ltd, Re
Atlantic Computer Systems Plc, Re [1990] B.C.C. 454, Ch D (Companies Ct)
*Approved* 14/1756
Atlantic Electronics Ltd v Revenue and Customs Commissioners see Revenue and Customs Commissioners v Atlantic Electronics Ltd
Atlas Property London Ltd v Revenue and Customs Commissioners [2014] UKFTT 674 (TC); [2014] S.T.I. 2664, FTT (Tax)
ATP Pension Service A/S v Skatteministeriet (C-464/12) [2014] Pens. L.R. 59, AGO

ATP Pension Service A/S v Skatteministeriet (C-464/12) see ATP PensionService A/S v Skatteministeriet (C-464/12)

ATP PensionService A/S v Skatteministeriet (C-464/12); *sub nom* ATP Pension Service A/S v Skatteministeriet (C-464/12) [2014] S.T.C. 2145; [2014] Pens. L.R. 223; [2014] B.V.C. 17; [2014] S.T.I. 1566, ECJ (5th Chamber)

Attorney General v Arthur Andersen & Co (UK) [1989] E.C.C. 224; Independent, March 31, 1988, CA (Civ Div); affirming Times, October 13, 1987, QBD ........... *Digested,* 88/**2929**: *Applied* 98/757: *Distinguished* 14/303: *Followed* 97/3904

Attorney General v Baines [2013] EWHC 4326 (Admin); [2014] A.C.D. 47, DC

Attorney General v Barker (Civil Proceedings Order) [2000] 1 F.L.R. 759; [2000] 2 F.C.R. 1; [2000] Fam. Law 400; (2000) 97(10) L.S.G. 37; Times, March 7, 2000, DC ........... *Digested,* 00/**631**: *Applied* 01/92, 05/339: *Approved* 14/1074

Attorney General v Beard see Attorney General v Davey

Attorney General v Blake [2001] 1 A.C. 268; [2000] 3 W.L.R. 625; [2000] 4 All E.R. 385; [2000] 2 All E.R. (Comm) 487; [2001] I.R.L.R. 36; [2001] Emp. L.R. 329; [2000] E.M.L.R. 949; (2000) 23(12) I.P.D. 23098; (2000) 97(32) L.S.G. 37; (2000) 150 N.L.J. 1230; (2000) 144 S.J.L.B. 242; Times, August 3, 2000; Independent, November 6, 2000, HL; affirming [1998] Ch. 439; [1998] 2 W.L.R. 805; [1998] 1 All E.R. 833; [1998] E.M.L.R. 309; (1998) 95(4) L.S.G. 33; (1998) 148 N.L.J. 15; (1998) 142 S.J.L.B. 35; Times, December 22, 1997; Independent, December 19, 1997, CA (Civ Div); reversing [1997] Ch. 84; [1996] 3 W.L.R. 741; [1996] 3 All E.R. 903; [1996] E.M.L.R. 382; [1996] F.S.R. 727; (1996) 19(7) I.P.D. 19066; Times, April 23, 1996, Ch D ........... *Digested,* 00/**797**: *Applied* 00/2132, 06/1018, 08/2669, 12/858, 14/2991: *Complaint upheld* 07/2224: *Considered* 03/717, 04/912, 05/956, 07/1054, 09/3956: *Followed* 10/1937

Attorney General v Dallas [2012] EWHC 156 (Admin); [2012] 1 W.L.R. 991; [2012] 1 Cr. App. R. 32; [2012] Crim. L.R. 694; [2012] A.C.D. 21; (2012) 109(6) L.S.G. 23; Times, February 13, 2012, DC ........... *Digested,* 12/**8**: *Applied* 14/14

Attorney General v Davey; *joined case* Attorney General v Beard [2013] EWHC 2317 (Admin); [2014] 1 Cr. App. R. 1; [2014] A.C.D. 5, DC ........... *Digested,* 14/**14**

Attorney General v Growfar see Attorney General v Times Newspapers Ltd

Attorney General v Leveller Magazine Ltd; *joined cases* Attorney General v Peace News Ltd; Attorney General v National Union of Journalists [1979] A.C. 440; [1979] 2 W.L.R. 247; [1979] 1 All E.R. 745; (1979) 68 Cr. App. R. 342; [1979] Crim. L.R. 247; (1979) 123 S.J. 129, HL; reversing [1979] Q.B. 31; [1978] 3 W.L.R. 395; [1978] 3 All E.R. 731; [1978] Crim. L.R. 627; (1978) 122 S.J. 541, DC ........... *Digested,* 79/**2120**: *Applied* 80/2120, 81/446, 87/679, 92/971, 94/5047, 98/75, 08/854, 14/664: *Cited* 04/1511: *Considered* 88/692, 89/784, 92/969, 93/736, 94/1084, 94/3754, 95/3545, 97/5066, 04/809, 09/4674, 11/599: *Followed* 96/674, 14/1693: *Referred to* 84/866

Attorney General v Mathieson [1907] 2 Ch. 383, CA
*Applied* 64/2599, 14/38: *Followed* 61/1002

Attorney General v National Assembly for Wales Commission; *sub nom* Local Government Byelaws (Wales) Bill 2012, Re [2012] UKSC 53; [2013] 1 A.C. 792; [2012] 3 W.L.R. 1294; [2013] 1 All E.R. 1013; Times, December 31, 2012, SC ........... *Digested,* 13/**1957**: *Followed* 14/573

Attorney General v National Union of Journalists see Attorney General v Leveller Magazine Ltd

Attorney General v Newspaper Publishing Plc see Attorney General v Times Newspapers Ltd

Attorney General v Observer and Guardian Newspapers see Attorney General v Times Newspapers Ltd

Attorney General v Peace News Ltd see Attorney General v Leveller Magazine Ltd

Attorney General v Pearson 36 E.R. 135; (1817) 3 Mer. 353, Ch D
*Applied* 14/38: *Distinguished* 81/226

Attorney General v Sunday Telegraph see Attorney General v Times Newspapers Ltd

Attorney General v Times Newspapers Ltd; *sub nom* Attorney General v Observer and Guardian Newspapers; *joined cases* Attorney General v Newspaper Publishing Plc; Attorney General v Growfar; Attorney General v Sunday Telegraph [1992] 1 A.C. 191; [1991] 2 W.L.R. 994; [1991] 2 All E.R. 398; (1991) 141 N.L.J. 528; (1991) 135 S.J.L.B. 508; Times, April 12, 1991; Independent, April 23, 1991; Guardian, April 12, 1991, HL; affirming Times, February 28, 1990, CA (Civ Div); affirming [1989] 1 F.S.R. 457; Times, May 9, 1989; Independent, May 9, 1989; Guardian, May 9, 1989, Ch D ....................... *Digested,* 91/**2809**: *Applied* 02/444, 03/773, 14/14: *Cited* 91/777: *Considered* 96/27, 01/18, 06/2880, 11/862, 12/469

Attorney General v Times Newspapers Ltd [1974] A.C. 273; [1973] 3 W.L.R. 298; [1973] 3 All E.R. 54; (1973) 117 S.J. 617, HL; reversing [1973] Q.B. 710; [1973] 2 W.L.R. 452; [1973] 1 All E.R. 815; (1973) 117 S.J. 188, CA (Civ Div); reversing [1972] 3 W.L.R. 855; [1972] 3 All E.R. 1136; [1973] Crim. L.R. 38; (1972) 116 S.J. 885, QBD ....................... *Digested,* 73/**2618**: *Applied* 73/2619, 78/2339, 79/2122, 81/2217, 86/2600, 88/666, 98/3094, 14/14: *Approved* 74/2143: *Complaint upheld* 80/1385: *Considered* 79/423, 82/2613, 86/2598, 88/771, 89/3108, 90/3588, 91/2805, 93/587: *Distinguished* 81/998, 82/2436, 95/3959: *Followed* 77/2309

Attorney General for England and Wales v Counsel General for Wales; *sub nom* Agricultural Sector (Wales) Bill, Re [2014] UKSC 43; [2014] 1 W.L.R. 2622; [2014] 4 All E.R. 789; Times, July 14, 2014, SC ....................... *Digested,* 14/**573**

Attorney General of Belize v Belize Telecom Ltd [2009] UKPC 10; [2009] 1 W.L.R. 1988; [2009] 2 All E.R. 1127; [2009] 2 All E.R. (Comm) 1; [2009] Bus. L.R. 1316; [2009] B.C.C. 433; [2009] 2 B.C.L.C. 148, PC (Bze) *Applied* 10/1117, 10/235, 10/2749, 12/2057, 12/2739, 13/587, 13/593, 14/2278: *Considered* 10/228, 10/2338, 10/239, 10/642, 11/1053, 11/2780, 12/2319, 12/516, 13/1878, 13/2454, 13/2833, 13/3791, 13/535, 13/537, 14/17, 14/1969: *Followed* 10/3045

Attorney General of Nigeria v Abacha see Compagnie Noga d'Importation et d'Exportation SA v Abacha (No.3)

Attorney General of Trinidad and Tobago v Matthews [2011] UKPC 38, PC (Trin) *Considered* 14/448

Attorney General's Reference (No.1 of 1985) [1986] Q.B. 491; [1986] 2 W.L.R. 733; [1986] 2 All E.R. 219; (1986) 83 Cr. App. R. 70; (1986) 150 J.P. 242; [1986] Crim. L.R. 476; (1986) 150 J.P.N. 287; (1986) 83 L.S.G. 1226; (1986) 130 S.J. 299, CA (Crim Div) ....................... *Digested,* 86/**933**: *Overruled* 14/79

Attorney General's Reference (No.2 of 1982); *sub nom* Attorney General's Reference (No.2 of 1983), Re [1984] Q.B. 624; [1984] 2 W.L.R. 447; [1984] 2 All E.R. 216; (1984) 1 B.C.C. 98973; (1984) 78 Cr. App. R. 131; [1985] Crim. L.R. 241; (1984) 81 L.S.G. 279; (1984) 128 S.J. 221; Times, November 25, 1983, CA (Crim Div) ....................... *Digested,* 84/**958**: *Considered* 90/1172: *Followed* 01/1084, 14/1807

Attorney General's Reference (No.2 of 1983), Re see Attorney General's Reference (No.2 of 1982)

Attorney General's Reference (No.9 of 2013); *sub nom* R. v Rees (Robert) [2013] EWCA Crim 597; [2014] 1 Cr. App. R. (S.) 3, CA (Crim Div) ....................... *Digested,* 14/**2704**

Attorney General's Reference (No.27 of 2013); *sub nom* R. v Burinskas (Gintas); *joined cases* R. v C; R. v Mathews (Michael Richard); R. v Smith (Paul Simon); R. v Donegan (David); R. v Hanson (John); R. v Ahmad (Goran Kamal); R. v P (Anthony) [2014] EWCA Crim 334; [2014] 1 W.L.R. 4209; [2014] 2 Cr. App. R. (S.) 45, CA (Crim Div) ....................... *Digested,* 14/**2613**

Attorney General's Reference (No.30 of 2013); *sub nom* R. v O [2013] EWCA Crim 1188, CA (Crim Div) *Applied* 14/2630

Attorney General's Reference (No.34 of 2014); *sub nom* R. v Jenkin (John) [2014] EWCA Crim 1394; [2014] 2 Cr. App. R. (S.) 84, CA (Crim Div)

Attorney General's Reference (No.37 of 2013); *sub nom* R. v Culpeper (Jason) [2013] EWCA Crim 1466; [2014] 1 Cr. App. R. (S.) 62, CA (Crim Div) ....................... *Digested,* 14/**2639**

Attorney General's Reference (No.38 of 2013); *sub nom* R. v Hall (James Stuart) [2013] EWCA Crim 1450; [2014] 1 Cr. App. R. (S.) 61, CA (Crim Div) ....................... *Digested,* 14/**2602**

Attorney General's Reference (No.41 of 2013); *sub nom* R. v Mohamoed (Mohammed Ali) (also known as Ali (Jamal)) [2013] EWCA Crim 1729; [2014] 1 Cr. App. R. (S.) 80, CA (Crim Div) ....................... *Digested,* 14/**2630**

Attorney General's Reference (No.51 of 2013); *sub nom* R. v Wright (Joseph) [2013] EWCA Crim 1927; [2014] 1 Cr. App. R. (S.) 83, CA (Crim Div) ....................... *Digested,* 14/**2638**

Attorney General's Reference (No.53 of 2013); *sub nom* R. v Wilson (Neil) [2013] EWCA Crim 2544; [2014] 2 Cr. App. R. (S.) 1, CA (Crim Div) ............ *Digested,* 14/**2606**

Attorney General's Reference (No.54 of 2011) [2011] EWCA Crim 2276; [2012] 1 Cr. App. R. (S.) 106; [2012] M.H.L.R. 87; [2012] Crim. L.R. 144, CA (Crim Div) ....... *Digested,* 12/**2946**: *Applied* 14/2649

Attorney General's Reference (No.55 of 2008); *sub nom* R. v C; *joined cases* R. v CD; R. v F; R. v A; R. v R; R. v W; R. v D; R. v P; R. v PC [2008] EWCA Crim 2790; [2009] 1 W.L.R. 2158; [2009] 2 All E.R. 867; [2009] 2 Cr. App. R. (S.) 22; [2009] Prison L.R. 353; [2009] Crim. L.R. 221; Times, December 4, 2008, CA (Crim Div) ............ *Digested,* 09/**3405**: *Applied* 09/3334, 11/2859: *Considered* 10/2839, 14/2664: *Followed* 11/2913

Attorney General's Reference (No.68 of 2008); *sub nom* R. v Myrie (Owen Anthony) [2008] EWCA Crim 3188; [2009] 2 Cr. App. R. (S.) 48, CA (Crim Div) ............ *Digested,* 09/**3337**: *Considered* 10/2837, 12/2836, 14/2590

Attorney General's Reference (No.69 of 2013); *sub nom* R. v McLoughlin (Ian); R. v Newell (Lee William) [2014] EWCA Crim 188; [2014] 1 W.L.R. 3964; [2014] 3 All E.R. 73; [2014] 2 Cr. App. R. (S.) 40; [2014] H.R.L.R. 7; [2014] Crim. L.R. 471; (2014) 158(8) S.J.L.B. 37; Times, February 24, 2014, CA (Crim Div) ......... *Digested,* 14/**2701**

Attorney General's Reference (Nos 3, 73 and 75 of 2010); *sub nom* R. v McGee (Mark Stuart); R. v Pyo (Hyung-Woo); R. v Anigbugu (Michael) [2011] EWCA Crim 633; [2011] 2 Cr. App. R. (S.) 100; [2011] Crim. L.R. 580; Times, March 28, 2011, CA (Crim Div) ............ *Digested,* 11/**3046**: *Applied* 13/2770: *Considered* 13/2629, 13/2772, 13/2774: *Explained* 14/2622

Attorney General's Reference (Nos 4, 5, 6, 7 and 8 of 2014); *sub nom* R. v Deacon (Nathan); R. v Deacon (Tafari); R. v Kumar (Durrell); R. v Wilson (Josiah); R. v Dawson (Timothy) [2014] EWCA Crim 651; [2014] 2 Cr. App. R. (S.) 51, CA (Crim Div) ............ *Digested,* 14/**2633**

Attorney General's Reference (Nos 7 and 8 of 2013); *sub nom* R. v Levene (Nicholas David); R. v Williams (Alexander Martin); R. v Kallakis (Achilleas Michalis) [2013] EWCA Crim 709; [2014] 1 Cr. App. R. (S.) 26; [2013] Lloyd's Rep. F.C. 417; [2013] Crim. L.R. 776, CA (Crim Div) ............ *Digested,* 13/**2598**

Attorney General's Reference (Nos 88, 89, 90 and 91 of 2006); *sub nom* R. v Meehan (Brian John); R. v McCallister (Gerard Martin); R. v Sangha (Bhovinder Singh); R. v Burch (David William) [2006] EWCA Crim 3254; [2007] 2 Cr. App. R. (S.) 28, CA (Crim Div) ............ *Digested,* 07/**3598**: *Applied* 08/3256, 08/3328: *Considered* 14/2600: *Distinguished* 08/3327

Attrill v Dresdner Kleinwort Ltd; *sub nom* Dresdner Kleinwort Ltd v Attrill [2013] EWCA Civ 394; [2013] 3 All E.R. 607; [2013] I.R.L.R. 548; [2013] I.C.R. D30, CA (Civ Div); affirming [2012] EWHC 1189 (QB); [2012] I.R.L.R. 553; (2012) 109(21) L.S.G. 18, QBD ............ *Digested,* 13/**953**: *Considered* 14/2263

Audit Gestion Revision et Expertise Comptable de L'Ocean Indien (Societe) v Gescore (Societe) [2014] E.C.C. 7, Cass (F)

Auriferous Properties Ltd (No.1), Re [1898] 1 Ch. 691, Ch D *Not followed* 14/1752

Austin v Commissioner of Police of the Metropolis [2009] UKHL 5; [2009] 1 A.C. 564; [2009] 2 W.L.R. 372; [2009] 3 All E.R. 455; [2009] H.R.L.R. 16; [2009] U.K.H.R.R. 581; 26 B.H.R.C. 642; [2009] Po. L.R. 66; (2009) 153(4) S.J.L.B. 29; Times, January 29, 2009, HL; affirming [2007] EWCA Civ 989; [2008] Q.B. 660; [2008] 2 W.L.R. 415; [2008] 1 All E.R. 564; [2008] H.R.L.R. 1; [2008] U.K.H.R.R. 205; [2007] Po. L.R. 182; (2007) 104(42) L.S.G. 32; (2007) 151 S.J.L.B. 1367; Times, October 29, 2007, CA (Civ Div); affirming [2005] EWHC 480 (QB); [2005] H.R.L.R. 20; [2005] U.K.H.R.R. 1039; [2005] Po. L.R. 68; (2005) 155 N.L.J. 515; Times, April 14, 2005, QBD ............ *Digested,* 09/**2033**: *Complaint dismissed* 12/1667: *Considered* 14/2468: *Followed* 11/2600, 12/1663, 12/2288

Austin v Miller Argent (South Wales) Ltd [2014] EWCA Civ 1012; [2014] 3 E.G.L.R. 1; [2014] L.L.R. 663; (2014) 164(7618) N.L.J. 20; (2014) 158(30) S.J.L.B. 41, CA (Civ Div); affirming [2013] EWHC 2622 (TCC), QBD (TCC)

Australian and New Zealand Banking Group v Bangadilly Pastoral Co (Unreported, 1978), HC (Aus) *Applied* 14/278

AV (Democratic Republic of Congo) v Secretary of State for the Home Department see R. (on the application of Akpinar) v Upper Tribunal (Immigration and Asylum Chamber)

AV Concepts Ltd v Revenue and Customs Commissioners [2013] UKFTT 646 (TC); [2014] S.T.I. 380, FTT (Tax)

AVENTIS PHARMACEUTICALS INC/Enhancers (T852/09) [2014] E.P.O.R. 4, EPO (Technical Bd App)

AVH v SI (Abduction: Child's Objection) [2014] EWHC 2938 (Fam); [2014] Fam. Law 1511, Fam Div

Avilkina v Russia (1585/09) 35 B.H.R.C. 208, ECHR

Aviva Investors Property Developments Ltd v Whitby (Valuation Officer); *joined case* PPG Southern Ltd v Mills (Valuation Officer) [2013] UKUT 430 (LC); [2014] R.A. 61, UT (Lands) ........ *Digested,* 14/**2486**

Avon Cosmetics Ltd v Revenue and Customs Commissioners [2014] UKFTT 172 (TC); [2014] S.F.T.D. 852; [2014] S.T.I. 1605, FTT (Tax)

Avon Freeholds Ltd v Regent Court RTM Co Ltd [2013] UKUT 213 (LC); [2013] L. & T.R. 23, UT (Lands) ........ *Digested,* 14/**2011**

Award Framers Int Ltd v Revenue and Customs Commissioners [2014] UKFTT 225 (TC); [2014] S.T.I. 1664, FTT (Tax)

Awareness Ltd v Plymouth City Council; *sub nom* Plymouth City Council's Trade Mark application (No.2547975), Re [2013] R.P.C. 34, App Person ........ *Digested,* 14/**1938**

AWG Group Ltd (formerly Anglian Water Plc) v Morrison; *sub nom* Morrison v AWG Group Ltd (formerly Anglian Water Plc) [2006] EWCA Civ 6; [2006] 1 W.L.R. 1163; [2006] 1 All E.R. 967; Independent, January 25, 2006, CA (Civ Div); reversing [2005] EWHC 2786 (Ch); (2006) 103(3) L.S.G. 27, Ch D ........ *Digested,* 06/**30**: *Applied* 10/486, 10/727, 14/1071: *Followed* 14/42

AX v Federal Tax Administration 16 I.T.L. Rep. 82, BG (Swi)

Axa Corporate Solutions Assurance SA v Refcomp SpA [2014] I.L.Pr. 12, Cass (F)

Axa Equity & Law Life Assurance Society Plc v National Westminster Bank Plc [1998] C.L.C. 1177, CA (Civ Div); affirming [1998] P.N.L.R. 433, Ch D ........ *Digested,* 98/**332**: *Considered* 14/383

AXA General Insurance Ltd v HM Advocate see AXA General Insurance Ltd, Petitioners

AXA General Insurance Ltd v Lord Advocate see AXA General Insurance Ltd, Petitioners

AXA General Insurance Ltd, Petitioners; *sub nom* AXA General Insurance Ltd v HM Advocate; AXA General Insurance Ltd v Lord Advocate [2011] UKSC 46; [2012] 1 A.C. 868; [2011] 3 W.L.R. 871; 2012 S.C. (U.K.S.C.) 122; 2011 S.L.T. 1061; [2012] H.R.L.R. 3; [2011] U.K.H.R.R. 1221; (2011) 122 B.M.L.R. 149; (2011) 108(41) L.S.G. 22; Times, October 19, 2011, SC; reversing in part [2011] CSIH 31; 2011 S.C. 662; 2011 S.L.T. 439; 2011 S.C.L.R. 305; 2011 G.W.D. 14-325; Times, May 3, 2011, IH (1 Div); reversing in part [2010] CSOH 2; 2010 S.L.T. 179; 2010 G.W.D. 7-118; Times, January 19, 2010, OH ........ *Digested,* 11/**473**: *Applied* 14/2444, 14/2964: *Cited* 14/3730: *Considered* 12/4206, 13/3703

AXA Insurance Ltd (formerly Winterthur Swiss Insurance Co) v Akther & Darby Solicitors [2009] EWCA Civ 1166; [2010] 1 W.L.R. 1662; [2009] 2 C.L.C. 793; 127 Con. L.R. 50; [2010] Lloyd's Rep. I.R. 393; [2010] Lloyd's Rep. P.N. 187; [2010] P.N.L.R. 10; (2009) 106(45) L.S.G. 16; (2009) 159 N.L.J. 1629; [2009] N.P.C. 129; Times, December 15, 2009, CA (Civ Div); affirming [2009] EWHC 635 (Comm); [2009] P.N.L.R. 25, QBD (Comm) ........ *Digested,* 10/**2284**: *Applied* 12/447: *Considered* 14/2523, 14/591: *Followed* 13/2087

AXA UK Plc v Revenue and Customs Commissioners; *sub nom* Revenue and Customs Commissioners v AXA UK Plc [2011] EWCA Civ 1607; [2012] S.T.C. 754; [2012] B.V.C. 1; [2012] S.T.I. 34, CA (Civ Div); reversing [2008] EWHC 1137 (Ch); [2008] S.T.C. 2091; [2008] B.T.C. 5485; [2008] B.V.C. 605; [2008] S.T.I. 1389, Ch D; affirming [2008] B.V.C. 2023; [2007] V. & D.R. 282; [2008] S.T.I. 204, V&DTr (London) ........ *Digested,* 12/**3415**: *Considered* 14/3046: *Preliminary ruling given* 11/3531

Ayerst (Inspector of Taxes) v C&K (Construction) Ltd [1976] A.C. 167; [1975] 3 W.L.R. 16; [1975] 2 All E.R. 537; [1975] S.T.C. 345; [1975] T.R. 117; (1975) 119 S.J. 424, HL; affirming [1975] 1 W.L.R. 191; [1975] 1 All E.R. 162; [1975] S.T.C. 1; [1974] T.R. 269; (1974) 119 S.J. 100, CA (Civ Div); affirming [1974] 1 All E.R. 676; [1974] S.T.C. 98; [1973] T.R. 303, Ch D ........ *Digested,* 75/**1677**: *Applied* 92/2572, 92/605, 14/2878: *Considered* 81/260, 81/263, 12/1845

Aylesbury Vale DC v Call A Cab Ltd [2013] EWHC 3765 (Admin); [2014] P.T.S.R. 523; [2014] R.T.R. 30; [2014] L.L.R. 261, DC ........ *Digested,* 14/**2585**

Ayliffe v DPP; *joined cases* Percy v DPP; Swain v DPP [2005] EWHC 684 (Admin); [2006] Q.B. 227; [2005] 3 W.L.R. 628; [2005] 3 All E.R. 330; [2005] Crim. L.R. 959; [2005] A.C.D. 86, DC ........ *Digested,* 05/**754**: *Affirmed* 06/835: *Applied* 14/667

Ayliffe v DPP see R. v Jones (Margaret)

Ayoola v St Christopher's Fellowship [2014] I.C.R. D37, EAT

Ayuntamiento de Sevilla v Recaudadores de Tributos de las Zonas Primera y Segunda (C-202/90) [1993] S.T.C. 659; [1991] E.C.R. I-4247; [1994] 1 C.M.L.R. 424, ECJ (5th Chamber)
*Applied* 98/4905, 09/4121: *Considered* 14/3044

AZ v Secretary of State for Communities and Local Government [2012] EWHC 3660 (Admin); [2014] P.T.S.R. 835; [2013] B.L.G.R. 444; [2013] J.P.L. 713, QBD (Admin) ........ *Digested,* 13/**2310**

AZ (A Child) (Recognising the Adoption of a Child), Re [2014] I.L.Pr. 5, Cass (F)

Azevedo v IMCOPA - Importacao, Exportaacao e Industria de Oleos Ltda [2013] EWCA Civ 364; [2014] 3 W.L.R. 1124; [2014] 2 All E.R. (Comm) 97; [2014] B.C.C. 611; [2014] 1 B.C.L.C. 72, CA (Civ Div); affirming [2012] EWHC 1849 (Comm), QBD (Comm) ........ *Digested,* 14/**275**: *Considered* 13/203

Azimi-Moayed v Secretary of State for the Home Department see Azimi-Moayed (Decisions Affecting Children: Onward Appeals), Re

Azimi-Moayed (Decisions Affecting Children: Onward Appeals), Re; *sub nom* Azimi-Moayed v Secretary of State for the Home Department [2013] UKUT 197 (IAC); [2013] Imm. A.R. 696; [2013] I.N.L.R. 693, UT (IAC) ........ *Digested,* 14/**1640**

Aziz v Aziz [2007] EWCA Civ 712; [2008] 2 All E.R. 501; [2007] Fam. Law 1047; Times, July 17, 2007, CA (Civ Div) ........ *Digested,* 07/**2699**: *Considered* 14/1949: *Followed* 13/1858

Azov Shipping Co v Baltic Shipping Co (No.1) [1999] 1 All E.R. 476; [1999] 1 Lloyd's Rep. 68; [1998] C.L.C. 1240, QBD (Comm) ........ *Digested,* 99/**226**: *Applied* 04/183, 14/123

Azov Shipping Co v Baltic Shipping Co (No.3) [1999] 2 All E.R. (Comm) 453; [1999] 2 Lloyd's Rep. 159; [1999] C.L.C. 1425, QBD (Comm) ........ *Digested,* 99/**4452**: *Applied* 10/351, 14/115

B v B (Abduction: BIIR) [2014] EWHC 1804 (Fam); [2014] Fam. Law 1225, Fam Div

B v B (Abduction: Habitual Residence); *sub nom* FB v IB (Abduction: Habitual Residence); M (Children), Re [2014] EWHC 759 (Fam); [2014] Fam. Law 1080, Fam Div

B v B (Brussels II Revised: Article 15) [2008] EWHC 2965 (Fam); [2009] 1 F.L.R. 517; [2009] Fam. Law 292, Fam Div ........ *Digested,* 09/**1600**: *Applied* 14/1287, 14/1355: *Considered* 13/1282

B v B (Mesher Order) [2002] EWHC 3106 (Fam); [2003] 2 F.L.R. 285; [2003] Fam. Law 462, Fam Div
*Applied* 14/1365: *Followed* 04/1519

B v C see HHH Employee Trust, Re

B v Croydon HA; *sub nom* LB v Croydon HA [1995] Fam. 133; [1995] 2 W.L.R. 294; [1995] 1 All E.R. 683; [1995] 1 F.L.R. 470; [1995] 1 F.C.R. 662; [1995] P.I.Q.R. P145; [1995] Fam. Law 244; (1994) 144 N.L.J. 1696; Times, December 1, 1994; Independent, November 30, 1994, CA (Civ Div); affirming [1995] 1 F.C.R. 332, QBD ........ *Digested,* 95/**3341**: *Applied* 09/4389: *Considered* 96/2979: *Distinguished* 14/2187

B v D; *sub nom* AB v CD [2014] EWCA Civ 229; [2014] 3 All E.R. 667; [2014] 2 All E.R. (Comm) 242; [2014] C.P. Rep. 27; [2014] 1 C.L.C. 899; [2014] B.L.R. 313; 153 Con. L.R. 70; [2014] C.I.L.L. 3497, CA (Civ Div); reversing [2014] EWHC 1 (QB), QBD ........ *Digested,* 14/**409**

B v Harrow LBC (No.1); *sub nom* B v Special Educational Needs Tribunal; F v Special Education Needs Tribunal; F v Harrow LBC [2000] 1 W.L.R. 223; [2000] 1 All E.R. 876; [2000] 3 F.C.R. 1; [2000] B.L.G.R. 162; [2000] Ed. C.R. 188; [2000] E.L.R. 109; (2000) 97(6) L.S.G. 34; (2000) 144 S.J.L.B. 83; Times, January 28, 2000; Independent, February 2, 2000, HL; reversing [1998] 3 F.C.R. 231; [1999] B.L.G.R. 144; [1998] Ed. C.R. 176; [1998] E.L.R. 351; (1998) 42 B.M.L.R. 88; (1998) 95(17) L.S.G. 32; (1998) 142 S.J.L.B. 134; Times, March 26, 1998, CA (Civ Div); reversing [1998] Ed. C.R. 1; Times, December 29, 1997, QBD ........ *Digested,* 00/**1946**: *Applied* 14/937: *Considered* 98/1983, 02/1165, 07/5121, 08/1083, 13/902, 14/938: *Explained* 11/986

B v Hungary see A v Hungary

B v I (Forced Marriage) [2010] 1 F.L.R. 1721; [2010] Fam. Law 348, Fam Div ........ *Digested,* 10/**1406**: *Not applied* 14/1392

B v IB (Order to set aside disposition under Insolvency Act) [2013] EWHC 3755 (Fam); [2014] 2 F.L.R. 273; [2014] B.P.I.R. 331; [2014] Fam. Law 287, Fam Div *Digested,* 14/**1372**

B v K (Abduction: Contempt); *sub nom* M (A Child), Re [2014] EWHC 1122 (Fam); [2014] Fam. Law 1079, Fam Div

B v Ministry of Defence; *sub nom* AB v Ministry of Defence; Ministry of Defence v AB [2012] UKSC 9; [2013] 1 A.C. 78; [2012] 2 W.L.R. 643; [2012] 3 All E.R. 673; [2012] P.I.Q.R. P13; [2012] Med. L.R. 306; (2012) 125 B.M.L.R. 69; (2012) 109(22) L.S.G. 19; (2012) 156(11) S.J.L.B. 31; Times, March 27, 2012, SC; affirming [2010] EWCA Civ 1317; (2011) 117 B.M.L.R. 101; Times, January 19, 2011, CA (Civ Div); reversing in part [2009] EWHC 1225 (QB); Times, June 10, 2009, QBD ........ *Digested,* 12/**448**: *Considered* 14/419: *Followed* 13/393

B v Revenue and Customs Commissioners [2014] UKFTT 256 (TC); [2014] S.T.I. 1982, FTT (Tax)

B v S [2009] EWHC 2491 (Fam); [2010] 1 F.L.R. 748; [2010] Fam. Law 9, Fam Div ..... *Digested,* 10/**1271**: *Considered* 14/1241

B v Special Educational Needs Tribunal see B v Harrow LBC (No.1)

B v X CC see P (Children) (Placement Orders: Parental Consent), Re

B (A Child) v Barnet and Chase Farm Hospital NHS Trust (Unreported, October 31, 2013), QBD [*Catriona Stirling, Barrister, Cloisters, 1 Pump Court, Temple*] ........ *Digested,* 14/**2312**

B (A Child) v DPP [2000] 2 A.C. 428; [2000] 2 W.L.R. 452; [2000] 1 All E.R. 833; [2000] 2 Cr. App. R. 65; [2000] Crim. L.R. 403; (2000) 97(11) L.S.G. 36; (2000) 144 S.J.L.B. 108; Times, February 25, 2000; Independent, April 10, 2000, HL; reversing [1999] 3 W.L.R. 116; [1998] 4 All E.R. 265; [1999] 1 Cr. App. R. 163; (1998) 148 N.L.J. 1177, DC ........ *Digested,* 00/**1002**: *Applied* 00/5063, 01/1070, 10/679, 14/674: *Considered* 04/751: *Followed* 05/758

B (A Child) (Care Order: Jurisdiction), Re see B (A Child) (Care Proceedings: Jurisdiction), Re

B (A Child) (Care Order: Proportionality: Criterion for Review), Re see B (A Child) (Care Proceedings: Appeal), Re

B (A Child) (Care Proceedings: Appeal), Re; *sub nom* B (A Child) (Care Proceedings: Threshold Criteria), Re; B (A Child) (Care Order: Proportionality: Criterion for Review), Re [2013] UKSC 33; [2013] 1 W.L.R. 1911; [2013] 3 All E.R. 929; [2013] 2 F.L.R. 1075; [2013] 2 F.C.R. 525; [2013] H.R.L.R. 29; [2013] Fam. Law 946; (2013) 157(24) S.J.L.B. 37, SC; affirming [2012] EWCA Civ 1475; [2013] 2 F.L.R. 388; [2013] Fam. Law 139, CA (Civ Div) ........ *Digested,* 13/**1213**: *Applied* 14/1238, 14/1247, 14/1250, 14/1283, 14/1323, 14/1346, 14/1672, 14/2444: *Considered* 14/1243, 14/1404: *Followed* 13/1221, 14/1232, 14/1245, 14/1579

B (A Child) (Care Proceedings: Appellate Judge's Power to Re-make Decision), Re see B (A Child) (Evaluation: Appellate Court's Function), Re

B (A Child) (Care Proceedings: Jurisdiction), Re; *sub nom* B (A Child) (Care Order: Jurisdiction), Re [2013] EWCA Civ 1434; [2014] Fam. 139; [2014] 2 W.L.R. 1384; [2014] 1 All E.R. 1045; [2014] 1 F.L.R. 900; [2014] 1 F.C.R. 87; [2014] Fam. Law 20; (2013) 157(47) S.J.L.B. 37, CA (Civ Div) ........ *Digested,* 14/**1417**

B (A Child) (Care Proceedings: Proportionality Evaluation), Re see B (A Child) (Evaluation: Appellate Court's Function), Re

B (A Child) (Care Proceedings: Threshold Criteria), Re see B (A Child) (Care Proceedings: Appeal), Re

B (A Child) (Disclosure), Re see Kent CC v B (A Child)

B (A Child) (Evaluation: Appellate Court's Function), Re; *sub nom* MB v Staffordshire CC; B (A Child) (Care Proceedings: Appellate Judge's Power to Re-make Decision), Re; B (A Child) (Care Proceedings: Proportionality Evaluation), Re [2014] EWCA Civ 565; [2014] 1 W.L.R. 4344; [2014] 3 F.C.R. 129; [2014] Fam. Law 1087, CA (Civ Div) ........ *Digested,* 14/**1348**

B (A Child) (Evidence: Passport Order), Re see B (A Child) (Wrongful Removal: Orders against Non-Parties), Re

B (A Child) (Hague Convention Proceedings), Re [2014] EWCA Civ 375; [2014] Fam. Law 942, CA (Civ Div)

B (A Child) (Immunisation: Parental Rights), Re see C (A Child) (Immunisation: Parental Rights), Re

B (A Child) (Looked After Child), Re; *sub nom* Redcar and Cleveland BC v B [2013] EWCA Civ 964; [2014] 1 F.L.R. 277; [2013] Fam. Law 1382, CA (Civ Div) ........ *Digested,* 14/**1434**

B (A Child) (Paternal Grandmother: Joinder as Party), Re [2012] EWCA Civ 737; [2012] 2 F.L.R. 1358; [2012] 2 F.C.R. 554; [2012] Fam. Law 1073; (2012) 162 N.L.J. 844, CA (Civ Div) ........ *Digested,* 12/**1344**: *Followed* 13/1271, 14/1251

B (A Child) (Removal from Jurisdiction: Removal of Family's Passports as Coercive Measure), Re see B (A Child) (Wrongful Removal: Orders against Non-Parties), Re

B (A Child) (Wrongful Removal: Orders against Non-Parties), Re; *sub nom* B (A Child) (Evidence: Passport Order), Re; B (A Child) (Removal from Jurisdiction: Removal of Family's Passports as Coercive Measure), Re [2014] EWCA Civ 843; [2014] 1 F.C.R. 75; [2014] Fam. Law 1250, CA (Civ Div)

B (A Child), Re; *sub nom* Southampton City Council v A Mother [2014] EWFC 16; [2014] Fam. Law 1378, Fam Div

B (A Child), Re see LB v Merton LBC

B (A Child), Re see Q v Q

B (A Minor) (Child Abduction: Consent), Re [1994] 2 F.L.R. 249; [1995] 2 F.C.R. 505; [1994] Fam. Law 606; (1994) 91(23) L.S.G. 27; (1994) 138 S.J.L.B. 109; Times, May 12, 1994; Independent, May 9, 1994, CA (Civ Div) .......... *Digested,* 95/**3447**: *Considered* 96/534, 97/401, 97/402, 06/1639, 09/1573, 14/1384: *Distinguished* 97/404, 03/1505: *Followed* 03/1504

B (Adoption Order: Jurisdiction to Set Aside), Re; *sub nom* B (Adoption: Setting Aside), Re [1995] Fam. 239; [1995] 3 W.L.R. 40; [1995] 3 All E.R. 333; [1995] 2 F.L.R. 1; [1995] 3 F.C.R. 671; [1995] Fam. Law 469; (1995) 92(27) L.S.G. 33; (1995) 139 S.J.L.B. 176; Times, April 6, 1995; Independent, March 22, 1995, CA (Civ Div); affirming [1995] 1 F.L.R. 1; [1994] 2 F.C.R. 1297; Independent, May 10, 1994; Guardian, May 13, 1994, Fam Div .......... *Digested,* 95/**3376**: *Applied* 09/1484, 13/1333: *Considered* 96/465, 14/1231

B (Adoption: Immigration Status), Re [2014] EWHC 1284 (Fam); [2014] Fam. Law 1084, Fam Div

B (Adoption: Setting Aside), Re see B (Adoption Order: Jurisdiction to Set Aside), Re

B (Child) (Private Law Proceedings: Evidence of Non-subject Child), Re; *sub nom* B (Private Law Proceedings: Child's Evidence), Re [2014] EWCA Civ 1015; [2014] Fam. Law 1386, CA (Civ Div)

B (Children) (Change of Name), Re see W (A Child) (Illegitimate Child: Change of Surname), Re

B (Children) (Foreign Adoption: Refusal of Recognition), Re see A County Council v M

B (Children) (Placement for Adoption: Grandmother's Objection), Re; *sub nom* B (Children) (Placement Order: Grandmother's Objection), Re [2012] EWCA Civ 1940; [2014] 3 F.C.R. 387; [2014] Fam. Law 411, CA (Civ Div)

B (Children) (Placement Order: Grandmother's Objection), Re see B (Children) (Placement for Adoption: Grandmother's Objection), Re

B (Children) (Residence Order: Implementation), Re [2012] EWCA Civ 1901; [2014] 3 F.C.R. 395, CA (Civ Div)

B (Children) (Sexual Abuse: Standard of Proof), Re; *sub nom* Local Authority X v B [2008] UKHL 35; [2009] 1 A.C. 11; [2008] 3 W.L.R. 1; [2008] 4 All E.R. 1; [2008] 2 F.L.R. 141; [2008] 2 F.C.R. 339; [2008] Fam. Law 619; [2008] Fam. Law 837; Times, June 12, 2008, HL; affirming [2008] EWCA Civ 282; [2008] 2 F.L.R. 168, CA (Civ Div); affirming [2007] EWHC 2395 (Fam); [2008] 2 F.L.R. 173, Fam Div .......... *Digested,* 08/**1501**: *Applied* 09/1553, 10/1330, 10/1355, 11/1335, 12/3259, 13/1215, 13/420, 14/1293: *Considered* 08/3774, 08/5003, 09/1519, 09/1611, 09/2649, 10/1305, 10/1327, 10/1416, 10/975: *Followed* 09/1096, 09/1523, 10/1317, 10/1325, 10/1428, 11/1346, 11/1451, 12/1347, 12/1354, 12/437, 13/1222, 13/1227

B (Children), Re; *sub nom* Wakefield City MDC v Media [2010] EWHC 262 (Fam); [2010] 1 F.L.R. 1708; [2010] 3 F.C.R. 296; [2010] Fam. Law 594, Fam Div (Leeds) .......... *Digested,* 10/**1731**: *Applied* 14/1436

B (Children), Re see X Council v B

B (Children: Long-term Foster Care), Re [2014] EWCA Civ 1172; [2014] 3 F.C.R. 500, CA (Civ Div)

B (Disclosure to Other Parties), Re [2001] 2 F.L.R. 1017; [2002] 2 F.C.R. 32; [2001] Fam. Law 798, Fam Div .......... *Digested,* 02/**1622**: *Applied* 14/2184: *Considered* 02/1621, 11/1328: *Followed* 11/1436

B (Private Law Proceedings: Child's Evidence), Re see B (Child) (Private Law Proceedings: Evidence of Non-subject Child), Re

B&Q Plc v Liverpool and Lancashire Properties Ltd (2001) 81 P. & C.R. 20; [2001] 1 E.G.L.R. 92; [2001] 15 E.G. 138; [2000] E.G. 101 (C.S.); (2000) 97(39) L.S.G. 41; Times, September 6, 2000, Ch D .......... *Digested,* 00/**4634**: *Applied* 12/2315, 14/2519

B-G (A Child) (Parental Orders: Domicile), Re [2014] EWHC 444 (Fam); [2014] 2 F.L.R. 968; [2014] Fam. Law 814, Fam Div

B-S (Children) (Adoption Order: Leave to Oppose), Re see B-S (Children) (Adoption: Leave to Oppose), Re

B-S (Children) (Adoption: Application of s.47(5)), Re see B-S (Children) (Adoption: Leave to Oppose), Re

B-S (Children) (Adoption: Leave to Oppose), Re; *sub nom* B-S (Children) (Adoption Order: Leave to Oppose), Re; B-S (Children) (Adoption: Application of s.47(5)), Re [2013] EWCA Civ 1146; [2014] 1 W.L.R. 563; [2014] 1 F.L.R. 1035; [2013] 3 F.C.R. 481; [2013] Fam. Law 1515; (2013) 157(36) S.J.L.B. 37, CA (Civ Div) .... *Digested,* 14/**1245**: *Applied* 14/1232, 14/1238, 14/1246, 14/1283, 14/1284: *Followed* 14/1243, 14/1247, 14/1248, 14/1252, 14/1254, 14/1291

B.J. Crabtree (Insulations) Limited v GPT Communication Systems Limited (Unreported, October 23, 1990), CA (Civ Div) *Applied* 14/407

B4U Network (Europe) Ltd v Performing Right Society Ltd see Performing Right Society Ltd v B4U Network (Europe) Ltd

BAA Ltd v Competition Commission [2012] EWCA Civ 1077, CA (Civ Div); affirming [2012] CAT 3; [2012] Comp. A.R. 134; Times, February 22, 2012, CAT ............ *Digested,* 12/**547**: *Considered* 14/547: *Followed* 14/535

Babajanov v Secretary of State for the Home Department see Babajanov (Continuity of Residence: Immigration (EEA) Regulations 2006), Re

Babajanov (Continuity of Residence: Immigration (EEA) Regulations 2006), Re; *sub nom* Babajanov v Secretary of State for the Home Department [2013] UKUT 513 (IAC); [2014] Imm. A.R. 196; [2014] I.N.L.R. 444, UT (IAC) ........................ *Digested,* 14/**1735**

Babcock v Lawson (1880) 5 Q.B.D. 284, CA; affirming (1879) 4 Q.B.D. 394, QBD *Considered* 14/273

Babcock International Ltd v National Grid Co Plc see Fairchild v Glenhaven Funeral Services Ltd (t/a GH Dovener & Son)

Bache v Zurich Insurance Plc [2014] EWHC 2430 (TCC); [2014] Lloyd's Rep. I.R. 663; [2014] C.I.L.L. 3545, QBD (TCC)

Backaldrin Osterreich The Kornspitz Co GmbH v Pfahnl Backmittel GmbH (C-409/12) [2014] Bus. L.R. 320; [2014] E.T.M.R. 30, ECJ (3rd Chamber)

Bacon v Automattic Inc [2011] EWHC 1072 (QB); [2012] 1 W.L.R. 753; [2011] 2 All E.R. (Comm) 852, QBD ........................................................................ *Digested,* 12/**471**: *Applied* 12/470, 14/1278

Badre v Italy [2014] EWHC 614 (Admin); [2014] A.C.D. 93, QBD (Admin)

BAE Systems (Operations) Ltd v Konczak; *joined case* Konczak v BAE Systems (Operations) Ltd [2014] I.R.L.R. 676, EAT ........................................................ *Digested,* 14/**1039**

BAE Systems Surface Ships Ltd v Assessor for Glasgow; *sub nom* BAE Systems Surface Ships Ltd v Glasgow Assessor 2014 S.L.T. (Lands Tr) 2; [2014] R.V.R. 12; 2013 G.W.D. 35-700, Lands Tr (Scot) ........................................................ *Digested,* 14/**3675**

BAE Systems Surface Ships Ltd v Glasgow Assessor see BAE Systems Surface Ships Ltd v Assessor for Glasgow

Baho v Meerza [2014] EWCA Civ 669; [2014] 4 Costs L.R. 620, CA (Civ Div) ............. *Digested,* 14/**391**

Bailey v Angove's Pty Ltd see D&D Wines International Ltd (In Liquidation), Re

Bailey v Brent LBC see R. (on the application of Bailey) v Brent LBC

Bailey v R&R Plant (Peterborough) Ltd; *sub nom* R&R Plant (Peterborough) Ltd v Bailey [2012] EWCA Civ 410; [2012] I.R.L.R. 503, CA (Civ Div); affirming UKEAT/0370/10/ZT, EAT ........................................................................ *Digested,* 12/**1179**: *Followed* 14/1134

Bailey v Warren [2006] EWCA Civ 51; [2006] C.P. Rep. 26; [2006] M.H.L.R. 211; [2006] W.T.L.R. 753; Times, February 20, 2006, CA (Civ Div); affirming [2005] P.I.Q.R. P15, QBD ........................................................................ *Digested,* 06/**483**: *Applied* 12/319: *Considered* 13/2199, 14/435

Baines v Nursing and Midwifery Council see Adesina v Nursing and Midwifery Council

Baird v Hastings (t/a Hastings and Co Solicitors) [2013] NIQB 143; [2014] P.N.L.R. 17, QBD (NI) ........................................................................ *Digested,* 14/**3216**

Baka v Hungary (20261/12) 37 B.H.R.C. 366, ECHR

Baker v Hallam Estates Ltd [2013] EWHC 2668 (QB); [2013] 6 Costs L.O. 959, QBD .. *Digested,* 14/**396**

Baker v Rowe [2009] EWCA Civ 1162; [2010] 2 Costs L.R. 175; [2010] 1 F.L.R. 761; [2010] 1 F.C.R. 413; [2010] Fam. Law 17; (2009) 153(44) S.J.L.B. 33, CA (Civ Div) ........................................................................ *Digested,* 10/**1284**: *Applied* 11/1323: *Considered* 13/1302: *Followed* 14/1337

Baker v Secretary of State for Communities and Local Government see R. (on the application of Baker) v Secretary of State for Communities and Local Government

Baker v West Reading Social Club; *sub nom* West Reading Social Club, Re [2014] EWHC 3033 (Ch); [2014] B.C.C. 575, Ch D

Bakewell Management Ltd v Brandwood; *sub nom* Brandwood v Bakewell Management Ltd [2004] UKHL 14; [2004] 2 A.C. 519; [2004] 2 W.L.R. 955; [2004] 2 All E.R. 305; [2004] R.T.R. 26; [2005] 1 P. & C.R. 1; [2004] 2 E.G.L.R. 15; [2004] 20 E.G. 168; [2004] 15 E.G. 104 (C.S.); (2004) 101(18) L.S.G. 34; (2004) 154 N.L.J. 553; (2004) 148 S.J.L.B. 418; [2004] N.P.C. 53; [2004] 2 P. & C.R. DG6; Times, April 2, 2004; Independent, April 6, 2004, HL; reversing [2003] EWCA Civ 23; [2003] 1 W.L.R. 1429; [2003] R.T.R. 30; [2003] 1 P. & C.R. 27; [2003] 1 E.G.L.R. 17; [2003] 09 E.G. 198; [2003] 6 E.G. 146 (C.S.); (2003) 100(11) L.S.G. 33; [2003] N.P.C. 12; [2003] 1 P. & C.R. DG22; Times, February 5, 2003; Independent, February 7, 2003, CA (Civ Div); affirming [2002] EWHC 472 (Ch); [2003] J.P.L. 75; [2002] 14 E.G. 124 (C.S.); (2002) 99(19) L.S.G. 30; (2002) 146 S.J.L.B. 102; Times, April 19, 2002, Ch D ........... *Digested,* 04/**3224**: *Applied* 14/2488: *Followed* 05/3404

Baldwin (t/a Ventnor Towers Hotel) v Revenue and Customs Commissioners [2014] UKFTT 489 (TC); [2014] S.T.I. 2097, FTT (Tax)

Balfour Beatty Construction v Serco Ltd [2004] EWHC 3336 (TCC), QBD (TCC) *Applied* 09/657, 10/553, 10/560, 13/519: *Considered* 09/659, 14/576: *Followed* 07/726

Balfour Beatty Construction Ltd v Lambeth LBC [2002] EWHC 597 (TCC); [2002] B.L.R. 288; [2002] T.C.L.R. 25; 84 Con. L.R. 1; (2002) 18 Const. L.J. 405, QBD (TCC) ........................................ *Digested,* 02/**662**: *Applied* 05/644, 10/557, 14/586: *Considered* 12/583

Ball v Secretary of State for Communities and Local Government [2014] EWCA Civ 372; [2014] J.P.L. 1016, CA (Civ Div) ........................................ *Digested,* 14/**2415**

Ballast Nedam NV v European Commission (C-612/12 P) [2014] 4 C.M.L.R. 26, ECJ (5th Chamber)

Balog v Birmingham City Council see Birmingham City Council v Balog

Bamber v United Kingdom (130/10) see Vinter v United Kingdom (66069/09)

Bampton Property Group Ltd v King (Revenue Officer) see R. (on the application of Bampton Property Group Ltd) v King

Banco Santander SA v Deutscher Sparkassen- und Giroverband eV (C-218/13) see Oberbank AG v Deutscher Sparkassen- und Giroverband eV (C-217/13)

Bank Mellat v HM Treasury [2013] UKSC 39; [2014] A.C. 700; [2013] 3 W.L.R. 179; [2013] 4 All E.R. 533; [2013] H.R.L.R. 30; [2013] Lloyd's Rep. F.C. 580, SC; reversing [2011] EWCA Civ 1; [2012] Q.B. 101; [2011] 3 W.L.R. 714; [2011] 2 All E.R. 802; [2011] H.R.L.R. 13; [2011] U.K.H.R.R. 208; [2011] Lloyd's Rep. F.C. 168, CA (Civ Div); affirming [2010] EWHC 1332 (QB); [2010] Lloyd's Rep. F.C. 504, QBD ........................................ *Digested,* 13/**194**: *Considered* 14/2744, 14/545

Bank Mellat v HM Treasury [2013] UKSC 38; [2014] A.C. 700; [2013] 4 All E.R. 495; [2013] Lloyd's Rep. F.C. 557, SC ........................................ *Digested,* 14/**48**: *Applied* 14/2102, 14/45: *Followed* 14/663

Bank of Credit and Commerce International (Overseas) Ltd (In Liquidation) v Ernst & Whinney see Bank of Credit and Commerce International (Overseas) Ltd (In Liquidation) v Price Waterhouse (No.3)

Bank of Credit and Commerce International (Overseas) Ltd (In Liquidation) v Price Waterhouse (No.3); *joined case* Bank of Credit and Commerce International (Overseas) Ltd (In Liquidation) v Ernst & Whinney [1998] Ch. 84; [1997] 3 W.L.R. 849; [1997] 4 All E.R. 781; [1997] 6 Bank. L.R. 216; [1998] B.C.C. 511; Times, June 25, 1997, Ch D ........................................ *Digested,* 97/**316**: *Considered* 14/762: *Doubted* 00/274, 07/439

Bank of Credit and Commerce International SA (In Liquidation) v Ali (No.1) [2001] UKHL 8; [2002] 1 A.C. 251; [2001] 2 W.L.R. 735; [2001] 1 All E.R. 961; [2001] I.C.R. 337; [2001] I.R.L.R. 292; [2001] Emp. L.R. 359; (2001) 98(15) L.S.G. 32; (2001) 151 N.L.J. 351; (2001) 145 S.J.L.B. 67; (2001) 145 S.J.L.B. 70; Times, March 6, 2001, HL; affirming [2000] 3 All E.R. 51; [2000] I.C.R. 1410; [2000] I.R.L.R. 398; Times, May 10, 2000, CA (Civ Div); reversing [1999] 2 All E.R. 1005; [1999] I.C.R. 1068; [1999] I.R.L.R. 226; (1999) 96(7) L.S.G. 35; (1999) 149 N.L.J. 53; Times, January 25, 1999, Ch D ........................................ *Digested,* 01/**2228**: *Applied* 02/207, 02/217, 03/2723, 06/203, 06/2411, 07/2760, 08/663, 12/2023, 14/381: *Considered* 07/2500, 08/2178, 08/2195, 08/648, 09/722, 10/613, 12/2389, 13/578, 14/3354: *Distinguished* 02/703

Bank of Credit and Commerce International SA (In Liquidation) (No.15), Re see Morris v Bank of India

Bank of India v Morris see Morris v Bank of India

Bank of Ireland v Colliers International UK Plc (In Administration); *sub nom* Colliers International UK Plc (In Administration), Re [2012] EWHC 2942 (Ch); [2013] Ch. 422; [2013] 2 W.L.R. 895; [2012] B.P.I.R. 1099, Ch D (Companies Ct) ........ *Digested,* 13/**1670**: *Applied* 14/1790: *Considered* 14/3194

Bank of Ireland v Faithful & Gould Ltd [2014] EWHC 2217 (TCC); [2014] T.C.L.R. 7; [2014] P.N.L.R. 28, QBD (TCC) ........ *Digested,* 14/**2217**

Bank of Ireland v Gill [2013] EWHC 2996 (Ch); [2014] B.P.I.R. 156, Ch D ........ *Digested,* 14/**485**

Bank of Ireland v Philip Pank Partnership [2014] EWHC 284 (TCC); [2014] 2 Costs L.R. 301, QBD (TCC) ........ *Digested,* 14/**353**

Bank of Scotland v Bennett see Royal Bank of Scotland Plc v Etridge (No.2)

Bank of Scotland Plc v Forrester [2014] EWHC 2036 (Ch); [2014] 2 P. & C.R. DG19, Ch D

Bank of Scotland Plc v Joseph [2014] EWCA Civ 28; [2014] 1 P. & C.R. 18; [2014] 1 E.G.L.R. 21, CA (Civ Div) ........ *Digested,* 14/**2511**

Bank of Scotland Plc v Owners of the Union Emerald see Bank of Scotland Plc v Owners of the Union Gold

Bank of Scotland Plc v Owners of the Union Gold; *sub nom* Bank of Scotland Plc v Owners of the Union Silver; Bank of Scotland Plc v Owners of the Union Emerald; Bank of Scotland Plc v Owners of the Union Pluto [2013] EWHC 1696 (Admlty); [2014] 1 Lloyd's Rep. 53; [2013] 2 C.L.C. 36, QBD (Admlty) ........ *Digested,* 14/**2729**

Bank of Scotland Plc v Owners of the Union Pluto see Bank of Scotland Plc v Owners of the Union Gold

Bank of Scotland Plc v Owners of the Union Silver see Bank of Scotland Plc v Owners of the Union Gold

Bank of Scotland Plc v Targetfollow Properties Holdings Ltd [2010] EWHC 3606 (Ch); [2013] B.C.C. 817, Ch D ........ *Digested,* 14/**1759**

Bank St Petersburg v Arkhangelsky; *sub nom* Arkhangelsky v Bank St Petersburg [2014] EWCA Civ 593; [2014] 1 W.L.R. 4360; [2014] 1 C.L.C. 670; Times, June 5, 2014, CA (Civ Div); reversing in part [2013] EWHC 3529 (Ch), Ch D ........ *Digested,* 14/**417**

Banks v Goodfellow (1869-70) L.R. 5 Q.B. 549, QB
*Applied* 47-51/10958, 01/5165, 01/5167, 02/4328, 05/3971, 06/4093, 06/4094, 06/4096, 06/4108, 07/3958, 08/3619, 10/3214, 12/3192, 13/2968, 13/2982, 14/2839, 14/2841, 14/2843: *Considered* 78/351.u, 10/3213, 13/2985: *Followed* 14/2838

Banks v Kingston upon Thames RLBC [2008] EWCA Civ 1443; [2009] P.T.S.R. 1354; [2009] H.L.R. 29; [2009] B.L.G.R. 536; Times, March 10, 2009, CA (Civ Div) .... *Digested,* 09/**1899**: *Applied* 12/1623, 14/1603, 14/1613: *Followed* 14/1602

Bannai v Erez [2013] EWHC 4287 (Comm); [2014] B.P.I.R. 1369, QBD (Comm)

Bannai v Erez [2013] EWHC 3689 (Comm); [2014] B.P.I.R. 4, QBD (Comm) ........ *Digested,* 14/**301**

Banner Homes Holdings Ltd (formerly Banner Homes Group Plc) v Luff Developments Ltd [2000] Ch. 372; [2000] 2 W.L.R. 772; [2000] 2 All E.R. 117; [2000] 2 B.C.L.C. 269; [2000] W.T.L.R. 473; (1999-2000) 2 I.T.E.L.R. 525; [2000] E.G. 15 (C.S.); (2000) 97(6) L.S.G. 37; (2000) 97(6) L.S.G. 35; (2000) 144 S.J.L.B. 83; (2000) 79 P. & C.R. D29; Times, February 17, 2000; Independent, February 11, 2000, CA (Civ Div) ........ *Digested,* 00/**2327**: *Applied* 05/3379, 10/3443: *Considered* 05/695, 12/2024: *Followed* 14/2493

Banque Financiere de la Cite SA v Parc (Battersea) Ltd [1999] 1 A.C. 221; [1998] 2 W.L.R. 475; [1998] 1 All E.R. 737; [1998] C.L.C. 520; [1998] E.G. 36 (C.S.); (1998) 95(15) L.S.G. 31; (1998) 148 N.L.J. 365; (1998) 142 S.J.L.B. 101; Times, March 2, 1998, HL; reversing CHANF 95/0221/B, CA (Civ Div) ........ *Digested,* 98/**2521**: *Applied* 01/3793, 03/3610, 03/3613, 04/3242, 04/3267, 06/3509, 09/991, 13/2472: *Cited* 00/3550: *Considered* 08/2170: *Followed* 11/2716, 12/2768, 14/2529: *Referred to* 00/1460

Barbados Trust Co Ltd (formerly CI Trustees (Asia Pacific) Ltd) v Bank of Zambia [2007] EWCA Civ 148; [2007] 2 All E.R. (Comm) 445; [2007] 1 Lloyd's Rep. 495; [2007] 1 C.L.C. 434; (2006-07) 9 I.T.E.L.R. 689, CA (Civ Div); reversing in part [2006] EWHC 222 (Comm); [2006] 1 Lloyd's Rep. 723; [2006] 1 C.L.C. 311; (2005-06) 8 I.T.E.L.R. 739, QBD (Comm) ........ *Digested,* 07/**305**: *Considered* 14/591

Barber v Guardian Royal Exchange Assurance Group (C-262/88) [1991] 1 Q.B. 344; [1991] 2 W.L.R. 72; [1990] 2 All E.R. 660; [1990] E.C.R. I-1889; [1990] 2 C.M.L.R. 513; [1990] I.C.R. 616; [1990] I.R.L.R. 240; [1990] Pens. L.R. 95; [1990] 1 P.L.R. 103; (1990) 140 N.L.J. 925; Times, May 18, 1990; Independent, May 23, 1990; Financial Times, May 25, 1990; Guardian, July 12, 1990, ECJ ... *Digested,* 90/**1915**: *Applied* 91/1636, 91/1669, 92/1979, 93/1751, 95/1997, 95/1998, 95/2001, 98/2240, 98/4133, 01/2277, 01/2281, 02/1367, 02/3380, 04/2799, 05/3000, 14/1087, 14/1120: *Cited* 92/1940, 92/1968, 95/2095, 00/4382, 10/389, 11/2343: *Considered* 94/4814, 94/4822, 94/4826, 95/2000, 95/2039, 96/2629, 96/4609, 97/5378, 01/4605, 05/1257, 06/2960, 06/2987, 06/2993, 07/3043, 08/2743, 09/2798: *Followed* 00/2159, 14/2258: *Referred to* 97/2214, 97/3947, 14/2271

Barber v Staffordshire CC [1996] I.C.R. 379; [1996] I.R.L.R. 209; (1996) 140 S.J.L.B. 43; Times, January 29, 1996; Independent, February 2, 1996, CA (Civ Div) ...... *Digested,* 96/**2578**: *Applied* 97/2241, 01/2278, 02/1354: *Considered* 98/2162, 98/2190, 02/1309, 06/1319: *Distinguished* 02/1357: *Followed* 14/387

Barclay Pharmaceuticals Ltd v Waypharm LP [2013] EWHC 503 (Comm); [2014] 2 All E.R. (Comm) 82; [2013] 2 B.C.L.C. 551, QBD (Comm) ..................................... *Digested,* 14/**1818**

Barclays Bank Ltd v Quistclose Investments Ltd; *sub nom* Quistclose Investments Ltd v Rolls Razor Ltd (In Voluntary Liquidation) [1970] A.C. 567; [1968] 3 W.L.R. 1097; [1968] 3 All E.R. 651; (1968) 112 S.J. 903, HL; affirming [1968] Ch. 540; [1968] 2 W.L.R. 478; [1968] 1 All E.R. 613; (1967) 118 N.L.J. 13; (1968) 112 S.J. 85; Times, December 18, 1967, CA (Civ Div); reversing [1967] Ch. 910; [1967] 2 W.L.R. 1064; [1967] 1 All E.R. 864; (1967) 111 S.J. 190, Ch D ........... *Digested,* 68/**459**: *Applied* 84/332, 87/345, 89/178, 94/489, 05/2325, 10/1876, 14/1689: *Considered* 75/160, 79/153, 95/2938, 99/294, 00/437, 01/3835, 08/3710: *Distinguished* 69/2281, 69/3367, 78/142, 95/4151, 03/2427: *Followed* 14/3028: *Referred to* 08/2169

Barclays Bank Ltd v TOSG Trust Fund Ltd [1984] A.C. 626; [1984] 2 W.L.R. 650; [1984] 1 All E.R. 1060; (1984) 1 B.C.C. 99081; (1984) 81 L.S.G. 1360; (1984) 134 N.L.J. 656; (1984) 128 S.J. 261, HL; affirming [1984] 2 W.L.R. 49; [1984] 1 All E.R. 628; (1984) 1 B.C.C. 99017; (1983) 127 S.J. 730, CA (Civ Div) ............ *Digested,* 84/**330**: *Applied* 14/1751: *Considered* 92/2048

Barclays Bank Plc v Coleman see Royal Bank of Scotland Plc v Etridge (No.2)

Barclays Bank Plc v Harris see Royal Bank of Scotland Plc v Etridge (No.2)

Barclays Bank Plc v O'Brien [1994] 1 A.C. 180; [1993] 3 W.L.R. 786; [1993] 4 All E.R. 417; [1994] 1 F.L.R. 1; [1994] 1 F.C.R. 357; (1994) 26 H.L.R. 75; (1994) 13 Tr. L.R. 165; [1994] C.C.L.R. 94; [1994] Fam. Law 78; [1993] E.G. 169 (C.S.); (1993) 143 N.L.J. 1511; (1993) 137 S.J.L.B. 240; [1993] N.P.C. 135; Times, October 22, 1993; Independent, October 22, 1993, HL; affirming [1993] Q.B. 109; [1992] 3 W.L.R. 593; [1992] 4 All E.R. 983; [1993] 1 F.L.R. 124; [1993] 1 F.C.R. 97; (1993) 25 H.L.R. 7; (1993) 66 P. & C.R. 135; (1992) 11 Tr. L.R. 153; [1992] C.C.L.R. 37; [1993] Fam. Law 62; (1992) 89(27) L.S.G. 34; (1992) 142 N.L.J. 1040; (1992) 136 S.J.L.B. 175; [1992] N.P.C. 74; Times, June 3, 1992; Independent, June 17, 1992; Financial Times, June 10, 1992, CA (Civ Div) ...... *Digested,* 94/**3300**: *Applied* 94/3294, 95/2443, 95/2451, 96/419, 98/4363, 99/6431, 01/4878, 01/4880, 03/2379, 12/1824, 14/2588: *Cited* 98/305, 00/4644, 00/4662, 01/2653: *Considered* 94/2246, 95/2196, 95/2444, 95/2446, 95/2449, 95/2450, 95/4659, 96/411, 96/4967, 96/4970, 96/4973, 97/4232, 97/4240, 97/4244, 99/3715, 99/4377, 00/2333, 00/4664, 00/6670, 01/669, 10/224, 11/2688: *Disapproved* 97/6087: *Distinguished* 94/5914, 04/1526: *Explained* 98/4358: *Followed* 97/4238, 99/4390, 00/4273, 02/3839: *Not followed* 94/5881, 96/6577: *Referred to* 95/2447, 99/310

Barclays Bank Plc v Revenue and Customs Commissioners see Accenture Services Ltd v Revenue and Customs Commissioners

Barclays Bank Plc v Unicredit Bank AG (formerly Bayerische Hypo-und Vereinsbank AG) [2014] EWCA Civ 302; [2014] 2 All E.R. (Comm) 115; [2014] 2 Lloyd's Rep. 59; [2014] 1 B.C.L.C. 417; [2014] 1 C.L.C. 342; [2014] Bus. L.R. D15, CA (Civ Div); affirming [2012] EWHC 3655 (Comm); [2013] 2 Lloyd's Rep. 1; [2014] 1 B.C.L.C. 342; [2013] Bus. L.R. D78, QBD (Comm) .......................................... *Digested,* 14/**266**

Barclays De Zoete Wedd Services Ltd v Secretary of State for Social Security see Tullett & Tokyo Forex International Ltd v Secretary of State for Social Security

Barclays Mercantile Business Finance Ltd v Mawson (Inspector of Taxes); *sub nom* ABC Ltd v M (Inspector of Taxes) [2004] UKHL 51; [2005] 1 A.C. 684; [2004] 3 W.L.R. 1383; [2005] 1 All E.R. 97; [2005] S.T.C. 1; 76 T.C. 446; [2004] B.T.C. 414; 7 I.T.L. Rep. 383; [2004] S.T.I. 2435; (2004) 154 N.L.J. 1830; (2004) 148 S.J.L.B. 1403; Times, November 27, 2004, HL; affirming [2002] EWCA Civ 1853; [2003] S.T.C. 66; [2003] B.T.C. 81; [2002] S.T.I. 1809; (2003) 100(9) L.S.G. 29; Times, December 27, 2002; Independent, December 18, 2002, CA (Civ Div); reversing [2002] EWHC 1527 (Ch); [2002] S.T.C. 1068; [2002] B.T.C. 388; [2002] S.T.I. 1066; (2002) 99(38) L.S.G. 34; Times, August 26, 2002, Ch D; affirming [2002] S.T.C. (S.C.D.) 78; [2002] S.T.I. 47, Sp Comm .................... *Digested,* 05/**3988**: *Applied* 06/4213, 07/3992, 07/4085, 08/3662, 08/3840, 09/3754, 09/3755, 09/3849, 09/3876, 11/3277, 12/3234: *Considered* 06/4257, 08/3765, 09/3916, 10/3390, 11/3285, 11/3347, 14/2851: *Distinguished* 06/4125: *Followed* 05/4022, 10/3249, 10/3329, 11/3383, 13/3095, 14/2873

Barclays Mercantile Industrial Finance Ltd v Melluish (Inspector of Taxes) [1990] S.T.C. 314; 63 T.C. 95; [1990] B.T.C. 209; (1990) 87(12) L.S.G. 42; Times, February 22, 1990, Ch D .................... *Digested,* 91/**585**: *Considered* 14/2867

Barclays Wealth Trustees (Jersey) Ltd v Erimus Housing Ltd; *joined case* Erimus Housing Ltd v Barclays Wealth Trustees (Jersey) Ltd [2014] EWCA Civ 303; [2014] 2 P. & C.R. 4; [2014] L. & T.R. 23; [2014] 2 P. & C.R. DG3, CA (Civ Div); reversing [2013] EWHC 2699 (Ch); [2014] L. & T.R. 1, Ch D .................... *Digested,* 14/**1977**

Barella v Zacharia (t/a Seacrest Fish Bar) (Unreported, February 20, 2014), CC (Nottingham) [*Express Solicitors, Resolution House, 317-319 Palatine Road, Manchester*] .................... *Digested,* 14/**464**

Barkas v North Yorkshire CC see R. (on the application of Barkas) v North Yorkshire CC

Barker v Bajjon; *sub nom* Barker (A Bankrupt), Re [2008] B.P.I.R. 771, Ch D .................... *Digested,* 09/**2266**: *Considered* 14/3198

Barker (A Bankrupt), Re see Barker v Bajjon

Barking and Dagenham LBC v SS [2014] EWHC 3338 (Fam); [2014] Fam. Law 1676, Fam Div

Barlin Associates Ltd v Revenue and Customs Commissioners [2014] UKFTT 957 (TC); [2014] S.T.I. 3179, FTT (Tax)

Barlow v Stone [2012] I.R.L.R. 898; [2012] Eq. L.R. 861, EAT .................... *Digested,* 12/**1070**: *Applied* 14/1078

Barn Properties Ltd v Secretary of State for Scotland 1995 S.C. 145; 1996 S.L.T. 964; 1995 S.C.L.R. 113, IH (Ex Div) .................... *Digested,* 95/**6449**: *Considered* 14/2376

Barnes v Eastenders Cash & Carry Plc see Crown Prosecution Service v Eastenders Group

Barnes v Eastenders Group see Crown Prosecution Service v Eastenders Group

Barnes v Revenue and Customs Commissioners [2014] EWCA Civ 31; [2014] B.T.C. 5, CA (Civ Div); affirming [2012] UKUT 273 (TCC); [2012] S.T.C. 1904; [2012] B.T.C. 1688; [2012] S.T.I. 2595, UT (Tax); affirming [2011] UKFTT 95 (TC); [2011] S.F.T.D. 443; [2011] S.T.I. 1622, FTT (Tax) .................... *Digested,* 14/**2976**

Barnet v Crozier [1987] 1 W.L.R. 272; [1987] 1 All E.R. 1041; (1987) 84 L.S.G. 658; (1987) 131 S.J. 298, CA (Civ Div) .................... *Digested,* 87/**2301**: *Applied* 04/939, 10/842, 14/840: *Considered* 97/4857

Barnetson v Framlington Group Ltd; *sub nom* Framlington Group Ltd v Barnetson [2007] EWCA Civ 502; [2007] 1 W.L.R. 2443; [2007] 3 All E.R. 1054; [2007] C.P. Rep. 42; [2007] I.C.R. 1439; [2007] I.R.L.R. 598; (2007) 23 Const. L.J. 665; Times, June 11, 2007, CA (Civ Div) .................... *Digested,* 07/**343**: *Followed* 14/1008

Barnett v Barnett [2014] EWHC 2678 (Fam); [2014] Fam. Law 1518, Fam Div

Barnett v Lambeth LBC see Kay v Lambeth LBC

Barnsley MBC v Yerrakalva see Yerrakalva v Barnsley MBC

Barnwell Enterprises Ltd v ECP Africa FII Investments LLC [2013] EWHC 2517 (Comm); [2014] 1 Lloyd's Rep. 171, QBD (Comm) .................... *Digested,* 14/**113**

Barnwell Manor Wind Energy Ltd v East Northamptonshire DC see East Northamptonshire DC v Secretary of State for Communities and Local Government

Barras v Aberdeen Steam Trawling & Fishing Co Ltd [1933] A.C. 402; [1933] All E.R. Rep. 52; (1933) 45 Ll. L. Rep. 199; 1933 S.C. (H.L.) 21; 1933 S.L.T. 338, HL; affirming (1932) 42 Ll. L. Rep. 58; 1932 S.C. 432; 1932 S.L.T. 293, IH (1 Div) *Applied* 14/2936: *Considered* 47-51/9934, 83/538

Barratt v Robinson [2014] UKUT 322 (LC); [2014] 3 E.G.L.R. 42, UT (Lands)

Barry v Butlin 12 E.R. 1089; (1838) 2 Moo. P.C. 480, PC
*Applied* 47-51/7915, 59/3451, 06/4107, 13/2982, 14/2841: *Considered* 66/5003, 73/3494, 02/4338, 11/3257, 11/3267

Barthelemy v F&C Alternative Investments (Holdings) Ltd see F&C Alternative Investments (Holdings) Ltd v Barthelemy (Costs)

Bartholomew v Hackney LBC [1999] I.R.L.R. 246, CA (Civ Div) .................................. *Digested,* 99/**2108**:
*Applied* 01/2254: *Considered* 12/1080, 14/1062

Bartkauskaite v Bartkauskiene see Tasleem v Beverley

Basch v Stekel [2001] L. & T.R. 1; (2001) 81 P. & C.R. DG1, CA (Civ Div)
*Followed* 14/1972

Bassano v Toft [2014] EWHC 377 (QB); [2014] E.C.C. 14; [2014] C.T.L.C. 117; [2014] Bus. L.R. D9, QBD .................................. *Digested,* 14/**273**

Bastrust Corp Ltd v MF see Shinorvic Trust, Re

BAT Industries Plc v Windward Prospects Ltd [2013] EWHC 4087 (Comm); [2014] 2 All E.R. (Comm) 757; [2014] 1 Lloyd's Rep. 559, QBD (Comm) .......................... *Digested,* 14/**559**

Bate v Aviva Insurance UK Ltd [2014] EWCA Civ 334; [2014] Lloyd's Rep. I.R. 527, CA (Civ Div); affirming [2013] EWHC 1687 (Comm); [2013] Lloyd's Rep. I.R. 492, QBD (Comm) .................................. *Digested,* 14/**1836**

Bates van Winkelhof v Clyde & Co LLP; *joined case* Clyde & Co LLP v Bates van Winkelhof [2014] UKSC 32; [2014] 1 W.L.R. 2047; [2014] 3 All E.R. 225; [2014] I.C.R. 730; [2014] I.R.L.R. 641; Times, June 4, 2014, SC; reversing [2012] EWCA Civ 1207; [2013] 1 All E.R. 844; [2013] I.C.R. 883; [2012] I.R.L.R. 992; (2012) 109(38) L.S.G. 19; (2012) 156(37) S.J.L.B. 31, CA (Civ Div); reversing in part [2012] I.R.L.R. 548, EAT .................................. *Digested,* 14/**1067**:
*Applied* 13/1075

Bateson v Bateson see Batesons Hotels (1958), Re

Batesons Hotels (1958), Re; *sub nom* Bateson v Bateson [2013] EWHC 2530 (Ch); [2014] 1 B.C.L.C. 507, Ch D (Manchester) .................................. *Digested,* 14/**521**

Bath and North East Somerset DC v Mowlem Plc [2004] EWCA Civ 115; [2004] B.L.R. 153; 100 Con. L.R. 1; (2004) 148 S.J.L.B. 265, CA (Civ Div)
*Followed* 14/409

Bath Society v Secretary of State for the Environment [1991] 1 W.L.R. 1303; [1992] 1 All E.R. 28; 89 L.G.R. 834; (1991) 4 Admin. L.R. 77; (1991) 62 P. & C.R. 565; [1991] 2 P.L.R. 51; [1991] J.P.L. 663; [1991] C.O.D. 427; [1991] E.G. 14 (C.S.); (1991) 135 S.J. 382; Times, February 14, 1991, CA (Civ Div) .......................... *Digested,* 92/**4184**:
*Applied* 14/2388: *Cited* 95/4751: *Considered* 91/3446, 92/4186, 94/43

Batsanina v Russia (3932/02) (2014) 58 E.H.R.R. 16, ECHR

Baumbast v Secretary of State for the Home Department (C-413/99) [2002] E.C.R. I-7091; [2002] 3 C.M.L.R. 23; [2003] I.C.R. 1347; [2003] I.N.L.R. 1; Times, October 8, 2002, ECJ .................................. *Digested,* 02/**2628**:
*Applied* 07/1611, 07/3824, 11/1793: *Considered* 06/1589, 08/1847, 09/3622, 10/1250, 13/1523, 14/1739: *Distinguished* 05/3856: *Explained* 11/1794: *Followed* 05/2204

Baxter v Camden LBC (No.2) see Southwark LBC v Mills

Bayat v Cecil see Cecil v Bayat

Bayer AG v Paranova A/S (C-436/93) see Bristol Myers Squibb Co v Paranova A/S (C-427/93)

Bayer Pharma AG v Genentech Inc see Regeneron Pharmaceuticals Inc v Genentech Inc

BAYER/Ethinylestradiol and drospirenone (T598/12) [2014] E.P.O.R. 18, EPO (Technical Bd App)

Bayerische Motorenwerke AG v Ronayne (T/A BMW Care) [2013] IEHC 612; [2014] E.T.M.R. 29, HC (Irl)

Bayley v SG Associates [2014] EWHC 782 (Ch); [2014] W.T.L.R. 1315, Ch D ............ *Digested,* 14/**3026**

Baynes v Hedger [2009] EWCA Civ 374; [2009] 2 F.L.R. 767; [2009] 2 F.C.R. 183; [2009] W.T.L.R. 759; (2008-09) 11 I.T.E.L.R. 987; [2009] Fam. Law 666; (2009) 106(20) L.S.G. 19, CA (Civ Div); affirming [2008] EWHC 1587 (Ch); [2008] 2 F.L.R. 1805; [2008] 3 F.C.R. 151; [2008] W.T.L.R. 1719; (2008-09) 11 I.T.E.L.R. 71; [2008] Fam. Law 1087, Ch D .................................. *Digested,* 09/**3718**:
*Applied* 14/2825: *Considered* 10/3208

Bayoil SA, Re; *sub nom* Seawind Tankers Corp v Bayoil SA [1999] 1 W.L.R. 147; [1999] 1 All E.R. 374; [1999] 1 Lloyd's Rep. 211; [1998] B.C.C. 988; [1999] 1 B.C.L.C. 62; (1998) 142 S.J.L.B. 251; Times, October 12, 1998, CA (Civ Div) ... *Digested,* 98/**3324**:
*Applied* 99/3351, 00/3486, 02/2723, 06/2399: *Considered* 99/3254, 99/3350, 04/2180, 05/2346, 09/2271, 11/1900: *Followed* 13/1720, 14/1788

BB (A Child), Re; *sub nom* Wiltshire CC v F [2013] EWHC 2747 (Fam); [2014] 2 F.L.R. 336; [2014] Fam. Law 299, Fam Div

BBC v Johns [1965] Ch. 32; [1964] 2 W.L.R. 1071; [1964] 1 All E.R. 923; [1964] R.V.R. 579; 10 R.R.C. 239; 41 T.C. 471; (1964) 43 A.T.C. 38; [1964] T.R. 45; (1964) 108 S.J. 217, CA; reversing [1963] R.A. 337; [1963] R.V.R. 695; 10 R.R.C. 164; (1963) 42 A.T.C. 341; [1963] T.R. 369, Ch D ................................ *Digested,* 64/**1831**: *Applied* 90/4790, 14/17: *Considered* 88/3845

BBC, Re; *sub nom* A v BBC; A v Secretary of State for the Home Department [2014] UKSC 25; [2014] 2 W.L.R. 1243; [2014] 2 All E.R. 1037; 2014 S.C. (U.K.S.C.) 151; 2014 S.L.T. 613; 2014 S.C.L.R. 593; [2014] E.M.L.R. 25; 37 B.H.R.C. 664; 2014 G.W.D. 15-266; Times, May 15, 2014, SC; affirming [2013] CSIH 43; 2013 S.C. 533; 2013 S.L.T. 749; 2013 G.W.D. 19-377, IH (1 Div) ..................... *Digested,* 14/**43**: *Applied* 14/3433: *Considered* 14/790

BC v IA see N (Adoption Order), Re

BCCI SA, Re see Malik v Bank of Credit and Commerce International SA (In Liquidation)

BCEN-Eurobank (now known as VTB Bank (France) SA) v Vostokrybprom Co Ltd (The Phoenix) [2014] 1 Lloyd's Rep. 449, Sup Ct (OECS)

BDMS Ltd v Rafael Advanced Defence Systems [2014] EWHC 451 (Comm); [2014] 1 Lloyd's Rep. 576, QBD (Admin)

BDV Hungary Trading Kft (In Liquidation) v Nemzeti Ado- es Vamhivatal Kozep-magyarorszagi Regionalis Ado Foigazgatosaga (C-563/12) [2014] S.T.C. 1015; [2014] B.V.C. 3, ECJ (5th Chamber)

BDW Trading Ltd v South Anglia Housing Ltd [2013] EWHC 2169 (Ch); [2014] 1 W.L.R. 920; [2014] H.L.R. 2; [2013] L. & T.R. 25; [2013] 3 E.G.L.R. 139; [2013] 30 E.G. 78 (C.S.), Ch D ........................................................................ *Digested,* 14/**2012**

BE v DE (Evidence: Without Prejudice Privilege) [2014] EWHC 2318 (Fam); [2014] Fam. Law 1387, Fam Ct

Beach v Secretary of State for the Environment, Transport and the Regions [2001] EWHC Admin 381; [2002] J.P.L. 185, QBD (Admin) ......................................... *Digested,* 02/**3645**: *Applied* 14/2354

Beacon Insurance Co Ltd v Maharaj Bookstore Ltd [2014] UKPC 21; [2014] 4 All E.R. 418; [2014] 2 All E.R. (Comm) 558, PC (Trin)

Beard (formerly Coleman) v Williams; *sub nom* Coleman v Williams [1986] 1 E.G.L.R. 148; (1986) 278 E.G. 1087, CA (Civ Div) .......................................................... *Digested,* 86/**1882**: *Followed* 14/1976

Beary v Pall Mall Investments [2005] EWCA Civ 415; [2005] P.N.L.R. 35, CA (Civ Div); affirming [2004] EWHC 1608 (Ch), Ch D ................................................... *Digested,* 05/**2863**: *Considered* 14/2197

Beauty Star Ltd v Janmohamed [2014] EWCA Civ 451; [2014] C.P. Rep. 34, CA (Civ Div) ..................................................................................................................... *Digested,* 14/**390**

Beazley Underwriting Ltd v Al Ahleia Insurance Co [2013] EWHC 677 (Comm); [2013] Lloyd's Rep. I.R. 561, QBD (Comm) .................................................................. *Digested,* 14/**1857**

Becker v Finanzamt Munster-Innenstadt (8/81) [1982] E.C.R. 53; [1982] 1 C.M.L.R. 499, ECJ ........................................................................................................ *Digested,* 82/**1333**: *Applied* 91/3640, 98/2111, 99/4984, 00/5321, 03/4559, 03/4568, 07/1565, 07/4351, 14/3057: *Cited* 00/5317: *Considered* 92/4815, 06/4475: *Followed* 04/1206: *Referred to* 13/3190

Beckett Investment Management Group Ltd v Hall [2007] EWCA Civ 613; [2007] I.C.R. 1539; [2007] I.R.L.R. 793; (2007) 151 S.J.L.B. 891; Times, July 11, 2007, CA (Civ Div); reversing [2007] EWHC 241 (QB), QBD ............................. *Digested,* 07/**1327**: *Considered* 07/351, 14/1032

Bedale Golf Club Ltd v Revenue and Customs Commissioners [2014] UKUT 99 (TCC); [2014] B.V.C. 512; [2014] S.T.I. 878, UT (Tax) ....................................... *Digested,* 14/**3088**

Bedford v Bedfordshire CC [2013] EWHC 1717 (QB); [2014] P.T.S.R. 351; [2013] H.R.L.R. 33; [2014] B.L.G.R. 44; [2014] Med. L.R. 89, QBD ............................. *Digested,* 14/**1638**

Bedfordshire Constabulary v RU [2013] EWHC 2350 (Fam); [2014] Fam. 69; [2014] 2 W.L.R. 780; [2014] 1 All E.R. 1068; [2014] 1 F.L.R. 286; [2014] 1 F.C.R. 383; [2013] Fam. Law 1526, Fam Div .......................................................................... *Digested,* 14/**1391**

Bedfordshire Police Authority v Constable; *sub nom* Constable v Bedfordshire Police Authority [2009] EWCA Civ 64; [2009] 2 All E.R. (Comm) 200; [2009] Lloyd's Rep. I.R. 607; [2009] Po. L.R. 90, CA (Civ Div); affirming [2008] EWHC 1375 (Comm); [2009] Lloyd's Rep. I.R. 39; [2008] Po. L.R. 240, QBD (Comm) ........... *Digested,* 09/**2294**: *Considered* 14/2448

Beechwood Birmingham Ltd v Hoyer Group UK Ltd [2010] EWCA Civ 647; [2011] Q.B. 357; [2010] 3 W.L.R. 1677; [2011] 1 All E.R. (Comm) 460; [2010] Bus. L.R. 1562; [2010] R.T.R. 33, CA (Civ Div) .......................................................... *Digested,* 11/**858**: *Considered* 14/826

Beeres v Crown Prosecution Service (West Midlands) [2014] EWHC 283 (Admin); [2014] 2 Cr. App. R. 8; (2014) 178 J.P. 477; [2014] Crim. L.R. 668; [2014] A.C.D. 70, QBD (Admin) ........ *Digested,* 14/**646**

Beezadhur v Independent Commission Against Corruption [2014] UKPC 27; (2014) 158(34) S.J.L.B. 37, PC (Mau)

Beghal v DPP [2013] EWHC 2573 (Admin); [2014] Q.B. 607; [2014] 2 W.L.R. 150; [2014] 1 All E.R. 529; [2014] A.C.D. 29; (2013) 157(34) S.J.L.B. 40, DC ........ *Digested,* 14/**701**: *Applied* 14/703

Begraj v Heer Manak Solicitors [2014] I.C.R. 1020; [2014] I.R.L.R. 689, EAT ........ *Digested,* 14/**1071**

Begum v Tower Hamlets LBC; *sub nom* Tower Hamlets LBC v Begum (Runa) [2003] UKHL 5; [2003] 2 A.C. 430; [2003] 2 W.L.R. 388; [2003] 1 All E.R. 731; [2003] H.R.L.R. 16; [2003] U.K.H.R.R. 419; 14 B.H.R.C. 400; [2003] H.L.R. 32; [2003] B.L.G.R. 205; 2003 Hous. L.R. 20; [2003] A.C.D. 41; (2003) 100(13) L.S.G. 28; (2003) 147 S.J.L.B. 232; [2003] N.P.C. 21; Times, February 17, 2003; Independent, February 18, 2003, HL; affirming [2002] EWCA Civ 239; [2002] 1 W.L.R. 2491; [2002] 2 All E.R. 668; [2002] H.R.L.R. 24; [2002] U.K.H.R.R. 1014; [2002] H.L.R. 29; [2002] B.L.G.R. 417; [2002] A.C.D. 72; (2002) 99(16) L.S.G. 37; (2002) 146 S.J.L.B. 67; [2002] N.P.C. 35; Times, April 4, 2002; Independent, March 14, 2002; Daily Telegraph, March 6, 2002, CA (Civ Div) .... *Digested,* 03/**55**: *Applied* 03/3446, 03/4104, 03/4975, 06/1812, 07/3915, 09/1906, 09/2652, 12/1625, 13/744: *Considered* 02/3740, 03/2073, 03/2632, 07/2772, 08/2449, 09/1836, 10/1691, 10/1694, 10/2197, 10/3180, 14/2025: *Followed* 14/1612

Begum (Nipa) v Tower Hamlets LBC; *sub nom* Tower Hamlets LBC v Begum (Nipa) [2000] 1 W.L.R. 306; (2000) 32 H.L.R. 445; [2000] C.O.D. 31; (1999) 96(44) L.S.G. 41; (1999) 143 S.J.L.B. 277; [1999] N.P.C. 131; Times, November 9, 1999; Independent, December 20, 1999, CA (Civ Div) ........ *Digested,* 99/**3051**: *Considered* 14/2025: *Not followed* 08/1845

Behague v Revenue and Customs Commissioners [2013] UKFTT 596 (TC); [2014] W.T.L.R. 187; [2013] S.T.I. 3577, FTT (Tax) ........ *Digested,* 14/**2934**

Beheersmaatschappij Van Ginkel Waddinxveen BV v Inspecteur der Omzetbelasting (C-163/91); *joined case* Reisen Passagebureau van Ginkel BV v Inspecteur der Omzetbelasting, Utrecht [1996] S.T.C. 825; [1992] E.C.R. I-5723, ECJ (3rd Chamber) ........ *Digested,* 93/**4410**: *Applied* 14/3073

Behrami v France (Admissibility) (71412/01); *joined case* Saramati v France (Admissibility) (78166/01) 22 B.H.R.C. 477; (2007) 45 E.H.R.R. SE10, ECHR ... *Digested,* 08/**1881**: *Applied* 14/1893: *Distinguished* 08/1964

Belcher v Dartmoor National Park Authority [2014] P.A.D. 41, Planning Inspector

Belchikova v Russia (2408/06) (Unreported, March 25, 2010), ECHR *Considered* 14/1968

Belfast City Council v Miss Behavin' Ltd [2007] UKHL 19; [2007] 1 W.L.R. 1420; [2007] 3 All E.R. 1007; [2007] N.I. 89; [2007] H.R.L.R. 26; [2008] B.L.G.R. 127; [2007] L.L.R. 312; (2007) 104(19) L.S.G. 27; (2007) 151 S.J.L.B. 575; Times, May 1, 2007, HL ........ *Digested,* 07/**2816**: *Applied* 08/3582, 09/4215: *Considered* 09/3007, 12/2330, 14/2444: *Followed* 12/1301

Belgacom NV v Interkommunale voor Teledistributie van het Gewest Antwerpen (Integan) (C-221/12) [2014] P.T.S.R. 650; [2014] 2 C.M.L.R. 23, ECJ (10th Chamber)

Belgium v Recolta Recycling SPRL (C-440/04) see Kittel v Belgium (C-439/04)

Bell v Peter Browne & Co [1990] 2 Q.B. 495; [1990] 3 W.L.R. 510; [1990] 3 All E.R. 124; (1990) 140 N.L.J. 701; Independent, May 9, 1990, CA (Civ Div) ........ *Digested,* 91/**2343**: *Applied* 02/3304, 09/2735, 10/2283, 10/381, 11/349, 12/447: *Considered* 93/2997, 94/2912, 00/2621, 08/382, 14/1840, 14/591: *Distinguished* 05/443: *Followed* 10/2282

Bell Electric Ltd v Aweco Appliance Systems GmbH & Co KG (Application to Stay Appeal) [2002] EWCA Civ 1501; [2003] 1 All E.R. 344; [2003] C.P. Rep. 18; Times, November 20, 2002, CA (Civ Div) ........ *Digested,* 02/**381**: *Applied* 14/432: *Considered* 09/443

Beller v Linton see Legal Equitable Securities, Re

Bellinger v Mercer Ltd; *sub nom* Mercer Ltd v Ballinger [2014] EWCA Civ 996; [2014] 1 W.L.R. 3597; [2014] Pens. L.R. 669; (2014) 158(31) S.J.L.B. 37, CA (Civ Div); reversing in part [2014] EWHC 372 (Ch), Ch D ........ *Digested,* 14/**426**

Bellingham v Dhillon [1973] Q.B. 304; [1972] 3 W.L.R. 730; [1973] 1 All E.R. 20; (1972) 116 S.J. 566, QBD ........ *Digested,* 72/**826**: *Applied* 14/827: *Considered* 83/1071

Bellis v Merthyr Tydfil CBC [2014] P.A.D. 50, Planning Inspector

Bello v Salford City Council see R. (on the application of Mensah) v Salford City Council

Belmont Finance Corp Ltd v Williams Furniture Ltd [1979] Ch. 250; [1978] 3 W.L.R. 712; [1979] 1 All E.R. 118; (1978) 122 S.J. 743, CA (Civ Div) ........................... *Digested,* 78/**242**: *Applied* 84/958: *Considered* 82/1199, 85/306, 86/170, 90/1993, 95/2193, 95/4535: *Followed* 14/1807

Ben Hashem v Ali Shayif [2008] EWHC 2380 (Fam); [2009] 1 F.L.R. 115; [2008] Fam. Law 1179, Fam Div ........................... *Digested,* 09/**1489**: *Applied* 13/1300, 14/1371: *Considered* 11/324, 12/1312, 12/1431: *Distinguished* 14/2494

Ben Nevis (Holdings) Ltd v Revenue and Customs Commissioners see Revenue and Customs Commissioners v Ben Nevis (Holdings) Ltd

Benedetti v Sawiris; *sub nom* Sawiris v Benedetti [2013] UKSC 50; [2014] A.C. 938; [2013] 3 W.L.R. 351; [2013] 4 All E.R. 253; [2013] 2 All E.R. (Comm) 801; 149 Con. L.R. 1, SC; reversing in part [2010] EWCA Civ 1427, CA (Civ Div); reversing in part [2009] EWHC 1330 (Ch), Ch D ........................... *Digested,* 13/**2473**: *Applied* 14/3079

Benham v United Kingdom (19380/92) (1996) 22 E.H.R.R. 293; Times, June 24, 1996; Independent, June 19, 1996, ECHR; no effect (1994) 18 E.H.R.R. CD105, Eur Comm HR ........................... *Digested,* 96/**3155**: *Applied* 97/2765, 06/2157, 07/948: *Cited* 96/16: *Considered* 09/1098, 13/1239, 14/321: *Followed* 00/3221

Beninca v European Commission (T-561/12) [2014] 4 C.M.L.R. 15, GC (5th Chamber)

Benjamin, Re; *sub nom* Neville v Benjamin [1902] 1 Ch. 723, Ch D *Applied* 57/1121, 62/2791: *Considered* 85/261, 13/1664, 14/3030

Benkharbouche v Embassy of Sudan; *joined case* Janah v Libya [2014] 1 C.M.L.R. 40; [2014] I.C.R. 169; [2013] I.R.L.R. 918; (2013) 163(7580) N.L.J. 32, EAT ..... *Digested,* 14/**1123**

Bennett v Bristol Alliance Nominee (No.1) Ltd see A/Wear UK Ltd (In Administration), Re

Bennett v FMK Construction Ltd [2005] EWHC 1268 (TCC); 101 Con. L.R. 92, QBD (TCC) *Applied* 14/577

Bennett v Ogston 15 T.C. 374, Unknown court *Applied* 47-51/4759, 58/1548, 14/2909

Bentine v Bentine; *joined case* Official Solicitor v Wilsons Solicitors LLP (Costs) [2013] EWHC 3098 (Ch); [2014] 1 All E.R. 983; [2014] C.P. Rep. 2; [2013] 6 Costs L.R. 934; [2014] W.T.L.R. 197, Ch D ........................... *Digested,* 14/**332**: *Considered* 14/329

Bentley-Thomas v Winkfield PC [2013] EWHC 356 (Admin); [2014] L.L.R. 413; [2013] Env. L.R. D7, DC

Bentleys Stokes & Lowless v Beeson (Inspector of Taxes) [1952] 2 All E.R. 82; [1952] 1 T.L.R. 1529; 45 R. & I.T. 461; 33 T.C. 491; (1952) 31 A.T.C. 229; [1952] T.R. 239; [1952] W.N. 280; (1952) 96 S.J. 345, CA; affirming [1951] 2 All E.R. 667; [1951] 2 T.L.R. 592; 44 R. & I.T. 606; [1951] W.N. 453; (1951) 95 S.J. 515, Ch D ........................... *Digested,* 52/**1654**: *Applied* 65/1940, 70/1304, 80/396: *Considered* 14/2870: *Distinguished* 81/2842, 85/1784: *Followed* 13/3026, 13/3080

Benyon v Customs and Excise Commissioners see Beynon v Customs and Excise Commissioners

Berent v Family Mosaic Housing [2012] EWCA Civ 961; [2012] B.L.R. 488; [2012] C.I.L.L. 3213, CA (Civ Div); reversing in part [2011] EWHC 1353 (TCC), QBD (TCC) ........................... *Digested,* 13/**2084**: *Followed* 14/2206

Berezovsky v Forbes Inc (No.1); *sub nom* Glouchkov v Michaels; Berezovsky v Michaels; *joined case* Glouchkov v Forbes Inc [2000] 1 W.L.R. 1004; [2000] 2 All E.R. 986; [2001] I.L.Pr. 21; [2000] E.M.L.R. 643; (2000) 97(22) L.S.G. 44; (2000) 150 N.L.J. 741; Times, May 16, 2000; Independent, May 18, 2000, HL; affirming [1999] I.L.Pr. 358; [1999] E.M.L.R. 278; Times, November 27, 1998, CA (Civ Div); reversing Times, January 19, 1998, QBD ........................... *Digested,* 00/**769**: *Applied* 01/1825, 05/974, 05/978, 14/841: *Considered* 12/474: *Distinguished* 99/750

Berezovsky v Michaels see Berezovsky v Forbes Inc (No.1)

Berezovsky (Deceased), Re see Wood v Gorbunova

Berger v Berger [2013] EWCA Civ 1305; [2014] W.T.L.R. 35, CA (Civ Div) ........................... *Digested,* 14/**2824**

Berger & Co v Gill & Duffus SA see Gill & Duffus SA v Berger & Co Inc

Berkeley Applegate (Investment Consultants) Ltd (No.1), Re; *joined case* Harris v Conway [1989] Ch. 32; [1988] 3 W.L.R. 95; [1988] 3 All E.R. 71; (1988) 4 B.C.C. 274; [1989] B.C.L.C. 28; [1989] P.C.C. 261; (1988) 132 S.J. 896, Ch D (Companies Ct) ........ *Digested,* 88/**362**: *Cited* 04/2170: *Considered* 14/2493: *Referred to* 11/1898

Berkley v Poulett [1977] 1 E.G.L.R. 86; (1977) 241 E.G. 911; (1976) 120 S.J. 836; Times, November 4, 1976, CA (Civ Div) ........ *Digested,* 76/**2303**: *Applied* 96/4748, 12/3364: *Considered* 96/4999, 14/2505

Berkvens v Netherlands (Admissibility) (18485/14) (2014) 59 E.H.R.R. SE6, ECHR

Bernh Larsen Holding AS v Norway (24117/08) (2014) 58 E.H.R.R. 8; 35 B.H.R.C. 224, ECHR

Berntsen v Tait see Coniston Hotel (Kent) LLP (In Liquidation), Re

Berrier v Revenue and Customs Commissioners [2014] UKFTT 457 (TC); [2014] S.T.I. 2658, FTT (Tax)

Berrill (t/a Cobweb Antiques) v Hill (Valuation Officer) [2000] R.A. 194, Lands Tr ........ *Digested,* 00/**4600**: *Considered* 01/4832, 14/2136

Berriman v Delabole Slate Ltd; *sub nom* Delabole Slate Ltd v Berriman [1985] I.C.R. 546; [1985] I.R.L.R. 305, CA (Civ Div); affirming [1984] I.C.R. 636; [1984] I.R.L.R. 394; (1984) 81 L.S.G. 1678, EAT ........ *Digested,* 85/**1275**: *Applied* 12/1159: *Considered* 11/1145, 14/1128: *Followed* 14/1140

Berry v Revenue and Customs Commissioners [2011] UKUT 81 (TCC); [2011] S.T.C. 1057; [2011] B.T.C. 1623; [2011] S.T.I. 636, UT (Tax); affirming [2009] UKFTT 386 (TC); [2010] S.T.I. 1449, FTT (Tax) ........ *Digested,* 11/**3366**: *Applied* 14/2878: *Considered* 14/2975: *Followed* 13/3088

Bessant v South Cone Inc see REEF Trade Mark

Besselink v Council of the European Union (T-331/11) [2014] 1 C.M.L.R. 28, GC (5th Chamber)

Best v Chief Land Registrar see R. (on the application of Best) v Chief Land Registrar

Best v Revenue and Customs Commissioners [2014] UKFTT 77 (TC); [2014] W.T.L.R. 409, FTT (Tax) ........ *Digested,* 14/**2935**

Bestuur van het Algemeen Burgerlijk Pensioenfonds v Beune (C-7/93) [1994] E.C.R. I-4471; [1995] 3 C.M.L.R. 30; [1995] All E.R. (E.C.) 97; [1995] I.R.L.R. 103, ECJ ........ *Digested,* 95/**1996**: *Applied* 04/2800: *Considered* 02/3362, 14/1120

Betriu Montull v Instituto Nacional de la Seguridad Social (INSS) (C-5/12); *sub nom* Montull v Instituto Nacional de la Seguridad Social (INSS) (C-5/12) [2014] 1 C.M.L.R. 35; [2014] C.E.C. 675; [2013] I.C.R. 1323; [2013] I.R.L.R. 976; [2013] Eq. L.R. 1078, ECJ (4th Chamber)

Betterment Properties (Weymouth) Ltd v Dorset CC; *sub nom* Taylor v Betterment Properties (Weymouth) Ltd [2012] EWCA Civ 250; [2012] 2 P. & C.R. 3; [2012] 11 E.G. 93 (C.S.), CA (Civ Div); affirming [2010] EWHC 3045 (Ch); [2011] 1 E.G.L.R. 129; [2010] 48 E.G. 84 (C.S.); [2010] N.P.C. 115, Ch D ........ *Digested,* 12/**2763**: *Affirmed* 14/2507

Betterment Properties (Weymouth) Ltd v Dorset CC see Paddico (267) Ltd v Kirklees Metropolitan Council

Bexley LBC v V [2014] EWHC 2187 (Fam); [2014] Fam. Law 1396, Fam Div

Beynon v Customs and Excise Commissioners; *sub nom* Benyon v Customs and Excise Commissioners [2004] UKHL 53; [2005] 1 W.L.R. 86; [2004] 4 All E.R. 1091; [2005] S.T.C. 55; [2004] B.T.C. 5794; [2005] B.V.C. 3; [2004] S.T.I. 2434; (2004) 148 S.J.L.B. 1404; Times, November 26, 2004, HL; reversing [2002] EWCA Civ 1870; [2003] S.T.C. 169; [2003] B.T.C. 5071; [2003] B.V.C. 127; [2003] S.T.I. 31; Times, January 15, 2003, CA (Civ Div); reversing [2002] EWHC 518 (Ch); [2002] S.T.C. 699; [2002] B.T.C. 5366; [2002] B.V.C. 494; [2002] S.T.I. 401, Ch D; affirming [2001] B.V.C. 2331; [2001] S.T.I. 1323, V&DTr ........ *Digested,* 05/**4397**: *Considered* 06/4449, 14/3102: *Distinguished* 08/4061: *Followed* 14/3050

Beyond Retro Ltd v Office for Harmonisation in the Internal Market (Trade Marks and Designs) (OHIM) (T-170/12) [2014] E.T.M.R. 54, GC (9th Chamber)

BGC Brokers LP v Tullett Prebon Plc see Tullett Prebon Plc v BGC Brokers LP

BGZ Leasing sp z oo v Dyrektor Izby Skarbowej w Warszawie (C-224/11) [2013] S.T.C. 2162; [2013] S.T.I. 295, ECJ (6th Chamber) *Applied* 13/3229: *Followed* 14/3050

BH v Lord Advocate see H v Lord Advocate

Bhamjee v Forsdick [2003] EWCA Civ 1113; [2004] 1 W.L.R. 88; [2003] C.P. Rep. 67; [2003] B.P.I.R. 1252; (2003) 100(36) L.S.G. 41; Times, July 31, 2003; Independent, July 29, 2003, CA (Civ Div) ........ *Digested,* 03/**482**: *Applied* 04/282, 10/355: *Considered* 04/281, 07/368, 14/67: *Followed* 10/272

Bhatia Best Ltd v Lord Chancellor [2014] EWHC 746 (QB); [2014] 1 W.L.R. 3487; [2014] 3 All E.R. 573; (2014) 164(7600) N.L.J. 28; (2014) 158(14) S.J.L.B. 37, QBD ........ *Digested,* 14/**2025**

Bhatnagar v General Medical Council [2013] EWHC 3412 (Admin); [2014] Med. L.R. 27, QBD (Admin) ........ *Digested,* 14/**1501**

Bhatt v Revenue and Customs Commissioners [2014] UKFTT 430 (TC); [2014] S.T.I. 2047, FTT (Tax)

Bhura v Bhura [2014] EWHC 727 (Fam); [2014] Fam. Law 1116, Fam Div

Biagioli v San Marino (Admissibility) (8162/13) (2014) 59 E.H.R.R. SE13, ECHR

Biasci v Ministero dell'Interno (C-660/11); *joined case* Rainone v Ministero dell'Interno (C-8/12) [2014] 1 C.M.L.R. 30, ECJ (3rd Chamber)

Bibby ACF Ltd v Agate [2013] B.P.I.R. 685, Ch D ........ *Digested,* 14/**1831**

Bibi v Secretary of State for the Home Department see R. (on the application of Aguilar Quila) v Secretary of State for the Home Department

Bicici v Turkey (30357/05) (2014) 58 E.H.R.R. 12, ECHR

Bicioc v Romania [2014] EWHC 628 (Admin); [2014] A.C.D. 91, QBD (Admin)

Bickford v South Staffordshire Council [2014] P.A.D. 36, Planning Inspector

Biddle & Co v Tetra Pak Ltd; *sub nom* Tetra Pak Ltd v Biddle & Co [2010] EWHC 54 (Ch); [2010] 1 W.L.R. 1466, Ch D ........ *Digested,* 10/**391**: *Considered* 14/427

Bigos v Bousted [1951] 1 All E.R. 92, KBD ........ *Digested,* 47-51/**1751**: *Applied* 13/216: *Not followed* 14/264

Billington v Cole see Cole v Billington

Billsop Properties Ltd (In Administration), Re see Black Ant Co Ltd (In Administration), Re

Bilta (UK) Ltd (In Liquidation) v Nazir; *sub nom* Jetivia SA v Bilta (UK) Ltd (In Liquidation) [2013] EWCA Civ 968; [2014] Ch. 52; [2013] 3 W.L.R. 1167; [2014] 1 All E.R. 168; [2014] 1 All E.R. (Comm) 176; [2014] 1 Lloyd's Rep. 113; [2013] S.T.C. 2298; [2013] B.C.C. 655; [2014] 1 B.C.L.C. 302; [2013] Lloyd's Rep. F.C. 620; [2014] B.V.C. 33; [2013] S.T.I. 2677, CA (Civ Div); affirming [2012] EWHC 2163 (Ch); [2013] 2 W.L.R. 825; [2013] 1 All E.R. 375; [2012] S.T.C. 2424; [2013] B.C.C. 235; [2012] S.T.I. 2554; Times, October 15, 2012, Ch D .... *Digested,* 14/**1807**: *Followed* 14/510

Bimbo SA v Office for Harmonisation in the Internal Market (Trade Marks and Designs) (OHIM) (C-591/12 P) [2014] E.T.M.R. 41, ECJ (2nd Chamber)

Binder v Germany [2014] EWHC 133 (Admin); [2014] A.C.D. 73, QBD (Admin)

Binns v Firstplus Financial Group Plc [2013] EWHC 2436 (QB); [2014] Bus. L.R. 110; (2013) 157(38) S.J.L.B. 41, QBD ........ *Digested,* 14/**296**

Birch v Ministry of Defence [2013] EWCA Civ 676; [2014] P.I.Q.R. P1, CA (Civ Div); reversing [2012] EWHC 2267 (QB), QBD (Manchester)

Birch v Treasury Solicitor [1951] Ch. 298; [1950] 2 All E.R. 1198; [1951] 1 T.L.R. 225; (1950) 94 S.J. 838, CA ........ *Digested,* 47-51/**4312**: *Applied* 14/2817: *Considered* 90/1995, 91/3707

Birch v University College London Hospital NHS Foundation Trust [2008] EWHC 2237 (QB); (2008) 104 B.M.L.R. 168; (2008) 105(39) L.S.G. 19, QBD ........ *Digested,* 09/**2842**: *Considered* 14/2198

Bircham & Co Nominees (No.2) Ltd v Clarke see Earl Cadogan v Sportelli

Bird v Jones 115 E.R. 668; (1845) 7 Q.B. 742, KB *Applied* 14/2468

Birkdale School, Sheffield v Revenue and Customs Commissioners [2008] EWHC 409 (Ch); [2008] S.T.C. 2002; [2008] B.T.C. 5274; [2008] B.V.C. 397; [2008] S.T.I. 431; (2008) 158 N.L.J. 415; Times, April 23, 2008, Ch D; reversing [2007] B.V.C. 2426, V&DTr (Manchester) ........ *Digested,* 08/**4035**: *Considered* 14/3046

Birkett v James [1978] A.C. 297; [1977] 3 W.L.R. 38; [1977] 2 All E.R. 801; (1977) 121 S.J. 444, HL ........ *Digested,* 77/**2410**: *Applied* 78/2237, 78/2426, 78/310.u, 81/113, 81/1966, 83/2209, 83/3068, 84/2739, 89/3075, 92/3495, 93/1764, 93/3336, 94/2902, 95/2963, 96/366, 96/900, 97/785, 00/616, 09/4867: *Considered* 77/2407, 77/2408, 77/2411, 77/516u, 78/265u, 78/306u, 78/313u, 79/1663, 79/1665, 79/2191, 79/41u, 80/293u, 81/2201, 82/1849, 82/2461, 82/2553, 82/628u, 83/3073, 85/2683, 85/2728, 87/133, 87/2985, 88/2934, 89/2963, 89/3070, 89/3071, 91/2971, 92/190, 92/2813, 92/3610, 92/3611, 93/3338, 94/3644, 94/3788, 94/3904, 95/3891, 97/1314, 97/3024, 97/489, 97/644, 97/759, 97/761, 98/611, 98/612, 98/613, 98/619, 00/348, 00/4656, 06/5096, 07/3957, 08/4576, 14/452: *Distinguished* 78/1848, 78/2425, 80/2194, 81/868, 88/2838, 90/3644, 94/3635, 95/3888, 96/909, 98/614: *Followed* 78/2423, 78/311.u, 96/898, 97/1007, 99/3356: *Referred to* 97/1037, 97/754, 00/605, 00/617: *Superseded* 99/367, 00/626

Birmingham Children's NHS Trust v B [2014] EWHC 531 (Fam); (2014) 137 B.M.L.R. 222, Fam Div
Birmingham City Council v AB [2014] EWHC 3090 (Fam); [2014] Fam. Law 1663, Fam Div (Birmingham)
Birmingham City Council v Ali see Ali v Birmingham City Council
Birmingham City Council v Ali see R. (on the application of Aweys) v Birmingham City Council
Birmingham City Council v Aweys see R. (on the application of Aweys) v Birmingham City Council
Birmingham City Council v Balog; *sub nom* Balog v Birmingham City Council [2013] EWCA Civ 1582; [2014] H.L.R. 14, CA (Civ Div) ............ *Digested,* 14/**1592**
Birmingham City Council v Beech (aka Howell) [2014] EWCA Civ 830; [2014] H.L.R. 38; [2014] 2 P. & C.R. DG20, CA (Civ Div); affirming [2013] EWHC 518 (QB), QBD ............ *Digested,* 14/**1965**
Birmingham City Council v Emery [2014] E.L.R. 203, EAT ............ *Digested,* 14/**952**
Birmingham City Council v Frisby see Hounslow LBC v Powell
Birmingham City Council v James [2013] EWCA Civ 552; [2014] 1 W.L.R. 23; (2013) 177 J.P. 425, CA (Civ Div) ............ *Digested,* 13/**372**
Birmingham Corp v Sowsbery [1970] R.T.R. 84; (1969) 113 S.J. 877, QBD ............ *Digested,* 69/**890**: *Applied* 11/858: *Cited* 00/350: *Considered* 93/1582, 14/826: *Distinguished* 01/1535: *Not applied* 06/1016
Birmingham Hippodrome Theatre Trust Ltd v Revenue and Customs Commissioners [2014] EWCA Civ 684; [2014] 1 W.L.R. 3867; [2014] S.T.C. 2222; [2014] B.V.C. 27; [2014] S.T.I. 2223; Times, July 10, 2014, CA (Civ Div); affirming [2013] UKUT 57 (TCC); [2013] S.T.C. 1079; [2013] B.V.C. 1743; [2013] S.T.I. 489, UT (Tax); affirming [2011] UKFTT 117 (TC); [2011] S.F.T.D. 473, FTT (Tax) ............ *Digested,* 14/**3057**: *Considered* 13/3207
Bishop v Golstein see Golstein v Bishop
Bishop v Golstein see Golstein v Bishop
Bishop's Stortford Civic Federation v East Hertfordshire DC see R. (on the application of Bishop's Stortford Civic Federation) v East Hertfordshire DC
BJ v MJ (Financial Order: Overseas Trust) [2011] EWHC 2708 (Fam); [2012] 1 F.L.R. 667; [2012] W.T.L.R. 395; 14 I.T.E.L.R. 572; [2012] Fam. Law 277, Fam Div .... *Digested,* 12/**1440**: *Applied* 13/1303, 14/1371
BJ (Incapacitated Adult), Re; *sub nom* Salford City Council v BJ (Incapacitated Adult) [2009] EWHC 3310 (Fam); [2010] 1 F.L.R. 1373; (2010) 13 C.C.L. Rep. 65; [2010] M.H.L.R. 283; [2010] Fam. Law 242, Fam Div ............ *Digested,* 10/**2264**: *Applied* 14/2187
BKK Mobil Oil Korperschaft des offentlichen Rechts v Zentrale zur Bekampfung unlauteren Wettbewerbs eV (C-59/12) [2014] 2 C.M.L.R. 1; [2014] C.E.C. 516, ECJ (1st Chamber)
Black v R. 2014 TCC 12; 16 I.T.L. Rep. 573, Tax Ct (Can)
Black v Sumitomo Corp [2001] EWCA Civ 1819; [2002] 1 W.L.R. 1562; [2003] 3 All E.R. 643; [2002] 1 Lloyd's Rep. 693; [2002] C.P.L.R. 148; Times, January 25, 2002; Independent, December 13, 2001, CA (Civ Div); reversing (Unreported, July 26, 2001), QBD (Comm) ............ *Digested,* 02/**422**: *Applied* 02/426, 05/456, 06/430, 06/431, 07/500, 07/503, 08/356, 08/402, 09/397, 09/434: *Considered* 07/502, 08/401, 08/403: *Followed* 10/398, 14/438
Black Ant Co Ltd (In Administration), Re; *sub nom* Urban Ventures Ltd v Thomas; *joined case* Billsop Properties Ltd (In Administration), Re [2014] EWHC 1161 (Ch); [2014] 2 E.G.L.R. 179, Ch D (Companies Ct)
Blackbay Ventures Ltd (t/a Chemistree) v Gahir [2014] I.C.R. 747; [2014] I.R.L.R. 416, EAT ............ *Digested,* 14/**1096**
Blackburn (t/a Cornish Moorland Honey) v Revenue and Customs Commissioners [2013] UKFTT 525 (TC); [2014] S.F.T.D. 195; [2013] S.T.I. 3404; [2013] S.T.I. 3437, FTT (Tax) ............ *Digested,* 14/**3099**
Blackpool BC v Cargill; *joined case* Blackpool BC v Morris [2013] UKUT 377 (LC); [2014] L. & T.R. 2, UT (Lands) ............ *Digested,* 14/**2014**
Blackpool BC v Morris see Blackpool BC v Cargill
Blackwell v Revenue and Customs Commissioners [2014] UKFTT 103 (TC); [2014] S.T.I. 1581, FTT (Tax)
Blake v Associated Newspapers Ltd JS/01/0206, QBD *Disapproved* 14/38
Blake v Waltham Forest LBC see R. (on the application of Blake) v Waltham Forest LBC
Blanco v Agenzia delle Entrate - Direzione Provinciale I di Roma - Ufficio Controlli (C-344/13) [2014] S.T.I. 3173, ECJ (3rd Chamber)

Blanco v Scottish Ministers see Somerville v Scottish Ministers
Blanco Settlements, Re see Colour Trusts, Re
Blankley v Central Manchester and Manchester Children's University Hospitals NHS Trust [2014] EWHC 168 (QB); [2014] 1 W.L.R. 2683; [2014] 2 All E.R. 1104; [2014] 2 Costs L.R. 320; (2014) 138 B.M.L.R. 30, QBD .................................... *Digested,* 14/**2053**
Blemain Finance Ltd v Cugley [2014] B.P.I.R. 20, CC (Bristol) .................................... *Digested,* 14/**1769**
Blemain Finance Ltd v Goulding [2013] EWCA Civ 1630; [2014] 1 P. & C.R. DG16, CA (Civ Div)
Blomqvist v Rolex SA [2014] E.T.M.R. 38, HR (DK)
Blomqvist v Rolex SA (C-98/13) [2014] Bus. L.R. 356; [2014] E.T.M.R. 25; [2014] E.C.D.R. 10, ECJ (2nd Chamber)
Bloom v HM Senior Coroner for the Western District of London [2014] EWHC 2698 (Admin); [2014] Med. L.R. 490, DC
Bloom v Pensions Regulator; *sub nom* Lehman Companies, Re; Nortel Companies, Re; Nortel GmbH (In Administration), Re; Nortel Networks UK Pension Trust Ltd, Re; Lehman Brothers International (Europe) (In Administration), Re; *joined case* Lomas v Pensions Regulator [2013] UKSC 52; [2014] A.C. 209; [2013] 3 W.L.R. 504; [2013] 4 All E.R. 887; [2013] Bus. L.R. 1056; [2013] B.C.C. 624; [2013] 2 B.C.L.C. 135; [2013] B.P.I.R. 866; [2013] Pens. L.R. 299, SC; reversing [2011] EWCA Civ 1124; [2012] 1 All E.R. 1455; [2012] Bus. L.R. 818; [2012] B.C.C. 83; [2012] 1 B.C.L.C. 248; [2011] Pens. L.R. 397, CA (Civ Div); affirming [2010] EWHC 3010 (Ch); [2011] Bus. L.R. 766; [2011] B.C.C. 277; [2011] Pens. L.R. 37; Times, March 4, 2011, Ch D (Companies Ct) .................. *Digested,* 13/**2138**:
*Applied* 13/287, 14/1773: *Considered* 14/1752
Bloor Homes v Cheshire East Council [2014] P.A.D. 22, Planning Inspector
Bloy v Motor Insurers' Bureau [2013] EWCA Civ 1543; [2014] Lloyd's Rep. I.R. 75; [2014] P.I.Q.R. P9; (2013) 157(47) S.J.L.B. 37, CA (Civ Div); affirming 0MA90403, QBD (Manchester) .......................................................................... *Digested,* 14/**2559**
BLP Group Plc v Customs and Excise Commissioners (C-4/94) [1996] 1 W.L.R. 174; [1995] S.T.C. 424; [1995] E.C.R. I-983; [1995] 2 C.M.L.R. 750; [1995] All E.R. (E.C.) 401; [1995] B.V.C. 159; Times, April 17, 1995, ECJ (5th Chamber) ......... *Digested,* 95/**5059**:
*Applied* 00/5309, 01/5585, 03/4551, 03/4556, 04/3990, 04/3994, 06/4456, 08/3990, 08/4013, 09/4059, 12/3396, 13/3245: *Considered* 98/4932, 99/5015, 11/3553, 14/3089: *Distinguished* 96/5869, 99/4994: *Followed* 96/5866, 97/5003, 01/5606, 12/3426: *Referred to* 00/5337
Blue Chip Trading Ltd v Helbawi [2009] I.R.L.R. 128, EAT .......................................... *Digested,* 09/**1171**:
*Considered* 14/1119
Blue Holding (1) Pte Ltd v United States; *sub nom* United States v Abacha [2014] EWCA Civ 1291; Times, November 10, 2014, CA (Civ Div) .............................. *Digested,* 14/**406**
BLUE HORIZON/Handling unit (T1635/10) [2014] E.P.O.R. 46, EPO (Technical Bd App)
Blue Tropic Ltd v Chkhartishvili [2014] EWHC 2243 (Ch); [2014] I.L.Pr. 33, Ch D ......... *Digested,* 14/**560**
Bluewater Energy Services BV v Mercon Steel Structures BV [2014] EWHC 2132 (TCC); 155 Con. L.R. 85, QBD (TCC)
Blum v Revenue and Customs [2013] UKUT 304 (LC); [2014] R.V.R. 137, UT (Lands) *Digested,* 14/**2856**
Blunt v Jackson see I Fit Global Ltd, Re
BMC Properties and Management Ltd v Jackson (Valuation Officer) [2014] UKUT 93 (LC); [2014] R.A. 309, UT (Lands) ...................................................................... *Digested,* 14/**2127**
BMG (Mansfield) Ltd v Galliford Try Construction Ltd [2013] EWHC 3183 (TCC); [2014] C.P. Rep. 3; [2014] C.I.L.L. 3437, QBD (TCC) ........................................ *Digested,* 14/**291**
BMI Healthcare Ltd v Competition Commission [2013] CAT 24; [2014] Comp. A.R. 8, CAT
*Applied* 14/551
BMI Healthcare Ltd v Competition Commission [2014] CAT 1; [2014] Comp. A.R. 199, CAT
BN v MA (Maintenance Pending Suit: Prenuptial Agreement) [2013] EWHC 4250 (Fam); [2014] Fam. Law 443, Fam Div
BNP Paribas v Mezzotero [2004] I.R.L.R. 508; (2004) 148 S.J.L.B. 666, EAT ............. *Digested,* 04/**1289**:
*Applied* 14/1008: *Explained* 10/1054
BNP Paribas, Re 16 I.T.L. Rep. 898, CE (F)

BNY Corporate Trustee Services Ltd v Eurosail-UK 2007-3BL Plc; *joined case* BNY Corporate Trustee Services Ltd v v Neuberger Berman Europe Ltd [2013] UKSC 28; [2013] 1 W.L.R. 1408; [2013] 3 All E.R. 271; [2013] 2 All E.R. (Comm) 531; [2013] Bus. L.R. 715; [2013] B.C.C. 397; [2013] 1 B.C.L.C. 613, SC; affirming [2011] EWCA Civ 227; [2011] 1 W.L.R. 2524; [2011] 3 All E.R. 470; [2011] Bus. L.R. 1359; [2011] B.C.C. 399; [2011] 2 B.C.L.C. 1; Times, March 14, 2011, CA (Civ Div); affirming [2010] EWHC 2005 (Ch); [2011] 1 W.L.R. 1200; [2010] Bus. L.R. 1731; Times, September 23, 2010, Ch D ........... *Digested,* 13/**1704**: *Considered* 12/1833: *Followed* 14/1793

BNY Corporate Trustee Services Ltd v v Neuberger Berman Europe Ltd see BNY Corporate Trustee Services Ltd v Eurosail-UK 2007-3BL Plc

BOARD OF REGENTS, UNIVERSITY OF TEXAS/Cancer treatment (T1780/12) [2014] E.P.O.R. 28, EPO (Technical Bd App)

Board of the Pension Protection Fund v Trustees of the West of England Ship Owners Insurance Services Ltd Retirement Benefits Scheme see West of England Ship Owners Insurance Services Ltd Retirement Benefits Scheme, Re

Boardman v Phipps; *sub nom* Phipps v Boardman [1967] 2 A.C. 46; [1966] 3 W.L.R. 1009; [1966] 3 All E.R. 721; (1966) 110 S.J. 853, HL; affirming [1965] Ch. 992; [1965] 2 W.L.R. 839; [1965] 1 All E.R. 849; (1965) 109 S.J. 197, CA; affirming [1964] 1 W.L.R. 993; [1964] 2 All E.R. 187; (1964) 108 S.J. 619, Ch D ............. *Digested,* 66/**11052**: *Applied* 72/361, 72/487, 78/3060, 81/2624, 94/2083, 01/5525, 03/520, 04/456, 05/2812, 05/4307, 07/1536, 07/575, 10/1239, 13/71: *Considered* 77/2708, 78/328, 84/388, 87/3552, 87/3553, 89/459, 90/487, 01/951, 13/1787, 13/3791: *Distinguished* 88/311, 04/3940: *Followed* 14/512

Bocacina Ltd v Boca Cafes Ltd [2014] EWHC 26 (IPEC); [2014] F.S.R. 33, IPEC ........ *Digested,* 14/**364**

Bock v Air France SA (C-432/07) see Sturgeon v Condor Flugdienst GmbH (C-402/07)

Boddington v British Transport Police [1999] 2 A.C. 143; [1998] 2 W.L.R. 639; [1998] 2 All E.R. 203; (1998) 162 J.P. 455; (1998) 10 Admin. L.R. 321; (1998) 148 N.L.J. 515; Times, April 3, 1998, HL; affirming [1997] C.O.D. 3; (1996) 140 S.J.L.B. 185; Times, July 23, 1996; Independent, July 12, 1996, QBD .............. *Digested,* 98/**89**: *Applied* 03/776, 09/2160, 13/1960: *Considered* 02/873, 09/341, 14/2376: *Distinguished* 02/3708, 06/328: *Followed* 01/81, 02/4201

Bodhaniya v Crown Prosecution Service [2013] EWHC 1743 (Admin); (2014) 178 J.P. 1, QBD (Admin) ........................................................................................ *Digested,* 14/**660**

Body Corporate 83501 v Christchurch City Council [2014] Lloyd's Rep. I.R. 89, HC (NZ)

Boedeker v Schlecker (t/a Firma Anton Schlecker) (C-64/12) see Schlecker (t/a Firma Anton Schlecker) v Boedeker (C-64/12)

Boggis v Natural England see R. (on the application of Boggis) v Natural England

Bogle (Neil William) see R. v Baybasin (Mehmet Sirin)

Bogusz (Deceased), Re see Vallee v Birchwood

Bohning v United States [2005] EWHC 2613 (Admin); [2007] 1 W.L.R. 362; [2006] 3 All E.R. 394; [2005] Extradition L.R. 121, DC ..................................................... *Digested,* 06/**1610**: *Considered* 14/1228

Bolam v Friern Hospital Management Committee [1957] 1 W.L.R. 582; [1957] 2 All E.R. 118; [1955-95] P.N.L.R. 7; (1957) 101 S.J. 357, QBD ................................ *Digested,* 57/**2431**: *Applied* 67/2729, 83/2548, 84/2322, 84/2326, 85/2318, 87/2601, 87/2605, 91/2654, 93/2999, 94/3399, 95/3679, 97/3797, 99/3997, 00/2779, 00/4250, 01/4513, 02/1120, 04/2742, 04/996, 05/2839, 05/2854, 06/2869, 06/2872, 07/2926, 08/2659, 08/2763, 09/2842, 09/2844, 09/2849, 09/73, 10/2273, 10/2396, 11/2245: *Approved* 75/245: *Cited* 00/4248, 00/4283, 03/1161: *Considered* 88/2453, 89/3044, 93/2712, 94/3359, 95/3714, 96/3580, 97/3789, 02/1637, 03/2958, 04/2705, 07/2953, 13/3892, 14/2198: *Distinguished* 74/265, 92/3242, 93/233, 96/4469: *Followed* 97/2142, 98/3986, 99/4056, 99/789, 14/2299: *Not applied* 99/3992, 99/3995

Bolitho (Deceased) v City and Hackney HA [1998] A.C. 232; [1997] 3 W.L.R. 1151; [1997] 4 All E.R. 771; [1998] P.I.Q.R. P10; [1998] Lloyd's Rep. Med. 26; (1998) 39 B.M.L.R. 1; [1998] P.N.L.R. 1; (1997) 94(47) L.S.G. 30; (1997) 141 S.J.L.B. 238; Times, November 27, 1997, HL; affirming [1993] P.I.Q.R. P334; [1993] 4 Med. L.R. 381, CA (Civ Div) ............................................................................. *Digested,* 97/**3789**: *Applied* 98/3977, 99/3994, 01/4263, 01/4542, 02/3294, 03/5826, 04/2698, 06/2869, 07/2917, 07/2926, 08/2644, 08/2763, 09/2840, 09/2842, 09/2844, 09/73, 14/2197: *Considered* 96/4459, 98/3986, 03/2989, 07/2923, 07/3068: *Distinguished* 98/3969, 05/2863: *Followed* 98/3963, 99/3989

Bolkiah v KPMG; *sub nom* HRH Prince Jefri Bolkiah v KPMG [1999] 2 A.C. 222; [1999] 2 W.L.R. 215; [1999] 1 All E.R. 517; [1999] 1 B.C.L.C. 1; [1999] C.L.C. 175; [1999] P.N.L.R. 220; (1999) 149 N.L.J. 16; (1999) 143 S.J.L.B. 35; Times, April 20, 1999; Independent, January 12, 1999, HL; reversing (1998) 95(42) L.S.G. 33; (1998) 148 N.L.J. 1602; (1998) 142 S.J.L.B. 268; Times, October 22, 1998; Independent, October 22, 1998, CA (Civ Div); reversing Times, September 25, 1998, Ch D ........ *Digested,* 99/**1**:
*Applied* 00/2504, 00/4008, 02/216, 02/3108, 04/2569, 05/2724, 12/2097, 14/2060: *Considered* 99/2, 99/3796, 00/4007, 03/2821, 06/1042, 11/287, 12/1051, 12/1140, 12/334: *Distinguished* 12/418: *Followed* 00/2469, 10/1379

Bollacke v K + K Klaas & Kock BV & Co KG (C-118/13) [2014] All E.R. (EC) 1011; [2014] I.C.R. 828; [2014] I.R.L.R. 732, ECJ (1st Chamber)

Bolsover DC v Dennis Rye Ltd see Dennis Rye Ltd v Bolsover DC

Bolton v Godwin-Austen; *joined case* St Anselm Development Co Ltd v Bolton [2014] EWCA Civ 27; [2014] H.L.R. 15; [2014] 1 P. & C.R. 15; [2014] L. & T.R. 11; [2014] 1 E.G.L.R. 137, CA (Civ Div) ........ *Digested,* 14/**1983**

Bolton v Law Society [1994] 1 W.L.R. 512; [1994] 2 All E.R. 486; [1994] C.O.D. 295; Times, December 8, 1993, CA (Civ Div) ........ *Digested,* 94/**4220**:
*Applied* 98/3724, 03/1724, 05/1807, 05/3349, 09/1000, 09/2587, 10/1545: *Approved* 03/1733: *Considered* 07/2800, 10/1539: *Followed* 97/3375, 05/1805, 13/1952, 14/2056, 14/2057

Bolton School v Evans [2006] EWCA Civ 1653; [2007] I.C.R. 641; [2007] I.R.L.R. 140; (2006) 103(46) L.S.G. 30; (2006) 150 S.J.L.B. 1532, CA (Civ Div); affirming [2006] I.R.L.R. 500; [2006] E.L.R. 255, EAT ........ *Digested,* 07/**1438**:
*Followed* 14/1093

Bombay Province v Bombay Municipal Corp [1947] A.C. 58; 62 T.L.R. 643; [1947] L.J.R. 380, PC (Ind) ........ *Digested,* 47-51/**1656**:
*Applied* 07/875, 14/17: *Considered* 86/1934: *Distinguished* 88/3845: *Followed* 49/4357

Bonafonte v Grupo Torras SA see Grupo Torras SA v Al-Sabah (No.5)

Bonas Group Pension Scheme, Re see Michel Van De Wiele NV v Pensions Regulator

Bond v Hackney Citizens Advice Bureau see Rhys-Harper v Relaxion Group Plc

Bondi v Bank of America NA (C-341/04) see Eurofood IFSC Ltd, Re (C-341/04)

Bone v North Essex Partnership NHS Foundation Trust see North Essex Partnership NHS Foundation Trust v Bone

Bongrain SA's Trade Mark Application (No.2134604) [2004] EWCA Civ 1690; [2005] E.T.M.R. 47; [2005] R.P.C. 14, CA (Civ Div); affirming [2003] EWHC 531 (Ch), Ch D ........ *Digested,* 05/**2532**:
*Considered* 14/1932

Bonham-Carter v Situ Ventures Ltd; *sub nom* Situ Ventures Ltd v Bonham-Carter [2013] EWCA Civ 47; [2014] B.C.C. 125, CA (Civ Div); reversing [2012] EWHC 230 (Ch); [2012] B.C.C. 717, Ch D ........ *Digested,* 14/**519**

Bonifacti v Italy (C-9/90) see Francovich v Italy (C-6/90)

Bonik EOOD v Direktor na Direktsia Obzhalvane i upravlenie na izpalnenieto - Varna pri Tsentralno upravlenie na Natsionalnata agentsia za prihodite (C-285/11) [2013] S.T.C. 773; [2013] S.T.I. 64, ECJ (3rd Chamber)
*Applied* 14/3070: *Cited* 14/3810

Boodhoo v Secretary of State for the Home Department see Boodhoo (EEA Regs: Relevant Evidence), Re

Boodhoo (EEA Regs: Relevant Evidence), Re; *sub nom* Boodhoo v Secretary of State for the Home Department [2013] UKUT 346 (IAC); [2013] Imm. A.R. 1135; [2014] I.N.L.R. 285, UT (IAC) ........ *Digested,* 14/**1731**:
*Considered* 14/1676

Bookit Ltd v Customs and Excise Commissioners; *sub nom* Bookit Ltd v Customs and Excise Commissioners [2006] EWCA Civ 550; [2006] S.T.C. 1367; [2006] B.T.C. 5535; [2006] B.V.C. 605; [2006] L.L.R. 680; [2006] S.T.I. 1513, CA (Civ Div); affirming [2005] EWHC 1689 (Ch); [2005] S.T.C. 1481; [2005] B.T.C. 5581; [2005] B.V.C. 612; [2005] S.T.I. 1337, Ch D; reversing [2004] B.V.C. 2229; [2004] V. & D.R. 421; [2004] S.T.I. 1949, V&DTr (London) ........ *Digested,* 06/**4435**:
*Applied* 07/5568, 08/3993, 14/3046: *Distinguished* 08/4041

Bookit Ltd v Customs and Excise Commissioners see Bookit Ltd v Customs and Excise Commissioners

Bookit Ltd v Revenue and Customs Commissioners [2014] UKFTT 856 (TC); [2014] S.T.I. 2907, FTT (Tax)

Booth v Bradford MDC see Bradford MDC v Booth

Booth v Mirror Group Newspapers Plc [1992] S.T.C. 615; Times, July 10, 1992, QBD . *Digested,* 93/**2287**:
*Considered* 14/2894

Booth v Parole Board see Reilly's Application for Judicial Review, Re

Bootle v HM Inspector of Taxes (Unreported, December 14, 1995), Sp Comm
*Approved* 14/2894: *Considered* 08/3846

Bophuthatswana National Commercial Corp v Customs and Excise Commissioners [1993] S.T.C. 702, CA (Civ Div); affirming [1992] S.T.C. 741, QBD .................. *Digested,* 94/**4617**: *Applied* 14/3102

Borax Europe Ltd v General State Administration 17 I.T.L. Rep. 452, Trib Sup (Sp)

Borealis AB v Geogas Trading SA [2010] EWHC 2789 (Comm); [2011] 1 Lloyd's Rep. 482, QBD (Comm) .................. *Digested,* 11/**529**: *Applied* 13/400, 14/617: *Considered* 13/1741

BOREALIS/Polymer composition for pipes (T59/08) [2014] E.P.O.R. 19, EPO (Technical Bd App)

Borovsky v Slovakia (24528/02) (2014) 59 E.H.R.R. 25, ECHR

Borshchevskiy v Russia (14853/03) (Unreported, February 12, 2007), ECHR
*Applied* 14/59

Boss Holdings Ltd v Grosvenor West End Properties Ltd; *joined case* Mallett & Sons (Antiques) Ltd v Grosvenor West End Properties Ltd [2008] UKHL 5; [2008] 1 W.L.R. 289; [2008] 2 All E.R. 759; [2008] H.L.R. 29; [2008] 2 P. & C.R. 20; [2008] L. & T.R. 10; [2008] 1 E.G.L.R. 51; [2008] 15 E.G. 174; [2008] R.V.R. 313; [2008] 5 E.G. 167 (C.S.); (2008) 152(6) S.J.L.B. 31; [2008] N.P.C. 9; Times, February 4, 2008, HL; reversing [2006] EWCA Civ 594; [2006] 1 W.L.R. 2848; [2006] L. & T.R. 16; [2006] 2 E.G.L.R. 43; [2006] 26 E.G. 156; [2006] 13 E.G. 140 (C.S.); Times, May 26, 2006, CA (Civ Div) .................. *Digested,* 08/**2450**: *Considered* 12/3423, 13/2439: *Followed* 10/2716, 14/1770

Botham v Ministry of Defence see Edwards v Chesterfield Royal Hospital NHS Foundation Trust

Botham v Ministry of Defence see Lawson v Serco Ltd

Bothma (t/a DAB Builders) v Mayhaven Healthcare Ltd [2006] EWHC 2601 (QB), QBD
*Affirmed* 08/587: *Considered* 14/582

Bothma (t/a DAB Builders) v Mayhaven Healthcare Ltd [2007] EWCA Civ 527; 114 Con. L.R. 131, CA (Civ Div) .................. *Digested,* 08/**587**: *Considered* 12/586: *Followed* 14/114

Bottomley v Todmorden Cricket Club [2003] EWCA Civ 1575; [2004] P.I.Q.R. P18; (2003) 100(48) L.S.G. 18; (2003) 147 S.J.L.B. 1309; Times, November 13, 2003, CA (Civ Div) .................. *Digested,* 03/**2990**: *Considered* 07/2935: *Distinguished* 04/2707: *Followed* 14/2996

Bouanich v Directeur des services fiscaux de la Drome (C-375/12) [2014] B.T.C. 9; [2014] S.T.I. 1575, ECJ (5th Chamber)

Bournemouth University Higher Education Corp v Buckland; *sub nom* Buckland v Bournemouth University Higher Education Corp [2010] EWCA Civ 121; [2011] Q.B. 323; [2010] 3 W.L.R. 1664; [2010] 4 All E.R. 186; [2010] I.C.R. 908; [2010] I.R.L.R. 445; (2010) 154(8) S.J.L.B. 28; Times, May 3, 2010, CA (Civ Div); reversing in part [2009] I.C.R. 1042; [2009] I.R.L.R. 606, EAT .................. *Digested,* 10/**1032**: *Applied* 14/3500: *Considered* 12/1063, 14/1021: *Followed* 14/1024

Bouygues UK Ltd v Dahl-Jensen UK Ltd [2001] 1 All E.R. (Comm) 1041; [2001] C.L.C. 927; [2000] B.L.R. 522; (2001) 3 T.C.L.R. 2; 73 Con. L.R. 135; (2000) 97(35) L.S.G. 36; Times, August 17, 2000, CA (Civ Div); affirming [2000] B.L.R. 49; (2000) 2 T.C.L.R. 308; 70 Con. L.R. 41; Independent, February 7, 2000, QBD (TCC) .................. *Digested,* 00/**3489**: *Applied* 02/654, 03/667, 05/644, 06/333, 10/566, 10/845, 10/847, 12/600, 14/578, 14/581: *Considered* 02/655, 11/486: *Distinguished* 10/556: *Followed* 01/6289, 10/558, 10/846

Bowen-West v Secretary of State for Communities and Local Government [2012] EWCA Civ 321; [2012] Env. L.R. 22; [2012] J.P.L. 1128, CA (Civ Div); affirming [2011] EWHC 2930 (Admin); [2012] J.P.L. 450, QBD (Admin) .................. *Digested,* 12/**2585**: *Considered* 13/2365: *Followed* 14/1187

Bown v Gould & Swayne [1996] P.N.L.R. 130; [1996] N.P.C. 5, CA (Civ Div) .................. *Digested,* 96/**4498**: *Applied* 99/308: *Considered* 14/3216: *Distinguished* 99/4051

Bowring v Revenue and Customs Commissioners [2013] UKFTT 366 (TC); [2014] S.F.T.D. 347; [2013] S.T.I. 2889, FTT (Tax) .................. *Digested,* 14/**2974**

Bowring v Secretary of State for Communities and Local Government [2013] EWHC 1115 (Admin); [2013] J.P.L. 1417, QBD (Admin) .................. *Digested,* 13/**2303**: *Applied* 14/2385

Boxmoor Construction Ltd v Revenue and Customs Commissioners [2014] UKFTT 833 (TC); [2014] S.T.I. 2770, FTT (Tax)

Boxus v Region Wallonne (C-128/09) [2011] E.C.R. I-9711; [2012] C.E.C. 414; [2012] Env. L.R. 14, ECJ (Grand Chamber)
*Followed* 14/1201

Boyd v Incommunities Ltd [2013] EWCA Civ 756; [2013] H.L.R. 44, CA (Civ Div) ......... *Digested,* 14/**1999**

Boyle v SCA Packaging Ltd see SCA Packaging Ltd v Boyle

Boys v Chaplin; *sub nom* Chaplin v Boys [1971] A.C. 356; [1969] 3 W.L.R. 322; [1969] 2 All E.R. 1085; [1969] 2 Lloyd's Rep. 487; (1969) 113 S.J. 608, HL; affirming [1968] 2 Q.B. 1; [1968] 2 W.L.R. 328; [1968] 1 All E.R. 283; (1967) 111 S.J. 968; Times, December 7, 1967, CA (Civ Div); affirming [1967] 3 W.L.R. 266; [1967] 2 All E.R. 665; (1967) 111 S.J. 297, QBD ......... *Digested,* 69/**469**:
*Applied* 76/2174, 92/477, 04/568, 06/635: *Considered* 78/26u, 89/3528, 92/1916, 95/4724, 95/4736, 02/634, 05/608, 06/641, 14/825: *Explained* 92/3456: *Followed* 83/360, 00/1463

BP Plc v AON Ltd (No.1) [2005] EWHC 2554 (Comm); [2006] 1 Lloyd's Rep. 549, QBD (Comm) ......... *Digested,* 06/**648**:
*Applied* 14/426

BP Properties Ltd v Buckler (1988) 55 P. & C.R. 337; (1987) 284 E.G. 375; (1987) 137 N.L.J. 899, CA (Civ Div) ......... *Digested,* 88/**2155**:
*Applied* 01/578, 06/3453: *Considered* 05/3439, 14/1588: *Followed* 01/4842

BP Supergas Anonimos Etairia Geniki Emporiki Viomichaniki Kai Antiprossopeion v Greece (C-62/93) [1995] S.T.C. 805; [1995] E.C.R. I-1883; [1995] All E.R. (E.C.) 684, ECJ (6th Chamber) ......... *Digested,* 95/**5063**:
*Applied* 14/3057: *Followed* 02/4737

BPC Hotels Ltd v Brooke North (A Firm) see Chandra v Brooke North (A Firm)

BPE Solicitors v Gabriel see Gabriel v Little

BPP University College of Professional Studies v Revenue and Customs Commissioners; *sub nom* Revenue and Customs Commissioners v BPP Holdings Ltd [2014] UKUT 496 (TCC); [2014] B.V.C. 544, UT (Tax); reversing [2014] UKFTT 644 (TC); [2014] S.T.I. 2598, FTT (Tax)

Brabon, Re; *sub nom* Treharne v Brabon [2000] B.C.C. 1171; [2001] 1 B.C.L.C. 11; [2000] B.P.I.R. 537; [2000] E.G. 38 (C.S.); [2000] N.P.C. 21, Ch D ......... *Digested,* 00/**3450**:
*Applied* 13/1707, 14/1809: *Distinguished* 05/135, 06/65

Bracking v Secretary of State for Work and Pensions see R. (on the application of Bracking) v Secretary of State for Work and Pensions

Bracknell Forest BC v Adams see Adams v Bracknell Forest BC

Bradburn v Great Western Railway Co (1874-75) L.R. 10 Ex. 1, Ex Ct
*Applied* 47-51/2525, 47-51/2543, 63/2456, 66/8472, 71/3091, 72/836, 73/740, 79/2472, 14/827: *Approved* 69/906: *Considered* 63/951, 94/2687, 99/793

Bradford MDC v Booth; *sub nom* Booth v Bradford MDC (2000) 164 J.P. 485; (2001) 3 L.G.L.R. 8; [2001] L.L.R. 151; [2000] C.O.D. 338; (2000) 164 J.P.N. 801; Times, May 31, 2000, DC ......... *Digested,* 00/**395**:
*Applied* 06/2761, 06/2778, 07/2800, 07/2802, 09/371, 10/746, 14/2131: *Not applied* 12/533

Bradshaw v University College of Wales (Aberystwyth) [1988] 1 W.L.R. 190; [1987] 3 All E.R. 200; (1988) 132 S.J. 51, Ch D ......... *Digested,* 87/**293**:
*Considered* 88/271, 14/285

Brady v Environmental Protection Agency (C-113/12) [2014] 2 C.M.L.R. 3; [2014] Env. L.R. 13, ECJ (4th Chamber)

Bramston v Haut [2012] EWCA Civ 1637; [2013] 1 W.L.R. 1720; [2013] B.P.I.R. 25, CA (Civ Div); reversing [2012] EWHC 1279 (Ch); [2012] B.P.I.R. 672, Ch D (Bankruptcy Ct) ......... *Digested,* 13/**1700**:
*Applied* 14/1795, 14/1796: *Considered* 14/1832

Bramston v Oraki [2014] EWHC 2982 (Ch); [2014] B.P.I.R. 1374, Ch D

Bramston v Riaz [2014] B.P.I.R. 42, CC (Wakefield) ......... *Digested,* 14/**1830**

Brandeaux Advisers (UK) Ltd v Chadwick [2010] EWHC 3241 (QB); [2011] I.R.L.R. 224, QBD ......... *Digested,* 11/**1068**:
*Considered* 14/1022

Brandwood v Bakewell Management Ltd see Bakewell Management Ltd v Brandwood

Brannigan v Davison [1997] A.C. 238; [1996] 3 W.L.R. 859; 2 B.H.R.C. 395; (1996) 140 S.J.L.B. 231, PC (NZ) ......... *Digested,* 97/**1168**:
*Applied* 00/315: *Considered* 14/539

Bratt Auto Services Ltd v Revenue and Customs Commissioners [2014] UKFTT 676 (TC); [2014] S.F.T.D. 1120; [2014] S.T.I. 2666, FTT (Tax) ......... *Digested,* 14/**3076**

Braun v Land Baden-Wurttemberg (C-524/13) [2014] B.T.C. 36, ECJ (2nd Chamber)

Breadner v Granville-Grossman (Costs) [2006] W.T.L.R. 411; [2001] W.T.L.R. 377, Ch D ......... *Digested,* 01/**5526**:
*Considered* 14/374

Bremer Vulcan Schiffbau und Maschinenfabrik v South India Shipping Corp see Bremer Vulkan Schiffbau und Maschinenfabrik v South India Shipping Corp Ltd

Bremer Vulkan Schiffbau und Maschinenfabrik v South India Shipping Corp Ltd; *sub nom* Bremer Vulcan Schiffbau und Maschinenfabrik v South India Shipping Corp; *joined case* Gregg v Raytheon [1981] A.C. 909; [1981] 2 W.L.R. 141; [1981] 1 All E.R. 289; [1981] 1 Lloyd's Rep. 253; [1981] Com. L.R. 19; [1981] E.C.C. 151; (1981) 125 S.J. 114, HL; affirming [1980] 2 W.L.R. 905; [1980] 1 All E.R. 420; [1980] 1 Lloyd's Rep. 255; (1980) 124 S.J. 396; Times, November 28, 1979, CA (Civ Div); affirming [1979] 3 W.L.R. 471; [1979] 3 All E.R. 194; (1979) 76 L.S.G. 834; (1979) 123 S.J. 504, QBD ........ *Digested,* 81/**119**: *Applied* 81/106, 81/99, 82/139, 83/142, 88/131, 92/189, 95/179: *Considered* 80/98, 81/113, 85/116, 87/133, 87/147, 98/244, 01/5711, 02/294, 08/4086: *Distinguished* 93/151, 14/1022: *Referred to* 80/2461, 81/281, 81/79

Brendoncare Foundation v Sevenoaks DC [2014] P.A.D. 34, Planning Inspector

Brennan v Prior see Devillebichot (Deceased), Re

Brent LBC v Risk Management Partners Ltd; *sub nom* Risk Management Partners Ltd v Brent LBC [2011] UKSC 7; [2011] 2 A.C. 34; [2011] 2 W.L.R. 166; [2011] 2 All E.R. 209; [2011] P.T.S.R. 481; [2011] 2 C.M.L.R. 26; [2011] Eu. L.R. 615; [2011] B.L.G.R. 169; (2011) 155(6) S.J.L.B. 31; Times, February 10, 2011, SC; reversing [2009] EWCA Civ 490; [2010] P.T.S.R. 349; [2010] B.L.G.R. 99, CA (Civ Div) ........ *Digested,* 11/**2635**: *Applied* 10/1692, 11/2137, 12/3686: *Considered* 10/2672, 11/2633: *Followed* 14/1619

Brent LBC v Shulem B Association Ltd [2011] EWHC 1663 (Ch); [2011] 1 W.L.R. 3014; [2011] 4 All E.R. 778; [2011] L. & T.R. 22; [2011] 27 E.G. 77 (C.S.); [2011] N.P.C. 69, Ch D ........ *Digested,* 12/**2066**: *Considered* 12/2065, 14/2013

Bressol v Gouvernement de la Communaute Francaise (C-73/08) [2010] 3 C.M.L.R. 20; [2011] C.E.C. 80, ECJ (Grand Chamber) *Applied* 11/3177: *Considered* 14/1102

Brewster v Northern Ireland Local Government Officers' Superannuation Committee [2013] NICA 54; [2014] Pens. L.R. 103, CA (NI) ........ *Digested,* 14/**3226**

Brewster's Application for Judicial Review, Re [2012] NIQB 85; [2013] Pens. L.R. 165, QBD (NI) ........ *Digested,* 13/**3395**: *Reversed* 14/3226

Breyer Group Plc v Department of Energy and Climate Change; *joined cases* Touch Solar Ltd v Department of Energy and Climate Change; Homesun Holdings Ltd v Department of Energy and Climate Change; Free Power for Schools LP v Department of Energy and Climate Change [2014] EWHC 2257 (QB); [2014] J.P.L. 1346, QBD

Brezec v Croatia (7177/10) [2014] H.L.R. 3, ECHR *Considered* 14/1968

Brick Farm Management Ltd v Richmond Housing Partnership Ltd; *sub nom* Richmond Housing Partnership Ltd v Brick Farm Management Ltd [2005] EWHC 1650 (QB); [2005] 1 W.L.R. 3934; [2006] H.L.R. 3; [2005] 3 E.G.L.R. 57; [2005] 48 E.G. 224; (2005) 155 N.L.J. 1483; [2005] N.P.C. 108; [2006] 1 P. & C.R. DG5; Times, August 30, 2005, QBD ........ *Digested,* 05/**3385**: *Applied* 14/2018

Brickfield Properties Ltd v Botten [2013] UKUT 133 (LC); [2013] 2 E.G.L.R. 70; [2013] 2 P. & C.R. DG8, UT (Lands) ........ *Digested,* 14/**1992**

Bridport and West Dorset Golf Club Ltd v Revenue and Customs Commissioners (C-495/12) see Revenue and Customs Commissioners v Bridport and West Dorset Golf Club Ltd (C-495/12)

Briels v Minister van Infrastructuur en Milieu (C-521/12) [2014] P.T.S.R. 1120, ECJ (2nd Chamber)

Briess v Rosher see Briess v Woolley

Briess v Woolley; *sub nom* Briess v Rosher [1954] A.C. 333; [1954] 2 W.L.R. 832; [1954] 1 All E.R. 909; (1954) 98 S.J. 286, HL; reversing [1953] 2 Q.B. 218; [1953] 2 W.L.R. 608; [1953] 1 All E.R. 717; (1953) 97 S.J. 209, CA ........ *Digested,* 54/**468**: *Applied* 14/2201: *Approved* 66/9912

Briggs v Gleeds see Gleeds Retirement Benefits Scheme, Re

Bright v Motor Insurers' Bureau [2014] EWHC 1557 (QB); [2014] 4 Costs L.R. 643; [2014] R.T.R. 24, QBD ........ *Digested,* 14/**2047**

Brighton University v Dovehouse Interiors Ltd; *sub nom* University of Brighton v Dovehouse Interiors Ltd [2014] EWHC 940 (TCC); [2014] B.L.R. 432; 153 Con. L.R. 147, QBD (TCC) ........ *Digested,* 14/**577**

Brightsolid Online Technology Ltd v Revenue and Customs Commissioners [2014] UKFTT 1040 (TC); [2014] S.T.I. 3557, FTT (Tax)
Brilliant Independent Media Specialists Ltd (In Liquidation), Re see Maxwell v Brookes
Bristol & West Building Society v Fancy & Jackson [1997] 4 All E.R. 582; [1997] N.P.C. 109, Ch D ........ *Digested,* 98/**4027**: *Considered* 01/4529, 14/2195: *Followed* 99/4036, 99/4379, 13/1950: *Not applied* 11/2259
Bristol & West Building Society v Mothew (t/a Stapley & Co); *sub nom* Mothew v Bristol & West Building Society [1998] Ch. 1; [1997] 2 W.L.R. 436; [1996] 4 All E.R. 698; [1997] P.N.L.R. 11; (1998) 75 P. & C.R. 241; [1996] E.G. 136 (C.S.); (1996) 146 N.L.J. 1273; (1996) 140 S.J.L.B. 206; [1996] N.P.C. 126; Times, August 2, 1996, CA (Civ Div) ........ *Digested,* 96/**4503**: *Applied* 97/3822, 97/3823, 98/859, 99/458, 00/2334, 03/3015, 04/2569, 07/797, 11/2707, 11/3470: *Considered* 97/3827, 98/2298, 99/3796, 00/2323, 00/5270, 00/649, 05/2873, 06/4389, 10/1118, 12/275, 12/3345, 13/1305, 14/2195: *Distinguished* 08/3897: *Followed* 99/3814, 99/4037, 03/5827, 11/2259, 12/57, 14/2055
Bristol & West Plc v Revenue and Customs Commissioners [2014] UKUT 73 (TCC); [2014] S.T.C. 1048; [2014] B.T.C. 507; [2014] S.T.I. 869, UT (Tax); reversing in part [2013] UKFTT 216 (TC); [2013] S.F.T.D. 1027; [2013] S.T.I. 2220, FTT (Tax) ........ *Digested,* 14/**2970**
Bristol Alliance Nominee (No.1) Ltd v Bennett see A/Wear UK Ltd (In Administration), Re
Bristol City Council v A Mother; *sub nom* SB (Minors), Re [2012] EWHC 2548 (Fam); [2013] 2 F.L.R. 1153; [2012] Fam. Law 1448, Fam Div ........ *Digested,* 14/**1340**: *Considered* 14/1288
Bristol City Council v AA [2014] EWHC 1022 (Fam); [2014] Fam. Law 965, Fam Div
Bristol City Council v Digs (Bristol) Ltd [2014] EWHC 869 (Admin); [2014] H.L.R. 30; [2014] 2 E.G.L.R. 169; [2014] L.L.R. 679, QBD (Admin) ........ *Digested,* 14/**1606**
Bristol Corp v Ross see McPhail v Persons, Names Unknown
Bristol Myers Squibb Co v Paranova A/S (C-427/93); *joined cases* CH Boehringer Sohn v Paranova A/S (C-429/93); Bayer AG v Paranova A/S (C-436/93) [2003] Ch. 75; [2002] 3 W.L.R. 1746; [1996] E.C.R. I-3457; [1997] 1 C.M.L.R. 1151; [1996] C.E.C. 716; [1996] E.T.M.R. 1; [1997] F.S.R. 102; (1997) 34 B.M.L.R. 59, ECJ; no effect [1996] E.C.R. I-3457; [1996] F.S.R. 225, AGO ........ *Digested,* 97/**4879**: *Applied* 97/3892, 98/3506, 00/3706, 00/3709, 04/2400, 08/2392, 08/2398, 09/2459, 13/1818: *Cited* 00/3703: *Considered* 98/3514, 98/3544, 99/3560, 02/2916, 03/2641, 14/1925: *Distinguished* 98/3426: *Followed* 99/3558, 04/2411: *Referred to* 05/2444
Brit UW Ltd v Imperial Marine Co see Starlight Shipping Co v Allianz Marine & Aviation Versicherungs AG
Brit UW Ltd v Imperial Marine Co see Starlight Shipping Co v Allianz Marine & Aviation Versicherungs AG
Brit UW Ltd v Starlight Shipping Co see Starlight Shipping Co v Allianz Marine & Aviation Versicherungs AG
Brit UW Ltd v Starlight Shipping Co see Starlight Shipping Co v Allianz Marine & Aviation Versicherungs AG
Brit UW Ltd v Starlight Shipping Co see Starlight Shipping Co v Allianz Marine & Aviation Versicherungs AG
British Airways Pension Trustees Ltd v British Airways Plc see Stevens v Bell
British Airways Plc v Fox see Fox v British Airways Plc
British Airways Plc v Sindicato Espanol de Pilotos de Lineas Aereas [2013] EWHC 1657 (Comm); [2013] 2 C.L.C. 65; [2013] I.L.Pr. 45, QBD (Comm) ........ *Digested,* 14/**555**
British Airways Plc v Valencia [2014] I.R.L.R. 683; [2014] I.C.R. D29, EAT ........ *Digested,* 14/**1138**
British American Insurance (Kenya) Ltd v Matelec SAL [2013] EWHC 3278 (Comm); [2014] Lloyd's Rep. I.R. 287, QBD (Comm) ........ *Digested,* 14/**117**
British American Nickel Corp Ltd v MJ O'Brien Ltd [1927] A.C. 369, PC (Can) *Applied* 71/1238: *Considered* 14/275
British American Tobacco Denmark A/S v Exel Europe Ltd see British American Tobacco Switzerland SA v Exel Europe Ltd
British American Tobacco International Ltd v Belgium (C-435/03); *sub nom* British American Tobacco International Ltd v Ministerie van Financien (C-435/03) [2006] S.T.C. 158; [2005] E.C.R. I-7077; [2005] 3 C.M.L.R. 33; [2005] B.T.C. 5724; [2005] B.V.C. 755; [2005] S.T.I. 1256, ECJ (3rd Chamber) ........ *Digested,* 06/**4488**: *Applied* 14/3082
British American Tobacco International Ltd v Ministerie van Financien (C-435/03) see British American Tobacco International Ltd v Belgium (C-435/03)

British American Tobacco Switzerland SA v Exel Europe Ltd; *joined case* British American Tobacco Denmark A/S v Exel Europe Ltd [2013] EWCA Civ 1319; [2014] 1 W.L.R. 4526; [2014] 1 Lloyd's Rep. 503; [2013] 2 C.L.C. 683; [2014] R.T.R. 12, CA (Civ Div); reversing [2012] EWHC 694 (Comm); [2013] 1 W.L.R. 397; [2012] 2 Lloyd's Rep. 1; [2012] 1 C.L.C. 549, QBD (Comm) ....................... *Digested,* 14/**3011**

British Coal Corp v Keeble [1997] I.R.L.R. 336, EAT ....................... *Digested,* 97/**2266**: *Applied* 98/2195: *Considered* 05/1301, 08/1133: *Referred to* 14/1040

British Credit Trust Ltd v Revenue and Customs Commissioners [2014] UKFTT 744 (TC); [2014] S.T.I. 2735, FTT (Tax)

British Film Institute v Revenue and Customs Commissioners [2013] UKFTT 72 (TC); [2013] S.F.T.D. 629; [2013] S.T.I. 429, FTT (Tax) ....................... *Digested,* 13/**3190**: *Affirmed* 14/3043

British Gas Plc v Stockport MBC see Transco Plc v Stockport MBC

British Gas Trading Ltd v Oak Cash and Carry Ltd [2014] EWHC 4058 (QB); [2014] 6 Costs L.R. 1122, QBD

British Malleable Iron Co Ltd v Revelan (IOM) Ltd [2013] EWHC 1954 (Ch); [2013] 3 E.G.L.R. 23, Ch D ....................... *Digested,* 14/**2521**

British Printing Industries Federation v Revenue and Customs Commissioners [2014] UKFTT 150 (TC); [2014] S.T.I. 951, FTT (Tax)

British Red Ash Collieries Ltd, Re [1920] 1 Ch. 326, CA *Considered* 14/1973

British Seafood Ltd v Kruk [2008] EWHC 1528 (QB), QBD *Considered* 14/1289

British Sky Broadcasting Group Plc v Duarte (t/a Crispin Inn) [2014] EWHC 111 (Ch); [2014] F.S.R. 32, Ch D (Patents Ct) ....................... *Digested,* 14/**1860**

British Sky Broadcasting Ltd v Office of Communications; *joined case* British Telecommunications Plc v Office of Communications [2014] EWCA Civ 133; [2014] 4 All E.R. 673; [2014] 2 All E.R. (Comm) 973; [2014] Bus. L.R. 713, CA (Civ Div); reversing in part [2012] CAT 20, CAT ....................... *Digested,* 14/**552**

British Telecommunications Plc v Office of Communications [2012] EWCA Civ 1051, CA (Civ Div); affirming [2011] CAT 5, CAT *Considered* 14/545

British Telecommunications Plc v Office of Communications see British Sky Broadcasting Ltd v Office of Communications

British Telecommunications Plc v One in a Million Ltd; *joined cases* Ladbroke Group Plc v One in a Million Ltd; J Sainsbury Plc v One in a Million Ltd; Virgin Enterprises Ltd v One in a Million Ltd; Marks & Spencer Plc v One in a Million Ltd [1999] 1 W.L.R. 903; [1998] 4 All E.R. 476; [1999] E.T.M.R. 61; [1997-98] Info. T.L.R. 423; [1998] I.T.C.L.R. 146; [2001] E.B.L.R. 2; [1999] F.S.R. 1; [1998] Masons C.L.R. 165; (1998) 95(37) L.S.G. 37; (1998) 148 N.L.J. 1179; Times, July 29, 1998; Independent, July 31, 1998, CA (Civ Div); affirming [1997-98] Info. T.L.R. 316; [1998] I.T.C.L.R. 7; [1998] F.S.R. 265; (1997) 16 Tr. L.R. 554; [1998] Masons C.L.R. 116; (1998) 21(2) I.P.D. 21016; (1997) 147 N.L.J. 1809; Times, December 2, 1997, Ch D ....................... *Digested,* 98/**3520**: *Applied* 04/2272, 06/2593, 07/2545, 14/1025: *Considered* 98/3501, 00/3592, 01/5357, 02/2782, 02/2891, 03/2648, 07/2674: *Followed* 11/1943: *Referred to* 99/3587

British Telecommunications Plc v Revenue and Customs Commissioners see Revenue and Customs Commissioners v GMAC UK Plc

British Telecommunications Plc v Telefonica O2 UK Ltd see Telefonica O2 UK Ltd v British Telecommunications Plc

British Union for the Abolition of Vivisection (BUAV) v Secretary of State for the Home Department [2014] EWHC 43 (Admin); [2014] A.C.D. 69, QBD (Admin)

British Waterways Board v Severn Trent Water Ltd [2001] EWCA Civ 276; [2002] Ch. 25; [2001] 3 W.L.R. 613; [2001] 3 All E.R. 673; [2001] Env. L.R. 45; [2002] E.H.L.R. 1; (2001) 98(16) L.S.G. 34; (2001) 98(13) L.S.G. 43; [2001] N.P.C. 53; Times, March 23, 2001; Independent, March 14, 2001, CA (Civ Div); reversing [2001] Ch. 32; [2000] 3 W.L.R. 1; [2000] 1 All E.R. 347; [2000] Env. L.R. 284; (1999) 96(42) L.S.G. 41; (1999) 143 S.J.L.B. 249; [1999] N.P.C. 120; Times, October 26, 1999; Independent, November 29, 1999, Ch D ....................... *Digested,* 01/**5632**: *Approved* 14/3034: *Considered* 07/2961, 12/3374: *Followed* 13/3182

British Westinghouse Electric & Manufacturing Co Ltd v Underground Electric Railways Co of London Ltd (No.2) [1912] A.C. 673, HL; reversing [1912] 3 K.B. 128, CA
*Applied* 47-51/431, 53/3775, 55/2483, 56/936, 65/993, 69/3313, 70/748, 72/826, 78/312, 78/704, 79/658, 00/2566: *Approved* 66/3146: *Considered* 75/18.u, 75/248, 76/59.u, 79/849, 85/1860, 91/1503, 91/3194, 94/3438, 95/4510, 97/1808, 01/894, 11/538, 14/827: *Distinguished* 90/1565: *Followed* 95/3704, 97/3843, 14/2210

Briton Medical and General Life Assurance Association, Re (1886) 32 Ch. D. 503, Ch D
*Considered* 14/1808

Broadland DC v Trott [2011] EWCA Civ 301, CA (Civ Div); reversing [2011] J.P.L. 62, QBD
*Considered* 11/2549, 14/2376

Brock v Wollams [1949] 2 K.B. 388; [1949] 1 All E.R. 715; (1949) 93 S.J. 319, CA ....... *Digested,* 47-51/**8806**:
*Applied* 47-51/8457, 47-51/8812, 47-51/8813, 53/3133, 78/1818, 10/1703: *Approved* 67/1858: *Considered* 64/3153, 65/3406, 73/106.u, 81/1323, 86/1932, 90/2827, 14/2008: *Distinguished* 47-51/8810: *Followed* 47-51/8817

Brockenhurst College v Revenue and Customs Commissioners [2013] UKFTT 153 (TC); [2013] S.T.I. 1523, FTT (Tax)
*Affirmed* 14/3042

Brockton Capital LLP v Atlantic-Pacific Capital Inc [2014] EWHC 1459 (Comm); [2014] 2 Lloyd's Rep. 275, QBD (Comm) ........ *Digested,* 14/**131**

Broderip v Salomon see Salomon v Salomon & Co Ltd

Brodziak v Poland; *sub nom* Madej v Poland; Marczuk v Poland; Dunec v Poland [2013] EWHC 3394 (Admin); [2014] A.C.D. 59, QBD (Admin)

Brogan v United Kingdom (11209/84) see Brogan v United Kingdom (A/145-B)

Brogan v United Kingdom (A/145-B); *sub nom* Tracey v United Kingdom; Brogan v United Kingdom (11209/84); *joined cases* McFadden v United Kingdom (11365/85); Coyle v United Kingdom (11266/84) (1989) 11 E.H.R.R. 117; Times, November 30, 1988; Independent, November 30, 1988; Guardian, December 7, 1988, ECHR; no effect (1987) 9 E.H.R.R. CD378, Eur Comm HR *Digested,* 88/**1804**:
*Applied* 03/2157, 05/2130, 07/2231, 08/1967: *Considered* 14/2464: *Followed* 98/3073

Brogden v Investec Bank Plc [2014] EWHC 2785 (Comm); [2014] I.R.L.R. 924, QBD (Comm)

Brogsitter v Fabrication de Montres Normandes EURL (C-548/12) [2014] Q.B. 753; [2014] 2 W.L.R. 1600; [2014] 1 All E.R. (Comm) 965; [2014] I.L.Pr. 20, ECJ (7th Chamber)

Bromarin AB v IMD Investments Ltd [1999] S.T.C. 301; [1999] B.T.C. 74, CA (Civ Div); reversing [1998] S.T.C. 244; [1998] B.T.C. 3, Ch D ........ *Digested,* 99/**4662**:
*Applied* 14/2508

Bromley LBC v Special Educational Needs Tribunal (No.2) [1999] 3 All E.R. 587; (1999) 1 L.G.L.R. 970; [1999] B.L.G.R. 747; [1999] Ed. C.R. 907; [1999] E.L.R. 260; (1999) 2 C.C.L. Rep. 239; [1999] C.O.D. 409; Times, June 14, 1999; Independent, June 17, 1999, CA (Civ Div); affirming (Unreported, December 18, 1998), QBD ........ *Digested,* 99/**1890**:
*Applied* 02/1167, 07/1266, 14/943: *Considered* 03/1123, 07/1262, 12/993

Bronester v Priddle [1961] 1 W.L.R. 1294; [1961] 3 All E.R. 471; (1961) 105 S.J. 683, CA ........ *Digested,* 61/**56**:
*Followed* 14/2873

Brook v Reed; *sub nom* Brook, Re [2011] EWCA Civ 331; [2012] 1 W.L.R. 419; [2011] 3 All E.R. 743; [2011] B.C.C. 423; [2012] 1 B.C.L.C. 379; [2011] 4 Costs L.R. 622; [2011] B.P.I.R. 583; (2011) 108(14) L.S.G. 21; (2011) 161 N.L.J. 473; [2011] N.P.C. 34, CA (Civ Div) ........ *Digested,* 11/**1897**:
*Applied* 14/1781: *Considered* 11/1852

Brook, Re see Brook v Reed

Brooke v Purton see Huntley (Deceased), Re

Brooks v Blackpool BC [2013] EWHC 3735 (Admin); (2014) 178 J.P. 79; [2014] R.T.R. 13, QBD (Admin) ........ *Digested,* 14/**2564**

Brooks v Commissioner of Police of the Metropolis [2005] UKHL 24; [2005] 1 W.L.R. 1495; [2005] 2 All E.R. 489; [2005] Po. L.R. 157; (2005) 155 N.L.J. 653; Times, April 26, 2005, HL; reversing [2002] EWCA Civ 407; [2002] Po. L.R. 88; Daily Telegraph, April 11, 2002, CA (Civ Div) ........ *Digested,* 05/**3342**:
*Applied* 07/2934, 08/2641, 14/2203: *Considered* 06/2880, 10/3420: *Distinguished* 06/2171: *Followed* 08/2646, 13/2387

Broomleigh Housing Association Ltd v Okonkwo [2010] EWCA Civ 1113; [2011] C.P. Rep. 4; [2011] H.L.R. 5; [2010] 42 E.G. 104 (C.S.); (2010) 107(41) L.S.G. 22; Times, November 18, 2010, CA (Civ Div) ........ *Digested,* 11/**336**: *Considered* 14/391

Brosa v Germany (5709/09) 37 B.H.R.C. 354, ECHR

Brown v Bennett [1999] B.C.C. 525; [1999] 1 B.C.L.C. 649, CA (Civ Div); affirming [1999] B.C.C. 91; [1998] 2 B.C.L.C. 97; Times, January 3, 1998, Ch D ........ *Digested,* 99/**3288**: *Applied* 07/3438: *Considered* 14/2991

Brown v City of London Corp; *sub nom* Satelscoop BV, Re; Sobam BV, Re [1996] 1 W.L.R. 1070; [1996] B.C.C. 351; [1996] 1 B.C.L.C. 446; [1996] 1 E.G.L.R. 139; [1996] 22 E.G. 118; [1996] R.A. 93; [1995] E.G. 189 (C.S.); [1995] N.P.C. 180, Ch D ........ *Digested,* 96/**4917**: *Considered* 14/1972

Brown v Davies [2013] EWHC 3523 (Fam); [2014] Fam. Law 148, Fam Div

Brown v HM Coroner for Norfolk [2014] EWHC 187 (Admin); [2014] 1 W.L.R. 3191; (2014) 178 J.P. 462; [2014] A.C.D. 66, QBD (Admin) ........ *Digested,* 14/**34**

Brown v InnovatorOne Plc [2012] EWHC 1321 (Comm), QBD (Comm) *Applied* 14/1459, 14/299

Brown v Rentokil Ltd (C-394/96) [1998] E.C.R. I-4185; [1998] 2 C.M.L.R. 1049; [1998] All E.R. (EC) 791; [1998] C.E.C. 829; [1998] I.C.R. 790; [1998] I.R.L.R. 445; [1998] 2 F.L.R. 649; [1999] 1 F.C.R. 49; (1999) 48 B.M.L.R. 126; [1998] Fam. Law 597; Times, July 2, 1998, ECJ ........ *Digested,* 98/**2148**: *Applied* 99/2115, 14/1117

Brown v South Cambridgeshire DC [2014] P.A.D. 2, Planning Inspector

Brown v Stephenson [2013] EWHC 2531 (Ch); [2013] W.T.L.R. 1675; [2014] 1 P. & C.R. DG2, Ch D ........ *Digested,* 14/**3032**

Brown v United Kingdom (986/04, 26/10/04) (Unreported, October 26, 2004), ECHR *Applied* 14/2233

Browne v Associated Newspapers Ltd [2007] EWCA Civ 295; [2008] Q.B. 103; [2007] 3 W.L.R. 289; [2007] C.P. Rep. 29; [2007] E.M.L.R. 20; (2007) 157 N.L.J. 671, CA (Civ Div); reversing in part [2007] EWHC 202 (QB); [2007] E.M.L.R. 19; (2007) 157 N.L.J. 670, QBD ........ *Digested,* 07/**2893**: *Considered* 11/2199: *Followed* 14/790

Browning v Information Commissioner [2014] EWCA Civ 1050; [2014] 1 W.L.R. 3848; [2014] H.R.L.R. 25; Times, August 14, 2014, CA (Civ Div) ........ *Digested,* 14/**400**

Brownlee's Application for Judicial Review, Re [2014] UKSC 4; [2014] N.I. 188, SC; reversing [2013] NICA 57, CA (NI); reversing [2013] NIQB 36, QBD (NI) ........ *Digested,* 14/**2040**

Brudenell-Bruce v Moore [2013] EWHC 4408 (Ch); [2014] W.T.L.R. 559, Ch D ........ *Digested,* 14/**428**

Brumby (Inspector of Taxes) v Milner; *sub nom* Day v Quick [1976] 1 W.L.R. 1096; [1976] 3 All E.R. 636; [1976] S.T.C. 534; 51 T.C. 583; [1976] T.R. 249; (1976) 120 S.J. 754, HL; affirming [1976] 1 W.L.R. 29; [1975] 3 All E.R. 1004; [1975] S.T.C. 644; [1975] T.R. 249; (1975) 119 S.J. 728, CA (Civ Div); affirming [1975] 1 W.L.R. 958; [1975] 2 All E.R. 773; [1975] S.T.C. 215; [1974] T.R. 397; (1974) 119 S.J. 257; Times, December 20, 1974, Ch D ........ *Digested,* 76/**1441**: *Considered* 87/2034, 88/1929, 89/2025: *Followed* 86/1760, 12/3300, 14/1792

Brunel University v Webster see Wong v Igen Ltd (formerly Leeds Careers Guidance)

Brunswick Properties Ltd v Revenue and Customs Commissioners [2014] UKFTT 601 (TC); [2014] S.T.I. 2426, FTT (Tax)

Brutus v Cozens [1973] A.C. 854; [1972] 3 W.L.R. 521; [1972] 2 All E.R. 1297; (1972) 56 Cr. App. R. 799; [1973] Crim. L.R. 56; (1972) 116 S.J. 647, HL; reversing [1972] 1 W.L.R. 484; [1972] 2 All E.R. 1; (1972) 116 S.J. 217, QBD ........ *Digested,* 72/**706**: *Applied* 73/602, 73/655, 74/2726, 79/2532, 93/4067, 93/977, 98/4669, 04/770, 05/796, 07/863, 11/1239, 14/412: *Considered* 73/602, 74/2726, 82/632, 86/1238, 89/3395, 89/3602, 90/4372, 91/2373, 93/4067, 95/5119, 96/1506, 03/4560, 11/687, 14/673: *Distinguished* 90/4372: *Followed* 97/2863, 11/3510: *Referred to* 95/5116

Bryers v. Canadian Pacific Steamships Ltd see Canadian Pacific Steamships Ltd v Bryers

BS v Dundee City Council see S v Dundee City Council

BS (Bangladesh) v Secretary of State for the Home Department see Sarkar v Secretary of State for the Home Department

BS Design & Management Ltd v Revenue and Customs Commissioners [2014] UKFTT 496 (TC); [2014] S.T.I. 2100, FTT (Tax)

BT Fleet Ltd v McKenna [2005] EWHC 387 (Admin); (2005) 102(21) L.S.G. 33; Times, April 5, 2005, QBD (Admin) *Considered* 14/1575

BT Pension Scheme Trustees Ltd v British Telecommunications Plc; *sub nom* Secretary of State for Culture, Media and Sport v BT Pension Scheme Trustees Ltd [2014] EWCA Civ 958; [2014] Pens. L.R. 647, CA (Civ Div); affirming in part [2010] EWHC 2642 (Ch); [2010] Pens. L.R. 487, Ch D ............ *Digested,* 11/**2345**

BT/Internet telephony (T484/11) [2014] E.P.O.R. 17, EPO (Technical Bd App)

Bucci v Carman see Casa Estates (UK) Ltd (In Liquidation), Re

Buchanan v McLean see McLean v Buchanan

Buckingham (Inspector of Taxes) v Securities Properties [1980] 1 W.L.R. 380; [1980] S.T.C. 166; 53 T.C. 292; [1979] T.R. 415; (1980) 124 S.J. 17; Times, December 7, 1979, Ch D ........ *Digested,* 82/**473**: *Approved* 98/4600: *Considered* 14/2882

Buckingham Bingo Ltd v Revenue and Customs Commissioners; *joined cases* Buckingham Hunts Cross Ltd v Revenue and Customs Commissioners; Buckingham Middleton Ltd v Revenue and Customs Commissioners; Buckingham Huyton Ltd v Revenue and Customs Commissioners; Hamblins Leisure Services Ltd v Revenue and Customs Commissioners [2013] UKFTT 713 (TC); [2014] S.T.I. 387, FTT (Tax)

Buckingham Hunts Cross Ltd v Revenue and Customs Commissioners see Buckingham Bingo Ltd v Revenue and Customs Commissioners

Buckingham Huyton Ltd v Revenue and Customs Commissioners see Buckingham Bingo Ltd v Revenue and Customs Commissioners

Buckingham International Plc (In Liquidation) (No.2), Re; *sub nom* Mitchell v Buckingham International Plc (In Liquidation); Mitchell v Carter (No.2) [1998] B.C.C. 943; [1998] 2 B.C.L.C. 369, CA (Civ Div); affirming Times, November 20, 1997, Ch D ........ *Digested,* 99/**3305**: *Applied* 11/1827: *Considered* 09/2206, 14/1829: *Distinguished* 01/3750

Buckingham Middleton Ltd v Revenue and Customs Commissioners see Buckingham Bingo Ltd v Revenue and Customs Commissioners

Buckinghamshire CC v HW [2013] UKUT 470 (AAC); [2013] E.L.R. 519, UT (AAC) ..... *Digested,* 14/**906**

Buckinghamshire CC v ST [2013] UKUT 468 (AAC); [2013] E.L.R. 528, UT (AAC) ...... *Digested,* 14/**946**

Buckland v Bournemouth University Higher Education Corp see Bournemouth University Higher Education Corp v Buckland

Buckland v United Kingdom (40060/08) (2013) 56 E.H.R.R. 16; [2013] H.L.R. 2; (2012) 162 N.L.J. 1257, ECHR ........ *Digested,* 13/**1560**: *Considered* 14/1968

Buckstone Group Ltd v Oldham LBC [2013] UKUT 265 (LC); [2014] R.V.R. 74, UT (Lands) ........ *Digested,* 14/**481**

Buckton v Buckton see Buckton (Costs), Re

Buckton (Costs), Re; *sub nom* Buckton v Buckton [1907] 2 Ch. 406, Ch D *Applied* 02/378, 10/321: *Considered* 98/481, 01/455, 01/5522, 02/379, 03/4470, 12/2384, 12/389, 13/441, 14/2815, 14/374

Bucnys v Lithuania see Lithuania v Bucnys

Budayeva v Russia (15339/02) (2014) 59 E.H.R.R. 2, ECHR

Budejovicky Budvar Narodni Podnik v Anheuser-Busch Inc [2012] EWCA Civ 880; [2012] 3 All E.R. 1405; [2012] E.T.M.R. 48; [2013] R.P.C. 12; (2012) 109(29) L.S.G. 29, CA (Civ Div); reversing [2008] EWHC 263 (Ch); [2008] R.P.C. 21; (2008) 31(3) I.P.D. 31015; (2008) 152(9) S.J.L.B. 29, Ch D ........ *Digested,* 12/**1982**: *Considered* 14/1926

Bugeja v Customs and Excise Commissioners (No.2) see Lex Services Plc v Customs and Excise Commissioners

Bull v Hall see Hall v Bull

Bullitt Mobile Ltd v Sonim Technologies [2013] EWHC 3367 (IPEC); [2014] F.S.R. 23, IPEC ........ *Digested,* 14/**473**

Bundesdruckerei GmbH v Stadt Dortmund (C-549/13) [2014] I.R.L.R. 980, ECJ (9th Chamber)

Bundeswettbewerbsbehorde v Schenker & Co AG (C-681/11) [2013] Bus. L.R. 1176; [2013] 5 C.M.L.R. 25; [2014] All E.R. (EC) 573; [2014] C.E.C. 197, ECJ (Grand Chamber)

Bundswettbewerbsbehorde (Federal Competition Authority) v T GmbH [2014] E.C.C. 24, OGH (A)

Bunge SA v Nibulon Trading BV [2013] EWHC 3936 (Comm); [2014] 1 Lloyd's Rep. 393, QBD (Comm) ........ *Digested,* 14/**112**

Bunge SA v Nidera BV (formerly Nidera Handelscompagnie BV) [2013] EWCA Civ 1628; [2014] 1 Lloyd's Rep. 404; [2014] 1 C.L.C. 27, CA (Civ Div); affirming [2013] EWHC 84 (Comm); [2013] 1 Lloyd's Rep. 621; [2013] 1 C.L.C. 325, QBD (Comm) ........ *Digested,* 14/**2587**: *Referred to* 13/1862

BUPA Australia Pty Ltd v Shaw [2013] VSC 507; [2014] Lloyd's Rep. I.R. 151, Sup Ct (Vic)
BUPA Insurance Ltd v Revenue and Customs Commissioners [2014] UKUT 262 (TCC); [2014] S.T.C. 2615; [2014] B.T.C. 519; [2014] S.T.I. 2408, UT (Tax) ...... *Digested,* 14/**2878**
Burca v Parkinson (Inspector of Taxes) [2001] S.T.C. 1298; 74 T.C. 125; [2002] B.T.C. 64; [2001] S.T.I. 1016, Ch D ...... *Digested,* 02/**4357**: *Considered* 14/2852
Burchell v Raj Properties Ltd [2013] UKUT 443 (LC); [2014] L. & T.R. 3; [2013] 3 E.G.L.R. 62; [2013] 43 E.G. 127 (C.S.), UT (Lands) ...... *Digested,* 14/**1989**
Burdge v Pyne [1969] 1 W.L.R. 364; [1969] 1 All E.R. 467; 45 T.C. 320; [1968] T.R. 383; (1968) 112 S.J. 947, Ch D ...... *Digested,* 69/**1720**: *Considered* 14/1386
Burdis v Livsey see Lagden v O'Connor
Burgess v Hawes; *sub nom* Burgess's Estate, Re; Hawes v Burgess [2013] EWCA Civ 94; [2013] W.T.L.R. 453, CA (Civ Div); affirming [2012] W.T.L.R. 423, CC (Central London) ...... *Digested,* 13/**2985**: *Applied* 14/2843: *Considered* 13/2984: *Followed* 14/2840
Burgess's Estate, Re see Burgess v Hawes
Burgo Group SpA v Illochroma SA (C-327/13) EU:C:2014:2158; [2014] I.L.Pr. 42, ECJ (1st Chamber)
Burkett, Re see R. (on the application of Burkett) v Hammersmith and Fulham LBC (No.1)
Burman v Mount Cook Land Ltd [2001] EWCA Civ 1712; [2002] Ch. 256; [2002] 2 W.L.R. 1172; [2002] 1 All E.R. 144; [2002] H.L.R. 45; [2002] L. & T.R. 19; [2002] 1 E.G.L.R. 61; [2002] 06 E.G. 156; [2001] 48 E.G. 128 (C.S.); (2001) 98(46) L.S.G. 37; (2002) 99(3) L.S.G. 26; (2002) 146 S.J.L.B. 12; [2001] N.P.C. 166; [2002] 1 P. & C.R. DG16; Independent, November 30, 2001, CA (Civ Div); reversing [2001] 1 E.G.L.R. 62; [2001] 10 E.G. 164, CC (Central London) ...... *Digested,* 01/**4174**: *Applied* 03/2745, 05/2652, 10/2695, 14/1983
Burnden Group Plc v Northstar Systems Ltd (In Liquidation) see Ultraframe (UK) Ltd v Fielding
Burnip v Birmingham City Council; *joined cases* Gorry v Wiltshire CC; Trengove v Walsall MBC [2012] EWCA Civ 629; [2013] P.T.S.R. 117; [2012] H.R.L.R. 20; [2012] Eq. L.R. 701; [2013] H.L.R. 1; [2012] B.L.G.R. 954; Times, August 21, 2012, CA (Civ Div) ...... *Digested,* 12/**3111**: *Applied* 14/2757: *Followed* 13/2885
Burns v Burns [2007] EWHC 2492 (Fam); [2008] 1 F.L.R. 813; [2008] Fam. Law 119, Fam Div ...... *Digested,* 08/**1566**: *Applied* 09/1617, 14/1394
Burntcopper Ltd (t/a Contemporary Design Unit) v International Travel Catering Association Ltd [2014] EWHC 148 (Comm); [2014] 2 All E.R. (Comm) 1055, QBD (Comm)
Burrell v Micheldever Tyre Services Ltd; *sub nom* Micheldever Tyre Services Ltd v Burrell [2014] EWCA Civ 716; [2014] I.C.R. 935; [2014] I.R.L.R. 630; [2014] Eq. L.R. 418; (2014) 158(23) S.J.L.B. 41, CA (Civ Div); reversing [2013] Eq. L.R. 695, EAT ...... *Digested,* 14/**1059**
Burridge v Breckland DC see R. (on the application of Burridge) v Breckland DC
Burrow Down Support Services Ltd v Rossiter [2008] I.C.R. 1172, EAT ...... *Digested,* 08/**1177**: *Applied* 10/1120, 14/1091, 14/1092: *Considered* 11/1100
Burrows v Brent LBC [1996] 1 W.L.R. 1448; [1996] 4 All E.R. 577; [1997] 1 F.L.R. 178; [1997] 2 F.C.R. 43; (1997) 29 H.L.R. 167; [1997] 1 E.G.L.R. 32; [1997] 11 E.G. 150; [1997] Fam. Law 246; (1996) 93(43) L.S.G. 26; (1996) 146 N.L.J. 1616; (1996) 140 S.J.L.B. 239; [1996] N.P.C. 149; Times, November 4, 1996; Independent, November 8, 1996, HL; reversing (1995) 27 H.L.R. 748; (1996) 72 P. & C.R. 261; [1995] E.G. 128 (C.S.); [1995] N.P.C. 124; Times, July 21, 1995; Independent, August 22, 1995, CA (Civ Div) ...... *Digested,* 96/**3829**: *Applied* 00/4297, 03/2769, 03/2770, 06/2714, 06/2717, 06/2719: *Considered* 97/2713, 10/2074: *Distinguished* 96/3834, 01/4146: *Explained* 06/2705: *Followed* 14/2003
Burry & Knight Ltd v Knight see Burry & Knight Ltd, Re
Burry & Knight Ltd, Re; *sub nom* Burry & Knight Ltd v Knight; Hoburne Ltd, Re [2014] EWCA Civ 604; [2014] 1 W.L.R. 4046; [2014] B.C.C. 393, CA (Civ Div); reversing in part 1763 & 1764/2012, Ch D (Companies Ct) ...... *Digested,* 14/**518**
Businessman v Revenue and Customs Commissioners [2008] S.T.C. (S.C.D.) 1151; [2008] S.T.I. 1991, Sp Comm ...... *Digested,* 09/**3891**: *Considered* 14/2890

Butlers Ship Stores Ltd v Revenue and Customs Commissioners [2013] UKUT 564 (TCC); [2014] S.T.C. 732, UT (Tax); affirming [2012] UKFTT 371 (TC), FTT (Tax) ..................... *Digested,* 14/**823**

Butlin v Butlin (Rectification) see Butlin's Settlement Trusts (Rectification), Re

Butlin's Settlement Trusts (Rectification), Re; *sub nom* Butlin v Butlin (Rectification) [1976] Ch. 251; [1976] 2 W.L.R. 547; [1976] 2 All E.R. 483; (1975) 119 S.J. 794, Ch D ..................... *Digested,* 76/**2508**:
*Applied* 98/4873, 01/5510, 11/3502: *Considered* 07/4247, 13/3171, 13/3178, 14/3029: *Followed* 01/4595

Butt v Revenue and Customs Commissioners [2014] UKFTT 490 (TC); [2014] S.T.I. 2097, FTT (Tax)

Buttes Gas & Oil Co v Hammer (No.3); *joined case* Occidental Petroleum Corp v Buttes Gas & Oil Co (No.2) [1982] A.C. 888; [1981] 3 W.L.R. 787; [1981] 3 All E.R. 616; [1981] Com. L.R. 257; (1981) 125 S.J. 776; Times, October 31, 1981, HL; reversing [1981] Q.B. 223; [1980] 3 W.L.R. 668; [1980] 3 All E.R. 475; (1980) 124 S.J. 630, CA (Civ Div) ..................... *Digested,* 81/**1473**:
*Applied* 87/3060, 96/3659, 06/2396: *Cited* 93/3224: *Considered* 84/2700, 92/203, 92/3479, 93/3224, 96/1086, 96/681, 99/723, 00/1756, 00/5107, 03/4204, 05/212, 06/501, 08/358, 09/399, 13/40: *Distinguished* 85/2651, 90/3689: *Explained* 14/38: *Not followed* 89/1699

Button v Salama [2013] EWHC 2972 (Fam); [2014] 2 F.L.R. 479; [2014] Fam. Law 25, Fam Div ..................... *Digested,* 14/**1332**

Button v Salama [2013] EWHC 2474 (Fam); [2014] 2 F.L.R. 471; [2014] Fam. Law 24, Fam Div

Button v Salama [2013] EWHC 4152 (Fam); [2014] 2 F.L.R. 488; [2014] Fam. Law 434, Fam Div ..................... *Digested,* 14/**1334**

Buzzoni v Revenue and Customs Commissioners; *sub nom* Kamhi (Deceased), Re [2013] EWCA Civ 1684; [2014] 1 W.L.R. 3040; [2014] 1 E.G.L.R. 181; [2014] B.T.C. 1; [2014] W.T.L.R. 421, CA (Civ Div); reversing [2012] UKUT 360 (TCC); [2013] S.T.C. 262; [2012] B.T.C. 1727; [2013] W.T.L.R. 47; [2013] S.T.I. 61, UT (Tax); affirming [2011] UKFTT 267 (TC); [2011] S.F.T.D. 771; [2011] W.T.L.R. 1163; [2011] S.T.I. 1946, FTT (Tax) ..................... *Digested,* 14/**2938**

Byrne v Motor Insurers' Bureau [2008] EWCA Civ 574; [2009] Q.B. 66; [2008] 3 W.L.R. 1421; [2008] 4 All E.R. 476; [2008] R.T.R. 26; [2008] 3 C.M.L.R. 4; [2008] Eu. L.R. 732; [2008] Lloyd's Rep. I.R. 705; [2008] P.I.Q.R. P14; (2008) 158 N.L.J. 860; (2008) 152(22) S.J.L.B. 31; Times, July 2, 2008, CA (Civ Div); affirming [2007] EWHC 1268 (QB); [2008] 2 W.L.R. 234; [2007] 3 All E.R. 499; [2008] R.T.R. 1; [2007] 3 C.M.L.R. 15; [2007] Eu. L.R. 739; [2008] Lloyd's Rep. I.R. 61; [2007] P.I.Q.R. P25; (2007) 104(25) L.S.G. 38; (2007) 157 N.L.J. 858; (2007) 151 S.J.L.B. 811; Times, June 15, 2007, QBD ..................... *Digested,* 08/**2212**:
*Considered* 09/2292, 11/1750, 11/1923, 14/1853

Bywater Properties Investments LLP v Oswestry Town Council [2014] EWHC 310 (Ch); [2014] 2 P. & C.R. 1, Ch D ..................... *Digested,* 14/**2005**

C v A (A Minor) [2011] EWHC 4033 (Fam), Fam Div
*Applied* 14/1304

C v C (Court of Protection: Disclosure); *sub nom* RC v CC [2014] EWHC 131 (COP); [2014] 1 W.L.R. 2731; [2014] C.O.P.L.R. 351; (2014) 17 C.C.L. Rep. 127, CP ... *Digested,* 14/**2184**

C v Chief Constable of Northern Ireland see C's Application for Judicial Review, Re

C v D [2009] EWHC 1942 (Fam); [2010] 1 F.L.R. 583; [2009] Fam. Law 1038, Fam Div ..................... *Digested,* 10/**1306**:
*Applied* 13/1346: *Considered* 14/1434

C v D (Abduction: Grave Risk of Harm) [2013] EWHC 2989 (Fam); [2014] 2 F.L.R. 724; [2014] Fam. Law 404, Fam Div

C v H; *sub nom* SC v BH (Passport Order) [2014] EWHC 1584 (Fam); [2014] Fam. Law 1115, Fam Div

C v H see C (A Child) (Prohibited Steps Order: Procedural Irregularity), Re

C v M (Wrongful Retention: Habitual Residence) (C-376/14 PPU) EU:C:2014:2268; [2014] Fam. Law 1674, ECJ (3rd Chamber)

C v North Cumbria University Hospitals NHS Trust [2014] EWHC 61 (QB); [2014] Med. L.R. 189, QBD ..................... *Digested,* 14/**2299**

C v Nottingham and Newark Magistrates' Court [2013] EWHC 3790 (Admin); [2014] A.C.D. 55, DC

C v South East Coast Ambulance Service NHS Foundation Trust (Unreported, May 22, 2014), QBD [*Devonshires Solicitors, 30 Finsbury Circus, London*] ..................... *Digested,* 14/**2317**

C v W [2008] EWCA Civ 1459; [2009] 4 All E.R. 1129; [2009] C.P. Rep. 20; [2009] 1 Costs L.R. 123; [2009] R.T.R. 17; (2009) 159 N.L.J. 73, CA (Civ Div) ..................... *Digested,* 09/**2563**:
*Applied* 12/2079: *Considered* 14/2047

C v W; *sub nom* JPC v SLW [2007] EWHC 1349 (Fam); [2007] 2 F.L.R. 900; [2007] 3 F.C.R. 243; [2007] Fam. Law 886, Fam Div ........ *Digested,* 07/**1745**: *Applied* 14/1310: *Considered* 12/1368

C (A Child) v Great Western Hospitals NHS Foundation Trust (Unreported, January 9, 2014), CC (Swindon) [*Withy King Solicitors, 5-6 Northumberland Passage, Queen Square, Bath*] ........ *Digested,* 14/**2331**

C (A Child) v Hull and East Yorkshire Hospitals NHS Trust (Unreported, February 3, 2014), QBD [*Stamp, Jackson & Procter LLP, 5 Parliament Street, Hull*] ........ *Digested,* 14/**2316**

C (A Child) (Adoption Proceedings: Change of Circumstances), Re see C (A Child) (Adoption: Placement Order), Re

C (A Child) (Adoption: Leave to Oppose), Re see C (A Child) (Adoption: Placement Order), Re

C (A Child) (Adoption: Placement Order), Re; *sub nom* C (A Child) (Adoption: Leave to Oppose), Re; C (A Child) (Adoption Proceedings: Change of Circumstances), Re [2013] EWCA Civ 431; [2013] 1 W.L.R. 3720; [2013] 2 F.L.R. 1393; [2014] 1 F.C.R. 50; [2013] Fam. Law 785, CA (Civ Div) ........ *Digested,* 14/**1234**: *Not followed* 14/1245

C (A Child) (Appeal from Care and Placement Orders), Re see C (A Child) (Placement for Adoption: Judicial Approach), Re

C (A Child) (Care and Placement: Long-term Welfare Decision), Re see C (A Child) (Placement for Adoption: Judicial Approach), Re

C (A Child) (Care Proceedings: Deaf Parent), Re; *sub nom* C (Care Proceedings: Parents with Disabilities), Re [2014] EWCA Civ 128; [2014] 1 W.L.R. 2495; [2014] 3 F.C.R. 627; [2014] Fam. Law 1088, CA (Civ Div) ........ *Digested,* 14/**1272**

C (A Child) (Immunisation: Parental Rights), Re; *sub nom* C (Welfare of Child: Immunisation), Re; B (A Child) (Immunisation: Parental Rights), Re; *joined case* F (A Child) (Immunisation: Parental Rights), Re [2003] EWCA Civ 1148; [2003] 2 F.L.R. 1095; [2003] 3 F.C.R. 156; (2003) 73 B.M.L.R. 152; [2003] Fam. Law 731; (2003) 147 S.J.L.B. 934; Times, August 15, 2003; Independent, October 15, 2003, CA (Civ Div); affirming [2003] EWHC 1376 (Fam); [2003] 2 F.L.R. 1054; (2003) 100(31) L.S.G. 31; Times, June 26, 2003, Fam Div ........ *Digested,* 03/**1777**: *Followed* 14/1304

C (A Child) (Parental Order), Re [2013] EWHC 2408 (Fam); [2014] 1 F.L.R. 757; [2013] Fam. Law 1535, Fam Div ........ *Digested,* 14/**1416**

C (A Child) (Parental Order), Re; *sub nom* AB v DE [2013] EWHC 2413 (Fam); [2014] 1 F.L.R. 654; [2014] Fam. Law 33, Fam Div ........ *Digested,* 14/**1414**

C (A Child) (Placement for Adoption: Judicial Approach), Re; *sub nom* C (A Child) (Care and Placement: Long-term Welfare Decision), Re; C (A Child) (Appeal from Care and Placement Orders), Re [2013] EWCA Civ 1257; [2014] 1 W.L.R. 2247; [2014] 2 F.L.R. 131; [2014] 1 F.C.R. 173; [2014] Fam. Law 16; (2013) 157(41) S.J.L.B. 39, CA (Civ Div) ........ *Digested,* 14/**1238**

C (A Child) (Placement Order: Appeal), Re [2014] EWCA Civ 70; [2014] 2 F.L.R. 1327; [2014] Fam. Law 419, CA (Civ Div)

C (A Child) (Practice: Setting Aside Consent Order in Abduction Proceedings), Re [2013] EWCA Civ 204; [2013] 2 F.L.R. 1300; [2013] Fam. Law 811, CA (Civ Div) ........ *Digested,* 14/**1312**

C (A Child) (Private Law: Public Funding), Re see Q v Q

C (A Child) (Prohibited Steps Order: Procedural Irregularity), Re; *sub nom* C (Family Proceedings: Practice), Re; C v H; C (Due Process), Re [2013] EWCA Civ 1412; [2014] 1 W.L.R. 2182; [2014] 1 F.L.R. 1239; [2014] 1 F.C.R. 239; [2014] Fam. Law 461, CA (Civ Div) ........ *Digested,* 14/**1351**

C (A Minor) (Care Proceedings: Disclosure), Re; *sub nom* EC (Disclosure of Material), Re; EC (A Minor) (Care Proceedings: Disclosure), Re [1997] Fam. 76; [1997] 2 W.L.R. 322; [1996] 2 F.L.R. 725; [1996] 3 F.C.R. 521; [1997] Fam. Law 160; Times, October 22, 1996, CA (Civ Div); reversing in part [1996] 2 F.L.R. 123; [1996] Fam. Law 603, Fam Div ........ *Digested,* 96/**1347**: *Applied* 02/1619, 02/1620, 03/1518, 06/499, 08/1449, 08/1540, 09/1616, 10/1311, 10/1313: *Considered* 97/377, 98/2386, 00/7, 14/1330: *Followed* 99/2349, 11/1325, 12/1342

C (Abduction: Settlement) (No.1), Re see Cannon v Cannon

C (Adult Patient: Restriction of Publicity after Death), Re [1996] 2 F.L.R. 251; [1996] 1 F.C.R. 605; [1996] Fam. Law 610, Fam Div ........ *Digested,* 96/**2981**: *Considered* 14/21

C (An Infant), Re see J v C

C (Care Proceedings: Parents with Disabilities), Re see C (A Child) (Care Proceedings: Deaf Parent), Re

C (Children) (Permission to Relocate), Re [2014] EWCA Civ 705; [2014] Fam. Law 1255, CA (Civ Div)

C (Children) (Transcripts: Permission to Appeal), Re [2013] EWCA Civ 1158; [2014] 2 F.L.R. 147; [2014] Fam. Law 14, CA (Civ Div) .................................................. *Digested,* 14/**1338**

C (Due Process), Re see C (A Child) (Prohibited Steps Order: Procedural Irregularity), Re

C (Family Proceedings: Case Management), Re [2012] EWCA Civ 1489; [2013] 1 F.L.R. 1089; [2013] 3 F.C.R. 399; [2013] Fam. Law 380, CA (Civ Div) .............. *Digested,* 13/**1341**: *Applied* 14/1381

C (Family Proceedings: Practice), Re see C (A Child) (Prohibited Steps Order: Procedural Irregularity), Re

C (Welfare of Child: Immunisation), Re see C (A Child) (Immunisation: Parental Rights), Re

C (Zimbabwe) v Secretary of State for the Home Department; *sub nom* Chikwamba v Secretary of State for the Home Department [2008] UKHL 40; [2008] 1 W.L.R. 1420; [2009] 1 All E.R. 363; [2008] H.R.L.R. 39; [2008] U.K.H.R.R. 1008; [2008] Imm. A.R. 700; [2008] I.N.L.R. 502; (2008) 152(26) S.J.L.B. 31; Times, June 26, 2008, HL; reversing [2005] EWCA Civ 1779, CA (Civ Div) .................. *Digested,* 08/**2052**: *Applied* 10/1789, 12/1765: *Considered* 09/2163, 13/1633: *Followed* 14/1715

C and V (Minors) (Contact: Parental Responsibility Order), Re [1998] 1 F.L.R. 392; [1998] 1 F.C.R. 52; [1998] Fam. Law 10; Times, June 30, 1997, CA (Civ Div).... *Digested,* 97/**439**: *Followed* 14/1421

C's Application for Judicial Review, Re; *sub nom* M v Chief Constable of Northern Ireland; C v Chief Constable of Northern Ireland; McE v Prison Service of Northern Ireland; *joined cases* C, Re; M, Re; McE, Re [2009] UKHL 15; [2009] 1 A.C. 908; [2009] 2 W.L.R. 782; [2009] 4 All E.R. 335; [2009] N.I. 258; [2009] 2 Cr. App. R. 1; [2009] E.M.L.R. 19; [2009] H.R.L.R. 20; [2009] U.K.H.R.R. 853; [2009] Po. L.R. 114; [2009] Crim. L.R. 525; (2009) 153(11) S.J.L.B. 28; Times, March 12, 2009, HL (NI); affirming [2007] NIQB 101; [2008] N.I. 203, DC .......... *Digested,* 09/**4216**: *Considered* 11/1293: *Followed* 14/36

C, Re see C's Application for Judicial Review, Re

Cabinet Office v Beavan [2014] I.R.L.R. 434, EAT ....................................................... *Digested,* 14/**1142**

Cabvision Ltd v Revenue and Customs Commissioners [2013] UKFTT 721 (TC); [2014] S.T.I. 391, FTT (Tax)

Cadbury UK Ltd v Societe des Produits Nestle SA see Societe des Produits Nestle SA v Cadbury UK Ltd

Cadogan Hotel Partners Ltd v Ozog [2014] Eq. L.R. 691, EAT

Caffoor (Trustees of the Abdul Gaffoor Trust) v Income Tax Commissioner (Colombo); *sub nom* Trustees of Abdul Gaffoor Trust v Income Tax Commissioner, Colombo; Gaffoor (Abdul) Trustees v Ceylon Commissioner of Income Tax [1961] A.C. 584; [1961] 2 W.L.R. 794; [1961] 2 All E.R. 436; (1961) 40 A.T.C. 93; [1961] T.R. 97; (1961) 105 S.J. 383, PC (Cey) ............................................ *Digested,* 61/**943**: *Applied* 01/5291: *Considered* 66/5957, 70/158, 10/3536, 14/3079: *Distinguished* 07/4001: *Explained* 09/4053: *Followed* 88/247

Cahillane v National Asset Loan Management Ltd [2014] EWHC 1992 (Ch); [2014] B.P.I.R. 1093, Ch D ........................................................................................... *Digested,* 14/**1827**

Cain v Francis; *joined case* McKay v Hamlani [2008] EWCA Civ 1451; [2009] Q.B. 754; [2009] 3 W.L.R. 551; [2009] 2 All E.R. 579; [2009] C.P. Rep. 19; [2009] R.T.R. 18; [2009] LS Law Medical 82; (2009) 106(2) L.S.G. 20, CA (Civ Div) .... *Digested,* 09/**420**: *Applied* 09/2854: *Considered* 10/376, 11/860: *Followed* 14/421

Caixa d'Estalvis i Pensions de Barcelona v Generalidad de Cataluna (C-139/12) [2014] B.V.C. 21; [2014] S.T.I. 1573, ECJ (10th Chamber)

Caledonia Bureau Investment & Property v Caffrey [1998] I.C.R. 603; [1998] I.R.L.R. 110, EAT ........................................................................................................ *Digested,* 98/**5825**: *Considered* 08/1215: *Not followed* 14/1117

Caliendo v Mishcon de Reya [2014] EWHC 3414 (Ch); [2014] 6 Costs L.O. 935, Ch D

Calix v Attorney General of Trinidad and Tobago [2013] UKPC 15; [2013] 1 W.L.R. 3283; [2013] 4 All E.R. 401; 35 B.H.R.C. 416; Times, July 16, 2013, PC (Trin)

Callery v Gray (No.1); *sub nom* Callery v Gray (Nos.1 and 2); Callery v Gray (No.2); *joined case* Russell v Pal Pak Corrugated Ltd (No.1) [2002] UKHL 28; [2002] 1 W.L.R. 2000; [2002] 3 All E.R. 417; [2002] 2 Costs L.R. 205; [2003] R.T.R. 4; [2003] Lloyd's Rep. I.R. 203; [2002] P.I.Q.R. P32; (2002) 152 N.L.J. 1031; Times, July 2, 2002; Independent, July 2, 2002; Daily Telegraph, July 11, 2002, HL; affirming [2001] EWCA Civ 1117; [2001] 1 W.L.R. 2112; [2001] 3 All E.R. 833; [2001] 2 Costs L.R. 163; [2001] Lloyd's Rep. I.R. 743; [2001] P.I.Q.R. P32; (2001) 151 N.L.J. 1129; Times, July 18, 2001; Independent, July 24, 2001; Daily Telegraph, July 24, 2001, CA (Civ Div); reversing in part [2002] R.T.R. 10, CC (Chester) [*Amelans, Solicitors, Barlow House, 708-710 Wilmslow Road, Manchester*] ........ *Digested,* 02/**360**: *Applied* 02/322, 03/330, 03/332, 05/2704, 10/2117, 10/310: *Cited* 03/331: *Considered* 05/2703, 06/2739, 06/2740, 06/2741, 06/2742, 06/402, 07/389, 12/2079, 13/313, 14/1835: *Distinguished* 04/2552

Callery v Gray (No.2) see Callery v Gray (No.1)

Callery v Gray (Nos.1 and 2) see Callery v Gray (No.1)

Calltel Telecom Ltd v Revenue and Customs Commissioners see Mobilx Ltd (In Administration) v Revenue and Customs Commissioners

CalMac Ferries Ltd v Wallace [2014] I.C.R. 453; [2014] Eq. L.R. 115, EAT (SC) ........ *Digested,* 14/**3504**

Calmex Ltd, Re [1989] 1 All E.R. 485; (1988) 4 B.C.C. 761; [1989] B.C.L.C. 299; [1989] P.C.C. 233, Ch D (Companies Ct) ........ *Digested,* 89/**351**: *Considered* 14/1758: *Distinguished* 04/445

Calthorpe v Mcoscar see Anstruther Gough Calthorpe v McOscar

Calver v Thomas (Valuation Officer) [2013] UKUT 482 (LC); [2014] R.V.R. 71, UT (Lands) ........ *Digested,* 14/**2481**

Calyon v Michailaidis [2009] UKPC 34, PC (Gib) *Considered* 13/249, 14/288

Cam v Matrix Service Development and Training Ltd [2013] Eq. L.R. 1146, EAT ........ *Digested,* 14/**1108**

Cambra v Jones; *sub nom* Palacin Cambra v Jones (Contempt Proceedings: Child Joined as Party) [2014] EWHC 913 (Fam); [2014] Fam. Law 959, Fam Div

Cambra v Jones [2013] EWHC 88 (Fam); [2014] 1 F.L.R. 5; [2013] Fam. Law 520, Fam Div

Cambridge Water Co Ltd v Eastern Counties Leather Plc; *joined case* Cambridge Water Co Ltd v Hutchings & Harding Ltd [1994] 2 A.C. 264; [1994] 2 W.L.R. 53; [1994] 1 All E.R. 53; [1994] 1 Lloyd's Rep. 261; [1994] Env. L.R. 105; [1993] E.G. 211 (C.S.); (1994) 144 N.L.J. 15; (1994) 138 S.J.L.B. 24; Times, December 10, 1993; Independent, December 10, 1993, HL; reversing [1993] Env. L.R. 287; [1992] N.P.C. 147; Times, December 29, 1992, CA (Civ Div); reversing [1993] Env. L.R. 116; Times, October 23, 1991, QBD ........ *Digested,* 94/**3410**: *Applied* 97/3864, 00/4289, 01/3800, 06/4340, 08/2664, 11/2275: *Considered* 97/1032, 98/4042, 12/2312: *Followed* 02/3323, 14/2219

Cambridge Water Co Ltd v Hutchings & Harding Ltd see Cambridge Water Co Ltd v Eastern Counties Leather Plc

Cambridgeshire CC v PS see S (A Child) (Split Hearing: Fact Finding), Re

Camden LBC v PC see PC (A Child) (Brussels II Revised: Jurisdiction within United Kingdom), Re

Camille and Henry Dreyfus Foundation Inc v Inland Revenue Commissioners [1956] A.C. 39; [1955] 3 W.L.R. 451; [1955] 3 All E.R. 97; 1955 S.L.T. 335; 48 R. & I.T. 551; 36 T.C. 126; (1955) 34 A.T.C. 208; [1955] T.R. 229; (1955) 99 S.J. 560, HL; affirming [1954] Ch. 672; [1954] 3 W.L.R. 167; [1954] 2 All E.R. 466; 47 R. & I.T. 476; (1954) 33 A.T.C. 209; [1954] T.R. 211; (1954) 98 S.J. 455, CA; affirming 47 R. & I.T. 244; (1954) 33 A.T.C. 60; [1954] T.R. 69, Ch D ........ *Digested,* 55/**304**: *Applied* 14/2936: *Considered* 94/538: *Followed* 97/344

Campaign Against Arms Trade v BAE Systems Plc [2007] EWHC 330 (QB), QBD *Applied* 08/1424, 14/384

Campaign for Nuclear Disarmament v Prime Minister of the United Kingdom see R. (on the application of Campaign for Nuclear Disarmament) v Prime Minister

Campbell v Entry Clearance Officer, Kingston see Campbell (Exclusion: Zambrano), Re

Campbell v MGN Ltd see Campbell v Mirror Group Newspapers Ltd

Campbell v Mirror Group Newspapers Ltd; *sub nom* Campbell v MGN Ltd [2004] UKHL 22; [2004] 2 A.C. 457; [2004] 2 W.L.R. 1232; [2004] 2 All E.R. 995; [2004] E.M.L.R. 15; [2004] H.R.L.R. 24; [2004] U.K.H.R.R. 648; 16 B.H.R.C. 500; (2004) 101(21) L.S.G. 36; (2004) 154 N.L.J. 733; (2004) 148 S.J.L.B. 572; Times, May 7, 2004; Independent, May 11, 2004, HL; reversing [2002] EWCA Civ 1373; [2003] Q.B. 633; [2003] 2 W.L.R. 80; [2003] 1 All E.R. 224; [2003] E.M.L.R. 2; [2003] H.R.L.R. 2; (2002) 99(42) L.S.G. 38; (2002) 146 S.J.L.B. 234; Times, October 16, 2002; Independent, October 18, 2002, CA (Civ Div); reversing [2002] EWHC 499 (QB); [2002] E.M.L.R. 30; [2002] H.R.L.R. 28; (2002) 99(19) L.S.G. 28; (2002) 146 S.J.L.B. 107; Times, March 29, 2002; Daily Telegraph, April 11, 2002, QBD ........ *Digested,* 04/**2673**:
*Applied* 03/1217, 05/2121, 05/2812, 06/2853, 06/3400, 07/2189, 07/2247, 07/2510, 08/1886, 08/1999, 10/1280, 10/4, 11/339, 12/1656: *Considered* 03/2923, 06/2440, 07/2250, 07/2887, 08/1992, 09/3962, 09/929, 14/1758: *Distinguished* 07/2383: *Followed* 05/979, 06/2096, 06/456, 08/1984, 10/408, 14/247

Campbell v Mylchreest [1999] P.I.Q.R. Q17, CA (Civ Div); affirming [1998] P.I.Q.R. P20, QBD ........ *Digested,* 00/**1459**:
*Applied* 14/2305: *Considered* 11/2373, 13/2198

Campbell v Thomas Cook Tour Operations Ltd [2014] Eq. L.R. 655, CC (Sheffield)

Campbell v Thomas Cook Tour Operations Ltd [2014] Eq. L.R. 108, CC (Sheffield) ..... *Digested,* 14/**1587**

Campbell v United Kingdom (7511/76); *sub nom* Campbell v United Kingdom (A/48); *joined case* Cosans v United Kingdom (7743/76) (1982) 4 E.H.R.R. 293, ECHR
*Applied* 97/2787, 09/2000, 10/1025, 14/2164: *Considered* 03/1114, 12/1658: *Distinguished* 05/1019

Campbell v United Kingdom (A/48) see Campbell v United Kingdom (7511/76)

Campbell v Wardlaw (1883) 8 App. Cas. 641; (1883) 10 R. (H.L.) 65, HL
*Applied* 14/2982

Campbell (Exclusion: Zambrano), Re; *sub nom* Campbell v Entry Clearance Officer, Kingston [2013] UKUT 147 (IAC), UT (IAC)
*Applied* 14/1741

Campbell's Estate, Re 17 I.T.E.L.R. 470, HC (NZ)

Canada Steamship Lines Ltd v King, The [1952] A.C. 192; [1952] 1 All E.R. 305; [1952] 1 Lloyd's Rep. 1; [1952] 1 T.L.R. 261; (1952) 96 S.J. 72, PC (Can) ......... *Digested,* 52/**610**:
*Applied* 55/3036, 71/9949, 74/296, 74/447, 75/273, 78/3186, 80/359, 82/2909, 88/461, 90/636, 93/499, 95/778, 96/1216, 99/836, 01/947, 02/712, 10/3040, 13/574: *Cited* 99/3311: *Considered* 68/2647, 73/407, 81/110.u, 81/304, 81/3603, 82/403, 97/937, 00/5991, 00/895, 09/715, 10/621, 14/599: *Followed* 96/5302: *Referred to* 95/5571

Canadian Pacific Steamships Ltd v Bryers; *sub nom* Bryers v. Canadian Pacific Steamships Ltd [1958] A.C. 485; [1957] 3 W.L.R. 993; [1957] 3 All E.R. 572; [1957] 2 Lloyd's Rep. 387; (1957) 101 S.J. 957, HL; affirming [1957] 1 Q.B. 134; [1956] 3 W.L.R. 776; [1956] 3 All E.R. 560; [1956] 2 Lloyd's Rep. 394; (1956) 100 S.J. 816, CA; affirming [1956] 1 W.L.R. 1181; [1956] 3 All E.R. 242; [1956] 2 Lloyd's Rep. 252; (1956) 100 S.J. 635, Assizes (Liverpool) ................. *Digested,* 57/**2364**:
*Applied* 59/2185, 67/2678: *Followed* 14/2998

Canas Property Co v KL Television Services [1970] 2 Q.B. 433; [1970] 2 W.L.R. 1133; [1970] 2 All E.R. 795; (1970) 21 P. & C.R. 601; (1970) 114 S.J. 337, CA (Civ Div) ........ *Digested,* 70/**1518**:
*Applied* 85/1863, 89/2206: *Considered* 75/1863, 14/1969

Candolin v Vahinkovakuutusosakeyhtio Pohjola (C-537/03) [2005] E.C.R. I-5745; [2006] R.T.R. 1; [2005] 3 C.M.L.R. 17; [2006] Lloyd's Rep. I.R. 209, ECJ (1st Chamber) ........ *Digested,* 06/**2425**:
*Applied* 10/1927, 13/1724, 14/1853: *Considered* 10/1928

Canning's Application for Judicial Review, Re see Fox's Application for Judicial Review, Re

Cannon v Cannon; *sub nom* C (Abduction: Settlement) (No.1), Re [2004] EWCA Civ 1330; [2005] 1 W.L.R. 32; [2005] 1 F.L.R. 169; [2004] 3 F.C.R. 438; [2005] Fam. Law 8; (2004) 101(44) L.S.G. 31; Times, October 28, 2004, CA (Civ Div); reversing [2004] EWHC 1245 (Fam); [2005] 1 F.L.R. 127; [2004] Fam. Law 782, Fam Div ........ *Digested,* 05/**1539**:
*Applied* 07/1746, 09/1537, 09/4919, 14/1378: *Considered* 07/1736, 09/1539, 09/1643, 09/4902

Canonical UK Ltd v TST Millbank LLC [2012] EWHC 3710 (Ch); [2013] L. & T.R. 15; [2013] 2 E.G.L.R. 193, Ch D ........ *Digested,* 14/**1987**:
*Applied* 14/1969

Cantabrica Coach Holdings Ltd v Vehicle Inspectorate see Vehicle Inspectorate v Cantabrica Coach Holdings Ltd

Canterbury City Council v Ali [2013] EWHC 2360 (Admin); [2014] L.L.R. 1, QBD (Admin)

Canterbury Hockey Club v Revenue and Customs Commissioners (C-253/07) [2009] P.T.S.R. 853; [2008] S.T.C. 3351; [2008] E.C.R. I-7821; [2009] 1 C.M.L.R. 13; [2009] C.E.C. 252; [2008] B.T.C. 5707; [2008] B.V.C. 824; [2008] S.T.I. 2250; Times, November 4, 2008, ECJ (4th Chamber) ............ *Digested,* 09/**4048**: *Applied* 10/3482, 13/3190: *Considered* 09/4093, 14/3043: *Followed* 09/4047

Cantor Index Ltd v Lister [2002] C.P. Rep. 25, Ch D ............ *Digested,* 02/**471**: *Applied* 13/369: *Considered* 14/404

Cantrell (t/a Foxearth Lodge Nursing Home) v Customs and Excise Commissioners [2003] EWHC 404 (Ch); [2003] S.T.C. 486; [2003] B.T.C. 5140; [2003] B.V.C. 196; [2003] S.T.I. 325, Ch D; reversing [2003] S.T.I. 440, V&DTr *Applied* 13/3228, 14/3103

Cantrell (t/a Foxearth Lodge Nursing Home) v Customs and Excise Commissioners [2000] S.T.C. 100; [2000] B.T.C. 5044; [2000] B.V.C. 82; [2000] S.T.I. 103, QBD ............ *Digested,* 00/**5366**: *Applied* 14/3103

Caparo Industries Plc v Dickman [1990] 2 A.C. 605; [1990] 2 W.L.R. 358; [1990] 1 All E.R. 568; [1990] B.C.C. 164; [1990] B.C.L.C. 273; [1990] E.C.C. 313; [1955-95] P.N.L.R. 523; (1990) 87(12) L.S.G. 42; (1990) 140 N.L.J. 248; (1990) 134 S.J. 494; Times, February 12, 1990; Independent, February 16, 1990; Financial Times, February 13, 1990; Guardian, February 15, 1990; Daily Telegraph, February 15, 1990, HL; affirming [1989] Q.B. 653; [1989] 2 W.L.R. 316; [1989] 1 All E.R. 798; (1989) 5 B.C.C. 105; [1989] B.C.L.C. 154; [1989] P.C.C. 125; (1988) 138 N.L.J. Rep. 289; (1989) 133 S.J. 221; Times, August 8, 1988; Independent, August 10, 1988; Financial Times, August 5, 1988; Daily Telegraph, August 26, 1988, CA (Civ Div); reversing in part (1988) 4 B.C.C. 144; [1988] B.C.L.C. 387, QBD ............ *Digested,* 90/**3266**: *Applied* 90/3265, 90/3281, 91/2650, 91/2652, 92/1915, 92/2605, 93/2982, 94/3365, 95/2906, 95/3668, 95/3686, 95/3701, 95/4519, 95/4730, 96/4440, 96/4484, 97/331, 97/3778, 97/3816, 98/3997, 99/3956, 99/3963, 99/3966, 99/4025, 99/5435, 00/4201, 00/4246, 00/4249, 00/6162, 00/6586, 00/679, 01/1509, 01/1989, 01/4462, 01/4464, 01/4541, 04/2119, 04/2704, 04/658, 05/2845, 05/2848, 05/2851, 05/2861, 05/2868, 06/2885, 06/4380, 06/684, 07/1682, 08/2644, 08/4861, 09/2725, 09/2726, 09/2727, 09/2848, 10/4300, 11/2553, 11/4482, 14/2203: *Cited* 00/4218, 07/1755: *Considered* 91/2657, 91/35, 93/2044, 93/2958, 93/2983, 93/2994, 93/2997, 95/3452, 95/3652, 95/3667, 95/3721, 98/3921, 98/3951, 98/3999, 99/3953, 00/4205, 01/550, 03/5821, 04/386, 04/5103, 05/2891, 06/2880, 06/5590, 06/5600, 07/2937, 07/2952, 07/733, 08/2653, 08/4946, 08/4947, 08/4949, 09/4702, 10/2281, 10/81, 11/2370, 11/4485, 12/4236, 12/4257, 13/2087, 13/565: *Distinguished* 91/2653: *Followed* 93/5553, 97/4087, 97/424, 98/3930, 98/3987, 99/3959, 99/4015, 00/4219, 00/4224, 01/4470, 09/265, 10/2278, 11/2254, 11/2255, 11/2256, 12/2294, 12/2297, 14/2202, 14/2205, 14/2210: *Referred to* 92/6078, 94/6386, 95/5841, 99/4023

Capernwray Missionary Fellowship of Torchbearers v Revenue and Customs Commissioners [2014] UKFTT 626 (TC); [2014] S.F.T.D. 1051, FTT (Tax) ........ *Digested,* 14/**3040**

Capewell v Customs and Excise Commissioners; *sub nom* Capewell v Revenue and Customs Commissioners [2007] UKHL 2; [2007] 1 W.L.R. 386; [2007] 2 All E.R. 370; [2007] 2 Costs L.R. 287; [2007] B.P.I.R. 678; (2007) 104(7) L.S.G. 26; (2007) 157 N.L.J. 223; (2007) 151 S.J.L.B. 198; Times, February 1, 2007, HL; reversing [2005] EWCA Civ 964; [2006] C.P. Rep. 5; [2005] B.P.I.R. 1266; Times, September 20, 2005, CA (Civ Div) ............ *Digested,* 07/**1014**: *Applied* 14/802: *Considered* 11/260, 12/465

Capewell v Revenue and Customs Commissioners see Capewell v Customs and Excise Commissioners

Capita ATL Pension Trustees Ltd v Zurkinskas [2010] EWHC 3365 (Ch); [2011] 1 W.L.R. 1274; [2011] Pens. L.R. 99, Ch D ............ *Digested,* 11/**2342**: *Applied* 14/2271

Capital & Counties Properties Plc, Re see Liberty International Plc, Re

Capital and City Holdings Ltd v Dean Warburg Ltd (1989) 58 P. & C.R. 346; [1989] 25 E.G. 97; [1988] E.G. 174 (C.S.), CA (Civ Div) ............ *Digested,* 89/**2206**: *Applied* 14/1987: *Followed* 14/1969

Capital Bank Cashflow Finance Ltd v Southall [2004] EWCA Civ 817; [2004] 2 All E.R. (Comm) 675, CA (Civ Div) ............ *Digested,* 04/**228**: *Applied* 14/637

Card Protection Plan Ltd v Customs and Excise Commissioners [2001] UKHL 4; [2002] 1 A.C. 202; [2001] 2 W.L.R. 329; [2001] 2 All E.R. 143; [2001] 1 All E.R. (Comm) 438; [2001] S.T.C. 174; [2001] 2 C.M.L.R. 2; [2001] B.T.C. 5083; [2001] B.V.C. 158; [2001] S.T.I. 151; (2001) 98(9) L.S.G. 41; (2001) 145 S.J.L.B. 60; Times, February 6, 2001, HL; reversing [1994] S.T.C. 199; [1994] 1 C.M.L.R. 756, CA (Civ Div); affirming [1992] S.T.C. 797, QBD .......................... *Digested,* 01/**5600**:
*Applied* 94/4602, 04/3992, 06/4449: *Considered* 98/4961, 07/5568, 11/3567, 14/3058: *Preliminary ruling given* 99/4972: *Referred to* 95/5039, 95/5093

Card Protection Plan Ltd v Customs and Excise Commissioners (C-349/96) [1999] 2 A.C. 601; [1999] 3 W.L.R. 203; [1999] S.T.C. 270; [1999] E.C.R. I-973; [1999] 2 C.M.L.R. 743; [1999] All E.R. (E.C.) 339; [1999] C.E.C. 133; [1999] B.T.C. 5121; [1999] B.V.C. 155; Times, March 18, 1999, ECJ (6th Chamber) .............. *Digested,* 99/**4972**:
*Applied* 00/5343, 00/5346, 00/5369, 02/4745, 02/4750, 02/4782, 03/4538, 03/4545, 03/4576, 03/4580, 04/3968, 04/4009, 05/4354, 05/4355, 05/4397, 06/4449, 06/4476, 06/4514, 07/4341, 07/4342, 08/4025, 08/4035, 08/4040, 08/4048, 09/4098, 11/3562: *Considered* 01/5599, 03/4537, 03/4558, 04/3977, 04/4018, 04/4020, 05/4419, 06/4438, 06/4490, 08/3999, 08/4061, 09/4041, 09/4135, 09/5224, 11/1465, 11/3550, 14/3102: *Distinguished* 00/5294, 01/5564, 05/4394: *Explained* 12/3431: *Followed* 99/4983, 00/5344, 04/3981, 06/4501, 10/3519, 12/3387, 13/3221, 13/3227, 14/3050

Caresse Navigation Ltd v Office National de L'Electricite (The Channel Ranger) [2013] EWHC 3081 (Comm); [2014] 1 Lloyd's Rep. 337; [2013] 2 C.L.C. 480, QBD (Comm) .......................................................................................................... *Digested,* 14/**2707**

Caresse Navigation Ltd v Office National de l'Electricite see Caresse Navigation Ltd v Zurich Assurances MAROC

Caresse Navigation Ltd v Zurich Assurances MAROC; *sub nom* Caresse Navigation Ltd v Office National de l'Electricite [2014] EWCA Civ 1366; Times, December 4, 2014, CA (Civ Div)

Caribeenne de Dietetique et Sante (Societe) v Pierre Fabre Dermo-Cosmetique (Societe) [2014] E.C.C. 6, Cass (F)

Carillion Construction Ltd v Devonport Royal Dockyard Ltd [2005] EWCA Civ 1358; [2006] B.L.R. 15; 104 Con. L.R. 1; (2005) 102(47) L.S.G. 26; Times, November 24, 2005, CA (Civ Div); affirming [2005] EWHC 778 (TCC); [2005] B.L.R. 310; 102 Con. L.R. 167, QBD (TCC) .......................................................................... *Digested,* 06/**670**:
*Applied* 07/395, 07/728, 09/658, 10/845, 11/490, 14/581: *Considered* 09/4839, 10/556, 10/558, 10/563, 10/580: *Distinguished* 09/651: *Followed* 06/666, 13/1719

Carinthia v S [2014] 2 C.M.L.R. 34, VfGH (A)

Carl Zeiss Stiftung v Rayner & Keeler Ltd; *joined case* Rayner & Keeler Ltd v Courts & Co [1967] 1 A.C. 853; [1966] 3 W.L.R. 125; [1966] 2 All E.R. 536; [1967] R.P.C. 497; (1966) 110 S.J. 425, HL; reversing [1965] Ch. 596; [1965] 2 W.L.R. 277; [1965] 1 All E.R. 300; [1965] R.P.C. 141; (1965) 109 S.J. 51; Times, December 18, 1964; Guardian, December 18, 1964, CA; reversing [1964] R.P.C. 299, Ch D (RPC) ............................................................................................................ *Digested,* 66/**1665**:
*Applied* 85/1291, 86/2689, 87/1441, 87/3091, 04/373: *Considered* 71/3476, 77/2399, 79/791, 80/2609, 84/2704, 90/2860, 90/610, 00/785, 10/337: *Followed* 83/138, 96/1102, 96/853, 10/2029, 13/266, 14/564: *Referred to* 95/6225

Carlill v Carbolic Smoke Ball Co [1893] 1 Q.B. 256, CA; affirming [1892] 2 Q.B. 484, QBD
*Applied* 57/592, 67/1745, 73/1529, 95/799, 14/275: *Approved* 66/3146: *Considered* 64/3479, 67/1745, 80/1888, 88/2020, 91/474: *Distinguished* 52/2194, 73/3095

Carltona Ltd v Commissioners of Works [1943] 2 All E.R. 560, CA
*Applied* 47-51/1530, 47-51/8203, 54/46, 61/7385, 68/3426, 69/276, 76/279, 96/7374, 02/2593, 02/3761, 03/4042, 07/717: *Cited* 07/2811: *Considered* 83/2708, 87/4112, 91/1981, 93/1662, 00/5396, 07/5436, 14/2568, 14/808: *Distinguished* 97/4123: *Followed* 90/4713, 96/2961

Carman v Bucci see Casa Estates (UK) Ltd (In Liquidation), Re

Carman v Letchford; *sub nom* Hollier (A Bankrupt), Re [2010] EWHC 3155 (Ch); [2014] B.P.I.R. 927, Ch D

Carnoustie Golf Course Committee v Inland Revenue Commissioners 1929 S.C. 419; 1929 S.L.T. 366, IH (1 Div)
*Applied* 14/2849

Carpet Decor (Guildford) v Secretary of State for the Environment (1982) 261 E.G. 56; [1981] J.P.L. 806, Unknown court .......................................................................... *Digested,* 81/**2679**:
*Considered* 85/1928, 14/2408

Carpetright Plc v Ray (Valuation Officer) [2014] UKUT 145 (LC); [2014] R.A. 417, UT (Lands)

Carratu v Poste Italiane SpA (C-361/12) [2014] 2 C.M.L.R. 27; [2014] I.C.R. 291, ECJ (3rd Chamber)

Carrimore Six Wheelers Ltd v Inland Revenue Commissioners 26 T.C. 301, Unknown court
*Applied* 01/5200, 14/2914: *Considered* 99/4663

Carroll v Egg Banking Plc see Andrew v Barclays Bank Plc

Carson v Secretary of State for Work and Pensions see R. (on the application of Carson) v Secretary of State for Work and Pensions

Carter v Ahsan; *sub nom* Watt (formerly Carter) v Ahsan; Labour Party v Ahsan; Ashan v Watt (formerly Carter) [2007] UKHL 51; [2008] 1 A.C. 696; [2008] 2 W.L.R. 17; [2008] 1 All E.R. 869; [2008] I.C.R. 82; [2008] I.R.L.R. 243; (2007) 157 N.L.J. 1694; Times, November 27, 2007, HL; reversing [2005] EWCA Civ 990; [2005] I.C.R. 1817; Times, August 23, 2005, CA (Civ Div); reversing [2004] I.C.R. 938, EAT ............ *Digested,* 08/**379**:
*Considered* 09/1202, 09/188, 13/1, 14/1698

Cartier parfums - lunettes SAS v Ziegler France SA (C-1/13) [2014] C.E.C. 1051; [2014] I.L.Pr. 25, ECJ (3rd Chamber)

Cartwright v Registrar of Companies see Globespan Airways Ltd (In Liquidation), Re

Carvill v Inland Revenue Commissioners (Transfer Purpose) [2000] S.T.C. (S.C.D.) 143; [2000] S.T.I. 584, Sp Comm ............ *Digested,* 00/**5021**:
*Considered* 05/4041, 14/2916

Cary v Commissioner of Police of the Metropolis [2014] EWCA Civ 987; [2014] C.P. Rep. 42; [2014] Eq. L.R. 707, CA (Civ Div) ............ *Digested,* 14/**378**

Casa Estates (UK) Ltd (In Liquidation), Re; *sub nom* Bucci v Carman; Carman v Bucci [2014] EWCA Civ 383; [2014] B.C.C. 269; [2014] 2 B.C.L.C. 49; [2014] B.P.I.R. 523, CA (Civ Div); affirming [2013] EWHC 2371 (Ch), Ch D (Companies Ct) ... *Digested,* 14/**1793**

Casio Computer Co Ltd v Sayo (No.3) [2001] EWCA Civ 661; [2001] I.L.Pr. 43, CA (Civ Div); affirming (2001) 98(6) L.S.G. 45; Times, February 6, 2001, Ch D ...... *Digested,* 01/**809**:
*Applied* 07/659, 14/2991: *Followed* 06/630

Caster v Finanzamt Essen-Sud (C-326/12) see van Caster v Finanzamt Essen-Sud (C-326/12)

Castle v Commissioner of Police of the Metropolis; *sub nom* R. (on the application of Castle) v Commissioner of Police of the Metropolis [2011] EWHC 2317 (Admin); [2012] 1 All E.R. 953; (2011) 108(36) L.S.G. 18; (2011) 161 N.L.J. 1252, DC ............ *Digested,* 12/**1663**:
*Considered* 14/1596

Castle v Crown Prosecution Service; *sub nom* Castle v DPP [2014] EWHC 587 (Admin); [2014] 1 W.L.R. 4279; (2014) 178 J.P. 285; [2014] R.T.R. 19, DC ....... *Digested,* 14/**2568**

Castle v DPP see Castle v Crown Prosecution Service

Castleford Homes Ltd v Secretary of State for the Environment, Transport and the Regions [2001] EWHC Admin 77; [2001] P.L.C.R. 29; [2001] J.P.L. 1217 (Note); [2001] 7 E.G. 160 (C.S.); (2001) 98(7) L.S.G. 42; [2001] N.P.C. 25, QBD (Admin) ............ *Digested,* 02/**3730**:
*Applied* 04/3080, 10/2564: *Considered* 03/3430, 14/2411

Castro v Secretary of State for the Home Department see Castro (Removals: S.47 (as Amended))

Castro (Removals: S.47 (as Amended)); *sub nom* Castro v Secretary of State for the Home Department [2014] UKUT 234 (IAC); [2014] Imm. A.R. 950, UT (IAC)

Caterpillar (NI) Ltd (formerly FG Wilson (Engineering) Ltd) v John Holt & Co (Liverpool) Ltd see FG Wilson (Engineering) Ltd v John Holt & Co (Liverpool) Ltd

Catholic Child Welfare Society v Various Claimants see Various Claimants v Institute of the Brothers of the Christian Schools

Catling v Catling [2014] EWHC 180 (Ch); [2014] W.T.L.R. 955, Ch D ............ *Digested,* 14/**2830**

Cavendish Munro Professional Risks Management Ltd v Geduld [2010] I.C.R. 325; [2010] I.R.L.R. 38, EAT ............ *Digested,* 10/**1106**:
*Applied* 14/1024, 14/1094, 14/1095

Cavendish Square Holdings BV v Makdessi see Makdessi v Cavendish Square Holdings BV

CB v CB (Abduction: Child's Objections) [2013] EWHC 2092 (Fam); [2014] 1 F.L.R. 663; [2013] Fam. Law 1357, Fam Div

CBS Songs Ltd v Amstrad Consumer Electronics Plc [1988] A.C. 1013; [1988] 2 W.L.R. 1191; [1988] 2 All E.R. 484; [1988] 2 F.T.L.R. 168; [1988] R.P.C. 567; (1988) 132 S.J. 789; Times, May 13, 1988; Independent, May 17, 1988; Financial Times, May 18, 1988; Guardian, May 19, 1988, HL; affirming [1988] Ch. 61; [1987] 3 W.L.R. 144; [1987] 3 All E.R. 151; [1987] 1 F.T.L.R. 488; [1987] R.P.C. 429; (1987) 84 L.S.G. 1243, CA (Civ Div); reversing Times, May 9, 1986, Ch D ........ *Digested,* 88/**503**: *Applied* 02/4544: *Considered* 89/2805, 99/3462, 09/2451, 09/442: *Distinguished* 03/310, 13/1773: *Followed* 00/3576, 10/1945, 14/1924: *Referred to* 93/3041, 00/3570

CC v DD see Q (A Child) (Parental Order: Domicile), Re

CC v NC (Maintenance Pending Suit) [2014] EWHC 703 (Fam); [2014] Fam. Law 967, Fam Div

CD v Revenue and Customs Commissioners [2014] I.C.R. D1, EAT

CD v ST (C-167/12) [2014] 3 C.M.L.R. 15; [2014] I.R.L.R. 551; [2014] Eq. L.R. 298; [2014] I.C.R. D26, ECJ (Grand Chamber)

CECA SA v European Commission (T-24/10) see Arkema France v European Commission (T-23/10)

Cecil v Bayat; *sub nom* Bayat v Cecil [2011] EWCA Civ 135; [2011] 1 W.L.R. 3086; [2011] C.P. Rep. 25, CA (Civ Div); reversing [2010] EWHC 641 (Comm), QBD (Comm) ........ *Digested,* 11/**385**: *Applied* 12/471, 13/100, 14/478: *Considered* 12/313, 12/472, 12/473: *Followed* 11/387, 12/470, 14/476

Celanese International Corp v BP Chemicals Ltd [1999] R.P.C. 203; (1999) 22(1) I.P.D. 22002; Times, November 5, 1998, Ch D (Patents Ct) ........ *Digested,* 98/**3469**: *Considered* 14/1887: *Followed* 12/1941: *Not applied* 13/1818

CELANESE INTERNATIONAL CORP/Vinyl acetate ethylene emulsion (T2441/09) [2014] E.P.O.R. 15, EPO (Technical Bd App)

CELANESE/Method of removing organic iodides (T291/08) [2014] E.P.O.R. 10, EPO (Technical Bd App)

Celine, Re 17 I.T.L. Rep. 115, CE (F)

Celtic Road Group (Dundalk) Ltd v Commissioner of Valuation see Celtic Roads Group (Dundalk) Ltd v Commissioner of Valuation

Celtic Roads Group (Dundalk) Ltd v Commissioner of Valuation; *sub nom* Westlink Toll Bridge Ltd v Commissioner of Valuation; Celtic Road Group (Dundalk) Ltd v Commissioner of Valuation; *joined case* West-Link Toll Bridge Ltd v Commissioner of Valuation [2013] IESC 42; [2014] R.A. 233, Sup Ct (Irl); reversing in part [2008] IEHC 255; [2008] R.A. 395, HC (Irl)

Central Association of Carers in Finland v Finland (70/2011) (2014) 58 E.H.R.R. SE7, ECSR

Central Bank of Nigeria v Williams see Williams v Central Bank of Nigeria

Central Examining Court, Madrid v Sander see R. (on the application of United States) v Bow Street Magistrates' Court

Central London Community Healthcare NHS Trust v Information Commissioner [2013] UKUT 551 (AAC); (2014) 136 B.M.L.R. 61, UT (AAC); affirming (2013) 130 B.M.L.R. 135, FTT ........ *Digested,* 14/**61**

Central Sussex College v Revenue and Customs Commissioners [2014] UKFTT 1058 (TC); [2014] S.T.I. 3558, FTT (Tax)

Central Trading & Exports Ltd v Fioralba Shipping Co [2014] EWHC 2397 (Comm); [2014] 2 Lloyd's Rep. 449; (2014) 164(7616) N.L.J. 21; [2014] Bus. L.R. D19, QBD (Comm) ........ *Digested,* 14/**123**

Centre for Legal Resources v Romania (47848/08) 37 B.H.R.C. 423, ECHR

Centre Public d'Aide Sociale, Courcelles v Lebon (316/85) [1987] E.C.R. 2811; [1989] 1 C.M.L.R. 337; Times, September 9, 1987, ECJ ........ *Digested,* 90/**2209**: *Applied* 10/1823, 10/3129, 12/1279, 14/1685: *Considered* 95/4617, 07/1652: *Followed* 97/4605: *Not followed* 04/3597

Centrica India Offshore Private Ltd v Commissioner of Income Tax 16 I.T.L. Rep. 957, HC (Ind)

Centro Hospitalar de Setubal EPE v Eurest (Portugal) - Sociedade Europeia de Restaurantes Lda (C-574/12) [2014] P.T.S.R. 1174; (2014) 158(26) S.J.L.B. 37, ECJ (5th Chamber)

Centrotherm Systemtechnik GmbH v Office for Harmonisation in the Internal Market (Trade Marks and Designs) (OHIM) (C-610/11 P) [2014] E.T.M.R. 7, ECJ (4th Chamber)

Century National Merchant Bank & Trust Co Ltd v Davies [1998] A.C. 628; [1998] 2 W.L.R. 779; (1998) 142 S.J.L.B. 110, PC (Jam) ........ *Digested,* 98/**281**: *Considered* 14/548

Cerep III TW Sarl v Kendrick (Valuation Officer) [2014] R.V.R. 331, VT

Cetelem SA v Roust Holdings Ltd [2005] EWCA Civ 618; [2005] 1 W.L.R. 3555; [2005] 4 All E.R. 52; [2005] 2 All E.R. (Comm) 203; [2005] 2 Lloyd's Rep. 494; [2005] 1 C.L.C. 821; Times, June 13, 2005, CA (Civ Div); affirming [2004] EWHC 3175 (QB), QBD ........ *Digested,* 05/**325**: *Applied* 08/277: *Considered* 07/233, 08/361, 11/368, 13/105, 14/139: *Distinguished* 07/249

CF v Secretary of State for the Home Department see Secretary of State for the Home Department v CC

CF v Security Service; *joined case* Mohamed v Foreign and Commonwealth Office [2013] EWHC 3402 (QB); [2014] 1 W.L.R. 1699; [2014] 2 All E.R. 378, QBD ..... *Digested,* 14/**316**

CF Asset Finance Ltd v Okonji [2014] EWCA Civ 870; [2014] E.C.C. 23; [2014] C.T.L.C. 218, CA (Civ Div) ........ *Digested,* 14/**628**

CH Boehringer Sohn v Paranova A/S (C-429/93) see Bristol Myers Squibb Co v Paranova A/S (C-427/93)

Chabauty v France (57412/08) (2014) 58 E.H.R.R. 38, ECHR

Chadwick v Hollingsworth [2010] EWHC 2718 (QB); [2011] 6 Costs L.R. 931, QBD *Considered* 14/2297

Chadwick v Nash [2012] B.P.I.R. 70, Ch D ........ *Digested,* 12/**1816**: *Considered* 14/1796

Chai v Peng [2014] EWHC 750 (Fam); [2014] 2 F.L.R. 1189; [2014] Fam. Law 809, Fam Div

Chai v Peng [2014] EWHC 1519 (Fam); [2014] Fam. Law 1101, Fam Div

Chakrabarty v Ipswich Hospital NHS Trust [2014] EWHC 2735 (QB); [2014] Med. L.R. 379, QBD ........ *Digested,* 14/**1554**

Chakravarti's Application for Judicial Review, Re see McLarnon's Application for Judicial Review, Re

Chakravorty v Revenue and Customs Commissioners [2014] UKUT 184 (LC); [2014] R.V.R. 274, UT (Lands)

Challinor v Juliet Bellis & Co [2013] EWHC 620 (Ch), Ch D *Applied* 14/408

Chambelin Solicitors v Emokpae see Wong v Igen Ltd (formerly Leeds Careers Guidance)

Champion v North Norfolk DC see R. (on the application of Champion) v North Norfolk DC

Chandler v Cape Plc [2012] EWCA Civ 525; [2012] 1 W.L.R. 3111; [2012] 3 All E.R. 640; [2012] I.C.R. 1293; [2012] P.I.Q.R. P17, CA (Civ Div); affirming [2011] EWHC 951 (QB); (2011) 108(19) L.S.G. 20, QBD ........ *Digested,* 12/**2400**: *Followed* 14/2202

Chandra v Brooke North (A Firm); *joined case* BPC Hotels Ltd v Brooke North (A Firm) [2013] EWCA Civ 1559; [2014] T.C.L.R. 1; 151 Con. L.R. 113; [2013] 50 E.G. 102 (C.S.), CA (Civ Div); reversing [2013] EWHC 417 (QB), QBD ........ *Digested,* 14/**427**: *Considered* 14/426

Changtel Solutions UK Ltd (formerly Enta Technologies Ltd) v Revenue and Customs Commissioners see Enta Technologies Ltd, Re

Chaplin v Boys see Boys v Chaplin

Chaplin v United Kingdom (59842/10) see Eweida v United Kingdom (48420/10)

Chaplin Patents Holdings Co Inc v Group Lotus Plc Times, January 12, 1994; Independent, January 10, 1994, CA (Civ Div) ........ *Digested,* 94/**3452**: *Applied* 11/399, 14/493: *Considered* 96/4543, 01/3882

Chapman v Belgium (Admissibility) (39619/06) (2014) 58 E.H.R.R. SE12, ECHR

Chapman v Powys CC [2014] P.A.D. 14, Planning Inspector

Chapman v United Kingdom (27238/95) (2001) 33 E.H.R.R. 18; 10 B.H.R.C. 48; Times, January 30, 2001, ECHR; no effect (1998) 25 E.H.R.R. CD64, Eur Comm HR ........ *Digested,* 01/**4744**: *Applied* 02/3684, 03/3380, 03/3485, 05/3285, 06/2823, 09/3018, 13/1582: *Considered* 02/3686, 03/3424, 04/1376, 04/3040, 04/3095, 06/3331, 07/2137, 07/2879, 07/3293, 08/2918, 08/4302, 09/3007, 10/2608, 14/2744: *Distinguished* 02/3069, 04/1992, 09/1941: *Followed* 06/3381

Chappell v Revenue and Customs Commissioners [2014] UKUT 344 (TCC); [2014] B.T.C. 523; [2014] S.T.I. 2581, UT (Tax); reversing in part [2013] UKFTT 98 (TC); [2013] S.F.T.D. 733; [2013] S.T.I. 1720, FTT (Tax) ........ *Digested,* 13/**3096**

Chappell v Times Newspapers Ltd [1975] 1 W.L.R. 482; [1975] 2 All E.R. 233; [1975] I.C.R. 145; [1975] I.R.L.R. 90; 18 Man. Law 5; (1975) 119 S.J. 82, CA (Civ Div) *Digested,* 75/**1095**: *Applied* 93/536: *Considered* 77/959, 85/1181, 08/4750, 14/1026

Charity Commission for England and Wales v Framjee [2014] EWHC 2507 (Ch); [2014] W.T.L.R. 1489; 17 I.T.E.L.R. 271, Ch D ........ *Digested,* 14/**286**

Charles Church Developments Ltd v Stent Foundations Ltd [2007] EWHC 855 (TCC); [2007] C.I.L.L. 2477, QBD (TCC)
*Considered* 14/439

Charman v Charman [2005] EWCA Civ 1606; [2006] 1 W.L.R. 1053; [2006] 2 F.L.R. 422; [2006] W.T.L.R. 1; (2006-07) 9 I.T.E.L.R. 43; [2006] Fam. Law 516; (2006) 103(5) L.S.G. 28; Independent, January 13, 2006, CA (Civ Div); affirming [2005] EWHC 2406 (Fam), Fam Div .......... *Digested,* 06/**1625**:
*Applied* 09/1494, 09/1495, 11/1301, 11/1307, 12/1439, 14/1373, 14/1374: *Followed* 12/1440

Chartbrook Ltd v Persimmon Homes Ltd [2009] UKHL 38; [2009] 1 A.C. 1101; [2009] 3 W.L.R. 267; [2009] 4 All E.R. 677; [2010] 1 All E.R. (Comm) 365; [2009] Bus. L.R. 1200; [2009] B.L.R. 551; 125 Con. L.R. 1; [2010] 1 P. & C.R. 9; [2009] 3 E.G.L.R. 119; [2009] C.I.L.L. 2729; [2009] 27 E.G. 91 (C.S.); (2009) 153(26) S.J.L.B. 27; [2009] N.P.C. 87; [2009] N.P.C. 86; Times, July 2, 2009, HL; reversing [2008] EWCA Civ 183; [2008] 2 All E.R. (Comm) 387; [2008] 11 E.G. 92 (C.S.); [2008] N.P.C. 30, CA (Civ Div); affirming [2007] EWHC 409 (Ch); [2007] 1 All E.R. (Comm) 1083; [2007] 2 P. & C.R. 9; [2007] 11 E.G. 160 (C.S.), Ch D .......... *Digested,* 09/**722**:
*Applied* 10/1038, 10/2709, 11/236, 11/505, 11/550, 12/2042, 12/2057, 13/1886, 13/3185, 13/571, 14/2707: *Considered* 10/1920, 10/574, 10/578, 10/622, 10/623, 11/175, 11/187, 11/2704, 12/516, 13/2454, 14/2279, 14/2503: *Followed* 10/516, 12/1797, 12/2759, 12/626, 12/627

Chartwell Estate Agents Ltd v Fergies Properties SA [2014] EWCA Civ 506; [2014] C.P. Rep. 36; [2014] 3 Costs L.R. 588; [2014] C.I.L.L. 3513, CA (Civ Div); affirming [2014] EWHC 438 (QB); [2014] 2 Costs L.R. 353, QBD .......... *Digested,* 14/**461**:
*Followed* 14/447

Chase v News Group Newspapers Ltd; *sub nom* Chase v Newsgroup Newspapers Ltd [2002] EWCA Civ 1772; [2003] E.M.L.R. 11; (2002) 146 S.J.L.B. 279; Times, December 31, 2002, CA (Civ Div); affirming [2002] EWHC 1101 (QB), QBD .......... *Digested,* 03/**953**:
*Considered* 14/833

Chase v Newsgroup Newspapers Ltd see Chase v News Group Newspapers Ltd

Chaudhary v Chaudhary [2013] EWCA Civ 758; [2013] 2 F.L.R. 1526; [2013] Fam. Law 1257, CA (Civ Div) .......... *Digested,* 14/**2490**

Chauhan v General Medical Council [2010] EWHC 2093 (Admin), QBD (Admin)
*Applied* 14/1495

Chawda, Re; *sub nom* Lemon v Chawda [2014] B.P.I.R. 49, Ch D (Bankruptcy Ct) .......... *Digested,* 14/**1203**

Cheapside Land Development Co Ltd v Messels Service Co see United Scientific Holdings Ltd v Burnley BC

Chekiang, The see Admiralty Commissioners v Owners of the SS Chekiang

Chekiang, The see Admiralty Commissioners v Owners of the SS Chekiang

Chelmsford County Court v Ramet [2014] EWHC 56 (Fam); [2014] 2 F.L.R. 1081; [2014] 3 F.C.R. 328; [2014] Fam. Law 435, Fam Div .......... *Digested,* 14/**13**

Chelsea Building Society v Nash [2010] EWCA Civ 1247; [2011] B.P.I.R. 381, CA (Civ Div) .......... *Digested,* 11/**213**:
*Applied* 14/1826

Chem Orchid, The [2014] 1 Lloyd's Rep. 520, HC (Sing)

Chemische Fabrik Kreussler & Co GmbH v Sunstar Deutschland GmbH (formerly John O Butler GmbH) (C-308/11) (Unreported, September 6, 2012), ECJ
*Applied* 14/1528

Chemistree Homecare Ltd v AbbVie Ltd [2013] EWCA Civ 1338; [2014] U.K.C.L.R. 1; [2014] E.C.C. 1, CA (Civ Div); affirming [2013] EWHC 264 (Ch); [2013] U.K.C.L.R. 135; [2013] 4 Costs L.O. 510, Ch D .......... *Digested,* 14/**530**

Chen v Office for Harmonisation in the Internal Market (Trade Marks and Designs) (OHIM) (T-55/12) [2014] E.C.D.R. 2, GC (7th Chamber)

Chen v Secretary of State for the Home Department (C-200/02); *joined case* Zhu v Secretary of State for the Home Department (C-200/02) [2005] Q.B. 325; [2004] 3 W.L.R. 1453; [2004] E.C.R. I-9925; [2004] 3 C.M.L.R. 48; [2005] All E.R. (EC) 129; [2004] C.E.C. 503; [2004] Imm. A.R. 754; [2005] I.N.L.R. 1; Times, October 21, 2004, ECJ; no effect [2004] E.C.R. I-9925; [2004] Imm. A.R. 333, AGO .......... *Digested,* 05/**2207**:
*Applied* 07/1611, 08/1345: *Considered* 06/1589, 07/1652, 07/2367, 08/2095, 11/3791, 14/1734: *Distinguished* 07/2368: *Followed* 12/3596

Cherry v Boultbee 41 E.R. 171; (1839) 4 My. & C. 442, Ch D
*Applied* 06/2359, 10/1868: *Considered* 04/3952, 12/1790, 13/1706: *Not applied* 14/1752

Cherry Tree Investments Ltd v Landmain Ltd [2012] EWCA Civ 736; [2013] Ch. 305; [2013] 2 W.L.R. 481; [2013] 1 B.C.L.C. 484; [2012] 2 P. & C.R. 10; [2012] 2 E.G.L.R. 141; [2012] 23 E.G. 97 (C.S.), CA (Civ Div) ....... *Digested,* 13/**2454**: *Distinguished* 14/2278: *Followed* 14/2521

Cherry Tree Machine Co Ltd v Dawson see Shell Tankers UK Ltd v Jeromson

Cheruvier (t/a Fleur Estelle Belly Dance School) v Revenue and Customs Commissioners [2014] UKFTT 7 (TC); [2014] S.T.I. 538, FTT (Tax)

Cheshire West and Chester Council v P; *sub nom* P v Cheshire West and Chester Council; P v Surrey CC; *joined case* Surrey CC v P [2014] UKSC 19; [2014] A.C. 896; [2014] 2 W.L.R. 642; [2014] 2 All E.R. 585; [2014] P.T.S.R. 460; [2014] 2 F.C.R. 71; [2014] C.O.P.L.R. 313; [2014] H.R.L.R. 13; (2014) 17 C.C.L. Rep. 5; [2014] Med. L.R. 321; (2014) 137 B.M.L.R. 16; (2014) 158(13) S.J.L.B. 37; Times, April 1, 2014, SC; reversing [2011] EWCA Civ 1257; [2012] P.T.S.R. 1447; [2012] 1 F.L.R. 693; (2012) 15 C.C.L. Rep. 48; [2013] Med. L.R. 421; [2011] M.H.L.R. 430; [2012] Fam. Law 137, CA (Civ Div); reversing [2011] EWHC 1330 (Fam), CP ....... *Digested,* 14/**2189**: *Considered* 12/2267, 12/2279

Chester v Afshar [2004] UKHL 41; [2005] 1 A.C. 134; [2004] 3 W.L.R. 927; [2004] 4 All E.R. 587; [2005] P.I.Q.R. P12; [2005] Lloyd's Rep. Med. 109; (2005) 81 B.M.L.R. 1; [2005] P.N.L.R. 14; (2004) 101(43) L.S.G. 34; (2004) 154 N.L.J. 1589; (2004) 148 S.J.L.B. 1215; Times, October 19, 2004, HL; affirming [2002] EWCA Civ 724; [2003] Q.B. 356; [2002] 3 W.L.R. 1195; [2002] 3 All E.R. 552; [2002] Lloyd's Rep. Med. 305; (2002) 67 B.M.L.R. 66; (2002) 99(29) L.S.G. 33; (2002) 146 S.J.L.B. 167; Times, June 13, 2002; Daily Telegraph, June 13, 2002, CA (Civ Div); affirming 1997 C No. 198, HQ 9902422, QBD ....... *Digested,* 05/**2841**: *Applied* 09/2842: *Considered* 12/1535, 14/2198: *Distinguished* 05/2863: *Followed* 06/2866

Chester v Secretary of State for Justice see R. (on the application of Chester) v Secretary of State for Justice

Chester Hall Precision Engineering Ltd v Service Centres Aero France [2014] EWHC 2529 (QB); [2014] I.L.Pr. 38, QBD ....... *Digested,* 14/**568**

Chevron Petroleum (UK) Ltd v BP Petroleum Development Ltd [1981] S.T.C. 689; 57 T.C. 137, Ch D ....... *Digested,* 82/**1605**: *Applied* 13/3087, 14/2920

Cheyne Finance Plc (In Receivership), Re [2007] EWHC 2402 (Ch); [2008] 2 All E.R. 987; [2008] Bus. L.R. 1562; [2008] B.C.C. 182; [2008] 1 B.C.L.C. 741, Ch D (Companies Ct) ....... *Digested,* 08/**2152**: *Applied* 14/1793: *Approved* 13/1704: *Considered* 10/236, 11/216

Chhabra v West London Mental Health NHS Trust; *sub nom* West London Mental Health NHS Trust v Chhabra [2013] UKSC 80; [2014] 1 All E.R. 943; [2014] I.C.R. 194; [2014] I.R.L.R. 227; [2014] Med. L.R. 111; (2014) 136 B.M.L.R. 1, SC; reversing [2013] EWCA Civ 11; [2013] I.R.L.R. 398; [2013] Med. L.R. 33, CA (Civ Div); reversing [2012] EWHC 1735 (QB); [2012] Med. L.R. 489, QBD .. *Digested,* 14/**1555**: *Followed* 14/1052

Chief Constable of Bedfordshire v Liversidge; *sub nom* Liversidge v Chief Constable of Bedfordshire [2002] EWCA Civ 894; [2002] I.C.R. 1135; [2002] I.R.L.R. 651; [2002] Emp. L.R. 998; [2002] Po. L.R. 146, CA (Civ Div); affirming [2002] I.R.L.R. 15, EAT ....... *Digested,* 02/**1397**: *Considered* 02/1415, 03/1298: *Followed* 14/1099

Chief Constable of Hertfordshire v Van Colle see Van Colle v Chief Constable of Hertfordshire

Chief Constable of Lincolnshire v Stubbs [1999] I.C.R. 547; [1999] I.R.L.R. 81, EAT .... *Digested,* 00/**2211**: *Considered* 14/1135

Chief Constable of Merseyside v Husain see Yearwood v Commissioner of Police of the Metropolis

Chief Constable of West Yorkshire v Homer see Homer v Chief Constable of West Yorkshire

Chief Constable of West Yorkshire v Vento (No.2) see Vento v Chief Constable of West Yorkshire

Chief Justice of the Cayman Islands v Governor of the Cayman Islands [2012] UKPC 39; [2014] A.C. 198; [2013] 3 W.L.R. 457, PC (CI)

Chief Land Registrar v Silkstone see Silkstone v Tatnall

Chiemgauer Membran und Zeltbau GmbH (formerly Koch Hightex GmbH) v New Millennium Experience Co Ltd (formerly Millennium Central Ltd) (No.2); *sub nom* Chiemguaer Membran und Zeltbau GmbH (formerly Koch Hightex GmbH) v New Millennium Experience Co Ltd (formerly Millennium Central Ltd) [2002] B.P.I.R. 42; (2001) 98(5) L.S.G. 36; Times, January 16, 2001, Ch D ....... *Digested,* 01/**948**: *Not followed* 14/119

Chiemguaer Membran und Zeltbau GmbH (formerly Koch Hightex GmbH) v New Millennium Experience Co Ltd (formerly Millennium Central Ltd) see Chiemgauer Membran und Zeltbau GmbH (formerly Koch Hightex GmbH) v New Millennium Experience Co Ltd (formerly Millennium Central Ltd) (No.2)

Chikwamba v Secretary of State for the Home Department see C (Zimbabwe) v Secretary of State for the Home Department

Chilcott v Revenue and Customs Commissioners [2010] EWCA Civ 1538; [2011] S.T.C. 456; 81 T.C. 28; [2011] B.T.C. 1; [2010] S.T.I. 3244, CA (Civ Div); affirming [2009] EWHC 3287 (Ch); [2010] S.T.C. 453; [2010] S.T.I. 395, Ch D; affirming [2009] S.T.C. (S.C.D.) 148; [2009] S.T.I. 220, Sp Comm .................... *Digested,* 11/**3380**: *Applied* 12/3127

Child Poverty Action Group v Secretary of State for Work and Pensions see R. (on the application of Child Poverty Action Group) v Secretary of State for Work and Pensions

Children's Rights Alliance for England v Secretary of State for Justice see R. (on the application of Children's Rights Alliance for England) v Secretary of State for Justice

China National Chartering Co Ltd v Daiichii Chuo Kisen Kaisha see Gard Marine & Energy Ltd v China National Chartering Co Ltd

Chinnock v Rea see Schumann v Veale Wasbrough

Chiriboga v International Bank for Reconstruction and Development 616 F.Supp. 963, US Court
*Considered* 14/2892

Chishimba v Kensington and Chelsea RLBC [2013] EWCA Civ 786; [2014] P.T.S.R. 49; [2013] H.L.R. 34; [2013] B.L.G.R. 656, CA (Civ Div) .................................... *Digested,* 13/**1534**: *Considered* 14/1597

Christie v Leachinsky; *sub nom* Leachinsky v Christie [1947] A.C. 573; [1947] 1 All E.R. 567; 63 T.L.R. 231; (1947) 111 J.P. 224; [1947] L.J.R. 757; 176 L.T. 443, HL; affirming [1946] K.B. 124; [1945] 2 All E.R. 395, CA .................................. *Digested,* 47-51/**6152**: *Applied* 71/10199, 75/2960, 75/2964, 80/2304, 82/2715, 86/638, 04/891, 07/2292, 10/669, 14/2192: *Considered* 68/3982, 76/402, 80/2312, 81/2328, 90/4323, 98/4286: *Distinguished* 47-51/6159: *Followed* 81/2090: *Referred to* 93/4889

Christmas v Hampshire CC (Duty of Care) see X (Minors) v Bedfordshire CC

Christofides v Seddon [2014] W.T.L.R. 215, CC (Central London)

Christoforou v Standard Apartments Ltd [2013] UKUT 586 (LC); [2014] L. & T.R. 12, UT (Lands) .................................................................................................. *Digested,* 14/**1988**

Christopher Moran Holdings Ltd v Bairstow see Park Air Services Plc, Re

Christou v Haringey LBC [2013] EWCA Civ 178; [2014] Q.B. 131; [2013] 3 W.L.R. 796; [2014] 1 All E.R. 135; [2013] I.C.R. 1007; [2013] I.R.L.R. 379; (2013) 163 N.L.J. 323, CA (Civ Div); affirming [2012] I.R.L.R. 622, EAT .............................. *Digested,* 13/**979**

CHS Tour Services GmbH v Team4 Travel GmbH (C-435/11) [2014] 1 All E.R. (Comm) 96; [2013] Bus. L.R. 1302; [2014] 1 C.M.L.R. 38; [2014] C.E.C. 76; (2013) 157(37) S.J.L.B. 37, ECJ (1st Chamber)

Church Commissioners for England v Hampshire CC; *sub nom* R. (on the application of Church Commissioners for England) v Hampshire CC [2014] EWCA Civ 634; [2014] 1 W.L.R. 4555; [2014] B.L.G.R. 706; [2014] 2 E.G.L.R. 203, CA (Civ Div); reversing in part [2013] EWHC 1933 (Admin); [2014] A.C.D. 21, QBD (Admin) ........................................................................................................ *Digested,* 14/**2525**

Church of England Building Society v Piskor [1954] Ch. 553; [1954] 2 W.L.R. 952; [1954] 2 All E.R. 85; (1954) 98 S.J. 316, CA; affirming [1954] J.P.L. 189, Ch D . *Digested,* 54/**2109**: *Applied* 89/468: *Considered* 14/2505: *Followed* 68/403: *Overruled* 90/707

Church of Jesus Christ of Latter-Day Saints v Gallagher (Valuation Officer) see Gallagher (Valuation Officer) v Church of Jesus Christ of Latter-Day Saints

Church of Jesus Christ of Latter-Day Saints v United Kingdom (7552/09) (2014) 59 E.H.R.R. 18; [2014] R.A. 322; Times, March 19, 2014, ECHR ........................... *Digested,* 14/**2134**

Church of Scientology Religious Education College Inc v Revenue and Customs Commissioners [2014] UKFTT 1064 (TC); [2014] S.T.I. 3561, FTT (Tax)

Churchill v Roach [2002] EWHC 3230 (Ch); [2004] 2 F.L.R. 989; [2004] 3 F.C.R. 744; [2003] W.T.L.R. 779; [2004] Fam. Law 720, Ch D ............................................. *Digested,* 03/**4469**: *Applied* 14/2822

Chweidan v Mishcon de Reya [2014] EWHC 2685 (QB); [2014] I.R.L.R. 871, QBD

Cichopek v Poland (Admissibility) (15189/10) (2014) 58 E.H.R.R. SE1, ECHR

CIMFRA (China) Ltd v State Tax Bureau of Pucheng County, Shaanxi Province 17 I.T.L. Rep. 506, Unknown court

Cine Bes Filmcheck ve Yapimcilik AS v United International Pictures see United International Pictures v Cine Bes Filmcilik ve Yapimcilik AS

CIP Properties (AIPT) Ltd v Galliford Try Infrastructure Ltd [2014] EWHC 3546 (TCC); 156 Con. L.R. 202; [2014] 6 Costs L.R. 1026, QBD (TCC)

Circle Thirty Three Housing Trust Ltd v Nelson see Nelson v Circle Thirty Three Housing Trust Ltd
Cisco Systems Inc v European Commission (T-79/12) [2014] 4 C.M.L.R. 20, GC (4th Chamber)
Citifinancial Europe Plc v Davidson [2014] Pens. L.R. 625, Ch D
Citroen Belux NV v Federatie voor Verzekerings- en Financiele Tussenpersonen (FvF) (C-265/12) [2014] 1 All E.R. (Comm) 214; [2014] 1 C.M.L.R. 26; [2013] All E.R. (EC) 1098; [2014] C.E.C. 596, ECJ (1st Chamber)
City & County Properties Ltd v Yeats [2012] UKUT 227 (LC); [2013] R.V.R. 47, UT (Lands) .......... *Digested,* 13/**1884**: *Considered* 14/1981
City and County of Swansea v XZ [2014] EWHC 212 (Fam); [2014] 2 F.L.R. 1091; [2014] Fam. Law 972, Fam Div
City Branch Group Ltd, Re see Gross v Rackind
City Facilities Management (UK) Ltd v Ling [2014] Eq. L.R. 399, EAT .......... *Digested,* 14/**1043**
City of Edinburgh Council v Lothian Valuation Appeal Committee; *sub nom* Edinburgh City Council's Appeal, Re [2014] CSIH 32; [2014] R.A. 410; 2014 G.W.D. 14-262, IH (Ex Div) .......... *Digested,* 14/**3651**
Citybranch Group Ltd, Re see Gross v Rackind
CJ CGV Co Ltd's Application, Re [2013] VSC 656; 16 I.T.L. Rep. 814, Sup Ct (Vic)
CJD v Royal Bank of Scotland see D v Royal Bank of Scotland
Claim against Iran, Re (1963) 45 I.L.R. 57, BverfG (Ger) *Applied* 81/285: *Considered* 14/1056
Claim for Legal Fees in Infringement Proceedings, Re (I ZR 194/12) [2014] I.L.Pr. 13, BGH (Ger)
Clamp's Estate, Re 17 I.T.E.L.R. 159, HC (NZ)
Clark v Ardington Electrical Services see Lagden v O'Connor
Clark v Clark Construction Initiatives Ltd [2008] EWCA Civ 1446; [2009] I.C.R. 718, CA (Civ Div); affirming [2009] B.C.C. 665; [2008] I.C.R. 635; [2008] I.R.L.R. 364, EAT .......... *Digested,* 09/**1202**: *Applied* 09/1199: *Considered* 14/1110
Clark v In Focus Asset Management & Tax Solutions Ltd [2014] EWCA Civ 118; [2014] 1 W.L.R. 2502; [2014] 3 All E.R. 313; [2014] 2 All E.R. (Comm) 159; [2014] 1 C.L.C. 170; [2014] Lloyd's Rep. I.R. 437; [2014] P.N.L.R. 19, CA (Civ Div); reversing [2012] EWHC 3669 (QB); [2013] P.N.L.R. 14, QBD .......... *Digested,* 14/**1449**
Clark v Midland Packaging Ltd; *sub nom* Midland Packaging Ltd v Clark [2005] 2 All E.R. 266, EAT .......... *Digested,* 14/**1057**: *Disapproved* 05/1244
Clark v Tull (t/a Ardington Electrical Services) see Lagden v O'Connor
Clark v University of Lincolnshire and Humberside [2000] 1 W.L.R. 1988; [2000] 3 All E.R. 752; [2000] Ed. C.R. 553; [2000] E.L.R. 345; [2000] C.O.D. 293; (2000) 150 N.L.J. 616; (2000) 144 S.J.L.B. 220; Times, May 3, 2000; Independent, May 3, 2000, CA (Civ Div) .......... *Digested,* 00/**2001**: *Applied* 05/2497, 06/1227, 07/1281, 13/913: *Considered* 07/51, 09/1056, 09/341, 13/909: *Followed* 14/916
Clark (Inspector of Taxes) v Oceanic Contractors Inc [1983] 2 A.C. 130; [1983] 2 W.L.R. 94; [1983] 1 All E.R. 133; [1983] S.T.C. 35; 56 T.C. 183; (1982) 13 A.T.R. 901; (1983) 133 N.L.J. 62; (1983) 127 S.J. 54, HL; reversing [1982] 1 W.L.R. 222; [1982] S.T.C. 66; [1982] E.C.C. 224; [1981] T.R. 463; (1980) 124 S.J. 34; Times, November 11, 1981, CA (Civ Div); reversing [1981] 1 W.L.R. 59; [1980] S.T.C. 656; [1980] E.C.C. 485; [1980] T.R. 341; (1980) 124 S.J. 595, Ch D .......... *Digested,* 85/**1766**: *Applied* 87/209, 05/4104, 05/685, 10/3362, 14/2894: *Considered* 88/190, 04/3758, 06/4228, 10/763: *Distinguished* 85/318
Clarke v Barclays Bank Plc [2014] EWHC 505 (Ch); [2014] 3 Costs L.R. 440, Ch D ..... *Digested,* 14/**292**
Clarke v Crown Prosecution Service [2013] EWHC 366 (Admin); (2014) 178 J.P. 7, DC .......... *Digested,* 14/**2566**
Clarke v Edinburgh & District Tramways Co Ltd 1919 S.C. (H.L.) 35; (1919) 1 S.L.T. 247, HL *Applied* 01/6217, 03/5252: *Followed* 13/6, 14/1579
Classica Shipping Co Ltd v CMA CGM SA see CMA CGM SA v Classica Shipping Co Ltd (The CMA Djakarta)
Claussen v Yeates see Cranfield v Bridgegrove Ltd
Claymore Services Ltd v Nautilus Properties Ltd [2007] EWHC 805 (TCC); [2007] B.L.R. 452, QBD (TCC) .......... *Digested,* 08/**608**: *Applied* 11/1863, 13/339, 14/2210, 14/408
Clayton v Army Board of the Defence Council [2014] EWHC 1651 (Admin); [2014] A.C.D. 110, QBD (Admin)

Clayton v Clayton [2006] EWCA Civ 878; [2006] Fam. 83; [2006] 3 W.L.R. 599; [2007] 1 All E.R. 1197; [2007] E.M.L.R. 3; [2007] 1 F.L.R. 11; [2006] 2 F.C.R. 405; [2006] H.R.L.R. 34; [2007] U.K.H.R.R. 264; [2006] Fam. Law 926; (2006) 103(28) L.S.G. 28; (2006) 156 N.L.J. 1101; (2006) 150 S.J.L.B. 890; Times, July 4, 2006; Independent, June 29, 2006, CA (Civ Div); reversing [2005] EWHC 3451 (Fam), Fam Div ........ *Digested,* 06/**1687**: *Applied* 08/1443: *Considered* 08/1540, 10/1731, 11/1331, 14/46: *Followed* 07/1732

Clayton v Clayton 16 I.T.E.L.R. 44, HC (NZ)

Clearbrook Property Holdings Ltd v Verrier [1974] 1 W.L.R. 243; [1973] 3 All E.R. 614; (1974) 27 P. & C.R. 430; (1974) 118 S.J. 117, Ch D ........ *Digested,* 73/**1875**: *Applied* 85/389, 90/3701, 14/2512: *Considered* 87/2111: *Distinguished* 74/2022, 91/2976: *Followed* 89/459

Cleary v Monmouthshire CC [2014] P.A.D. 27, Planning Inspector

Cleeve Link Ltd v Bryla [2014] I.C.R. 264; [2014] I.R.L.R. 86, EAT ........ *Digested,* 14/**1141**

Clemens v Peter Richards (t/a John Bryan) [1977] I.R.L.R. 332, EAT *Applied* 13/1082: *Considered* 14/1090

Clements v Lloyds Banking Plc [2014] I.C.R. D22, EAT

Clenaware Leasing Ltd, Re see Harris v Secretary of State for Business, Innovation and Skills

Clenaware Systems Ltd, Re see Harris v Secretary of State for Business, Innovation and Skills

Clibbery v Allan; *sub nom* Cliberry v Allan [2002] EWCA Civ 45; [2002] Fam. 261; [2002] 2 W.L.R. 1511; [2002] 1 All E.R. 865; [2002] 1 F.L.R. 565; [2002] 1 F.C.R. 385; [2002] U.K.H.R.R. 697; [2002] Fam. Law 260; (2002) 99(11) L.S.G. 37; (2002) 152 N.L.J. 222; (2002) 146 S.J.L.B. 38; Times, February 5, 2002; Independent, February 5, 2002, CA (Civ Div); affirming [2001] 2 F.L.R. 819; [2001] 2 F.C.R. 577; [2001] Fam. Law 654; (2001) 98(27) L.S.G. 40; (2001) 151 N.L.J. 969; (2001) 145 S.J.L.B. 160; Times, July 2, 2001; Independent, July 30, 2001, Fam Div ........ *Digested,* 02/**1695**: *Applied* 14/1353: *Considered* 04/185: *Followed* 12/22

Cliberry v Allan see Clibbery v Allan

ClientEarth v European Commission (T-111/11) [2014] Env. L.R. 11, GC (6th Chamber)

ClientEarth v European Food Safety Authority (EFSA) (T-214/11) [2014] 1 C.M.L.R. 34, GC (6th Chamber)

Clift v United Kingdom (7205/07) Times, July 21, 2010, ECHR *Considered* 14/2234

Clift v Welsh Office [1999] 1 W.L.R. 796; [1998] 4 All E.R. 852; (1999) 78 P. & C.R. 32; [1998] R.V.R. 303; (1998) 95(36) L.S.G. 31; (1998) 76 P. & C.R. D46; Times, August 24, 1998; Independent, July 29, 1998, CA (Civ Div); affirming [1997] R.V.R. 12, Lands Tr ........ *Digested,* 98/**4041**: *Distinguished* 14/2219

Clingham v Kensington and Chelsea RLBC see R. (on the application of McCann) v Manchester Crown Court

Cloburn Quarry Co Ltd v Revenue and Customs Commissioners [2013] CSOH 203; [2014] S.T.C. 1073; 2014 S.L.T. 303; 2014 G.W.D. 2-35, OH ........ *Digested,* 14/**3803**

Closegate Hotel Development (Durham Ltd) v McLean [2013] EWHC 3237 (Ch); [2014] Bus. L.R. 405, Ch D (Companies Ct) ........ *Digested,* 14/**1760**

CLP Holding Co Ltd v Singh [2014] EWCA Civ 1103; [2014] 3 E.G.L.R. 101; [2014] B.V.C. 40; [2014] S.T.I. 3023, CA (Civ Div) ........ *Digested,* 14/**632**

Club Co (UK) Ltd v Revenue and Customs Commissioners [2014] UKFTT 576 (TC); [2014] S.T.I. 2253, FTT (Tax)

Clyde & Co LLP v Bates van Winkelhof see Bates van Winkelhof v Clyde & Co LLP

Clydesdale Bank Plc v Workman [2014] P.N.L.R. 18, Ch D ........ *Digested,* 14/**3025**

Clymo v Shell-Mex BP 187 E.G. 19; [1963] R.A. 191; [1963] R.V.R. 471; 10 R.R.C. 85; [1963] J.P.L. 668, CA; affirming [1962] R.A. 576; [1962] R.V.R. 651; [1962] J.P.L. 809, Lands Tr ........ *Digested,* 63/**2965**: *Applied* 14/2129: *Considered* 06/3349

CM v Bexley LBC [2011] UKUT 215 (AAC); [2011] E.L.R. 413, UT (AAC) ........ *Digested,* 11/**986**: *Applied* 13/902, 14/938

CM v Surrey CC (SEN) [2014] UKUT 4 (AAC); [2014] E.L.R. 91, UT (AAC) ........ *Digested,* 14/**944**

CM v Westminster Magistrates' Court see R. (on the application of B) v Westminster Magistrates' Court

CM (EM Country Guidance: Disclosure: Zimbabwe), Re; *sub nom* CM (Zimbabwe) v Secretary of State for the Home Department [2013] EWCA Civ 1303; [2014] Imm. A.R. 326, CA (Civ Div); affirming [2013] UKUT 59 (IAC), UT (IAC) ........ *Digested,* 14/**1664**

CM (Zimbabwe) v Secretary of State for the Home Department see CM (EM Country Guidance: Disclosure: Zimbabwe), Re

CMA CGM SA v Classica Shipping Co Ltd (The CMA Djakarta); *sub nom* Classica Shipping Co Ltd v CMA CGM SA [2004] EWCA Civ 114; [2004] 1 All E.R. (Comm) 865; [2004] 1 Lloyd's Rep. 460; [2004] 1 C.L.C. 468; (2004) 101(11) L.S.G. 36; Times, February 27, 2004, CA (Civ Div); reversing in part [2003] EWHC 641 (Comm); [2003] 2 All E.R. (Comm) 21; [2003] 2 Lloyd's Rep. 50, QBD (Comm) ........ *Digested,* 04/**3487**: *Considered* 09/3580, 14/2732

Co-operative Bank Plc v Phillips [2014] EWHC 2862 (Ch); [2014] 5 Costs L.R. 830; [2014] B.P.I.R. 1430; [2014] C.T.L.C. 293, Ch D ........ *Digested,* 14/**338**

Co-Operative Bank Plc, Re [2013] EWHC 4074 (Ch); [2014] B.C.C. 457, Ch D ........ *Digested,* 14/**1824**

Co-operative Group Ltd v Birse Developments Ltd [2014] EWCA Civ 707; [2014] B.L.R. 477, CA (Civ Div); affirming [2013] EWHC 3145 (TCC), QBD (TCC) ........ *Digested,* 14/**425**

Co-operative Group Ltd v Birse Developments Ltd (In Liquidation) [2014] EWHC 530 (TCC); [2014] B.L.R. 359; 153 Con. L.R. 103; [2014] P.N.L.R. 21, QBD (TCC) .. *Digested,* 14/**591**

Coal Authority v Newbold see Newbold v Coal Authority

Coal Consumers Association, Re (1876) 4 Ch. D. 625, Ch D *Disapproved* 14/1756

Coard v National Westminster Bank Ltd see Salmon (Deceased), Re

Coastal (Bermuda) Petroleum Ltd v VTT Vulcan Petroleum SA (No.2) (The Marine Star) [1996] 2 Lloyd's Rep. 383; [1996] C.L.C. 1510, CA (Civ Div); reversing [1994] 2 Lloyd's Rep. 629; [1994] C.L.C. 1019, QBD (Comm) ........ *Digested,* 96/**5369**: *Considered* 14/2716

Cobbold v Greenwich LBC (Unreported, August 9, 1999), CA (Civ Div) *Applied* 05/454, 09/419: *Considered* 04/270: *Doubted* 11/389: *Followed* 12/303, 14/299

Cobham Hire Services Ltd v Eeles see Eeles v Cobham Hire Services Ltd

COCA COLA COMPANY/Correction (T1869/12) [2014] E.P.O.R. 32, EPO (Technical Bd App)

Cocking v Sandhurst (Stationers) Ltd [1974] I.C.R. 650; (1975) 10 I.T.R. 6, NIRC; reversing (Unreported, 1947), IT ........ *Digested,* 75/**1119**: *Applied* 77/1165, 83/1240, 00/2151, 13/1082, 14/1070: *Considered* 89/78, 95/2114: *Distinguished* 93/1760

Cockram v Air Products Plc [2014] I.C.R. 1065; [2014] I.R.L.R. 672, EAT ........ *Digested,* 14/**1021**

Coco v AN Clark (Engineers) Ltd [1968] F.S.R. 415; [1969] R.P.C. 41, Ch D ........ *Digested,* 68/**1458**: *Applied* 88/3403, 99/3437, 01/4415, 03/1217, 07/4190, 09/2049, 13/1776, 13/1804, 14/1864: *Considered* 03/2923, 08/60, 08/71

Codemasters Software Co Ltd v Automobile Club de l'Ouest [2009] EWHC 3194 (Ch); [2010] F.S.R. 13, Ch D (Patents Ct) ........ *Digested,* 10/**253**: *Considered* 14/256

Codona v Mid-Bedfordshire DC [2004] EWCA Civ 925; [2005] H.L.R. 1; [2005] B.L.G.R. 241; [2005] A.C.D. 10; (2004) 148 S.J.L.B. 910; [2004] N.P.C. 120; Times, July 21, 2004, CA (Civ Div) ........ *Digested,* 04/**1890**: *Applied* 12/1626: *Considered* 08/1840: *Explained* 14/1605

Coflexip SA v Stolt Comex Seaway MS Ltd [2001] 1 All E.R. 952 (Note); [2001] R.P.C. 9; (2000) 23(10) I.P.D. 23081, CA (Civ Div); affirming [1999] 2 All E.R. 593; [1999] F.S.R. 473; (1999) 22(4) I.P.D. 22035; (1999) 22(4) I.P.D. 22036; (1999) 149 N.L.J. 196; Times, February 4, 1999; Independent, February 3, 1999, Ch D (Patents Ct) ........ *Digested,* 02/**2840**: *Applied* 14/1929

Cohen v Snelling see Lubovsky v Snelling

Colaingrove Ltd v Revenue and Customs Commissioners [2013] UKFTT 343 (TC); [2013] S.F.T.D. 1182; [2013] S.T.I. 2349, FTT (Tax) ........ *Digested,* 14/**3102**

Colaingrove Ltd v Revenue and Customs Commissioners; *sub nom* Revenue and Customs Commissioners v Colaingrove Ltd [2014] UKUT 132 (TCC); [2014] S.T.C. 1457; [2014] B.V.C. 519; [2014] S.T.I. 1767, UT (Tax); affirming in part [2013] UKFTT 312 (TC); [2013] S.F.T.D. 1110; [2013] S.T.I. 2183, FTT (Tax) ... *Digested,* 14/**3101**

Colchester v Revenue and Customs Commissioners [2014] UKUT 83 (TCC); [2014] S.T.C. 2078; [2014] 3 E.G.L.R. 105; [2014] B.V.C. 513; [2014] S.T.I. 871, UT (Tax); affirming [2013] UKFTT 45 (TC); [2013] S.F.T.D. 435; [2013] S.T.I. 336, FTT (Tax) ........ *Digested,* 14/**3103**

Cole v Billington; *sub nom* Billington v Cole [2013] EWCA Civ 502; [2014] B.P.I.R. 350, CA (Civ Div)

Cole v Lambeth LBC see Kay v Lambeth LBC

Colefax v First Tier Tribunal (Social Entitlement Chamber) see R. (on the application of Colefax) v First Tier Tribunal (Social Entitlement Chamber)

Coleman v Attridge Law (A Firm) (C-303/06) [2008] E.C.R. I-5603; [2008] 3 C.M.L.R. 27; [2008] All E.R. (EC) 1105; [2008] C.E.C. 986; [2008] I.C.R. 1128; [2008] I.R.L.R. 722; Times, July 29, 2008, ECJ (Grand Chamber) ............................... *Digested,* 09/**1176**: *Applied* 10/1049: *Considered* 09/1233, 11/1057, 14/1038: *Not applied* 11/4224

Coleman v Williams see Beard (formerly Coleman) v Williams

Coles v Hetherton [2013] EWCA Civ 1704; [2014] 3 All E.R. 377; [2014] 2 All E.R. (Comm) 223; [2014] Lloyd's Rep. I.R. 367, CA (Civ Div); affirming [2012] EWHC 1599 (Comm); [2013] 1 All E.R. (Comm) 453; [2012] R.T.R. 33; [2013] Lloyd's Rep. I.R. 9; (2012) 162 N.L.J. 873, QBD (Comm) ................................. *Digested,* 14/**1852**: *Applied* 14/829

Coll v Floreat Merchant Banking Ltd [2014] EWHC 1741 (QB); (2014) 158(24) S.J.L.B. 53, QBD

Collection (Management) Ltd v Jackson (Valuation Officer) [2013] UKUT 166 (LC); [2013] R.A. 311, UT (Lands) ........................................................................ *Digested,* 14/**2129**

Collector of Stamp Revenue v Arrowtown Assets Ltd 6 I.T.L. Rep. 454, CFA (HK) *Applied* 07/3992, 09/3825, 14/2878: *Considered* 05/4084, 09/3755

College of Estate Management v Customs and Excise Commissioners; *sub nom* College of Estate Management v Revenue and Customs Commissioners [2005] UKHL 62; [2005] 1 W.L.R. 3351; [2005] 4 All E.R. 933; [2005] S.T.C. 1957; [2006] 2 C.M.L.R. 3; [2005] B.T.C. 5673; [2005] B.V.C. 704; [2005] S.T.I. 1753; (2005) 102(44) L.S.G. 32; [2005] N.P.C. 118; Times, October 26, 2005, HL; reversing [2004] EWCA Civ 1086; [2004] S.T.C. 1471; [2004] B.T.C. 5754; [2004] B.V.C. 813; [2004] S.T.I. 1972; (2004) 101(37) L.S.G. 36; (2004) 148 S.J.L.B. 1030; Times, October 11, 2004, CA (Civ Div); reversing [2003] EWHC 2712 (Ch); [2004] S.T.C. 235; [2004] B.T.C. 5335; [2004] B.V.C. 395; [2004] S.T.I. 1867; [2003] S.T.I. 2119, Ch D; affirming [2003] V. & D.R. 165; [2003] S.T.I. 1087, V&DTr .............................................................................................. *Digested,* 06/**4449**: *Applied* 08/4035, 08/4041, 08/4048, 09/4098, 14/3050: *Considered* 06/4437, 11/3567, 14/3102

College of Estate Management v Revenue and Customs Commissioners see College of Estate Management v Customs and Excise Commissioners

Collegewood Street Ltd's Trade Mark Application, Re [2014] E.T.M.R. 12, PO (Irl)

Collier v Williams; *joined cases* Marshall v Maggs; Leeson v Marsden; Glass v Surrendran [2006] EWCA Civ 20; [2006] 1 W.L.R. 1945; [2007] 1 All E.R. 991; [2006] C.P. Rep. 22; [2006] P.I.Q.R. P18; (2006) 103(7) L.S.G. 23; (2006) 150 S.J.L.B. 128; Times, February 3, 2006, CA (Civ Div) ......................................... *Digested,* 06/**348**: *Applied* 07/464, 08/359, 09/392, 10/274, 12/443: *Considered* 07/480, 10/319, 10/415, 11/345, 11/61: *Followed* 10/275, 11/1260, 14/439

Colliers International UK Plc (In Administration), Re see Bank of Ireland v Colliers International UK Plc (In Administration)

Collins v Secretary of State for Business Innovation and Skills [2014] EWCA Civ 717; [2014] C.P. Rep. 39; [2014] P.I.Q.R. P19; [2014] Med. L.R. 291, CA (Civ Div); affirming [2013] EWHC 1117 (QB), QBD ......................................................... *Digested,* 14/**419**

Collins v Secretary of State for Communities and Local Government [2013] EWCA Civ 1193; [2013] P.T.S.R. 1594, CA (Civ Div); affirming [2012] EWHC 2760 (Admin), QBD (Admin) ........................................................................................ *Digested,* 14/**2437**: *Applied* 14/1596

Collins v Wilcock [1984] 1 W.L.R. 1172; [1984] 3 All E.R. 374; (1984) 79 Cr. App. R. 229; (1984) 148 J.P. 692; [1984] Crim. L.R. 481; (1984) 81 L.S.G. 2140; (1984) 128 S.J. 660, DC .......................................................................................... *Digested,* 84/**506**: *Applied* 88/2276, 08/753, 11/2580, 14/2468: *Considered* 86/3464, 86/479

Collins Stewart Ltd v Financial Times Ltd (No.2) [2005] EWHC 262 (QB); [2006] E.M.L.R. 5, QBD ........................................................................................... *Digested,* 06/**1040**: *Applied* 10/838, 14/832

Colloseum Holding AG v Levi Strauss & Co (C-12/12) [2013] Bus. L.R. 768; [2013] E.T.M.R. 34, ECJ (5th Chamber) *Followed* 14/1937

Colon v Netherlands (49458/06 (2012) 55 E.H.R.R. SE5, ECHR *Considered* 14/2461

Colonial Bank v Whinney (1886) 11 App. Cas. 426, HL; reversing (1885) 30 Ch. D. 261, CA *Applied* 14/2528

Coloroll Pension Trustees Ltd v Russell (C-200/91) see Ten Oever v Stichting Bedrijfspensioenfonds voor het Glazenwassers- en Schoonmaakbedrijf (C-109/91)

Colour Trusts, Re; *sub nom* Blanco Settlements, Re; Wilson v Monaghan 16 I.T.E.L.R. 323, Royal Ct (Gue)

Colquhoun v Harris; *sub nom* 16 & 18 Alexandra Road, Mitcham, Surrey, CR4 3LT, Re [2010] EWHC 3963 (Ch), Ch D
*Considered* 14/2509
Comic Enterprise Ltd v Twentieth Century Fox Film Corp [2014] EWHC 2286 (Ch); [2014] E.T.M.R. 51, Ch D ..... *Digested,* 14/**1923**
Comic Enterprises Ltd v Twentieth Century Fox Film Corp [2014] EWHC 185 (Ch); [2014] E.T.M.R. 46; [2014] F.S.R. 35, Ch D ..... *Digested,* 14/**1928**
Commerzbank AG v Brehm [2014] B.P.I.R. 359, Ch D (Bankruptcy Ct)
Commission of the European Communities v AssiDoman Kraft Products AB (C-310/97 P) [1999] E.C.R. I-5363; [1999] 5 C.M.L.R. 1253; [1999] All E.R. (EC) 737; Times, October 19, 1999, ECJ ..... *Digested,* 99/**2223**:
*Applied* 12/538, 14/550: *Considered* 13/492: *Distinguished* 06/1548
Commission of the European Communities v European Parliament (C-299/05) [2007] E.C.R. I-8695, ECJ
*Considered* 14/2780: *Followed* 11/3131
Commission of the European Communities v France (C60/96) [1999] S.T.C. 480; [1997] E.C.R. I-3827, ECJ (6th Chamber) ..... *Digested,* 99/**4971**:
*Applied* 14/3052
Commission of the European Communities v Germany (29/84); *sub nom* Nursing Directives, Re (29/84) [1985] E.C.R. 1661; [1986] 3 C.M.L.R. 579, ECJ ..... *Digested,* 87/**1521**:
*Applied* 09/1164, 14/1222
Commission of the European Communities v Germany (C-319/05) [2007] E.C.R. I-9811; [2008] 1 C.M.L.R. 36, ECJ (1st Chamber) ..... *Digested,* 08/**1335**:
*Applied* 09/1403, 14/1528: *Considered* 09/2408
Commission of the European Communities v Ireland (C-215/06) [2008] E.C.R. I-4911; [2009] Env. L.R. D3, ECJ (2nd Chamber)
*Applied* 10/2617: *Followed* 14/2424
Commission of the European Communities v Ireland (C-427/07); *sub nom* Transposition of Directive 85/337, Re (C-427/07) [2009] E.C.R. I-6277; [2011] 3 C.M.L.R. 46; [2010] Env. L.R. 8, ECJ (2nd Chamber)
*Applied* 14/1222: *Considered* 11/2562, 11/4020
Commission of the European Communities v Italy (C-104/86); *sub nom* Repayment of Illegal Taxes, Re (C-104/86) [1988] E.C.R. 1799; [1989] 3 C.M.L.R. 25, ECJ .... *Digested,* 91/**4034**:
*Distinguished* 14/3098
Commission of the European Communities v Netherlands (235/85) [1987] E.C.R. 1471; [1988] 2 C.M.L.R. 921, ECJ ..... *Digested,* 89/**1682**:
*Applied* 09/4121: *Cited* 97/4967: *Considered* 14/3044
Commission of the European Communities v Spain (C-124/96) [1998] S.T.C. 1237; [1998] E.C.R. I-2501, ECJ (6th Chamber) ..... *Digested,* 99/**4984**:
*Applied* 13/3190: *Considered* 14/3043
Commission of the European Communities v Spain (C-227/01) [2004] E.C.R. I-8253; [2005] Env. L.R. 20, ECJ ..... *Digested,* 05/**1365**:
*Considered* 09/1319: *Distinguished* 14/1187
Commission of the European Communities v Spain (C-88/07); *sub nom* Marketing of Herbal Medicines, Re (C-88/07) [2009] E.C.R. I-1353; [2009] 2 C.M.L.R. 52, ECJ (1st Chamber) ..... *Digested,* 09/**1403**:
*Applied* 14/1528
Commission of the European Communities v United Kingdom (C98/04) [2006] E.C.R. I-4003, ECJ
*Considered* 14/2377
Commissioner for the South African Revenue Service v Krok 16 I.T.L. Rep. 838, HC (SA)
Commissioner of Police of the Metropolis v Bangs [2014] EWHC 546 (Admin); (2014) 178 J.P. 158, DC ..... *Digested,* 14/**663**
Commissioner of Police of the Metropolis v Kay see Kay v Commissioner of Police of the Metropolis
Commissioner of Police of the Metropolis v Keohane [2014] I.C.R. 1073; [2014] Eq. L.R. 386, EAT ..... *Digested,* 14/**1118**
Commissioner of Police of the Metropolis v Miller see Yearwood v Commissioner of Police of the Metropolis
Commissioner of Police of the Metropolis v Police Medical Appeal Board see R. (on the application of Commissioner of Police of the Metropolis) v Police Medical Appeal Board
Commissioner of Police of the Metropolis v Raissi see Raissi v Commissioner of Police of the Metropolis
Commissioner of Police of the Metropolis v Times Newspapers Ltd [2011] EWHC 2705 (QB); [2014] E.M.L.R. 1, QBD
*Considered* 12/335

Commissioner of Police of the Metropolis v Woolway (Valuation Officer) [2014] UKUT 183 (LC); [2014] R.A. 455, UT (Lands)
Commissioner of Taxation v Resource Capital Fund III LP see Resource Capital Fund III LP v Commissioner of Taxation
Commissioners of Crown Lands v Page see Crown Lands Commissioners v Page
Commonwealth Institute (In Members' Voluntary Liquidation), Re; *sub nom* Setchim v Secretary of State for Foreign and Commonwealth Affairs [2014] EWHC 2218 (Ch); [2014] W.T.L.R. 1621, Ch D (Companies Ct) ........ *Digested,* 14/**1813**
Compagnie Noga d'Importation et d'Exportation SA v Abacha (No.3); *sub nom* Compagnie Noga d'Importation et d'Exportation SA v Russia; Compagnie Noga d'Importation et d'Exportation SA v Australia and New Zealand Banking Group Ltd; *joined case* Attorney General of Nigeria v Abacha [2002] EWCA Civ 1142; [2003] 1 W.L.R. 307; [2003] C.P. Rep. 5, CA (Civ Div); affirming in part [2002] C.L.C. 207, QBD (Comm) ........ *Digested,* 02/**292**: *Applied* 10/1990, 14/37
Compagnie Noga d'Importation et d'Exportation SA v Australia and New Zealand Banking Group Ltd see Compagnie Noga d'Importation et d'Exportation SA v Abacha (No.3)
Compagnie Noga d'Importation et d'Exportation SA v Russia see Compagnie Noga d'Importation et d'Exportation SA v Abacha (No.3)
Compania Naviera Micro SA v Shipley International Inc (The Parouth) [1982] 2 Lloyd's Rep. 351, CA (Civ Div) ........ *Digested,* 82/**379**: *Applied* 87/3132: *Followed* 14/115
Compania Naviera Sota y Aznar v Ralli Bros see Ralli Bros v Compania Naviera Sota y Aznar
Company (No.000359 of 1987), Re; *sub nom* International Westminster Bank v Okeanos Maritime Corp [1988] Ch. 210; [1987] 3 W.L.R. 339; [1987] 3 All E.R. 137; (1987) 3 B.C.C. 160; [1987] B.C.L.C. 450; [1988] P.C.C. 64; (1987) 84 L.S.G. 1811; (1987) 131 S.J. 938, Ch D (Companies Ct) ........ *Digested,* 87/**375**: *Applied* 97/3090, 14/1783: *Considered* 92/2579, 99/3350, 99/3351
Company (No.000709 of 1992), Re see O'Neill v Phillips
Company (No.005685 of 1988) (No.2), Re see Ringtower Holdings, Re
Company (No.0005945 of 2006), Re [2006] EWHC 3436 (Ch); [2007] B.P.I.R. 1; (2006) 150 S.J.L.B. 1153, Ch D ........ *Digested,* 07/**2461**: *Considered* 14/1987
Company (No.007466 of 2003), Re; *sub nom* Company (No.1389920), Re [2004] EWHC 60 (Ch); [2004] 1 W.L.R. 1357; [2004] B.C.C. 288; [2004] 2 B.C.L.C. 434; (2004) 101(7) L.S.G. 34; Times, February 2, 2004, Ch D (Companies Ct) . *Digested,* 04/**390**: *Considered* 14/1758
Company (No.1389920), Re see Company (No.007466 of 2003), Re
Compaq Computer Ltd v Abercorn Group Ltd (t/a Osiris) [1991] B.C.C. 484; [1993] B.C.L.C. 603, Ch D
*Considered* 94/2598, 14/2586
Complaint of Surveillance, Re [2014] 2 All E.R. 576, IPT ........ *Digested,* 14/**666**
Comptroller of Income Tax v AZP [2012] SGHC 112; 14 I.T.L. Rep. 1155, HC (Sing)
*Considered* 14/2893
Comptroller of Income Tax v BJY [2013] SGHC 173; 16 I.T.L. Rep. 324, HC (Sing)
Comptroller of Income Tax v BKW [2013] SGHC 205; 16 I.T.L. Rep. 344, HC (Sing)
Concept Multi Car Ltd v Revenue and Customs Commissioners [2014] UKFTT 110 (TC); [2014] S.T.I. 801, FTT (Tax)
Conde Nast Publications Ltd v Revenue and Customs Commissioners see Fleming (t/a Bodycraft) v Customs and Excise Commissioners
Condogianis v Guardian Assurance Co Ltd [1921] 2 A.C. 125; (1921) 7 Ll. L. Rep. 155, PC (Aus)
*Considered* 14/1846
Condon Ex p. James, Re (1873-74) L.R. 9 Ch. App. 609; [1874-80] All E.R. Rep. 388, CA in Chancery
*Applied* 70/310, 72/189, 74/357, 75/170, 09/399: *Considered* 99/3258, 00/3433, 05/2261, 11/187, 14/608: *Distinguished* 72/197, 82/195, 87/3806, 88/3612, 02/2655: *Not applied* 99/3230
Conductive Inkjet Technology Ltd v Uni-Pixel Displays Inc [2013] EWHC 2968 (Ch); [2014] 1 All E.R. (Comm) 654; [2014] F.S.R. 22, Ch D (Patents Ct) ........ *Digested,* 14/**477**
Confetra - Confederazione Generale Italiana dei Trasporti e della Logistica v Ministero delle Infrastrutture e dei Trasporti (C-187/13) see API - Anonima Petroli Italiana SpA v Ministero delle Infrastrutture e dei Trasporti (C-184/13)
Confidential v Commissioner of Taxation 17 I.T.L. Rep. 400, AAT (Aus)

Conister Trust Ltd v John Hardman & Co; *sub nom* John Hardman & Co v Conister Trust Ltd [2008] EWCA Civ 841; [2008] C.T.L.C. 152; (2008) 158 N.L.J. 1113, CA (Civ Div)
*Considered* 14/610

Coniston Hotel (Kent) LLP (In Liquidation), Re; *sub nom* Berntsen v Tait [2013] EWHC 93 (Ch); [2013] 2 B.C.L.C. 405, Ch D (Companies Ct) ........ *Digested,* 14/**1765**

Conlon v Black Horse Ltd [2012] C.T.L.C. 193, QBD ........ *Digested,* 13/**550**: *Affirmed* 14/609

Conlon v Black Horse Ltd see Plevin v Paragon Personal Finance Ltd

Conlon v Simms; *sub nom* Simms v Conlon [2006] EWCA Civ 1749; [2008] 1 W.L.R. 484; [2007] 3 All E.R. 802; Times, January 17, 2007, CA (Civ Div); reversing [2006] EWHC 401 (Ch); [2006] 2 All E.R. 1024; (2006) 103(13) L.S.G. 25, Ch D ........ *Digested,* 07/**339**: *Considered* 07/471, 14/297

Connery v Williams Business College Ltd [2014] NSWSC 154; 17 I.T.E.L.R. 251, Sup Ct (NSW)

Conor Medsystems Inc v Angiotech Pharmaceuticals Inc; *sub nom* Angiotech Pharmaceuticals Inc's Patent (No.706376); Angiotech Pharmaceuticals Inc v Conor Medsystems Inc [2008] UKHL 49; [2008] 4 All E.R. 621; [2008] R.P.C. 28; (2008) 103 B.M.L.R. 100; (2008) 31(8) I.P.D. 31049; (2008) 105(28) L.S.G. 16; (2008) 152(29) S.J.L.B. 31, HL; reversing [2007] EWCA Civ 5; [2007] R.P.C. 20; (2007) 94 B.M.L.R. 122; (2007) 30(5) I.P.D. 30031, CA (Civ Div); affirming [2006] EWHC 260 (Pat); [2006] R.P.C. 28; (2006) 29(5) I.P.D. 29042, Ch D (Patents Ct) ........ *Digested,* 08/**2325**: *Applied* 09/2394, 10/1967: *Considered* 14/1896: *Followed* 12/1948

Conseil national de l'ordre des medecins v Ministre de l'Enseignement superieur et de la Recherche (C-492/12) [2014] 1 C.M.L.R. 36; [2014] C.E.C. 707, ECJ (4th Chamber)

Constable v Bedfordshire Police Authority see Bedfordshire Police Authority v Constable

Constantine v Lambeth LBC see Kay v Lambeth LBC

Constantinides v Constantinides [2013] EWHC 3688 (Fam); [2014] 1 W.L.R. 1934; [2014] 2 F.L.R. 736; [2014] Fam. Law 440, Fam Div ........ *Digested,* 14/**1368**

Constantinides v Law Society [2006] EWHC 725 (Admin); (2006) 156 N.L.J. 680, DC
*Considered* 14/2472

Constructora Principado SA v Menendez Alvarez (C-226/12) [2014] 1 All E.R. (Comm) 385, ECJ (1st Chamber)

Consultant Services Group Ltd v Revenue and Customs Commissioners [2014] UKFTT 197 (TC); [2014] S.T.I. 1609, FTT (Tax)

Contour Aerospace Ltd v Virgin Atlantic Airways Ltd see Virgin Atlantic Airways Ltd v Jet Airways (India) Ltd

Contrarian Funds LLC v Lomas see Lehman Brothers International (Europe) (In Administration), Re

Conway v Jam Factory Freehold Ltd [2013] UKUT 592 (LC); [2014] 1 E.G.L.R. 111, UT (Lands)

Cook v Deeks [1916] 1 A.C. 554, PC (Can)
*Applied* 78/241: *Considered* 06/543, 14/2991

Cook v Mortgage Business Plc see North East Property Buyers Litigation, Re

Cooke v DPP see R. (on the application of Cooke) v DPP

Cooke v MGN Ltd [2014] EWHC 2831 (QB); [2014] E.M.L.R. 31, QBD ........ *Digested,* 14/**834**

Coolatinney Developments Ltd v Revenue and Customs Commissioners; *joined cases* Northam House 1129 Ltd v Revenue and Customs Commissioners; Northam House 1130 Ltd v Revenue and Customs Commissioners; Northam House 1131 Ltd v Revenue and Customs Commissioners; Northam House 1136 Ltd v Revenue and Customs Commissioners [2011] UKFTT 252 (TC); [2011] S.T.I. 1908, FTT (Tax)
*Applied* 14/2978

Coombs v Dorset NHS Primary Care Trust; *sub nom* North Dorset NHS Primary Care Trust v Coombs [2013] EWCA Civ 471; [2014] 1 W.L.R. 111; [2013] 4 All E.R. 429; (2013) 16 C.C.L. Rep. 376; [2013] P.I.Q.R. P16; [2013] M.H.L.R. 194, CA (Civ Div); affirming [2012] EWHC 521 (QB); [2012] Med. L.R. 438; [2012] M.H.L.R. 144, QBD ........ *Digested,* 13/**2060**

Cooper v Isle of Wight College [2007] EWHC 2831 (QB); [2008] I.R.L.R. 124, QBD ..... *Digested,* 08/**1184**: *Applied* 14/1124

Cooper-Hohn v Hohn [2014] EWHC 2314 (Fam); [2014] Fam. Law 1528, Fam Div

Copley v Lawn; *joined case* Maden v Haller [2009] EWCA Civ 580; [2010] 1 All E.R. (Comm) 890; [2010] Bus. L.R. 83; [2009] R.T.R. 24; [2009] Lloyd's Rep. I.R. 496; [2009] P.I.Q.R. P21; Times, July 15, 2009, CA (Civ Div); reversing 8XQ51030, CC (Leeds) ........ *Digested,* 09/**970**: *Applied* 12/1898: *Considered* 12/1902, 12/859: *Followed* 14/1852

Copol Clothing v Hindmarch (Inspector of Taxes) [1984] 1 W.L.R. 411; [1984] S.T.C. 33; 57 T.C. 575; (1984) 81 L.S.G. 124; (1984) 128 S.J. 65; Times, November 24, 1983, CA (Civ Div); affirming [1982] S.T.C. 421; [1982] B.T.C. 164; (1982) 126 S.J. 313, Ch D ........ *Digested,* 84/**452**: *Applied* 92/2470, 95/5126: *Followed* 14/2882

Coppage v Safety Net Security Ltd see Safetynet Security Ltd v Coppage

Copthorn Holdings Ltd v Revenue and Customs Commissioners [2013] UKFTT 190 (TC); [2014] S.F.T.D. 1; [2013] S.T.I. 1679, FTT (Tax) ........ *Digested,* 14/**3054**

Core Issues Trust v Transport for London see R. (on the application of Core Issues Trust) v Transport for London

Corelogic Ltd v Bristol City Council [2013] EWHC 2088 (TCC); 149 Con. L.R. 225, QBD (TCC) ........ *Digested,* 14/**430**

Corey's Application for Judicial Review, Re; *sub nom* Corey, Re [2013] UKSC 76; [2014] A.C. 516; [2013] 3 W.L.R. 1612; [2014] 1 All E.R. 863, SC ........ *Digested,* 14/**2230**

Corey's Application for Judicial Review, Re [2012] NICA 57; [2014] N.I. 49, CA (NI); reversing [2012] NIQB 56, QBD (NI)

Corey, Re see Corey's Application for Judicial Review, Re

Corkish (Listing Officer) v Wright [2014] EWHC 237 (Admin); [2014] R.V.R. 233, QBD (Admin) ........ *Digested,* 14/**2086**

Corman-Collins SA v La Maison du Whisky SA (C-9/12) [2014] Q.B. 431; [2014] 2 W.L.R. 494; [2014] 1 All E.R. (Comm) 882; [2014] C.E.C. 820; [2014] I.L.Pr. 15, ECJ (1st Chamber)

Cornell v Wiltshire Council [2014] P.A.D. 10, Planning Inspector

Coroin Ltd, Re; *sub nom* McKillen v Misland (Cyprus) Investments Ltd; McKillen v Barclay [2013] EWCA Civ 781; [2014] B.C.C. 14; [2013] 2 B.C.L.C. 583, CA (Civ Div); affirming [2012] EWHC 2343 (Ch), Ch D (Companies Ct) ........ *Digested,* 14/**515**: *Considered* 14/523

Corscombe Close Block 8 RTM Co Ltd v Roseleb Ltd [2013] UKUT 81 (LC); [2013] L. & T.R. 16; [2013] 10 E.G. 147 (C.S.), UT (Lands) ........ *Digested,* 14/**2018**

Cosans v United Kingdom (7743/76) see Campbell v United Kingdom (7511/76)

Coshott v Prentice [2014] FCAFC 88; 17 I.T.E.L.R. 555, Fed Ct (Aus) (Full Ct)

Cosmetic Warriors Ltd v Amazon.co.uk Ltd [2013] EWHC 2470 (Ch); [2014] F.S.R. 15, Ch D ........ *Digested,* 14/**1936**

Cosmetic Warriors Ltd v Amazon.co.uk Ltd [2014] EWHC 181 (Ch); [2014] E.C.C. 28; [2014] F.S.R. 31, Ch D ........ *Digested,* 14/**1927**

Cosmichome Ltd v Southampton City Council [2013] EWHC 1378 (Ch); [2013] 1 W.L.R. 2436; [2013] 2 P. & C.R. 13; [2014] 1 E.G.L.R. 171, Ch D ........ *Digested,* 13/**2459**

Cosmo Leisure Ltd v Revenue and Customs Commissioners [2012] UKFTT 733 (TC); [2013] L.L.R. 320, FTT (Tax)

*Not followed* 14/2847

Cosmotrade SA v Kairos Shipping Ltd; *sub nom* Kairos Shipping Ltd v Enka & Co LLC [2014] EWCA Civ 217; [2014] 1 W.L.R. 3883; [2014] 1 All E.R. (Comm) 909; [2014] 1 Lloyd's Rep. 586; [2014] C.P. Rep. 28; [2014] 1 C.L.C. 293; 2014 A.M.C. 686, CA (Civ Div); reversing [2013] EWHC 1904 (Comm); [2013] 2 Lloyd's Rep. 535; [2013] 2 C.L.C. 82, QBD (Comm) ........ *Digested,* 14/**2732**

Cotswold Grange Country Park LLP v Secretary of State for Communities and Local Government [2014] EWHC 1138 (Admin); [2014] J.P.L. 981, QBD (Admin)

Cotter v Revenue and Customs Commissioners see Revenue and Customs Commissioners v Cotter

Cottonex Anstalt v Patriot Spinning Mills Ltd [2014] EWHC 236 (Comm); [2014] 1 Lloyd's Rep. 615, QBD (Comm) ........ *Digested,* 14/**116**

Coty Germany GmbH v First Note Perfumes NV (C-360/12) [2014] Bus. L.R. 1294; [2014] E.T.M.R. 49, ECJ (4th Chamber)

Council for the Regulation of Health Care Professionals v General Medical Council; *sub nom* Ruscillo v Council for the Regulation of Health Care Professionals; Council for the Regulation of Health Care Professionals v Truscott; *joined case* Council for the Regulation of Health Care Professionals v Nursing and Midwifery Council [2004] EWCA Civ 1356; [2005] 1 W.L.R. 717; [2005] Lloyd's Rep. Med. 65; [2005] A.C.D. 69; [2005] A.C.D. 99; (2004) 148 S.J.L.B. 1248; Times, October 27, 2004; Independent, October 28, 2004, CA (Civ Div); affirming [2004] EWHC 527 (Admin); [2004] 1 W.L.R. 2068; [2004] Lloyd's Rep. Med. 365; [2005] A.C.D. 46; (2004) 101(16) L.S.G. 28; Times, April 8, 2004, QBD (Admin) ........ *Digested,* 05/**1796**: *Applied* 05/1801, 05/1919, 07/1953, 10/1540, 11/1540, 14/1518: *Followed* 14/1497

Council for the Regulation of Health Care Professionals v Nursing and Midwifery Council see Council for the Regulation of Health Care Professionals v General Medical Council

Council for the Regulation of Health Care Professionals v Truscott see Council for the Regulation of Health Care Professionals v General Medical Council

Council of the European Union v Access Info Europe (C-280/11) [2014] 2 C.M.L.R. 6, ECJ (1st Chamber)

County Ltd v Girozentrale Securities [1996] 3 All E.R. 834; [1996] 1 B.C.L.C. 653, CA (Civ Div) ........ *Digested,* 96/**1248**: *Applied* 14/617: *Considered* 08/160

County Personnel (Employment Agency) Ltd v Alan R Pulver & Co [1987] 1 W.L.R. 916; [1987] 1 All E.R. 289; [1986] 2 E.G.L.R. 246; (1987) 84 L.S.G. 1409; (1986) 136 N.L.J. 1138; (1987) 131 S.J. 474; Times, October 29, 1986, CA (Civ Div) ........ *Digested,* 87/**3551**: *Applied* 91/1315, 91/1319, 93/2989, 00/1483, 07/2947, 10/2286, 11/537: *Considered* 89/1197, 89/1199, 90/1567, 92/1533, 94/1758, 96/4502, 99/4031, 14/2214: *Distinguished* 98/4018, 05/2866: *Followed* 98/3959, 98/4025

Courtwell Properties Ltd v Greencore PF (UK) Ltd [2014] EWHC 184 (TCC); [2014] 2 Costs L.O. 289; [2014] C.I.L.L. 3481, QBD (TCC) ........ *Digested,* 14/**334**

Covanta Energy Ltd v Merseyside Waste Disposal Authority [2013] EWHC 2964 (TCC); 151 Con. L.R. 135, QBD (TCC) ........ *Digested,* 14/**484**

Covanta Energy Ltd v Merseyside Waste Disposal Authority [2013] EWHC 2922 (TCC); 151 Con. L.R. 146, QBD (TCC) ........ *Digested,* 14/**2477**

Coventry v Coventry see Coventry (Deceased), Re

Coventry v Lawrence; *sub nom* Lawrence v Coventry (t/a RDC Promotions); Lawrence v Fen Tigers Ltd [2014] UKSC 46; [2014] 3 W.L.R. 555; [2014] 4 All E.R. 517; [2014] P.T.S.R. 1014; [2014] 5 Costs L.O. 759; [2014] H.L.R. 42; [2014] 2 P. & C.R. 19; [2014] 3 E.G.L.R. 71, SC ........ *Digested,* 14/**2221**

Coventry v Lawrence see Coventry (t/a RDC Promotions) v Lawrence

Coventry (Deceased), Re; *sub nom* Coventry v Coventry [1980] Ch. 461; [1979] 3 W.L.R. 802; [1979] 3 All E.R. 815; (1979) 123 S.J. 606, CA (Civ Div); affirming [1979] 2 W.L.R. 853; [1979] 2 All E.R. 408; (1979) 123 S.J. 406; Times, November 14, 1978, Ch D ........ *Digested,* 79/**2807**: *Applied* 81/2887, 83/3919, 83/3920, 95/5147, 03/4123, 08/3610, 11/3247, 14/2822: *Considered* 82/206, 82/3385, 83/3921, 84/2464, 84/3665, 86/3549, 92/4584, 95/2355, 07/4112: *Followed* 96/5551, 10/3209

Coventry (t/a RDC Promotions) v Lawrence; *sub nom* Coventry v Lawrence; Lawrence v Coventry (t/a RDC Promotions); Lawrence v Fen Tigers Ltd [2014] UKSC 13; [2014] A.C. 822; [2014] 2 W.L.R. 433; [2014] 2 All E.R. 622; [2014] P.T.S.R. 384; [2014] B.L.R. 271; 152 Con. L.R. 1; [2014] Env. L.R. 25; [2014] H.L.R. 21; [2014] 2 P. & C.R. 2; [2014] 1 E.G.L.R. 147; [2014] L.L.R. 423; (2014) 158(9) S.J.L.B. 37, SC; reversing [2012] EWCA Civ 26; [2012] 1 W.L.R. 2127; [2012] 3 All E.R. 168; [2012] P.T.S.R. 1505; 141 Con. L.R. 79; [2012] Env. L.R. 28; [2012] 1 E.G.L.R. 165; [2012] L.L.R. 343; [2012] 10 E.G. 88 (C.S.); (2012) 109(11) L.S.G. 21; (2012) 156(9) S.J.L.B. 31, CA (Civ Div) ........ *Digested,* 14/**2223**: *Applied* 14/2526: *Followed* 13/2101

Coventry City Council v B; *joined case* Coventry City Council v Y [2012] EWHC 4014 (Fam); [2014] Fam. Law 954, Fam Div

Coventry City Council v CC see A (A Child) (Adoption), Re

Coventry City Council v Y see Coventry City Council v B

Coventry Permanent Economic Building Society v Jones [1951] 1 All E.R. 901; [1951] 1 T.L.R. 739; [1951] W.N. 218, Ch D ........ *Digested,* 47-51/**6346**: *Approved* 90/707: *Considered* 53/2309, 14/2505: *Distinguished* 47-51/6347, 47-51/6348, 54/2109

Coventry School Foundation Trustees v Whitehouse [2013] EWCA Civ 885; [2014] 1 P. & C.R. 4; [2013] 3 E.G.L.R. 85; [2013] 2 P. & C.R. DG24, CA (Civ Div); reversing [2012] EWHC 2351 (Ch); [2012] 3 E.G.L.R. 151, Ch D ...................... *Digested,* 14/**2514**

Coventry University v Mian [2014] EWCA Civ 1275; [2014] E.L.R. 455; [2014] Med. L.R. 502, CA (Civ Div)

Coward v Phaestos Ltd [2014] EWCA Civ 1256; [2014] 6 Costs L.O. 843, CA (Civ Div); affirming [2013] EWHC 2612 (Ch), Ch D

Cox v Ergo Versicherung AG (formerly Victoria); *sub nom* Cox (Deceased), Re [2014] UKSC 22; [2014] A.C. 1379; [2014] 2 W.L.R. 948; [2014] 2 All E.R. 926; [2014] 1 C.L.C. 430; [2014] R.T.R. 20; Times, April 14, 2014, SC; affirming [2012] EWCA Civ 854, CA (Civ Div) ...................... *Digested,* 14/**825**

Cox v Ministry of Justice [2014] EWCA Civ 132; [2014] 3 W.L.R. 1036; [2014] I.C.R. 713; [2014] P.I.Q.R. P17, CA (Civ Div) ...................... *Digested,* 14/**2343**

Cox (Deceased), Re see Cox v Ergo Versicherung AG (formerly Victoria)

Coyle v United Kingdom (11266/84) see Brogan v United Kingdom (A/145-B)

CP-Credit Prive SA v Kyrgyz Mobil Tel Ltd see AK Investment CJSC v Kyrgyz Mobil Tel Ltd

CPL v CH-W see L-W (Children) (Enforcement and Committal: Contact), Re

CR v MZ (Financial Remedies: Beneficial Ownership) [2013] EWHC 295 (Fam); [2014] 1 F.L.R. 22; [2014] W.T.L.R. 233; [2013] Fam. Law 1377, Fam Div ......... *Digested,* 14/**2494**

CR v SR (Financial Remedies: Permission to Appeal) [2013] EWHC 1155 (Fam); [2014] 1 F.L.R. 186; [2013] Fam. Law 938, Fam Div

Craigdallie v Aikman 3 E.R. 601; (1813) 1 Dow 1, HL
*Applied* 14/38: *Considered* 01/5501

Cramaso LLP v Earl of Seafield see Cramaso LLP v Viscount Reidhaven's Trustees

Cramaso LLP v Ogilvie-Grant see Cramaso LLP v Viscount Reidhaven's Trustees

Cramaso LLP v Viscount Reidhaven's Trustees; *sub nom* Cramaso LLP v Earl of Seafield; Cramaso LLP v Ogilvie-Grant [2014] UKSC 9; [2014] A.C. 1093; [2014] 2 W.L.R. 317; [2014] 2 All E.R. 270; [2014] 1 All E.R. (Comm) 830; 2014 S.C. (U.K.S.C.) 121; 2014 S.L.T. 521; 2014 S.C.L.R. 484; (2014) 158(7) S.J.L.B. 37; Times, February 20, 2014, SC; reversing [2011] CSIH 81; 2012 S.C. 240; 2012 G.W.D. 1-11, IH (2 Div); affirming [2010] CSOH 62; 2010 G.W.D. 20-403, OH ...................... *Digested,* 14/**2201**

Cranfield v Bridgegrove Ltd; *joined cases* Smith v Hughes; Murphy v Staples UK Ltd; McManus v Sharif; Claussen v Yeates [2003] EWCA Civ 656; [2003] 1 W.L.R. 2441; [2003] 3 All E.R. 129; [2003] C.P. Rep. 54; [2003] 21 E.G. 191 (C.S.); (2003) 147 S.J.L.B. 599; [2003] N.P.C. 66; Times, May 16, 2003, CA (Civ Div) . *Digested,* 03/**455**:
*Applied* 05/467, 05/485, 07/371: *Considered* 06/347: *Followed* 14/472

Cravecrest Ltd v Sixth Duke of Westminster; *sub nom* Cravecrest Ltd v Trustees of the Will of the Second Duke of Westminster [2013] EWCA Civ 731; [2014] Ch. 301; [2014] 2 W.L.R. 679; [2013] 4 All E.R. 456; [2013] H.L.R. 43; [2013] 2 P. & C.R. 16; [2013] L. & T.R. 26; [2013] 3 E.G.L.R. 47; [2013] 26 E.G. 107 (C.S.), CA (Civ Div); affirming [2012] UKUT 68 (LC), UT (Lands) ...................... *Digested,* 13/**2428**

Cravecrest Ltd v Trustees of the Will of the Second Duke of Westminster see Cravecrest Ltd v Sixth Duke of Westminster

Crawford v Department for Employment and Learning [2014] NICA 26; [2014] I.R.L.R. 626, CA (NI) ...................... *Digested,* 14/**3143**

Crawford v Jenkins [2014] EWCA Civ 1035; [2014] E.M.L.R. 29, CA (Civ Div) ............ *Digested,* 14/**2992**

Crawford Adjusters (Cayman) Ltd v Sagicor General Insurance (Cayman) Ltd [2013] UKPC 17; [2014] A.C. 366; [2013] 3 W.L.R. 927; [2013] 4 All E.R. 8; [2013] 6 Costs L.O. 826, PC (CI)

CRC Credit Fund Ltd v GLG Investments Plc Sub-Fund: European Equity Fund see Lehman Brothers International (Europe) (In Administration), Re

Cream Holdings Ltd v Banerjee [2004] UKHL 44; [2005] 1 A.C. 253; [2004] 3 W.L.R. 918; [2004] 4 All E.R. 617; [2005] E.M.L.R. 1; [2004] H.R.L.R. 39; [2004] U.K.H.R.R. 1071; 17 B.H.R.C. 464; (2005) 28(2) I.P.D. 28001; (2004) 101(42) L.S.G. 29; (2004) 154 N.L.J. 1589; (2004) 148 S.J.L.B. 1215; Times, October 15, 2004, HL; reversing [2003] EWCA Civ 103; [2003] Ch. 650; [2003] 3 W.L.R. 999; [2003] 2 All E.R. 318; [2003] E.M.L.R. 16; [2003] H.R.L.R. 18; (2003) 100(15) L.S.G. 25; Times, February 28, 2003; Independent, April 7, 2003, CA (Civ Div) ...................... *Digested,* 05/**2041**:
*Applied* 04/1924, 05/4191, 06/1037, 06/454, 07/2189, 07/2672, 07/2887, 07/2893, 10/1743, 10/1939, 11/339: *Considered* 05/970, 06/456, 08/2379, 09/4260: *Followed* 11/2200, 11/341, 14/1864: *Not applied* 04/928

Credit and Mercantile Plc v Kaymuu Ltd [2014] EWHC 1746 (Ch); [2014] B.P.I.R. 1127, Ch D ...................... *Digested,* 14/**2493**

Credit Suisse v Beegas Nominees Ltd [1994] 4 All E.R. 803; (1995) 69 P. & C.R. 177; [1994] 12 E.G. 189; [1994] 11 E.G. 151; [1993] E.G. 157 (C.S.); [1993] N.P.C. 123; Independent, September 15, 1993, Ch D ............ *Digested,* 95/**2982**: *Applied* 99/3738: *Approved* 14/1978: *Considered* 99/3695

Credit Suisse AG v Arabian Aircraft & Equipment Leasing Co EC [2013] EWCA Civ 1169; [2014] C.P. Rep. 4, CA (Civ Div); reversing [2013] EWHC 1094 (Comm), QBD (Comm) ............ *Digested,* 14/**431**

Credit Suisse London Nominees Ltd v Fairfield Sentry Ltd (In Liquidation) see Fairfield Sentry Ltd (In Liquidation) v Migani

Creditsights Ltd v Dhunna see Dhunna v Creditsights Ltd

Creed-Miles v Southwark LBC see R. (on the application of Creed-Miles) v Southwark LBC

Crema v Cenkos Securities Plc [2010] EWCA Civ 1444; [2011] 1 W.L.R. 2066; [2011] 2 All E.R. (Comm) 676; [2011] Bus. L.R. 943; [2010] 2 C.L.C. 963; [2011] C.I.L.L. 2980, CA (Civ Div); reversing [2010] EWHC 461 (Comm); [2010] 2 All E.R. (Comm) 1; [2010] Bus. L.R. D105, QBD (Comm) ............ *Digested,* 11/**221**: *Applied* 12/2057, 14/594: *Followed* 12/1905, 12/246

Crest Homes Plc v Marks [1987] A.C. 829; [1987] 3 W.L.R. 293; [1987] 2 All E.R. 1074; [1988] R.P.C. 21; (1987) 84 L.S.G. 2362; (1987) 137 N.L.J. 662; (1987) 131 S.J. 1003, HL; affirming [1987] 3 W.L.R. 48; [1987] F.S.R. 305; (1987) 84 L.S.G. 2048; (1987) 137 N.L.J. 318, CA (Civ Div) ............ *Digested,* 87/**2885**: *Applied* 88/2837, 93/4265, 96/5659, 98/471, 01/554, 09/330, 14/382: *Considered* 88/2833, 92/3475, 93/3211, 96/762, 09/400: *Distinguished* 96/689, 00/309: *Followed* 97/465, 99/321, 04/258

Criminal Injuries Compensation Authority v First-Tier Tribunal (Social Entitlement Chamber) [2014] EWCA Civ 65; [2014] P.I.Q.R. P10; (2014) 158(6) S.J.L.B. 37; Times, February 21, 2014, CA (Civ Div) ............ *Digested,* 14/**54**

Criminal Practice Directions Amendment No.1 see Practice Direction (Criminal Proceedings: Various Changes)

Criminal Proceedings against Bernaldez (C-129/94) [1996] E.C.R. I-1829; [1996] 2 C.M.L.R. 889; [1996] All E.R. (EC) 741; Times, May 6, 1996, ECJ (5th Chamber) ............ *Digested,* 96/**3614**: *Applied* 14/1853: *Considered* 07/3458, 10/1927, 10/1928, 12/1899, 12/1903, 13/1742: *Followed* 00/3547

Criminal Proceedings against D (C-358/13); *joined case* Criminal Proceedings against G (C-181/14) [2014] P.T.S.R. 1217, ECJ (4th Chamber)

Criminal Proceedings against G (C-181/14) see Criminal Proceedings against D (C-358/13)

Criminal Proceedings against Galli (31/74) [1975] E.C.R. 47; [1975] 1 C.M.L.R. 211, ECJ ............ *Digested,* 75/**1200**: *Considered* 14/1473

Criminal Proceedings against Hoffmann (C-144/00); *sub nom* Hoffmann (C-144/00) [2004] S.T.C. 740; [2003] E.C.R. I-2921; [2004] 1 C.M.L.R. 37; [2005] B.T.C. 5010; [2005] B.V.C. 41; [2003] S.T.I. 587; Times, April 17, 2003, ECJ (6th Chamber) ............ *Digested,* 03/**4527**: *Applied* 09/4048, 13/3190: *Considered* 14/3043

Criminal Proceedings against International Jet Management GmbH (C-628/11) [2014] 3 C.M.L.R. 22, ECJ (Grand Chamber)

Criminal Proceedings against Keck (C-267/91); *joined case* Criminal Proceedings against Mithouard (C-268/91) [1993] E.C.R. I-6097; [1995] 1 C.M.L.R. 101; Times, November 25, 1993; Financial Times, November 30, 1993, ECJ ............ *Digested,* 94/**4885**: *Applied* 05/500, 06/1557, 06/1559, 06/1561, 08/1331, 09/1404: *Considered* 95/4907, 95/642, 96/2801, 01/2486, 03/1455, 12/4151, 14/3647: *Distinguished* 05/1449: *Followed* 98/3855, 00/4165, 04/636

Criminal Proceedings against Lundberg (C-317/12) [2014] R.T.R. 2, ECJ

Criminal Proceedings against Mithouard (C-268/91) see Criminal Proceedings against Keck (C-267/91)

Crinion v IG Markets Ltd see IG Markets Ltd v Crinion

Crociani v Crociani [2014] UKPC 40; 17 I.T.E.L.R. 624, PC (Jer)

Crocker Enterprises Ltd v Giordano Poultry-Plast SpA [2013] EWHC 2491 (Ch); [2013] F.S.R. 44, Ch D (Patents Ct) ............ *Digested,* 14/**493**

Croesus Financial Services Ltd v Bradshaw [2013] EWHC 3685 (QB), QBD (Admin) *Considered* 14/1032

Croft Vets Ltd v Butcher [2013] Eq. L.R. 1170, EAT ............ *Digested,* 14/**1049**

Crofts v Veta Ltd see Lawson v Serco Ltd

Croke v Hydro Aluminium Worcester Ltd [2007] I.C.R. 1303, EAT ............ *Digested,* 07/**1344**: *Applied* 10/1107, 14/1068: *Considered* 09/1224

Crono Service scarl v Roma Capitale (C-419/12) [2014] 3 C.M.L.R. 5, ECJ (3rd Chamber)
Cross v Revenue and Customs Commissioners [2014] UKFTT 907 (TC); [2014] S.T.I. 2984, FTT (Tax)
Cross-Border Personnel Leasing, Re (VwGH 2009/13/0031) 16 I.T.L. Rep. 598, VwGH (A)
Crossland v OCS Group Ltd [2014] EWCA Civ 678; [2014] 5 Costs L.R. 791, CA (Civ Div) ........ *Digested,* 14/**361**
Crouch & Lyndon (A Firm) v IPG Finance Australia Pty Ltd [2013] QCA 220; [2014] P.N.L.R. 3, CA (Qld)
Crown Lands Commissioners v Page; *sub nom* Commissioners of Crown Lands v Page [1960] 2 Q.B. 274; [1960] 3 W.L.R. 446; [1960] 2 All E.R. 726; (1960) 104 S.J. 642, CA; affirming (1959) 174 E.G. 7, HC ........ *Digested,* 60/**1719**:
*Applied* 14/2508: *Considered* 77/376, 78/315, 05/2644: *Followed* 85/1869
Crown Prosecution Service v D [2006] EWHC 2738 (Admin), QBD (Admin)
*Considered* 14/723
Crown Prosecution Service v Eastenders Group; *sub nom* Barnes v Eastenders Group; Eastenders Cash & Carry Plc v Crown Prosecution Service; Barnes v Eastenders Cash & Carry Plc [2014] UKSC 26; [2014] 2 W.L.R. 1269; [2014] 3 All E.R. 1; [2014] 2 Cr. App. R. 19; [2014] H.R.L.R. 15; [2014] Lloyd's Rep. F.C. 461; [2014] B.P.I.R. 867; Times, May 30, 2014, SC; reversing in part [2012] EWCA Crim 2436; [2013] 1 W.L.R. 1494; [2013] 2 All E.R. 437; [2013] 1 Cr. App. R. 24; [2013] Lloyd's Rep. F.C. 235, CA (Crim Div) ........ *Digested,* 14/**802**:
*Considered* 13/756
Crown Prosecution Service v Fraser; *joined case* Fraser v Crown Prosecution Service [2014] Eq. L.R. 535; [2014] I.C.R. D18, EAT ........ *Digested,* 14/**1051**
Crown Prosecution Service v J see Jennings v Crown Prosecution Service
Crown Prosecution Service v Nelson see R. v Nelson (John Stanley)
Crown Prosecution Service v Pathak see R. v Nelson (John Stanley)
Crown Prosecution Service v Picton [2006] EWHC 1108 (Admin); (2006) 170 J.P. 567; (2006) 170 J.P.N. 954, DC ........ *Digested,* 06/**988**:
*Applied* 09/944: *Considered* 07/1029: *Distinguished* 14/710
Crown Prosecution Service v Sykes; *sub nom* Sykes v Crown Prosecution Service [2013] EWHC 3600 (Admin); [2014] Crim. L.R. 542, QBD (Admin)
Croydon LBC v U [2014] EWHC 823 (Fam); [2014] Fam. Law 960, Fam Div
Cruddas v Calvert [2013] EWCA Civ 748; [2014] E.M.L.R. 5, CA (Civ Div); reversing [2013] EWHC 1427 (QB); [2014] E.M.L.R. 4, QBD ........ *Digested,* 14/**837**
Cruz City 1 Mauritius Holdings v Unitech Ltd [2014] EWHC 3131 (Comm); [2014] Bus. L.R. D25, QBD (Comm)
Cruz City 1 Mauritius Holdings v Unitech Ltd [2013] EWHC 1323 (Comm); [2013] 2 All E.R. (Comm) 1137, QBD (Comm) ........ *Digested,* 14/**305**
Crystal Imports Ltd v Certain Underwriters at Lloyd's of London [2014] Lloyd's Rep. I.R. 379, HC (NZ)
Crystal Palace FC Ltd v Kavanagh see Kavanagh v Crystal Palace FC 2000 Ltd
CSG (Stratford) Ltd v Newham LBC [2013] EWHC 2868 (TCC); [2014] 1 P. & C.R. DG6, QBD (TCC)
Csonka v Magyar Allam (C-409/11) [2014] 1 C.M.L.R. 14; [2014] C.E.C. 763, ECJ (1st Chamber)
*Considered* 14/1853
CTL (Children) (Welfare Hearing: Expert Report), Re [2013] EWHC 2134 (Fam); [2014] 1 F.L.R. 762; [2014] 3 F.C.R. 181; [2013] Fam. Law 1368, Fam Div ........ *Digested,* 14/**1237**
CU v Westminster Magistrates' Court see R. (on the application of B) v Westminster Magistrates' Court
Cuadrench More v Koninklijke Luchtvaart Maatschappij NV (C-139/11) [2013] 2 All E.R. (Comm) 1152; [2013] 1 Lloyd's Rep. 341; [2013] 2 C.M.L.R. 4, ECJ (3rd Chamber)
*Applied* 14/165: *Cited* 14/3319
Cudak v Lithuania (15869/02) (2010) 51 E.H.R.R. 15; 30 B.H.R.C. 157, ECHR (Grand Chamber)
*Applied* 14/1123: *Considered* 14/1056
Cukurova Holding AS v Sonera Holding BV [2014] UKPC 15; [2014] 1 C.L.C. 643; 155 Con. L.R. 1, PC (BVI)
Culla Park Ltd v Richards [2007] EWHC 1687 (QB), QBD
*Considered* 14/457
Cumbria CC v M [2014] EWHC 2596 (Fam); [2014] Fam. Law 1529, Fam Div (Carlisle)
Cummings v Official Receiver [2002] EWHC 2894 (Ch), Ch D
*Considered* 14/1750

Cummins Engine Co Ltd v Davis Freight Forwarding (Hull) Ltd [1981] 1 W.L.R. 1363; [1981] 3 All E.R. 567; [1981] 2 Lloyd's Rep. 402; [1981] Com. L.R. 229; [1982] R.T.R. 60; (1981) 125 S.J. 775, CA (Civ Div); affirming [1981] 2 Lloyd's Rep. 106, QBD (Comm) ............ *Digested,* 81/**218**: *Applied* 86/269: *Considered* 12/559, 14/3011

Currie v Revenue and Customs Commissioners [2014] UKFTT 882 (TC); [2014] S.T.I. 3362, FTT (Tax)

Cusack v Harrow LBC; *sub nom* Harrow LBC v Cusack [2013] UKSC 40; [2013] 1 W.L.R. 2022; [2013] 4 All E.R. 97; [2013] P.T.S.R. 921; [2013] R.T.R. 26; [2013] H.R.L.R. 26; [2013] 3 E.G.L.R. 29; [2014] R.V.R. 148; [2013] 26 E.G. 106 (C.S.); Times, July 23, 2013, SC; reversing in part [2011] EWCA Civ 1514; [2012] P.T.S.R. 970; [2012] R.T.R. 19; [2012] 1 E.G.L.R. 43; [2012] 10 E.G. 90; [2012] J.P.L. 738; [2011] 50 E.G. 59 (C.S.); [2011] N.P.C. 127; Times, January 10, 2012, CA (Civ Div); reversing in part [2011] EWHC 460 (QB), QBD ............ *Digested,* 13/**2506**

Cussens v Realreed Ltd; *sub nom* Realreed Ltd v Cussens [2013] EWHC 1229 (QB); [2014] 1 W.L.R. 275; [2013] 22 E.G. 93 (C.S.); [2013] 2 P. & C.R. DG10, QBD . *Digested,* 14/**413**

Customs and Excise Commissioners v Arena Corp Ltd (In Provisional Liquidation); *sub nom* Arena Corp Ltd (In Provisional Liquidation) v Customs and Excise Commissioners; Arena Corp Ltd, Re; *joined case* Arena Corp Ltd (In Provisional Liquidation) v Schroeder [2004] EWCA Civ 371; [2005] Eu. L.R. 15; [2004] B.P.I.R. 415, CA (Civ Div); affirming [2003] EWHC 3032 (Ch); [2004] B.P.I.R. 375, Ch D ............ *Digested,* 04/**902**: *Applied* 14/1833, 14/823: *Considered* 05/2348: *Followed* 09/958

Customs and Excise Commissioners v British United Provident Association Ltd see Customs and Excise Commissioners v Wellington Private Hospital Ltd

Customs and Excise Commissioners v East Midlands Aggregates Ltd see East Midlands Aggregates Ltd v Customs and Excise Commissioners

Customs and Excise Commissioners v Leicester University Student Union see Customs and Excise Commissioners v Leicester University Students Union

Customs and Excise Commissioners v Leicester University Students Union; *sub nom* Customs and Excise Commissioners v Leicester University Student Union; Customs and Excise Commissioners v University of Leicester Students Union [2001] EWCA Civ 1972; [2002] S.T.C. 147; [2002] E.L.R. 347; [2002] B.T.C. 5064; [2002] B.V.C. 269; [2002] S.T.I. 38; (2002) 99(10) L.S.G. 33; Times, January 25, 2002, CA (Civ Div); affirming [2001] S.T.C. 550; [2001] B.T.C. 5187; [2001] B.V.C. 252; [2001] S.T.I. 599, Ch D; reversing [2001] B.V.C. 2102; [2001] S.T.I. 53, V&DTr ............ *Digested,* 02/**4741**: *Considered* 14/3041, 14/3045

Customs and Excise Commissioners v Lex Services Plc see Lex Services Plc v Customs and Excise Commissioners

Customs and Excise Commissioners v Parkwood Landfill Ltd see Parkwood Landfill Ltd v Customs and Excise Commissioners

Customs and Excise Commissioners v Pegasus Birds Ltd see Pegasus Birds Ltd v Customs and Excise Commissioners

Customs and Excise Commissioners v Redrow Group Plc [1999] 1 W.L.R. 408; [1999] 2 All E.R. 1; [1999] S.T.C. 161; [1999] B.T.C. 5062; [1999] B.V.C. 96; [1999] E.G. 20 (C.S.); (1999) 96(9) L.S.G. 32; (1999) 143 S.J.L.B. 58; [1999] N.P.C. 18; Times, February 18, 1999; Independent, February 18, 1999, HL; reversing [1997] S.T.C. 1053; [1997] B.T.C. 5347; [1997] B.V.C. 461; [1997] E.G. 92 (C.S.); Times, July 3, 1997; Independent, July 14, 1997, CA (Civ Div); reversing [1996] S.T.C. 365; [1995] E.G. 202 (C.S.), QBD; affirming [1995] V. & D.R. 115, VAT Tr (Manchester) ............ *Digested,* 99/**4994**: *Applied* 02/4774, 04/3992, 05/4346, 05/4375, 06/5741, 07/4310, 08/4018, 14/3061: *Considered* 03/4529, 13/3209: *Distinguished* 05/4379, 06/4468: *Explained* 08/4020: *Followed* 10/3515, 11/3542, 13/3204

Customs and Excise Commissioners v School of Finance and Management (London) Ltd see School of Finance and Management (London) Ltd v Customs and Excise Commissioners

Customs and Excise Commissioners v St Martin's Hospital see Customs and Excise Commissioners v Wellington Private Hospital Ltd

Customs and Excise Commissioners v United Biscuits (UK) Ltd [1992] S.T.C. 325; 1992 S.C. 308; 1992 S.L.T. 781, IH (Ex Div) ............ *Digested,* 92/**6530**: *Applied* 04/4018: *Considered* 11/56, 14/3102

Customs and Excise Commissioners v University of Leicester Students Union see Customs and Excise Commissioners v Leicester University Students Union

Customs and Excise Commissioners v Wellington Private Hospital Ltd; *joined cases* Customs and Excise Commissioners v British United Provident Association Ltd; Customs and Excise Commissioners v St Martin's Hospital [1997] S.T.C. 445; [1997] B.T.C. 5140; [1997] B.V.C. 251; Times, February 11, 1997, CA (Civ Div); reversing [1995] S.T.C. 628; Independent, May 30, 1995, QBD ................ *Digested,* 97/**5057**: *Applied* 01/5604, 06/4438, 14/3102: *Doubted* 14/3050: *Followed* 99/4978

Cutting v Islam [2014] EWHC 1515 (QB); [2014] 4 Costs L.O. 652, QBD .................... *Digested,* 14/**2297**

CW v East Riding of Yorkshire Council see SC v East Riding of Yorkshire Council

CW v SG see DW (A Child) (Termination of Parental Responsibility), Re

CYC v PC see York City Council v C

Cyganik v Agulian; *sub nom* Agulian v Cyganik [2006] EWCA Civ 129; [2006] 1 F.C.R. 406; [2006] W.T.L.R. 565; (2005-06) 8 I.T.E.L.R. 762, CA (Civ Div); reversing [2005] EWHC 444 (Ch); [2005] W.T.L.R. 1049; (2004-05) 7 I.T.E.L.R. 831, Ch D .................... *Digested,* 06/**4082**: *Applied* 08/1528, 11/3243: *Considered* 07/4068, 08/2137, 14/1325: *Followed* 10/3207, 13/1194

Cyprus v Turkey (25781/94) (2014) 59 E.H.R.R. 16; 37 B.H.R.C. 543; (2014) 59 E.H.R.R. SE4, ECHR (Grand Chamber)

D v D see D (A Child) (Abduction: Rights of Custody), Re

D v Durham CC see Durham CC v D

D v K [2014] EWHC 700 (Fam); [2014] Fam. Law 1094, Fam Div (Bristol)

D v Royal Bank of Scotland; *sub nom* CJD v Royal Bank of Scotland [2013] CSIH 86; [2014] I.R.L.R. 25; 2013 G.W.D. 35-691, IH (Ex Div) .................... *Digested,* 14/**3505**

D (A Child) v Chesterfield Royal Hospital NHS Foundation Trust (Unreported, February 25, 2014), QBD [*Withy King LLP, Midland Bridge House, Midland Bridge Road, Bath*] .................... *Digested,* 14/**2340**

D (A Child) (Abduction: Foreign Custody Right), Re see D (A Child) (Abduction: Rights of Custody), Re

D (A Child) (Abduction: Rights of Custody), Re; *sub nom* D v D; D (A Child) (Abduction: Foreign Custody Right), Re [2006] UKHL 51; [2007] 1 A.C. 619; [2006] 3 W.L.R. 989; [2007] 1 All E.R. 783; [2007] 1 F.L.R. 961; [2007] 1 F.C.R. 1; [2007] Fam. Law 102; (2006) 103(46) L.S.G. 29; (2006) 156 N.L.J. 1803; (2006) 150 S.J.L.B. 1532; Times, November 17, 2006; Independent, November 21, 2006, HL; reversing [2006] EWCA Civ 830, CA (Civ Div) .................... *Digested,* 07/**1775**: *Applied* 07/1743, 08/1460, 09/1641, 10/1341, 14/1323: *Considered* 07/1736, 09/1573, 09/1635, 11/1349: *Followed* 09/1539, 11/1348, 14/1310

D (A Child) (Fact-finding Hearing), Re; *sub nom* A Local Authority v B [2014] EWHC 121 (Fam); [2014] Fam. Law 421, Fam Div

D (A Child) (Leave to Oppose Making of Adoption Order), Re [2013] EWCA Civ 1480; [2014] 2 F.L.R. 866; [2014] 1 F.C.R. 602; [2014] Fam. Law 273, CA (Civ Div) ... *Digested,* 14/**1248**

D (A Child) (Nigerian Fertility Clinic: Fact-Finding), Re [2012] EWHC 4231 (Fam); [2013] 2 F.L.R. 1417; [2013] Fam. Law 943, Fam Div .................... *Digested,* 14/**1430**

D (A Child) (Parental Responsibility: Removal), Re see DW (A Child) (Termination of Parental Responsibility), Re

D (A Child) (Surrogacy), Re [2014] EWHC 2121 (Fam); [2014] Fam. Law 1402, Fam Div (Leeds)

D (A Child) (Transfer of Proceedings), Re; *sub nom* M (Brussels II Revised: Art.15), Re; *joined case* Nottingham City Council v LM [2014] EWCA Civ 152; [2014] 2 F.L.R. 1372; [2014] 2 F.C.R. 585; [2014] Fam. Law 966, CA (Civ Div); reversing [2013] EWHC 4078 (Fam); [2014] 2 F.L.R. 496; [2014] Fam. Law 280, Fam Div .................... *Digested,* 14/**1287**

D (A Child) (Withdrawal of Parental Responsibility), Re see DW (A Child) (Termination of Parental Responsibility), Re

D (Brussels II Revised: Contact), Re [2007] EWHC 822 (Fam); [2008] 1 F.L.R. 516; [2008] Fam. Law 205, Fam Div .................... *Digested,* 08/**1548**: *Applied* 14/1432

D (Children) (CAFCASS: Safeguarding Checks), Re [2014] EWHC 2376 (Fam); [2014] Fam. Law 1516, Fam Div

D (Domestic Violence: Court Orders), Re see P v D

D (Minors) (Adoption Reports: Confidentiality), Re [1996] A.C. 593; [1995] 3 W.L.R. 483; [1995] 4 All E.R. 385; [1995] 2 F.L.R. 687; [1996] 1 F.C.R. 205; [1996] Fam. Law 8; (1995) 145 N.L.J. 1612, HL; reversing [1995] 1 W.L.R. 356; [1995] 1 F.L.R. 631; (1995) 139 S.J.L.B. 13; Times, December 8, 1994; Independent, December 6, 1994; Guardian, December 5, 1994, CA (Civ Div) .................... *Digested,* 96/**474**: *Applied* 96/508, 97/356, 99/2360, 99/6065, 00/2534, 02/1609, 06/1671, 10/1312, 11/1327, 13/1189, 14/2184: *Considered* 08/922, 11/1328: *Distinguished* 99/6064: *Followed* 13/1223

D (Recognition and Enforcement of Romanian Order), Re; *sub nom* MD v AA [2014] EWHC 2756 (Fam); [2014] Fam. Law 1531, Fam Div

D Borough Council v B [2011] EWHC 101 (Fam); [2012] Fam. 36; [2011] 3 W.L.R. 1257; [2011] 3 All E.R. 435; [2011] 2 F.L.R. 72; [2011] 3 F.C.R. 62; (2011) 14 C.C.L. Rep. 189; [2011] Fam. Law 472; (2011) 161 N.L.J. 254, CP .................. *Digested,* 11/**2204**: *Applied* 14/2175: *Referred to* 14/2172

D&D Wines International Ltd (In Liquidation), Re; *sub nom* Angove Pty Ltd v Bailey; Bailey v Angove's Pty Ltd [2014] EWCA Civ 215; [2014] 2 B.C.L.C. 129; [2014] B.P.I.R. 902, CA (Civ Div); reversing [2013] EWHC 215 (Ch), Ch D (Manchester) .................. *Digested,* 14/**78**

D&H Travel Ltd v Foster [2006] I.C.R. 1537, EAT .................. *Digested,* 07/**1382**: *Considered* 14/1081

D'Souza v Lambeth LBC (No.2) see Rhys-Harper v Relaxion Group Plc

D, Re [2013] EWHC 3294 (Fam); [2014] Fam. Law 149, Fam Div

D.Jacobson & Sons v Crocs Inc [2014] EWHC 987 (Ch); [2014] E.C.C. 16, Ch D .......... *Digested,* 14/**1863**

Da Conceicao Mateus v Portugal (Admissibility) (62235/12) (2014) 58 E.H.R.R. SE4, ECHR

Da Rocha-Afodu v Mortgage Express Ltd [2014] EWCA Civ 454; [2014] 2 P. & C.R. DG10, CA (Civ Div)

Dacorum BC v Sims see Sims v Dacorum BC

Dadouch v Malta (38816/07) (2014) 59 E.H.R.R. 34, ECHR

Daejan Investments Ltd v Benson [2013] UKSC 14; [2013] 1 W.L.R. 854; [2013] 2 All E.R. 375; [2013] H.L.R. 21; [2013] 2 P. & C.R. 2; [2013] L. & T.R. 17; [2013] 2 E.G.L.R. 45; [2013] R.V.R. 164; [2013] 11 E.G. 80 (C.S.); (2013) 157(10) S.J.L.B. 31; Times, April 11, 2013, SC; reversing [2011] EWCA Civ 38; [2011] 1 W.L.R. 2330; [2011] H.L.R. 21; [2011] 2 P. & C.R. 2; [2011] L. & T.R. 14; [2011] 2 E.G.L.R. 113; [2011] 5 E.G. 105 (C.S.); Times, April 5, 2011, CA (Civ Div); affirming [2009] UKUT 233 (LC); [2010] 2 P. & C.R. 8; [2010] L. & T.R. 11, UT (Lands) .................. *Digested,* 13/**1879**: *Applied* 13/1897: *Followed* 12/2062, 14/1981

Dafis v Ceredigion CC [2014] P.A.D. 17, Planning Inspector

Dahabshiil Transfer Services Ltd v Barclays Bank Plc; *joined case* Harada Ltd v Barclays Bank Plc [2013] EWHC 3379 (Ch); [2014] U.K.C.L.R. 215, Ch D .......... *Digested,* 14/**527**

Daiichi Sankyo Co Ltd v DEMO Anonimos Viomikhaniki kai Emporiki Etairia Farmakon (C-414/11) [2014] Bus. L.R. 1, ECJ (Grand Chamber)

Daintrey Ex p. Holt, Re [1893] 2 Q.B. 116, QBD *Applied* 86/1517, 04/1289: *Considered* 84/1946: *Distinguished* 02/312: *Explained* 14/1008

Dale v de Soissons [1950] 2 All E.R. 460; 66 T.L.R. (Pt. 2) 223; 43 R. & I.T. 886; 32 T.C. 118; [1950] T.R. 221; [1950] W.N. 354; (1950) 94 S.J. 455, CA; affirming [1950] 1 All E.R. 912; 66 T.L.R. (Pt. 1) 1099, Ch D .................. *Digested,* 47-51/**4784**: *Applied* 97/2974, 14/2913: *Considered* 01/5274

Daley v Strathclyde RC [1977] I.R.L.R. 414, IT *Applied* 13/1082: *Considered* 14/1090

Dallah Real Estate & Tourism Holding Co v Ministry of Religious Affairs see Dallah Real Estate & Tourism Holding Co v Pakistan

Dallah Real Estate & Tourism Holding Co v Pakistan; *sub nom* Dallah Real Estate & Tourism Holding Co v Ministry of Religious Affairs [2010] UKSC 46; [2011] 1 A.C. 763; [2010] 3 W.L.R. 1472; [2011] 1 All E.R. 485; [2011] 1 All E.R. (Comm) 383; [2011] Bus. L.R. 158; [2010] 2 Lloyd's Rep. 691; [2010] 2 C.L.C. 793; 133 Con. L.R. 1; (2010) 160 N.L.J. 1569; Times, November 5, 2010, SC; affirming [2009] EWCA Civ 755; [2010] 2 W.L.R. 805; [2010] 1 All E.R. 592; [2010] 1 All E.R. (Comm) 917; [2010] Bus. L.R. 384; [2010] 1 Lloyd's Rep. 119; [2009] 2 C.L.C. 84; [2010] B.L.R. 1; 125 Con. L.R. 37; [2009] 30 E.G. 67 (C.S.); Times, August 24, 2009, CA (Civ Div); affirming [2008] EWHC 1901 (Comm); [2009] 1 All E.R. (Comm) 505; [2008] 2 Lloyd's Rep. 535; 121 Con. L.R. 138; (2008) 105(33) L.S.G. 21, QBD (Comm) .................. *Digested,* 11/**142**: *Followed* 11/125, 14/124, 14/140

Dalmia Dairy Industries v National Bank of Pakistan [1978] 2 Lloyd's Rep. 223; (1977) 121 S.J. 442, CA (Civ Div) .................. *Digested,* 78/**92**: *Followed* 14/128

Dalriada Trustees Ltd v Nidd Vale Trustees Ltd see PI Consulting (Trustee Services) Ltd v Pensions Regulator

Dalton (Deceased), Re see Yates v Revenue and Customs Commissioners

Damjanovic v Bosnia and Herzegovina (34179/08) see Maktouf v Bosnia and Herzegovina (2312/08)

Damon Compania Naviera SA v Hapag-Lloyd International SA (The Blankenstein) [1985] 1 W.L.R. 435; [1985] 1 All E.R. 475; [1985] 1 Lloyd's Rep. 93; (1985) 82 L.S.G. 1644; (1985) 129 S.J. 218, CA (Civ Div); affirming [1983] 3 All E.R. 510; [1983] 2 Lloyd's Rep. 522; [1983] Com. L.R. 204, QBD (Comm) ........................ *Digested,* 85/**403**: *Considered* 12/2723: *Followed* 14/2735

Danescroft RTM Co Ltd v Inspired Holdings Ltd [2014] L. & T.R. 4; [2013] 3 E.G.L.R. 155, LVT ........................ *Digested,* 14/**2009**

Daniel v Revenue and Customs Commissioners [2014] UKFTT 173 (TC), FTT (Tax) *Applied* 14/2890

Daniel v Trinidad and Tobago [2014] UKPC 3; [2014] A.C. 1290; [2014] 2 W.L.R. 1154; [2014] 2 All E.R. 461; [2014] 1 Cr. App. R. 32; Times, April 22, 2014, PC (Trin)

Daniels v Commissioner of Police of the Metropolis [2005] EWCA Civ 1312; [2006] C.P. Rep. 9; (2005) 102(44) L.S.G. 30; Times, October 28, 2005, CA (Civ Div) . *Digested,* 06/**397**: *Followed* 14/345

Danilenkov v Russia (67336/01) (2014) 58 E.H.R.R. 19, ECHR

Danks v Qinetiq Holdings Ltd [2012] EWHC 570 (Ch); [2012] Pens. L.R. 131, Ch D .... *Digested,* 12/**2383**: *Considered* 14/2283

Dano v Jobcenter Leipzig (C-333/13) (2014) 158(44) S.J.L.B. 37; Times, November 18, 2014, ECJ (Grand Chamber)

Dansk Jurist- og Okonomforbund v Indenrigs- og Sundhedsministeriet (C-546/11); *sub nom* Toftgaard v Indenrigs- og Sundhedsministeriet (C-546/11) [2014] 1 C.M.L.R. 41; [2014] I.C.R. 1; [2014] I.R.L.R. 37; [2013] Eq. L.R. 1099, ECJ (2nd Chamber)

Dany Lions Ltd v Bristol Cars Ltd [2014] EWHC 817 (QB); [2014] 2 All E.R. (Comm) 403; [2014] Bus. L.R. D11, QBD ........................ *Digested,* 14/**630**

Dany Lions Ltd v Bristol Cars Ltd [2013] EWHC 2997 (QB); [2014] 1 Lloyd's Rep. 281, QBD ........................ *Digested,* 14/**619**

Danzan 2003 Trust v Assessor for Lothian 2014 S.L.T. (Lands Tr) 4; [2014] R.V.R. 36; 2013 G.W.D. 35-699, Lands Tr (Scot) ........................ *Digested,* 14/**3677**: *Cited* 14/3666

Dar Al Arkan Real Estate Development Co v Al-Refai [2014] EWCA Civ 715; [2014] 1 C.L.C. 855, CA (Civ Div); affirming [2013] EWHC 4112 (QB); [2014] 1 C.L.C. 813, QBD (Comm)

Darbishire v Warran [1963] 1 W.L.R. 1067; [1963] 3 All E.R. 310; [1963] 2 Lloyd's Rep. 187; (1963) 107 S.J. 631, CA ........................ *Digested,* 63/**941**: *Considered* 91/3194: *Distinguished* 71/3157: *Doubted* 14/1852: *Followed* 99/2504: *Not followed* 12/1902

Darby v National Trust for Places of Historic Interest or Natural Beauty [2001] EWCA Civ 189; (2001) 3 L.G.L.R. 29; [2001] P.I.Q.R. P27; Times, February 23, 2001, CA (Civ Div) ........................ *Digested,* 01/**4504**: *Applied* 14/2208: *Considered* 05/4196

Darby & Darby v Joyce; *sub nom* Joyce v Darby & Darby [2014] EWCA Civ 677; [2014] 3 E.G.L.R. 49, CA (Civ Div)

Dardana Ltd v Yukos Oil Co (No.1); *sub nom* Yukos Oil Co v Dardana Ltd; Petroalliance Services Co Ltd v Yukos Oil Co [2002] EWCA Civ 543; [2002] 1 All E.R. (Comm) 819; [2002] 2 Lloyd's Rep. 326; [2002] C.L.C. 1120, CA (Civ Div); reversing in part [2002] 1 Lloyd's Rep. 225, QBD (Comm) ........................ *Digested,* 03/**196**: *Considered* 05/463, 09/188, 14/122

Data Marketing & Secretarial Ltd v S&S Enterprises Ltd [2014] EWHC 1499 (IPEC); [2014] E.C.C. 22, IPEC ........................ *Digested,* 14/**1939**

Data Power Systems Ltd v Safehosts (London) Ltd [2013] EWHC 2479 (Ch); [2013] B.C.C. 721, Ch D (Birmingham) ........................ *Digested,* 14/**1753**

Data Select Ltd v Revenue and Customs Commissioners [2012] UKUT 187 (TCC); [2012] S.T.C. 2195; [2012] B.V.C. 1743; [2012] S.T.I. 2185, UT (Tax); affirming [2011] UKFTT 535 (TC), FTT (Tax) ........................ *Digested,* 12/**3428**: *Applied* 13/2996, 14/2983

Datema Hellmann Worldwide Logistics BV v Staatssecretaris van Financien (C-130/13) see Kamino International Logistics BV v Staatssecretaris van Financien (C-129/13)

Daventry DC v Daventry and District Housing Ltd [2011] EWCA Civ 1153; [2012] 1 W.L.R. 1333; [2012] 2 All E.R. (Comm) 142; [2012] Bus. L.R. 485; [2012] Pens. L.R. 57; [2012] 1 P. & C.R. 5; [2011] 42 E.G. 120 (C.S.), CA (Civ Div); reversing [2010] EWHC 1935 (Ch), Ch D ........................ *Digested,* 12/**626**: *Applied* 12/2042, 12/2371, 13/571, 14/1991

David v Nemzeti Ado- es Vamhivatal Eszak-alfoldi Regionalis Ado Foigazgatosaga (C-142/11) see Mahageben kft v Nemzeti Ado- es Vamhivatal Del-dunantuli Regionalis Ado Foigazgatosaga (C-80/11)

David McLean Housing Contractors Ltd v Swansea Housing Association Ltd [2002] B.L.R. 125, QBD (TCC) ........ *Digested,* 02/**661**: *Considered* 09/659, 10/844, 14/576

David T Morrison & Co Ltd (t/a Gael Home Interiors) v ICL Plastics Ltd [2014] UKSC 48; 2014 S.C. (U.K.S.C.) 222; 2014 S.L.T. 791; 2014 S.C.L.R. 711; [2014] C.I.L.L. 3561; 2014 G.W.D. 25-504, SC; reversing [2013] CSIH 19; 2013 S.C. 391; 2013 S.L.T. 413; 2013 S.C.L.R. 674; 2013 G.W.D. 11-237, IH (Ex Div); reversing [2012] CSOH 44; 2012 S.L.T. 813; 2012 Rep. L.R. 118; 2012 G.W.D. 12-236, OH ........ *Digested,* 14/**2470**

Davidson v Aegis Defence Services (BVI) Ltd [2013] EWHC 590 (QB), QBD *Affirmed* 14/421

Davidson v Aegis Defence Services (BVI) Ltd [2013] EWCA Civ 1586; [2014] 2 All E.R. 216; [2014] C.P. Rep. 17, CA (Civ Div) ........ *Digested,* 14/**421**

Davidson's Trustees v Ogilvie see Simpson (Davidson's Trustees) v Ogilvie

Davies v Davies [2014] EWCA Civ 568; [2014] Fam. Law 1252; [2014] 2 P. & C.R. DG12, CA (Civ Div)

Davies v Esure Insurance Ltd (Unreported, August 4, 2014), CC (Blackwood) [*Mooneerams Solicitors, 2 Cae Gwyrdd, 2 Greenmeadow Springs Business Park, Cardiff*] ........ *Digested,* 14/**2337**

Davies v Haringey LBC [2014] EWHC 3393 (QB); [2014] B.L.G.R. 743, QBD

Davies v Rees (1886) 17 Q.B.D. 408, CA *Applied* 14/273

Davies v Secretary of State for Energy and Climate Change [2012] EWCA Civ 1380, CA (Civ Div) *Considered* 13/393, 14/419

Davies v Sumner; *sub nom* Sumner v Davies [1984] 1 W.L.R. 1301; [1984] 3 All E.R. 831; (1985) 149 J.P. 110; [1985] R.T.R. 95; 84 L.G.R. 123; (1985) 149 J.P.N. 11; (1985) 82 L.S.G. 45; (1984) 128 S.J. 814; (1985) 4 Tr. L. 1, HL; affirming [1984] 1 W.L.R. 405; (1984) 81 L.S.G. 360; (1984) 128 S.J. 18; Times, August 11, 1983, QBD ........ *Digested,* 84/**3100**: *Applied* 88/3168, 91/3183, 14/273: *Considered* 96/7320, 99/4406, 06/715: *Referred to* 00/3570

Davis v DPP [1988] R.T.R. 156; [1988] Crim. L.R. 249, DC ........ *Digested,* 88/**3075**: *Applied* 93/3494, 94/3976: *Considered* 90/3973, 93/3504, 14/660

Davis v Price; *sub nom* Price v Davis [2014] EWCA Civ 26; [2014] 1 W.L.R. 2129; [2014] B.P.I.R. 494, CA (Civ Div); affirming [2013] EWHC 323 (Ch); [2013] B.P.I.R. 200, Ch D ........ *Digested,* 14/**1800**: *Considered* 14/1799

Davis v Richards and Wallington Industries Ltd [1990] 1 W.L.R. 1511; [1991] 2 All E.R. 563; [1990] Pens. L.R. 141, Ch D ........ *Digested,* 91/**1727**: *Considered* 14/2279

Davis & Dann Ltd v Revenue and Customs Commissioners [2013] UKUT 374 (TCC); [2014] S.T.C. 39; [2013] B.V.C. 1707; [2013] S.T.I. 2860, UT (Tax) ........ *Digested,* 13/**3213**

Davis Pneumatic Systems Ltd (In Administration), Re see Parmeko Holdings Ltd (In Administration), Re

Davisons Solicitors v Nationwide Building Society see Nationwide Building Society v Davisons Solicitors

Dawnay Day & Co Ltd v Cantor Fitzgerald International [2000] R.P.C. 669; (1999) 22(9) I.P.D. 22091; Times, July 14, 1999, CA (Civ Div); affirming Times, January 26, 1998, Ch D ........ *Digested,* 99/**600**: *Applied* 11/2004, 14/1872

Daws Hill Neighbourhood Forum v Wycombe DC see R. (on the application of Daws Hill Neighbourhood Forum) v Wycombe DC

Dawson v Cherry Tree Machine Co Ltd see Shell Tankers UK Ltd v Jeromson

Dawson v Paul 16 I.T.E.L.R. 876, HC (NZ)

Dawson v Thomson Airways Ltd [2014] EWCA Civ 845; [2014] 4 All E.R. 832; [2014] 2 Lloyd's Rep. 399; [2014] 1 C.L.C. 1018; [2014] 3 C.M.L.R. 35; (2014) 164(7612) N.L.J. 18, CA (Civ Div) ........ *Digested,* 14/**165**

Dawson v Wearmouth [1999] 2 A.C. 308; [1999] 2 W.L.R. 960; [1999] 2 All E.R. 353; [1999] 1 F.L.R. 1167; [1999] 1 F.C.R. 625; [1999] Fam. Law 378; (1999) 96(17) L.S.G. 24; (1999) 143 S.J.L.B. 114; Times, March 26, 1999; Independent, May 10, 1999, HL; affirming [1998] Fam. 75; [1998] 2 W.L.R. 392; [1998] 1 All E.R. 271; [1997] 2 F.L.R. 629; [1998] 1 F.C.R. 31; [1998] Fam. Law 15; (1997) 94(35) L.S.G. 34; (1997) 141 S.J.L.B. 200; Times, August 22, 1997; Independent, October 9, 1997, CA (Civ Div) ........ *Digested,* 99/**2377**: *Applied* 01/2609: *Considered* 98/2431, 02/1652, 08/1465, 14/1303: *Followed* 99/2375

Dawsons Ltd v Bonnin [1922] 2 A.C. 413; (1922) 12 Ll. L. Rep. 237; 1922 S.C. (H.L.) 156; 1922 S.L.T. 444, HL; affirming 1921 S.C. 511; 1921 1 S.L.T. 324, IH (2 Div)
*Applied* 96/7091: *Followed* 13/1736, 14/1846

Day v Day [2013] EWCA Civ 280; [2014] Ch. 114; [2013] 3 W.L.R. 556; [2013] 3 All E.R. 661; [2013] W.T.L.R. 817; [2013] 2 P. & C.R. DG1, CA (Civ Div) .............. *Digested,* 13/**3178**: *Considered* 14/3029

Day v Harris see Day v Royal College of Music

Day v Hosebay Ltd; *sub nom* Hosebay Ltd v Day; Lexgorge Ltd v Howard de Walden Estates Ltd; *joined case* Howard de Walden Estates Ltd v Lexgorge Ltd [2012] UKSC 41; [2012] 1 W.L.R. 2884; [2012] 4 All E.R. 1347; [2012] H.L.R. 48; [2013] 1 P. & C.R. 9; [2013] L. & T.R. 3; [2012] 3 E.G.L.R. 33; [2012] 43 E.G. 116; [2012] R.V.R. 359; [2012] 42 E.G. 132 (C.S.); (2012) 156(39) S.J.L.B. 31; Times, October 26, 2012, SC; reversing [2010] EWCA Civ 748; [2010] 1 W.L.R. 2317; [2010] 4 All E.R. 36; [2010] H.L.R. 41; [2010] L. & T.R. 20; [2010] 3 E.G.L.R. 66; [2010] 38 E.G. 106; [2010] R.V.R. 329; (2010) 154(27) S.J.L.B. 29; (2010) 154(26) S.J.L.B. 30; [2010] N.P.C. 73; Times, August 10, 2010, CA (Civ Div) .............. *Digested,* 13/**2439**: *Considered* 14/1982: *Followed* 12/2031

Day v Quick see Brumby (Inspector of Taxes) v Milner

Day v Royal College of Music; *sub nom* Day v Harris [2013] EWCA Civ 191; [2014] Ch. 211; [2013] 3 W.L.R. 1560; [2013] W.T.L.R. 591; 16 I.T.E.L.R. 111; (2013) 157(12) S.J.L.B. 35, CA (Civ Div); reversing [2012] EWHC 2041 (Ch), Ch D ..... *Digested,* 13/**2962**

Day v Shaw [2014] EWHC 36 (Ch); [2014] 2 P. & C.R. DG1, Ch D

Days Healthcare UK Ltd (formerly Days Medical Aids Ltd) v Pihsiang Machinery Manufacturing Co Ltd [2006] EWHC 1444 (QB); [2006] 4 All E.R. 233; [2007] C.P. Rep. 1; [2006] 5 Costs L.R. 788, QBD
*Considered* 14/467

Days Medical Aids Ltd v Pihsiang Machinery Manufacturing Co Ltd [2004] EWCA Civ 993, CA (Civ Div)
*Applied* 14/432

Dazmonda Ltd (t/a Sugar and Spice) v Revenue and Customs Commissioners [2014] UKFTT 337 (TC); [2014] S.T.I. 1920, FTT (Tax)

DB v AB (Contact: Alternative Families) [2014] EWHC 384 (Fam); [2014] 2 F.L.R. 1197, Fam Div (Leeds)

DB Group Services (UK) Ltd v Revenue and Customs Commissioners see UBS AG v Revenue and Customs Commissioners

DB Schenker Rail (UK) Ltd v Schunk GmbH [2014] CAT 2; [2014] Comp. A.R. 205, CAT .............. *Digested,* 14/**534**

DB UK Bank Ltd v Edmunds & Co [2014] P.N.L.R. 12, Ch D (Cardiff) .............. *Digested,* 14/**2055**

DCC Holdings (UK) Ltd v Revenue and Customs Commissioners; *sub nom* Revenue and Customs Commissioners v DCC Holdings (UK) Ltd [2010] UKSC 58; [2011] 1 W.L.R. 44; [2011] 1 All E.R. 537; [2011] S.T.C. 326; 80 T.C. 301; [2011] B.T.C. 13; [2011] S.T.I. 133, SC; affirming [2009] EWCA Civ 1165; [2010] S.T.C. 80; [2009] B.T.C. 724; [2009] S.T.I. 2933, CA (Civ Div); reversing [2008] EWHC 2429 (Ch); [2009] S.T.C. 77; [2008] B.T.C. 755; [2008] S.T.I. 2319, Ch D; reversing [2007] S.T.C. (S.C.D.) 592; [2007] S.T.I. 1649, Sp Comm .............. *Digested,* 11/**3311**: *Applied* 12/2385: *Considered* 14/2972

DD (Afghanistan) v Secretary of State for the Home Department see Al-Sirri v Secretary of State for the Home Department

DE v AB (Permission Hearing: Publicity Protection) [2014] EWCA Civ 1064; [2014] Fam. Law 1530, CA (Civ Div)

De Dampierre v De Dampierre [1988] A.C. 92; [1987] 2 W.L.R. 1006; [1987] 2 All E.R. 1; [1987] 2 F.L.R. 300; [1987] Fam. Law 418; (1987) 84 L.S.G. 1493; (1987) 131 S.J. 471, HL; reversing [1987] 1 F.L.R. 511; [1986] Fam. Law 361, CA (Civ Div) .............. *Digested,* 87/**399**: *Applied* 92/475, 95/2334, 99/2403, 02/628, 03/1554, 05/1623: *Considered* 94/3256, 97/2453, 07/1810, 09/1497: *Followed* 92/5695, 13/1274, 14/567: *Referred to* 95/2303

De Keyser Ltd v Wilson; *sub nom* Wilson v De Keyser Ltd [2001] I.R.L.R. 324; [2001] Emp. L.R. 767, EAT .............. *Digested,* 01/**2271**: *Applied* 04/1252, 13/1001: *Considered* 14/1043

De L v H see R (A Child) (Abduction: Child's Objections), Re

De Meyere v Belgium (A/43) see Le Compte v Belgium (A/43)

De Reneville (otherwise Sheridan) v De Reneville [1948] P. 100; [1948] 1 All E.R. 56; 64 T.L.R. 82; [1948] L.J.R. 1761, CA; affirming [1947] P. 168; [1947] 2 All E.R. 112; 63 T.L.R. 490; 177 L.T. 408; (1948) 92 S.J. 83, PDAD ............................ *Digested,* 47-51/**3143**:
*Applied* 47-51/3120, 47-51/3121, 47-51/3186, 52/541, 58/1072, 63/470, 65/543, 71/3603, 72/424, 14/1394: *Considered* 58/1062, 63/467: *Distinguished* 53/576, 65/3815

De Souza Ribeiro v France (22689/07) (2014) 59 E.H.R.R. 10, ECHR

De Wilde v Belgium (No.1) (A/12) (1979-80) 1 E.H.R.R. 373, ECHR
*Applied* 02/3869, 03/3067, 08/2690, 14/2233: *Considered* 09/1960, 09/2761, 09/2768

Dear v Jackson see Jackson v Dear

Debtor v Johnston see Debtor (No.87 of 1999), Re

Debtor (No.87 of 1999), Re; *sub nom* Debtor v Johnston [2000] B.P.I.R. 589; (2000) 97(7) L.S.G. 40; Times, February 14, 2000, Ch D ............................ *Digested,* 00/**3486**:
*Applied* 14/1788: *Considered* 01/3780, 09/2271

Debtor (No.544/SD/98), Re [2000] B.C.L.C. 103, CA (Civ Div); affirming Independent, July 5, 1999, Ch D ............................ *Digested,* 00/**3447**:
*Considered* 14/1788

Debtor (No.657/SD/1991), Re; *sub nom* Morley v Inland Revenue Commissioners [1992] S.T.C. 751; [1993] B.C.L.C. 180; [1996] B.P.I.R. 452; 65 T.C. 127, Ch D *Digested,* 93/**2358**:
*Applied* 14/1826

Decadent Vapours Ltd v Bevan (Unreported, February 18, 2014), Ch D (Cardiff)
*Reversed* 14/454

Decadent Vapours Ltd v Bevan see Denton v TH White Ltd

Deckmyn v Vandersteen (C-201/13) [2014] Bus. L.R. 1368; [2014] E.C.D.R. 21, ECJ (Grand Chamber)

Decro-Wall International SA v Practitioners in Marketing [1971] 1 W.L.R. 361; [1971] 2 All E.R. 216; (1970) 115 S.J. 171, CA (Civ Div) ............................ *Digested,* 71/**1838**:
*Applied* 73/2659, 74/1350, 13/2839, 14/623: *Considered* 88/446

Deeny v Gooda Walker Ltd (Duty of Care) see Henderson v Merrett Syndicates Ltd (No.1)

Deep Vein Thrombosis and Air Travel Group Litigation, Re [2005] UKHL 72; [2006] 1 A.C. 495; [2005] 3 W.L.R. 1320; [2006] 1 All E.R. 786; [2006] 1 All E.R. (Comm) 313; [2006] 1 Lloyd's Rep. 231; [2005] 2 C.L.C. 1083; [2006] P.I.Q.R. P14; (2006) 87 B.M.L.R. 1; (2006) 103(3) L.S.G. 26; (2005) 155 N.L.J. 1925; (2006) 150 S.J.L.B. 29; Times, December 12, 2005; Independent, December 13, 2005, HL; affirming [2003] EWCA Civ 1005; [2004] Q.B. 234; [2003] 3 W.L.R. 956; [2004] 1 All E.R. 445; [2004] 1 All E.R. (Comm) 459; [2004] 1 Lloyd's Rep. 316; [2003] 2 C.L.C. 884; [2003] P.I.Q.R. P35; (2004) 76 B.M.L.R. 38; (2003) 100(35) L.S.G. 34; (2003) 147 S.J.L.B. 869; Times, July 14, 2003; Independent, July 8, 2003, CA (Civ Div); affirming [2002] EWHC 2825 (QB); [2003] 1 All E.R. 935; [2003] 1 All E.R. (Comm) 418; (2003) 71 B.M.L.R. 82; Times, January 17, 2003, QBD ............................ *Digested,* 06/**252**:
*Applied* 08/208, 09/258, 14/152: *Considered* 10/2029

Defty v Prestwood [2014] B.P.I.R. 373, Ch D

Del Rio Prada v Spain (42750/09) (2014) 58 E.H.R.R. 37, ECHR

Delabole Slate Ltd v Berriman see Berriman v Delabole Slate Ltd

Delaney v Secretary of State for Transport [2014] EWHC 1785 (QB); [2014] R.T.R. 25; [2014] 3 C.M.L.R. 32; [2014] Lloyd's Rep. I.R. 575; [2014] P.I.Q.R. P22; (2014) 164(7610) N.L.J. 18, QBD ............................ *Digested,* 14/**1853**

Delfi AS v Estonia (64569/09) (2014) 58 E.H.R.R. 29, ECHR

Delphi Trust Ltd, Re 16 I.T.E.L.R. 885, HC (IoM)

Deltafina SpA v European Commission (C-578/11 P) [2014] 5 C.M.L.R. 12, ECJ (2nd Chamber)

Demir v Turkey (34503/97) [2009] I.R.L.R. 766; (2009) 48 E.H.R.R. 54, ECHR ........... *Digested,* 09/**1938**:
*Applied* 13/1057: *Considered* 11/4384, 12/1155, 14/1016, 14/1627

Demirkan v Germany (C-221/11) [2014] 1 C.M.L.R. 39, ECJ (Grand Chamber)

Denkavit International BV v Kamer van Koophandel en Fabrieken voor Midden-Gelderland (C2/94) [1996] E.C.R. I-2827; [1996] 3 C.M.L.R. 504, ECJ
*Considered* 14/2377: *Followed* 97/3983

Dennard v Plant see Lagden v O'Connor

Dennis v Lloyds Bank Plc see Dennis (Deceased), Re

Dennis (Deceased), Re; *sub nom* Dennis v Lloyds Bank Plc [1981] 2 All E.R. 140; (1980) 124 S.J. 885; Times, November 14, 1980, Ch D ............................ *Digested,* 81/**2887**:
*Applied* 03/4123, 14/2825: *Considered* 00/2528, 07/4112

Dennis Rye Ltd v Bolsover DC; *sub nom* Bolsover DC v Dennis Rye Ltd [2009] EWCA Civ 372; [2009] 4 All E.R. 1140; [2010] B.C.C. 248; [2009] B.P.I.R. 778; [2009] R.A. 202; [2009] Bus. L.R. D115; Times, May 19, 2009, CA (Civ Div) ................ *Digested,* 09/**2271**: *Applied* 11/355: *Distinguished* 14/1778

Denteh v South London and Maudsley NHS Foundation Trust [2014] I.C.R. D21, EAT

Denton v TH White Ltd 7BS90560, QBD (Bristol) *Reversed* 14/454

Denton v TH White Ltd; *joined cases* Decadent Vapours Ltd v Bevan; Utilise TDS Ltd v Cranstoun Davies [2014] EWCA Civ 906; [2014] 1 W.L.R. 3926; [2014] C.P. Rep. 40; [2014] B.L.R. 547; 154 Con. L.R. 1; [2014] 4 Costs L.R. 752; [2014] C.I.L.L. 3568; (2014) 164(7614) N.L.J. 17, CA (Civ Div) .................................... *Digested,* 14/**454**: *Applied* 14/453: *Considered* 14/2983, 14/838: *Followed* 14/330

Department for the Environment, Food and Rural Affairs v Robertson see Robertson v Department for the Environment, Food and Rural Affairs

Department of Constitutional Affairs v O'Brien; *sub nom* Ministry of Justice v O'Brien; O'Brien v Ministry of Justice; O'Brien v Department of Constitutional Affairs [2013] UKSC 6; [2013] 1 W.L.R. 522; [2013] 2 All E.R. 1; [2013] I.C.R. 499; [2013] I.R.L.R. 315; [2013] Pens. L.R. 129; Times, February 22, 2013, SC; reversing [2008] EWCA Civ 1448; [2009] 2 C.M.L.R. 15; [2009] I.C.R. 593; [2009] I.R.L.R. 294; (2009) 159 N.L.J. 74; Times, February 10, 2009, CA (Civ Div); reversing UKEAT/0139/ZT, EAT ................................................................ *Digested,* 13/**998**: *Applied* 14/2021

Deputy Commissioner of Taxation v Hickey [1999] FCA 259, Fed Ct (Aus) (Full Ct) *Considered* 14/404

Deputy Director of Income Tax (International Taxation) v AP Moller-Maersk A/S 16 I.T.L. Rep. 392, ITAT (Ind)

Derby & Co Ltd v Weldon (No.7) [1990] 1 W.L.R. 1156; [1990] 3 All E.R. 161, Ch D .... *Digested,* 91/**2859**: *Applied* 07/470: *Considered* 91/781, 14/1804: *Reversed in part* 91/2921

Derbyshire CC v F; *sub nom* F (Habitual Residence: Peripatetic Existence), Re [2014] EWFC 26; [2014] Fam. Law 1522, Fam Ct

Derwent Holdings Ltd v Trafford BC see R. (on the application of Derwent Holdings Ltd) v Trafford BC

Desnousse v Newham LBC [2006] EWCA Civ 547; [2006] Q.B. 831; [2006] 3 W.L.R. 349; [2007] 2 All E.R. 547; [2006] H.L.R. 38; [2007] B.L.G.R. 368; [2006] N.P.C. 58; Times, June 28, 2006; Independent, May 19, 2006, CA (Civ Div) ..... *Digested,* 06/**2046**: *Followed* 14/1625

Deugi v Tower Hamlets LBC see Tower Hamlets LBC v Deugi

Deutsche Bahn AG v Morgan Advanced Materials Plc [2013] CAT 31; [2014] Comp. A.R. 197, CAT

Deutsche Bahn AG v Morgan Advanced Materials Plc [2013] CAT 28; [2014] Comp. A.R. 75, CAT

Deutsche Bahn AG v Morgan Advanced Materials Plc (formerly Morgan Crucible Co Plc) [2013] CAT 23; [2014] Comp. A.R. 6, CAT

Deutsche Bahn AG v Morgan Advanced Materials Plc (formerly Morgan Crucible Co Plc) [2013] EWCA Civ 1484; [2014] C.P. Rep. 10; [2014] U.K.C.L.R. 238, CA (Civ Div); affirming [2013] CAT 18; [2013] Comp. A.R. 388, CAT ...................... *Digested,* 14/**542**

Deutsche Bahn AG v Morgan Advanced Materials Plc (formerly Morgan Crucible Co Plc) [2013] CAT 20; [2013] Comp. A.R. 428, CAT ............................................ *Digested,* 14/**311**

Deutsche Bahn AG v Morgan Advanced Materials Plc (formerly Morgan Crucible Co Plc) [2013] CAT 22; [2014] Comp. A.R. 1, CAT

Deutsche Bahn AG v Morgan Advanced Materials Plc (formerly Morgan Crucible Co Plc) see Deutsche Bahn AG v Morgan Crucible Co Plc

Deutsche Bahn AG v Morgan Crucible Co Plc; *sub nom* Deutsche Bahn AG v Morgan Advanced Materials Plc (formerly Morgan Crucible Co Plc) [2014] UKSC 24; [2014] 2 All E.R. 785; [2014] 2 All E.R. (Comm) 545; [2014] Bus. L.R. 377; [2014] U.K.C.L.R. 667; [2014] 4 C.M.L.R. 33; [2014] E.C.C. 29, SC; reversing [2012] EWCA Civ 1055; [2013] Bus. L.R. 125; [2012] U.K.C.L.R. 279, CA (Civ Div); reversing [2011] CAT 16; [2011] Comp. A.R. 569, CAT ............................ *Digested,* 14/**550**

Deutsche Bank AG v Sebastian Holdings Inc [2014] EWHC 2073 (Comm); [2014] 4 Costs L.R. 711, QBD (Comm) ............................................................................ *Digested,* 14/**368**

Deutsche Bank AG v Sebastian Holdings Inc [2014] EWHC 112 (Comm); [2014] 1 All E.R. (Comm) 733, QBD (Comm) ...................................................................... *Digested,* 14/**478**

Deutsche Bank AG v Unitech Global Ltd; *joined case* Deutsche Bank AG v Unitech Ltd [2013] EWHC 2793 (Comm); [2014] 2 All E.R. (Comm) 268; [2013] 2 Lloyd's Rep. 629; [2014] U.K.C.L.R. 15, QBD (Comm) ..................................... *Digested,* 14/**238**

Deutsche Bank AG v Unitech Ltd see Deutsche Bank AG v Unitech Global Ltd

Deutsche Bank Group Services (UK) Ltd v Revenue and Customs Commissioners see UBS AG v Revenue and Customs Commissioners

Deutsche Lufthansa AG v Flughafen Frankfurt-Hahn GmbH (C-284/12) [2014] 2 C.M.L.R. 20, ECJ (2nd Chamber)
*Considered* 14/3803
Deutsche Umwelthilfe eV v Germany (C-515/11) [2013] 1 W.L.R. 3764; [2014] Env. L.R. 8, ECJ (2nd Chamber)
Devenish v Tester (Unreported, April 9, 2014), CC (Northampton) [*Isaac Hogarth, Barrister, 12 King's Bench Walk, London*] ........ *Digested,* 14/**2351**
Devillebichot (Deceased), Re; *sub nom* Brennan v Prior [2013] EWHC 2867 (Ch); [2013] W.T.L.R. 1701, Ch D ........ *Digested,* 14/**2845**
Devon CC v Celtic Bioenergy Ltd [2014] EWHC 309 (TCC); [2014] 4 Costs L.R. 609; [2014] C.I.L.L. 3465, QBD (TCC) ........ *Digested,* 14/**359**
Devon CC v Celtic Composting Systems Ltd [2014] EWHC 552 (TCC); [2014] C.I.L.L. 3501, QBD (TCC)
Devon CC v TR see AC v Devon CC
Dewji v Banwaitt [2013] EWHC 3746 (QB); [2014] B.P.I.R. 63, QBD ........ *Digested,* 14/**1814**
DGFP Zeta, Re 16 I.T.L. Rep. 930, CE (F)
DH v CL [2014] EWHC 1836 (Fam); [2014] Fam. Law 1247, Fam Div
DH (Jamaica) v Secretary of State for the Home Department see Harrison v Secretary of State for the Home Department
DH Edmonds Ltd v East Sussex Police Authority Times, July 15, 1988, CA (Civ Div) ... *Digested,* 88/**765**: *Considered* 09/3075, 14/2448
DHL Express France SAS v Chronopost SA (C-235/09) [2012] C.E.C. 22; [2011] E.T.M.R. 33; [2011] F.S.R. 38, ECJ (Grand Chamber)
*Applied* 14/1929
Dhooharika v DPP [2014] UKPC 11; [2014] 3 W.L.R. 1081; (2014) 158(18) S.J.L.B. 37; Times, May 6, 2014, PC (Mau)
Dhunna v Creditsights Ltd; *sub nom* Creditsights Ltd v Dhunna [2014] EWCA Civ 1238; [2014] I.R.L.R. 953, CA (Civ Div); reversing [2013] I.C.R. 909, EAT ........ *Digested,* 13/**1075**
Di Marco v Morshead Mansions Ltd; *sub nom* Morshead Mansions Ltd v Di Marco [2014] EWCA Civ 96; [2014] 1 W.L.R. 1799; [2014] 2 All E.R. 773; [2014] C.P. Rep. 22; [2014] H.L.R. 28; [2014] 1 P. & C.R. 20; [2014] L. & T.R. 13; [2014] 2 E.G.L.R. 31, CA (Civ Div); reversing [2013] EWHC 1068 (Ch); [2013] L. & T.R. 27, Ch D ........ *Digested,* 14/**2015**
Diag Human SE v Czech Republic [2014] EWHC 1639 (Comm); [2014] 2 Lloyd's Rep. 283; [2014] 1 C.L.C. 750, QBD (Comm) ........ *Digested,* 14/**125**
Diag Human SE v Czech Republic [2013] EWHC 3190 (Comm); [2014] 1 All E.R. (Comm) 605; [2014] 1 Lloyd's Rep. 288, QBD (Comm) ........ *Digested,* 14/**127**
Diageo North America Inc v Intercontinental Brands (ICB) Ltd [2010] EWCA Civ 920; [2011] 1 All E.R. 242; [2012] Bus. L.R. 401; [2010] E.T.M.R. 57; [2011] R.P.C. 2; (2010) 154(31) S.J.L.B. 29, CA (Civ Div); affirming [2010] EWHC 17 (Ch); [2010] 3 All E.R. 147; [2010] E.T.M.R. 17; [2010] R.P.C. 12; (2010) 33(3) I.P.D. 33015; (2010) 154(5) S.J.L.B. 29, Ch D ........ *Digested,* 11/**1961**: *Considered* 13/1793: *Followed* 14/1889
Diakite v Commissaire General aux Refugies et aux Apatrides (C-285/12) [2014] 1 W.L.R. 2477; [2014] Imm. A.R. 631; [2014] I.N.L.R. 719, ECJ (4th Chamber)
Diamond Build Ltd v Clapham Park Homes Ltd [2008] EWHC 1439 (TCC); 119 Con. L.R. 32; [2008] C.I.L.L. 2601, QBD (TCC) ........ *Digested,* 09/**676**: *Considered* 14/592
Diamond Jewellers Ltd v Mittal (t/a Mittal Trading Co) [2014] EWHC 2395 (QB); [2014] B.V.C. 39, QBD ........ *Digested,* 14/**634**
Diamond Resorts (Europe) Ltd, Re [2012] EWHC 3576 (Ch); [2013] B.C.C. 275, Ch D (Companies Ct) ........ *Digested,* 13/**474**: *Distinguished* 13/473: *Followed* 14/501
Dick's Trustees v Robertson; *sub nom* Dick's Trustees, Special Case (1901) 3 F. 1021; (1901) 9 S.L.T. 115, IH (2 Div)
*Applied* 14/2982
Dick's Trustees, Special Case see Dick's Trustees v Robertson
Dickinson v Kilmorie (Aldridge) Downes see Ransom (Inspector of Taxes) v Higgs
Dickinson (Inspector of Taxes) v Downes see Ransom (Inspector of Taxes) v Higgs
Dickinson (t/a John Dickinson Equipment Finance) v Rushmer (t/a FJ Associates) (Costs) [2002] 1 Costs L.R. 128; (2002) 152 N.L.J. 58, Ch D ........ *Digested,* 02/**339**: *Followed* 14/2934
Diesel SpA v Montex Holdings Ltd [2014] E.T.M.R. 4, PO (Irl)
Dietz v Lennig Chemicals Ltd [1969] 1 A.C. 170; [1967] 3 W.L.R. 165; [1967] 2 All E.R. 282; (1967) 111 S.J. 354, HL; affirming [1966] 1 W.L.R. 1349; [1966] 2 All E.R. 962; (1966) 110 S.J. 448, CA ........ *Digested,* 67/**3106**: *Distinguished* 99/1422: *Followed* 04/417, 14/435

Digital Rights Ireland Ltd v Minister for Communications, Marine and Natural Resources (C-293/12); *joined case* Proceedings Brought by Karntner Landesregierung (C-594/12) [2014] 3 W.L.R. 1607; [2014] 2 All E.R. (Comm) 1; [2014] 3 C.M.L.R. 44; [2014] All E.R. (EC) 775, ECJ (Grand Chamber)

Digital Satellite Warranty Cover Ltd v Financial Services Authority see Digital Satellite Warranty Cover Ltd, Re

Digital Satellite Warranty Cover Ltd, Re; *sub nom* Freeman (t/a Satellite Services) v Financial Services Authority; Digital Satellite Warranty Cover Ltd v Financial Services Authority; *joined cases* Freeman (t/a Satellite Services), Re; Nationwide Digital Satellite Warranty Services Ltd, Re [2013] UKSC 7; [2013] 1 W.L.R. 605; [2013] 2 All E.R. 202; [2013] 1 All E.R. (Comm) 625; [2013] Bus. L.R. 292; [2013] 1 C.L.C. 378; [2013] Lloyd's Rep. I.R. 236; (2013) 163 N.L.J. 207, SC; affirming [2011] EWCA Civ 1413; [2012] 2 All E.R. (Comm) 38; [2012] Bus. L.R. 990; [2012] 1 C.L.C. 39; [2012] Lloyd's Rep. I.R. 112, CA (Civ Div); affirming [2011] EWHC 122 (Ch); [2011] Bus. L.R. 981; [2011] 1 C.L.C. 249, Ch D (Companies Ct) ........ *Digested,* 13/**1367**: *Applied* 14/1439

Dillard v F&C Commercial Property Holdings Ltd [2014] EWHC 1219 (QB); [2014] C.I.L.L. 3517, QBD

Dimond v Lovell [2002] 1 A.C. 384; [2000] 2 W.L.R. 1121; [2000] 2 All E.R. 897; [2000] R.T.R. 243; [2000] C.C.L.R. 57; 2000 Rep. L.R. 62; (2000) 97(22) L.S.G. 47; (2000) 150 N.L.J. 740; Times, May 12, 2000; Independent, May 17, 2000, HL; affirming [2000] Q.B. 216; [1999] 3 W.L.R. 561; [1999] 3 All E.R. 1; [1999] R.T.R. 297; [1999] C.C.L.R. 46; (1999) 96(21) L.S.G. 40; (1999) 149 N.L.J. 681; (1999) 143 S.J.L.B. 181; Times, May 3, 1999, CA (Civ Div); reversing (Unreported, May 1, 1998), CC (Sheffield) [*Cottrill Stone Lawless Solicitors, 18 Lloyd Street, Albert Square, Manchester*] ........ *Digested,* 00/**2566**: *Applied* 99/2470, 99/2471, 99/2475, 99/2478, 00/2570, 00/2587, 01/1527, 01/881, 01/900, 07/2497, 12/1898, 13/3033, 14/1852, 14/829: *Cited* 99/2458, 99/2461, 99/2476, 99/2499, 00/2574, 00/2580, 00/2592, 00/2593, 01/3830, 01/896, 01/899, 02/685: *Considered* 99/2453, 99/2454, 99/2459, 99/2460, 99/2465, 99/2466, 99/2467, 99/2468, 99/2477, 99/2479, 99/2481, 99/2496, 99/532, 00/2589, 00/311, 00/425, 01/885, 01/888, 01/890, 01/898, 06/702, 09/683, 09/970, 11/2258, 14/3473: *Distinguished* 99/2452, 99/2482, 99/2491, 99/2504, 99/535, 00/2578, 00/2585, 00/2597, 01/893, 01/894, 02/932, 04/630: *Followed* 99/2463, 99/2489, 00/2565, 00/2577, 00/2579, 01/657, 01/887, 01/901, 04/628, 12/1902, 12/2812, 14/610: *Referred to* 99/2451, 99/2464, 99/2472, 99/2473, 99/2474, 99/2483, 99/2485, 99/2487, 99/2490, 00/2562, 01/1542

Din (Taj) v Wandsworth LBC [1983] 1 A.C. 657; [1981] 3 W.L.R. 918; [1981] 3 All E.R. 881; (1981-82) 1 H.L.R. 73; 78 L.G.R. 113; (1981) 125 S.J. 828; Times, November 27, 1981, HL; reversing Times, June 30, 1981, CA (Civ Div) ........ *Digested,* 82/**1472**: *Applied* 95/2580, 96/3049, 98/3000, 04/1889: *Approved* 97/2666: *Considered* 84/1638, 85/1615, 85/1621, 87/1878, 93/2064, 03/2056: *Distinguished* 84/1641: *Followed* 97/2665, 98/3011, 11/1650, 14/1599

Dingmar v Dingmar [2006] EWCA Civ 942; [2007] Ch. 109; [2006] 3 W.L.R. 1183; [2007] 2 All E.R. 382; [2007] 1 F.L.R. 210; [2006] 2 F.C.R. 595; [2006] W.T.L.R. 1171; [2006] Fam. Law 1025; [2006] N.P.C. 83, CA (Civ Div) ........ *Digested,* 06/**4088**: *Considered* 14/2823

Dinsdale Moorland Services Ltd v Evans [2014] EWHC 2 (Ch); [2014] 2 Costs L.R. 217, Ch D (Leeds) ........ *Digested,* 14/**1034**

Dion Investments Pty Ltd, Re [2013] NSWSC 1941; [2014] W.T.L.R. 1333; 16 I.T.E.L.R. 627, Sup Ct (NSW)

Direct Cosmetics Ltd v Customs and Excise Commissioners (C-138/86); *joined case* Laughtons Photographs Ltd v Customs and Excise Commissioners [1988] S.T.C. 540; [1988] E.C.R. 3937; [1988] 3 C.M.L.R. 333; Times, September 2, 1988, ECJ ........ *Digested,* 89/**1676**: *Applied* 92/4546, 14/3081: *Considered* 96/5877

Direct Line Insurance Plc v Khan [2001] EWCA Civ 1794; [2002] Lloyd's Rep. I.R. 364, CA (Civ Div); affirming HQ0005988, QBD ........ *Digested,* 02/**2739**: *Considered* 05/2359, 09/2281: *Followed* 14/1838

Director General of Fair Trading v First National Bank Plc [2001] UKHL 52; [2002] 1 A.C. 481; [2001] 3 W.L.R. 1297; [2002] 1 All E.R. 97; [2001] 2 All E.R. (Comm) 1000; [2002] 1 Lloyd's Rep. 489; [2002] E.C.C. 22; (2001) 151 N.L.J. 1610; Times, November 1, 2001; Daily Telegraph, October 30, 2001, HL; reversing [2000] Q.B. 672; [2000] 2 W.L.R. 1353; [2000] 2 All E.R. 759; [2000] 1 All E.R. (Comm) 371; [2000] Lloyd's Rep. Bank. 130; [2000] C.C.L.R. 31; (2000) 97(7) L.S.G. 39; Times, March 14, 2000, CA (Civ Div); reversing [2000] 1 W.L.R. 98; [2000] 1 All E.R. 240; [1999] Lloyd's Rep. Bank. 427; [2000] E.C.C. 169; (1999) 18 Tr. L.R. 245; Times, September 21, 1999; Independent, November 8, 1999, Ch D ........ *Digested,* 01/**910**: *Applied* 01/3832, 03/664, 04/618, 07/766, 08/214, 08/2484, 09/179, 09/682, 09/702, 09/703, 10/2064, 10/609, 14/595: *Considered* 03/2456, 05/194, 09/178, 11/568, 13/3553, 14/608: *Followed* 05/721

Director of Income Tax v e-Funds IT Solution 16 I.T.L. Rep. 686, HC (Ind)

Director of Land Valuation v Banks [2014] R.V.R. 93, CA (Ber); affirming [2013] R.V.R. 3, Sup Ct (Ber)

Director of the Assets Recovery Agency v Jackson [2007] EWHC 2553 (QB), QBD *Applied* 10/271, 14/440

Director of the Assets Recovery Agency v Olupitan; *sub nom* Olupitan v Director of the Assets Recovery Agency [2008] EWCA Civ 104; [2008] C.P. Rep. 24; [2008] Lloyd's Rep. F.C. 253; (2008) 105(10) L.S.G. 29; [2008] N.P.C. 23, CA (Civ Div); affirming [2007] EWHC 162 (QB); (2007) 157 N.L.J. 258; [2007] N.P.C. 17, QBD ........ *Digested,* 08/**292**: *Applied* 10/270, 10/271: *Considered* 09/830, 14/440: *Followed* 12/467

Director of the Serious Fraud Office v B see Director of the Serious Fraud Office v O'Brien

Director of the Serious Fraud Office v O'Brien; *sub nom* R. v O'Brien; OB v Director of the Serious Fraud Office; Director of the Serious Fraud Office v B [2014] UKSC 23; [2014] A.C. 1246; [2014] 2 W.L.R. 902; [2014] 2 All E.R. 798; [2014] Lloyd's Rep. F.C. 401; Times, April 11, 2014, SC; affirming [2012] EWCA Crim 67; [2012] 1 W.L.R. 3170; [2012] 3 All E.R. 999; [2012] Lloyd's Rep. F.C. 389, CA (Crim Div) ........ *Digested,* 14/**15**

District Court Bratislava Iii Slovakia v Katrencik see Slovakia v Katrencik

Divall v Divall [2014] EWHC 95 (Fam); [2014] 2 F.L.R. 1104; [2014] Fam. Law 781, Fam Div

Dix (Deceased), Re see Gully v Dix

Dixie v British Polythene Industries Plc see Aktas v Adepta

Dixon v Spain [2014] UKPC 38; 37 B.H.R.C. 688, PC (Gib)

Dixons Retail Plc v Revenue and Customs Commissioners [2012] UKFTT 666 (TC); [2013] S.F.T.D. 72; [2012] S.T.I. 3179, FTT (Tax) *Preliminary ruling given* 14/3082

Dixons Retail Plc v Revenue and Customs Commissioners (C-494/12) [2014] Ch. 326; [2014] 2 W.L.R. 893; [2014] S.T.C. 375; [2014] B.V.C. 2; [2013] S.T.I. 3573, ECJ (2nd Chamber) ........ *Digested,* 14/**3082**: *Considered* 14/3067

DJ&C Withers (Farms) Ltd v Ambic Equipment Ltd see English v Emery Reimbold & Strick Ltd

DL v EL (Hague Abduction Convention: Effect of Reversal of Return Order on Appeal); *sub nom* L (A Child) (Custody: Habitual Residence), Re; KL (A Child) (Abduction: Habitual Residence: Inherent Jurisdiction), Re [2013] UKSC 75; [2014] A.C. 1017; [2013] 3 W.L.R. 1597; [2014] 1 All E.R. 999; [2014] 1 F.L.R. 772; [2014] 1 F.C.R. 69; [2014] Fam. Law 266, SC; reversing [2013] EWCA Civ 865; [2014] 1 F.L.R. 570; [2013] 3 F.C.R. 69; [2013] Fam. Law 1513; (2013) 157(29) S.J.L.B. 31, CA (Civ Div); affirming [2013] EWHC 49 (Fam); [2013] 2 F.L.R. 163; [2013] Fam. Law 521, Fam Div ........ *Digested,* 14/**1380**: *Considered* 14/1381

DLA Piper UK LLP v BDO LLP [2013] EWHC 3970 (Admin); [2014] 1 W.L.R. 4425, QBD (Admin)

DMC Beteiligungsgesellschaft mbH v Finanzamt Hamburg-Mitte (C-164/12) [2014] S.T.C. 1345; [2014] 2 C.M.L.R. 47; [2014] B.T.C. 16, ECJ (1st Chamber)

DMWSHNZ Ltd v Revenue and Customs Commissioners [2014] UKUT 98 (TCC); [2014] S.T.C. 1440; [2014] B.T.C. 509; [2014] S.T.I. 880, UT (Tax); affirming [2013] UKFTT 37 (TC); [2013] S.F.T.D. 648; [2013] S.T.I. 1504, FTT (Tax) ....... *Digested,* 14/**2855**

DNick Holding Plc, Re see Eckerle v Wickeder Westfalenstahl GmbH

Do v Immigration Appeal Tribunal see R. (on the application of Ullah) v Special Adjudicator

DO v LP see S (A Child) (Adoption Order or Special Guardianship Order), Re

Do v Secretary of State for the Home Department see R. (on the application of Ullah) v Special Adjudicator
Dobie v Burns International Security Services (UK) Ltd [1985] 1 W.L.R. 43; [1984] 3 All E.R. 333; [1984] I.C.R. 812; [1984] I.R.L.R. 329; (1985) 82 L.S.G. 517; (1984) 134 N.L.J. 832; (1984) 128 S.J. 872, CA (Civ Div); affirming [1983] I.C.R. 478; [1983] I.R.L.R. 278, EAT ........ *Digested,* 84/**1310**:
*Applied* 86/1170, 86/1278, 09/1260, 10/1149, 13/969: *Considered* 85/1255: *Doubted* 14/1061: *Followed* 86/1221, 14/1112
Docker v Rose [2013] EWHC 4512 (Ch); [2014] B.P.I.R. 535, Ch D ........ *Digested,* 14/**1775**
Dolca v Romania (59282/11) (2014) 59 E.H.R.R. 26, ECHR
Doleman v Shaw see Shaw v Doleman
Dolphin Maritime & Aviation Services Ltd v Sveriges Angartygs see Dolphin Maritime & Aviation Services Ltd v Sveriges Angfartygs Assurans Forening
Dolphin Maritime & Aviation Services Ltd v Sveriges Angfartygs Assurans Forening; *sub nom* Dolphin Maritime & Aviation Services Ltd v Sveriges Angartygs [2009] EWHC 716 (Comm); [2010] 1 All E.R. (Comm) 473; [2009] 2 Lloyd's Rep. 123; [2009] 1 C.L.C. 460; [2009] I.L.Pr. 52, QBD (Comm) ........ *Digested,* 09/**618**:
*Applied* 14/556
Dombo Beheer BV v Netherlands (A/274-A) (1994) 18 E.H.R.R. 213, ECHR ........ *Digested,* 95/**2621**:
*Applied* 97/2811, 98/3112: *Considered* 08/1284, 11/411, 14/2221
Dominique v Queen, The [2013] UKPC 32; [2013] 1 W.L.R. 3884, PC (Bah) ........ *Digested,* 14/**2663**
Don King Productions Inc v Warren (No.1) [2000] Ch. 291; [1999] 3 W.L.R. 276; [1999] 2 All E.R. 218; [1999] 1 Lloyd's Rep. 588; [2000] 1 B.C.L.C. 607; [1999] E.M.L.R. 402; Times, February 9, 1999; Independent, January 25, 1999, CA (Civ Div); affirming [1998] 2 All E.R. 608; [1998] 2 Lloyd's Rep. 176; [1998] 2 B.C.L.C. 132; [1998] R.P.C. 817; (1998) 95(21) L.S.G. 24; (1998) 142 S.J.L.B. 162; Times, April 13, 1998, Ch D ........ *Digested,* 99/**4092**:
*Applied* 00/3864: *Considered* 06/268, 14/591
Donald v Suckling (1865-66) L.R. 1 Q.B. 585, QB
*Considered* 14/273
Donaldson v O'Sullivan [2008] EWCA Civ 879; [2009] 1 W.L.R. 924; [2009] 1 All E.R. 1087; [2009] B.C.C. 99; [2008] B.P.I.R. 1288; (2008) 158 N.L.J. 1226; Times, October 6, 2008, CA (Civ Div); affirming [2008] EWHC 387 (Ch); [2008] B.C.C. 328; [2008] B.P.I.R. 288, Ch D (Bristol) ........ *Digested,* 08/**2130**:
*Applied* 14/1754: *Considered* 11/1845
DONALDSON COMPANY/Admissibility of appeal (J22/12) [2014] E.P.O.R. 29, EPO (Legal Bd App)
Doncaster MBC v Haigh [2014] EWHC 724 (Fam); [2014] Fam. Law 808, Fam Div
Dong v National Crime Agency [2014] UKFTT 369 (TC); [2014] S.T.I. 2092, FTT (Tax)
Donoghue v Poplar Housing & Regeneration Community Association Ltd see Poplar Housing & Regeneration Community Association Ltd v Donoghue
Donovan v Gwentoys Ltd [1990] 1 W.L.R. 472; [1990] 1 All E.R. 1018; (1990) 87(15) L.S.G. 40; (1990) 134 S.J. 910; Times, March 23, 1990; Independent, March 23, 1990; Guardian, March 28, 1990, HL; reversing Times, June 7, 1989, CA (Civ Div) ........ *Digested,* 90/**2960**:
*Applied* 94/5183, 99/464, 09/420: *Considered* 92/2811, 97/667, 99/476, 00/512, 01/601, 14/419: *Followed* 04/2719, 14/421
Donovan v Rana [2014] EWCA Civ 99; [2014] 1 P. & C.R. 23; [2014] 2 E.G.L.R. 1, CA (Civ Div) ........ *Digested,* 14/**2520**
Doosan Babcock Ltd v Comercializadora de Equipos y Materiales Mabe Lda (formerly Mabe Chile Lda) [2013] EWHC 3010 (TCC); [2014] 1 Lloyd's Rep. 464, QBD (TCC) ........ *Digested,* 14/**410**
Doosan Babcock Ltd v Comercializadora de Equipos y Materiales Mabe Lda (formerly Mabe Chile Lda) [2013] EWHC 3201 (TCC); [2014] B.L.R. 33, QBD (TCC) ........ *Digested,* 14/**411**
Douglas v Hello! Ltd (No.6); *sub nom* Douglas v Hello! Ltd (Trial Action: Breach of Confidence) (No.3) [2005] EWCA Civ 595; [2006] Q.B. 125; [2005] 3 W.L.R. 881; [2005] 4 All E.R. 128; [2005] E.M.L.R. 28; [2005] 2 F.C.R. 487; [2005] H.R.L.R. 27; (2005) 28(8) I.P.D. 28057; (2005) 155 N.L.J. 828; Times, May 24, 2005; Independent, May 26, 2005, CA (Civ Div); reversing in part [2003] EWHC 786 (Ch); [2003] 3 All E.R. 996; [2003] E.M.L.R. 31; (2003) 153 N.L.J. 595; Independent, June 16, 2003, Ch D ........ *Digested,* 05/**2812**:
*Applied* 03/1217, 05/4188, 07/2510: *Approved* 04/1391: *Considered* 06/2440, 14/415, 14/842: *Reversed* 07/4190
Douglas v Hello! Ltd (Trial Action: Breach of Confidence) (No.3) see Douglas v Hello! Ltd (No.6)
Douglas v Hello! Ltd see OBG Ltd v Allan
Dow Chemical Co v European Commission (C-179/12 P) [2014] Bus. L.R. 119; [2014] 4 C.M.L.R. 6, ECJ (9th Chamber)

Dow Chemical Co v European Commission (C-499/11 P) [2014] 4 C.M.L.R. 1, ECJ (1st Chamber)
Dow Jones & Co Inc v Jameel see Jameel v Dow Jones & Co Inc
Dowden v Stack see Stack v Dowden
Down (Inspector of Taxes) v Compston [1937] 2 All E.R. 475, KBD
*Considered* 14/1386: *Distinguished* 69/1720
Downsview Nominees Ltd v First City Corp Ltd; *sub nom* First City Corp Ltd v Downsview Nominees Ltd [1993] A.C. 295; [1993] 2 W.L.R. 86; [1993] 3 All E.R. 626; [1993] B.C.C. 46; [1994] 2 B.C.L.C. 49; (1992) 89(45) L.S.G. 26; (1992) 136 S.J.L.B. 324; Times, December 15, 1992; Independent, December 14, 1992, PC (NZ); reversing in part [1990] 3 N.Z.L.R. 265, CA (NZ) ................ *Digested,* 93/**2881**:
*Applied* 96/4988, 02/3834, 03/3938, 14/278: *Considered* 00/4657, 01/4541, 03/3583, 06/3491, 13/481
Dowson & Mason v Potter [1986] 1 W.L.R. 1419; [1986] 2 All E.R. 418; (1986) 83 L.S.G. 3429; (1986) 130 S.J. 841, CA (Civ Div) ................ *Digested,* 86/**972**:
*Followed* 14/2989: *Referred to* 94/3437
Doyle v United Kingdom (Admissibility) (30158/06) (2007) 45 E.H.R.R. SE3, ECHR
*Considered* 14/1633
DP (India) v Secretary of State for the Home Department see SA (Pakistan) v Secretary of State for the Home Department
DP (Revocation of Lasting Power of Attorney), Re; *sub nom* Public Guardian v JM [2014] C.O.P.L.R. 188; [2014] W.T.L.R. 979, CP ................ *Digested,* 14/**2170**
DPAS Ltd v Revenue and Customs Commissioners [2013] UKFTT 676 (TC); [2014] S.T.I. 385, FTT (Tax)
DPP v Armstrong see Armstrong v DPP
DPP v Bhagwan see R. v Bhagwan (Dharam Singh)
DPP v Clarke; *joined cases* DPP v O'Keefe; DPP v O'Connell; DPP v Lewis (1992) 94 Cr. App. R. 359; (1992) 156 J.P. 267; [1992] Crim. L.R. 60; [1992] C.O.D. 103; (1991) 135 S.J. 135; Times, August 27, 1991; Independent, September 18, 1991; Guardian, August 28, 1991, QBD ................ *Digested,* 93/**977**:
*Considered* 14/673
DPP v Denning [1991] 2 Q.B. 532; [1991] 3 W.L.R. 235; [1991] 3 All E.R. 439; (1992) 94 Cr. App. R. 272; (1991) 155 J.P. 1003; [1991] R.T.R. 271; [1991] Crim. L.R. 699; [1991] C.O.D. 358; (1991) 155 J.P.N. 426; (1991) 135 S.J. 506; Times, April 9, 1991; Independent, April 17, 1991, QBD ................ *Digested,* 91/**844**:
*Considered* 11/825, 14/750
DPP v Gowing [2013] EWHC 4614 (Admin); (2014) 178 J.P. 181, DC ................ *Digested,* 14/**810**
DPP v Hammond see Hammond v DPP
DPP v Haw [2007] EWHC 1931 (Admin); [2008] 1 W.L.R. 379; [2007] H.R.L.R. 43; [2007] U.K.H.R.R. 1194; [2008] Crim. L.R. 562; (2007) 104(33) L.S.G. 26; (2007) 157 N.L.J. 1198; Times, September 11, 2007, DC ................ *Digested,* 07/**2811**:
*Followed* 14/808
DPP v Hawkins [1996] R.T.R. 160, CA (Civ Div) ................ *Digested,* 96/**5088**:
*Considered* 14/2561
DPP v Hussain (1994) 158 J.P. 602; (1994) 158 J.P.N. 570; Times, June 1, 1994, QBD ................ *Digested,* 94/**1032**:
*Considered* 14/810
DPP v Issler [2014] EWHC 669 (Admin); [2014] 1 W.L.R. 3686; [2014] R.T.R. 21; (2014) 137 B.M.L.R. 129; [2014] A.C.D. 105; (2014) 158(16) S.J.L.B. 57, DC ... *Digested,* 14/**2561**
DPP v Jarman [2013] EWHC 4391 (Admin); (2014) 178 J.P. 89; [2014] A.C.D. 54, QBD (Admin) ................ *Digested,* 14/**764**
DPP v Lewis see DPP v Clarke
DPP v Mahon [2012] NICA 50; [2014] N.I. 19, CA (NI)
DPP v O'Connell see DPP v Clarke
DPP v O'Keefe see DPP v Clarke
DPP v Radziwilowicz [2014] EWHC 2283 (Admin); (2014) 178 J.P. 432, DC ................ *Digested,* 14/**710**
DPP v Regional Pool Promotions [1964] 2 Q.B. 244; [1964] 2 W.L.R. 209; [1964] 1 All E.R. 65; (1964) 128 J.P. 150; 62 L.G.R. 82; (1963) 107 S.J. 984, DC ................ *Digested,* 64/**1626**:
*Applied* 14/3048
DPP v Schildkamp; *sub nom* R. v Schildkamp [1971] A.C. 1; [1970] 2 W.L.R. 279; [1969] 3 All E.R. 1640; (1970) 54 Cr. App. R. 90; (1969) 119 N.L.J. 1116; (1970) 114 S.J. 54; Times, November 28, 1969, HL; affirming [1969] 1 W.L.R. 818; [1969] 2 All E.R. 835; (1969) 113 S.J. 486, CA (Crim Div) ................ *Digested,* 70/**303**:
*Applied* 79/848, 83/680: *Considered* 88/322, 14/723

DPP v Withers (Ian Douglas); *sub nom* R. v Gearing (Helen); R. v Withers (Ian Douglas); *joined cases* R. v Withers (Phyllis May); R. v Withers (Helen); R. v Withers (Stuart Robert) [1975] A.C. 842; [1974] 3 W.L.R. 751; [1974] 3 All E.R. 984; (1974) 60 Cr. App. R. 85; [1975] Crim. L.R. 95; (1974) 118 S.J. 862, HL; reversing [1974] Q.B. 414; [1974] 2 W.L.R. 26; [1974] 1 All E.R. 100; (1974) 58 Cr. App. R. 187; Times, October 20, 1973, CA (Crim Div) ................................ *Digested,* 75/**524**: *Considered* 14/772

DPP of Northern Ireland v Maxwell; *sub nom* Maxwell v DPP of Northern Ireland; R. v Maxwell (James Charles) [1978] 1 W.L.R. 1350; [1978] 3 All E.R. 1140; (1979) 68 Cr. App. R. 128; [1978] Crim. L.R. 40; (1978) 122 S.J. 758, HL; affirming [1978] 1 W.L.R. 1363; [1978] Crim. L.R. 422, CA (NI) ....................................... *Digested,* 78/**394**: *Applied* 88/2526, 90/1131, 14/683: *Considered* 84/2369, 93/917, 95/1278: *Referred to* 88/2241

DPP's Application for Judicial Review, Re see Millar's Application for Judicial Review, Re

DR v GR (Financial Remedy: Variation of Overseas Trust) [2013] EWHC 1196 (Fam); [2013] 2 F.L.R. 1534; [2013] W.T.L.R. 1123; 16 I.T.E.L.R. 281, Fam Div ........... *Digested,* 13/**1303**

DR v MB see AB (A Child) (Abduction: Art.15: Procedure and Evidence), Re

Drake Insurance Plc (In Provisional Liquidation) v Provident Insurance Plc [2003] EWCA Civ 1834; [2004] Q.B. 601; [2004] 2 W.L.R. 530; [2004] 2 All E.R. (Comm) 65; [2004] 1 Lloyd's Rep. 268; [2004] 1 C.L.C. 574; [2004] R.T.R. 19; [2004] Lloyd's Rep. I.R. 277, CA (Civ Div); reversing [2003] EWHC 109 (Comm); [2003] 1 All E.R. (Comm) 759; [2004] R.T.R. 11; [2003] Lloyd's Rep. I.R. 781; Independent, March 31, 2003, QBD (Comm) ...................................... *Digested,* 04/**2228**: *Applied* 14/1850: *Approved* 03/2476: *Considered* 04/192, 08/2386

Dramatico Entertainment Ltd v British Sky Broadcasting Ltd [2012] EWHC 1152 (Ch); [2012] 3 C.M.L.R. 15; [2012] E.C.D.R. 24; [2012] Info. T.L.R. 219; (2012) 109(20) L.S.G. 25, Ch D ........................................................................................ *Digested,* 12/**1908**: *Applied* 13/1752, 13/1763, 14/1868

Draper v Lincolnshire CC [2014] EWHC 2388 (Admin); [2014] B.L.G.R. 673, QBD (Admin) ............................................................................................................ *Digested,* 14/**2149**

Drax Holdings Ltd, Re; *joined case* InPower Ltd, Re [2003] EWHC 2743 (Ch); [2004] 1 W.L.R. 1049; [2004] 1 All E.R. 903; [2004] B.C.C. 334; [2004] 1 B.C.L.C. 10, Ch D (Companies Ct) ......................................................................................... *Digested,* 04/**2190**: *Applied* 06/2361, 14/1820, 14/1821, 14/500: *Considered* 06/550, 07/2448

Draycott v Hannells Letting Ltd (t/a Hannells Letting Agents) [2010] EWHC 217 (QB); [2011] 1 W.L.R. 1606; [2010] 3 All E.R. 411; [2010] H.L.R. 27; [2010] L. & T.R. 12; [2010] N.P.C. 18, QBD ................................................................................. *Digested,* 10/**2045**: *Approved* 11/2076: *Superseded* 14/2016

Dresdner Kleinwort Ltd v Attrill see Attrill v Dresdner Kleinwort Ltd

Dresser-Rand SA v Agenzia delle Entrate, Direzione Provinciale, Ufficio Controlli di Genova (C-606/12) [2014] B.V.C. 15; [2014] S.T.I. 1631, ECJ (7th Chamber)

Drew v Walsall Healthcare NHS Trust [2013] Eq. L.R. 1051, EAT ................................ *Digested,* 14/**1113**

Drilling Global Consultant LLP v Revenue and Customs Commissioners [2014] UKFTT 888 (TC); [2014] S.T.I. 3363, FTT (Tax)

Drinkall v Whitwood [2003] EWCA Civ 1547; [2004] 1 W.L.R. 462; [2004] 4 All E.R. 378; (2003) 100(47) L.S.G. 21; (2003) 147 S.J.L.B. 1308; Times, November 13, 2003, CA (Civ Div) ............................................................................................. *Digested,* 04/**417**: *Applied* 07/489: *Considered* 14/435

Drown v Revenue and Customs Commissioners [2014] UKFTT 892 (TC); [2014] S.T.I. 3707, FTT (Tax)

Drozdovs v Baltikums AAS (C-277/12) [2014] R.T.R. 14; [2014] Lloyd's Rep. I.R. 230, ECJ (2nd Chamber)

Drummond v Revenue and Customs Commissioners [2009] EWCA Civ 608; [2009] S.T.C. 2206; 79 T.C. 793; [2009] B.T.C. 312; [2009] S.T.I. 2021, CA (Civ Div); affirming [2008] EWHC 1758 (Ch); [2008] S.T.C. 2707; [2008] B.T.C. 473; [2008] S.T.I. 1875, Ch D; reversing [2007] S.T.C. (S.C.D.) 682; [2007] S.T.I. 1818, Sp Comm ........................................................................................... *Digested,* 10/**3248**: *Applied* 09/3741, 09/3849, 14/2868: *Followed* 10/3344: *Referred to* 13/2088, 13/3006

Drysdale v Department of Transport (Maritime and Coastguard Agency) [2014] EWCA Civ 1083; [2014] C.P. Rep. 43; [2014] I.R.L.R. 892, CA (Civ Div); affirming UKEAT/0171/12/LA, EAT ..................................................................................... *Digested,* 14/**1083**

DSM Nutritional Products v Assessor for Ayrshire Valuation Joint Board 2014 S.L.T. (Lands Tr) 7; [2014] R.V.R. 100; 2014 G.W.D. 1-30, Lands Tr (Scot) ................. *Digested,* 14/**3673**

DTE Financial Services Ltd v Wilson (Inspector of Taxes) [2001] EWCA Civ 455; [2001] S.T.C. 777; 74 T.C. 14; [2001] B.T.C. 159; [2001] S.T.I. 670; (2001) 98(21) L.S.G. 40; Times, May 3, 2001; Daily Telegraph, April 10, 2001, CA (Civ Div); affirming [1999] S.T.C. 1061; [1999] B.T.C. 415; (1999) 96(44) L.S.G. 41; (1999) 143 S.J.L.B. 270; Times, November 9, 1999, Ch D; affirming [1999] S.T.C. (S.C.D.) 121, Sp Comm ........ *Digested,* 01/**5237**: *Applied* 07/4085, 08/3671, 13/3094: *Considered* 14/3807: *Distinguished* 03/4233

Duarte Hueros v Autociba SA (C-32/12) [2014] 1 All E.R. (Comm) 267; [2014] 1 C.M.L.R. 53; [2014] C.E.C. 310, ECJ (1st Chamber)

Dubai Aluminium Co Ltd v Amhurst Brown Martin & Nicholson see Dubai Aluminium Co Ltd v Salaam

Dubai Aluminium Co Ltd v Salaam; *joined case* Dubai Aluminium Co Ltd v Amhurst Brown Martin & Nicholson [2002] UKHL 48; [2003] 2 A.C. 366; [2002] 3 W.L.R. 1913; [2003] 1 All E.R. 97; [2003] 2 All E.R. (Comm) 451; [2003] 1 Lloyd's Rep. 65; [2003] 1 B.C.L.C. 32; [2003] 1 C.L.C. 1020; [2003] I.R.L.R. 608; [2003] W.T.L.R. 163; (2003) 100(7) L.S.G. 36; (2002) 146 S.J.L.B. 280; Times, December 6, 2002; Independent, December 10, 2002, HL; reversing [2001] Q.B. 113; [2000] 3 W.L.R. 910; [2000] 2 Lloyd's Rep. 168; [2000] Lloyd's Rep. P.N. 497; [2000] P.N.L.R. 578; Times, April 21, 2000, CA (Civ Div); reversing [1999] 1 Lloyd's Rep. 415; (1998) 148 N.L.J. 1301; Times, September 4, 1998, QBD (Comm) ........ *Digested,* 03/**3046**: *Applied* 01/4267, 03/3033, 03/3045, 05/4199, 05/4200, 06/1337, 06/2915, 06/543, 07/4248, 08/3897, 08/3906: *Considered* 08/3953, 12/3344, 14/2991: *Distinguished* 03/3613: *Followed* 09/265, 11/3476

Dubai Islamic Bank PJSC v PSI Energy Holding Co BSC see Plantation Holdings (FZ) LLC v Dubai Islamic Bank PJSC

Dufoo v Tolaini see Quiet Moments Ltd, Re

Dukali v Lamrani [2012] EWHC 1748 (Fam); [2012] 2 F.L.R. 1099; [2012] 2 F.C.R. 574; [2012] Fam. Law 1205, Fam Div ........ *Digested,* 12/**1443**: *Approved* 13/1299: *Considered* 14/2008

Dumez France SA v Hessische Landesbank (220/88) [1990] E.C.R. I-49; [1990] I.L.Pr. 299, ECJ (6th Chamber) *Applied* 09/618, 10/3410, 14/556: *Considered* 91/3931, 06/646: *Explained* 14/542

Dumrul v Standard Chartered Bank [2010] EWHC 2625 (Comm); [2010] 2 C.L.C. 661, QBD (Comm) ........ *Digested,* 11/**382**: *Applied* 14/407

Dunamenti Eromu Zrt v European Commission (T-179/09) [2014] 3 C.M.L.R. 36, GC (6th Chamber)

Dunbartonshire, Argyll and Bute Assessor v Akram see Assessor for Dunbartonshire, Argyll and Bute v Akram

Duncan v Duncan [2013] EWCA Civ 1407; [2014] 2 F.L.R. 624; [2014] Fam. Law 289, CA (Civ Div) ........ *Digested,* 14/**2050**

Duncan v Revenue and Customs Commissioners [2014] UKFTT 1013 (TC); [2014] S.T.I. 3440, FTT (Tax)

Dunec v Poland see Brodziak v Poland

Dunham v United States [2014] EWHC 334 (Admin); [2014] A.C.D. 94, QBD (Admin)

Dunhill v Burgin [2014] UKSC 18; [2014] 1 W.L.R. 933; [2014] 2 All E.R. 364; [2014] R.T.R. 16; [2014] C.O.P.L.R. 199; (2014) 17 C.C.L. Rep. 203; [2014] P.I.Q.R. P13; (2014) 137 B.M.L.R. 1; (2014) 164(7599) N.L.J. 20; (2014) 158(12) S.J.L.B. 41; Times, March 28, 2014, SC; affirming [2012] EWCA Civ 397; [2012] C.P. Rep. 29; [2012] P.I.Q.R. P15, CA (Civ Div); reversing [2011] EWHC 464 (QB), QBD (Manchester) ........ *Digested,* 14/**435**: *Considered* 14/625

Dunhill v Burgin [2012] EWHC 3163 (QB); [2012] 1 W.L.R. 3739; [2013] 1 All E.R. 482; [2013] P.I.Q.R. P5; Times, January 17, 2013, QBD (Manchester) ........ *Digested,* 13/**2199**: *Affirmed* 14/435

Dunlop v Revenue and Customs Commissioners [2014] UKFTT 1054 (TC); [2014] S.T.I. 3558, FTT (Tax)

Dunlop Pneumatic Tyre Co Ltd v New Garage & Motor Co Ltd [1915] A.C. 79, HL *Applied* 47-51/1721, 52/1550, 61/3908, 61/3909, 62/1397, 62/2842, 62/850, 63/1643, 72/501, 76/1618, 82/407, 98/111, 00/2115, 04/667, 06/678, 06/745, 06/768, 08/674, 09/3583, 09/5040, 14/642: *Considered* 54/1463, 66/3146, 95/493, 08/1126, 11/223: *Followed* 96/6701, 11/534, 14/1141

Dunoon Developments v Secretary of State for the Environment and Poole BC (1993) 65 P. & C.R. 101; [1992] 2 P.L.R. 128; [1992] J.P.L. 936; [1992] E.G. 24 (C.S.); [1992] N.P.C. 22, CA (Civ Div) ........ *Digested,* 93/**3943**: *Considered* 14/2408

Dunsfold Park Ltd v Secretary of State for Communities and Local Government [2014] EWCA Civ 627; [2014] J.P.L. 1106, CA (Civ Div); affirming [2013] EWHC 1878 (Admin); [2013] B.L.G.R. 861; [2013] J.P.L. 1568, QBD (Admin) ........................ *Digested,* 14/**2356**

Dunster Properties Ltd v First Secretary of State [2007] EWCA Civ 236; [2007] 2 P. & C.R. 26; [2007] J.P.L. 1464; (2007) 151 S.J.L.B. 336, CA (Civ Div); reversing [2006] EWHC 2079 (Admin), QBD (Admin) ........................ *Digested,* 07/**3278**: *Applied* 14/2066: *Considered* 07/3283: *Followed* 12/2602, 13/2349

Duomatic Ltd, Re [1969] 2 Ch. 365; [1969] 2 W.L.R. 114; [1969] 1 All E.R. 161; (1968) 112 S.J. 922, Ch D ........................ *Digested,* 69/**412**: *Applied* 74/321, 80/268, 80/269, 99/607, 00/654, 01/748, 03/540, 04/472, 07/572, 07/588, 11/409, 11/413, 14/510, 14/512: *Considered* 98/704, 02/556, 04/458, 05/470, 08/3792, 08/494: *Distinguished* 90/487, 07/321

Durham CC v D; *sub nom* D v Durham CC [2012] EWCA Civ 1654; [2013] 1 W.L.R. 2305; [2013] 2 All E.R. 213; [2013] C.P. Rep. 15; [2013] B.L.G.R. 315; [2013] Fam. Law 795, CA (Civ Div) ........................ *Digested,* 13/**359**: *Applied* 14/2184

Durkin v DSG Retail Ltd [2014] UKSC 21; [2014] 1 W.L.R. 1148; [2014] 2 All E.R. 715; [2014] 1 All E.R. (Comm) 929; 2014 S.C. (U.K.S.C.) 139; 2014 S.L.T. 468; 2014 S.C.L.R. 403; [2014] E.C.C. 20; 2014 G.W.D. 12-211; Times, April 4, 2014, SC; reversing [2010] CSIH 49; 2010 S.C. 662; 2011 S.L.T. 114; 2010 S.C.L.R. 692; [2010] C.T.L.C. 252; 2010 G.W.D. 28-574, IH (1 Div) ........................ *Digested,* 14/**613**

Durrani v Secretary of State for the Home Department see Durrani (Entrepreneurs: Bank Letters: Evidential Flexibility), Re

Durrani (Entrepreneurs: Bank Letters: Evidential Flexibility), Re; *sub nom* Durrani v Secretary of State for the Home Department [2014] UKUT 295 (IAC); [2014] Imm. A.R. 1019, UT (IAC)

Durrant v Branksome Urban DC [1897] 2 Ch. 291, CA
*Considered* 14/3034: *Distinguished* 01/5632: *Followed* 99/5036, 12/3374

Durrant v Chief Constable of Avon and Somerset [2013] EWCA Civ 1624; [2014] 1 W.L.R. 4313; [2014] 2 All E.R. 757; [2014] C.P. Rep. 11; [2014] 1 Costs L.R. 130, CA (Civ Div) ........................ *Digested,* 14/**463**: *Applied* 14/462, 14/9: *Considered* 14/451, 14/461: *Followed* 14/457

Dusza v Powys Teaching Local Health Board; *sub nom* Powys Teaching Local Health Board v Dusza [2014] EWHC 339 (Admin); [2014] Med. L.R. 147; (2014) 138 B.M.L.R. 160, QBD (Admin) ........................ *Digested,* 14/**1490**

DV3 RS Limited Partnership v Revenue and Customs Commissioners; *sub nom* Revenue and Customs Commissioners v DV3 RS Limited Partnership [2013] EWCA Civ 907; [2014] 1 W.L.R. 1136; [2013] S.T.C. 2150; [2013] 3 E.G.L.R. 159; [2013] B.T.C. 661; [2013] S.T.I. 2570; [2013] 31 E.G. 51 (C.S.), CA (Civ Div); reversing [2012] UKUT 399 (TCC); [2013] S.T.C. 430; [2012] B.T.C. 1753, UT (Tax); affirming [2011] UKFTT 138 (TC); [2011] S.F.T.D. 531; [2011] S.T.I. 1626, FTT (Tax) ........................ *Digested,* 13/**3130**

DW (A Child) (Termination of Parental Responsibility), Re; *sub nom* D (A Child) (Parental Responsibility: Removal), Re; D (A Child) (Withdrawal of Parental Responsibility), Re; CW v SG [2014] EWCA Civ 315; [2014] 3 F.C.R. 314; [2014] Fam. Law 971, CA (Civ Div); affirming [2013] EWHC 854 (Fam); [2013] 2 F.L.R. 655; [2013] Fam. Law 796, Fam Div ........................ *Digested,* 14/**1424**: *Considered* 14/1425

Dwyer v Westminster City Council; *sub nom* Westminster City Council v Dwyer [2014] EWCA Civ 153; [2014] 2 P. & C.R. 7; [2014] 2 E.G.L.R. 5; [2014] 2 P. & C.R. DG4, CA (Civ Div) ........................ *Digested,* 14/**2518**

Dymny v Lambeth LBC see Kay v Lambeth LBC

Dyson v Leeds City Council (No.2) see Fairchild v Glenhaven Funeral Services Ltd (t/a GH Dovener & Son)

Dyson Ltd v Registrar of Trade Marks (C-321/03) [2007] Bus. L.R. 787; [2007] E.C.R. I-687; [2007] 2 C.M.L.R. 14; [2007] C.E.C. 223; [2007] E.T.M.R. 34; [2007] R.P.C. 27, ECJ (3rd Chamber) ........................ *Digested,* 07/**1580**: *Applied* 13/1758: *Considered* 14/1934

Dyson Technology Ltd v Strutt [2007] EWHC 1756 (Ch); [2007] 4 Costs L.R. 597, Ch D ........................ *Digested,* 07/**388**: *Applied* 14/348

Dzhamayeva v Russia (26980/06) (2014) 59 E.H.R.R. 6, ECHR

E v B (C-436/13) [2014] 3 W.L.R. 1750; [2014] Fam. Law 1675; (2014) 158(38) S.J.L.B. 37; Times, October 30, 2014, ECJ (2nd Chamber)

E v Channel Four Television Corp [2005] EWHC 1144 (Fam); [2005] E.M.L.R. 30; [2005] 2 F.L.R. 913; [2005] U.K.H.R.R. 789; [2005] Fam. Law 866, Fam Div ..... *Digested,* 06/**454**: *Applied* 14/436

E v Refugee Applications Commissioner (C-493/10) see R. (on the application of NS) v Secretary of State for the Home Department (C-411/10)

E v Secretary of State for the Home Department see Secretary of State for the Home Department v F

E (A Child) (Adoption Order: Proportionality of Outcome to Circumstances), Re; *sub nom* E (A Child) (Adoption: Proportionate Outcome), Re [2013] EWCA Civ 1614; [2014] 2 F.L.R. 514; [2014] 3 F.C.R. 240; [2014] Fam. Law 272, CA (Civ Div) ........ *Digested,* 14/**1232**

E (A Child) (Adoption: Proportionate Outcome), Re see E (A Child) (Adoption Order: Proportionality of Outcome to Circumstances), Re

E (A Child) (Brussels II Revised: Vienna Convention: Reporting Restriction), Re see E (A Child) (Care Proceedings: European Dimension), Re

E (A Child) (Care Order: Change of Care Plan), Re; *sub nom* Father v SBC; E (A Child) (Child under Care Order: Injunction under Human Rights Act 1998), Re [2014] EWFC 6; [2014] 3 W.L.R. 1733; [2014] Fam. Law 1230; (2014) 164(7611) N.L.J. 19, Fam Ct

E (A Child) (Care Proceedings: European Dimension), Re; *sub nom* E (A Child) (Care Proceedings: Jurisdiction), Re; E (A Child) (Brussels II Revised: Vienna Convention: Reporting Restriction), Re [2014] EWHC 6 (Fam); [2014] 1 W.L.R. 2670; [2014] 2 F.L.R. 151; [2014] 2 F.C.R. 264; [2014] Fam. Law 425, Fam Div *Digested,* 14/**1344**

E (A Child) (Care Proceedings: Jurisdiction), Re see E (A Child) (Care Proceedings: European Dimension), Re

E (A Child) (Child under Care Order: Injunction under Human Rights Act 1998), Re see E (A Child) (Care Order: Change of Care Plan), Re

E (A Minor) v Dorset CC (Appeal) see X (Minors) v Bedfordshire CC

E (Alleged Patient), Re see Sheffield City Council v E

E (Assisted Reproduction: Parent), Re; *sub nom* AB v CD [2013] EWHC 1418 (Fam); [2013] 2 F.L.R. 1357; [2013] 3 F.C.R. 532; [2013] Fam. Law 962; (2013) 163(7563) N.L.J. 19, Fam Div ........ *Digested,* 14/**1408**

E Friz GmbH v Von der Heyden (C-215/08) [2010] 3 C.M.L.R. 23, ECJ (1st Chamber) *Followed* 14/611

E Pfeiffer Weinkellerei-Weineinkauf GmbH & Co v Arbuthnot Factors Ltd [1988] 1 W.L.R. 150; (1987) 3 B.C.C. 608; [1987] B.C.L.C. 522; Times, March 11, 1987, QBD ........ *Digested,* 88/**3178**: *Considered* 14/2586: *Distinguished* 92/489

E, Re; *sub nom* N v E [2014] EWCOP 27; [2014] Med. L.R. 417, CP ........ *Digested,* 14/**2158**

E-Clear (UK) Plc (In Liquidation) v Elia [2013] EWCA Civ 1114; [2013] 2 B.C.L.C. 455; [2014] 1 P. & C.R. DG4, CA (Civ Div); reversing [2012] EWHC 1256 (Ch), Ch D ........ *Digested,* 14/**489**

E-Squared Ltd, Re see Nygate v E-Squared Ltd

E. ON Global Commodities SE v Agentia Nationala de Administrare Fiscala (C-323/12) [2014] B.V.C. 20; [2014] S.T.I. 750, ECJ (10th Chamber)

E.Surv Ltd v Goldsmith Williams Solicitors [2014] EWHC 1104 (Ch); [2014] P.N.L.R. 25, Ch D (Manchester) ........ *Digested,* 14/**2215**

EA v AP (Schedule I Proceedings: Jurisdiction: Stay) [2013] EWHC 2344 (Fam); [2014] I.L.Pr. 17; [2014] Fam. Law 32, Fam Div ........ *Digested,* 14/**1385**

Ealing LBC v Connors [2013] EWHC 3493 (Fam); [2014] 2 F.L.R. 328; [2014] Fam. Law 151, Fam Div ........ *Digested,* 14/**317**

Ealing LBC v P see P v Ealing LBC

Ealing LBC v Surdonja see Mohamed v Hammersmith and Fulham LBC

Earl Cadogan v 27/29 Sloane Gardens Ltd see Earl Cadogan v Sportelli

Earl Cadogan v 27/29 Sloane Gardens Ltd see Pitts v Earl Cadogan

Earl Cadogan v Atlantic Telecasters Ltd see Pitts v Earl Cadogan

Earl Cadogan v Grandeden Property Management Ltd see Earl Cadogan v Sportelli

Earl Cadogan v Grandeden Property Management Ltd see Pitts v Earl Cadogan

Earl Cadogan v Pitts see Pitts v Earl Cadogan

Earl Cadogan v Sportelli; *joined cases* Bircham & Co Nominees (No.2) Ltd v Clarke; Howard de Walden Estates Ltd v Maybury Court Freehold Co Ltd; Earl Cadogan v Grandeden Property Management Ltd; Earl Cadogan v 27/29 Sloane Gardens Ltd [2007] EWCA Civ 1042; [2008] 1 W.L.R. 2142; [2008] 2 All E.R. 220; [2008] L. & T.R. 13; [2008] 1 E.G.L.R. 137; [2007] R.V.R. 314; [2007] 44 E.G. 180 (C.S.); (2007) 151 S.J.L.B. 1402; [2007] N.P.C. 110, CA (Civ Div); affirming [2007] 1 E.G.L.R. 153; [2006] R.V.R. 382, Lands Tr ........ *Digested,* 07/**2743**: *Applied* 08/2452, 09/3127, 13/1884, 14/1981: *Cited* 08/2442: *Considered* 09/2528, 09/3155, 09/402, 10/2062, 12/2032: *Distinguished* 10/2056: *Followed* 08/2451: *Reversed in part* 09/2519

Earl Cadogan v Sportelli see Pitts v Earl Cadogan

Earl of Ellesmere v Wallace [1929] 2 Ch. 1, CA
*Applied* 67/1745, 90/1992, 91/502: *Followed* 14/3048
Earlsferry Thistle Golf Club v Revenue and Customs Commissioners; *sub nom* Revenue and Customs Commissioners v Earlsferry Thistle Golf Club [2014] UKUT 250 (TCC); [2014] S.T.C. 2498; [2014] B.V.C. 520; [2014] S.T.I. 2221, UT (Tax); reversing [2013] UKFTT 187 (TC); [2013] S.T.I. 1678, FTT (Tax)
Earp v Kurd; *sub nom* Kurd, Re [2013] B.P.I.R. 965, Ch D ............ *Digested,* 14/**1825**
Earthshine Ltd v Revenue and Customs Commissioners [2014] UKUT 271 (TCC); [2014] B.V.C. 522; [2014] S.T.I. 2290, UT (Tax); affirming [2011] UKFTT 667 (TC), FTT (Tax) ............ *Digested,* 14/**3065**
Easingwood v Cockcroft 2013 BCCA 182; 16 I.T.E.L.R. 364, CA (BC)
East England Schools CIC (t/a 4MySchools) v Palmer [2013] EWHC 4138 (QB); [2014] I.R.L.R. 191, QBD ............ *Digested,* 14/**1030**
East Midlands Aggregates Ltd v Customs and Excise Commissioners; *sub nom* Customs and Excise Commissioners v East Midlands Aggregates Ltd [2004] EWHC 856 (Ch); [2004] S.T.C. 1582; [2005] 1 P. & C.R. 11; [2004] B.T.C. 8107; [2004] S.T.I. 1085; [2004] N.P.C. 66; Times, May 24, 2004, Ch D; affirming [2004] 2 P. & C.R. 1; [2003] V. & D.R. 460, V&DTr (Manchester) ........ *Digested,* 04/**3684**:
*Applied* 10/3226, 14/2846
East Northamptonshire DC v Secretary of State for Communities and Local Government; *joined case* Barnwell Manor Wind Energy Ltd v East Northamptonshire DC [2014] EWCA Civ 137; [2014] 1 P. & C.R. 22; [2014] 2 E.G.L.R. 85; [2014] J.P.L. 731; [2014] A.C.D. 80, CA (Civ Div); affirming [2013] EWHC 473 (Admin); [2013] 2 P. & C.R. 5; [2013] J.P.L. 1128; [2013] 12 E.G. 78 (C.S.), QBD (Admin) ............ *Digested,* 14/**2388**
Eastenders Cash & Carry Plc v Crown Prosecution Service see Crown Prosecution Service v Eastenders Group
Eastenders Cash & Carry Plc v Revenue and Customs Commissioners see R. (on the application of Eastenders Cash & Carry Plc) v Revenue and Customs Commissioners
Eastenders Cash & Carry Plc v South Western Magistrates' Court see R. (on the application of Eastenders Cash & Carry Plc) v South Western Magistrates' Court
Eastern Holdings Establishment of Vaduz v Singer & Friedlander Ltd [1967] 1 W.L.R. 1017; [1967] 2 All E.R. 1192; (1967) 111 S.J. 253, Ch D ............ *Digested,* 67/**505**:
*Considered* 69/411, 14/1808
Eastwood (Deceased), Re; *sub nom* Lloyds Bank Ltd v Eastwood [1975] Ch. 112; [1974] 3 W.L.R. 454; [1974] 3 All E.R. 603; [1997] Costs L.R. (Core Vol.) 50; (1974) 118 S.J. 533, CA (Civ Div); reversing [1973] 3 W.L.R. 795; [1973] 3 All E.R. 1079; (1973) 117 S.J. 487, Ch D ............ *Digested,* 74/**2927**:
*Applied* 76/2129, 81/837, 94/4556, 95/4019, 99/393, 00/390, 10/3986, 14/1073:
*Considered* 83/2915
Eaton v Caulfield [2013] EWHC 2214 (Ch); [2014] B.C.C. 653, Ch D (Companies Ct)
Eaton v Natural England [2013] EWCA Civ 628; [2013] Env. L.R. 37, CA (Civ Div) ...... *Digested,* 14/**339**
Eaton Mansions (Westminster) Ltd v Stinger Compania de Inversion SA [2013] EWCA Civ 1308; [2014] C.P. Rep. 12; [2014] H.L.R. 4; [2014] 1 P. & C.R. 5; [2014] 1 E.G.L.R. 89; [2013] 45 E.G. 74 (C.S.), CA (Civ Div); affirming [2012] EWHC 3354 (Ch); [2012] 49 E.G. 66 (C.S.), Ch D ............ *Digested,* 14/**824**
EB v United Kingdom (Admissibility) (63019/10) (2014) 59 E.H.R.R. SE7, ECHR
EB (Kosovo) v Secretary of State for the Home Department; *joined cases* FI (Nigeria) v Secretary of State for the Home Department; HB (Ethiopia) v Secretary of State for the Home Department; JL (Sierra Leone) v Secretary of State for the Home Department [2008] UKHL 41; [2009] 1 A.C. 1159; [2008] 3 W.L.R. 178; [2008] 4 All E.R. 28; [2008] H.R.L.R. 40; [2008] U.K.H.R.R. 1087; 25 B.H.R.C. 228; [2008] Imm. A.R. 713; [2008] I.N.L.R. 516; (2008) 105(26) L.S.G. 21; (2008) 158 N.L.J. 968; (2008) 152(26) S.J.L.B. 30; Times, June 30, 2008, HL; reversing in part [2006] EWCA Civ 1713; [2007] Imm. A.R. 396; [2007] I.N.L.R. 150; (2007) 104(1) L.S.G. 12, CA (Civ Div) ............ *Digested,* 08/**2037**:
*Applied* 08/2075, 09/2141, 11/1770, 14/1671: *Considered* 10/1777, 10/1806, 11/1790, 13/3776, 14/1650: *Followed* 09/2163, 10/1761, 10/1790, 11/1735, 11/1789, 13/1618
Ebhogiaye v Solicitors Regulation Authority [2013] EWHC 2445 (Admin); [2014] A.C.D. 13, QBD (Admin)
Ebury (Valuation Officer), Re [2003] R.A. 261, Lands Tr ............ *Digested,* 04/**3179**:
*Considered* 14/2132
EC (A Minor) (Care Proceedings: Disclosure), Re see C (A Minor) (Care Proceedings: Disclosure), Re
EC (Disclosure of Material), Re see C (A Minor) (Care Proceedings: Disclosure), Re

Eckerle v Wickeder Westfalenstahl GmbH; *sub nom* DNick Holding Plc, Re [2013] EWHC 68 (Ch); [2014] Ch. 196; [2013] 3 W.L.R. 1316; [2014] B.C.C. 1; Times, April 9, 2013, Ch D ........ *Digested,* 13/**480**

Eclairs Group Ltd v JKX Oil & Gas Plc; *joined cases* Glengary Overseas Ltd v JKX Oil & Gas Plc; JKX Oil & Gas Plc v Eclairs Group Ltd [2014] EWCA Civ 640; [2014] 4 All E.R. 463; [2014] 2 All E.R. (Comm) 1018; [2014] Bus. L.R. 835; [2014] 2 B.C.L.C. 164; Times, May 29, 2014, CA (Civ Div); reversing [2013] EWHC 2631 (Ch); [2014] Bus. L.R. 18; [2014] 1 B.C.L.C. 202, Ch D ........ *Digested,* 14/**520**

Eclipse Film Partners No.35 LLP v Revenue and Customs Commissioners [2013] UKUT 639 (TCC); [2014] S.T.C. 1114; [2014] B.T.C. 503, UT (Tax); reversing in part [2012] UKFTT 270 (TC); [2012] S.F.T.D. 823; [2012] S.T.I. 1607, FTT (Tax) ........ *Digested,* 14/**2981**

Eclipse Film Partners No.35 LLP v Revenue and Customs Commissioners; *sub nom* Revenue and Customs Commissioners v Eclipse Film Partners No.35 LLP [2014] EWCA Civ 184; [2014] C.P. Rep. 26; [2014] B.T.C. 10; [2014] S.T.I. 742, CA (Civ Div); affirming [2013] UKUT 141 (TCC); [2013] S.T.C. 1618; [2013] B.T.C. 1786; [2013] S.T.I. 1909, UT (Tax) ........ *Digested,* 14/**2888**

Eco-Energy (GB) Ltd v First Secretary of State [2004] EWCA Civ 1566; [2005] 2 P. & C.R. 5; [2005] 2 P.L.R. 33; [2005] J.P.L. 1079; (2004) 148 S.J.L.B. 1368, CA (Civ Div) ........ *Digested,* 06/**3319**:
*Applied* 13/2355: *Considered* 07/536, 11/2562, 14/2401

EcoChilla v Cornwall Council [2014] P.A.D. 31, Planning Inspector

Ecologistas en Accion-CODA v Ayuntamiento de Madrid (C-142/07) [2009] P.T.S.R. 458; [2008] E.C.R. I-6097; [2009] Env. L.R. D4, ECJ (3rd Chamber)
*Considered* 09/3032, 10/2605: *Distinguished* 14/1187

Econometric Ltd v Greater London Authority [2013] UKUT 219 (LC); [2014] R.V.R. 251, UT (Lands)

Ecotrade SpA v Agenzia delle Entrate - Ufficio di Genova 3 (C-95/07); *sub nom* Ecotrade SpA v Agenzia delle Entrate - Ufficio di Genova 3 (C-96/07) [2008] S.T.C. 2626; [2008] E.C.R. I-3457; [2008] 3 C.M.L.R. 1; [2008] C.E.C. 1007; [2010] B.V.C. 235; [2008] S.T.I. 1327, ECJ (3rd Chamber) ........ *Digested,* 08/**1308**:
*Applied* 13/3224, 14/3057

Ecotrade SpA v Agenzia delle Entrate - Ufficio di Genova 3 (C-96/07) see Ecotrade SpA v Agenzia delle Entrate - Ufficio di Genova 3 (C-95/07)

Ecotricity (Next Generation) Ltd v Secretary of State for Communities and Local Government [2014] EWHC 2699 (Admin); [2014] J.P.L. 1338, QBD (Admin)

ED&F Man Sugar Ltd v Unicargo Transportgesellschaft GmbH [2013] EWCA Civ 1449; [2014] 1 Lloyd's Rep. 412; [2013] 2 C.L.C. 938, CA (Civ Div); affirming [2012] EWHC 2879 (Comm); [2013] 1 All E.R. (Comm) 955; [2012] 2 Lloyd's Rep. 660, QBD (Comm) ........ *Digested,* 14/**2713**

EDF Energy Powerlink Ltd v National Union of Rail, Maritime and Transport Workers [2009] EWHC 2852 (QB); [2010] I.R.L.R. 114, QBD ........ *Digested,* 10/**1097**:
*Complaint dismissed* 14/1627

EDG v RR (Enforcement of Foreign Maintenance Order) [2014] EWHC 816 (Fam); [2014] Fam. Law 1104, Fam Div

Edgar v Edgar [1980] 1 W.L.R. 1410; [1980] 3 All E.R. 887; (1981) 2 F.L.R. 19; (1980) 11 Fam. Law 20; (1980) 124 S.J. 809; Times, July 24, 1980, CA (Civ Div) ........ *Digested,* 80/**791**:
*Applied* 91/1794, 95/2340, 95/2344, 96/2857, 07/1708, 12/1437: *Cited* 04/1514: *Considered* 82/1490, 82/907, 83/2622, 87/1743, 94/2166, 95/2336, 03/1580, 07/1830, 09/1583: *Distinguished* 83/1100, 96/2875, 97/2477, 99/4635: *Followed* 84/1118, 05/1688, 14/1387: *Referred to* 87/1750, 93/5228

Edgehill v Secretary of State for the Home Department [2014] EWCA Civ 402; [2014] Imm. A.R. 883, CA (Civ Div) ........ *Digested,* 14/**1707**

Edgerton v Edgerton [2012] EWCA Civ 181; [2012] 1 W.L.R. 2655; [2012] C.P. Rep. 17; [2012] 2 F.L.R. 273; [2012] 1 F.C.R. 421; [2012] Fam. Law 798; Times, April 18, 2012, CA (Civ Div) ........ *Digested,* 12/**1314**:
*Considered* 14/496

Edgeskill Ltd v Revenue and Customs Commissioners [2014] UKUT 38 (TCC); [2014] S.T.C. 1174; [2014] B.V.C. 506; [2014] S.T.I. 691, UT (Tax); affirming [2011] UKFTT 393 (TC), FTT (Tax) ........ *Digested,* 14/**3069**:
*Considered* 14/3067

Edinburgh City Council's Appeal, Re see City of Edinburgh Council v Lothian Valuation Appeal Committee

Editorial Board of Pravoye Delo v Ukraine (33014/05) (2014) 58 E.H.R.R. 28, ECHR

Edmond de Rothschild Securities (UK) Ltd v Exillon Energy Plc [2014] EWHC 2165 (Comm); [2014] 5 Costs L.O. 749, QBD (Comm) ........ *Digested,* 14/**631**

Edmondson, Re see Thomas v Edmondson

Edwards v Chesterfield Royal Hospital NHS Foundation Trust; *joined case* Botham v Ministry of Defence [2011] UKSC 58; [2012] 2 A.C. 22; [2012] 2 W.L.R. 55; [2012] 2 All E.R. 278; [2012] I.C.R. 201; [2012] I.R.L.R. 129; [2012] Med. L.R. 93; (2012) 124 B.M.L.R. 51; (2012) 162 N.L.J. 30; (2011) 155(48) S.J.L.B. 31; Times, January 23, 2012, SC; reversing [2010] EWCA Civ 571; [2011] Q.B. 339; [2010] 3 W.L.R. 1285; [2010] I.C.R. 1181; [2010] I.R.L.R. 702; [2010] Med. L.R. 307; (2010) 107(23) L.S.G. 19; (2010) 154(21) S.J.L.B. 28, CA (Civ Div); reversing [2009] EWHC 2011 (QB); [2009] I.R.L.R. 822, QBD .......................... *Digested,* 12/**1167**: *Applied* 13/1486: *Considered* 11/1531: *Followed* 13/434, 14/1052

Edwards v Environment Agency (C-260/11) see R. (on the application of Edwards) v Environment Agency (C-260/11)

Edwards v Environment Agency see R. (on the application of Edwards) v Environment Agency

Edwards v Flamingo Land Ltd [2013] EWCA Civ 801; [2013] Eq. L.R. 888; [2014] L.L.R. 693, CA (Civ Div) .......................... *Digested,* 13/**1510**

Edwards v United States [2013] EWHC 1906 (Admin); [2014] 1 W.L.R. 1532; [2013] 4 All E.R. 871; [2014] A.C.D. 9, QBD (Admin) .......................... *Digested,* 14/**1229**

Edwards (Inspector of Taxes) v Bairstow; *joined case* Edwards (Inspector of Taxes) v Harrison [1956] A.C. 14; [1955] 3 W.L.R. 410; [1955] 3 All E.R. 48; 48 R. & I.T. 534; 36 T.C. 207; (1955) 34 A.T.C. 198; [1955] T.R. 209; (1955) 99 S.J. 558, HL; reversing (1954) 47 R. & I.T. 340; (1954) 33 A.T.C. 131; [1954] T.R. 155, CA; affirming 46 R. & I.T. 177; (1954) 33 A.T.C. 58; [1954] T.R. 65, QBD .......... *Digested,* 55/**417**: *Applied* 56/4272, 59/1529, 62/1506, 66/6154, 67/1949, 71/3949, 71/999, 74/320, 76/250, 77/2446, 82/1617, 82/1647, 82/476, 83/1225, 83/1976, 84/460, 89/125, 89/3189, 90/2675, 90/754, 92/3364, 93/2274, 95/391, 95/876, 98/2137, 98/2140, 98/4622, 99/3066, 99/6471, 03/4251, 06/4189, 06/4278, 07/4068, 09/4532, 11/3390, 14/2849, 14/2981: *Considered* 56/4853, 74/1834, 74/1873, 74/2097, 74/283.u, 74/485, 82/3282, 84/3218, 84/3253, 87/3193, 90/1864, 91/2373, 92/164, 94/357, 94/7, 95/155, 95/5020, 95/7, 95/896, 98/4604, 99/4660, 99/4663, 06/215, 06/4118, 07/4348, 08/160, 14/1453: *Followed* 03/4190, 10/3096, 10/3509, 14/3105: *Referred to* 74/1816

Edwards (Inspector of Taxes) v Harrison see Edwards (Inspector of Taxes) v Bairstow

Edwards-Tubb v JD Wetherspoon Plc [2011] EWCA Civ 136; [2011] 1 W.L.R. 1373; [2011] C.P. Rep. 27; [2011] P.I.Q.R. P16; (2011) 121 B.M.L.R. 70; (2011) 155(9) S.J.L.B. 31, CA (Civ Div) .......................... *Digested,* 11/**327**: *Applied* 14/291

Edwin H Bradley & Sons v Secretary of State for the Environment (1984) 47 P. & C.R. 374; (1982) 266 E.G. 926; (1982) 266 E.G. 264; [1982] J.P.L. 43, QBD ............ *Digested,* 86/**3745**: *Applied* 86/3389: *Considered* 14/2373

Eeles v Cobham Hire Services Ltd; *sub nom* Cobham Hire Services Ltd v Eeles [2009] EWCA Civ 204; [2010] 1 W.L.R. 409; [2009] C.P. Rep. 29; [2009] P.I.Q.R. P15; [2009] LS Law Medical 274; (2009) 106(13) L.S.G. 17; (2009) 153(11) S.J.L.B. 30, CA (Civ Div); reversing [2008] EWHC 2369 (QB), QBD ..... *Digested,* 09/**414**: *Applied* 10/2397, 11/2373, 12/2404, 12/853, 14/2305: *Followed* 11/2374, 12/2407, 12/2408, 13/2198

Egg Stores (Stamford Hill) v Leibovici [1977] I.C.R. 260; [1976] I.R.L.R. 376; (1976) 11 I.T.R. 289, EAT .......................... *Digested,* 77/**951**: *Applied* 77/952: *Considered* 91/1695, 14/1089

Eghan v Secretary of State for the Home Department see Alam v Secretary of State for the Home Department

Egyptian Hotels Ltd v James Mitchell see Mitchell (Surveyor of Taxes) v Egyptian Hotels Ltd

EH v X LBC see A (Children), Re

EI du Pont de Nemours & Co v European Commission (C-172/12 P) [2014] 4 C.M.L.R. 7; [2014] C.E.C. 440, ECJ (9th Chamber)

EI DU PONT/Fine denier yarn (T1799/08) [2014] E.P.O.R. 3, EPO (Technical Bd App)

Eichner v Midland Bank Executor and Trustee Co [1970] 1 W.L.R. 1120; [1970] 2 All E.R. 597; (1970) 21 P. & C.R. 503; (1970) 114 S.J. 373, CA (Civ Div) .............. *Digested,* 70/**1532**: *Considered* 74/152.u: *Followed* 14/1976

Eilbeck (Inspector of Taxes) v Rawling see WT Ramsay Ltd v Inland Revenue Commissioners

EK (Article 4 ECHR: Anti-Trafficking Convention: Tanzania), Re; *sub nom* EK (Tanzania) v Secretary of State for the Home Department [2013] UKUT 313 (IAC); [2013] Imm. A.R. 895; [2014] I.N.L.R. 166, UT (IAC) .......................... *Digested,* 14/**1728**: *Approved* 14/1700

EK (Tanzania) v Secretary of State for the Home Department see EK (Article 4 ECHR: Anti-Trafficking Convention: Tanzania), Re

El Hogar Perfecto del Siglo XXI SL v Office for Harmonisation in the Internal Market (Trade Marks and Designs) (OHIM) (T-337/12) [2014] E.C.D.R. 1, GC (6th Chamber)

El Makdessi v Cavendish Square Holdings BV see Makdessi v Cavendish Square Holdings BV

Electrosteel Castings Ltd v Scan Trans Shipping & Chartering Sdn Bhd [2002] EWHC 1993 (Comm); [2002] 2 All E.R. (Comm) 1064; [2003] 1 Lloyd's Rep. 190; 87 Con. L.R. 50, QBD (Comm) ........ *Digested,* 03/**3908**: *Applied* 14/123

Elefanten Schuh GmbH v Jacqmain (C-150/80) [1981] E.C.R. 1671; [1982] 3 C.M.L.R. 1, ECJ ........ *Digested,* 82/**1259**: *Applied* 89/4512, 92/3508, 94/475, 14/542

Elek v Bar-Tur [2013] EWCA Civ 1774, CA (Civ Div); affirming [2013] EWHC 207 (Ch); [2013] 2 E.G.L.R. 159; [2013] 8 E.G. 107 (C.S.), Ch D ........ *Digested,* 14/**622**

Eli Lilly & Co v Human Genome Sciences Inc [2012] EWCA Civ 1185; [2013] R.P.C. 22; (2012) 109(35) L.S.G. 23, CA (Civ Div) ........ *Digested,* 13/**1808**: *Applied* 14/1900

Eli Lilly & Co v Janssen Alzheimer Immunotherapy [2013] EWHC 1737 (Pat); [2014] R.P.C. 1, Ch D (Patents Ct) ........ *Digested,* 14/**1900**

Eli Lilly & Co Ltd v Human Genome Sciences Inc (C-493/12) [2014] R.P.C. 21, ECJ (3rd Chamber)

Eliades v City of London Common Council see Nolton Business Centres Ltd, Re

Elias v Secretary of State for Defence see R. (on the application of Elias) v Secretary of State for Defence

Ella v Ella [2007] EWCA Civ 99; [2007] 2 F.L.R. 35; [2007] 3 F.C.R. 768; [2007] Fam. Law 483; (2007) 104(5) L.S.G. 31; (2007) 151 S.J.L.B. 125, CA (Civ Div) ........ *Digested,* 07/**1810**: *Applied* 14/1326

Ellaway v Cardiff CC [2014] EWHC 836 (Admin); [2014] P.T.S.R. D12, QBD (Admin)

Ellerman Lines Ltd v Read [1928] 2 K.B. 144; 64 A.L.R. 1128, CA
*Considered* 14/417

Elliot v Salford City Council [2014] P.A.D. 24, Planning Inspector

Elliott v LRC Products Ltd; *sub nom* LUV Trade Mark; Elliott's Trade Mark Application [2014] R.P.C. 13, App Person

Elliott v Secretary of State for Communities and Local Government [2013] EWCA Civ 703; [2014] Env. L.R. 1, CA (Civ Div) ........ *Digested,* 14/**2398**

Elliott's Trade Mark Application see Elliott v LRC Products Ltd

Ellis v Cabinet Office [2014] EWHC 2049 (Ch); [2014] Pens. L.R. 681, Ch D

Ellis v Ministry of Defence see Smith v Ministry of Defence

Ellis v Rowbotham [1900] 1 Q.B. 740, CA
*Applied* 61/8058: *Considered* 70/1518, 79/159u, 14/1969: *Followed* 10/1835

Elmdene Estates Ltd v White [1960] A.C. 528; [1960] 2 W.L.R. 359; [1960] 1 All E.R. 306; (1960) 104 S.J. 126, HL; affirming [1960] 1 Q.B. 1; [1959] 3 W.L.R. 185; [1959] 2 All E.R. 605; (1959) 103 S.J. 656, CA ........ *Digested,* 60/**2754**: *Applied* 78/1795, 80/1598, 14/2016: *Considered* 71/10007

Elmi v United Kingdom (11449/07) see Sufi v United Kingdom (8319/07)

Elosta v Commissioner of Police of the Metropolis see R. (on the application of Elosta) v Commissioner of Police of the Metropolis

Else Refining & Recycling Ltd v Revenue and Customs Commissioners [2014] UKUT 8 (TCC); [2014] S.T.C. 1401; [2014] B.V.C. 503; [2014] S.T.I. 437, UT (Tax); affirming [2012] UKFTT 470 (TC), FTT (Tax) ........ *Digested,* 14/**3066**

Elsevier Ltd v Munro [2014] EWHC 2728 (QB); [2014] 5 Costs L.O. 797, QBD ........ *Digested,* 14/**423**

Elsevier Ltd v Munro [2014] EWHC 2648 (QB); [2014] I.R.L.R. 766, QBD ........ *Digested,* 14/**1033**

Elvington Park Ltd v York City Council [2009] EWHC 1805 (Admin); [2010] Env. L.R. 10; [2010] L.L.R. 279; [2010] J.P.L. 331, QBD (Admin) ........ *Digested,* 10/**2298**: *Considered* 14/2226

Elwood v Goodman; *joined case* Goodman v Elwood [2013] EWCA Civ 1103; [2014] Ch. 442; [2014] 2 W.L.R. 967; [2013] 4 All E.R. 1077; [2014] 1 P. & C.R. 8; (2013) 157(35) S.J.L.B. 41; [2014] 1 P. & C.R. DG1; Times, October 16, 2013, CA (Civ Div); reversing in part [2012] EWHC 3624 (Ch), Ch D (Companies Ct) . *Digested,* 13/**2435**

Elys v Marks & Spencer Plc [2014] I.C.R. 1091, EAT ........ *Digested,* 14/**1080**

EM (Eritrea) v Secretary of State for the Home Department see R. (on the application of EM (Eritrea)) v Secretary of State for the Home Department

EM (Lebanon) v Secretary of State for the Home Department [2008] UKHL 64; [2009] 1 A.C. 1198; [2008] 3 W.L.R. 931; [2009] 1 All E.R. 559; [2008] 2 F.L.R. 2067; [2009] 1 F.C.R. 441; [2009] H.R.L.R. 6; [2009] U.K.H.R.R. 22; [2009] Imm. A.R. 189; [2009] I.N.L.R. 123; [2008] Fam. Law 1190; (2008) 105(42) L.S.G. 21; (2008) 158 N.L.J. 1531; (2008) 152(41) S.J.L.B. 30; Times, October 24, 2008, HL; reversing [2006] EWCA Civ 1531; [2007] 1 F.L.R. 991; [2007] 3 F.C.R. 1; [2007] U.K.H.R.R. 1; [2007] Imm. A.R. 347; [2007] Fam. Law 398; (2006) 150 S.J.L.B. 1570; Times, November 29, 2006, CA (Civ Div) .................................... *Digested,* 08/**2038**: *Distinguished* 14/1692

Eman v College van Burgemeester en Wethouders van den Haag (C-300/04) [2006] E.C.R. I-8055; [2007] 1 C.M.L.R. 4; [2007] All E.R. (EC) 486, ECJ .................... *Digested,* 07/**1582**: *Applied* 12/1030: *Considered* 14/976

Embassy of Brazil v de Castro Cerqueira [2014] 1 W.L.R. 3718; [2014] I.C.R. 703, EAT .................................... *Digested,* 14/**1139**

Emblaze Mobility Solutions Ltd v Revenue and Customs Commissioners [2014] UKFTT 679 (TC); [2014] S.F.T.D. 1133; [2014] S.T.I. 2667, FTT (Tax)

Emerald, The see Owners of No.7 Steam Sand Pump Dredger v Owners of Steamship Greta Holme

Emerging Markets Series of DFA Investment Trust Co v Dyrektor Izby Skarbowej w Bydgoszczy (C-190/12) [2014] S.T.C. 1660; [2014] 3 C.M.L.R. 46; [2014] B.T.C. 18, ECJ (1st Chamber)

Emerson Electric Co v Mersen UK Portslade Ltd (formerly Le Carbone (Great Britain) Ltd); *sub nom* Emerson Electric Co v Morgan Crucible Co Plc [2012] EWCA Civ 1559; [2013] Bus. L.R. 342; [2013] U.K.C.L.R. 81, CA (Civ Div) .................. *Digested,* 13/**491**: *Followed* 14/549

Emerson Electric Co v Morgan Crucible Co Plc see Emerson Electric Co v Mersen UK Portslade Ltd (formerly Le Carbone (Great Britain) Ltd)

EMI (IP) Ltd v British Sky Broadcasting Group Plc see Starbucks (UK) Ltd v British Sky Broadcasting Group Plc

EMI Group Electronics Ltd v Coldicott (Inspector of Taxes); *sub nom* Thorn EMI Electronics Ltd v Coldicott (Inspector of Taxes) [2000] 1 W.L.R. 540; [1999] S.T.C. 803; [1999] I.R.L.R. 630; 71 T.C. 455; [1999] B.T.C. 294; (1999) 96(32) L.S.G. 34; (1999) 143 S.J.L.B. 220; Independent, October 11, 1999, CA (Civ Div); affirming [1997] S.T.C. 1372; [1997] B.T.C. 532; (1997) 94(43) L.S.G. 29; (1997) 141 S.J.L.B. 222; Times, November 14, 1997; Independent, November 10, 1997, Ch D; affirming [1996] S.T.C. (S.C.D.) 455, Sp Comm ........................ *Digested,* 99/**4729**: *Considered* 01/5274, 14/2908: *Followed* 12/3311

EMI Records Ltd v British Sky Broadcasting Ltd [2013] EWHC 379 (Ch); [2013] Bus. L.R. 884; [2013] E.C.D.R. 8; [2013] F.S.R. 31; Times, April 23, 2013, Ch D ....... *Digested,* 13/**1752**: *Applied* 13/1763, 14/1868

Emilio Pucci (Societe) v H&M Hennes and Mauritz AB [2014] I.L.Pr. 21, Cass (F)

Emirates Trading Agency LLC v Prime Mineral Exports Private Ltd [2014] EWHC 2104 (Comm); [2014] 2 Lloyd's Rep. 457; (2014) 164(7615) N.L.J. 19, QBD (Comm) .................................... *Digested,* 14/**629**

Emmett v Sisson [2014] EWCA Civ 64; [2014] 2 P. & C.R. 3, CA (Civ Div) .................. *Digested,* 14/**2519**

Emmott v Attorney General (C-208/90) see Emmott v Minister for Social Welfare (C-208/90)

Emmott v Minister for Social Welfare (C-208/90); *joined case* Emmott v Attorney General (C-208/90) [1991] E.C.R. I-4269; [1991] 3 C.M.L.R. 894; [1993] I.C.R. 8; [1991] I.R.L.R. 387, ECJ .................................... *Digested,* 92/**4840**: *Considered* 95/2112, 96/2573, 96/2577, 06/4028, 07/2490, 14/3077: *Distinguished* 95/4639, 97/3983, 99/5284, 07/1639, 07/1640, 09/1407: *Followed* 92/1974

Emokpae v Chamberlin Solicitors see Wong v Igen Ltd (formerly Leeds Careers Guidance)

Empresa Exportadora De Azucar (CUBAZUCAR) v Industria Azucarera Nacional SA (IANSA) (The Playa Larga and Marble Islands) [1983] 2 Lloyd's Rep. 171; [1983] Com. L.R. 58; Times, December 13, 1982, CA (Civ Div); affirming [1982] Com. L.R. 171, QBD (Comm) .................................... *Digested,* 83/**411**: *Applied* 94/4066: *Considered* 94/1758, 96/1219, 14/557

Emre v Switzerland (5056/10) (2014) 59 E.H.R.R. 11, ECHR

Emrek v Sabranovic (C-218/12) [2014] Bus. L.R. 104; [2014] C.E.C. 888; [2014] I.L.Pr. 39, ECJ (3rd Chamber)

EMS (Independent Accident Management Services) Ltd v Revenue and Customs Commissioners [2014] UKFTT 891 (TC); [2014] S.T.I. 3429, FTT (Tax)

Emslie v Scottish Ministers 2014 S.L.T. (Lands Tr) 39; [2014] R.V.R. 302; 2014 G.W.D. 6-132, Lands Tr (Scot) .................................... *Digested,* 14/**3725**

Emslie & Simpson Ltd v City of Aberdeen DC 1995 S.L.T. 355; [1994] 1 E.G.L.R. 33; [1994] 18 E.G. 136, IH (1 Div) .......... *Digested,* 94/**5474**: *Applied* 02/3828: *Considered* 14/2357

EN v Westminster Magistrates' Court see R. (on the application of B) v Westminster Magistrates' Court

Enderby v Frenchay HA (C-127/92) [1994] 1 All E.R. 495; [1993] E.C.R. I-5535; [1994] 1 C.M.L.R. 8; [1994] I.C.R. 112; [1993] I.R.L.R. 591; Times, November 12, 1993; Financial Times, November 2, 1993, ECJ (1st Chamber) .......... *Digested,* 94/**4813**: *Applied* 05/1268, 06/1364, 14/1103: *Considered* 96/2550, 97/5226, 06/1368, 09/1206, 12/1101, 12/1144, 13/1012: *Distinguished* 94/1979, 04/1254: *Followed* 96/5713, 03/1275

Endowment Fund for the Rehabilitation of Tigray v Chubb see Mengiste v Endowment Fund for the Rehabilitation of Tigray

Enel Maritsa Iztok 3 AD v Direktor Obzhalvane i Upravlenie na Izpalnenieto NAP (C-107/10) (Unreported, May 12, 2011), ECJ *Applied* 14/3077

Ener-G Holdings Plc v Hormell [2012] EWCA Civ 1059; [2013] 1 All E.R. (Comm) 1162; [2012] C.P. Rep. 47; 144 Con. L.R. 43; [2012] 3 E.G.L.R. 61; [2012] 45 E.G. 96, CA (Civ Div); affirming [2011] EWHC 3290 (Comm); [2012] 1 All E.R. (Comm) 466, QBD (Comm) .......... *Digested,* 13/**575**: *Considered* 14/270

Energy Financing Team Ltd v Director of the Serious Fraud Office see R. (on the application of Energy Financing Team Ltd) v Bow Street Magistrates Court

Energy Renewals Ltd v Borg [2014] EWHC 2166 (Ch); [2014] I.R.L.R. 713, Ch D

Enfield LBC v Hutchinson 3G UK Ltd [2013] R.A. 429, MC .......... *Digested,* 14/**2140**

Enfield LBC v Outdoor Plus Ltd [2012] EWCA Civ 608; [2012] C.P. Rep. 35; [2012] 2 E.G.L.R. 105; [2012] 29 E.G. 86, CA (Civ Div) .......... *Digested,* 12/**860**: *Applied* 14/824

Engel v Netherlands (A/22) (1979-80) 1 E.H.R.R. 647, ECHR *Applied* 88/2973, 98/3119, 00/3235, 02/3349, 03/4604, 03/866, 03/925, 05/2909, 05/4164, 06/4640, 07/2172, 07/2226, 08/1956, 08/1958, 09/2008, 10/975, 12/2288, 12/3127: *Considered* 01/98, 02/2470, 02/2619, 03/2141, 04/2777, 04/3144, 06/5128, 07/2171, 07/54, 07/953, 09/1098, 09/1934, 09/2033, 11/1691, 14/2657

Engel v Peri; *sub nom* Peri v Engel [2002] EWHC 799 (Ch); [2002] B.P.I.R. 961; (2002) 99(23) L.S.G. 27; (2002) 146 S.J.L.B. 135, Ch D .......... *Digested,* 03/**2376**: *Applied* 05/2210, 08/2132, 14/1754: *Considered* 10/1903

England v Magill see Porter v Magill

English v Emery Reimbold & Strick Ltd; *joined cases* DJ&C Withers (Farms) Ltd v Ambic Equipment Ltd; Verrechia (t/a Freightmaster Commercials) v Commissioner of Police of the Metropolis [2002] EWCA Civ 605; [2002] 1 W.L.R. 2409; [2002] 3 All E.R. 385; [2002] C.P.L.R. 520; [2003] I.R.L.R. 710; [2002] U.K.H.R.R. 957; (2002) 99(22) L.S.G. 34; (2002) 152 N.L.J. 758; (2002) 146 S.J.L.B. 123; Times, May 10, 2002; Independent, May 7, 2002, CA (Civ Div) .......... *Digested,* 02/**301**: *Applied* 02/371, 04/2698, 05/1212, 05/1256, 05/950, 06/1335, 06/4090, 06/498, 07/1434, 07/249, 09/1747, 11/1107, 11/217, 12/1357, 12/2040: *Considered* 03/1544, 03/847, 05/2213, 06/2226, 06/468, 07/2453, 07/466, 08/283, 13/1280, 13/1536, 13/312: *Distinguished* 05/1138: *Followed* 12/1347, 13/112, 13/1442, 14/3059: *Referred to* 11/1142

English & American Insurance Co Ltd, Re [2013] EWHC 3360 (Ch); [2014] W.T.L.R. 57; [2014] 1 P. & C.R. DG11, Ch D .......... *Digested,* 14/**3030**

English Bridge Union Ltd v Revenue and Customs Commissioners [2014] UKFTT 181 (TC); [2014] S.F.T.D. 843; [2014] S.T.I. 1608, FTT (Tax)

English Cities Fund (General Partners) Ltd v Grace (Valuation Officer) [2013] R.A. 215, VT .......... *Digested,* 13/**2404**: *Applied* 14/2132: *Doubted* 14/2083

English Welsh & Scottish Railway Ltd v Enron Coal Services Ltd (In Liquidation) see Enron Coal Services Ltd (In Liquidation) v English Welsh & Scottish Railway Ltd

Ennis v Lovell [2014] R.P.C. 32, App Person

Enron Coal Services Ltd (In Liquidation) v English Welsh & Scottish Railway Ltd; *sub nom* English Welsh & Scottish Railway Ltd v Enron Coal Services Ltd (In Liquidation) [2009] EWCA Civ 647; [2010] Bus. L.R. 28; [2009] U.K.C.L.R. 816; Times, July 21, 2009, CA (Civ Div); reversing [2009] CAT 7, CAT .......... *Digested,* 09/**549**: *Applied* 11/431: *Considered* 10/481, 11/442: *Followed* 11/437, 14/541

Enron Coal Services Ltd (In Liquidation) v English Welsh & Scottish Railway Ltd [2011] EWCA Civ 2; [2011] U.K.C.L.R. 303; (2011) 108(5) L.S.G. 18, CA (Civ Div); affirming [2009] CAT 36; [2010] Comp. A.R. 108; [2010] E.C.C. 7, CAT .... *Digested,* 11/**431**: *Followed* 11/437, 12/523, 13/494, 14/541

Enta Technologies Ltd v Revenue and Customs Commissioners see Enta Technologies Ltd, Re

Enta Technologies Ltd, Re; *sub nom* Changtel Solutions UK Ltd (formerly Enta Technologies Ltd) v Revenue and Customs Commissioners; Revenue and Customs Commissioners v Changtel Solutions UK Ltd (formerly Enta Technologies Ltd); Enta Technologies Ltd v Revenue and Customs Commissioners [2014] EWHC 548 (Ch); [2014] B.C.C. 683; [2014] B.P.I.R. 543; [2014] B.V.C. 22, Ch D (Companies Ct) .... *Digested,* 14/**1833**

Enterprise Holdings Inc v Europcar Group UK Ltd [2014] EWHC 2498 (Ch); [2014] E.T.M.R. 50, Ch D .... *Digested,* 14/**1935**

Entrust Pension Ltd v Prospect Hospice Ltd [2012] EWHC 1666 (Ch); [2012] Pens. L.R. 341, Ch D .... *Digested,* 12/**2372**: *Applied* 14/2278

Entry Clearance Officer, Madrid v Yarce see Yarce (Adequate Maintenance: Benefits: Spain), Re

Entry Clearance Officer, Manila v Lim see Lim (EEA: Dependency: Malaysia)

Entry Clearance Officer, New York v F see F (Para 320(8): Type of Leave: USA), Re

Environment Agency v Campbell see Holmes v Campbell

Environment Agency v Donnelly [2014] Eq. L.R. 13, EAT .... *Digested,* 14/**1046**

Environment Agency v Milford Haven Port Authority (The Sea Empress); *sub nom* R. v Milford Haven Port Authority [2000] 2 Cr. App. R. (S.) 423; [2000] Env. L.R. 632; [2000] J.P.L. 943, CA (Crim Div); reversing in part [1999] 1 Lloyd's Rep. 673, Crown Ct (Cardiff) .... *Digested,* 00/**2291**: *Considered* 07/3655, 08/3288, 11/1632, 14/2632

Environment Agency v Rowan [2008] I.C.R. 218; [2008] I.R.L.R. 20, EAT .... *Digested,* 08/**1134**: *Applied* 11/1058, 12/1064, 12/1066, 13/974, 13/975, 14/1044: *Considered* 09/1178, 10/1046, 13/968: *Followed* 12/1065

Environmental Manufacturing LLP v Office for Harmonisation in the Internal Market (Trade Marks and Designs) (OHIM) (C-383/12) (Unreported, November 14, 2013), ECJ *Applied* 14/1921

Environmental Recycling Technologies Plc v Stillwell [2012] EWHC 2097 (Pat), Ch D (Patents Ct) *Considered* 14/493

Envoygate (Installations) Ltd v Revenue and Customs Commissioners [2014] UKFTT 221 (TC); [2014] S.T.I. 1661, FTT (Tax)

Equality and Human Rights Commission v Earle [2014] I.R.L.R. 845, EAT .... *Digested,* 14/**1027**

Equitas Ltd v Walsham Bros & Co Ltd [2013] EWHC 3264 (Comm); [2014] Lloyd's Rep. I.R. 398; [2014] P.N.L.R. 8; [2014] Bus. L.R. D7, QBD (Comm) .... *Digested,* 14/**1840**

Equoland Soc coop arl v Agenzia delle Dogane - Ufficio delle Dogane di Livorno (C-272/13) [2014] S.T.C. 2487; [2014] B.V.C. 36, ECJ (6th Chamber)

Eremia v Moldova (3564/11) (2014) 58 E.H.R.R. 2; [2013] Eq. L.R. 911, ECHR

Erimus Housing Ltd v Barclays Wealth Trustees (Jersey) Ltd see Barclays Wealth Trustees (Jersey) Ltd v Erimus Housing Ltd

Erkapic v Croatia (51198/08) 35 B.H.R.C. 564, ECHR

Erlanger v New Sombrero Phosphate Co; *sub nom* New Sombrero Phosphate Co v Erlanger (1878) 3 App. Cas. 1218, HL; affirming (1877) 5 Ch. D. 73, CA *Applied* 53/2071, 71/1318, 77/1207, 84/388, 95/842, 06/743: *Considered* 96/4972, 07/799, 14/511

Erste Group Bank AG (London) v JSC (VMZ Red October) [2013] EWHC 2926 (Comm); [2014] B.P.I.R. 81, QBD (Comm) .... *Digested,* 14/**479**: *Applied* 14/562

Erven Warnink BV v J Townend & Sons (Hull) Ltd (No.1) [1979] A.C. 731; [1979] 3 W.L.R. 68; [1979] 2 All E.R. 927; [1979] F.S.R. 397; [1980] R.P.C. 31; (1979) 123 S.J. 47, HL; reversing [1978] F.S.R. 473, CA (Civ Div); reversing [1978] F.S.R. 1, Ch D .... *Digested,* 79/**2690**: *Applied* 80/2728, 81/2789, 84/3531, 94/4293, 95/4938, 95/6459, 98/3523, 02/2770, 11/2010: *Considered* 83/475, 84/3534, 84/3536, 90/4319, 96/3637, 96/3638, 07/2674: *Followed* 99/6314, 10/1955, 11/1961, 13/1793, 14/1889: *Referred to* 94/4290, 97/4902

ES (Iran) v Secretary of State for the Home Department see JD (Congo) v Secretary of State for the Home Department

Esdaile v Payne see Lane v Esdaile

Esparon (t/a Middle West Residential Care Home ) v Slavikovska [2014] I.C.R. 1037; [2014] I.R.L.R. 598, EAT ........ *Digested,* 14/**1091**

Esporta Ltd v Revenue and Customs Commissioners; *sub nom* Revenue and Customs Commissioners v Esporta Ltd [2014] EWCA Civ 155; [2014] S.T.C. 1548; [2014] B.V.C. 28; [2014] L.L.R. 483; [2014] S.T.I. 741, CA (Civ Div); affirming [2013] UKUT 173 (TCC); [2013] S.T.C. 2139; [2013] B.V.C. 1663; [2013] S.T.I. 3454, UT (Tax); reversing [2011] UKFTT 633 (TC), FTT (Tax) ...... *Digested,* 14/**3090**

Essa v Secretary of State for the Home Department see Essa (EEA: Rehabilitation/Integration), Re

Essa (EEA: Rehabilitation/Integration), Re; *sub nom* Essa v Secretary of State for the Home Department [2013] UKUT 316 (IAC); [2013] Imm. A.R. 980, UT (IAC) ..... *Digested,* 14/**1676**: *Approved* 14/1670

Esso Societe anonyme francaise v European Commission (T-540/08) [2014] 5 C.M.L.R. 15, GC (3rd Chamber)

Essop v Home Office (UK Border Agency) [2014] I.C.R. 871; [2014] I.R.L.R. 592; [2014] Eq. L.R. 377, EAT ........ *Digested,* 14/**1103**

Estate Agency Affairs Board v Auction Alliance (Pty) Ltd 36 B.H.R.C. 443, Const Ct (SA)

ET v TZ (Recognition and Enforcement of Foreign Residence Order) [2013] EWHC 2621 (Fam); [2014] 2 F.L.R. 373; [2014] Fam. Law 36, Fam Div ........ *Digested,* 14/**1432**

ET Agrokonsulting-04-Velko Stoyanov v Izpalnitelen direktor na Darzhaven fond 'Zemedelie' - Razplashtatelna agentsia (C-93/12) [2014] 1 C.M.L.R. 3, ECJ (3rd Chamber)

ETC (East Anglia) Ltd v Revenue and Customs Commissioners [2014] UKFTT 98 (TC); [2014] S.T.I. 800, FTT (Tax)

EU (Afghanistan) v Secretary of State for the Home Department see KA (Afghanistan) v Secretary of State for the Home Department

Euro Foods Group v Cumbria CC [2013] EWHC 2659 (Admin); (2013) 177 J.P. 614, DC ........ *Digested,* 14/**766**

Euro-Asian Oil SA v Abilo (UK) Ltd [2013] EWHC 485 (Comm); [2014] 1 All E.R. (Comm) 162, QBD (Comm) ........ *Digested,* 14/**476**

Eurofood IFSC Ltd, Re (C-341/04); *sub nom* Bondi v Bank of America NA (C-341/04) [2006] Ch. 508; [2006] 3 W.L.R. 309; [2006] E.C.R. I-3813; [2006] B.C.C. 397; [2007] 2 B.C.L.C. 151; [2006] All E.R. (EC) 1078; [2006] I.L.Pr. 23; [2006] B.P.I.R. 661, ECJ; no effect [2006] E.C.R. I-3813; [2005] B.C.C. 1021, AGO ..... *Digested,* 07/**2428**: *Applied* 07/2411, 08/1284, 09/2192, 10/1873, 11/1823, 11/1873, 14/1808: *Considered* 08/4023, 13/108, 13/1693: *Followed* 14/1817

Europa Oil and Gas Ltd v Secretary of State for Communities and Local Government [2014] EWCA Civ 825; [2014] P.T.S.R. 1471; [2014] J.P.L. 1259, CA (Civ Div); affirming [2013] EWHC 2643 (Admin); [2014] 1 P. & C.R. 3; [2014] J.P.L. 21, QBD (Admin) ........ *Digested,* 14/**2381**: *Considered* 14/2394

European Action of the Disabled (AEH) v France (81/2012) (2014) 58 E.H.R.R. SE13, ECSR

European Commission v Belgium (C-296/12) [2014] 2 C.M.L.R. 48; [2014] B.T.C. 6, ECJ (10th Chamber)

European Commission v Belgium (C-383/10) [2013] 3 C.M.L.R. 48; [2014] C.E.C. 559; [2013] B.V.C. 218, ECJ (5th Chamber)

European Commission v Council of the European Union (C-114/12) [2014] E.C.D.R. 18, AGO

European Commission v Council of the European Union (C-137/12) [2014] 2 C.M.L.R. 14, ECJ (Grand Chamber)

European Commission v Dimosia Epicheirisi Ilektrismou AE (DEI) (C-553/12 P) [2014] 5 C.M.L.R. 19, ECJ (3rd Chamber)

European Commission v EnBW Energie Baden-Wurttemberg AG (C-365/12 P) [2014] 4 C.M.L.R. 30, ECJ (3rd Chamber)

European Commission v European Parliament (C-427/12) [2014] 3 C.M.L.R. 23, ECJ (Grand Chamber)

European Commission v Germany (C-95/12) [2014] 2 C.M.L.R. 12; [2014] C.E.C. 903, ECJ (Grand Chamber)

European Commission v Hungary (C-288/12) [2014] 3 C.M.L.R. 42; [2014] All E.R. (EC) 895, ECJ (Grand Chamber)

European Commission v Ireland (C-272/12 P) [2014] 2 C.M.L.R. 29, ECJ (Grand Chamber)

European Commission v Italy (C-312/11) (Unreported, July 4, 2013), ECJ *Considered* 14/1038

European Commission v Kadi (C-584/10 P) [2014] 1 C.M.L.R. 24; [2014] All E.R. (EC) 123; (2013) 163(7578) N.L.J. 20, ECJ (Grand Chamber)

European Commission v Lithuania (C-61/12) [2014] 3 C.M.L.R. 25, ECJ (5th Chamber)
European Commission v Netherlands (C-224/12 P) [2014] 3 C.M.L.R. 41, ECJ (2nd Chamber)
European Commission v Netherlands (C-576/10) [2014] 1 C.M.L.R. 12, ECJ (1st Chamber)
European Commission v Poland (C-569/10) [2014] 1 C.M.L.R. 4, ECJ (4th Chamber)
European Commission v Poland (C-639/11) [2014] 3 C.M.L.R. 26, ECJ (5th Chamber)
European Commission v Siemens AG Osterreich (C-231/11 P) [2014] 5 C.M.L.R. 1, ECJ (4th Chamber)
European Commission v United Kingdom (C-112/14) [2014] B.T.C. 51; [2014] S.T.I. 3297, ECJ (8th Chamber)
European Commission v United Kingdom (C-172/13) [2014] B.T.C. 49, AGO
European Commission v United Kingdom (C-530/11) [2014] Q.B. 988; [2014] 3 W.L.R. 853; [2014] 3 C.M.L.R. 6; [2014] Env. L.R. D2, ECJ (2nd Chamber) ................. *Digested,* 14/**1222**
European Confederation of Police (EuroCOP) v Ireland (2014) 59 E.H.R.R. SE10, ECSR
European Drinks SA v Office for Harmonisation in the Internal Market (Trade Marks and Designs) (OHIM) (T-495/12) [2014] E.T.M.R. 43, GC (9th Chamber)
European Medicines Agency (EMA) v AbbVie Inc (C-389/13 P(R)) [2014] 2 C.M.L.R. 21, ECJ
European Risk Insurance Co hf v McManus (t/a McManus Seddon Runhams) see McManus v European Risk Insurance Co hf
European Tour Operators Association v Revenue and Customs Commissioners [2014] UKFTT 213 (TC); [2014] S.T.I. 1658, FTT (Tax)
Euroption Strategic Fund Ltd v Skandinaviska Enskilda Banken AB [2012] EWHC 584 (Comm); [2013] 1 B.C.L.C. 125; [2013] Bus. L.R. D67, QBD (Comm) ............... *Digested,* 13/**217**: *Applied* 14/242
Evans v Bremridge 69 E.R. 741; (1855) 2 Kay & J. 174, Ct of Chancery
*Applied* 14/637
Evans v Cig Mon Cymru Ltd [2008] EWCA Civ 390; [2008] 1 W.L.R. 2675; [2008] P.I.Q.R. P17, CA (Civ Div) ........................................................................ *Digested,* 09/**353**: *Applied* 14/418: *Distinguished* 14/430
Evans v Finance-U-Ltd [2013] EWCA Civ 869; [2014] R.T.R. 8; [2013] E.C.C. 26; [2013] B.P.I.R. 1001; [2014] C.T.L.C. 133, CA (Civ Div) ................................... *Digested,* 13/**549**
Evans v Royal Wolverhampton Hospitals NHS Foundation Trust [2014] EWHC 3185 (QB); [2014] 6 Costs L.O. 899, QBD
Evans v Wimbledon and Putney Commons Conservators [2014] EWCA Civ 940; [2014] 2 P. & C.R. 17, CA (Civ Div); affirming [2013] EWHC 3411 (Admin); [2013] 46 E.G. 109 (C.S.), QBD (Admin) ........................................................ *Digested,* 14/**2498**
Evans Marshall & Co v Bertola SA (No.1) [1973] 1 W.L.R. 349; [1973] 1 All E.R. 992; [1973] 1 Lloyd's Rep. 453; (1972) 117 S.J. 225, CA (Civ Div) ............................ *Digested,* 73/**2659**: *Applied* 10/362: *Considered* 74/2784, 14/409
Evialis SA v SIAT [2003] EWHC 863 (Comm); [2003] 2 Lloyd's Rep. 377; [2003] 2 C.L.C. 802; [2003] I.L.Pr. 43; [2004] Lloyd's Rep. I.R. 187, QBD (Comm) .......... *Digested,* 03/**609**: *Applied* 08/562: *Considered* 05/614: *Disapproved* 14/565
Evn AG v Austria (C-448/01) [2003] E.C.R. I-14527; [2004] 1 C.M.L.R. 22, ECJ (6th Chamber) ..................................................................................................... *Digested,* 04/**3163**: *Applied* 11/2109, 14/2475
Eweida v United Kingdom (48420/10); *joined cases* Chaplin v United Kingdom (59842/10); Ladele v United Kingdom (51671/10); McFarlane v United Kingdom (36516/10) [2013] I.R.L.R. 231; (2013) 57 E.H.R.R. 8; 34 B.H.R.C. 519; [2013] Eq. L.R. 264; (2013) 163 N.L.J. 70; Times, February 4, 2013, ECHR ................ *Digested,* 13/**1548**: *Considered* 14/3099: *Followed* 13/1568
Examination of clarity of amended claims by Opposition Divisions and Boards of Appeal (T373/12) [2014] E.P.O.R. 27, EPO (Technical Bd App)
Excalibur Ventures LLC v Texas Keystone Inc [2014] EWHC 3436 (Comm); [2014] 6 Costs L.O. 975, QBD (Comm)
Excel RTI Solutions Ltd v Revenue and Customs Commissioners see Universal Enterprises (EU) Ltd v Revenue and Customs Commissioners
Excelsior Commercial & Industrial Holdings Ltd v Salisbury Hamer Aspden & Johnson (Costs); *sub nom* Excelsior Commercial & Industrial Holdings Ltd v Salisbury Hammer Aspden & Johnson [2002] EWCA Civ 879; [2002] C.P. Rep. 67; [2002] C.P.L.R. 693; Independent, June 18, 2002, CA (Civ Div) ........................ *Digested,* 02/**353**: *Applied* 07/399, 09/373, 10/1283, 11/285, 11/288, 13/309: *Considered* 06/380, 07/398, 08/318, 09/374, 10/290: *Followed* 14/1337

Excelsior Commercial & Industrial Holdings Ltd v Salisbury Hammer Aspden & Johnson see Excelsior Commercial & Industrial Holdings Ltd v Salisbury Hamer Aspden & Johnson (Costs)
Executors of Verdegaal's Estate v Revenue and Customs Commissioners [2014] UKFTT 878 (TC); [2014] S.T.I. 3242, FTT (Tax)
EXIQON/Bi-cyclic nucleoside analogues (T2165/08) [2014] E.P.O.R. 34, EPO (Technical Bd App)
Explora Group Ltd v Trading Force Ltd see Explora Group Plc v Hesco Bastion Ltd
Explora Group Plc v Hesco Bastion Ltd; *joined case* Explora Group Ltd v Trading Force Ltd [2005] EWCA Civ 646; (2005) 149 S.J.L.B. 924, CA (Civ Div); reversing [2004] EWHC 1863 (QB), QBD
*Considered* 14/2529
Exton v West Dorset DC [2014] P.A.D. 11, Planning Inspector
Extreme Oyster v Guildford BC see R. (on the application of Extreme Oyster) v Guildford BC
EY v EZ [2013] EWHC 4403 (Fam); [2014] Fam. Law 785, Fam Div (Leeds)
Eyedial Ltd v Revenue and Customs Commissioners [2013] UKUT 432 (TCC); [2014] S.T.C. 520; [2013] B.V.C. 1802; [2013] S.T.I. 3056, UT (Tax); affirming [2011] UKFTT 47 (TC), FTT (Tax) ........ *Digested,* 14/**3064**
Eyitene v Wirral MBC [2014] EWCA Civ 1243; [2014] I.R.L.R. 944, CA (Civ Div)

F v B see F (Abduction: Consent), Re
F v F (MMR Vaccine); *sub nom* F v F (Welfare of Children: Immunisation) [2013] EWHC 2683 (Fam); [2014] 1 F.L.R. 1328; (2014) 136 B.M.L.R. 105; [2014] Fam. Law 29, Fam Div ........ *Digested,* 14/**1304**
F v F (Welfare of Children: Immunisation) see F v F (MMR Vaccine)
F v Harrow LBC see B v Harrow LBC (No.1)
F v Premier ministre (C-168/13 PPU) [2014] 2 C.M.L.R. 19, ECJ (2nd Chamber)
F v Shears (Unreported, June 5, 2013), QBD [*Fletchers Solicitors, Dukes House, 34 Hoghton Street, Southport*] ........ *Digested,* 14/**2313**
F v Special Education Needs Tribunal see B v Harrow LBC (No.1)
F v Wychavon DC see K v Wolverhampton City Council
F v Y (Abduction: Acquiescence) [2014] 2 F.L.R. 875; [2014] Fam. Law 406, Fam Div
F (A Child) (Abduction: Art.13(b): Psychiatric Assessment), Re [2014] EWCA Civ 275; [2014] 2 F.L.R. 1115; [2014] Fam. Law 767, CA (Civ Div)
F (A Child) (Appeal from Placement Order), Re; *sub nom* F (A Child) (Placement Order: Best Interests), Re [2013] EWCA Civ 1277; [2014] 1 F.C.R. 415; [2014] Fam. Law 161, CA (Civ Div) ........ *Digested,* 14/**1253**
F (A Child) (Care Proceedings: Habitual Residence), Re [2014] EWCA Civ 789; [2014] Fam. Law 1244, CA (Civ Div)
F (A Child) (Family Proceedings: Costs), Re [2008] EWCA Civ 938; [2008] 2 F.L.R. 1662; [2008] Fam. Law 981, CA (Civ Div) ........ *Digested,* 09/**1594**:
*Followed* 14/1335
F (A Child) (Immunisation: Parental Rights), Re see C (A Child) (Immunisation: Parental Rights), Re
F (A Child) (Placement Order: Best Interests), Re see F (A Child) (Appeal from Placement Order), Re
F (A Child) (Return Order: Power to Revoke), Re; *sub nom* TF v PJ (Reversal of Judgment) [2014] EWHC 1780 (Fam); [2014] 1 W.L.R. 4375; [2014] Fam. Law 1226, Fam Div
F (Abduction: Consent), Re; *sub nom* F v B [2014] EWHC 484 (Fam); [2014] Fam. Law 768, Fam Div
F (Adult Patient), Re see F (Adult: Court's Jurisdiction), Re
F (Adult: Court's Jurisdiction), Re; *sub nom* F (Adult Patient), Re [2001] Fam. 38; [2000] 3 W.L.R. 1740; [2000] 2 F.L.R. 512; [2000] 3 F.C.R. 30; [2000] U.K.H.R.R. 712; (2000) 3 C.C.L. Rep. 210; [2000] Lloyd's Rep. Med. 381; (2000) 55 B.M.L.R. 81; [2000] M.H.L.R. 120; [2000] Fam. Law 709; (2000) 97(35) L.S.G. 37; (2000) 97(36) L.S.G. 41; Times, July 25, 2000; Independent, July 6, 2000, CA (Civ Div) ........ *Digested,* 00/**4171**:
*Applied* 01/2662, 04/3648: *Considered* 11/2220: *Followed* 07/3911, 14/436
F (Habitual Residence: Peripatetic Existence), Re see Derbyshire CC v F
F (Mental Capacity: Interim Jurisdiction), Re [2010] 2 F.L.R. 28; (2009) 12 C.C.L. Rep. 530; [2009] M.H.L.R. 196; [2009] W.T.L.R. 1309; [2010] Fam. Law 243, CP ...... *Digested,* 10/**1587**:
*Applied* 11/2221, 14/2159
F (Para 320(8): Type of Leave: USA), Re; *sub nom* Entry Clearance Officer, New York v F [2013] UKUT 309 (IAC); [2013] Imm. A.R. 839, UT (IAC) ........ *Digested,* 14/**1687**

F&C Alternative Investments (Holdings) Ltd v Barthelemy (Costs); *sub nom* Barthelemy v F&C Alternative Investments (Holdings) Ltd; *joined case* F&C Partners LLP, Re [2012] EWCA Civ 843; [2013] 1 W.L.R. 548; [2012] 4 All E.R. 1096; [2013] Bus. L.R. 186; [2013] 1 Costs L.R. 35, CA (Civ Div); reversing [2011] EWHC 2807 (Ch); [2012] Bus. L.R. 891; Times, December 1, 2011, Ch D ........ *Digested,* 13/**320**:
*Applied* 14/343, 14/371: *Considered* 14/445: *Distinguished* 13/323: *Followed* 13/349

F&C Partners LLP, Re see F&C Alternative Investments (Holdings) Ltd v Barthelemy (Costs)

F-K v Poland see R. (on the application of HH) v Westminster City Magistrates' Court

FA (Iraq) v Secretary of State for the Home Department [2011] UKSC 22; [2011] 4 All E.R. 503; [2011] 3 C.M.L.R. 23; (2011) 108(24) L.S.G. 18, SC; no effect [2010] EWCA Civ 696; [2010] 1 W.L.R. 2545; [2011] 1 All E.R. 270; [2010] 3 C.M.L.R. 39, CA (Civ Div) ........ *Digested,* 11/**1750**:
*Applied* 12/1184, 14/1642: *Followed* 11/1711

Faci SpA v European Commission (T-46/10) [2014] 4 C.M.L.R. 27, GC (3rd Chamber)

Factortame Ltd v Secretary of State for the Environment, Transport and the Regions (Costs) (No.2); *sub nom* R. (on the application of Factortame Ltd) v Secretary of State for Transport, Local Government and the Regions (Costs: Champertous Agreement) [2002] EWCA Civ 932; [2003] Q.B. 381; [2002] 3 W.L.R. 1104; [2002] 4 All E.R. 97; [2003] B.L.R. 1; [2002] 3 Costs L.R. 467; (2002) 99(35) L.S.G. 34; (2002) 152 N.L.J. 1313; (2002) 146 S.J.L.B. 178; Times, July 9, 2002; Independent, July 10, 2002; Daily Telegraph, July 11, 2002, CA (Civ Div) ........ *Digested,* 02/**321**:
*Applied* 03/3919, 06/392, 09/369, 14/2032: *Considered* 04/288, 10/2114, 11/2098, 12/623: *Followed* 12/349

Fadairo v Suit Supply UK Lime Street Ltd [2014] I.C.R. D11, EAT

Fagan v Papanicola see Papanicola v Fagan

Fage UK Ltd v Chobani UK Ltd [2014] EWCA Civ 5; [2014] E.T.M.R. 26; [2014] F.S.R. 29; [2014] C.T.L.C. 49, CA (Civ Div); affirming [2013] EWHC 630 (Ch); [2013] E.T.M.R. 28; [2013] F.S.R. 32; (2013) 157(14) S.J.L.B. 31, Ch D ........ *Digested,* 14/**1889**

FAI General Insurance Co Ltd, Re see HIH Casualty & General Insurance Ltd, Re

FAI Insurances Ltd, Re see HIH Casualty & General Insurance Ltd, Re

Fairchild v Glenhaven Funeral Services Ltd (t/a GH Dovener & Son); *joined cases* Matthews v British Uralite Plc; Babcock International Ltd v National Grid Co Plc; Fox v Spousal (Midlands) Ltd; Matthews v Associated Portland Cement Manufacturers (1978) Ltd; Dyson v Leeds City Council (No.2); Pendleton v Stone & Webster Engineering Ltd [2002] UKHL 22; [2003] 1 A.C. 32; [2002] 3 W.L.R. 89; [2002] 3 All E.R. 305; [2002] I.C.R. 798; [2002] I.R.L.R. 533; [2002] P.I.Q.R. P28; [2002] Lloyd's Rep. Med. 361; (2002) 67 B.M.L.R. 90; (2002) 152 N.L.J. 998; Times, June 21, 2002; Independent, June 25, 2002; Daily Telegraph, June 27, 2002, HL; reversing [2001] EWCA Civ 1881; [2002] 1 W.L.R. 1052; [2002] I.C.R. 412; [2002] I.R.L.R. 129; [2002] P.I.Q.R. P27; Times, December 13, 2001; Independent, December 21, 2001; Daily Telegraph, December 20, 2001, CA (Civ Div); affirming 00/TLQ/1284, QBD ...... *Digested,* 02/**2225**:
*Applied* 04/2693, 04/2755, 06/2867, 07/5100, 08/2764, 10/2269: *Considered* 02/3245, 02/3247, 03/2990, 05/2841, 05/4199, 09/2723, 09/2835, 09/2837, 09/425, 11/1905, 11/350, 12/2291, 13/1726: *Explained* 12/1884: *Followed* 06/2866, 11/2249, 14/2996

Fairfield Sentry Ltd (In Liquidation) v Migani; *joined cases* Lombard, Odier & Cie v Fairfield Sentry Ltd (In Liquidation); Credit Suisse London Nominees Ltd v Fairfield Sentry Ltd (In Liquidation); Quilvest Finance Ltd v Fairfield Sentry Ltd (In Liquidation); UBS AG New York v Fairfield Sentry Ltd (In Liquidation) [2014] UKPC 9; [2014] 1 C.L.C. 611; Times, May 1, 2014, PC (BVI)

Fairford Group Ltd Plc (In Liquidation) v Revenue and Customs Commissioners; *sub nom* Revenue and Customs Commissioners v Fairford Partnership Ltd (In Liquidation); Revenue and Customs Commissioners v Fairford Group Plc (In Liquidation) [2014] UKUT 329 (TCC); [2014] B.V.C. 529, UT (Tax); affirming [2014] UKFTT 319 (TC), FTT (Tax) ........ *Digested,* 14/**3063**

Fairhold (Yorkshire) Ltd v Trinity Wharf (SE16) RTM Co Ltd [2013] UKUT 502 (LC); [2014] L. & T.R. 6; [2014] 1 P. & C.R. DG10, UT (Lands) ........ *Digested,* 14/**2516**

Fairhold Mercury Ltd v HQ (Block 1) Action Management Co Ltd [2013] UKUT 487 (LC); [2014] L. & T.R. 5; [2013] 44 E.G. 99 (C.S.); [2014] 1 P. & C.R. DG7, UT (Lands) ........ *Digested,* 14/**2515**

Fairhurst Ward Abbots Ltd v Botes Building Ltd see Fairhurst Ward Abbotts Ltd v Botes Building Ltd

Fairhurst Ward Abbotts Ltd v Botes Building Ltd; *sub nom* Fairhurst Ward Abbots Ltd v Botes Building Ltd [2004] EWCA Civ 83; [2004] I.C.R. 919; [2004] I.R.L.R. 304; (2004) 148 S.J.L.B. 235; Times, February 26, 2004; Independent, February 17, 2004, CA (Civ Div); affirming (2003) 100(22) L.S.G. 29; Times, April 16, 2003, EAT ........ *Digested,* 04/**1298**: *Applied* 08/1197, 14/1131

Fairstar Heavy Transport NV v Adkins [2013] EWCA Civ 886; [2013] 2 C.L.C. 272; [2014] E.M.L.R. 12; [2014] F.S.R. 8; [2014] Bus. L.R. D2, CA (Civ Div); reversing [2012] EWHC 2952 (TCC); [2012] 2 C.L.C. 795; [2012] Info. T.L.R. 39; [2013] C.I.L.L. 3273; [2013] Bus. L.R. D73, QBD (TCC) ........ *Digested,* 14/**80**

Fajemisin v General Dental Council [2013] EWHC 3501 (Admin); [2014] 1 W.L.R. 1169, QBD (Admin) ........ *Digested,* 14/**1493**

Falkonera Shipping Co v Arcadia Energy Pte Ltd [2014] EWCA Civ 713; [2014] 2 Lloyd's Rep. 406; [2014] 1 C.L.C. 931, CA (Civ Div); affirming [2012] EWHC 3678 (Comm); [2013] 1 Lloyd's Rep. 582; [2013] 1 C.L.C. 280, QBD (Comm) ... *Digested,* 14/**2742**

Falmouth and Truro Port HA v South West Water Ltd see R. v Falmouth and Truro Port HA Ex p. South West Water Ltd

Famosa Shipping Co Ltd v Armada Bulk Carriers Ltd (The Fanis) [1994] 1 Lloyd's Rep. 633, QBD (Comm) ........ *Digested,* 95/**4510**: *Applied* 14/827: *Considered* 11/3114: *Followed* 96/5314

Fantask A/S v Industriministeriet (Erhvervsministeriet) (C188/95); *sub nom* Fantask A/S v Ministry of Industry and Trade (C188/95) [1997] E.C.R. I-6783; [1998] 1 C.M.L.R. 473; [1998] All E.R. (E.C.) 1; [1998] C.E.C. 359, ECJ ........ *Digested,* 98/**655**: *Applied* 99/5284, 00/4462, 14/3077: *Considered* 08/4016: *Followed* 13/3132

Fantask A/S v Ministry of Industry and Trade (C188/95) see Fantask A/S v Industriministeriet (Erhvervsministeriet) (C188/95)

Farah v Hillingdon LBC [2014] EWCA Civ 359; [2014] H.L.R. 24, CA (Civ Div) ........ *Digested,* 14/**1594**

Fareham BC v Revenue and Customs Commissioners [2014] UKFTT 1033 (TC); [2014] S.T.I. 3552, FTT (Tax)

Farimani v Gates [1984] 2 E.G.L.R. 66; (1984) 271 E.G. 887; (1984) 81 L.S.G. 1999; (1984) 128 S.J. 615, CA (Civ Div) ........ *Digested,* 84/**1900**: *Considered* 91/2227, 05/2639, 14/1840

Farr v Millerson's Investments (1971) 22 P. & C.R. 1055; [1971] J.P.L. 523, Lands Tr *Applied* 14/2358: *Considered* 10/2696

Farraj v King's Healthcare NHS Trust [2009] EWCA Civ 1203; [2010] 1 W.L.R. 2139; [2010] P.T.S.R. 1176; [2010] P.I.Q.R. P7; [2010] Med. L.R. 1; (2010) 11 B.M.L.R. 131; (2009) 106(46) L.S.G. 19, CA (Civ Div); reversing [2008] EWHC 2468 (QB), QBD ........ *Digested,* 10/**2272**: *Applied* 12/2297: *Approved* 14/2200

Farrell v Whitty (C-356/05) [2007] E.C.R. I-3067; [2007] 2 C.M.L.R. 46; [2007] C.E.C. 718; [2007] Lloyd's Rep. I.R. 525, ECJ ........ *Digested,* 07/**1565**: *Applied* 14/1853: *Considered* 09/2292: *Distinguished* 08/2211

Farrelly (M&E) Building Services Ltd v Byrne Brothers (Formwork) Ltd [2013] EWHC 1186 (TCC); [2013] Bus. L.R. 1413; [2013] C.I.L.L. 3378, QBD (TCC) ........ *Digested,* 14/**586**

Farrugia v Burtenshaw [2014] EWHC 1036 (QB); [2014] Med. L.R. 153, QBD ........ *Digested,* 14/**2306**

Father v SBC see E (A Child) (Care Order: Change of Care Plan), Re

Fazenda Publica v Banco Mais SA (C-183/13) [2014] S.T.C. 2325; [2014] B.V.C. 37; [2014] S.T.I. 2472, ECJ (4th Chamber)

Fazliyski v Bulgaria (40908/05) 35 B.H.R.C. 583, ECHR

FB v IB (Abduction: Habitual Residence) see B v B (Abduction: Habitual Residence)

FB v West Sussex CC see S (Children) (Care Proceedings: Fact-finding Hearing), Re

Federal Commerce & Navigation Co Ltd v Molena Alpha Inc (The Nanfri); *joined cases* Federal Commerce & Navigation Co Ltd v Molena Beta Inc (The Benfri); Federal Commerce & Navigation Co Ltd v Molena Gamma Inc (The Lorfri) [1979] A.C. 757; [1978] 3 W.L.R. 991; [1979] 1 All E.R. 307; [1979] 1 Lloyd's Rep. 201; (1978) 122 S.J. 843; Times, November 29, 1978, HL; affirming in part [1978] Q.B. 927; [1978] 3 W.L.R. 309; [1978] 3 All E.R. 1066; [1978] 2 Lloyd's Rep. 132; (1978) 122 S.J. 347, CA (Civ Div); reversing [1978] 1 Lloyd's Rep. 581, QBD (Comm) ........ *Digested,* 79/**2452**: *Applied* 79/342, 80/1627, 80/2457, 81/2484, 94/4062, 01/941, 10/1241, 11/1251, 11/3117, 13/2839: *Considered* 79/100, 79/156, 80/2460, 80/2792, 85/2604, 85/3203, 93/2495, 94/2797, 97/3366, 08/676, 11/2678: *Distinguished* 83/3413: *Followed* 10/3048, 11/1943, 14/1779, 14/623: *Referred to* 80/99

Federal Commerce & Navigation Co Ltd v Molena Beta Inc (The Benfri) see Federal Commerce & Navigation Co Ltd v Molena Alpha Inc (The Nanfri)

Federal Commerce & Navigation Co Ltd v Molena Gamma Inc (The Lorfri) see Federal Commerce & Navigation Co Ltd v Molena Alpha Inc (The Nanfri)

Federal-Mogul Asbestos Personal Injury Trust v Federal-Mogul Ltd (formerly T&N Plc) [2014] EWHC 2002 (Comm); [2014] Lloyd's Rep. I.R. 671, QBD (Comm)
Federation Against Copyright Theft Ltd v Ashton [2013] EWHC 1923 (Admin); [2014] 1 W.L.R. 1322; [2014] L.L.R. 9, DC ........ *Digested,* 14/**1861**
Federation internationale de football association (FIFA) v European Commission (C-204/11 P) [2014] 1 C.M.L.R. 19, ECJ (3rd Chamber)
Federation internationale de football association (FIFA) v European Commission (C-205/11 P) [2014] 1 C.M.L.R. 20, ECJ (3rd Chamber)
Federation Regionale des Syndicats d'Exploitants Agricoles de la Region Bretagne (FRSEA Bretagne) v Compagnie Financiere et de Participations Roullier CFPR [2014] 5 C.M.L.R. 20, Trib Gde Inst (F)
Feeney v Harvie [2014] HCJAC 84; 2014 S.C.L. 677; 2014 S.C.C.R. 504; [2014] L.L.R. 701; 2014 G.W.D. 25-485, HCJ ........ *Digested,* 14/**3406**
Feeney v Secretary of State for Transport [2013] EWHC 1238 (Admin); [2013] Env. L.R. 34; [2013] A.C.D. 119, QBD (Admin) ........ *Digested,* 13/**2335**: *Considered* 14/2426
Feest v South West SHA [2014] EWHC 177 (QB); [2014] 1 Lloyd's Rep. 419, QBD (Merc) (Bristol) ........ *Digested,* 14/**2309**
Feld v Secretary of State for Business, Innovation and Skills see Secretary of State for Business, Innovation and Skills v Feld
Felixstowe Dock and Railway Co Ltd v Revenue and Customs Commissioners [2014] UKFTT 452 (TC); [2014] S.F.T.D. 955; [2014] S.T.I. 2524, FTT (Tax) ........ *Digested,* 14/**2880**
Felixstowe Dock and Railway Co Ltd v Revenue and Customs Commissioners [2011] UKFTT 838 (TC); [2012] S.F.T.D. 366; 14 I.T.L. Rep. 394; [2012] S.T.I. 285, FTT (Tax) ........ *Digested,* 12/**3252**: *Preliminary ruling given* 14/2881
Felixstowe Dock and Railway Co Ltd v Revenue and Customs Commissioners (C-80/12) [2014] S.T.C. 1489; [2014] 3 C.M.L.R. 31; [2014] All E.R. (EC) 925; [2014] B.T.C. 19; [2014] S.T.I. 1630, ECJ (Grand Chamber) ........ *Digested,* 14/**2881**
Fellowes & Son v Fisher [1976] Q.B. 122; [1975] 3 W.L.R. 184; [1975] 2 All E.R. 829; (1975) 119 S.J. 390, CA (Civ Div) ........ *Digested,* 75/**2642**: *Applied* 14/2477: *Considered* 79/327u: *Not followed* 92/4143: *Referred to* 76/404.u
Fellowes International Holdings Ltd v Kyrgyz Mobil Tel Ltd see AK Investment CJSC v Kyrgyz Mobil Tel Ltd
Feltham v Freer Bouskell [2013] EWHC 1952 (Ch); 152 Con. L.R. 124; [2014] P.N.L.R. 2; [2013] W.T.L.R. 1363, Ch D ........ *Digested,* 13/**2094**
Feltham v Freer Bouskell (Costs) [2013] EWHC 3086 (Ch); [2014] 1 Costs L.O. 29, Ch D ........ *Digested,* 14/**424**
Feltrim Underwriting Agencies Ltd v Arbuthnott see Henderson v Merrett Syndicates Ltd (No.1)
Fenech v Serious Organised Crime Agency [2013] UKFTT 555 (TC); [2014] Lloyd's Rep. F.C. 68, FTT (Tax) ........ *Digested,* 14/**2929**
Fengije v Austria [2014] 2 C.M.L.R. 28, VfGH (A)
Fennelly v Connex South Eastern Ltd [2001] I.R.L.R. 390; Independent, January 22, 2001, CA (Civ Div) ........ *Digested,* 02/**4555**: *Considered* 12/3344, 14/3000
Fenton's Trustee v Inland Revenue Commissioners see Paton v Inland Revenue Commissioners
Fenty v Arcadia Group Brands Ltd (t/a Topshop) [2013] EWHC 2310 (Ch); [2014] E.C.D.R. 3; [2014] F.S.R. 5, Ch D ........ *Digested,* 14/**1890**
Fercometal Sarl v MSC Mediterranean Shipping Co SA (The Simona) [1989] A.C. 788; [1988] 3 W.L.R. 200; [1988] 2 All E.R. 742; [1988] 2 Lloyd's Rep. 199; (1988) 138 N.L.J. Rep. 178; (1988) 132 S.J. 966, HL; affirming [1987] 2 Lloyd's Rep. 236; [1987] 2 F.T.L.R. 254; Times, June 1, 1987, CA (Civ Div); affirming [1986] 1 Lloyd's Rep. 171, QBD (Comm) ........ *Digested,* 88/**3202**: *Applied* 14/119
Ferguson v Revenue and Customs Commissioners [2014] UKFTT 433 (TC); [2014] S.F.T.D. 934; [2014] S.T.I. 2474, FTT (Tax)
Fern Advisers Ltd v Burford [2014] EWHC 762 (QB); [2014] B.P.I.R. 581, QBD ........ *Digested,* 14/**506**
Fern Computer Consultancy Ltd v Intergraph Cadworx & Analysis Solutions Inc [2014] EWHC 2908 (Ch); [2014] Bus. L.R. 1397, Ch D
Fernandez Martinez v Spain (56030/07) 37 B.H.R.C. 1; [2014] E.L.R. 467, ECHR (Grand Chamber)
FG Skerritt Ltd v Caledonian Building Systems Ltd [2013] EWHC 1898 (TCC); [2014] B.P.I.R. 393, QBD (TCC) ........ *Digested,* 14/**579**

FG Whitley & Sons Co Ltd v Secretary of State for Wales (1992) 64 P. & C.R. 296; [1992] 3 P.L.R. 72; [1992] J.P.L. 856; [1992] E.G. 46 (C.S.); [1992] N.P.C. 45; Times, April 2, 1992, CA (Civ Div); affirming (1990) 60 P. & C.R. 185; [1990] 2 P.L.R. 44; [1990] J.P.L. 678; Times, October 24, 1989, QBD .......... *Digested*, 93/**3941**: *Applied* 00/4452, 03/3431, 09/3045, 12/2576, 14/2356: *Considered* 96/4755, 99/4259, 00/4510, 06/3344, 10/360, 11/2555: *Distinguished* 06/3354, 09/3043

FG Wilson (Engineering) Ltd v John Holt & Co (Liverpool) Ltd; *sub nom* Caterpillar (NI) Ltd (formerly FG Wilson (Engineering) Ltd) v John Holt & Co (Liverpool) Ltd [2013] EWCA Civ 1232; [2014] 1 W.L.R. 2365; [2014] 1 All E.R. 785; [2014] 1 All E.R. (Comm) 393; [2014] 1 Lloyd's Rep. 180; [2013] 2 C.L.C. 501; [2014] B.L.R. 103; [2014] B.P.I.R. 1104, CA (Civ Div); reversing [2012] EWHC 2477 (Comm); [2013] 1 All E.R. (Comm) 223; [2012] 2 Lloyd's Rep. 479; [2012] B.L.R. 468; 146 Con. L.R. 94, QBD (Comm) .......... *Digested*, 14/**2586**: *Applied* 13/1812

FH Brundle v Perry [2014] EWHC 979 (IPEC); [2014] 4 Costs L.O. 576, IPEC .......... *Digested*, 14/**1884**

FHR European Ventures LLP v Cedar Capital Partners LLC; *sub nom* FHR European Ventures LLP v Mankarious [2014] UKSC 45; [2014] 3 W.L.R. 535; [2014] 4 All E.R. 79; [2014] 2 All E.R. (Comm) 425; [2014] 2 Lloyd's Rep. 471; [2014] 2 B.C.L.C. 145; [2014] Lloyd's Rep. F.C. 617; [2014] 3 E.G.L.R. 119; [2014] W.T.L.R. 1135, SC; affirming [2013] EWCA Civ 17; [2014] Ch. 1; [2013] 3 W.L.R. 466; [2013] 3 All E.R. 29; [2013] 2 All E.R. (Comm) 257; [2013] 1 Lloyd's Rep. 416; [2013] 2 B.C.L.C. 1; [2013] 2 E.G.L.R. 169; [2013] W.T.L.R. 631; 15 I.T.E.L.R. 902; [2013] 1 P. & C.R. DG24, CA (Civ Div); reversing [2011] EWHC 2999 (Ch), Ch D .......... *Digested*, 14/**79**: *Applied* 14/2588

FHR European Ventures LLP v Mankarious see FHR European Ventures LLP v Cedar Capital Partners LLC

FI (Nigeria) v Secretary of State for the Home Department see EB (Kosovo) v Secretary of State for the Home Department

Fibria Celulose S/A v Pan Ocean Co Ltd see Pan Ocean Co Ltd, Re

Fidex Ltd v Revenue and Customs Commissioners [2014] UKUT 454 (TCC); [2014] B.T.C. 530; [2014] S.T.I. 3425, UT (Tax); reversing [2013] UKFTT 212 (TC); [2013] S.F.T.D. 964, FTT (Tax) .......... *Digested*, 13/**3048**

Figurasin v Central Capital Ltd [2014] EWCA Civ 504; [2014] 2 All E.R. (Comm) 257, CA (Civ Div) .......... *Digested*, 14/**1455**

Finance and Business Training Ltd v Revenue and Customs Commissioners [2013] UKUT 594 (TCC); [2014] S.T.C. 900; [2013] B.V.C. 1860; [2014] S.T.I. 438, UT (Tax); affirming [2012] UKFTT 382 (TC); [2012] S.T.I. 2739, FTT (Tax) .......... *Digested*, 14/**3045**

Finance and Business Training Ltd v Revenue and Customs Commissioners [2014] EWCA Civ 1412; [2014] B.V.C. 48, CA (Civ Div)

Financial Conduct Authority v Asset LI Inc see Financial Services Authority v Asset LI Inc (t/a Asset Land Investment Inc)

Financial Conduct Authority v Capital Alternatives Ltd [2014] EWHC 144 (Ch); [2014] 3 All E.R. 780; [2014] 2 All E.R. (Comm) 481; [2014] Bus. L.R. 1452, Ch D .......... *Digested*, 14/**1439**

Financial Conduct Authority v Hobbs; *sub nom* Hobbs v Financial Conduct Authority; Hobbs v Financial Services Authority [2013] EWCA Civ 918; [2013] Bus. L.R. 1290; [2013] Lloyd's Rep. F.C. 504, CA (Civ Div); reversing [2013] Lloyd's Rep. F.C. 460, UT (Tax) .......... *Digested*, 13/**1366**: *Applied* 14/2247

Financial Services Authority v Asset LI Inc (t/a Asset Land Investment Inc); *sub nom* Financial Conduct Authority v Asset LI Inc; Asset Land Investment Plc v Financial Conduct Authority (formerly The Financial Services Authority) [2014] EWCA Civ 435; [2014] Bus. L.R. 993; [2014] 2 B.C.L.C. 545, CA (Civ Div); affirming [2013] EWHC 178 (Ch); [2013] 2 B.C.L.C. 480, Ch D .......... *Digested*, 14/**1459**: *Applied* 14/1439

Financial Services Authority v Fradley (t/a Top Bet Placement Services); *sub nom* Financial Services Authority v Woodward [2005] EWCA Civ 1183; [2006] 2 B.C.L.C. 616; [2006] L.L.R. 35; Times, December 1, 2005, CA (Civ Div); reversing in part [2004] EWHC 3008 (Ch); [2005] 1 B.C.L.C. 479; [2005] L.L.R. 55; (2004) 101(45) L.S.G. 31; Times, November 8, 2004, Ch D .......... *Digested*, 06/**1736**: *Followed* 14/1459

Financial Services Authority v Rourke (t/a JE Rourke & Co) [2002] C.P. Rep. 14; (2001) 98(46) L.S.G. 36; Times, November 12, 2001, Ch D .......... *Digested*, 01/**543**: *Applied* 10/2751, 10/593, 14/2224: *Considered* 11/1869, 12/591, 13/1730: *Followed* 06/2443

Financial Services Authority v Woodward see Financial Services Authority v Fradley (t/a Top Bet Placement Services)

Financings v Stimson [1962] 1 W.L.R. 1184; [1962] 3 All E.R. 386, CA ......................... *Digested,* 62/**1407**: *Approved* 66/3146: *Considered* 01/880: *Followed* 14/628

Finanzamt Dortmund-West v Klinikum Dortmund gGmbH (C-366/12) [2014] S.T.C. 2197; [2014] B.V.C. 10; [2014] S.T.I. 1564, ECJ (3rd Chamber)

Finanzamt Dusseldorf-Mitte v Ibero Tours GmbH (C-300/12) [2014] Ch. 335; [2014] 2 W.L.R. 1105; [2014] B.V.C. 4; [2014] S.T.I. 628, ECJ (1st Chamber)

Finanzamt Freistadt Rohrbach Urfahr v Unabhangiger Finanzsenat Aussenstelle Linz (C-219/12) [2014] S.T.C. 114; [2014] C.E.C. 231; [2013] B.V.C. 269; [2013] S.T.I. 2300, ECJ (2nd Chamber)

Finanzamt Saarlouis v Malburg (C-204/13) [2014] S.T.C. 1916; [2014] B.V.C. 12; [2014] S.T.I. 1570, ECJ (6th Chamber)

Findlay v Secretary of State for the Home Department see Findlay, Re

Findlay, Re; *sub nom* Findlay v Secretary of State for the Home Department [1985] A.C. 318; [1984] 3 W.L.R. 1159; [1984] 3 All E.R. 801; [1985] Crim. L.R. 154; (1985) 82 L.S.G. 38; (1984) 128 S.J. 816, HL; affirming Times, July 7, 1984, CA (Civ Div); affirming Times, May 23, 1984, DC ............................................ *Digested,* 84/**2756**: *Applied* 94/4983, 99/5221, 00/4490, 07/4378: *Cited* 94/2469: *Considered* 87/20, 87/3617, 94/43, 95/3098, 95/3099, 95/3252, 99/2684, 06/2224, 10/2595: *Followed* 97/3934, 14/2234

Findley v Jones (Unreported, January 13, 2009), Sup Ct Costs Office *Doubted* 14/2053

Fine & Country Ltd v Okotoks Ltd (formerly Spicerhaart Ltd); *sub nom* Okotoks Ltd (formerly Spicerhaart Ltd) v Fine & Country Ltd [2013] EWCA Civ 672; [2014] F.S.R. 11, CA (Civ Div); affirming [2012] EWHC 2230 (Ch); (2012) 109(34) L.S.G. 24, Ch D ........................................................................................ *Digested,* 14/**1872**

Finelvet AG v Vinava Shipping Co Ltd (The Chrysalis) [1983] 1 W.L.R. 1469; [1983] 2 All E.R. 658; [1983] 1 Lloyd's Rep. 503; [1983] Com. L.R. 126; (1983) 80 L.S.G. 2684; (1983) 127 S.J. 680, QBD ........................................................................ *Digested,* 83/**3415**: *Applied* 06/203, 13/2838: *Considered* 11/129, 14/2738: *Followed* 06/740

Finesse Group Ltd v Bryson Products (A Firm) [2013] EWHC 3273 (TCC); [2013] 6 Costs L.R. 991, QBD (TCC) .................................................................... *Digested,* 14/**2204**

Finglands Coachways Ltd v O'Hare [2014] EWHC 1513 (QB); [2014] 4 Costs L.O. 668, QBD ................................................................................................. *Digested,* 14/**331**

Finmeccanica Group Services SpA v Revenue and Customs Commissioners [2014] UKFTT 224 (TC); [2014] S.T.I. 1663, FTT (Tax)

Finn v Revenue and Customs Commissioners [2014] UKFTT 426 (TC); [2014] S.T.I. 2294, FTT (Tax)

Finnamore (t/a Hanbidge Storage Services) v Revenue and Customs Commissioners; *sub nom* Revenue and Customs Commissioners v Finnamore (t/a Hanbidge Storage Services) [2014] UKUT 336 (TCC); [2014] S.T.C. 2754; [2014] B.V.C. 530; [2014] S.T.I. 2580, UT (Tax); reversing [2011] UKFTT 216 (TC); [2011] S.F.T.D. 551; [2011] S.T.I. 1555, FTT (Tax) ....................................................... *Digested,* 14/**3052**: *Considered* 12/3414

Finnigan v Chief Constable of Northumbria [2013] EWCA Civ 1191; [2014] 1 W.L.R. 445; [2013] Eq. L.R. 1201; (2013) 134 B.M.L.R. 1, CA (Civ Div) ......................... *Digested,* 14/**2465**

Fiona Trust & Holding Corp v Privalov; *sub nom* Premium Nafta Products Ltd v Fili Shipping Co Ltd [2007] UKHL 40; [2007] 4 All E.R. 951; [2007] 2 All E.R. (Comm) 1053; [2007] Bus. L.R. 1719; [2008] 1 Lloyd's Rep. 254; [2007] 2 C.L.C. 553; 114 Con. L.R. 69; [2007] C.I.L.L. 2528; (2007) 104(42) L.S.G. 34; (2007) 151 S.J.L.B. 1364; Times, October 25, 2007, HL; affirming [2007] EWCA Civ 20; [2007] 1 All E.R. (Comm) 891; [2007] Bus. L.R. 686; [2007] 2 Lloyd's Rep. 267; [2007] 1 C.L.C. 144; (2007) 23 Const. L.J. 307; (2007) 104(6) L.S.G. 33; Times, January 29, 2007, CA (Civ Div); reversing [2006] EWHC 2583 (Comm); [2007] 1 All E.R. (Comm) 81, QBD (Comm) .............................. *Digested,* 07/**792**: *Applied* 08/154, 09/620, 10/371, 11/75, 12/481: *Considered* 07/529, 08/249, 08/425, 08/670, 09/176, 09/607, 09/733, 10/173, 10/351, 10/563, 11/873, 13/2803, 13/99, 14/557: *Followed* 09/619, 10/353, 10/420, 12/105, 12/114, 13/250, 13/96, 14/133

FIRIN OOD v Direktor na Direktsia 'Obzhalvane i danachno-osiguritelna praktika' (C-107/13) [2014] S.T.C. 1581; [2014] B.V.C. 13; [2014] S.T.I. 1577, ECJ (2nd Chamber)

Firodi Shipping Ltd v Griffon Shipping LLC see Griffon Shipping LLC v Firodi Shipping Ltd (The Griffon)

First City Corp Ltd v Downsview Nominees Ltd see Downsview Nominees Ltd v First City Corp Ltd

First Class Communications Ltd v Revenue and Customs Commissioners [2014] UKUT 244 (TCC); [2014] B.V.C. 521, UT (Tax); affirming [2013] UKFTT 342 (TC), FTT (Tax) ........................................................................................ *Digested,* 14/**3095**

First Nationwide v Revenue and Customs Commissioners; *sub nom* Revenue and Customs Commissioners v First Nationwide [2012] EWCA Civ 278; [2012] S.T.C. 1261; 81 T.C. 738; [2012] B.T.C. 99; [2012] S.T.I. 1372, CA (Civ Div); affirming [2011] UKUT 174 (TCC); [2011] S.T.C. 1540; [2011] B.T.C. 1640; [2011] S.T.I. 1618, UT (Tax); affirming [2010] UKFTT 24 (TC); [2010] S.F.T.D. 408; [2010] S.T.I. 1522, FTT (Tax) ........ *Digested,* 12/**3246**

Fiscale eenheid PPG Holdings BV cs te Hoogezand v Inspecteur van de Belastingdienst/Noord/kantoor Groningen (C-26/12) [2014] S.T.C. 175; [2013] Pens. L.R. 273; [2013] B.V.C. 372; [2013] S.T.I. 2560, ECJ (4th Chamber); no effect [2013] Pens. L.R. 177, AGO

Fischer v Diffley [2013] EWHC 4567 (Ch); [2014] C.O.P.L.R. 212; [2014] W.T.L.R. 757, Ch D ........ *Digested,* 14/**2843**

Fish Legal v Information Commissioner (C-279/12) [2014] Q.B. 521; [2014] 2 W.L.R. 568; [2014] 2 C.M.L.R. 36; [2014] Env. L.R. 18, ECJ (Grand Chamber) ........ *Digested,* 14/**1178**

Fisher v Peterborough City Council [2014] P.A.D. 29, Planning Inspector

Fisher v Revenue and Customs Commissioners [2014] UKFTT 804 (TC); [2014] S.F.T.D. 1341; 17 I.T.L. Rep. 141; [2014] S.T.I. 3128, FTT (Tax) ........ *Digested,* 14/**2916**

Fisscher v Voorhuis Hengelo BV (C-128/93) see Vroege v NCIV Instituut voor Volkshuisvesting BV (C-57/93)

Fitzpatrick v Sarcon (No 177) Ltd [2012] NICA 58; [2014] N.I. 35, CA (NI); reversing [2012] NICh 10, Ch D (NI)

Fitzpatrick v Sterling Housing Association Ltd [2001] 1 A.C. 27; [1999] 3 W.L.R. 1113; [1999] 4 All E.R. 705; [2000] 1 F.L.R. 271; [1999] 2 F.L.R. 1027; [2000] 1 F.C.R. 21; [2000] U.K.H.R.R. 25; 7 B.H.R.C. 200; (2000) 32 H.L.R. 178; [2000] L. & T.R. 44; [2000] Fam. Law 14; [1999] E.G. 125 (C.S.); (1999) 96(43) L.S.G. 3; [1999] N.P.C. 127; (2000) 79 P. & C.R. D4; Times, November 2, 1999; Independent, November 2, 1999, HL; reversing [1998] Ch. 304; [1998] 2 W.L.R. 225; [1997] 4 All E.R. 991; [1998] 1 F.L.R. 6; [1998] 1 F.C.R. 417; (1998) 30 H.L.R. 576; [1997] Fam. Law 784; [1997] E.G. 122 (C.S.); (1997) 147 N.L.J. 1275; [1997] N.P.C. 118; Times, July 31, 1997; Independent, July 29, 1997, CA (Civ Div) ........ *Digested,* 99/**3715**:
*Applied* 00/4147, 02/1824, 05/2118, 06/4089, 11/1649, 13/1640, 14/2008:
*Considered* 99/24, 02/914, 04/2538, 10/1703, 13/1868

Fitzpatrick's Application for Judicial Review, Re; *joined case* Shiels' Application for Judicial Review, Re [2013] NICA 66; [2014] N.I. 277, CA (NI)

FK (Kenya) v Secretary of State for the Home Department see Kamau (Kenya) v Secretary of State for the Home Department

FKI Engineering Ltd v Stribog Ltd; *sub nom* Stribog Ltd v FKI Engineering Ltd [2011] EWCA Civ 622; [2011] 1 W.L.R. 3264; [2012] 1 All E.R. (Comm) 549; [2011] Bus. L.R. 1410; [2011] 2 Lloyd's Rep. 387; [2011] C.P. Rep. 33; [2011] 1 C.L.C. 1005; (2011) 108(23) L.S.G. 17, CA (Civ Div); reversing [2010] EWHC 1160 (Comm); [2010] 2 All E.R. (Comm) 906; [2010] 2 Lloyd's Rep. 524; [2010] 1 C.L.C. 752; [2010] I.L.Pr. 39, QBD (Comm) ........ *Digested,* 11/**392**:
*Considered* 13/442, 14/565

Flame SA v Glory Wealth Shipping Pte Ltd [2013] EWHC 3153 (Comm); [2014] Q.B. 1080; [2014] 2 W.L.R. 1405; [2014] 1 All E.R. (Comm) 1043; [2013] 2 Lloyd's Rep. 653; [2013] 2 C.L.C. 527, QBD (Comm) ........ *Digested,* 14/**119**

Flanagan v Greenbanks Ltd (t/a Lazenby Insulation) [2013] EWCA Civ 1702; [2014] T.C.L.R. 2; 151 Con. L.R. 98, CA (Civ Div) ........ *Digested,* 14/**617**

Flanagan v Revenue and Customs Commissioners [2014] UKFTT 175 (TC); 82 T.C. 392; [2014] S.F.T.D. 881; [2014] S.T.I. 1772, FTT (Tax)

Fleming v Ireland [2013] IESC 19; 35 B.H.R.C. 155; (2013) 132 B.M.L.R. 1, Sup Ct (Irl); affirming [2013] IEHC 2; (2013) 131 B.M.L.R. 30, HC (Irl)

Fleming (t/a Bodycraft) v Customs and Excise Commissioners; *sub nom* Fleming (t/a Bodycraft) v Revenue and Customs Commissioners; *joined case* Conde Nast Publications Ltd v Revenue and Customs Commissioners [2008] UKHL 2; [2008] 1 W.L.R. 195; [2008] 1 All E.R. 1061; [2008] S.T.C. 324; [2008] 1 C.M.L.R. 48; [2008] Eu. L.R. 455; [2008] B.T.C. 5096; [2008] B.V.C. 221; [2008] S.T.I. 181; (2008) 158 N.L.J. 182; (2008) 152(5) S.J.L.B. 30; [2008] N.P.C. 5; Times, January 25, 2008, HL; affirming [2006] EWCA Civ 70; [2006] S.T.C. 864; [2006] Eu. L.R. 864; [2006] B.T.C. 5241; [2006] B.V.C. 310; [2006] S.T.I. 457; (2006) 103(10) L.S.G. 25; Times, March 1, 2006; Independent, February 17, 2006, CA (Civ Div); reversing [2005] EWHC 232 (Ch); [2005] S.T.C. 707; [2005] Eu. L.R. 735; [2005] B.T.C. 5215; [2005] B.V.C. 246, Ch D; affirming in part [2004] V. & D.R. 172; [2004] S.T.I. 1560, V&DTr (London) ........ *Digested,* 08/**4016**:
*Applied* 06/4465, 10/3507, 12/3381: *Cited* 12/3430: *Considered* 07/4360, 08/3676, 09/4070, 10/2672, 10/3491, 14/3038: *Followed* 05/4367, 11/3519

Fleming (t/a Bodycraft) v Revenue and Customs Commissioners see Fleming (t/a Bodycraft) v Customs and Excise Commissioners

Fleming Agri-Products Ltd v Revenue and Customs Commissioners [2014] UKFTT 965 (TC); [2014] S.T.I. 3217, FTT (Tax)

Fletcher v Chief Constable of Leicestershire [2013] EWHC 3357 (Admin); [2014] Lloyd's Rep. F.C. 60, QBD (Admin) ........ *Digested,* 14/**767**

Fletcher v Vooght [2000] B.P.I.R. 435; (2000) 97(12) L.S.G. 39; (2000) 144 S.J.L.B. 135, Ch D
*Considered* 05/2309, 14/1799

Flogas Britain Ltd v Calor Gas Ltd [2013] EWHC 3060 (Ch); [2014] F.S.R. 34, Ch D ... *Digested,* 14/**2989**

Florence v South Africa 37 B.H.R.C. 492, Const Ct (SA)

FLS Plast A/S v European Commission (C-243/12 P) [2014] 5 C.M.L.R. 14, ECJ (1st Chamber)

FLSmidth & Co A/S v European Commission (C-238/12 P) [2014] 4 C.M.L.R. 32, ECJ (1st Chamber)

Fluff Ltd (t/a Mag-it) v Customs and Excise Commissioners [2001] S.T.C. 674; [2001] B.T.C. 5477; [2001] B.V.C. 489; [2000] S.T.I. 752; Independent, June 19, 2000, QBD; affirming [1999] B.V.C. 2121, V&DTr ........ *Digested,* 01/**5625**: *Followed* 14/3100

flyLAL-Lithuanian Airlines AS v Starptautiska lidosta Riga VAS (C-302/13) [2014] 5 C.M.L.R. 27, ECJ (3rd Chamber)

Flynn v Secretary of State for Communities and Local Government see R. (on the application of Flynn) v Secretary of State for Communities and Local Government

FN v Sweden (28774/09) (2014) 59 E.H.R.R. 32, ECHR

FNM Corp Ltd v Drammock International Ltd [2009] EWHC 1294 (Pat), Ch D (Patents Ct)
*Considered* 14/1879

Fofana v Thubin [2006] EWHC 744 (Admin); [2006] Extradition L.R. 102, DC
*Applied* 12/1280: *Considered* 12/1281, 14/1228

Fogarty v United Kingdom (37112/97) [2002] I.R.L.R. 148; (2002) 34 E.H.R.R. 12; 12 B.H.R.C. 132; Times, November 26, 2001, ECHR ........ *Digested,* 02/**2398**: *Considered* 06/2642, 14/1056

Fogarty (Filled Products) Ltd v Revenue and Customs Commissioners [2014] UKFTT 936 (TC); [2014] S.T.I. 3095, FTT (Tax)

Folien Fischer AG v Ritrama SpA (C-133/11) [2013] Q.B. 523; [2013] 2 W.L.R. 373; [2014] 1 All E.R. (Comm) 569; [2013] C.E.C. 727; [2013] I.L.Pr. 1, ECJ (1st Chamber)

Fondazione Enasarco v Lehman Brothers Finance SA [2014] EWHC 34 (Ch); [2014] 2 B.C.L.C. 662, Ch D (Companies Ct)

Fonderie 2A v Ministre de l'Economie et des Finances (C-446/13) [2014] B.V.C. 45; [2014] S.T.I. 3024, ECJ (2nd Chamber)

Fonecomp Ltd v Revenue and Customs Commissioners [2013] UKUT 599 (TCC); [2014] S.T.C. 956; [2014] B.V.C. 502, UT (Tax); affirming [2012] UKFTT 102 (TC), FTT (Tax) ........ *Digested,* 14/**3070**: *Considered* 14/3067, 14/3069

Foneshops Ltd v Revenue and Customs Commissioners [2013] UKFTT 675 (TC); [2014] S.F.T.D. 607, FTT (Tax)

Fonnship A/S v Svenska Transportarbetareforbundet (C-83/13) [2014] All E.R. (EC) 1083, ECJ (Grand Chamber)

FoodCo UK LLP (t/a Muffin Break) v Henry Boot Developments Ltd [2010] EWHC 358 (Ch), Ch D
*Approved* 14/639

Football Association Premier League Ltd v British Sky Broadcasting Ltd [2013] EWHC 2058 (Ch); [2013] E.C.D.R. 14, Ch D ........ *Digested,* 13/**1763**: *Applied* 14/1868

Football Association Premier League Ltd v QC Leisure (C-403/08); *joined case* Murphy v Media Protection Services Ltd (C-429/08) [2012] Bus. L.R. 1321; [2011] E.C.R. I-9083; [2012] 1 C.M.L.R. 29; [2012] All E.R. (EC) 629; [2012] C.E.C. 242; [2012] E.C.D.R. 8; [2012] F.S.R. 1; (2011) 108(40) L.S.G. 22; (2011) 161 N.L.J. 1415; Times, November 23, 2011, ECJ (Grand Chamber); no effect [2011] E.C.D.R. 11, AGO ........ *Digested,* 12/**1924**: *Applied* 12/1920, 12/1925, 13/1769: *Considered* 13/1762, 13/3542, 14/1860, 14/3349, 14/3354: *Followed* 12/1928

Force India Formula One Team Ltd v 1 Malaysia Racing Team Sdn Bhd; *sub nom* Force India Formula One Team Ltd v Aerolab Srl [2013] EWCA Civ 780; [2013] R.P.C. 36, CA (Civ Div); affirming [2012] EWHC 616 (Ch); [2012] R.P.C. 29, Ch D ........ *Digested,* 14/**624**: *Applied* 14/247, 14/2989: *Considered* 14/2989

Force India Formula One Team Ltd v Aerolab Srl see Force India Formula One Team Ltd v 1 Malaysia Racing Team Sdn Bhd

Ford v Malaysian Airline Systems Berhad [2013] EWCA Civ 1163; [2014] 1 Lloyd's Rep. 301, CA (Civ Div) ........ *Digested,* 14/**152**

Forde & McHugh Ltd v Revenue and Customs Commissioners; *sub nom* Revenue and Customs Commissioners v Forde & McHugh Ltd [2014] UKSC 14; [2014] 1 W.L.R. 810; [2014] 2 All E.R. 356; [2014] S.T.C. 724; [2014] I.C.R. 403; [2014] Pens. L.R. 203; 82 T.C. 165; [2014] B.T.C. 8; [2014] S.T.I. 739, SC; reversing [2012] EWCA Civ 692; [2012] 3 All E.R. 1256; [2012] S.T.C. 1872; [2013] I.C.R. 467; [2012] Pens. L.R. 381; [2012] B.T.C. 194; [2012] S.T.I. 1919, CA (Civ Div); reversing [2011] UKUT 78 (TCC); [2011] S.T.C. 1428; [2011] B.T.C. 1614; [2011] S.T.I. 593, UT (Tax) ........ *Digested,* 14/**2950**

Fordent Holdings Ltd v Secretary of State for Communities and Local Government [2013] EWHC 2844 (Admin); [2014] 2 P. & C.R. 12; [2014] J.P.L. 226; (2013) 157(43) S.J.L.B. 53, QBD (Admin) ........ *Digested,* 14/**2394**

Forest House Estates Ltd v Al-Harthi [2013] UKUT 479 (LC); [2014] J.P.L. 137, UT (Lands)

Forest of Dean Friends of the Earth v Forest of Dean DC [2013] EWHC 1567 (Admin); [2014] Env. L.R. 3, QBD (Admin) ........ *Digested,* 14/**2372**

Forestships International Ltd v Armonia Shipping & Finance Corp (The Ira) [1995] 1 Lloyd's Rep. 103; Lloyd's List, September 23, 1994, QBD (Comm) *Applied* 13/2836: *Doubted* 14/2740

Forstater v Python (Monty) Pictures Ltd [2013] EWHC 3759 (Ch); [2014] 1 Costs L.R. 36, Ch D ........ *Digested,* 14/**343**: *Considered* 14/838

Forster v Outred & Co [1982] 1 W.L.R. 86; [1982] 2 All E.R. 753; (1981) 125 S.J. 309, CA (Civ Div) ........ *Digested,* 82/**1849**: *Applied* 81/1621, 83/1765, 85/2012, 88/2154, 89/2585, 91/2343, 01/4526, 01/4527, 04/2740, 05/437, 09/2735, 09/426, 11/2246, 13/2093: *Considered* 82/1845, 83/1071, 84/1104, 84/1579, 85/1689, 93/2997, 94/2912, 00/2621, 01/946, 06/474, 14/591: *Distinguished* 85/2291, 88/2158, 02/3276: *Doubted* 83/2215: *Followed* 05/2865

Forsyth v Revenue and Customs Commissioners [2014] UKFTT 915 (TC); [2014] S.T.I. 3430, FTT (Tax)

Forty-Five Holdings Ltd v Grosvenor (Mayfair) Estate [2009] UKUT 234 (LC); [2010] L. & T.R. 21; [2010] 2 E.G. 84 (C.S.), UT (Lands) ........ *Digested,* 11/**2668**: *Applied* 14/1985

Foscolo Mango & Co Ltd v Stag Line Ltd see Stag Line Ltd v Foscolo Mango & Co Ltd

Foscolo, Mango & Co Ltd, v Stag Line Ltd see Stag Line Ltd v Foscolo Mango & Co Ltd

Foscolo, Mango & Co Ltd, and HC Vivian Ltd v Stag Line Ltd see Stag Line Ltd v Foscolo Mango & Co Ltd

Foscolo, Mango & Co Ltd, and HC Vivian Ltd v Stag Line Ltd see Stag Line Ltd v Foscolo Mango & Co Ltd

Foster v British Gas Plc (C-188/89) [1991] 1 Q.B. 405; [1991] 2 W.L.R. 258; [1990] 3 All E.R. 897; [1990] E.C.R. I-3313; [1990] 2 C.M.L.R. 833; [1991] I.C.R. 84; [1990] I.R.L.R. 353; [1990] Pens. L.R. 189; Times, July 13, 1990, ECJ *Applied* 92/1977, 95/2070, 95/5037, 98/2111, 07/1565, 07/2496: *Approved* 91/1673: *Considered* 95/2031, 06/2108, 14/1018: *Followed* 96/2625: *Referred to* 97/2277

Foster v DPP [2013] EWHC 2039 (Admin); (2014) 178 J.P. 15, DC ........ *Digested,* 14/**785**

Foster v Information Commissioner (2014) 136 B.M.L.R. 193, FTT (GRC) ........ *Digested,* 14/**74**

Foster v Mackinnon (1868-69) L.R. 4 C.P. 704, CCP *Considered* 69/526, 14/628

Foulser v Revenue and Customs Commissioners [2014] UKFTT 483 (TC); [2014] S.T.I. 2764, FTT (Tax)

Fowles v Heathrow Airport Ltd [2008] EWCA Civ 1270; [2009] 1 P. & C.R. DG8, CA (Civ Div); affirming [2008] EWHC 219 (Ch); [2008] N.P.C. 19; [2008] 1 P. & C.R. DG24, Ch D *Followed* 14/1976

Fox v British Airways Plc; *sub nom* British Airways Plc v Fox; Fox (Deceased), Re [2013] EWCA Civ 972; [2013] I.C.R. 1257; [2013] I.R.L.R. 812; [2013] Pens. L.R. 347, CA (Civ Div); affirming [2013] I.C.R. 51, EAT ...................................... *Digested,* 13/**1069**: *Followed* 14/2302

Fox v Foundation Piling Ltd [2011] EWCA Civ 790; [2011] C.P. Rep. 41; [2011] 6 Costs L.R. 961, CA (Civ Div) .................................................................... *Digested,* 12/**352**: *Applied* 14/371: *Considered* 12/353, 13/339: *Followed* 13/290

Fox v Jewell [2013] EWCA Civ 1152; [2014] W.T.L.R. 283, CA (Civ Div) ..................... *Digested,* 14/**310**

Fox v Spousal (Midlands) Ltd see Fairchild v Glenhaven Funeral Services Ltd (t/a GH Dovener & Son)

Fox (Deceased), Re see Fox v British Airways Plc

Fox Strategic Land and Property v Cheshire East Council [2014] P.A.D. 4, Planning Inspector

Fox's Application for Judicial Review, Re; *joined case* Canning's Application for Judicial Review, Re [2013] NICA 19; [2014] N.I. 221, CA (NI)

Fra.bo SpA v Deutsche Vereinigung des Gas- und Wasserfaches eV (DVGW) - Technisch-Wissenschaftlicher Verein (C-171/11) [2013] Q.B. 187; [2013] 2 W.L.R. 1; [2012] 3 C.M.L.R. 38, ECJ (4th Chamber) *Applied* 14/555

Framlington Group Ltd v Barnetson see Barnetson v Framlington Group Ltd

France v European Commission (C-115/12 P) [2014] P.T.S.R. 152; [2014] 1 C.M.L.R. 46, ECJ (4th Chamber)

France v European Commission (C-559/12 P) [2014] 3 C.M.L.R. 39, ECJ (1st Chamber)

France (A Bankrupt), Re; *sub nom* Nutting v France [2014] EWHC 2123 (Ch); [2014] B.P.I.R. 1448, Ch D (Leeds)

Francis v Brent Housing Partnership Ltd [2013] EWCA Civ 912; [2013] H.L.R. 47; [2013] 32 E.G. 56 (C.S.), CA (Civ Div) ................................................................ *Digested,* 14/**2003**

Francovich v Italy (C-6/90); *joined case* Bonifacti v Italy (C-9/90) [1991] E.C.R. I-5357; [1993] 2 C.M.L.R. 66; [1995] I.C.R. 722; [1992] I.R.L.R. 84; Times, November 20, 1991, ECJ ........................................................................................ *Digested,* 92/**4815**: *Applied* 98/2570, 98/3396, 99/3620, 08/2208, 13/1581: *Cited* 00/2380: *Considered* 92/2904, 94/3046, 94/4842, 95/2031, 96/2566, 96/2596, 96/2597, 96/2629, 96/2792, 96/2803, 97/4627, 07/2490, 14/2987: *Distinguished* 09/1379: *Followed* 97/2265, 02/1571, 11/1717

Frankice (Golders Green) Ltd (In Administration), Re [2010] EWHC 1229 (Ch); [2010] Bus. L.R. 1608; Times, June 14, 2010, Ch D ...................................................... *Digested,* 11/**1821**: *Considered* 14/3194

Franklin v Barnet LBC [2014] P.A.D. 26, Planning Inspector

Frans Maas Logistics (UK) Ltd v CDR Trucking BV [1999] 1 All E.R. (Comm) 737; [1999] 2 Lloyd's Rep. 179, QBD (Comm) .......................................................... *Digested,* 99/**732**: *Approved* 01/5419: *Considered* 09/3972, 14/3011

Fraser v Crown Prosecution Service see Crown Prosecution Service v Fraser

Fraser v Revenue and Customs Commissioners [2012] UKFTT 189 (TC), FTT (Tax) *Applied* 14/2955

Fred Perry (Holdings) Ltd v Brands Plaza Trading Ltd (t/a Brands Plaza) [2012] EWCA Civ 224; [2012] 6 Costs L.R. 1007; [2012] F.S.R. 28, CA (Civ Div); reversing in part [2011] EWHC 1030 (Ch), Ch D ................................................ *Digested,* 12/**484**: *Applied* 13/342, 13/440: *Considered* 13/405, 14/394: *Followed* 14/459

Free Grammar School of John Lyon v Helman see Helman v John Lyon Free Grammar School

Free Power for Schools LP v Department of Energy and Climate Change see Breyer Group Plc v Department of Energy and Climate Change

Freeman & Lockyer v Buckhurst Park Properties (Mangal) Ltd [1964] 2 Q.B. 480; [1964] 2 W.L.R. 618; [1964] 1 All E.R. 630; (1964) 108 S.J. 96, CA .................. *Digested,* 64/**444**: *Applied* 73/420, 74/30, 77/2890, 84/27, 85/21, 95/775, 05/517, 13/2092, 14/1924: *Considered* 67/33, 72/1649, 80/14, 81/43.u, 83/202, 00/4024, 12/3787: *Distinguished* 94/362: *Followed* 94/5374, 01/6105

Freeman (t/a Satellite Services) v Financial Services Authority see Digital Satellite Warranty Cover Ltd, Re

Freeman (t/a Satellite Services), Re see Digital Satellite Warranty Cover Ltd, Re

French v Carter Lemon Camerons LLP [2012] EWCA Civ 1180; [2012] 6 Costs L.O. 879; [2013] P.N.L.R. 2; (2012) 162 N.L.J. 1155; (2012) 156(34) S.J.L.B. 27, CA (Civ Div); affirming [2011] EWHC 3252 (QB), QBD ............................................ *Digested,* 13/**1947**: *Considered* 14/724

French v Hartman [2014] EWHC 1682 (QB); [2014] 6 Costs L.O. 829, QBD

French v Portugal [2013] UKPC 16; [2014] A.C. 40; [2013] 3 W.L.R. 907, PC (Gib)

Freud (Deceased), Re; *sub nom* Rawstron v Freud [2014] EWHC 2577 (Ch); [2014] W.T.L.R. 1453; 17 I.T.E.L.R. 479, Ch D ........ *Digested,* 14/**2834**

Friends Life Co Ltd v Alexander (Valuation Officer) [2012] R.A. 263, VT ........ *Digested,* 12/**2524**: *Doubted* 14/2083

Friends Life Ltd v Siemens Hearing Instruments Ltd see Siemens Hearing Instruments Ltd v Friends Life Ltd

Friends Life Management Services Ltd v A&A Express Building Ltd [2014] EWHC 1463 (Ch); [2014] 2 E.G.L.R. 53; [2014] 2 P. & C.R. DG17, Ch D

Frisby v Birmingham City Council see Hounslow LBC v Powell

Frith Accountants Ltd v Law [2014] I.C.R. 805; [2014] I.R.L.R. 510, EAT ........ *Digested,* 14/**1136**

Frontier Systems Ltd (t/a Voiceflex) v Frip Finishing Ltd [2014] EWHC 1907 (TCC); [2014] B.L.R. 563, QBD (TCC) ........ *Digested,* 14/**2985**

Frost v Wokingham DC see Maltedge and Frost v Wokingham DC

Frost (Deceased), Re; *sub nom* Kloosman v Aylen [2013] EWHC 435 (Ch); [2014] W.T.L.R. 77; [2013] W.T.L.R. 673, Ch D ........ *Digested,* 13/**2972**

Fryett v Revenue and Customs Commissioners [2014] UKFTT 220 (TC); [2014] S.F.T.D. 979; [2014] S.T.I. 1914, FTT (Tax)

FS v Bromley LBC [2013] UKUT 529 (AAC); [2014] E.L.R. 1, UT (AAC) ........ *Digested,* 14/**938**

FSS PEnsion Trustees Ltd v Board of the Pension Protection Fund see FSS Pension Trustees Ltd, Re

FSS Pension Trustees Ltd, Re; *sub nom* FSS PEnsion Trustees Ltd v Board of the Pension Protection Fund [2014] EWHC 1397 (Ch); [2014] Pens. L.R. 303, Ch D ........ *Digested,* 14/**2264**

FU (Afghanistan) v Secretary of State for the Home Department see KA (Afghanistan) v Secretary of State for the Home Department

Fuerta Ltd, Re [2014] IEHC 12; [2014] B.C.C. 281, HC (Irl)

Fuglers LLP v Solicitors Regulation Authority; *sub nom* Fuglers LLP v Solicitors Regulatory Authority [2014] EWHC 179 (Admin); [2014] B.P.I.R. 610, QBD (Admin) ........ *Digested,* 14/**2056**

Fuglers LLP v Solicitors Regulatory Authority see Fuglers LLP v Solicitors Regulation Authority

Fujitsu Services Ltd v IBM United Kingdom Ltd [2014] EWHC 752 (TCC); [2014] 1 C.L.C. 353; 153 Con. L.R. 203, QBD (TCC) ........ *Digested,* 14/**618**

Fulfilment Logistics Ltd v May (Valuation Officer) see Total Fulfilment Logistics Ltd v May (Valuation Officer)

Fuller v Redbridge LBC (2013) 134 B.M.L.R. 183, EAT ........ *Digested,* 14/**1044**

Fulton v AIB Group (UK) Plc [2014] NICh 8; [2014] B.P.I.R. 1169, Ch D (NI) ........ *Digested,* 14/**3194**

Fulton Shipping Inc of Panama v Globalia Business Travel SAU (formerly Travelplan SAU) of Spain [2014] EWHC 1547 (Comm); [2014] 2 Lloyd's Rep. 230; [2014] 1 C.L.C. 711; 154 Con. L.R. 183, QBD (Comm) ........ *Digested,* 14/**827**

Furlonger v Lalatta [2014] EWHC 37 (Ch); [2014] L. & T.R. 14, Ch D ........ *Digested,* 14/**2006**

Furstlich Castell'sches Domanenamt Albrecht Furst zu Castell-Castell v Office for Harmonisation in the Internal Market (Trade Marks and Designs) (OHIM) (T-320/10) [2014] E.T.M.R. 13, GC (6th Chamber)

Futter v Futter see Pitt v Holt

Futter v Revenue and Customs Commissioners see Pitt v Holt

FV (Italy) v Secretary of State for the Home Department see Secretary of State for the Home Department v FV (Italy)

fx LIFE SCIENCES/Standardised plant extraction (T475/10) [2014] E.P.O.R. 14, EPO (Technical Bd App)

Fyfe v Watts; *joined case* Watts v Watts [2013] EWHC 1374 (Ch); [2014] 1 Costs L.O. 1; [2013] W.T.L.R. 1169, Ch D ........ *Digested,* 13/**311**

Fyfe (WAP) v Fife Assessor see WAP Fyfe v Assessor for Fife Council

Fyffes Group Ltd v Reefer Express Lines Pty Ltd [1996] 2 Lloyd's Rep. 171, QBD (Comm) ........ *Digested,* 96/**5377**: *Considered* 14/2716

Fyffes Group Ltd v Templeman [2000] 2 Lloyd's Rep. 643; (2000) 97(25) L.S.G. 40; Times, June 14, 2000, QBD (Comm) ........ *Digested,* 00/**5104**: *Considered* 14/2991

Fynes v St George's Hospital NHS Trust [2014] EWHC 756 (QB); (2014) 138 B.M.L.R. 170, QBD

Fynn v Inland Revenue Commissioners [1958] 1 W.L.R. 585; [1958] 1 All E.R. 270; 51 R. & I.T. 142; 37 T.C. 629; (1957) 36 A.T.C. 313; [1957] T.R. 323; (1958) 102 S.J. 381, Ch D ........ *Digested,* 58/**1570**: *Considered* 14/2916

FZ v Secretary of State for the Home Department [2003] UKIAT 31; [2003] Imm. A.R. 633, IAT
*Applied* 14/1664

FZ (Democratic Republic of Congo) v Secretary of State for the Home Department; *sub nom* Zoumbas v Secretary of State for the Home Department [2013] UKSC 74; [2013] 1 W.L.R. 3690; [2014] 1 All E.R. 638; 2014 S.C. (U.K.S.C.) 75; [2014] 1 F.C.R. 141; [2014] Imm. A.R. 479; [2014] I.N.L.R. 262, SC; affirming [2012] CSIH 87; 2012 G.W.D. 40-785, IH (Ex Div); affirming [2012] CSOH 47; 2012 G.W.D. 13-259, OH ........ *Digested,* 14/**1650**: *Applied* 14/1651

G v B (Financial Remedies: Asset Beneficiaries) [2013] EWHC 3414 (Fam); [2014] 2 F.L.R. 292; [2014] Fam. Law 290, Fam Div ........ *Digested,* 14/**1374**

G v E (Costs); *sub nom* Manchester City Council v G (Costs); G v Manchester City Council (Costs) [2011] EWCA Civ 939; [2011] C.P. Rep. 45; [2011] 2 F.L.R. 1297; (2011) 14 C.C.L. Rep. 725; [2011] M.H.L.R. 381; [2014] W.T.L.R. 449; [2011] Fam. Law 1196; (2011) 155(31) S.J.L.B. 31, CA (Civ Div); affirming [2010] EWHC 3385 (Fam); [2011] 1 F.L.R. 1566; (2011) 14 C.C.L. Rep. 140; [2011] Fam. Law 473, CP ........ *Digested,* 12/**364**

G v G (Minors: Custody Appeal) [1985] 1 W.L.R. 647; [1985] 2 All E.R. 225; [1985] F.L.R. 894; [1985] Fam. Law 321; (1985) 82 L.S.G. 2010; (1985) 83 L.S.G. 2010; (1985) 135 N.L.J. 439; (1985) 129 S.J. 315, HL ........ *Digested,* 85/**2594**: *Applied* 86/2145, 86/2196, 87/1773, 87/2489, 87/2490, 87/2519, 87/2527, 91/2553, 92/3032, 95/3372, 95/3390, 95/3469, 95/3486, 95/3489, 95/3493, 95/3561, 96/563, 96/604, 96/607, 96/614, 96/6976, 02/3270, 02/498, 06/1670, 07/1800, 08/2128, 09/1572, 09/1639, 10/1310, 14/1323: *Approved* 98/2398: *Considered* 86/2142, 86/2182, 88/2357, 88/2952, 89/2410, 89/2459, 90/3125, 95/3386, 95/3498, 95/3532, 95/67, 96/608, 97/384, 00/2489, 04/2134, 07/4550: *Distinguished* 88/2935, 09/2217: *Explained* 87/2439: *Followed* 86/1099, 86/2068, 86/2201, 96/560, 96/609, 09/1226, 10/1308, 10/1437, 11/1379: *Referred to* 86/3641, 94/3220

G v Manchester City Council (Costs) see G v E (Costs)

G v Mental Health Tribunal for Scotland; *sub nom* G v Scottish Ministers [2013] UKSC 79; 2014 S.C. (U.K.S.C.) 84; 2014 S.L.T. 247; 2014 S.C.L.R. 415, SC; affirming [2011] CSIH 55; 2012 S.C. 138; 2011 S.C.L.R. 770; [2011] M.H.L.R. 387; 2011 G.W.D. 29-638, IH (2 Div) ........ *Digested,* 14/**2180**

G v R (Pre-Nuptial Contract) see Radmacher v Granatino

G v Scottish Ministers see G v Mental Health Tribunal for Scotland

G v Sheffield Health and Social Care NHS Foundation Trust (Unreported, June 14, 2013), QBD (Sheffield) [*Tim Meakin, Barrister, 7 Bedford Row Chambers, 7 Bedford Row, London*] ........ *Digested,* 14/**2323**

G v Staatssecretaris van Veiligheid en Justitie (C-383/13 PPU); *sub nom* MG v Staatssecretaris van Veiligheid en Justitie (C-383/13 PPU) [2014] 1 C.M.L.R. 27, ECJ (2nd Chamber)

G (A Child) (Adoption: Leave to Oppose), Re see G (A Child) (Non-relative Carer: Joinder to Adoption Proceedings), Re

G (A Child) (Adoption: Unmarried Couple), Re see P (A Child) (Adoption: Unmarried Couples), Re

G (A Child) (Care Proceedings: Welfare Balancing Exercise: Proportionality), Re see G (A Child) (Care Proceedings: Welfare Evaluation), Re

G (A Child) (Care Proceedings: Welfare Evaluation), Re; *sub nom* G (A Child) (Care Proceedings: Welfare Balancing Exercise: Proportionality), Re [2013] EWCA Civ 965; [2014] 1 F.L.R. 670; [2013] 3 F.C.R. 293; [2013] Fam. Law 1246; (2013) 157(31) S.J.L.B. 31, CA (Civ Div) ........ *Digested,* 14/**1346**: *Applied* 14/1238, 14/1247, 14/1250, 14/1323: *Explained* 14/1348: *Followed* 14/1245, 14/1277

G (A Child) (Interim Care Order: Residential Assessment), Re; *sub nom* Kent CC v G; G (A Child) (Interim Care Orders: Inpatient Assessment), Re [2005] UKHL 68; [2006] 1 A.C. 576; [2005] 3 W.L.R. 1166; [2006] 1 All E.R. 706; [2006] 1 F.L.R. 601; [2005] 3 F.C.R. 621; [2006] Fam. Law 91; (2005) 102(47) L.S.G. 28; Times, November 25, 2005; Independent, November 29, 2005, HL; reversing [2004] EWCA Civ 24; [2004] 1 F.L.R. 876; [2004] 1 F.C.R. 317; [2004] Fam. Law 325; (2004) 101(9) L.S.G. 31; Times, January 29, 2004, CA (Civ Div) ........ *Digested,* 06/**1654**: *Applied* 07/1725: *Considered* 11/1336, 14/1284: *Distinguished* 07/1751: *Followed* 09/1527

G (A Child) (Interim Care Orders: Inpatient Assessment), Re see G (A Child) (Interim Care Order: Residential Assessment), Re

G (A Child) (Intractable Contact Dispute), Re [2013] EWHC 2948 (Fam); [2014] Fam. Law 23, Fam Div

G (A Child) (Jurisdiction: Brussels II Revised), Re; *sub nom* G (Jurisdiction: Art 19 BIIR), Re; I v G [2014] EWCA Civ 680; [2014] Fam. Law 1111; (2014) 158(21) S.J.L.B. 37, CA (Civ Div); affirming [2013] EWHC 4017 (Fam); [2014] 2 F.L.R. 746; [2014] Fam. Law 455, Fam Div

G (A Child) (Leave to Apply for Residence Order: Non-relative), Re see G (A Child) (Non-relative Carer: Joinder to Adoption Proceedings), Re

G (A Child) (Non-relative Carer: Joinder to Adoption Proceedings), Re; *sub nom* G (A Child) (Adoption: Leave to Oppose), Re; G (A Child) (Leave to Apply for Residence Order: Non-relative), Re [2014] EWCA Civ 432; [2014] 3 W.L.R. 1719; [2014] 2 F.L.R. 525; [2014] 2 F.C.R. 151; [2014] Fam. Law 946; (2014) 158(15) S.J.L.B. 37, CA (Civ Div) ........ *Digested,* 14/**1251**

G (A Child) (Same-sex Relationship: Family Life Declaration), Re; *sub nom* L v C (Applications by Non-Biological Mother) [2014] EWFC 1; [2014] Fam. Law 1095, Fam Div

G (An Adult) (Costs), Re [2014] EWCOP 5; [2014] C.O.P.L.R. 432, CP ........ *Digested,* 14/**346**

G (An Adult), Re; *joined case* Redbridge LBC v G [2014] EWCOP 1361; [2014] C.O.P.L.R. 416, CP ........ *Digested,* 14/**436**

G (Care: Challenge to Local Authority's Decision), Re [2003] EWHC 551 (Fam); [2003] 2 F.L.R. 42; [2003] Fam. Law 389, Fam Div ........ *Digested,* 03/**1521**: *Applied* 09/1516, 14/1264: *Considered* 05/1530, 10/1358: *Distinguished* 05/318

G (Children) (Contact Proceedings: Costs), Re [2013] EWCA Civ 1017; [2014] 1 F.L.R. 517; [2014] Fam. Law 26, CA (Civ Div) ........ *Digested,* 14/**1335**

G (Children) (Recognition of Brazilian Adoption), Re [2014] EWHC 2605 (Fam); [2014] Fam. Law 1520, Fam Div

G (Children) (Residence: Same Sex Partner), Re [2005] EWCA Civ 462; [2005] 2 F.L.R. 957; [2006] 1 F.C.R. 436; Times, April 29, 2005, CA (Civ Div) ........ *Digested,* 05/**1579**: *Applied* 08/1586: *Considered* 14/1422

G (Children) (Shared Residence Order: Biological Mother of Donor Egg), Re see G (Children) (Shared Residence Order: Biological Non-Birth Mother), Re

G (Children) (Shared Residence Order: Biological Non-Birth Mother), Re; *sub nom* G (Children) (Shared Residence Order: Biological Mother of Donor Egg), Re [2014] EWCA Civ 336; [2014] 2 F.L.R. 897; [2014] 2 F.C.R. 395; [2014] Fam. Law 970, CA (Civ Div) ........ *Digested,* 14/**1422**

G (Jurisdiction: Art 19 BIIR), Re see G (A Child) (Jurisdiction: Brussels II Revised), Re

G (Parental Orders), Re [2014] EWHC 1561 (Fam); [2014] Fam. Law 1114, Fam Div

G-C (A Child) (Contact Order: Staying Contact with Father), Re [2013] EWCA Civ 301; [2013] 2 F.L.R. 1307; [2013] Fam. Law 794, CA (Civ Div) ........ *Digested,* 14/**1410**

Gabriel v Little; *joined cases* BPE Solicitors v Gabriel; Gabriel v Little (t/a High Tech Design & Build Ltd) [2013] EWCA Civ 1513; 16 I.T.E.L.R. 567, CA (Civ Div); reversing in part [2012] EWHC 1193 (Ch); [2013] 1 B.C.L.C. 750; [2013] W.T.L.R. 419; 15 I.T.E.L.R. 387, Ch D ........ *Digested,* 14/**2195**

Gabriel v Little (t/a High Tech Design & Build Ltd) see Gabriel v Little

GAF Corp v Amchem Products Inc [1975] 1 Lloyd's Rep. 601, CA (Civ Div) ........ *Digested,* 75/**363**: *Applied* 14/477

Gaffoor (Abdul) Trustees v Ceylon Commissioner of Income Tax see Caffoor (Trustees of the Abdul Gaffoor Trust) v Income Tax Commissioner (Colombo)

Gaines-Cooper v Revenue and Customs Commissioners [2008] EWCA Civ 1502; 81 T.C. 61, CA (Civ Div) ........ *Digested,* 12/**3270**

Galaxy Energy International Ltd v Murco Petroleum Ltd (The Seacrown) [2013] EWHC 3720 (Comm); [2013] 2 C.L.C. 1007, QBD (Comm) ........ *Digested,* 14/**620**

Galaxy Special Maritime Enterprise v Prima Ceylon Ltd (The Olympic Galaxy) [2006] EWCA Civ 528; [2006] 2 All E.R. (Comm) 902; [2006] 2 Lloyd's Rep. 27; [2006] 1 C.L.C. 772, CA (Civ Div); reversing [2005] EWHC 3285 (Comm), QBD (Comm) ........ *Digested,* 06/**632**: *Followed* 14/567

Gale v Serious Organised Crime Agency see Serious Organised Crime Agency v Gale

Galileo International Technology LLC v Office for Harmonisation in the Internal Market (Trade Marks and Designs) (OHIM) (T-450/11) [2014] E.T.M.R. 59, GC (9th Chamber)

Gallagher (Valuation Officer) v Church of Jesus Christ of Latter-Day Saints; *sub nom* Church of Jesus Christ of Latter-Day Saints v Gallagher (Valuation Officer) [2008] UKHL 56; [2008] 1 W.L.R. 1852; [2008] 4 All E.R. 640; [2008] H.R.L.R. 46; [2008] R.A. 317; (2008) 158 N.L.J. 1179; [2008] N.P.C. 92; [2008] 2 P. & C.R. DG25; Times, August 7, 2008, HL; affirming [2006] EWCA Civ 1598; [2007] R.A. 1; (2006) 150 S.J.L.B. 1572; [2006] N.P.C. 126; [2007] 2 P. & C.R. DG6, CA (Civ Div); affirming [2006] R.A. 1, Lands Tr ........................................ *Digested,* 08/**2596**:
*Applied* 10/2686: *Complaint dismissed* 14/2134: *Followed* 11/2187

Gallagher Homes Ltd v Solihull MBC; *sub nom* Solihull MBC v Gallagher Homes Ltd [2014] EWCA Civ 1610, CA (Civ Div); reversing in part [2014] EWHC 1283 (Admin); [2014] J.P.L. 1117, QBD (Birmingham)

Gallaher Group Ltd v Office of Fair Trading see Somerfield Stores Ltd v Office of Fair Trading

Gallaher Group Ltd v Office of Fair Trading see Somerfield Stores Ltd v Office of Fair Trading

Gallie v Lee see Saunders v Anglia Building Society (formerly Northampton Town and County Building Society)

Gallop v Newport City Council [2013] EWCA Civ 1583; [2014] I.R.L.R. 211; [2014] Eq. L.R. 141, CA (Civ Div); reversing [2013] I.R.L.R. 23; [2012] Eq. L.R. 998, EAT .. *Digested,* 14/**1041**

Galp Energia Espana SA v Europe Commission (T-462/07) [2014] 4 C.M.L.R. 9, GC (8th Chamber)
*Applied* 14/550

Games Station Ltd, Re see Jervis v Pillar Denton Ltd

Gandia Blasco SA v Office for Harmonisation in the Internal Market (Trade Marks and Designs) (OHIM) (T-339/12) [2014] E.C.D.R. 15, GC (7th Chamber)

Ganusaukas v Lithuania (47922/99) [1999] Prison L.R. 124, ECHR
*Applied* 14/2233

Garantovana as v European Commission (C-90/13) see 1 garantovana as v European Commission (C-90/13 P)

Garcha v Charity Commission for England and Wales [2014] EWHC 2754 (Ch); [2014] P.T.S.R. D28, Ch D

Garcia v Commissioner of Internal Revenue 16 I.T.L. Rep. 61, US Court

Gard Marine & Energy Ltd v China National Chartering Co Ltd; *joined case* China National Chartering Co Ltd v Daiichii Chuo Kisen Kaisha [2013] EWHC 2199 (Comm); [2013] 2 All E.R. (Comm) 1058; [2014] 1 Lloyd's Rep. 59; [2013] 2 C.L.C. 322, QBD (Comm) .................................................................................. *Digested,* 14/**2726**

Gardiner v Merton LBC see Merton LBC v Gardiner

Gardiner v Smith see Gardiner (William), Re

Gardiner (William), Re; *sub nom* Gardiner v Smith [1901] 1 Ch. 697, Ch D
*Considered* 64/1007, 14/2982

Gardner v Chief Constable of the West Midlands [2014] Eq. L.R. 23, EAT .................. *Digested,* 14/**1047**

Garfield v Maddocks [1974] Q.B. 7; [1973] 2 W.L.R. 888; [1973] 2 All E.R. 303; (1973) 57 Cr. App. R. 372; [1973] Crim. L.R. 231; (1973) 117 S.J. 145, QBD .............. *Digested,* 73/**470**:
*Applied* 79/2293, 79/2313, 86/539, 90/861, 94/943: *Considered* 79/392, 85/2095, 89/680, 14/785

Garlicki v Poland (36921/07) (2014) 58 E.H.R.R. 34, ECHR

Garnaga v Ukraine (20390/07) 36 B.H.R.C. 212, ECHR

Garner (Inspector of Taxes) v Pounds see Garner (Inspector of Taxes) v Pounds Shipowners & Shipbreakers Ltd

Garner (Inspector of Taxes) v Pounds Shipowners & Shipbreakers Ltd; *sub nom* Pounds Shipowners & Shipbreakers Ltd v Garner (Inspector of Taxes); *joined case* Garner (Inspector of Taxes) v Pounds [2000] 1 W.L.R. 1107; [2000] 3 All E.R. 218; [2000] S.T.C. 420; [2000] 2 E.G.L.R. 69; [2000] 34 E.G. 84; 72 T.C. 561; [2000] B.T.C. 190; [2000] S.T.I. 783; [2000] E.G. 62 (C.S.); (2000) 97(23) L.S.G. 41; [2000] N.P.C. 58; Times, May 19, 2000; Independent, May 24, 2000, HL; affirming [1999] S.T.C. 19; [1998] B.T.C. 495; [1998] E.G. 172 (C.S.); Times, December 1, 1998, CA (Civ Div); reversing [1997] S.T.C. 551; [1997] B.T.C. 223; (1997) 94(11) L.S.G. 35; (1997) 141 S.J.L.B. 71; Times, March 6, 1997; Independent, April 21, 1997, Ch D ........................................................... *Digested,* 00/**4922**:
*Applied* 02/4357: *Considered* 12/3233, 14/2852

Garrod v North Hertfordshire DC [2014] P.A.D. 35, Planning Inspector

Gas v France (25951/07) (2014) 59 E.H.R.R. 22, ECHR

Gascogne Sack Deutschland GmbH v European Commission (C-40/12 P) [2014] 4 C.M.L.R. 12, ECJ (Grand Chamber)

Gater Assets Ltd v Nak Naftogaz Ukrainiy [2007] EWCA Civ 988; [2008] 1 All E.R. (Comm) 209; [2008] Bus. L.R. 388; [2007] 2 Lloyd's Rep. 588; [2008] C.P. Rep. 4; [2007] 2 C.L.C. 567, CA (Civ Div); reversing [2007] EWHC 697 (Comm); [2007] 2 All E.R. (Comm) 208; [2007] 1 Lloyd's Rep. 522, QBD (Comm) .......... *Digested,* 08/**413**: *Considered* 12/392, 14/127

Gater Assets Ltd v Nak Naftogaz Ukrainiy [2008] EWHC 1108 (Comm); [2009] 1 All E.R. (Comm) 667; [2009] Bus. L.R. 396; [2008] 2 Lloyd's Rep. 295, QBD (Comm) .......... *Digested,* 08/**171**: *Applied* 14/128

Gateshead Jewish Nursery v Revenue and Customs Commissioners [2014] UKFTT 685 (TC); [2014] S.T.I. 2668, FTT (Tax)

Gateway Plaza Ltd v White [2014] EWCA Civ 555; [2014] 2 E.G.L.R. 191; [2014] 2 P. & C.R. DG15, CA (Civ Div)

Gatt v Malta (28221/08) (2014) 58 E.H.R.R. 32, ECHR

Gaughran's Application for Judicial Review, Re [2012] NIQB 88; [2014] N.I. 1, QBD (NI)

Gaydarov v Direktor na Glavna Direktsia Ohranitelna Politsia pri Ministerstvo na Vatreshnite Raboti (C-430/10) [2011] E.C.R. I-11637, ECJ *Applied* 14/1223

Gayhurst Community School v ER [2013] UKUT 558 (AAC); [2014] E.L.R. 103, UT (AAC) .......... *Digested,* 14/**934**

Gaynor v Central West London Buses Ltd [2006] EWCA Civ 1120; [2007] 1 W.L.R. 1045; [2007] 1 All E.R. 84; [2007] 1 Costs L.R. 33; (2006) 156 N.L.J. 1324; Times, August 25, 2006; Independent, October 5, 2006, CA (Civ Div) .......... *Digested,* 06/**2738**: *Applied* 14/2032

GB Housley Ltd v Revenue and Customs Commissioners; *sub nom* Revenue and Customs Commissioners v GB Housley Ltd [2014] UKUT 320 (TCC); [2014] S.T.C. 2733; [2014] B.V.C. 528, UT (Tax); affirming [2013] UKFTT 150 (TC); [2013] S.F.T.D. 1196; [2013] S.T.I. 1442, FTT (Tax) .......... *Digested,* 14/**3060**

GD Construction (St Albans) Ltd v Scottish & Newcastle Plc see Scottish & Newcastle Plc v GD Construction (St Albans) Ltd

GE v KE (Nigerian Customary Marriage and Divorce) [2013] EWHC 1938 (Fam); [2014] Fam. Law 1113, Fam Div

GE Properties (Wales) Ltd v Swansea City Council [2014] P.A.D. 55, Planning Inspector

Gebhard v Consiglio dell'Ordine degli Avvocati e Procuratori di Milano (C-55/94) [1995] E.C.R. I-4165; [1996] 1 C.M.L.R. 603; [1996] All E.R. (EC) 189; [1996] C.E.C. 175; Times, December 13, 1995, ECJ .......... *Digested,* 96/**3902**: *Applied* 07/1624, 09/3938: *Considered* 10/1249, 13/2531, 14/1102: *Followed* 02/1571, 05/1462, 05/1468

Gebremariam v Ethiopian Airlines Enterprise (t/a Ethiopian Airlines) [2014] I.R.L.R. 354, EAT .......... *Digested,* 14/**1024**

Geden Operations Ltd v Dry Bulk Handy Holdings Inc (The Bulk Uruguay) [2014] EWHC 885 (Comm); [2014] 2 All E.R. (Comm) 196; [2014] 2 Lloyd's Rep. 66; (2014) 164(7601) N.L.J. 20, QBD (Comm) .......... *Digested,* 14/**2738**

Gee v Shell UK Ltd [2002] EWCA Civ 1479; [2003] I.R.L.R. 82; (2002) 99(49) L.S.G. 19; (2002) 146 S.J.L.B. 245; Times, November 4, 2002, CA (Civ Div) .......... *Digested,* 02/**1353**: *Applied* 14/1083: *Considered* 05/1220, 05/1318

Geldard v Depuy International Ltd (Unreported, April 10, 2012), CC (Leeds) [*Thompsons Solicitors, 17 Wellington Street, Leeds*] .......... *Digested,* 14/**2327**

Gelley v Shephard [2013] EWCA Civ 1172; [2014] 1 P. & C.R. DG5, CA (Civ Div)

Gemeente 's-Hertogenbosch v Staatssecretaris van Financien (C-92/13) [2014] B.V.C. 41; [2014] S.T.I. 2928, ECJ (4th Chamber)

Gemeinde Altrip v Land Rheinland-Pfalz (C-72/12) [2014] P.T.S.R. 311, ECJ (2nd Chamber)

GENENTECH/File exclusion (T2522/10) [2014] E.P.O.R. 42, EPO (Technical Bd App)

General Dental Council v Jamous [2013] EWHC 1428 (Admin); (2013) 134 B.M.L.R. 79; [2013] A.C.D. 115, DC .......... *Digested,* 14/**1486**

General Healthcare Group Ltd v Revenue and Customs Commissioners [2014] UKFTT 353 (TC); [2014] S.F.T.D. 1026; [2014] S.T.I. 1921, FTT (Tax) .......... *Digested,* 14/**3053**

General Medical Council v Hiew [2007] EWCA Civ 369; [2007] 1 W.L.R. 2007; [2007] 4 All E.R. 473; [2007] LS Law Medical 309; Times, June 15, 2007, CA (Civ Div); affirming [2006] EWHC 2699 (Admin), QBD (Admin) .......... *Digested,* 07/**1951**: *Applied* 13/1441, 14/1494: *Considered* 10/1542

General Motors Acceptance Corp (UK) Plc v Revenue and Customs Commissioners [2007] B.V.C. 2302, V&DTr (London) *Considered* 11/3551, 14/3075

Generics (UK) Ltd (t/a Mylan) v Yeda Research & Development Co Ltd [2013] EWCA Civ 925; [2013] Bus. L.R. 1329; [2014] R.P.C. 4, CA (Civ Div); affirming [2012] EWHC 1848 (Pat), Ch D (Patents Ct) ........ *Digested,* 14/**1896**: *Considered* 14/1900

Genesis Housing Association Ltd v Liberty Syndicate Management Ltd [2013] EWCA Civ 1173; [2013] Bus. L.R. 1399; [2013] 2 C.L.C. 444; [2013] B.L.R. 565; 151 Con. L.R. 81; [2014] Lloyd's Rep. I.R. 318; [2013] C.I.L.L. 3417; [2013] 42 E.G. 124 (C.S.), CA (Civ Div); affirming [2012] EWHC 3105 (TCC); [2012] 2 C.L.C. 837; [2013] B.L.R. 28, QBD (TCC) ........ *Digested,* 14/**1846**

Genil 48 SL v Bankinter SA (C-604/11) [2013] Bus. L.R. 1132; [2013] 3 C.M.L.R. 43; [2014] C.E.C. 95, ECJ (4th Chamber)

Genovese v Malta (53124/09) [2012] 1 F.L.R. 10; (2014) 58 E.H.R.R. 25; [2011] Eq. L.R. 1282; [2012] Fam. Law 20, ECHR

George v Inland Revenue Commissioners see Inland Revenue Commissioners v George

George v Secretary of State for the Home Department see R. (on the application of George) v Secretary of State for the Home Department

Georgian American Alloys Inc v White and Case LLP [2014] EWHC 94 (Comm); [2014] 1 C.L.C. 86, QBD (Comm) ........ *Digested,* 14/**2060**

Georgiou (t/a Marios Chippery) v Customs and Excise Commissioners; *sub nom* Marios Chippery, Re [1996] S.T.C. 463, CA (Civ Div); affirming [1995] S.T.C. 1101; Times, October 19, 1995, QBD; affirming [1994] V.A.T.T.R. 125, VAT Tr (Manchester) ........ *Digested,* 96/**5905**: *Applied* 07/4283, 11/3533, 13/779, 14/3065: *Complaint dismissed* 01/3522: *Considered* 10/3469: *Followed* 10/3496

Germany v Italy (Unreported, February 3, 2012), ICJ *Considered* 14/1632

Germany v Puid (C-4/11) [2014] Q.B. 346; [2014] 2 W.L.R. 98; [2014] I.N.L.R. 458, ECJ (Grand Chamber)

Gestevision Telecinco SA v Youtube LLC [2014] 2 C.M.L.R. 13, Aud (Sp)

Geys v Societe Generale; *sub nom* Societe Generale (London Branch) v Geys [2012] UKSC 63; [2013] 1 A.C. 523; [2013] 2 W.L.R. 50; [2013] 1 All E.R. 1061; [2013] I.C.R. 117; [2013] I.R.L.R. 122; Times, January 28, 2013, SC; reversing in part [2011] EWCA Civ 307; [2011] I.R.L.R. 482, CA (Civ Div); reversing in part [2010] EWHC 648 (Ch); [2010] I.R.L.R. 950, Ch D ........ *Digested,* 13/**1056**: *Considered* 14/1026, 14/952

Ghaidan v Godin-Mendoza; *sub nom* Godin-Mendoza v Ghaidan; Ghaidan v Mendoza; Mendoza v Ghaidan [2004] UKHL 30; [2004] 2 A.C. 557; [2004] 3 W.L.R. 113; [2004] 3 All E.R. 411; [2004] 2 F.L.R. 600; [2004] 2 F.C.R. 481; [2004] H.R.L.R. 31; [2004] U.K.H.R.R. 827; 16 B.H.R.C. 671; [2004] H.L.R. 46; [2005] 1 P. & C.R. 18; [2005] L. & T.R. 3; [2004] 2 E.G.L.R. 132; [2004] Fam. Law 641; [2004] 27 E.G. 128 (C.S.); (2004) 101(27) L.S.G. 30; (2004) 154 N.L.J. 1013; (2004) 148 S.J.L.B. 792; [2004] N.P.C. 100; [2004] 2 P. & C.R. DG17; Times, June 24, 2004, HL; affirming [2002] EWCA Civ 1533; [2003] Ch. 380; [2003] 2 W.L.R. 478; [2002] 4 All E.R. 1162; [2002] 3 F.C.R. 591; [2003] U.K.H.R.R. 254; 13 B.H.R.C. 608; [2003] H.L.R. 35; [2003] L. & T.R. 14; [2003] A.C.D. 12; [2003] Fam. Law 87; [2002] 46 E.G. 197 (C.S.); (2003) 100(1) L.S.G. 24; (2002) 152 N.L.J. 1718; (2002) 146 S.J.L.B. 253; [2002] N.P.C. 138; [2003] 1 P. & C.R. DG14; Times, November 14, 2002; Independent, November 22, 2002, CA (Civ Div) ........ *Digested,* 04/**2538**: *Applied* 04/1889, 05/2118, 05/2641, 06/4484, 07/3293, 07/4358, 08/3137, 09/2528, 09/4294, 10/1049, 11/594, 13/1629, 14/1016, 14/1063, 14/2008, 14/823: *Considered* 04/1312, 04/707, 05/2129, 06/1004, 06/1649, 06/4470, 06/871, 07/5431, 09/2106, 09/3765, 13/1868: *Followed* 13/947, 13/991, 14/1123, 14/1262, 14/2864

Ghaidan v Mendoza see Ghaidan v Godin-Mendoza

Ghana v Gambrah [2014] EWHC 1569 (Admin); [2014] 1 W.L.R. 4464; [2014] A.C.D. 114, DC

Ghelanis Superstore and Cash & Carry Ltd v Revenue and Customs Commissioners [2014] UKFTT 111 (TC); [2014] S.F.T.D. 835; [2014] S.T.I. 1582, FTT (Tax) ..... *Digested,* 14/**2866**

Giambrone v JMC Holidays Ltd (formerly t/a Sunworld Holidays Ltd) (Costs) [2002] EWHC 2932 (QB); [2003] 1 All E.R. 982; [2003] 2 Costs L.R. 189; (2003) 153 N.L.J. 58, QBD ........ *Digested,* 03/**347**: *Applied* 14/331

Gibbon v Manchester City Council; *joined case* LG Blower Specialist Bricklayer Ltd v Reeves [2010] EWCA Civ 726; [2010] 1 W.L.R. 2081; [2011] 2 All E.R. 258; [2010] C.P. Rep. 40; [2010] 5 Costs L.R. 828; [2010] P.I.Q.R. P16; [2010] 3 E.G.L.R. 85; [2010] 36 E.G. 120; [2010] 27 E.G. 84 (C.S.), CA (Civ Div) ........... *Digested,* 10/**387**: *Applied* 11/359, 14/371: *Considered* 13/401: *Followed* 11/297, 13/290, 13/295

Gibbs v Revenue and Customs Commissioners [2013] UKFTT 236 (TC), FTT (Tax) *Considered* 14/2862

Gibbs Gillespie (A Partnership) v Sturch [2014] EWCA Civ 392; [2014] E.C.C. 31, CA (Civ Div)

Gibraltar European Elections, Re (C-145/04) see Spain v United Kingdom (C-145/04)

Gibson v Revenue and Customs Commissioners [2013] UKFTT 636 (TC); [2014] S.T.I. 440, FTT (Tax)

Gidrxslme Shipping Co Ltd v Tantomar Transportes Maritimos Lda (The Naftilos) [1995] 1 W.L.R. 299; [1994] 4 All E.R. 507; [1994] 2 Lloyd's Rep. 392; [1994] C.L.C. 544; (1994) 91(27) L.S.G. 37; (1994) 138 S.J.L.B. 127; Times, May 27, 1994, QBD (Comm) .......... *Digested,* 96/**844**: *Applied* 14/305: *Considered* 03/397

Gielen v Ministerraad (C-299/13) [2014] B.T.C. 47; [2014] S.T.I. 3125, ECJ (5th Chamber)

Giersch v Luxembourg (C-20/12) [2014] 1 C.M.L.R. 2; [2014] C.E.C. 349, ECJ (5th Chamber)

Gilbert (Valuation Officer) v S Hickinbottom & Sons Ltd [1956] 2 Q.B. 40; [1956] 2 W.L.R. 952; [1956] 2 All E.R. 101; (1956) 120 J.P. 288; 54 L.G.R. 215; 1 R.R.C. 46; (1956) 49 R. & I.T. 231; (1956) 100 S.J. 301, CA; affirming 165 E.G. 440; 48 R. & I.T. 170; [1955] J.P.L. 373, Lands Tr .......... *Digested,* 56/**7297**: *Applied* 97/4033, 08/3041, 08/3051, 09/2683: *Considered* 61/6117, 61/7484, 86/2788, 91/2374, 11/2646: *Distinguished* 61/7481: *Followed* 11/2649, 12/2685, 13/2410, 14/2137

Gilbert Ash (Northern) Ltd v Modern Engineering (Bristol) Ltd; *sub nom* Modern Engineering (Bristol) Ltd v Gilbert Ash (Northern) Ltd [1974] A.C. 689; [1973] 3 W.L.R. 421; [1973] 3 All E.R. 195; 1 B.L.R. 73; 72 L.G.R. 1; (1973) 117 S.J. 745, HL; reversing 71 L.G.R. 162, CA (Civ Div) .......... *Digested,* 73/**262**: *Applied* 74/268, 81/188, 85/218, 88/461, 92/312, 93/2361, 08/680, 11/546, 13/2830: *Considered* 75/3180, 85/2604, 93/2519, 94/2797, 07/5011, 11/505: *Distinguished* 74/267, 84/2722: *Followed* 82/3441, 83/3961, 86/202, 93/301, 10/625, 13/960, 14/618

Gilchrist v Revenue and Customs Commissioners [2014] UKUT 169 (TCC); [2014] 4 All E.R. 943; [2014] S.T.C. 1713; [2014] B.T.C. 513; [2014] W.T.L.R. 1209; [2014] S.T.I. 1875, UT (Tax) .......... *Digested,* 14/**2939**

Giles v Royal National Institute for the Blind; *sub nom* Giles v Royal National Institute of Blind People [2014] EWHC 1373 (Ch); [2014] S.T.C. 1631; [2014] B.T.C. 24; [2014] W.T.L.R. 1347; 17 I.T.E.L.R. 170; [2014] S.T.I. 1910, Ch D .......... *Digested,* 14/**2831**

Giles v Royal National Institute of Blind People see Giles v Royal National Institute for the Blind

Gill v Quinn [2004] EWHC 883 (Ch); [2005] B.P.I.R. 129, Ch D *Considered* 06/2331, 14/1781

Gill v RSPCA see Gill v Woodall

Gill v Woodall; *sub nom* Gill v RSPCA [2010] EWCA Civ 1430; [2011] Ch. 380; [2011] 3 W.L.R. 85; [2011] W.T.L.R. 251; [2010] N.P.C. 126; Times, February 1, 2011, CA (Civ Div); affirming [2009] EWHC 3778 (Ch), Ch D (Leeds) .......... *Digested,* 11/**3268**: *Applied* 13/2985, 14/2843: *Considered* 14/2840: *Followed* 14/2841

Gill & Duffus SA v Berger & Co Inc; *sub nom* Berger & Co v Gill & Duffus SA [1984] A.C. 382; [1984] 2 W.L.R. 95; [1984] 1 All E.R. 438; [1984] 1 Lloyd's Rep. 227; (1984) 81 L.S.G. 429; (1984) 128 S.J. 47, HL; reversing [1983] 1 Lloyd's Rep. 622; [1983] Com. L.R. 122, CA (Civ Div); reversing [1981] 2 Lloyd's Rep. 233; [1981] Com. L.R. 253, QBD (Comm) .......... *Digested,* 84/**403**: *Considered* 14/119

Gillan v United Kingdom (4158/05) (2010) 50 E.H.R.R. 45; 28 B.H.R.C. 420; [2010] Crim. L.R. 415; (2010) 160 N.L.J. 104; Times, January 15, 2010, ECHR .......... *Digested,* 10/**1746**: *Applied* 12/2663: *Considered* 14/2461, 14/701

Gillett v Holt [2001] Ch. 210; [2000] 3 W.L.R. 815; [2000] 2 All E.R. 289; [2000] 2 F.L.R. 266; [2000] 1 F.C.R. 705; [2000] W.T.L.R. 195; [2000] Fam. Law 714; (2000) 97(12) L.S.G. 40; (2000) 144 S.J.L.B. 141; [2000] N.P.C. 25; (2000) 80 P. & C.R. D3; Times, March 17, 2000, CA (Civ Div); reversing [1998] 3 All E.R. 917; [1998] 2 F.L.R. 470; [1998] Fam. Law 596; (1998) 95(26) L.S.G. 31; Times, June 18, 1998, Ch D ........ *Digested,* 00/**2321**: *Applied* 03/3592, 04/1520, 04/3676, 06/3494, 09/1363, 14/3024: *Considered* 01/4859, 02/4319, 06/4092, 09/2318, 09/3723, 13/1162: *Distinguished* 05/3384, 12/1266: *Followed* 01/5158, 02/3843

Gillingham Football Club Ltd v McCammon; *joined case* Scally v McCammon [2014] Eq. L.R. 4, EAT ........ *Digested,* 14/**1106**

Gimex International Groupe Import Export v Chill Bag Co Ltd [2012] EWPCC 34; [2012] 6 Costs L.R. 1069, PCC ........ *Digested,* 13/**1810**: *Considered* 13/1811, 14/356

Giorgi v Italy (23563/07) (2014) 59 E.H.R.R. 31, ECHR

Girobank Plc v Clarke (Inspector of Taxes) [1998] 1 W.L.R. 942; [1998] 4 All E.R. 312; [1998] S.T.C. 182; 70 T.C. 387; [1998] B.T.C. 24; (1998) 95(6) L.S.G. 25; (1998)142 S.J.L.B. 43; Times, January 6, 1998; Independent, January 26, 1998, CA (Civ Div); affirming [1996] S.T.C. 540; 70 T.C. 387; [1996] E.G. 45 (C.S.); (1996) 93(16) L.S.G. 32; (1996) 140 S.J.L.B. 100; Times, March 21, 1996, Ch D ........ *Digested,* 98/**4600**: *Considered* 14/2882

Girotra v Revenue and Customs Commissioners [2014] UKFTT 775 (TC); [2014] S.T.I. 2767, FTT (Tax)

Gisda Cyf v Barratt [2010] UKSC 41; [2010] 4 All E.R. 851; [2010] I.C.R. 1475; [2010] I.R.L.R. 1073; (2010) 160 N.L.J. 1457; (2010) 154(39) S.J.L.B. 30; Times, October 19, 2010, SC; affirming [2009] EWCA Civ 648; [2009] I.C.R. 1408; [2009] I.R.L.R. 934, CA (Civ Div); affirming UKEAT/0173/08/ZT, EAT ........ *Digested,* 10/**1142**: *Applied* 13/987: *Considered* 11/1122, 14/3506

GJ v Foundation Trust see J v Foundation Trust

GKN Bolts & Nuts Ltd (Automotive Division) Birmingham Works Sports & Social Club, Re; *sub nom* Leek v Donkersley [1982] 1 W.L.R. 774; [1982] 2 All E.R. 855; (1982) 79 L.S.G. 953; (1982) 126 S.J. 327, Ch D ........ *Digested,* 82/**283**: *Applied* 07/4264: *Considered* 14/526

Gladehurst Properties Ltd v Hashemi; *sub nom* Hashemi v Gladehurst Properties Ltd [2011] EWCA Civ 604; [2011] 4 All E.R. 556; [2011] H.L.R. 36; [2011] L. & T.R. 25; [2011] 2 E.G.L.R. 19; [2011] 29 E.G. 90; [2011] 2 P. & C.R. DG17, CA (Civ Div) ........ *Digested,* 11/**2074**: *Considered* 11/2075: *Superseded* 14/2016

Gladman Commercial Properties v Fisher Hargreaves Proctor [2013] EWCA Civ 1466; [2014] C.P. Rep. 13; [2014] P.N.L.R. 11; [2013] 47 E.G. 128 (C.S.), CA (Civ Div); affirming [2013] EWHC 25 (Ch), Ch D ........ *Digested,* 14/**2993**

Gladman Development Ltd v Wokingham BC [2014] EWHC 2320 (Admin); [2014] P.T.S.R. D24, QBD

Gladman Developments Ltd v Stroud DC [2014] P.A.D. 43, Planning Inspector

Glantz v Finland (37394/11) [2014] S.T.C. 2263, ECHR

Glapwell Football Club Ltd v Revenue and Customs Commissioners [2013] UKFTT 516 (TC); [2014] S.F.T.D. 485; [2013] S.T.I. 3777, FTT (Tax) ........ *Digested,* 14/**2875**

Glasgow Airport Ltd v Assessor for Renfrewshire Valuation Joint Board 2014 S.L.T. (Lands Tr) 46; [2014] R.V.R. 34; 2013 G.W.D. 36-710, Lands Tr (Scot) ........ *Digested,* 14/**3672**

Glasgow City Council v Fox Cross Claimants; *sub nom* Glasgow City Council v Unison; *joined cases* Unison v Glasgow City Council; GMB v Glasgow City Council [2014] CSIH 27; 2014 S.C. 610; 2014 S.L.T. 716; [2014] I.R.L.R. 532; [2014] Eq. L.R. 271; 2014 G.W.D. 18-341, IH (Ex Div); affirming [2013] I.C.R. 954; [2013] Eq. L.R. 460, EAT (SC) ........ *Digested,* 14/**3503**

Glasgow City Council v Marshall [2000] 1 W.L.R. 333; [2000] 1 All E.R. 641; 2000 S.C. (H.L.) 67; 2000 S.L.T. 429; 2000 S.C.L.R. 889; [2000] I.C.R. 196; [2000] I.R.L.R. 272; (2000) 2 L.G.L.R. 679; [2000] B.L.G.R. 229; (2000) 97(7) L.S.G. 39; (2000) 144 S.J.L.B. 101; Times, February 8, 2000; Independent, March 27, 2000, HL; affirming 1998 S.C. 274; 1998 S.L.T. 799; 1998 S.C.L.R. 33; 1997 G.W.D. 40-2089, IH (1 Div) ........ *Digested,* 00/**6214**: *Applied* 06/1368, 10/1083, 11/1116, 14/3504: *Considered* 10/1084: *Followed* 04/1255, 12/1100

Glasgow City Council v Unison see Glasgow City Council v Fox Cross Claimants

Glass v Surrendran see Collier v Williams

Glass v United Kingdom (61827/00) [2004] 1 F.L.R. 1019; [2004] 1 F.C.R. 553; (2004) 39 E.H.R.R. 15; (2005) 8 C.C.L. Rep. 16; (2004) 77 B.M.L.R. 120; [2004] Fam. Law 410; Times, March 11, 2004, ECHR ........ *Digested,* 04/**1994**: *Applied* 10/1744, 14/1516: *Considered* 04/1692, 05/1812

Glatzel v Freistaat Bayern (C-356/12) [2014] R.T.R. 26; [2014] 3 C.M.L.R. 52; [2014] All E.R. (EC) 1018, ECJ (5th Chamber)

Glaxo Group Ltd v Genentech Inc [2008] EWCA Civ 23; [2008] Bus. L.R. 888; [2008] F.S.R. 18; (2008) 31(4) I.P.D. 31024; Times, February 21, 2008, CA (Civ Div); affirming [2007] EWHC 1416 (Pat); [2007] F.S.R. 35; (2007) 30(7) I.P.D. 30048, Ch D (Patents Ct) ........ *Digested,* 08/**2271**: *Applied* 08/2272: *Considered* 12/1939: *Followed* 10/1964, 14/1903: *Referred to* 13/1806

GlaxoSmithKline Biological SA v Comptroller-General of Patents, Designs and Trade Marks [2013] EWHC 619 (Pat); [2013] R.P.C. 26, Ch D (Patents Ct) ........ *Digested,* 13/**1783**: *Preliminary ruling given* 14/1899

Glaxosmithkline Biologicals SA v Comptroller-General of Patents, Designs and Trade Marks (C-210/13) [2014] R.P.C. 17, ECJ (8th Chamber) ........ *Digested,* 14/**1899**

Gleeds Retirement Benefits Scheme, Re; *sub nom* Briggs v Gleeds [2014] EWHC 1178 (Ch); [2014] 3 W.L.R. 1469; [2014] Pens. L.R. 265; (2014) 158(18) S.J.L.B. 37, Ch D ........ *Digested,* 14/**2262**

Gleeson v J Wippell & Co Ltd [1977] 1 W.L.R. 510; [1977] 3 All E.R. 54; [1977] F.S.R. 301; (1977) 121 S.J. 157, Ch D ........ *Digested,* 77/**2399**: *Applied* 98/3385, 98/618, 08/2125, 13/419, 14/1878: *Cited* 00/346: *Considered* 82/2514, 93/3153

Gleeson Developments Ltd v Secretary of State for Communities and Local Government see R. (on the application of Gleeson Developments Ltd) v Secretary of State for Communities and Local Government

Glencore Energy UK Ltd v Cirrus Oil Services Ltd [2014] EWHC 87 (Comm); [2014] 1 All E.R. (Comm) 513; [2014] 2 Lloyd's Rep. 1, QBD (Comm) ........ *Digested,* 14/**643**

Glendalough Associated SA v Harris Calnan Construction Co Ltd [2013] EWHC 3142 (TCC); [2014] 1 W.L.R. 1751; [2013] 3 E.G.L.R. 115; [2014] C.I.L.L. 3441, QBD (TCC) ........ *Digested,* 14/**583**

Glengary Overseas Ltd v JKX Oil & Gas Plc see Eclairs Group Ltd v JKX Oil & Gas Plc

Glinski v McIver [1962] A.C. 726; [1962] 2 W.L.R. 832; [1962] 1 All E.R. 696; (1962) 106 S.J. 261, HL; affirming [1960] Crim. L.R. 428; Times, February 6, 1960, CA; reversing [1959] Crim. L.R. 56; Times, November 1, 1958, QBD ........ *Digested,* 62/**1887**: *Applied* 66/7586, 00/470, 14/2447: *Considered* 64/2337

Global Container Lines Ltd v Bonyad Shipping Co (No.1) [1998] 1 Lloyd's Rep. 528, QBD (Comm) ........ *Digested,* 98/**4442**: *Followed* 14/618

Global Mailing Ltd v Revenue and Customs Commissioners see 288 Group Ltd v Revenue and Customs Commissioners

Global Process Systems Inc v Syarikat Takaful Malaysia Bhd (The Cendor Mopu); *sub nom* Syarikat Takaful Malaysia Bhd v Global Process Systems Inc [2011] UKSC 5; [2011] 1 All E.R. 869; [2012] 1 All E.R. (Comm) 111; [2011] Bus. L.R. 537; [2011] 1 Lloyd's Rep. 560; [2011] 1 C.L.C. 1; [2011] Lloyd's Rep. I.R. 302; 2011 A.M.C. 305; Times, February 9, 2011, SC; affirming [2009] EWCA Civ 1398; [2010] 3 All E.R. 248; [2010] 2 All E.R. (Comm) 224; [2010] 1 Lloyd's Rep. 243; [2009] 2 C.L.C. 1056; [2010] Lloyd's Rep. I.R. 221; Times, March 2, 2010, CA (Civ Div); reversing [2009] EWHC 637 (Comm); [2009] 2 All E.R. (Comm) 795; [2009] 2 Lloyd's Rep. 72; [2009] Lloyd's Rep. I.R. 511, QBD (Comm) ........ *Digested,* 11/**1915**: *Followed* 13/1740, 14/1851

Global Radio Holdings Ltd v Competition Commission [2013] CAT 26; [2014] Comp. A.R. 51, CAT ........ *Digested,* 14/**547**

Globespan Airways Ltd (In Liquidation), Re; *sub nom* Cartwright v Registrar of Companies [2012] EWCA Civ 1159; [2013] 1 W.L.R. 1122; [2012] 4 All E.R. 1124; [2013] B.C.C. 252; [2013] 1 B.C.L.C. 339; (2012) 109(33) L.S.G. 18; (2012) 162 N.L.J. 1124; Times, November 19, 2012, CA (Civ Div); reversing [2012] EWHC 359 (Ch); [2012] 2 All E.R. 1234; [2012] B.C.C. 479; Times, June 4, 2012, Ch D (Manchester) ........ *Digested,* 13/**1668**: *Followed* 14/1811

Glouchkov v Forbes Inc see Berezovsky v Forbes Inc (No.1)

Glouchkov v Michaels see Berezovsky v Forbes Inc (No.1)

Glyn v Revenue and Customs Commissioners [2013] UKFTT 645 (TC); [2014] S.T.I. 630, FTT (Tax)

GMAC UK Plc v Revenue and Customs Commissioners see Revenue and Customs Commissioners v GMAC UK Plc
GMB v Glasgow City Council see Glasgow City Council v Fox Cross Claimants
Godin-Mendoza v Ghaidan see Ghaidan v Godin-Mendoza
Gogay v Hertfordshire CC [2000] I.R.L.R. 703; [2001] 1 F.L.R. 280; [2001] 1 F.C.R. 455; (2001) 3 L.G.L.R. 14; [2000] Fam. Law 883; (2000) 97(37) L.S.G. 40; Times, October 3, 2000, CA (Civ Div) ........ *Digested,* 00/**4890**: *Considered* 03/1246, 14/2263: *Followed* 13/956
Gohil v Gohil [2014] EWCA Civ 274; [2014] 3 W.L.R. 717; [2014] 2 F.C.R. 455; [2014] Fam. Law 1103, CA (Civ Div) ........ *Digested,* 14/**1369**
Gold Harp Properties Ltd v MacLeod see MacLeod v Gold Harp Properties Ltd
Gold Standard Telecom Ltd v Revenue and Customs Commissioners [2014] UKFTT 577 (TC); [2014] S.T.I. 2254, FTT (Tax)
Goldacre (Offices) Ltd v Nortel Networks UK Ltd (In Administration) [2009] EWHC 3389 (Ch); [2010] Ch. 455; [2010] 3 W.L.R. 171; [2010] Bus. L.R. 870; [2010] B.C.C. 299; [2010] 2 B.C.L.C. 248; [2010] 1 E.G.L.R. 25; [2010] 9 E.G. 168, Ch D (Companies Ct) ........ *Digested,* 10/**1835**: *Applied* 12/1794: *Considered* 11/4392: *Overruled* 14/1756
Goldbet Sportwetten GmbH v Sperindeo (C-144/12) [2013] Bus. L.R. 1115; [2014] C.E.C. 331; [2014] I.L.Pr. 1, ECJ (3rd Chamber)
Golden Balls Ltd v Office for Harmonisation in the Internal Market (Trade Marks and Designs) (OHIM) (T-437/11) [2014] E.T.M.R. 1, GC (1st Chamber)
Golden Strait Corp v Nippon Yusen Kubishika Kaisha (The Golden Victory) [2007] UKHL 12; [2007] 2 A.C. 353; [2007] 2 W.L.R. 691; [2007] 3 All E.R. 1; [2007] 2 All E.R. (Comm) 97; [2007] Bus. L.R. 997; [2007] 2 Lloyd's Rep. 164; [2007] 1 C.L.C. 352; (2007) 157 N.L.J. 518; (2007) 151 S.J.L.B. 468; Times, March 30, 2007, HL; affirming [2005] EWCA Civ 1190; [2006] 1 W.L.R. 533; [2006] 1 All E.R. (Comm) 235; [2005] 2 Lloyd's Rep. 747; [2005] 2 C.L.C. 576; (2005) 102(43) L.S.G. 31; Times, October 21, 2005, CA (Civ Div); affirming [2005] EWHC 161 (Comm); [2005] 1 All E.R. (Comm) 467; [2005] 1 Lloyd's Rep. 443; [2005] 1 C.L.C. 138; Times, March 4, 2005, QBD (Comm) ........ *Digested,* 07/**3816**: *Applied* 10/616, 13/579, 14/119: *Considered* 08/2147, 11/3113, 13/2554: *Followed* 10/3003
Golden Trust, Re; *sub nom* Megerisi v Protec Trust Management Establishment 16 I.T.E.L.R. 665, Grand Ct (CI)
Goldsmiths (Jewellers) Ltd v Customs and Excise Commissioners (C-330/95) [1997] S.T.C. 1073; [1997] E.C.R. I-3801; [1997] 3 C.M.L.R. 978; [1997] B.T.C. 5380; [1997] B.V.C. 494; Times, July 25, 1997, ECJ (6th Chamber) ........ *Digested,* 97/**4974**: *Applied* 11/3519, 12/3381, 14/3038: *Considered* 07/4323
Golfa v Secretary of State for the Home Department see R. (on the application of Golfa) v Secretary of State for the Home Department
Gollop v Pryke (Unreported, November 29, 2011), Ch D *Applied* 14/362
Golstein v Bishop; *sub nom* Bishop v Golstein [2014] EWCA Civ 10; [2014] Ch. 455; [2014] 2 W.L.R. 1448; [2014] 3 All E.R. 397, CA (Civ Div); affirming [2013] EWHC 881 (Ch); [2014] Ch. 131; [2013] 3 W.L.R. 572, Ch D ........ *Digested,* 14/**2227**
Golstein v Bishop; *joined case* Bishop v Golstein [2013] EWHC 1706 (Ch); [2013] B.P.I.R. 708, Ch D ........ *Digested,* 14/**1798**
Gomba Holdings (UK) Ltd v Minories Finance Ltd (No.2) [1993] Ch. 171; [1992] 3 W.L.R. 723; [1992] 4 All E.R. 588; [1992] B.C.C. 877; (1992) 136 S.J.L.B. 54; [1992] N.P.C. 12, CA (Civ Div); reversing in part [1992] B.C.L.C. 851, Ch D ...... *Digested,* 92/**3432**: *Applied* 97/3248, 06/698, 09/3165, 14/338
Gomes Viana Novo v Fundo de Garantia Salarial IP (C-309/12) [2014] I.C.R. 372, ECJ (5th Chamber)
Gooda Walker Ltd v Deeny see Henderson v Merrett Syndicates Ltd (No.1)
Goodbrand (Inspector of Taxes) v Loffland Bros North Sea Inc; *sub nom* Poseidon Inc v Inspector of Taxes; Loffland Brothers North Sea Inc v Goodbrand (Inspector of Taxes) [1998] S.T.C. 930; [1998] B.T.C. 297; Times, July 15, 1998; Independent, July 2, 1998, CA (Civ Div); affirming [1997] S.T.C. 102; [1997] B.T.C. 100; Times, January 24, 1997, Ch D; reversing [1996] S.T.C. (S.C.D.) 273, Sp Comm ........ *Digested,* 98/**4619**: *Considered* 14/2852
Goodchild-Simpson v General Medical Council [2014] EWHC 1343 (Admin); (2014) 139 B.M.L.R. 128, QBD (Admin)
Goode v Marks and Spencer Plc UKEAT/0442/09/DM, EAT *Applied* 14/1095

Goode v Martin [2001] EWCA Civ 1899; [2002] 1 W.L.R. 1828; [2002] 1 All E.R. 620; [2002] C.P. Rep. 16; [2002] C.P.L.R. 74; [2002] C.L.C. 420; [2002] P.I.Q.R. P24; (2002) 152 N.L.J. 109; Times, January 24, 2002; Independent, January 16, 2002, CA (Civ Div); reversing [2001] 3 All E.R. 562, QBD (Admlty) ............. *Digested,* 02/**487**: *Applied* 07/350, 07/491: *Considered* 02/486: *Distinguished* 01/419: *Followed* 14/426

Goodfellow v Nelson Line (Liverpool) Ltd [1912] 2 Ch. 324, Ch D *Considered* 14/275

Goodman v Central Capital Ltd [2012] EWHC 8 (QB); [2012] C.T.L.C. 158, QBD (Merc) (Birmingham) ............. *Digested,* 13/**225**: *Considered* 14/1455

Goodman v Elwood see Elwood v Goodman

Goodman v Goodman [2013] EWHC 758 (Ch); [2014] Ch. 186; [2013] 3 W.L.R. 1551; [2013] 3 All E.R. 490; [2013] W.T.L.R. 1181, Ch D ............. *Digested,* 13/**2961**

Goodrich Corp v Revenue and Customs Commissioners [2014] UKFTT 1029 (TC); [2014] S.T.I. 3550, FTT (Tax)

Goodwin v United Kingdom (28957/95) [2002] I.R.L.R. 664; [2002] 2 F.L.R. 487; [2002] 2 F.C.R. 577; (2002) 35 E.H.R.R. 18; 13 B.H.R.C. 120; (2002) 67 B.M.L.R. 199; [2002] Fam. Law 738; (2002) 152 N.L.J. 1171; Times, July 12, 2002, ECHR ............. *Digested,* 02/**2532**: *Applied* 03/1310, 11/3155, 14/2294: *Considered* 04/1261, 04/2814, 07/2261: *Followed* 02/1419, 03/2169

Google France Sarl v Centre National de Recherche en Relations Humaines (CNRRH) Sarl (C-238/08) see Google France Sarl v Louis Vuitton Malletier SA (C-236/08)

Google France Sarl v Louis Vuitton Malletier SA (C-236/08); *joined cases* Google France Sarl v Viaticum SA (C-237/08); Google France Sarl v Centre National de Recherche en Relations Humaines (CNRRH) Sarl (C-238/08) [2011] Bus. L.R. 1; [2010] E.C.R. I-2417; [2011] All E.R. (EC) 411; [2010] E.T.M.R. 30; [2010] R.P.C. 19; 3 A.L.R. Int'l 867; Times, June 8, 2010, ECJ (Grand Chamber) ............. *Digested,* 10/**2005**: *Applied* 12/1973, 13/1831: *Followed* 14/1927

Google France Sarl v Viaticum SA (C-237/08) see Google France Sarl v Louis Vuitton Malletier SA (C-236/08)

Google Inc v Vidal-Hall see Vidal-Hall v Google Inc

Google Spain SL v Agencia Espanola de Proteccion de Datos (AEPD) (C-131/12) [2014] Q.B. 1022; [2014] 3 W.L.R. 659; [2014] 2 All E.R. (Comm) 301; [2014] 3 C.M.L.R. 50; [2014] All E.R. (EC) 717; [2014] E.C.D.R. 16; [2014] E.M.L.R. 27; 36 B.H.R.C. 589; (2014) 164(7607) N.L.J. 20, ECJ (Grand Chamber)

Gordon v Legister see Wright-Gordon v Legister

Gordon v Omgate Ltd; *sub nom* Omgate Ltd v Gordon; Gordon, Re [2001] B.P.I.R. 909, Ch D ............. *Digested,* 02/**2652**: *Considered* 14/1790

Gordon, Re see Gordon v Omgate Ltd

Gore v Revenue and Customs Commissioners [2014] UKFTT 904 (TC); [2014] S.T.I. 2956, FTT (Tax)

Gore v Stannard (t/a Wyvern Tyres); *sub nom* Stannard (t/a Wyvern Tyres) v Gore [2012] EWCA Civ 1248; [2014] Q.B. 1; [2013] 3 W.L.R. 623; [2013] 1 All E.R. 694; [2013] Env. L.R. 10; [2012] 3 E.G.L.R. 129; [2012] 42 E.G. 133 (C.S.), CA (Civ Div) ............. *Digested,* 13/**3143**

Gorman v Lambeth LBC see Kay v Lambeth LBC

Gorry v Wiltshire CC see Burnip v Birmingham City Council

Gough v DPP [2013] EWHC 3267 (Admin); (2013) 177 J.P. 669; [2014] Crim. L.R. 371; [2014] A.C.D. 49, QBD (Admin) ............. *Digested,* 14/**673**

Gough v United Kingdom (49327/11) Times, December 3, 2014, ECHR

Gould v Advent Computer Training Ltd; *sub nom* Advent Computer Training Ltd, Re [2010] EWHC 1042 (Ch); [2011] B.C.C. 52, Ch D (Birmingham) ............. *Digested,* 11/**1829**: *Applied* 14/1764

Government of the French Community v Flemish Government (C-212/06) [2008] E.C.R. I-1683; [2008] 2 C.M.L.R. 31; [2009] All E.R. (EC) 187, ECJ (Grand Chamber) ............. *Digested,* 08/**1361**: *Considered* 14/2916

Govsha v Belarus (1790/2008) 35 B.H.R.C. 1, UN HRC

GP Aviation Group International Ltd, Re; *sub nom* Williams v Glover [2013] EWHC 1447 (Ch); [2014] 1 W.L.R. 166; [2014] 2 All E.R. 448; [2014] 1 B.C.L.C. 474; [2013] B.P.I.R. 576, Ch D ............. *Digested,* 13/**1709**

GPE (Hanover Square) Ltd v Transport for London; *sub nom* Hanover Square Ltd v Transport for London [2012] UKUT 417 (LC); [2014] R.V.R. 77; [2013] J.P.L. 1334, UT (Lands) ........ *Digested,* 14/**2502**

GPS (Great Britain) Ltd v Bird (Valuation Officer) [2013] UKUT 527 (LC); [2014] R.A. 145, UT (Lands) ........ *Digested,* 14/**2136**

Grace v Black Horse Ltd [2014] EWCA Civ 1413; [2014] C.T.L.C. 312, CA (Civ Div)

Graffiti Busters Ltd v Revenue and Customs Commissioners [2014] UKFTT 61 (TC); [2014] S.T.I. 544, FTT (Tax)

Graham v Every [2014] EWCA Civ 191; [2014] B.C.C. 376, CA (Civ Div) ........ *Digested,* 14/**523**

Graham v Green (Inspector of Taxes) [1925] 2 K.B. 37; 43 A.L.R. 791, KBD
*Considered* 14/1386: *Distinguished* 52/1666, 69/1720

Graham (t/a Xs & Os Amusements (formerly t/a Satellite Amusements)) v Revenue and Customs Commissioners [2014] UKUT 75 (TCC); [2014] B.V.C. 509, UT (Tax); affirming [2012] UKFTT 644 (TC), FTT (Tax)

Granada UK Rental & Retail Ltd v Pension Regulator see Granada UK Rental & Retail Ltd v Pensions Regulator

Granada UK Rental & Retail Ltd v Pensions Regulator; *sub nom* ITV Plc v Pensions Regulator; Granada UK Rental & Retail Ltd v Pension Regulator [2014] Pens. L.R. 17, UT (Tax) ........ *Digested,* 14/**2247**

Grand Entertainments Co v Revenue and Customs Commissioners [2014] UKFTT 610 (TC); [2014] S.T.I. 2428, FTT (Tax)

Grant v Hayes [2014] EWHC 2646 (Ch); [2014] B.P.I.R. 1455, Ch D

Grant v McDermott 16 I.T.E.L.R. 977, HC (NZ)

Grant (Inspector of Taxes) v Downes Settlement Trustees see Ransom (Inspector of Taxes) v Higgs

Granton Advertising BV v Inspecteur van de Belastingdienst Haaglanden/kantoor Den Haag (C-461/12) [2014] S.T.C. 2375; [2014] B.V.C. 31; [2014] S.T.I. 2113, ECJ (5th Chamber)

Grattan Plc v Revenue and Customs Commissioners (C-310/11) [2013] S.T.C. 502; [2013] S.T.I. 292, ECJ (2nd Chamber) ........ *Digested,* 13/**1171**: *Considered* 14/3079

Grauel Ruffer v Pokorna (C-322/13) see Ruffer v Pokorna (C-322/13)

Graves v Capital Home Loans Ltd [2014] EWCA Civ 1297; [2014] C.T.L.C. 233, CA (Civ Div)

Gray v Smith [2013] EWHC 4136 (Comm); [2014] 2 All E.R. (Comm) 359, QBD (Comm) ........ *Digested,* 14/**2588**

Gray v Thames Trains Ltd [2009] UKHL 33; [2009] 1 A.C. 1339; [2009] 3 W.L.R. 167; [2009] 4 All E.R. 81; [2009] P.I.Q.R. P22; [2009] LS Law Medical 409; (2009) 108 B.M.L.R. 205; [2009] M.H.L.R. 73; [2009] Po. L.R. 229; (2009) 159 N.L.J. 925; (2009) 153(24) S.J.L.B. 33; Times, June 19, 2009, HL; reversing in part [2008] EWCA Civ 713; [2009] 2 W.L.R. 351; [2008] P.I.Q.R. P20; [2008] M.H.L.R. 180; (2008) 105(26) L.S.G. 22; Times, July 9, 2008, CA (Civ Div); reversing [2007] EWHC 1558 (QB), QBD ........ *Digested,* 09/**2836**:
*Applied* 12/2415, 13/2195: *Considered* 10/2293, 10/3411, 13/1797, 14/2994, 14/3718: *Followed* 10/2285, 12/2417

Grayan Building Services Ltd (In Liquidation), Re; *sub nom* Secretary of State for Trade and Industry v Gray [1995] Ch. 241; [1995] 3 W.L.R. 1; [1995] B.C.C. 554; [1995] 1 B.C.L.C. 276; (1995) 92(1) L.S.G. 36; (1994) 138 S.J.L.B. 227; Times, November 24, 1994; Independent, December 12, 1994, CA (Civ Div) .... *Digested,* 95/**582**:
*Applied* 00/660, 07/2418, 07/566: *Considered* 96/985, 99/610, 09/2530: *Followed* 97/824, 13/477, 14/508

Graziani-Weiss v Austria (31950/06) (2014) 58 E.H.R.R. 22, ECHR

Great Elephant Corp v Trafigura Beheer BV [2013] EWCA Civ 905; [2013] 2 All E.R. (Comm) 992; [2014] 1 Lloyd's Rep. 1; [2013] 2 C.L.C. 185, CA (Civ Div); reversing [2012] EWHC 1745 (Comm); [2013] 1 All E.R. (Comm) 415; [2012] 2 Lloyd's Rep. 503; [2012] 2 C.L.C. 505, QBD (Comm) ........ *Digested,* 14/**2716**

Great Peace Shipping Ltd v Tsavliris Salvage (International) Ltd [2002] EWCA Civ 1407; [2003] Q.B. 679; [2002] 3 W.L.R. 1617; [2002] 4 All E.R. 689; [2002] 2 All E.R. (Comm) 999; [2002] 2 Lloyd's Rep. 653; [2003] 2 C.L.C. 16; (2002) 99(43) L.S.G. 34; (2002) 152 N.L.J. 1616; [2002] N.P.C. 127; Times, October 17, 2002; Independent, October 22, 2002, CA (Civ Div); affirming (2001) 151 N.L.J. 1696, QBD (Comm) ........ *Digested,* 02/**720**:
*Applied* 04/383, 04/472, 08/2743, 12/1285: *Considered* 05/516, 08/360, 09/3565, 10/2748: *Followed* 14/619

Great Portland Estates Plc v Westminster City Council see Westminster City Council v Great Portland Estates Plc

Great Western Hospitals NHS Foundation Trust v AA [2014] EWHC 166 (Fam); [2014] 2 F.L.R. 1206; [2014] Fam. Law 412, Fam Div

Great Western Hospitals NHS Foundation Trust v AA [2014] EWHC 132 (Fam); [2014] 2 F.L.R. 1209; [2014] Fam. Law 412, Fam Div

Greater Glasgow Health Board v Baxter Clark & Paul 1990 S.C. 237; 1992 S.L.T. 35, OH ............ Digested, 92/**6209**: *Approved* 96/6667: *Cited* 97/5682: *Considered* 96/6666: *Distinguished* 00/6638: *Overruled* 14/2470

Greater London Council v Cleveland Bridge and Engineering Co Ltd 34 B.L.R. 50; 8 Con. L.R. 30, CA (Civ Div); affirming [1984] C.I.L.L. 106, HC ............ Digested, 87/**245**: *Applied* 14/627: *Considered* 00/826, 12/595: *Followed* 12/595

Greaves v H Montlake & Co see Greaves v Stolkin

Greaves v Stolkin; *sub nom* Stolkin (Deceased), Re; *joined case* Greaves v H Montlake & Co [2013] EWHC 1140 (Ch); [2013] W.T.L.R. 1793, Ch D ............ Digested, 14/**2840**: *Applied* 14/2843

Grebenshikova v Office for Harmonisation in the Internal Market (Trade Marks and Designs) (OHIM) (T-394/10) [2014] E.T.M.R. 22, GC (3rd Chamber)

Green v Astor [2013] EWHC 1857 (Ch); [2013] 6 Costs L.O. 911; [2013] W.T.L.R. 1489, Ch D ............ Digested, 14/**2815**

Green v Austin [2014] B.P.I.R. 1176, CC (Kingston on Thames)

Green v Revenue and Customs Commissioners [2014] UKFTT 396 (TC); [2014] S.T.I. 2235, FTT (Tax)

Green v Royal Bank of Scotland Plc [2014] Bus. L.R. 596, SC

Green v Royal Bank of Scotland Plc [2013] EWCA Civ 1197; [2014] Bus. L.R. 168; [2013] 2 C.L.C. 634; [2014] P.N.L.R. 6, CA (Civ Div); affirming [2012] EWHC 3661 (QB), QBD (Merc) (Manchester) ............ Digested, 14/**241**

Greenacre Publishing Group v Manson Group see Greenacre Publishing Ltd, Re

Greenacre Publishing Ltd, Re; *sub nom* Greenacre Publishing Group v Manson Group [2000] B.C.C. 11; Times, December 17, 1998, Ch D ............ Digested, 99/**3348**: *Considered* 14/1788

Greenalls Management Ltd v Customs and Excise Commissioners [2005] UKHL 34; [2005] 1 W.L.R. 1754; [2005] 4 All E.R. 274; [2005] 2 C.M.L.R. 40; [2005] Eu. L.R. 839; [2005] L.L.R. 401; (2005) 102(23) L.S.G. 28; Times, May 16, 2005; Independent, May 19, 2005, HL; reversing [2003] EWCA Civ 896; [2003] 1 W.L.R. 2609; (2003) 100(32) L.S.G. 34; (2003) 147 S.J.L.B. 814; Times, July 2, 2003, CA (Civ Div); reversing in part [2002] EWHC 1691 (Ch); [2002] 1 W.L.R. 3333; [2002] V. & D.R. 33, Ch D ............ Digested, 05/**947**: *Applied* 04/902, 14/823: *Considered* 08/881

Greenclose Ltd v National Westminster Bank Plc [2014] EWHC 1156 (Ch); [2014] 2 Lloyd's Rep. 169; [2014] 2 B.C.L.C. 486; [2014] 1 C.L.C. 562; (2014) 158(17) S.J.L.B. 37, Ch D ............ Digested, 14/**270**

Greene King Plc v Revenue and Customs Commissioners [2014] UKUT 178 (TCC); [2014] S.T.C. 2439; [2014] B.T.C. 515, UT (Tax); affirming [2012] UKFTT 385 (TC); [2012] S.F.T.D. 1085; [2012] S.T.I. 2595, FTT (Tax) ............ Digested, 14/**2883**

Greene King Plc v Stanley [2001] EWCA Civ 1966; [2002] B.P.I.R. 491, CA (Civ Div) .. Digested, 03/**2379**: *Applied* 14/1826

Greener v DPP (1996) 160 J.P. 265; [1996] C.O.D. 200; (1996) 160 J.P.N. 255; Times, February 15, 1996, DC ............ Digested, 96/**1458**: *Considered* 14/679

Greenock Corp v Arbuckle Smith & Co Ltd see Arbuckle Smith & Co Ltd v Greenock Corp

Greenpeace of New Zealand Inc, Re [2014] NZSC 105; 17 I.T.E.L.R. 296, Sup Ct (NZ)

Greens v United Kingdom (60041/08) (2011) 53 E.H.R.R. 21; [2010] 2 Prison L.R. 22; (2010) 160 N.L.J. 1685; Times, November 24, 2010, ECHR ............ Digested, 11/**1703**: *Applied* 11/1687, 14/976: *Considered* 11/1702

Greenwich Millennium Village Ltd v Essex Services Group Plc (formerly Essex Electrical Group Ltd) [2014] EWHC 1099 (TCC); [2014] T.C.L.R. 4, QBD (TCC) Digested, 14/**371**

Greenwich Millennium Village Ltd v Essex Services Group Plc (formerly Essex Electrical Group Ltd); *sub nom* HS Environment Services Ltd v DG Robson Mechanical Services Ltd [2014] EWCA Civ 960; [2014] 1 W.L.R. 3517; 156 Con. L.R. 1; [2014] 3 E.G.L.R. 111, CA (Civ Div); affirming [2013] EWHC 3059 (TCC); 151 Con. L.R. 1, QBD (TCC) ............ Digested, 14/**599**

Greenwood v Bennett [1973] Q.B. 195; [1972] 3 W.L.R. 691; [1972] 3 All E.R. 586; [1972] R.T.R. 535; (1972) 116 S.J. 762, CA (Civ Div) ............ Digested, 72/**3137**: *Considered* 14/2529: *Distinguished* 93/69

Greenwood (Automatic Deportation: Order of Events), Re; *sub nom* Secretary of State for the Home Department v Greenwood [2014] UKUT 342 (IAC); [2014] Imm. A.R. 1288, UT (IAC)

Gregg v Raytheon see Bremer Vulkan Schiffbau und Maschinenfabrik v South India Shipping Corp Ltd
Greville Bathe Fund Trust, Re 17 I.T.E.L.R. 221, Royal Ct (Jer)
Grey (t/a Citytax) v Swansea City and County Council [2013] EWCA Civ 1057; [2013] P.T.S.R. 1366; [2014] R.T.R. 3; [2014] L.L.R. 296, CA (Civ Div) ........................ *Digested,* 14/**2554**
Griffin v Plymouth Hospital NHS Trust [2014] EWCA Civ 1240; [2014] I.R.L.R. 962; [2014] Pens. L.R. 689, CA (Civ Div); affirming UKEAT/0554/12/LA, EAT
Griffin (t/a K&D Contractors) v Midas Homes Ltd 78 Con. L.R. 152; (2002) 18 Const. L.J. 67, QBD (TCC) ........................ *Digested,* 02/**663**:
*Applied* 14/577: *Considered* 08/595, 14/582
Griffiths v JP Harrison (Watford) Ltd; *sub nom* JP Harrison (Watford) Ltd v Griffiths [1963] A.C. 1; [1962] 2 W.L.R. 909; [1962] 1 All E.R. 909; 40 T.C. 281; (1962) 41 A.T.C. 36; [1962] T.R. 33; (1962) 106 S.J. 281, HL; affirming (1961) 40 A.T.C. 132; [1961] T.R. 121; (1961) 105 S.J. 425, CA; affirming 53 R. & I.T. 739; (1960) 39 A.T.C. 287; [1960] T.R. 265, HC ........................ *Digested,* 62/**1506**:
*Applied* 65/1935, 67/533, 68/1891, 69/1664, 14/2849: *Considered* 69/1667:
*Distinguished* 66/6072, 67/1985, 69/1725: *Followed* 64/1816, 66/5971, 82/485
Griffiths v Secretary of State for Work and Pensions [2014] Eq. L.R. 545, EAT ............ *Digested,* 14/**1048**
Griffon Shipping LLC v Firodi Shipping Ltd (The Griffon); *sub nom* Firodi Shipping Ltd v Griffon Shipping LLC [2013] EWCA Civ 1567; [2014] 1 All E.R. (Comm) 593; [2014] 1 Lloyd's Rep. 471; [2014] 1 C.L.C. 1, CA (Civ Div); affirming [2013] EWHC 593 (Comm); [2013] 2 All E.R. (Comm) 246; [2013] 2 Lloyd's Rep. 50; [2013] 1 C.L.C. 741, QBD (Comm) ........................ *Digested,* 14/**2735**
Groarke v Fontaine [2014] EWHC 1676 (QB); [2014] 4 Costs L.R. 670; [2014] R.T.R. 31; (2014) 164(7609) N.L.J. 17, QBD ........................ *Digested,* 14/**299**
Grocholewska-Mullins v Mullins [2014] EWCA Civ 148; [2014] Fam. Law 444, CA (Civ Div)
Gross v Rackind; *sub nom* Rackind v Gross; City Branch Group Ltd, Re; Citybranch Group Ltd, Re [2004] EWCA Civ 815; [2005] 1 W.L.R. 3505; [2004] 4 All E.R. 735; [2005] B.C.C. 11; (2004) 148 S.J.L.B. 661, CA (Civ Div); affirming [2003] EWHC 3298 (Ch), Ch D (Companies Ct) ........................ *Digested,* 05/**530**:
*Applied* 14/523: *Considered* 06/566, 08/484
Gross v Switzerland (67810/10) [2013] 3 F.C.R. 608; (2014) 58 E.H.R.R. 7; 35 B.H.R.C. 187; (2013) 134 B.M.L.R. 37, ECHR
*Considered* 14/672
Grosvenor v Aylesford School Governors; *joined case* Lawson v Governing Body of Aylesford School [2014] EWCA Civ 491; [2014] C.P. Rep. 32, CA (Civ Div); affirming UKEAT/0001/08/LA, UKEAT/0002/08/LA, UKEAT/0003/08/LA, EAT ... *Digested,* 14/**37**
Ground Rents (Regisport) Ltd v Dowlen [2014] UKUT 144 (LC); [2014] 3 E.G.L.R. 7, UT (Lands)
Group M UK Ltd v Cabinet Office [2014] EWHC 3863 (TCC); [2014] 6 Costs L.R. 1090, QBD (TCC)
Group Seven Ltd v Allied Investment Corp Ltd [2013] EWHC 1509 (Ch); [2014] 1 W.L.R. 735, Ch D ........................ *Digested,* 14/**403**:
*Approved* 14/405
Group Seven Ltd v Allied Investment Corp Ltd [2013] EWHC 1423 (Ch), Ch D
*Considered* 14/1804
Groupe Eurotunnel SA v Competition Commission; *joined case* Societe Cooperative de Production Sea France SA v Competition Commission [2013] CAT 21; [2013] Comp. A.R. 432, CAT ........................ *Digested,* 14/**538**
Groupe Eurotunnel SA v Competition Commission; *joined case* Societe Cooperative de Production Sea France SA v Competition Commission [2013] CAT 30; [2014] Comp. A.R. 77, CAT ........................ *Digested,* 14/**545**
Groupe Gascogne SA v European Commission (C-58/12 P) [2014] 4 C.M.L.R. 14, ECJ (Grand Chamber)
Groupement des cartes bancaires (CB) v European Commission (C-67/13 P) [2014] 5 C.M.L.R. 22, ECJ (3rd Chamber)
Grovedeck Ltd v Capital Demolition Ltd [2000] B.L.R. 181; (2000) 2 T.C.L.R. 689; Independent, May 8, 2000, QBD (TCC)
*Doubted* 14/583
Grundig Italiana SpA v Ministero delle Finanze (C-255/00) [2002] E.C.R. I-8003; [2003] 1 C.M.L.R. 36; [2003] All E.R. (EC) 176; [2003] C.E.C. 178, ECJ (6th Chamber) ........................ *Digested,* 03/**1454**:
*Applied* 05/4377: *Considered* 05/4367, 08/4016, 14/2885: *Distinguished* 06/4470

Grupo Torras SA v Al-Sabah (No.5); *sub nom* Al-Sabah v Grupo Torras SA; *joined case* Bonafonte v Grupo Torras SA [2001] Lloyd's Rep. Bank. 36; [2001] C.L.C. 221; [2001] Lloyd's Rep. P.N. 117, CA (Civ Div); reversing [1999] C.L.C. 1469, QBD (Comm) ........ *Digested,* 01/**721**:
*Applied* 01/809, 14/2991
GSM Export (UK) Ltd v Revenue and Customs Commissioners [2014] UKUT 529 (TCC); [2014] B.V.C. 547, UT (Tax)
GSM Export (UK) Ltd (In Administration) v Revenue and Customs Commissioners [2014] UKUT 457 (TCC); [2014] B.V.C. 539, UT (Tax)
GSTS Pathology Services LLP v Revenue and Customs Commissioners [2014] UKFTT 211 (TC); [2014] S.T.I. 1610, FTT (Tax)
GT v United Kingdom (Admissibility) (63339/12) see IR v United Kingdom (Admissibility) (14876/12)
Guardian News and Media Ltd v AB Times, June 18, 2014, CA (Crim Div) ........ *Digested,* 14/**44**
Guardian News and Media Ltd v City of Westminster Magistrates' Court see R. (on the application of Guardian News and Media Ltd) v City of Westminster Magistrates' Court
Guardian News and Media Ltd v Incedal [2014] EWCA Crim 1861; [2014] H.R.L.R. 28; Times, October 29, 2014, CA (Crim Div) ........ *Digested,* 14/**45**
Guardian News and Media Ltd v United States see R. (on the application of Guardian News and Media Ltd) v City of Westminster Magistrates' Court
Guardian News and Media Ltd, Re; *sub nom* Ahmed v HM Treasury; Al-Ghabra v HM Treasury; HM Treasury v Youssef [2010] UKSC 1; [2010] 2 A.C. 697; [2010] 2 W.L.R. 325; [2010] 2 All E.R. 799; [2010] E.M.L.R. 15; [2010] H.R.L.R. 14; [2010] U.K.H.R.R. 181; (2010) 107(6) L.S.G. 18; (2010) 154(4) S.J.L.B. 29; [2010] N.P.C. 8; Times, January 28, 2010, SC ........ *Digested,* 10/**4**:
*Applied* 11/4, 11/599: *Considered* 10/1068, 10/1716, 11/373, 13/246:
*Followed* 11/1733, 11/868, 13/757, 14/790
Gudanaviciene v Director of Legal Aid Casework [2014] EWCA Civ 1622, CA (Civ Div); reversing in part [2014] EWHC 1840 (Admin); [2014] A.C.D. 123, QBD (Admin)
Guide Dogs for the Blind Association v Revenue and Customs Commissioners [2012] UKFTT 687 (TC); [2012] S.T.I. 3302, FTT (Tax)
*Considered* 14/3076
Guidezone Ltd, Re; *joined case* Kaneria v Kaneria [2014] EWHC 1165 (Ch); [2014] 1 W.L.R. 3728; [2014] 3 Costs L.R. 554, Ch D (Companies Ct) ........ *Digested,* 14/**398**:
*Approved* 14/397
Gulbenkian's Settlement Trusts (No.1), Re; *sub nom* Hacobian v Maun; Whishaw v Stephens [1970] A.C. 508; [1968] 3 W.L.R. 1127; [1968] 3 All E.R. 785; (1968) 112 S.J. 882, HL; affirming [1968] Ch. 126; [1967] 3 W.L.R. 1112; [1967] 3 All E.R. 15; (1967) 111 S.J. 686, CA (Civ Div) ........ *Digested,* 68/**3031**:
*Applied* 68/3586, 69/2770, 70/2635, 72/3163, 73/2597: *Cited* 72/3163:
*Considered* 69/2775, 76/2492, 86/2804: *Distinguished* 79/2813:
*Followed* 68/4068, 14/2257
Gully v Dix; *sub nom* Dix (Deceased), Re [2004] EWCA Civ 139; [2004] 1 W.L.R. 1399; [2004] 1 F.L.R. 918; [2004] 1 F.C.R. 453; [2004] W.T.L.R. 331; [2004] Fam. Law 334; (2004) 101(6) L.S.G. 32; (2004) 148 S.J.L.B. 116; Times, January 28, 2004, CA (Civ Div) ........ *Digested,* 04/**3663**:
*Applied* 14/2820, 14/2822
Gulshan (Article 8: New Rules: Correct Approach); *sub nom* Secretary of State for the Home Department v Gulshan [2013] UKUT 640 (IAC); [2014] Imm. A.R. 489, UT (IAC) ........ *Digested,* 14/**1710**
Guna Designs Ltd v Sonole Designs Ltd [2014] E.T.M.R. 61, PO (Irl)
Gurgur v Enfield LBC [2013] EWHC 3483 (Admin); [2014] L.L.R. 306, QBD (Admin)
Gurneville Securities Ltd v Thomson (Inspector of Taxes) see Thomson (Inspector of Taxes) v Gurneville Securities Ltd
Gurney (Inspector of Taxes) v Petch see Petch v Gurney (Inspector of Taxes)
Gustovarac v Croatia (Admissibility) (60223/09) [2014] H.L.R. 29, ECHR
GW v RW (Financial Provision: Departure from Equality) [2003] EWHC 611 (Fam); [2003] 2 F.L.R. 108; [2003] 2 F.C.R. 289; [2003] Fam. Law 386, Fam Div ........ *Digested,* 03/**1587**:
*Applied* 04/4216: *Considered* 14/1360: *Doubted* 03/1571: *Overruled* 11/1300
GW Plowman & Son Ltd v Ash; *sub nom* Plowman (GW) & Son v Ash [1964] 1 W.L.R. 568; [1964] 2 All E.R. 10; (1964) 108 S.J. 216, CA ........ *Digested,* 64/**1334**:
*Applied* 70/751, 70/924, 90/1933, 14/1029: *Distinguished* 94/1925:
*Followed* 86/4022, 89/4294
GW, Re; *sub nom* Haringey LBC v CM [2014] W.T.L.R. 1689, CP

H v B (Wardship: Jurisdiction); *sub nom* H (Children) (Abduction: Jurisdiction: Habitual Residence), Re [2014] EWCA Civ 1101; [2014] 3 F.C.R. 405; [2014] Fam. Law 1523; Times, August 8, 2014, CA (Civ Div); affirming [2013] EWHC 2950 (Fam); [2014] Fam. Law 38, Fam Div ........ *Digested,* 14/**1381**

H v F (Relocation) [2014] EWFC 11; [2014] Fam. Law 1401, Fam Ct

H v G (Adoption: Appeal) [2013] EWHC 2136 (Fam); [2014] 1 F.L.R. 691; [2013] Fam. Law 1358, Fam Div ........ *Digested,* 14/**1235**

H v H (Periodical Payments: Variation: Clean Break) [2014] EWCA Civ 1523, CA (Civ Div); reversing [2014] EWHC 760 (Fam); [2014] 2 F.L.R. 1338; [2014] Fam. Law 1105, Fam Div

H v K CC; *sub nom* H v Kent CC [2011] EWCA Civ 709; [2011] B.L.G.R. 798; [2011] E.L.R. 433, CA (Civ Div); affirming [2010] UKUT 376 (AAC), UT (AAC) ........ *Digested,* 11/**981**: *Followed* 14/938

H v Kent CC see H v K CC

H v Lord Advocate; *sub nom* Howes, Re; BH v Lord Advocate; *joined case* KAS v Lord Advocate [2012] UKSC 24; [2013] 1 A.C. 413; [2012] 3 W.L.R. 151; [2012] 4 All E.R. 600; 2012 S.C. (U.K.S.C.) 308; 2012 S.L.T. 799; 2012 S.C.L. 635; 2012 S.C.C.R. 562; [2012] H.R.L.R. 24; (2012) 109(27) L.S.G. 19; 2012 G.W.D. 21-432; Times, July 3, 2012, SC; affirming [2011] HCJAC 77; 2011 S.C.L. 978; 2012 S.C.C.R. 1; 2011 G.W.D. 26-587, HCJ; reversing in part 2008 G.W.D. 14-263, Sh Ct (Lothian) ........ *Digested,* 12/**1289**: *Applied* 13/1187: *Considered* 14/1650

H v W (Cap on Wife's Share of Bonus Payments); *sub nom* P v P [2013] EWHC 4105 (Fam); [2014] Fam. Law 445, Fam Div

H v W (Cap on Wife's Share of Bonus Payments: Costs) [2014] EWHC 2846 (Fam); [2014] Fam. Law 1519, Fam Div

H v Warrington BC see WH v Warrington BC

H (A Child) v McGine (Unreported, June 26, 2014), CC (Woolwich) [*Joseph England, Barrister, 3 Paper Buildings, Temple, London*] ........ *Digested,* 14/**2336**

H (A Child) v Mocko (Unreported, January 8, 2014), CC (Canterbury) [*Robert Golin, Barrister, Farrar's Building, Temple, London*] ........ *Digested,* 14/**2333**

H (A Child) (Abduction: Habitual Residence: Agreement), Re [2013] EWCA Civ 148; [2013] 2 F.L.R. 1426; [2013] Fam. Law 783, CA (Civ Div) ........ *Digested,* 14/**1377**

H (A Child) (Interim Contact Order: Relaxation of Restrictions), Re see H (A Child) (Interim Contact: Domestic Violence Allegations), Re

H (A Child) (Interim Contact: Domestic Violence Allegations), Re; *sub nom* H (A Child) (Interim Contact Order: Relaxation of Restrictions), Re [2013] EWCA Civ 72; [2014] 1 F.L.R. 41; [2014] 2 F.C.R. 378; [2013] Fam. Law 532, CA (Civ Div) ..... *Digested,* 14/**1322**

H (A Debtor) (No.38-SD of 1997), Re see Regional Collection Services Ltd v Heald

H (Abduction: Consent: Acquiescence), Re [2013] EWHC 3857 (Fam); [2014] 2 F.L.R. 385; [2014] Fam. Law 265, Fam Div ........ *Digested,* 14/**1383**

H (Care Proceedings: Appeal from Care Order), Re; *sub nom* H (Children), Re [2014] EWCA Civ 536; [2014] Fam. Law 1089, CA (Civ Div)

H (Children) (Abduction: Jurisdiction: Habitual Residence), Re see H v B (Wardship: Jurisdiction)

H (Children) (Adoption Order: Application for Permission for Leave to Oppose), Re see W (A Child) (Adoption Order: Leave to Oppose), Re

H (Children) (Contact: Domestic Violence), Re see L (A Child) (Contact: Domestic Violence), Re

H (Children), Re see H (Care Proceedings: Appeal from Care Order), Re

H (In Bankruptcy), Re see Regional Collection Services Ltd v Heald

H (Minors) (Adoption: Putative Father's Rights) (No.3), Re see H (Minors) (Local Authority: Parental Rights) (No.3), Re

H (Minors) (Child Abuse: Threshold Conditions), Re see H (Minors) (Sexual Abuse: Standard of Proof), Re

H (Minors) (Local Authority: Parental Rights) (No.3), Re; *sub nom* H (Minors) (Adoption: Putative Father's Rights) (No.3), Re [1991] Fam. 151; [1991] 2 W.L.R. 763; [1991] 2 All E.R. 185; [1991] 1 F.L.R. 214; [1991] F.C.R. 361; 89 L.G.R. 537; [1991] Fam. Law 306; (1991) 135 S.J. 16; Times, November 21, 1990, CA (Civ Div) ........ *Digested,* 91/**2500**: *Applied* 94/3194, 95/3531, 95/3533, 98/2437, 03/1538, 14/1422: *Considered* 93/2832, 95/3532, 96/592, 96/594, 98/2425, 99/2382: *Distinguished* 92/3113

H (Minors) (Sexual Abuse: Standard of Proof), Re; *sub nom* H (Minors) (Child Abuse: Threshold Conditions), Re; H and R (Child Sexual Abuse: Standard of Proof), Re [1996] A.C. 563; [1996] 2 W.L.R. 8; [1996] 1 All E.R. 1; [1996] 1 F.L.R. 80; [1996] 1 F.C.R. 509; [1996] Fam. Law 74; (1995) 145 N.L.J. 1887; (1996) 140 S.J.L.B. 24; Times, December 15, 1995; Independent, January 17, 1996, HL; affirming [1995] 1 F.L.R. 643; [1995] 2 F.C.R. 384; [1995] Fam. Law 401; (1995) 159 J.P.N. 338, CA (Civ Div) ........ *Digested,* 96/**632**:
*Applied* 96/490, 96/496, 98/2401, 00/949, 01/1975, 01/2566, 02/1636, 04/1463, 04/1481, 05/1529, 05/1559, 05/1560, 05/4191, 05/570, 06/1043, 06/2435, 06/2859, 06/4107, 07/2680, 08/1440, 10/1236, 12/2415, 13/1216, 14/2832: *Considered* 96/482, 96/556, 96/610, 01/2549, 01/721, 06/1680, 08/1457, 09/1097, 09/1553, 11/1371, 12/1352: *Distinguished* 01/2550: *Explained* 10/1329: *Followed* 02/1105, 04/1458, 05/2825, 08/1501, 08/1502, 08/4142, 10/1305, 10/1325, 11/1442, 12/437

H and R (Child Sexual Abuse: Standard of Proof), Re see H (Minors) (Sexual Abuse: Standard of Proof), Re

H Gautzsch Grosshandel GmbH & Co KG v Munchener Boulevard Mobel Joseph Duna GmbH (C-479/12) [2014] Bus. L.R. 391; [2014] E.C.D.R. 14; [2014] R.P.C. 28, ECJ (3rd Chamber)

H Trust, Re see X Trust Co Ltd v RW

H Waites Ltd v Hambledon Court Ltd [2014] EWHC 651 (Ch); [2014] 1 E.G.L.R. 119, Ch D

H-L (A Child) (Care Proceedings: Expert Evidence), Re; *sub nom* H-L (A Child) (Expert Evidence: Test for Permission), Re [2013] EWCA Civ 655; [2014] 1 W.L.R. 1160; [2013] 2 F.L.R. 1434; [2013] Fam. Law 1252, CA (Civ Div) ........ *Digested,* 14/**1341**

H-L (A Child) (Expert Evidence: Test for Permission), Re see H-L (A Child) (Care Proceedings: Expert Evidence), Re

HA (A Child), Re [2012] EWHC 1068 (COP), CP
*Considered* 14/2159

HA (Capacity to Change), Re; *sub nom* A Local Authority v A Mother [2013] EWHC 3634 (Fam); [2014] 2 F.L.R. 540; [2014] Fam. Law 277, Fam Div ........ *Digested,* 14/**1291**

Haas v Switzerland (31322/07) (2011) 53 E.H.R.R. 33, ECHR
*Considered* 12/1517, 14/672

Haasova v Petrik (C-22/12) [2014] R.T.R. 15, ECJ (2nd Chamber)

Habas Sinai Ve Tibbi Gazlar Istihsal Endustrisi v VSC Steel Co Ltd [2013] EWHC 4071 (Comm); [2014] 1 Lloyd's Rep. 479, QBD (Comm) ........ *Digested,* 14/**115**

Habib Bank Ltd v Central Bank of Sudan [2006] EWHC 1767 (Comm); [2007] 1 W.L.R. 470; [2007] 1 All E.R. (Comm) 53; [2006] 2 Lloyd's Rep. 412; [2006] 2 C.L.C. 176; Times, September 11, 2006, QBD (Comm) ........ *Digested,* 06/**504**:
*Applied* 14/1139: *Considered* 07/522

Habib Bank Ltd v Jaffer [2000] C.P.L.R. 438; (2000) 97(17) L.S.G. 34; (2000) 144 S.J.L.B. 187; Times, April 5, 2000, CA (Civ Div) ........ *Digested,* 00/**344**:
*Applied* 14/487

Hachette Filipacchi Associates v France (71111/01) (2009) 49 E.H.R.R. 23, ECHR ..... *Digested,* 09/**1945**:
*Considered* 14/664

Hackney Empire Ltd v Aviva Insurance UK Ltd (formerly t/a Norwich Union Insurance Ltd) [2013] EWHC 2212 (TCC); 149 Con. L.R. 213, QBD (TCC) ........ *Digested,* 14/**408**

Hacobian v Maun see Gulbenkian's Settlement Trusts (No.1), Re

Haderer v Finanzamt Wilmersdorf (C-445/05) [2008] S.T.C. 2171; [2007] E.C.R. I-4841; [2007] 3 C.M.L.R. 17; [2007] C.E.C. 881; [2010] B.V.C. 306; [2007] S.T.I. 1734, ECJ (3rd Chamber) ........ *Digested,* 08/**3999**:
*Applied* 13/3193: *Followed* 14/3051

Hadi Jemaldeen v A-Z Law Solicitors; *sub nom* Jemaldeen v A-Z Law Solicitors [2012] EWCA Civ 1431; [2013] C.P. Rep. 8; (2012) 156(44) S.J.L.B. 31, CA (Civ Div) . *Digested,* 13/**38**:
*Considered* 14/1347

Hadley v Baxendale 156 E.R. 145; (1854) 9 Ex. 341, Ex Ct
*Applied* 47-51/5368, 47-51/5562, 53/3775, 55/2559, 56/50, 66/11174, 66/12340, 66/3146, 67/3623, 77/2881, 79/2391, 80/640, 81/138, 86/980, 90/2764, 91/1316, 93/4846, 93/517, 98/4384, 99/1379, 01/1507, 03/5438, 05/959, 08/3443, 09/3561: *Cited* 14/643: *Considered* 47-51/9490, 61/2343, 67/3615, 68/1013, 69/881, 73/3466, 74/427, 87/2429, 90/670, 94/5413, 96/1196, 96/401, 97/3839, 97/6165, 97/989, 00/5981, 07/1064, 10/626, 11/533, 13/783: *Distinguished* 47-51/2561, 47-51/2566, 47/2561, 85/1282, 99/3946: *Followed* 67/3527, 69/3379, 88/1065, 98/1472, 10/832: *Referred to* 76/155.u, 83/4027

Haider v Syed [2013] EWHC 4079 (Ch); [2014] W.T.L.R. 387, Ch D ........ *Digested,* 14/**2832**

Haile v Waltham Forest LBC [2014] EWCA Civ 792; [2014] P.T.S.R. 1376; [2014] H.L.R. 37; [2014] 2 P. & C.R. DG18, CA (Civ Div) ........ *Digested,* 14/**1599**

Hainsworth v Ministry of Defence [2014] EWCA Civ 763; [2014] 3 C.M.L.R. 43; [2014] I.R.L.R. 728; [2014] Eq. L.R. 553, CA (Civ Div) ... *Digested,* 14/**1038**
Hainsworth v Ministry of Defence [2013] Eq. L.R. 1159, EAT
*Affirmed* 14/1038
Hajigeorgiou v Vasiliou see Vasiliou v Hajigeorgiou
Hakki v Secretary of State for Work and Pensions [2014] EWCA Civ 530; [2014] B.T.C. 22; [2014] L.L.R. 704; [2014] Fam. Law 1238, CA (Civ Div) ... *Digested,* 14/**1386**
Haleemudeen v Secretary of State for the Home Department [2014] EWCA Civ 558; [2014] Imm. A.R. 1087, CA (Civ Div)
Halifax Plc v Customs and Excise Commissioners (C-255/02) [2006] Ch. 387; [2006] 2 W.L.R. 905; [2006] S.T.C. 919; [2006] E.C.R. I-1609; [2006] 2 C.M.L.R. 36; [2006] C.E.C. 690; [2006] B.T.C. 5308; [2006] B.V.C. 377; [2006] S.T.I. 501; Times, February 27, 2006, ECJ ... *Digested,* 06/**4467**:
*Applied* 06/4462, 07/4308, 08/4007, 08/4014, 08/741, 08/878, 09/4112, 10/132, 10/1803, 10/3515, 10/823, 11/3535, 11/3559, 13/3205, 14/3087: *Considered* 06/5131, 07/4159, 08/3694, 09/1434, 09/4063, 10/1256, 10/3486, 10/3526, 11/3557, 11/3570: *Distinguished* 08/5106: *Followed* 10/3486, 10/3522, 11/3561, 12/3394
Hall v Beckenham Corp [1949] 1 K.B. 716; [1949] 1 All E.R. 423; 65 T.L.R. 146; (1949) 113 J.P. 179; 47 L.G.R. 291; 42 R. & I.T. 247; [1949] L.J.R. 965; (1949) 93 S.J. 219, KBD ... *Digested,* 47-51/**6987**:
*Considered* 13/2470, 14/2526
Hall v Bull; *sub nom* Bull v Hall; Preddy v Bull [2013] UKSC 73; [2013] 1 W.L.R. 3741; [2014] 1 All E.R. 919; [2014] H.R.L.R. 4; 36 B.H.R.C. 190; [2014] Eq. L.R. 76; (2013) 157(46) S.J.L.B. 37, SC; affirming [2012] EWCA Civ 83; [2012] 1 W.L.R. 2514; [2012] 2 All E.R. 1017; [2012] H.R.L.R. 11; [2012] Eq. L.R. 338; [2012] L.L.R. 311; (2012) 162 N.L.J. 329; Times, April 2, 2012, CA (Civ Div); affirming [2011] Eq. L.R. 283, CC (Bristol) ... *Digested,* 14/**1639**:
*Followed* 13/1568
Hall v Herbert [1993] 2 S.C.R. 159, Sup Ct (Can)
*Considered* 14/2994
Hall v Leeds City Council see Hounslow LBC v Powell
Hall v Oliver (Unreported, May 21, 2014), CC (Cardiff) [*James Bentley, Barrister, Guildhall Chambers, 5-8 Broad Street, Bristol*] ... *Digested,* 14/**2342**
Hall v Woolston Hall Leisure Ltd [2001] 1 W.L.R. 225; [2000] 4 All E.R. 787; [2001] I.C.R. 99; [2000] I.R.L.R. 578; (2000) 97(24) L.S.G. 39; (2000) 150 N.L.J. 833; Times, May 31, 2000; Independent, June 8, 2000, CA (Civ Div); reversing [1998] I.C.R. 651, EAT ... *Digested,* 00/**2205**:
*Applied* 04/1278, 04/665, 04/671, 09/1171: *Considered* 03/1218, 04/1202, 08/1209, 12/1055: *Followed* 04/1201, 12/1173, 14/1119
Hallam Estates Ltd v Baker [2014] EWCA Civ 661; [2014] C.P. Rep. 38; [2014] 4 Costs L.R. 660; (2014) 164(7608) N.L.J. 19, CA (Civ Div); reversing [2012] EWHC 1046 (QB), QBD ... *Digested,* 14/**397**
Hallam-Eames v Merrett Syndicates Ltd see Henderson v Merrett Syndicates Ltd (No.1)
Halliburton Energy Services Inc v Smith International (North Sea) Ltd [2006] EWCA Civ 1715; (2007) 30(2) I.P.D. 30009, CA (Civ Div); affirming [2005] EWHC 1623 (Pat); [2005] Info. T.L.R. 323; [2006] R.P.C. 2, Ch D (Patents Ct) ... *Digested,* 05/**2441**:
*Applied* 06/2468, 07/2632, 10/1962: *Considered* 06/2535, 12/1946, 14/1879
Halliburton Manufacturing & Services Ltd v Ravat see Ravat v Halliburton Manufacturing & Services Ltd
Halligen v Secretary of State for the Home Department see Pomiechowski v Poland
Halpern v Greater London Authority [2014] UKUT 116 (LC); [2014] R.V.R. 166, UT (Lands) ... *Digested,* 14/**2361**
Halsall v Brizell [1957] Ch. 169; [1957] 2 W.L.R. 123; [1957] 1 All E.R. 371; (1957) 101 S.J. 88, Ch D ... *Digested,* 57/**3005**:
*Applied* 67/2196, 78/787, 14/2510: *Cited* 13/2435: *Considered* 66/10313, 94/576, 98/4345
Halsey v Milton Keynes General NHS Trust; *joined case* Steel v Joy [2004] EWCA Civ 576; [2004] 1 W.L.R. 3002; [2004] 4 All E.R. 920; [2004] C.P. Rep. 34; [2004] 3 Costs L.R. 393; (2005) 81 B.M.L.R. 108; (2004) 101(22) L.S.G. 31; (2004) 154 N.L.J. 769; (2004) 148 S.J.L.B. 629; Times, May 27, 2004; Independent, May 21, 2004, CA (Civ Div) ... *Digested,* 04/**291**:
*Applied* 06/393, 06/397, 09/391, 11/295, 13/291, 14/1403: *Considered* 04/255, 04/266, 05/356, 08/1084, 08/307, 12/2304, 12/382, 13/1364: *Followed* 14/345, 14/375
Halsted v Halsted see Halsted's Will Trusts, Re

Halsted's Will Trusts, Re; *sub nom* Halsted v Halsted [1937] 2 All E.R. 570, Ch D
*Applied* 58/3107, 14/3027: *Considered* 61/8141, 62/2800, 09/1608
Ham v Ham [2013] EWCA Civ 1301; [2014] W.T.L.R. 255, CA (Civ Div) ........................ *Digested,* 14/**2229**
Hamalainen v Finland (37359/09) 37 B.H.R.C. 55, ECHR (Grand Chamber)
Hamblett v Godfrey (Inspector of Taxes) [1987] 1 W.L.R. 357; [1987] 1 All E.R. 916; [1987] S.T.C. 60; (1987) 84 L.S.G. 658; (1987) 131 S.J. 361, CA (Civ Div); affirming [1986] 1 W.L.R. 839; [1986] 2 All E.R. 513; [1986] S.T.C. 213; (1986) 83 L.S.G. 1063; (1986) 130 S.J. 485, Ch D ........................ *Digested,* 87/**2034**:
*Considered* 88/1929, 91/2092, 95/2766, 11/3359, 14/2908:
*Distinguished* 89/2028, 90/2646
Hamblins Leisure Services Ltd v Revenue and Customs Commissioners see Buckingham Bingo Ltd v Revenue and Customs Commissioners
Hamill v Chelmsford Magistrates' Court see R. (on the application of Hamill) v Chelmsford Magistrates' Court
Hamilton v Hamilton [2013] EWCA Civ 13; [2013] Fam. 292; [2013] 2 W.L.R. 1440; [2014] 1 F.L.R. 55; [2013] 2 F.C.R. 343; [2013] Fam. Law 539; (2013) 157(4) S.J.L.B. 43, CA (Civ Div) ........................ *Digested,* 13/**1294**
Hamilton v Official Receiver [1998] B.P.I.R. 602, Ch D ........................ *Digested,* 99/**3278**:
*Considered* 14/1750
Hamilton & Kinneil (Archerfield) Ltd v Revenue and Customs Commissioners; *sub nom* Revenue and Customs Commissioners v Hamilton & Kinneil (Archerfield) Ltd [2014] UKFTT 350 (TC); [2014] S.F.T.D. 1008; [2014] S.T.I. 2234, FTT (Tax) ........................ *Digested,* 14/**2887**
Hammerton v Hammerton [2007] EWCA Civ 248; [2007] 2 F.L.R. 1133; [2007] 3 F.C.R. 107; [2007] Fam. Law 798; Times, April 12, 2007, CA (Civ Div) ........................ *Digested,* 07/**948**:
*Considered* 08/296, 14/13, 14/321: *Followed* 14/2043
Hammond v Bristow Helicopters Ltd see King v Bristow Helicopters Ltd
Hammond v DPP; *sub nom* DPP v Hammond [2004] EWHC 69 (Admin); (2004) 168 J.P. 601; (2004) 168 J.P.N. 877; Times, January 28, 2004, DC ........................ *Digested,* 04/**770**:
*Applied* 06/828: *Considered* 11/687, 14/673
Hammond v Osborn [2002] EWCA Civ 885; [2002] W.T.L.R. 1125; (2002) 99(34) L.S.G. 29; (2002) 146 S.J.L.B. 176; [2002] 2 P. & C.R. DG20; Times, July 18, 2002, CA (Civ Div); reversing HQ0004566, QBD ........................ *Digested,* 02/**4314**:
*Applied* 03/3556, 03/4124, 04/3671: *Followed* 14/2836
Hammond Suddards Solicitors v Agrichem International Holdings Ltd [2001] EWCA Civ 2065; [2002] C.P. Rep. 21, CA (Civ Div) ........................ *Digested,* 02/**383**:
*Applied* 02/303, 02/381, 14/432: *Considered* 09/443, 12/477:
*Distinguished* 03/306: *Followed* 10/412
Hamnett v Essex CC [2014] EWHC 246 (Admin); [2014] 1 W.L.R. 2562; [2014] R.T.R. 22; [2014] A.C.D. 83, QBD (Admin) ........................ *Digested,* 14/**2580**
Hampshire CC v Beazley see R. v Beazley (Rosemary)
Hampshire CC v Broadway (Valuation Officer) [1982] R.A. 309; [1983] J.P.L. 122, Lands Tr
*Applied* 14/2479
Hampshire CC v Supportways Community Services Ltd see R. (on the application of Supportways Community Services Ltd) v Hampshire CC
Hampshire Land Co (No.2), Re [1896] 2 Ch. 743, Ch D
*Applied* 54/2993, 99/3382, 08/2648, 12/3401, 14/1807, 14/510:
*Considered* 95/4535, 96/3568, 09/2733, 10/446, 11/414: *Distinguished* 00/5348:
*Referred to* 76/34.u
Hampton Fuel Allotment Charity, Re; *sub nom* Richmond upon Thames LBC v Rogers [1989] Ch. 484; [1988] 3 W.L.R. 513; [1988] 2 All E.R. 761; (1988) 152 L.G. Rev. 971; (1988) 85(32) L.S.G. 34, CA (Civ Div) ........................ *Digested,* 88/**271**:
*Applied* 03/268, 14/285: *Considered* 94/368
Hanchett-Stamford v Attorney General [2008] EWHC 330 (Ch); [2009] Ch. 173; [2009] 2 W.L.R. 405; [2008] 4 All E.R. 323; [2009] P.T.S.R. 1; [2008] 2 P. & C.R. 5; [2009] W.T.L.R. 101; (2008) 158 N.L.J. 371, Ch D (Bristol) ........................ *Digested,* 08/**3970**:
*Considered* 14/526
Hancock v Revenue and Customs Commissioners [2014] UKFTT 695 (TC); [2014] S.F.T.D. 1163; [2014] S.T.I. 2978, FTT (Tax) ........................ *Digested,* 14/**2851**
Handels- og Kontorfunktionaerernes Forbund Danmark (HK) v Experian A/S (C-476/11) see HK Danmark v Experian A/S (C-476/11)
Handelswekerij GJ Bier BV v Mines de Potasse d'Alsace SA (21/76) [1978] Q.B. 708; [1977] 3 W.L.R. 479; [1976] E.C.R. 1735; [1977] 1 C.M.L.R. 284; (1977) 121 S.J. 677; Times, December 6, 1976, ECJ ........................ *Digested,* 77/**1283**:
*Applied* 07/672, 10/3410, 14/556: *Considered* 92/2790, 96/7098, 06/646, 07/666:
*Distinguished* 02/629: *Followed* 95/705, 98/770, 06/631: *Referred to* 97/895

Hanily v Minister of Local Government and Planning [1951] 2 K.B. 917; [1951] 2 All E.R. 749; (1951) 115 J.P. 547; 49 L.G.R. 769; (1951-52) 2 P. & C.R. 161; (1951) 95 S.J. 577, CA ........ *Digested,* 47-51/**1492**: *Applied* 53/1992: *Considered* 14/2401

Hankinson v Revenue and Customs Commissioners [2011] EWCA Civ 1566; [2012] 1 W.L.R. 2322; [2012] S.T.C. 485; 81 T.C. 424; [2012] B.T.C. 1; [2012] S.T.I. 29, CA (Civ Div); affirming [2010] UKUT 361 (TCC); [2010] S.T.C. 2640; [2010] B.T.C. 1691; [2010] S.T.I. 2642, UT (Tax); affirming [2009] UKFTT 384 (TC); [2010] S.T.I. 1368, FTT (Tax) ........ *Digested,* 12/**3268**: *Approved* 11/3317: *Considered* 11/3356, 12/3223: *Followed* 12/3269, 14/2890

Hannam v Financial Conduct Authority [2014] UKUT 233 (TCC); [2014] Lloyd's Rep. F.C. 704, UT (Tax)

Hannan v Newham LBC [2014] EWHC 1424 (Admin); [2014] J.P.L. 1101, QBD (Admin)

Hanningfield v Chief Constable of Essex [2013] EWHC 243 (QB); [2013] 1 W.L.R. 3632, QBD ........ *Digested,* 14/**2458**

Hanoman v Southwark LBC [2009] UKHL 29; [2009] 1 W.L.R. 1367; [2009] 4 All E.R. 585; [2009] P.T.S.R. 1059; [2010] H.L.R. 5; [2009] 24 E.G. 84 (C.S.); [2009] N.P.C. 74; [2009] 2 P. & C.R. DG14; Times, June 16, 2009, HL; affirming [2008] EWCA Civ 624; [2009] 1 W.L.R. 374; [2009] P.T.S.R. 69; [2009] H.L.R. 6; [2008] 24 E.G. 140 (C.S.); (2008) 105(29) L.S.G. 34; [2008] N.P.C. 64; [2008] 2 P. & C.R. DG14; Times, June 24, 2008, CA (Civ Div) ........ *Digested,* 09/**2541**: *Applied* 14/2016

Hanover Square Ltd v Transport for London see GPE (Hanover Square) Ltd v Transport for London

Hansford v Southampton Magistrates' Court [2008] EWHC 67 (Admin); [2008] 4 All E.R. 432; [2008] B.P.I.R. 379; Times, March 19, 2008, DC ........ *Digested,* 08/**2176**: *Considered* 14/732

Hanson v Church Commissioners for England; *sub nom* Hanson v London Rent Assessment Committee; *joined case* R. v London Rent Assessment Committee Ex p. Hanson [1978] Q.B. 823; [1977] 2 W.L.R. 848; [1977] 3 All E.R. 404; (1977) 34 P. & C.R. 158; (1976) 241 E.G. 683; [1977] J.P.L. 245; (1976) 120 S.J. 837; Times, November 8, 1976, CA (Civ Div); reversing [1976] Q.B. 394; [1976] 2 W.L.R. 318; [1976] 1 All E.R. 245; (1976) 31 P. & C.R. 286; (1975) 119 S.J. 867; Times, November 12, 1975, QBD ........ *Digested,* 77/**2520**: *Applied* 78/2507, 14/2010: *Considered* 87/2145

Hanson v London Rent Assessment Committee see Hanson v Church Commissioners for England

Hanson v Mercredi; *sub nom* Lubberts' Estate, Re 17 I.T.E.L.R. 438, CA (Alta)

Hanson Quarry Products Europe Ltd v Competition Commission see Lafarge Tarmac Holdings Ltd v Competition Commission

Happy Dragon Restaurants Ltd v Director of Lands [2014] R.V.R. 286, HC (HK)

Harada Ltd v Barclays Bank Plc see Dahabshiil Transfer Services Ltd v Barclays Bank Plc

Harb v Aziz [2014] EWHC 1807 (Ch); [2014] 1 W.L.R. 4437; [2014] H.R.L.R. 16, Ch D *Digested,* 14/**1949**

Harcourt v FEF Griffin [2007] EWHC 1500 (QB); [2008] Lloyd's Rep. I.R. 386; [2007] P.I.Q.R. Q9, QBD ........ *Digested,* 07/**511**: *Considered* 14/465: *Not followed* 08/352

Harding v Revenue and Customs Commissioners [2013] UKUT 575 (TCC); [2014] S.T.C. 891; [2013] B.T.C. 2088; [2013] S.T.I. 3773, UT (Tax) ........ *Digested,* 14/**2927**

Harding v Van Lee (Unreported, December 16, 2013), CC (Southampton) [*Katie Henry, Barrister, No 18 Chambers, 1 Rownhams House, Rownhams, Southampton*] ........ *Digested,* 14/**2321**

Harding v Wealands [2006] UKHL 32; [2007] 2 A.C. 1; [2006] 3 W.L.R. 83; [2006] 4 All E.R. 1; [2006] 2 C.L.C. 193; [2006] R.T.R. 35; (2006) 156 N.L.J. 1136; (2006) 150 S.J.L.B. 917; Times, July 6, 2006, HL; reversing [2004] EWCA Civ 1735; [2005] 1 W.L.R. 1539; [2005] 1 All E.R. 415; [2005] 2 C.L.C. 411; [2005] R.T.R. 20; (2005) 155 N.L.J. 59; Times, January 5, 2005, CA (Civ Div); reversing [2004] EWHC 1957 (QB), QBD ........ *Digested,* 06/**635**: *Applied* 09/611, 14/2559: *Considered* 06/641, 12/564, 14/825

Hare v Schurek [1993] C.C.L.R. 47; Times, May 28, 1993, CA (Civ Div) ........ *Digested,* 93/**465**: *Followed* 14/273

Hargreaves v Revenue and Customs Commissioners [2014] UKUT 395 (TCC); [2014] B.T.C. 526, UT (Tax) ........ *Digested,* 14/**2890**

Haringey LBC v CM see GW, Re

Haringey LBC v Musa [2014] EWHC 962 (Fam); [2014] Fam. Law 949, Fam Div

Haringey LBC v Musa [2014] EWHC 1200 (Fam); [2014] Fam. Law 951, Fam Div

Haringey LBC v Musa [2014] EWHC 1341 (Fam); [2014] Fam. Law 952, Fam Div

Harman v Home Office see Home Office v Harman
Harris v Conway see Berkeley Applegate (Investment Consultants) Ltd (No.1), Re
Harris v Rothery 16 I.T.E.L.R. 681, Sup Ct (NSW)
Harris v Secretary of State for Business, Innovation and Skills; *sub nom* Clenaware Systems Ltd, Re; Tivg Ltd, Re; Clenaware Leasing Ltd, Re [2013] EWHC 2514 (Ch); [2014] 1 B.C.L.C. 447, Ch D ........ *Digested,* 14/**507**
Harrison v Black Horse Ltd [2011] EWCA Civ 1128; [2012] E.C.C. 7; [2012] Lloyd's Rep. I.R. 521; [2011] C.T.L.C. 105; (2011) 155(39) S.J.L.B. 31, CA (Civ Div); affirming [2010] EWHC 3152 (QB); [2011] Lloyd's Rep. I.R. 455; [2011] C.T.L.C. 1, QBD (Merc) ........ *Digested,* 12/**614**: *Applied* 13/225, 13/550, 14/609
Harrison v Laidlaw [2014] EWHC 35 (Ch); [2014] C.P. Rep. 20, Ch D ........ *Digested,* 14/**433**
Harrison v Secretary of State for the Home Department; *sub nom* DH (Jamaica) v Secretary of State for the Home Department; *joined case* AB (Morocco) v Secretary of State for the Home Department [2012] EWCA Civ 1736; [2013] 2 C.M.L.R. 23; [2013] Imm. A.R. 622; [2013] I.N.L.R. 416, CA (Civ Div) ........ *Digested,* 13/**1597**: *Applied* 14/1612
Harrison v Secretary of State for the Home Department see Sanade (British Children: Zambrano: Dereci), Re
Harrison v Shepherd Homes Ltd [2014] EWHC 2786 (TCC); 156 Con. L.R. 158; [2014] 5 Costs L.R. 797, QBD (TCC) ........ *Digested,* 14/**373**
Harrison v Technical Sign Co Ltd; *sub nom* Active Commercial Interiors Ltd v Cluttons LLP [2013] EWCA Civ 1569; [2014] P.N.L.R. 15, CA (Civ Div); reversing [2012] EWHC 2887 (TCC); [2013] B.L.R. 244, QBD (TCC) ........ *Digested,* 14/**2205**
Harrison v United Kingdom (Admissibility) (44301/13) (2014) 59 E.H.R.R. SE1, ECHR
Harrod's Ltd v Harrod's (Buenos Aires) Ltd (Costs); *sub nom* Harrods Ltd v Harrods (Buenos Aires) Ltd (Costs) [2014] 6 Costs L.R. 975, Ch D
Harrods Ltd v Harrodian School [1996] R.P.C. 697; (1996) 19(10) I.P.D. 19090; Times, April 3, 1996, CA (Civ Div) ........ *Digested,* 96/**5717**: *Applied* 97/4905, 14/1890
Harrods Ltd v Harrods (Buenos Aires) Ltd (Costs) see Harrod's Ltd v Harrod's (Buenos Aires) Ltd (Costs)
Harrow LBC v A [2014] EWHC 303 (Fam); [2014] Fam. Law 436, Fam Div
Harrow LBC v Cusack see Cusack v Harrow LBC
Harrow LBC v Johnstone [1997] 1 W.L.R. 459; [1997] 1 All E.R. 929; [1997] 1 F.L.R. 887; [1997] 2 F.C.R. 225; (1997) 29 H.L.R. 475; [1997] Fam. Law 478; (1997) 161 J.P. Rep. 580; [1997] E.G. 41 (C.S.); (1997) 94(15) L.S.G. 26; (1997) 147 N.L.J. 413; [1997] N.P.C. 40; Times, March 14, 1997, HL; reversing [1995] 2 F.L.R. 191; [1995] 3 F.C.R. 132; (1996) 28 H.L.R. 83; 93 L.G.R. 435; [1995] Fam. Law 550; [1995] E.G. 53 (C.S.); [1995] N.P.C. 47; Times, March 31, 1995, CA (Civ Div) ........ *Digested,* 97/**2703**: *Considered* 00/2529, 14/496
Harry & Garry Ltd v (1) Mahesh Jariwalla (2) Shaunak Jariwalla (3) Hasmukh Jethalal Shah (Unreported, June 16, 1988), CA (Civ Div) *Not followed* 14/2586
Hart v Burbidge; *joined case* Samways v Burbidge [2014] EWCA Civ 992; [2014] W.T.L.R. 1361, CA (Civ Div); affirming [2013] EWHC 1628 (Ch); [2013] W.T.L.R. 1191; [2013] 2 P. & C.R. DG20, Ch D ........ *Digested,* 14/**1207**
Hart (RN) v AR Marshall & Sons (Bulwell) [1977] 1 W.L.R. 1067; [1978] 2 All E.R. 413; [1977] I.C.R. 539; [1977] I.R.L.R. 61; (1977) 12 I.T.R. 190; (1977) 121 S.J. 677, EAT ........ *Digested,* 77/**952**: *Considered* 14/1089
Hart Investments Ltd v Fidler [2006] EWHC 2857 (TCC); [2007] B.L.R. 30; [2007] T.C.L.R. 1; 109 Con. L.R. 67; [2006] C.I.L.L. 2397, QBD (TCC) ........ *Digested,* 07/**433**: *Applied* 11/494, 13/522, 14/583
Hartley v Magill see Porter v Magill
Harvest Finance Ltd (In Liquidation), Re see Jackson v Cannons Law Practice LLP
Harvest Finance Ltd (In Liquidation), Re see Jackson v Cannons Law Practice LLP
Harvest Finance Ltd (In Liquidation), Re see Jackson v Cannons Law Practice LLP
Harvey v Dunbar Assets Plc [2013] EWCA Civ 952; [2013] B.P.I.R. 722; [2013] 32 E.G. 57 (C.S.), CA (Civ Div); reversing [2012] EWHC 2890 (Ch); [2013] B.P.I.R. 66, Ch D (Newcastle) ........ *Digested,* 14/**637**
Harvey's Jersey Cream Ltd v Revenue and Customs Commissioners [2013] UKFTT 663 (TC); [2014] S.F.T.D. 599; [2014] S.T.I. 589, FTT (Tax) ........ *Digested,* 14/**2853**
Harwood v Baker 13 E.R. 117; (1840) 3 Moo. P.C. 282, PC (UK) *Applied* 47-51/10958, 01/5165: *Considered* 10/3214, 11/3267: *Followed* 14/2838
Harwood Construction Ltd v Lantrode Ltd (Unreported, November 24, 2000), QBD *Considered* 14/581

Hashemi v Gladehurst Properties Ltd see Gladehurst Properties Ltd v Hashemi
Hashtroodi v Hancock [2004] EWCA Civ 652; [2004] 1 W.L.R. 3206; [2004] 3 All E.R. 530; [2005] C.P. Rep. 17; Times, June 4, 2004; Independent, June 16, 2004, CA (Civ Div) ........ *Digested,* 04/**284**:
*Applied* 05/466, 06/348, 10/415, 14/445: *Considered* 05/403, 11/354, 13/405: *Followed* 11/384
Haslemere Estates v Baker [1982] 1 W.L.R. 1109; [1982] 3 All E.R. 525; (1982) 126 S.J. 463, Ch D ........ *Digested,* 82/**281**:
*Considered* 87/293, 88/271, 94/368, 14/285: *Distinguished* 03/268
Haslen (t/a Racer MX) v Revenue and Customs Commissioners [2013] UKFTT 658 (TC); [2014] S.T.I. 381, FTT (Tax)
Hassan v United Kingdom (29750/09) Times, October 16, 2014, ECHR
Hatton v United Kingdom (36022/97) (2003) 37 E.H.R.R. 28; 15 B.H.R.C. 259; Times, July 10, 2003, ECHR (Grand Chamber) ........ *Digested,* 04/**1984**:
*Applied* 04/1373, 08/1977: *Considered* 04/2763, 04/3042, 14/1635: *Distinguished* 07/3256
Hauck GmbH & Co KG v Stokke A/S (C-205/13) [2014] Bus. L.R. 1284; [2014] E.T.M.R. 60, ECJ (2nd Chamber)
Haulader v Secretary of State for the Home Department see Oboh v Secretary of State for the Home Department
Hauptzollamt Itzehoe v HJ Repenning GmbH (183/85) [1986] E.C.R. 1873; [1987] 2 C.M.L.R. 34, ECJ (3rd Chamber)
*Distinguished* 14/816
Hausgaard v Prime Minister (199/2012) [2014] 3 C.M.L.R. 16, HR (DK)
Haward v Fawcetts (A Firm) [2006] UKHL 9; [2006] 1 W.L.R. 682; [2006] 3 All E.R. 497; [2006] P.N.L.R. 25; [2006] 10 E.G. 154 (C.S.); [2006] N.P.C. 25; Times, March 3, 2006, HL; reversing [2004] EWCA Civ 240; [2004] P.N.L.R. 34; (2004) 148 S.J.L.B. 355, CA (Civ Div); reversing [2003] P.N.L.R. 36, QBD ........ *Digested,* 06/**472**:
*Considered* 07/475, 08/381, 11/2633: *Followed* 11/352, 13/391, 14/2212
Hawes v Burgess see Burgess v Hawes
Hawk Insurance Co Ltd, Re [2001] EWCA Civ 241; [2002] B.C.C. 300; [2001] 2 B.C.L.C. 480, CA (Civ Div); reversing [2001] B.C.C. 57, Ch D (Companies Ct) .. *Digested,* 02/**2714**:
*Applied* 02/2715, 03/2440, 07/2448, 14/1820: *Considered* 06/2362, 06/2381: *Followed* 05/2333
Hawkes v Cuddy; *sub nom* Neath Rugby Ltd, Re [2009] EWCA Civ 291; [2010] B.C.C. 597; [2009] 2 B.C.L.C. 427, CA (Civ Div) ........ *Digested,* 10/**452**:
*Applied* 14/2202
Hawkins v Newham LBC; *sub nom* Newham LBC v Hawkins [2005] EWCA Civ 451; [2005] H.L.R. 42; [2005] B.L.G.R. 750; [2005] 2 E.G.L.R. 51; [2005] 29 E.G. 100; [2005] N.P.C. 55; [2005] 2 P. & C.R. DG16; Times, May 3, 2005; Independent, April 29, 2005, CA (Civ Div) ........ *Digested,* 06/**2714**:
*Applied* 14/2003
Haxton v Philips Electronics UK Ltd [2014] EWCA Civ 4; [2014] 1 W.L.R. 2721; [2014] 2 All E.R. 225; [2014] P.I.Q.R. P11; (2014) 164(7592) N.L.J. 16, CA (Civ Div) ... *Digested,* 14/**2302**
Hay v Aynsley [2013] NSWSC 1689; 17 I.T.E.L.R. 238, Sup Ct (NSW)
Hay v Credit agricole mutuel de Charente-Maritime et des Deux-Sevres (C-267/12) [2014] 2 C.M.L.R. 32; [2014] C.E.C. 740, ECJ (5th Chamber)
Hayat v Secretary of State for the Home Department; *sub nom* Secretary of State for the Home Department v Hayat; *joined case* Treebhowan v Secretary of State for the Home Department [2012] EWCA Civ 1054; [2013] Imm. A.R. 15; [2013] I.N.L.R. 17, CA (Civ Div) ........ *Digested,* 13/**1633**:
*Considered* 14/1715
Haydon v Strudwick (Unreported, April 9, 2010), Sen Cts Costs Office
*Considered* 14/343
Hayes v Chief Constable of Merseyside [2011] EWCA Civ 911; [2012] 1 W.L.R. 517; [2011] 2 Cr. App. R. 30; [2012] Crim. L.R. 35; Times, August 19, 2011, CA (Civ Div) ........ *Digested,* 11/**2597**:
*Applied* 14/2458
Hayes v Hayes [2014] EWHC 2694 (Ch); [2014] Bus. L.R. 1238; [2014] B.P.I.R. 1212, Ch D ........ *Digested,* 14/**1788**
Hayim v Citibank NA [1987] A.C. 730; [1987] 3 W.L.R. 83; (1987) 84 L.S.G. 1573; (1987) 131 S.J. 660, PC (HK) ........ *Digested,* 87/**1425**:
*Applied* 08/351, 08/3959: *Considered* 14/3026
Hayloft Plants Ltd v Revenue and Customs Commissioners see 288 Group Ltd v Revenue and Customs Commissioners
Haynes v Department for Business, Innovation and Skills [2014] EWHC 643 (QB); [2014] 3 Costs L.R. 475, QBD ........ *Digested,* 14/**348**

Haywood v Senior (Unreported, February 18, 2014), CC (Sheffield) [*Stephen Garner, Barrister, Old Square Chambers, 10-11 Bedford Row, London*] ........................ *Digested,* 14/**2345**
Hazel v Manchester College see Manchester College v Hazel
HB (Ethiopia) v Secretary of State for the Home Department see EB (Kosovo) v Secretary of State for the Home Department
HC STARCK INC/Low oxygen refractory metal powder (T389/11) [2014] E.P.O.R. 7, EPO (Technical Bd App)
Head (Valuation Officer) v Tower Hamlets LBC [2005] R.A. 177, Lands Tr .................. *Digested,* 05/**3361**: *Applied* 14/2129: *Distinguished* 09/2679
Healey Sports Cars Switzerland Ltd v Jensen Cars Ltd [2014] EWHC 24 (Pat); [2014] E.T.M.R. 18; [2014] Bus. L.R. D3, Ch D (Patents Ct) ........................................ *Digested,* 14/**1931**
Health and Safety Executive v Polyflor Ltd; *sub nom* Polyflor Ltd v Health and Safety Executive [2014] EWCA Crim 1522; [2014] I.C.R. 1142, CA (Crim Div) ............ *Digested,* 14/**2296**
Healthcare at Home Ltd v Common Services Agency [2014] UKSC 49; [2014] 4 All E.R. 210; [2014] P.T.S.R. 1081; 2014 S.C. (U.K.S.C.) 247; 2014 S.L.T. 769; 2014 G.W.D. 25-505; Times, August 7, 2014, SC; affirming [2013] CSIH 22; 2013 S.C. 411; 2013 G.W.D. 13-291, IH (2 Div); affirming [2012] CSOH 75; [2012] Eu. L.R. 684; 2012 G.W.D. 18-359, OH .................................................. *Digested,* 14/**2475**
Hearst Holdings Inc v AVELA Inc [2014] EWHC 1553 (Ch); [2014] E.T.M.R. 39; [2014] I.L.Pr. 32, Ch D (Patents Ct) .......................................................................... *Digested,* 14/**1920**
Hearst Holdings Inc v AVELA Inc [2014] EWHC 439 (Ch); [2014] E.T.M.R. 34; [2014] F.S.R. 36, Ch D ........................................................................................... *Digested,* 14/**1922**
Heart of England NHS Foundation Trust v JB [2014] EWHC 342 (COP); (2014) 137 B.M.L.R. 232, CP
Heating Electrical Lighting and Piping Ltd (In Liquidation) v Ross [2012] EWHC 3764 (Ch); [2012] B.P.I.R. 1122, Ch D ............................................................................ *Digested,* 13/**1685**: *Followed* 14/1773
Heaton (Inspector of Taxes) v Bell [1970] A.C. 728; [1969] 2 W.L.R. 735; [1969] 2 All E.R. 70; (1969) 48 A.T.C. 73; [1969] T.R. 77; (1969) 113 S.J. 245, HL; reversing [1968] 1 W.L.R. 1385; [1968] 2 All E.R. 1156; [1968] T.R. 147, CA (Civ Div); reversing [1968] 1 W.L.R. 263; [1968] 1 All E.R. 857; [1967] T.R. 199; (1967) 111 S.J. 586; Times, July 12, 1967, Ch D ................................................ *Digested,* 69/**1743**: *Applied* 90/2659, 14/2912
Heavan, Ex p. see Lundy Granite Co, Re
Hedley Byrne & Co Ltd v Heller & Partners Ltd [1964] A.C. 465; [1963] 3 W.L.R. 101; [1963] 2 All E.R. 575; [1963] 1 Lloyd's Rep. 485; (1963) 107 S.J. 454, HL; affirming [1962] 1 Q.B. 396; [1961] 3 W.L.R. 1225; [1961] 3 All E.R. 891; (1961) 105 S.J. 910, CA; affirming Times, December 21, 1960, QBD .......................... *Digested,* 63/**2416**: *Applied* 63/330, 67/2677, 70/1493, 70/1880, 71/8000, 71/9949, 72/2364, 72/38, 73/2307, 73/2309, 73/325, 74/2597, 76/1868, 76/341, 77/2886, 78/1512, 78/1695, 78/2822, 79/1859, 79/213, 80/363, 81/1849, 81/1860, 81/2752, 83/2574, 85/2304, 85/2324, 89/56, 90/3266, 94/3362, 95/3701, 97/3787, 97/3818, 01/1508, 02/3277, 02/4542, 02/6000, 05/2868, 06/5156, 08/3904, 09/2725, 09/4393, 14/1062: *Cited* 14/241: *Considered* 65/2671, 66/8304, 66/9394, 68/3054, 69/1998, 69/2462, 69/2463, 69/882, 70/1849, 72/173, 72/2363, 72/2396, 74/158, 74/3638, 75/2326, 76/1343, 77/1452, 77/157, 77/2032, 77/370.u, 79/1864, 79/1884, 80/1898, 80/362, 83/1734, 83/2534, 86/215, 87/2579, 87/2580, 87/2591, 87/2619, 88/1710, 88/2433, 88/2444, 88/2456, 88/3409, 89/2543, 89/2566, 89/2585, 89/469, 90/4312, 91/2661, 91/3370, 92/3192, 93/2983, 93/2997, 93/2999, 94/4234, 94/5029, 94/5216, 95/3667, 95/3689, 95/4838, 95/770, 96/4531, 98/3920, 00/4200, 00/4205, 02/5421, 04/2706, 06/2880, 08/4947, 08/4949, 09/4142, 10/2281, 10/3422, 11/2270: *Distinguished* 64/3468, 65/3076, 67/2731, 71/10472, 71/11921, 71/7804, 72/2349, 72/2352, 73/2312, 87/2576, 98/3922: *Explained* 72/107, 94/1918: *Followed* 64/2565, 65/2727, 74/2576, 75/419, 92/6091, 96/1012, 96/4439, 96/4488, 98/3951, 98/3987, 02/6008, 10/2278, 13/540, 13/565: *Referred to* 81/1852, 88/4958, 95/5841
Heesom v Public Services Ombudsman for Wales [2014] EWHC 1504 (Admin); [2014] 4 All E.R. 269; [2014] B.L.G.R. 509, QBD (Admin) ............................................ *Digested,* 14/**2102**
Heininger v Bayerische Hypo- und Vereinsbank AG (C-481/99) [2001] E.C.R. I-9945; [2003] 2 C.M.L.R. 42; [2004] All E.R. (EC) 1; [2004] C.E.C. 202, ECJ (6th Chamber) ............................................................................................................ *Digested,* 03/**698**: *Applied* 06/697: *Distinguished* 09/681: *Followed* 14/611
Heinisch v Germany (28274/08) [2011] I.R.L.R. 922; (2014) 58 E.H.R.R. 31; 32 B.H.R.C. 252, ECHR
Heintz van Landewijck Sarl v Staatssecretaris van Financien (C-494/04) [2006] E.C.R. I-5381; [2010] B.V.C. 538, ECJ (3rd Chamber) *Applied* 14/823
Heis v Attestor Value Master Fund LP see MF Global UK Ltd (In Administration), Re

Heis v Attestor Value Master Fund LP see MF Global UK Ltd (In Special Administration), Re
Helander v Finland (10410/10) (2014) 58 E.H.R.R. SE5, ECHR
Helena Housing Ltd v Pinder see Lambeth LBC v O'Kane
Helianthus (London) Ltd v Revenue and Customs Commissioners [2014] UKFTT 52 (TC); [2014] S.T.I. 543, FTT (Tax)
Helioslough Ltd v Department for Communities and Local Government [2014] P.A.D. 42, Planning Inspector
Hellard v Chadwick [2014] EWHC 2158 (Ch); [2014] B.P.I.R. 1234, Ch D (Bankruptcy Ct) ........ *Digested,* 14/**1774**
Hellard v Chadwick [2014] B.P.I.R. 163, Ch D ........ *Digested,* 14/**1773**
Hellard v De Brito Carvalho see HLC Environmental Projects Ltd, Re
Hellard v Kapoor see Kapoor (In Bankruptcy), Re
Hellas Communications (Luxembourg) II SCA, Re [2014] B.P.I.R. 179, Ch D ........ *Digested,* 14/**1754**
Hellas Telecommunications (Luxembourg) II SCA, Re; *sub nom* Hosking v Nautadutilh Avocats Luxembourg [2013] B.P.I.R. 756, Ch D (Companies Ct) ........ *Digested,* 14/**1805**
Hellenic Hull Mutual Association Plc v Starlight Shipping Co see Starlight Shipping Co v Allianz Marine & Aviation Versicherungs AG
Hellyer v Hellyer (Lump sum payments) [1996] 2 F.L.R. 579; [1997] 1 F.C.R. 340; [1997] B.P.I.R. 85; [1997] Fam. Law 14, CA (Civ Div) ........ *Digested,* 97/**2483**: *Followed* 14/1363
Helman v John Lyon Free Grammar School; *sub nom* Free Grammar School of John Lyon v Helman [2014] EWCA Civ 17; [2014] 1 W.L.R. 2451; [2014] B.P.I.R. 406; [2014] H.L.R. 26; [2014] 1 P. & C.R. 16; [2014] L. & T.R. 15; [2014] 1 E.G.L.R. 49, CA (Civ Div); reversing [2013] 16 E.G. 106 (C.S.), CC (Central London) ........ *Digested,* 14/**1984**
Hemming's Estate, Re see Raymond Saul & Co v Holden
Henderson v All Around The World Recordings Ltd (Costs) [2013] EWPCC 19; [2013] F.S.R. 42, PCC ........ *Digested,* 14/**356**: *Applied* 14/1884: *Considered* 14/493
Henderson v Foxworth Investments Ltd; *sub nom* Liquidator of Letham Grange Development Co Ltd v Foxworth Investments Ltd [2014] UKSC 41; [2014] 1 W.L.R. 2600; 2014 S.C. (U.K.S.C.) 203; 2014 S.L.T. 775; 2014 S.C.L.R. 692; (2014) 158(27) S.J.L.B. 37; 2014 G.W.D. 23-437, SC; reversing [2013] CSIH 13; 2013 S.L.T. 445; 2013 G.W.D. 10-218, IH (Ex Div); reversing [2011] CSOH 66; 2011 S.L.T. 1152; 2011 G.W.D. 14-341, OH ........ *Digested,* 14/**1579**
Henderson v Henderson [1843-60] All E.R. Rep. 378; 67 E.R. 313; (1843) 3 Hare 100, Ct of Chancery
*Applied* 65/100, 67/1498, 91/1736, 97/461, 97/997, 98/2162, 98/2163, 98/3454, 98/80, 99/3313, 99/4025, 00/5111, 01/4678, 02/419, 03/470, 04/264, 05/2505, 06/2531, 09/2742, 09/431, 14/368: *Considered* 75/2463, 82/946, 84/2704, 89/1534, 94/3285, 94/3746, 95/3894, 96/1105, 98/244, 98/4067, 98/518, 98/618, 99/3732, 99/620, 00/604, 00/785, 01/410, 01/6474, 03/466, 04/425, 06/1319, 08/271, 10/458, 11/1077, 11/1136, 14/1449, 14/1790: *Distinguished* 47-51/3681, 99/4384, 99/549, 00/2605, 00/349: *Followed* 99/3952, 00/2322, 05/329, 14/2865: *Not applied* 99/1376: *Referred to* 99/4014
Henderson v Merrett Syndicates Ltd (No.1); *sub nom* Gooda Walker Ltd v Deeny; McLarnon Deeney v Gooda Walker Ltd; Arbuthnott v Fagan; *joined cases* Hallam-Eames v Merrett Syndicates Ltd; Hughes v Merrett Syndicates Ltd; Feltrim Underwriting Agencies Ltd v Arbuthnott; Deeny v Gooda Walker Ltd (Duty of Care) [1995] 2 A.C. 145; [1994] 3 W.L.R. 761; [1994] 3 All E.R. 506; [1994] 2 Lloyd's Rep. 468; [1994] C.L.C. 918; (1994) 144 N.L.J. 1204; Times, July 26, 1994; Independent, August 3, 1994, HL; affirming [1994] C.L.C. 55; [1994] E.C.C. 537; Times, December 30, 1993; Independent, December 14, 1993, CA (Civ Div); affirming [1994] 2 Lloyd's Rep. 193; Times, October 20, 1993, QBD (Comm) ........ *Digested,* 94/**3362**:
*Applied* 95/3667, 98/795, 01/1508, 01/4487, 01/4490, 03/499, 04/3240, 06/2881, 06/2882, 07/752, 08/4949, 09/2725, 09/4393, 11/2270, 14/1840: *Cited* 00/4218: *Considered* 95/2906, 95/3701, 95/4838, 96/2993, 96/3580, 97/692, 98/3920, 03/2475, 04/619, 06/2880, 10/3422: *Distinguished* 04/600: *Followed* 96/1133, 99/3984, 10/619, 11/3472: *Referred to* 99/4023
Henderson v Scottish Ministers see Somerville v Scottish Ministers
Henderson's Estate, Re see Nouvion v Freeman
Henderson, Re see Nouvion v Freeman
Hendrick v Knight [2014] E.T.M.R. 58, App Person
Hendy v Ministry of Justice [2014] EWHC 2535 (Ch); [2014] I.R.L.R. 856, Ch D ........ *Digested,* 14/**1052**

Henley v Murray (Inspector of Taxes) [1950] 1 All E.R. 908; 31 T.C. 351; [1950] T.R. 25; [1950] W.N. 241, CA; reversing 42 R. & I.T. 501; [1949] T.R. 335; (1949) 93 S.J. 792, HC ........ *Digested*, 47-51/**4783**: *Applied* 14/2913: *Considered* 11/3359: *Distinguished* 47-51/4784, 84/1800
Hensman v Ministry of Defence [2014] Eq. L.R. 670, EAT
Henwood v Barlow Clowes International Ltd (In Liquidation) [2008] EWCA Civ 577; [2008] B.P.I.R. 778; [2008] N.P.C. 61; Times, June 18, 2008, CA (Civ Div); reversing [2007] EWHC 1579 (Ch); [2007] B.P.I.R. 1329, Ch D (Bankruptcy Ct) *Digested*, 08/**2137**: *Applied* 11/3243, 14/1325
Heritage Oil and Gas Ltd v Tullow Uganda Ltd see Tullow Uganda Ltd v Heritage Oil and Gas Ltd
Herman v Revenue and Customs Commissioners [2007] S.T.C. (S.C.D.) 571; [2007] W.T.L.R. 1201; [2007] S.T.I. 1441, Sp Comm ........ *Digested*, 07/**3991**: *Applied* 14/2974
Heron v Sefton MBC [2014] Eq. L.R. 130, EAT ........ *Digested*, 14/**1013**
Heron v TNT (UK) Ltd [2013] EWCA Civ 469; [2014] 1 W.L.R. 1277; [2013] 3 All E.R. 479; [2013] 4 Costs L.R. 551; [2013] P.N.L.R. 21, CA (Civ Div); affirming (Unreported, April 23, 2012), CC (Guildford) ........ *Digested*, 13/**317**
Herridge v Parker [2014] Lloyd's Rep. I.R. 177, CC (Cardiff) ........ *Digested*, 14/**1835**
Hershaw v Sheffield City Council [2014] I.C.R. 1120; [2014] I.R.L.R. 919, EAT ........ *Digested*, 14/**1035**
Hertfordshire CC v B; *sub nom* A Local Authority v NB [2013] EWHC 4100 (Fam); [2014] Fam. Law 416, Fam Div
Hertfordshire CC v H [2013] EWHC 4049 (Fam); [2014] Fam. Law 422, Fam Div
Hertfordshire CC v Secretary of State for Communities and Local Government [2012] EWCA Civ 1473; [2013] J.P.L. 560, CA (Civ Div); affirming [2012] EWHC 277 (Admin); [2012] J.P.L. 836, QBD (Admin) ........ *Digested*, 13/**2322**: *Considered* 14/2438
Hervis Sport- es Divatkereskedelmi Kft v Nemzeti Ado- es Vamhivatal Kozep-dunantuli Regionalis Ado Foigazgatosaga (C-385/12) [2014] 3 C.M.L.R. 2; [2014] B.T.C. 15, ECJ (Grand Chamber)
Hewage v Grampian Health Board [2012] UKSC 37; [2012] 4 All E.R. 447; 2013 S.C. (U.K.S.C.) 54; 2013 S.L.T. 1191; [2012] I.C.R. 1054; [2012] I.R.L.R. 870; [2012] Eq. L.R. 884; 2012 G.W.D. 25-521; Times, October 29, 2012, SC; affirming [2011] CSIH 4; 2011 S.C. 397; 2011 S.L.T. 319; 2011 G.W.D. 4-127, IH (2 Div); reversing UKEATS/0016/08/MT, EAT (SC) ........ *Digested*, 12/**1072**: *Followed* 14/1024, 14/1100
Hewitt v Leicester City Council see Hewitt v Leicester Corp
Hewitt v Leicester Corp; *sub nom* Hewitt v Leicester City Council [1969] 1 W.L.R. 855; [1969] 2 All E.R. 802; (1969) 133 J.P. 452; 67 L.G.R. 436; (1969) 20 P. & C.R. 629; 210 E.G. 459; (1969) 113 S.J. 346, CA (Civ Div); affirming (1968) 19 P. & C.R. 809; [1968] J.P.L. 407, Lands Tr ........ *Digested*, 69/**445**: *Applied* 72/2830, 89/2125: *Considered* 89/2127, 90/2859: *Distinguished* 71/9926: *Not applied* 14/2379
HF (Iraq) v Secretary of State for the Home Department; *joined cases* HM (Iraq) v Secretary of State for the Home Department; RM (Iraq) v Secretary of State for the Home Department; MK (Iraq) v Secretary of State for the Home Department [2013] EWCA Civ 1276; [2014] 1 W.L.R. 1329, CA (Civ Div) ........ *Digested*, 14/**1645**
HH v Italy see R. (on the application of HH) v Westminster City Magistrates' Court
HHH Employee Trust, Re; *sub nom* B v C 16 I.T.E.L.R. 1, Royal Ct (Jer)
Hi Hotel HCF SARL v Spoering (C-387/12) [2014] 1 W.L.R. 1912; [2014] E.C.D.R. 24; [2014] I.L.Pr. 26, ECJ (4th Chamber)
Hibberd v DPP; *sub nom* Hibberd v Muddle CO 2614/96, QBD ........ *Digested*, 97/**1251**: *Considered* 14/667
Hibberd v Muddle see Hibberd v DPP
Hibbert Pownall & Newton (A Firm) v Whitehead see Whitehead v Searle
Hickey v Secretary of State for Communities and Local Government [2013] EWHC 3163 (QB); [2014] I.R.L.R. 22, QBD ........ *Digested*, 14/**1127**
Hicks v Coal Authority [2013] UKUT 388 (LC); [2014] R.V.R. 340, UT (Lands)
Hide v Steeplechase Co (Cheltenham) Ltd [2013] EWCA Civ 545; [2014] 1 All E.R. 405; [2014] I.C.R. 326; [2013] P.I.Q.R. P22; [2013] L.L.R. 697; (2013) 163(7562) N.L.J. 16, CA (Civ Div) ........ *Digested*, 13/**1506**: *Considered* 13/3897
Highbury Pension Fund Management Co v Zirfin Investments Ltd [2013] EWCA Civ 1283; [2014] Ch. 359; [2014] 2 W.L.R. 1129; [2014] 1 All E.R. 674; [2014] 1 B.C.L.C. 118; [2014] 1 P. & C.R. 13, CA (Civ Div); reversing [2013] EWHC 238 (Ch); [2013] 3 All E.R. 327; [2013] 2 B.C.L.C. 331; Times, April 22, 2013, Ch D *Digested*, 14/**1205**
Higson v Guenault [2014] EWCA Civ 703; [2014] 2 P. & C.R. DG13, CA (Civ Div)

HIH Casualty & General Insurance Ltd, Re; *sub nom* McGrath v Riddell; McMahon v McGrath; *joined cases* FAI Insurances Ltd, Re; World Marine & General Insurances Pty Ltd, Re; FAI General Insurance Co Ltd, Re [2008] UKHL 21; [2008] 1 W.L.R. 852; [2008] 3 All E.R. 869; [2008] Bus. L.R. 905; [2008] B.C.C. 349; [2012] 2 B.C.L.C. 655; [2008] B.P.I.R. 581; [2008] Lloyd's Rep. I.R. 756; (2008) 105(16) L.S.G. 26; (2008) 152(16) S.J.L.B. 30; Times, April 11, 2008, HL; reversing [2006] EWCA Civ 732; [2007] 1 All E.R. 177; [2007] Bus. L.R. 250; [2007] B.C.C. 335; Times, July 5, 2006, CA (Civ Div); affirming [2005] EWHC 2125 (Ch); [2006] 2 All E.R. 671, Ch D (Companies Ct) ........................ *Digested,* 08/**2158**: *Applied* 06/2367, 10/1872, 10/1875, 12/1810: *Considered* 10/1871, 11/1885, 11/201, 13/1696: *Followed* 14/1766

Hill v Chief Constable of West Yorkshire [1989] A.C. 53; [1988] 2 W.L.R. 1049; [1988] 2 All E.R. 238; (1988) 152 L.G. Rev. 709; (1988) 85(20) L.S.G. 34; (1988) 138 N.L.J. Rep. 126; (1988) 132 S.J. 700, HL; affirming [1988] Q.B. 60; [1987] 2 W.L.R. 1126; [1987] 1 All E.R. 1173; (1987) 151 L.G. Rev. 729; (1987) 84 L.S.G. 982; (1987) 137 N.L.J. 222; (1987) 131 S.J. 626, CA (Civ Div); affirming (1986) 136 N.L.J. 238, QBD ........................ *Digested,* 88/**2435**: *Applied* 90/3278, 92/3354, 93/2958, 94/3384, 95/3452, 95/3652, 99/3963, 08/2641, 08/2767, 12/2629, 14/2203: *Considered* 87/2580, 90/5493, 92/3209, 94/4296, 95/3649, 95/3652, 96/4441, 99/3970, 99/4009, 05/3342, 08/2645, 10/3420, 11/2585: *Disapproved* 98/3102: *Distinguished* 95/3686, 99/3972, 99/5434, 00/4229, 06/2171: *Followed* 01/4479, 08/2646, 13/2387

Hillcrest Homes Ltd v Beresford & Curbishley Ltd [2014] EWHC 280 (TCC); 153 Con. L.R. 179; [2014] C.I.L.L. 3506, QBD (TCC) ........................ *Digested,* 14/**582**

Hillingdon LBC v AO [2014] EWHC 75 (Fam); [2014] Fam. Law 775, Fam Div

Hills v Revenue and Customs Commissioners [2014] UKFTT 646 (TC); [2014] S.T.I. 2600, FTT (Tax)

Hills Contractors and Construction Ltd v Struth [2013] EWHC 1693 (TCC); [2014] 1 W.L.R. 1, QBD (TCC) ........................ *Digested,* 14/**472**

Hindawi v Secretary of State for the Home Department see R. (on the application of Clift) v Secretary of State for the Home Department

Hindcastle Ltd v Barbara Attenborough Associates Ltd [1997] A.C. 70; [1996] 2 W.L.R. 262; [1996] 1 All E.R. 737; [1996] B.C.C. 636; [1996] 2 B.C.L.C. 234; [1996] B.P.I.R. 595; [1996] 1 E.G.L.R. 94; [1996] 15 E.G. 103; [1996] E.G. 32 (C.S.); (1996) 93(12) L.S.G. 29; (1996) 140 S.J.L.B. 84; [1996] N.P.C. 28; Times, February 23, 1996, HL; affirming [1995] Q.B. 95; [1994] 3 W.L.R. 1100; [1994] 4 All E.R. 129; [1994] B.C.C. 705; [1994] 2 B.C.L.C. 728; (1995) 70 P. & C.R. 29; [1994] 43 E.G. 154; [1994] E.G. 109 (C.S.); [1994] N.P.C. 86; Times, July 6, 1994; Independent, July 18, 1994, CA (Civ Div) ........................ *Digested,* 96/**3704**: *Applied* 98/3650, 98/3651, 04/2194, 04/2511, 06/3469: *Distinguished* 98/3620: *Followed* 09/2514, 14/1972

Hindes v Northern Ireland Housing Executive [2014] R.V.R. 204, Lands Tr (NI)

Hindley v Braintree DC; *joined case* McGregor v Braintree DC [2014] P.A.D. 49, Planning Inspector

Hines v Lambeth LBC [2014] EWCA Civ 660; [2014] 1 W.L.R. 4112; [2014] H.L.R. 32; Times, June 19, 2014, CA (Civ Div) ........................ *Digested,* 14/**1612**

Hiri v Secretary of State for the Home Department [2014] EWHC 254 (Admin); [2014] A.C.D. 97, QBD (Admin)

Hirst v United Kingdom (74025/01) (2006) 42 E.H.R.R. 41; 19 B.H.R.C. 546; [2006] 1 Prison L.R. 220; (2005) 155 N.L.J. 1551; Times, October 10, 2005, ECHR (Grand Chamber) ........................ *Digested,* 06/**2150**: *Applied* 11/1702, 11/1703, 14/976: *Considered* 07/5431, 10/1730, 11/2294, 14/3703: *Distinguished* 13/1544

Hiscox v Outhwaite (No.3) [1991] 2 Lloyd's Rep. 524, QBD (Comm) ........................ *Digested,* 92/**2619**: *Approved* 04/2242: *Considered* 14/1844

Historic Scotland Executive Agency v Highland and Western Isles Valuation Joint Board Assessor 2014 S.L.T. (Lands Tr) 50; [2014] R.V.R. 14; 2013 G.W.D. 37-723, Lands Tr (Scot) ........................ *Digested,* 14/**3674**

HJ (A Child) (Transfer of Proceedings), Re [2013] EWHC 1867 (Fam); [2014] 1 F.L.R. 430; [2013] Fam. Law 1255, Fam Div ........................ *Digested,* 14/**1286**: *Applied* 14/1356

HK (Afghanistan) v Secretary of State for the Home Department [2012] EWCA Civ 315, CA (Civ Div)
*Applied* 14/1657: *Followed* 13/1579

HK Danmark v Dansk almennyttigt Boligselskab (C-335/11); *sub nom* Ring v Dansk Almennyttigt Boligselskab DAB (C-335/11); *joined case* HK Danmark v Dansk Arbejdsgiverforening (C-337/11) [2013] 3 C.M.L.R. 21; [2014] All E.R. (EC) 1161; [2013] I.C.R. 851; [2013] I.R.L.R. 571; [2013] Eq. L.R. 528; (2013) 132 B.M.L.R. 58, ECJ (2nd Chamber)
*Applied* 13/966: *Considered* 14/1038

HK Danmark v Dansk Arbejdsgiverforening (C-337/11) see HK Danmark v Dansk almennyttigt Boligselskab (C-335/11)

HK Danmark v Experian A/S (C-476/11); *sub nom* Handels- og Kontorfunktionaerernes Forbund Danmark (HK) v Experian A/S (C-476/11) [2014] 1 C.M.L.R. 42; [2014] I.C.R. 27; [2013] Eq. L.R. 1117; [2013] Pens. L.R. 397, ECJ (2nd Chamber)

HL v United Kingdom (45508/99); *sub nom* L v United Kingdom (45508/99) (2005) 40 E.H.R.R. 32; 17 B.H.R.C. 418; (2004) 7 C.C.L. Rep. 498; [2005] Lloyd's Rep. Med. 169; (2005) 81 B.M.L.R. 131; [2004] M.H.L.R. 236; Times, October 19, 2004, ECHR ........ *Digested,* 05/**2109**:
*Applied* 07/3913, 14/2189: *Considered* 11/3225, 12/2280

HLC Environmental Projects Ltd, Re; *sub nom* Hellard v De Brito Carvalho [2013] EWHC 2876 (Ch); [2014] B.C.C. 337, Ch D (Companies Ct) ........ *Digested,* 14/**509**

HLH Warenvertriebs GmbH v Germany (C-211/03) [2005] E.C.R. I-5141, ECJ
*Applied* 08/1335: *Followed* 14/1528

HM v Sweden (3/2011) 37 B.H.R.C. 87, UN CRPD

HM (A Child), Re; *sub nom* SM v HM [2014] Med. L.R. 40; [2012] Med. L.R. 449; [2012] W.T.L.R. 281, CP ........ *Digested,* 12/**2287**

HM (Article 15(c): Iraq), Re; *sub nom* HM (Iraq) v Secretary of State for the Home Department [2012] UKUT 409 (IAC), UT (IAC)
*Affirmed* 14/1645

HM (Iraq) v Secretary of State for the Home Department see HF (Iraq) v Secretary of State for the Home Department

HM (Iraq) v Secretary of State for the Home Department see HM (Article 15(c): Iraq), Re

HM Treasury v Ahmed see A v HM Treasury

HM Treasury v Al-Ghabra see A v HM Treasury

HM Treasury v Youssef see Guardian News and Media Ltd, Re

HN v Minister for Justice, Equality and Law Reform (C-604/12) see N v Minister for Justice, Equality and Law Reform (C-604/12)

Hobbs v Financial Conduct Authority see Financial Conduct Authority v Hobbs

Hobbs v Financial Services Authority see Financial Conduct Authority v Hobbs

Hobson (t/a Windmill Dental Suite) v Revenue and Customs Commissioners [2013] UKFTT 689 (TC); [2014] S.T.I. 387, FTT (Tax)

Hoburne Ltd, Re see Burry & Knight Ltd, Re

Hochstrasser (Inspector of Taxes) v Mayes; *joined case* Jennings v Kinder (Inspector of Taxes) [1960] A.C. 376; [1960] 2 W.L.R. 63; [1959] 3 All E.R. 817; 53 R. & I.T. 12; 38 T.C. 673; (1959) 38 A.T.C. 360; [1959] T.R. 355, HL; affirming [1959] Ch. 22; [1958] 3 W.L.R. 215; [1958] 3 All E.R. 285; 51 R. & I.T. 767; (1958) 37 A.T.C. 205; [1958] T.R. 237; (1958) 102 S.J. 546, CA; affirming [1958] 2 W.L.R. 982; [1958] 1 All E.R. 369; 51 R. & I.T. 321; (1957) 36 A.T.C. 356; [1957] T.R. 365; (1958) 102 S.J. 419, Ch D ........ *Digested,* 59/**1543**:
*Applied* 64/1836, 76/1441, 78/1675, 82/1636, 89/2028, 90/2646, 91/2092, 99/4729, 05/4071, 10/3290: *Considered* 65/1946, 87/2034, 95/2766, 10/3323, 11/3326, 11/3359, 12/3115, 12/3299, 14/2908: *Distinguished* 76/1438, 86/1762: *Followed* 09/3825

Hochtief Ltd v Revenue and Customs Commissioners [2009] UKFTT 321 (TC); [2010] S.F.T.D. 268; [2010] S.T.I. 396, FTT (Tax) ........ *Digested,* 10/**3226**:
*Applied* 14/2846

Hockin v Marsden; *sub nom* London & Westcountry Estates Ltd, Re [2014] EWHC 763 (Ch); [2014] Bus. L.R. 441; [2014] 2 B.C.L.C. 531; [2014] B.P.I.R. 637, Ch D (Companies Ct) ........ *Digested,* 14/**1750**

Hocking v Revenue and Customs Commissioners [2014] UKFTT 1034 (TC); [2014] S.T.I. 3553, FTT (Tax)

Hockley v Essex CC [2013] EWHC 4051 (Admin); [2014] Env. L.R. 24, QBD (Admin) . *Digested,* 14/**2427**

Hoddinott v Persimmon Homes (Wessex) Ltd [2007] EWCA Civ 1203; [2008] 1 W.L.R. 806; [2008] C.P. Rep. 9; (2007) 104(47) L.S.G. 25; Times, December 28, 2007, CA (Civ Div) ........ *Digested,* 08/**359**:
*Applied* 10/274: *Considered* 11/385, 13/405, 14/476: *Distinguished* 08/2680: *Followed* 11/384

Hodgkinson & Corby Ltd v Wards Mobility Services Ltd (No.1) [1994] 1 W.L.R. 1564; [1995] F.S.R. 169; (1995) 14 Tr. L.R. 79; Times, August 3, 1994; Independent, October 17, 1994, Ch D ........ *Digested,* 95/**4739**:
*Applied* 14/1890: *Considered* 96/5706: *Referred to* 98/3516

Hoff v Atherton [2004] EWCA Civ 1554; [2005] W.T.L.R. 99, CA (Civ Div); affirming [2004] EWHC 177 (Ch), Ch D ........ *Digested,* 05/**3971**:
*Applied* 08/3619, 09/3733: *Considered* 10/3213, 11/3267: *Followed* 14/2838, 14/2841

Hoffer v Germany (397/07) (2014) 58 E.H.R.R. 40; 29 B.H.R.C. 674, ECHR

Hoffmann (C-144/00) see Criminal Proceedings against Hoffmann (C-144/00)

Hogarth v Alexander Miller, Brother & Co (The Westfalia) [1891] A.C. 48; (1890) 18 R. (H.L.) 10, HL; affirming (1889) 16 R. 599, IH (2 Div)
*Applied* 74/3559: *Considered* 09/3582: *Followed* 14/2740

Hok Ltd v Revenue and Customs Commissioners; *sub nom* Revenue and Customs Commissioners v Hok Ltd [2012] UKUT 363 (TCC); [2013] S.T.C. 225; 81 T.C. 540; [2012] B.T.C. 1711; [2012] S.T.I. 3402, UT (Tax); reversing [2011] UKFTT 433 (TC); [2011] W.T.L.R. 1583, FTT (Tax) ........ *Digested,* 13/**3073**:
*Applied* 13/3199: *Considered* 13/3121: *Followed* 13/3218

Holden Vale (Conference Centre) Ltd v Whitehead (Valuation Officer) [2013] UKUT 237 (LC); [2014] R.A. 10, UT (Lands) ........ *Digested,* 14/**2482**

Holden-Hindley v Holden-Hindley [2013] EWHC 3053 (Ch); [2014] W.T.L.R. 275, Ch D ........ *Digested,* 14/**3027**

Holder v Gedling BC see R. (on the application of Holder) v Gedling BC

Holding Slovenske elektrarne doo (HSE) v European Commission (T-399/09) [2014] 4 C.M.L.R. 21, GC (3rd Chamber)

Holland v Revenue and Customs Commissioners see Revenue and Customs Commissioners v Holland

Hollier (A Bankrupt), Re see Carman v Letchford

Hollinger Print Ltd v Revenue and Customs Commissioners [2013] UKFTT 739 (TC); [2014] S.T.I. 451, FTT (Tax)

Hollington v F Hewthorn & Co Ltd [1943] K.B. 587; [1943] 2 All E.R. 35, CA; affirming in part [1943] K.B. 27, KBD
*Applied* 67/759, 84/1531, 87/1669, 93/2525, 03/509, 11/2165, 14/1787: *Approved* 66/11738: *Considered* 47-51/6522, 58/957, 67/1608, 67/3246, 69/2418, 70/1018, 70/1024, 80/2609, 93/3153, 96/1410, 04/192, 06/2926, 07/339, 09/336, 14/288: *Disapproved* 07/826: *Distinguished* 56/2546, 93/3038: *Followed* 66/7003

Hollister Inc v Medik Ostomy Supplies Ltd [2012] EWCA Civ 1419; [2013] Bus. L.R. 428; [2013] E.T.M.R. 10; [2013] F.S.R. 24; (2013) 129 B.M.L.R. 173, CA (Civ Div); reversing in part [2011] EWPCC 40; [2012] F.S.R. 17; (2012) 124 B.M.L.R. 107, PCC ........ *Digested,* 13/**1818**:
*Followed* 14/1887

Holloway v DCM Optical Ltd (Quantum) 1UC14165, CC (Central London) [*Devonshires Solicitors, 30 Finsbury Circus, London*] ........ *Digested,* 14/**2350**

Holman v Johnson 98 E.R. 1120; (1775) 1 Cowp. 341, KB
*Applied* 53/535, 55/412, 62/480, 14/264: *Cited* 12/1055: *Considered* 67/1836, 94/551, 08/2649: *Distinguished* 56/1512, 80/1306

Holme v Brunskill (1878) 3 Q.B.D. 495, CA
*Applied* 64/1640, 95/3013, 10/634: *Considered* 86/1595, 05/703, 12/594, 13/218, 13/532, 13/542, 14/256: *Followed* 14/1980: *Referred to* 95/3014

Holmes v Campbell; *sub nom* Environment Agency v Campbell (1998) 162 J.P. 655; (1998) 162 J.P.N. 523; (1998) 95(23) L.S.G. 26; (1998) 142 S.J.L.B. 171; [1999] Env. L.R. D4; Times, May 18, 1998, DC ........ *Digested,* 98/**1040**:
*Considered* 14/764

Holmes v Scottish Legal Life Assurance Society (1932) 48 T.L.R. 306, KBD
*Applied* 14/1846

Holmes-Moorhouse v Richmond upon Thames LBC [2009] UKHL 7; [2009] 1 W.L.R. 413; [2009] 3 All E.R. 277; [2009] P.T.S.R. 698; [2009] 1 F.L.R. 904; [2009] 2 F.C.R. 277; [2009] H.L.R. 34; [2009] B.L.G.R. 730; [2009] Fam. Law 391; (2009) 153(5) S.J.L.B. 28; [2009] N.P.C. 22; Times, February 5, 2009, HL; reversing [2007] EWCA Civ 970; [2008] 1 W.L.R. 1289; [2008] 1 F.L.R. 1061; [2007] 3 F.C.R. 736; [2008] H.L.R. 19; [2008] B.L.G.R. 1; [2008] Fam. Law 22; [2007] N.P.C. 104; Times, November 19, 2007, CA (Civ Div) ........ *Digested,* 09/**1900**:
*Applied* 11/1662, 14/2182: *Considered* 13/1535, 14/1592: *Distinguished* 11/1669: *Followed* 11/1651, 11/3220, 12/1639, 14/1600

Holt v Attorney General [2014] UKPC 4; [2014] 2 All E.R. 397; [2014] Lloyd's Rep. F.C. 335, PC (IoM)

Holt v Reading BC; *sub nom* Reading BC v Holt [2013] EWCA Civ 641; [2014] P.T.S.R. 444; [2013] H.L.R. 40; [2014] L. & T.R. 7; [2013] 25 E.G. 108 (C.S.), CA (Civ Div) .......... *Digested,* 13/**1540**

Home Office v Harman; *sub nom* Harman v Home Office [1983] 1 A.C. 280; [1982] 2 W.L.R. 338; [1982] 1 All E.R. 532; (1982) 126 S.J. 136, HL; affirming [1981] Q.B. 534; [1981] 2 W.L.R. 310; [1981] 2 All E.R. 349; (1981) 125 S.J. 149, CA (Civ Div); affirming Times, November 28, 1980, QBD .......... *Digested,* 82/**2433**: *Applied* 86/1505, 86/3480: *Considered* 84/2560, 84/2625, 87/2885, 88/2833, 92/3475, 93/4265, 12/469, 14/381, 14/762

Home Office v Lownds see Lownds v Home Office

Home Office v Robinson [1982] I.C.R. 31; [1981] I.R.L.R. 524, EAT .......... *Digested,* 82/**1117**: *Considered* 14/1135

Home Treat Ltd, Re [1991] B.C.C. 165; [1991] B.C.L.C. 705, Ch D (Companies Ct) .......... *Digested,* 91/**2125**: *Applied* 14/512

Homer v Chief Constable of West Yorkshire; *sub nom* Chief Constable of West Yorkshire v Homer [2012] UKSC 15; [2012] 3 All E.R. 1287; [2012] I.C.R. 704; [2012] I.R.L.R. 601; [2012] Eq. L.R. 594; (2012) 162 N.L.J. 652; (2012) 156(17) S.J.L.B. 31; Times, April 30, 2012, SC; reversing in part [2010] EWCA Civ 419; [2010] I.C.R. 987; [2010] I.R.L.R. 619; (2010) 107(19) L.S.G. 24; (2010) 154(17) S.J.L.B. 29, CA (Civ Div); affirming [2009] I.C.R. 223; [2009] I.R.L.R. 262, EAT .......... *Digested,* 12/**1034**: *Applied* 14/1102, 14/1111

Homesun Holdings Ltd v Department of Energy and Climate Change see Breyer Group Plc v Department of Energy and Climate Change

Honda Motor Europe Ltd v Powell [2014] EWCA Civ 437; [2014] Pens. L.R. 255, CA (Civ Div); affirming [2013] EWHC 3149 (Ch); [2013] Pens. L.R. 417, Ch D .......... *Digested,* 14/**2279**

Honda Motor Europe Ltd, Re [2013] EWHC 2842 (Ch); [2013] B.C.C. 767, Ch D .......... *Digested,* 14/**502**

Honduras Wharf Ltd v Revenue and Customs Commissioners [2014] UKFTT 581 (TC); [2014] S.T.I. 2425, FTT (Tax)

Hone v Abbey Forwarding Ltd (In Liquidation); *sub nom* Abbey Forwarding Ltd (In Liquidation) v Hone [2014] EWCA Civ 711; [2014] 3 W.L.R. 1676, CA (Civ Div); reversing in part [2012] EWHC 4060 (Ch), Ch D

Honeysuckle Properties v Fletcher see Tiensia v Vision Enterprises Ltd (t/a Universal Estates)

Honeywell International (Middle East) Ltd v Meydan Group LLP [2014] B.L.R. 599, QBD (TCC) .......... *Digested,* 14/**126**

Honeywell International Middle East Ltd v Meydan Group LLC [2014] EWHC 1344 (TCC); [2014] 2 Lloyd's Rep. 133; [2014] B.L.R. 401; 154 Con. L.R. 113; [2014] Bus. L.R. D13, QBD (TCC) .......... *Digested,* 14/**138**

Hongkong Fir Shipping Co Ltd v Kawasaki Kisen Kaisha Ltd (The Hongkong Fir) [1962] 2 Q.B. 26; [1962] 2 W.L.R. 474; [1962] 1 All E.R. 474; [1961] 2 Lloyd's Rep. 478; (1961) 106 S.J. 35, CA; affirming [1961] 2 W.L.R. 716; [1961] 2 All E.R. 257; [1961] 1 Lloyd's Rep. 159; (1961) 105 S.J. 347, QBD (Comm) .......... *Digested,* 62/**2838**: *Applied* 71/1838, 75/3041, 78/2636, 79/2387, 99/3700, 00/874, 00/899, 14/623: *Considered* 70/362, 74/3426, 80/2393, 99/838, 00/3532: *Distinguished* 66/1818, 68/1777, 83/262: *Explained* 81/2433: *Followed* 10/625, 13/533

Honourable Society of Middle Temple v Revenue and Customs Commissioners; *sub nom* Revenue and Customs Commissioners v Honourable Society of Middle Temple [2013] UKUT 250 (TCC); [2013] S.T.C. 1998; [2013] B.V.C. 1690; [2013] S.T.I. 2218; (2013) 163(7567) N.L.J. 21, UT (Tax); reversing [2011] UKFTT 390 (TC); [2011] S.F.T.D. 1088, FTT (Tax) .......... *Digested,* 13/**3229**: *Applied* 14/3052

Hoogendijk v Netherlands (Admissibility) (58641/00) (2005) 40 E.H.R.R. SE22, ECHR *Applied* 14/2744

Hook v British Airways Plc; *joined case* Stott v Thomas Cook Tour Operators Ltd [2014] UKSC 15; [2014] A.C. 1347; [2014] 2 W.L.R. 521; [2014] 2 All E.R. 461; [2014] 1 All E.R. (Comm) 849; [2014] 2 Lloyd's Rep. 207; [2014] 3 C.M.L.R. 7; [2014] Eq. L.R. 287; (2014) 158(10) S.J.L.B. 37; Times, March 13, 2014, SC; affirming [2012] EWCA Civ 66; [2012] 2 All E.R. (Comm) 1265; [2012] 1 Lloyd's Rep. 386; [2012] Eq. L.R. 351, CA (Civ Div); affirming [2011] EWHC 379 (QB); [2011] 1 All E.R. (Comm) 1128; [2011] Eq. L.R. 351, QBD .......... *Digested,* 14/**161**: *Considered* 14/165

Hooper v Oates [2013] EWCA Civ 91; [2014] Ch. 287; [2014] 2 W.L.R. 743; [2013] 3 All E.R. 211; [2013] 1 E.G.L.R. 93; [2013] 16 E.G. 108; [2013] 9 E.G. 93 (C.S.); (2013) 157(8) S.J.L.B. 31; [2013] 1 P. & C.R. DG22, CA (Civ Div) .......... *Digested,* 13/**2445**

Hope v Ireland [2014] EWHC 3854 (Ch); [2014] S.T.I. 3705, Ch D

Hope v Premierpace (Europe) Ltd [1999] B.P.I.R. 695, Ch D .......... *Digested,* 99/**3233**: *Considered* 11/1855, 14/1779: *Explained* 12/1819: *Followed* 12/1817

Hopkins Developments Ltd v Secretary of State for Communities and Local Government; *joined case* Secretary of State for Communities and Local Government v Hopkins Development Ltd [2014] EWCA Civ 470; [2014] P.T.S.R. 1145; [2014] 2 E.G.L.R. 91; [2014] J.P.L. 1000, CA (Civ Div); reversing [2013] EWHC 1783 (Admin), QBD (Admin) ........ *Digested,* 14/**2411**

Horizon Security Services Ltd v Ndeze [2014] I.R.L.R. 854; [2014] I.C.R. D31, EAT .... *Digested,* 14/**1058**

Horn Linie GmbH & Co v Panamericana Formas e Impresos SA (The Hornbay) [2006] EWHC 373 (Comm); [2006] 2 All E.R. (Comm) 924; [2006] 2 Lloyd's Rep. 44, QBD (Comm) ........ *Digested,* 06/**639**: *Applied* 09/617: *Considered* 14/301

Horne and Meredith Properties Ltd v Cox [2014] EWCA Civ 423; [2014] 2 P. & C.R. 18; [2014] L. & T.R. 24; [2014] 2 E.G.L.R. 175; [2014] 2 P. & C.R. DG8, CA (Civ Div) ........ *Digested,* 14/**1976**

Horsfold v Bird see Horsford v Bird

Horsford v Bird; *sub nom* Horsfold v Bird [2006] UKPC 3; [2006] 1 E.G.L.R. 75; [2006] 15 E.G. 136; (2006) 22 Const. L.J. 187; (2006) 103(6) L.S.G. 34, PC (Ant) ....... *Digested,* 06/**1031**: *Applied* 14/824: *Considered* 07/1060, 11/859

Horton v Young (Inspector of Taxes) [1972] Ch. 157; [1971] 3 W.L.R. 348; [1971] 3 All E.R. 412; 47 T.C. 60; [1971] T.R. 181; (1971) 115 S.J. 388, CA (Civ Div); affirming [1971] 2 W.L.R. 236; [1971] 2 All E.R. 351; [1970] T.R. 319; (1970) 114 S.J. 954; Times, December 2, 1970, Ch D ........ *Digested,* 71/**5757**: *Considered* 03/4222, 04/3759: *Distinguished* 14/2932

Hosebay Ltd v Day see Day v Hosebay Ltd

Hosier v Goodall [1962] 2 Q.B. 401; [1962] 2 W.L.R. 157; [1962] 1 All E.R. 30; (1962) 126 J.P. 52; 60 L.G.R. 500; (1961) 105 S.J. 1085, DC ........ *Digested,* 62/**2699**: *Considered* 90/2782, 14/1712: *Distinguished* 66/11845: *Followed* 65/3492, 95/5622

Hosking v Nautadutilh Avocats Luxembourg see Hellas Telecommunications (Luxembourg) II SCA, Re

Hospital Medical Group Ltd v Westwood [2012] EWCA Civ 1005; [2013] I.C.R. 415; [2012] I.R.L.R. 834, CA (Civ Div); affirming UKEAT/0232/11/LA, EAT ........ *Digested,* 12/**1083**: *Approved* 14/1067

Hostgilt Ltd v Megahart Ltd [1999] S.T.C. 141; [1999] B.T.C. 5057; [1999] B.V.C. 78; (1999) 77 P. & C.R. D34; Times, January 5, 1999, Ch D ........ *Digested,* 99/**4969**: *Considered* 14/632

Hotak v Southwark LBC [2013] EWCA Civ 515; [2013] P.T.S.R. 1338; [2013] H.L.R. 32; [2013] B.L.G.R. 781; Times, July 4, 2013, CA (Civ Div) ........ *Digested,* 13/**1542**: *Applied* 14/1601

Hotel Cipriani Srl v Fred 250 Ltd (formerly Cipriani (Grosvenor Street) Ltd) [2013] EWHC 70 (Ch); [2013] E.C.C. 11; [2013] E.T.M.R. 18; [2013] F.S.R. 34, Ch D .. *Digested,* 13/**1757**: *Considered* 14/1929

Hotel Company 42 The Calls Ltd, Re; *sub nom* Whitfield v Al Jaber [2013] EWHC 3925 (Ch); [2014] B.C.C. 136, Ch D ........ *Digested,* 14/**1761**

Hoteles Pinero Canarias SL v Keefe [2013] EWHC 4279 (QB); [2014] Lloyd's Rep. I.R. 455, QBD ........ *Digested,* 14/**553**

Hounga v Allen see Allen v Hounga

Hounslow LBC v Powell; *sub nom* Powell v Hounslow LBC; Hall v Leeds City Council; Frisby v Birmingham City Council; Mushin v Manchester City Council; Mullen v Salford City Council; *joined cases* Salford City Council v Mullen; Leeds City Council v Hall; Birmingham City Council v Frisby [2011] UKSC 8; [2011] 2 A.C. 186; [2011] 2 W.L.R. 287; [2011] 2 All E.R. 129; [2011] P.T.S.R. 512; [2011] H.R.L.R. 18; [2011] U.K.H.R.R. 548; [2011] H.L.R. 23; [2011] B.L.G.R. 363; [2011] 1 P. & C.R. 20; [2011] 9 E.G. 164 (C.S.); (2011) 155(8) S.J.L.B. 31; [2011] N.P.C. 24; Times, March 1, 2011, SC; reversing in part [2010] EWCA Civ 336; [2011] 1 All E.R. 119; [2010] H.L.R. 35; [2010] B.L.G.R. 559; [2010] 15 E.G. 95 (C.S.); [2010] N.P.C. 43, CA (Civ Div) ........ *Digested,* 11/**2069**: *Applied* 14/1997, 14/3635: *Considered* 13/1892, 14/1625: *Followed* 12/1645, 12/2055, 13/1562, 13/1890, 13/3806, 14/2524

Housden v Conservators of Wimbledon and Putney Commons [2008] EWCA Civ 200; [2008] 1 W.L.R. 1172; [2008] 3 All E.R. 1038; [2008] 2 E.G.L.R. 107; [2008] 12 E.G. 97 (C.S.); [2008] N.P.C. 35, CA (Civ Div); reversing [2007] EWHC 1171 (Ch); [2007] 1 W.L.R. 2543; [2008] 1 All E.R. 397; Times, June 4, 2007, Ch D .. *Digested,* 08/**3067**: *Followed* 14/2498

House of Spring Gardens Ltd v Waite (No.2) [1991] 1 Q.B. 241; [1990] 3 W.L.R. 347; [1990] 2 All E.R. 990, CA (Civ Div) ........ *Digested,* 90/**610**: *Applied* 95/688: *Considered* 14/125: *Distinguished* 01/4882

HouseLetDirect v Newham LBC see K v Portsmouth City Council

Howard de Walden Estates Ltd v Lexgorge Ltd see Day v Hosebay Ltd

Howard de Walden Estates Ltd v Maybury Court Freehold Co Ltd see Earl Cadogan v Sportelli

Howden Joinery Group Plc v Revenue and Customs Commissioners [2014] UKFTT 257 (TC); [2014] S.F.T.D. 1186; [2014] S.T.I. 2015, FTT (Tax)

Howe v Secretary of State for Business, Enterprise and Regulatory Reform see Secretary of State for Business, Enterprise and Regulatory Reform v Neufeld

Howell v Trippier (Inspector of Taxes); *sub nom* Red Discretionary Trustees v Inspector of Taxes [2004] EWCA Civ 885; [2004] S.T.C. 1245; 76 T.C. 415; [2004] B.T.C. 305; [2004] W.T.L.R. 839; [2004] S.T.I. 1654; (2004) 148 S.J.L.B. 881; Times, August 17, 2004, CA (Civ Div); affirming [2004] S.T.C. (S.C.D.) 132; [2004] W.T.L.R. 437; [2004] S.T.I. 314, Sp Comm ........ *Digested,* 04/**3825**: *Considered* 14/2939: *Followed* 10/3451

Howes, Re see H v Lord Advocate

Howkins & Harrison v Tyler [2001] Lloyd's Rep. P.N. 1; [2001] P.N.L.R. 27; [2000] E.G. 91 (C.S.); Times, August 8, 2000, CA (Civ Div); affirming [2001] P.N.L.R. 26; [2000] E.G. 30 (C.S.); (2000) 97(10) L.S.G. 38; [2000] N.P.C. 20, Ch D ...... *Digested,* 00/**1448**: *Applied* 01/609, 14/549: *Cited* 02/469

Hoyle v Rogers see Rogers v Hoyle

HRH Prince Jefri Bolkiah v KPMG see Bolkiah v KPMG

HS Environment Services Ltd v DG Robson Mechanical Services Ltd see Greenwich Millennium Village Ltd v Essex Services Group Plc (formerly Essex Electrical Group Ltd)

HS2 Action Alliance Ltd v Secretary of State for Transport see R. (on the application of Buckinghamshire CC) v Secretary of State for Transport

HSBC Asia Holdings BV v Gillespie [2011] I.C.R. 192; [2011] I.R.L.R. 209; [2011] Eq. L.R. 25, EAT ........ *Digested,* 11/**1117**: *Applied* 14/1101

HSBC Bank Plc v Tambrook Jersey Ltd see Tambrook Jersey Ltd, Re

HSBC Holdings Plc v Revenue and Customs Commissioners [2012] UKFTT 163 (TC); 81 T.C. 663; [2012] S.F.T.D. 913, FTT (Tax) ........ *Digested,* 12/**3330**

HSM Law Ltd v Revenue and Customs Commissioners [2014] UKFTT 830 (TC); [2014] S.T.I. 2768, FTT (Tax)

HTC Corp v Gemalto NV see HTC Corp v Gemalto SA

HTC Corp v Gemalto SA; *joined case* HTC Corp v Gemalto NV [2014] EWCA Civ 1335, CA (Civ Div); affirming [2013] EWHC 1876 (Pat); [2014] R.P.C. 9, Ch D (Patents Ct) ........ *Digested,* 14/**1897**

HTC Corp v Nokia Corp [2013] EWCA Civ 1759; [2014] R.P.C. 31, CA (Civ Div)

HTC Corp v Nokia Corp [2013] EWHC 3778 (Pat); [2014] Bus. L.R. 217; [2014] R.P.C. 30, Ch D (Patents Ct) ........ *Digested,* 14/**1895**

HTC Corp v Nokia Corp [2013] EWHC 3247 (Pat); [2014] R.P.C. 19, Ch D (Patents Ct) ........ *Digested,* 14/**1901**

HTC Europe Co Ltd v Apple Inc; *joined case* Apple Inc v HTC Corp [2013] EWCA Civ 451; [2013] R.P.C. 30, CA (Civ Div); reversing in part [2012] EWHC 1789 (Pat); [2012] Info. T.L.R. 225, Ch D (Patents Ct) ........ *Digested,* 13/**1795**: *Followed* 14/1897

Hua Tyan Development Ltd v Zurich Insurance Co Ltd (The Ho Feng 7) [2014] 2 Lloyd's Rep. 637, CFA (HK); affirming [2013] 2 Lloyd's Rep. 468; [2014] Lloyd's Rep. I.R. 1, CA (HK)

Huang v Secretary of State for the Home Department; *joined cases* Kashmiri v Secretary of State for the Home Department; Abu-Qulbain v Secretary of State for the Home Department [2007] UKHL 11; [2007] 2 A.C. 167; [2007] 2 W.L.R. 581; [2007] 4 All E.R. 15; [2007] 1 F.L.R. 2021; [2007] H.R.L.R. 22; [2007] U.K.H.R.R. 759; 24 B.H.R.C. 74; [2007] Imm. A.R. 571; [2007] I.N.L.R. 314; [2007] Fam. Law 587; (2007) 151 S.J.L.B. 435; Times, March 22, 2007, HL; reversing in part [2005] EWCA Civ 105; [2006] Q.B. 1; [2005] 3 W.L.R. 488; [2005] 3 All E.R. 435; [2005] H.R.L.R. 15; [2005] U.K.H.R.R. 651; [2005] Imm. A.R. 240; [2005] I.N.L.R. 247; (2005) 102(20) L.S.G. 30; (2005) 149 S.J.L.B. 297; Times, March 16, 2005, CA (Civ Div) ........ *Digested,* 07/**2340**: *Applied* 05/2179, 05/2193, 05/2211, 06/2224, 06/2249, 07/2307, 07/2308, 07/2330, 07/2364, 08/2039, 08/2075, 09/2102, 09/2132, 10/765, 11/1762, 11/1770, 12/1655, 12/1775, 12/3593, 14/1703, 14/2444: *Considered* 05/2213, 07/2289, 07/2298, 08/2036, 08/2052, 09/2101, 10/1266, 10/1821, 10/356, 10/795, 11/1778, 12/1004, 12/1767, 12/2330: *Explained* 06/2264: *Followed* 08/2036, 09/4361, 10/1761, 10/1790, 13/1618, 14/1678, 14/1715, 14/1718

Huawei Technologies Co Ltd v ZTE Corp ZTE Deutschland GmbH [2014] E.C.C. 13, LG (Ger)

Hubbard v Bank of Scotland Plc (t/a Birmingham Midshires) [2014] EWCA Civ 648; [2014] P.N.L.R. 23, CA (Civ Div) ........ *Digested,* 14/**2218**

Huckfield, Re see R. v Manchester Crown Court Ex p. DPP
Hudson v Leigh; *joined case* Leigh v Hudson [2009] EWHC 1306 (Fam); [2013] Fam. 77; [2013] 2 W.L.R. 632; [2009] 2 F.L.R. 1129; [2009] 3 F.C.R. 401; [2009] Fam. Law 810; Times, July 17, 2009, Fam Div .......... *Digested,* 09/**1617**: *Applied* 10/1406, 12/1444, 12/1446, 13/1322, 14/2190
Hudson's Concrete Products v Evans (DB) (Bilston) (1961) 105 S.J. 281, CA .......... *Digested,* 61/**1173**: *Considered* 14/1814
Hufford v Samsung Electronics (UK) Ltd [2014] EWHC 2956 (TCC); [2014] B.L.R. 633, QBD (TCC)
Hughes v Esure Insurance Ltd (Unreported, May 13, 2014), CC (Blackwood) [*BDE Law, First Floor, 25-26 Neptune Court, Vanguard Way, Cardiff*] .......... *Digested,* 14/**2348**
Hughes v Merrett Syndicates Ltd see Henderson v Merrett Syndicates Ltd (No.1)
Hulm & Lewis, Re [1892] 2 Q.B. 261, QBD
*Considered* 14/136
Humber Ironworks & Shipbuilding Co, Re; *sub nom* Warrant Finance Co's Case (No.1) (1868-69) L.R. 4 Ch. App. 643, CA in Chancery
*Applied* 55/373, 14/1752: *Followed* 82/335
Humphreys v Revenue and Customs Commissioners [2012] UKSC 18; [2012] 1 W.L.R. 1545; [2012] 4 All E.R. 27; [2012] P.T.S.R. 1024; [2012] 3 F.C.R. 403; [2012] H.R.L.R. 21; [2012] Eq. L.R. 714; [2012] S.T.I. 1664; (2012) 162 N.L.J. 712; (2012) 156(20) S.J.L.B. 31; Times, May 26, 2012, SC; affirming [2010] EWCA Civ 56; [2010] 1 F.C.R. 630; [2010] U.K.H.R.R. 497, CA (Civ Div) .......... *Digested,* 12/**3093**: *Applied* 14/2757: *Considered* 11/3159: *Followed* 13/2885
Hunston Properties Ltd v Secretary of State for Communities and Local Government; *sub nom* St Albans City and District Council v Hunston Properties Ltd [2013] EWCA Civ 1610; [2014] 1 E.G.L.R. 79; [2014] J.P.L. 599, CA (Civ Div); affirming [2013] EWHC 2678 (Admin); [2014] J.P.L. 240, QBD (Admin) .......... *Digested,* 14/**2432**: *Considered* 14/2430
Hunt v Conwy CBC [2013] EWHC 1154 (Ch); [2014] 1 W.L.R. 254; [2013] B.P.I.R. 790, Ch D .......... *Digested,* 14/**1816**
Hunt v Hosking see Ovenden Colbert Printers Ltd (In Liquidation), Re
Hunt v North Somerset Council; *sub nom* R. (on the application of Hunt) v North Somerset Council [2013] EWCA Civ 1320; [2014] B.L.G.R. 1; (2013) 16 C.C.L. Rep. 502, CA (Civ Div); reversing in part [2012] EWHC 1928 (Admin); [2012] Eq. L.R. 951; (2012) 15 C.C.L. Rep. 625, QBD (Admin) .......... *Digested,* 14/**2111**: *Considered* 14/2106
Hunt v North Somerset Council (Costs); *sub nom* R. (on the application of Hunt) v North Somerset Council (Costs) [2013] EWCA Civ 1483; (2013) 16 C.C.L. Rep. 530, CA (Civ Div) .......... *Digested,* 14/**324**
Hunt v Optima (Cambridge) Ltd [2014] EWCA Civ 714; [2014] B.L.R. 613; 155 Con. L.R. 29; [2014] P.N.L.R. 29; [2014] 3 E.G.L.R. 169; Times, August 19, 2014, CA (Civ Div); reversing [2013] EWHC 681 (TCC); 148 Con. L.R. 27, QBD (TCC) .......... *Digested,* 14/**2207**
Hunt v Salliss see Salliss v Hunt
Hunt v Yearwood-Grazette [2009] EWHC 2112 (Ch); [2009] B.P.I.R. 810, Ch D .......... *Digested,* 09/**2267**: *Considered* 14/3198
Hunter v Newcastle Crown Court [2013] EWHC 191 (Admin); [2014] Q.B. 94; [2013] 3 W.L.R. 918; [2013] 2 Costs L.R. 348; [2013] A.C.D. 45, DC .......... *Digested,* 13/**702**
Huntley (Deceased), Re; *sub nom* Brooke v Purton [2014] EWHC 547 (Ch); [2014] W.T.L.R. 745, Ch D .......... *Digested,* 14/**2833**
Hurley Palmer Flatt Ltd v Barclays Bank Plc [2014] EWHC 3042 (TCC); [2014] B.L.R. 713; 156 Con. L.R. 213; [2014] C.I.L.L. 3577, QBD (TCC)
Hurlingham Estates Ltd v Wilde & Partners [1997] 1 Lloyd's Rep. 525; [1997] S.T.C. 627; [1997] B.T.C. 240; (1997) 147 N.L.J. 453; Times, January 3, 1997; Independent, February 17, 1997, Ch D .......... *Digested,* 97/**3842**: *Considered* 14/2211: *Referred to* 00/4255
Hurst v Bryk [2002] 1 A.C. 185; [2000] 2 W.L.R. 740; [2000] 2 All E.R. 193; [2000] 2 B.C.L.C. 117; [2000] E.G. 49 (C.S.); (2000) 97(17) L.S.G. 35; (2000) 150 N.L.J. 511; (2000) 144 S.J.L.B. 189; Times, April 4, 2000, HL; affirming [1999] Ch. 1; [1998] 2 W.L.R. 269; [1997] 2 All E.R. 283; Times, March 20, 1997; Independent, February 7, 1997, CA (Civ Div); affirming (Unreported, April 7, 1995), Ch D .......... *Digested,* 00/**4317**: *Considered* 00/4320, 03/3047, 06/2340, 13/2102, 14/2227
Hurst v Kelly [2013] I.C.R. 1225, EAT .......... *Digested,* 14/**1078**
Hurst & Middleton Ltd, Re [1912] 2 Ch. 520, CA
*Considered* 14/136

Hurstanger Ltd v Wilson [2007] EWCA Civ 299; [2007] 1 W.L.R. 2351; [2007] 4 All E.R. 1118; [2007] 2 All E.R. (Comm) 1037; [2008] Bus. L.R. 216; [2007] C.T.L.C. 59; (2007) 104(16) L.S.G. 23; (2007) 157 N.L.J. 555; (2007) 151 S.J.L.B. 467; [2007] N.P.C. 41; Times, May 11, 2007, CA (Civ Div); reversing in part [2007] C.T.L.C. 9, CC (Coventry) .......... *Digested,* 07/**765**: *Applied* 14/138: *Followed* 12/57

Hussain v Bradford Community Housing Ltd [2009] EWCA Civ 763; [2010] H.L.R. 16, CA (Civ Div) .......... *Digested,* 10/**2093**: *Considered* 14/1996

Hussain v King Edward VII Hospital [2013] EWCA Civ 1863; (2014) 136 B.M.L.R. 54, CA (Civ Div); affirming [2012] EWHC 3441 (QB), QBD .......... *Digested,* 14/**2298**

Hussain v Secretary of State for the Home Department see Pokhriyal v Secretary of State for the Home Department

Hussein v General Medical Council [2013] EWHC 3535 (Admin); (2014) 136 B.M.L.R. 202, QBD (Admin) .......... *Digested,* 14/**1504**

Hussey v Eels [1990] 2 Q.B. 227; [1990] 2 W.L.R. 234; [1990] 1 All E.R. 449; [1990] 19 E.G. 77; [1989] E.G. 168 (C.S.); (1990) 140 N.L.J. 53, CA (Civ Div) .......... *Digested,* 90/**1565**: *Applied* 03/938, 14/827: *Considered* 91/1503, 01/4152: *Followed* 97/3843

Hussman (Europe) Ltd v Al Ameen Development & Trade Co see Hussmann (Europe) Ltd v Al Ameen Development & Trade Co

Hussmann (Europe) Ltd v Al Ameen Development & Trade Co; *sub nom* Hussman (Europe) Ltd v Al Ameen Development & Trade Co [2000] 2 Lloyd's Rep. 83; [2000] C.L.C. 1243, QBD (Comm) .......... *Digested,* 00/**228**: *Applied* 14/118

Hutchings v Islington LBC [1998] 1 W.L.R. 1629; [1998] 3 All E.R. 445; [1998] I.C.R. 1230; (1999) 1 L.G.L.R. 1; [1998] Pens. L.R. 239; Times, May 6, 1998, CA (Civ Div) .......... *Digested,* 98/**4129**: *Applied* 14/413: *Considered* 03/1265

Hutchinson v Birmingham City Council 1303038.11, ET *Considered* 14/952

Hutchison 3G UK Ltd v Edwards [2014] Eq. L.R. 525, EAT .......... *Digested,* 14/**1050**

Huzar v Jet2.com Ltd see Jet2.com Ltd v Huzar

Huzrat v Hounslow LBC [2013] EWCA Civ 1865; [2014] H.L.R. 17, CA (Civ Div) .......... *Digested,* 14/**1596**

HW v GK see K (Children) (Contact: Interim Care Order), Re

Hyde v Cogan 99 E.R. 445; (1781) 2 Doug. K.B. 699, KB *Applied* 14/2448

Hyder Consulting (UK) Ltd v Carillion Construction Ltd [2011] EWHC 1810 (TCC); 138 Con. L.R. 212, QBD (TCC) .......... *Digested,* 12/**583**: *Considered* 14/576

HYDRO QUEBEC/Petition for review (R14/12) [2014] E.P.O.R. 21, EPO (Enlarged Bd App)

Hyundai Merchant Marine Co Ltd v Furness Withy (Australia) Pty (The Doric Pride) [2006] EWCA Civ 599; [2006] 2 All E.R. (Comm) 188; [2006] 2 Lloyd's Rep. 175; [2007] 2 C.L.C. 1042, CA (Civ Div); affirming [2005] EWHC 945 (Comm); [2005] 2 Lloyd's Rep. 470; [2005] 1 C.L.C. 780, QBD (Comm) .......... *Digested,* 06/**3917**: *Considered* 08/3468, 08/3474: *Followed* 14/2739

Hyundai Motor UK Ltd v Revenue and Customs Commissioners see 288 Group Ltd v Revenue and Customs Commissioners

I v G see G (A Child) (Jurisdiction: Brussels II Revised), Re

I (A Child) (Contact Application: Jurisdiction), Re; *sub nom* Y v I [2009] UKSC 10; [2010] 1 A.C. 319; [2009] 3 W.L.R. 1299; [2010] 1 All E.R. 445; [2010] I.L.Pr. 19; [2010] 1 F.L.R. 361; [2010] 1 F.C.R. 200; [2010] Fam. Law 237; (2009) 159 N.L.J. 1736; (2009) 153(46) S.J.L.B. 32; Times, December 4, 2009, SC; reversing [2009] EWCA Civ 965; [2009] Fam. Law 1134, CA (Civ Div); affirming [2009] EWHC 1378 (Fam); [2009] Fam. Law 805, Fam Div .......... *Digested,* 10/**1413**: *Applied* 14/1381: *Considered* 11/1402: *Followed* 13/1282, 13/1335, 14/1287

I Fit Global Ltd, Re; *sub nom* Blunt v Jackson [2013] EWHC 2090 (Ch); [2014] 2 B.C.L.C. 116, Ch D (Companies Ct) .......... *Digested,* 14/**522**

IA (A Child) (Fact-finding: Welfare: Single Hearing: Experts' Reports), Re [2013] EWHC 2499 (Fam); (2013) 134 B.M.L.R. 61, Fam Div .......... *Digested,* 14/**1274**

IA (Iran) v Secretary of State for the Home Department; *sub nom* A v Secretary of State for the Home Department [2014] UKSC 6; [2014] 1 W.L.R. 384; [2014] 1 All E.R. 1015; 2014 S.C. (U.K.S.C.) 105; 2014 S.L.T. 598; 2014 S.C.L.R. 366; [2014] Imm. A.R. 613; [2014] I.N.L.R. 559; 2014 G.W.D. 4-86; Times, February 4, 2014, SC; affirming [2011] CSIH 28; 2011 S.C. 625; 2011 S.L.T. 706; 2011 G.W.D. 14-344, IH (Ex Div) .......... *Digested,* 14/**1659**

IAG New Zealand Ltd v Jackson [2013] NZCA 302; [2014] Lloyd's Rep. I.R. 97, CA (NZ)

IBA Health Ltd v Office of Fair Trading; *sub nom* Office of Fair Trading v IBA Healthcare Ltd [2004] EWCA Civ 142; [2004] 4 All E.R. 1103; [2005] 1 All E.R. (Comm) 147; [2004] U.K.C.L.R. 683; [2005] E.C.C. 1; [2004] I.C.R. 1364; (2004) 101(11) L.S.G. 33; (2004) 154 N.L.J. 352; Times, February 25, 2004; Independent, March 29, 2004, CA (Civ Div); affirming [2003] CAT 27; [2004] Comp. A.R. 235, CAT ........ *Digested,* 04/**531**: *Applied* 06/614, 08/542, 10/491, 11/955: *Considered* 11/436, 14/547: *Distinguished* 06/570: *Followed* 10/496

IBM United Kingdom Holdings Ltd v Dalgleish [2014] EWHC 980 (Ch); [2014] Pens. L.R. 335, Ch D ........ *Digested,* 14/**2263**

Ibrahim v Birmingham City Council see Ali v Birmingham City Council

IBSolution GmbH v Office for Harmonisation in the Internal Market (Trade Marks and Designs) (OHIM) (T-533/12) [2014] E.T.M.R. 19, GC (5th Chamber)

Icebreaker 1 LLP v Revenue and Customs Commissioners [2010] UKUT 477 (TCC); [2011] S.T.C. 1078; [2011] B.T.C. 1579; [2011] S.T.I. 372, UT (Tax); reversing in part [2010] UKFTT 6 (TC); [2010] S.T.I. 1520, FTT (Tax) ........ *Digested,* 11/**3347**: *Followed* 14/2975

Ichin v Ukraine (28189/04) (2014) 58 E.H.R.R. 24, ECHR

ICM Computer Group Ltd v Stribley [2013] EWHC 2995 (Ch); [2013] Pens. L.R. 409, Ch D ........ *Digested,* 14/**2278**

Icopal AS, Re [2013] EWHC 3469 (Ch); [2014] 2 All E.R. (Comm) 1183; [2014] 2 B.C.L.C. 110, Ch D ........ *Digested,* 14/**1819**

Iddenden v Secretary of State for the Environment [1972] 1 W.L.R. 1433; [1972] 3 All E.R. 883; 71 L.G.R. 20; (1973) 26 P. & C.R. 553; (1972) 116 S.J. 665, CA (Civ Div); affirming [1972] 3 All E.R. 722, DC ........ *Digested,* 72/**3339**: *Applied* 14/2378: *Considered* 76/2697, 93/3837: *Distinguished* 91/3449

Idess Ltd v Revenue and Customs Commissioners [2014] UKFTT 511 (TC); [2014] S.T.I. 2101, FTT (Tax)

Idrodinamica Spurgo Velox srl v Acquedotto Pugliese SpA (C-161/13) [2014] P.T.S.R. 935, ECJ (5th Chamber)

IE Contractors Ltd v Lloyds Bank Plc; *joined case* IE Contractors Ltd v Rafidain Bank [1990] 2 Lloyd's Rep. 496; 51 B.L.R. 5; Financial Times, July 17, 1990, CA (Civ Div); reversing in part [1989] 2 Lloyd's Rep. 205, QBD (Comm) ........ *Digested,* 91/**256**: *Applied* 14/265: *Distinguished* 05/703

IE Contractors Ltd v Rafidain Bank see IE Contractors Ltd v Lloyds Bank Plc

IFE Fund SA v Goldman Sachs International [2007] EWCA Civ 811; [2007] 2 Lloyd's Rep. 449; [2007] 2 C.L.C. 134; (2007) 104(32) L.S.G. 24, CA (Civ Div); affirming [2006] EWHC 2887 (Comm); [2007] 1 Lloyd's Rep. 264; [2006] 2 C.L.C. 1043, QBD (Comm) ........ *Digested,* 08/**3904**: *Applied* 14/640: *Considered* 10/619

IFG International Trust Co Ltd v French [2014] W.T.L.R. 1191; [2013] W.T.L.R. 251; 16 I.T.E.L.R. 499, HC (IoM)

IFX Investment Co Ltd v Revenue and Customs Commissioners see Revenue and Customs Commissioners v IFX Investment Co Ltd

IG Communications Ltd v Office for Harmonisation in the Internal Market (Trade Marks and Designs) (OHIM) (T-301/09) [2013] E.T.M.R. 17, GC (5th Chamber) *Followed* 14/1937

IG Index Ltd v Cloete [2014] EWCA Civ 1128; [2014] C.P. Rep. 44; (2014) 158(32) S.J.L.B. 41, CA (Civ Div); reversing [2013] EWHC 3789 (QB), QBD ........ *Digested,* 14/**380**

IG Markets Ltd v Crinion; *sub nom* Crinion v IG Markets Ltd [2013] EWCA Civ 587; [2013] C.P. Rep. 41; Times, July 31, 2013, CA (Civ Div); affirming 1BM40042; 1BM40043, QBD (Merc) (Birmingham) ........ *Digested,* 13/**387**: *Followed* 14/1263

Igen Ltd (formerly Leeds Careers Guidance) v Wong see Wong v Igen Ltd (formerly Leeds Careers Guidance)

Ignaoua v United Kingdom (Admissibility) (46706/08) (2014) 59 E.H.R.R. SE2, ECHR

Igroup Ltd v Ocwen; *sub nom* IGroup Ltd, Re [2003] EWHC 2431 (Ch); [2004] 1 W.L.R. 451; [2003] 4 All E.R. 1063; [2003] B.C.C. 993; [2004] 2 B.C.L.C. 61; (2003) 100(46) L.S.G. 24; Times, November 4, 2003, Ch D (Companies Ct) ..... *Digested,* 04/**445**: *Considered* 14/1758

IGroup Ltd, Re see Igroup Ltd v Ocwen

IH (A Child) (Permission to Apply for Adoption), Re [2013] EWHC 1235 (Fam); [2014] 1 F.L.R. 70; [2013] Fam. Law 935, Fam Div ........ *Digested,* 14/**1241**

Iida v Stadt Ulm (C-40/11) [2013] Fam. 121; [2013] 2 W.L.R. 788; [2013] 1 C.M.L.R. 47; [2014] All E.R. (EC) 619, ECJ (3rd Chamber) *Considered* 13/1597

Ikbal v Sterling Law [2013] EWHC 3291 (Ch); [2014] P.N.L.R. 9, Ch D .......................... *Digested,* 14/**2059**

Iles v Revenue and Customs Commissioners [2014] UKFTT 436 (TC); [2014] S.T.I. 2523, FTT (Tax)

Iliffe News & Media Ltd v Revenue and Customs Commissioners [2012] UKFTT 696 (TC); [2014] F.S.R. 6; [2013] S.F.T.D. 309; [2013] S.T.I. 388, FTT (Tax) ........... *Digested,* 13/**3045**

Ilott v Mitson [2014] EWHC 542 (Fam); [2014] W.T.L.R. 575; [2014] Fam. Law 789, Fam Div .......................... *Digested,* 14/**2819**

IM v LM (Capacity to Consent to Sexual Relations) see M (An Adult) (Capacity: Consent to Sexual Relations), Re

IM (Nigeria) v Secretary of State for the Home Department see R. (on the application of Muaza) v Secretary of State for the Home Department

IM Properties Development Ltd v Lichfield DC see R. (on the application of IM Properties Development Ltd) v Lichfield DC

Imam-Sadeque v Bluebay Asset Management (Services) Ltd [2012] EWHC 3511 (QB); [2013] I.R.L.R. 344, QBD .......................... *Digested,* 13/**960**: *Applied* 14/1025

Imerman v Imerman see Tchenguiz v Imerman

Imerman v Tchenguiz see Tchenguiz v Imerman

Imfeld v Belgium (C-303/12) [2014] S.T.I. 258, ECJ (5th Chamber)

Impeller Flow Meter (X ZR 48/03) (Unreported), BGH (Ger) *Considered* 14/1877

Imperial Group Pension Trust Ltd v Imperial Tobacco Ltd [1991] 1 W.L.R. 589; [1991] 2 All E.R. 597; [1991] I.C.R. 524; [1991] I.R.L.R. 66; [1990] Pens. L.R. 263; [1990] P.L.R. 239; (1991) 88(9) L.S.G. 39; (1991) 141 N.L.J. 55; Independent, December 4, 1990; Financial Times, December 5, 1990; Guardian, December 11, 1990, Ch D .......................... *Digested,* 91/**2725**: *Applied* 13/2169: *Considered* 14/2263: *Followed* 97/3997

Imperial Loan Co Ltd v Stone [1892] 1 Q.B. 599, CA *Considered* 13/2199, 14/435, 14/625

Inco Europe Ltd v First Choice Distribution [2000] 1 W.L.R. 586; [2000] 2 All E.R. 109; [2000] 1 All E.R. (Comm) 674; [2000] 1 Lloyd's Rep. 467; [2000] C.L.C. 1015; [2000] B.L.R. 259; (2000) 2 T.C.L.R. 487; 74 Con. L.R. 55; (2000) 97(12) L.S.G. 39; (2000) 144 S.J.L.B. 134; [2000] N.P.C. 22; Times, March 10, 2000; Independent, March 15, 2000, HL; affirming [1999] 1 W.L.R. 270; [1999] 1 All E.R. 820; [1999] C.L.C. 165; (1999) 1 T.C.L.R. 169; (1998) 95(41) L.S.G. 45; (1998) 142 S.J.L.B. 269; Times, October 22, 1998; Independent, October 12, 1998, CA (Civ Div) .......................... *Digested,* 00/**220**: *Applied* 02/3792, 02/5549, 03/1962, 07/2810, 08/3316, 08/7, 12/7, 14/1063, 14/1770: *Considered* 05/2742, 07/848, 11/4269, 11/4270, 11/4452, 12/2092: *Followed* 03/5952, 12/831, 13/2160, 14/799

Independent News and Media Ltd v A; *sub nom* A v Independent News and Media Ltd [2010] EWCA Civ 343; [2010] 1 W.L.R. 2262; [2010] 3 All E.R. 32; [2010] E.M.L.R. 22; [2010] 2 F.L.R. 1290; [2010] 2 F.C.R. 187; [2010] U.K.H.R.R. 713; (2010) 13 C.C.L. Rep. 262; (2010) 113 B.M.L.R. 162; [2010] M.H.L.R. 154; [2010] Fam. Law 705; Times, April 30, 2010, CA (Civ Div); affirming [2009] EWHC 2858 (Fam); [2010] 1 F.L.R. 916; [2009] M.H.L.R. 336; [2010] W.T.L.R. 55; [2010] Fam. Law 357; Times, November 17, 2009, Fam Div .......................... *Digested,* 10/**332**: *Applied* 11/2209, 12/407, 14/2191: *Considered* 13/2066: *Followed* 11/2210, 12/15

Industrie du bois de Vielsalm & Cie (IBV) SA v Region wallonne (C-195/12) [2014] 1 C.M.L.R. 43, ECJ (4th Chamber)

Industry-Wide Coal Staff Superannuation Scheme Co-ordinator Ltd v Industry-Wide Coal Staff Superannuation Scheme Trustees Ltd [2012] EWHC 3712 (Ch); [2013] Pens. L.R. 55, Ch D .......................... *Digested,* 13/**2160**: *Considered* 14/2278

INEOS SALES (UK) LTD/Polymer treatment (T935/12) [2014] E.P.O.R. 36, EPO (Technical Bd App)

Infederation Ltd v Google Inc; *sub nom* Infederation Ltd v Google Ireland Ltd [2013] EWHC 2295 (Ch); [2014] 1 All E.R. 325; [2013] U.K.C.L.R. 773; [2014] 1 C.M.L.R. 13; [2013] E.C.C. 31; [2014] Bus. L.R. D5, Ch D .......................... *Digested,* 14/**529**

Infederation Ltd v Google Ireland Ltd see Infederation Ltd v Google Inc

Infopaq International A/S v Danske Dagblades Forening (C-5/08) [2012] Bus. L.R. 102; [2009] E.C.R. I-6569; [2009] E.C.D.R. 16; [2010] F.S.R. 20, ECJ (4th Chamber) *Applied* 12/1917, 12/1920, 12/1923, 13/1768, 13/1769, 14/1870: *Considered* 10/1942: *Followed* 11/1950

Information and Privacy Commissioner of Alberta v United Food and Commercial Workers Local 401 2013 SCC 62; 36 B.H.R.C. 745, Sup Ct (Can)

ING Intermediate Holdings Ltd v Revenue and Customs Commissioners [2014] UKFTT 938 (TC); [2014] S.T.I. 3096, FTT (Tax)

Ingenieurburo Eulitz GbR Thomas und Marion Eulitz v Finanzamt Dresden I (C-473/08) [2010] B.V.C. 728, ECJ
*Applied* 13/3193: *Followed* 14/3051

Ingram v Inland Revenue Commissioners [2000] 1 A.C. 293; [1999] 2 W.L.R. 90; [1999] 1 All E.R. 297; [1999] S.T.C. 37; [1999] L. & T.R. 85; [1998] B.T.C. 8047; [1998] E.G. 181 (C.S.); (1999) 96(3) L.S.G. 33; (1999) 143 S.J.L.B. 52; [1998] N.P.C. 160; Times, December 16, 1998; Independent, December 15, 1998, HL; reversing [1997] 4 All E.R. 395; [1997] S.T.C. 1234; [1997] B.T.C. 8009; (1997) 94(34) L.S.G. 29; (1997) 141 S.J.L.B. 204; [1997] N.P.C. 129; Times, September 11, 1997, CA (Civ Div); reversing [1995] 4 All E.R. 334; [1995] S.T.C. 564; (1995) 92(23) L.S.G. 33; (1995) 139 S.J.L.B. 128; [1995] N.P.C. 92; Times, May 23, 1995; Independent, June 5, 1995, Ch D .................. *Digested,* 99/**4740**:
*Applied* 12/2151, 12/3234, 14/2938: *Considered* 03/4270, 13/3102: *Followed* 11/3394, 14/1809

Inland Revenue Commissioners v Banco do Brasil SA see Inland Revenue Commissioners v Commerzbank AG

Inland Revenue Commissioners v Bland [2003] EWHC 1068 (Ch); [2003] B.P.I.R. 1274, Ch D .................. *Digested,* 04/**2156**:
*Considered* 14/1799

Inland Revenue Commissioners v Brebner [1967] 2 A.C. 18; [1967] 2 W.L.R. 1001; [1967] 1 All E.R. 779; 1967 S.C. (H.L.) 31; 1967 S.L.T. 113; 43 T.C. 705; (1967) 46 A.T.C. 17; [1967] T.R. 21; (1967) 111 S.J. 216, HL; affirming 1966 S.L.T. 208; (1966) 45 A.T.C. 228; [1966] T.R. 203, IH (1 Div) .................. *Digested,* 67/**1978**:
*Applied* 79/1485, 03/4323, 09/3848, 10/3343, 10/3382, 14/2972: *Considered* 68/1912, 95/2753, 13/3045: *Distinguished* 69/1750

Inland Revenue Commissioners v Commerzbank AG; *joined case* Inland Revenue Commissioners v Banco do Brasil SA [1990] S.T.C. 285; (1990) 87(13) L.S.G. 44; Times, February 22, 1990; Independent, February 26, 1990, Ch D .................. *Digested,* 91/**588**:
*Applied* 06/4163, 10/3236, 12/3272, 14/2892: *Considered* 96/1307

Inland Revenue Commissioners v George; *sub nom* George v Inland Revenue Commissioners; Stedman's Executors v Inland Revenue Commissioners [2003] EWCA Civ 1763; [2004] S.T.C. 147; 75 T.C. 735; [2004] B.T.C. 8003; [2004] W.T.L.R. 75; [2003] S.T.I. 2276; (2004) 101(3) L.S.G. 34; Times, December 9, 2003; Independent, December 11, 2003, CA (Civ Div); reversing [2003] EWHC 318 (Ch); [2003] S.T.C. 468; [2003] B.T.C. 8037; [2003] W.T.L.R. 471; [2003] S.T.I. 297; (2003) 100(17) L.S.G. 29; Times, March 18, 2003, Ch D; reversing [2002] S.T.C. (S.C.D.) 358; [2002] W.T.L.R. 1357; [2002] S.T.I. 1155, Sp Comm .................. *Digested,* 04/**3791**:
*Applied* 06/4237, 09/3856, 12/3220, 13/3098, 13/3099: *Considered* 06/4238: *Distinguished* 09/4532: *Followed* 11/3390, 14/2935

Inland Revenue Commissioners v Kahn see Toshoku Finance UK Plc (In Liquidation), Re

Inland Revenue Commissioners v McGuckian; *joined case* McGuckian v Inland Revenue Commissioners [1997] 1 W.L.R. 991; [1997] 3 All E.R. 817; [1997] S.T.C. 908; [1997] N.I. 157; 69 T.C. 1; [1997] B.T.C. 346; (1997) 94(27) L.S.G. 23; (1997) 141 S.J.L.B. 153; Times, June 20, 1997; Independent, July 28, 1997, HL (NI); reversing [1994] S.T.C. 888; [1994] N.I. 1, CA (NI) .................. *Digested,* 97/**2979**:
*Applied* 00/5043, 01/5205: *Considered* 99/4709, 12/3322, 14/2916

Inland Revenue Commissioners v Metrolands (Property Finance) Ltd [1982] 1 W.L.R. 341; [1982] 2 All E.R. 557; [1982] S.T.C. 259; 80 L.G.R. 553; 54 T.C. 679; [1982] J.P.L. 570; (1982) 126 S.J. 188, HL; reversing [1981] 1 W.L.R. 637; [1981] 2 All E.R. 166; [1981] S.T.C. 193; 79 L.G.R. 358; [1980] T.R. 457; (1981) 125 S.J. 19, Ch D .................. *Digested,* 82/**3135**:
*Applied* 92/344: *Approved* 99/4704: *Considered* 14/2970: *Referred to* 95/529

Inland Revenue Commissioners v Pratt [1982] S.T.C. 756; 57 T.C. 1; (1982) 79 L.S.G. 1444, Unknown court .................. *Digested,* 82/**1644**:
*Considered* 14/2916

Inland Revenue Commissioners v Rossminster Ltd see R. v Inland Revenue Commissioners Ex p. Rossminster Ltd

Inland Revenue Commissioners v Test Claimants in the Franked Investment Income Group Litigation see Test Claimants in the FII Group Litigation v Inland Revenue Commissioners

Innerspaces Self Storage Ltd v Harding [2014] EWCA Civ 46; [2014] L. & T.R. 16; [2014] 1 P. & C.R. DG20, CA (Civ Div) .................. *Digested,* 14/**1971**

InnoLux Corp v European Commission (T-91/11) [2014] 4 C.M.L.R. 23, GC (6th Chamber)

Innospec Ltd v Walker [2014] I.C.R. 645; [2014] I.R.L.R. 334; [2014] Eq. L.R. 192; [2014] Pens. L.R. 237, EAT ........ *Digested,* 14/**1120**

Innoweb BV v Wegener ICT Media BV (C-202/12) [2014] Bus. L.R. 308, ECJ (5th Chamber)

InPower Ltd, Re see Drax Holdings Ltd, Re

Insight Group Ltd v Kingston Smith (A Firm) [2012] EWHC 3644 (QB); [2014] 1 W.L.R. 1448; [2013] 3 All E.R. 518; [2013] 1 C.L.C. 90; [2013] P.N.L.R. 13, QBD ........ *Digested,* 13/**445**

Inspecteur van de Belastingdienst Holland-Noord/kantoor Zaandam v MSA International Holdings BV (C-41/13) see Inspecteur van de Belastingdienst/Noord/kantoor Groningen v SCA Group Holding BV (C-39/13)

Inspecteur van de Belastingdienst Holland-Noord/kantoor Zaandam v MSA International Holdings BV (C-41/13) see Inspecteur van de Belastingdienst/Noord/kantoor Groningen v SCA Group Holding BV (C-39/13)

Inspecteur van de Belastingdienst/Noord/kantoor Groningen v SCA Group Holding BV (C-39/13); *joined cases* Inspecteur van de Belastingdienst Holland-Noord/kantoor Zaandam v MSA International Holdings BV (C-41/13); X AG v Inspecteur van de Belastingdienst Amsterdam (C-40/13) [2014] S.T.C. 2107; [2014] S.T.I. 2115, ECJ (2nd Chamber)

Inspecteur van de Belastingdienst/Noord/kantoor Groningen v SCA Group Holding BV (C-39/13); *sub nom* X AG v Inspecteur van de Belastingdienst Amsterdam (C-40/13); Inspecteur van de Belastingdienst Holland-Noord/kantoor Zaandam v MSA International Holdings BV (C-41/13) [2014] B.T.C. 14, AGO

Institut professionnel des agents immobiliers (IPI) v Englebert (C-473/12) [2014] 2 C.M.L.R. 9; [2014] C.E.C. 719, ECJ (3rd Chamber)

Institute of Chartered Accountants in England and Wales v Customs and Excise Commissioners [1999] 1 W.L.R. 701; [1999] 2 All E.R. 449; [1999] S.T.C. 398; [1999] 2 C.M.L.R. 1333; [1999] B.T.C. 5165; [1999] B.V.C. 215; (1999) 96(20) L.S.G. 40; (1999) 149 N.L.J. 559; (1999) 143 S.J.L.B. 131; Times, March 29, 1999; Independent, April 14, 1999, HL; affirming [1998] 1 W.L.R. 315; [1998] 4 All E.R. 115; [1997] S.T.C. 1155; [1997] B.T.C. 5355; [1997] B.V.C. 469; (1997) 94(25) L.S.G. 34; (1997) 141 S.J.L.B. 128; Times, May 19, 1997; Independent, May 22, 1997, CA (Civ Div); affirming [1996] S.T.C. 799; Times, February 19, 1996, QBD; affirming [1995] V. & D.R. 87, VAT Tr (London) ........ *Digested,* 99/**4990**: *Applied* 03/4606, 05/4383, 09/5227, 14/3085: *Considered* 10/1139

Insular Council of Fuerteventura (Canary Islands) v Spain [2014] 3 C.M.L.R. 40, Trib Sup (Sp)

Insurance Co of Africa v Scor (UK) Reinsurance Co Ltd [1985] 1 Lloyd's Rep. 312, CA (Civ Div); reversing in part [1983] 1 Lloyd's Rep. 541; [1983] Com. L.R. 81, QBD (Comm) ........ *Digested,* 85/**1803**: *Applied* 96/3624, 04/2242, 07/2504, 14/1844: *Approved* 09/2296: *Considered* 86/366, 88/413, 94/2697

Insurance Co of the State of Pennsylvania v Equitas Insurance Ltd [2013] EWHC 3713 (Comm); [2014] Lloyd's Rep. I.R. 195, QBD (Comm) ........ *Digested,* 14/**303**

Intel Corp v European Commission (T-286/09) EU:T:2014:547; [2014] 5 C.M.L.R. 9, GC (7th Chamber)

Intelligent Managed Services Ltd v Revenue and Customs Commissioners [2013] UKFTT 741 (TC); [2014] S.T.I. 452, FTT (Tax)

Inter-Environnement Bruxelles ASBL v Region de Bruxelles-Capitale (C-567/10) [2012] 2 C.M.L.R. 30; [2012] Env. L.R. 30, ECJ (4th Chamber) *Considered* 13/3703: *Followed* 14/1201

Intercontainer Interfrigo SC (ICF) v Balkenende Oosthuizen BV (C-133/08) [2010] Q.B. 411; [2010] 3 W.L.R. 24; [2010] 1 All E.R. (Comm) 613; [2010] Bus. L.R. 808; [2010] 2 Lloyd's Rep. 400; [2009] E.C.R. I-9687; [2010] 2 C.L.C. 396; [2010] All E.R. (EC) 1; [2010] C.E.C. 310; [2010] I.L.Pr. 3, ECJ (Grand Chamber) ........ *Digested,* 11/**466**: *Applied* 12/56, 14/2711: *Followed* 11/174

Interfish Ltd v Revenue and Customs Commissioners [2014] EWCA Civ 876; [2014] B.T.C. 34; [2014] S.T.I. 2286, CA (Civ Div); affirming [2013] UKUT 336 (TCC); [2014] S.T.C. 79; [2013] B.T.C. 1946; [2013] S.T.I. 3028; (2013) 163(7576) N.L.J. 19, UT (Tax); affirming [2010] UKFTT 219 (TC); [2010] S.T.I. 2397, FTT (Tax) ........ *Digested,* 14/**2870**

Interflora Inc v Marks & Spencer Plc [2014] EWCA Civ 1403, CA (Civ Div); reversing [2013] EWHC 1291 (Ch); [2013] E.T.M.R. 35; [2013] F.S.R. 33; (2013) 157(21) S.J.L.B. 31, Ch D ........ *Digested,* 13/**1831**: *Applied* 14/1917, 14/1926, 14/1928

Interflora Inc v Marks & Spencer Plc [2013] EWHC 1683 (Ch); [2014] F.S.R. 3, Ch D .. *Digested,* 14/**1885**

Interflora Inc v Marks & Spencer Plc; *sub nom* Marks & Spencer Plc v Interflora Inc [2012] EWCA Civ 1501; [2013] 2 All E.R. 663; [2013] E.T.M.R. 11; [2013] F.S.R. 21; [2013] Bus. L.R. D46, CA (Civ Div); reversing [2012] EWHC 1722 (Ch); [2012] F.S.R. 32, Ch D ........ *Digested,* 13/**1830**: *Applied* 14/1935: *Considered* 13/1793, 14/1936, 14/289

Interflora Inc v Marks & Spencer Plc [2013] EWHC 1484 (Ch); [2014] F.S.R. 2, Ch D .. *Digested,* 14/**1929**

Interflora Inc v Marks & Spencer Plc [2013] EWCA Civ 319; [2013] F.S.R. 26, CA (Civ Div); reversing [2013] EWHC 273 (Ch), Ch D ........ *Digested,* 13/**1828**: *Considered* 14/289: *Followed* 14/1936

International Federation for Human Rights (FIDH) v Belgium (75/2011) (2014) 59 E.H.R.R. SE14, ECSR

International Federation for Human Rights (FIDH) v Greece (72/2011) (2014) 59 E.H.R.R. SE3, ECSR

International Leisure Ltd v First National Trustee Co UK Ltd [2012] EWHC 1971 (Ch); [2013] Ch. 346; [2013] 2 W.L.R. 466; [2012] B.C.C. 738; [2014] 1 B.C.L.C. 128; [2012] P.N.L.R. 34, Ch D ........ *Digested,* 13/**481**

International Planned Parenthood Federation - European Network (IPPF EN) v Italy (87/2012) (2014) 58 E.H.R.R. SE17, ECSR

International Stem Cell Corp v Comptroller General of Patents [2013] EWHC 807 (Ch); [2013] 3 C.M.L.R. 14; [2014] R.P.C. 2, Ch D (Patents Ct) ........ *Digested,* 13/**1751**

International Westminster Bank v Okeanos Maritime Corp see Company (No.000359 of 1987), Re

Interpretation of a Foreign Enforcement Order, Re (IX ZB 44/12) [2014] I.L.Pr. 45, BGH (Ger)

Interprods Ltd v De La Rue International Ltd [2014] EWHC 68 (Comm); [2014] 1 Lloyd's Rep. 540, QBD (Comm) ........ *Digested,* 14/**133**

Inuit Tapiriit Kanatami v European Parliament (C-583/11 P) [2014] Q.B. 648; [2014] 2 W.L.R. 1462; [2014] 1 C.M.L.R. 54; [2014] All E.R. (EC) 1, ECJ (Grand Chamber)

Investment Trust Companies (In Liquidation) v Revenue and Customs Commissioners [2012] EWHC 458 (Ch); [2012] S.T.C. 1150; [2012] Eu. L.R. 470; [2012] B.V.C. 109; [2012] S.T.I. 1373; [2013] S.T.I. 1488, Ch D ........ *Digested,* 12/**3430**: *Applied* 13/2472, 14/2529

Investor v Investment Adviser (10 7/12 Ob) [2014] E.C.C. 17, OGH (A)

Investors Compensation Scheme Ltd v Hopkin & Sons see Investors Compensation Scheme Ltd v West Bromwich Building Society (No.1)

Investors Compensation Scheme Ltd v West Bromwich Building Society (No.1); *joined cases* Investors Compensation Scheme Ltd v Hopkin & Sons; Alford v West Bromwich Building Society; Armitage v West Bromwich Building Society [1998] 1 W.L.R. 896; [1998] 1 All E.R. 98; [1998] 1 B.C.L.C. 531; [1997] C.L.C. 1243; [1997] P.N.L.R. 541; (1997) 147 N.L.J. 989; Times, June 24, 1997, HL; reversing [1998] 1 B.C.L.C. 521; [1997] C.L.C. 348; [1997] P.N.L.R. 166; [1997] N.P.C. 104; Times, November 8, 1996, CA (Civ Div); affirming [1998] 1 B.C.L.C. 493; Times, October 10, 1996, Ch D ........ *Digested,* 97/**2537**: *Applied* 99/3420, 99/5795, 99/852, 00/900, 01/375, 01/4272, 01/4950, 01/5508, 01/959, 02/207, 02/3028, 02/3821, 03/2460, 03/2723, 03/500, 03/530, 03/671, 04/2215, 04/2223, 04/273, 04/3255, 04/4614, 04/653, 04/670, 05/2402, 05/288, 05/469, 05/718, 06/203, 06/2411, 07/1327, 07/2494, 07/3028, 07/741, 07/779, 07/806, 07/811, 08/2195, 08/2438, 08/3783, 08/660, 08/663, 08/667, 09/1663, 09/2527, 09/2538, 09/722, 10/1040, 10/163, 10/2713, 10/622, 11/2696, 11/3565, 12/1039, 12/1876, 12/2023, 12/2042, 12/2389, 12/3364, 13/1051, 13/1709, 13/1897, 13/572, 13/587, 13/944, 14/1973: *Cited* 99/2489, 07/1841: *Considered* 99/2480, 00/3686, 00/5932, 00/878, 01/2430, 02/4683, 04/2205, 04/2407, 04/4988, 07/1323, 09/3154, 09/3755, 09/3841, 10/2338, 10/574, 10/578, 11/187, 12/2078, 12/3048, 13/1736, 14/412: *Followed* 98/807, 00/2173, 10/3006, 11/3300, 13/218, 13/2435, 13/2454, 14/117, 14/1775, 14/2006, 14/2521

Invicta UK v International Brands Ltd [2013] EWHC 1564 (QB); [2013] E.C.C. 30, QBD ........ *Digested,* 14/**82**

Ioannou v Secretary of State for Communities and Local Government; *joined case* Secretary of State for Communities and Local Government v Ioannou [2014] EWCA Civ 1432, CA (Civ Div); reversing [2013] EWHC 3945 (Admin); [2014] 1 E.G.L.R. 83; [2014] J.P.L. 608, QBD (Admin) ........ *Digested,* 14/**2402**

IPC Media Ltd v Media 10 Ltd [2014] EWCA Civ 1439, CA (Civ Div); affirming [2013] EWHC 3796 (IPEC); [2014] F.S.R. 25, IPEC ........ *Digested,* 14/**1926**

IPCO (Nigeria) Ltd v Nigerian National Petroleum Corp [2014] EWHC 576 (Comm); [2014] 1 Lloyd's Rep. 625, QBD (Comm) ........ *Digested,* 14/**137**

IPCom GmbH & Co KG v HTC Europe Co Ltd [2013] EWCA Civ 1496; [2014] Bus. L.R. 187; [2014] R.P.C. 12, CA (Civ Div); affirming [2013] EWHC 2880 (Ch), Ch D (Patents Ct) ........ *Digested,* 14/**1903**

IR v United Kingdom (Admissibility) (14876/12); *joined case* GT v United Kingdom (Admissibility) (63339/12) (2014) 58 E.H.R.R. SE14, ECHR

Irvine v Commissioner of Police of the Metropolis (Costs) [2005] EWCA Civ 129; [2005] C.P. Rep. 19; [2005] 3 Costs L.R. 380; (2005) 149 S.J.L.B. 182, CA (Civ Div) ........ *Digested,* 05/**359**: *Followed* 14/373

Irvine v Talksport Ltd [2002] EWHC 367 (Ch); [2002] 1 W.L.R. 2355; [2002] 2 All E.R. 414; [2002] E.M.L.R. 32; [2002] F.S.R. 60; (2002) 25(6) I.P.D. 25039; (2002) 99(18) L.S.G. 38; (2002) 152 N.L.J. 553; (2002) 146 S.J.L.B. 85, Ch D ........ *Digested,* 02/**2783**: *Applied* 14/1890: *Considered* 07/2674, 10/1990

Irving v Revenue and Customs Commissioners [2008] EWCA Civ 6; [2008] S.T.C. 597; [2008] Pens. L.R. 197; 79 T.C. 836; [2008] B.T.C. 36; [2008] S.T.I. 186, CA (Civ Div); affirming [2007] EWHC 147 (Ch); [2007] S.T.C. 1712; [2007] B.T.C. 269; [2007] S.T.I. 339; Times, March 8, 2007, Ch D; affirming [2006] S.T.C. (S.C.D.) 241; [2006] S.T.I. 1270, Sp Comm ........ *Digested,* 08/**3772**: *Followed* 13/3084: *Referred to* 14/2926

Isaghehi v Nursing and Midwifery Council [2014] EWHC 127 (Admin); [2014] A.C.D. 76, QBD (Admin)

Isis Investments Ltd v Oscatello Investments Ltd [2013] EWCA Civ 1493; [2014] Bus. L.R. 341; [2014] C.P. Rep. 14, CA (Civ Div); affirming [2013] EWHC 7 (Ch), Ch D ........ *Digested,* 14/**495**

Islamic Investment Co of the Gulf (Bahamas) Ltd v Symphony Gems NV [2008] EWCA Civ 389; Times, April 4, 2008, CA (Civ Div) ........ *Digested,* 08/**433**: *Considered* 14/391: *Followed* 11/336

Islamic Republic of Iran Shipping Lines v Denby [1987] 1 Lloyd's Rep. 367; [1987] 1 F.T.L.R. 30; (1986) 136 N.L.J. 1162, QBD (Comm) ........ *Digested,* 87/**3553**: *Overruled* 14/79

Island Records Ltd v Tring International Plc [1996] 1 W.L.R. 1256; [1995] 3 All E.R. 444; [1995] F.S.R. 560; Times, April 28, 1995, Ch D ........ *Digested,* 95/**849**: *Applied* 07/2530: *Cited* 10/417: *Considered* 14/1923: *Followed* 97/1031, 13/1774: *Referred to* 96/1276

Isle of Wight Council v Revenue and Customs Commissioners [2014] UKUT 446 (TCC); [2014] B.V.C. 538, UT (Tax)

Islington BC v Secretary of State for Communities and Local Government [2014] EWHC 62 (Admin); [2014] L.L.R. 494, QBD (Admin)

Islington LBC v Ladele see Ladele v Islington LBC

Islington LBC v O [2008] EWHC 2297 (Admin), QBD (Admin) *Applied* 14/943: *Considered* 14/941

Islington LBC v QR [2014] EWCOP 26; (2014) 17 C.C.L. Rep. 344, CP

Islington LBC v Secretary of State for Communities and Local Government; *sub nom* Ashburton Trading Ltd v Secretary of State for Communities and Local Government [2014] EWCA Civ 378, CA (Civ Div); affirming [2013] EWHC 2320 (Admin); [2014] J.P.L. 206, QBD (Admin) ........ *Digested,* 14/**2384**

Islington LBC v Unite Group Plc [2013] EWHC 508 (Admin); [2013] P.T.S.R. 1078; [2013] H.L.R. 33; [2013] 14 E.G. 86 (C.S.), QBD (Admin) ........ *Digested,* 13/**1530**: *Considered* 14/1606

Ismail v Entry Clearance Officer see Mahad (Ethiopia) v Entry Clearance Officer

Ismail v Secretary of State for Defence [2013] EWHC 3032 (Admin); [2014] A.C.D. 34, QBD (Admin)

Ismail v United Kingdom (Admissibility) (48078/09) (2014) 58 E.H.R.R. SE6, ECHR

Isocom Ltd v Revenue and Customs Commissioners [2014] UKFTT 571 (TC); [2014] S.T.I. 2792, FTT (Tax)

Istituto Nazionale della Previdenza Sociale (INPS) v Bruno (C-395/08); *joined case* Istituto Nazionale della Previdenza Sociale (INPS) v Lotti (C-396/08) [2010] 3 C.M.L.R. 45; [2011] C.E.C. 352; [2010] I.R.L.R. 890, ECJ (2nd Chamber) *Considered* 14/1087

Istituto Nazionale della Previdenza Sociale (INPS) v Lotti (C-396/08) see Istituto Nazionale della Previdenza Sociale (INPS) v Bruno (C-395/08)

Itau BBA International Ltd, Re [2012] EWHC 1783 (Ch); [2013] Bus. L.R. 490; [2013] B.C.C. 225; Times, September 11, 2012, Ch D ........ *Digested,* 12/**499**: *Considered* 14/503

Itchen Sash Window Renovation Ltd v Revenue and Customs Commissioners [2014] UKFTT 518 (TC); [2014] S.T.I. 2163, FTT (Tax)

ITN News Ltd, Re see R. v ITN News

ITT Schaub Lorenz Vertriebsgesellschaft mbH v Birkart Johann Internationale Spedition GmbH & Co KG [1988] 1 Lloyd's Rep. 487; [1988] F.T.L.R. 463, CA (Civ Div) ........ *Digested,* 88/**265**: *Applied* 99/4944: *Considered* 12/559, 14/3011

ITV Broadcasting Ltd v TV Catchup Ltd (C-607/11); *sub nom* ITV Broadcasting Ltd v TVCatchup Ltd (C-607/11) [2013] Bus. L.R. 1020; [2013] 3 C.M.L.R. 1; [2014] C.E.C. 663; [2013] E.C.D.R. 9; [2013] F.S.R. 36, ECJ (4th Chamber) ........ *Digested,* 13/**1762**: *Followed* 13/1763

ITV Broadcasting Ltd v TVCatchup Ltd (C-607/11) see ITV Broadcasting Ltd v TV Catchup Ltd (C-607/11)

ITV Plc v Pensions Regulator see Granada UK Rental & Retail Ltd v Pensions Regulator

ITV Services Ltd v Revenue and Customs Commissioners [2013] EWCA Civ 867; [2014] S.T.C. 325; [2013] B.T.C. 633; [2013] S.T.I. 2563, CA (Civ Div); affirming [2012] UKUT 47 (TCC); [2012] S.T.C. 1213; [2012] B.T.C. 1561; [2012] S.T.I. 1661, UT (Tax); affirming [2010] UKFTT 586 (TC); [2011] S.F.T.D. 261; [2011] S.T.I. 1342, FTT (Tax) ........ *Digested,* 13/**3114**

ITW v Z see M (Statutory Will), Re

Ivashchenko v Ukraine (760/03) (2014) 58 E.H.R.R. 41, ECHR

IVD GmbH & Co KG v Arztekammer Westfalen-Lippe (C-526/11) [2014] 1 C.M.L.R. 31; [2014] C.E.C. 453, ECJ (5th Chamber)

Iveco Ltd v Revenue and Customs Commissioners [2014] UKFTT 451 (TC); [2014] S.T.I. 2050, FTT (Tax)

Iveco Ltd v Revenue and Customs Commissioners [2013] UKFTT 763 (TC); [2014] S.F.T.D. 661; [2014] S.T.I. 537, FTT (Tax) ........ *Digested,* 14/**3075**

Ivelda v Yates see Ivleva (formerly Yates) v Yates

Ivey v Genting Casinos UK Ltd (t/a Crockfords Club) [2014] EWHC 3394 (QB); (2014) 158(46) S.J.L.B. 37, QBD

Ivleva (formerly Yates) v Yates; *sub nom* Ivelda v Yates [2014] EWHC 554 (Fam); [2014] 2 F.L.R. 1126; [2014] Fam. Law 783, Fam Div

IW (A Child), Re see ML v KW (Contact: Finding of Fact Hearing)

J v C; *sub nom* C (An Infant), Re [1970] A.C. 668; [1969] 2 W.L.R. 540; [1969] 1 All E.R. 788; (1969) 113 S.J. 164, HL ........ *Digested,* 69/**1802**: *Applied* 74/2417, 76/1752, 76/219.u, 77/1944, 77/1951, 77/1952, 81/1786, 84/2188, 04/1924, 14/1346: *Considered* 76/1785, 77/257u, 77/333u, 77/347u, 79/176.u, 83/1861, 86/1509, 87/2498, 88/2343: *Distinguished* 75/2164, 06/1695: *Followed* 76/1773, 85/2235, 06/1694

J v Commissioner of Police of the Metropolis; *sub nom* AKJ v Commissioner of Police of the Metropolis; *joined case* A v Commissioner of Police of the Metropolis [2013] EWHC 32 (QB); [2013] 1 W.L.R. 2734, QBD ........ *Digested,* 13/**2380**: *Reversed in part* 14/36

J v Crown Prosecution Service see Jennings v Crown Prosecution Service

J v DLA Piper UK LLP [2010] I.C.R. 1052; [2010] I.R.L.R. 936; [2010] Eq. L.R. 164; (2010) 115 B.M.L.R. 107; (2010) 154(24) S.J.L.B. 37, EAT ........ *Digested,* 10/**1043**: *Applied* 14/1043

J v Foundation Trust; *sub nom* GJ v Foundation Trust [2009] EWHC 2972 (Fam); [2010] Fam. 70; [2010] 3 W.L.R. 840; [2010] 1 F.L.R. 1251; (2009) 12 C.C.L. Rep. 600; [2010] Med. L.R. 167; [2010] M.H.L.R. 13; [2010] Fam. Law 139, CP *Digested,* 10/**2254**: *Applied* 12/2286, 14/2187

J v G (Parental Orders) [2013] EWHC 1432 (Fam); [2014] 1 F.L.R. 297; [2013] Fam. Law 972, Fam Div ........ *Digested,* 14/**1415**

J v South Staffordshire DC see K v Wolverhampton City Council

J (A Child) (Appeal from Care Order), Re see J (A Child) (Final Care Order: Threshold Criteria), Re

J (A Child) (Care Proceedings: Appeal), Re [2014] EWFC 4; [2014] Fam. Law 1232, Fam Ct

J (A Child) (Care Proceedings: Contra Mundum Injunction), Re see J (A Child) (Reporting Restriction: Internet: Video), Re

J (A Child) (Final Care Order: Threshold Criteria), Re; *sub nom* J (A Child) (Appeal from Care Order), Re [2013] EWCA Civ 1685; [2014] 2 F.L.R. 1351; [2014] 1 F.C.R. 221; [2014] Fam. Law 423, CA (Civ Div) ........ *Digested,* 14/**1271**

J (A Child) (Reporting Restriction: Internet: Video), Re; *sub nom* J (A Child) (Care Proceedings: Contra Mundum Injunction), Re [2013] EWHC 2694 (Fam); [2014] E.M.L.R. 7; [2014] 1 F.L.R. 523; [2014] 2 F.C.R. 284; [2013] Fam. Law 1389, Fam Div ........ *Digested,* 14/**1278**: *Applied* 14/1344, 14/1436

J (A Child) (Residence and Contact Dispute), Re [2012] EWCA Civ 1231; [2013] 1 F.L.R. 716; [2013] Fam. Law 381, CA (Civ Div) .......... *Digested,* 13/**1278**: *Considered* 14/1347

J (A Child) (Vulnerable Witness: Sexual Abuse: Fact Finding), Re see A (A Child) (Vulnerable Witness: Fact Finding), Re

J (A Child: Disclosure), Re see A (A Child) (Disclosure of Third Party Information), Re

J (A Minor) (Prohibited Steps Order: Circumcision), Re; *sub nom* U (A Minor) (Specific Issue Orders: Muslim Upbringing and Circumcision), Re; J (Specific Issue Orders: Child's Religious Upbringing and Circumcision), Re [2000] 1 F.L.R. 571; [2000] 1 F.C.R. 307; (2000) 52 B.M.L.R. 82; [2000] Fam. Law 246; (1999) 96(47) L.S.G. 30; Times, December 22, 1999, CA (Civ Div); affirming [1999] 2 F.L.R. 678; [1999] 2 F.C.R. 345; [1999] Fam. Law 543; Times, June 1, 1999; Independent, June 28, 1999, Fam Div .......... *Digested,* 00/**2484**: *Applied* 05/1580, 07/3906: *Considered* 14/1692: *Followed* 03/1777

J (Abduction: Children's Objections), Re; *sub nom* AJ v JJ [2011] EWCA Civ 1448; [2012] 1 F.L.R. 457; [2012] 1 F.C.R. 161; [2012] Fam. Law 257, CA (Civ Div) ... *Digested,* 12/**1368**: *Applied* 14/1310

J (Children) (Care Proceedings: Past Possible Perpetrators in New Family Unit), Re see J (Children) (Care Proceedings: Threshold Criteria), Re

J (Children) (Care Proceedings: Threshold Criteria), Re; *sub nom* J (Children) (Care Proceedings: Past Possible Perpetrators in New Family Unit), Re; J (Children) (Non-Accidental Injury: Past Possible Perpetrator in New Family), Re [2013] UKSC 9; [2013] 1 A.C. 680; [2013] 2 W.L.R. 649; [2013] 3 All E.R. 1; [2013] 1 F.L.R. 1373; [2013] 2 F.C.R. 149; [2013] Fam. Law 375; (2013) 157(8) S.J.L.B. 31; Times, February 26, 2013, SC; affirming [2012] EWCA Civ 380; [2012] 3 W.L.R. 952; [2012] 2 F.L.R. 842; [2012] 2 F.C.R. 1; [2012] Fam. Law 790; (2012) 156(14) S.J.L.B. 31, CA (Civ Div) .......... *Digested,* 13/**1216**: *Applied* 14/1405

J (Children) (Non-Accidental Injury: Past Possible Perpetrator in New Family), Re see J (Children) (Care Proceedings: Threshold Criteria), Re

J (Children) (Placement of Children outside Family), Re see A Local Authority v A Mother

J (Children) (Private Law), Re [2014] EWHC 330 (Fam); [2014] Fam. Law 818, Fam Div

J (Specific Issue Orders: Child's Religious Upbringing and Circumcision), Re see J (A Minor) (Prohibited Steps Order: Circumcision), Re

J Bews and Sons v Revenue and Customs Commissioners [2014] UKFTT 1014 (TC); [2014] S.T.I. 3441, FTT (Tax)

J Bollinger SA v Costa Brava Wine Co Ltd (No.4) [1961] 1 W.L.R. 277; [1961] 1 All E.R. 561; [1961] R.P.C. 116; (1961) 105 S.J. 180; Times, December 17, 1960, Ch D .......... *Digested,* 61/**8885**: *Applied* 10/1955, 14/1889: *Considered* 72/3429, 73/3328, 75/3430

J Lauritzen AS v Wijsmuller BV (The Super Servant Two) [1990] 1 Lloyd's Rep. 1; Times, October 17, 1989; Independent, October 30, 1989; Financial Times, October 24, 1989, CA (Civ Div); affirming [1989] 1 Lloyd's Rep. 148, QBD (Comm) .......... *Digested,* 90/**4065**: *Applied* 14/2053: *Considered* 06/754, 08/668

J Murphy & Sons Ltd v Johnston Precast Ltd [2008] EWHC 3024 (TCC), QBD (TCC) *Applied* 14/362

J Rosenthal & Sons v Esmail (t/a HMH Esmail & Sons) [1965] 1 W.L.R. 1117; [1965] 2 All E.R. 860; [1965] 2 Lloyd's Rep. 171; (1965) 109 S.J. 553, HL; affirming [1964] 2 Lloyd's Rep. 447; (1964) 108 S.J. 839, CA .......... *Digested,* 65/**3530**: *Applied* 14/119: *Referred to* 75/447.u

J Sainsbury Plc v O'Connor (Inspector of Taxes) [1991] 1 W.L.R. 963; [1991] S.T.C. 529; [1991] S.T.C. 318; 64 T.C. 208; [1991] B.T.C. 181; [1991] S.T.I. 529; (1991) 135 S.J.L.B. 46; Times, May 29, 1991; Financial Times, June 12, 1991, CA (Civ Div); affirming [1990] S.T.C. 516, Ch D .......... *Digested,* 92/**605**: *Applied* 97/3276, 14/2878: *Considered* 91/557, 05/2380

J Sainsbury Plc v One in a Million Ltd see British Telecommunications Plc v One in a Million Ltd

J-M (A Child) (Contact Proceedings: Balance of Harm), Re [2014] EWCA Civ 434; [2014] Fam. Law 957, CA (Civ Div)

J1 v Secretary of State for the Home Department [2013] EWCA Civ 279, CA (Civ Div) *Applied* 14/1645

JA (Afghanistan) v Secretary of State for the Home Department [2014] EWCA Civ 450; [2014] 1 W.L.R. 4291, CA (Civ Div)

Jabre v Financial Services Authority (Unreported, July 10, 2006), FSMT *Applied* 14/2247

Jack v Craig see London Scottish Finance Ltd (In Administration), Re
Jack Wills Ltd v House of Fraser (Stores) Ltd [2014] EWHC 110 (Ch); [2014] E.T.M.R. 28; [2014] F.S.R. 39, Ch D ........ *Digested,* 14/**1921**
Jackson v Cannons Law Practice LLP; *sub nom* Harvest Finance Ltd (In Liquidation), Re [2013] B.P.I.R. 1020, Ch D ........ *Digested,* 14/**1806**
Jackson v Cannons Law Practice LLP; *sub nom* Harvest Finance Ltd (In Liquidation), Re [2013] B.P.I.R. 1020, Ch D (Companies Ct) ........ *Digested,* 14/**1804**
Jackson v Cannons Law Practice LLP; *sub nom* Harvest Finance Ltd (In Liquidation), Re [2013] B.P.I.R. 1020, Ch D (Companies Ct) ........ *Digested,* 14/**1802**
Jackson v Dear; *sub nom* Dear v Jackson [2013] EWCA Civ 89; [2014] 1 B.C.L.C. 186, CA (Civ Div); reversing [2012] EWHC 2060 (Ch), Ch D
JACKSON FOUNDATION/Correction of application (J5/12) [2014] E.P.O.R. 22, EPO (Legal Bd App)
Jacobs v Chaudhuri [1968] 2 Q.B. 470; [1968] 2 W.L.R. 1098; [1968] 2 All E.R. 124; (1968) 19 P. & C.R. 286; (1968) 112 S.J. 135, CA (Civ Div) ........ *Digested,* 68/**2191**: *Applied* 75/1868, 78/1784: *Followed* 14/1995
Jacobs v Motor Insurers Bureau [2010] EWCA Civ 1208; [2011] 1 W.L.R. 2609; [2011] 1 All E.R. 844; [2011] 1 All E.R. (Comm) 445; [2011] R.T.R. 2; [2011] Lloyd's Rep. I.R. 355, CA (Civ Div); reversing [2010] EWHC 231 (QB); [2010] 1 All E.R. (Comm) 1128; [2010] R.T.R. 35; [2010] Lloyd's Rep. I.R. 244, QBD ........ *Digested,* 11/**1922**: *Applied* 14/2559
Jacobs E&C Ltd v Laker Vent Engineering Ltd see Laker Vent Engineering Ltd v Jacobs E&C Ltd
Jacobsohn v Blake 134 E.R. 1164; (1844) 6 Man. & G. 919, CCP
*Applied* 14/820
Jafri v Lincoln College [2014] EWCA Civ 449; [2014] 3 W.L.R. 933; [2014] 3 All E.R. 709; [2014] I.C.R. 920; [2014] I.R.L.R. 544, CA (Civ Div) ........ *Digested,* 14/**1061**: *Followed* 14/1059
Jaggard v Sawyer [1995] 1 W.L.R. 269; [1995] 2 All E.R. 189; [1995] 1 E.G.L.R. 146; [1995] 13 E.G. 132; [1994] E.G. 139 (C.S.); [1994] N.P.C. 116; Independent, August 22, 1994, CA (Civ Div); affirming [1993] 1 E.G.L.R. 197, CC (Weymouth) ........ *Digested,* 95/**4142**: *Applied* 05/3434, 07/3425, 09/2744: *Cited* 01/1549: *Considered* 98/4341, 00/5127, 04/912, 06/1018, 07/1060, 12/855: *Followed* 14/1895
Jama v Germany [2013] EWHC 3276 (Admin); [2014] 1 W.L.R. 1843, DC ........ *Digested,* 14/**1227**
Jameel v Dow Jones & Co Inc; *sub nom* Dow Jones & Co Inc v Jameel [2005] EWCA Civ 75; [2005] Q.B. 946; [2005] 2 W.L.R. 1614; [2005] E.M.L.R. 16; (2005) 149 S.J.L.B. 181; Times, February 14, 2005; Independent, February 10, 2005, CA (Civ Div) ........ *Digested,* 05/**974**: *Applied* 09/975, 10/834, 10/838, 11/870, 13/792, 13/795, 14/841: *Considered* 06/1041, 09/986, 11/869, 12/432, 12/864, 14/415: *Followed* 12/869, 13/800
James v Aintree University Hospitals NHS Foundation Trust see Aintree University Hospitals NHS Foundation Trust v James
James v Greenwich LBC [2008] EWCA Civ 35; [2008] I.C.R. 545; [2008] I.R.L.R. 302, CA (Civ Div); affirming [2007] I.C.R. 577; [2007] I.R.L.R. 168, EAT ........ *Digested,* 08/**1149**: *Applied* 07/1344, 11/1072: *Considered* 07/4073, 08/1125, 10/1070: *Followed* 14/1064
James v United Kingdom (25119/09); *joined cases* Wells v United Kingdom (57715/09); Lee v United Kingdom (57877/09) (2013) 56 E.H.R.R. 12; 33 B.H.R.C. 617; (2012) 109(37) L.S.G. 20, ECHR ........ *Digested,* 13/**1558**: *Considered* 13/2112, 13/2113, 13/3878, 14/2234: *Followed* 14/3702
James v United Kingdom (8793/79) see James v United Kingdom (A/98)
James v United Kingdom (A/98); *sub nom* James v United Kingdom (8793/79); Trustees of the Duke of Westminster's Estate v United Kingdom (8793/79) (1986) 8 E.H.R.R. 123; [1986] R.V.R. 139, ECHR; no effect (1983) 5 E.H.R.R. 440; (1983) 5 E.H.R.R. CD491, Eur Comm HR; no effect (1984) 6 E.H.R.R. CD475, Eur Comm HR ........ *Digested,* 86/**1650**: *Applied* 03/2171, 05/2027, 06/2187, 06/2193, 07/3977, 08/1920, 08/1925, 08/1949, 09/2030, 10/211, 11/1701, 11/1703, 13/2469: *Considered* 96/1118, 97/2796, 01/1844, 03/2095, 03/2838, 03/3485, 03/5819, 04/1376, 05/3376, 06/2089, 06/2185, 07/2773, 08/3860, 13/3417, 14/1635, 14/2221: *Followed* 98/4201, 02/3803, 11/473
James (t/a P&C James Properties) v Welsh Assembly Government [2013] UKUT 422 (LC); [2014] R.V.R. 48, UT (Lands) ........ *Digested,* 14/**2360**

James Graham & Co (Timber) Ltd v Southgate-Sands [1986] Q.B. 80; [1985] 2 W.L.R. 1044; [1985] 2 All E.R. 344; [1985] Fin. L.R. 194; (1985) 82 L.S.G. 1408; (1985) 35 N.L.J. 290; (1985) 129 S.J. 331, CA (Civ Div) .................................... *Digested,* 85/**1590**: *Applied* 04/228, 14/637: *Distinguished* 13/588

Jamieson v Jamieson [1952] A.C. 525; [1952] 1 All E.R. 875; 1952 S.C. (H.L.) 44; 1952 S.L.T. 257; [1952] 1 T.L.R. 833; (1952) 116 J.P. 226, HL; reversing 1951 S.C. 286; 1951 S.L.T. 174, IH (1 Div) .................................... *Digested,* 52/**985**: *Applied* 52/984, 54/950, 54/951, 55/782, 55/788, 56/2542, 60/951, 62/911, 62/921, 94/6150, 95/6163, 00/6599, 06/5122, 06/5150, 06/5156, 08/4861, 08/4976, 09/5081, 10/3997, 11/4481: *Considered* 73/886, 12/3821, 12/3842, 14/3354: *Distinguished* 54/943: *Followed* 57/1025, 01/6252, 03/5278

Jamieson (Valuation Officer) v Eon UK Plc [2013] UKUT 369 (LC); [2014] R.A. 97, UT (Lands) .................................... *Digested,* 14/**2137**

Janah v Libya see Benkharbouche v Embassy of Sudan

Janowiec v Russia (55508/07) (2014) 58 E.H.R.R. 30, ECHR (Grand Chamber) *Considered* 14/62

Janowski v Poland (2000) 29 E.H.R.R. 705; 5 B.H.R.C. 672, ECHR .................................... *Digested,* 99/**3108**: *Applied* 14/2102

Janvey v Wastell see Stanford International Bank Ltd (In Receivership), Re

Japan Leasing (Europe) Plc, Re see Wallace v Shoa Leasing (Singapore) PTE Ltd

Japp v Virgin Holidays Ltd [2013] EWCA Civ 1371; [2014] P.I.Q.R. P8, CA (Civ Div) ... *Digested,* 14/**2303**

Jasim v Secretary of State for the Home Department [2006] EWCA Civ 342; Times, May 17, 2006, CA (Civ Div) .................................... *Digested,* 06/**2231**: *Considered* 14/1645

Jasinskis v Latvia (45744/08) (2014) 58 E.H.R.R. 21, ECHR

Jauch v Pensionsversicherungsanstalt der Arbeiter (C-215/99) [2001] E.C.R. I-1901, ECJ *Applied* 06/1572, 08/1359: *Considered* 14/2780

Javad v Aqil [1991] 1 W.L.R. 1007; [1991] 1 All E.R. 243; (1991) 61 P. & C.R. 164; [1990] 41 E.G. 61; [1990] E.G. 69 (C.S.); (1990) 140 N.L.J. 1232, CA (Civ Div) . *Digested,* 91/**2218**: *Applied* 00/4670, 02/3029: *Considered* 91/122, 92/3091, 01/4162, 14/1977: *Not applied* 98/3683

Jawad v Newham LBC [2014] P.A.D. 28, Planning Inspector

JB Trustees Ltd v Secretary of State for Communities and Local Government [2013] EWHC 3555 (Admin); [2014] J.P.L. 656; [2013] 48 E.G. 124 (C.S.), QBD (Admin) .................................... *Digested,* 14/**2419**

JC v Central Criminal Court see R. (on the application of JC) v Central Criminal Court

JC v Shropshire Council [2014] R.V.R. 164, VT .................................... *Digested,* 14/**2093**

JD (Congo) v Secretary of State for the Home Department; *joined cases* MR (Bangladesh) v Secretary of State for the Home Department; ES (Iran) v Secretary of State for the Home Department; WN (Gambia) v Secretary of State for the Home Department [2012] EWCA Civ 327; [2012] 1 W.L.R. 3273; [2012] Imm. A.R. 719; [2012] I.N.L.R. 412; Times, May 28, 2012, CA (Civ Div) .. *Digested,* 12/**457**: *Considered* 14/50

JD Wetherspoon Plc v Harris [2013] EWHC 1088 (Ch); [2013] 1 W.L.R. 3296, Ch D .... *Digested,* 14/**2990**

JD Wetherspoon Plc v Revenue and Customs Commissioners [2012] UKUT 42 (TCC); [2012] S.T.C. 1450; 81 T.C. 588; [2012] B.T.C. 1578; [2012] L.L.R. 641; [2012] S.T.I. 1382, UT (Tax); reversing in part [2009] UKFTT 374 (TC); [2010] S.T.I. 1292, FTT (Tax) .................................... *Digested,* 12/**3222**

JD Wetherspoon Plc v Van De Berg & Co Ltd [2007] EWHC 1044 (Ch); [2007] P.N.L.R. 28, Ch D .................................... *Digested,* 07/**471**: *Applied* 10/432, 14/2523

JE (Jamaica) v Secretary of State for the Home Department [2014] EWCA Civ 192; [2014] C.P. Rep. 24, CA (Civ Div) .................................... *Digested,* 14/**327**

Jefferson v O'Connor [2014] EWCA Civ 38; [2014] 2 F.L.R. 759; [2014] 2 F.C.R. 112; [2014] Fam. Law 456, CA (Civ Div) .................................... *Digested,* 14/**1324**

Jeffery v Jeffery [2013] EWHC 1942 (Ch); [2013] W.T.L.R. 1509, Ch D .................................... *Digested,* 14/**2841**

Jeffrey v Commissioner of Police of the Metropolis see Yearwood v Commissioner of Police of the Metropolis

JEG v IS (Sexual Abuse Allegations) [2014] EWHC 287 (Fam); [2014] Fam. Law 955, Fam Div

Jelbert v Davies; *sub nom* Jelbert v Davis [1968] 1 W.L.R. 589; [1968] 1 All E.R. 1182; (1968) 19 P. & C.R. 383; (1968) 112 S.J. 172, CA (Civ Div) .................................... *Digested,* 68/**1315**: *Applied* 93/1623: *Considered* 77/115.u: *Distinguished* 87/1233: *Followed* 10/2743, 14/2521

Jelbert v Davis see Jelbert v Davies

Jemaldeen v A-Z Law Solicitors see Hadi Jemaldeen v A-Z Law Solicitors

Jenkins v Livesey (formerly Jenkins) [1985] A.C. 424; [1985] 2 W.L.R. 47; [1985] 1 All E.R. 106; [1985] F.L.R. 813; [1985] Fam. Law 310; (1985) 82 L.S.G. 517; (1985) 134 N.L.J. 55, HL; reversing [1985] Fam. Law 180, CA (Civ Div) ........... *Digested,* 85/**1049**: *Applied* 93/1905, 08/1551, 09/764: *Considered* 85/1053, 85/1076, 86/1083, 86/1102, 93/1877, 94/2165, 10/3683, 12/1312, 14/1369: *Followed* 95/2342, 14/1366

Jennings v Crown Prosecution Service; *sub nom* J v Crown Prosecution Service; Crown Prosecution Service v J [2008] UKHL 29; [2008] 1 A.C. 1046; [2008] 2 W.L.R. 1148; [2008] 4 All E.R. 113; [2008] 2 Cr. App. R. 29; [2008] Lloyd's Rep. F.C. 421; (2008) 152(21) S.J.L.B. 29; Times, May 19, 2008, HL; affirming [2005] EWCA Civ 746; [2006] 1 W.L.R. 182; [2005] 4 All E.R. 391; Times, July 12, 2005; Independent, June 30, 2005, CA (Civ Div) ........................................ *Digested,* 08/**858**: *Applied* 07/3615, 09/932, 10/709, 11/848, 12/755, 14/727: *Considered* 08/3271, 11/722, 12/758: *Followed* 09/834, 09/848, 10/734, 11/723, 12/469, 14/728

Jennings v Kinder (Inspector of Taxes) see Hochstrasser (Inspector of Taxes) v Mayes

Jeromson v Shell Tankers UK Ltd see Shell Tankers UK Ltd v Jeromson

Jervis v Pillar Denton Ltd; *sub nom* Games Station Ltd, Re; Pillar Denton Ltd v Jervis [2014] EWCA Civ 180; [2014] 3 W.L.R. 901; [2014] 3 All E.R. 519; [2014] 2 All E.R. (Comm) 826; [2014] B.C.C. 165; [2014] 2 B.C.L.C. 204; [2014] 2 E.G.L.R. 9; Times, April 16, 2014, CA (Civ Div); reversing [2013] EWHC 2171 (Ch); [2013] B.C.C. 618, Ch D ........................................ *Digested,* 14/**1756**

Jessemey v Rowstock Ltd see Rowstock Ltd v Jessemey

Jet2.com Ltd v Blackpool Airport Ltd [2012] EWCA Civ 417; [2012] 2 All E.R. (Comm) 1053; [2012] 1 C.L.C. 605; 142 Con. L.R. 1; [2012] C.I.L.L. 3165, CA (Civ Div); affirming [2011] EWHC 1529 (Comm); [2011] 2 All E.R. (Comm) 988; [2011] C.I.L.L. 3033, QBD (Comm) ........................................ *Digested,* 12/**158**: *Followed* 14/630

Jet2.com Ltd v Huzar; *sub nom* Huzar v Jet2.com Ltd [2014] EWCA Civ 791; [2014] 4 All E.R. 581; [2014] 2 All E.R. (Comm) 914; [2014] Bus. L.R. 1324; [2014] 2 Lloyd's Rep. 368; [2014] 1 C.L.C. 969, CA (Civ Div) ........................................ *Digested,* 14/**166**

Jetair NV v FOD Financien (C-599/12) [2014] S.T.C. 1088; [2014] B.V.C. 16; [2014] S.T.I. 1562, ECJ (8th Chamber)

Jetivia SA v Bilta (UK) Ltd (In Liquidation) see Bilta (UK) Ltd (In Liquidation) v Nazir

Jeynes v News Magazines Ltd [2008] EWCA Civ 130, CA (Civ Div) *Applied* 13/795, 13/796, 13/798, 14/839: *Considered* 14/836

JG v Lord Chancellor see JG (A Child) v Legal Services Commission

JG (A Child) v Legal Services Commission; *sub nom* JG v Lord Chancellor [2014] EWCA Civ 656; [2014] 5 Costs L.O. 708; [2014] 2 F.L.R. 1218; [2014] 3 F.C.R. 567; [2014] H.R.L.R. 18; [2014] Fam. Law 1097, CA (Civ Div); reversing [2013] EWHC 804 (Admin); [2013] 2 F.L.R. 1174; [2013] Fam. Law 1125, QBD (Admin) ........................................ *Digested,* 14/**1342**

JGD Construction Ltd v Mills [2013] EWHC 572 (Ch); [2013] B.P.I.R. 811, Ch D (Bristol) ........................................ *Digested,* 14/**492**

Jif Lemon case see Reckitt & Colman Products Ltd v Borden Inc (No.3)

JIH v News Group Newspapers Ltd [2011] EWCA Civ 42; [2011] 1 W.L.R. 1645; [2011] 2 All E.R. 324; [2011] C.P. Rep. 17; [2011] E.M.L.R. 15; [2011] 2 F.C.R. 95; (2011) 108(7) L.S.G. 18; (2011) 161 N.L.J. 211; Times, February 7, 2011, CA (Civ Div); reversing in part [2010] EWHC 2818 (QB); [2011] E.M.L.R. 9; (2010) 154(43) S.J.L.B. 34, QBD ........................................ *Digested,* 11/**373**: *Applied* 11/1302, 11/375, 12/331: *Considered* 11/1677: *Distinguished* 12/15: *Followed* 14/790

Jim Ennis Construction Ltd v Premier Asphalt Ltd [2009] EWHC 1906 (TCC); 125 Con. L.R. 141; [2009] 3 E.G.L.R. 7; [2009] 41 E.G. 116; [2009] C.I.L.L. 2745, QBD (TCC) ........................................ *Digested,* 10/**555**: *Considered* 14/358: *Not followed* 13/535

Jindal Iron & Steel Co Ltd v Islamic Solidarity Shipping Co Jordan Inc; *joined case* TCI Trans Commodities AG v Islamic Solidarity Shipping Co Jordan Inc [2004] UKHL 49; [2005] 1 W.L.R. 1363; [2005] 1 All E.R. 175; [2005] 1 All E.R. (Comm) 1; [2005] 1 Lloyd's Rep. 57; [2004] 2 C.L.C. 1172; 2005 A.M.C. 1; (2004) 148 S.J.L.B. 1405; Times, November 26, 2004, HL; affirming [2003] EWCA Civ 144; [2003] 1 All E.R. (Comm) 747; [2003] 2 Lloyd's Rep. 87; [2003] 1 C.L.C. 885, CA (Civ Div); reversing in part [2002] EWHC 1268 (Comm); [2002] 2 All E.R. (Comm) 364, QBD (Comm) ........................................ *Digested,* 05/**3787**: *Applied* 14/2705

JJ Food Service Ltd v Zulhayir [2013] EWCA Civ 1304; [2014] C.P. Rep. 15, CA (Civ Div) ........................................ *Digested,* 14/**357**

JJ Food Service Ltd v Zulhayir see Zulhayir v JJ Food Services Ltd

JK v KC see AB v CD
JK v Secretary of State for Work and Pensions [2013] UKUT 218 (AAC); [2013] 3 C.M.L.R. 32, UT (AAC) ........ *Digested,* 14/**2780**
JKN v JCN (Divorce: Forum) [2010] EWHC 843 (Fam); [2011] 1 F.L.R. 826; [2011] 2 F.C.R. 33; [2010] Fam. Law 796, Fam Div ........ *Digested,* 11/**1402**: *Applied* 13/1274, 14/1326
JKX Oil & Gas Plc v Eclairs Group Ltd see Eclairs Group Ltd v JKX Oil & Gas Plc
JL v Secretary of State for the Home Department see JL (Medical Reports: Credibility: China), Re
JL (Medical Reports: Credibility: China), Re; *sub nom* JL v Secretary of State for the Home Department [2013] UKUT 145 (IAC); [2013] Imm. A.R. 727, UT (IAC) ..... *Digested,* 14/**1647**
JL (Sierra Leone) v Secretary of State for the Home Department see EB (Kosovo) v Secretary of State for the Home Department
JM v CZ (Costs: Ex Parte Order) [2014] EWHC 1125 (Fam); [2014] Fam. Law 1099, Fam Div
JM Finn & Co Ltd v Holliday [2013] EWHC 3450 (QB); [2014] I.R.L.R. 102, QBD ........ *Digested,* 14/**1028**
JMCB v LE (C-400/10 PPU) see McB v E (C-400/10 PPU)
JO v GO see O (Court of Protection: Jurisdiction), Re
JO (Uganda) v Secretary of State for the Home Department; *joined case* JT (Ivory Coast) v Secretary of State for the Home Department [2010] EWCA Civ 10; [2010] 1 W.L.R. 1607; [2010] Imm. A.R. 421; [2010] I.N.L.R. 545; (2010) 107(6) L.S.G. 18; Times, February 8, 2010, CA (Civ Div) ........ *Digested,* 10/**1773**: *Applied* 11/1789, 14/1678: *Considered* 10/1777, 12/1743: *Followed* 11/1728, 13/1618
Jobserve Ltd v Network Multimedia Television Ltd (Restored Injunction Hearing); *sub nom* Network Multimedia Television Ltd (t/a Silicon.com) v Jobserve Ltd (Restored Injunction Hearing) [2001] EWCA Civ 2021; [2002] U.K.C.L.R. 184; [2002] Masons C.L.R. 17, CA (Civ Div); affirming [2001] U.K.C.L.R. 814; (2001) 24(6) I.P.D. 24039, Ch D ........ *Digested,* 02/**600**: *Followed* 14/527
Jobsin Co UK Plc (t/a Internet Recruitment Solutions) v Department of Health; *sub nom* Jobsin.co.uk Plc v Department of Health [2001] EWCA Civ 1241; [2002] 1 C.M.L.R. 44; [2001] Eu. L.R. 685; (2001) 98(33) L.S.G. 29; Times, October 2, 2001, CA (Civ Div) ........ *Digested,* 01/**4406**: *Applied* 10/2672, 10/2675: *Considered* 14/69: *Distinguished* 11/2107: *Followed* 11/2095, 11/2631
Jobsin.co.uk Plc v Department of Health see Jobsin Co UK Plc (t/a Internet Recruitment Solutions) v Department of Health
Jobson v Johnson [1989] 1 W.L.R. 1026; [1989] 1 All E.R. 621; (1988) 4 B.C.C. 488, CA (Civ Div) ........ *Digested,* 88/**353**: *Considered* 07/3420, 13/568, 14/642
John v Rees; *joined cases* Martin v Davis; Rees v John [1970] Ch. 345; [1969] 2 W.L.R. 1294; [1969] 2 All E.R. 274; (1969) 113 S.J. 487, Ch D ........ *Digested,* 69/**353**: *Applied* 09/2086, 09/440, 14/2162: *Approved* 71/6934: *Considered* 79/15, 83/2969, 11/376, 14/946: *Distinguished* 09/442: *Not applied* 78/219
JOHN BEAN TECHNOLOGIES/Right to be heard in oral proceedings (R11/12) [2014] E.P.O.R. 1, EPO (Enlarged Bd App)
John Hardman & Co v Conister Trust Ltd see Conister Trust Ltd v John Hardman & Co
John Kay Ltd v Kay [1952] 2 Q.B. 258; [1952] 1 All E.R. 813; [1952] 1 T.L.R. 766; (1952) 96 S.J. 212, CA; affirming (1951) 102 L.J. 123, CC (Norwich) ........ *Digested,* 52/**1958**: *Applied* 14/1994: *Considered* 52/1960, 77/1753
John Laing & Son v Kingswood Assessment Committee [1949] 1 K.B. 344; [1949] 1 All E.R. 224; 65 T.L.R. 80; (1949) 113 J.P. 111; 47 L.G.R. 64; 42 R. & I.T. 15; (1949) 93 S.J. 26, CA; affirming [1948] 2 K.B. 116; [1948] 1 All E.R. 943; 64 T.L.R. 407, KBD ........ *Digested,* 47-51/**8292**: *Applied* 55/2275, 56/7264, 60/2685, 70/2414, 98/4319, 05/3370, 07/3342, 09/3111, 13/1999, 13/2416, 14/2140: *Considered* 77/2453, 82/2642, 84/2913, 85/2924, 85/2926, 87/3181, 88/3029, 88/3035, 90/3917, 12/2157, 12/2696: *Distinguished* 75/2776, 99/4333: *Followed* 99/4335, 01/4821
John Mander Pension Scheme Trustees Ltd v Revenue and Customs Commissioners [2013] EWCA Civ 1683; [2014] 1 W.L.R. 2209; [2014] S.T.C. 2136; [2014] Pens. L.R. 135; [2014] B.T.C. 2; [2014] S.T.I. 255, CA (Civ Div); affirming [2013] UKUT 51 (TCC); [2013] S.T.C. 1453; [2013] B.T.C. 1623; [2013] S.T.I. 385, UT (Tax); affirming [2011] UKFTT 686 (TC); [2012] S.F.T.D. 322; [2011] S.T.I. 3335, FTT (Tax) ........ *Digested,* 14/**2947**
John Martin Holdings Ltd v Revenue and Customs Commissioners [2013] UKFTT 714 (TC); [2014] S.T.I. 388, FTT (Tax)

John Pimblett and Sons v Customs and Excise Commissioners [1988] S.T.C. 358, CA (Civ Div); affirming [1987] S.T.C. 202, QBD; reversing [1987] S.T.C. 202; [1985] V.A.T.T.R. 210, VAT Tr ........ *Digested,* 88/**3636**:
*Distinguished* 11/3582: *Doubted* 13/3245, 14/3098: *Referred to* 95/5116

Johnson v County Bideford Ltd [2012] UKUT 457 (LC); [2013] L. & T.R. 18, UT (Lands) ........ *Digested,* 14/**2013**

Johnson v Davies [1999] Ch. 117; [1998] 3 W.L.R. 1299; [1998] 2 All E.R. 649; [1999] B.C.C. 275; [1998] 2 B.C.L.C. 252; [1998] B.P.I.R. 607; (2000) 79 P. & C.R. 14; [1998] L. & T.R. 69; [1998] 3 E.G.L.R. 72; [1998] 49 E.G. 153; (1998) 95(19) L.S.G. 23; (1998) 142 S.J.L.B. 141; [1998] N.P.C. 50; Times, March 31, 1998, CA (Civ Div); affirming [1997] 1 W.L.R. 1511; [1997] 1 All E.R. 921; [1997] 1 B.C.L.C. 580; [1997] B.P.I.R. 221; [1997] 1 E.G.L.R. 42; [1997] 19 E.G. 157; (1996) 146 N.L.J. 1814, Ch D ........ *Digested,* 98/**3351**:
*Applied* 03/2442, 07/2422, 11/1818, 11/213, 14/1826: *Considered* 99/3336, 00/3884

Johnson v Gore Wood & Co (No.1); *sub nom* Johnson v Gore Woods & Co [2002] 2 A.C. 1; [2001] 2 W.L.R. 72; [2001] 1 All E.R. 481; [2001] C.P.L.R. 49; [2001] B.C.C. 820; [2001] 1 B.C.L.C. 313; [2001] P.N.L.R. 18; (2001) 98(1) L.S.G. 24; (2001) 98(8) L.S.G. 46; (2000) 150 N.L.J. 1889; (2001) 145 S.J.L.B. 29; Times, December 22, 2000; Independent, February 7, 2001, HL; reversing in part [1999] C.P.L.R. 155; [1999] B.C.C. 474; [1999] Lloyd's Rep. P.N. 91; [1999] P.N.L.R. 426; [1998] N.P.C. 151, CA (Civ Div) ........ *Digested,* 01/**410**:
*Applied* 99/3313, 01/746, 02/280, 02/281, 02/3286, 02/3310, 03/291, 03/4600, 03/470, 04/265, 04/459, 05/2448, 05/2505, 05/520, 05/533, 06/2591, 06/320, 07/346, 08/271, 08/383, 09/2225, 09/2742, 09/696, 10/1889, 10/3225, 10/3528, 10/426, 11/1136, 11/1955, 13/1010, 13/1523, 14/1787: *Considered* 01/5710, 01/675, 01/708, 06/1042, 06/562, 07/2677, 10/458, 11/378, 12/1171, 13/266: *Distinguished* 02/565, 04/2338, 10/256, 10/425: *Followed* 01/749, 04/2733, 04/425, 05/483, 10/1, 10/257, 10/826, 11/1077, 11/354, 13/1309, 13/434, 13/783, 14/1878

Johnson v Gore Woods & Co see Johnson v Gore Wood & Co (No.1)

Johnson v Ministry of Defence [2012] EWCA Civ 1505; [2013] P.I.Q.R. P7, CA (Civ Div) ........ *Digested,* 13/**2203**:
*Applied* 14/419

Johnson v Official Receiver [2014] EWHC 2609 (Ch); [2014] B.P.I.R. 1245, Ch D

Johnson v Unisys Ltd [2001] UKHL 13; [2003] 1 A.C. 518; [2001] 2 W.L.R. 1076; [2001] 2 All E.R. 801; [2001] I.C.R. 480; [2001] I.R.L.R. 279; [2001] Emp. L.R. 469; Times, March 23, 2001; Independent, March 29, 2001, HL; affirming [1999] 1 All E.R. 854; [1999] I.C.R. 809; [1999] I.R.L.R. 90, CA (Civ Div) ........ *Digested,* 01/**2253**:
*Applied* 03/1216, 03/1332, 03/1337, 05/1340, 06/1283, 07/1317, 08/1124, 08/1206, 08/3841, 09/1741, 10/1142, 10/1153, 12/1167: *Considered* 03/1246, 03/1333, 04/1183, 04/1303, 04/1307, 06/1288, 06/1290, 07/3990, 08/4751, 10/1055, 10/1118, 11/1049, 11/1531: *Distinguished* 02/5565: *Followed* 02/1313, 05/1326, 13/434, 14/1024

Johnson v Westminster City Council [2013] EWCA Civ 773; [2013] H.L.R. 45, CA (Civ Div) ........ *Digested,* 14/**1604**

Johnson (Valuation Officer) v H&B Foods Ltd [2013] UKUT 539 (LC); [2014] R.A. 490, UT (Lands)

Johnston & Sons Ltd v Holland [1988] 1 E.G.L.R. 264; [1988] E.G. 24 (C.S.), CA (Civ Div) ........ *Digested,* 88/**478**:
*Applied* 97/3302, 02/3034, 09/3151: *Considered* 09/2538, 14/2508

Joint Selling of the Media Rights to the FA Premier League, Re (COMP/C-2/38.173) [2007] C.E.C. 2138, CEC ........ *Digested,* 08/**544**:
*Applied* 14/528

Joint Stock Asset Management Co Ingosstrakh-Investments v BNP Paribas SA [2012] EWCA Civ 644; [2012] 1 Lloyd's Rep. 649; [2012] 2 C.L.C. 312, CA (Civ Div) ... *Digested,* 12/**313**:
*Considered* 14/305

Joint Stock Co Aeroflot - Russian Airlines v Berezovsky [2014] EWCA Civ 20; [2014] 1 C.L.C. 53, CA (Civ Div); reversing [2012] EWHC 3017 (Ch), Ch D ........ *Digested,* 14/**564**

Joint Stock Co Aeroflot Russian Airlines v Berezovsky see Aeroflot - Russian Airlines v Berezovsky

Jolly v Jay [2002] EWCA Civ 277; Times, April 3, 2002; Independent, March 15, 2002, CA (Civ Div) ........ *Digested,* 02/**297**:
*Considered* 03/453: *Followed* 02/299: *Referred to* 14/395

Jones v 3M Healthcare Ltd (No.1) see Rhys-Harper v Relaxion Group Plc

Jones v F Sirl & Son (Furnishers) Ltd [1997] I.R.L.R. 493, EAT ........ *Digested,* 97/**2206**:
*Doubted* 14/3500

Jones v Financial Conduct Authority [2013] EWHC 2731 (Ch); [2013] B.P.I.R. 1033, Ch D ..... *Digested,* 14/**1826**

Jones v Financial Services Authority [2013] B.P.I.R. 589, CC (Leeds) *Affirmed* 14/1826

Jones v First Great Western Ltd; *sub nom* Jones v First Greater Western Ltd [2014] EWCA Civ 301, CA (Civ Div); affirming [2013] EWHC 1485 (Ch); [2014] L.L.R. 16, Ch D (Bristol)

Jones v First Greater Western Ltd see Jones v First Great Western Ltd

Jones v First-tier Tribunal (Social Entitlement Chamber) see R. (on the application of Jones) v First-tier Tribunal (Social Entitlement Chamber)

Jones v Kernott; *sub nom* Kernott v Jones [2011] UKSC 53; [2012] 1 A.C. 776; [2011] 3 W.L.R. 1121; [2012] 1 All E.R. 1265; [2012] 1 F.L.R. 45; [2011] 3 F.C.R. 495; [2011] B.P.I.R. 1653; [2012] H.L.R. 14; [2012] W.T.L.R. 125; 14 I.T.E.L.R. 491; [2011] Fam. Law 1338; [2011] 46 E.G. 104 (C.S.); (2011) 155(43) S.J.L.B. 35; [2011] N.P.C. 116; [2012] 1 P. & C.R. DG9; Times, November 10, 2011, SC; reversing [2010] EWCA Civ 578; [2010] 1 W.L.R. 2401; [2010] 3 All E.R. 423; [2010] 2 F.L.R. 1631; [2010] 2 F.C.R. 372; [2010] B.P.I.R. 853; [2011] 1 P. & C.R. 9; [2010] W.T.L.R. 1583; 13 I.T.E.L.R. 275; [2010] Fam. Law 806; [2010] 22 E.G. 106 (C.S.); (2010) 154(21) S.J.L.B. 30; [2010] N.P.C. 62, CA (Civ Div); reversing [2009] EWHC 1713 (Ch); [2010] 1 All E.R. 947; [2010] 1 F.L.R. 38; [2009] B.P.I.R. 1380; [2009] W.T.L.R. 1771; [2009] Fam. Law 1043; [2010] 1 P. & C.R. DG4, Ch D ..... *Digested,* 12/**2705**:
*Applied* 12/1438, 12/2322, 13/2421: *Considered* 12/2024, 13/2422:
*Followed* 14/2489

Jones v Ministry of the Interior Al-Mamlaka Al-Arabiya AS Saudiya see Jones v Saudi Arabia

Jones v National Coal Board [1957] 2 Q.B. 55; [1957] 2 W.L.R. 760; [1957] 2 All E.R. 155; (1957) 101 S.J. 319, CA ..... *Digested,* 57/**2871**:
*Applied* 13/38: *Considered* 14/1347

Jones v Parkin see Meek, Re

Jones v Saudi Arabia; *sub nom* Jones v Ministry of the Interior Al-Mamlaka Al-Arabiya AS Saudiya; *joined case* Mitchell v Al-Dali [2006] UKHL 26; [2007] 1 A.C. 270; [2006] 2 W.L.R. 1424; [2007] 1 All E.R. 113; [2006] H.R.L.R. 32; [2007] U.K.H.R.R. 24; 20 B.H.R.C. 621; (2006) 156 N.L.J. 1025; (2006) 150 S.J.L.B. 811; Times, June 15, 2006; Independent, June 22, 2006, HL; reversing in part [2004] EWCA Civ 1394; [2005] Q.B. 699; [2005] 2 W.L.R. 808; [2005] U.K.H.R.R. 57; [2005] A.C.D. 50; (2004) 101(44) L.S.G. 31; (2004) 154 N.L.J. 1655; (2004) 148 S.J.L.B. 1286; Times, November 1, 2004; Independent, November 3, 2004, CA (Civ Div); reversing in part (Unreported, July 30, 2003), QBD ..... *Digested,* 06/**2644**:
*Applied* 06/2642: *Complaint dismissed* 14/1632

Jones v Secretary of State for Energy and Climate Change; *joined case* Secretary of State for Energy and Climate Change v Jones [2014] EWCA Civ 363; [2014] 3 All E.R. 956; [2014] C.P. Rep. 33; [2014] 3 Costs L.O. 541, CA (Civ Div); affirming [2013] EWHC 1023 (QB); [2013] 3 All E.R. 1014, QBD ..... *Digested,* 14/**335**

Jones v Stroud DC [1986] 1 W.L.R. 1141; [1988] 1 All E.R. 5; 34 B.L.R. 27; 8 Con. L.R. 23; 84 L.G.R. 886; [1986] 2 E.G.L.R. 133; (1986) 279 E.G. 213; (1986) 2 Const. L.J. 185; (1986) 130 S.J. 469, CA (Civ Div) ..... *Digested,* 86/**1993**:
*Applied* 87/242, 01/885, 02/690, 14/829: *Cited* 00/2592: *Considered* 00/2587:
*Doubted* 01/1527: *Followed* 99/2504, 12/1902: *Referred to* 01/1542

Jones v United Kingdom (34356/06); *joined case* Mitchell v United Kingdom (40528/06) (2014) 59 E.H.R.R. 1; 36 B.H.R.C. 81, ECHR ..... *Digested,* 14/**1632**

Jones v Wealth Management (UK) Ltd [2014] EWHC 842 (Ch); [2014] B.P.I.R. 948, Ch D ..... *Digested,* 14/**444**

Jones v Wentworth Securities see Jones v Wrotham Park Settled Estates

Jones v Whalley [2006] UKHL 41; [2007] 1 A.C. 63; [2006] 3 W.L.R. 179; [2006] 4 All E.R. 113; [2007] 1 Cr. App. R. 2; [2007] Crim. L.R. 74; (2006) 150 S.J.L.B. 1020; Times, July 31, 2006; Independent, October 6, 2006, HL; reversing [2005] EWHC 931 (Admin); (2005) 169 J.P. 466; [2006] Crim. L.R. 67; (2005) 169 J.P.N. 679, QBD (Admin) ..... *Digested,* 06/**973**:
*Considered* 09/827, 09/900, 10/777, 14/798

Jones v Wrotham Park Settled Estates; *sub nom* Jones v Wentworth Securities [1980] A.C. 74; [1979] 2 W.L.R. 132; [1979] 1 All E.R. 286; (1979) 38 P. & C.R. 77; (1979) 123 S.J. 34, HL; reversing [1978] 3 W.L.R. 585; [1978] 3 All E.R. 527; (1979) 37 P. & C.R. 289; (1978) 246 E.G. 223; (1978) 122 S.J. 557, CA (Civ Div); reversing (1977) 33 P. & C.R. 304; (1976) 240 E.G. 804; [1977] J.P.L. 36, Lands Tr ..... *Digested,* 79/**1610**:
*Applied* 03/1962, 09/2528: *Considered* 99/5209, 13/2428, 14/2970

Jones (Alleged Contempt of Court), Re see Solicitor General v Jones
Jones (Deceased), Re see Kershaw v Roberts
Jopling v Leavesley [2013] EWCA Civ 1605; [2014] W.T.L.R. 807, CA (Civ Div) .......... *Digested,* 14/**370**
Jordan v United Kingdom (24746/94) (2003) 37 E.H.R.R. 2; 11 B.H.R.C. 1; [2001] Inquest L.R. 101; Times, May 18, 2001, ECHR .......... *Digested,* 01/**3575**: *Applied* 02/3779, 04/4066, 06/18, 06/2126, 07/13: *Considered* 03/2167, 03/4910, 04/37, 07/2234, 07/2980, 08/1975, 10/1722, 14/47
Jorgensen (Listing Officer) v Gomperts; *sub nom* R. (on the application of Jorgensen (Listing Officer)) v Gomports [2006] EWHC 1885 (Admin); [2006] R.A. 300; [2006] N.P.C. 93, QBD (Admin) .......... *Digested,* 07/**2835**: *Cited* 14/2086: *Followed* 13/2397
Joseph Hill & Co Solicitors, Re; *sub nom* R. v X (Wasted Costs Order), Re [2013] EWCA Crim 775; [2014] 1 W.L.R. 786; [2013] 2 Cr. App. R. 20; [2013] P.N.L.R. 31, CA (Crim Div) .......... *Digested,* 13/**771**
Josife v Summertrot Holdings Ltd [2014] EWHC 996 (Ch); [2014] B.P.I.R. 1250, Ch D *Digested,* 14/**625**
Jovanovic v Serbia (21794/08) 35 B.H.R.C. 666, ECHR
Joyce v Darby & Darby see Darby & Darby v Joyce
Joyce v Joyce [2013] EWHC 1353 (Fam); [2014] 1 F.L.R. 1338; [2014] Fam. Law 150, Fam Div
Joyce v O'Brien [2013] EWCA Civ 546; [2014] 1 W.L.R. 70; [2013] Lloyd's Rep. I.R. 523; [2013] P.I.Q.R. P23, CA (Civ Div); affirming [2012] EWHC 1324 (QB); [2012] Lloyd's Rep. I.R. 553; [2012] P.I.Q.R. P18; (2012) 156(21) S.J.L.B. 31, QBD .......... *Digested,* 13/**2195**
JP v LP (Surrogacy Arrangement: Wardship) [2014] EWHC 595 (Fam); [2014] Fam. Law 813, Fam Div
JP v NP (Financial Remedies: Costs) see P v P (Divorce: Financial Remedy Order)
JP v South London and Maudsley NHS Foundation Trust [2012] UKUT 486 (AAC); [2013] M.H.L.R. 148, UT (AAC) .......... *Digested,* 14/**2164**
JP Harrison (Watford) Ltd v Griffiths see Griffiths v JP Harrison (Watford) Ltd
JP Morgan Chase Bank NA v Northern Rock (Asset Management) Plc [2014] EWHC 291 (Ch); [2014] 1 W.L.R. 2197; [2014] C.T.L.C. 33, Ch D .......... *Digested,* 14/**607**
JP Morgan Europe Ltd v Primacom AG [2005] EWHC 508 (Comm); [2005] 2 All E.R. (Comm) 764; [2005] 2 Lloyd's Rep. 665; [2005] 1 C.L.C. 493; [2006] I.L.Pr. 11, QBD (Comm) .......... *Digested,* 06/**647**: *Applied* 14/416
JP Morgan Fleming Claverhouse Investment Trust Plc v Revenue and Customs Commissioners (C-363/05) [2008] S.T.C. 1180; [2007] E.C.R. I-5517; [2007] 3 C.M.L.R. 32; [2008] C.E.C. 42; [2007] Pens. L.R. 265; [2010] B.V.C. 337; [2007] S.T.I. 1765, ECJ (3rd Chamber) .......... *Digested,* 08/**4002**: *Applied* 09/4040, 10/3478, 14/3044: *Considered* 08/3994: *Referred to* 12/3417
JPC v SLW see C v W
JS v KB [2014] EWHC 483 (COP); [2014] C.O.P.L.R. 275; [2014] W.T.L.R. 991, CP ... *Digested,* 14/**2160**
JS (A Child), Re [2012] EWHC 1370 (Fam), Fam Div *Applied* 14/1340
JS (Afghanistan) v Secretary of State for the Home Department see JS (Former Unaccompanied Child: Durable Solution: Afghanistan), Re
JS (Former Unaccompanied Child: Durable Solution: Afghanistan), Re; *sub nom* JS (Afghanistan) v Secretary of State for the Home Department [2013] UKUT 568 (IAC); [2014] I.N.L.R. 1, UT (IAC)
JSC Bank of Moscow v Kekhman; *sub nom* Kekhman, Re [2014] B.P.I.R. 959, Ch D (Bankruptcy Ct) .......... *Digested,* 14/**1783**
JSC BTA Bank v Ablyazov [2012] EWCA Civ 1411; [2013] 1 W.L.R. 1331; [2013] 2 All E.R. 515; Times, January 8, 2013, CA (Civ Div); affirming [2012] EWHC 237 (Comm), QBD (Comm) .......... *Digested,* 13/**454**: *Considered* 14/457
JSC BTA Bank v Ablyazov [2013] EWCA Civ 928; [2014] 1 W.L.R. 1414; [2014] 1 All E.R. (Comm) 700; [2014] 1 Lloyd's Rep. 195; [2013] 2 C.L.C. 286, CA (Civ Div); affirming [2012] EWHC 1819 (Comm); [2012] 2 All E.R. (Comm) 1243; [2012] 2 C.L.C. 641; (2012) 109(31) L.S.G. 20, QBD (Comm) .......... *Digested,* 14/**404**: *Considered* 14/405
JSC BTA Bank v Kythreotis see JSC BTA Bank v Solodchenko
JSC BTA Bank v Solodchenko; *sub nom* JSC BTA Bank v Kythreotis [2010] EWCA Civ 1436; [2011] 1 W.L.R. 888; [2011] 4 All E.R. 1240; [2011] 2 All E.R. (Comm) 1063; [2010] 2 C.L.C. 925; [2011] 1 P. & C.R. DG21; Times, February 23, 2011, CA (Civ Div) .......... *Digested,* 11/**333**: *Followed* 14/405
JSC BTA Bank v Usarel Investments Ltd [2013] EWHC 1780 (Ch); [2014] 1 B.C.L.C. 407, Ch D .......... *Digested,* 14/**516**

JSC Zestafoni G Nikoladze Ferroalloy Plant v Ronly Holdings Ltd [2004] EWHC 245 (Comm); [2004] 2 Lloyd's Rep. 335; [2004] 1 C.L.C. 1146, QBD (Comm) ......... *Digested,* 05/**196**: *Applied* 14/115

JT v Suffolk CC; *sub nom* MRJ (Reconsideration of Order), Re [2014] W.T.L.R. 1243, CP

JT (Ivory Coast) v Secretary of State for the Home Department see JO (Uganda) v Secretary of State for the Home Department

Julian Hernandez v Spain (C-198/13) [2014] All E.R. (EC) 971, ECJ (5th Chamber)

Junaideen v Secretary of State for the Home Department see Secretary of State for the Home Department v Pankina

Juncal v United Kingdom (Admissibility) (32357/09) (2014) 58 E.H.R.R. SE2, ECHR

JW (China) v Secretary of State for the Home Department [2013] EWCA Civ 1526; [2014] Imm. A.R. 501, CA (Civ Div) ........ *Digested,* 14/**1725**

JW Dwyer Ltd v Metropolitan Police District Receiver [1967] 2 Q.B. 970; [1967] 3 W.L.R. 731; [1967] 2 All E.R. 1051; [1967] 2 Lloyd's Rep. 29; (1967) 131 J.P. 416; (1967) 111 S.J. 372, QBD ........ *Digested,* 67/**864**: *Applied* 14/2448: *Considered* 09/3075

JW Spear & Sons Ltd v Zynga Inc; *sub nom* SCRABBLE Trade Mark [2013] EWCA Civ 1175; [2014] 1 All E.R. 1093; [2014] Bus. L.R. 148; [2013] E.C.C. 34; [2014] E.T.M.R. 5; [2014] F.S.R. 14, CA (Civ Div); affirming [2012] EWHC 3345 (Ch); [2013] F.S.R. 28, Ch D ........ *Digested,* 14/**1934**

JW Spear & Sons Ltd v Zynga Inc [2013] EWHC 3348 (Ch); [2014] F.S.R. 19, Ch D .... *Digested,* 14/**1915**

JXMX (A Child) v Dartford and Gravesham NHS Trust [2013] EWHC 3956 (QB); (2014) 135 B.M.L.R. 180, QBD ........ *Digested,* 14/**300**

K v A Local Authority; *sub nom* K v LBX [2012] EWCA Civ 79; [2012] 1 F.C.R. 441; (2012) 15 C.C.L. Rep. 112; (2012) 109(8) L.S.G. 17, CA (Civ Div) ........ *Digested,* 12/**2283**: *Applied* 13/2069: *Followed* 14/2182

K v A Local Authority [2013] UKUT 624 (AAC); [2014] E.L.R. 295, UT (AAC) ........ *Digested,* 14/**932**

K v B (Abduction: Child's Objection to Return) [2014] Fam. Law 768, Fam Div

K v Brent LBC see S (A Child), Re

K v Crown Prosecution Service [2014] EWHC 1606 (Admin); (2014) 178 J.P. 259; [2014] Fam. Law 1251, DC ........ *Digested,* 14/**2463**

K v D (Committal: Application to Strike Out); *sub nom* SK v HD [2013] EWHC 796 (Fam); [2014] Fam. Law 22, Fam Div

K v K (Children: Permanent Removal from Jurisdiction); *sub nom* MK v CK; K v K (Relocation: Shared Care Arrangement) [2011] EWCA Civ 793; [2012] Fam. 134; [2012] 2 W.L.R. 941; [2012] 2 F.L.R. 880; [2011] 3 F.C.R. 111; [2011] Fam. Law 1078, CA (Civ Div) ........ *Digested,* 11/**1382**: *Applied* 13/1248: *Considered* 14/1311

K v K (Relocation: Shared Care Arrangement) see K v K (Children: Permanent Removal from Jurisdiction)

K v Kingswood Centre Hospital Managers [2014] EWCA Civ 1332; [2014] Med. L.R. 497; Times, November 20, 2014, CA (Civ Div); affirming [2014] EWHC 2271 (Admin), QBD (Admin)

K v LBX see K v A Local Authority

K v Portsmouth City Council; *joined case* HouseLetDirect v Newham LBC [2014] R.V.R. 165, VT ........ *Digested,* 14/**2091**

K v Wolverhampton City Council; *joined cases* J v South Staffordshire DC; F v Wychavon DC [2014] R.V.R. 160, VT ........ *Digested,* 14/**2098**

K & H (Children), Re [2006] EWCA Civ 1898; [2007] 1 F.L.R. 2043; [2007] Fam. Law 485; (2007) 151 S.J.L.B. 24, CA (Civ Div) ........ *Digested,* 07/**1714**: *Applied* 10/1307, 13/1208: *Followed* 14/1263

K (A Child) v Nguyen (Unreported, February 25, 2014), CC (Clerkenwell) [*Robert Golin, Barrister, Farrar's Building, Temple, London*] ........ *Digested,* 14/**2347**

K (A Child) v Whittington Hospital NHS Trust (Unreported, May 6, 2014), QBD [*Withy King LLP, Midland Bridge House, Midland Bridge Road, Bath*] ........ *Digested,* 14/**2339**

K (A Child) (Abduction: Case Management), Re [2010] EWCA Civ 1546; [2011] 1 F.L.R. 1268; [2011] Fam. Law 336, CA (Civ Div) ........ *Digested,* 11/**1347**: *Considered* 12/1362, 14/1379

K (A Child) (Abduction: Inchoate Rights), Re see K (A Child) (Abduction: Rights of Custody), Re

K (A Child) (Abduction: Rights of Custody), Re; *sub nom* K (A Child) (Abduction: Inchoate Rights), Re; VK v CC [2014] UKSC 29; [2014] A.C. 1401; [2014] 2 W.L.R. 1304; [2014] 3 All E.R. 149; [2014] N.I. 315; [2014] 2 F.L.R. 629; [2014] 2 F.C.R. 231; [2014] Fam. Law 943, SC; reversing [2014] NICA 15, CA (NI) ...... *Digested,* 14/**1384**

K (A Child) (Brussels II Revised: Art.15), Re see T (A Child) (Care Proceedings: Request to Assume Jurisdiction), Re

K (A Child) (Care Proceedings: Jurisdiction), Re see T (A Child) (Care Proceedings: Request to Assume Jurisdiction), Re

K (A Child) (Return Order: Failure to Comply: Committal: Appeal), Re; *sub nom* MB v GK; M (A Child) (Habitual Residence: Temporary Placement), Re; K (A Child) (Wardship: Committal for Breach of Return Orders), Re [2014] EWCA Civ 905; [2014] 3 F.C.R. 428; [2014] Fam. Law 1384, CA (Civ Div)

K (A Child) (Wardship: Committal for Breach of Return Orders), Re see K (A Child) (Return Order: Failure to Comply: Committal: Appeal), Re

K (A Child) (Wardship: Publicity), Re [2013] EWHC 3748 (Fam); [2014] 2 F.L.R. 310; [2014] Fam. Law 164, Fam Div (Coventry) ........ *Digested,* 14/**1436**

K (A Child) (Wardship: Publicity), Re [2013] EWHC 2684 (Fam); [2014] 1 F.L.R. 548; [2014] 3 F.C.R. 362; [2013] Fam. Law 1534, Fam Div ........ *Digested,* 14/**1268**

K (A Minor) (Removal from Jurisdiction: Practice), Re [1999] 2 F.L.R. 1084; [1999] 3 F.C.R. 673; [1999] Fam. Law 754; (1999) 96(33) L.S.G. 29; Times, July 29, 1999, CA (Civ Div) ........ *Digested,* 99/**2384**: *Followed* 11/1375, 14/1313

K (Abduction: Consent), Re [1997] 2 F.L.R. 212; [1998] 1 F.C.R. 311; [1997] Fam. Law 532, Fam Div ........ *Digested,* 97/**389**: *Applied* 10/1337, 13/1315, 14/1383

K (Children) (Breakdown of Arrangements: Urgent Hearing), Re see K (Children) (Contact: Interim Care Order), Re

K (Children) (Contact: Interim Care Order), Re; *sub nom* K (Children) (Breakdown of Arrangements: Urgent Hearing), Re; HW v GK [2014] EWCA Civ 1195; [2014] 3 F.C.R. 261; [2014] Fam. Law 1515, CA (Civ Div) ........ *Digested,* 14/**1331**

K (Children) (Risk Posed by Father), Re [2013] EWCA Civ 1776; [2014] 2 F.L.R. 1140; [2014] Fam. Law 786, CA (Civ Div)

K (Infants), Re see Official Solicitor v K

KA (Adequacy of Maintenance: Pakistan), Re see KA (Pakistan) v Secretary of State for the Home Department

KA (Afghanistan) v Secretary of State for the Home Department; *sub nom* SA (Afghanistan) v Secretary of State for the Home Department; SU (Afghanistan) v Secretary of State for the Home Department; FU (Afghanistan) v Secretary of State for the Home Department; QA (Afghanistan) v Secretary of State for the Home Department; AK (Afghanistan) v Secretary of State for the Home Department; EU (Afghanistan) v Secretary of State for the Home Department; AR (Afghanistan) v Secretary of State for the Home Department [2012] EWCA Civ 1014; [2013] 1 W.L.R. 615; [2012] Imm. A.R. 1054; [2013] I.N.L.R. 149, CA (Civ Div) ........ *Digested,* 13/**1579**: *Applied* 14/1657: *Followed* 13/1580

KA (Pakistan) v Secretary of State for the Home Department; *sub nom* KA (Adequacy of Maintenance: Pakistan), Re [2006] UKAIT 65; [2007] Imm. A.R. 155, AIT ...... *Digested,* 07/**2326**: *Applied* 08/2053, 08/2055, 14/1689: *Considered* 11/1744

KA (Pakistan) v Secretary of State for the Home Department see Sapkota v Secretary of State for the Home Department

KAB v Sweden (886/11) [2014] Imm. A.R. 371, ECHR

Kadhim v Brent LBC Housing Benefit Board see R. (on the application of Kadhim) v Brent LBC Housing Benefit Review Board

Kahn v Inland Revenue Commissioners see Toshoku Finance UK Plc (In Liquidation), Re

Kainz v Pantherwerke AG (C-45/13) [2014] 3 W.L.R. 1292; [2014] 1 All E.R. (Comm) 433; [2014] C.E.C. 954; [2014] I.L.Pr. 16, ECJ (4th Chamber)

Kairos Shipping Ltd v Enka & Co LLC see Cosmotrade SA v Kairos Shipping Ltd

Kalmneft v Glencore International AG; *sub nom* AOOT Kalmneft v Glencore International AG [2002] 1 All E.R. 76; [2001] 2 All E.R. (Comm) 577; [2002] 1 Lloyd's Rep. 128; [2001] C.L.C. 1805; Times, November 20, 2001, QBD (Comm) ........ *Digested,* 01/**337**: *Applied* 03/206, 09/3561, 10/166, 13/95, 14/123: *Considered* 06/196, 08/173, 12/102

Kalu v Brighton and Sussex University Hospitals NHS Trust [2014] Eq. L.R. 488, EAT *Digested,* 14/**1101**

Kamau (Kenya) v Secretary of State for the Home Department; *sub nom* FK (Kenya) v Secretary of State for the Home Department [2010] EWCA Civ 1302, CA (Civ Div) *Followed* 14/1739

Kambadzi v Secretary of State for the Home Department see R. (on the application of Kambadzi) v Secretary of State for the Home Department

Kamhi (Deceased), Re see Buzzoni v Revenue and Customs Commissioners

Kamino International Logistics BV v Staatssecretaris van Financien (C-129/13); *joined case* Datema Hellmann Worldwide Logistics BV v Staatssecretaris van Financien (C-130/13) [2014] S.T.C. 2704, ECJ (5th Chamber)
Kaneira v English and Wales Cricket Board Ltd (ECB) see Kaneria v England and Wales Cricket Board Ltd (ECB)
Kaneria v England and Wales Cricket Board Ltd (ECB); *sub nom* Kaneira v English and Wales Cricket Board Ltd (ECB) [2014] EWHC 1348 (Comm); (2014) 164(7606) N.L.J. 16, QBD (Comm)
Kaneria v Kaneria see Guidezone Ltd, Re
Kanji v Attorney General of Canada 16 I.T.E.L.R. 345, CJ (Ont)
Kanu v Southwark LBC [2014] EWCA Civ 1085; [2014] P.T.S.R. 1197; [2014] H.L.R. 40; [2014] B.L.G.R. 785, CA (Civ Div) ........ *Digested,* 14/**1601**
Kapenova v Department of Health [2014] I.C.R. 884; [2014] Eq. L.R. 501, EAT ........ *Digested,* 14/**1102**
Kaplan, Re [2010] W.T.L.R. 1171; (2009-10) 12 I.T.E.L.R. 693, Royal Ct (Jer)
*Considered* 14/2893
Kapoor (In Bankruptcy), Re; *sub nom* Hellard v Kapoor [2013] EWHC 2204 (Ch); [2013] B.P.I.R. 745, Ch D ........ *Digested,* 14/**1796**
Kapri v Albania see Kapri v Lord Advocate
Kapri v Lord Advocate; *sub nom* Kapri v Albania [2013] UKSC 48; [2013] 1 W.L.R. 2324; [2013] 4 All E.R. 599; 2013 S.C. (U.K.S.C.) 311; 2013 S.L.T. 743; 2013 S.C.L. 653; 2013 S.C.C.R. 430; [2013] H.R.L.R. 31; 36 B.H.R.C. 136; 2013 G.W.D. 25-493, SC ........ *Digested,* 13/**1187**
Karaman v Germany (17103/10) 36 B.H.R.C. 37, ECHR
Karbhari v Ahmed [2013] EWHC 4042 (QB); [2014] 1 Costs L.R. 151, QBD (Preston) . *Digested,* 14/**475**: *Considered* 14/451
Kareem v Secretary of State for the Home Department see Kareem (Proxy Marriages: EU Law), Re
Kareem (Proxy Marriages: EU Law), Re; *sub nom* Kareem v Secretary of State for the Home Department [2014] UKUT 24 (IAC); [2014] Imm. A.R. 573, UT (IAC)
Karen Millen Fashions Ltd v Dunnes Stores (C-345/13) [2014] Bus. L.R. 756, ECJ (2nd Chamber)
Karen Millen Fashions Ltd v Dunnes Stores (C-345/13) [2014] E.C.D.R. 17, AGO
Karpov v Browder [2013] EWHC 3071 (QB); [2014] E.M.L.R. 8, QBD ........ *Digested,* 14/**841**
KAS v Lord Advocate see H v Lord Advocate
Kashmiri v Secretary of State for the Home Department see Huang v Secretary of State for the Home Department
Kasler v OTP Jelzalogbank Zrt (C-26/13) [2014] 2 All E.R. (Comm) 443; [2014] Bus. L.R. 664, ECJ (4th Chamber)
Kasumu v Arrow Global (Guernsey) Ltd [2013] EWHC 789 (Ch); [2013] B.P.I.R. 1047, Ch D ........ *Digested,* 14/**1790**
KASY v Advocate General for Scotland see N v Advocate General for Scotland
Katsora v Belarus (1836/2008) 35 B.H.R.C. 41, UN HRC
Katz v Bradney see MK Airlines Ltd (In Liquidation), Re
Kaupthing HF v Kaupthing Singer & Friedlander Ltd (In Administration) see Kaupthing Singer & Friedlander Ltd (In administration), Re
Kaupthing Singer & Friedlander Ltd (In administration), Re; *sub nom* Kaupthing HF v Kaupthing Singer & Friedlander Ltd (In Administration) [2012] EWHC 2235 (Ch); [2014] 1 B.C.L.C. 13, Ch D
*Applied* 14/1808
Kaur v Dhaliwal [2014] EWHC 1991 (Ch); [2014] W.T.L.R. 1381; [2014] Fam. Law 1241, Ch D ........ *Digested,* 14/**2820**
Kaur v S Russell & Sons Ltd [1973] Q.B. 336; [1973] 2 W.L.R. 147; [1973] 1 All E.R. 617; (1972) 117 S.J. 91; Times, December 19, 1972, CA (Civ Div); reversing [1972] 3 W.L.R. 663; [1972] 3 All E.R. 305; (1972) 116 S.J. 446, QBD ........ *Digested,* 73/**1964**: *Applied* 73/1156, 82/2480, 94/393: *Considered* 07/477, 12/439: *Distinguished* 74/1321, 83/1311, 97/2914: *Followed* 14/420: *Not followed* 82/1092: *Referred to* 13/2061
Kaur v Walsall MBC (Unreported, July 8, 2014), CC (Walsall) [*DBS Law, Broadway, Broad Street, Birmingham, West Midlands*] ........ *Digested,* 14/**2341**
Kavanagh v Crystal Palace FC 2000 Ltd; *sub nom* Crystal Palace FC Ltd v Kavanagh [2013] EWCA Civ 1410; [2014] 1 All E.R. 1033; [2014] B.C.C. 664; [2014] 2 B.C.L.C. 438; [2014] I.C.R. 251; [2014] I.R.L.R. 139; (2013) 157(45) S.J.L.B. 37, CA (Civ Div); reversing [2013] I.R.L.R. 291, EAT ........ *Digested,* 14/**1130**

Kay v Commissioner of Police of the Metropolis; *sub nom* Commissioner of Police of the Metropolis v Kay; R. (on the application of Kay) v Commissioner of Police of the Metropolis [2008] UKHL 69; [2008] 1 W.L.R. 2723; [2009] 2 All E.R. 935; [2009] R.T.R. 16; [2009] H.R.L.R. 10; (2008) 105(47) L.S.G. 19; (2008) 152(46) S.J.L.B. 31; Times, November 27, 2008, HL; reversing [2007] EWCA Civ 477; [2007] 1 W.L.R. 2915; [2007] 4 All E.R. 31; [2008] R.T.R. 3; [2007] Po. L.R. 135; (2007) 104(23) L.S.G. 34; Times, June 13, 2007, CA (Civ Div); reversing [2006] EWHC 1536 (Admin); [2006] R.T.R. 39; [2006] Po. L.R. 111; [2006] A.C.D. 86; (2006) 150 S.J.L.B. 919; Times, July 3, 2006, DC ............................ *Digested,* 09/**1994**: *Considered* 09/1162, 14/699

Kay v Lambeth LBC; *sub nom* Leeds City Council v Price; Lambeth LBC v Kay; *joined cases* Gorman v Lambeth LBC; Constantine v Lambeth LBC; Barnett v Lambeth LBC; Cole v Lambeth LBC; Dymny v Lambeth LBC; Price v Leeds City Council [2006] UKHL 10; [2006] 2 A.C. 465; [2006] 2 W.L.R. 570; [2006] 4 All E.R. 128; [2006] 2 F.C.R. 20; [2006] H.R.L.R. 17; [2006] U.K.H.R.R. 640; 20 B.H.R.C. 33; [2006] H.L.R. 22; [2006] B.L.G.R. 323; [2006] 2 P. & C.R. 25; [2006] L. & T.R. 8; [2006] 11 E.G. 194 (C.S.); (2006) 150 S.J.L.B. 365; [2006] N.P.C. 29; Times, March 10, 2006; Independent, March 14, 2006, HL; affirming [2004] EWCA Civ 926; [2005] Q.B. 352; [2004] 3 W.L.R. 1396; [2004] H.L.R. 56; Times, July 26, 2004, CA (Civ Div) ............................ *Digested,* 06/**2173**: *Applied* 06/2708, 06/499, 07/2247, 07/2403, 08/1978, 08/2467, 09/1560, 09/2534, 09/2544, 10/2063, 10/2080: *Complaint upheld* 11/1699: *Considered* 05/3424, 07/2242, 07/3867, 07/543, 07/855, 08/2449, 10/2059, 10/2076, 13/66: *Distinguished* 07/2816: *Followed* 09/2533, 09/3173, 10/1705, 10/2061, 13/1562, 14/2234, 14/3702: *Not followed* 11/2066, 13/412

Kaye v South Oxfordshire DC [2013] EWHC 4165 (Ch); [2014] 2 All E.R. 1019; [2014] Bus. L.R. 597; [2014] B.C.C. 143; [2014] 2 B.C.L.C. 383; [2014] B.P.I.R. 416; [2014] R.A. 123, Ch D (Manchester) ............................ *Digested,* 14/**1794**

Kazakhstan Kagazy Plc v Arip see Kazakhstan Kagazy Plc v Zhunus

Kazakhstan Kagazy Plc v Zhunus; *sub nom* Kazakhstan Kagazy Plc v Arip [2014] EWCA Civ 381; [2014] 1 C.L.C. 451, CA (Civ Div); affirming [2013] EWHC 3618 (Comm), QBD (Comm)

Kaziu v Secretary of State for the Home Department see R. (on the application of Kaziu) v Secretary of State for the Home Department

Kazmunaygaz Trading AG (formerly Vector Energy AG) v OMV Supply and Trading AG see OMV Supply and Trading AG v Kazmunaygaz Trading AG (formerly Vector Energy AG)

Kear v Forest of Dean DC [2014] P.A.D. 16, Planning Inspector

Keary Developments Ltd v Tarmac Construction Ltd [1995] 3 All E.R. 534; [1995] 2 B.C.L.C. 395; 73 B.L.R. 115, CA (Civ Div) ............................ *Digested,* 96/**724**: *Applied* 96/692, 96/704, 98/450, 07/416, 07/512, 09/443, 12/395, 12/523, 14/469: *Considered* 95/4009, 04/329, 14/468: *Followed* 97/563, 10/412, 13/423

Keating v Bromley LBC (No.2) see X (Minors) v Bedfordshire CC

Kedebe v Secretary of State for Business, Innovation and Skills see R. (on the application of Kebede) v Secretary of State for Business, Innovation and Skills

Keene v Wellcom London Ltd [2014] EWHC 134 (Ch); [2014] W.T.L.R. 1011, Ch D .... *Digested,* 14/**526**

Keep Streets Live Campaign Ltd v Camden LBC [2014] EWHC 607 (Admin); [2014] B.L.G.R. 286; [2014] L.L.R. 502; [2014] A.C.D. 101, QBD (Admin) ............................ *Digested,* 14/**2065**

Kekhman, Re see JSC Bank of Moscow v Kekhman

Kelderman v Valuation Office Agency [2014] EWHC 1592 (Admin); [2014] R.V.R. 323, QBD (Admin)

Kellie v Wheatley & Lloyd Architects Ltd [2014] EWHC 2886 (TCC); [2014] B.L.R. 644; [2014] 5 Costs L.R. 854, QBD (TCC) ............................ *Digested,* 14/**362**

Kellogg Estate, Re; *sub nom* Rouches v Kellogg 2013 BCSC 2292; 16 I.T.E.L.R. 717, Sup Ct (BC)

Kelly v NGRID Intellectual Property Ltd [2014] E.T.M.R. 21, PO (Irl)

Kelly v Revenue and Customs Commissioners [2014] UKFTT 1012 (TC); [2014] S.T.I. 3438, FTT (Tax)

Kemeh v Ministry of Defence see Ministry of Defence v Kemeh

Kemsley v Barclays Bank Plc [2013] EWHC 1274 (Ch); [2013] B.P.I.R. 839, Ch D (Bankruptcy Ct) ............................ *Digested,* 14/**302**

Kendall, Ex parte 34 E.R. 199; (1811) 17 Ves. Jr. 514, Ct of Chancery *Applied* 14/1205: *Considered* 13/1160

Kendrick v Revenue and Customs Commissioners see Kendricks Planning Ltd v Revenue and Customs Commissioners

Kendrick (Valuation Officer) v Mayday Optical Co Ltd see Mayday Optical Co Ltd v Kendrick (Valuation Officer)

Kendricks Planning Ltd v Revenue and Customs Commissioners; *joined case* Kendrick v Revenue and Customs Commissioners [2014] UKFTT 767 (TC); [2014] S.T.I. 2737, FTT (Tax)

Kendrion NV v European Commission (C-50/12 P) [2014] 4 C.M.L.R. 13, ECJ (Grand Chamber)

Kennedy v Charity Commission see Kennedy v Information Commissioner

Kennedy v Information Commissioner; *sub nom* Kennedy v Charity Commission [2014] UKSC 20; [2014] 2 W.L.R. 808; [2014] 2 All E.R. 847; [2014] E.M.L.R. 19; [2014] H.R.L.R. 14; (2014) 158(13) S.J.L.B. 37; Times, April 2, 2014, SC; affirming [2012] EWCA Civ 317; [2012] 1 W.L.R. 3524; [2012] E.M.L.R. 20, CA (Civ Div); reversing in part [2010] EWHC 475 (Admin); [2010] 1 W.L.R. 1489, QBD (Admin) ........ *Digested,* 14/**58**

Kennemer Golf & Country Club v Inspecteur Belastingdienst Particulieren/Ondernemingen Haarlem (C-174/00) see Kennemer Golf & Country Club v Staatssecretaris van Financien (C-174/00)

Kennemer Golf & Country Club v Staatssecretaris van Financien (C-174/00); *sub nom* Kennemer Golf & Country Club v Inspecteur Belastingdienst Particulieren/Ondernemingen Haarlem (C-174/00) [2002] Q.B. 1252; [2002] 3 W.L.R. 829; [2002] S.T.C. 502; [2002] E.C.R. I-3293; [2002] 2 C.M.L.R. 12; [2002] All E.R. (EC) 480; [2002] C.E.C. 330; [2002] B.T.C. 5205; [2002] B.V.C. 395; [2002] S.T.I. 354; Times, April 11, 2002, ECJ (5th Chamber) ........ *Digested,* 02/**4756**: *Applied* 07/4284, 07/4292, 13/3241, 14/3090: *Considered* 05/4358: *Followed* 02/4758, 09/4107

Kent CC v A-K see A (A Child) (Adoption: Placement Outside Jurisdiction), Re

Kent CC v B (A Child); *sub nom* B (A Child) (Disclosure), Re [2004] EWHC 411 (Fam); [2004] 2 F.L.R. 142; [2004] 3 F.C.R. 1; [2004] Lloyd's Rep. Med. 303; [2004] Fam. Law 493; (2004) 154 N.L.J. 498, Fam Div ........ *Digested,* 04/**1459**: *Applied* 06/445, 07/1711, 07/1732, 08/1444: *Considered* 10/1299, 14/1436

Kent CC v C [2014] EWHC 604 (Fam); [2014] Fam. Law 770, Fam Div

Kent CC v G see G (A Child) (Interim Care Order: Residential Assessment), Re

Kent CC v IS [2013] EWHC 2308 (Fam); [2014] 1 F.L.R. 787; [2013] Fam. Law 1366, Fam Div ........ *Digested,* 14/**1270**

Kenya Aid Programme v Sheffield City Council; *sub nom* Sheffield City Council v Kenya Aid Programme; *joined case* R. (on the application of Kenya Aid Programme) v Sheffield Magistrates' Court [2013] EWHC 54 (Admin); [2014] Q.B. 62; [2013] 3 W.L.R. 422; [2013] 2 E.G.L.R. 138; [2013] R.A. 75; [2013] A.C.D. 56, DC ........ *Digested,* 13/**2035**: *Followed* 13/236

Kenyon-Brown v Desmond Banks & Co (Undue Influence) (No.2) see Royal Bank of Scotland Plc v Etridge (No.2)

Keppel Bus Co v Sa'ad bin Ahmad [1974] 1 W.L.R. 1082; [1974] 2 All E.R. 700; [1974] R.T.R. 504; 17 K.I.R. 90; (1974) 118 S.J. 531, PC (Sing) ........ *Digested,* 74/**1231**: *Considered* 14/3000: *Distinguished* 95/3735

Keppel Seghers UK Ltd v Hinds [2014] I.C.R. 1105; [2014] I.R.L.R. 754, EAT ........ *Digested,* 14/**1068**

Keramag Keramische Werke AG v European Commission (T-379/10); *joined case* Sanitec Europe Oy v European Commission (T-381/10) [2014] 4 C.M.L.R. 3, GC (4th Chamber)

Kernott v Jones see Jones v Kernott

Kerrouche v Secretary of State for the Home Department (No.1) see R. v Secretary of State for the Home Department Ex p. Kerrouche (No.1)

Kershaw v Roberts; *sub nom* Jones (Deceased), Re [2014] EWHC 1037 (Ch); [2014] 3 Costs L.R. 536; [2014] W.T.L.R. 1395; (2014) 158(16) S.J.L.B. 57, Ch D ........ *Digested,* 14/**309**

Kesabo v African Barrick Gold Plc [2013] EWHC 3198 (QB); [2013] 6 Costs L.R. 954, QBD ........ *Digested,* 14/**393**

Kevern v Ayres [2014] EWHC 165 (Ch); [2014] W.T.L.R. 441, Ch D ........ *Digested,* 14/**2816**

Keyu v Secretary of State for Foreign and Commonwealth Affairs see R. (on the application of Keyu) v Secretary of State for Foreign and Commonwealth Affairs

KH (Care: Non-Accidental Death: Placement of Siblings), Re [2013] EWHC 165 (Fam); [2013] 2 F.L.R. 565; [2013] Fam. Law 527, Fam Div ........ *Digested,* 14/**1276**

Khaira v Shergill; *sub nom* Shergill v Khaira [2014] UKSC 33; [2014] 3 W.L.R. 1; [2014] 3 All E.R. 243; [2014] P.T.S.R. 907; [2014] W.T.L.R. 1729; Times, June 18, 2014, SC; reversing [2012] EWCA Civ 983; [2012] P.T.S.R. 1697; [2012] W.T.L.R. 1795; (2012) 162 N.L.J. 1001, CA (Civ Div) ........ *Digested,* 14/**38**

Khan v Harrow LBC [2013] EWHC 2687 (TCC); [2013] B.L.R. 611; [2013] C.I.L.L. 3421, QBD (TCC) ........ *Digested,* 14/**2206**

Khan v Inland Revenue Commissioners see Toshoku Finance UK Plc (In Liquidation), Re

Khan v Royal Mail Group Ltd [2014] EWCA Civ 1082; [2014] I.R.L.R. 947; [2014] Eq. L.R. 700, CA (Civ Div); affirming UKEAT/0160/11/DM, EAT

Khan v Secretary of State for the Home Department see R. (on the application of Khan) v Secretary of State for the Home Department

Khan v United Kingdom (Admissibility) (11987/11) (2014) 58 E.H.R.R. SE15, ECHR

Khans Solicitors v Chifuntwe [2013] EWCA Civ 481; [2014] 1 W.L.R. 1185; [2013] 4 All E.R. 367; [2013] 4 Costs L.R. 564; [2013] P.N.L.R. 29; (2013) 157(19) S.J.L.B. 35, CA (Civ Div); reversing in part [2012] EWHC 2108 (QB); [2012] 6 Costs L.R. 1047, QBD; affirming CC 1106668, Sen Cts Costs Office ................ *Digested,* 13/**332**

Khanum v Secretary of State for the Home Department see Khanum (Paragraph 353B), Re

Khanum (Paragraph 353B), Re; *sub nom* Khanum v Secretary of State for the Home Department [2013] UKUT 311 (IAC); [2013] Imm. A.R. 858, UT (IAC) ................ *Digested,* 14/**1727**

Kharug v Upper Tribunal (Immigration and Asylum Chamber); *joined cases* Yassin v Secretary of State for the Home Department; Olufunmilaya v Secretary of State for the Home Department [2014] EWHC 2037 (Admin); [2014] A.C.D. 122, QBD (Admin)

Khatel v Secretary of State for the Home Department see Secretary of State for the Home Department v Raju

Khatel (S.85A: Effect of Continuing Application), Re see Secretary of State for the Home Department v Raju

Khawaja v Revenue and Customs Commissioners [2013] UKUT 353 (TCC); [2014] S.T.C. 150; [2013] B.T.C. 1995; [2013] S.T.I. 2886, UT (Tax); reversing in part [2012] UKFTT 183 (TC); [2012] S.T.I. 1843, FTT (Tax) .................................... *Digested,* 14/**2954**

Khodorkovskiy v Russia (11082/06); *joined case* Lebedev v Russia (13772/05) (2014) 59 E.H.R.R. 7, ECHR

Khreino v Khreino (No.2) [2000] 1 F.C.R. 80, CA (Civ Div) .......................................... *Digested,* 00/**2529**: *Considered* 14/1372: *Followed* 11/1298

Kidd v Cheshire East Council [2014] P.A.D. 20, Planning Inspector

Kilic v Turkey (22492/93) (2001) 33 E.H.R.R. 58, ECHR ............................................. *Digested,* 02/**2489**: *Applied* 14/2460

Kilmarnock Equitable Cooperative Society Ltd v Inland Revenue Commissioners 1966 S.L.T. 224; 42 T.C. 675; (1966) 45 A.T.C. 205; [1966] T.R. 185, IH (1 Div) ........ *Digested,* 66/**5884**: *Considered* 96/5565, 08/3647: *Distinguished* 98/4603, 06/4158, 14/2882: *Followed* 81/333

Kilmorie (Aldridge) Ltd v Dickinson (Inspector of Taxes) see Ransom (Inspector of Taxes) v Higgs

Kim v Chasewood Park Residents Ltd [2013] EWCA Civ 239; [2013] H.L.R. 24; [2013] 2 P. & C.R. DG4, CA (Civ Div) ........................................................................ *Digested,* 13/**1161**: *Applied* 14/1760

Kim v Fibria Celulose S/A see Pan Ocean Co Ltd, Re

Kinderis v Kinderene [2014] EWHC 693 (Fam); [2014] Fam. Law 1082, Fam Div

Kinderis v Kineriene [2013] EWHC 4139 (Fam); [2014] Fam. Law 1081, Fam Div

King v Ahmed (Unreported, August 28, 2013), CC (Bromley) [*Robert Mackenzie, Barrister, Temple Gate Chambers, 4th Floor, 218 Strand, London*] ................... *Digested,* 14/**2311**

King v American Airlines Inc (Unreported, 2002), US Court *Considered* 14/161

King v Bristow Helicopters Ltd; *sub nom* Hammond v Bristow Helicopters Ltd; *joined case* Morris v KLM Royal Dutch Airlines [2002] UKHL 7; [2002] 2 A.C. 628; [2002] 2 W.L.R. 578; [2002] 2 All E.R. 565; [2002] 1 All E.R. (Comm) 385; [2002] 1 Lloyd's Rep. 745; 2002 S.C. (H.L.) 59; 2002 S.L.T. 378; 2002 S.C.L.R. 499; [2002] C.L.C. 820; [2002] P.I.Q.R. P29; (2002) 99(13) L.S.G. 25; (2002) 146 S.J.L.B. 61; 2002 G.W.D. 9-274; Times, March 1, 2002; Independent, March 5, 2002; Daily Telegraph, March 7, 2002, HL; reversing [2001] 1 Lloyd's Rep. 95; 2001 S.C. 54; 2001 S.L.T. 126; 2001 S.C.L.R. 393; 2000 G.W.D. 25-923; Times, October 25, 2000, IH (1 Div); reversing 1999 S.L.T. 919; 1998 G.W.D. 40-2028, OH .............................................................................. *Digested,* 02/**5305**: *Applied* 08/208, 09/258, 10/200, 14/2309: *Considered* 03/3123, 14/2732: *Not followed* 01/5385

King v Crown Energy Trading AG [2003] EWHC 163 (Comm); [2003] 2 C.L.C. 540; [2003] I.L.Pr. 28; Times, March 14, 2003, QBD (Comm) .................................... *Digested,* 03/**484**: *Doubted* 14/514

King v Dubrey [2014] EWHC 2083 (Ch); [2014] W.T.L.R. 1411, Ch D .......................... *Digested,* 14/**2817**

King v United Kingdom (Admissibility) (No.2) (13881/02) [2004] S.T.C. 911; [2007] B.T.C. 74; 6 I.T.L. Rep. 872; [2004] S.T.I. 1117, ECHR ..................................... *Digested,* 04/**1949**: *Applied* 06/4188, 07/4358: *Considered* 14/2954

King v Victoria Insurance Co Ltd [1896] A.C. 250, PC (Aus)
*Applied* 57/1763, 64/3384: *Considered* 00/311, 02/935, 14/610: *Distinguished* 00/1460

King (A Child), Re; *sub nom* Portsmouth City Council v King [2014] EWHC 2964 (Fam); [2014] 2 F.L.R. 855; [2014] Fam. Law 1400, Fam Div ............ *Digested*, 14/**1420**

King's College Hospital NHS Foundation Trust v T [2014] EWHC 3315 (Fam); [2014] Fam. Law 1678, Fam Div

King's Lynn and West Norfolk BC v Bunning [2013] EWHC 3390 (QB); [2014] 2 All E.R. 1095; [2014] 1 Costs L.O. 85, QBD ............ *Digested*, 14/**2043**: *Applied* 14/1517: *Cited* 14/13

Kingsley v Orban [2014] EWHC 2991 (Ch); [2014] B.P.I.R. 1468, Ch D

Kingstons Solicitors v Reiss Solicitors [2014] EWCA Civ 172; [2014] 6 Costs L.R. 998, CA (Civ Div)

Kirk Care Housing Association Ltd v Crerar and Partners 1996 S.L.T. 150, OH ............ *Digested*, 96/**6666**: *Overruled* 14/2470

Kirker v Ambitions Personnel (Nottinghamshire) Ltd see Rhys-Harper v Relaxion Group Plc

Kirker v British Sugar Plc see Rhys-Harper v Relaxion Group Plc

Kirklees Council v RE [2014] EWHC 3182 (Fam); [2014] Fam. Law 1679, Fam Div

Kirkpatrick v Snoozebox Ltd [2014] B.C.C. 477, QBD ............ *Digested*, 14/**1812**

Kisoka v Ratnpinyotip (t/a Rydevale Day Nursery) [2014] I.C.R. D17, EAT

Kitechnology BV v Unicor GmbH Plastmaschinen [1994] I.L.Pr. 568; [1995] F.S.R. 765, CA (Civ Div); reversing [1994] I.L.Pr. 560, Ch D ............ *Digested*, 96/**1219**: *Followed* 14/415

Kittel v Belgium (C-439/04); *joined case* Belgium v Recolta Recycling SPRL (C-440/04) [2008] S.T.C. 1537; [2006] E.C.R. I-6161; [2008] B.T.C. 5439; [2008] B.V.C. 559; [2006] S.T.I. 1851, ECJ (3rd Chamber) ............ *Digested*, 08/**4052**:
*Applied* 07/4317, 07/4318, 09/4061, 09/4063, 09/4064, 09/4078, 10/3495, 11/3533, 11/3556, 12/3402, 12/3405, 14/3066, 14/3070: *Considered* 07/4312, 09/4077, 09/4126, 09/4131, 10/3497, 12/3404, 14/3810: *Followed* 10/3502, 12/3401, 14/3065, 14/3067, 14/3069, 14/3071, 14/3092: *Referred to* 09/4079

Kizhakudan v Secretary of State for the Home Department [2012] EWCA Civ 566; [2012] Imm. A.R. 886; [2013] I.N.L.R. 38, CA (Civ Div) ............ *Digested*, 13/**1627**: *Distinguished* 14/1728

KL (A Child) (Abduction: Habitual Residence: Inherent Jurisdiction), Re see DL v EL (Hague Abduction Convention: Effect of Reversal of Return Order on Appeal)

Klein v Austria (57028/00) (2014) 59 E.H.R.R. 14, ECHR

Kleinwort Benson (Jersey) Trustees Ltd v Pinto; *sub nom* Pinto's Voluntary Settlement, Re [2004] W.T.L.R. 879, Royal Ct (Jer)
*Considered* 14/3027

Kleinwort Benson Ltd v Birmingham City Council see Kleinwort Benson Ltd v Lincoln City Council

Kleinwort Benson Ltd v Kensington and Chelsea RLBC see Kleinwort Benson Ltd v Lincoln City Council

Kleinwort Benson Ltd v Lincoln City Council; *joined cases* Kleinwort Benson Ltd v Kensington and Chelsea RLBC; Kleinwort Benson Ltd v Southwark LBC; Kleinwort Benson Ltd v Birmingham City Council [1999] 2 A.C. 349; [1998] 3 W.L.R. 1095; [1998] 4 All E.R. 513; [1998] Lloyd's Rep. Bank. 387; [1999] C.L.C. 332; (1999) 1 L.G.L.R. 148; (1999) 11 Admin. L.R. 130; [1998] R.V.R. 315; (1998) 148 N.L.J. 1674; (1998) 142 S.J.L.B. 279; [1998] N.P.C. 145; Times, October 30, 1998; Independent, November 4, 1998, HL ............ *Digested*, 98/**2297**:
*Applied* 99/2218, 03/4142, 04/383, 07/3973, 09/307: *Considered* 99/532, 03/1579, 05/4129, 07/1052, 10/3512, 12/3078: *Followed* 14/2262: *Not applied* 04/3173

Kleinwort Benson Ltd v Southwark LBC see Kleinwort Benson Ltd v Lincoln City Council

KLM Royal Dutch Airlines NV v Flughafen Frankfurt/Main AG (IV/34.801) [1998] 4 C.M.L.R. 779, CEC
*Considered* 11/430, 14/528

Klockner Holdings GmbH v Klockner Beteiligungs GmbH [2005] EWHC 1453 (Comm), QBD (Comm)
*Applied* 14/303: *Considered* 11/125

Kloosman v Aylen see Frost (Deceased), Re

Knapp v Ecclesiastical Insurance Group Plc [1998] Lloyd's Rep. I.R. 390; [1998] P.N.L.R. 172; Times, November 17, 1997, CA (Civ Div) ............ *Digested*, 97/**645**:
*Applied* 01/4526, 03/3003, 08/384, 09/2735, 10/2283: *Cited* 99/3365: *Considered* 00/2621, 14/591: *Distinguished* 05/443: *Followed* 10/2282

Knauf UK GmbH v British Gypsum Ltd (No.1) [2001] EWCA Civ 1570; [2002] 1 W.L.R. 907; [2002] 2 All E.R. 525; [2001] 2 All E.R. (Comm) 960; [2002] 1 Lloyd's Rep. 199; [2002] C.L.C. 239; [2002] I.L.Pr. 30; (2001) 145 S.J.L.B. 259; Times, November 15, 2001; Independent, November 7, 2001, CA (Civ Div); reversing [2001] 2 All E.R. (Comm) 332; [2001] C.L.C. 1141, QBD (Comm) ..................... *Digested,* 01/**828**:
*Considered* 04/411, 06/507, 06/510, 06/515, 07/244, 14/478

Kneale v Barclays Bank Plc (t/a Barclaycard) [2010] EWHC 1900 (Comm); [2010] C.T.L.C. 233, QBD (Comm)
*Overruled in part* 14/438

Knight v Frost [1999] B.C.C. 819; [1999] 1 B.C.L.C 364, Ch D .................................... *Digested,* 99/**628**:
*Applied* 13/479, 14/512

KNN Colburn LLP v GD City Holdings Ltd [2013] EWHC 2879 (TCC); [2013] T.C.L.R. 10, QBD (TCC) ......................................................................................... *Digested,* 14/**585**

KNS Industrial Services (Birmingham) Ltd v Sindall Ltd (2001) 3 T.C.L.R. 10; 75 Con. L.R. 71; (2001) 17 Const. L.J. 170, QBD (TCC) ................................................ *Digested,* 01/**858**:
*Applied* 10/569, 14/130: *Considered* 03/667

Koch v Germany (497/09) [2013] 1 F.C.R. 595; (2013) 56 E.H.R.R. 6, ECHR
*Considered* 14/672

Koch Marine Inc v d'Amica Societa di Navigazione arl (The Elena d'Amico) [1980] 1 Lloyd's Rep. 75, QBD (Comm) ........................................................................... *Digested,* 80/**640**:
*Applied* 11/3114, 14/827: *Considered* 11/3113

Kochar v Commissioner of Police of the Metropolis see Yearwood v Commissioner of Police of the Metropolis

Kohler Mira Ltd v Bristan Group Ltd [2013] EWPCC 2; [2014] F.S.R. 1, PCC .............. *Digested,* 14/**1873**

Kohli v Avtar Lit see Sunrise Radio Ltd, Re

Kohli v Lit [2012] EWHC 1338 (Ch), Ch D
*Affirmed* 14/525

Kohli v Lit see Sunrise Radio Ltd, Re

Kohli v Lit see Sunrise Radio Ltd, Re

Kolevi v Bulgaria (1108/02) (2014) 59 E.H.R.R. 23, ECHR

Konan v Secretary of State for the Home Department IATRF 2000/0020/C, CA (Civ Div)
*Followed* 14/1664

Konczak v BAE Systems (Operations) Ltd see BAE Systems (Operations) Ltd v Konczak

Kone AG v OBB-Infrastruktur AG (C-557/12) EU:C:2014:1317; [2014] 5 C.M.L.R. 5, ECJ (5th Chamber)

Kone Oyj v European Commission (C-510/11 P) [2014] 4 C.M.L.R. 10, ECJ (10th Chamber)

Kong Wah Holdings Ltd, Re [2007] 4 H.K.L.R.D. 620, CFI (HK)
*Considered* 14/1339

Koninklijke KPN Nederland NV v Benelux-Merkenbureau (C-363/99) [2006] Ch. 1; [2005] 3 W.L.R. 649; [2004] E.C.R. I-1619; [2005] 2 C.M.L.R. 10; [2005] All E.R. (EC) 19; [2005] C.E.C. 216; [2004] E.T.M.R. 57, ECJ (6th Chamber) ......... *Digested,* 05/**2437**:
*Applied* 05/2529, 07/2647, 07/2648, 08/2343, 08/2396, 11/1998, 12/1976:
*Considered* 05/2532, 14/1872: *Followed* 13/1834

Koninklijke Philips Electronics NV v Remington Consumer Products Ltd (C-299/99); *sub nom* Philips Electronics NV v Remington Consumer Products Ltd (C-299/99) [2003] Ch. 159; [2003] 2 W.L.R. 294; [2002] E.C.R. I-5475; [2002] 2 C.M.L.R. 52; [2002] All E.R. (EC) 634; [2002] C.E.C. 525; [2002] E.T.M.R. 81; [2003] R.P.C. 2; (2002) 25(9) I.P.D. 25060; Times, June 20, 2002; Daily Telegraph, June 27, 2002, ECJ; no effect [2002] E.C.R. I-5475; [2001] E.T.M.R. 48; [2001] R.P.C. 38, AGO .................................................................. *Digested,* 02/**2903**:
*Applied* 03/2632, 05/2438, 07/1580, 07/2637, 08/2402, 09/2437:
*Considered* 03/2613, 03/2631, 05/2533, 06/2598, 14/1932: *Followed* 05/2548, 06/2610, 09/2411

Konkola Copper Mines Plc v U&M Mining Zambia Ltd [2014] EWHC 2146 (Comm); [2014] 2 Lloyd's Rep. 507, QBD (Comm)

Konkola Copper Mines Plc v U&M Mining Zambia Ltd [2014] EWHC 2374 (Comm); [2014] 2 Lloyd's Rep. 649; [2014] Bus. L.R. D21, QBD (Comm)

Konkurrenten.no AS v EFTA Surveillance Authority (E-5/12) see Risdal Touring AS v EFTA Surveillance Authority (E-4/12)

Konstantinides, Re (C-475/11) see Proceedings against Konstantinides (C-475/11)

Kookmin Bank v Rainy Sky SA see Rainy Sky SA v Kookmin Bank

Koretskyy v Ukraine (40269/02) (2014) 59 E.H.R.R. 5, ECHR

Kosta v Carnwath; *sub nom* Kosta v Trustees of the Phillimore Estate [2014] UKUT 319 (LC); [2014] L. & T.R. 25, UT (Lands)

Kosta v Trustees of the Phillimore Estate see Kosta v Carnwath

Kotke v Saffarini [2005] EWCA Civ 221; [2005] 2 F.L.R. 517; [2005] 1 F.C.R. 642; [2005] P.I.Q.R. P26; [2005] Fam. Law 535; (2005) 155 N.L.J. 414; Independent, March 16, 2005, CA (Civ Div) .......... *Digested*, 05/**55**: *Applied* 10/3208, 14/2822

Koushkaki v Germany (C-84/12) [2014] 2 C.M.L.R. 38; [2014] C.E.C. 973, ECJ (Grand Chamber)

KP (A Child) (Abduction: Child's Objections), Re see A (Abduction: Child's Objections to Return), Re

KP (A Child) (Abduction: Judge Meeting Child: Conduct of Interview), Re see A (Abduction: Child's Objections to Return), Re

KP (A Child) (Abduction: Rights of Custody), Re see A (Abduction: Child's Objections to Return), Re

Kraal v Earthquake Commission [2014] Lloyd's Rep. I.R. 596, HC (NZ)

Krebs v NHS Commissioning Board; *sub nom* Krebs v NHS Commissioning Board (As Successor Body to Salford Primary Care Trust) [2014] EWCA Civ 1540, CA (Civ Div); affirming [2013] EWHC 3474 (Admin); [2014] Med. L.R. 70; (2014) 136 B.M.L.R. 84, QBD .......... *Digested*, 14/**1492**

Krebs v NHS Commissioning Board (As Successor Body to Salford Primary Care Trust) see Krebs v NHS Commissioning Board

Krejci Lager & Umschlagbetriebs GmbH v Olbrich Transport und Logistik GmbH (C-469/12) [2014] C.E.C. 654; [2014] I.L.Pr. 8, ECJ (10th Chamber)

Krishevsky v DPP [2014] EWHC 1755 (Admin); (2014) 178 J.P. 369, DC

Kronhofer v Maier (C168/02) [2004] 2 All E.R. (Comm) 759; [2005] 1 Lloyd's Rep. 284; [2004] E.C.R. I-6009; [2004] All E.R. (EC) 939; [2004] I.L.Pr. 27, ECJ (2nd Chamber) .......... *Digested*, 05/**603**: *Applied* 14/556

Kronos International Inc v Finanzamt Leverkusen (C-47/12) [2014] B.T.C. 45; [2014] S.T.I. 2974, ECJ (1st Chamber)

Kruppa v Benedetti [2014] EWHC 1887 (Comm); [2014] 2 All E.R. (Comm) 617; [2014] Bus. L.R. 1104; [2014] 2 Lloyd's Rep. 421, QBD (Comm) .......... *Digested*, 14/**132**

KS v Bradford MDC [2014] EWHC 11 (Admin); [2014] 3 F.C.R. 164; [2014] Fam. Law 458, QBD (Admin) .......... *Digested*, 14/**1308**

KS v Neath Port Talbot CBC [2014] EWCA Civ 941; [2014] Fam. Law 1396, CA (Civ Div)

KS Energy Services Ltd v BR Energy (M) Sdn Bhd [2014] SGCA 16; [2014] B.L.R. 658, CA (Sing)

KU (A Child) v Liverpool City Council see U (A Child) v Liverpool City Council

Kubrik v Ucar see Sofra Bakery Ltd (In Liquidation), Re

Kudla v Poland (30210/96) (2002) 35 E.H.R.R. 11; 10 B.H.R.C. 269; [2000] Prison L.R. 380, ECHR .......... *Digested*, 01/**3543**: *Applied* 06/2127, 07/2198, 07/2227, 07/2230, 07/2231, 08/1916, 09/1964, 12/1670: *Considered* 08/4653, 12/1711, 14/1680

Kuen v Director of Lands [2014] R.V.R. 280, CA (HK)

Kulibaba v United States [2014] EWHC 176 (Admin); [2014] Lloyd's Rep. F.C. 383, DC .......... *Digested*, 14/**1228**

Kulikowski v Poland (18353/03) (2014) 58 E.H.R.R. 23, ECHR

Kumar v AGF Insurance Ltd [1999] 1 W.L.R. 1747; [1998] 4 All E.R. 788; [1999] Lloyd's Rep. I.R. 147; [1999] P.N.L.R. 269, QBD (Comm) .......... *Digested*, 99/**3420**: *Applied* 14/1846: *Considered* 13/1736

Kumara v Jalal see Kumari v Jalal

Kumari v Jalal; *sub nom* Kumara v Jalal [1997] 1 W.L.R. 97; [1996] 4 All E.R. 65; [1996] 2 F.L.R. 588; [1997] 1 F.C.R. 422; [1997] Fam. Law 13; (1996) 146 N.L.J. 1349; Times, October 15, 1996, CA (Civ Div) .......... *Digested*, 96/**17**: *Considered* 12/1367: *Followed* 14/1333

Kumon Educational UK Co Ltd v Revenue and Customs Commissioners [2014] UKFTT 109 (TC); [2014] S.T.I. 800, FTT (Tax)

Kumon Educational UK Co Ltd v Revenue and Customs Commissioners [2014] UKFTT 772 (TC); [2014] S.T.I. 2766, FTT (Tax)

Kurd, Re see Earp v Kurd

KUREHA/Process for producing microcapsules (T1550/05) [2014] E.P.O.R. 13, EPO (Technical Bd App)

Kuwait Airways Corp v Iraq Airways Co (No.6) see Kuwait Airways Corp v Iraqi Airways Co (No.6)

Kuwait Airways Corp v Iraqi Airways Co (Disclosure: Fraud Exception) [2005] EWCA Civ 286; [2005] 1 W.L.R. 2734; [2005] C.P. Rep. 32; (2005) 102(21) L.S.G. 33; (2005) 155 N.L.J. 468; Times, April 25, 2005, CA (Civ Div); affirming [2005] EWHC 367 (Comm), QBD (Comm) .......... *Digested*, 05/**294**: *Considered* 14/1804

Kuwait Airways Corp v Iraqi Airways Co (No.5) see Kuwait Airways Corp v Iraqi Airways Co (No.6)

Kuwait Airways Corp v Iraqi Airways Co (No.6); *sub nom* Kuwait Airways Corp v Iraq Airways Co (No.6); *joined case* Kuwait Airways Corp v Iraqi Airways Co (No.5) [2002] UKHL 19; [2002] 2 A.C. 883; [2002] 2 W.L.R. 1353; [2002] 3 All E.R. 209; [2002] 1 All E.R. (Comm) 843; [2003] 1 C.L.C. 183; Times, May 21, 2002, HL; affirming [2001] 3 W.L.R. 1117; [2001] 1 All E.R. (Comm) 557; [2001] 1 Lloyd's Rep. 161; [2001] C.L.C. 262; (2000) 97(48) L.S.G. 37; (2001) 145 S.J.L.B. 5; Times, November 21, 2000; Daily Telegraph, November 21, 2000, CA (Civ Div); reversing in part [2000] 2 All E.R. (Comm) 360; (2000) 97(23) L.S.G. 44; Times, May 31, 2000, QBD (Comm) ........ *Digested,* 02/**4540**: *Applied* 04/1277, 09/3578, 09/615, 10/2392: *Considered* 04/2249, 04/734, 05/212, 06/2451, 10/2016, 10/3414, 11/1071, 12/120, 12/1290, 14/825: *Followed* 04/427, 10/3409

Kuwait Airways Corp v Kuwait Insurance Co (No.3) [2000] 1 All E.R. (Comm) 972; [2001] C.P. Rep. 60; [2000] Lloyd's Rep. I.R. 678, QBD (Comm) ........ *Digested,* 00/**3523**: *Applied* 01/4936, 14/408

Kuwait Asia Bank EC v National Mutual Life Nominees Ltd [1991] 1 A.C. 187; [1990] 3 W.L.R. 297; [1990] 3 All E.R. 404; [1990] 2 Lloyd's Rep. 95; [1990] B.C.C. 567; [1990] B.C.L.C. 868, PC (NZ) ........ *Digested,* 90/**520**: *Considered* 14/2202: *Followed* 93/5553: *Not followed* 95/2199

Kuwait Oil Tanker Co SAK v Al-Bader (No.3) [2000] 2 All E.R. (Comm) 271; (2000) 97(23) L.S.G. 44; Times, May 30, 2000; Independent, June 26, 2000, CA (Civ Div); affirming Independent, January 11, 1999, QBD (Comm) ........ *Digested,* 00/**5106**: *Applied* 04/451, 05/4190, 06/2435: *Considered* 04/7, 10/1876, 10/510: *Followed* 14/479

Kuwait Petroleum (GB) Ltd v Customs and Excise Commissioners see Lex Services Plc v Customs and Excise Commissioners

Kuwait Petroleum Corp v European Commission (C-581/12 P) [2014] 4 C.M.L.R. 11, ECJ (10th Chamber)

KY (Somalia) v Secretary of State for the Home Department see N v Advocate General for Scotland

Kyrgystan v Finrep GmbH see Kyrgyz Republic Ministry of Transport Department of Civil Aviation v Finrep GmbH

Kyrgyz Republic Ministry of Transport Department of Civil Aviation v Finrep GmbH; *sub nom* Kyrgystan v Finrep GmbH [2006] EWHC 1722 (Comm); [2006] 2 C.L.C. 402; [2007] Bus. L.R. D17, QBD (Comm) ........ *Digested,* 07/**244**: *Considered* 12/313, 14/305

L v C (Applications by Non-Biological Mother) see G (A Child) (Same-sex Relationship: Family Life Declaration), Re

L v M (A Child) see Murphy v Murphy

L v United Kingdom (45508/99) see HL v United Kingdom (45508/99)

L (A Child) (Application Hearing: Legal Representation), Re [2013] EWCA Civ 267; [2013] 2 F.L.R. 1444; [2013] Fam. Law 798, CA (Civ Div) ........ *Digested,* 14/**1350**

L (A Child) (Brussels II Revised), Re see L (A Child) (Recognition of Foreign Order), Re

L (A Child) (Care: Threshold Criteria), Re [2007] 1 F.L.R. 2050; [2007] Fam. Law 297, Fam Div ........ *Digested,* 08/**1502**: *Considered* 10/1329, 14/1281

L (A Child) (Case Management: Child's Evidence), Re [2013] EWCA Civ 1778; [2014] 2 F.L.R. 972; [2014] Fam. Law 780, CA (Civ Div) ........ *Digested,* 14/**1309**

L (A Child) (Contact: Domestic Violence), Re; *joined cases* H (Children) (Contact: Domestic Violence), Re; V (A Child) (Contact: Domestic Violence), Re; M (A Child) (Contact: Domestic Violence), Re [2001] Fam. 260; [2001] 2 W.L.R. 339; [2000] 4 All E.R. 609; [2000] 2 F.L.R. 334; [2000] 2 F.C.R. 404; [2000] Fam. Law 603; (2000) 164 J.P.N. 918; (2000) 144 S.J.L.B. 222; Times, June 21, 2000; Independent, June 22, 2000, CA (Civ Div) ........ *Digested,* 00/**2475**: *Applied* 01/2564, 06/1673, 09/1641, 11/1396: *Considered* 03/1541, 05/1587, 06/1672, 14/1321, 14/1411

L (A Child) (Custody: Habitual Residence), Re see DL v EL (Hague Abduction Convention: Effect of Reversal of Return Order on Appeal)

L (A Child) (Family Proceedings: Practice and Procedure), Re; *sub nom* NL (A Child) (Appeal: Interim Care Order: Facts and Reasons), Re [2014] EWHC 270 (Fam); [2014] 1 W.L.R. 2795; [2014] 1 F.L.R. 1384; [2014] 3 F.C.R. 464; [2014] Fam. Law 427, Fam Div ........ *Digested,* 14/**1263**: *Considered* 14/1284

L (A Child) (Interim Care Order: Mother's Imprisonment), Re see L (A Child) (Interim Care Order: Prison Mother and Baby Unit), Re

L (A Child) (Interim Care Order: Prison Mother and Baby Unit), Re; *sub nom* L (A Child) (Interim Care Order: Mother's Imprisonment), Re [2013] EWCA Civ 489; [2014] 1 F.L.R. 807; [2013] 3 F.C.R. 90; [2013] Fam. Law 940, CA (Civ Div) ..... *Digested,* 13/**1208**

L (A Child) (Leave to Oppose Making of Adoption Order), Re [2013] EWCA Civ 1481; [2014] 2 F.L.R. 913; [2014] 1 F.C.R. 613; [2014] Fam. Law 275, CA (Civ Div) ... *Digested,* 14/**1247**

L (A Child) (Parental Order: Foreign Surrogacy), Re; *sub nom* L (Commercial Surrogacy), Re [2010] EWHC 3146 (Fam); [2011] Fam. 106; [2011] 2 W.L.R. 1006; [2011] 1 F.L.R. 1423; [2011] Fam. Law 241, Fam Div ..... *Digested,* 11/**1457**: *Applied* 12/1454, 13/1334, 14/1413, 14/1415

L (A Child) (Recognition of Foreign Order), Re; *sub nom* L (A Child) (Brussels II Revised), Re [2012] EWCA Civ 1157; [2013] Fam. 94; [2013] 2 W.L.R. 152; [2013] 1 F.L.R. 430; [2013] 2 F.C.R. 195; [2012] Fam. Law 1458, CA (Civ Div); reversing [2012] EWHC 983 (Fam); [2013] 1 F.L.R. 796; [2012] Fam. Law 952, Fam Div ..... *Digested,* 13/**1284**: *Applied* 14/1432

L (Care Proceedings: Human Rights Claims), Re [2003] EWHC 665 (Fam); [2003] 2 F.L.R. 160; [2004] 1 F.C.R. 289; [2003] Fam. Law 466, Fam Div ..... *Digested,* 03/**1519**: *Applied* 04/1460, 14/2182: *Approved* 04/1461: *Considered* 08/1438

L (Children) (Preliminary Finding: Power to Reverse), Re see L-B (Children) (Care Proceedings: Power to Revise Judgment), Re

L (Commercial Surrogacy), Re see L (A Child) (Parental Order: Foreign Surrogacy), Re

L Batley Pet Products Ltd v North Lanarkshire Council [2014] UKSC 27; [2014] 3 All E.R. 64; [2014] Bus. L.R. 615; 2014 S.C. (U.K.S.C.) 174; 2014 S.L.T. 593; 2014 S.C.L.R. 501; [2014] 2 P. & C.R. 9; Times, May 12, 2014, SC; reversing [2012] CSIH 83; 2012 G.W.D. 37-745, IH (Ex Div); reversing [2012] CSOH 209; 2012 G.W.D. 4-73, OH ..... *Digested,* 14/**1978**

L Inc v S GmbH [2014] E.C.C. 25, OGH (A)

L'Oreal SA v eBay International AG (C-324/09) [2012] Bus. L.R. 1369; [2012] All E.R. (EC) 501; [2011] E.T.M.R. 52; [2012] E.M.L.R. 6; [2011] R.P.C. 27; Times, July 19, 2011, ECJ (Grand Chamber) *Applied* 12/1922, 13/1772, 13/1829: *Followed* 14/1927

L-A (Children) (Care: Chronic Neglect), Re [2009] EWCA Civ 822; [2010] 1 F.L.R. 80; [2009] Fam. Law 1025, CA (Civ Div) ..... *Digested,* 10/**1307**: *Applied* 10/1303, 10/1304, 10/1308, 11/1338: *Considered* 10/1358, 14/1331: *Followed* 14/1263

L-B (Children) (Care Proceedings: Power to Revise Judgment), Re; *sub nom* L (Children) (Preliminary Finding: Power to Reverse), Re; L-B (Children) (Reversal of Judgment), Re [2013] UKSC 8; [2013] 1 W.L.R. 634; [2013] 2 All E.R. 294; [2013] 2 F.L.R. 859; [2013] 2 F.C.R. 19; [2013] Fam. Law 664, SC; reversing [2012] EWCA Civ 984; [2013] 1 F.L.R. 209; [2012] 2 F.C.R. 591; [2012] Fam. Law 1318; (2012) 156(29) S.J.L.B. 27, CA (Civ Div) ..... *Digested,* 13/**1231**: *Explained* 14/427

L-B (Children) (Reversal of Judgment), Re see L-B (Children) (Care Proceedings: Power to Revise Judgment), Re

L-W (Children) (Contact Order: Committal), Re see L-W (Children) (Enforcement and Committal: Contact), Re

L-W (Children) (Enforcement and Committal: Contact), Re; *sub nom* CPL v CH-W; L-W (Children) (Contact Order: Committal), Re [2010] EWCA Civ 1253; [2011] 1 F.L.R. 1095; [2011] 1 F.C.R. 78; [2011] Fam. Law 14, CA (Civ Div) ..... *Digested,* 11/**1444**: *Applied* 14/1323: *Followed* 12/1400

LA v ML see MP (Fact-finding Hearing: Care Proceedings: Art.15), Re

La Mer Technology Inc v Laboratoires Goemar SA (C-259/02); *sub nom* Laboratories Goemar SA's Trade Marks (Nos.1338514 and 1402537) (C-259/02) [2004] E.C.R. I-1159; [2004] E.T.M.R. 47; [2004] F.S.R. 38, ECJ (3rd Chamber) ..... *Digested,* 04/**2417**: *Applied* 05/2518, 05/2582: *Followed* 14/1931

La Redoute (Societe), Re [2014] E.C.C. 33, Cass (F)

Laboratoires Boiron SA v Agence Centrale des Organismes de Securite Sociale (ACOSS) (C-526/04) see Laboratoires Boiron SA v Union de Recouvrement des Cotisations de Securite Sociale et d'Allocations Familiales (URSSAF) de Lyon (C-526/04)

Laboratoires Boiron SA v Union de Recouvrement des Cotisations de Securite Sociale et d'Allocations Familiales (URSSAF) de Lyon (C-526/04); *sub nom* Laboratoires Boiron SA v Agence Centrale des Organismes de Securite Sociale (ACOSS) (C-526/04) [2006] E.C.R. I-7529; [2006] 3 C.M.L.R. 50; [2007] C.E.C. 77, ECJ (2nd Chamber) ........ *Digested,* 07/**649**: *Considered* 14/3803

Laboratoires CTRS v European Commission (T-301/12) [2014] All E.R. (EC) 300; (2013) 134 B.M.L.R. 133, GC (5th Chamber)

Laboratoires Lyocentre v Laakealan turvallisuus- ja kehittamiskeskus (C-109/12) (Unreported, October 3, 2013), ECJ *Considered* 14/1528

Laboratories Goemar SA's Trade Marks (Nos.1338514 and 1402537) (C-259/02) see La Mer Technology Inc v Laboratoires Goemar SA (C-259/02)

Labour Party v Ahsan see Carter v Ahsan

Lace International Ltd v Mayor's Office for Policing and Crime see Mitsui Sumitomo Insurance Co (Europe) Ltd v Mayor's Office for Policing and Crime

Laceys (Wholesale) Footwear Ltd v Bowler International Freight Ltd [1997] 2 Lloyd's Rep. 369; Times, May 12, 1997, CA (Civ Div) ........ *Digested,* 97/**4287**: *Applied* 98/4807, 05/3455, 14/278: *Considered* 07/4215

Ladak v DRC Locums Ltd [2014] I.R.L.R. 851; [2014] I.C.R. D39, EAT ........ *Digested,* 14/**1073**

Ladbroke Group Plc v One in a Million Ltd see British Telecommunications Plc v One in a Million Ltd

Ladbrokes Betting & Gaming Ltd v Edwards [2013] EWHC 1446 (QB); [2014] L.L.R. 721, QBD

Ladbrokes Betting and Gaming Ltd v Edwards [2013] EWHC 1365 (QB); [2014] L.L.R. 715, QBD

Ladd v Marshall [1954] 1 W.L.R. 1489; [1954] 3 All E.R. 745; (1954) 98 S.J. 870, CA .. *Digested,* 54/**2507**: *Applied* 61/6769, 67/3202, 68/1544, 68/1545, 69/572, 71/3489, 73/2097, 79/318.u, 84/1737, 88/2128, 91/2927, 91/2928, 92/604, 93/1855, 95/3922, 95/504, 96/5321, 96/654, 96/656, 97/2869, 98/3200, 00/302, 01/632, 01/633, 02/2859, 02/309, 03/2235, 03/274, 03/4116, 03/943, 04/255, 05/2208, 05/2224, 05/2494, 06/310, 06/314, 06/441, 07/3364, 08/268, 09/2083, 10/1332, 10/251, 10/350, 11/239, 12/456: *Considered* 63/1013, 67/1339, 74/113.u, 74/163.u, 74/199.u, 74/226.u, 74/227.u, 74/252.u, 75/230.u, 75/374.u, 79/355.u, 80/380u, 81/361u, 82/2382, 83/2702, 83/3016, 85/1256, 86/1853, 86/2017, 87/2494, 90/1552, 91/471, 93/555, 94/2623, 94/3746, 95/3442, 95/3532, 96/2994, 96/3242, 96/5722, 96/680, 97/2865, 97/4903, 98/322, 00/305, 00/306, 00/3292, 00/562, 01/3621, 01/634, 02/270, 02/271, 02/506, 03/2242, 03/2597, 04/2030, 05/290, 05/464, 07/3387, 08/1432, 10/252, 11/1299, 11/1303, 11/2518, 11/346, 13/1576, 13/1677, 14/2000: *Distinguished* 61/2556, 61/6677, 63/603, 90/3542, 92/2059, 96/756, 97/3366, 99/3546: *Followed* 59/2147, 83/2860, 92/3290, 97/458, 12/1415: *Not applied* 97/3000, 00/3710: *Referred to* 76/470.u, 99/3153, 99/3256, 99/4014

Ladele v Islington LBC; *sub nom* Islington LBC v Ladele [2009] EWCA Civ 1357; [2010] 1 W.L.R. 955; [2010] P.T.S.R. 982; [2010] I.C.R. 532; [2010] I.R.L.R. 211; [2010] B.L.G.R. 690, CA (Civ Div); affirming [2009] I.C.R. 387; [2009] I.R.L.R. 154; [2009] B.L.G.R. 305, EAT ........ *Digested,* 10/**1115**: *Applied* 12/1682: *Complaint dismissed* 13/1548: *Considered* 10/1114, 14/1113: *Followed* 10/1114, 11/1425

Ladele v United Kingdom (51671/10) see Eweida v United Kingdom (48420/10)

Lady & Kid A/S v Skatteministeriet (C-398/09) [2012] S.T.C. 854; [2012] 1 C.M.L.R. 14; [2012] All E.R. (EC) 410; [2012] C.E.C. 517; [2012] B.V.C. 83, ECJ (Grand Chamber) *Applied* 14/3079: *Followed* 14/2874

LADYBIRD/Petition for review (R15/13) [2014] E.P.O.R. 16, EPO (Enlarged Bd App)

Lafarge Tarmac Holdings Ltd v Competition and Markets Authority [2014] CAT 5; [2014] Comp. A.R. 306, CAT ........ *Digested,* 14/**535**

Lafarge Tarmac Holdings Ltd v Competition Commission; *joined case* Hanson Quarry Products Europe Ltd v Competition Commission [2013] CAT 27; [2014] Comp. A.R. 69, CAT ........ *Digested,* 14/**544**

Lafferty v Revenue and Customs Commissioners [2014] UKFTT 358 (TC); [2014] S.T.I. 1923, FTT (Tax)

Lagden v O'Connor; *sub nom* Clark v Tull (t/a Ardington Electrical Services); *joined cases* Clark v Ardington Electrical Services; Dennard v Plant; Sen v Steelform Engineering Co Ltd; Burdis v Livsey [2003] UKHL 64; [2004] 1 A.C. 1067; [2003] 3 W.L.R. 1571; [2004] 1 All E.R. 277; [2004] R.T.R. 24; [2004] Lloyd's Rep. I.R. 315; (2003) 153 N.L.J. 1869; (2003) 147 S.J.L.B. 1430; Times, December 5, 2003, HL; affirming [2002] EWCA Civ 510; [2003] Q.B. 36; [2002] 3 W.L.R. 762; [2003] R.T.R. 3; [2002] Lloyd's Rep. I.R. 524, CA (Civ Div); reversing in part [2002] Lloyd's Rep. I.R. 138, CC (Oxford) .............................. *Digested,* 04/**630**: *Applied* 06/5246, 06/703, 07/1066, 08/896, 14/829: *Cited* 02/687, 11/4036: *Considered* 07/2497, 07/767, 14/3473, 14/830: *Distinguished* 11/4192, 11/858: *Followed* 06/1033, 11/858, 12/1898, 12/1902, 12/2812, 14/2302

Lai's Ltd v Revenue and Customs Commissioners [2014] UKFTT 212 (TC); [2014] S.T.I. 1657, FTT (Tax)

Laing v Manchester City Council [2006] I.C.R. 1519; [2006] I.R.L.R. 748, EAT ............ *Digested,* 06/**1349**: *Applied* 11/1119, 14/1011: *Approved* 07/1401

Laing v Queen, The [2013] UKPC 14; [2013] 1 W.L.R. 2670; [2014] 1 Cr. App. R. 2, PC (Ber)

Laing v Taylor Walton (A Firm); *sub nom* Taylor Walton (A Firm) v Laing [2007] EWCA Civ 1146; [2008] B.L.R. 65; [2008] P.N.L.R. 11; [2007] 47 E.G. 169 (C.S.); (2007) 104(46) L.S.G. 27, CA (Civ Div); reversing [2007] EWHC 196 (QB); [2007] 9 E.G. 202 (C.S.), QBD .............................................................. *Digested,* 08/**272**: *Applied* 14/1842: *Followed* 14/2209

Laing O'Rourke Construction Ltd (formerly Laing O'Rourke Northern Ltd) v Healthcare Support (Newcastle) Ltd [2014] EWHC 2595 (TCC); [2014] B.L.R. 722; 155 Con. L.R. 148; [2014] C.I.L.L. 3549, QBD (TCC)

Laithwaite v Revenue and Customs Commissioners [2014] UKFTT 759 (TC); [2014] S.T.I. 3083, FTT (Tax)

Lakatamia Shipping Co Ltd v Su [2014] EWHC 275 (Comm); [2014] 2 Costs L.R. 307, QBD (Comm) .............................................................. *Digested,* 14/**449**

Lakatamia Shipping Co Ltd v Su [2014] EWHC 796 (Comm); [2014] 3 Costs L.R. 532, QBD (Comm) .............................................................. *Digested,* 14/**341**

Lakatamia Shipping Co Ltd v Su [2014] EWCA Civ 636; [2014] C.P. Rep. 37; [2014] 1 C.L.C. 688, CA (Civ Div); affirming [2013] EWHC 1814 (Comm), QBD (Comm) *Digested,* 14/**405**

Lake District National Park Authority v Grace (Valuation Officer) [2014] R.A. 81, VT .... *Digested,* 14/**2479**

Lakeport Navigation Co Panama SA v Anonima Petroli Italiana SpA (The Olympic Brilliance) [1982] 2 Lloyd's Rep. 205, CA (Civ Div); affirming [1981] 2 Lloyd's Rep. 176; [1981] Com. L.R. 203, QBD (Comm) ........................................ *Digested,* 82/**2860**: *Applied* 14/2714

Laker Vent Engineering Ltd v Jacobs E&C Ltd; *joined case* Jacobs E&C Ltd v Laker Vent Engineering Ltd [2014] EWHC 1058 (TCC); 154 Con. L.R. 77, QBD (TCC) .............................................................. *Digested,* 14/**114**

Lamb v Revenue and Customs Prosecutions Office see Pigott, Re

Lambert v Barratt Homes Ltd [2010] EWCA Civ 681; [2010] B.L.R. 527; 131 Con. L.R. 29; [2011] H.L.R. 1; [2010] 2 E.G.L.R. 59; [2010] 33 E.G. 72; [2010] J.P.L. 1625; [2010] 25 E.G. 103 (C.S.); [2010] N.P.C. 69; [2010] Env. L.R. D8, CA (Civ Div); reversing in part [2009] EWHC 744 (QB); [2009] 2 E.G.L.R. 63; [2009] 32 E.G. 70; [2009] Env. L.R. D14, QBD (Leeds) .............................. *Digested,* 10/**2300**: *Considered* 14/2220

Lambert v Lewis; *sub nom* Lexmead (Basingstoke) Ltd v Lewis [1982] A.C. 225; [1981] 2 W.L.R. 713; [1981] 1 All E.R. 1185; [1981] 2 Lloyd's Rep. 17; [1981] R.T.R. 346; (1981) 125 S.J. 310, HL; reversing [1980] 2 W.L.R. 299; [1980] 1 All E.R. 978; [1980] 1 Lloyd's Rep. 311; [1980] R.T.R. 152; (1980) 124 S.J. 50, CA (Civ Div); reversing in part [1978] 1 Lloyd's Rep. 610; [1979] R.T.R. 61; (1981) 78 L.S.G. 597, QBD .............................................................. *Digested,* 81/**1841**: *Applied* 85/2331: *Considered* 14/617: *Referred to* 88/3408

Lambeth LBC v Johnston [2008] EWCA Civ 690; [2009] H.L.R. 10; [2008] N.P.C. 70; Times, June 30, 2008, CA (Civ Div) .............................................................. *Digested,* 08/**1846**: *Applied* 09/1899, 12/1623: *Followed* 11/1656, 14/1602

Lambeth LBC v Kay see Kay v Lambeth LBC

Lambeth LBC v Loveridge; *sub nom* Loveridge v Lambeth LBC [2014] UKSC 65; [2014] 1 W.L.R. 4516; Times, December 11, 2014, SC; reversing [2013] EWCA Civ 494; [2013] 1 W.L.R. 3390; [2013] 3 All E.R. 261; [2013] H.L.R. 31; [2013] 21 E.G. 106 (C.S.); [2013] 2 P. & C.R. DG13, CA (Civ Div) .............................. *Digested,* 13/**1896**

Lambeth LBC v O'Kane; *joined case* Helena Housing Ltd v Pinder [2005] EWCA Civ 1010; [2006] H.L.R. 2; [2005] 32 E.G. 67 (C.S.); [2005] N.P.C. 110; Times, September 22, 2005, CA (Civ Div) .............................................................. *Digested,* 06/**2719**: *Applied* 14/2003

Lambeth LBC v Rumbelow HC2000 00723, Ch D
*Applied* 14/1588

Lambeth Overseers v London CC; *sub nom* London CC v Lambeth Overseers [1897] A.C. 625, HL; affirming [1896] 2 Q.B. 25, CA; reversing [1895] 2 Q.B. 511, QBD
*Applied* 47-51/6987, 57/2963, 61/7463: *Considered* 85/2889, 14/2526: *Distinguished* 61/7444: *Followed* 52/2890

Lambourn v McLellan [1903] 2 Ch. 268, CA; affirming [1903] 1 Ch. 806, Ch D
*Considered* 14/1973

Lamichhane v Secretary of State for the Home Department [2012] EWCA Civ 260; [2012] 1 W.L.R. 3064; [2012] Imm. A.R. 683; Times, May 30, 2012, CA (Civ Div) ........ *Digested,* 12/**1730**:
*Applied* 12/1760: *Considered* 13/1599, 14/1679

Lammerzahl GmbH v Freie Hansestadt Bremen (C-241/06) [2007] E.C.R. I-8415; [2008] 1 C.M.L.R. 19, ECJ (3rd Chamber) ........ *Digested,* 08/**3019**:
*Applied* 11/2634: *Considered* 14/2475

Lamovec v Slovenia (Admissibility) (31765/08) (2014) 59 E.H.R.R. SE8, ECHR

Lanarkshire Valuation Joint Board Assessor v Jane Norman Ltd see Assessor for Lanarkshire Valuation Joint Board v Jane Norman Ltd

Lancashire CC v Lord (Valuation Officer) [1987] R.A. 153, Lands Tr ........ *Digested,* 87/**3172**:
*Applied* 14/2479

Lancashire CC v R; *sub nom* N (A Child) (Fact-finding Hearing: Accidental Injury), Re [2013] EWHC 3064 (Fam); (2014) 135 B.M.L.R. 153; [2014] Fam. Law 28, Fam Div (Liverpool) ........ *Digested,* 14/**1406**

Lancashire CC v SB see W (A Child) (Care Proceedings: ABE Interviews), Re

Lancaster City Council v Thomas Newell Ltd see Thomas Newall Ltd v Lancaster City Council

Land Baden-Wurttemberg v Tsakouridis (C-145/09) [2011] 2 C.M.L.R. 11; [2013] All E.R. (EC) 183; [2011] C.E.C. 714; [2011] Imm. A.R. 276; [2011] I.N.L.R. 415, ECJ (Grand Chamber)
*Considered* 13/1647: *Followed* 12/1708, 13/1595, 14/1675, 14/1676

Land Berlin v Beneficiaries of Land Restitution (BGH V ZR 232/1) [2014] I.L.Pr. 44, BGH (Ger)

Land Securities Plc v Revenue and Customs Commissioners [2013] UKUT 124 (TCC); [2013] S.T.C. 1043; 81 T.C. 843; [2013] B.T.C. 1773; [2013] S.T.I. 1493, UT (Tax); affirming [2011] UKFTT 599 (TC); [2012] S.F.T.D. 215, FTT (Tax) ........ *Digested,* 13/**3028**

Landelijke Vereniging tot Behoud van de Waddenzee v Staatssecretaris van Landbouw, Natuurbeheer en Visserij (C-127/02) [2004] E.C.R. I-7405; [2005] 2 C.M.L.R. 31; [2005] All E.R. (EC) 353; [2005] Env. L.R. 14; [2004] N.P.C. 136, ECJ ........ *Digested,* 05/**1439**:
*Applied* 09/1353, 10/1189: *Considered* 08/2967, 10/1227, 14/1188

Landesbank Hessen-Thuringen Girozentrale v Bayerische Landesbank (London Branch) [2014] EWHC 1404 (Comm); [2014] 2 B.C.L.C. 681, QBD (Comm)

Lane v Esdaile; *sub nom* Esdaile v Payne [1891] A.C. 210, HL; affirming (1889) 40 Ch. D. 520, CA
*Applied* 83/2997, 86/91, 88/2894, 92/3505, 06/204, 13/455, 14/10: *Distinguished* 90/3733: *Followed* 60/1949, 00/360: *Not applied* 98/381

Lanes Group Plc v Galliford Try Infrastructure Ltd (t/a Galliford Try Rail) [2011] EWCA Civ 1617; [2012] Bus. L.R. 1184; [2012] 1 C.L.C. 129; [2012] B.L.R. 121; 141 Con. L.R. 46; [2012] 1 E.G.L.R. 27; [2012] 13 E.G. 92; [2012] C.I.L.L. 3116, CA (Civ Div) ........ *Digested,* 12/**581**:
*Considered* 14/577

Langhorne v Revenue and Customs Commissioners [2014] UKFTT 533 (TC); [2014] S.T.I. 2163, FTT (Tax)

Langton v Secretary of State for Health [2014] I.C.R. D2, EAT

Laskar v Laskar [2008] EWCA Civ 347; [2008] 1 W.L.R. 2695; [2008] 2 F.L.R. 589; [2008] 2 P. & C.R. 14; [2008] 2 E.G.L.R. 70; [2008] 21 E.G. 140; [2008] Fam. Law 638; [2008] 7 E.G. 142 (C.S.); Times, March 4, 2008, CA (Civ Div) ........ *Digested,* 08/**3104**:
*Considered* 11/3500: *Distinguished* 14/2492

Latreefers Inc, Re see Stocznia Gdanska SA v Latreefers Inc

Laughtons Photographs Ltd v Customs and Excise Commissioners see Direct Cosmetics Ltd v Customs and Excise Commissioners (C-138/86)

Lavarack v Woods of Colchester [1967] 1 Q.B. 278; [1966] 3 W.L.R. 706; [1966] 3 All E.R. 683; 1 K.I.R. 312; (1966) 110 S.J. 770, CA ........ *Digested,* 66/**4415**:
*Applied* 84/1014, 98/2098, 14/827: *Distinguished* 73/1140, 03/1216, 05/1212: *Followed* 97/6006

Lavelle v Lavelle [2004] EWCA Civ 223; [2004] 2 F.C.R. 418; Times, March 9, 2004, CA (Civ Div)
*Applied* 14/2490

Laverty v British Gas Trading Ltd [2014] EWHC 2721 (Ch); [2014] B.C.C. 701, Ch D (Companies Ct)

Lavrov v Estonia see Lithuania v Bucnys

Law Society v Beller [2014] EWHC 3923 (Ch); [2014] 5 Costs L.O. 683; [2014] B.P.I.R. 1480, Ch D

Law Society v Kordowski [2011] EWHC 3185 (QB); [2014] E.M.L.R. 2; [2011] Info. T.L.R. 221; (2012) 109(1) L.S.G. 13, QBD

Law Society v Sephton & Co [2006] UKHL 22; [2006] 2 A.C. 543; [2006] 2 W.L.R. 1091; [2006] 3 All E.R. 401; [2006] P.N.L.R. 31; (2006) 156 N.L.J. 844; (2006) 150 S.J.L.B. 669; [2006] N.P.C. 56; Times, May 11, 2006, HL; affirming [2004] EWCA Civ 1627; [2005] Q.B. 1013; [2005] 3 W.L.R. 212; [2005] P.N.L.R. 21; (2005) 102(5) L.S.G. 29; (2005) 149 S.J.L.B. 56; Times, January 11, 2005, CA (Civ Div); reversing in part [2004] EWHC 544 (Ch); [2004] P.N.L.R. 27, Ch D .... *Digested,* 06/**474**:
*Applied* 08/384, 13/391: *Considered* 07/2490, 08/382, 09/2735, 14/2523, 14/591: *Distinguished* 08/2651, 10/2284: *Explained* 09/426: *Followed* 07/479, 13/2087

Law Society (Solicitors Regulation Authority) v Emeana [2013] EWHC 2130 (Admin); [2014] A.C.D. 14; (2013) 157(30) S.J.L.B. 31, QBD (Admin)

Lawal v Northern Spirit Ltd [2003] UKHL 35; [2004] 1 All E.R. 187; [2003] I.C.R. 856; [2003] I.R.L.R. 538; [2003] H.R.L.R. 29; [2003] U.K.H.R.R. 1024; (2003) 100(28) L.S.G. 30; (2003) 153 N.L.J. 1005; (2003) 147 S.J.L.B. 783; Times, June 27, 2003, HL; reversing [2002] EWCA Civ 1218; [2003] C.P. Rep. 21; [2002] I.C.R. 1507; [2002] I.R.L.R. 714; [2002] H.R.L.R. 46; [2003] U.K.H.R.R. 238; (2002) 99(46) L.S.G. 33; Times, November 7, 2002, CA (Civ Div); affirming [2002] I.C.R. 486; [2002] I.R.L.R. 228; Times, January 29, 2002, EAT *Digested,* 03/**1251**:
*Applied* 05/2908, 08/834, 10/1722, 12/3336: *Considered* 04/1904, 06/207, 11/4135: *Distinguished* 14/42

Lawless v Ireland (No.3) (A/3) (1979-80) 1 E.H.R.R. 15, ECHR .................................... *Digested,* 79/**1172**:
*Considered* 14/2464

Lawrence v Coventry (t/a RDC Promotions) see Coventry (t/a RDC Promotions) v Lawrence

Lawrence v Coventry (t/a RDC Promotions) see Coventry v Lawrence

Lawrence v Fen Tigers Ltd see Coventry (t/a RDC Promotions) v Lawrence

Lawrence v Fen Tigers Ltd see Coventry v Lawrence

Lawrence v Regent Office Care Ltd (C-320/00) [2002] E.C.R. I-7325; [2002] 3 C.M.L.R. 27; [2003] I.C.R. 1092; [2002] I.R.L.R. 822; [2002] Emp. L.R. 1248; Times, October 10, 2002, ECJ .............................................................................. *Digested,* 02/**1363**:
*Applied* 05/1258, 13/1011: *Considered* 04/1253, 04/1258, 09/1206, 14/3503

Lawson v Governing Body of Aylesford School see Grosvenor v Aylesford School Governors

Lawson v Serco Ltd; *sub nom* Serco Ltd v Lawson; *joined cases* Crofts v Veta Ltd; Botham v Ministry of Defence [2006] UKHL 3; [2006] 1 All E.R. 823; [2006] I.C.R. 250; [2006] I.R.L.R. 289; (2006) 103(6) L.S.G. 36; (2006) 156 N.L.J. 184; (2006) 150 S.J.L.B. 131; Times, January 27, 2006, HL; reversing [2004] EWCA Civ 12; [2004] 2 All E.R. 200; [2004] I.C.R. 204; [2004] I.R.L.R. 206; (2004) 148 S.J.L.B. 148; Times, January 30, 2004, CA (Civ Div); reversing EAT/0018/02TM, EAT ........................................................................................ *Digested,* 06/**1390**:
*Applied* 05/1210, 05/1329, 07/1355, 08/1171, 08/1214, 10/1146, 11/1134, 12/1181: *Considered* 08/1201, 08/17, 11/4227, 12/1143, 12/1176, 13/1075, 14/1077: *Followed* 09/1264, 10/1036, 10/1145, 11/1070: *Not followed* 03/1264

Layard Horsfall Ltd v Legal Ombudsman [2013] EWHC 4137 (QB); [2014] 2 Costs L.O. 277; (2014) 164(7590) N.L.J. 20, QBD (Admin) ........................................ *Digested,* 14/**2054**

Layher AB v Mon.Zon Sverige AB [2014] E.T.M.R. 14, HR (Swe)

LB v Croydon HA see B v Croydon HA

LB v Merton LBC; *sub nom* B (A Child), Re [2013] EWCA Civ 476; [2014] 1 F.L.R. 1066; [2013] Fam. Law 941, CA (Civ Div)

LB Holdings Intermediate 2 Ltd (In Administration), Re see Lehman Brothers International (Europe) (In Administration), Re

LB RE Financing No.1 Ltd v Trustees of the Lehman Brothers Pension Scheme see Trustees of the Lehman Brothers Pension Scheme v Pensions Regulator

LBX v TT [2014] EWCOP 24; [2014] C.O.P.L.R. 561, CP

LC (Children) (Abduction: Habitual Residence: State of Mind of Child), Re see LC (Children) (International Abduction: Child's Objections to Return), Re

LC (Children) (Habitual Residence: Grave Risk of Harm), Re; *sub nom* M v F [2014] EWFC 8; [2014] Fam. Law 1377, Fam Div

LC (Children) (International Abduction: Child's Objections to Return), Re; *sub nom* LC (Children) (Abduction: Habitual Residence: State of Mind of Child), Re; LCG v RL (Abduction: Habitual Residence and Child's Objection) [2014] UKSC 1; [2014] A.C. 1038; [2014] 2 W.L.R. 124; [2014] 1 All E.R. 1181; [2014] 1 F.L.R. 1486; [2014] 1 F.C.R. 491; [2014] Fam. Law 408; (2014) 158(4) S.J.L.B. 49; Times, January 21, 2014, SC; reversing [2013] EWCA Civ 1058; [2014] 1 F.L.R. 1458; [2014] Fam. Law 9, CA (Civ Div); reversing [2013] EWHC 1383 (Fam); [2014] 1 F.L.R. 307; [2013] Fam. Law 1119, Fam Div ............................ *Digested,* 14/**1378**: *Considered* 14/1381: *Followed* 14/1310

LCG v RL (Abduction: Habitual Residence and Child's Objection) see LC (Children) (International Abduction: Child's Objections to Return), Re

LCL Le Credit Lyonnais SA v Kalhan (C-565/12) [2014] 3 C.M.L.R. 29, ECJ (4th Chamber)

LE (Jamaica) v Secretary of State for the Home Department see R. (on the application of LE (Jamaica)) v Secretary of State for the Home Department

Le Compte v Belgium (A/43); *joined cases* De Meyere v Belgium (A/43); Van Leuven v Belgium (A/43) [1982] E.C.C. 240; (1982) 4 E.H.R.R. 1, ECHR; reversing [1980] E.C.C. 294, Eur Comm HR
*Applied* 97/2811, 98/3120, 98/3156, 00/2212, 05/2734, 08/1931, 14/287: *Considered* 07/1951, 09/1739, 11/1061

Le Credit Lyonnais v Ministre du Budget, des Comptes publics et de la Reforme de l'Etat (C-388/11) [2014] S.T.C. 245; [2014] C.E.C. 382; [2013] B.V.C. 460; [2013] S.T.I. 3568, ECJ (1st Chamber)

Le Rayon d'Or Sarl v Ministre de l'Economie et des Finances (C-151/13) [2014] S.T.C. 1165; [2014] B.V.C. 25; [2014] S.T.I. 1579, ECJ (6th Chamber)

Leach v Office of Communications; *sub nom* A v B [2012] EWCA Civ 959; [2012] I.C.R. 1269; [2012] I.R.L.R. 839, CA (Civ Div); affirming [2010] I.R.L.R. 844, EAT ............................................ *Digested,* 12/**1175**: *Followed* 14/1137

Leachinsky v Christie see Christie v Leachinsky

Leander v Sweden (9248/81) see Leander v Sweden (A/116)

Leander v Sweden (A/116); *sub nom* Leander v Sweden (9248/81) (1987) 9 E.H.R.R. 433; Times, April 25, 1987, ECHR; no effect (1985) 7 E.H.R.R. CD557, Eur Comm HR; no effect (1984) 6 E.H.R.R. CD541, Eur Comm HR ........................ *Digested,* 87/**1919**: *Applied* 98/3096, 02/1835, 02/57, 07/2249, 07/2258, 11/1082, 11/599, 14/436: *Considered* 00/3248, 10/1079, 10/332, 12/1657

Lebedev v Russia (13772/05) see Khodorkovskiy v Russia (11082/06)

Ledger v Revenue and Customs Commissioners [2014] UKFTT 962 (TC); [2014] S.T.I. 3216, FTT (Tax)

Ledger v Wootton [2007] EWHC 2599 (Ch); [2008] W.T.L.R. 235, Ch D (Birmingham) *Digested,* 08/**3617**: *Applied* 14/2841

Ledra Fisheries Ltd v Turner [2003] EWHC 1049 (Ch), Ch D
*Applied* 14/303

Lee v United Kingdom (57877/09) see James v United Kingdom (25119/09)

Leeds City Council v Hall see Hounslow LBC v Powell

Leeds City Council v Price see Kay v Lambeth LBC

Leeds City Council v Revenue and Customs Commissioners [2013] UKUT 596 (TCC); [2014] S.T.C. 789; [2014] B.V.C. 501, UT (Tax) ............................ *Digested,* 14/**3077**

Leeds City Council v Revenue and Customs Commissioners [2014] UKUT 350 (TCC); [2014] B.V.C. 531, UT (Tax) ............................ *Digested,* 14/**2983**

Leeds Dental Team Ltd v Rose [2014] I.C.R. 94; [2014] I.R.L.R. 8, EAT .................... *Digested,* 14/**1023**

Leeds Design Innovation Centre Ltd v Revenue and Customs Commissioners [2014] UKFTT 9 (TC); [2014] S.F.T.D. 681; [2014] S.T.I. 693, FTT (Tax) .................... *Digested,* 14/**2909**

Leeds Permanent Building Society v United Kingdom (21449/93) see National & Provincial Building Society v United Kingdom (21319/93)

Leeds Shipping Co v Societe Francaise Bunge SA (The Eastern City) [1958] 2 Lloyd's Rep. 127, CA; affirming [1957] 2 Lloyd's Rep. 153; Times, July 17, 1957, QBD (Comm) ............................ *Digested,* 58/**3144**: *Applied* 77/2760, 95/4517: *Approved* 79/2445: *Considered* 69/3301, 78/2723, 07/3817, 10/3045: *Followed* 14/2726

Leeds United Football Club Ltd v Chief Constable of West Yorkshire [2013] EWCA Civ 115; [2014] Q.B. 168; [2013] 3 W.L.R. 539; [2013] 2 All E.R. 760, CA (Civ Div); affirming [2012] EWHC 2113 (QB); [2013] L.L.R. 380, QBD ............................ *Digested,* 13/**2388**

Leek v Donkersley see GKN Bolts & Nuts Ltd (Automotive Division) Birmingham Works Sports & Social Club, Re

Lees v Solihull Magistrates' Court [2013] EWHC 3779 (Admin); [2014] Lloyd's Rep. F.C. 233, DC ............................ *Digested,* 14/**805**

Leeson v Marsden see Collier v Williams

Legal Equitable Securities, Re; *sub nom* Beller v Linton [2010] EWHC 2046 (Ch); [2011] B.C.C. 354; [2010] B.P.I.R. 1151, Ch D .................................................. *Digested,* 11/**328**: *Applied* 11/1876, 14/1757

Lego Juris A/S v Office for Harmonisation in the Internal Market (Trade Marks and Designs) (OHIM) (C-48/09 P) [2010] E.C.R. I-8403; [2010] E.T.M.R. 63, ECJ (Grand Chamber) *Considered* 14/1932

Lehman Brothers International (Europe) (In Administration) v CRC Credit Fund Ltd see Lehman Brothers International (Europe) (In Administration), Re

Lehman Brothers International (Europe) (In Administration) v Lehman Brothers Finance SA see Lehman Brothers International (Europe) (In Administration), Re

Lehman Brothers International (Europe) (In Administration), Re [2013] EWHC 1664 (Ch); [2014] B.C.C. 132, Ch D .................................................. *Digested,* 14/**480**

Lehman Brothers International (Europe) (In Administration), Re [2012] EWHC 2997 (Ch); [2014] 2 B.C.L.C. 295, Ch D (Companies Ct)

Lehman Brothers International (Europe) (In Administration), Re [2009] EWCA Civ 1161; [2010] Bus. L.R. 489; [2010] B.C.C. 272; [2010] 1 B.C.L.C. 496; Times, November 12, 2009, CA (Civ Div); affirming [2009] EWHC 2141 (Ch), Ch D (Companies Ct) .................................................. *Digested,* 10/**1893**: *Applied* 14/500

Lehman Brothers International (Europe) (In Administration), Re; *sub nom* Contrarian Funds LLC v Lomas [2014] EWHC 1687 (Ch); [2014] Bus. L.R. 1186; [2014] 2 B.C.L.C. 651; [2014] B.P.I.R. 1259, Ch D (Companies Ct) .................................................. *Digested,* 14/**1757**

Lehman Brothers International (Europe) (In Administration), Re; *sub nom* Lomas v Rab Market Cycles (Master) Fund Ltd [2009] EWHC 2545 (Ch), Ch D (Companies Ct) *Considered* 10/1835, 11/187, 14/1755

Lehman Brothers International (Europe) (In Administration), Re; *sub nom* Lehman Brothers International (Europe) (In Administration) v Lehman Brothers Finance SA [2013] EWCA Civ 188; [2014] 2 B.C.L.C. 451, CA (Civ Div); reversing [2012] EWHC 1072 (Ch), Ch D (Companies Ct)

Lehman Brothers International (Europe) (In Administration), Re; *sub nom* Lehman Brothers International (Europe) (In Administration) v CRC Credit Fund Ltd; CRC Credit Fund Ltd v GLG Investments Plc Sub-Fund: European Equity Fund [2012] UKSC 6; [2012] 3 All E.R. 1; [2012] Bus. L.R. 667; [2012] 1 B.C.L.C. 487; [2012] W.T.L.R. 1355; (2012) 162 N.L.J. 364; Times, March 12, 2012, SC; affirming [2010] EWCA Civ 917; [2011] Bus. L.R. 277; [2011] 2 B.C.L.C. 184; [2011] 1 C.M.L.R. 27, CA (Civ Div); reversing in part [2009] EWHC 3228 (Ch); [2010] 2 B.C.L.C. 301, Ch D (Companies Ct) .................................................. *Digested,* 12/**1786**: *Considered* 13/223, 13/3791, 14/1751

Lehman Brothers International (Europe) (In Administration), Re; *joined cases* LB Holdings Intermediate 2 Ltd (In Administration), Re; Lehman Brothers Ltd (In Administration), Re [2014] EWHC 704 (Ch); [2014] 3 W.L.R. 466; [2014] B.C.C. 193, Ch D (Companies Ct) .................................................. *Digested,* 14/**1752**

Lehman Brothers International (Europe) (In Administration), Re see Bloom v Pensions Regulator

Lehman Brothers Ltd (In Administration), Re see Lehman Brothers International (Europe) (In Administration), Re

Lehman Companies, Re see Bloom v Pensions Regulator

Leicester City Council v Chhatbar [2014] EWHC 830 (Fam); [2014] 2 F.L.R. 1365; [2014] Fam. Law 802, Fam Div

Leicester City Council v S [2014] EWHC 1575 (Fam); [2014] Fam. Law 1245, Fam Div

Leicester City Council v Shearer [2013] EWCA Civ 1467; [2014] H.L.R. 8, CA (Civ Div) .................................................. *Digested,* 14/**1622**

Leidseplein Beheer BV v Red Bull GmbH (C-65/12) [2014] Bus. L.R. 280; [2014] E.T.M.R. 24, ECJ (1st Chamber)

Leigh v Certibilt Investments [1988] 04 E.G. 127, Unknown court .................................................. *Digested,* 88/**2071**: *Considered* 14/2004

Leigh v Hudson see Hudson v Leigh

Leigh v London Ambulance Service NHS Trust [2014] EWHC 286 (QB); [2014] Med. L.R. 134, QBD

Leigh v London Ambulance Service NHS Trust (Quantum) (Unreported, February 20, 2014), QBD [*Russell-Cooke LLP, 2 Putney Hill, Putney, London*] .................................................. *Digested,* 14/**2349**

Leighton v Charlambous see Leighton v Michael

Leighton v Michael; *joined case* Leighton v Charlambous [1995] I.C.R. 1091; [1996] I.R.L.R. 67; Times, October 26, 1995, EAT .................................................. *Digested,* 95/**2045**: *Applied* 98/2227, 14/1119: *Approved* 00/2205: *Considered* 03/1218

Leisure (Norwich) II Ltd v Luminar Lava Ignite Ltd (In Administration); *sub nom* Luminar Oceana Ltd, Re; Luminar Lava Gems Ltd, Re; Luminar Liquid Ltd, Re; Luminar Lava Ignite Ltd, Re; *joined cases* X-Scape Milton Keynes Ltd v Luminar Oceana Ltd; XL (Maidstone) Ltd v Luminar Gems Ltd; XL (Maidstone) Ltd v Luminar Liquid Ltd [2012] EWHC 951 (Ch); [2014] Ch. 165; [2013] 3 W.L.R. 1132; [2012] 4 All E.R. 894; [2012] B.C.C. 497; [2013] 2 B.C.L.C. 115; [2012] L. & T.R. 29, Ch D ........ *Digested,* 12/**1794**: *Overruled* 14/1756

Lemon v Chawda see Chawda, Re

Lemonious v Church Commissioners UKEAT/0253/12/KN, EAT *Applied* 14/1133

Lennon v Birmingham City Council [2001] EWCA Civ 435; [2001] I.R.L.R. 826, CA (Civ Div) ........ *Digested,* 02/**1354**: *Considered* 02/1309: *Followed* 14/387

Les Laboratoires Servier v Apotex Inc [2014] UKSC 55; [2014] 3 W.L.R. 1257; [2014] Bus. L.R. 1217; Times, November 17, 2014, SC; affirming [2012] EWCA Civ 593; [2013] Bus. L.R. 80; [2013] R.P.C. 21, CA (Civ Div) ........ *Digested,* 13/**1797**

Lesoochranarske Zoskupenie VLK v Ministerstvo Zivotneho Prostredia Slovenskej Republiky (C-240/09) [2012] Q.B. 606; [2012] 3 W.L.R. 278; [2012] P.T.S.R. 822; [2011] 2 C.M.L.R. 43; [2012] All E.R. (EC) 1; [2011] Env. L.R. 28, ECJ (Grand Chamber) *Cited* 14/339

Letterstedt v Broers; *sub nom* Vicomtesse Montmort v Broers (1884) 9 App. Cas. 371; [1881-85] All E.R. Rep. 882, PC (Cape) *Applied* 07/3956, 10/3449, 14/2818, 14/3276: *Considered* 85/3131

Letting International Ltd v Newham LBC [2007] EWCA Civ 1522; [2008] Eu. L.R. 517, CA (Civ Div) *Considered* 11/2627: *Followed* 14/2477

LEVEL 3/Tracking electronic content (T901/10) [2014] E.P.O.R. 43, EPO (Technical Bd App)

Leventoglu Abdulkadiroglu v Turkey (7971/07) 36 B.H.R.C. 223, ECHR

Levob Verzekeringen BV v Staatssecretaris van Financien (C-41/04) [2006] S.T.C. 766; [2005] E.C.R. I-9433; [2006] 2 C.M.L.R. 8; [2006] C.E.C. 424; [2007] B.T.C. 5186; [2007] B.V.C. 155; [2005] S.T.I. 1777, ECJ (1st Chamber) ........ *Digested,* 06/**4501**: *Applied* 07/4332, 07/4341, 08/4035, 08/4048, 09/4098, 09/4099, 09/4106, 13/3229: *Considered* 12/3420: *Distinguished* 12/3438: *Followed* 08/4041, 09/4100, 10/3519, 13/3221, 14/3050

Lewis v Associated Newspapers Ltd see Rubber Improvement Ltd v Daily Telegraph Ltd

Lewis v Condon [2013] NSWCA 204; 17 I.T.E.L.R. 185, CA (NSW)

Lewis v Daily Telegraph Ltd see Rubber Improvement Ltd v Daily Telegraph Ltd

Lewis v Lewis [2014] EWCA Civ 412; [2014] W.T.L.R. 1021, CA (Civ Div) ........ *Digested,* 14/**434**

Lewis v Three Rivers DC [2013] EWHC 3250 (Admin); [2014] J.P.L. 636, DC ........ *Digested,* 14/**2435**

Lewisham LBC v South London Healthcare NHS Trust Special Administrator see R. (on the application of Lewisham LBC) v Secretary of State for Health

Lex Services Plc v Customs and Excise Commissioners; *sub nom* Customs and Excise Commissioners v Lex Services Plc; *joined cases* Kuwait Petroleum (GB) Ltd v Customs and Excise Commissioners; Bugeja v Customs and Excise Commissioners (No.2); Littlewoods Organisation Plc v Customs and Excise Commissioners [2003] UKHL 67; [2004] 1 W.L.R. 1; [2004] 1 All E.R. 434; [2004] S.T.C. 73; [2004] R.T.R. 18; [2003] B.T.C. 5658; [2004] B.V.C. 53; [2003] S.T.I. 2274; (2004) 101(3) L.S.G. 34; (2003) 147 S.J.L.B. 1430; Times, December 5, 2003, HL; affirming [2001] EWCA Civ 1542; [2001] S.T.C. 1568; [2002] R.T.R. 16; [2001] B.T.C. 5608; [2002] B.V.C. 71; [2001] S.T.I. 1381; (2001) 98(46) L.S.G. 36; (2001) 145 S.J.L.B. 254; (2001) 145 S.J.L.B. 255; Times, November 7, 2001, CA (Civ Div); affirming [2000] S.T.C. 697; [2001] R.T.R. 9; [2000] B.T.C. 5305; [2000] B.V.C. 338; [2000] S.T.I. 1061; Times, October 17, 2000; Independent, October 30, 2000, Ch D (Companies Ct); affirming [1999] B.V.C. 2307; [1999] V. & D.R. 156, V&DTr ........ *Digested,* 04/**4016**: *Applied* 04/4006, 06/4514, 08/4028: *Considered* 02/4783, 11/3572, 14/3081: *Distinguished* 04/3973: *Followed* 14/3079

Lexgorge Ltd v Howard de Walden Estates Ltd see Day v Hosebay Ltd

Lexmead (Basingstoke) Ltd v Lewis see Lambert v Lewis

Leyton Sixth Form College v Revenue and Customs Commissioners [2013] UKFTT 660 (TC); [2014] S.T.I. 384, FTT (Tax)

LG Blower Specialist Bricklayer Ltd v Reeves see Gibbon v Manchester City Council

LG CHEM LTD/Method for making lithium battery (T1766/13) [2014] E.P.O.R. 37, EPO (Technical Bd App)

LG Display Co Ltd v European Commission (T-128/11) [2014] 4 C.M.L.R. 24, GC (6th Chamber)

LH (Nigeria) v Secretary of State for the Home Department [2013] EWCA Civ 26; [2013] Imm. A.R. 769, CA (Civ Div) ........ *Digested,* 14/**1673**

Libert v Gouvernement Flamand (C-197/11); *joined case* All Projects & Developments NV v Vlaamse Regering (C-203/11) [2013] 3 C.M.L.R. 35; [2014] All E.R. (EC) 424, ECJ (1st Chamber)

Libertarian Investments Ltd v Hall 17 I.T.E.L.R. 1, CA (HK)

Libertel Groep BV v Benelux-Merkenbureau (C-104/01) [2004] Ch. 83; [2004] 2 W.L.R. 1081; [2003] E.C.R. I-3793; [2005] 2 C.M.L.R. 45; [2003] E.T.M.R. 63; [2004] F.S.R. 4; Times, May 12, 2003, ECJ; no effect [2003] E.C.R. I-3793; [2003] E.T.M.R. 41, AGO ........ *Digested,* 03/**2599**:
*Applied* 04/2370, 05/2529, 05/2533: *Considered* 05/2532, 07/2673, 13/1758:
*Explained* 14/1933: *Followed* 05/2553, 13/1821

Liberty International Plc, Re; *joined case* Capital & Counties Properties Plc, Re [2010] EWHC 1060 (Ch); [2010] 2 B.C.L.C. 665; [2011] Bus. L.R. D17, Ch D (Companies Ct) ........ *Digested,* 11/**421**:
*Applied* 14/517: *Considered* 12/3861

Liberty Mercian Ltd v Cuddy Civil Engineering Ltd [2013] EWHC 2688 (TCC); [2014] 1 All E.R. (Comm) 761; [2014] B.L.R. 179; [2013] T.C.L.R. 9; 150 Con. L.R. 124, QBD (TCC) ........ *Digested,* 13/**571**

Liberty Mercian Ltd v Cuddy Civil Engineering Ltd [2013] EWHC 4110 (TCC); [2014] C.I.L.L. 3469, QBD (TCC)

Liberty Mercian Ltd v Cuddy Civil Engineering Ltd [2014] EWHC 3584 (TCC); 157 Con. L.R. 72; [2014] C.I.L.L. 3583, QBD (TCC)

Lictor Anstalt v Mir Steel UK Ltd [2014] EWHC 3316 (CH); [2014] 6 Costs L.O. 918, Ch D

Lidl (UK) GmbH v Ryder (Valuation Officer) [2013] UKUT 348 (LC); [2014] R.A. 23, UT (Lands) ........ *Digested,* 14/**2484**

Lie v Mohile [2014] EWCA Civ 728; [2014] 2 P. & C.R. 13, CA (Civ Div) ........ *Digested,* 14/**1995**

Lifeline Europe Ltd v Revenue and Customs Commissioners [2014] UKUT 135 (TCC); [2014] S.T.C. 1974; [2014] B.V.C. 514, UT (Tax); affirming [2012] UKFTT 424 (TC), FTT (Tax) ........ *Digested,* 14/**3067**

Lifeline Europe Ltd v Revenue and Customs Commissioners see Universal Enterprises (EU) Ltd v Revenue and Customs Commissioners

Lifestyle Supplies VoF v Ultimate Nutrition Inc (R 1462/2012-G) [2014] E.T.M.R. 27, OHIM (Grand Bd App)

Liggett v Northern Bank Ltd [2013] B.P.I.R. 595, Ch D (NI) ........ *Digested,* 14/**3195**

Lim v Royal Wolverhampton Hospitals NHS Trust [2011] EWHC 2178 (QB); [2012] Med. L.R. 146; (2011) 122 B.M.L.R. 43, QBD ........ *Digested,* 12/**1527**:
*Not followed* 14/1554

Lim v Walia [2014] EWCA Civ 1076; [2014] 3 F.C.R. 284; [2014] Fam. Law 1517, CA (Civ Div) ........ *Digested,* 14/**2823**

Lim (EEA: Dependency: Malaysia); *sub nom* Entry Clearance Officer, Manila v Lim [2013] UKUT 437 (IAC); [2014] Imm. A.R. 358; [2014] I.N.L.R. 484, UT (IAC) ... *Digested,* 14/**1685**

Lincolnshire CC v Mouchel Business Services Ltd [2014] EWHC 352 (TCC); [2014] B.L.R. 347; [2014] T.C.L.R. 3; [2014] C.I.L.L. 3484, QBD (TCC) ........ *Digested,* 14/**439**

Lindsay v London School of Economics and Political Science see London School of Economics and Political Science v Lindsay

Lindum Construction Co Ltd v Office of Fair Trading [2014] EWHC 1613 (Ch); [2014] Bus. L.R. 681, Ch D ........ *Digested,* 14/**548**

Line v Baker [2014] EWHC 1368 (Ch); [2014] 2 P. & C.R. DG14, Ch D

Lines Bros (In Liquidation), Re [1983] Ch. 1; [1982] 2 W.L.R. 1010; [1982] 2 All E.R. 183; [1982] Com. L.R. 81; (1982) 126 S.J. 197, CA (Civ Div); reversing [1981] Com. L.R. 214; (1981) 125 S.J. 426, HC ........ *Digested,* 82/**335**:
*Applied* 04/2192: *Considered* 84/323, 87/365, 93/2626, 14/1752

Link Financial Ltd v Wilson [2014] EWHC 252 (Ch); [2014] C.T.L.C. 145, Ch D ........ *Digested,* 14/**616**

Linklaters Business Services v Sir Robert McAlpine Ltd [2010] EWHC 2931 (TCC); 133 Con. L.R. 211, QBD (TCC) ........ *Digested,* 11/**496**:
*Considered* 14/591

Linklaters Business Services v Sir Robert McAlpine Ltd [2010] EWHC 3123 (TCC), QBD (TCC)
*Applied* 14/371

Linnett v Halliwells LLP [2009] EWHC 319 (TCC); [2009] 1 C.L.C. 157; [2009] B.L.R. 312; 123 Con. L.R. 104; [2009] C.I.L.L. 2704; (2009) 159 N.L.J. 396; [2009] N.P.C. 32, QBD (TCC) ........ *Digested,* 09/**991**:
*Applied* 13/524, 14/577

Lipkin Gorman v Karpnale Ltd [1991] 2 A.C. 548; [1991] 3 W.L.R. 10; [1992] 4 All E.R. 512; (1991) 88(26) L.S.G. 31; (1991) 141 N.L.J. 815; (1991) 135 S.J.L.B. 36; Times, June 7, 1991; Independent, June 18, 1991; Financial Times, June 11, 1991; Guardian, June 13, 1991, HL; reversing [1989] 1 W.L.R. 1340; [1992] 4 All E.R. 409; [1989] B.C.L.C. 756; [1989] Fin. L.R. 137; (1990) 87(4) L.S.G. 40; (1989) 139 N.L.J. 76; (1990) 134 S.J. 234; Times, November 19, 1988; Independent, October 17, 1988; Financial Times, October 19, 1988; Daily Telegraph, October 28, 1988, CA (Civ Div); reversing in part [1987] 1 W.L.R. 987; [1992] 4 All E.R. 331; [1987] B.C.L.C. 159; [1986] F.L.R. 271; (1986) 136 N.L.J. 659; (1987) 131 S.J. 940, QBD ........ *Digested,* 91/**502**:
*Applied* 94/3911, 95/4336, 95/855, 00/2320, 02/4667, 03/257, 03/3610, 04/3264, 04/3267, 09/312, 12/2766, 14/1451: *Considered* 88/177, 00/2331, 01/2434, 04/4117, 12/3291: *Followed* 96/3453, 98/1472, 03/2418, 04/3265: *Referred to* 96/5556

Lippens v Kortekaas (C-170/11) [2013] C.E.C. 613; [2012] I.L.Pr. 42, ECJ (1st Chamber)
*Applied* 14/539

Liquidator of Letham Grange Development Co Ltd v Foxworth Investments Ltd see Henderson v Foxworth Investments Ltd

Liquidator of West Mercia Safetywear Ltd v Dodd; *sub nom* West Mercia Safetywear Ltd (In Liquidation) v Dodd (1988) 4 B.C.C. 30; [1988] B.C.L.C. 250; [1988] P.C.C. 212, CA (Civ Div) ........ *Digested,* 88/**308**:
*Applied* 03/521, 07/2429, 13/479: *Followed* 14/509

Lister v Hesley Hall Ltd [2001] UKHL 22; [2002] 1 A.C. 215; [2001] 2 W.L.R. 1311; [2001] 2 All E.R. 769; [2001] I.C.R. 665; [2001] I.R.L.R. 472; [2001] Emp. L.R. 819; [2001] 2 F.L.R. 307; [2001] 2 F.C.R. 97; (2001) 3 L.G.L.R. 49; [2001] E.L.R. 422; [2001] Fam. Law 595; (2001) 98(24) L.S.G. 45; (2001) 151 N.L.J. 728; (2001) 145 S.J.L.B. 126; [2001] N.P.C. 89; Times, May 10, 2001; Independent, June 11, 2001; Daily Telegraph, May 8, 2001, HL; reversing Times, October 13, 1999; Independent, November 22, 1999, CA (Civ Div) ........ *Digested,* 01/**5359**:
*Applied* 02/1531, 03/3033, 03/3046, 03/432, 04/655, 05/4199, 05/4200, 06/1337, 07/4201, 08/3906, 09/5104, 10/2296, 10/4499: *Cited* 02/5360, 03/2975: *Considered* 05/5573, 06/476, 06/5592, 07/5427, 08/385, 12/2298, 12/3344: *Followed* 10/379, 11/3476, 14/3000

Lister v Narla Engineering and Imports Ltd (Quantum) (Unreported, December 20, 2013), CC (Leeds) [*Quality Solicitors, Oliver & Co, Douglas House, 117 Foregate Street, Chester*] ........ *Digested,* 14/**2328**

Lister & Co v Stubbs (1890) 45 Ch. D. 1, CA
*Applied* 87/3553, 11/3499: *Considered* 80/2156: *Disapproved* 94/2083: *Distinguished* 55/361, 81/2158, 05/3443: *Overruled* 14/79

Lithuania v Bucnys; *sub nom* Bucnys v Lithuania; *joined cases* Sakalis v Lithuania; Lavrov v Estonia [2013] UKSC 71; [2014] A.C. 480; [2013] 3 W.L.R. 1485; [2014] 2 All E.R. 235, SC; reversing in part [2012] EWHC 2771 (Admin); [2013] 1 All E.R. 1220, DC ........ *Digested,* 14/**1226**

Little v Richmond Pharmacology Ltd [2014] I.C.R. 85; [2013] Eq. L.R. 1153, EAT ........ *Digested,* 14/**1115**

Little France Ltd v Ealing LBC [2013] EWHC 2144 (Admin); [2014] L.L.R. 92, QBD (Admin)

Littlewoods Organisation Plc v Customs and Excise Commissioners see Lex Services Plc v Customs and Excise Commissioners

Littlewoods Retail Ltd v Revenue and Customs Commissioners [2014] EWHC 868 (Ch); [2014] S.T.C. 1761; [2014] B.V.C. 23, Ch D ........ *Digested,* 14/**3079**

Littlewoods Retail Ltd v Revenue and Customs Commissioners (C-591/10) [2012] S.T.C. 1714; [2012] S.T.I. 2359, ECJ (Grand Chamber)
*Considered* 13/3219: *Followed* 14/2874, 14/3079

Liu v Secretary of State for the Home Department; *joined cases* Wang v Secretary of State for the Home Department; Ahmed v Secretary of State for the Home Department; Mouloungui v Secretary of State for the Home Department [2007] EWCA Civ 1275; [2008] 1 C.M.L.R. 27; [2008] Eu. L.R. 347; [2008] Imm. A.R. 273, CA (Civ Div) ........ *Digested,* 08/**2095**:
*Applied* 14/1734: *Followed* 14/1739

Live Wire Telecom Ltd v Revenue and Customs Commissioners see Livewire Telecom Ltd v Revenue and Customs Commissioners

Liverpool City Council v SG [2014] EWCOP 10; [2014] C.O.P.L.R. 585; [2014] P.T.S.R. D20, CP

Liversidge v Chief Constable of Bedfordshire see Chief Constable of Bedfordshire v Liversidge

Liversidge v Owen Mumford Ltd [2012] EWPCC 40; [2012] 6 Costs L.R. 1076; [2013] F.S.R. 38, PCC ........ *Digested,* 13/**1811**: *Applied* 14/1884

Livewire Telecom Ltd v Revenue and Customs Commissioners; *sub nom* Live Wire Telecom Ltd v Revenue and Customs Commissioners; Revenue and Customs Commissioners v Livewire Telecom Ltd; *joined case* Olympia Technology Ltd v Revenue and Customs Commissioners [2009] EWHC 15 (Ch); [2009] S.T.C. 643; [2009] B.T.C. 5173; [2009] B.V.C. 172; [2009] S.T.I. 190, Ch D; affirming [2008] B.V.C. 2208; [2008] V. & D.R. 131; [2008] S.T.I. 1161, V&DTr (London) . *Digested,* 09/**4064**: *Applied* 09/4077, 09/4078, 14/3070: *Considered* 09/4063, 09/4126, 10/3496, 10/3497, 11/3556, 12/3402, 14/3069

Livingstone v Adjudication Panel for England [2006] EWHC 2533 (Admin); [2006] H.R.L.R. 45; [2006] B.L.G.R. 799; [2007] A.C.D. 22; (2006) 156 N.L.J. 1650; Times, November 9, 2006, QBD (Admin) ........ *Digested,* 06/**2833**: *Considered* 13/2012, 14/2102

Ljungkvist v Sweden [2013] EWHC 1682 (Admin); [2014] A.C.D. 60, QBD (Admin)

Lloyd v Browning [2013] EWCA Civ 1637; [2014] 1 P. & C.R. 11; [2014] 1 E.G.L.R. 73, CA (Civ Div) ........ *Digested,* 14/**639**

Lloyd v Lewisham LBC [2013] EWCA Civ 923; [2013] P.T.S.R. 1442; [2013] H.L.R. 48, CA (Civ Div) ........ *Digested,* 14/**2758**

Lloyd v McMahon [1987] A.C. 625; [1987] 2 W.L.R. 821; [1987] 1 All E.R. 1118; 85 L.G.R. 545; [1987] R.V.R. 58; (1987) 84 L.S.G. 1240; (1987) 137 N.L.J. 265; (1987) 131 S.J. 409, HL; affirming 85 L.G.R. 348; [1986] R.V.R. 188, CA (Civ Div) ........ *Digested,* 87/**3162**: *Applied* 94/66, 00/538, 06/345: *Considered* 94/3835, 94/6012, 95/162, 95/3252, 95/4668, 00/6628, 03/1057, 06/1712: *Explained* 14/2162

Lloyd v Sadler [1978] Q.B. 774; [1978] 2 W.L.R. 721; [1978] 2 All E.R. 529; (1978) 35 P. & C.R. 78; (1978) 245 E.G. 479; (1978) 122 S.J. 111, CA (Civ Div) ........ *Digested,* 78/**1806**: *Applied* 85/43, 97/3303: *Considered* 86/1644, 86/41, 88/2077, 14/1995: *Referred to* 88/2043

Lloyd v Secretary of State for Communities and Local Government [2014] EWCA Civ 839; [2014] J.P.L. 1247, CA (Civ Div); affirming [2013] EWHC 3076 (Admin), QBD (Admin)

Lloyd Schuhfabrik Meyer & Co GmbH v Klijsen Handel BV (C-342/97) [1999] E.C.R. I-3819; [1999] 2 C.M.L.R. 1343; [1999] All E.R. (EC) 587; [1999] C.E.C. 285; [1999] E.T.M.R. 690; [2000] F.S.R. 77; (1999) 22(11) I.P.D. 22111; Times, June 30, 1999, ECJ; no effect [1999] E.C.R. I-3819; [1999] E.T.M.R. 10; [1999] F.S.R. 627, AGO ........ *Digested,* 99/**3538**: *Applied* 01/4056, 01/5881, 04/2375, 07/1560, 07/2639, 07/2641, 08/2346, 08/2372, 08/2407: *Considered* 04/2380, 05/2509, 05/2514, 06/2546, 06/2557, 06/2585, 07/2640, 08/2397, 14/1872: *Followed* 00/3773

Lloyd-Owen v Spire Healthcare Ltd [2013] EWHC 3542 (QB); [2014] Med. L.R. 268, QBD ........ *Digested,* 14/**1566**

Lloyds Bank Ltd v Eastwood see Eastwood (Deceased), Re

Lloyds Bank Plc v Rosset [1991] 1 A.C. 107; [1990] 2 W.L.R. 867; [1990] 1 All E.R. 1111; [1990] 2 F.L.R. 155; (1990) 22 H.L.R. 349; (1990) 60 P. & C.R. 311; (1990) 140 N.L.J. 478, HL; reversing [1989] Ch. 350; [1988] 3 W.L.R. 1301; [1988] 3 All E.R. 915; [1989] 1 F.L.R. 51; (1989) 57 P. & C.R. 62; [1988] Fam. Law 472; (1989) 86(1) L.S.G. 39; (1988) 138 N.L.J. Rep. 149; (1988) 132 S.J. 1698; Times, May 23, 1988; Independent, June 3, 1988; Guardian, June 9, 1988; Daily Telegraph, June 9, 1988, CA (Civ Div) ........ *Digested,* 90/**706**: *Applied* 92/2034, 96/4993, 01/5503, 02/1670, 02/1684, 02/3823, 02/4317, 03/3592, 03/4479, 04/3233, 04/3948, 05/3379, 07/3363, 07/3392, 09/3119, 09/3146, 09/3719, 11/1837, 13/2421: *Approved* 90/707: *Considered* 89/467, 92/2031, 96/4950, 96/4995, 97/4937, 10/3442, 11/1292: *Distinguished* 02/4342: *Followed* 95/2187, 96/4943, 13/1692, 14/2489

Lloyds Banking Group Plc v Revenue and Customs Commissioners see Standard Chartered Plc v Revenue and Customs Commissioners

Lloyds TSB Bank Plc v Markandan & Uddin (A Firm) [2012] EWCA Civ 65; [2012] 2 All E.R. 884; [2012] P.N.L.R. 20; (2012) 162 N.L.J. 328, CA (Civ Div); affirming [2010] EWHC 2517 (Ch); [2011] P.N.L.R. 6; (2010) 107(42) L.S.G. 19; [2011] 1 P. & C.R. DG11, Ch D ........ *Digested,* 12/**2757**: *Applied* 13/227: *Approved* 13/689: *Considered* 14/2055: *Followed* 13/1951, 13/2444, 14/2059

Lloyds TSB General Insurance Holdings Ltd v Lloyds Bank Group Insurance Co Ltd; *joined case* Abbey National Plc v Lee [2003] UKHL 48; [2003] 4 All E.R. 43; [2003] 2 All E.R. (Comm) 665; [2004] 1 C.L.C. 116; [2003] Lloyd's Rep. I.R. 623; [2003] Pens. L.R. 315; (2003) 153 N.L.J. 1270; (2003) 147 S.J.L.B. 935, HL; reversing [2001] EWCA Civ 1643; [2002] 1 All E.R. (Comm) 42; [2002] C.L.C. 287; [2002] Lloyd's Rep. I.R. 113; [2002] Lloyd's Rep. P.N. 211; [2001] Pens. L.R. 325, CA (Civ Div); affirming [2001] 1 All E.R. (Comm) 13; [2001] Lloyd's Rep. I.R. 237; [2001] Lloyd's Rep. P.N. 28, QBD (Comm) ..................... *Digested,* 03/**2454**: *Applied* 14/1844: *Considered* 12/1904

LM (A Child) (Transfer of Irish Proceedings), Re see M (A Child) (Foreign Care Proceedings: Transfer),Re

LM (Article 8: Married Appellant: Proportionality: Jamaica), Re; *sub nom* LM (Jamaica) v Secretary of State for the Home Department [2010] UKUT 379 (IAC), UT (IAC) *Considered* 14/1715

LM (Jamaica) v Secretary of State for the Home Department see LM (Article 8: Married Appellant: Proportionality: Jamaica), Re

LM Ferro Ltd v Revenue and Customs Commissioners [2013] UKFTT 463 (TC); 82 T.C. 214; [2013] S.T.I. 3468, FTT (Tax)

Local Authority X v B see B (Children) (Sexual Abuse: Standard of Proof), Re

Local Authority X v M; *sub nom* A Local Authority v MM; MM (An Adult), Re [2007] EWHC 2003 (Fam); [2009] 1 F.L.R. 443; [2008] 3 F.C.R. 788; (2008) 11 C.C.L. Rep. 119; [2008] Fam. Law 213, Fam Div .......................................................... *Digested,* 08/**3568**: *Applied* 08/1437, 08/756, 10/3212, 11/2204, 14/2175: *Considered* 09/806: *Referred to* 14/2172

Local Government Byelaws (Wales) Bill 2012, Re see Attorney General v National Assembly for Wales Commission

Lock v British Gas Trading Ltd (C-539/12) [2014] 3 C.M.L.R. 53; [2014] All E.R. (EC) 1194; [2014] I.C.R. 813; [2014] I.R.L.R. 648, ECJ (1st Chamber)

Lockwood v Department of Work and Pensions [2013] EWCA Civ 1195; [2014] 1 All E.R. 250; [2014] I.C.R. 1257; [2013] I.R.L.R. 941; [2013] Eq. L.R. 1190, CA (Civ Div); affirming [2013] Eq. L.R. 206, EAT ..................................................... *Digested,* 14/**1014**

Loffland Brothers North Sea Inc v Goodbrand (Inspector of Taxes) see Goodbrand (Inspector of Taxes) v Loffland Bros North Sea Inc

Lok'nstore Group Plc v Revenue and Customs Commissioners; *joined case* Revenue and Customs Commissioners v Lok'nstore Group Plc [2014] UKUT 288 (TCC); [2014] B.V.C. 523; [2014] S.T.I. 2404, UT (Tax); reversing [2012] UKFTT 589 (TC); [2012] S.T.I. 2940, FTT (Tax) ................................................................... *Digested,* 14/**3089**

Lomas v AK see AK (Gift Application), Re

Lomas v Parle [2003] EWCA Civ 1804; [2004] 1 W.L.R. 1642; [2004] 1 All E.R. 1173; [2004] 1 F.L.R. 812; [2004] 1 F.C.R. 97; [2004] Fam. Law 243; Times, January 13, 2004, CA (Civ Div) ......................................................................................... *Digested,* 04/**1502**: *Applied* 09/356: *Considered* 05/1621, 05/343, 06/3671: *Followed* 14/13

Lomas v Pensions Regulator see Bloom v Pensions Regulator

Lomas v Rab Market Cycles (Master) Fund Ltd see Lehman Brothers International (Europe) (In Administration), Re

Lomax (Inspector of Taxes) v Peter Dixon & Son Ltd [1943] K.B. 671; [1943] 2 All E.R. 255; 25 T.C. 353, CA *Applied* 74/1855, 84/1782, 14/2909: *Considered* 82/1623: *Followed* 11/3367

Lombard North Central Plc v Blower [2014] EWHC 2267 (Ch); [2014] I.L.Pr. 46; [2014] B.P.I.R. 1501, Ch D

Lombard, Odier & Cie v Fairfield Sentry Ltd (In Liquidation) see Fairfield Sentry Ltd (In Liquidation) v Migani

Lombard-Knight v Rainstorm Pictures Inc see Rainstorm Pictures Inc v Lombard-Knight

London & Westcountry Estates Ltd, Re see Hockin v Marsden

London CC v Lambeth Overseers see Lambeth Overseers v London CC

London CC v Robinson & Lambeth BC 66 E.G. 9; 48 R. & I.T. 455; [1955] J.P.L. 607; 105 L.J. 460, Lands Tr *Applied* 14/2479

London Christian Radio Ltd v Radio Advertising Clearance Centre see R. (on the application of London Christian Radio Ltd) v Radio Advertising Clearance Centre

London College of Computing Ltd v Revenue and Customs Commissioners [2013] UKUT 404 (TCC); [2014] S.T.C. 404; [2013] B.V.C. 1764, UT (Tax); affirming [2012] UKFTT 342 (TC); [2012] S.T.I. 2515, FTT (Tax) ..................................... *Digested,* 14/**3041**: *Considered* 14/3045

London Corp, The [1935] P. 70; (1935) 51 Ll. L. Rep. 67, CA; affirming (1934) 50 Ll. L. Rep. 14, PDAD
*Applied* 67/1021, 14/829: *Followed* 99/2504

London School of Economics and Political Science v Lindsay; *joined case* Lindsay v London School of Economics and Political Science [2013] EWCA Civ 1650; [2014] I.R.L.R. 218; [2014] Eq. L.R. 150, CA (Civ Div); affirming [2013] Eq. L.R. 10, EAT ........ *Digested,* 14/**1105**

London Scottish Finance Ltd (In Administration), Re; *sub nom* Jack v Craig [2013] EWHC 4047 (Ch); [2014] Bus. L.R. 424; [2013] C.T.L.C. 231, Ch D (Companies Ct) ........ *Digested,* 14/**608**

London Steam Ship Owners Mutual Insurance Association Ltd v Spain; *sub nom* London Steamship Owners' Mutual Insurance Association Ltd v Spain [2013] EWHC 3188 (Comm); [2014] 1 Lloyd's Rep. 309; [2013] 2 C.L.C. 562, QBD (Comm) ........ *Digested,* 14/**129**

London Steam Ship Owners Mutual Insurance Association Ltd v Spain (The Prestige) [2013] EWHC 2840 (Comm); [2014] 1 All E.R. (Comm) 300; [2014] 1 Lloyd's Rep. 137; 150 Con. L.R. 181, QBD (Comm) ........ *Digested,* 14/**140**

London Steamship Owners' Mutual Insurance Association Ltd v Spain see London Steam Ship Owners Mutual Insurance Association Ltd v Spain

London Underground Ltd v Strouthos; *sub nom* Strouthos v London Underground Ltd [2004] EWCA Civ 402; [2004] I.R.L.R. 636, CA (Civ Div); reversing EAT/0016/03/ZT, EAT ........ *Digested,* 05/**1332**:
*Applied* 14/1495

Long v Farrer & Co [2004] EWHC 1774 (Ch); [2004] B.P.I.R. 1218, Ch D ........ *Digested,* 05/**2294**:
*Applied* 14/1787

Long v Value Properties Ltd see 1,3 and 5 Argall Avenue, Re

Longridge on the Thames v Revenue and Customs Commissioners; *sub nom* Revenue and Customs Commissioners v Longridge on the Thames [2014] UKUT 504 (TCC); [2014] B.V.C. 546; [2014] S.T.I. 3428, UT (Tax); affirming [2013] UKFTT 158 (TC); [2013] S.T.I. 1527, FTT (Tax)

Lonsdale Sports Ltd v Erol [2013] EWHC 2956 (Pat); [2013] E.C.C. 33; [2014] R.P.C. 15, Ch D (Patents Ct) ........ *Digested,* 14/**1937**

Loose v Lynn Shellfish Ltd [2014] EWCA Civ 846; (2014) 158(26) S.J.L.B. 37, CA (Civ Div); reversing in part [2013] EWHC 901 (Ch); [2013] L.L.R. 713, Ch D

Lord Carlile of Berriew v Secretary of State for the Home Department see R. (on the application of Lord Carlile of Berriew QC) v Secretary of State for the Home Department

Lord Chancellor v Ahmed [2013] EWHC 3642 (QB); [2014] 1 Costs L.R. 21, QBD ........ *Digested,* 14/**2034**

Lord Chancellor v McLarty and Co Solicitors [2011] EWHC 3182 (QB); [2012] 1 Costs L.R. 190; Times, January 2, 2012, QBD ........ *Digested,* 12/**2081**:
*Applied* 14/2036

Lord Chancellor v Michael J Reed Ltd [2009] EWHC 2981 (QB); [2010] 1 Costs L.R. 72, QBD ........ *Digested,* 10/**329**:
*Applied* 14/2036: *Considered* 11/748, 12/2081: *Followed* 10/2103, 10/2105, 14/752

Lord Howard of Henderskelfe's Executors v Revenue and Customs Commissioners; *sub nom* Revenue and Customs Commissioners v Lord Howard of Henderskelfe's Executors [2014] EWCA Civ 278; [2014] 1 W.L.R. 3902; [2014] 3 All E.R. 50; [2014] S.T.C. 1100; [2014] B.T.C. 12; [2014] W.T.L.R. 791; [2014] S.T.I. 1560, CA (Civ Div); affirming [2013] UKUT 129 (TCC); [2013] 3 All E.R. 817; [2013] S.T.C. 1025; [2013] B.T.C. 1750; [2013] S.T.I. 1501, UT (Tax); reversing [2011] UKFTT 493 (TC); [2011] S.F.T.D. 1194; [2011] S.T.I. 2702, FTT (Tax) ........ *Digested,* 14/**2854**

Lord McAlpine of West Green v Bercow [2013] EWHC 981 (QB); [2014] E.M.L.R. 3, QBD ........ *Digested,* 14/**839**

Lord-Castle v DPP [2009] EWHC 87 (Admin), DC
*Applied* 14/2561

Lordsvale Finance Plc v Bank of Zambia [1996] Q.B. 752; [1996] 3 W.L.R. 688; [1996] 3 All E.R. 156; [1996] C.L.C. 1849; Times, April 8, 1996, QBD ........ *Digested,* 96/**773**:
*Applied* 08/674, 14/642: *Considered* 04/667, 06/776

Loring v Woodland Trust; *sub nom* Woodland Trust v Loring [2014] EWCA Civ 1314; [2014] S.T.I. 3239, CA (Civ Div); affirming [2013] EWHC 4400 (Ch); [2014] 2 All E.R. 836; [2014] B.T.C. 26; [2014] W.T.L.R. 593, Ch D ........ *Digested,* 14/**2937**

Lothian Valuation Joint Board Assessor v Over The Counter Ltd see Assessor for Lothian Valuation Joint Board v Over The Counter Ltd

Loughborough Students' Union v Revenue and Customs Commissioners [2013] UKUT 517 (TCC); [2014] S.T.C. 357; [2013] B.V.C. 1873; [2013] S.T.I. 3452, UT (Tax); reversing in part [2012] UKFTT 331 (TC); [2012] S.T.I. 2336, FTT (Tax) ........ *Digested,* 14/**3047**

Loughlin v Dal Singh see Loughlin v Singh

Loughlin v Singh; *sub nom* Loughlin v Dal Singh [2013] EWHC 1641 (QB); [2013] Med. L.R. 513, QBD ........ *Digested,* 14/**2330**

Louis Vuitton Malletier v Office for Harmonisation in the Internal Market (Trade Marks and Designs) (OHIM) (C-97/12 P) [2014] E.T.M.R. 42; [2014] Bus. L.R. D17, ECJ (8th Chamber)

Love v Halfords Ltd [2014] EWHC 1057 (QB); [2014] R.T.R. 32; [2014] P.I.Q.R. P20, QBD ........ *Digested,* 14/**2295**

Lovell Partnerships Ltd v Merton Priory Homes [2014] EWHC 1615 (TCC); [2014] Bus. L.R. 954; [2014] B.L.R. 541; [2014] C.I.L.L. 3521, QBD (TCC) ........ *Digested,* 14/**641**

Loveridge v Lambeth LBC see Lambeth LBC v Loveridge

Low v Bouverie [1891] 3 Ch. 82, CA
*Applied* 47-51/1739, 47-51/9471, 61/3264, 91/1735: *Approved* 72/495: *Considered* 14/1760: *Distinguished* 55/2537: *Followed* 13/1161

Lowe v Quayle Munro Ltd 1997 S.C. 346; 1997 S.L.T. 1168; 1997 S.C.L.R. 701; 1997 G.W.D. 10-438, OH ........ *Digested,* 97/**6179**: *Approved* 14/1978

Lownds v Home Office; *sub nom* Home Office v Lownds; Lownds v Secretary of State for the Home Department [2002] EWCA Civ 365; [2002] 1 W.L.R. 2450; [2002] 4 All E.R. 775; [2002] C.P. Rep. 43; [2002] C.P.L.R. 328; [2002] 2 Costs L.R. 279; (2002) 99(19) L.S.G. 28; (2002) 146 S.J.L.B. 86; Times, April 5, 2002, CA (Civ Div) ........ *Digested,* 02/**333**:
*Applied* 03/259, 03/347, 04/293, 04/301, 04/303, 04/316, 04/320, 05/331, 05/372, 06/2421, 11/284, 12/388: *Considered* 04/319, 06/556, 07/389, 10/283, 10/284, 14/331: *Followed* 08/336, 11/270, 13/299

Lownds v Secretary of State for the Home Department see Lownds v Home Office

Loxley v BAE Systems Land Systems (Munitions & Ordnance) Ltd [2008] I.C.R. 1348; [2008] I.R.L.R. 853; [2008] Pens. L.R. 353, EAT ........ *Digested,* 08/**1115**:
*Applied* 11/1127, 14/1014: *Considered* 09/1163, 10/1020, 11/1030

LPA Umbrella Trust, Re; *sub nom* Pensions Regulator v A Admin Ltd [2014] EWHC 1378 (Ch); [2014] Pens. L.R. 319, Ch D ........ *Digested,* 14/**2257**

LRP (A Child) (Care Proceedings: Placement Order), Re [2013] EWHC 3974 (Fam); [2014] 2 F.L.R. 399; [2014] Fam. Law 278, Fam Div ........ *Digested,* 14/**1252**

LRP (A Child) (Leave to Oppose Adoption Application), Re [2014] EWHC 3311 (Fam); [2014] Fam. Law 1662, Fam Div

LS v Oxfordshire CC [2013] UKUT 135 (AAC); [2013] E.L.R. 429, UT (AAC) ........ *Digested,* 14/**943**

LTJ Diffusion SA v Sadas Vertbaudet SA (C-291/00) [2003] E.C.R. I-2799; [2003] C.E.C. 283; [2003] E.T.M.R. 83; [2003] F.S.R. 34; Times, March 26, 2003, ECJ; no effect [2003] E.C.R. I-2799; [2002] E.T.M.R. 40; [2003] F.S.R. 1, AGO *Digested,* 03/**2611**:
*Applied* 04/2394, 04/2402, 07/2663, 14/1926: *Considered* 02/2907

Lu v Nottingham University Hospitals NHS Trust [2014] EWHC 690 (QB); (2014) 137 B.M.L.R. 172, QBD

Lubberts' Estate, Re see Hanson v Mercredi

Lubovsky v Snelling; *joined case* Cohen v Snelling [1944] K.B. 44; [1943] 2 All E.R. 577; (1944) 77 Ll. L. Rep. 57, CA; reversing (1943) 75 Ll. L. Rep. 165, KBD
*Considered* 14/2715: *Distinguished* 57/3327

Lubrizol Corp v Esso Petroleum Co Ltd (No.5) [1998] R.P.C. 727; (1998) 21(8) I.P.D. 21081, CA (Civ Div); affirming [1997] R.P.C. 195, Ch D (Patents Ct) ........ *Digested,* 99/**3507**:
*Applied* 06/2531: *Considered* 05/2505, 14/1879

Luca v Italy (33354/96) (2003) 36 E.H.R.R. 46; [2001] Crim. L.R. 747, ECHR ........ *Digested,* 03/**2125**:
*Applied* 06/1611, 09/2014, 12/657: *Cited* 05/888: *Considered* 08/691, 08/697, 14/287

Luckwell v Limata [2014] EWHC 536 (Fam); [2014] 2 F.L.R. 1252; [2014] Fam. Law 794, Fam Div

Luckwell v Limata [2014] EWHC 502 (Fam); [2014] 2 F.L.R. 168; [2014] Fam. Law 792, Fam Div ........ *Digested,* 14/**1375**

Luckwell v Limata [2014] EWHC 1035 (Fam); [2014] Fam. Law 962, Fam Div

Ludlow v Commissioner of Police of the Metropolis; *sub nom* R. v Ludlow (Edward Alexander); Ludlow v Metropolitan Police Commissioner [1971] A.C. 29; [1970] 2 W.L.R. 521; [1970] 1 All E.R. 567; (1970) 54 Cr. App. R. 233; (1970) 114 S.J. 148, HL; affirming [1970] 1 Q.B. 101; [1969] 3 W.L.R. 640; [1969] 3 All E.R. 701; (1969) 53 Cr. App. R. 563; (1969) 113 S.J. 812, CA (Crim Div) ........ *Digested,* 70/**458**:
*Applied* 80/1744, 80/520, 80/559, 82/629, 91/683: *Considered* 81/388, 86/624, 94/935, 96/1566, 03/4723: *Followed* 83/698, 14/774

Ludlow v Metropolitan Police Commissioner see Ludlow v Commissioner of Police of the Metropolis
Lukaszewski v Poland see Pomiechowski v Poland
Lumba v Secretary of State for the Home Department see R. (on the application of Lumba) v Secretary of State for the Home Department
Luminar Lava Gems Ltd, Re see Leisure (Norwich) II Ltd v Luminar Lava Ignite Ltd (In Administration)
Luminar Lava Ignite Ltd, Re see Leisure (Norwich) II Ltd v Luminar Lava Ignite Ltd (In Administration)
Luminar Liquid Ltd, Re see Leisure (Norwich) II Ltd v Luminar Lava Ignite Ltd (In Administration)
Luminar Oceana Ltd, Re see Leisure (Norwich) II Ltd v Luminar Lava Ignite Ltd (In Administration)
Lumsdon v Legal Services Board see R. (on the application of Lumsdon) v Legal Services Board
Lundy Granite Co, Re; *sub nom* Heavan, Ex p. (1870-71) L.R. 6 Ch. App. 462, CA in Chancery
*Applied* 74/356, 11/1818, 13/1706, 14/1756: *Considered* 10/1835, 11/4392
Lunn Poly Ltd v Liverpool & Lancashire Properties Ltd [2006] EWCA Civ 430; [2007] L. & T.R. 6; [2006] 2 E.G.L.R. 29; [2006] 25 E.G. 210; [2006] 12 E.G. 222 (C.S.); Times, April 18, 2006, CA (Civ Div) .......... *Digested*, 06/**1019**:
*Applied* 12/858, 14/824
Lupofresh Ltd v Sapporo Breweries Ltd see Sapporo Breweries Ltd v Lupofresh Ltd
Lurcott v Wakeley & Wheeler [1911] 1 K.B. 905; [1911-13] All E.R. Rep. 41, CA
*Applied* 55/2354, 64/2094, 68/3365, 79/599, 82/1748, 84/1958, 98/3628, 14/2509:
*Approved* 65/2200: *Considered* 69/2024, 79/1599, 86/1854:
*Distinguished* 63/1958
Luton BC v Zeb [2014] EWHC 732 (Admin); [2014] L.L.R. 527, QBD (Admin)
LUV Trade Mark see Elliott v LRC Products Ltd
Luxembourg v Linster (C287/98) [2000] E.C.R. I-6917; [2001] Env. L.R. D3; Times, October 5, 2000, ECJ .......... *Digested*, 00/**2354**:
*Considered* 14/1201
LVK - 56 EOOD v Direktor na Direktsia 'Obzhalvane i upravlenie na izpalnenieto' (C-643/11) (Unreported, January 31, 2013), ECJ
*Applied* 14/3070
Lydd Airport Action Group v Secretary of State for Communities and Local Government see Royal Society for the Protection of Birds v Secretary of State for Communities and Local Government
Lymington Marina Ltd v Macnamara [2007] EWCA Civ 151; [2007] 2 All E.R. (Comm) 825; [2007] N.P.C. 27; [2007] Bus. L.R. D29, CA (Civ Div); affirming [2006] EWHC 704 (Ch); [2006] 2 All E.R. (Comm) 200; [2006] N.P.C. 43, Ch D .......... *Digested*, 06/**763**:
*Considered* 14/2006
Lynch v Secretary of State for the Environment, Transport and the Regions [1999] J.P.L. 354, QBD .......... *Digested*, 99/**4176**:
*Applied* 02/3645, 10/2564, 14/2354
Lyons v Central Commercial London Properties Ltd see Lyons v Central Commercial Properties Ltd
Lyons v Central Commercial Properties Ltd; *sub nom* Lyons v Central Commercial London Properties Ltd [1958] 1 W.L.R. 869; [1958] 2 All E.R. 767, CA .......... *Digested*, 58/**1812**:
*Applied* 70/1532, 14/1994: *Followed* 14/1976
Lyons v DWP Jobcentre Plus [2014] I.C.R. 668, EAT .......... *Digested*, 14/**1117**
Lyreco Belgium NV v Rogiers (C-588/12) [2014] I.R.L.R. 656, ECJ (3rd Chamber)
Lysville v Price (Inspector of Taxes) see Minsham Properties v Price (Inspector of Taxes)

M v B (Application for Permission to Relocate to Abu Dhabi) [2014] EWHC 2686 (Fam); [2014] Fam. Law 1533, Fam Ct
M v Bulgaria (41416/08) (2014) 58 E.H.R.R. 20, ECHR
M v Chief Constable of Northern Ireland see C's Application for Judicial Review, Re
M v Croydon LBC; *sub nom* R. (on the application of M) v Croydon LBC [2012] EWCA Civ 595; [2012] 1 W.L.R. 2607; [2012] 3 All E.R. 1237; [2012] 4 Costs L.R. 689; [2012] 3 F.C.R. 179; [2012] B.L.G.R. 822, CA (Civ Div) .......... *Digested*, 12/**343**:
*Considered* 12/399: *Explained* 14/64: *Followed* 13/1963, 13/329, 13/330
M v Director of Legal Aid Casework [2014] EWHC 1354 (Admin); [2014] A.C.D. 124, QBD (Admin)
M v F (Declaration of Parentage: Circumstances of Conception) see M v F (Legal Paternity)

M v F (Legal Paternity); *sub nom* M v F (Declaration of Parentage: Circumstances of Conception) [2013] EWHC 1901 (Fam); [2014] 1 F.L.R. 352; [2014] 1 F.C.R. 456; [2013] Fam. Law 1386, Fam Div ........ *Digested,* 14/**1409**
M v F see LC (Children) (Habitual Residence: Grave Risk of Harm), Re
M v M [2013] EWHC 2534 (Fam); [2014] 1 F.L.R. 439; [2013] W.T.L.R. 1725; 16 I.T.E.L.R. 391; [2013] Fam. Law 1525, Fam Div ........ *Digested,* 14/**1358**
M v M (Costs) [2013] EWHC 3372 (Fam); [2014] 1 F.L.R. 499, Fam Div ........ *Digested,* 14/**1337**
M v M (Divorce: Jurisdiction: Validity of Marriage); *sub nom* A-M v A-M (Divorce: Jurisdiction: Validity of Marriage) [2001] 2 F.L.R. 6; [2001] Fam. Law 495, Fam Div ........ *Digested,* 01/**2615**: *Applied* 02/4310, 09/1617, 12/1444, 14/2190: *Considered* 09/1573
M v M (Maintenance Pending Suit: Enforcement on Dismissal of Suit) [2009] EWCA Civ 1427; [2010] 1 F.L.R. 1413; [2010] Fam. Law 443; [2010] Fam. Law 335; (2009) 106(42) L.S.G. 23, CA (Civ Div); affirming [2008] EWHC 2153 (Fam); [2009] 1 F.L.R. 790; [2009] Fam. Law 8, Fam Div ........ *Digested,* 10/**1289**: *Doubted* 14/1388
M v M (Short Marriage: Clean Break) see Miller v Miller
M v M (Stay of Proceedings: Return of Children) [2005] EWHC 1159 (Fam); [2006] 1 F.L.R. 138; [2005] Fam. Law 853, Fam Div *Applied* 07/1790: *Followed* 13/1282: *Not applied* 14/1355
M v M see AB v CB (Divorce and Maintenance: Discretion to Stay)
M v S (Property Ownership: Preliminary Issue) [2013] EWHC 2080 (Fam); [2014] Fam. Law 446, Fam Div
M v Times Newspapers Ltd see PNM v Times Newspapers Ltd
M v W (Appliction After New Zealand Financial Agreement) [2014] EWHC 925 (Fam); [2014] Fam. Law 1107, Fam Div
M v Warwickshire CC see Warwickshire CC v M
M v Wells Unit West London Mental Health Trust see R. (on the application of M) v Kingston Crown Court
M (A Child) (Abduction: Paternity: DNA Testing), Re [2013] EWCA Civ 1131; [2014] 1 F.L.R. 695; [2013] Fam. Law 1514; (2013) 161(7577) N.L.J. 17, CA (Civ Div) .... *Digested,* 14/**1426**
M (A Child) (Breach of Undertakings: Committal), Re [2013] EWCA Civ 743; [2014] 1 F.L.R. 588; [2013] Fam. Law 1250, CA (Civ Div) ........ *Digested,* 14/**318**
M (A Child) (Care and Placement Orders: Guardian's Evidence), Re; *sub nom* M (A Child) (Guardian's Appeal from Care Proceedings), Re [2014] EWCA Civ 226; [2014] Fam. Law 776, CA (Civ Div)
M (A Child) (Care Order: Findings against Father), Re [2013] EWCA Civ 1819; [2014] Fam. Law 415, CA (Civ Div)
M (A Child) (Contact: Domestic Violence), Re see L (A Child) (Contact: Domestic Violence), Re
M (A Child) (Foreign Care Proceedings: Transfer),Re; *sub nom* LM (A Child) (Transfer of Irish Proceedings), Re [2013] EWHC 646 (Fam); [2013] Fam. 308; [2013] 3 W.L.R. 1463; [2013] 2 F.L.R. 708; [2013] Fam. Law 806, Fam Div ........ *Digested,* 13/**1234**: *Applied* 14/1286, 14/1356: *Considered* 14/1285
M (A Child) (Guardian's Appeal from Care Proceedings), Re see M (A Child) (Care and Placement Orders: Guardian's Evidence), Re
M (A Child) (Habitual Residence: Temporary Placement), Re; *sub nom* MB v GK [2014] EWHC 963 (Fam); [2014] Fam. Law 963, Fam Div
M (A Child) (Habitual Residence: Temporary Placement), Re see K (A Child) (Return Order: Failure to Comply: Committal: Appeal), Re
M (A Child) (Parental Responsibility Order), Re; *sub nom* M (A Child) (Parental Responsibility: Welfare: Status); PM v MB [2013] EWCA Civ 969; [2014] 1 F.L.R. 339; [2014] 2 F.C.R. 46; [2013] Fam. Law 1256, CA (Civ Div) ........ *Digested,* 14/**1419**: *Considered* 14/1422
M (A Child) (Parental Responsibility: Welfare: Status) see M (A Child) (Parental Responsibility Order), Re
M (A Child) (Removal from Jurisdiction: Adjournment), Re [2010] EWCA Civ 888; [2011] 1 F.L.R. 1943; [2010] Fam. Law 1068, CA (Civ Div) ........ *Digested,* 11/**1375**: *Followed* 14/1313
M (A Child), Re see B v K (Abduction: Contempt)
M (A Minor) v Newham LBC see X (Minors) v Bedfordshire CC
M (Adult Patient) (Minimally Conscious State: Withdrawal of Treatment), Re; *sub nom* W v M [2011] EWHC 2443 (Fam); [2012] 1 W.L.R. 1653; [2012] 1 All E.R. 1313; [2012] P.T.S.R. 1040; [2012] 1 F.L.R. 495; [2012] 1 F.C.R. 1; (2011) 14 C.C.L. Rep. 689; [2011] Med. L.R. 584; (2011) 122 B.M.L.R. 67; [2011] Fam. Law 1330; (2011) 108(39) L.S.G. 18; (2011) 156 N.L.J. 1368; Times, December 1, 2011, CP ........ *Digested,* 12/**1558**: *Considered* 12/2282, 14/494

M (An Adult) (Capacity: Consent to Sexual Relations), Re; *sub nom* IM v LM (Capacity to Consent to Sexual Relations) [2014] EWCA Civ 37; [2014] 3 W.L.R. 409; [2014] 3 All E.R. 491; [2014] 2 F.C.R. 13; [2014] C.O.P.L.R. 246; (2014) 17 C.C.L. Rep. 39; [2014] Med. L.R. 345; (2014) 158(5) S.J.L.B. 37, CA (Civ Div) .. *Digested,* 14/**2175**: *Considered* 14/693

M (Best Interests: Deprivation of Liberty), Re [2013] EWHC 3456 (COP); [2014] C.O.P.L.R. 35; (2014) 135 B.M.L.R. 189, CP .......... *Digested,* 14/**2193**

M (Brussels II Revised: Art.15), Re see D (A Child) (Transfer of Proceedings), Re

M (Children) (Contact Refusal: Appeal), Re [2013] EWCA Civ 1147; [2014] 2 F.L.R. 685; [2014] Fam. Law 148, CA (Civ Div) .......... *Digested,* 14/**1411**

M (Children) (Placement Order), Re see Warwickshire CC v M

M (Children), Re [2013] EWCA Civ 388, CA (Civ Div) *Applied* 14/1383

M (Children), Re see B v B (Abduction: Habitual Residence)

M (Minors) (Access: Contempt: Committal), Re; *sub nom* M (Minors) (Breach of Undertaking), Re [1991] 1 F.L.R. 355; [1991] F.C.R. 272; [1991] Crim. L.R. 265, CA (Civ Div) .......... *Digested,* 92/**3408**: *Considered* 14/321

M (Minors) (Breach of Undertaking), Re see M (Minors) (Access: Contempt: Committal), Re

M (Notification of Step-parent Adoption), Re; *sub nom* A v P Council [2014] EWHC 1128 (Fam); [2014] Fam. Law 1085, Fam Div

M (Schedule I Provision), Re see M-M (A Child) (Financial Provision: Father Resident Abroad), Re

M (Statutory Will), Re; *sub nom* ITW v Z [2009] EWHC 2525 (Fam); [2011] 1 W.L.R. 344; [2010] 3 All E.R. 682; (2009) 12 C.C.L. Rep. 635; [2010] M.H.L.R. 304; [2009] W.T.L.R. 1791, CP .......... *Digested,* 10/**3212**: *Applied* 11/3216, 11/3266, 13/2978: *Considered* 13/2069, 13/2074, 14/1267

M Children's Hospital NHS Foundation Trust v Y [2014] EWHC 2651 (Fam); [2014] Fam. Law 1527, Fam Div

M Wheeler & Co Ltd v Warren [1928] Ch. 840, CA *Applied* 14/1968

M, Re see C's Application for Judicial Review, Re

M-F (Children) (Appeal:Case Management: Necessary Delay), Re see M-F (Children) (Care Proceedings: Extension of Time Limit), Re

M-F (Children) (Care Proceedings: Extension of Time Limit), Re; *sub nom* M-F (Children) (Appeal:Case Management: Necessary Delay), Re [2014] EWCA Civ 991; (2014) 158(30) S.J.L.B. 41, CA (Civ Div)

M-M (A Child) (Financial Provision: Father Resident Abroad), Re; *sub nom* M (Schedule I Provision), Re [2014] EWCA Civ 276; [2014] 2 F.L.R. 1391; [2014] 2 F.C.R. 412; [2014] Fam. Law 1100, CA (Civ Div) .......... *Digested,* 14/**1360**

M3 Property Ltd v ZedHomes Ltd [2012] EWHC 780 (TCC); [2012] C.I.L.L. 3174, QBD (TCC) *Considered* 14/407

MA v Entry Clearance Officer, Istanbul see MA (Zambrano: EU Children outside EU: Iran), Re

MA v Secretary of State for Health [2012] UKUT 474 (AAC); [2013] M.H.L.R. 56, UT (AAC) .......... *Digested,* 14/**2181**

MA v Secretary of State for the Home Department (C-648/11); *sub nom* R. (on the application of MA (Eritrea)) v Secretary of State for the Home Department (C-648/11); *joined cases* R. (on the application of DA (Iraq)) v Secretary of State for the Home Department (C-648/11); R. (on the application of BT (Eritrea)) v Secretary of State for the Home Department (C-648/11) [2013] 1 W.L.R. 2961; [2013] 3 C.M.L.R. 49; [2014] All E.R. (EC) 181; [2014] Imm. A.R. 20; [2013] I.N.L.R. 587, ECJ (4th Chamber) .......... *Digested,* 14/**1658**

MA (Afghanistan) v Secretary of State for the Home Department see TN (Afghanistan) v Secretary of State for the Home Department

MA (Eritrea) v Secretary of State for the Home Department see R. (on the application of EM (Eritrea)) v Secretary of State for the Home Department

MA (Zambrano: EU Children outside EU: Iran), Re; *sub nom* SM v Entry Clearance Officer, Bangkok; MA v Entry Clearance Officer, Istanbul [2013] UKUT 380 (IAC); [2013] Imm. A.R. 1142, UT (IAC) .......... *Digested,* 14/**1741**

MA Lloyd & Sons Ltd (t/a KPM Marine) v PPC International Ltd (t/a Professional Powercraft) [2014] EWHC 41 (QB); [2014] 2 Costs L.R. 256, QBD .......... *Digested,* 14/**451**

MABN v Advocate General for Scotland see N v Advocate General for Scotland

Maccabi Rishon Lezion Basketball Amuta (Society) v Rehovot Assessment Officer 16 I.T.L. Rep. 25, District Ct (Tel Aviv)

MacCulloch v Imperial Chemical Industries Plc [2008] I.C.R. 1334; [2008] I.R.L.R. 846; (2008) 152(34) S.J.L.B. 31, EAT ............ *Digested,* 09/**1161**: *Applied* 12/1036, 14/1014

MacDermid Offshore Solutions LLC v Niche Products Ltd see Niche Products Ltd v MacDermid Offshore Solutions LLC

MacDermott, Re see R. (on the application of Adams) v Secretary of State for Justice

MacDonald v Fernandez see McDonald v Fernandez

Mace v Ponders End International Ltd [2014] I.R.L.R. 697, EAT ............ *Digested,* 14/**1084**

Mackay v Dick (1881) 6 App. Cas. 251; (1881) 8 R. (H.L.) 37, HL *Applied* 54/2992, 74/3930, 76/2547, 80/349, 86/222, 09/709, 10/1954, 12/2319, 14/638: *Considered* 58/3137, 93/550: *Distinguished* 57/3137: *Followed* 09/717: *Not applied* 92/3947

Mackay v Kaupthing Singer & Friedlander Ltd (In Administration) see UK Housing Alliance (North West) Ltd (In Administration), Re

Mackellar v Griffin [2014] EWHC 2644 (Ch); [2014] B.P.I.R. 1516, Ch D

MacKinlay (Inspector of Taxes) v Arthur Young McClelland Moores & Co [1990] 2 A.C. 239; [1989] 3 W.L.R. 1245; [1990] 1 All E.R. 45; [1990] S.T.C. 898; 62 T.C. 704; (1989) 139 N.L.J. 1671; (1989) 134 S.J. 22, HL; reversing [1989] Ch. 454; [1988] 2 W.L.R. 1117; [1988] 2 All E.R. 1; [1988] S.T.C. 116; [1988] 1 F.T.L.R. 381; (1988) 85(9) L.S.G. 46; (1988) 138 N.L.J. Rep. 30; (1988) 132 S.J. 266, CA (Civ Div); reversing [1986] 1 W.L.R. 1468; [1986] S.T.C. 491; (1986) 83 L.S.G. 1037; (1986) 136 N.L.J. 3513; (1986) 130 S.J. 822, Ch D ....... *Digested,* 90/**2667**: *Applied* 13/3027, 14/2870: *Followed* 11/3372, 12/3295

Macklin v Revenue and Customs Commissioners [2013] UKFTT 554 (TC); [2014] S.F.T.D. 290; 16 I.T.L. Rep. 355, FTT (Tax) ............ *Digested,* 14/**2892**

Maclaine Watson & Co Ltd v International Tin Council (No.2) [1989] Ch. 286; [1988] 3 W.L.R. 1190; [1988] 3 All E.R. 257; (1988) 85(41) L.S.G. 44; (1988) 132 S.J. 1495; Times, May 5, 1988; Independent, May 10, 1988, CA (Civ Div); affirming [1987] 1 W.L.R. 1711; [1987] 3 All E.R. 886; [1987] B.C.L.C. 653; (1988) 85(2) L.S.G. 36; (1987) 131 S.J. 1659, Ch D ............ *Digested,* 89/**2989**: *Considered* 89/3024: *Followed* 11/320, 14/305

Maclaverty Cooper Atkins v Lord Chancellor [2014] EWHC 1387 (QB); [2014] 4 Costs L.R. 629, QBD ............ *Digested,* 14/**2036**

MacLennan v Morgan Sindall (Infrastructure) Plc [2013] EWHC 4044 (QB); [2014] 1 W.L.R. 2462; (2014) 158(2) S.J.L.B. 37, QBD ............ *Digested,* 14/**308**

MacLeod v Gold Harp Properties Ltd; *sub nom* Gold Harp Properties Ltd v MacLeod [2014] EWCA Civ 1084; [2014] 3 E.G.L.R. 133, CA (Civ Div)

MacMahon's Application for Judicial Review, Re [2012] NIQB 93; [2014] N.I. 28, QBD (NI)

Macmillan Inc v Bishopsgate Investment Trust Plc (No.3) [1996] 1 W.L.R. 387; [1996] 1 All E.R. 585; [1996] B.C.C. 453; (1995) 139 S.J.L.B. 225; Times, November 7, 1995; Independent, December 11, 1995, CA (Civ Div); affirming [1995] 1 W.L.R. 978; [1995] 3 All E.R. 747, Ch D ............ *Digested,* 95/**693**: *Applied* 00/777, 09/611, 10/509, 11/1922, 14/2588: *Considered* 07/677, 10/237, 10/510

Macmillan Inc v Bishopsgate Investment Trust Plc (No.4); *sub nom* MCC Proceeds Inc v Bishopsgate Investment Trust Plc (No.4) [1999] C.L.C. 417; Times, December 7, 1998, CA (Civ Div) ............ *Digested,* 99/**728**: *Applied* 14/633

Maco Door & Window Hardware (UK) Ltd v Revenue and Customs Commissioners; *sub nom* Revenue and Customs Commissioners v Maco Door & Window Hardware (UK) Ltd [2008] UKHL 54; [2008] 1 W.L.R. 1790; [2008] 3 All E.R. 1020; [2008] Bus. L.R. 1425; [2008] S.T.C. 2594; 79 T.C. 287; [2008] B.T.C. 486; [2008] S.T.I. 1918; (2008) 105(32) L.S.G. 18; Times, September 2, 2008, HL; reversing [2007] EWCA Civ 545; [2007] Bus. L.R. 1686; [2007] S.T.C. 1442; [2007] B.T.C. 607; [2007] S.T.I. 1773; (2007) 151 S.J.L.B. 861; [2007] N.P.C. 73, CA (Civ Div); reversing [2006] EWHC 1832 (Ch); [2007] S.T.C. 721; [2006] B.T.C. 829; [2006] S.T.I. 1919; Times, August 11, 2006, Ch D; reversing [2006] S.T.C. (S.C.D.) 1; [2005] S.T.I. 1996, Sp Comm ............ *Digested,* 08/**3647**: *Considered* 14/2882

Macob Civil Engineering Ltd v Morrison Construction Ltd [1999] C.L.C. 739; [1999] B.L.R. 93; (1999) 1 T.C.L.R. 113; 64 Con. L.R. 1; [1999] 3 E.G.L.R. 7; [1999] 37 E.G. 173; (1999) 15 Const. L.J. 300; (1999) 96(10) L.S.G. 28; Times, March 11, 1999; Independent, March 1, 1999, QBD (TCC) ............ *Digested,* 99/**794**: *Applied* 02/662, 03/643, 03/667, 06/333, 10/560, 11/487, 13/1719, 14/130, 14/581: *Approved* 00/806: *Considered* 11/131: *Distinguished* 00/807: *Referred to* 99/795

Madami v Secretary of State for the Home Department see R. (on the application of Lumba) v Secretary of State for the Home Department
Madarassy v Nomura International Plc [2007] EWCA Civ 33; [2007] I.C.R. 867; [2007] I.R.L.R. 246, CA (Civ Div); affirming UKEAT/0326/31/ILB, EAT ........................ *Digested,* 07/**1401**: *Applied* 07/1184, 09/4267, 11/1119, 12/1125: *Approved* 12/1072: *Considered* 12/1033, 13/1032: *Followed* 10/1122, 14/1100: *Referred to* 13/986
Madej v Poland see Brodziak v Poland
Maden v Haller see Copley v Lawn
Madoff Securities International Ltd (In Liquidation) v Raven [2013] EWHC 3147 (Comm); [2014] Lloyd's Rep. F.C. 95, QBD (Comm) ........................................ *Digested,* 14/**510**
Maeda Corp v Hong Kong [2014] B.L.R. 22, CA (HK)
Magic Memories Group (UK) Ltd v Revenue and Customs Commissioners [2013] UKFTT 730 (TC); [2014] S.T.I. 447, FTT (Tax)
Magill v Porter see Porter v Magill
Magill v Weeks see Porter v Magill
Magmatic Ltd v PMS International Group Plc see Magmatic Ltd v PMS International Ltd
Magmatic Ltd v PMS International Ltd; *sub nom* Magmatic Ltd v PMS International Group Plc [2014] EWCA Civ 181; [2014] E.C.D.R. 20; [2014] R.P.C. 24, CA (Civ Div); reversing [2013] EWHC 1925 (Pat); [2013] E.C.C. 29; [2014] R.P.C. 23, Ch D (Patents Ct) ........................................ *Digested,* 14/**1908**
Magyar Kereszteny Mennonita Egyhaz v Hungary (70945/11) 37 B.H.R.C. 187, ECHR
Magyar Telecom BV, Re [2013] EWHC 3800 (Ch); [2014] B.C.C. 448; (2013) 163(7588) N.L.J. 20, Ch D ........................................ *Digested,* 14/**500**: *Applied* 14/1783
Mahad (Ethiopia) v Entry Clearance Officer; *sub nom* Muhumed v Entry Clearance Officer; Sakthivel v Entry Clearance Officer; Ismail v Entry Clearance Officer; Ali v Entry Clearance Officer; *joined cases* MI (Somalia) v Entry Clearance Officer; VS (Sri Lanka) v Entry Clearance Officer; MB (Pakistan) v Entry Clearance Officer; SA (Somalia) v Entry Clearance Officer; AM (Ethiopia) v Entry Clearance Officer [2009] UKSC 16; [2010] 1 W.L.R. 48; [2010] 2 All E.R. 535; [2010] Imm. A.R. 203; [2010] I.N.L.R. 268; (2009) 153(48) S.J.L.B. 34; Times, December 21, 2009, SC; reversing [2008] EWCA Civ 1082; [2009] Imm. A.R. 254; (2008) 105(41) L.S.G. 19, CA (Civ Div) ........................................ *Digested,* 10/**1822**: *Applied* 10/1781, 10/1782, 11/1744, 12/1741, 13/1649, 14/1707: *Considered* 10/1805, 11/1744, 14/1689, 14/1703
Mahageben kft v Nemzeti Ado- es Vamhivatal Del-dunantuli Regionalis Ado Foigazgatosaga (C-80/11); *joined case* David v Nemzeti Ado- es Vamhivatal Eszak-alfoldi Regionalis Ado Foigazgatosaga (C-142/11) [2012] S.T.C. 1934; [2013] C.E.C. 306; [2012] S.T.I. 2733, ECJ (3rd Chamber) *Applied* 14/3070: *Cited* 14/3810: *Considered* 14/3069
Mahamdia v Algeria (C-154/11) [2014] All E.R. (EC) 96; [2013] C.E.C. 452; [2012] I.L.Pr. 41; [2013] I.C.R. 1; Times, October 16, 2012, ECJ (Grand Chamber)
Maher v Groupama Grand Est [2009] EWCA Civ 1191; [2010] 1 W.L.R. 1564; [2010] 2 All E.R. 455; [2010] 2 All E.R. (Comm) 843; [2009] 2 C.L.C. 852; [2010] R.T.R. 10; [2010] Lloyd's Rep. I.R. 543, CA (Civ Div); affirming [2009] EWHC 38 (QB); [2009] 1 W.L.R. 1752; [2009] 1 All E.R. 1116; [2009] 1 All E.R. (Comm) 793; [2009] 1 C.L.C. 22; [2009] R.T.R. 20; [2009] I.L.Pr. 45; [2009] Lloyd's Rep. I.R. 659; (2009) 159 N.L.J. 158, QBD ........................................ *Digested,* 10/**509**: *Considered* 10/2408, 11/471, 14/553: *Followed* 10/510
Mahmud v Bank of Credit and Commerce International SA (In Liquidation) see Malik v Bank of Credit and Commerce International SA (In Liquidation)
Maier v ASOS Plc [2014] EWHC 123 (Ch); [2014] E.T.M.R. 36, Ch D ........................ *Digested,* 14/**1916**
Maier v ASOS Plc [2013] EWHC 2831 (Ch); [2014] E.T.M.R. 35; [2014] F.S.R. 16, Ch D ........................................ *Digested,* 14/**1913**
Maierhofer v Finanzamt Augsburg-Land (C-315/00) [2003] S.T.C. 564; [2003] E.C.R. I-563; [2003] 2 C.M.L.R. 37; [2003] C.E.C. 192; [2003] B.T.C. 5269; [2003] B.V.C. 325; [2003] S.T.I. 88, ECJ (5th Chamber) ........................................ *Digested,* 03/**4532**: *Applied* 05/4421, 14/3052: *Considered* 05/4403: *Followed* 12/3414, 13/3194
Mail and Guardian Media Ltd v Chipu 36 B.H.R.C. 714, Const Ct (SA)
Mainstream Properties Ltd v Young see OBG Ltd v Allan
Mairs (Inspector of Taxes) v Haughey [1994] 1 A.C. 303; [1993] 3 W.L.R. 393; [1993] 3 All E.R. 801; [1993] S.T.C. 569; [1993] I.R.L.R. 551; 66 T.C. 273; [1993] B.T.C. 339; Times, July 23, 1993; Independent, August 16, 1993, HL (NI); affirming [1992] S.T.C. 495, CA (NI) ........................................ *Digested,* 93/**2275**: *Applied* 05/4071, 14/2911: *Considered* 99/4729, 10/3322, 10/3323, 14/2908: *Distinguished* 97/2974, 11/3359: *Followed* 11/3354

Mak v Revenue and Customs Commissioners [2013] UKFTT 417 (TC); [2013] S.F.T.D. 1250; [2013] S.T.I. 3302, FTT (Tax) .......... *Digested,* 14/**2858**

Makanjuola v Secretary of State for Communities and Local Government [2013] EWHC 3528 (Admin); [2014] J.P.L. 439, QBD (Admin) .......... *Digested,* 14/**2385**

Makdessi v Cavendish Square Holdings BV; *sub nom* El Makdessi v Cavendish Square Holdings BV; Cavendish Square Holdings BV v Makdessi [2013] EWCA Civ 1539; [2014] 2 All E.R. (Comm) 125; [2013] 2 C.L.C. 968; [2014] B.L.R. 246, CA (Civ Div); reversing [2012] EWHC 3582 (Comm); [2013] 1 All E.R. (Comm) 787, QBD (Comm) .......... *Digested,* 14/**642**

Maks Pen EOOD v Direktor na Direktsia 'Obzhalvane i danachno-osiguritelna praktika' Sofia (C-18/13) [2014] B.V.C. 14; [2014] S.T.I. 752, ECJ (7th Chamber)
*Considered* 14/3067

Maktouf v Bosnia and Herzegovina (2312/08); *joined case* Damjanovic v Bosnia and Herzegovina (34179/08) (2014) 58 E.H.R.R. 11, ECHR (Grand Chamber)

Makudi v Baron Triesman of Tottenham see Makudi v Triesman

Makudi v Triesman; *sub nom* Makudi v Baron Triesman of Tottenham [2014] EWCA Civ 179; [2014] Q.B. 839; [2014] 2 W.L.R. 1228; [2014] 3 All E.R. 36; [2014] E.M.L.R. 17; (2014) 164(7597) N.L.J. 17, CA (Civ Div); affirming [2013] EWHC 142 (QB), QBD .......... *Digested,* 14/**843**

Malekia v Secretary of State for the Home Department see Secretary of State for the Home Department v Pankina

Malekout v Secretary of State for Work and Pensions [2010] EWCA Civ 162, CA (Civ Div)
*Applied* 14/2758

Maletic v lastminute.com GmbH (C-478/12) [2014] Q.B. 424; [2014] 2 W.L.R. 260; [2014] 1 All E.R. (Comm) 745; [2014] C.E.C. 732; [2014] I.L.Pr. 9; (2013) 157(45) S.J.L.B. 37, ECJ (8th Chamber)

Malik v Bank of Credit and Commerce International SA (In Liquidation); *sub nom* Mahmud v Bank of Credit and Commerce International SA (In Liquidation); BCCI SA, Re [1998] A.C. 20; [1997] 3 W.L.R. 95; [1997] 3 All E.R. 1; [1997] I.C.R. 606; [1997] I.R.L.R. 462; (1997) 94(25) L.S.G. 33; (1997) 147 N.L.J. 917; Times, June 13, 1997; Independent, June 20, 1997, HL; reversing [1995] 3 All E.R. 545; [1996] I.C.R. 406; [1995] I.R.L.R. 375; (1995) 145 N.L.J. 593; Times, April 12, 1995; Independent, March 17, 1995, CA (Civ Div); affirming [1994] I.R.L.R. 282; Times, February 23, 1994; Independent, March 21, 1994, Ch D ... *Digested,* 97/**2192**:
*Applied* 99/2010, 01/2305, 03/1216, 04/1193, 04/1196, 04/2215, 05/1209, 08/1120, 09/1255, 10/1034, 10/4168, 13/1016: *Considered* 96/2673, 98/2106, 99/2030, 99/2149, 01/2253, 03/1246, 07/1320, 09/1228, 10/613, 11/1101: *Distinguished* 11/1049: *Explained* 99/2111: *Followed* 10/1026, 11/73, 12/3974, 14/1023

Malik v Fassenfelt [2013] EWCA Civ 798; [2013] 3 E.G.L.R. 99; [2013] 28 E.G. 84 (C.S.); (2013) 157(27) S.J.L.B. 31, CA (Civ Div) .......... *Digested,* 14/**2524**

Malik v Manchester Crown Court see R. (on the application of Malik) v Manchester Crown Court

Mallalieu v Drummond (Inspector of Taxes) [1983] 2 A.C. 861; [1983] 3 W.L.R. 409; [1983] 2 All E.R. 1095; [1983] S.T.C. 665; 55 T.C. 330; (1983) 80 L.S.G. 2368; (1983) 133 N.L.J. 869; (1983) 127 S.J. 538, HL; reversing [1983] 1 W.L.R. 252; [1983] 1 All E.R. 801; [1983] S.T.C. 124; (1983) 127 S.J. 37, CA (Civ Div); affirming [1981] 1 W.L.R. 908; [1981] S.T.C. 391; [1981] T.R. 105; (1981) 125 S.J. 205, Ch D .......... *Digested,* 83/**1983**:
*Applied* 85/1784, 13/3027, 14/2870, 14/2932: *Considered* 90/2667, 99/4701: *Distinguished* 97/2945: *Followed* 96/3356, 13/3080, 14/2975

Mallett & Sons (Antiques) Ltd v Grosvenor West End Properties Ltd see Boss Holdings Ltd v Grosvenor West End Properties Ltd

Maltedge and Frost v Wokingham DC; *sub nom* Frost v Wokingham DC (1992) 64 P. & C.R. 487; [1992] 3 P.L.R. 137; [1993] Crim. L.R. 400; [1992] C.O.D. 501; Times, May 21, 1992, DC .......... *Digested,* 93/**3865**:
*Considered* 14/2379

Malzy v Eichholz see Malzy v Eicholz

Malzy v Eicholz; *sub nom* Malzy v Eichholz [1916] 2 K.B. 308, CA
*Applied* 14/2221: *Distinguished* 97/3302

Mamatkulov v Turkey (46827/99); *joined case* Askarov v Turkey (46951/99) (2005) 41 E.H.R.R. 25; 18 B.H.R.C. 203; Times, March 8, 2005, ECHR (Grand Chamber) *Digested,* 05/**2076**:
*Applied* 12/1726, 12/1727: *Considered* 08/2038, 09/2101, 13/1184, 13/1187, 14/1651

Mammadov v Azerbaijan (4762/05) (2014) 58 E.H.R.R. 18; [2011] Inquest L.R. 137, ECHR

Man Enterprise SAL v Al-Waddan Hotel Ltd [2013] EWHC 2356 (TCC); [2014] 1 Lloyd's Rep. 217, QBD (TCC) ........ *Digested,* 14/**134**

Man Nutzfahrzeuge AG v Ernst & Young see Man Nutzfahrzeuge AG v Freightliner Ltd

Man Nutzfahrzeuge AG v Freightliner Ltd; *sub nom* Man Nutzfahrzeuge AG v Ernst & Young [2007] EWCA Civ 910; [2007] B.C.C. 986; [2008] 2 B.C.L.C. 22; [2007] 2 C.L.C. 455; [2008] Lloyd's Rep. F.C. 77; [2008] P.N.L.R. 6; (2007) 104(37) L.S.G. 35; (2007) 151 S.J.L.B. 1229, CA (Civ Div); affirming [2005] EWHC 2347 (Comm), QBD (Comm) ........ *Digested,* 08/**2642**: *Considered* 08/648, 14/1099

Man O'War Station Ltd v Auckland City Council (No.1) [2002] UKPC 28, PC (NZ) *Applied* 14/42

Manchester City Council v G (Costs) see G v E (Costs)

Manchester City Council v JW [2014] UKUT 168 (AAC); [2014] E.L.R. 304, UT (AAC) . *Digested,* 14/**941**

Manchester City Council v Pinnock [2011] UKSC 6; [2011] 2 W.L.R. 220; [2011] 2 All E.R. 586; 31 B.H.R.C. 699; (2011) 155(6) S.J.L.B. 31; [2011] N.P.C. 16, SC ..... *Digested,* 11/**2067**: *Followed* 13/412, 14/2524

Manchester City Council v Pinnock; *sub nom* Pinnock v Manchester City Council [2010] UKSC 45; [2011] 2 A.C. 104; [2010] 3 W.L.R. 1441; [2011] 1 All E.R. 285; [2011] P.T.S.R. 61; [2011] H.R.L.R. 3; [2010] U.K.H.R.R. 1213; 31 B.H.R.C. 670; [2011] H.L.R. 7; [2010] B.L.G.R. 909; [2011] L. & T.R. 2; [2010] 3 E.G.L.R. 113; [2010] 45 E.G. 93 (C.S.); (2010) 107(44) L.S.G. 16; (2011) 108(8) L.S.G. 20; (2010) 154(42) S.J.L.B. 30; [2010] N.P.C. 109; Times, November 4, 2010, SC; affirming in part [2009] EWCA Civ 852; [2010] 1 W.L.R. 713; [2010] 3 All E.R. 201; [2010] P.T.S.R. 423; [2010] H.L.R. 7; [2009] B.L.G.R. 869; [2009] 32 E.G. 68 (C.S.), CA (Civ Div) ........ *Digested,* 11/**2066**: *Applied* 11/2069, 14/1997, 14/3635: *Considered* 13/1892, 14/1625: *Distinguished* 12/2599: *Followed* 10/1705, 12/1301, 12/1645, 12/2055, 13/1562, 13/1890, 14/2000

Manchester College v Hazel; *sub nom* Hazel v Manchester College [2014] EWCA Civ 72; [2014] I.C.R. 989; [2014] I.R.L.R. 392, CA (Civ Div); affirming UKEAT/0642/11/RN, UKEAT/0136/12/RN, EAT ........ *Digested,* 14/**1140**

Manchester Ship Canal Co Ltd v United Utilities Water Plc [2014] UKSC 40; [2014] 1 W.L.R. 2576; [2014] 4 All E.R. 40; [2014] 3 E.G.L.R. 81; Times, July 8, 2014, SC; reversing [2013] EWCA Civ 40; [2013] 1 W.L.R. 2570; [2013] 2 All E.R. 642; [2013] Env. L.R. 20, CA (Civ Div); reversing [2012] EWHC 232 (Ch); [2012] Env. L.R. 31, Ch D ........ *Digested,* 14/**3034**

Manchester, Sheffield and Lincolnshire Railway Co v Anderson [1898] 2 Ch. 394, CA *Applied* 61/7524, 14/2508: *Considered* 05/2644

Mandalia v Secretary of State for the Home Department see Secretary of State for the Home Department v Rodriguez

Mander v Commercial Union Assurance Co Plc; *joined cases* Mander v Gyngell Dobinson Gregory Co Ltd; Mander v Prudential Assurance Co Ltd [1998] Lloyd's Rep. I.R. 93, QBD (Comm) ........ *Digested,* 98/**3394**: *Considered* 14/1843

Mander v Gyngell Dobinson Gregory Co Ltd see Mander v Commercial Union Assurance Co Plc

Mander v Prudential Assurance Co Ltd see Mander v Commercial Union Assurance Co Plc

Mann v Mann [2014] EWHC 537 (Fam); [2014] 1 W.L.R. 2807; [2014] 2 F.L.R. 928; [2014] Fam. Law 795; (2014) 158(11) S.J.L.B. 37, Fam Div ........ *Digested,* 14/**1403**

Mann v Nijar see Nijar v Mann

Mann Singh v France (1928/2010) 36 B.H.R.C. 675, UN HRC

Mannai Investment Co Ltd v Eagle Star Life Assurance Co Ltd [1997] A.C. 749; [1997] 2 W.L.R. 945; [1997] 3 All E.R. 352; [1997] C.L.C. 1124; [1997] 1 E.G.L.R. 57; [1997] 25 E.G. 138; [1997] 24 E.G. 122; (1997) 16 Tr. L.R. 432; [1997] E.G. 82 (C.S.); (1997) 94(30) L.S.G. 30; (1997) 147 N.L.J. 846; (1997) 141 S.J.L.B. 130; [1997] N.P.C. 81; Times, May 26, 1997, HL; reversing [1995] 1 W.L.R. 1508; [1996] 1 All E.R. 55; (1996) 71 P. & C.R. 129; [1996] 1 E.G.L.R. 69; [1996] 06 E.G. 140; [1995] E.G. 124 (C.S.); (1995) 139 S.J.L.B. 179; [1995] N.P.C. 117; Times, July 19, 1995, CA (Civ Div) ........ *Digested,* 97/**3256**: *Applied* 98/3598, 00/5612, 01/4156, 01/4182, 02/3008, 03/2723, 04/2243, 04/2497, 04/670, 05/2646, 05/523, 06/284, 07/2728, 07/807, 08/2438, 11/2060, 12/3364, 14/1996, 14/2970: *Considered* 03/2758, 05/475, 07/2754, 09/5040, 10/4356, 12/4124: *Distinguished* 98/3033, 98/3608, 00/3910, 04/2488, 08/2437, 12/2022: *Explained* 06/2703: *Followed* 98/3614, 00/3885, 00/4421, 10/2049, 14/1970, 14/2226

Manolete Partners Plc v Hastings BC [2014] EWCA Civ 562; [2014] 1 W.L.R. 4030; [2014] B.L.R. 389; [2014] 2 E.G.L.R. 145; Times, May 28, 2014, CA (Civ Div); affirming [2013] EWHC 842 (TCC); [2013] B.L.R. 361; [2013] 2 E.G.L.R. 17; [2013] R.V.R. 241, QBD (TCC) ........ *Digested,* 14/**2113**

Manorgate Ltd v First Scottish Property Services Ltd [2013] CSOH 108; [2014] P.N.L.R. 1; 2013 G.W.D. 25-491, OH ........ *Digested,* 14/**3687**

Manson v Smith (Liquidator of Thomas Christy Ltd) [1997] 2 B.C.L.C. 161, CA (Civ Div) ........ *Digested,* 98/**3341**: *Applied* 13/1707, 14/1809: *Considered* 04/2172

Manzi v Capitaneria di Porto di Genova (C-537/11) [2014] 1 Lloyd's Rep. 496, ECJ (4th Chamber)

MAP v RAP (Consent Order: Appeal: Incapacity) [2013] EWHC 4784 (Fam); [2014] Fam. Law 1671, Fam Div

Marcan Shipping (London) Ltd v Kefalas [2007] EWCA Civ 463; [2007] 1 W.L.R. 1864; [2007] 3 All E.R. 365; [2007] C.P. Rep. 41; [2007] 1 C.L.C. 785; (2007) 104(22) L.S.G. 23, CA (Civ Div) ........ *Digested,* 08/**285**: *Considered* 11/400: *Followed* 13/1007, 14/2002

Marcel v Commissioner of Police of the Metropolis; *joined case* Anchor Brewhouse Developments v Jaggard [1992] Ch. 225; [1992] 2 W.L.R. 50; [1992] 1 All E.R. 72; (1992) 4 Admin. L.R. 309; (1991) 141 N.L.J. 1224; (1991) 135 S.J.L.B. 125; Times, August 7, 1991; Independent, July 24, 1991; Guardian, August 28, 1991, CA (Civ Div); reversing in part [1991] 2 W.L.R. 1118; [1991] 1 All E.R. 845; Times, December 5, 1990, Ch D ........ *Digested,* 92/**3581**: *Applied* 92/2580, 00/934: *Considered* 03/3481, 10/2661, 10/270, 14/762: *Referred to* 92/3494, 93/3108, 95/3069

Marcus Webb Golf Professional v Revenue and Customs Commissioners [2013] EWCA Civ 1225; [2013] B.V.C. 504, CA (Civ Div); affirming [2012] UKUT 378 (TCC); [2013] S.T.C. 574; [2012] B.V.C. 1944; [2012] S.T.I. 3232, UT (Tax); affirming [2009] UKFTT 388 (TC), FTT (Tax) ........ *Digested,* 14/**3051**

Marczuk v Poland see Brodziak v Poland

Maredelanto Compania Naviera SA v Bergbau-Handel GmbH (The Mihalis Angelos) [1971] 1 Q.B. 164; [1970] 3 W.L.R. 601; [1970] 3 All E.R. 125; [1970] 2 Lloyd's Rep. 43; (1970) 114 S.J. 548, CA (Civ Div); reversing [1970] 2 W.L.R. 907; [1970] 1 All E.R. 673; [1970] 1 Lloyd's Rep. 118, QBD (Comm) ........ *Digested,* 70/**357**: *Applied* 14/119: *Considered* 76/2547, 07/3816: *Followed* 98/811, 00/4702

Marengo v Daily Sketch and Daily Graphic Ltd [1992] F.S.R. 1, CA *Applied* 14/1890: *Followed* 92/4143

Marex Financial Ltd v Creative Finance Ltd [2013] EWHC 2155 (Comm); [2014] 1 All E.R. (Comm) 122, QBD (Comm) ........ *Digested,* 14/**242**

Margan v Commonwealth of Australia [2013] FCA 109; 35 B.H.R.C. 147, Fed Ct (Aus) (Sgl judge)

Marghia (Procedural Fairness); *sub nom* Secretary of State for the Home Department v Marghia [2014] UKUT 366 (IAC); [2014] Imm. A.R. 1308, UT (IAC)

Marinari v Lloyds Bank Plc (C-364/93) [1996] Q.B. 217; [1996] 2 W.L.R. 159; [1995] E.C.R. I-2719; [1996] 5 Bank. L.R. 84; [1996] All E.R. (E.C.) 84; [1996] C.E.C. 14; [1995] I.L.Pr. 737; Times, October 19, 1995, ECJ ........ *Digested,* 95/**705**: *Applied* 08/418, 14/556: *Considered* 06/646

Marine A v Judge Advocate General see R. v Marine A

Marine Investment Finland Oy, Re see Zodiac Pool Solutions SAS, Re

Mariner v Revenue and Customs Commissioners [2013] UKFTT 657 (TC); [2014] S.F.T.D. 504; [2014] W.T.L.R. 293; [2014] S.T.I. 588, FTT (Tax) ........ *Digested,* 14/**2979**

Marios Chippery, Re see Georgiou (t/a Marios Chippery) v Customs and Excise Commissioners

Mark Rowlands Ltd v Berni Inns Ltd [1986] Q.B. 211; [1985] 3 W.L.R. 964; [1985] 3 All E.R. 473; [1985] 2 Lloyd's Rep. 437; [1985] 2 E.G.L.R. 92; (1985) 276 E.G. 191, CA (Civ Div); affirming (1984) 134 N.L.J. 236, HC ........ *Digested,* 86/**1787**: *Considered* 94/120, 98/3619, 14/1855: *Distinguished* 90/411, 94/4086, 96/3751: *Followed* 94/5930: *Referred to* 89/2093

Marketing of Herbal Medicines, Re (C-88/07) see Commission of the European Communities v Spain (C-88/07)

Markou v Goodwin [2013] EWHC 4570 (Ch); [2014] W.T.L.R. 605, Ch D ........ *Digested,* 14/**2839**

Marks & Spencer Plc v Assessor for Highland and Western Isles Valuation Joint Board [2013] CSIH 96; 2014 S.L.T. 241; [2014] R.A. 171; 2013 G.W.D. 40-768, LVAC ........ *Digested,* 14/**3670**

Marks & Spencer Plc v BNP Paribas Securities Services Trust Co (Jersey) Ltd [2014] EWCA Civ 603; [2014] L. & T.R. 26; [2014] 2 E.G.L.R. 48; [2014] 2 P. & C.R. DG16, CA (Civ Div); reversing [2013] EWHC 1279 (Ch); [2013] L. & T.R. 31; [2013] 22 E.G. 92 (C.S.), Ch D ........ *Digested,* 14/**1969**

Marks & Spencer Plc v Customs and Excise Commissioners (C-309/06) [2008] S.T.C. 1408; [2008] E.C.R. I-2283; [2008] 2 C.M.L.R. 42; [2009] C.E.C. 358; [2008] B.T.C. 5457; [2008] B.V.C. 577; [2008] S.T.I. 1194, ECJ (3rd Chamber) ........... *Digested,* 08/**4060**: *Applied* 09/4046, 12/3388, 13/3245: *Considered* 09/4070, 13/3220, 14/3074

Marks & Spencer Plc v Customs and Excise Commissioners (C-62/00) [2003] Q.B. 866; [2003] 2 W.L.R. 665; [2002] S.T.C. 1036; [2002] E.C.R. I-6325; [2002] 3 C.M.L.R. 9; [2002] C.E.C. 572; [2002] B.T.C. 5477; [2002] B.V.C. 622; [2002] S.T.I. 1009; Times, July 20, 2002, ECJ (5th Chamber) ........................................ *Digested,* 02/**4775**: *Applied* 04/3987, 05/4377, 06/4442, 06/4470, 09/3771, 10/3483, 11/3570, 13/3244, 14/3038: *Considered* 05/4367, 06/4460, 06/4487, 08/4016, 08/4065, 09/4070, 10/3507, 14/2885

Marks & Spencer Plc v Customs and Excise Commissioners (No.5); *joined case* Sussex University v Customs and Excise Commissioners [2009] UKHL 8; [2009] 1 All E.R. 939; [2009] S.T.C. 452; [2009] B.T.C. 5106; [2009] B.V.C. 106; [2009] S.T.I. 474, HL; reversing [2003] EWCA Civ 1448; [2004] S.T.C. 1; [2004] 1 C.M.L.R. 8; [2004] Eu. L.R. 170; [2004] B.T.C. 5091; [2004] B.V.C. 151; [2003] S.T.I. 1848; (2003) 100(45) L.S.G. 30; Times, October 27, 2003; Independent, October 24, 2003, CA (Civ Div) ........................................ *Digested,* 09/**4134**: *Applied* 06/4442: *Considered* 14/3075: *Distinguished* 11/3551

Marks & Spencer Plc v Interflora Inc see Interflora Inc v Marks & Spencer Plc

Marks & Spencer Plc v One in a Million Ltd see British Telecommunications Plc v One in a Million Ltd

Marks & Spencer Plc v Revenue and Customs Commissioners; *sub nom* Revenue and Customs Commissioners v Marks & Spencer Plc [2013] UKSC 30; [2013] 1 W.L.R. 1586; [2013] 3 All E.R. 835; [2013] S.T.C. 1262; [2013] 3 C.M.L.R. 36; [2013] B.T.C. 162; [2013] S.T.I. 1899, SC; affirming in part [2011] EWCA Civ 1156; [2012] S.T.C. 231; [2012] 1 C.M.L.R. 33; [2012] Eu. L.R. 275; [2011] B.T.C. 589; [2011] S.T.I. 2843; [2011] N.P.C. 103, CA (Civ Div) ........................ *Digested,* 13/**3035**: *Affirmed* 14/2877: *Considered* 13/3034

Marks & Spencer Plc v Revenue and Customs Commissioners [2014] UKSC 11; [2014] 1 W.L.R. 711; [2014] 2 All E.R. 331; [2014] S.T.C. 819; [2014] B.T.C. 7; [2014] S.T.I. 682, SC .................................................................................. *Digested,* 14/**2877**

Marleasing SA v La Comercial Internacional de Alimentacion SA (C-106/89) [1990] E.C.R. I-4135; [1993] B.C.C. 421; [1992] 1 C.M.L.R. 305, ECJ (6th Chamber) *Applied* 97/2383, 00/5520, 02/4402, 07/1370, 07/27, 08/1171, 08/3137, 08/4063, 08/509, 08/510, 09/2160, 10/1049, 10/1927, 13/947, 14/82: *Cited* 10/2352: *Considered* 03/2647, 05/4411, 06/4484, 07/2496, 08/4062, 09/2292, 09/3954, 13/2146, 13/986: *Distinguished* 95/2938: *Followed* 12/2679, 14/2874: *Referred to* 13/977

Marley v Rawlings [2014] UKSC 2; [2014] 2 W.L.R. 213; [2014] 1 All E.R. 807; [2014] 2 F.L.R. 555; [2014] W.T.L.R. 299; 16 I.T.E.L.R. 642; [2014] Fam. Law 466; (2014) 158(4) S.J.L.B. 49; Times, January 28, 2014, SC; reversing [2012] EWCA Civ 61; [2013] Ch. 271; [2013] 2 W.L.R. 205; [2012] 4 All E.R. 630; [2012] 2 F.L.R. 556; [2012] W.T.L.R. 639; 14 I.T.E.L.R. 843; [2012] Fam. Law 403, CA (Civ Div); affirming [2011] EWHC 161 (Ch); [2011] 1 W.L.R. 2146; [2011] 2 All E.R. 103; [2011] 1 F.L.R. 2052; [2012] 1 F.C.R. 615; [2011] W.T.L.R. 595; [2011] Fam. Law 477, Ch D ........................................................ *Digested,* 14/**2835**: *Followed* 14/2833, 14/2834

Marley v Rawlings (Costs) [2014] UKSC 51; [2014] 3 W.L.R. 1015; [2014] 4 All E.R. 619; [2014] 5 Costs L.R. 905; [2014] W.T.L.R. 1511; [2014] Fam. Law 1682, SC .................................................................................................. *Digested,* 14/**351**

Marlwood Commercial Inc v Kozeny see Omega Group Holdings Ltd v Kozeny

Maronier v Larmer [2002] EWCA Civ 774; [2003] Q.B. 620; [2002] 3 W.L.R. 1060; [2003] 3 All E.R. 848; [2003] 1 All E.R. (Comm) 225; [2002] C.L.C. 1281; [2002] I.L.Pr. 39; (2002) 99(28) L.S.G. 30; (2002) 146 S.J.L.B. 161; Times, June 13, 2002; Independent, June 21, 2002, CA (Civ Div) .............................................. *Digested,* 02/**636**: *Explained* 14/564: *Followed* 12/565

Marper v United Kingdom (30566/04) see S v United Kingdom (30562/04)

Marquez Samohano v Universitat Pompeu Fabra (C-190/13) [2014] I.C.R. 609; [2014] I.R.L.R. 459, ECJ (8th Chamber)

Marren (Inspector of Taxes) v Ingles [1980] 1 W.L.R. 983; [1980] 3 All E.R. 95; [1980] S.T.C. 500; 54 T.C. 76; [1980] T.R. 335; (1980) 124 S.J. 562, HL; affirming [1979] 1 W.L.R. 1131; [1979] S.T.C. 637; (1979) 123 S.J. 373, CA (Civ Div); reversing in part [1979] S.T.C. 58; [1978] T.R. 233; (1978) 122 S.J. 594; Times, July 13, 1978, Ch D .................................................................................. *Digested,* 80/**1456**: *Considered* 88/253, 96/431: *Followed* 80/1446, 14/2873

Marsden v Crown Prosecution Service [2014] EWHC 3359 (Admin); (2014) 178 J.P. 497, QBD (Admin)

Marshall v Bourneville [2013] NZCA 271; 16 I.T.E.L.R. 522, CA (NZ)
Marshall v Harland & Wolff Ltd [1972] 1 W.L.R. 899; [1972] 2 All E.R. 715; [1972] 1 R.L.R. 90; [1972] I.C.R. 101; [1972] I.R.L.R. 90; (1972) 7 I.T.R. 150; (1972) 116 S.J. 484, NIRC ........ *Digested,* 72/**1219**:
*Applied* 74/1250, 75/1097, 95/1979, 98/2108: *Considered* 14/1089: *Explained* 74/1283
Marshall v Maggs see Collier v Williams
Marshall (Inspector of Taxes) v Kerr [1995] 1 A.C. 148; [1994] 3 W.L.R. 299; [1994] 3 All E.R. 106; [1994] S.T.C. 638; 67 T.C. 81; (1994) 91(30) L.S.G. 32; (1994) 138 S.J.L.B. 155; Times, July 5, 1994; Independent, July 18, 1994, HL; reversing [1993] S.T.C. 360; 67 T.C. 73; [1993] S.T.I. 353; (1993) 90(14) L.S.G. 45; Times, March 8, 1993; Independent, April 26, 1993, CA (Civ Div); reversing [1991] S.T.C. 686; 67 T.C. 56; (1992) 89(3) L.S.G. 33; Times, November 13, 1991; Independent, December 2, 1991, Ch D ........ *Digested,* 94/**359**:
*Applied* 06/4117, 09/3714, 13/3130: *Considered* 96/438, 99/4704, 07/3988, 09/3847, 14/570: *Followed* 04/2733, 12/3306: *Referred to* 95/529
Martin v Davis see John v Rees
Martin v Devonshires Solicitors [2011] I.C.R. 352; [2011] Eq. L.R. 108, EAT ........ *Digested,* 11/**1063**:
*Applied* 12/1130, 13/1035, 14/1093: *Considered* 13/1045: *Not followed* 14/1107
Martin v Most see Martin (Sean) v HM Advocate
Martin v Revenue and Customs Commissioners; *joined case* Revenue and Customs Commissioners v Martin [2014] UKUT 429 (TCC); [2014] B.T.C. 527; [2014] S.T.I. 3021, UT (Tax); affirming [2013] UKFTT 40 (TC); [2013] S.F.T.D. 417; [2013] S.T.I. 1505, FTT (Tax) ........ *Digested,* 14/**2913**
Martin v Secretary of State for Work and Pensions [2009] EWCA Civ 1289; [2010] W.T.L.R. 671; Times, February 17, 2010, CA (Civ Div) ........ *Digested,* 10/**512**:
*Considered* 14/566
Martin (Sean) v HM Advocate; *sub nom* Martin v Most; *joined case* Miller (Ross) v HM Advocate [2010] UKSC 10; 2010 S.C. (U.K.S.C.) 40; 2010 S.L.T. 412; 2010 S.C.L. 476; 2010 S.C.C.R. 401; Times, March 9, 2010, SC ........ *Digested,* 10/**533**:
*Applied* 13/1957: *Followed* 14/573
Martin Retail Group Ltd v Crawley BC [2014] L. & T.R. 17; [2014] 1 E.G.L.R. 42, CC (Central London) ........ *Digested,* 14/**1979**
Martin Y Paz Diffusion SA v Depuydt (C-661/11) [2014] Bus. L.R. 329; [2014] E.T.M.R. 6, ECJ (3rd Chamber)
Martineau Galleries No.1 Ltd v Birmingham City Council [2013] EWHC 3018 (Ch); [2014] 1 P. & C.R. 6, Ch D (Birmingham) ........ *Digested,* 14/**2004**
Martrade Shipping & Transport GmbH v United Enterprises Corp [2014] EWHC 1884 (Comm); [2014] 2 Lloyd's Rep. 198; [2014] 1 C.L.C. 985, QBD (Comm) ........ *Digested,* 14/**2711**
Marwaha v Singh [2013] EWCA Civ 1878; [2014] P.T.S.R. 1166; (2013) 157(44) S.J.L.B. 37, CA (Civ Div) ........ *Digested,* 14/**326**
Maryland Estates Ltd v Abbathure Flat Management Co Ltd [1999] 1 E.G.L.R. 100; [1999] 06 E.G. 177, Lands Tr ........ *Digested,* 99/**3688**:
*Applied* 11/2668: *Explained* 14/2497
Marzillier, Dr Meier & Dr Guntner Rechtsanwaltsgesellschaft mbH v AMT Futures Ltd see AMT Futures Ltd v Marzillier, Dr Meier & Dr Guntner Rechtsanwaltsgesellschaft mbH
Masco Corp v European Commission (T-378/10) [2014] 4 C.M.L.R. 2, GC (4th Chamber)
Masih v Yousaf; *sub nom* R. (on the application of Masih) v Yousaf [2014] EWCA Civ 234; [2014] H.L.R. 27; [2014] L. & T.R. 18, CA (Civ Div) ........ *Digested,* 14/**1998**
Maskhadova v Russia (18071/05) 36 B.H.R.C. 364, ECHR
Maslov v Austria (1638/03) [2009] I.N.L.R. 47, ECHR (Grand Chamber) ........ *Digested,* 09/**2070**:
*Applied* 10/1772, 10/1773, 11/1731, 11/1734, 12/1676, 13/1566, 13/1596, 14/1678: *Considered* 12/1677, 12/1775, 13/1620, 14/1717
Mason v Mason see Mason, Re
Mason, Re; *sub nom* Mason v Mason [1891] 3 Ch. 467, Ch D
*Considered* 14/2982
Masri v Consolidated Contractors International Co SAL [2009] UKHL 43; [2010] 1 A.C. 90; [2009] 3 W.L.R. 385; [2009] 4 All E.R. 847; [2010] 1 All E.R. (Comm) 220; [2009] Bus. L.R. 1269; [2009] 2 Lloyd's Rep. 473; [2009] C.P. Rep. 47; [2010] B.C.C. 25; [2009] 2 B.C.L.C. 382; [2009] 2 C.L.C. 366; [2009] B.P.I.R. 1029; (2009) 159 N.L.J. 1137; (2009) 159 N.L.J. 1250; Times, August 13, 2009, HL; reversing [2008] EWCA Civ 876; [2009] 2 W.L.R. 699; [2009] Bus. L.R. 246; [2009] 1 Lloyd's Rep. 42; [2008] C.P. Rep. 42; [2008] 2 C.L.C. 126; [2009] I.L.Pr. 9; [2008] B.P.I.R. 1524, CA (Civ Div) ........ *Digested,* 09/**408**:
*Considered* 10/268, 10/404, 13/248, 14/3345, 14/539: *Distinguished* 14/305

Massachusetts Institute of Technology, Re (C-431/04) see Proceedings Brought by Massachusetts Institute of Technology (C-431/04)
Masstech Corp Ltd v Revenue and Customs Commissioners see Universal Enterprises (EU) Ltd v Revenue and Customs Commissioners
MasterCard Inc v European Commission (C-382/12 P) [2014] 5 C.M.L.R. 23, ECJ (3rd Chamber)
Masterfoods Ltd (t/a Mars Ireland) v HB Ice Cream Ltd (C-344/98) [2000] E.C.R. I-11369; [2001] 4 C.M.L.R. 14; [2001] All E.R. (EC) 130; Times, February 2, 2001, ECJ ........ *Digested,* 01/**762**:
*Applied* 06/585, 09/3113, 09/454, 13/436: *Considered* 10/349, 13/500, 14/486: *Followed* 08/543
Masterman-Lister v Brutton & Co see Masterman-Lister v Jewell
Masterman-Lister v Jewell; *joined case* Masterman-Lister v Brutton & Co [2002] EWCA Civ 1889; [2003] 1 W.L.R. 1511; [2003] 3 All E.R. 162; [2003] C.P. Rep. 29; (2004) 7 C.C.L. Rep. 5; [2003] P.I.Q.R. P20; [2003] Lloyd's Rep. Med. 244; (2003) 73 B.M.L.R. 1; [2003] M.H.L.R. 166; [2003] W.T.L.R. 259; (2003) 147 S.J.L.B. 60; Times, December 28, 2002, CA (Civ Div); affirming [2002] EWHC 417 (QB); [2002] Lloyd's Rep. Med. 239; [2002] M.H.L.R. 161; [2002] W.T.L.R. 563, QBD ........ *Digested,* 03/**311**:
*Applied* 06/482, 06/483, 07/811, 08/2468, 08/3568, 09/2737, 12/319: *Approved* 14/435: *Considered* 03/4492, 07/484, 09/2200, 13/2055, 13/2199: *Followed* 05/473
Masters v Barclays Bank Plc [2013] EWHC 2166 (Ch); [2013] B.P.I.R. 1058, Ch D ........ *Digested,* 14/**1789**
Masters v Furber [2013] EWHC 3023 (Ch); [2014] B.P.I.R. 263, Ch D (Birmingham) ... *Digested,* 14/**1801**
Mather v Revenue and Customs Commissioners [2014] UKFTT 1062 (TC); [2014] S.T.I. 3560, FTT (Tax)
Matratzen Concord AG v Hukla Germany SA (C421/04) [2006] E.C.R. I-2303; [2006] C.E.C. 621; [2006] E.T.M.R. 48, ECJ (1st Chamber) ........ *Digested,* 06/**2588**:
*Considered* 14/1102
Matthews v Associated Portland Cement Manufacturers (1978) Ltd see Fairchild v Glenhaven Funeral Services Ltd (t/a GH Dovener & Son)
Matthews v British Uralite Plc see Fairchild v Glenhaven Funeral Services Ltd (t/a GH Dovener & Son)
Matthews v Matthews [2013] EWCA Civ 1874; [2014] 2 F.L.R. 1259; [2014] Fam. Law 962, CA (Civ Div)
Matthews v Revenue and Customs Commissioners; *joined case* Sidwick v Revenue and Customs Commissioners [2012] UKUT 229 (TCC); [2014] S.T.C. 297; [2013] B.T.C. 1916; [2013] S.T.I. 3570, Ch D
Matthews v Surrey CC [2014] P.A.D. 6, Planning Inspector
Mattis v Pollock (t/a Flamingos Nightclub) [2003] EWCA Civ 887; [2003] 1 W.L.R. 2158; [2004] 4 All E.R. 85; [2003] I.C.R. 1335; [2003] I.R.L.R. 603; [2004] P.I.Q.R. P3; [2003] L.L.R. 718; (2003) 147 S.J.L.B. 816; Times, July 16, 2003, CA (Civ Div); reversing [2002] EWHC 2177 (QB); [2003] L.L.R. 41, QBD ........ *Digested,* 03/**3033**:
*Applied* 08/3906: *Considered* 12/3344, 14/3000
Matyjek v Poland (Admissibility) (38184/03) (Unreported, May 30, 2006), ECHR
*Considered* 14/2102: *Distinguished* 09/2008
Maughan (Formerly Wilmot) v Wilmot [2014] EWHC 1288 (Fam); [2014] Fam. Law 1108, Fam Div
Mawcon, Ltd, Re see Mawcon, Re
Mawcon, Re; *sub nom* Mawcon, Ltd, Re [1969] 1 W.L.R. 78; [1969] 1 All E.R. 188; (1968) 112 S.J. 1004, Ch D ........ *Digested,* 69/**418**:
*Applied* 72/390, 14/1784
Maxwell v Brookes; *sub nom* Brilliant Independent Media Specialists Ltd (In Liquidation), Re [2014] B.P.I.R. 1395, Ch D (Companies Ct)
Maxwell v DPP of Northern Ireland see DPP of Northern Ireland v Maxwell
May v Gosport BC [2013] UKUT 632 (LC); [2014] R.V.R. 140, UT (Lands) ........ *Digested,* 14/**2358**
May v Rother DC [2014] EWHC 456 (Admin); [2014] L.L.R. 535, QBD (Admin)
Mayday Optical Co Ltd v Kendrick (Valuation Officer); *sub nom* Kendrick (Valuation Officer) v Mayday Optical Co Ltd [2013] UKUT 548 (LC); [2014] R.A. 45, UT (Lands); reversing [2012] R.V.R. 235, VT ........ *Digested,* 14/**2128**
Maye's Application for Judicial Review, Re [2013] NIQB 39; [2014] N.I. 62, QBD (NI)
Mayes v Revenue and Customs Commissioners; *sub nom* Revenue and Customs Commissioners v Mayes [2011] EWCA Civ 407; [2011] S.T.C. 1269; 81 T.C. 247; [2011] B.T.C. 261; [2011] S.T.I. 1444, CA (Civ Div); affirming [2009] EWHC 2443 (Ch); [2010] S.T.C. 1; [2009] B.T.C. 617; [2009] S.T.I. 2747, Ch D; reversing [2009] S.T.C. (S.C.D.) 181; [2009] S.T.I. 476, Sp Comm ........ *Digested,* 11/**3383**:
*Considered* 11/3285, 11/3366, 14/2868: *Followed* 12/3261

Mayflower Theatre Trust Ltd v Revenue and Customs Commissioners [2007] EWCA Civ 116; [2007] S.T.C. 880; [2007] B.T.C. 5221; [2007] B.V.C. 190; [2007] S.T.I. 413; (2007) 104(10) L.S.G. 30; (2007) 151 S.J.L.B. 294; [2007] N.P.C. 24, CA (Civ Div); affirming [2006] EWHC 706 (Ch); [2006] S.T.C. 1607; [2007] B.T.C. 5018; [2007] B.V.C. 41; [2006] S.T.I. 1150, Ch D; reversing [2006] B.V.C. 2199; [2006] S.T.I. 279, V&DTr (London) ............ *Digested,* 08/**4013**: *Considered* 14/3089: *Distinguished* 08/4012

MB v GK see K (A Child) (Return Order: Failure to Comply: Committal: Appeal), Re

MB v GK see M (A Child) (Habitual Residence: Temporary Placement), Re

MB v Secretary of State for Work and Pensions [2014] EWCA Civ 1112; [2014] I.C.R. 1129; [2014] H.R.L.R. 27; Times, August 12, 2014, CA (Civ Div) ............ *Digested,* 14/**2294**

MB v Staffordshire CC see B (A Child) (Evaluation: Appellate Court's Function), Re

MB (Caesarean Section), Re; *sub nom* MB (Medical Treatment), Re [1997] 2 F.L.R. 426; [1997] 2 F.C.R. 541; [1997] 8 Med. L.R. 217; (1997) 38 B.M.L.R. 175; [1997] Fam. Law 542; (1997) 147 N.L.J. 600; Times, April 18, 1997; Independent, April 8, 1997, CA (Civ Div) ............ *Digested,* 97/**2594**: *Applied* 03/1718, 03/58, 06/2868, 08/1437, 08/3568: *Considered* 04/1690, 06/2860: *Followed* 14/2188

MB (Medical Treatment), Re see MB (Caesarean Section), Re

MB (Pakistan) v Entry Clearance Officer see Mahad (Ethiopia) v Entry Clearance Officer

Mba v Merton LBC [2013] EWCA Civ 1562; [2014] 1 W.L.R. 1501; [2014] 1 All E.R. 1235; [2014] I.C.R. 357; [2014] I.R.L.R. 145; [2014] Eq. L.R. 51; (2013) 157(48) S.J.L.B. 37, CA (Civ Div); affirming [2013] I.C.R. 658; [2013] Eq. L.R. 209; (2013) 157(3) S.J.L.B. 31, EAT ............ *Digested,* 14/**1112**

MCashback Software 6 LLP v Revenue and Customs Commissioners [2013] UKFTT 679 (TC); [2014] S.F.T.D. 510; [2014] S.T.I. 796, FTT (Tax) ............ *Digested,* 14/**2862**

McB v E (C-400/10 PPU); *sub nom* JMCB v LE (C-400/10 PPU) [2011] Fam. 364; [2011] 3 W.L.R. 699; [2011] All E.R. (EC) 379; [2011] I.L.Pr. 24; [2011] 1 F.L.R. 518; [2011] 2 F.C.R. 382; [2011] Fam. Law 8, ECJ (3rd Chamber) ............ *Digested,* 11/**1372**: *Considered* 14/1384

MCC Proceeds Inc v Bishopsgate Investment Trust Plc (No.4) see Macmillan Inc v Bishopsgate Investment Trust Plc (No.4)

McCabe v Greater Glasgow Health Board [2014] I.C.R. D41, EAT (SC)

McCall v Revenue and Customs Commissioners [2009] NICA 12; [2009] S.T.C. 990; [2009] N.I. 245; 79 T.C. 758; [2009] B.T.C. 8059; [2011] W.T.L.R. 1823; [2009] S.T.I. 1124, CA (NI); affirming [2008] S.T.C. (S.C.D.) 752; [2008] W.T.L.R. 865; [2008] S.T.I. 1256, Sp Comm ............ *Digested,* 09/**4532**: *Applied* 12/3220, 14/2935: *Considered* 11/3390

McCambridge Ltd v Joseph Brennan Bakeries [2014] IEHC 269; [2014] E.T.M.R. 44, HC (Irl)

McCann v McCann [2013] NICh 7; [2014] N.I. 201, Ch D (NI)

McCarthy and Stone (Developments) Ltd v Revenue and Customs Commissioners [2013] UKFTT 727 (TC); [2014] S.F.T.D. 625; [2014] S.T.I. 445, FTT (Tax) ....... *Digested,* 14/**3058**

McCartney, Re see R. (on the application of Adams) v Secretary of State for Justice

McCaughey v United Kingdom (43098/09) (2014) 58 E.H.R.R. 13; (2013) 163(7572) N.L.J. 20; Times, October 4, 2013, ECHR ............ *Digested,* 14/**1634**

McCaughey's Application for Judicial Review, Re [2011] UKSC 20; [2012] 1 A.C. 725; [2011] 2 W.L.R. 1279; [2011] 3 All E.R. 607; [2011] N.I. 122; [2011] H.R.L.R. 25; [2011] U.K.H.R.R. 720; [2011] Inquest L.R. 22; (2011) 155(20) S.J.L.B. 35; Times, May 20, 2011, SC; reversing [2010] NICA 13, CA (NI); affirming [2009] NIQB 77; [2009] Inquest L.R. 244, QBD (NI) ............ *Digested,* 11/**1695**: *Complaint upheld* 14/1634: *Considered* 14/62

McClennan Architects Ltd v Jones see McLennan Architects Ltd v Jones

McConnell Dowell Constructors (Aust) Pty Ltd v National Grid Gas Plc (formerly Transco Plc) [2006] EWHC 2551 (TCC); [2007] B.L.R. 92, QBD (TCC) ............ *Digested,* 07/**731**: *Applied* 14/579

McDaid v Nursing and Midwifery Council [2014] EWHC 1862 (Admin); [2014] Med. L.R. 368, QBD (Admin) ............ *Digested,* 14/**1517**

McDaniel & Co v Clarke [2014] EWHC 3826 (QB); [2014] 6 Costs L.R. 963, QBD

McDonald v Department for Communities and Local Government; *sub nom* National Grid Electricity Transmission Plc v McDonald (Deceased); McDonald (Deceased) v National Grid Electricity Transmission Plc [2014] UKSC 53; [2014] 3 W.L.R. 1197; [2014] I.C.R. 1172, SC; affirming [2013] EWCA Civ 1346; [2014] P.I.Q.R. P7, CA (Civ Div) ............ *Digested,* 14/**2998**

McDonald v Fernandez; *sub nom* MacDonald v Fernandez [2003] EWCA Civ 1219; [2004] 1 W.L.R. 1027; [2003] 4 All E.R. 1033; [2004] H.L.R. 13; [2004] L. & T.R. 5; [2003] 3 E.G.L.R. 22; [2003] 42 E.G. 128; (2003) 100(34) L.S.G. 33; (2003) 147 S.J.L.B. 995; [2003] N.P.C. 107; [2004] 1 P. & C.R. DG3; Times, October 9, 2003, CA (Civ Div) .......... *Digested,* 03/**2712**: *Considered* 08/2437, 14/1996: *Explained* 06/2703

McDonald v Graham [1994] R.P.C. 407; Times, January 12, 1994, CA (Civ Div) .......... *Digested,* 95/**861**: *Applied* 14/1902: *Considered* 12/1956

McDonald v Kensington and Chelsea RLBC see R. (on the application of McDonald) v Kensington and Chelsea RLBC

McDonald v McDonald [2014] EWCA Civ 1049; [2014] B.P.I.R. 1270; [2014] H.L.R. 43; [2014] 2 P. & C.R. 20; [2014] 3 E.G.L.R. 30, CA (Civ Div) .......... *Digested,* 14/**1968**

McDonald v United Kingdom (4241/12) 37 B.H.R.C. 130; (2014) 17 C.C.L. Rep. 187; Times, June 13, 2014, ECHR .......... *Digested,* 14/**1635**

McDonald (Deceased) v National Grid Electricity Transmission Plc see McDonald v Department for Communities and Local Government

McDonnell v Walker [2009] EWCA Civ 1257; [2010] C.P. Rep. 14; [2010] P.I.Q.R. P5; (2009) 106(47) L.S.G. 18; (2009) 153(45) S.J.L.B. 29, CA (Civ Div) .......... *Digested,* 10/**376**: *Considered* 14/421

McE v Prison Service of Northern Ireland see C's Application for Judicial Review, Re

McE, Re see C's Application for Judicial Review, Re

McFadden v United Kingdom (11365/85) see Brogan v United Kingdom (A/145-B)

McFarlane v McFarlane see Miller v Miller

McFarlane v United Kingdom (36516/10) see Eweida v United Kingdom (48420/10)

McGeoch v Lord President of the Council [2011] CSIH 67; 2012 S.C. 410; 2012 S.L.T. 224; [2012] Eu. L.R. 345; 2011 G.W.D. 38-773, IH (Ex Div); affirming [2011] CSOH 65; 2011 S.L.T. 633; 2011 G.W.D. 14-320, OH .......... *Digested,* 12/**3970**: *Affirmed* 14/976

McGeoch v Lord President of the Council see R. (on the application of Chester) v Secretary of State for Justice

McGivney v Golderslea Ltd (2001) 17 Const. L.J. 454, CA (Civ Div) .......... *Digested,* 02/**4548**: *Considered* 14/2303

McGowan v B [2011] UKSC 54; [2011] 1 W.L.R. 3121; 2012 S.C. (U.K.S.C.) 182; 2012 S.L.T. 37; 2012 S.C.L. 85; 2012 S.C.C.R. 109; [2012] H.R.L.R. 7; (2011) 155(45) S.J.L.B. 31; Times, November 25, 2011, SC .......... *Digested,* 12/**3909**: *Considered* 12/771, 14/662: *Followed* 12/3875, 12/743, 14/3458

McGraddie v McGraddie [2013] UKSC 58; [2013] 1 W.L.R. 2477; 2014 S.C. (U.K.S.C.) 12; 2013 S.L.T. 1212; 2013 G.W.D. 25-471, SC; reversing [2012] CSIH 23; 2012 G.W.D. 15-310, IH (Ex Div); reversing [2010] CSOH 60; 2010 G.W.D. 21-404, OH .......... *Digested,* 13/**6**: *Followed* 14/1579

McGrath v Riddell see HIH Casualty & General Insurance Ltd, Re

McGraw-Hill International (UK) Ltd v Deutsche Apotheker- und Arztebank EG [2014] EWHC 2436 (Comm); [2014] 2 Lloyd's Rep. 523, QBD (Comm)

McGregor v Braintree DC see Hindley v Braintree DC

McGuckian v Inland Revenue Commissioners see Inland Revenue Commissioners v McGuckian

McGuire v Rose [2013] EWCA Civ 429; [2014] B.P.I.R. 650, CA (Civ Div)

McIntosh v McIntosh [2013] W.T.L.R. 1565, CC (Luton) .......... *Digested,* 14/**2825**

McIntyre v United States [2014] EWHC 1886 (Admin); [2014] A.C.D. 115, DC

McKay v Hamlani see Cain v Francis

McKeen (Deceased), Re (Costs) see Viva! Campaigns Ltd v Scott (Costs)

McKenna v Crown Prosecution Service [2014] EWHC 2060 (Admin); [2014] A.C.D. 68, QBD (Admin)

McKeown's Application for Judicial Review, Re see McLarnon's Application for Judicial Review, Re

McKerr's Application for Judicial Review, Re; *sub nom* McKerr, Re [2004] UKHL 12; [2004] 1 W.L.R. 807; [2004] 2 All E.R. 409; [2004] N.I. 212; [2004] H.R.L.R. 26; [2004] U.K.H.R.R. 385; 17 B.H.R.C. 68; [2004] Lloyd's Rep. Med. 263; [2004] Inquest L.R. 35; (2004) 101(13) L.S.G. 33; (2004) 148 S.J.L.B. 355; Times, March 12, 2004, HL (NI); reversing [2003] NICA 1; [2003] N.I. 117, CA (NI) ...... *Digested,* 04/**1976**: *Applied* 06/17, 06/2932, 06/4528: *Considered* 05/17, 08/1975, 10/3545, 12/2336: *Doubted* 11/1695: *Followed* 07/27, 14/62

McKerr, Re see McKerr's Application for Judicial Review, Re

McKillen v Barclay see Coroin Ltd, Re

McKillen v Misland (Cyprus) Investments Ltd see Coroin Ltd, Re

McKinnon v Graham [2013] EWHC 2870 (Ch); [2013] B.P.I.R. 1070, Ch D .......... *Digested,* 14/**1766**

McKinnon v Redbridge LBC see Redbridge LBC v Dhinsa

McKnight (Inspector of Taxes) v Sheppard; *sub nom* Sheppard v McKnight (Inspector of Taxes) [1999] 1 W.L.R. 1333; [1999] 3 All E.R. 491; [1999] S.T.C. 669; 71 T.C. 419; [1999] B.T.C. 236; (1999) 96(27) L.S.G. 34; (1999) 149 N.L.J. 966; (1999) 143 S.J.L.B. 188; Times, June 18, 1999; Independent, June 23, 1999, HL; affirming [1997] S.T.C. 846; [1997] B.T.C. 328; (1997) 94(21) L.S.G. 32; (1997) 141 S.J.L.B. 115; Times, May 12, 1997; Independent, May 13, 1997, CA (Civ Div); reversing [1996] S.T.C. 627; (1996) 140 S.J.L.B. 140; Times, May 21, 1996; Independent, July 8, 1996, Ch D .......... *Digested,* 99/**4701**: *Followed* 14/2869

McLaren Racing Ltd v Revenue and Customs Commissioners; *sub nom* Revenue and Customs Commissioners v McLaren Racing Ltd [2014] UKUT 269 (TCC); [2014] S.T.C. 2417; 82 T.C. 345; [2014] B.T.C. 518; [2014] S.T.I. 2288, UT (Tax); reversing [2012] UKFTT 601 (TC); [2013] S.F.T.D. 18, FTT (Tax) .......... *Digested,* 14/**2869**

McLarnon Deeney v Gooda Walker Ltd see Henderson v Merrett Syndicates Ltd (No.1)

McLarnon's Application for Judicial Review, Re; *joined cases* Chakravarti's Application for Judicial Review, Re; McKeown's Application for Judicial Review, Re [2013] NIQB 40; [2014] N.I. 73, QBD (NI)

McLaughlin v Dacorum BC [2014] P.A.D. 30, Planning Inspector

McLean v Buchanan; *sub nom* Buchanan v McLean [2001] UKPC D 3; [2001] 1 W.L.R. 2425; 2002 S.C. (P.C.) 1; 2001 S.L.T. 780; 2001 S.C.C.R. 475; [2001] H.R.L.R. 51; [2001] U.K.H.R.R. 793; (2001) 98(28) L.S.G. 44; (2001) 145 S.J.L.B. 158; 2001 G.W.D. 19-720; Times, June 4, 2001, PC (Sc); affirming 2000 J.C. 603; 2000 S.L.T. 928; 2000 S.C.C.R. 682; [2000] U.K.H.R.R. 598; 2000 G.W.D. 22-850; Times, August 11, 2000, HCJ .......... *Digested,* 01/**6760**: *Applied* 13/3810: *Considered* 06/918, 12/4137, 14/2040: *Distinguished* 02/5619: *Followed* 02/5490, 11/4426

McLeish (Deceased), Re see Whitehead v Searle

McLennan Architects Ltd v Jones; *sub nom* McClennan Architects Ltd v Jones [2014] EWHC 2604 (TCC); [2014] T.C.L.R. 6, QBD (TCC) .......... *Digested,* 14/**407**

McMahon v McGrath see HIH Casualty & General Insurance Ltd, Re

McManus v European Risk Insurance Co hf; *sub nom* European Risk Insurance Co hf v McManus (t/a McManus Seddon Runhams) [2013] EWCA Civ 1545; [2014] Lloyd's Rep. I.R. 169, CA (Civ Div); affirming [2013] EWHC 18 (Ch); [2013] Lloyd's Rep. I.R. 533, Ch D .......... *Digested,* 14/**1841**

McManus v Sharif see Cranfield v Bridgegrove Ltd

McMillan v Airedale NHS Foundation Trust [2014] EWCA Civ 1031; [2014] I.R.L.R. 803, CA (Civ Div) .......... *Digested,* 14/**1054**

McMonagle v Westminster City Council [1990] 2 A.C. 716; [1990] 2 W.L.R. 823; [1990] 1 All E.R. 993; (1990) 154 J.P. 854; [1990] Crim. L.R. 732; [1990] C.O.D. 363; (1990) 154 J.P.N. 546; (1990) 154 L.G. Rev. 594; (1990) 87(19) L.S.G. 41; (1990) 134 S.J. 785, HL; affirming 87 L.G.R. 486; [1989] Crim. L.R. 455; (1989) 86(15) L.S.G. 39; (1989) 133 S.J. 422, DC .......... *Digested,* 90/**2933**: *Considered* 14/814

McNeill v Aberdeen City Council see Aberdeen City Council v McNeill

McNicholas Construction Co Ltd v Customs and Excise Commissioners [2000] S.T.C. 553; [2000] B.T.C. 5225; [2000] B.V.C. 255; [2000] S.T.I. 889; Independent, July 24, 2000, QBD .......... *Digested,* 00/**5348**: *Applied* 05/2307, 08/2648: *Approved* 03/4601: *Considered* 02/4732, 14/1807: *Followed* 12/3401

McNicol v Balfour Beatty Rail Maintenance Ltd; *joined case* Rugamer v Sony Music Entertainment UK Ltd [2002] EWCA Civ 1074; [2002] I.C.R. 1498; [2002] I.R.L.R. 711; [2002] Emp. L.R. 1097; (2003) 71 B.M.L.R. 1; (2002) 99(38) L.S.G. 33; (2002) 146 S.J.L.B. 201; Times, August 26, 2002, CA (Civ Div); affirming [2002] I.C.R. 381; [2001] I.R.L.R. 644; [2001] Emp. L.R. 1318, EAT .... *Digested,* 02/**1322**: *Applied* 08/1132, 09/1174, 10/1043, 10/1051, 14/1043

McNulty v McNulty [2002] EWHC 123 (Ch); [2002] W.T.L.R. 737, Ch D .......... *Digested,* 02/**4309**: *Applied* 14/2821

McPhail v Persons, Names Unknown; *joined case* Bristol Corp v Ross [1973] Ch. 447; [1973] 3 W.L.R. 71; [1973] 3 All E.R. 393; 72 L.G.R. 93; (1973) 117 S.J. 448, CA (Civ Div) .......... *Digested,* 73/**2800**: *Applied* 75/1072, 75/475, 87/2183, 07/543: *Considered* 74/5.u, 10/2079, 10/2726: *Followed* 74/3008, 86/464: *Not followed* 14/2524

McPherson v BNP Paribas SA (London Branch) [2004] EWCA Civ 569; [2004] 3 All E.R. 266; [2004] 4 Costs L.R. 596; [2004] I.C.R. 1398; [2004] I.R.L.R. 558; Times, May 31, 2004; Independent, May 20, 2004, CA (Civ Div); reversing EAT/0916/02 ILB, EAT .......... *Digested,* 04/**1314**: *Applied* 05/1220, 13/969: *Considered* 12/1091, 14/946: *Followed* 11/1097

McTear v Englehard [2014] EWHC 722 (Ch); [2014] 3 Costs L.R. 493, Ch D ............. *Digested,* 14/**462**
McWhinnie v Revenue and Customs Commissioners [2013] UKFTT 588 (TC); [2014] Pens. L.R. 1, FTT (Tax) ............. *Digested,* 14/**2907**
MD v AA see D (Recognition and Enforcement of Romanian Order), Re
MD v CT (Parental Responsibility Order: Recognition and Enforcement of Foreign Judgment) [2014] EWHC 871 (Fam); [2014] I.L.Pr. 31; [2014] Fam. Law 975, Fam Div ............. *Digested,* 14/**1289**
MD v Mersey Care NHS Trust [2013] UKUT 127 (AAC); [2013] M.H.L.R. 164, UT (AAC) ............. *Digested,* 14/**2163**
MDA Renewables Ltd v Pembrokeshire CC [2014] P.A.D. 48, Planning Inspector
ME v Refugee Applications Commissioner (C-493/10) see R. (on the application of NS) v Secretary of State for the Home Department (C-411/10)
Meadows Indemnity Co Ltd v Insurance Corp of Ireland Plc; *sub nom* Meadows Indemnity Co Ltd v International Commercial Bank Plc [1989] 2 Lloyd's Rep. 298; Times, May 23, 1989, CA (Civ Div); reversing [1989] 1 Lloyd's Rep. 181; Times, June 3, 1988; Independent, July 5, 1988, QBD (Comm) ............. *Digested,* 90/**3640**: *Applied* 96/1144, 06/2324: *Followed* 98/92, 14/567
Meadows Indemnity Co Ltd v International Commercial Bank Plc see Meadows Indemnity Co Ltd v Insurance Corp of Ireland Plc
Med Marine v Castillo Schiffahrts GmbH & Co KG [2014] EWHC 1064 (Comm); [2014] 2 Lloyd's Rep. 162, QBD (Comm) ............. *Digested,* 14/**561**
Medcalf v Mardell (Wasted Costs Order); *sub nom* Medcalf v Weatherill [2002] UKHL 27; [2003] 1 A.C. 120; [2002] 3 W.L.R. 172; [2002] 3 All E.R. 721; [2002] C.P. Rep. 70; [2002] C.P.L.R. 647; [2002] 3 Costs L.R. 428; [2002] P.N.L.R. 43; (2002) 99(31) L.S.G. 34; (2002) 152 N.L.J. 1032; (2002) 146 S.J.L.B. 175; [2002] N.P.C. 89; Times, June 28, 2002, HL; reversing [2001] C.P.L.R. 140; [2001] Lloyd's Rep. P.N. 146; [2001] P.N.L.R. 14; (2001) 98(5) L.S.G. 36; Times, January 2, 2001, CA (Civ Div) ............. *Digested,* 02/**405**: *Applied* 01/5354, 03/383, 08/1173, 08/341, 09/386: *Considered* 04/325, 11/313, 14/1036: *Followed* 12/403
Medcalf v Weatherill see Medcalf v Mardell (Wasted Costs Order)
Mediaset SpA v Ministero dello Sviluppo economico (C-69/13) [2014] 3 C.M.L.R. 8, ECJ (2nd Chamber)
MedImmune Ltd v Novartis Pharmaceuticals UK Ltd; *joined case* Novartis Pharmaceuticals UK Ltd v MedImmune Ltd [2012] EWCA Civ 1234; [2013] R.P.C. 27, CA (Civ Div) *Applied* 13/1801: *Followed* 13/1807, 14/1897
Medis ehf v Eli Lilly & Co see Actavis Group hf v Eli Lilly & Co
Medison Co Ltd v Victor (Far East) Ltd HCCT 4/2000, CFI (HK) *Considered* 14/122
Mediterranean Salvage & Towage Ltd v Seamar Trading & Commerce Inc (The Reborn) [2009] EWCA Civ 531; [2010] 1 All E.R. (Comm) 1; [2009] 2 Lloyd's Rep. 639; [2009] 1 C.L.C. 909; (2009) 159 N.L.J. 898, CA (Civ Div); affirming [2008] EWHC 1875 (Comm); [2009] 1 All E.R. (Comm) 411; [2008] 2 Lloyd's Rep. 628; [2008] 2 C.L.C. 381, QBD (Comm) ............. *Digested,* 10/**3045**: *Applied* 12/2319, 14/636: *Considered* 11/2780, 13/2833: *Followed* 10/516
Medway Council v A Mother; *sub nom* Medway Council v M [2014] EWHC 308 (Fam); [2014] 2 F.L.R. 982; [2014] Fam. Law 777, Fam Div
Medway Council v M see Medway Council v A Mother
Meek, Re; *sub nom* Jones v Parkin [2014] EWCOP 1; [2014] C.O.P.L.R. 535; [2014] W.T.L.R. 1155, CP ............. *Digested,* 14/**2829**: *Considered* 14/21
Mega Brands International v Office for Harmonisation in the Internal Market (Trade Marks and Designs) (OHIM) (T-604/11) [2014] E.T.M.R. 45, GC (2nd Chamber)
Megerisi v Protec Trust Management Establishment see Golden Trust, Re
Megtian Ltd (In Administration) v Revenue and Customs Commissioners [2010] EWHC 18 (Ch); [2010] S.T.C. 840; [2010] B.V.C. 314; [2010] S.T.I. 232; [2010] Bus. L.R. D93; Times, February 2, 2010, Ch D ............. *Digested,* 10/**3496**: *Applied* 14/3071: *Considered* 14/3065
Mehjoo v Harben Barker (A Firm) [2014] EWCA Civ 358; [2014] 4 All E.R. 806; [2014] S.T.C. 1470; [2014] P.N.L.R. 24; [2014] B.T.C. 17; [2014] S.T.I. 1627, CA (Civ Div); reversing [2013] EWHC 1500 (QB); [2013] B.T.C. 509, QBD ............. *Digested,* 14/**2211**

Meikle v Nottinghamshire CC; *sub nom* Nottinghamshire CC v Meikle [2004] EWCA Civ 859; [2004] 4 All E.R. 97; [2005] I.C.R. 1; [2004] I.R.L.R. 703; (2004) 80 B.M.L.R. 129; (2004) 148 S.J.L.B. 908; Times, July 15, 2004; Independent, July 14, 2004, CA (Civ Div); affirming EAT/0033/03 RN, EAT ............................ *Digested,* 04/**1193**:
*Applied* 05/1227, 06/1282, 08/1122, 10/1034, 14/3500: *Considered* 06/1300:
*Followed* 14/1023

Meiklejohn v St George's Healthcare NHS Trust [2014] EWCA Civ 120; [2014] Med. L.R. 122; (2014) 137 B.M.L.R. 56, CA (Civ Div); affirming [2013] EWHC 469 (QB); [2013] Med. L.R. 191; (2013) 131 B.M.L.R. 202, QBD ............................ *Digested,* 14/**2198**

Meister v Speech Design Carrier Systems GmbH (C-415/10) [2012] 2 C.M.L.R. 39; [2014] All E.R. (EC) 231; [2012] C.E.C. 1290; [2012] I.C.R. 1006; [2012] Eq. L.R. 602; Times, August 20, 2012, ECJ (2nd Chamber)

Melanesian Mission Trust Board v Australian Mutual Provident Society (1997) 74 P. & C.R. 297; [1997] 2 E.G.L.R. 128; [1997] 41 E.G. 153; [1996] N.P.C. 188, PC (NZ) ............................ *Digested,* 97/**3324**:
*Considered* 04/4988, 14/2005: *Followed* 97/3319

Melik & Co v Norwich Union Fire Insurance Society [1980] 1 Lloyd's Rep. 523, QBD ... *Digested,* 80/**1530**:
*Applied* 14/1837: *Considered* 11/1910

Mellin v White see White v Mellin

Mellor v Secretary of State for Communities and Local Government (C-75/08) see R. (on the application of Mellor) v Secretary of State for Communities and Local Government (C-75/08)

Melville Dundas Ltd (In Receivership) v George Wimpey UK Ltd [2007] UKHL 18; [2007] 1 W.L.R. 1136; [2007] 3 All E.R. 889; [2007] Bus. L.R. 1182; 2007 S.C. (H.L.) 116; 2007 S.L.T. 413; 2007 S.C.L.R. 429; [2007] B.L.R. 257; 112 Con. L.R. 1; [2007] C.I.L.L. 2469; (2007) 104(19) L.S.G. 25; (2007) 151 S.J.L.B. 571; 2007 G.W.D. 14-276; Times, May 8, 2007, HL; reversing 2006 S.C. 310; 2006 S.L.T. 95; 2006 S.C.L.R. 356; [2006] B.L.R. 164; 2006 G.W.D. 2-26, IH (Ex Div); reversing 2005 S.L.T. 24; 2005 S.C.L.R. 116, OH ............................ *Digested,* 06/**5149**:
*Applied* 07/744, 14/641: *Considered* 08/598, 11/486: *Followed* 11/4059

Menarys Retail Ltd v Commissioner of Valuation [2013] R.V.R. 264, Lands Tr (NI) ...... *Digested,* 14/**3213**

Mendaro v World Bank (Unreported, 1983), US Court
*Considered* 14/2892

Mendoza v Ghaidan see Ghaidan v Godin-Mendoza

Menelaou v Bank of Cyprus Plc; *sub nom* Menelaou v Bank of Cyprus UK Ltd [2013] EWCA Civ 1960; [2014] 1 W.L.R. 854; [2013] 2 P. & C.R. 21, CA (Civ Div); reversing [2012] EWHC 1991 (Ch), Ch D ............................ *Digested,* 13/**2472**

Menelaou v Bank of Cyprus UK Ltd see Menelaou v Bank of Cyprus Plc

Mengiste v Endowment Fund for the Rehabilitation of Tigray; *sub nom* Endowment Fund for the Rehabilitation of Tigray v Chubb; Tigray v Chubb [2013] EWCA Civ 1003; [2014] C.P. Rep. 5; [2013] 5 Costs L.R. 841; [2014] P.N.L.R. 4; (2013) 157(34) S.J.L.B. 40, CA (Civ Div); reversing in part [2012] EWHC 2782 (Ch), Ch D ............................ *Digested,* 13/**262**

Menier v Hooper's Telegraph Works (1873-74) L.R. 9 Ch. App. 350, CA in Chancery
*Considered* 14/275

Mensah v East Hertfordshire NHS Trust [1998] I.R.L.R. 531; Independent, June 18, 1998, CA (Civ Div) ............................ *Digested,* 98/**2165**:
*Applied* 14/1083: *Considered* 03/1260, 10/1070

Mensah v Salford City Council see R. (on the application of Mensah) v Salford City Council

Menson v United Kingdom (Admissibility) (47916/99) [2003] Inquest L.R. 146; [2003] Po. L.R. 155; (2003) 37 E.H.R.R. CD220, ECHR
*Applied* 14/35: *Considered* 10/3922

Mental Health Trust v DD [2014] EWCOP 11; (2014) 140 B.M.L.R. 118; [2014] Fam. Law 1380, CP

Mentmore Towers Ltd v Packman Lucas Ltd [2010] EWHC 457 (TCC); [2010] C.P. Rep. 34; [2010] B.L.R. 393; [2010] C.I.L.L. 2846; [2010] Bus. L.R. D114, QBD (TCC) ............................ *Digested,* 10/**849**:
*Considered* 14/3360

MEPC Holdings Ltd v Taylor (Inspector of Taxes) see Taylor (Inspector of Taxes) v MEPC Holdings Ltd

Mercedes-Benz Financial Services UK Ltd v Revenue and Customs Commissioners [2014] UKUT 200 (TCC); [2014] S.T.C. 2558; [2014] B.V.C. 515; [2014] S.T.I. 1950, UT (Tax); reversing [2013] UKFTT 381 (TC); [2013] S.F.T.D. 1134; [2013] S.T.I. 2606, FTT (Tax) ............................ *Digested,* 14/**3086**

Mercer Ltd v Ballinger see Bellinger v Mercer Ltd

Merchant International Co Ltd v Natsionalna Aktsionerna Kompaniia Naftogaz Ukrainy [2014] EWCA Civ 1603, CA (Civ Div); affirming [2014] EWHC 391 (Comm); [2014] 1 C.L.C. 271, QBD (Comm) ........ *Digested,* 14/**491**

Merchant International Co Ltd v Natsionalna Aktsionerna Kompaniya Naftogaz Ukrayiny [2012] EWCA Civ 196; [2012] 1 W.L.R. 3036; [2012] 2 All E.R. (Comm) 1; [2012] C.P. Rep. 25; [2012] 1 C.L.C. 396; Times, April 23, 2012, CA (Civ Div); affirming [2011] EWHC 1820 (Comm); [2011] 2 All E.R. (Comm) 755; [2011] 2 C.L.C. 711, QBD (Comm) ........ *Digested,* 12/**565**: *Followed* 14/124, 14/564

Merck Sharp Dohme Corp v Teva Pharma BV [2013] EWHC 1958 (Pat); [2014] F.S.R. 13; (2013) 133 B.M.L.R. 177, Ch D (Patents Ct) ........ *Digested,* 13/**1778**

Mercredi v Chaffe (C-497/10 PPU) [2012] Fam. 22; [2011] 3 W.L.R. 1229; [2011] I.L.Pr. 23; [2011] 1 F.L.R. 1293; [2011] Fam. Law 351, ECJ (1st Chamber) ........ *Digested,* 11/**1429**: *Applied* 12/1349, 13/1246, 13/1336, 14/1349: *Considered* 11/1431, 12/1371, 13/1244, 13/1316: *Followed* 13/1284, 14/1378

Merlin Financial Consultants Ltd v Cooper [2014] EWHC 1196 (QB); [2014] I.R.L.R. 610, QBD ........ *Digested,* 14/**1032**

Mermec UK Ltd v Network Rail Infrastructure Ltd [2011] EWHC 1847 (TCC), QBD (TCC) *Considered* 14/430

Mersey Docks and Harbour Board v Owners of the SS Marpessa (The Marpessa) [1907] A.C. 241, HL; affirming [1906] P. 95, CA; affirming [1906] P. 14, PDAD *Considered* 69/890, 14/826

Merthyr Tydfil Car Auction Ltd v Thomas see Thomas v Merthyr Tydfil Car Auction Ltd

Merton LBC v Gardiner; *sub nom* Gardiner v Merton LBC [1981] Q.B. 269; [1981] 2 W.L.R. 232; [1981] I.C.R. 186; [1980] I.R.L.R. 472; 79 L.G.R. 374; (1981) 125 S.J. 97; Times, November 26, 1980, CA (Civ Div); affirming [1980] I.R.L.R. 302, EAT ........ *Digested,* 81/**815**: *Considered* 90/1957, 13/3679, 14/3503

Messenger Newspaper Group Ltd v National Graphical Association (NGA) [1984] I.R.L.R. 397, QBD *Distinguished* 06/1040: *Not followed* 14/824

Messier Dowty Ltd v Sabena SA [2000] 1 W.L.R. 2040; [2001] 1 All E.R. 275; [2000] 1 All E.R. (Comm) 833; [2000] 1 Lloyd's Rep. 428; [2000] C.P. Rep. 72; [2000] C.L.C. 889; [2001] I.L.Pr. 5; (2000) 97(10) L.S.G. 36; (2000) 144 S.J.L.B. 124; Times, March 14, 2000; Independent, February 29, 2000, CA (Civ Div) ........ *Digested,* 00/**778**: *Considered* 07/2555, 10/2393: *Distinguished* 06/631: *Followed* 01/543, 04/566, 14/1894

MET v HAT (Interim Maintenance) [2014] EWHC 717 (Fam); [2014] Fam. Law 1110, Fam Div

MET v HAT (Interim Maintenance) [2013] EWHC 4247 (Fam); [2014] 2 F.L.R. 692; [2014] Fam. Law 447, Fam Div ........ *Digested,* 14/**1389**

Metacom AG v Rechtsanwalte Zipper & Collegen (E-6/13) [2014] 1 C.M.L.R. 50, EFTA

Metalfer Corp v Pan Ocean Shipping Co Ltd [1998] 2 Lloyd's Rep. 632; [1997] C.L.C. 1574, QBD (Comm) ........ *Digested,* 98/**253**: *Applied* 12/112, 14/561

Metall Market OOO v Vitorio Shipping Co Ltd [2013] EWCA Civ 650; [2014] Q.B. 760; [2014] 2 W.L.R. 979; [2013] 2 All E.R. (Comm) 585; [2013] 2 Lloyd's Rep. 541; [2013] 1 C.L.C. 979, CA (Civ Div); reversing in part [2012] EWHC 844 (Comm); [2012] 2 All E.R. (Comm) 577; [2012] 2 Lloyd's Rep. 73, QBD (Comm) ........ *Digested,* 13/**2801**

Metis Apartments Ltd v Grace (Valuation Officer) [2014] R.A. 222, VT ........ *Digested,* 14/**2132**: *Doubted* 14/2083

Metock v Minister for Justice, Equality and Law Reform (C-127/08) [2009] Q.B. 318; [2009] 2 W.L.R. 821; [2008] E.C.R. I-6241; [2008] 3 C.M.L.R. 39; [2009] All E.R. (EC) 40; [2009] C.E.C. 286; [2008] 3 F.C.R. 425; [2009] Imm. A.R. 113; [2009] I.N.L.R. 75, ECJ (Grand Chamber) ........ *Digested,* 09/**1412**: *Applied* 10/3129, 12/1776, 14/1732, 14/1738, 14/1740: *Considered* 10/1248: *Followed* 09/2169

Metropol Spielstatten Unternehmergesellschaft (haftungsbeschrankt) v Finanzamt Hamburg-Bergedorf (C-440/12) [2014] S.T.C. 505; [2013] B.V.C. 514; [2013] S.T.I. 3398, ECJ (1st Chamber)

Metropolis Inmobiliarias y Restauraciones SL v Office for Harmonisation in the Internal Market (Trade Marks and Designs) (OHIM) (T-284/11) [2014] E.T.M.R. 15, GC (8th Chamber)

Metropolitan Bank v Heiron (1880) 5 Ex. D. 319, CA *Applied* 11/3499: *Considered* 87/3553: *Disapproved* 94/2083: *Overruled* 14/79

Metso Paper Bender Forrest Ltd v Revenue and Customs Commissioners [2013] UKFTT 674 (TC); [2014] S.F.T.D. 529; [2014] S.T.I. 694, FTT (Tax) ................. *Digested,* 14/**2884**

Meux's Brewery Co v City of London Electric Lighting Co see Shelfer v City of London Electric Lighting Co (No.1)

MF v Brent LBC; *sub nom* P-M (A Child), Re [2013] EWHC 1838 (Fam); [2014] 1 F.L.R. 195; [2013] Fam. Law 1244, Fam Div ................. *Digested,* 14/**1236**

MF (Albania) v Secretary of State for the Home Department [2014] EWCA Civ 902; [2014] Imm. A.R. 1170, CA (Civ Div)

MF (Article 8: New Rules: Nigeria), Re; *sub nom* MF (Nigeria) v Secretary of State for the Home Department [2012] UKUT 393 (IAC); [2013] Imm. A.R. 256, UT (IAC) *Digested,* 13/**1620**: *Affirmed* 14/1669: *Applied* 13/1618: *Referred to* 14/1674

MF (Nigeria) v Secretary of State for the Home Department [2013] EWCA Civ 1192; [2014] 1 W.L.R. 544; [2014] 2 All E.R. 543; [2014] Imm. A.R. 211; [2014] I.N.L.R. 18; Times, December 17, 2013, CA (Civ Div) ................. *Digested,* 14/**1669**: *Applied* 14/1678, 14/1710

MF (Nigeria) v Secretary of State for the Home Department see MF (Article 8: New Rules: Nigeria), Re

MF Global UK Ltd (In Administration), Re; *sub nom* Heis v Attestor Value Master Fund LP [2013] EWHC 92 (Ch); [2013] Bus. L.R. 1030, Ch D (Companies Ct) .......... *Digested,* 13/**223**: *Considered* 14/1751

MF Global UK Ltd (In Special Administration), Re [2014] EWHC 2222 (Ch); [2014] Bus. L.R. 1156; (2014) 158(28) S.J.L.B. 37, Ch D (Companies Ct)

MF Global UK Ltd (In Special Administration), Re; *sub nom* Heis v Attestor Value Master Fund LP [2013] EWHC 2556 (Ch); [2014] 1 W.L.R. 1558; [2014] 1 B.C.L.C. 91, Ch D ................. *Digested,* 14/**1751**

MF Global UK Ltd (In Special Administration), Re [2013] EWHC 1655 (Ch); [2013] 1 W.L.R. 3874; [2013] 2 B.C.L.C. 426; [2013] W.T.L.R. 1239, Ch D (Companies Ct) ................. *Digested,* 13/**1664**: *Considered* 14/3030

MG v A Local Authority [2011] EWCA Civ 745; [2011] 2 F.L.R. 955; [2011] Fam. Law 927, CA (Civ Div) ................. *Digested,* 12/**1324**: *Followed* 14/1331

MG v Germany (8577/08) see Schwabe v Germany (8080/08)

MG v Staatssecretaris van Veiligheid en Justitie (C-383/13 PPU) see G v Staatssecretaris van Veiligheid en Justitie (C-383/13 PPU)

MG (EU deportation: Article 28(3): Imprisonment: Portugal), Re; *sub nom* Secretary of State for the Home Department v MG (Portugal) [2012] UKUT 268 (IAC); [2013] 1 C.M.L.R. 20, UT (IAC) ................. *Digested,* 13/**1590**: *Preliminary ruling given* 14/1666

MG Rover Group Ltd (In Creditors Voluntary Liquidation) v Revenue and Customs Commissioners [2014] UKFTT 327 (TC); [2014] S.F.T.D. 1218, FTT (Tax)

MGN Ltd v United Kingdom (39401/04); *sub nom* Mirror Group Newspapers Ltd v United Kingdom (39401/04) [2011] 1 Costs L.O. 84; [2011] E.M.L.R. 20; (2011) 53 E.H.R.R. 5; 29 B.H.R.C. 686; Times, January 20, 2011, ECHR ................. *Digested,* 11/**1680**: *Considered* 14/2221

MH v United Kingdom (11577/06) (2014) 58 E.H.R.R. 35; (2014) 136 B.M.L.R. 17, ECHR

MH Investments v Cayman Islands Tax Information Authority 16 I.T.L. Rep. 274, Grand Ct (CI)

MI (A Child) (Care Proceedings), Re [2013] EWHC 1073 (Fam); [2014] 1 F.L.R. 208; [2013] Fam. Law 1248, Fam Div ................. *Digested,* 14/**1281**

MI (Pakistan) v Secretary of State for the Home Department [2014] EWCA Civ 826; [2014] Imm. A.R. 1043, CA (Civ Div)

MI (Somalia) v Entry Clearance Officer see Mahad (Ethiopia) v Entry Clearance Officer

Mi-Space (UK) Ltd v Lend Lease Construction (EMEA) Ltd [2013] EWHC 2001 (TCC); [2013] B.L.R. 600; [2013] C.I.L.L. 3405, QBD (TCC) ................. *Digested,* 14/**437**

Michael v Middleton [2013] 6 Costs L.R. 899, Ch D (Birmingham) ................. *Digested,* 14/**458**

Michael v Miller [2004] EWCA Civ 282; [2004] 2 E.G.L.R. 151; (2004) 148 S.J.L.B. 387; [2004] N.P.C. 46; [2004] 2 P. & C.R. DG5; Times, March 30, 2004, CA (Civ Div) ................. *Digested,* 04/**3259**: *Considered* 13/230: *Explained* 14/277

Michael v Official Receiver [2013] EWHC 4286 (Ch); [2014] B.P.I.R. 666, Ch D

Michaud v France (12323/11) (2014) 59 E.H.R.R. 9, ECHR

Michel Van De Wiele NV v Pensions Regulator; *sub nom* Bonas Group Pension Scheme, Re; Pensions Regulator v Michel Van De Wiele NV [2011] Pens. L.R. 109; (2011) 161 N.L.J. 289, UT (Tax) ................. *Digested,* 11/**2310**: *Applied* 14/2247

Micheldever Tyre Services Ltd v Burrell see Burrell v Micheldever Tyre Services Ltd
MICROSOFT CORP/Lossless adaptive encoding (T1162/13) [2014] E.P.O.R. 39, EPO (Technical Bd App)
Mid-East Sales Ltd v United Engineering and Trading Co (PVT) Ltd [2014] EWHC 1457 (Comm); [2014] 2 All E.R. (Comm) 623; [2014] 4 Costs L.O. 605, QBD (Comm) ............ *Digested,* 14/**448**: *Applied* 14/447
Middleton v Vosper Thorneycroft (UK) Ltd 6SO05696, CC (Winchester) *Considered* 14/330
Midland Bank Plc v Wallace see Royal Bank of Scotland Plc v Etridge (No.2)
Midland Bank Trust Co Ltd v Hett Stubbs & Kemp [1979] Ch. 384; [1978] 3 W.L.R. 167; [1978] 3 All E.R. 571; [1955-95] P.N.L.R. 95; (1977) 121 S.J. 830; Times, December 2, 1977, Ch D ............ *Digested,* 78/**2822**: *Applied* 97/3809, 99/1889, 99/4034, 03/3018, 11/2265: *Approved* 83/3610, 94/3362: *Considered* 89/2585, 93/2997, 97/3829, 97/649, 03/5827, 14/3216: *Distinguished* 91/2343, 02/3304, 11/349: *Followed* 93/2980, 96/4498, 97/3825: *Referred to* 81/1852
Midland Expressway Ltd v Carillion Construction Ltd (No.3) [2006] EWHC 1505 (TCC); [2006] B.L.R. 325; 107 Con. L.R. 205; [2006] C.I.L.L. 2386, QBD (TCC) *Digested,* 06/**674**: *Applied* 14/586
Midland Packaging Ltd v Clark see Clark v Midland Packaging Ltd
Midlands Co-operative Society Ltd v Revenue and Customs Commissioners [2008] EWCA Civ 305; [2008] Bus. L.R. 1187; [2008] S.T.C. 1803; [2008] B.T.C. 5292; [2008] B.V.C. 414; [2008] S.T.I. 1199; Times, April 22, 2008, CA (Civ Div); affirming [2007] EWHC 1432 (Ch); [2008] S.T.C. 421; [2007] B.T.C. 5685; [2007] B.V.C. 653; [2007] S.T.I. 1767; Times, June 29, 2007, Ch D; reversing [2005] S.T.I. 1737, V&DTr ............ *Digested,* 08/**2522**: *Applied* 12/3427, 13/3244: *Followed* 14/3097
MIG, Re see Surrey CC v CA
Mighty v Secretary of State for the Home Department see R. (on the application of Lumba) v Secretary of State for the Home Department
Migration Services International Ltd, Re; *sub nom* Webster v Official Receiver [2000] B.C.C. 1095; [2000] 1 B.C.L.C. 666; (1999) 96(47) L.S.G. 29; Times, December 2, 1999; Independent, January 17, 2000, Ch D (Companies Ct) ....... *Digested,* 00/**668**: *Applied* 14/508
Mihaj v Sodexho Ltd [2014] I.C.R. D25, EAT
Mike Haynes Ltd v Revenue and Customs Commissioners [2014] UKFTT 279 (TC); [2014] S.T.I. 2091, FTT (Tax)
Mikhaylenko v Ukraine (49069/11) 35 B.H.R.C. 555, ECHR
Mikolajova v Slovakia (4479/03) (Unreported, January 18, 2011), ECHR *Applied* 14/2971
Milanovic v Serbia (44614/07) (2014) 58 E.H.R.R. 33, ECHR
Milebush Properties Ltd v Tameside MBC [2011] EWCA Civ 270; [2011] P.T.S.R. 1654; [2012] 1 P. & C.R. 3; [2011] 2 E.G.L.R. 143; [2011] 12 E.G. 114 (C.S.); [2011] N.P.C. 31; [2011] 2 P. & C.R. DG5, CA (Civ Div); affirming [2010] EWHC 1022 (Ch); [2010] 2 E.G.L.R. 93; [2010] 30 E.G. 64; [2010] J.P.L. 1303; [2010] 20 E.G. 145 (C.S.); [2010] N.P.C. 58, Ch D ............ *Digested,* 12/**2612**: *Considered* 14/2224
Miles v Wakefield MBC [1987] A.C. 539; [1987] 2 W.L.R. 795; [1987] 1 All E.R. 1089; [1987] I.C.R. 368; [1987] I.R.L.R. 193; [1987] 1 F.T.L.R. 533; 85 L.G.R. 649; (1987) 84 L.S.G. 1239; (1987) 137 N.L.J. 266; (1987) 131 S.J. 408, HL; reversing [1985] 1 W.L.R. 822; [1985] 1 All E.R. 905; [1985] I.C.R. 363; [1985] I.R.L.R. 108; 84 L.G.R. 335; (1985) 82 L.S.G. 1166; (1985) 129 S.J. 299, CA (Civ Div); reversing [1984] I.C.R. 332; 83 L.G.R. 395; Times, November 22, 1983, QBD ............ *Digested,* 87/**1380**: *Applied* 84/1191, 07/1436, 08/1169, 08/1184: *Considered* 96/2638, 96/2673, 11/2162, 14/1032, 14/1124
Millar's Application for Judicial Review, Re; *joined case* DPP's Application for Judicial Review, Re [2013] NIQB 57; [2014] N.I. 246, QBD (NI)
Millbank Financial Services Ltd v Crawford [2014] I.R.L.R. 18, EAT ............ *Digested,* 14/**1094**
Millenium Energy Trading Ltd v Revenue and Customs Commissioners [2014] UKFTT 884 (TC); [2014] S.T.I. 2951, FTT (Tax)
Miller v McFeely [2012] EWHC 4409 (Ch); [2014] B.P.I.R. 1529, Ch D

Miller v Miller; *sub nom* M v M (Short Marriage: Clean Break); *joined case* McFarlane v McFarlane [2006] UKHL 24; [2006] 2 A.C. 618; [2006] 2 W.L.R. 1283; [2006] 3 All E.R. 1; [2006] 1 F.L.R. 1186; [2006] 2 F.C.R. 213; [2006] Fam. Law 629; (2006) 103(23) L.S.G. 28; (2006) 156 N.L.J. 916; (2006) 150 S.J.L.B. 704; Times, May 25, 2006; Independent, May 26, 2006, HL; affirming [2005] EWCA Civ 984; [2006] 1 F.L.R. 151; [2005] 2 F.C.R. 713; [2005] Fam. Law 766; (2005) 102(33) L.S.G. 24, CA (Civ Div); affirming [2005] EWHC 528 (Fam); [2005] 2 F.L.R. 533; [2005] Fam. Law 537, Fam Div .......... *Digested,* 06/**1629**: *Applied* 06/4090, 07/1695, 07/1700, 08/1419, 08/1434, 08/1564, 09/1488, 09/1495, 09/1510, 12/3188, 13/1310: *Cited* 07/1694, 08/1423, 12/1316: *Considered* 06/1627, 07/1691, 07/1697, 07/1704, 08/1422, 10/1296, 11/1290, 11/1297, 11/1309, 11/1311, 12/1427, 12/1440: *Distinguished* 06/1717, 14/1367: *Followed* 07/1706, 10/1297, 11/1300, 11/1302, 13/1309: *Referred to* 08/1552

Miller v Network Rail Infrastructure Ltd [2014] UKUT 264 (LC); [2014] R.V.R. 305; [2014] J.P.L. 1270, UT (Lands)

Miller (Ross) v HM Advocate see Martin (Sean) v HM Advocate

Miller-Mead v Minister of Housing and Local Government [1963] 2 Q.B. 196; [1963] 2 W.L.R. 225; [1963] 1 All E.R. 459; (1963) 127 J.P. 122; 61 L.G.R. 152; (1963) 14 P. & C.R. 266; [1963] J.P.L. 151; (1962) 106 S.J. 1052, CA; reversing in part [1962] 2 Q.B. 555; [1962] 3 W.L.R. 654; [1962] 3 All E.R. 99; (1962) 126 J.P. 457; 60 L.G.R. 340; (1962) 13 P. & C.R. 425; (1962) 106 S.J. 492, QBD .... *Digested,* 63/**3406**: *Applied* 64/3580, 64/3584, 65/3828, 66/11738, 66/11846, 68/3830, 71/11427, 74/3740, 76/2696, 76/2697, 78/2877, 86/3266, 87/3604, 91/3470, 99/4249, 02/3675, 07/3233, 11/2549, 14/2378: *Considered* 69/3453, 69/3470, 70/2775, 79/2625, 86/3268, 86/3273, 90/4360, 90/4367, 91/3520, 94/2219, 95/4867, 96/4798: *Distinguished* 63/3358: *Followed* 94/4439: *Not followed* 98/4183

Mills v General Dental Council [2014] EWHC 89 (Admin); [2014] A.C.D. 77, QBD (Admin)

Milton Furniture Ltd v Brit Insurance Ltd [2014] EWHC 965 (QB); [2014] Lloyd's Rep. I.R. 540, QBD .......... *Digested,* 14/**1837**

MIM Construction v Revenue and Customs Commissioners [2014] UKFTT 371 (TC); [2014] S.T.I. 1923, FTT (Tax)

Minerva Navigation Inc v Oceana Shipping AG; *joined case* Oceana Shipping AG v Transatlantica Commodities SA [2013] EWCA Civ 1273; [2014] 1 All E.R. (Comm) 552; [2013] 2 Lloyd's Rep. 673; [2013] 2 C.L.C. 614, CA (Civ Div); reversing [2012] EWHC 3608 (Comm); [2013] 2 All E.R. (Comm) 28; [2013] 1 Lloyd's Rep. 145; [2013] 1 C.L.C. 226, QBD (Comm) .......... *Digested,* 14/**2740**

Mining Services Ltd, Re see UK Coal Operations Ltd, Re

Minister Finansow v MDDP sp z oo Akademia Biznesu sp komandytowa (C-319/12) [2014] S.T.C. 699; [2014] B.V.C. 11; [2013] S.T.I. 3775, ECJ (3rd Chamber)

Minister Finansow v RR Donnelley Global Turnkey Solutions Poland sp z oo (C-155/12) [2014] S.T.C. 131; [2013] B.V.C. 342; [2013] S.T.I. 2473, ECJ (1st Chamber)

Minister of Transport v Pettitt; *sub nom* Pettit v Minister of Transport 67 L.G.R. 449; (1969) 20 P. & C.R. 344; (1969) 113 S.J. 36; Times, December 14, 1968, CA (Civ Div); reversing in part (1968) 19 P. & C.R. 112; [1967] J.P.L. 718, Lands Tr .......... *Digested,* 69/**429**: *Applied* 71/1467, 04/3207: *Approved* 72/49: *Considered* 92/439: *Distinguished* 14/2359

Minister voor Immigratie en Asiel v X (C-199/12); *joined cases* Minister voor Immigratie en Asiel v Y (C-200/12); Z v Minister voor Immigratie en Asiel (C-201/12) [2014] Q.B. 1111; [2014] 3 W.L.R. 770; [2014] 2 C.M.L.R. 16; [2014] Imm. A.R. 440; [2014] I.N.L.R. 827, ECJ (4th Chamber)

Minister voor Immigratie en Asiel v Y (C-200/12) see Minister voor Immigratie en Asiel v X (C-199/12)

Minister voor Immigratie, Integratie en Asiel v B (C-456/12) see O v Minister voor Immigratie, Integratie en Asiel (C-456/12)

Minister voor Immigratie, Integratie en Asiel v G (C-457/12) see S v Minister voor Immigratie, Integratie en Asiel (C-457/12)

Ministeriet for Forskning, Innovation og Videregaende Uddannelser v Manova A/S (C-336/12) [2014] P.T.S.R. 254, ECJ (10th Chamber)

Ministerio de Defensa v Concello de Ferrol (C-522/13) [2014] S.T.I. 3080, ECJ (2nd Chamber)

Ministero dello Sviluppo economico v SOA Nazionale Costruttori - Organismo di Attestazione SpA (C-327/12) [2014] P.T.S.R. D10, ECJ (4th Chamber)

Ministre de l'Economie, des Finances et de l'Industrie v Carrefour France (Societe) [2014] E.C.C. 19, Cass (F)

Ministry of Defence v AB see B v Ministry of Defence

Ministry of Defence v Allbutt see Smith v Ministry of Defence
Ministry of Defence v Assessor for Fife Council; *sub nom* Ministry of Defence v Fife Assessor 2014 S.L.T. (Lands Tr) 34; [2014] R.V.R. 128; 2014 G.W.D. 1-28, Lands Tr (Scot) ........ *Digested,* 14/**3668**
Ministry of Defence v Ellis see Smith v Ministry of Defence
Ministry of Defence v Fife Assessor see Ministry of Defence v Assessor for Fife Council
Ministry of Defence v Grampian Assessor 2014 S.L.T. (Lands Tr) 44; [2014] R.V.R. 102; 2014 G.W.D. 1-27, Lands Tr (Scot) ........ *Digested,* 14/**3667**
Ministry of Defence v Kemeh; *sub nom* Kemeh v Ministry of Defence [2014] EWCA Civ 91; [2014] I.C.R. 625; [2014] I.R.L.R. 377; [2014] Eq. L.R. 259; Times, March 11, 2014, CA (Civ Div); affirming [2013] Eq. L.R. 605, EAT ........ *Digested,* 14/**1099**
Ministry of Justice v O'Brien; *sub nom* O'Brien v Ministry of Justice [2014] I.C.R. 773; [2014] I.R.L.R. 440, EAT ........ *Digested,* 14/**1087**
Ministry of Justice v O'Brien see Department of Constitutional Affairs v O'Brien
Minnesota Mining & Manufacturing Co v Johnson & Johnson Ltd (No.3) [1976] F.S.R. 139; [1976] R.P.C. 671, CA (Civ Div) ........ *Digested,* 76/**344.u**: *Applied* 10/1965: *Followed* 14/1885
Minsham Properties v Price (Inspector of Taxes); *joined case* Lysville v Price (Inspector of Taxes) [1990] S.T.C. 718; 63 T.C. 570; Times, November 13, 1990, Unknown court ........ *Digested,* 91/**594**: *Applied* 14/2909
Mirage Studios v Counter-Feat Clothing Co Ltd [1991] F.S.R. 145, Ch D ........ *Digested,* 92/**4433**: *Applied* 14/1890: *Referred to* 97/4884
Miramar Maritime Corp v Holborn Oil Trading (The Miramar) [1984] A.C. 676; [1984] 3 W.L.R. 1; [1984] 2 All E.R. 326; [1984] 2 Lloyd's Rep. 129; (1984) 81 L.S.G. 2000; (1984) 128 S.J. 414, HL; affirming [1984] 1 Lloyd's Rep. 142, CA (Civ Div); affirming [1983] 2 Lloyd's Rep. 319, QBD (Comm) ........ *Digested,* 84/**3156**: *Applied* 14/2705: *Considered* 95/4502
Miranda v Secretary of State for the Home Department see R. (on the application of Miranda) v Secretary of State for the Home Department
Mirror Group Newspapers Ltd v United Kingdom (39401/04) see MGN Ltd v United Kingdom (39401/04)
Mirror Group Newspapers Plc v Maxwell (No.1) [1998] B.C.C. 324; [1998] 1 B.C.L.C. 638; Times, July 15, 1997, Ch D ........ *Digested,* 97/**3072**: *Applied* 07/2443, 10/1903, 11/1828: *Considered* 05/352, 11/1897, 14/1754
Mirza v Secretary of State for the Home Department see R. (on the application of Mirza) v Secretary of State for the Home Department
Mitchell v Al-Dali see Jones v Saudi Arabia
Mitchell v Buckingham International Plc (In Liquidation) see Buckingham International Plc (In Liquidation) (No.2), Re
Mitchell v Carter (No.2) see Buckingham International Plc (In Liquidation) (No.2), Re
Mitchell v News Group Newspapers Ltd [2013] EWCA Civ 1537; [2014] 1 W.L.R. 795; [2014] 2 All E.R. 430; [2014] B.L.R. 89; [2013] 6 Costs L.R. 1008; [2014] E.M.L.R. 13; [2014] C.I.L.L. 3452; (2013) 163(7587) N.L.J. 20, CA (Civ Div); affirming [2013] EWHC 2355 (QB), QBD ........ *Digested,* 14/**445**: *Applied* 14/1757, 14/292, 14/341, 14/379, 14/395, 14/448, 14/449, 14/450, 14/451, 14/462, 14/475, 14/9: *Considered* 14/2983, 14/330, 14/397, 14/446: *Distinguished* 14/456: *Explained* 14/454: *Followed* 14/299, 14/353, 14/391, 14/447, 14/452, 14/455, 14/457, 14/460, 14/461, 14/463: *Not applied* 14/398: *Referred to* 14/343
Mitchell v United Kingdom (40528/06) see Jones v United Kingdom (34356/06)
Mitchell (Surveyor of Taxes) v Egyptian Hotels Ltd; *sub nom* Egyptian Hotels Ltd v James Mitchell [1915] A.C. 1022, HL; affirming [1914] 3 K.B. 118, CA *Applied* 14/2905
Mitchells (A Firm) v Funkwerk Information Technologies York Ltd [2008] P.N.L.R. 29, EAT ........ *Digested,* 08/**1173**: *Considered* 14/1036
Mitie Group v Mullineaux UKEAT/0708/04/DM, EAT *Applied* 14/1129
Mitsubishi Electric Corp v European Commission (C-489/11 P) see Siemens AG v European Commission (C-239/11 P)
MITSUBISHI/Images (T2231/09) [2014] E.P.O.R. 48, EPO (Technical Bd App)

Mitsui Sumitomo Insurance Co (Europe) Ltd v Mayor's Office for Policing and Crime; *sub nom* Lace International Ltd v Mayor's Office for Policing and Crime; Royal and Sun Alliance Insurance Plc v Mayor's Office for Policing and Crime [2014] EWCA Civ 682; [2014] 3 W.L.R. 576; [2014] 4 All E.R. 540; [2014] 2 All E.R. (Comm) 785; [2014] Lloyd's Rep. I.R. 612, CA (Civ Div); reversing in part [2013] EWHC 2734 (Comm); [2014] 1 All E.R. 422; [2014] 1 All E.R. (Comm) 225; [2014] Lloyd's Rep. I.R. 20; (2013) 157(37) S.J.L.B. 37, QBD (Comm)....... *Digested,* 14/**2448**

Mittal v RP Capital Explorer Master Fund [2014] B.P.I.R. 1537, Ch D

MJ v Secretary of State for the Home Department see MJ (Singh v Belgium: Tanveer Ahmed Unaffected) Afghanistan, Re

MJ (Singh v Belgium: Tanveer Ahmed Unaffected) Afghanistan, Re; *sub nom* MJ v Secretary of State for the Home Department [2013] UKUT 253 (IAC); [2013] Imm. A.R. 799, UT (IAC) ....... *Digested,* 14/**1726**

MJ Gleeson Group Plc v Axa Corporate Solutions Assurance SA [2013] Lloyd's Rep. I.R. 677, QBD (TCC) ....... *Digested,* 14/**1856**

MK v CK see K v K (Children: Permanent Removal from Jurisdiction)

MK v Secretary of State for the Home Department [2012] UKUT 126 (IAC), UT (IAC) *Affirmed* 14/1645

MK (Best Interests of Child: India), Re; *sub nom* Secretary of State for the Home Department v MK (India) [2011] UKUT 475 (IAC); [2012] Imm. A.R. 325; [2012] I.N.L.R. 292, UT (IAC) ....... *Digested,* 12/**1738**: *Approved* 14/1725

MK (Iraq) v Secretary of State for the Home Department see HF (Iraq) v Secretary of State for the Home Department

MK (Somalia) v Entry Clearance Officer [2008] EWCA Civ 1453; [2009] 2 F.L.R. 138; [2009] Imm. A.R. 386; [2009] Fam. Law 196; Times, March 11, 2009, CA (Civ Div) ....... *Digested,* 09/**2112**: *Applied* 12/1713, 12/1714: *Considered* 14/1684

MK Airlines Ltd (In Liquidation), Re; *sub nom* Katz v Bradney [2012] EWHC 1018 (Ch); [2012] 3 All E.R. 781; [2013] Bus. L.R. 169; [2014] B.C.C. 87; [2013] 1 B.C.L.C. 9, Ch D (Companies Ct) ....... *Digested,* 12/**1845**: *Considered* 14/1761

MK Airlines Ltd (In Liquidation), Re; *sub nom* MK Airlines Property Ltd (In Administration) v Katz [2012] EWHC 2764 (Ch); [2013] Bus. L.R. 243; [2014] B.C.C. 103, Ch D (Companies Ct) ....... *Digested,* 13/**1706**

MK Airlines Property Ltd (In Administration) v Katz see MK Airlines Ltd (In Liquidation), Re

ML v KW (Contact: Finding of Fact Hearing); *sub nom* IW (A Child), Re [2013] EWHC 341 (Fam); [2014] 1 F.L.R. 224; [2013] Fam. Law 663, Fam Div ....... *Digested,* 14/**1431**

Mladina dd Ljubljana v Slovenia (20981/10) 37 B.H.R.C. 342, ECHR

MM v Nottinghamshire Healthcare NHS Trust [2013] UKUT 107 (AAC); [2013] M.H.L.R. 161, UT (AAC) ....... *Digested,* 14/**2166**

MM v Secretary of State for Work and Pensions; *sub nom* Secretary of State for Work and Pensions v R. (on the application of MM) [2013] EWCA Civ 1565; [2014] 1 W.L.R. 1716; [2014] 2 All E.R. 289; [2014] Eq. L.R. 34, CA (Civ Div); reversing in part [2013] UKUT 259 (AAC); [2013] Eq. L.R. 754, UT (AAC) ....... *Digested,* 14/**2751**

MM v United Kingdom (24029/07) Times, January 16, 2013, ECHR *Applied* 14/1637: *Considered* 13/1564

MM (A Child) (Long Term Fostering: Placement with Family Members: Wishes and Feelings), Re [2013] EWHC 2697 (Fam); [2014] 1 F.L.R. 1342; [2014] Fam. Law 17, Fam Div ....... *Digested,* 14/**1282**

MM (An Adult), Re see Local Authority X v M

MM (Iran) v Secretary of State for the Home Department [2010] EWCA Civ 1457; [2011] I.N.L.R. 206, CA (Civ Div) ....... *Digested,* 11/**1720**: *Considered* 11/4380, 14/1659

MM (Sudan) v Secretary of State for the Home Department see MM (Unfairness: E&R: Sudan)

MM (Unfairness: E&R: Sudan); *sub nom* MM (Sudan) v Secretary of State for the Home Department [2014] UKUT 105 (IAC); [2014] I.N.L.R. 576, UT (IAC)

MN v Hackney LBC see R. (on the application of MN) v Hackney LBC

MN (Ahmadis: Country Conditions: Risk: Pakistan), Re; *sub nom* MN (Pakistan) v Secretary of State for the Home Department [2012] UKUT 389 (IAC), UT (IAC) *Applied* 14/1677

MN (Pakistan) v Secretary of State for the Home Department see MN (Ahmadis: Country Conditions: Risk: Pakistan), Re

MN (Somalia) v Secretary of State for the Home Department see N v Advocate General for Scotland

MN, Re [2010] EWHC 1926 (Fam); [2010] W.T.L.R. 1355, Fam Div ............................ *Digested,* 11/**2239**: *Followed* 14/2186

MO (Date of Decision: Applicable Rules: Nigeria), Re see Odelola v Secretary of State for the Home Department

MO (Nigeria) v Secretary of State for the Home Department see Odelola v Secretary of State for the Home Department

Moat Housing Group-South Ltd v Harris [2005] EWCA Civ 287; [2006] Q.B. 606; [2005] 3 W.L.R. 691; [2005] 4 All E.R. 1051; [2005] 2 F.L.R. 551; [2005] 3 F.C.R. 123; [2005] H.L.R. 33; [2005] Fam. Law 544; [2005] N.P.C. 40; Times, March 23, 2005, CA (Civ Div) ............................ *Digested,* 05/**324**: *Applied* 11/1298, 14/1999

Mobilx Ltd (In Administration) v Revenue and Customs Commissioners; *joined cases* Revenue and Customs Commissioners v Blue Sphere Global Ltd; Calltel Telecom Ltd v Revenue and Customs Commissioners [2010] EWCA Civ 517; [2010] S.T.C. 1436; [2010] Lloyd's Rep. F.C. 445; [2010] B.V.C. 638; [2010] S.T.I. 1589; Times, June 2, 2010, CA (Civ Div) ............................ *Digested,* 10/**3502**: *Applied* 11/3533, 14/3066, 14/3070: *Considered* 11/3538, 11/3556, 12/3398, 14/3071, 14/3810: *Followed* 11/3554, 12/3401, 12/3402, 12/3404, 12/3405, 14/3065, 14/3067, 14/3069, 14/3092

Modern Engineering (Bristol) Ltd v Gilbert Ash (Northern) Ltd see Gilbert Ash (Northern) Ltd v Modern Engineering (Bristol) Ltd

Mohamed v Foreign and Commonwealth Office see CF v Security Service

Mohamed v Hammersmith and Fulham LBC; *sub nom* Surdonja v Ealing LBC; Mohammed v Hammersmith and Fulham LBC; *joined case* Ealing LBC v Surdonja [2001] UKHL 57; [2002] 1 A.C. 547; [2001] 3 W.L.R. 1339; [2002] 1 All E.R. 176; [2002] 1 F.C.R. 183; [2002] H.L.R. 7; (2001) 98(45) L.S.G. 26; (2001) 151 N.L.J. 1664; (2001) 145 S.J.L.B. 253; [2001] N.P.C. 154; Times, November 2, 2001; Independent, November 8, 2001; Daily Telegraph, November 6, 2001, HL; affirming [2001] Q.B. 97; [2000] 3 W.L.R. 481; [2000] 2 All E.R. 597; (2000) 32 H.L.R. 481; [2000] N.P.C. 5; Times, February 11, 2000, CA (Civ Div) ............................ *Digested,* 01/**3419**: *Applied* 05/2008, 07/3910, 12/2278, 13/2058, 14/1603, 14/2806: *Considered* 03/2050, 08/1848, 08/1872, 13/2956: *Distinguished* 06/2045: *Followed* 11/1669

Mohamed v Kensington and Chelsea RLBC see Mohamed v Manek

Mohamed v Manek; *joined case* Mohamed v Kensington and Chelsea RLBC (1995) 27 H.L.R. 439; 94 L.G.R. 211; (1995) 159 L.G. Rev. 869; (1995) 139 S.J.L.B. 130; [1995] N.P.C. 56; Times, April 28, 1995; Independent, April 19, 1995, CA (Civ Div) ............................ *Digested,* 95/**2531**: *Considered* 06/2046: *Distinguished* 05/2660: *Followed* 14/1625

Mohamed v Secretary of State for the Home Department see Secretary of State for the Home Department v CC

Mohammed v Hammersmith and Fulham LBC see Mohamed v Hammersmith and Fulham LBC

Mohammed v Islington LBC [2013] EWCA Civ 739; [2013] H.L.R. 41, CA (Civ Div) ...... *Digested,* 14/**1600**

Mohamoud v Birmingham City Council [2014] EWCA Civ 227; [2014] H.L.R. 22; (2014) 158(11) S.J.L.B. 37, CA (Civ Div) ............................ *Digested,* 14/**1602**

Mohamud v WM Morrison Supermarkets Plc [2014] EWCA Civ 116; [2014] 2 All E.R. 990; [2014] I.R.L.R. 386; [2014] I.C.R. D19, CA (Civ Div) ............................ *Digested,* 14/**3000**

Mohan v Mohan [2013] EWCA Civ 586; [2013] C.P. Rep. 36; [2014] 1 F.L.R. 717; [2014] 1 F.C.R. 40; [2013] Fam. Law 959, CA (Civ Div) ............................ *Digested,* 13/**1289**

MOL Magyar Olaj- es Gazipari Nyrt v Office for Harmonisation in the Internal Market (Trade Marks and Designs) (OHIM) (T-367/12) [2014] E.T.M.R. 2, GC (7th Chamber)

Molinos Rio de la Plata SA v Revenue Service 16 I.T.L. Rep. 616, Tax court of Argentina

Molton Builders Ltd v Westminster City Council (1975) 30 P. & C.R. 182; (1975) 238 E.G. 411; (1975) 119 S.J. 627, CA (Civ Div); affirming [1974] J.P.L. 600, HC .... *Digested,* 75/**3347**: *Applied* 09/3151, 14/2508: *Considered* 88/478

Momax Logistik GmbH v Bundesamt fur Justiz (C-528/12) [2014] 3 C.M.L.R. 3, ECJ (10th Chamber)

Mona Oil Equipment & Supply Co Ltd v Rhodesia Railways Ltd [1949] 2 All E.R. 1014; (1949-50) 83 Ll. L. Rep. 178; [1950] W.N. 10, KBD ............................ *Digested,* 47-51/**1765**: *Applied* 14/638

Mond v Hammond Suddards (No.1) [1996] 2 B.C.L.C. 470, Ch D ............................ *Digested,* 97/**3095**: *Applied* 09/2225: *Considered* 05/2345, 14/1769

Money v Cadogan Holdings Ltd [2013] UKUT 211 (LC); [2013] 3 E.G.L.R. 145, UT (Lands) ........ *Digested,* 14/**2497**: *Applied* 14/1985

Monk v Cann Hall Primary School [2013] EWCA Civ 826; [2013] I.R.L.R. 732; [2014] P.I.Q.R. P3, CA (Civ Div); reversing [2012] EWHC 3819 (QB), QBD ........ *Digested,* 13/**434**

Monkey Tower Ltd v Ability International Ltd [2014] EWHC 18 (Pat); [2014] Bus. L.R. 291, Ch D (Patents Ct)

Montross Associated Investments SA v Moussaieff (1992) 63 P. & C.R. 31; [1992] 1 E.G.L.R. 55; [1992] 05 E.G. 160; [1991] E.G. 69 (C.S.); [1991] N.P.C. 84, CA (Civ Div); affirming (1991) 61 P. & C.R. 437; [1990] 2 E.G.L.R. 61; [1990] 45 E.G. 109; [1990] E.G. 88 (C.S.), Ch D ........ *Digested,* 92/**2669**: *Considered* 14/1994

Montull v Instituto Nacional de la Seguridad Social (INSS) (C-5/12) see Betriu Montull v Instituto Nacional de la Seguridad Social (INSS) (C-5/12)

Moore v British Columbia (Ministry of Education) 2012 SCC 81; 37 B.H.R.C. 114, Sup Ct (Can)

Moore v Moore [2007] EWCA Civ 361; [2007] I.L.Pr. 36; [2007] 2 F.L.R. 339; [2007] 2 F.C.R. 353; [2007] Fam. Law 698; (2007) 151 S.J.L.B. 573; Times, April 25, 2007, CA (Civ Div) ........ *Digested,* 07/**1697**: *Applied* 14/1385: *Considered* 08/1424, 11/1297

Moore v Revenue and Customs Commissioners [2011] UKUT 239 (TCC); [2011] S.T.C. 1784; [2011] B.T.C. 1793; [2011] S.T.I. 2602, UT (Tax); affirming [2010] UKFTT 271 (TC), FTT (Tax) ........ *Digested,* 11/**3355**: *Applied* 14/2891: *Considered* 12/3269, 13/3133

Moore v Secretary of State for Communities and Local Government [2013] EWCA Civ 1194; [2014] J.P.L. 362, CA (Civ Div); affirming [2012] EWHC 3192 (Admin); [2013] J.P.L. 672; [2012] 48 E.G. 63 (C.S.), QBD (Admin) ........ *Digested,* 14/**2383**

Moore v Secretary of State for Communities and Local Government [2012] EWCA Civ 1202; [2012] 3 E.G.L.R. 91; [2012] 46 E.G. 122; [2013] J.P.L. 192; [2013] A.C.D. 19, CA (Civ Div); affirming [2012] EWHC 1092 (Admin), QBD (Admin) ... *Digested,* 13/**2314**: *Applied* 14/2423

Moore v United Kingdom (3896/10) see Vinter v United Kingdom (66069/09)

Moore Stephens (A Firm) v Stone & Rolls Ltd (In Liquidation) see Stone & Rolls Ltd (In Liquidation) v Moore Stephens (A Firm)

Moorthy v Revenue and Customs Commissioners [2014] UKFTT 834 (TC); [2014] Eq. L.R. 640; [2014] S.T.I. 3241, FTT (Tax)

Moran v Ideal Cleaning Services Ltd [2014] 2 C.M.L.R. 37; [2014] I.C.R. 442; [2014] I.R.L.R. 172, EAT ........ *Digested,* 14/**1065**

Moran v Manchester City Council see Ali v Birmingham City Council

Moran v Manchester City Council see R. (on the application of Aweys) v Birmingham City Council

Moran Yacht & Ship Inc v Pisarev [2014] EWHC 1098 (Comm); [2014] 2 Lloyd's Rep. 88, QBD (Comm) ........ *Digested,* 14/**2728**

Morfee v Revenue and Customs Commissioners [2014] UKFTT 642 (TC); [2014] S.T.I. 2597, FTT (Tax)

Morgan v Hinton Organics (Wessex) Ltd [2009] EWCA Civ 107; [2009] C.P. Rep. 26; [2010] 1 Costs L.R. 1; [2009] Env. L.R. 30; [2009] 2 P. & C.R. 4; [2009] J.P.L. 1335, CA (Civ Div) ........ *Digested,* 09/**369**: *Applied* 11/334: *Followed* 11/279, 14/442

Morgan v New Forest National Park Authority [2014] P.A.D. 39, Planning Inspector

Morgan v Scott see Scott v Scott

Morgan v Staffordshire University [2002] I.C.R. 475; [2002] I.R.L.R. 190, EAT ........ *Digested,* 02/**1328**: *Applied* 05/1224, 14/1043

Morgan Stanley & Co International Plc v TAEL One Partners Ltd see TAEL One Partners Ltd v Morgan Stanley & Co International Plc

Morgan Stanley Dean Witter Bank Ltd v Visa International Service Association (Unreported, May 2, 2001), Unknown court *Applied* 14/529: *Considered* 09/454

Morge v Hampshire CC see R. (on the application of Morge) v Hampshire CC

Morley v Inland Revenue Commissioners see Debtor (No.657/SD/1991), Re

Morningside (Leicester) Ltd's Application, Re [2014] UKUT 70 (LC); [2014] J.P.L. 674; [2014] 2 P. & C.R. DG2, UT (Lands) ........ *Digested,* 14/**2513**

Moroccanoil Israel Ltd v Aldi Stores Ltd [2014] EWHC 1686 (IPEC); [2014] E.T.M.R. 55, IPEC ........ *Digested,* 14/**1888**

Moroney v Anglo-European College of Chiropractice [2009] EWCA Civ 1560, CA (Civ Div); affirming [2008] EWHC 2633 (QB); [2009] E.L.R. 111, QBD ........ *Digested,* 09/**1056**: *Considered* 13/909, 14/916

Moroni v Collo GmbH (C-110/91) see Ten Oever v Stichting Bedrijfspensioenfonds voor het Glazenwassers- en Schoonmaakbedrijf (C-109/91)

Morris v Bank of India; *sub nom* Bank of India v Morris; Bank of Credit and Commerce International SA (In Liquidation) (No.15), Re [2005] EWCA Civ 693; [2005] B.C.C. 739; [2005] 2 B.C.L.C. 328; [2005] B.P.I.R. 1067; Times, July 19, 2005, CA (Civ Div); affirming [2004] EWHC 528 (Ch); [2005] 1 All E.R. (Comm) 209; [2004] B.C.C. 404; [2004] 2 B.C.L.C. 279, Ch D (Companies Ct) ........................ *Digested,* 05/**2307**: *Applied* 08/2648: *Considered* 14/1807: *Followed* 12/3401

Morris v Banque Arabe et Internationale d'Investissement SA (No.1) [2000] C.P. Rep. 65; [2001] I.L.Pr. 37; (1999-2000) 2 I.T.E.L.R. 492; (2000) 97(1) L.S.G. 24; Times, December 23, 1999, Ch D (Companies Ct) ........................ *Digested,* 00/**315**: *Applied* 14/539

Morris v Director of the Serious Fraud Office [1993] Ch. 372; [1993] 3 W.L.R. 1; [1993] 1 All E.R. 788; [1992] B.C.C. 934; [1993] B.C.L.C. 580; Independent, September 11, 1992, Ch D (Companies Ct) ........................ *Digested,* 93/**2357**: *Considered* 14/762

Morris v DPP [2014] EWHC 105 (Admin); [2014] 2 Cr. App. R. 21, QBD (Admin) ......... *Digested,* 14/**811**

Morris v KLM Royal Dutch Airlines see King v Bristow Helicopters Ltd

Morris Homes (West Midlands) Ltd v Keay [2013] EWHC 932 (TCC); [2013] B.L.R. 370; 152 Con. L.R. 105, QBD (TCC) ........................ *Digested,* 13/**109**

Morrison v AWG Group Ltd (formerly Anglian Water Plc) see AWG Group Ltd (formerly Anglian Water Plc) v Morrison

Morrison v Revenue and Customs Commissioners see Revenue and Customs Commissioners v Morrison

Morrison Facilities Services Ltd v Norwich City Council [2010] EWHC 487 (Ch), Ch D *Applied* 11/2631, 14/2477

Morshead Mansions Ltd v Di Marco see Di Marco v Morshead Mansions Ltd

Mortgage Business Plc v Cook see North East Property Buyers Litigation, Re

Mortgage Business Plc v O'Shaughnessy see North East Property Buyers Litigation, Re

Mortimer v Motor Insurance Bureau [2010] EWCA Civ 959, CA (Civ Div) *Applied* 14/1292

Morton-Norwich Products Inc v Customs and Excise Commissioners see Norwich Pharmacal Co v Customs and Excise Commissioners

Moseley v Solicitors Regulation Authority [2013] EWHC 2108 (Admin); [2013] B.P.I.R. 855; (2013) 157(27) S.J.L.B. 31, QBD (Admin) ........................ *Digested,* 14/**2057**

Moses v Sussex Pharmaceuticals Ltd see Nygate v E-Squared Ltd

Moses-Taiga v Taiga; *sub nom* Taiga v Taiga [2005] EWCA Civ 1013; [2006] 1 F.L.R. 1074; [2008] 1 F.C.R. 696; [2006] Fam. Law 266, CA (Civ Div) ........................ *Digested,* 06/**1632**: *Applied* 07/1701, 07/1707, 08/1425: *Considered* 11/1412, 14/1388: *Distinguished* 14/1364: *Followed* 09/1501, 10/1289

Mosley v News Group Newspapers Ltd [2008] EWHC 1777 (QB); [2008] E.M.L.R. 20; (2008) 158 N.L.J. 1112; Times, July 30, 2008, QBD ........................ *Digested,* 08/**1992**: *Considered* 14/415

Mothew v Bristol & West Building Society see Bristol & West Building Society v Mothew (t/a Stapley & Co)

Motley v Higgs Trustees see Ransom (Inspector of Taxes) v Higgs

Motley (Inspector of Taxes) v Higgs Settlement Trustees see Ransom (Inspector of Taxes) v Higgs

Mott MacDonald Ltd v London & Regional Properties Ltd [2007] EWHC 1055 (TCC); 113 Con. L.R. 33; [2007] C.I.L.L. 2481, QBD (TCC) ........................ *Digested,* 07/**730**: *Applied* 11/492: *Considered* 14/583

Motto v Trafigura Ltd [2011] EWCA Civ 1150; [2012] 1 W.L.R. 657; [2012] 2 All E.R. 181; [2011] 6 Costs L.R. 1028; Times, November 22, 2011, CA (Civ Div) .......... *Digested,* 12/**388**: *Considered* 14/331

Mouat v DPP see R. (on the application of Ebrahim) v Feltham Magistrates Court

Mouloungui v Secretary of State for the Home Department see Liu v Secretary of State for the Home Department

Mount Cook Land Ltd v Westminster City Council see R. (on the application of Mount Cook Land Ltd) v Westminster City Council

Mount Eden Land Ltd v Speechly Bircham LLP [2014] EWHC 169 (QB); [2014] 2 Costs L.R. 337, QBD ........................ *Digested,* 14/**347**

Mountain v Hastings (1993) 25 H.L.R. 427; [1993] 29 E.G. 96; [1993] N.P.C. 56; Times, April 1, 1993; Independent, April 16, 1993, CA (Civ Div) ........................ *Digested,* 93/**2447**: *Applied* 04/2486, 14/1998

Mountney v Treharne; *sub nom* Mountney, Re [2002] EWCA Civ 1174; [2003] Ch. 135; [2002] 3 W.L.R. 1760; [2002] 2 F.L.R. 930; [2002] 3 F.C.R. 97; [2002] B.P.I.R. 1126; [2002] Fam. Law 809; (2002) 99(39) L.S.G. 38; Times, September 9, 2002, CA (Civ Div); reversing [2002] 2 F.L.R. 406; [2002] B.P.I.R. 556; [2002] Fam. Law 658; [2002] N.P.C. 6, Ch D .......... *Digested,* 02/**2676**:
*Applied* 14/3199: *Considered* 09/2208: *Followed* 04/2129

Mountney, Re see Mountney v Treharne

Moyna v Secretary of State for Social Security see Moyna v Secretary of State for Work and Pensions

Moyna v Secretary of State for Work and Pensions; *sub nom* Moyna v Secretary of State for Social Security [2003] UKHL 44; [2003] 1 W.L.R. 1929; [2003] 4 All E.R. 162; (2003) 73 B.M.L.R. 201; Times, August 11, 2003; Independent, October 2, 2003, HL; reversing [2002] EWCA Civ 408, CA (Civ Div) .......... *Digested,* 03/**4000**:
*Applied* 05/796, 14/412: *Considered* 11/1581: *Followed* 11/3510

Moynihan v Moynihan (Nos.1 and 2); *sub nom* Moynihan, Re [1997] 1 F.L.R. 59; [1997] Fam. Law 88; Independent, October 7, 1996, Fam Div .......... *Digested,* 97/**2450**:
*Applied* 08/1529, 14/1353

Moynihan, Re see Moynihan v Moynihan (Nos.1 and 2)

MP (Fact-finding Hearing: Care Proceedings: Art.15), Re; *sub nom* LA v ML [2013] EWHC 2063 (Fam); [2014] 1 F.L.R. 702; [2013] Fam. Law 1370, Fam Div .......... *Digested,* 14/**1356**

MP (Sri Lanka) v Secretary of State for the Home Department [2014] EWCA Civ 829; Times, July 3, 2014, CA (Civ Div) .......... *Digested,* 14/**1665**

MR (A Child) (Welfare Hearing), Re [2013] EWHC 1156 (Fam); [2013] 2 F.L.R. 1566; [2013] Fam. Law 939, Fam Div .......... *Digested,* 14/**1418**

MR (Bangladesh) v Secretary of State for the Home Department see JD (Congo) v Secretary of State for the Home Department

MRI Trading AG v Erdenet Mining Corp LLC [2013] EWCA Civ 156; [2013] 1 Lloyd's Rep. 638; [2013] 1 C.L.C. 423, CA (Civ Div); affirming [2012] EWHC 1988 (Comm); [2013] 1 All E.R. (Comm) 1; [2012] 2 Lloyd's Rep. 465, QBD (Comm) . *Digested,* 13/**566**:
*Applied* 14/112

MRJ (Reconsideration of Order), Re see JT v Suffolk CC

MS v North East London Foundation Trust [2013] UKUT 92 (AAC); [2013] M.H.L.R. 158, UT (AAC) .......... *Digested,* 14/**2168**

MS (Uganda) v Secretary of State for the Home Department [2014] EWCA Civ 50; [2014] 1 W.L.R. 2766; [2014] Imm. A.R. 745, CA (Civ Div) .......... *Digested,* 14/**1642**

MSS v Belgium (30696/09) (2011) 53 E.H.R.R. 2; 31 B.H.R.C. 313; [2011] I.N.L.R. 533, ECHR (Grand Chamber)
*Applied* 12/1696, 13/1578, 14/1652: *Distinguished* 13/1551

MT v T (Marriage: Strike-Out) [2013] EWHC 2061 (Fam); [2014] 1 F.L.R. 1352; [2014] Fam. Law 460, Fam Div .......... *Digested,* 14/**1388**

MT Hojgaard A/S v E.ON Climate and Renewables UK Robin Rigg East Ltd [2014] EWHC 1088 (TCC); [2014] B.L.R. 450, QBD (TCC)

MT Hojgaard A/S v E.On Climate and Renewables UK Robin Rigg East Ltd [2014] EWCA Civ 710; [2014] C.I.L.L. 3523, CA (Civ Div); affirming [2013] EWHC 967 (TCC); [2013] C.I.L.L. 3356, QBD (TCC)

MTV Europe v BMG Records (UK) Ltd [1997] 1 C.M.L.R. 867; [1997] Eu. L.R. 100, CA (Civ Div); affirming [1995] 1 C.M.L.R. 437; [1995] E.C.C. 216, Ch D .......... *Digested,* 97/**855**:
*Applied* 14/529: *Considered* 96/2806, 97/861, 01/442

Mubarak v Mubarak (No.2) [2002] EWHC 2171 (Fam); [2003] 2 F.L.R. 553; [2003] Fam. Law 560, Fam Div .......... *Digested,* 03/**1600**:
*Considered* 14/321

Muckian v Hoey [2014] NICh 11; [2014] W.T.L.R. 1255, Ch D (NI) .......... *Digested,* 14/**3276**

Muhumed v Entry Clearance Officer see Mahad (Ethiopia) v Entry Clearance Officer

Mul v Hutton Construction Ltd [2014] EWHC 1797 (TCC); [2014] B.L.R. 529; 154 Con. L.R. 159; [2014] C.I.L.L. 3529, QBD (TCC) .......... *Digested,* 14/**597**

Muledal v Norway (22703/10) see Vilnes v Norway (52806/09)

Mullen v Salford City Council see Hounslow LBC v Powell

Mullins v Laughton [2002] EWHC 2761 (Ch); [2003] Ch. 250; [2003] 2 W.L.R. 1006; [2003] 4 All E.R. 94; [2003] B.P.I.R. 674; (2003) 100(5) L.S.G. 30; (2003) 147 S.J.L.B. 56; Times, December 27, 2002, Ch D .......... *Digested,* 03/**3047**:
*Applied* 13/2102: *Considered* 14/2227

Multiplex Constructions (UK) Ltd v Cleveland Bridge UK Ltd [2008] EWHC 2280 (TCC); 122 Con. L.R. 88; [2009] 1 Costs L.R. 55; (2008) 105(39) L.S.G. 23, QBD (TCC) .......... *Digested,* 09/**378**:
*Applied* 11/273, 12/346, 13/290, 13/323, 13/349, 14/343: *Considered* 11/272, 12/354, 13/340: *Not followed* 13/324

Mundeba v Entry Clearance Officer, Nairobi see Mundeba (S.55 and Para 297(i)(f)), Re

Mundeba v Secretary of State for the Home Department see Mundeba (S.55 and Para 297(i)(f)), Re

Mundeba (S.55 and Para 297(i)(f)), Re; *sub nom* Mundeba v Secretary of State for the Home Department; Mundeba v Entry Clearance Officer, Nairobi [2013] UKUT 88 (IAC); [2014] I.N.L.R. 36, UT (IAC) *Applied* 14/1741

Muqtaar v Secretary of State for the Home Department see R. (on the application of Muqtaar) v Secretary of State for the Home Department

Murad v Al-Saraj; *joined case* Murad v Westwood Business Inc [2005] EWCA Civ 959; [2005] W.T.L.R. 1573; (2005) 102(32) L.S.G. 31, CA (Civ Div); affirming [2004] EWHC 1235 (Ch), Ch D ........ *Digested,* 06/**1513**: *Applied* 14/2991

Murad v Westwood Business Inc see Murad v Al-Saraj

Murex Energy Ltd v Mid-Devon DC [2014] P.A.D. 7, Planning Inspector

Murphy v Brentwood DC [1991] 1 A.C. 398; [1990] 3 W.L.R. 414; [1990] 2 All E.R. 908; [1990] 2 Lloyd's Rep. 467; 50 B.L.R. 1; 21 Con. L.R. 1; (1990) 22 H.L.R. 502; 89 L.G.R. 24; (1991) 3 Admin. L.R. 37; (1990) 6 Const. L.J. 304; (1990) 154 L.G. Rev. 1010; [1990] E.G. 105 (C.S.); (1990) 87(30) L.S.G. 15; (1990) 134 S.J. 1076; Times, July 27, 1990; Independent, July 27, 1990, HL; reversing [1990] 2 W.L.R. 944; [1990] 2 All E.R. 269; 88 L.G.R. 333; (1990) 87(5) L.S.G. 42; (1990) 134 S.J. 458; Times, December 27, 1989; Independent, January 26, 1990, CA (Civ Div); affirming 13 Con. L.R. 96, OR ........ *Digested,* 91/**2661**: *Applied* 91/2660, 94/2881, 96/4433, 00/4227, 01/4509, 02/3291, 03/2995, 04/600, 09/2726, 13/1880: *Considered* 92/3219, 93/2987, 93/2994, 93/2997, 94/4517, 95/3648, 95/3667, 95/4189, 95/4519, 96/2993, 96/4438, 96/4448, 96/7223, 97/3816, 05/436, 10/3422, 10/432, 14/2204: *Distinguished* 92/3199, 96/1156, 97/1752, 97/3776, 99/1409: *Followed* 98/3955, 11/2253, 11/2270: *Not followed* 98/3924: *Referred to* 94/6386

Murphy v Ireland (44179/98) (2004) 38 E.H.R.R. 13, ECHR ........ *Digested,* 04/**1922**: *Applied* 08/440, 12/3593, 14/1629: *Considered* 07/546

Murphy v Media Protection Services Ltd [2007] EWHC 3091 (Admin); [2008] 1 W.L.R. 1869; [2008] Bus. L.R. 1454; [2008] E.C.D.R. 9; [2008] F.S.R. 15; [2008] L.L.R. 332; [2008] A.C.D. 30; (2008) 31(3) I.P.D. 31018, DC ........ *Digested,* 08/**2248**: *Considered* 14/1861

Murphy v Media Protection Services Ltd [2012] EWHC 529 (Admin); [2013] 1 Costs L.R. 16; [2012] 3 C.M.L.R. 3; [2012] F.S.R. 13; [2013] L.L.R. 400, DC ........ *Digested,* 12/**360**: *Considered* 14/1861

Murphy v Media Protection Services Ltd [2008] EWHC 1666 (Admin); [2008] U.K.C.L.R. 427; [2008] F.S.R. 33, DC ........ *Digested,* 09/**2319**: *Considered* 10/1948, 14/1861: *Preliminary ruling given* 12/1924

Murphy v Media Protection Services Ltd (C-429/08) see Football Association Premier League Ltd v QC Leisure (C-403/08)

Murphy v Murphy; *sub nom* Murphy (A Child) v Holland; L v M (A Child) [2003] EWCA Civ 1862; [2004] 1 F.C.R. 1; [2004] Lloyd's Rep. I.R. 744; [2004] W.T.L.R. 239, CA (Civ Div) ........ *Digested,* 04/**3664**: *Applied* 14/2823: *Considered* 08/2122

Murphy v Murphy [2014] EWHC 2263 (Fam); [2014] Fam. Law 1520, Fam Div

Murphy v Rayner; *sub nom* Rayner v Lord Chancellor [2013] EWHC 3878 (Ch); [2014] 1 W.L.R. 677; [2014] 1 Costs L.R. 59, Ch D ........ *Digested,* 14/**376**

Murphy v Staples UK Ltd see Cranfield v Bridgegrove Ltd

Murphy v Sun Alliance and London Insurance Plc see Murphy v Young & Co's Brewery Plc

Murphy v Young & Co's Brewery Plc; *joined case* Murphy v Sun Alliance and London Insurance Plc [1997] 1 W.L.R. 1591; [1997] 1 All E.R. 518; [1997] 1 Lloyd's Rep. 236; [1997] C.L.C. 469; [1998] 1 Costs L.R. 94; [1997] 6 Re. L.R. 113; Times, January 8, 1997; Independent, December 6, 1996, CA (Civ Div); affirming [1996] L.R.L.R. 60; Lloyd's List, August 16, 1995, QBD ........ *Digested,* 97/**3113**: *Applied* 99/3422, 99/388, 00/413: *Considered* 97/3159, 01/5712, 14/1835: *Distinguished* 99/405: *Followed* 99/392

Murphy (A Child) v Holland see Murphy v Murphy

Murray v Associated Newspapers Ltd [2014] EWHC 1170 (QB); [2014] E.M.L.R. 23, QBD ........ *Digested,* 14/**840**

Murray v Big Pictures (UK) Ltd see Murray v Express Newspapers Plc

Murray v Express Newspapers Plc; *sub nom* Murray v Big Pictures (UK) Ltd [2008] EWCA Civ 446; [2009] Ch. 481; [2008] 3 W.L.R. 1360; [2008] E.C.D.R. 12; [2008] E.M.L.R. 12; [2008] 2 F.L.R. 599; [2008] 3 F.C.R. 661; [2008] H.R.L.R. 33; [2008] U.K.H.R.R. 736; [2008] Fam. Law 732; (2008) 105(20) L.S.G. 23; (2008) 158 N.L.J. 706; (2008) 152(19) S.J.L.B. 31, CA (Civ Div); reversing [2007] EWHC 1908 (Ch); [2007] E.C.D.R. 20; [2007] E.M.L.R. 22; [2008] 1 F.L.R. 704; [2007] 3 F.C.R. 331; [2007] H.R.L.R. 44; [2007] U.K.H.R.R. 1322; [2007] Fam. Law 1073; (2007) 157 N.L.J. 1199; Times, May 7, 2008, Ch D ...... *Digested,* 08/**1984**: *Applied* 10/1742: *Considered* 12/335, 13/1563, 13/2042: *Followed* 11/341, 14/842

Murray v Revenue and Customs Commissioners [2014] UKFTT 338 (TC); [2014] S.T.I. 2118, FTT (Tax)

Murray Group Holdings Ltd v Revenue and Customs Commissioners; *sub nom* Revenue and Customs Commissioners v Murray Group Holdings Ltd [2014] UKUT 292 (TCC); [2014] B.T.C. 521; [2014] S.T.I. 2409, UT (Tax); reversing in part [2012] UKFTT 692 (TC); [2013] S.F.T.D. 149; [2013] S.T.I. 492, FTT (Tax) *Digested,* 14/**2910**

Murrills v Berlanda [2014] EWCA Civ 6; [2014] C.P. Rep. 21; [2014] I.L.Pr. 41, CA (Civ Div) .......... *Digested,* 14/**471**

Mushin v Manchester City Council see Hounslow LBC v Powell

Mussellwhite v Youssefi see Youssefi v Mussellwhite

Mustafa (t/a Orsi Deli Foods) v Revenue and Customs Commissioners [2014] UKFTT 975 (TC); [2014] S.T.I. 3377, FTT (Tax)

Muster Inns Ltd v Revenue and Customs Commissioners [2014] UKFTT 563 (TC); [2014] S.F.T.D. 1035; [2014] S.T.I. 2250, FTT (Tax)

MVV Environment Devonport Ltd v Devon CC [2014] P.A.D. 5, Planning Inspector

MW (A Child) (Leave to Apply for Adoption), Re [2014] EWHC 385 (Fam); [2014] 2 F.L.R. 978; [2014] Fam. Law 772, Fam Div (Leeds) .......... *Digested,* 14/**1240**

MWH UK Ltd v Wise (Inspector of Health and Safety) [2014] EWHC 427 (Admin); [2014] A.C.D. 96, QBD (Admin) .......... *Digested,* 14/**1575**

MXB v East Sussex Hospitals NHS Trust [2012] EWHC 3279 (QB); (2013) 177 J.P. 31; [2013] 1 F.L.R. 1152; [2013] Med. L.R. 13; (2013) 130 B.M.L.R. 44; [2013] Crim. L.R. 417; [2013] Fam. Law 147, QBD .......... *Digested,* 13/**256**: *Considered* 14/801

My Kinda Town Ltd (t/a Chicago Pizza Pie Factory) v Soll and Grunts Investments [1983] R.P.C. 407, CA (Civ Div); reversing [1981] Com. L.R. 194; [1982] F.S.R. 147; [1983] R.P.C. 15, Ch D .......... *Digested,* 84/**3533**: *Followed* 14/1887

Myton v Wood Times, July 12, 1980, CA (Civ Div) .......... *Digested,* 80/**861**: *Approved* 14/2200

N v Advocate General for Scotland; *sub nom* KASY v Advocate General for Scotland; MABN v Advocate General for Scotland; Secretary of State for the Home Department v MN; Secretary of State for the Home Department v KY; MN (Somalia) v Secretary of State for the Home Department; KY (Somalia) v Secretary of State for the Home Department; *joined case* Y v Advocate General for Scotland [2014] UKSC 30; [2014] 1 W.L.R. 2064; [2014] 4 All E.R. 443; 2014 S.C. (U.K.S.C.) 183; 2014 S.L.T. 669; [2014] Imm. A.R. 981; [2014] I.N.L.R. 590; 2014 G.W.D. 17-325; Times, June 6, 2014, SC; affirming [2013] CSIH 68; 2013 S.L.T. 1143; 2013 G.W.D. 37-721, IH (Ex Div) .......... *Digested,* 14/**1641**

N v B (Adoption by Grandmother) [2013] EWHC 820 (Fam); [2014] 1 F.L.R. 369; [2013] Fam. Law 1359, Fam Div .......... *Digested,* 14/**1239**

N v Belgium 17 I.T.L. Rep. 340, RB (B)

N v E see E, Re

N v Governing Body of a School [2014] EWHC 1238 (Admin); [2014] A.C.D. 113, QBD (Admin)

N v K (Jurisdiction: International Liaison) [2014] EWHC 507 (Fam); [2014] 2 F.L.R. 1147; [2014] Fam. Law 806, Fam Div

N v Minister for Justice, Equality and Law Reform (C-604/12); *sub nom* HN v Minister for Justice, Equality and Law Reform (C-604/12) EU:C:2014:302; [2014] 1 W.L.R. 3371, ECJ (4th Chamber)

N v N (Jurisdiction: Maintenance) [2014] Fam. Law 159, Fam Div

N v N (Periodical Payments: Non-Disclosure) [2014] EWCA Civ 314; [2014] Fam. Law 1243, CA (Civ Div)

N v Newham LBC see R. (on the application of N) v Newham LBC

N v United Kingdom (26565/05) (2008) 47 E.H.R.R. 39; 25 B.H.R.C. 258; [2008] Imm. A.R. 657; [2008] I.N.L.R. 335; Times, June 6, 2007, ECHR (Grand Chamber) ... *Digested,* 08/**1909**: *Applied* 13/1551, 14/1665: *Considered* 09/2033: *Distinguished* 09/2082: *Followed* 09/2085

N & M Walkingshaw Ltd v Revenue and Customs Commissioners [2013] UKFTT 269 (TC); [2013] S.F.T.D. 1160; [2013] S.T.I. 1876, FTT (Tax) ................................ *Digested,* 14/**3081**
N (A Child) (Fact-finding Hearing: Accidental Injury), Re see Lancashire CC v R
N (A Minor) (Abduction: Brussels II Revised), Re [2014] EWHC 749 (Fam); [2014] Fam. Law 947, Fam Div
N (A Minor), Re see A v N (Committal: Refusal of Contact)
N (Adoption Order), Re; *sub nom* BC v IA [2014] EWFC 1491; [2014] Fam. Law 1086, Fam Ct
N (Children) (Care and Placement Orders: Sufficiency of Welfare Determination), Re [2014] EWCA Civ 1226; [2014] 3 F.C.R. 493, CA (Civ Div)
N (Death of a Child in DRC: Fact Finding), Re; *sub nom* SA v BN [2013] EWHC 4417 (Fam); [2014] Fam. Law 955, Fam Div (Birmingham)
N (Death of a Child in DRC: Order for Return: Contempt), Re; *sub nom* SA v BN [2014] EWHC 337 (Fam); [2014] Fam. Law 956, Fam Div
N (Kenya) v Secretary of State for the Home Department; *sub nom* R. (on the application of N) v Secretary of State for the Home Department [2004] EWCA Civ 1094; [2004] I.N.L.R. 612; (2004) 101(37) L.S.G. 36; Times, September 13, 2004, CA (Civ Div)
*Applied* 08/2046, 09/2081: *Considered* 12/1705: *Distinguished* 11/1732: *Followed* 14/1670: *Superseded* 11/1730
N (Leave to Remove from Jurisdiction), Re [2014] Fam. Law 976, Fam Div (Manchester)
N (Placement Order: Appeal), Re [2013] EWCA Civ 1534; [2014] Fam. Law 271, CA (Civ Div)
N&D (London) Ltd v Gadson (1992) 24 H.L.R. 64; [1992] 1 E.G.L.R. 112; [1992] 02 E.G. 176, QBD ................................ *Digested,* 92/**2756**: *Applied* 14/2016
NA v Secretary of State for the Home Department see NA (UT Rule 45: Singh v Belgium: Iran)
NA (UT Rule 45: Singh v Belgium: Iran); *sub nom* NA v Secretary of State for the Home Department [2014] UKUT 205 (IAC); [2014] Imm. A.R. 895, UT (IAC)
Nadreph Ltd v Willmett & Co; *sub nom* Nadreth v Willmett & Co [1978] 1 W.L.R. 1537; [1978] 1 All E.R. 746; (1978) 122 S.J. 744, Ch D ................................ *Digested,* 78/**715**: *Applied* 14/827: *Considered* 83/1071, 98/4025
Nadreth v Willmett & Co see Nadreph Ltd v Willmett & Co
Naeem v Secretary of State for Justice [2014] I.C.R. 472; [2014] I.R.L.R. 520; [2014] Eq. L.R. 206, EAT ................................ *Digested,* 14/**1111**
Nagarajan v London Regional Transport; *sub nom* Swiggs v Nagarajan (No.2); *joined case* Nagarajan v Swiggs (No.2) [2000] 1 A.C. 501; [1999] 3 W.L.R. 425; [1999] 4 All E.R. 65; [1999] I.C.R. 877; [1999] I.R.L.R. 572; (1999) 96(31) L.S.G. 36; (1999) 149 N.L.J. 1109; (1999) 143 S.J.L.B. 219; Times, July 19, 1999; Independent, October 11, 1999, HL; reversing [1998] I.R.L.R. 73, CA (Civ Div) ................................ *Digested,* 99/**2093**: *Applied* 02/1332, 02/1415, 05/1290, 05/2162, 06/1368, 07/1402, 08/1190: *Cited* 07/1404: *Considered* 01/2301, 07/266, 09/1210, 09/1228, 09/1229, 12/1150: *Followed* 03/1354, 11/1103, 14/1104
Nagarajan v Swiggs (No.2) see Nagarajan v London Regional Transport
Nagulananthan v Secretary of State for the Home Department see Subesh v Secretary of State for the Home Department
Naik v Secretary of State for the Home Department see R. (on the application of Naik) v Secretary of State for the Home Department
Naismith v Naismith see Naismith's Trustees v Naismith
Naismith's Trustees v Naismith; *sub nom* Naismith v Naismith 1909 S.C. 1380; 1909 2 S.L.T. 127, IH (2 Div)
*Applied* 14/2982
NAP Anglia Ltd v Sun-Land Development Co Ltd (Costs) [2012] EWHC 51 (TCC); [2012] B.L.R. 195; 141 Con. L.R. 247; [2012] 4 Costs L.O. 485, QBD (TCC) ..... *Digested,* 12/**349**: *Applied* 14/359
Napoli v Ministero della Giustizia, Dipartimento dell'Amministrazione penitenziaria (C-595/12) [2014] I.C.R. 486; [2014] Eq. L.R. 465, ECJ (1st Chamber)
Napp Pharmaceutical Holdings Ltd v Director General of Fair Trading (No.3) [2001] CAT 3; [2001] Comp. A.R. 33; [2002] E.C.C. 3, CCAT ................................ *Digested,* 02/**585**: *Applied* 10/475: *Considered* 04/515, 14/2247: *Followed* 05/565
Napp Pharmaceutical Holdings Ltd v Director General of Fair Trading (No.4) [2002] CAT 1; [2002] Comp. A.R. 13; [2002] E.C.C. 13; (2002) 64 B.M.L.R. 165, CCAT ................................ *Digested,* 02/**597**: *Applied* 04/542, 05/570, 08/525, 08/540: *Approved* 07/621: *Considered* 14/2247: *Followed* 05/572, 08/534

Narandas-Girdhar v Bradstock [2014] EWHC 1321 (Ch); [2014] B.P.I.R. 1014, Ch D ... *Digested,* 14/**1799**

Nasiopoulos v Ipourgos Igias kai Pronoias (C-575/11) [2014] 1 C.M.L.R. 7; [2014] C.E.C. 247, ECJ (1st Chamber)

Nasser v United Bank of Kuwait (Security for Costs) [2001] EWCA Civ 556; [2002] 1 W.L.R. 1868; [2002] 1 All E.R. 401; [2001] C.P. Rep. 105, CA (Civ Div) ............ *Digested,* 02/**385**: *Applied* 04/330, 05/465: *Considered* 02/384, 04/274, 10/411, 12/393, 13/421: *Explained* 14/433: *Followed* 11/382, 12/392

Nathaniel & Co Solicitors v Revenue and Customs Commissioners [2010] UKFTT 472 (TC), FTT (Tax)
*Considered* 14/3076

National & Provincial Building Society v United Kingdom (21319/93); *joined cases* Yorkshire Building Society v United Kingdom (21675/93); Leeds Permanent Building Society v United Kingdom (21449/93) [1997] S.T.C. 1466; (1998) 25 E.H.R.R. 127; 69 T.C. 540; [1997] B.T.C. 624; [1998] H.R.C.D. 34; Times, November 6, 1997, ECHR; no effect (1995) 19 E.H.R.R. CD56, Eur Comm HR *Digested,* 97/**2756**: *Applied* 05/2084, 08/1925, 14/2964: *Distinguished* 06/2146

National Bank Ltd, Re [1966] 1 W.L.R. 819; [1966] 1 All E.R. 1006; (1966) 110 S.J. 226, Ch D ............ *Digested,* 66/**1305**: *Applied* 00/683, 02/2715, 05/2334, 12/498: *Considered* 00/684, 07/2447, 12/512: *Followed* 09/475, 14/1822

National Commercial Bank Jamaica Ltd v Olint Corp Ltd [2009] UKPC 16; [2009] 1 W.L.R. 1405; [2009] Bus. L.R. 1110; [2009] 1 C.L.C. 637; Times, May 6, 2009, PC (Jam)
*Applied* 11/2637, 14/2477: *Considered* 12/1142, 12/556

National Credit Regulator v Opperman 35 B.H.R.C. 330, Const Ct (SA)

National Crime Agency v Szepietowski see Serious Organised Crime Agency v Szepietowski

National Crime Agency (formerly Serious Organised Crime Agency) v Namli see Serious Organised Crime Agency v Namli

National Exhibition Centre Ltd v Revenue and Customs Commissioners; *sub nom* Revenue and Customs Commissioners v National Exhibition Centre Ltd [2013] UKFTT 289 (TC); [2014] S.F.T.D. 107; [2013] S.T.I. 2003, FTT (Tax) ............ *Digested,* 14/**3046**

National Grid Electricity Transmission Plc v ABB Ltd [2009] EWHC 1326 (Ch); [2009] U.K.C.L.R. 838, Ch D ............ *Digested,* 09/**454**: *Applied* 13/436, 14/486, 14/529: *Considered* 10/349, 13/500

National Grid Electricity Transmission Plc v ABB Ltd [2013] EWHC 822 (Ch); [2013] U.K.C.L.R. 177; [2013] I.L.Pr. 39, Ch D ............ *Digested,* 13/**248**: *Affirmed* 14/539

National Grid Electricity Transmission Plc v ABB Ltd see Secretary of State for Health v Servier Laboratories Ltd

National Grid Electricity Transmission Plc v Anthony White Estates Ltd see Arnold White Estates Ltd v National Grid Electricity Transmission Plc

National Grid Electricity Transmission Plc v Arnold White Estates Ltd see Arnold White Estates Ltd v National Grid Electricity Transmission Plc

National Grid Electricity Transmission Plc v McDonald (Deceased) see McDonald v Department for Communities and Local Government

National Guild of Removers and Storers Ltd v Milner (t/a Intransit Removals and Storage) [2014] EWHC 670 (IPEC); [2014] F.S.R. 38, IPEC ............ *Digested,* 14/**1924**

National Museums and Galleries on Merseyside Board of Trustees v AEW Architects and Designers Ltd [2013] EWHC 3025 (TCC); [2014] 1 Costs L.O. 39, QBD (TCC) ............ *Digested,* 14/**325**

National Oilwell (UK) Ltd v Davy Offshore Ltd (Unreported, July 28, 1993), QBD (Comm) ............ *Digested,* 94/**4086**: *Applied* 04/2205, 07/740: *Considered* 14/1855

National Semiconductors (UK) Ltd v UPS Ltd and Inter City Trucks [1996] 2 Lloyd's Rep. 212, QBD (Comm) ............ *Digested,* 96/**5745**: *Applied* 14/278

National Union of Rail, Maritime and Transport Workers v United Kingdom (31045/10) [2014] I.R.L.R. 467; 37 B.H.R.C. 145; Times, April 30, 2014, ECHR ............ *Digested,* 14/**1627**

National Westminster Bank Plc v Gill see Royal Bank of Scotland Plc v Etridge (No.2)

National Westminster Bank Plc v King [2008] EWHC 280 (Ch); [2008] Ch. 385; [2008] 2 W.L.R. 1279; [2008] C.P. Rep. 23; [2008] 2 P. & C.R. 9; [2008] N.P.C. 22; Times, April 14, 2008, Ch D ............ *Digested,* 08/**346**: *Followed* 14/1902

National Westminster Bank Plc v Lucas; *sub nom* Savile's Estate, Re [2014] EWHC 653 (Ch); [2014] B.P.I.R. 551; [2014] W.T.L.R. 637, Ch D ............ *Digested,* 14/**2818**

Nationwide Anglia Building Society v Ahmed and Balakrishnan (1995) 70 P. & C.R. 381; [1995] N.P.C. 77, CA (Civ Div) ........ *Digested,* 96/**4953**: *Applied* 96/4951, 12/2734: *Considered* 14/2505

Nationwide Building Society v Davisons Solicitors; *sub nom* Davisons Solicitors v Nationwide Building Society [2012] EWCA Civ 1626; [2013] 3 Costs L.O. 464; [2013] P.N.L.R. 12; [2013] 1 E.G.L.R. 73; [2013] 10 E.G. 148; [2013] W.T.L.R. 393; (2012) 156(48) S.J.L.B. 31, CA (Civ Div); reversing (Unreported, April 24, 2012), QBD ........ *Digested,* 13/**2444**: *Applied* 13/227, 14/2059: *Followed* 13/1951

Nationwide Building Society v Dunlop Haywards (DHL) Ltd (t/a Dunlop Heywood Lorenz) [2009] EWHC 254 (Comm); [2010] 1 W.L.R. 258; [2009] 2 All E.R. (Comm) 715; [2009] 1 Lloyd's Rep. 447; [2010] Lloyd's Rep. P.N. 68; [2009] P.N.L.R. 20, QBD (Comm) ........ *Digested,* 09/**969**: *Applied* 11/266: *Considered* 14/2217

Nationwide Digital Satellite Warranty Services Ltd, Re see Digital Satellite Warranty Cover Ltd, Re

NATS (Services) Ltd v Gatwick Airport Ltd [2014] EWHC 3133 (TCC); [2014] B.L.R. 697; 156 Con. L.R. 177, QBD (TCC)

Natsvlishvili v Georgia (9043/05) 37 B.H.R.C. 593, ECHR

Naturally Yours Cosmetics Ltd v Customs and Excise Commissioners (C-230/87) [1988] S.T.C. 879; [1988] E.C.R. 6365; [1989] 1 C.M.L.R. 797; Times, November 29, 1988; Daily Telegraph, December 31, 1988, ECJ ........ *Digested,* 89/**1683**: *Applied* 91/3668, 97/4975, 97/4976, 98/4936, 00/5319, 01/5597, 05/4347, 09/4097, 14/3081: *Considered* 00/5347, 01/5556, 01/5598, 01/5599: *Distinguished* 11/3572: *Followed* 05/4406

Navitaire Inc v EasyJet Airline Co Ltd (No.3) [2004] EWHC 1725 (Ch); [2005] E.C.C. 30; [2005] E.C.D.R. 17; [2005] Info. T.L.R. 1; [2006] R.P.C. 3, Ch D ........ *Digested,* 05/**2427**: *Applied* 07/2514, 11/1948, 13/1768, 14/1870

Nayif v High Commission of Brunei Darussalam [2014] EWCA Civ 1521, CA (Civ Div); reversing [2013] EWHC 3938 (QB); [2014] Eq. L.R. 136, QBD ........ *Digested,* 14/**387**

NB (Pakistan) v Secretary of State for the Home Department see SA (Pakistan) v Secretary of State for the Home Department

NC v Leicestershire CC [2012] UKUT 85 (AAC); [2012] E.L.R. 365, UT (AAC) ........ *Digested,* 12/**995**: *Applied* 13/904, 14/943: *Considered* 14/941

ND v KP (Freezing Order: Ex Parte Application) [2011] EWHC 457 (Fam); [2011] 2 F.L.R. 662; [2011] Fam. Law 677; (2011) 161 N.L.J. 702, Fam Div ........ *Digested,* 11/**1298**: *Applied* 14/496

Ndikumana v Netherlands (Admissibility) (4714/06) (2014) 59 E.H.R.R. SE5, ECHR

Neath v Hugh Steeper Ltd (C-152/91) see Ten Oever v Stichting Bedrijfspensioenfonds voor het Glazenwassers- en Schoonmaakbedrijf (C-109/91)

Neath Rugby Ltd, Re see Hawkes v Cuddy

Nedbank Ltd v Mendelow NA 16 I.T.E.L.R. 552, Sup Ct (SA)

Needler Financial Services Ltd v Taber [2002] 3 All E.R. 501; [2002] Lloyd's Rep. P.N. 32; [2001] Pens. L.R. 253; (2001) 98(37) L.S.G. 39; (2001) 151 N.L.J. 1283; (2001) 145 S.J.L.B. 219; Times, August 9, 2001, Ch D ........ *Digested,* 01/**4593**: *Considered* 14/827

NEF Telecom Co BV, Re [2012] EWHC 2944 (Ch); [2014] B.C.C. 417, Ch D (Companies Ct)

Nelder v CPS Times, June 11, 1998; Independent, June 8, 1998, DC ........ *Digested,* 98/**1039**: *Considered* 14/667

Nelson v Circle Thirty Three Housing Trust Ltd; *sub nom* Circle Thirty Three Housing Trust Ltd v Nelson [2014] EWCA Civ 106; [2014] 3 Costs L.O. 355, CA (Civ Div) ........ *Digested,* 14/**2002**

Nelson v Deutsche Lufthansa AG (C-581/10); *joined case* R. (on the application of TUI Travel Plc) v Civil Aviation Authority (C-629/10) [2013] 1 All E.R. (Comm) 385; [2013] 1 Lloyd's Rep. 49; [2013] 1 C.M.L.R. 42; [2013] All E.R. (EC) 603, ECJ (Grand Chamber) *Applied* 14/165

Nelson v Greening & Sykes (Builders) Ltd [2007] EWCA Civ 1358; [2008] 1 E.G.L.R. 59; [2008] 8 E.G. 158; (2007-08) 10 I.T.E.L.R. 689; Times, January 22, 2008, CA (Civ Div) ........ *Digested,* 08/**3063**: *Applied* 14/3024

Nemeti v Sabre Insurance Co Ltd [2013] EWCA Civ 1555; [2014] C.P. Rep. 16; [2014] P.I.Q.R. P12, CA (Civ Div); affirming [2012] EWHC 3355 (QB), QBD ........ *Digested,* 14/**488**

Nemtsov v Russia (1774/11) 37 B.H.R.C. 312, ECHR

Nero v DPP see Richardson v DPP

Neste Oy v Lloyds Bank Plc [1983] 2 Lloyd's Rep. 658; [1983] Com. L.R. 145; (1983) 133 N.L.J. 597, QBD (Comm) ............ *Digested,* 83/**201**:
*Applied* 97/5578, 00/3433, 07/2388: *Considered* 92/489, 93/73, 14/78

Nestec SA v Dualit Ltd [2013] EWHC 923 (Pat); [2013] R.P.C. 32; (2013) 157(18) S.J.L.B. 31, Ch D (Patents Ct) ............ *Digested,* 14/**1877**

Netherlands v Russia (The Arctic Sunrise) [2014] 2 Lloyd's Rep. 20, Arbitration

Nethermere (St Neots) Ltd v Gardiner; *sub nom* Nethermere (St Neots) Ltd v Taverna [1984] I.C.R. 612; [1984] I.R.L.R. 240; (1984) 81 L.S.G. 2147; (1984) 134 N.L.J. 544, CA (Civ Div); affirming [1983] I.C.R. 319; [1983] I.R.L.R. 103; Times, November 17, 1982, EAT ............ *Digested,* 84/**1206**:
*Applied* 09/1198, 14/2912: *Considered* 98/2138, 01/2264: *Followed* 97/2195, 98/2137

Nethermere (St Neots) Ltd v Taverna see Nethermere (St Neots) Ltd v Gardiner

Netto Marken-Discount AG & Co KG v Deutsches Patent- und Markenamt (C-420/13) [2014] Bus. L.R. 981; [2014] E.T.M.R. 52, ECJ (3rd Chamber)

Netto Supermarkt GmbH & Co OHG v Finanzamt Malchin (C-271/06) [2008] S.T.C. 3280; [2008] E.C.R. I-771; [2009] B.T.C. 5158; [2009] B.V.C. 157; [2008] S.T.I. 315, ECJ (4th Chamber) ............ *Digested,* 09/**4045**:
*Applied* 09/4064, 14/823: *Considered* 09/4077, 12/3404

Network Multimedia Television Ltd (t/a Silicon.com) v Jobserve Ltd (Restored Injunction Hearing) see Jobserve Ltd v Network Multimedia Television Ltd (Restored Injunction Hearing)

Network Rail Infrastructure Ltd v Scottish Ministers [2013] CSIH 64; 2014 S.C. 15; [2014] R.V.R. 200; 2013 G.W.D. 24-463, IH (2 Div) ............ *Digested,* 14/**3724**

Neufeld v Secretary of State for Business, Enterprise and Regulatory Reform see Secretary of State for Business, Enterprise and Regulatory Reform v Neufeld

Neumans LLP v Andronikou see Portsmouth City Football Club Ltd (In Liquidation), Re

Neutrogena Corp v Golden Ltd (t/a Garnier) [1996] R.P.C. 473; (1996) 19(4) I.P.D. 19028, CA (Civ Div); affirming (Unreported, May 19, 1995), Ch D ............ *Digested,* 96/**5715**:
*Considered* 98/3516, 12/1972: *Followed* 14/1889: *Referred to* 98/3516

Neville v Benjamin see Benjamin, Re

New Deer Community Association v Revenue and Customs Commissioners [2014] UKFTT 1028 (TC); [2014] S.T.I. 3548, FTT (Tax)

New Sombrero Phosphate Co v Erlanger see Erlanger v New Sombrero Phosphate Co

New Yorker SHK Jeans GmbH & Co KG v Office for Harmonisation in the Internal Market (Trade Marks and Designs) (OHIM) (C-621/11 P) [2014] E.T.M.R. 10, ECJ (4th Chamber)

Newbigin (Valuation Officer) v SJ&J Monk (A Firm) see SJ&J Monk (A Firm) v Newbigin (Valuation Officer)

Newbold v Coal Authority; *sub nom* Coal Authority v Newbold [2013] EWCA Civ 584; [2014] 1 W.L.R. 1288; [2013] R.V.R. 247, CA (Civ Div); affirming [2012] UKUT 20 (LC); [2012] R.V.R. 157, UT (Lands) ............ *Digested,* 13/**2431**

Newcastle International Airport Ltd v Eversheds LLP [2013] EWCA Civ 1514; [2014] 1 W.L.R. 3073; [2014] 2 All E.R. 728; [2014] P.N.L.R. 13, CA (Civ Div); reversing [2012] EWHC 2648 (Ch); [2013] P.N.L.R. 5, Ch D ............ *Digested,* 14/**2216**

Newcastle upon Tyne Hospitals Foundation Trust v LM [2014] EWHC 454 (COP); (2014) 137 B.M.L.R. 226, CP
*Applied* 14/1525

Newcombe v Crown Prosecution Service [2013] EWHC 2160 (Admin); [2013] 6 Costs L.O. 905, DC ............ *Digested,* 14/**749**

Newey v Revenue and Customs Commissioners (C-653/11) see Revenue and Customs Commissioners v Newey (t/a Ocean Finance) (C-653/11)

Newham LBC v Ali; *sub nom* Ali v Newham LBC [2014] EWCA Civ 676; [2014] 1 W.L.R. 2743; [2014] B.L.G.R. 807; [2014] J.P.L. 1236; Times, June 11, 2014, CA (Civ Div); reversing in part [2013] EWHC 1715 (QB), QBD ............ *Digested,* 14/**2412**

Newham LBC v Hawkins see Hawkins v Newham LBC

Newland Shipping and Forwarding Ltd v Toba Trading FZC [2014] EWHC 1986 (Comm); [2014] 4 Costs L.R. 688, QBD (Comm) ............ *Digested,* 14/**447**

Newland Shipping and Forwarding Ltd v Toba Trading FZC [2014] EWHC 210 (Comm); [2014] 2 Costs L.R. 279; (2014) 164(7595) N.L.J. 17, QBD (Comm) ... *Digested,* 14/**450**:
*Considered* 14/449

Newman, Re [2014] EWHC 3136 (Fam); [2014] Fam. Law 1665, Fam Ct

Newman, Re [2014] EWHC 3399 (Fam); [2014] Fam. Law 1666, Fam Ct

Newsom v Robertson (Inspector of Taxes) [1953] Ch. 7; [1952] 2 All E.R. 728; [1952] 2 T.L.R. 636; 45 R. & I.T. 679; 33 T.C. 452; (1952) 31 A.T.C. 429; [1952] T.R. 401; (1952) 96 S.J. 696, CA; affirming [1952] 1 All E.R. 1290; [1952] 1 T.L.R. 1310; 45 R. & I.T. 384; (1952) 31 A.T.C. 261; [1952] T.R. 209; [1952] W.N. 256; (1952) 96 S.J. 313, Ch D ........ *Digested,* 52/**1663**: *Applied* 03/4222, 14/2932: *Considered* 04/3759: *Distinguished* 70/1305

Newspaper Licensing Agency Ltd v Meltwater Holdings BV (C-360/13) see Public Relations Consultants Association Ltd v Newspaper Licensing Agency Ltd (C-360/13)

Nexans SA v European Commission (C-37/13 P) [2014] 5 C.M.L.R. 13, ECJ (5th Chamber)

Next Distribution Ltd v Revenue and Customs Commissioners [2014] UKUT 227 (TCC); [2014] S.T.C. 2682; 82 T.C. 288; [2014] B.T.C. 516; [2014] S.T.I. 2229, UT (Tax); affirming [2012] UKFTT 405 (TC); [2012] S.T.I. 2838, FTT (Tax) ........ *Digested,* 14/**2882**

NF (Ghana) v Secretary of State for the Home Department [2008] EWCA Civ 906; [2009] Imm. A.R. 155; [2009] I.N.L.R. 93, CA (Civ Div) ........ *Digested,* 09/**2147**: *Considered* 09/1921, 09/2142, 14/1648

NHS v VT [2014] C.O.P.L.R. 44, CP ........ *Digested,* 14/**1527**

NHS Business Services Authority v Leeks [2014] EWHC 1446 (Ch); [2014] I.C.R. 948, Ch D ........ *Digested,* 14/**2281**

NHS Business Services Authority v Wheeler [2014] EWHC 2155 (Ch); [2014] Pens. L.R. 639, Ch D ........ *Digested,* 14/**2254**

NHS Commissioning Board (NHS England) v Bargain Dentist.Com; *joined cases* NHS Commissioning Board (NHS England) v Yellon; Yellon v NHS Commissioning Board (NHS England) [2014] EWHC 1994 (QB); [2014] Med. L.R. 301, QBD ........ *Digested,* 14/**1542**

NHS Commissioning Board (NHS England) v Yellon see NHS Commissioning Board (NHS England) v Bargain Dentist.Com

NHS Greater Glasgow and Clyde v Assessor for Renfrewshire 2014 S.L.T. (Lands Tr) 52; [2014] R.V.R. 32; 2013 G.W.D. 36-711, Lands Tr (Scot) ........ *Digested,* 14/**3671**

NHS Trust v FG [2014] EWCOP 30; [2014] C.O.P.L.R. 598; (2014) 17 C.C.L. Rep. 365; [2014] Med. L.R. 470, CP

Niche Products Ltd v MacDermid Offshore Solutions LLC [2013] EWHC 3540 (IPEC); [2014] E.M.L.R. 9; [2014] F.S.R. 24, IPEC ........ *Digested,* 14/**2995**

Niche Products Ltd v MacDermid Offshore Solutions LLC; *sub nom* MacDermid Offshore Solutions LLC v Niche Products Ltd [2013] EWHC 1493 (Ch); [2014] F.S.R. 21, Ch D; affirming [2013] EWPCC 11, PCC ........ *Digested,* 14/**567**

Nicholas v Penny; *sub nom* Penny v Nicholas [1950] 2 K.B. 466; [1950] 2 All E.R. 89; 66 T.L.R. (Pt. 1) 1122; (1950) 114 J.P. 335; 48 L.G.R. 535; 21 A.L.R.2d 1193; (1950) 94 S.J. 437, DC ........ *Digested,* 47-51/**9158**: *Applied* 14/2566

Nicholls v DPP [2013] EWHC 4365 (Admin); (2014) 178 J.P. 100; [2014] A.C.D. 53, DC ........ *Digested,* 14/**789**

Nicholls v Ladbrokes Betting & Gaming Ltd [2013] EWCA Civ 1963; [2014] P.I.Q.R. P4, CA (Civ Div) ........ *Digested,* 14/**2304**

Nicholson v Fayinka [2014] B.P.I.R. 692, Ch D (Bankruptcy Ct) ........ *Digested,* 14/**1776**

Nickel & Goeldner Spedition GmbH v "Kintra" UAB (C-157/13) [2014] 3 W.L.R. 1299, ECJ (1st Chamber)

Nicklinson v Ministry of Justice see R. (on the application of Nicklinson) v Ministry of Justice

Nicula v Administratia Finantelor Publice a Municipiului Sibiu (C-331/13) [2014] B.T.C. 46; [2014] S.T.I. 3127, ECJ (Grand Chamber)

Nidera BV v Venus International Free Zone for Trading and Marine Services SAE [2014] EWHC 2013 (Comm); [2014] 2 Lloyd's Rep. 425; [2014] 1 C.L.C. 1001, QBD (Comm) ........ *Digested,* 14/**1963**

Niederosterreichische Landes-Landwirtschaftskammer v Kuso (C-614/11) [2014] 1 C.M.L.R. 32; [2014] C.E.C. 608, ECJ (5th Chamber)

Niemietz v Germany (A/251-B) (1993) 16 E.H.R.R. 97, ECHR ........ *Digested,* 93/**2157**: *Applied* 98/3154, 08/1998: *Considered* 00/3248, 04/1304, 05/2116, 07/204, 09/2058, 09/2717, 11/1717, 14/799

Nierodzik v Samodzielny Publiczny Psychiatryczny Zaklad Opieki Zdrowotnej im dr Stanislawa Deresza w Choroszczy (C-38/13) [2014] 3 C.M.L.R. 14; [2014] I.C.R. 600, ECJ (8th Chamber)

Nightingale v Nightingale [2014] EWHC 77 (Fam); [2014] Fam. Law 796, Fam Div

Nijar v Mann; *sub nom* Mann v Nijar (2000) 32 H.L.R. 223; [1998] E.G. 188 (C.S.); (1999) 96(1) L.S.G. 25, CA (Civ Div) ........ *Digested,* 00/**3903**: *Applied* 14/2001

Ningbo Wentai Sports Equipment Co Ltd v Wang [2012] EWPCC 51; [2013] F.S.R. 40, PCC ........ *Digested,* 14/**1902**

Nintendo Co Ltd v PC Box Srl (C-355/12) [2014] E.C.D.R. 6, ECJ (4th Chamber)
NIPPON SHOKUNAI/Treating agent (T1526/10) [2014] E.P.O.R. 6, EPO (Technical Bd App)
Nipponkoa Insurance Co (Europe) Ltd v Inter-Zuid Transport BV (C-452/12) [2014] 1 All E.R. (Comm) 288; [2014] C.E.C. 751; [2014] I.L.Pr. 10, ECJ (3rd Chamber)
NJ v Wandsworth LBC [2013] EWCA Civ 1373; [2014] P.T.S.R. 497; [2014] H.L.R. 6, CA (Civ Div) ........ *Digested,* 14/**1613**: *Applied* 14/1603
NKM v Hungary (66529/11) [2013] S.T.C. 1104; 35 B.H.R.C. 355, ECHR
NL (A Child) (Appeal: Interim Care Order: Facts and Reasons), Re see L (A Child) (Family Proceedings: Practice and Procedure), Re
NM v Lambeth LBC [2011] UKUT 499 (AAC); [2012] E.L.R. 224, UT (AAC) ........ *Digested,* 12/**991**: *Considered* 14/906, 14/943
NML Capital Ltd v Chapman Freeborn Holdings Ltd [2013] EWCA Civ 589; [2013] 1 C.L.C. 968, CA (Civ Div) ........ *Digested,* 14/**384**
No.1 Deansgate (Residential) Ltd v No.1 Deansgate RTM Co Ltd [2013] UKUT 580 (LC); [2014] 1 P. & C.R. DG18, UT (Lands)
Noble v Revenue and Customs Commissioners [2014] UKUT 252 (TCC); [2014] B.V.C. 518; [2014] S.T.I. 2293, UT (Tax); affirming [2012] UKFTT 760 (TC); [2013] S.T.I. 202, FTT (Tax)
Noble Denton Middle East v Noble Denton International Ltd [2010] EWHC 2574 (Comm); [2011] 1 Lloyd's Rep. 387, QBD (Comm) ........ *Digested,* 11/**134**: *Applied* 14/134
Noel v Hillingdon LBC [2013] EWCA Civ 1602; [2014] H.L.R. 10, CA (Civ Div) ........ *Digested,* 14/**1597**
Nokia Corp v InterDigital Technology Corp (Application to Set Aside) [2006] EWCA Civ 1618; [2007] F.S.R. 23; (2007) 30(2) I.P.D. 30010, CA (Civ Div); affirming [2006] EWHC 802 (Pat); (2006) 29(7) I.P.D. 29053, Ch D (Patents Ct) ........ *Digested,* 07/**2555**: *Applied* 08/2334, 12/1265: *Followed* 14/1894
Nokia India Private Ltd v Additional Commissioner of Income Tax 16 I.T.L. Rep. 514, HC (Ind)
Nolton Business Centres Ltd, Re; *sub nom* Eliades v City of London Common Council [1996] B.C.C. 500; [1996] 1 B.C.L.C. 400; [1996] R.A. 116, Ch D ........ *Digested,* 96/**3499**: *Considered* 14/1794
Noma ApS v Homeenter AB [2014] E.C.C. 26, HR (DK)
Nomarchiaki Aftodioikisi Aitoloakarnanias v Ipourgos Perivallontos, Khorotaxias kai Dimosion Ergon (C-43/10) [2013] Env. L.R. 21, ECJ (Grand Chamber) *Followed* 14/1201
Nomura International Plc v Banca Monte Dei Paschi Di Siena SpA [2013] EWHC 3187 (Comm); [2014] 1 W.L.R. 1584, QBD (Comm) ........ *Digested,* 14/**416**
Noor v Revenue and Customs Commissioners; *sub nom* Revenue and Customs Commissioners v Noor [2013] UKUT 71 (TCC); [2013] S.T.C. 998; [2013] B.V.C. 1571; [2013] S.T.I. 481, UT (Tax); reversing [2011] UKFTT 349 (TC); [2011] S.T.I. 1950, FTT (Tax) ........ *Digested,* 13/**3199**: *Applied* 14/2926
Norbrook Laboratories (GB) Ltd v Shaw [2014] I.C.R. 540, EAT ........ *Digested,* 14/**1095**
Norbrook Laboratories Ltd v Axience SAS [2013] NIQB 62; [2014] I.L.Pr. 27, QBD (NI)
Nordea Bank Danmark A/S v Skatteministeriet (C-48/13) [2014] B.T.C. 38; [2014] S.T.I. 2520, ECJ (Grand Chamber)
Nordea Bank Norge ASA v Unicredit Corporate Banking SPA [2011] EWHC 30 (Comm), QBD (Comm) *Applied* 14/416
Nordecon AS v Rahandusministeerium (C-561/12) [2014] P.T.S.R. 343, ECJ (4th Chamber)
Norman v EC Harris Solutions Ltd UKEAT/0141/13/RN, EAT ........ *Digested,* 14/**1134**
Norseman Gold Plc v Revenue and Customs Commissioners [2014] UKFTT 573 (TC); [2014] S.T.I. 2252, FTT (Tax)
Nortel Companies, Re see Bloom v Pensions Regulator
Nortel GmbH (In Administration), Re see Bloom v Pensions Regulator
Nortel Networks UK Pension Trust Ltd, Re see Bloom v Pensions Regulator
North Australian Territory Co, Re [1892] 1 Ch. 322, CA *Considered* 11/3499: *Overruled* 14/79
North Dorset NHS Primary Care Trust v Coombs see Coombs v Dorset NHS Primary Care Trust

North East Property Buyers Litigation, Re; *sub nom* Mortgage Business Plc v O'Shaughnessy; Cook v Mortgage Business Plc; Tweddle v Southern Pacific Mortgages Ltd; Taylor v Southern Pacific Mortgages Ltd; Southern Pacific Mortgages Ltd v Scott; Mortgage Business Plc v Cook; Scott v Southern Pacific Mortgages Ltd [2014] UKSC 52; [2014] 3 W.L.R. 1163; [2014] H.L.R. 48; Times, October 28, 2014, SC; affirming [2012] EWCA Civ 17; [2012] 1 W.L.R. 1521; [2012] H.L.R. 21; [2012] 1 P. & C.R. 18; [2012] 1 E.G.L.R. 89; [2012] 15 E.G. 96; [2012] 5 E.G. 82 (C.S.), CA (Civ Div); affirming [2010] EWHC 2991 (Ch), Ch D (Newcastle) ........ *Digested,* 14/**2505**

North Essex Partnership NHS Foundation Trust v Bone; *sub nom* Bone v North Essex Partnership NHS Foundation Trust [2014] EWCA Civ 652; [2014] 3 All E.R. 964; [2014] I.C.R. 1053; [2014] I.R.L.R. 635, CA (Civ Div); reversing UKEAT/0352/12/GE, EAT ........ *Digested,* 14/**1125**

North Lincolnshire CC v Act Fast North Lincolnshire (CIC) [2013] EWHC 2890 (Admin); [2014] Env. L.R. 7; [2014] L.L.R. 562; [2014] J.P.L. 371, QBD (Admin) *Digested,* 14/**2226**

North Sea Energy Holdings NV v Petroleum Authority of Thailand [1999] 1 All E.R. (Comm.) 173; [1999] 1 Lloyd's Rep. 483, CA (Civ Div); affirming [1997] 2 Lloyd's Rep. 418, QBD (Comm) ........ *Digested,* 99/**859**: *Not followed* 14/119

North Somerset Council v O'Connell see Robert Sage Ltd (t/a Prestige Nursing Care Ltd) v O'Connell

North Staffordshire Railway Co, Ex p. see Traders' North Staffordshire Carrying Co, Re

North Western Bank Ltd v John Poynter Son & MacDonalds; *sub nom* North-Eastern Bank v Poynter & Co [1895] A.C. 56; (1894) 22 R. (H.L.) 1; (1894) 2 S.L.T. 311, HL; reversing (1894) 21 R. 513; (1894) 1 S.L.T. 509, IH (2 Div) *Considered* 14/273

North Wiltshire DC v Secretary of State for the Environment (1993) 65 P. & C.R. 137; [1992] 3 P.L.R. 113; [1992] J.P.L. 955; [1992] E.G. 65 (C.S.); [1992] N.P.C. 57; Times, April 21, 1992, CA (Civ Div); affirming [1991] 2 P.L.R. 67; [1991] E.G. 25 (C.S.), HC ........ *Digested,* 93/**3930**: *Applied* 00/4519, 14/2397: *Considered* 94/4437, 94/4464, 95/4875, 07/3276, 07/3283, 11/2165: *Distinguished* 96/4702: *Followed* 12/2602, 12/2751, 13/2349

North-Eastern Bank v Poynter & Co see North Western Bank Ltd v John Poynter Son & MacDonalds

Northam House 1129 Ltd v Revenue and Customs Commissioners see Coolatinney Developments Ltd v Revenue and Customs Commissioners

Northam House 1130 Ltd v Revenue and Customs Commissioners see Coolatinney Developments Ltd v Revenue and Customs Commissioners

Northam House 1131 Ltd v Revenue and Customs Commissioners see Coolatinney Developments Ltd v Revenue and Customs Commissioners

Northam House 1136 Ltd v Revenue and Customs Commissioners see Coolatinney Developments Ltd v Revenue and Customs Commissioners

Northampton Regional Livestock Centre Co v Cowling [2013] EWHC 1720 (QB); [2014] 1 Costs L.O. 15, QBD ........ *Digested,* 14/**468**

Northamptonshire Healthcare NHS Foundation Trust v ML [2014] EWCOP 2; [2014] C.O.P.L.R. 439, CP

Northern Ireland Housing Executive v Healthy Building (Ireland) Ltd [2014] NICA 27; 153 Con. L.R. 87, CA (NI) ........ *Digested,* 14/**3124**

Northern Ireland Housing Executive v Healthy Buildings Ltd [2013] NIQB 124, QBD (NI) *Affirmed* 14/3124

Northern Ireland Human Rights Commission's Application for Judicial Review, Re [2013] NICA 37; [2014] N.I. 263, CA (NI)

Northern Territory of Australia v Collins [2008] HCA 49, HC (Aus) *Considered* 14/1877

Northrop Grumman Mission Systems Europe Ltd v BAE Systems (Al Diriyah C4I) Ltd [2014] EWHC 3148 (TCC); [2014] T.C.L.R. 8; 156 Con. L.R. 141; [2014] 6 Costs L.O. 879; [2014] C.I.L.L. 3572, QBD (TCC) ........ *Digested,* 14/**345**

Northrop Grumman Mission Systems Europe Ltd v BAE Systems (Al Diriyah C4I) Ltd [2014] EWHC 2955 (TCC); 156 Con. L.R. 118, QBD (TCC)

Northstar Systems Ltd v Fielding (Costs) see Ultraframe (UK) Ltd v Fielding (Costs)

Northstar Systems Ltd (In Liquidation) v Fielding see Ultraframe (UK) Ltd v Fielding

Northumberland and Durham Property Trust Ltd v Ouaha [2014] EWCA Civ 571; [2014] H.L.R. 31, CA (Civ Div) ........ *Digested,* 14/**2008**

Northumbrian Water Ltd v Revenue and Customs Commissioners; *sub nom* Revenue and Customs Commissioners v Northumbrian Water Ltd [2013] UKFTT 337 (TC); [2014] S.F.T.D. 316; [2013] S.T.I. 3266, FTT (Tax) ........ *Digested,* 14/**2846**

Northumbrian Water Ltd v Sir Robert McAlpine Ltd [2014] EWCA Civ 685; [2014] B.L.R. 605; 154 Con. L.R. 26; [2014] Env. L.R. 28, CA (Civ Div); affirming [2013] EWHC 1940 (TCC); [2013] C.I.L.L. 3408, QBD (TCC) ............ *Digested,* 14/**2219**

Norwich and Peterborough Building Society v Steed (No.1) [1991] 1 W.L.R. 449; [1991] 2 All E.R. 880; (1993) 65 P. & C.R. 108; Times, March 14, 1991, CA (Civ Div) ............ *Digested,* 91/**2778**: *Applied* 91/2779, 93/4045, 98/243, 14/944: *Followed* 97/2939

Norwich Pharmacal Co v Customs and Excise Commissioners; *sub nom* Morton-Norwich Products Inc v Customs and Excise Commissioners [1974] A.C. 133; [1973] 3 W.L.R. 164; [1973] 2 All E.R. 943; [1973] F.S.R. 365; [1974] R.P.C. 101; (1973) 117 S.J. 567, HL; reversing [1972] 3 W.L.R. 870; [1972] 3 All E.R. 813; [1972] F.S.R. 405; [1972] R.P.C. 743; (1972) 116 S.J. 823, CA (Civ Div); reversing [1972] Ch. 566; [1972] 2 W.L.R. 864; [1972] 1 All E.R. 972; [1972] F.S.R. 1; (1971) 116 S.J. 315, Ch D ............ *Digested,* 73/**2643**: *Applied* 74/2936, 80/2132, 80/2136, 88/2832, 90/3660, 93/3348, 98/3508, 98/4872, 02/338, 02/425, 03/407, 03/424, 06/2096, 07/461, 08/389, 09/3159, 14/383: *Considered* 81/2115, 84/2596, 84/2625, 86/1501, 86/1503, 90/3581, 91/781, 92/3476, 93/3211, 95/4130, 96/553, 96/769, 97/2205, 98/332, 99/3444, 02/1884, 03/282, 10/1726: *Followed* 94/3552, 94/3738, 96/764, 00/5532: *Referred to* 99/319, 01/4413

Notcutt v Universal Equipment Co (London) [1986] 1 W.L.R. 641; [1986] 3 All E.R. 582; [1986] I.C.R. 414; [1986] I.R.L.R. 218; (1986) 83 L.S.G. 1314; (1986) 136 N.L.J. 393; (1986) 130 S.J. 392, CA (Civ Div) ............ *Digested,* 86/**1178**: *Followed* 14/1089

Notting Hill Housing Trust v Ealing LBC see A2Dominion Housing Group Ltd v Hammersmith and Fulham LBC

Notting Hill Housing Trust v Kensington and Chelsea RLBC see A2Dominion Housing Group Ltd v Hammersmith and Fulham LBC

Nottingham Building Society v Eurodynamics Systems Plc [1995] F.S.R. 605, CA (Civ Div); affirming [1993] F.S.R. 468, Ch D ............ *Digested,* 95/**773**: *Applied* 04/1135, 06/3486, 08/528, 14/1020: *Followed* 98/525

Nottingham City Council v LM see D (A Child) (Transfer of Proceedings), Re

Nottinghamshire CC v Meikle see Meikle v Nottinghamshire CC

Nottinghamshire Healthcare NHS Trust v RC [2014] EWCOP 1317; [2014] C.O.P.L.R. 468; [2014] Med. L.R. 260; (2014) 138 B.M.L.R. 147, CP ............ *Digested,* 14/**1525**

Nouri v Marvi [2010] EWCA Civ 1107; [2011] C.P. Rep. 6; [2011] P.N.L.R. 7; [2010] 3 E.G.L.R. 79; [2010] 50 E.G. 64; [2010] 42 E.G. 105 (C.S.), CA (Civ Div); affirming [2009] EWHC 2725 (Ch); [2010] P.N.L.R. 7, Ch D ............ *Digested,* 11/**349**: *Applied* 11/2246: *Considered* 14/1840

Nouvion v Freeman; *sub nom* Henderson's Estate, Re; Henderson, Re (1889) 15 App. Cas. 1, HL; affirming (1887) 37 Ch. D. 244, CA; reversing (1887) 35 Ch. D. 704, Ch D
*Applied* 52/537, 61/1319, 66/1641, 71/1589: *Considered* 66/1665: *Followed* 14/564

Novartis AG v Hospira UK Ltd [2013] EWCA Civ 583; [2014] 1 W.L.R. 1264; [2013] C.P. Rep. 37; [2014] R.P.C. 3, CA (Civ Div); reversing [2013] EWHC 1285 (Pat), Ch D (Patents Ct) ............ *Digested,* 13/**381**: *Followed* 14/1885

Novartis Pharmaceuticals UK Ltd v MedImmune Ltd see MedImmune Ltd v Novartis Pharmaceuticals UK Ltd

Novoship (UK) Ltd v Mikhaylyuk; *joined case* Novoship (UK) Ltd v Nikitin [2014] EWCA Civ 908; [2014] W.T.L.R. 1521; (2014) 158(28) S.J.L.B. 37, CA (Civ Div); reversing in part [2012] EWHC 3586 (Comm), QBD (Comm) ............ *Digested,* 14/**2991**

Novoship (UK) Ltd v Mikhaylyuk [2014] EWCA Civ 252; [2014] 1 All E.R. (Comm) 993; [2014] B.P.I.R. 698, CA (Civ Div); reversing [2013] EWHC 89 (Comm), QBD (Comm) ............ *Digested,* 14/**490**

Novoship (UK) Ltd v Nikitin see Novoship (UK) Ltd v Mikhaylyuk

NP v KRP (Recognition of Foreign Divorce) [2013] EWHC 694 (Fam); [2014] 2 F.L.R. 1; [2013] Fam. Law 1385, Fam Div ............ *Digested,* 14/**1327**

NRAM Plc v McAdam [2014] EWHC 4174 (Comm); [2014] C.T.L.C. 244, QBD (Comm)

NS v Secretary of State for the Home Department (C-411/10) see R. (on the application of NS) v Secretary of State for the Home Department (C-411/10)

NSL Ltd v Besagni see RR Donnelley Global Document Solutions Group Ltd v Besagni

Nuffield Health v Revenue and Customs Commissioners [2013] UKFTT 291 (TC); [2014] S.F.T.D. 164; [2013] S.T.I. 2004, FTT (Tax) ............ *Digested,* 14/**3050**

Nugent v Nugent [2013] EWHC 4095 (Ch); [2014] 3 W.L.R. 59; [2014] 2 All E.R. 313; [2014] 1 P. & C.R. 19; [2014] 1 E.G.L.R. 15, Ch D (Bristol) ............................... *Digested,* 14/**2512**

Nunez v Norway (55597/09) (2014) 58 E.H.R.R. 17, ECHR *Considered* 12/1775

Nunn v Chief Constable of Suffolk see R. (on the application of Nunn) v Chief Constable of Suffolk

Nursing and Midwifery Council v Kidd [2014] EWHC 847 (Admin); (2014) 158(15) S.J.L.B. 37, QBD (Admin)

Nursing Directives, Re (29/84) see Commission of the European Communities v Germany (29/84)

Nutro UK Ltd v Revenue and Customs Commissioners [2014] UKFTT 971 (TC); [2014] S.T.I. 3375, FTT (Tax)

Nutting v France see France (A Bankrupt), Re

NV (Sri Lanka) v Secretary of State for the Home Department see AS (Afghanistan) v Secretary of State for the Home Department

Nygate v E-Squared Ltd; *sub nom* Sussex Pharmaceutical Ltd, Re; E-Squared Ltd, Re; *joined case* Moses v Sussex Pharmaceuticals Ltd [2006] EWHC 532 (Ch); [2006] 1 W.L.R. 3414; [2006] 3 All E.R. 779; [2006] B.C.C. 379; [2006] 2 B.C.L.C. 277, Ch D ........................................................................................ *Digested,* 06/**2319**: *Applied* 14/1811: *Considered* 12/1793

NYK Bulkship (Atlantic) NV v Cargill International SA (The Global Santosh) [2014] EWCA Civ 403; [2014] 2 Lloyd's Rep. 103; [2014] 1 C.L.C. 515, CA (Civ Div); affirming [2013] EWHC 30 (Comm); [2013] 1 Lloyd's Rep. 455, QBD (Comm) ... *Digested,* 14/**2739**

Nykredit Mortgage Bank Plc v Edward Erdman Group Ltd (Interest on Damages) [1997] 1 W.L.R. 1627; [1998] 1 All E.R. 305; [1998] Lloyd's Rep. Bank. 39; [1998] C.L.C. 116; [1998] 1 Costs L.R. 108; [1998] P.N.L.R. 197; [1998] 1 E.G.L.R. 99; [1998] 05 E.G. 150; (1998) 95(1) L.S.G. 24; (1998) 142 S.J.L.B. 29; [1997] N.P.C. 165; (1998) 75 P. & C.R. D28; Times, December 3, 1997, HL *Digested,* 98/**1432**: *Applied* 99/4053, 01/4532, 02/465, 03/3003, 08/384: *Considered* 98/3917, 99/477, 99/557, 01/946, 06/474, 08/382, 09/2735, 09/426, 10/238, 12/2306, 14/2523: *Distinguished* 98/1472, 01/4527, 08/2651: *Followed* 98/4021, 98/4029, 02/3276, 10/2284, 13/2087, 13/2093, 14/2217

Nykredit Mortgage Bank Plc v Edward Erdman Group Ltd see South Australia Asset Management Corp v York Montague Ltd

Nyusti v Hungary (1/2010) 37 B.H.R.C. 99, UN CRPD

O v A; *sub nom* OPO v MLA [2014] EWCA Civ 1277; [2014] H.R.L.R. 31, CA (Civ Div)

O v Lewisham LBC [2007] EWHC 2130 (Admin); [2008] B.L.G.R. 765; [2007] E.L.R. 633; (2007) 104(37) L.S.G. 38, QBD (Admin) ........................................................ *Digested,* 08/**1083**: *Applied* 11/986, 14/937: *Considered* 13/902: *Followed* 11/983

O v Minister voor Immigratie, Integratie en Asiel (C-456/12); *sub nom* Minister voor Immigratie, Integratie en Asiel v B (C-456/12) [2014] Q.B. 1163; [2014] 3 W.L.R. 799; [2014] 3 C.M.L.R. 17; [2014] All E.R. (EC) 843; [2014] Imm. A.R. 828; [2014] I.N.L.R. 748, ECJ (Grand Chamber)

O v O (Child Abduction: Return to Third Country) [2013] EWHC 2970 (Fam); [2014] Fam. 87; [2014] 2 W.L.R. 1213; [2014] 1 F.L.R. 1406; [2014] Fam. Law 11, Fam Div ........................................................................................................ *Digested,* 14/**1382**

O v P (Sch.1 Application: Stay: Forum Conveniens) see S (A Minor), Re

O v Secretary of State for Education; *sub nom* R. (on the application of O) v Secretary of State for Education [2014] EWHC 22 (Admin); [2014] E.L.R. 232; [2014] A.C.D. 56, QBD (Admin)........................................................................................ *Digested,* 14/**951**

O (A Child) (Residence), Re [2012] EWCA Civ 1955; [2014] 1 F.L.R. 89; [2013] Fam. Law 968, CA (Civ Div)

O (Court of Protection: Jurisdiction), Re; *sub nom* JO v GO; PO, Re [2013] EWHC 3932 (COP); [2014] Fam. 197; [2014] 3 W.L.R. 453; [2014] C.O.P.L.R. 62; [2014] W.T.L.R. 337, CP ................................................................................ *Digested,* 14/**2186**

O Municipality (Ex p. Local Residents) v B [2014] I.L.Pr. 34, OL (DK)

O'Brien v Department of Constitutional Affairs see Department of Constitutional Affairs v O'Brien

O'Brien v Ministry of Justice see Department of Constitutional Affairs v O'Brien

O'Brien v Ministry of Justice see Ministry of Justice v O'Brien

O'Brien v South Cambridgeshire DC [2014] P.A.D. 32, Planning Inspector

O'Donnell v Bank of Ireland [2013] EWHC 489 (Ch); [2013] B.P.I.R. 1078, Ch D .......... *Digested,* 14/**290**

O'Donnell Developments Ltd v Build Ability Ltd [2009] EWHC 3388 (TCC); 128 Con. L.R. 141, QBD (TCC) ............................................................................ *Digested,* 10/**566**: *Considered* 14/586

O'Driscoll v Manchester Insurance Committee [1915] 3 K.B. 499, CA; affirming [1915] 1 K.B. 811, KBD
*Applied* 55/2162, 56/8878, 57/342, 13/3033, 14/491: *Distinguished* 47-51/7688, 52/227: *Followed* 14/2873

O'Farrell v O'Farrell [2012] EWHC 123 (QB); [2013] 1 F.L.R. 77; [2012] Fam. Law 514, QBD ........ *Digested,* 13/**1293**: *Applied* 14/496

O'Hara v Chief Constable of the Royal Ulster Constabulary [1997] A.C. 286; [1997] 2 W.L.R. 1; [1997] 1 All E.R. 129; [1996] N.I. 8; [1997] 1 Cr. App. R. 447; [1997] Crim. L.R. 432; (1997) 94(2) L.S.G. 26; (1996) 146 N.L.J. 1852; (1997) 141 S.J.L.B. 20; Times, December 13, 1996; Independent, December 18, 1996, HL
*Applied* 01/4780, 09/772, 12/2617: *Complaint upheld* 01/3560: *Considered* 14/2463: *Followed* 11/2612

O'Keeffe v Ireland (35810/09) (2014) 59 E.H.R.R. 15; 35 B.H.R.C. 601, ECHR (Grand Chamber)

O'Neil v Gale [2013] EWCA Civ 1554; [2014] Lloyd's Rep. F.C. 202, CA (Civ Div) ........ *Digested,* 14/**1451**

O'Neill v Phillips; *sub nom* Pectel Ltd, Re; Company (No.000709 of 1992), Re [1999] 1 W.L.R. 1092; [1999] 2 All E.R. 961; [1999] B.C.C. 600; [1999] 2 B.C.L.C. 1; (1999) 96(23) L.S.G. 33; (1999) 149 N.L.J. 805; Times, May 21, 1999, HL; affirming [1998] B.C.C. 405; [1997] 2 B.C.L.C. 739, CA (Civ Div) ........ *Digested,* 99/**634**:
*Applied* 00/691, 01/747, 02/5375, 05/39, 06/565, 07/563, 07/586, 09/539, 13/3679, 14/3503, 14/521: *Considered* 04/477, 04/478, 06/553, 06/567, 11/428, 12/517, 14/523: *Distinguished* 03/545, 13/486: *Followed* 14/522

O'Rorke v Revenue and Customs Commissioners; *sub nom* Revenue and Customs Commissioners v O'Rorke [2013] UKUT 499 (TCC); [2014] S.T.C. 279; [2013] B.T.C. 2096; [2014] S.T.I. 253, UT (Tax); reversing [2011] UKFTT 839 (TC); [2012] S.F.T.D. 553; [2012] S.T.I. 354, FTT (Tax) ........ *Digested,* 14/**2772**

O'Rourke (Inspector of Taxes) v Binks [1992] S.T.C. 703; Times, August 14, 1992; Independent, July 27, 1992, CA (Civ Div); reversing [1991] S.T.C. 455; Times, July 9, 1991, Ch D ........ *Digested,* 92/**322**:
*Applied* 97/337: *Considered* 14/2970: *Distinguished* 98/4687

O'Ryan v Revenue and Customs Commissioners [2014] UKFTT 838 (TC); [2014] S.T.I. 2905, FTT (Tax)

O'Sullivan v Loy [2014] B.P.I.R. 466, US Court

Oak Pits Colliery Co, Re (1882) 21 Ch. D. 322, CA
*Applied* 70/311, 74/356, 14/1756: *Considered* 93/2626

Oakapple Homes (Glossop) Ltd v DTR (2009) Ltd (In Liquidation) [2013] EWHC 2394 (TCC); 150 Con. L.R. 110; [2014] Lloyd's Rep. I.R. 103; [2013] 3 E.G.L.R. 1; (2013) 29 Const. L.J. 523, QBD (TCC) ........ *Digested,* 14/**590**

Oakley Inc v Animal Ltd [2005] EWCA Civ 1191; [2006] Ch. 337; [2006] 2 W.L.R. 294; [2006] 1 C.M.L.R. 22; [2006] Eu. L.R. 323; [2006] E.C.D.R. 7; [2006] R.P.C. 9; (2006) 29(2) I.P.D. 29010; Times, November 7, 2005, CA (Civ Div); reversing [2005] EWHC 419 (Pat); [2005] Eu. L.R. 713, Ch D (Patents Ct) ........ *Digested,* 06/**2460**:
*Applied* 07/69, 08/1197, 09/300, 10/1124: *Considered* 14/1109

Oakley Smith v Information Officer; *sub nom* Southern Pacific Personal Loans Ltd, Re; Smith v Information Officer [2013] EWHC 2485 (Ch); [2014] Ch. 426; [2014] 2 W.L.R. 1067; [2014] 1 All E.R. 98; [2014] B.C.C. 56; [2013] 2 B.C.L.C. 465; Times, October 10, 2013, Ch D (Companies Ct) ........ *Digested,* 13/**1710**: *Applied* 14/1812

Oakrock Ltd v Travelodge Hotels Ltd [2014] EWHC 1868 (TCC); [2014] B.L.R. 593, QBD (TCC) ........ *Digested,* 14/**594**

OAO Neftyanaya Kompaniya Yukos v Russia (Just Satisfaction) (14902/04) 37 B.H.R.C. 721; (2014) 59 E.H.R.R. SE12, ECHR

Oates v Revenue and Customs Commissioners [2014] UKUT 409 (LC); [2014] R.V.R. 337; [2014] B.T.C. 528, UT (Lands)

Oatley v Oatley; *sub nom* Oatley v Oatley Powney [2014] EWHC 1956 (Ch); [2014] W.T.L.R. 1433, Ch D ........ *Digested,* 14/**3029**

Oatley v Oatley Powney see Oatley v Oatley

OB v Director of the Serious Fraud Office see Director of the Serious Fraud Office v O'Brien

OB, Re; *sub nom* Public Guardian v AW [2014] EWCOP 28; [2014] W.T.L.R. 1705, CP

OBB-Personenverkehr AG v Schienen-Control Kommission (C-509/11) [2014] 1 C.M.L.R. 51; [2014] C.E.C. 787, ECJ (1st Chamber)

Oberbank AG v Deutscher Sparkassen- und Giroverband eV (C-217/13); *sub nom* Banco Santander SA v Deutscher Sparkassen- und Giroverband eV (C-218/13) [2014] Bus. L.R. 786; [2014] E.T.M.R. 56, ECJ (3rd Chamber)
*Considered* 14/1935

OBG Ltd v Allan; *sub nom* OBG Ltd v Allen; *joined cases* Douglas v Hello! Ltd; Mainstream Properties Ltd v Young [2007] UKHL 21; [2008] 1 A.C. 1; [2007] 2 W.L.R. 920; [2007] 4 All E.R. 545; [2008] 1 All E.R. (Comm) 1; [2007] Bus. L.R. 1600; [2007] I.R.L.R. 608; [2007] E.M.L.R. 12; [2007] B.P.I.R. 746; (2007) 30(6) I.P.D. 30037; [2007] 19 E.G. 165 (C.S.); (2007) 151 S.J.L.B. 674; [2007] N.P.C. 54; Times, May 4, 2007, HL; affirming [2005] EWCA Civ 106; [2005] Q.B. 762; [2005] 2 W.L.R. 1174; [2005] 2 All E.R. 602; [2005] 1 All E.R. (Comm) 639; [2005] 1 B.C.L.C. 711; [2005] B.L.R. 245; [2005] B.P.I.R. 928; [2005] P.N.L.R. 27; (2005) 102(14) L.S.G. 27; Times, February 24, 2005; Independent, February 18, 2005, CA (Civ Div); reversing (Unreported, February 18, 2004), Ch D (Manchester) .......... *Digested,* 07/**4190**:
*Applied* 09/3557, 09/3558, 10/1034, 10/3410, 13/488, 14/2528, 14/415: *Considered* 10/4134, 12/3347: *Followed* 08/3902, 11/369

OBG Ltd v Allen see OBG Ltd v Allan

Oboh v Secretary of State for the Home Department; *joined case* Haulader v Secretary of State for the Home Department [2013] EWCA Civ 1525; [2014] 1 W.L.R. 1680; [2014] Imm. A.R. 521, CA (Civ Div) .......... *Digested,* 14/**1732**

Obrascon Huarte Lain SA v Attorney General of Gibraltar [2014] EWHC 1028 (TCC); [2014] B.L.R. 484; [2014] C.I.L.L. 3536, QBD (TCC) .......... *Digested,* 14/**589**

Obrey v Secretary of State for Work and Pensions [2013] EWCA Civ 1584; [2014] H.L.R. 12, CA (Civ Div) .......... *Digested,* 14/**1615**

Occidental Petroleum Corp v Buttes Gas & Oil Co (No.2) see Buttes Gas & Oil Co v Hammer (No.3)

Oceana Shipping AG v Transatlantica Commodities SA see Minerva Navigation Inc v Oceana Shipping AG

Och-Ziff Management Europe Ltd v Och Capital LLP [2010] EWHC 2599 (Ch); [2011] Bus. L.R. 632; [2011] E.C.C. 5; [2011] E.T.M.R. 1; [2011] F.S.R. 11, Ch D .......... *Digested,* 11/**1999**:
*Applied* 11/2000, 13/1824, 14/1939

Ochranny svaz autorsky pro prava k dilum hudebnim os (OSA) v Lecebne lazne Marianske Lazne as (C-351/12) [2014] 4 C.M.L.R. 19; [2014] All E.R. (EC) 1050; [2014] E.C.D.R. 25, ECJ (4th Chamber)

Ochranny svaz autorsky pro prava k dilum hudebnim os (OSA) v Lecebne lazne Marianske Lazne as (C-351/12) [2014] E.C.D.R. 5, AGO

OCS Group Ltd v Taylor see Taylor v OCS Group Ltd

Odelola v Secretary of State for the Home Department; *sub nom* MO (Nigeria) v Secretary of State for the Home Department; MO (Date of Decision: Applicable Rules: Nigeria), Re [2009] UKHL 25; [2009] 1 W.L.R. 1230; [2009] 3 All E.R. 1061; [2010] Imm. A.R. 59; [2009] I.N.L.R. 401; Times, May 22, 2009, HL; affirming [2008] EWCA Civ 308; [2009] 1 W.L.R. 126; [2008] Imm. A.R. 632; [2008] I.N.L.R. 282; Times, June 2, 2008, CA (Civ Div); affirming [2007] UKAIT 57, AIT .......... *Digested,* 09/**2137**:
*Applied* 09/2166, 14/1686: *Considered* 12/1735, 14/1707

Odeniran v Southend on Sea BC; *sub nom* Southend-on-Sea BC v Odeniran [2013] EWHC 3888 (Admin); [2014] H.L.R. 11, QBD (Admin) .......... *Digested,* 14/**1616**

Odhams Leisure Group Ltd v Customs and Excise Commissioners [1992] S.T.C. 332; Independent, March 16, 1992, QBD .......... *Digested,* 92/**4562**:
*Considered* 07/4322, 14/3088

OFAB, Ostergotlands Fastigheter AB v Koot (C-147/12) [2014] 3 W.L.R. 1278; [2013] 2 All E.R. (Comm) 969; [2013] C.E.C. 1045; [2013] I.L.Pr. 38, ECJ (5th Chamber)

Office Angels v Rainer-Thomas [1991] I.R.L.R. 214; Times, April 15, 1991; Independent, May 14, 1991; Financial Times, March 27, 1991, CA (Civ Div); reversing Independent, February 4, 1991, QBD .......... *Digested,* 91/**447**:
*Applied* 98/2193, 12/1139: *Considered* 97/2257, 97/2258, 05/700, 06/1291, 14/1029, 14/1032: *Distinguished* 06/1292: *Followed* 14/1034

Office for Harmonisation in the Internal Market (Trade Marks and Designs) (OHIM) v National Lottery Commission (C-530/12 P) [2014] Bus. L.R. 583; [2014] E.T.M.R. 31; [2014] E.C.D.R. 19, ECJ (1st Chamber)

Office for Harmonisation in the Internal Market (Trade Marks and Designs) (OHIM) v Yoshida Metal Industry Co Ltd (C-338/12 P) see Pi-Design AG v Yoshida Metal Industry Co Ltd (C-337/12 P)

Office of Fair Trading v Gallaher Group Ltd see Somerfield Stores Ltd v Office of Fair Trading

Office of Fair Trading v IBA Healthcare Ltd see IBA Health Ltd v Office of Fair Trading

Office of Fair Trading v Somerfield Stores Ltd see Somerfield Stores Ltd v Office of Fair Trading

Officer L, Re [2007] UKHL 36; [2007] 1 W.L.R. 2135; [2007] 4 All E.R. 965; [2007] N.I. 277; [2007] H.R.L.R. 42; [2007] U.K.H.R.R. 1023; 26 B.H.R.C. 169; [2007] Inquest L.R. 214; (2007) 157 N.L.J. 1274; (2007) 151 S.J.L.B. 1061; Times, August 1, 2007, HL (NI); reversing [2007] NICA 8, CA (NI); affirming [2006] NIQB 75; [2006] Inquest L.R. 211, QBD (NI) ..................... *Digested,* 07/**544**:
*Applied* 08/767, 09/3680, 12/1671, 14/664: *Considered* 08/2645, 13/418

Official Liquidator v Molleson see Phosphate Sewage Co Ltd v Molleson (Res Judicata)

Official Receiver v Baker [2013] EWHC 4594 (Ch); [2014] B.P.I.R. 724, Ch D ............. *Digested,* 14/**1771**

Official Receiver v McKay [2009] EWCA Civ 467; [2010] Ch. 303; [2010] 2 W.L.R. 891; [2009] B.P.I.R. 1061, CA (Civ Div) ..................... *Digested,* 10/**1852**:
*Applied* 14/1781

Official Receiver v Parkins [2014] B.P.I.R. 1054, Ch D ..................... *Digested,* 14/**1767**

Official Receiver v Sinnamon [2013] NICh 11; [2013] B.P.I.R. 900, Ch D (NI) .............. *Digested,* 14/**3197**

Official Receiver for Northern Ireland v Gallagher [2014] NICh 6; [2014] B.P.I.R. 918, Ch D (NI) ..................... *Digested,* 14/**3199**

Official Receiver for Northern Ireland v Mallon [2013] B.P.I.R. 621, Ch D (NI) ............. *Digested,* 14/**3196**

Official Solicitor v K; *sub nom* K (Infants), Re [1965] A.C. 201; [1963] 3 W.L.R. 408; [1963] 3 All E.R. 191; (1963) 107 S.J. 616, HL; reversing [1963] Ch. 381; [1962] 3 W.L.R. 1517; [1962] 3 All E.R. 1000; (1962) 106 S.J. 900, CA; reversing [1962] 3 W.L.R. 752; [1962] 3 All E.R. 178; (1962) 106 S.J. 721, Ch D ..................... *Digested,* 63/**1807**:
*Applied* 63/1061, 63/1117, 64/2322, 72/2145, 85/2260, 94/3219, 94/3244, 95/3622, 99/2412, 14/2184: *Approved* 66/6287: *Considered* 69/1748, 69/295, 78/1989, 93/2747, 93/3209, 95/3562, 96/474, 03/1530, 10/276, 11/4302: *Distinguished* 63/1768, 70/1359: *Followed* 11/1328

Official Solicitor v Wilsons Solicitors LLP (Costs) see Bentine v Bentine

Ogbonna v Nursing and Midwifery Council [2010] EWCA Civ 1216, CA (Civ Div); reversing [2010] EWHC 272 (Admin); [2010] Med. L.R. 150, QBD (Admin)........ *Digested,* 10/**1660**:
*Considered* 12/304, 14/287

Ogieriakhi v Minister for Justice and Equality (C-244/13) [2014] 1 W.L.R. 3823; [2014] Imm. A.R. 1193, ECJ (2nd Chamber)

Okotoks Ltd (formerly Spicerhaart Ltd) v Fine & Country Ltd see Fine & Country Ltd v Okotoks Ltd (formerly Spicerhaart Ltd)

Oldham MBC v Worldwide Marketing Solutions Ltd [2014] EWHC 1910 (QB); [2014] P.T.S.R. 1072; [2014] B.L.G.R. 733, QBD ..................... *Digested,* 14/**497**

Oleynikov v Russia (36703/04) (2013) 57 E.H.R.R. 15; 35 B.H.R.C. 538, ECHR

Olotu v Crown Prosecution Service see Olotu v Secretary of State for the Home Department

Olotu v Home Office see Olotu v Secretary of State for the Home Department

Olotu v Secretary of State for the Home Department; *sub nom* Olotu v Crown Prosecution Service; Olotu v Home Office [1997] 1 W.L.R. 328; [1997] 1 All E.R. 385; (1997) 94(1) L.S.G. 24; (1997) 141 S.J.L.B. 14; Times, December 11, 1996; Independent, December 5, 1996, CA (Civ Div); affirming in part Times, May 8, 1996, QBD ..................... *Digested,* 97/**1299**:
*Applied* 02/4543, 06/2936, 13/253, 14/386

Olufunmilaya v Secretary of State for the Home Department see Kharug v Upper Tribunal (Immigration and Asylum Chamber)

Olupitan v Director of the Assets Recovery Agency see Director of the Assets Recovery Agency v Olupitan

Olympia & York Canary Wharf Ltd (No.1), Re; *sub nom* American Express Europe Ltd v Adamson [1993] B.C.C. 154; [1993] B.C.L.C. 453, Ch D (Companies Ct) ....... *Digested,* 93/**516**:
*Applied* 99/3264: *Considered* 94/2788, 14/3194: *Distinguished* 96/3519: *Followed* 96/7084

Olympia Technology Ltd v Revenue and Customs Commissioners see Livewire Telecom Ltd v Revenue and Customs Commissioners

Olympic Airlines SA, Re; *sub nom* Trustees of Olympic Airlines SA Pension and Life Assurance Scheme v Olympic Airlines SA [2013] EWCA Civ 643; [2014] 1 W.L.R. 1401; [2013] B.C.C. 728; [2013] 2 B.C.L.C. 171; [2013] B.P.I.R. 663; [2013] Pens. L.R. 281, CA (Civ Div); reversing [2012] EWHC 1413 (Ch); [2012] B.C.C. 841; [2013] 1 B.C.L.C. 415; [2012] I.L.Pr. 35; [2012] B.P.I.R. 1163, Ch D ..................... *Digested,* 13/**1697**

Olympus UK Ltd, Re [2014] EWHC 1350 (Ch); [2014] Bus. L.R. 816; [2014] 2 B.C.L.C. 402, Ch D (Companies Ct) ..................... *Digested,* 14/**503**

Omega Engineering Inc v Omega SA [2012] EWHC 3440 (Ch); [2013] F.S.R. 25, Ch D ..................... *Digested,* 13/**1834**:
*Applied* 14/1916

Omega Group Holdings Ltd v Kozeny; *joined case* Marlwood Commercial Inc v Kozeny [2004] EWCA Civ 798; [2005] 1 W.L.R. 104; [2004] 3 All E.R. 648; [2004] 2 C.L.C. 166; (2004) 148 S.J.L.B. 822, CA (Civ Div); affirming [2004] EWHC 189 (Comm), QBD (Comm) .......... *Digested,* 04/**344**: *Applied* 14/381, 14/382: *Considered* 09/400

Omega Proteins Ltd v Aspen Insurance UK Ltd [2010] EWHC 2280 (Comm); [2011] 1 All E.R. (Comm) 313; [2010] 2 C.L.C. 370; [2011] Lloyd's Rep. I.R. 183; (2010) 107(37) L.S.G. 17; (2010) 160 N.L.J. 1260, QBD (Comm) .......... *Digested,* 11/**1913**: *Considered* 14/1849

Omgate Ltd v Gordon see Gordon v Omgate Ltd

Omilaju v Waltham Forest LBC (No.2); *sub nom* Waltham Forest LBC v Omilaju (No.2) [2004] EWCA Civ 1493; [2005] 1 All E.R. 75; [2005] I.C.R. 481; [2005] I.R.L.R. 35; (2004) 148 S.J.L.B. 1370; Times, November 26, 2004, CA (Civ Div); reversing [2004] 3 All E.R. 129, EAT .......... *Digested,* 05/**1209**: *Applied* 07/1317: *Considered* 06/1321, 07/1319, 14/2227

OMV Petrom SA v Glencore International AG [2014] EWHC 242 (Comm); [2014] 2 Lloyd's Rep. 308, QBD (Comm) .......... *Digested,* 14/**297**

OMV Supply and Trading AG v Kazmunaygaz Trading AG (formerly Vector Energy AG); *joined case* Kazmunaygaz Trading AG (formerly Vector Energy AG) v OMV Supply and Trading AG [2014] EWCA Civ 75; [2014] 1 Lloyd's Rep. 647; [2014] 1 C.L.C. 113, CA (Civ Div); affirming [2013] EWHC 3941 (Comm), QBD (Comm) .......... *Digested,* 14/**626**

Onorati Settlement, Re; *sub nom* A v Confiance Ltd 17 I.T.E.L.R. 398, Royal Ct (Jer)

Onu v Akwiwu; *joined case* Akwiwu v Onu [2013] I.C.R. 1039; [2013] I.R.L.R. 523; [2013] Eq. L.R. 577; (2013) 157(19) S.J.L.B. 35, EAT .......... *Digested,* 13/**986**: *Affirmed* 14/1104: *Approved* 14/1063

Onu v Akwiwu see Taiwo v Olaigbe

Onuekwere v Secretary of State for the Home Department (C-378/12) [2014] 1 W.L.R. 2420; [2014] 2 C.M.L.R. 46; [2014] C.E.C. 1007; [2014] Imm. A.R. 551; [2014] I.N.L.R. 613, ECJ (2nd Chamber) .......... *Digested,* 14/**1737**

Onur v United Kingdom (27319/07) (2009) 49 E.H.R.R. 38, ECHR *Considered* 14/1678

Opal Glen Properties Ltd v Central Scotland Valuation Joint Board Assessor 2014 S.L.T. (Lands Tr) 22; [2014] R.V.R. 69; 2013 G.W.D. 38-741, Lands Tr (Scot) .. *Digested,* 14/**3679**

Open University v Revenue and Customs Commissioners [2013] UKFTT 326 (TC); [2013] S.F.T.D. 1228; [2013] S.T.I. 2252, FTT (Tax) .......... *Digested,* 14/**3044**

OPO v MLA see O v A

OR v Ealing LBC [2012] UKUT 211 (AAC); [2012] E.L.R. 436, UT (AAC) .......... *Digested,* 13/**900**: *Applied* 14/943

Oracle America Inc v M-Tech Data Ltd see Sun Microsystems Inc v M-Tech Data Ltd

Oraki v Dean & Dean [2013] EWCA Civ 1629; [2014] B.P.I.R. 266, CA (Civ Div); affirming [2012] EWHC 2885 (Ch); [2013] B.P.I.R. 88, Ch D (Bankruptcy Ct) ..... *Digested,* 14/**1780**

Orange Personal Communications Services Ltd v Office of Communications [2007] CAT 36, CAT *Applied* 10/493: *Considered* 14/545

Orford v S Three Staffing Ltd [2013] Eq. L.R. 1069, EAT .......... *Digested,* 14/**1070**

Oriental Press Group Ltd v Fevaworks Solutions Ltd [2014] E.M.L.R. 11, CFA (HK)

Oriflame UK Ltd v Revenue and Customs Commissioners [2014] UKFTT 454 (TC); [2014] S.T.I. 2050, FTT (Tax)

Orme v Charnwood BC [2014] R.V.R. 273, VT

Ormond Investments Co Ltd v Betts (Inspector of Taxes) [1928] A.C. 143, HL; reversing [1927] 2 K.B. 326, CA *Applied* 47-51/9922, 54/391: *Considered* 86/2164, 14/2887: *Followed* 55/1257

Orwell v Salford Royal NHS Trust Foundation [2013] EWHC 3245 (QB); (2014) 135 B.M.L.R. 137, QBD .......... *Digested,* 14/**2300**

Osborn v Cole [1999] B.P.I.R. 251, Ch D .......... *Digested,* 99/**382**: *Applied* 07/2444, 10/1902, 13/1700, 13/1703: *Approved* 07/2409: *Considered* 08/2131, 10/1903, 14/1832

Osborn v Parole Board see Reilly's Application for Judicial Review, Re

Oscroft v Benabo [1967] 1 W.L.R. 1087; [1967] 2 All E.R. 548; (1967) 111 S.J. 520, CA (Civ Div) .......... *Digested,* 67/**674**: *Considered* 88/2438, 14/2004: *Followed* 82/2399

Osman v United Kingdom (23452/94) [1999] 1 F.L.R. 193; (2000) 29 E.H.R.R. 245; 5 B.H.R.C. 293; (1999) 1 L.G.L.R. 431; (1999) 11 Admin. L.R. 200; [2000] Inquest L.R. 101; [1999] Crim. L.R. 82; [1998] H.R.C.D. 966; [1999] Fam. Law 86; (1999) 163 J.P.N. 297; Times, November 5, 1998, ECHR; no effect (1996) 22 E.H.R.R. CD137, Eur Comm HR ............ *Digested,* 98/**3102**: *Applied* 01/3476, 01/3571, 02/2489, 02/3236, 02/38, 03/2238, 04/13, 06/2171, 07/544, 08/2632, 08/2646, 09/2160, 09/2716, 09/2848, 09/4361, 10/1738, 11/1721, 13/1543, 13/1559, 13/3860, 14/1638, 14/2460: *Considered* 99/3966, 99/3982, 00/3170, 00/3239, 01/3459, 04/2039, 06/1607, 06/4806, 06/989, 07/2238, 07/2980, 08/2645, 09/22, 10/1739, 11/1684, 11/1700, 11/4487, 12/1671, 13/2387, 13/36, 14/1635: *Distinguished* 01/82

Osmani v Camden LBC [2004] EWCA Civ 1706; [2005] H.L.R. 22; (2005) 149 S.J.L.B. 61, CA (Civ Div) ............ *Digested,* 05/**1989**: *Applied* 06/2027, 09/1901: *Considered* 13/1542, 14/1600: *Followed* 13/1527

Osmani v Harrow LBC see Al-Ameri v Kensington and Chelsea RLBC

Osoba v Chief Constable of Hertfordshire [2013] Eq. L.R. 1072, EAT ............ *Digested,* 14/**1011**

Ostendorf v Germany (15598/08) 34 B.H.R.C. 738; [2013] Crim. L.R. 601, ECHR *Considered* 14/2464

Osterreichische Vereinigung zur Erhaltung, Starkung und Schaffung v Austria (39534/07) 36 B.H.R.C. 697, ECHR

Osterreichischer Gewerkschaftsbund v Wirtschaftskammer Osterreich - Fachverband Autobus-, Luftfahrt- und Schifffahrtsunternehmungen (C-328/13) [2014] I.C.R. 1152, ECJ (4th Chamber)

Otis Vehicle Rentals Ltd v Ciceley Commercials Ltd see Otis Vehicle Rentals Ltd (formerly Brandrick Hire (Birmingham) Ltd) v Ciceley Commercials Ltd (Damages)

Otis Vehicle Rentals Ltd (formerly Brandrick Hire (Birmingham) Ltd) v Ciceley Commercials Ltd (Damages); *sub nom* Otis Vehicle Rentals Ltd v Ciceley Commercials Ltd [2002] EWCA Civ 1064, CA (Civ Div) *Applied* 14/2586: *Followed* 13/2552

Ottica New Line di Accardi Vincenzo v Comune di Campobello di Mazara (C-539/11) [2014] 1 C.M.L.R. 44; [2014] C.E.C. 474, ECJ (4th Chamber)

Oughtred v Inland Revenue Commissioners [1960] A.C. 206; [1959] 3 W.L.R. 898; [1959] 3 All E.R. 623; (1959) 38 A.T.C. 317; [1959] T.R. 319; (1959) 103 S.J. 896, HL; affirming [1958] Ch. 678; [1958] 3 W.L.R. 64; [1958] 2 All E.R. 443; (1958) 37 A.T.C. 148; [1958] T.R. 177; (1958) 102 S.J. 468, CA; reversing [1958] Ch. 383; [1958] 2 W.L.R. 174; [1958] 1 All E.R. 252; (1957) 36 A.T.C. 291; [1957] T.R. 289; (1958) 102 S.J. 85, Ch D ............ *Digested,* 59/**3162**: *Applied* 62/2915, 04/3807: *Considered* 96/5781, 14/2505: *Distinguished* 62/2922, 67/1975

Our Communications Ltd v Revenue and Customs Commissioners; *sub nom* Revenue and Customs Commissioners v Our Communications Ltd [2013] UKUT 595 (TCC); [2014] S.T.C. 608; [2013] B.V.C. 1852, UT (Tax); reversing [2012] UKFTT 604 (TC); [2013] S.F.T.D. 55; [2012] S.T.I. 3027, FTT (Tax) ............ *Digested,* 14/**3080**

Ovenden Colbert Printers Ltd (In Liquidation), Re; *sub nom* Hunt v Hosking [2013] EWCA Civ 1408; [2014] 1 B.C.L.C. 291; [2014] B.P.I.R. 285, CA (Civ Div); affirming [2013] EWHC 311 (Ch); [2013] 2 B.C.L.C. 388; [2013] B.P.I.R. 370, Ch D (Companies Ct) ............ *Digested,* 14/**1809**

Owen v Revenue and Customs Commissioners [2014] UKFTT 245 (TC); [2014] S.T.I. 1664, FTT (Tax)

Owners - Strata Plan No.61288 v Brookfield Australia Investments Ltd; *sub nom* Owners Corp Strata Plan 61288 v Brookfield Multiplex Ltd [2014] HCA 36; 156 Con. L.R. 64, HC (Aus); reversing [2013] NSWCA 317; 152 Con. L.R. 206, CA (NSW)

Owners and/or Bailees of the Panamax Star v Owners of the Auk [2013] EWHC 4076 (Admlty); [2014] 1 Lloyd's Rep. 606, QBD (Admlty) ............ *Digested,* 14/**487**

Owners Corp Strata Plan 61288 v Brookfield Multiplex Ltd see Owners - Strata Plan No.61288 v Brookfield Australia Investments Ltd

Owners of Cargo Lately Laden on Board the Rewia v Caribbean Liners (Caribtainer) Ltd [1991] 2 Lloyd's Rep. 325; [1993] I.L.Pr. 507; Financial Times, July 12, 1991, CA (Civ Div); reversing [1991] 1 Lloyd's Rep. 69; Lloyd's List, September 21, 1990, QBD (Admlty) ............ *Digested,* 92/**3917**: *Applied* 03/484, 07/441: *Considered* 14/514

Owners of No.7 Steam Sand Pump Dredger v Owners of Steamship Greta Holme; *sub nom* Emerald, The [1897] A.C. 596, HL; reversing [1896] P. 192, CA *Applied* 61/8286, 11/858: *Considered* 52/893, 14/826: *Not applied* 06/1016

Owners of the Las Mercedes v Owners of the Abidin Daver [1984] A.C. 398; [1984] 2 W.L.R. 196; [1984] 1 All E.R. 470; [1984] 1 Lloyd's Rep. 339; (1984) 134 N.L.J. 235; (1984) 128 S.J. 99, HL; reversing [1983] 1 W.L.R. 884; [1983] 3 All E.R. 46; [1983] 2 Lloyd's Rep. 279; [1983] Com. L.R. 181, CA (Civ Div) .................... *Digested,* 84/**3151**:
*Applied* 85/1061, 87/3221, 06/632, 09/448: *Considered* 85/3131, 87/399, 92/3590, 09/456, 14/567: *Referred to* 91/5142

Owners of the Lord Citrine v Owners of the Hebridean Coast [1961] A.C. 545; [1961] 2 W.L.R. 48; [1961] 1 All E.R. 82; [1960] 2 Lloyd's Rep. 423; (1961) 105 S.J. 37, HL; affirming [1960] 3 W.L.R. 29; [1960] 2 All E.R. 85; [1960] 1 Lloyd's Rep. 227; (1960) 104 S.J. 507, CA; affirming [1959] 3 W.L.R. 569; [1959] 3 All E.R. 126; [1959] 2 Lloyd's Rep. 122; (1959) 103 S.J. 637, PDAD .............................. *Digested,* 61/**8286**:
*Applied* 11/858: *Approved* 69/3306: *Considered* 14/826: *Not applied* 06/1016

Owners of the Steamship Mediana v Owners of the Lightship Comet [1900] A.C. 113, HL; affirming [1899] P. 127, CA
*Applied* 47-51/2554, 03/943, 05/4193, 11/858: *Considered* 52/893, 78/44.u, 93/1415, 07/2497, 14/826

Owners of the Stolt Kestrel v Owners of the Niyazi S [2014] EWHC 1731 (Admlty); [2014] 2 Lloyd's Rep. 483; [2014] 1 C.L.C. 793, QBD (Admlty)

Owners of the Theresa Libra v Owners of the MSC Pamela [2013] EWHC 2792 (Admlty); [2013] 2 Lloyd's Rep. 596; [2013] 2 C.L.C. 429, QBD (Admlty) ........... *Digested,* 14/**2715**

Owusu v Jackson (t/a Villa Holidays Bal Inn Villas) (C-281/02) [2005] Q.B. 801; [2005] 2 W.L.R. 942; [2005] 2 All E.R. (Comm) 577; [2005] 1 Lloyd's Rep. 452; [2005] E.C.R. I-1383; [2005] 1 C.L.C. 246; [2005] I.L.Pr. 25; Times, March 9, 2005, ECJ .................................................................................................... *Digested,* 05/**604**:
*Applied* 09/455, 09/511, 10/371, 10/421, 14/560: *Considered* 06/329, 08/559, 10/1943, 10/501, 10/503, 11/469, 12/557, 13/1274, 14/1326: *Distinguished* 05/2406, 09/621: *Explained* 11/1402

Owusu v London Fire and Civil Defence Authority [1995] I.R.L.R. 574, EAT ................ *Digested,* 96/**2583**:
*Cited* 00/2183: *Considered* 97/2264, 14/1040

Oxborrow v West Suffolk Hospitals NHS Trust [2012] EWHC 1010 (QB); [2012] Med. L.R. 297, QBD .................................................................................... *Digested,* 12/**2408**:
*Considered* 14/2305

Oxford Diocesan Board of Finance v Secretary of State for Communities and Local Government; *sub nom* Wokingham BC v Oxford Diocesan Board of Finance [2013] EWCA Civ 1718; [2014] J.P.L. 530, CA (Civ Div); reversing [2013] EWHC 802 (Admin); [2013] J.P.L. 1285; [2013] A.C.D. 96; [2013] 17 E.G. 98 (C.S.), QBD (Admin) ............................................................................... *Digested,* 14/**2429**

Oxfordshire CC v B; *sub nom* Oxfordshire CC v GB; R. (on the application of GB) v Oxfordshire CC [2001] EWCA Civ 1358; [2002] B.L.G.R. 279; [2002] E.L.R. 8, CA (Civ Div); reversing in part [2001] EWHC Admin 378; [2001] E.L.R. 797, QBD (Admin) ..................................................................................... *Digested,* 02/**1165**:
*Considered* 07/5121, 08/1083, 10/988, 12/2040: *Followed* 11/981, 11/984, 14/938

Oxfordshire CC v GB see Oxfordshire CC v B

Ozen v Turkey (15672/08) (2014) 58 E.H.R.R. 27, ECHR

Oziegbe v Revenue and Customs Commissioners [2014] UKFTT 608 (TC); [2014] S.T.I. 2932, FTT (Tax)

P v Cheshire West and Chester Council see Cheshire West and Chester Council v P

P v D; *sub nom* D (Domestic Violence: Court Orders), Re [2014] EWHC 2355 (Fam); [2014] Fam. Law 1390, Fam Div

P v Ealing LBC; *sub nom* Ealing LBC v P [2013] EWCA Civ 1579; [2014] H.L.R. 5, CA (Civ Div) ........................................................................................... *Digested,* 14/**1598**

P v HM Attorney General for Gibraltar 35 B.H.R.C. 136, Sup Ct (Gib)

P v P (Divorce: Financial Remedy Order); *sub nom* JP v NP (Financial Remedies: Costs) [2014] EWHC 1101 (Fam); [2014] 1 W.L.R. 4607; [2014] Fam. Law 1106, Fam Div

P v P (Removal of Child to New Zealand) see Payne v Payne

P v P see H v W (Cap on Wife's Share of Bonus Payments)

P v Surrey CC see Cheshire West and Chester Council v P

P v Surrey CC see Surrey CC v CA

P v T see P (A Child) (Financial Provision), Re

P v United Kingdom (56547/00) [2002] 2 F.L.R. 631; [2002] 3 F.C.R. 1; (2002) 35 E.H.R.R. 31; 12 B.H.R.C. 615; [2002] Fam. Law 811; Times, August 16, 2002, ECHR ................................................................................................ *Digested,* 02/**2525**:
*Applied* 09/1533, 09/4291: *Considered* 03/1523, 04/1477, 07/1774, 14/1350

P v United Kingdom (Admissibility) (1529/10) (2014) 58 E.H.R.R. SE9, ECHR

P (A Child) v Service Insurance Co (Unreported, July 31, 2014), CC (Salisbury) [*Cordner Lewis Solicitors, 25-26 Neptune Court, Vanguard Way, Cardiff*] .......... *Digested,* 14/**2335**

P (A Child) v Tesco Stores Ltd (Unreported, December 20, 2013), CC (Kingston upon Hull) [*Joseph England, Barrister, 3 Paper Buildings, Temple, London*] .............. *Digested,* 14/**2319**

P (A Child) (Adoption Order: Leave to Oppose Making of Adoption Order), Re; *sub nom* P (A Child) (Adoption: Leave Proceedings), Re; P (A Child) (Adoption Proceedings), Re [2007] EWCA Civ 616; [2007] 1 W.L.R. 2556; [2007] 2 F.L.R. 1069; [2007] 2 F.C.R. 407; [2007] Fam. Law 889; (2007) 151 S.J.L.B. 894; Times, June 29, 2007, CA (Civ Div) .............. *Digested,* 07/**1684**: *Considered* 14/1248, 14/1251: *Explained* 07/1679: *Followed* 11/1282, 14/1245

P (A Child) (Adoption Proceedings), Re see P (A Child) (Adoption Order: Leave to Oppose Making of Adoption Order), Re

P (A Child) (Adoption: Leave Proceedings), Re see P (A Child) (Adoption Order: Leave to Oppose Making of Adoption Order), Re

P (A Child) (Adoption: Placement with non-UK Resident Family), Re see P (A Child) (Care Proceedings: Kinship Placement: Appeal), Re

P (A Child) (Adoption: Step-parent), Re; *sub nom* P (A Child) (Step-Parent Adoption), Re [2014] EWCA Civ 1174; [2014] 3 F.C.R. 193; [2014] Fam. Law 1512, CA (Civ Div)

P (A Child) (Adoption: Unmarried Couples), Re; *sub nom* G (A Child) (Adoption: Unmarried Couple), Re [2008] UKHL 38; [2009] 1 A.C. 173; [2008] 3 W.L.R. 76; [2008] N.I. 310; [2008] 2 F.L.R. 1084; [2008] 2 F.C.R. 366; [2008] H.R.L.R. 37; [2008] U.K.H.R.R. 1181; 24 B.H.R.C. 650; [2008] Fam. Law 977; (2008) 105(25) L.S.G. 25; Times, June 23, 2008, HL (NI); reversing [2007] NICA 20; [2007] N.I. 251, CA (NI) .............. *Digested,* 08/**4303**: *Applied* 11/3789, 13/240, 13/3334, 14/672: *Considered* 12/2336, 13/239

P (A Child) (Care and Placement: Child's Welfare), Re; *sub nom* P (Care and Placement Orders: Child Born Following Enforced Caesarean Section), Re [2014] 1 F.C.R. 636; [2014] Fam. Law 283, CC (Chelmsford)

P (A Child) (Care and Placement: Evidential Basis of Local Authority Case), Re; *sub nom* P (A Child) (Care Proceedings: Balancing Exercise), Re [2013] EWCA Civ 963; [2014] 1 F.L.R. 824; [2013] 3 F.C.R. 159; [2013] Fam. Law 1371, CA (Civ Div) .............. *Digested,* 13/**1221**: *Applied* 14/1346: *Followed* 14/1245

P (A Child) (Care Proceedings: Balancing Exercise), Re see P (A Child) (Care and Placement: Evidential Basis of Local Authority Case), Re

P (A Child) (Care Proceedings: Kinship Placement: Appeal), Re; *sub nom* P (A Child) (Adoption: Placement with non-UK Resident Family), Re [2014] EWCA Civ 888; [2014] 3 F.C.R. 349; [2014] Fam. Law 1382, CA (Civ Div)

P (A Child) (Enforced Caesarean: Adoption), Re [2014] EWHC 1146 (Fam); [2014] 2 F.L.R. 426; [2014] Fam. Law 949, Fam Div .............. *Digested,* 14/**1233**

P (A Child) (Enforced Caesarean: Reporting Restrictions), Re; *sub nom* P (A Child) (Reporting Restriction Order), Re [2013] EWHC 4048 (Fam); [2014] 2 F.L.R. 410; [2014] 2 F.C.R. 337; [2014] Fam. Law 414, Fam Div .............. *Digested,* 14/**1354**: *Applied* 14/1344

P (A Child) (Financial Provision), Re; *sub nom* P v T [2003] EWCA Civ 837; [2003] 2 F.L.R. 865; [2003] 2 F.C.R. 481; [2003] Fam. Law 717; (2003) 100(33) L.S.G. 27; Times, July 24, 2003; Independent, July 3, 2003, CA (Civ Div); reversing [2003] Fam. Law 303; Independent, December 11, 2002, Fam Div .............. *Digested,* 03/**1577**: *Applied* 05/1666, 08/1485, 09/1487, 09/1608, 14/1359, 14/1360: *Considered* 07/1688, 08/1429, 10/1281: *Distinguished* 05/1652: *Followed* 12/1433

P (A Child) (Prohibited Steps Order: Removal from Jurisdiction), Re [2013] EWCA Civ 1869; [2014] 2 F.L.R. 769; [2014] Fam. Law 788, CA (Civ Div)

P (A Child) (Reporting Restriction Order), Re see P (A Child) (Enforced Caesarean: Reporting Restrictions), Re

P (A Child) (Step-Parent Adoption), Re see P (A Child) (Adoption: Step-parent), Re

P (A Child), Re; *sub nom* An NHS Foundation Hospital v P [2014] EWHC 1650 (Fam); [2014] Fam. Law 1249, Fam Div

P (A Minor) (Residence Order: Child's Welfare), Re; *sub nom* P (Section 91(14) Guidelines: Residence and Religious Heritage), Re [2000] Fam. 15; [1999] 3 W.L.R. 1164; [1999] 3 All E.R. 734; [1999] 2 F.L.R. 573; [1999] 2 F.C.R. 289; [1999] Fam. Law 531; (1999) 163 J.P.N. 712; (1999) 96(21) L.S.G. 38; (1999) 149 N.L.J. 719; (1999) 143 S.J.L.B. 141; Times, May 11, 1999, CA (Civ Div) .... *Digested,* 99/**2389**: *Applied* 05/1587, 06/1681, 09/1588, 10/1394, 11/1342: *Considered* 02/1664, 03/47, 11/1396: *Followed* 07/1782, 14/1419

P (Care and Placement Orders: Child Born Following Enforced Caesarean Section), Re see P (A Child) (Care and Placement: Child's Welfare), Re

P (Children) (Adoption: Parental Consent), Re see P (Children) (Placement Orders: Parental Consent), Re

P (Children) (Findings of Fact), Re [2014] EWCA Civ 89; [2014] 1 F.C.R. 559; [2014] Fam. Law 439, CA (Civ Div) .......... *Digested,* 14/**1407**

P (Children) (Placement Orders: Parental Consent), Re; *sub nom* P (Children) (Adoption: Parental Consent), Re; B v X CC [2008] EWCA Civ 535; [2009] P.T.S.R. 150; [2008] 2 F.L.R. 625; [2008] 2 F.C.R. 185; Times, May 29, 2008, CA (Civ Div) .......... *Digested,* 08/**1575**: *Applied* 10/1272, 10/1425, 12/1297, 14/1341: *Considered* 11/1283, 11/4275, 14/1244, 14/1253: *Followed* 12/1296, 14/1243

P (Children) (Relocation: Appeal), Re [2014] EWCA Civ 852; [2014] Fam. Law 1393, CA (Civ Div)

P (Section 91(14) Guidelines: Residence and Religious Heritage), Re see P (A Minor) (Residence Order: Child's Welfare), Re

P (Statutory Will), Re [2009] EWHC 163 (Ch); [2010] Ch. 33; [2010] 2 W.L.R. 253; [2009] 2 All E.R. 1198; [2009] LS Law Medical 264; [2009] M.H.L.R. 146; [2009] W.T.L.R. 651; [2009] N.P.C. 24, CP .......... *Digested,* 09/**3727**: *Applied* 10/3212, 11/2219, 13/2978: *Considered* 13/2074, 14/2829

P (Terminating Parental Responsibility), Re [1995] 1 F.L.R. 1048; [1995] 3 F.C.R. 753; [1995] Fam. Law 471; (1995) 159 J.P.N. 675, Fam Div .......... *Digested,* 96/**591**: *Applied* 13/1337: *Considered* 14/1425: *Followed* 14/1424

P Oy v Veronsaajien oikeudenvalvontayksikko (C-6/12) [2014] 1 C.M.L.R. 15, ECJ (5th Chamber)

P Resources Ltd v Prest see Petrodel Resources Ltd v Prest

P&O Nedlloyd BV v Arab Metals Co (No.2) see P&O Nedlloyd BV v Arab Metals Co (The UB Tiger)

P&O Nedlloyd BV v Arab Metals Co (The UB Tiger); *sub nom* P&O Nedlloyd BV v Arab Metals Co (No.2) [2006] EWCA Civ 1717; [2007] 1 W.L.R. 2288; [2007] 2 All E.R. (Comm) 401; [2007] 2 Lloyd's Rep. 231; [2006] 2 C.L.C. 985; 116 Con. L.R. 200; Times, January 15, 2007, CA (Civ Div); reversing [2006] EWHC 2433 (Comm), QBD (Comm) .......... *Digested,* 07/**472**: *Considered* 10/2748: *Followed* 14/1393

P-J (Children) (Abduction: Habitual Residence: Consent), Re [2009] EWCA Civ 588; [2010] 1 W.L.R. 1237; [2009] 2 F.L.R. 1051; [2010] 1 F.C.R. 32; 2 A.L.R. Int'l 735; [2009] Fam. Law 786; (2009) 153(25) S.J.L.B. 29; Times, August 06, 2009, CA (Civ Div) .......... *Digested,* 09/**1541**: *Applied* 13/1313, 13/1315, 14/1383: *Considered* 12/1371: *Followed* 10/1336

P-M (A Child), Re see MF v Brent LBC

P-M (Parental Order: Payments to Surrogacy Agency), Re [2013] EWHC 2328 (Fam); [2014] 1 F.L.R. 725; [2013] Fam. Law 1388, Fam Div .......... *Digested,* 14/**1413**

P-S (Children) (Care Proceedings: Right to Give Evidence), Re see P-S (Children) (Family Proceedings: Evidence), Re

P-S (Children) (Child as Witness), Re see P-S (Children) (Family Proceedings: Evidence), Re

P-S (Children) (Family Proceedings: Evidence), Re; *sub nom* P-S (Children) (Care Proceedings: Right to Give Evidence), Re; P-S (Children) (Child as Witness), Re [2013] EWCA Civ 223; [2013] 1 W.L.R. 3831; [2014] 2 F.L.R. 27; [2013] 2 F.C.R. 299; [2013] Fam. Law 792, CA (Civ Div) .......... *Digested,* 13/**1247**

PA Holdings Ltd v Revenue and Customs Commissioners; *sub nom* Revenue and Customs Commissioners v PA Holdings Ltd [2011] EWCA Civ 1414; [2012] S.T.C. 582; 82 T.C. 1; [2011] B.T.C. 705; [2011] S.T.I. 3268; Times, December 30, 2011, CA (Civ Div); reversing [2010] UKUT 251 (TCC); [2010] S.T.C. 2343; [2010] B.T.C. 1626; [2010] S.T.I. 2274, UT (Tax); affirming [2009] UKFTT 95 (TC); [2009] S.F.T.D. 209; [2009] S.T.I. 1970, FTT (Tax) .......... *Digested,* 12/**3300**: *Applied* 12/3309: *Distinguished* 14/2921

Paal Wilson & Co A/S v Partenreederei Hannah Blumenthal (The Hannah Blumenthal) [1983] 1 A.C. 854; [1982] 3 W.L.R. 1149; [1983] 1 All E.R. 34; [1983] 1 Lloyd's Rep. 103; [1983] Com. L.R. 20; (1982) 126 S.J. 835, HL; affirming [1982] 3 W.L.R. 49; [1982] 3 All E.R. 394; [1982] 1 Lloyd's Rep. 582; [1982] Com. L.R. 117; (1982) 126 S.J. 292, CA (Civ Div); affirming [1981] 3 W.L.R. 823; [1982] 1 All E.R. 197; [1981] 2 Lloyd's Rep. 438; [1981] Com. L.R. 231; Times, July 10, 1981, QBD (Comm) .......... *Digested,* 82/**139**: *Applied* 82/80, 85/110, 88/131: *Considered* 86/1259, 87/133, 87/147, 90/4065: *Distinguished* 14/1022: *Referred to* 95/399

Pacific Molasses Co and United Molasses Trading Co v Entre Rios Compania Naviera SA (The San Nicholas) [1976] 1 Lloyd's Rep. 8, CA (Civ Div) .......... *Digested,* 76/**2530**: *Applied* 82/2858, 82/2888: *Considered* 95/4501, 14/2707

Paddico (267) Ltd v Adamson see Paddico (267) Ltd v Kirklees Metropolitan Council

Paddico (267) Ltd v Kirklees Metropolitan Council; *sub nom* Paddico (267) Ltd v Adamson; Adamson v Paddico (267) Ltd; Betterment Properties (Weymouth) Ltd v Dorset CC; *joined case* Taylor v Betterment Properties (Weymouth) Ltd [2014] UKSC 7; [2014] A.C. 1072; [2014] 2 W.L.R. 300; [2014] 2 All E.R. 1; [2014] B.L.G.R. 249; [2014] 1 P. & C.R. 24; [2014] 2 E.G.L.R. 109; [2014] J.P.L. 745; (2014) 164(7594) N.L.J. 19; (2014) 158(7) S.J.L.B. 37; Times, February 18, 2014, SC; reversing [2012] EWCA Civ 262; [2012] B.L.G.R. 617; [2012] 2 P. & C.R. 1; [2012] 11 E.G. 92 (C.S.), CA (Civ Div); reversing [2011] EWHC 1606 (Ch); [2011] B.L.G.R. 727; [2011] 26 E.G. 84 (C.S.); [2011] N.P.C. 66, Ch D ........ *Digested,* 14/**2507**

Padmore v Barry and Peggy High Foundation; *sub nom* Padmore v Official Custodian for Charities [2013] UKUT 646 (LC); [2014] 1 E.G.L.R. 129; [2014] R.V.R. 237, UT (Lands) ........ *Digested,* 14/**1985**

Padmore v Official Custodian for Charities see Padmore v Barry and Peggy High Foundation

Page v Hewetts Solicitors [2013] EWHC 2845 (Ch); [2014] W.T.L.R. 479, Ch D ........ *Digested,* 14/**420**: *Considered* 14/577

Pagel v Farman [2013] EWHC 2210 (Comm); [2013] W.T.L.R. 1575, QBD (Comm) .... *Digested,* 14/**1204**

Paget v Paget [1898] 1 Ch. 470, CA; affirming [1898] 1 Ch. 47, Ch D
*Applied* 14/1203: *Considered* 85/162, 85/2650

Pagnan SpA v Feed Products Ltd [1987] 2 Lloyd's Rep. 601, CA (Civ Div) ........ *Digested,* 88/**429**: *Applied* 96/5328, 02/676, 02/716, 04/602, 10/2830, 10/631: *Followed* 13/448, 14/636: *Referred to* 95/3947

Painter, Re [1895] 1 Q.B. 85, QBD
*Applied* 47-51/646, 14/1783: *Considered* 78/148: *Distinguished* 67/187

Pakhomova v Russia (22953/11) [2014] 2 F.L.R. 44; [2014] Fam. Law 156, ECHR

Pakistan v Dallah Real Estate and Tourism Holding Co 154 Con. L.R. 222, C d'A (Paris)

Paksas v Lithuania (34932/04) (2014) 59 E.H.R.R. 30, ECHR

Palacegate Properties Ltd v Camden LBC (2001) 3 L.G.L.R. 18; (2001) 82 P. & C.R. 17; [2000] 4 P.L.R. 59; [2001] J.P.L. 373 (Note); [2001] A.C.D. 23, DC ........ *Digested,* 01/**81**: *Considered* 14/2376

Palacin Cambra v Jones (Contempt Proceedings: Child Joined as Party) see Cambra v Jones

Palatial Leisure Ltd v Revenue and Customs Commissioners [2013] UKFTT 396 (TC); [2014] L.L.R. 103; [2013] S.T.I. 2867, FTT (Tax)

Palatine Graphic Arts Co v Liverpool City Council [1986] Q.B. 335; [1986] 2 W.L.R. 285; [1986] 1 All E.R. 366; (1986) 52 P. & C.R. 308; [1986] 1 E.G.L.R. 19; (1985) 277 E.G. 412; [1985] R.V.R. 211; [1986] J.P.L. 511; (1986) 83 L.S.G. 118; (1986) 136 N.L.J. 45; (1986) 130 S.J. 14; Times, December 6, 1985, CA (Civ Div); affirming [1985] R.V.R. 35, Lands Tr ........ *Digested,* 86/**350**: *Applied* 14/827: *Considered* 87/394

Palk v Mortgage Services Funding Plc [1993] Ch. 330; [1993] 2 W.L.R. 415; [1993] 2 All E.R. 481; (1993) 25 H.L.R. 56; (1993) 65 P. & C.R. 207; [1992] N.P.C. 114; Times, August 7, 1992; Independent, August 25, 1992; Guardian, August 19, 1992, CA (Civ Div) ........ *Digested,* 93/**2887**: *Applied* 97/4249: *Cited* 93/2882: *Considered* 11/243, 14/278: *Doubted* 96/5003: *Followed* 96/4980

Pall Mall Investments (London) Ltd v Gloucester City Council [2014] EWHC 2247 (Admin); [2014] P.T.S.R. 1184; [2014] 3 E.G.L.R. 95; [2014] R.A. 395, DC ........ *Digested,* 14/**2480**

Pall Mall Investments Ltd v Castle Point BC [2013] EWHC 4238 (Admin); [2014] R.V.R. 236, QBD (Admin) ........ *Digested,* 14/**2487**

Pall Mall Investments Ltd v Leeds City Council [2013] EWHC 3307 (Admin); [2013] R.V.R. 330, QBD (Admin) ........ *Digested,* 14/**2135**

Pallant v Morgan [1953] Ch. 43; [1952] 2 All E.R. 951; [1952] 2 T.L.R. 813, Ch D ........ *Digested,* 52/**3571**: *Applied* 00/2317, 10/3443, 12/2024, 14/2493: *Approved* 00/2327: *Considered* 05/695

Pallet Route Solutions Ltd v Morris [2014] I.C.R. 394, EAT ........ *Digested,* 14/**1081**

Palmer v Royal Bank of Scotland Plc [2014] I.C.R. 1288; [2014] Eq. L.R. 685, EAT

Palser v Grinling; *joined case* Property Holding Co v Mischeff [1948] A.C. 291; [1948] 1 All E.R. 1; 64 T.L.R. 2; [1948] L.J.R. 600; (1948) 92 S.J. 53, HL; affirming [1946] K.B. 631; [1946] 2 All E.R. 287, CA; affirming (Unreported, March 15, 1946), KBD ........ *Digested,* 47-51/**8586**: *Applied* 47-51/8467, 47-51/8560, 47-51/8574, 47-51/8576, 47-51/8584, 47-51/8589, 58/1804, 74/3181, 80/2766, 82/3306: *Considered* 68/3281, 69/3068, 69/3069, 74/134.u, 82/424, 93/2540, 11/107: *Followed* 14/547

Pan Ocean Co Ltd v Fibria Celulose S/A see Pan Ocean Co Ltd, Re

Pan Ocean Co Ltd, Re; *sub nom* Pan Ocean Co Ltd v Fibria Celulose S/A; Kim v Fibria Celulose S/A; Fibria Celulose S/A v Pan Ocean Co Ltd [2014] EWHC 2124 (Ch); [2014] Bus. L.R. 1041, Ch D (Companies Ct)

Panayiotou v Chief Constable of Hampshire see Panayiotou v Kernaghan

Panayiotou v Kernaghan; *sub nom* Panayiotou v Chief Constable of Hampshire [2014] I.R.L.R. 500; [2014] I.C.R. D23, EAT ........ *Digested,* 14/**1093**

Pancommerce SA v Veecheema BV [1983] 2 Lloyd's Rep. 304; [1983] Com. L.R. 230, CA (Civ Div); reversing [1982] 1 Lloyd's Rep. 645, QBD (Comm) ........ *Digested,* 83/**3343**: *Applied* 00/3848, 14/1964: *Considered* 13/1862, 13/2554

Panesar v Revenue and Customs Commissioners see R. (on the application of Panesar) v Central Criminal Court

Pankina v Secretary of State for the Home Department see Secretary of State for the Home Department v Pankina

Panter v Rowellian Football Social Club [2011] EWHC 1301 (Ch); [2012] Ch. 125; [2011] 3 W.L.R. 1147; [2014] B.C.C. 321; [2011] 2 B.C.L.C. 610, Ch D (Companies Ct) ........ *Digested,* 12/**1795**

Panton v Secretary of State for the Environment, Transport and the Regions (1999) 78 P. & C.R. 186; [1999] 1 P.L.R. 92; [1999] J.P.L. 461; [1999] N.P.C. 3; Times, January 21, 1999; Independent, January 18, 1999, QBD ........ *Digested,* 99/**4219**: *Considered* 01/4653, 14/2355

Papanicola v Fagan; *sub nom* Fagan v Papanicola [2008] EWHC 3348 (Ch); [2009] B.P.I.R. 320, Ch D ........ *Digested,* 09/**4010**: *Considered* 12/1825, 14/1831

Papanicola v Humphreys [2005] EWHC 335 (Ch); [2005] 2 All E.R. 418; [2006] B.P.I.R. 135; (2005) 102(19) L.S.G. 33; Times, April 28, 2005, Ch D (Bankruptcy Ct) ........ *Digested,* 05/**2277**: *Applied* 09/2217, 09/439, 11/1899, 12/1834, 13/1698, 14/1779, 14/290: *Considered* 10/1862, 11/1847

Papasavvas v O Fileleftheros Dimosia Etairia Ltd (C-291/13) (2014) 158(36) S.J.L.B. 37, ECJ (7th Chamber)

Paragon Finance Plc v DB Thakerar & Co; *joined case* Paragon Finance Plc v Thimbleby & Co [1999] 1 All E.R. 400; (1998) 95(35) L.S.G. 36; (1998) 142 S.J.L.B. 243; Times, August 7, 1998, CA (Civ Div) ........ *Digested,* 98/**536**: *Applied* 00/1452, 00/513, 03/519, 04/380, 06/470, 06/543, 06/561, 07/476, 07/491, 08/897, 14/426: *Considered* 98/383, 99/501, 00/520, 01/5505, 01/626, 07/4258, 10/394, 13/433, 14/2991: *Followed* 99/458

Paragon Finance Plc v Thimbleby & Co see Paragon Finance Plc v DB Thakerar & Co

Paramount Airways Ltd (No.2), Re; *sub nom* Powdrill v Hambros Bank (Jersey) Ltd [1993] Ch. 223; [1992] 3 W.L.R. 690; [1992] 3 All E.R. 1; [1992] B.C.C. 416; [1992] B.C.L.C. 710; (1992) 89(14) L.S.G. 31; (1992) 136 S.J.L.B. 97; [1992] N.P.C. 27; Times, March 5, 1992; Financial Times, March 10, 1992, CA (Civ Div); reversing [1992] Ch. 160; [1991] 3 W.L.R. 318; [1991] 4 All E.R. 267; [1991] B.C.C. 559; [1991] B.C.L.C. 767; (1991) 135 S.J.L.B. 76; [1991] N.P.C. 75; Times, June 20, 1991, Ch D (Companies Ct) ........ *Digested,* 92/**2528**: *Applied* 07/2407, 12/1869, 14/1807: *Considered* 98/529: *Followed* 10/1926, 12/1826

Paramount Home Entertainment International Ltd v British Sky Broadcasting Ltd [2013] EWHC 3479 (Ch); [2014] E.C.D.R. 7, Ch D ........ *Digested,* 14/**1868**

Paratus AMC Ltd v Fosuhene see Paratus AMC Ltd v Persons Unknown

Paratus AMC Ltd v Persons Unknown; *sub nom* Paratus AMC Ltd v Fosuhene [2013] EWCA Civ 827; [2014] H.L.R. 1; [2013] 2 P. & C.R. DG22, CA (Civ Div); affirming [2012] EWHC 3791 (Ch), Ch D ........ *Digested,* 14/**2001**

Park v Cho [2014] EWHC 55 (Ch); [2014] P.T.S.R. 769, Ch D

Park Air Services Plc, Re; *sub nom* Christopher Moran Holdings Ltd v Bairstow [2000] 2 A.C. 172; [1999] 2 W.L.R. 396; [1999] 1 All E.R. 673; [1999] B.C.C. 135; [1999] 1 B.C.L.C. 155; [1999] B.P.I.R. 786; [1999] L. & T.R. 289; [1999] 1 E.G.L.R. 1; [1999] 14 E.G. 149; [1999] E.G. 17 (C.S.); (1999) 149 N.L.J. 195; [1999] N.P.C. 12; Times, February 5, 1999; Independent, February 12, 1999, HL; reversing [1997] 1 W.L.R. 1376; [1997] 3 All E.R. 193; [1997] B.C.C. 712; [1997] 2 B.C.L.C. 75; (1998) 75 P. & C.R. 161; [1997] 2 E.G.L.R. 36; [1997] 30 E.G. 127; [1997] E.G. 68 (C.S.); (1997) 94(19) L.S.G. 25; (1997) 141 S.J.L.B. 112; [1997] N.P.C. 68; (1997) 74 P. & C.R. D23; Times, May 14, 1997, CA (Civ Div); reversing [1996] 1 W.L.R. 649; [1996] B.C.C. 556; [1996] 1 B.C.L.C. 547; [1996] B.P.I.R. 377; (1996) 72 P. & C.R. 174; [1996] 2 E.G.L.R. 49; [1996] 40 E.G. 136; [1995] N.P.C. 205, Ch D ........ *Digested,* 99/**3306**: *Followed* 99/3272, 14/1972

Park Cakes Ltd v Shumba see Shumba v Park Cakes Ltd

Park Valley Leisure Ltd v Maidstone BC [2014] P.A.D. 1, Planning Inspector
Parker v Thompson 2014 BCSC 1916; 17 I.T.E.L.R. 597, Sup Ct (BC)
Parker-Tweedale v Dunbar Bank (No.2) [1991] Ch. 26; [1990] 3 W.L.R. 780; [1990] 2 All E.R. 588; [1990] E.G. 19 (C.S.); (1990) 87(29) L.S.G. 33; (1990) 134 S.J. 1040; Times, February 23, 1990, CA (Civ Div) ........ *Digested,* 90/**3212**: *Followed* 00/3458, 14/2493
Parkes v Esso Petroleum Co Ltd see Parks v Esso Petroleum Co Ltd
Parks v Esso Petroleum Co Ltd; *sub nom* Parkes v Esso Petroleum Co Ltd [2000] E.C.C. 45; [2000] Eu. L.R. 25; (1999) 18 Tr. L.R. 232, CA (Civ Div); affirming [1999] 1 C.M.L.R. 455; [1998] Eu. L.R. 550, Ch D ........ *Digested,* 00/**120**: *Applied* 14/82: *Considered* 10/84, 10/86
Parkwell Investments Ltd v Wilson see Parkwell Investments Ltd, Re
Parkwell Investments Ltd, Re; *sub nom* Parkwell Investments Ltd v Wilson [2014] EWHC 3381 (Ch); [2014] B.C.C. 721, Ch D (Companies Ct)
Parkwood Landfill Ltd v Customs and Excise Commissioners; *sub nom* Customs and Excise Commissioners v Parkwood Landfill Ltd [2002] EWCA Civ 1707; [2003] 1 W.L.R. 697; [2003] 1 All E.R. 579; [2002] S.T.C. 1536; [2003] Env. L.R. 19; [2002] B.T.C. 8045; [2003] J.P.L. 861; [2002] S.T.I. 1653; (2003) 100(6) L.S.G. 26; (2002) 146 S.J.L.B. 278; [2002] N.P.C. 155; Times, December 4, 2002, CA (Civ Div); reversing [2002] EWHC 47 (Ch); [2002] S.T.C. 417; [2002] B.T.C. 8008; [2002] S.T.I. 156; (2002) 99(11) L.S.G. 38; (2002) 146 S.J.L.B. 45; [2002] N.P.C. 16; Times, February 12, 2002, Ch D; reversing [2002] E.H.L.R. Dig. 2, V&DTr ........ *Digested,* 03/**4278**: *Considered* 08/3818: *Distinguished* 14/2946
Parkwood Leisure Ltd v Laing O'Rourke Wales and West Ltd [2013] EWHC 2665 (TCC); [2013] B.L.R. 589; 150 Con. L.R. 93; [2013] 3 E.G.L.R. 6; [2013] C.I.L.L. 3413, QBD (TCC) ........ *Digested,* 14/**593**
Parmeko Holdings Ltd (In Administration), Re; *joined cases* RGS Plus Ltd (In Administration), Re; Davis Pneumatic Systems Ltd (In Administration), Re; Parmenko Group Ltd (In Administration), Re [2014] B.C.C. 159, Ch D (Birmingham) ........ *Digested,* 14/**1763**
Parmenko Group Ltd (In Administration), Re see Parmeko Holdings Ltd (In Administration), Re
Parry v Cleaver [1970] A.C. 1; [1969] 2 W.L.R. 821; [1969] 1 All E.R. 555; [1969] 1 Lloyd's Rep. 183; 6 K.I.R. 265; (1969) 113 S.J. 147, HL; reversing [1968] 1 Q.B. 195; [1967] 3 W.L.R. 739; [1967] 2 All E.R. 1168; 2 K.I.R. 844; (1967) 111 S.J. 415, CA (Civ Div) ........ *Digested,* 69/**906**: *Applied* 69/917, 69/919, 72/836, 73/729, 73/740, 74/814, 76/2517, 76/677, 79/2472, 85/942, 86/350, 87/1220, 88/1069, 89/1285, 92/2029, 94/2039, 01/6413, 14/1852: *Considered* 72/826, 72/834, 78/788, 80/630, 82/894, 83/1272, 85/11.u, 86/981, 87/1161, 87/394, 88/1070, 88/1710, 95/1616, 96/1218, 96/4529, 96/6896, 98/2099, 99/810, 00/5816, 09/5111: *Disapproved* 78/719: *Distinguished* 96/3603, 99/3410: *Explained* 14/827: *Followed* 77/773, 90/5070, 91/1327, 98/1468, 99/3411, 00/1488
Parry v Revenue and Customs Commissioners [2014] UKFTT 419 (TC); [2014] W.T.L.R. 1265; [2014] S.T.I. 2415, FTT (Tax)
Parsons Corp v CV Scheepvaartonderneming Happy Ranger [2002] EWCA Civ 694; [2002] 2 All E.R. (Comm) 24; [2002] 2 Lloyd's Rep. 357; [2003] 1 C.L.C. 122, CA (Civ Div); reversing [2002] 1 All E.R. (Comm) 176; [2001] 2 Lloyd's Rep. 530, QBD (Comm) ........ *Digested,* 02/**4090**: *Applied* 14/2706: *Considered* 02/4098: *Followed* 03/3897
Pasticceria e Confetteria Sant Ambroeus Srl v G&D Restaurant Associates Ltd; *sub nom* Pasticceria e Confetteria Sant Ambroeus Srl's Trade Mark Application (No.1317269) [2010] R.P.C. 28, App Person *Considered* 14/1931
Pasticceria e Confetteria Sant Ambroeus Srl's Trade Mark Application (No.1317269) see Pasticceria e Confetteria Sant Ambroeus Srl v G&D Restaurant Associates Ltd
Patel v Camden LBC [2013] EWHC 2459 (Admin); [2013] R.A. 439; [2014] A.C.D. 15, QBD (Admin) ........ *Digested,* 14/**2131**
Patel v Mirza [2014] EWCA Civ 1047; [2014] Lloyd's Rep. F.C. 561; [2014] W.T.L.R. 1567; Times, August 12, 2014, CA (Civ Div); reversing [2013] EWHC 1892 (Ch); [2013] Lloyd's Rep. F.C. 525; [2013] W.T.L.R. 1755; [2014] L.L.R. 110; [2013] 2 P. & C.R. DG23, Ch D ........ *Digested,* 14/**264**

Patel v Pirabakaran; *sub nom* Pirabakaran v Patel [2006] EWCA Civ 685; [2006] 1 W.L.R. 3112; [2006] 4 All E.R. 506; [2006] H.L.R. 39; [2006] 2 P. & C.R. 26; [2006] L. & T.R. 24; [2006] 3 E.G.L.R. 23; [2006] 36 E.G. 260; [2006] 23 E.G. 165 (C.S.); (2006) 103(24) L.S.G. 28; (2006) 150 S.J.L.B. 743; [2006] N.P.C. 63; Times, July 19, 2006; Independent, June 6, 2006, CA (Civ Div) ............... *Digested,* 06/**2708**: *Considered* 14/1625

Patel v Revenue and Customs Commissioners [2014] UKFTT 167 (TC); [2014] W.T.L.R. 1183, FTT (Tax) ............... *Digested,* 14/**2933**

Patel v Secretary of State for the Home Department; *joined cases* Anwar v Secretary of State for the Home Department; Alam v Secretary of State for the Home Department [2013] UKSC 72; [2014] A.C. 651; [2013] 3 W.L.R. 1517; [2014] 1 All E.R. 1157; [2014] Imm. A.R. 456; [2014] I.N.L.R. 205, SC; affirming [2012] EWCA Civ 741; [2013] 1 W.L.R. 63; [2012] 4 All E.R. 94; [2012] Imm. A.R. 898; [2012] I.N.L.R. 485; Times, August 30, 2012, CA (Civ Div) ............... *Digested,* 14/**1718**: *Considered* 14/1699

Patel, Re see R. v Patel (Hitendra) (Costs)

Patersons of Greenoakhill Ltd v Revenue and Customs Commissioners [2014] UKUT 225 (TCC); [2014] S.T.C. 2178; [2014] B.T.C. 517; [2014] S.T.I. 2232, UT (Tax); affirming [2014] UKFTT 334 (TC), FTT (Tax) ............... *Digested,* 14/**2946**

Patmalniece v Secretary of State for Work and Pensions [2011] UKSC 11; [2011] 1 W.L.R. 783; [2011] 3 All E.R. 1; [2011] P.T.S.R. 680; [2011] 2 C.M.L.R. 45; [2011] Eq. L.R. 508; (2011) 108(13) L.S.G. 23; (2011) 155(11) S.J.L.B. 31; Times, March 23, 2011, SC; affirming [2009] EWCA Civ 621; [2009] 4 All E.R. 738; [2010] P.T.S.R. 128; [2009] 3 C.M.L.R. 36, CA (Civ Div) ............... *Digested,* 11/**3177**: *Applied* 14/1104: *Cited* 11/1806: *Followed* 12/3117

Paton v Inland Revenue Commissioners; *sub nom* Fenton's Trustee v Inland Revenue Commissioners [1938] A.C. 341; [1938] 1 All E.R. 786, HL; affirming [1936] 2 K.B. 59; [1936] 1 All E.R. 116, CA
*Applied* 91/594, 14/2909

Patterson v Royal Society for the Prevention of Cruelty to Animals (RSPCA); *sub nom* R. (on the application of Patterson) v RSPCA [2013] EWHC 4531 (Admin); (2014) 178 J.P. 518, QBD (Admin)

Pattullo v Revenue and Customs Commissioners [2014] UKFTT 841 (TC); [2014] S.T.I. 3197, FTT (Tax)

Paulet v United Kingdom (6219/08) 37 B.H.R.C. 695; [2014] Lloyd's Rep. F.C. 484; [2014] Crim. L.R. 750; Times, May 19, 2014, ECHR ............... *Digested,* 14/**1631**

Paulley v First Group Plc [2014] EWCA Civ 1573, CA (Civ Div); reversing [2013] Eq. L.R. 1024, CC (Leeds) ............... *Digested,* 14/**3003**

Pavel v Sony Corp (No.1) [1993] F.S.R. 177, PCC ............... *Digested,* 93/**3027**: *Considered* 14/1877

Pavilion Property Trustees Ltd v Permira Advisers LLP [2014] EWHC 145 (Ch); [2014] 1 P. & C.R. 21; [2014] L. & T.R. 19, Ch D ............... *Digested,* 14/**1974**

Pavledes v Hadjisavva [2013] EWHC 124 (Ch); [2013] 2 E.G.L.R. 123, Ch D ............... *Digested,* 14/**2224**

Paycheck Services 3 Ltd, Re see Revenue and Customs Commissioners v Holland

Paymex Ltd v Revenue and Customs Commissioners [2011] UKFTT 350 (TC); [2012] B.P.I.R. 178; [2011] S.F.T.D. 1028; [2011] S.T.I. 1952, FTT (Tax) ............... *Digested,* 12/**3387**: *Applied* 14/3046

Payne v Payne; *sub nom* P v P (Removal of Child to New Zealand) [2001] EWCA Civ 166; [2001] Fam. 473; [2001] 2 W.L.R. 1826; [2001] 1 F.L.R. 1052; [2001] 1 F.C.R. 425; [2001] H.R.L.R. 28; [2001] U.K.H.R.R. 484; (2001) 165 J.P.N. 466; (2001) 98(10) L.S.G. 41; (2001) 145 S.J.L.B. 61; Times, March 9, 2001; Independent, February 22, 2001; Daily Telegraph, February 27, 2001, CA (Civ Div) ............... *Digested,* 01/**2596**: *Applied* 01/2597, 03/1545, 05/1590, 06/1626, 06/1688, 06/5363, 07/1794, 10/1359, 11/1373, 12/1389, 13/1248, 13/1252: *Considered* 05/1572, 05/1574, 05/1635, 06/1691, 07/1795, 11/1378, 11/1382, 12/4010, 14/1311: *Distinguished* 05/1575, 08/4780: *Followed* 11/1360, 11/1379, 11/1380, 13/1249: *Referred to* 08/1515

Payton v Brooks [1974] 1 Lloyd's Rep. 241; [1974] R.T.R. 169, CA (Civ Div) ............... *Digested,* 74/**841**: *Cited* 00/1484, 01/1543: *Considered* 98/1450: *Followed* 97/1815, 14/1852

PB v RB [2014] C.O.P.L.R. 481, CP ............... *Digested,* 14/**2161**

PB v SE see S (A Child) (Jurisdiction: Brussels IIR: Prorogation), Re

PB (India) v Secretary of State for the Home Department see SA (Pakistan) v Secretary of State for the Home Department

PC v City of York Council see York City Council v C

PC (A Child) (Brussels II Revised: Jurisdiction within United Kingdom), Re; *sub nom* Y (Children) (Care Proceedings: Transfer of Proceedings within UK Jurisdiction), Re; Camden LBC v PC [2013] EWHC 2336 (Fam); [2014] 1 F.L.R. 605; [2014] 3 F.C.R. 253; [2013] Fam. Law 1531, Fam Div ........ *Digested,* 14/**1285**

PCE Investors Ltd v Cancer Research UK [2012] EWHC 884 (Ch); [2012] 2 P. & C.R. 5; [2012] L. & T.R. 34; [2012] 17 E.G. 110 (C.S.), Ch D ........ *Digested,* 13/**1893**: *Applied* 14/1969, 14/2970: *Considered* 14/1987

PD Teesport Ltd, Re; *sub nom* PNPF Trust Co Ltd v Taylor [2009] EWHC 1693 (Ch); [2009] Pens. L.R. 263; [2009] W.T.L.R. 1215, Ch D ........ *Digested,* 09/**440**: *Considered* 14/1371

PE (Cameroon) v Secretary of State for the Home Department see R. (on the application of PE (Cameroon)) v Secretary of State for the Home Department

Peacock, Re [2012] UKSC 5; [2012] 1 W.L.R. 550; [2012] 2 All E.R. 257; [2012] 2 Cr. App. R. (S.) 81; [2012] Lloyd's Rep. F.C. 291; [2012] Crim. L.R. 472; Times, March 8, 2012, SC; affirming [2010] EWCA Civ 1465; [2011] Lloyd's Rep. F.C. 147, CA (Civ Div); affirming [2009] EWHC 3740 (Admin), QBD (Admin) ........ *Digested,* 12/**763**: *Followed* 14/741

Pearce v Beverley [2013] EWHC 2627 (Ch); [2014] W.T.L.R. 85, Ch D (Leeds) ........ *Digested,* 14/**2844**

Pearce & High Ltd v Baxter [1999] C.L.C. 749; [1999] B.L.R. 101; (1999) 1 T.C.L.R. 157; 66 Con. L.R. 110; Times, March 24, 1999; Independent, March 4, 1999, CA (Civ Div) ........ *Digested,* 99/**792**: *Applied* 02/671, 05/654, 14/597: *Considered* 11/531

Pearce's Appeal, Re [2014] UKUT 291 (LC); [2014] R.A. 341, UT (Lands)

Pearson v Revenue and Customs Commissioners [2014] UKFTT 890 (TC); [2014] S.T.I. 2952, FTT (Tax)

Pearson Driving Assessments Ltd v Minister for the Cabinet [2013] EWHC 2082 (TCC); 149 Con. L.R. 162, QBD (TCC) ........ *Digested,* 14/**2476**

Pectel Ltd, Re see O'Neill v Phillips

Pedro v Secretary of State for Work and Pensions [2009] EWCA Civ 1358; [2010] P.T.S.R. 1504; [2010] 2 C.M.L.R. 20; Times, January 5, 2010, CA (Civ Div); reversing CPC/1433/2008, SS Comm ........ *Digested,* 10/**3129**: *Applied* 14/1685

Peel Land and Property (Ports No.3) Ltd v TS Sheerness Steel Ltd [2014] EWCA Civ 100; [2014] 2 P. & C.R. 8; [2014] L. & T.R. 20; [2014] 2 E.G.L.R. 21; [2014] 2 P. & C.R. DG5, CA (Civ Div); reversing [2013] EWHC 1658 (Ch), Ch D ........ *Digested,* 14/**1973**

Pegasus Birds Ltd v Customs and Excise Commissioners; *sub nom* Customs and Excise Commissioners v Pegasus Birds Ltd [2004] EWCA Civ 1015; [2004] S.T.C. 1509; [2004] B.T.C. 5729; [2004] B.V.C. 788; [2004] S.T.I. 1759; (2004) 101(36) L.S.G. 35; (2004) 148 S.J.L.B. 945; Times, August 2, 2004, CA (Civ Div); reversing in part [2003] EWHC 2552 (Ch); [2004] S.T.C. 262; [2004] B.T.C. 5168; [2004] B.V.C. 228; [2003] S.T.I. 1938, Ch D; reversing [2003] S.T.I. 185, V&DTr ........ *Digested,* 04/**3972**: *Applied* 10/3469, 11/3517, 11/3573, 14/3037: *Cited* 06/4427: *Considered* 06/4425

Pegram Shopfitters Ltd v Tally Weijl (UK) Ltd; *sub nom* Pegram Shopfitters Ltd v Tally Wiejl (UK) Ltd [2003] EWCA Civ 1750; [2004] 1 W.L.R. 2082; [2004] 1 All E.R. 818; [2004] 1 All E.R. (Comm) 593; [2004] B.L.R. 65; 91 Con. L.R. 173, CA (Civ Div); reversing [2003] EWHC 984 (TCC); [2003] 1 W.L.R. 2990; [2003] 3 All E.R. 98; [2003] B.L.R. 296; 87 Con. L.R. 39, QBD (TCC) ........ *Digested,* 04/**589**: *Applied* 14/592: *Considered* 10/845, 11/4058

Pegram Shopfitters Ltd v Tally Wiejl (UK) Ltd see Pegram Shopfitters Ltd v Tally Weijl (UK) Ltd

Pelagic Freezing Ltd v Lovie Construction Ltd [2010] CSOH 145; 2010 G.W.D. 37-763, OH
*Doubted* 14/2470: *Followed* 11/4545

Pelckmans Turnhout NV v Walter Van Gastel Balen NV (C-483/12) [2014] 3 C.M.L.R. 49, ECJ (1st Chamber)

Pelipenko v Russia (69037/10) (2014) 58 E.H.R.R. SE11, ECHR

Pelix Ltd (in administration) v Revenue and Customs Commissioners see Universal Enterprises (EU) Ltd v Revenue and Customs Commissioners

Pell Frischmann Consultants Ltd v Prabhu [2013] EWHC 2203 (Ch); [2014] I.C.R. 153; [2013] Pens. L.R. 325, Ch D ........ *Digested,* 13/**441**

Pelling v Families Need Fathers Ltd [2001] EWCA Civ 1280; [2002] 2 All E.R. 440; [2002] 1 B.C.L.C. 645; (2001) 151 N.L.J. 1284, CA (Civ Div) ........ *Digested,* 02/**561**: *Applied* 14/518

Pembele v Secretary of State for the Home Department see Pembele (Paragraph 399(b)(i): Valid Leave: Meaning), Re

Pembele (Paragraph 399(b)(i): Valid Leave: Meaning), Re; *sub nom* Pembele v Secretary of State for the Home Department [2013] UKUT 310 (IAC); [2013] Imm. A.R. 845, UT (IAC) ........ *Digested,* 14/**1717**
Pender v DPP [2013] EWHC 2598 (Admin); (2013) 177 J.P. 662, DC ........ *Digested,* 14/**713**
Pendleton v Stone & Webster Engineering Ltd see Fairchild v Glenhaven Funeral Services Ltd (t/a GH Dovener & Son)
Pendragon Plc v Revenue and Customs Commissioners; *sub nom* Revenue and Customs Commissioners v Pendragon Plc [2013] EWCA Civ 868; [2014] S.T.C. 844; [2013] B.V.C. 414; [2013] S.T.I. 2568, CA (Civ Div); reversing [2012] UKUT 90 (TCC); [2012] S.T.C. 1638; [2012] B.V.C. 1644, UT (Tax); reversing [2009] UKFTT 192 (TC); [2010] B.V.C. 2019; [2010] S.F.T.D. 1; [2010] S.T.I. 1404, FTT (Tax) ........ *Digested,* 13/**3205**
Penny v Nicholas see Nicholas v Penny
Pension Regulator v Desmond see Pensions Regulator v Desmond
Pensions Regulator v A Admin Ltd see LPA Umbrella Trust, Re
Pensions Regulator v Desmond; *sub nom* Pension Regulator v Desmond [2013] NICA 62; [2014] Pens. L.R. 9, CA (NI) ........ *Digested,* 14/**3219**
Pensions Regulator v Michel Van De Wiele NV see Michel Van De Wiele NV v Pensions Regulator
Pensionsversicherungsanstalt v Brey (C-140/12) [2014] 1 W.L.R. 1080; [2014] 1 C.M.L.R. 37; [2014] All E.R. (EC) 534, ECJ (3rd Chamber)
*Applied* 14/1739
People v Germany [2014] 2 C.M.L.R. 18, BverwG (Ger)
Peoples Insurance Co of China (Hebei Branch) v Vysanthi Shipping Co Ltd (The Joanna V) [2003] EWHC 1655 (Comm); [2003] 2 Lloyd's Rep. 617, QBD (Comm) ........ *Digested,* 03/**206**:
*Applied* 14/123
Peracomo Inc v Telus Communications Co (The Realice) 2014 SCC 29; [2014] 2 Lloyd's Rep. 315, Sup Ct (Can)
Peratikou, (Yiannis) see R. v Bell (David)
Percival v Ealing LBC [2014] R.V.R. 271, VT
Percival v Revenue and Customs Commissioners [2013] UKFTT 240 (TC); [2014] S.F.T.D. 57; 15 I.T.L. Rep. 912; [2013] S.T.I. 2308, FTT (Tax) ........ *Digested,* 13/**3055**
Percy v DPP see Ayliffe v DPP
Percy v Hall [1997] Q.B. 924; [1997] 3 W.L.R. 573; [1996] 4 All E.R. 523; (1996) 160 J.P. Rep. 788; (1996) 93(23) L.S.G. 36; (1996) 140 S.J.L.B. 130; [1996] N.P.C. 74; Times, May 31, 1996, CA (Civ Div) ........ *Digested,* 96/**5688**:
*Applied* 97/4856, 13/253, 14/386: *Considered* 14/3344
Performing Right Society Ltd v B4U Network (Europe) Ltd; *sub nom* B4U Network (Europe) Ltd v Performing Right Society Ltd [2013] EWCA Civ 1236; [2014] Bus. L.R. 207; [2014] E.C.C. 3; [2014] F.S.R. 17; Times, October 25, 2013, CA (Civ Div); affirming [2012] EWHC 3010 (Ch); [2013] Bus. L.R. 664; [2013] F.S.R. 19, Ch D ........ *Digested,* 14/**1905**
Peri v Engel see Engel v Peri
Perinpanathan v City of Westminster Magistrates' Court see R. (on the application of Perinpanathan) v City of Westminster Magistrates' Court
Perks v United Kingdom (25277/94) (2000) 30 E.H.R.R. 33; [2000] R.A. 487, ECHR; no effect (1997) 24 E.H.R.R. CD35, Eur Comm HR ........ *Digested,* 00/**3221**:
*Considered* 05/2100, 14/2094
Perotti v Collyer-Bristow (A Firm) (Vexatious Litigant: Directions) [2004] EWCA Civ 639; [2004] 4 All E.R. 53, CA (Civ Div) ........ *Digested,* 05/**494**:
*Considered* 14/67
Perrett v Collins [1998] 2 Lloyd's Rep. 255; [1999] P.N.L.R. 77; Times, June 23, 1998, CA (Civ Div) ........ *Digested,* 98/**3923**:
*Applied* 05/2858: *Considered* 14/2205: *Distinguished* 06/2878: *Followed* 04/2710
Perrin v Revenue and Customs Commissioners [2014] UKFTT 223 (TC); [2014] S.F.T.D. 919; 16 I.T.L. Rep. 856, FTT (Tax)
Perry v Nursing and Midwifery Council [2013] EWCA Civ 145; [2013] 1 W.L.R. 3423; [2013] Med. L.R. 129; (2014) 135 B.M.L.R. 61, CA (Civ Div); affirming [2012] EWHC 2275 (Admin); [2012] Med. L.R. 723, QBD (Admin) ........ *Digested,* 13/**1441**
Persimmon Homes Teesside Ltd v Lewis see R. (on the application of Lewis) v Redcar and Cleveland BC
Petch v Gurney (Inspector of Taxes); *sub nom* Gurney (Inspector of Taxes) v Petch [1994] 3 All E.R. 731; [1994] S.T.C. 689; 66 T.C. 743; [1994] S.T.I. 678; (1994) 91(27) L.S.G. 37; Times, June 8, 1994; Independent, July 11, 1994, CA (Civ Div); affirming [1992] S.T.C. 892, Ch D ........ *Digested,* 94/**2529**:
*Applied* 95/2750, 05/2652: *Considered* 03/501, 09/2682, 14/1970:
*Distinguished* 09/2685

Peterborough City Council v Enterprise Managed Services Ltd [2014] EWHC 3193 (TCC); [2014] B.L.R. 735; 156 Con. L.R. 226; [2014] C.I.L.L. 3589, QBD (TCC)

Petillo v Unipol Assicurazioni SpA (C-371/12) [2014] 3 C.M.L.R. 1, ECJ (2nd Chamber)

Petroalliance Services Co Ltd v Yukos Oil Co see Dardana Ltd v Yukos Oil Co (No.1)

Petrochemical Industries Co (KSC) v Dow Chemical Co [2012] EWHC 2739 (Comm); [2012] 2 Lloyd's Rep. 691; [2013] 2 C.L.C. 864; [2012] C.I.L.L. 3269, QBD (Comm) .......... *Digested,* 13/**111**: *Applied* 14/118

Petrodel Resources Ltd v Prest; *sub nom* Prest v Petrodel Resources Ltd; P Resources Ltd v Prest; Prest v Prest [2013] UKSC 34; [2013] 2 A.C. 415; [2013] 3 W.L.R. 1; [2013] 4 All E.R. 673; [2013] B.C.C. 571; [2014] 1 B.C.L.C. 30; [2013] 2 F.L.R. 732; [2013] 3 F.C.R. 210; [2013] W.T.L.R. 1249; [2013] Fam. Law 953; (2013) 163(7565) N.L.J. 27; (2013) 157(24) S.J.L.B. 37; Times, June 24, 2013, SC; reversing [2012] EWCA Civ 1395; [2013] 2 W.L.R. 557; [2013] 1 All E.R. 795; [2013] 2 Costs L.O. 249; [2013] 2 F.L.R. 576; [2012] 3 F.C.R. 588; [2013] Fam. Law 150; Times, January 2, 2013, CA (Civ Div) .......... *Digested,* 13/**1300**: *Applied* 13/362, 13/685, 14/403: *Considered* 14/1372, 14/1388

Petru v Casa Judeteana de Asigurari de Sanatate Sibiu (C-268/13) (2014) 158(40) S.J.L.B. 37, ECJ (3rd Chamber)

Petterson v Ross see Ross (Deceased), Re

Pettit v Minister of Transport see Minister of Transport v Pettitt

Pfizer Ltd v Medimpex Jamaica Ltd [2014] UKPC 20; [2014] 4 All E.R. 431, PC (Jam)

Pfleger (C-390/12) see Proceedings Brought by Pfleger (C-390/12)

PG v TW (Child: Financial Provision) [2014] 1 F.L.R. 923; [2013] Fam. Law 1123, Fam Div .......... *Digested,* 14/**1359**

PG v TW (Child: Financial Provision: Legal Funding) [2012] EWHC 1892 (Fam); [2014] 1 F.L.R. 508; [2013] Fam. Law 1122, Fam Div

PGF II SA v OMFS Co 1 Ltd [2013] EWCA Civ 1288; [2014] 1 W.L.R. 1386; [2014] 1 All E.R. 970; [2014] C.P. Rep. 6; [2014] B.L.R. 1; 152 Con. L.R. 72; [2013] 6 Costs L.R. 973; [2013] 3 E.G.L.R. 16; [2013] 44 E.G. 98 (C.S.); (2013) 157(42) S.J.L.B. 37, CA (Civ Div); affirming [2012] EWHC 83 (TCC); [2012] 3 Costs L.O. 404, QBD (TCC) .......... *Digested,* 14/**375**

PH v Italy see R. (on the application of HH) v Westminster City Magistrates' Court

Pharmacia & Upjohn SA (formerly Upjohn SA) v Paranova A/S (C-379/97); *sub nom* Upjohn SA Danmark v Paranova A/S (C-379/97) [2000] Ch. 571; [2000] 3 W.L.R. 303; [1999] E.C.R. I-6927; [2000] 1 C.M.L.R. 51; [1999] All E.R. (EC) 880; [1999] C.E.C. 630; [1999] E.T.M.R. 937; [2000] F.S.R. 621; (2001) 62 B.M.L.R. 150; (2000) 18 Tr. L.R. 457, ECJ; no effect [1999] E.C.R. I-6927; [1999] E.T.M.R. 97, AGO .......... *Digested,* 00/**3709**: *Applied* 02/2917: *Considered* 03/2641, 14/1925

Philex Plc v Golban see Ridehalgh v Horsefield

Philips Electronics NV v Remington Consumer Products Ltd (C-299/99) see Koninklijke Philips Electronics NV v Remington Consumer Products Ltd (C-299/99)

Phillips v Magill see Porter v Magill

Phillips v Symes (A Bankrupt) (Expert Witnesses: Costs) [2004] EWHC 2330 (Ch); [2005] 1 W.L.R. 2043; [2005] 4 All E.R. 519; [2005] 2 All E.R. (Comm) 538; [2005] C.P. Rep. 12; [2005] 2 Costs L.R. 224; (2005) 83 B.M.L.R. 115; (2004) 101(44) L.S.G. 29; (2004) 154 N.L.J. 1615; Times, November 5, 2004, Ch D .... *Digested,* 05/**363**: *Considered* 14/1288

Phillips Petroleum Co (UK) Ltd v Enron (Europe) Ltd [1997] C.L.C. 329, CA (Civ Div) .. *Digested,* 97/**4951**: *Applied* 06/683, 12/639: *Considered* 08/2966, 09/719, 12/158: *Followed* 14/630

Philpott v Revenue and Customs Commissioners [2014] UKFTT 853 (TC); [2014] S.T.I. 3299, FTT (Tax)

Phipps v Boardman see Boardman v Phipps

Phoenix Kapitaldienst GmbH, Re see Schmitt v Deichmann

Phoenix Media Ltd v Cobweb Information Ltd HC.0002094, Ch D *Applied* 14/1886

Phoneer Ltd, Re [2002] 2 B.C.L.C. 241, Ch D .......... *Digested,* 03/**541**: *Applied* 14/523

Phosphate Sewage Co Ltd v Molleson (Res Judicata); *joined case* Official Liquidator v Molleson (1879) 4 App. Cas. 801; (1879) 6 R. (H.L.) 113, HL *Applied* 80/2609, 82/2382, 90/3542, 08/1432, 08/272, 14/2209

Photo Production Ltd v Securicor Transport Ltd [1980] A.C. 827; [1980] 2 W.L.R. 283; [1980] 1 All E.R. 556; [1980] 1 Lloyd's Rep. 545; (1980) 124 S.J. 147, HL; reversing [1978] 1 W.L.R. 856; [1978] 3 All E.R. 146; [1978] 2 Lloyd's Rep. 172; (1978) 122 S.J. 315, CA (Civ Div) ........ *Digested,* 80/**353**: *Applied* 81/303, 83/3330, 83/3440, 88/2388, 92/317, 05/2356, 08/393: *Considered* 82/403, 83/3314, 89/415, 95/179, 95/778, 02/4098, 12/2830: *Distinguished* 85/1863: *Followed* 10/627, 12/642, 14/618

PI Consulting (Trustee Services) Ltd v Pensions Regulator; *sub nom* Dalriada Trustees Ltd v Nidd Vale Trustees Ltd [2013] EWHC 3181 (Ch); [2013] Pens. L.R. 433, Ch D ........ *Digested,* 14/**2265**

Pi-Design AG v Yoshida Metal Industry Co Ltd (C-337/12 P); *joined case* Office for Harmonisation in the Internal Market (Trade Marks and Designs) (OHIM) v Yoshida Metal Industry Co Ltd (C-338/12 P) [2014] E.T.M.R. 32, ECJ (7th Chamber)

Pickard v Sears 112 E.R. 179; (1837) 6 Ad. & El. 469, KB *Considered* 09/5033, 14/1886

Pickenham Romford Ltd v Deville [2013] EWHC 2330 (Ch); [2014] 1 B.C.L.C. 380, Ch D ........ *Digested,* 14/**283**

Piepenbrock Dienstleistungen GmbH & Co KG v Kreis Duren (C-386/11) [2013] P.T.S.R. 1152; [2014] 1 C.M.L.R. 1; [2014] C.E.C. 148, ECJ (5th Chamber)

Pierce v Wood [2009] EWHC 3225 (Ch); [2010] W.T.L.R. 253, Ch D (Manchester) ...... *Digested,* 10/**3451**: *Not applied* 14/2939

Pieretti v Enfield LBC [2010] EWCA Civ 1104; [2011] 2 All E.R. 642; [2011] P.T.S.R. 565; [2010] Eq. L.R. 312; [2011] H.L.R. 3; [2010] B.L.G.R. 944; (2010) 13 C.C.L. Rep. 650; [2010] N.P.C. 98, CA (Civ Div) ........ *Digested,* 11/**1648**: *Applied* 14/1601: *Considered* 11/2168, 14/1596, 14/2017

Pierhead Purchasing Ltd v Revenue and Customs Commissioners [2014] UKUT 321 (TCC); [2014] B.V.C. 527, UT (Tax) ........ *Digested,* 14/**304**

Piggott (Inspector of Taxes) v Staines Investments Ltd [1995] S.T.C. 114; 68 T.C. 342; [1995] S.T.I. 213; (1995) 92(9) L.S.G. 41; Times, February 7, 1995, Ch D . *Digested,* 95/**876**: *Applied* 14/2878

Piglowska v Piglowski [1999] 1 W.L.R. 1360; [1999] 3 All E.R. 632; [1999] 2 F.L.R. 763; [1999] 2 F.C.R. 481; [1999] Fam. Law 617; (1999) 96(27) L.S.G. 34; (1999) 143 S.J.L.B. 190; Times, June 25, 1999, HL; reversing (Unreported, November 3, 1997), CA (Civ Div) ........ *Digested,* 99/**2421**: *Applied* 06/1633, 07/1766, 11/1344, 11/1445, 14/1283: *Considered* 00/2489, 01/2632, 01/4450, 09/603, 13/1280, 13/6, 14/1254: *Followed* 11/1332, 13/1224

Pigott, Re; *sub nom* Lamb v Revenue and Customs Prosecutions Office; Revenue and Customs Prosecutions Office v Pigott [2010] EWCA Civ 285; [2010] S.T.C. 1190; [2010] C.P. Rep. 31; [2010] Lloyd's Rep. F.C. 405; [2010] S.T.I. 797, CA (Civ Div); affirming [2008] EWHC 3245 (Admin), QBD (Admin) ........ *Digested,* 10/**738**: *Considered* 14/802

Pike v Revenue and Customs Commissioners [2014] EWCA Civ 824; [2014] S.T.C. 2549; [2014] B.T.C. 33; [2014] S.T.I. 2227, CA (Civ Div); affirming [2013] UKUT 225 (TCC); [2013] S.T.C. 2042; [2013] B.T.C. 1881; [2013] S.T.I. 1840, UT (Tax); affirming [2011] UKFTT 289 (TC); [2011] S.F.T.D. 830; [2011] S.T.I. 1990, FTT (Tax) ........ *Digested,* 14/**2920**: *Applied* 14/2909

Pilkington v Inland Revenue Commissioners; *sub nom* Pilkington v Pilkington; Pilkington's Will Trusts, Re [1964] A.C. 612; [1962] 3 W.L.R. 1051; [1962] 3 All E.R. 622; 40 T.C. 416; (1962) 41 A.T.C. 285; [1962] T.R. 265; (1962) 106 S.J. 834, HL; reversing [1961] Ch. 466; [1961] 2 W.L.R. 776; [1961] 2 All E.R. 330; (1961) 105 S.J. 422, CA; reversing [1959] Ch. 699; [1959] 3 W.L.R. 116; [1959] 2 All E.R. 623; (1959) 103 S.J. 528, Ch D ........ *Digested,* 62/**2800**: *Applied* 66/11045, 83/3364: *Considered* 70/2628, 74/993, 88/3683, 01/5507: *Distinguished* 67/4075: *Followed* 14/2974

Pilkington v Pilkington see Pilkington v Inland Revenue Commissioners

Pilkington Group Ltd v European Commission (C-278/13 P(R)) [2014] 4 C.M.L.R. 5, ECJ

Pilkington's Will Trusts, Re see Pilkington v Inland Revenue Commissioners

Pillar Denton Ltd v Jervis see Jervis v Pillar Denton Ltd

Pinckney v KDG Mediatech AG (C-170/12) [2013] Bus. L.R. 1313; [2014] C.E.C. 534; [2013] E.C.D.R. 15; [2014] I.L.Pr. 7; [2014] F.S.R. 18, ECJ (4th Chamber)

Pinevale Ltd v Revenue and Customs Commissioners; *sub nom* Revenue and Customs Commissioners v Pinevale Ltd [2014] UKUT 202 (TCC); [2014] S.T.C. 2217; [2014] B.V.C. 517; [2014] S.T.I. 1979, UT (Tax); reversing [2012] UKFTT 606 (TC); [2012] S.T.I. 3029, FTT (Tax) ........ *Digested,* 14/**3078**

Pineview Ltd v 83 Crampton Street RTM Co Ltd [2013] UKUT 598 (LC); [2014] 1 E.G.L.R. 65, UT (Lands)
Pinnington v Transport for London [2013] EWHC 3656 (Admin); [2014] L.L.R. 316, QBD (Admin)
Pinnock v Manchester City Council see Manchester City Council v Pinnock
Pinto's Voluntary Settlement, Re see Kleinwort Benson (Jersey) Trustees Ltd v Pinto
Pioneer Cladding Ltd v John Graham Construction Ltd [2013] EWHC 2954 (TCC); [2014] C.I.L.L. 3445, QBD (TCC)
Pioneer Hi Bred Switzerland v South Pyrenees Tax Authority 17 I.T.L. Rep. 431, Trib Ad (F)
PIP Breast Implant Litigation, Re see XYZ v Various Companies
Pipette System (Case X ZR 38/06) (Unreported), BGH (Ger)
*Considered* 14/1877
Pippi Longstocking Character (Infringement of a Copyright User's Rights), Re (I ZR 52/12) [2014] E.C.C. 27, BGH (Ger)
Pirabakaran v Patel see Patel v Pirabakaran
Pishbin v Hibbins (Valuation Officer) [2013] UKUT 180 (LC); [2013] R.V.R. 325, UT (Lands) ........ *Digested,* 14/**2483**
Pitalia v NHS Commissioning Board [2014] EWCA Civ 474; (2014) 138 B.M.L.R. 89, CA (Civ Div)
*Applied* 14/1542
Pitt v Holt; *joined cases* Futter v Futter; Futter v Revenue and Customs Commissioners; Pitt v Revenue and Customs Commissioners [2013] UKSC 26; [2013] 2 A.C. 108; [2013] 2 W.L.R. 1200; [2013] 3 All E.R. 429; [2013] S.T.C. 1148; [2013] Pens. L.R. 195; 81 T.C. 912; [2013] B.T.C. 126; [2013] W.T.L.R. 977; 15 I.T.E.L.R. 976; [2013] S.T.I. 1805; [2013] 2 P. & C.R. DG14; Times, June 10, 2013, SC; reversing in part [2011] EWCA Civ 197; [2012] Ch. 132; [2011] 3 W.L.R. 19; [2011] 2 All E.R. 450; [2011] S.T.C. 809; [2011] Pens. L.R. 175; [2011] B.T.C. 322; [2011] W.T.L.R. 623; 13 I.T.E.L.R. 749; [2011] S.T.I. 743; (2011) 108(12) L.S.G. 19; [2011] 2 P. & C.R. DG8, CA (Civ Div); reversing [2010] EWHC 45 (Ch); [2010] 1 W.L.R. 1199; [2010] 2 All E.R. 774; [2010] S.T.C. 901; [2010] B.T.C. 235; [2010] W.T.L.R. 269; (2009-10) 12 I.T.E.L.R. 807; [2010] S.T.I. 1443; Times, February 24, 2010, Ch D ........ *Digested,* 13/**3173**:
*Applied* 12/3364, 13/3178, 14/1204: *Considered* 12/1264
Pitt v Revenue and Customs Commissioners see Pitt v Holt
Pittoriou (A Bankrupt), Re see Pittortou (A Bankrupt), Re
Pittortou (A Bankrupt), Re; *sub nom* Pittoriou (A Bankrupt), Re [1985] 1 W.L.R. 58; [1985] 1 All E.R. 285, Ch D ........ *Digested,* 85/**162**:
*Applied* 14/1203: *Considered* 91/2655, 10/1853
Pitts v Earl Cadogan; *sub nom* Earl Cadogan v Pitts; Earl Cadogan v Sportelli; *joined cases* Earl Cadogan v Grandeden Property Management Ltd; Earl Cadogan v 27/29 Sloane Gardens Ltd; Earl Cadogan v Atlantic Telecasters Ltd [2008] UKHL 71; [2010] 1 A.C. 226; [2009] 2 W.L.R. 12; [2009] 3 All E.R. 365; [2009] 1 P. & C.R. 17; [2009] L. & T.R. 10; [2009] 1 E.G.L.R. 153; [2009] R.V.R. 42; [2008] 50 E.G. 72 (C.S.); (2009) 153(1) S.J.L.B. 33; [2008] N.P.C. 136; Times, December 17, 2008, HL; reversing in part [2007] EWCA Civ 1280; [2008] R.V.R. 244, CA (Civ Div); affirming [2007] 3 E.G.L.R. 86; [2007] 42 E.G. 296; [2007] R.V.R. 272, Lands Tr ........ *Digested,* 09/**2519**:
*Applied* 10/2696: *Considered* 12/2747, 13/2427, 14/1985, 14/2497:
*Distinguished* 13/2428
PJ Pipe & Valve Co Ltd v Audco India Ltd [2005] EWHC 1904 (QB); [2006] Eu. L.R. 368, QBD ........ *Digested,* 06/**61**:
*Applied* 09/87, 14/82: *Considered* 10/84
Plantation Holdings (FZ) LLC v Dubai Islamic Bank PJSC; *joined case* Dubai Islamic Bank PJSC v PSI Energy Holding Co BSC [2013] EWCA Civ 1229; [2014] C.P. Rep. 7, CA (Civ Div) ........ *Digested,* 14/**307**
Plasticos Espanoles SA (ASPLA) v European Commission (C-35/12 P) [2014] 5 C.M.L.R. 3, ECJ (6th Chamber)
Plastus Kreativ AB v Minnesota Mining & Manufacturing Co (Jurisdiction: Declaration) [1995] R.P.C. 438, Ch D (Patents Ct)
*Applied* 14/1894

Platform Home Loans Ltd v Oyston Shipways Ltd [2000] 2 A.C. 190; [1999] 2 W.L.R. 518; [1999] 1 All E.R. 833; [1999] C.L.C. 867; (1999) 1 T.C.L.R. 18; [1999] P.N.L.R. 469; [1999] 1 E.G.L.R. 77; [1999] 13 E.G. 119; [1999] E.G. 26 (C.S.); (1999) 96(10) L.S.G. 31; (1999) 149 N.L.J. 283; (1999) 143 S.J.L.B. 65; [1999] N.P.C. 21; Times, February 19, 1999; Independent, March 5, 1999, HL; reversing [1998] Ch. 466; [1998] 3 W.L.R. 94; [1998] 4 All E.R. 252; [1998] P.N.L.R. 512; [1998] 1 E.G.L.R. 108; [1998] 13 E.G. 148; [1997] E.G. 184 (C.S.); (1998) 95(1) L.S.G. 26; (1998) 142 S.J.L.B. 46; [1997] N.P.C. 185; Times, January 15, 1998, CA (Civ Div); reversing in part [1996] 2 E.G.L.R. 110; [1996] 49 E.G. 112; [1996] E.G. 146 (C.S.), Ch D ........ *Digested,* 99/**1389**: *Considered* 97/3846, 09/969, 14/2217: *Followed* 98/4005

Platinum Connect Ltd v Revenue and Customs Commissioners [2014] UKFTT 1032 (TC); [2014] S.T.I. 3551, FTT (Tax)

PlayUp Interactive Entertainment (UK) Pty Ltd v Givemefootball Ltd [2011] EWHC 1980 (Comm); [2011] Info. T.L.R. 289; (2011) 108(32) L.S.G. 16, QBD (Comm) *Digested,* 14/**621**

Plevin v Paragon Personal Finance Ltd; *joined case* Conlon v Black Horse Ltd [2014] UKSC 61; [2014] 1 W.L.R. 4222; [2014] Bus. L.R. 1257, SC; reversing in part [2013] EWCA Civ 1658; [2014] Bus. L.R. 553; [2014] E.C.C. 10; [2013] C.T.L.C. 209; (2014) 158(1) S.J.L.B. 37, CA (Civ Div) ........ *Digested,* 14/**609**

Plintal SA v 36-48A Edgewood Drive RTM Co Ltd LRX/16/2007, Lands Tr *Considered* 14/2011

Plowman (GW) & Son v Ash see GW Plowman & Son Ltd v Ash

Plummer, Re [2004] B.P.I.R. 767, Ch D (Bankruptcy Ct) ........ *Digested,* 05/**2275**: *Applied* 14/1784: *Considered* 14/1799

Plunkett v Coal Authority [2013] UKUT 212 (LC); [2014] R.V.R. 109, UT (Lands)

Plymouth City Council's Trade Mark application (No.2547975), Re see Awareness Ltd v Plymouth City Council

PM v MB see M (A Child) (Parental Responsibility Order), Re

PNM v Times Newspapers Ltd; *sub nom* M v Times Newspapers Ltd [2014] EWCA Civ 1132; [2014] C.P. Rep. 48; [2014] E.M.L.R. 30, CA (Civ Div); affirming [2013] EWHC 3177 (QB), QBD ........ *Digested,* 14/**790**

PNPF Trust Co Ltd v Taylor see PD Teesport Ltd, Re

PO, Re see O (Court of Protection: Jurisdiction), Re

Pohotovost' sro v Vasuta (C-470/12) [2014] 1 All E.R. (Comm) 1016, ECJ (3rd Chamber)

Pointe Gourde Quarrying & Transport Co v Sub-Intendent of Crown Lands [1947] A.C. 565; 63 T.L.R. 486, PC (Trin) ........ *Digested,* 47-51/**1435**: *Applied* 67/3806, 71/8984, 77/3265, 78/269, 89/361, 00/4426, 01/4666, 02/3656, 08/3072, 10/2548, 10/3423: *Cited* 14/2502: *Considered* 55/382, 64/485, 72/49, 74/371, 77/323, 78/272, 87/394, 90/582, 92/439, 95/3917, 95/666, 08/3071, 09/3135, 10/2543, 10/2551, 10/9, 11/2665: *Distinguished* 69/3481, 69/429, 69/436, 71/1493, 77/326: *Followed* 66/1529, 04/3033: *Not applied* 10/2550: *Referred to* 77/2967, 80/2907

Pointon York Group Plc v Poulton [2006] EWCA Civ 1001; [2007] 1 P. & C.R. 6; [2007] L. & T.R. 8; [2006] 3 E.G.L.R. 37; [2006] 38 E.G. 192; [2006] 29 E.G. 133 (C.S.); [2006] N.P.C. 86, CA (Civ Div) ........ *Digested,* 06/**2675**: *Followed* 14/1976

Pointstar Shipping & Finance Ltd v 7 Strathray Gardens Ltd see 7 Strathray Gardens Ltd v Pointstar Shipping & Finance Ltd

Pokhriyal v Secretary of State for the Home Department; *joined case* Hussain v Secretary of State for the Home Department [2013] EWCA Civ 1568; [2014] Imm. A.R. 711; [2014] I.N.L.R. 291; [2014] P.T.S.R. D4, CA (Civ Div) ........ *Digested,* 14/**1716**

Polyelectrolyte Producers Group GEIE (PPG) v European Chemicals Agency (ECHA) (C-625/11 P) [2014] 1 W.L.R. 158, ECJ (4th Chamber)

Polyelectrolyte Producers Group GEIE (PPG) v European Chemicals Agency (ECHA) (C-626/11 P); *sub nom* Polyelectrolyte Producers Group GEIE (PPG) v SNF SAS (C-626/11 P) [2014] 1 C.M.L.R. 47, ECJ (4th Chamber)

Polyelectrolyte Producers Group GEIE (PPG) v SNF SAS (C-626/11 P) see Polyelectrolyte Producers Group GEIE (PPG) v European Chemicals Agency (ECHA) (C-626/11 P)

Polyflor Ltd v Health and Safety Executive see Health and Safety Executive v Polyflor Ltd

Polymer Vision R&D Ltd v Van Dooren [2011] EWHC 2951 (Comm); [2012] I.L.Pr. 14, QBD (Comm) ........ *Digested,* 12/**563**: *Considered* 14/558

Pomiechowski v Poland; *joined cases* Halligen v Secretary of State for the Home Department; Lukaszewski v Poland; Ungureanu v Poland; Rozanski v Poland [2012] UKSC 20; [2012] 1 W.L.R. 1604; [2012] 4 All E.R. 667; [2012] H.R.L.R. 22; [2013] Crim. L.R. 147; (2012) 162 N.L.J. 749; Times, June 7, 2012, SC; reversing [2011] EWHC 2060 (Admin); [2012] 1 W.L.R. 391; [2012] A.C.D. 9, DC ........ *Digested,* 12/**1287**:
*Applied* 13/1490, 14/392

Ponomaryov v Bulgaria (5335/05) (2014) 59 E.H.R.R. 20; [2011] Eq. L.R. 883; [2011] E.L.R. 491, ECHR
*Considered* 12/1004, 13/864

Pontardawe Inn Ltd v Revenue and Customs Commissioners [2014] UKFTT 434 (TC); [2014] S.T.I. 2048, FTT (Tax)

Poole BC v W; *sub nom* W (Adoption Order), Re; SR (A Child), Re [2014] EWHC 1777 (Fam); [2014] Fam. Law 1228, Fam Div

Pooley v Whetham (1880) 15 Ch. D. 435, CA
*Applied* 88/2837, 12/469, 14/15: *Considered* 14/1230

Popeley v Popeley see Popely v Popely

Popely v Popely; *sub nom* Popeley v Popeley [2004] EWCA Civ 463; [2004] B.P.I.R. 778; (2004) 101(19) L.S.G. 29; (2004) 148 S.J.L.B. 569; Times, May 14, 2004; Independent, May 5, 2004, CA (Civ Div); affirming [2003] EWHC 2028 (Ch); [2003] B.P.I.R. 1398; (2003) 100(37) L.S.G. 33; Times, September 15, 2003, Ch D ........ *Digested,* 04/**2180**:
*Applied* 10/1858: *Considered* 07/2452, 07/2453: *Followed* 14/1788

Poplar Housing & Regeneration Community Association Ltd v Donaghue see Poplar Housing & Regeneration Community Association Ltd v Donoghue

Poplar Housing & Regeneration Community Association Ltd v Donoghue; *sub nom* Poplar Housing & Regeneration Community Association Ltd v Donaghue; Donoghue v Poplar Housing & Regeneration Community Association Ltd [2001] EWCA Civ 595; [2002] Q.B. 48; [2001] 3 W.L.R. 183; [2001] 4 All E.R. 604; [2001] 2 F.L.R. 284; [2001] 3 F.C.R. 74; [2001] U.K.H.R.R. 693; (2001) 33 H.L.R. 73; (2001) 3 L.G.L.R. 41; [2001] B.L.G.R. 489; [2001] A.C.D. 76; [2001] Fam. Law 588; [2001] 19 E.G. 141 (C.S.); (2001) 98(19) L.S.G. 38; (2001) 98(23) L.S.G. 38; (2001) 145 S.J.L.B. 122; [2001] N.P.C. 84; Times, June 21, 2001; Independent, May 2, 2001; Daily Telegraph, May 8, 2001, CA (Civ Div) .. *Digested,* 01/**4145**:
*Applied* 03/68, 06/4044, 08/860: *Considered* 02/2353, 02/3232:
*Followed* 02/3060, 14/1968

Porteous v West Dorset DC [2004] EWCA Civ 244; [2004] H.L.R. 30; [2004] B.L.G.R. 577; (2004) 148 S.J.L.B. 300; Independent, March 12, 2004, CA (Civ Div) ........ *Digested,* 04/**1893**:
*Followed* 14/1493

Porter v Magill; *sub nom* Magill v Weeks; Magill v Porter; *joined cases* Weeks v Magill; Hartley v Magill; England v Magill; Phillips v Magill [2001] UKHL 67; [2002] 2 A.C. 357; [2002] 2 W.L.R. 37; [2002] 1 All E.R. 465; [2002] H.R.L.R. 16; [2002] H.L.R. 16; [2002] B.L.G.R. 51; (2001) 151 N.L.J. 1886; [2001] N.P.C. 184; Times, December 14, 2001; Independent, February 4, 2002; Daily Telegraph, December 20, 2001, HL; reversing [2000] 2 W.L.R. 1420; (1999) 31 H.L.R. 823; (1999) 1 L.G.L.R. 523; [1999] B.L.G.R. 375; (1999) 11 Admin. L.R. 661; (1999) 163 J.P.N. 1025; (1999) 96(21) L.S.G. 39; (1999) 143 S.J.L.B. 147; Times, May 6, 1999, CA (Civ Div); reversing (1998) 30 H.L.R. 997, QBD .......... *Digested,* 02/**3185**:
*Applied* 03/1251, 03/1261, 03/319, 04/2652, 04/30, 05/13, 05/2153, 05/2908, 05/3279, 05/894, 06/207, 06/2755, 06/3339, 06/3346, 06/3987, 06/967, 07/1343, 07/1428, 07/31, 07/3252, 07/3264, 08/370, 08/834, 09/2456, 10/1722, 10/2144, 10/2805, 11/4221, 12/749, 13/760: *Considered* 02/294, 02/451, 05/646, 08/2935, 09/24, 12/2095, 12/970: *Followed* 03/5397, 04/1904, 04/4467, 10/1691, 10/768, 11/3598, 12/581, 13/262, 14/42

Porter Capital Corp v Masters [2014] 3 Costs L.R. 528, Ch D ........ *Digested,* 14/**467**

Portgas - Sociedade de Producao e Distribuicao de Gas SA v Ministerio da Agricultura, do Mar, do Ambiente e do Ordenamento do Territorio (C-425/12) [2014] 2 C.M.L.R. 30, ECJ (5th Chamber)

Portland Gas Storage Ltd v Revenue and Customs Commissioners [2014] UKUT 270 (TCC); [2014] S.T.C. 2589; [2014] B.T.C. 520; [2014] S.T.I. 2406, UT (Tax) ...... *Digested,* 14/**2978**

Portnykh v Nomura International Plc [2014] I.R.L.R. 251, EAT ........ *Digested,* 14/**1008**

Portnykh v Nomura International Plc (Costs) UKEAT/0448/13/LA, EAT
*Applied* 14/1058

Portsmouth City Council v King see King (A Child), Re

Portsmouth City Football Club Ltd (In Liquidation), Re; *sub nom* Neumans LLP v Andronikou [2013] EWCA Civ 916; [2014] 1 All E.R. 12; [2013] Bus. L.R. 1152; [2013] C.P. Rep. 45; [2013] B.C.C. 741; [2014] 1 B.C.L.C. 1; [2013] 6 Costs L.O. 934, CA (Civ Div); affirming [2012] EWHC 3088 (Ch); [2013] 1 All E.R. 975; [2013] Bus. L.R. 374; [2013] 1 B.C.L.C. 572; [2013] 2 Costs L.O. 313, Ch D (Companies Ct) ........ *Digested,* 14/**1792**: *Distinguished* 14/1755

Portugal v Goncalves (Unreported, 1982), Unknown court *Considered* 14/1056

Poseidon Inc v Inspector of Taxes see Goodbrand (Inspector of Taxes) v Loffland Bros North Sea Inc

Posteshop SpA - Divisione Franchising Kipoint v Autorita Garante della Concorrenza e del Mercato (C-52/13) [2014] 1 All E.R. (Comm) 753, ECJ (8th Chamber)

Potel v Yeung see Yeung v Potel

Potts Executors v Inland Revenue Commissioners [1951] A.C. 443; [1951] 1 All E.R. 76; [1951] 1 T.L.R. 152; 44 R. & I.T. 136; 32 T.C. 211; [1950] T.R. 379, HL; reversing [1949] 2 K.B. 706; [1949] 2 All E.R. 555; [1949] T.R. 257; (1949) 93 S.J. 663, CA; affirming 41 R. & I.T. 437; [1948] T.R. 297, HC ........ *Digested,* 47-51/**9946**: *Applied* 62/2619: *Considered* 67/4445, 13/3033, 14/2873: *Followed* 82/1641

Pounds Shipowners & Shipbreakers Ltd v Garner (Inspector of Taxes) see Garner (Inspector of Taxes) v Pounds Shipowners & Shipbreakers Ltd

Povse v Austria (3890/11) [2014] 1 F.L.R. 944; [2014] Fam. Law 31, ECHR

Powa (Jersey) Ltd v Revenue and Customs Commissioners [2013] EWCA Civ 225; [2014] B.V.C. 8, CA (Civ Div)

Powdrill v Hambros Bank (Jersey) Ltd see Paramount Airways Ltd (No.2), Re

Powell v Brent LBC [1988] I.C.R. 176; [1987] I.R.L.R. 446; (1988) 138 N.L.J. Rep. 33; Independent, August 10, 1987, CA (Civ Div) ........ *Digested,* 88/**1248**: *Considered* 90/1858, 09/509, 14/1026: *Distinguished* 91/1622: *Referred to* 91/1617

Powell v Evan Jones & Co [1905] 1 K.B. 11, CA *Considered* 11/3499: *Overruled* 14/79

Powell v Hounslow LBC see Hounslow LBC v Powell

Powell v OMV Exploration & Production Ltd [2014] I.C.R. 63; [2014] I.R.L.R. 80, EAT . *Digested,* 14/**1077**

Powell v Osbourne [1993] 1 F.L.R. 1001; [1993] 1 F.C.R. 797; [1993] Fam. Law 287; Times, December 3, 1992, CA (Civ Div) ........ *Digested,* 94/**4662**: *Considered* 06/4088, 14/2823

Power v Brown; *sub nom* Power, Re [2009] EWHC 9 (Ch); [2009] B.P.I.R. 340, Ch D . *Digested,* 09/**2225**: *Applied* 14/1769

Power v Godfrey [2013] EWHC 4359 (Ch); [2014] B.P.I.R. 484, Ch D ........ *Digested,* 14/**1782**

Power, Re see Power v Brown

Powlesland v DPP [2013] EWHC 3846 (Admin); [2014] 1 W.L.R. 2984; (2014) 178 J.P. 67; [2014] A.C.D. 50, DC ........ *Digested,* 14/**699**

Powys Teaching Local Health Board v Dusza see Dusza v Powys Teaching Local Health Board

Poyser v Mills see Poyser and Mills Arbitration, Re

Poyser and Mills Arbitration, Re; *sub nom* Poyser v Mills [1964] 2 Q.B. 467; [1963] 2 W.L.R. 1309; [1963] 1 All E.R. 612; (1963) 107 S.J. 115, QBD ........ *Digested,* 63/**43**: *Applied* 66/11724, 76/1349, 76/2725, 79/25, 84/3472, 85/2167, 86/3389, 92/4407, 97/2659, 97/2677, 12/1459, 13/112: *Considered* 82/3178, 86/3259, 86/3745, 93/2690, 95/1937, 95/2598, 14/2373: *Distinguished* 71/10036

Pozzoli SpA v BDMO SA [2007] EWCA Civ 588; [2007] F.S.R. 37; (2007) 30(8) I.P.D. 30051; [2007] Bus. L.R. D117, CA (Civ Div); affirming [2006] EWHC 1398 (Ch); (2006) 29(7) I.P.D. 29056, Ch D (Patents Ct) ........ *Digested,* 07/**2634**: *Applied* 08/2332, 09/2396, 09/2406, 09/2407, 10/1966, 10/1968, 10/1969, 10/1973, 10/1974, 10/1981, 10/2014, 11/1972, 11/1979: *Followed* 10/1980, 11/1956, 12/1940, 14/1897

PPG Southern Ltd v Mills (Valuation Officer) see Aviva Investors Property Developments Ltd v Whitby (Valuation Officer)

PR (Sri Lanka) v Secretary of State for the Home Department; *joined cases* TC (Zimbabwe) v Secretary of State for the Home Department; SS (Bangladesh) v Secretary of State for the Home Department [2011] EWCA Civ 988; [2012] 1 W.L.R. 73; [2011] C.P. Rep. 47; [2011] Imm. A.R. 904; [2012] I.N.L.R. 92, CA (Civ Div) ........ *Digested,* 12/**1770**: *Applied* 12/457: *Considered* 14/50

Practice Direction (CA (Crim Div): Criminal Proceedings: Amendment No.2); *sub nom* Practice Direction (CA (Crim Div): Criminal Proceedings: Various Changes) [2014] EWCA Crim 1569; [2014] 1 W.L.R. 3001, Sen Cts ........ *Digested,* 14/**796**

Practice Direction (CA (Crim Div): Criminal Proceedings: Costs: Amendment No.1) [2014] EWCA Crim 1570; [2014] 1 W.L.R. 3037, Sen Cts

Practice Direction (CA (Crim Div): Criminal Proceedings: General Matters); *sub nom* Practice Direction (Criminal Proceedings) (Sen Cts) [2013] EWCA Crim 1631; [2013] 1 W.L.R. 3164, CA (Crim Div) ........ *Digested,* 13/**747**: *Superseded in part* 14/795

Practice Direction (CA (Crim Div): Criminal Proceedings: Various Changes) see Practice Direction (CA (Crim Div): Criminal Proceedings: Amendment No.2)

Practice Direction (Ch D: Insolvency Proceedings) [2012] Bus. L.R. 643; [2012] B.C.C. 265; [2012] B.P.I.R. 409, Ch D ........ *Digested,* 12/**431**: *Considered* 14/1781: *Followed* 14/1828

Practice Direction (Criminal Proceedings) (Sen Cts) see Practice Direction (CA (Crim Div): Criminal Proceedings: General Matters)

Practice Direction (Criminal Proceedings: Costs); *sub nom* Practice Direction (Criminal Proceedings: Costs) [2013] EWCA Crim 1632; [2013] 1 W.L.R. 3255, Sen Cts . *Digested,* 14/**754**

Practice Direction (Criminal Proceedings: Costs) see Practice Direction (Criminal Proceedings: Costs)

Practice Direction (Criminal Proceedings: Various Changes); *sub nom* Criminal Practice Directions Amendment No.1 [2013] EWCA Crim 2328; [2014] 1 W.L.R. 35, CA (Crim Div) ........ *Digested,* 14/**795**

Practice Direction (EAT: Procedure 2013) [2013] I.C.R. 1382; [2014] I.R.L.R. 92, EAT *Digested,* 14/**1060**

Practice Direction (Fam Div: Adoption) [1976] 1 W.L.R. 1267; [1976] 3 All E.R. 864; (1976) 120 S.J. 788, Fam Div ........ *Digested,* 76/**1747**: *Considered* 83/2421: *Referred to* 14/1255

Practice Direction (Fam Div: Residence and Contact Orders: Domestic Violence and Harm) (No.2) [2009] 1 W.L.R. 251; [2009] 2 F.L.R. 1400; [2009] 1 F.C.R. 223, Fam Div ........ *Digested,* 10/**1428**: *Applied* 10/1397: *Considered* 10/1370, 10/1416, 10/314, 14/1321

Practice Direction (Fam Div: Use of Prescribed Documents) [2013] 2 F.L.R. 1582, Fam Div ........ *Digested,* 14/**1273**

Practice Direction (Sen Cts: Audio Recordings of Proceedings: Access) [2014] 1 W.L.R. 632; [2014] 2 All E.R. 330, Sen Cts ........ *Digested,* 14/**306**

Practice Direction (Sen Cts: Criminal Proceedings: Costs) [2010] 1 W.L.R. 2351; [2011] 1 Cr. App. R. 13, Sen Cts ........ *Digested,* 11/**800**: *Superseded* 14/754

PRACTICE DIRECTION: FAMILY DIVISION ADOPTION JURISDICTION APPLICATIONS) [1981] 2 All E.R. 1115, Fam Div ........ *Digested,* 14/**1255**

Practice Direction: Insolvency Proceedings [2014] B.C.C. 502; [2014] B.P.I.R. 1286, Ch D

Practice Guidance (CP: Deprivation of Liberty: Guidance for Providers of Children's Homes and Residential Special Schools) [2014] C.O.P.L.R. 243, CP ........ *Digested,* 14/**2171**

Practice Guidance (CP: Transparency in the Court of Protection: Publication of Judgments) [2014] 1 W.L.R. 235; [2014] E.M.L.R. 21; [2014] C.O.P.L.R. 78, CP ........ *Digested,* 14/**22**

Practice Guidance (Fam Ct: Duration of Ex Parte (Without Notice) Orders [2014] 3 F.C.R. 402, Fam Ct

Practice Guidance (Fam Div: Committal Proceedings: Open Court) [2013] 1 W.L.R. 1753; [2014] C.O.P.L.R. 76, Fam Div ........ *Digested,* 13/**279**

Practice Guidance (Fam Div: Transparency in the Family Courts: Publication of Judgments) [2014] 1 W.L.R. 230; [2014] E.M.L.R. 22; [2014] 1 F.L.R. 733; [2014] 2 F.C.R. 226, Fam Div ........ *Digested,* 14/**1345**

Practice Guidance (Sen Cts: Committal for Contempt of Court) see Practice Guidance (Sen Cts: Committal Proceedings: Open Court)

Practice Guidance (Sen Cts: Committal Proceedings: Open Court); *sub nom* Practice Guidance (Sen Cts: Committal for Contempt of Court) [2013] 1 W.L.R. 1316; [2014] C.O.P.L.R. 74, Sen Cts ........ *Digested,* 13/**280**: *Cited* 13/279

Practice Note (Fam Div: Final Orders) see Robinson v Robinson (Practice Note)

Prebble v Television New Zealand Ltd [1995] 1 A.C. 321; [1994] 3 W.L.R. 970; [1994] 3 All E.R. 407; (1994) 91(39) L.S.G. 38; (1994) 144 N.L.J. 1131; (1994) 138 S.J.L.B. 175; Times, July 13, 1994, PC (NZ) ........ *Digested,* 94/**3419**: *Applied* 09/75: *Considered* 04/927, 07/693, 11/484, 14/843: *Followed* 95/3132

Preddy v Bull see Hall v Bull

Premium Aircraft Interiors Ltd v Comptroller General of Patents see Virgin Atlantic Airways Ltd v Jet Airways (India) Ltd

Premium Nafta Products Ltd v Fili Shipping Co Ltd see Fiona Trust & Holding Corp v Privalov

President's Guidance (Fam Div: Allocation and Gatekeeping for Care, Supervision and Other Part 4 Proceedings) [2013] 2 F.L.R. 1578, Fam Div .......................... *Digested,* 14/**1352**
Press Association v Newcastle Upon Tyne Hospitals Foundation Trust [2014] EWCOP 6; [2014] C.O.P.L.R. 502, CP .......................................................................... *Digested,* 14/**21**
Prest v Petrodel Resources Ltd see Petrodel Resources Ltd v Prest
Prest v Prest see Petrodel Resources Ltd v Prest
Pretty v United Kingdom (2346/02); *sub nom* R. (on the application of Pretty) v DPP (2346/02) [2002] 2 F.L.R. 45; [2002] 2 F.C.R. 97; (2002) 35 E.H.R.R. 1; 12 B.H.R.C. 149; (2002) 66 B.M.L.R. 147; [2002] Fam. Law 588; (2002) 152 N.L.J. 707, ECHR .......................................................................... *Digested,* 02/**2528**:
*Applied* 04/2027, 06/2188, 06/3651, 09/2046, 10/1744, 13/619, 14/1516, 14/2237:
*Considered* 03/4070, 06/2217, 06/844, 07/2260, 12/1517, 12/1658, 14/672:
*Distinguished* 07/204: *Referred to* 04/2026
Price v Davis see Davis v Price
Price v Leeds City Council see Kay v Lambeth LBC
Price v Nunn [2013] EWCA Civ 1002, CA (Civ Div); affirming [2012] EWHC 1251 (Ch), Ch D (Bristol)
*Applied* 14/1842
Price v Price [2014] EWCA Civ 655; [2014] Fam. Law 1239, CA (Civ Div)
Price v Price (t/a Poppyland Headware) [2003] EWCA Civ 888; [2003] 3 All E.R. 911; [2004] P.I.Q.R. P6; (2003) 147 S.J.L.B. 813; Times, July 28, 2003; Independent, July 2, 2003, CA (Civ Div) .......................................................... *Digested,* 03/**392**:
*Applied* 13/440: *Considered* 13/2093, 14/394
Price v United Engineering Steels Ltd [1998] P.I.Q.R. P407, CA (Civ Div) .................... *Digested,* 99/**464**:
*Considered* 14/419: *Followed* 00/523
PricewaterhouseCoopers v Saad Investments Co Ltd [2014] UKPC 35; [2014] 1 W.L.R. 4482; [2014] 2 B.C.L.C. 583; Times, December 16, 2014, PC (Ber)
Primacom Holdings GmbH v Credit Agricole [2011] EWHC 3746 (Ch); [2013] B.C.C. 201, Ch D
*Considered* 14/1821
Primary Group (UK) Ltd v Royal Bank of Scotland Plc [2014] EWHC 1082 (Ch); [2014] 2 All E.R. (Comm) 1121; [2014] R.P.C. 26, Ch D ................................................ *Digested,* 14/**247**
Prime Sight Ltd v Lavarello [2013] UKPC 22; [2014] A.C. 436; [2014] 2 W.L.R. 84; [2013] 4 All E.R. 659; (2014) 158(2) S.J.L.B. 37, PC (Gib)
Primera Maritime (Hellas) Ltd v Jiangsu Eastern Heavy Industry Co Ltd [2013] EWHC 3066 (Comm); [2014] 1 All E.R. (Comm) 813; [2014] 1 Lloyd's Rep. 255; [2013] 2 C.L.C. 901, QBD (Comm) .......................................................................... *Digested,* 14/**118**
Primetrade AG v Ythan Ltd [2005] EWHC 2399 (Comm); [2006] 1 All E.R. 367; [2006] 1 All E.R. (Comm) 157; [2006] 1 Lloyd's Rep. 457; [2005] 2 C.L.C. 911, QBD (Comm) .......................................................................... *Digested,* 06/**3909**:
*Applied* 10/178, 14/115: *Considered* 14/123
Prince Abdulaziz v Apex Global Management Ltd; *sub nom* Apex Global Management Ltd v Fi Call Ltd [2014] UKSC 64; [2014] 1 W.L.R. 4495; Times, December 8, 2014, SC; affirming [2014] EWCA Civ 1106, CA (Civ Div)
Prince Abdulaziz Bin Mishal Bin Abdulaziz Al Saud v Apex Global Management Ltd see Apex Global Management Ltd v Fi Call Ltd
Princi London Ltd v Revenue and Customs Commissioners [2014] UKFTT 597 (TC); [2014] S.T.I. 2426, FTT (Tax)
Prinz v Region Hannover (C-523/11); *joined case* Seeberger v Studentenwerk Heidelberg (C-585/11) [2014] 1 C.M.L.R. 16; [2014] C.E.C. 258, ECJ (3rd Chamber)
Priory Events Ltd v Tandridge DC [2014] P.A.D. 44, Planning Inspector
Pro Med Logistik GmbH v Finanzamt Dresden-Sud (C-454/12) [2014] B.V.C. 18, ECJ (8th Chamber)
Proceedings against Balaz (C-60/12); *sub nom* Proceedings concerning Balaz (C-60/12) [2014] R.T.R. 7; [2014] 2 C.M.L.R. 17, ECJ (Grand Chamber)
Proceedings against Konstantinides (C-475/11); *sub nom* Konstantinides, Re (C-475/11) [2014] 1 C.M.L.R. 33; [2014] C.E.C. 621; (2013) 134 B.M.L.R. 148, ECJ (4th Chamber)
Proceedings Brought by A (C-523/07); *sub nom* A (Area of Freedom, Security and Justice), Re (C-523/07) [2010] Fam. 42; [2010] 2 W.L.R. 527; [2009] E.C.R. I-2805; [2009] I.L.Pr. 39; [2009] 2 F.L.R. 1; [2009] Fam. Law 568, ECJ ................ *Digested,* 09/**1552**:
*Considered* 11/1429, 13/1259, 13/1316: *Followed* 13/1284, 14/1378
Proceedings brought by K Oy (C-219/13) [2014] B.V.C. 44; [2014] S.T.I. 2930, ECJ (3rd Chamber)
Proceedings Brought by Karntner Landesregierung (C-594/12) see Digital Rights Ireland Ltd v Minister for Communications, Marine and Natural Resources (C-293/12)

Proceedings Brought by Massachusetts Institute of Technology (C-431/04); *sub nom* Massachusetts Institute of Technology, Re (C-431/04) [2006] E.C.R. I-4089; [2006] R.P.C. 34, ECJ (2nd Chamber) ........ *Digested,* 07/**2539**:
*Applied* 10/1983, 14/1899: *Considered* 09/2406: *Followed* 13/1783
Proceedings Brought by Penarroja Fa (C-372/09) [2011] 2 C.M.L.R. 49; [2012] C.E.C. 3, ECJ (4th Chamber)
*Applied* 14/1223
Proceedings Brought by Pfleger (C-390/12); *sub nom* Pfleger (C-390/12) [2014] 3 C.M.L.R. 47, ECJ (3rd Chamber)
Proceedings Brought by Schneider (C-386/12); *sub nom* Schneider, Re (C-386/12) [2014] Fam. 80; [2014] 2 W.L.R. 1048; [2014] C.E.C. 189; [2013] I.L.Pr. 44, ECJ (3rd Chamber)
Proceedings Brought by Sokoll-Seebacher (C-367/12) [2014] 3 C.M.L.R. 9, ECJ (4th Chamber)
Proceedings concerning Balaz (C-60/12) see Proceedings against Balaz (C-60/12)
Process Development Ltd v Hogg [1996] F.S.R. 45; (1996) 19(2) I.P.D. 19012, CA (Civ Div)
*Applied* 14/380
Procter & Gamble UK v Revenue and Customs Commissioners; *sub nom* Revenue and Customs Commissioners v Procter & Gamble UK [2009] EWCA Civ 407; [2009] S.T.C. 1990; [2009] B.T.C. 5462; [2009] B.V.C. 461; [2009] S.T.I. 1722, CA (Civ Div); reversing [2008] EWHC 1558 (Ch); [2008] S.T.C. 2650; [2008] B.T.C. 5617; [2008] B.V.C. 736; [2008] S.T.I. 1679; Times, July 18, 2008, Ch D; reversing [2007] S.T.I. 2251, V&DTr (London) ........ *Digested,* 09/**4129**:
*Applied* 10/61, 13/3205, 14/2910: *Distinguished* 10/3509
PROCTER & GAMBLE/Cooling compositions (T1080/10) [2014] E.P.O.R. 38, EPO (Technical Bd App)
PROCTOR & GAMBLE/Hair styling compositions (T287/11) [2014] E.P.O.R. 47, EPO (Technical Bd App)
Professional Golfers' Association Ltd v Revenue and Customs Commissioners [2013] UKFTT 605 (TC); [2014] S.T.I. 407, FTT (Tax)
Professional Standards Authority v General Chiropractic Council [2014] EWHC 2190 (Admin); [2014] Med. L.R. 363, QBD (Admin) ........ *Digested,* 14/**1518**
Professional Standards Authority for Health and Social Care v General Medical Council [2014] EWHC 1903 (Admin); [2014] Med. L.R. 311; [2014] A.C.D. 118, QBD (Admin) ........ *Digested,* 14/**1497**
Promociones y Construcciones BJ 200 SL (C-125/12) [2014] S.T.C. 237; [2013] B.V.C. 252; [2013] S.T.I. 3133, ECJ (6th Chamber)
Propend Finance Pty Ltd v Sing Times, May 2, 1997, CA (Civ Div) ........ *Digested,* 97/**3188**:
*Applied* 04/3849: *Considered* 14/1056
Property Holding Co v Mischeff see Palser v Grinling
Property Professionals + Ltd, Re [2013] EWHC 1903 (Ch); [2013] B.C.C. 606; [2014] 1 B.C.L.C. 466, Ch D (Birmingham) ........ *Digested,* 14/**1811**
Prophet Plc v Huggett [2014] EWCA Civ 1013; [2014] I.R.L.R. 797, CA (Civ Div); reversing [2014] EWHC 615 (Ch); [2014] I.R.L.R. 618, Ch D ........ *Digested,* 14/**1031**
ProRail BV v Xpedys NV (C-332/11) [2013] C.E.C. 879; [2013] I.L.Pr. 18, ECJ (1st Chamber)
*Explained* 14/539
Prospective Adopters v IA [2014] EWHC 331 (Fam); [2014] 2 F.L.R. 1158; [2014] Fam. Law 773, Fam Div
Prosser v Pembrokeshire Coast NPA [2014] P.A.D. 47, Planning Inspector
Proton Energy Group SA v Orlen Lietuva [2013] EWHC 2872 (Comm); [2014] 1 All E.R. (Comm) 972; [2014] 1 Lloyd's Rep. 100; 150 Con. L.R. 72, QBD (Comm) . *Digested,* 14/**636**
Provincie Antwerpen v Belgacom NV van publiek recht (C-256/13); *joined case* Provincie Antwerpen v Mobistar NV (C-264/13) [2014] B.T.C. 44, ECJ (3rd Chamber)
Provincie Antwerpen v Mobistar NV (C-264/13) see Provincie Antwerpen v Belgacom NV van publiek recht (C-256/13)
Proxima GR Properties Ltd v McGhee [2014] UKUT 59 (LC); [2014] 2 E.G.L.R. 27, UT (Lands)
Prudential Assurance Co Ltd v Revenue and Customs Commissioners [2013] EWHC 3249 (Ch); [2014] S.T.C. 1236; [2014] 2 C.M.L.R. 10; [2013] B.T.C. 751; [2013] S.T.I. 3391, Ch D ........ *Digested,* 14/**2874**
Prudential Assurance Co Ltd v Valuation Officer [2011] R.A. 490, VT ........ *Digested,* 12/**2697**:
*Doubted* 14/2083: *Referred to* 12/2524
PS (Incapacitated or Vulnerable Adult), Re see Sunderland City Council v P
PT Building Services Ltd v ROK Build Ltd [2008] EWHC 3434 (TCC), QBD (TCC)
*Applied* 14/583: *Considered* 14/130, 14/585

PT Perusahaan Gas Negara (Persero) TBK v CRW Joint Operation [2014] SGHC 146; 155 Con. L.R. 169, HC (Sing)
PTJ SPIERINGS/Fundamental violation of art.113 EPC and other fundamental procedural defects (R17/13) [2014] E.P.O.R. 2, EPO (Enlarged Bd App)
Public Guardian v AW see OB, Re
Public Guardian v Boff [2013] W.T.L.R. 1349, CP ........ *Digested,* 14/**2169**
Public Guardian v JM see DP (Revocation of Lasting Power of Attorney), Re
Public Guardian v MD see AB (Revocation of Enduring Power of Attorney), Re
Public Prosecution Service v Elliott see Public Prosecution Service v McKee
Public Prosecution Service v McKee; *sub nom* Public Prosecution Service of Northern Ireland v Elliott; *joined case* Public Prosecution Service v Elliott [2013] UKSC 32; [2013] 1 W.L.R. 1611; [2013] 3 All E.R. 365; [2013] N.I. 133; [2013] 2 Cr. App. R. 17; [2014] Crim. L.R. 77; Times, June 18, 2013, SC; affirming [2011] NICA 61; [2012] N.I. 154, CA (NI) ........ *Digested,* 13/**3289**
Public Prosecution Service of Northern Ireland v Elliott see Public Prosecution Service v McKee
Public Relations Consultants Association Ltd v Newspaper Licensing Agency Ltd (C-360/13); *sub nom* Newspaper Licensing Agency Ltd v Meltwater Holdings BV (C-360/13) EU:C:2014:1195; [2014] A.C. 1438; [2014] 3 W.L.R. 1025; [2014] 2 All E.R. (Comm) 657; [2014] Bus. L.R. 970; [2014] All E.R. (EC) 959; [2014] E.C.D.R. 22; [2014] E.M.L.R. 28, ECJ (4th Chamber)
Pugh v Pugh [1951] P. 482; [1951] 2 All E.R. 680; [1951] 2 T.L.R. 806; (1951) 95 S.J. 468, PDAD ........ *Digested,* 47-51/**3136**: *Considered* 14/1392: *Followed* 67/1319: *Not followed* 72/424
Pullan v Wilson [2014] EWHC 126 (Ch); [2014] W.T.L.R. 669; (2014) 158(10) S.J.L.B. 37; [2014] 1 P. & C.R. DG21, Ch D ........ *Digested,* 14/**3031**
Punj Lloyd Ltd v SABIC UK Petrochemicals Ltd (formerly Huntsman Petrochemicals (UK) Ltd) see SABIC UK Petrochemicals Ltd (formerly Huntsman Petrochemicals (UK) Ltd) v Punj Lloyd Ltd
Purdy v Cambran [2000] C.P. Rep. 67; [1999] C.P.L.R. 843, CA (Civ Div) ........ *Digested,* 00/**609**: *Applied* 02/498, 14/487
Purolite International Ltd v Revenue and Customs Commissioners [2012] UKFTT 475 (TC); 81 T.C. 562; [2012] S.T.I. 3068, FTT (Tax)
Purple Parking Ltd v Heathrow Airport Ltd [2011] EWHC 987 (Ch); [2011] U.K.C.L.R. 492, Ch D ........ *Digested,* 11/**430**: *Considered* 14/529
Pusa v Osuuspankkien Keskinainen Vakuutusyhtio (C-224/02) [2004] S.T.C. 1066; [2004] E.C.R. I-5763; [2004] 2 C.M.L.R. 23; [2004] All E.R. (EC) 797; [2004] S.T.I. 1167, ECJ (5th Chamber) ........ *Digested,* 05/**3002**: *Applied* 07/1610: *Considered* 07/1625, 14/821
Pwllbach Colliery Co Ltd v Woodman [1915] A.C. 634, HL
*Applied* 53/1165, 93/1615, 09/3151: *Considered* 64/1201, 68/1313, 70/823, 80/93.u: *Followed* 14/2520

Q v Q; *joined cases* B (A Child), Re; C (A Child) (Private Law: Public Funding), Re [2014] EWFC 31; [2014] Fam. Law 1398, Fam Ct
Q v Q (Funding of Representation and Expert Attendance) [2014] EWFC 7; [2014] Fam. Law 1248, Fam Ct
Q (A Child) (Parental Order: Domicile), Re; *sub nom* CC v DD [2014] EWHC 1307 (Fam); [2014] Fam. Law 1256, Fam Div
Q (Children), Re [2014] EWCA Civ 918; [2014] 3 F.C.R. 517; [2014] Fam. Law 1397, CA (Civ Div)
Q-ZAR Trade Mark see Quasar Manufacturing Ltd v Ricotti
QA (Afghanistan) v Secretary of State for the Home Department see KA (Afghanistan) v Secretary of State for the Home Department
QBE Management Services (UK) Ltd v Dymoke [2012] EWHC 80 (QB); [2012] I.R.L.R. 458; (2012) 162 N.L.J. 180, QBD ........ *Digested,* 12/**1141**: *Applied* 12/1142, 14/1025
Qdime Ltd v Bath Building (Swindon) Management Co Ltd [2014] UKUT 261 (LC); [2014] 3 E.G.L.R. 18, UT (Lands)
Qongwane v Secretary of State for the Home Department; *joined case* R. (on the application of Singh (India)) v Upper Tribunal (Immigration and Asylum Chamber) [2014] EWCA Civ 957; [2014] Imm. A.R. 1179, CA (Civ Div)
Quaintance v Tandan [2012] EWHC 4416 (Ch); [2014] W.T.L.R. 1609, Ch D
Quality Solicitors CMHT v Tunstall [2014] Eq. L.R. 679, EAT
Quasar Manufacturing Ltd v Ricotti; *sub nom* Ricotti v Quasar Manufacturing Ltd; Q-ZAR Trade Mark [2014] R.P.C. 25, App Person ........ *Digested,* 14/**1930**

Queens Moat Houses Plc, Re see Secretary of State for Trade and Industry v Bairstow

Quiet Moments Ltd, Re; *sub nom* Dufoo v Tolaini [2014] EWCA Civ 1536; [2014] 6 Costs L.R. 1106, CA (Civ Div); reversing in part [2013] EWHC 3806 (Ch), Ch D (Companies Ct)

Quietlynn Ltd v Southend BC (C23/89) [1991] 1 Q.B. 454; [1991] 2 W.L.R. 611; [1990] 3 All E.R. 207; [1990] E.C.R. I-3059; [1990] 3 C.M.L.R. 55; 88 L.G.R. 921; Times, July 19, 1990, ECJ (6th Chamber) .......... *Digested,* 91/**4068**: *Considered* 13/3837, 14/3647

Quila v Secretary of State for the Home Department see R. (on the application of Aguilar Quila) v Secretary of State for the Home Department

Quilvest Finance Ltd v Fairfield Sentry Ltd (In Liquidation) see Fairfield Sentry Ltd (In Liquidation) v Migani

Quirkco Investments Ltd v Aspray Transport Ltd [2011] EWHC 3060 (Ch); [2013] Lloyd's Rep. I.R. 55; [2012] L. & T.R. 19, Ch D (Leeds) .......... *Digested,* 12/**2023**: *Considered* 14/1987

Quistclose Investments Ltd v Rolls Razor Ltd (In Voluntary Liquidation) see Barclays Bank Ltd v Quistclose Investments Ltd

Qureshi v Brent LBC [2014] P.A.D. 52, Planning Inspector

R v A (Abduction: Habitual Residence) [2013] EWHC 692 (Fam); [2014] 1 F.L.R. 969; [2013] Fam. Law 932, Fam Div

R v C see S (Relocation: Parental Responsibility)

R v Collins Ex p Ian Stewart Brady [2000] Lloyd's Rep. Med. 355; (2001) 58 B.M.L.R. 173; [2000] M.H.L.R. 17, QBD .......... *Digested,* 00/**4172**: *Considered* 01/4431: *Distinguished* 14/2187

R v Criminal Injuries Compensation Authority (Unreported, October 22, 2013), FTT (SEC) [*Pannone LLP, 123 Deansgate, Manchester*] .......... *Digested,* 14/**2314**

R v R [2013] EWHC 4244 (Fam); [2014] 2 F.L.R. 699; [2014] Fam. Law 454, Fam Div *Digested,* 14/**1402**

R v R (Children Cases: Costs) see R (A Minor) (Legal Aid: Costs), Re

R v R (Divorce: Hemain Injunction) [2003] EWHC 2113 (Fam); [2005] 1 F.L.R. 386; [2005] Fam. Law 17, Fam Div .......... *Digested,* 05/**1623**: *Applied* 14/1326: *Considered* 10/1375

R v R see R (Parental Responsibility), Re

R v United Kingdom (35348/06) [2011] 2 F.L.R. 1236; (2012) 54 E.H.R.R. 2; [2011] Fam. Law 924, ECHR .......... *Digested,* 12/**1300**: *Applied* 14/2237

R (A Child) v Kent CC (Unreported, October 28, 2013), CC (Clerkenwell) [*Dowse & Co, 23-25 Dalston Lane, London*] .......... *Digested,* 14/**2320**

R (A Child) (Abduction: Child's Objections), Re; *sub nom* De L v H [2009] EWHC 3074 (Fam); [2010] 1 F.L.R. 1229; [2010] Fam. Law 328, Fam Div .......... *Digested,* 10/**1340**: *Considered* 12/1368, 14/1379

R (A Child) (Adoption: Father's Involvement), Re; *sub nom* S (A Child) (Adoption Proceedings: Joinder of Father), Re [2001] 1 F.L.R. 302; [2001] 1 F.C.R. 158; [2001] Fam. Law 91, CA (Civ Div) .......... *Digested,* 01/**2532**: *Distinguished* 14/1251

R (A Child) (Care Proceedings: Welfare Evaluation), Re see R (Care Proceedings: Welfare Analysis of Changed Circumstances), Re

R (A Child) (Habitual Residence), Re [2014] EWCA Civ 1032; [2014] Fam. Law 1526, CA (Civ Div)

R (A Child) (Prohibited Steps Order), Re; *sub nom* A (Prohibited Steps Order), Re [2013] EWCA Civ 1115; [2014] 1 F.L.R. 643; [2014] 1 F.C.R. 113; [2013] Fam. Law 1532, CA (Civ Div) .......... *Digested,* 14/**1313**

R (A Child) (Recognition of Indian Adoption), Re [2012] EWHC 2956 (Fam); [2013] 1 F.L.R. 1487; [2013] Fam. Law 274, Fam Div .......... *Digested,* 13/**1194**: *Applied* 14/1242

R (A Minor) (Legal Aid: Costs), Re; *sub nom* R v R (Children Cases: Costs) [1997] 2 F.L.R. 95; [1997] 1 F.C.R. 613; [1997] Fam. Law 391; (1997) 94(6) L.S.G. 27; Times, January 9, 1997, CA (Civ Div) .......... *Digested,* 97/**530**: *Considered* 99/2410, 10/1390: *Followed* 14/1335

R (Care Proceedings: Welfare Analysis of Changed Circumstances), Re; *sub nom* R (A Child) (Care Proceedings: Welfare Evaluation), Re [2014] EWCA Civ 597; [2014] 3 F.C.R. 152; [2014] Fam. Law 1091, CA (Civ Div) .......... *Digested,* 14/**1277**

R (Children) (Appeal from Placement Order: Change of Circumstances), Re [2013] EWCA Civ 1240; [2014] Fam. Law 162, CA (Civ Div)

R (Children) (Care and Placement Orders: Paternal Grandparents), Re [2013] EWCA Civ 1018; [2013] 3 F.C.R. 599, CA (Civ Div) .......... *Digested,* 14/**1244**: *Followed* 14/1245

R (Children) (Temporary Leave to Remove from Jurisdiction), Re [2014] EWHC 643 (Fam); [2014] 2 F.L.R. 1402; [2014] Fam. Law 817, Fam Div

R (Parental Responsibility), Re; *sub nom* R v R [2011] EWHC 1535 (Fam); [2011] 2 F.L.R. 1132; [2011] Fam. Law 939, Fam Div ........ *Digested,* 12/**1456**: *Considered* 14/1311

R&A Millett (Shops) Ltd v Leon Allan International Fashions [1989] 1 E.G.L.R. 138; [1989] 18 E.G. 107; [1988] E.G. 179 (C.S.); Independent, January 19, 1989, CA (Civ Div); affirming [1988] 13 E.G. 50, HC ........ *Digested,* 89/**2192**: *Followed* 14/2006

R&R Plant (Peterborough) Ltd v Bailey see Bailey v R&R Plant (Peterborough) Ltd

R-B (A Patient) v Official Solicitor see A (Mental Patient: Sterilisation), Re

R. v A [2014] EWCA Crim 299; [2014] 1 W.L.R. 2469; [2014] 2 Cr. App. R. 5, CA (Crim Div) ........ *Digested,* 14/**693**

R. v A [2014] EWCA Crim 567; [2014] 2 Cr. App. R. 7; Times, April 8, 2014, CA (Crim Div) ........ *Digested,* 14/**718**

R. v A see Attorney General's Reference (No.55 of 2008)

R. v Abdul (Jonathan); *joined cases* R. v Hamed (Ossama); R. v Mustafa (Imran) [2013] EWCA Crim 926; [2014] 1 Cr. App. R. (S.) 30, CA (Crim Div) ........ *Digested,* 14/**2669**

R. v Abdul (Zubar Hussain) [2012] EWCA Crim 1788, CA (Crim Div) *Distinguished* 14/775

R. v Ace (Peter John) (1990-91) 12 Cr. App. R. (S.) 533, CA (Crim Div) ........ *Digested,* 92/**1218**: *Considered* 96/1792, 14/2660: *Referred to* 94/1402

R. v Adamson (Michael Joseph) see R. v Nazari (Fazlollah)

R. v Adetukasi (Adeitan) [2013] EWCA Crim 851; [2014] 1 Cr. App. R. (S.) 11, CA (Crim Div) ........ *Digested,* 14/**2654**

R. v Afford (Christopher John) [2013] EWCA Crim 633; [2014] 1 Cr. App. R. (S.) 2, CA (Crim Div) ........ *Digested,* 14/**2662**

R. v Afonso (Americo Practicio); *joined cases* R. v Sajid (Mohammed); R. v Andrews (Douglas) [2004] EWCA Crim 2342; [2005] 1 Cr. App. R. (S.) 99; [2005] Crim. L.R. 73; (2004) 148 S.J.L.B. 1120; Times, October 14, 2004, CA (Crim Div) ...... *Digested,* 04/**3454**: *Applied* 06/3703, 10/2870, 12/2889: *Considered* 05/3700, 05/3748, 05/3751, 06/3695, 06/3704, 07/3633: *Distinguished* 05/3752, 07/3632: *Followed* 08/3278: *Not applied* 14/2622

R. v Afshar (Saeideh) see R. v Mateta (Koshi Pitshou)

R. v Ahmad (Goran Kamal) see Attorney General's Reference (No.27 of 2013)

R. v Ahmad (Shakeel); *joined cases* R. v Fields (Michael); R. v Ahmed (Syed Mubarak) [2014] UKSC 36; [2014] 3 W.L.R. 23; [2014] 4 All E.R. 767; [2014] 2 Cr. App. R. (S.) 75; [2014] Lloyd's Rep. F.C. 547; [2014] Crim. L.R. 756; Times, July 2, 2014, SC; reversing in part [2012] EWCA Crim 391; [2012] 1 W.L.R. 2335; [2012] 2 All E.R. 1137; [2012] S.T.C. 1239; [2012] 2 Cr. App. R. (S.) 85; [2012] Lloyd's Rep. F.C. 413; [2012] Crim. L.R. 468; [2012] S.T.I. 546; Times, May 29, 2012, CA (Crim Div) ........ *Digested,* 14/**728**: *Distinguished* 13/749: *Followed* 13/2595, 13/686

R. v Ahmed (Mohammed Mokshud) [2013] EWCA Crim 1393; (2013) 134 B.M.L.R. 20, CA (Crim Div) ........ *Digested,* 14/**2614**: *Applied* 14/2649

R. v Ahmed (Mushtaq) [2010] EWCA Crim 2899, CA (Crim Div) *Applied* 14/680: *Considered* 11/606

R. v Ahmed (Syed Mubarak) see R. v Ahmad (Shakeel)

R. v Ali (Sajid Pasha) see R. v Graham (Hemamali Krishna)

R. v Ali (Zaheer Iqbal) [2014] EWCA Crim 948; [2014] 2 Cr. App. R. 15, CA (Crim Div) *Digested,* 14/**779**

R. v All-Hilly (Salaam David) [2014] EWCA Crim 1614; [2014] 2 Cr. App. R. 33, CA (Crim Div) ........ *Digested,* 14/**652**

R. v Allen (Grant) [2013] EWCA Crim 976; [2014] 1 Cr. App. R. (S.) 28, CA (Crim Div)

R. v Alleyne (Rebekah) see R. v Boakye (Christiana)

R. v Allpress (Sylvia); *joined cases* R. v Martin (Stephen); R. v Morris (Paul Winter); R. v Casal (Miguel); R. v Symeou (Deborah) [2009] EWCA Crim 8; [2009] 2 Cr. App. R. (S.) 58; [2009] Lloyd's Rep. F.C. 242; [2009] Crim. L.R. 363, CA (Crim Div) ........ *Digested,* 10/**709**: *Applied* 14/727, 14/728: *Considered* 09/834, 10/734, 11/722

R. v AM; *joined cases* R. v MV; R. v RM; R. v MN [2010] EWCA Crim 2400; [2011] 1 Cr. App. R. 35, CA (Crim Div) ........ *Digested,* 11/**681**: *Considered* 13/656: *Followed* 14/696

R. v Andrews (Douglas) see R. v Afonso (Americo Practicio)

R. v Andukwa (Simon Ebunji) see R. v Mateta (Koshi Pitshou)

R. v Angell (Malcolm) [2014] EWCA Crim 1382; [2014] 2 Cr. App. R. (S.) 80, CA (Crim Div)

R. v Anh Kao (Tuan) see R. v Okedare (Charles)

R. v Banfield (Lynette) see R. v Banfield (Shirley)
R. v Banfield (Shirley); *joined case* R. v Banfield (Lynette) [2013] EWCA Crim 1394; [2014] Crim. L.R. 147, CA (Crim Div)
R. v Banfield (Shirley) [2014] EWCA Crim 1824; [2014] 5 Costs L.R. 896, CA (Crim Div) ........ *Digested,* 14/**2033**
R. v Barley (Louise Marie) [2014] EWCA Crim 1609; [2014] 2 Cr. App. R. (S.) 86, CA (Crim Div)
R. v Barnet LBC Ex p. Shah; *joined cases* R. v Shropshire CC Ex p. Abdullah; Ablack v Inner London Education Authority; Shah (Jitendra) v Barnet LBC; Shabpar v Barnet LBC; Abdullah v Shropshire CC; Akbarali v Brent LBC [1983] 2 A.C. 309; [1983] 2 W.L.R. 16; [1983] 1 All E.R. 226; 81 L.G.R. 305; (1983) 133 N.L.J. 61; (1983) 127 S.J. 36, HL; reversing [1982] Q.B. 688; [1982] 2 W.L.R. 474; [1982] 1 All E.R. 698; 80 L.G.R. 571; Times, November 12, 1981, CA (Civ Div); affirming [1981] 2 W.L.R. 86; [1980] 3 All E.R. 679; 79 L.G.R. 210; (1981) 125 S.J. 64, QBD ........ *Digested,* 83/**1157**: *Applied* 80/853, 84/3033, 85/1074, 85/1737, 86/1692, 86/703, 87/3489, 98/3007, 01/2612, 01/2617, 03/1127, 03/1556, 05/1627, 07/3910, 09/1541, 09/1802, 10/1041, 10/3333, 11/3371, 12/1371, 12/2278, 12/3416: *Considered* 82/973, 84/1173, 84/1178, 84/1645, 85/1107, 85/1108, 85/1127, 85/1771, 85/2165, 86/1136, 86/1703, 91/2372, 95/3206, 99/4564, 00/2778, 08/1692, 13/1250, 13/1645, 13/2956: *Distinguished* 83/1800, 04/1885: *Followed* 87/1928, 09/3829, 10/3179, 10/3332, 12/1392, 13/3011, 14/1729: *Not applied* 13/2058: *Referred to* 91/2373
R. v Barnett (Ian Stanley) [2011] EWCA Crim 2936; [2012] Lloyd's Rep. F.C. 157, CA (Crim Div) ........ *Digested,* 12/**757**: *Considered* 14/726
R. v Bashir (Sajid) see R. v Bestel (Jean Pierre)
R. v Bashir (Yasin) see R. v Mateta (Koshi Pitshou)
R. v Bate (Jonathan) [2013] EWCA Crim 1327; [2014] 1 Cr. App. R. (S.) 48, CA (Crim Div) ........ *Digested,* 14/**2637**
R. v Bava (Amrit) see R. v Patel (Sophia)
R. v Baverstock (Stephen Alan) [2013] EWCA Crim 1502; [2014] 1 Cr. App. R. (S.) 64, CA (Crim Div) ........ *Digested,* 14/**2628**
R. v Baybasin (Mehmet Sirin); *joined cases* Bogle (Neil William); R. v McMullen (Martin Anthony); R. v Molloy (Andrew) [2013] EWCA Crim 2357; [2014] 1 W.L.R. 2112; [2014] 1 Cr. App. R. 19; [2014] Crim. L.R. 528, CA (Crim Div) ...... *Digested,* 14/**777**
R. v Beazley (Rosemary); *sub nom* Hampshire CC v Beazley; *joined case* R. v Beazley (Scott) [2013] EWCA Crim 567; [2013] 1 W.L.R. 3331, CA (Crim Div) .. *Digested,* 14/**743**: *Applied* 14/733
R. v Beazley (Scott) see R. v Beazley (Rosemary)
R. v Beck (James) see R. v Cooke (John)
R. v Beckford (Kyle) [2014] EWCA Crim 1299; [2014] 2 Cr. App. R. (S.) 34, CA (Crim Div) ........ *Digested,* 14/**2658**
R. v Beckford (Luke Junior) [2013] EWCA Crim 2190; [2014] 2 Cr. App. R. (S.) 8, CA (Crim Div)
R. v Beedie (Thomas Sim) [1998] Q.B. 356; [1997] 3 W.L.R. 758; [1997] 2 Cr. App. R. 167; (1997) 161 J.P. 313; [1997] Crim. L.R. 747; (1997) 161 J.P.N. 531; (1997) 94(15) L.S.G. 26; (1997) 141 S.J.L.B. 83; Times, March 14, 1997; Independent, April 21, 1997, CA (Crim Div) ........ *Digested,* 97/**1317**: *Applied* 13/674: *Considered* 14/792: *Distinguished* 07/1022
R. v Bell (Colin James) see R. v Price (Patrick David)
R. v Bell (David); *joined cases* R. v Leigh (Kevin); R. v Bevan (Kenneth); R. v Middlecote (Andrew); Peratikou, (Yiannis) [2011] EWCA Crim 6, CA (Crim Div) *Applied* 14/727
R. v Bell (Mark Julian) see R. v Rogers (Bradley David)
R. v Bennett (Billy) see R. v Perkins (Robert)
R. v Benson (Joseph) see R. v Ezeemo (Godwin Chukwnaenya)
R. v Bergin (Peter) [2014] EWCA Crim 1228; [2014] 2 Cr. App. R. (S.) 71, CA (Crim Div)
R. v Bestel (Jean Pierre); *joined cases* R. v Bashir (Sajid); R. v Raza (Naim) [2013] EWCA Crim 1305; [2014] 1 W.L.R. 457; [2013] 2 Cr. App. R. 30; [2014] 1 Cr. App. R. (S.) 53; [2014] Crim. L.R. 607, CA (Crim Div) ........ *Digested,* 14/**731**: *Considered* 14/794
R. v Beswick (David) see R. v Blackshaw (Jordan Philip)
R. v Bevan (Kenneth) see R. v Bell (David)

R. v Bezzina (Anthony); *joined cases* R. v Elvin (Eric Everton); R. v Codling (Sadie) [1994] 1 W.L.R. 1057; [1994] 3 All E.R. 964; (1994) 99 Cr. App. R. 356; (1994) 158 J.P. 671; (1994) 158 J.P.N. 388; (1994) 91(5) L.S.G. 36; (1994) 138 S.J.L.B. 11; Times, December 7, 1993, CA (Crim Div) ........ *Digested,* 94/**1092**: *Applied* 09/785: *Considered* 14/3404, 14/679

R. v Bhagwan (Dharam Singh); *sub nom* DPP v Bhagwan [1972] A.C. 60; [1970] 3 W.L.R. 501; [1970] 3 All E.R. 97; (1970) 54 Cr. App. R. 460; (1970) 114 S.J. 683, HL; affirming [1970] 2 W.L.R. 837; [1970] 1 All E.R. 1129; (1970) 114 S.J. 166, CA (Crim Div) ........ *Digested,* 70/**187**: *Considered* 72/591, 14/772: *Distinguished* 92/2419: *Referred to* 99/2000

R. v Bieber (aka Coleman) (David Francis) see R. v Bieber (David Francis)

R. v Bieber (David Francis); *sub nom* R. v Bieber (aka Coleman) (David Francis) [2008] EWCA Crim 1601; [2009] 1 W.L.R. 223; [2009] 1 All E.R. 295; [2008] H.R.L.R. 43; [2010] 1 Prison L.R. 51; (2008) 105(31) L.S.G. 18; Times, August 11, 2008, CA (Crim Div) ........ *Digested,* 08/**3343**: *Considered* 12/2940, 14/2701: *Followed* 09/1473

R. v Bina (Arya) [2014] EWCA Crim 1444; [2014] 2 Cr. App. R. 30; (2014) 158(24) S.J.L.B. 53, CA (Crim Div) ........ *Digested,* 14/**690**

R. v Birch (Ben); *joined cases* R. v Tyrell (Andrew); R. v Davies (Aby) [2012] EWCA Crim 1000; [2013] 1 Cr. App. R. (S.) 16, CA (Crim Div) ........ *Digested,* 13/**2786**: *Applied* 14/2694

R. v Bird (Gary Kenneth) [1996] R.T.R. 22; [1995] Crim. L.R. 745, CA (Crim Div) ........ *Digested,* 96/**1617**: *Applied* 14/776

R. v Bird (Mark Leopold) [2013] EWCA Crim 1765; [2014] 1 Cr. App. R. (S.) 77, CA (Crim Div)

R. v BJ Electronics Ltd see R. v Ezeemo (Godwin Chukwnaenya)

R. v Blackman (Alexander Wayne) [2014] EWCA Crim 1029; [2014] 2 Cr. App. R. 18, CMAC ........ *Digested,* 14/**2657**

R. v Blackshaw (Jordan Philip); *joined cases* R. v Carter (Stephen); R. v Beswick (David); R. v Craven (Stephen); R. v Koyunco (Hassan); R. v McGrane (Lorraine); R. v Gillespie-Doyle (Michael); R. v Vanasco (Enrico); R. v Halloway (Hassan); R. v Sutcliffe (Perry John) [2011] EWCA Crim 2312; [2012] 1 W.L.R. 1126; [2012] 1 Cr. App. R. (S.) 114; [2012] Crim. L.R. 57; (2011) 108(42) L.S.G. 19; Times, October 25, 2011, CA (Crim Div) ........ *Digested,* 11/**3030**: *Applied* 13/2761: *Considered* 12/4259, 13/2649, 14/645

R. v Blackshaw (Paul James) see R. v Kenning (David Matthew)

R. v Blaydes (Matthew) [2014] EWCA Crim 798; [2014] 2 Cr. App. R. (S.) 55, CA (Crim Div) ........ *Digested,* 14/**2666**

R. v Bleazard (Daniel) see R. v Povey (Clive Richard)

R. v Boakye (Christiana); *joined cases* R. v Jagne (Shireen); R. v Latchman (Dona Narisa); R. v Nasri (Sbida); R. v Nwude (Ifeoma Kalistar); R. v Alleyne (Rebekah) [2012] EWCA Crim 838; [2013] 1 Cr. App. R. (S.) 2; [2012] Crim. L.R. 626, CA (Crim Div) ........ *Digested,* 13/**2620**: *Applied* 13/2617, 13/2625: *Considered* 13/2621, 13/2623, 14/2618

R. v Boal (Francis Steven) [1992] Q.B. 591; [1992] 2 W.L.R. 890; [1992] 3 All E.R. 177; [1992] B.C.L.C. 872; (1992) 95 Cr. App. R. 272; (1992) 156 J.P. 617; [1992] I.C.R. 495; [1992] I.R.L.R. 420; (1992) 156 L.G. Rev. 763; (1992) 136 S.J.L.B. 100; Times, March 16, 1992, CA (Crim Div) ........ *Digested,* 92/**2217**: *Applied* 13/656, 13/667: *Considered* 94/2514: *Followed* 14/696

R. v Bogacki (Steven); *joined cases* R. v Cox (Robert Charles); R. v Tillwach (Howard John) [1973] Q.B. 832; [1973] 2 W.L.R. 937; [1973] 2 All E.R. 864; (1973) 57 Cr. App. R. 593; [1973] R.T.R. 384; [1973] Crim. L.R. 385; (1973) 117 S.J. 355, CA (Crim Div) ........ *Digested,* 73/**648**: *Considered* 76/603, 77/663, 14/2554

R. v Bohannan (Mark Edward) [2010] EWCA Crim 2261; [2011] 1 Cr. App. R. (S.) 106, CA (Crim Div) ........ *Digested,* 11/**2946**: *Considered* 14/2652

R. v Bond (Richard) [2013] EWCA Crim 2713; [2014] 2 Cr. App. R. (S.) 3, CA (Crim Div)

R. v Booth (Jonathan) see R. v Pitts (Aaron)

R. v Borjanovic (Barislov) see R. v Searle (Terence)

R. v Botcher (Henrik) see R. v Greaves (Claude Clifford)

R. v Bott (Anthony) [2013] EWCA Crim 1553; [2014] L.L.R. 324, CA (Crim Div)

R. v Bouchereau (Pierre Roger) (30/77) [1978] Q.B. 732; [1978] 2 W.L.R. 250; [1981] 2 All E.R. 924; [1977] E.C.R. 1999; (1978) 66 Cr. App. R. 202; [1977] 2 C.M.L.R. 800; (1978) 122 S.J. 79, ECJ ........ *Digested,* 78/**629**: *Applied* 87/1938, 89/1108, 00/3345, 06/3723, 07/1559, 08/1344, 11/3790: *Considered* 83/1895, 93/5141, 94/2471, 97/2902, 12/3597, 13/2731, 14/2664: *Followed* 05/1462, 11/807: *Referred to* 83/806, 90/1405, 93/1108

R. v Boughton-Fox (Christopher) [2014] EWCA Crim 227; [2014] Lloyd's Rep. F.C. 343, CA (Crim Div) ........ *Digested,* 14/**744**

R. v Bow Street Metropolitan Stipendiary Magistrate Ex p. Pinochet Ugarte (No.3) [2000] 1 A.C. 147; [1999] 2 W.L.R. 827; [1999] 2 All E.R. 97; 6 B.H.R.C. 24; (1999) 96(17) L.S.G. 24; (1999) 149 N.L.J. 497; Times, March 25, 1999, HL; reversing in part Times, November 3, 1998; Independent, October 30, 1998, DC ........ *Digested,* 99/**2292**: *Applied* 06/2200, 14/1949: *Considered* 04/3849, 06/2644, 12/1290: *Reversed* 98/2354

R. v Bowden (Peter) see R. v Pitts (Aaron)

R. v Bowen (Carl Peter) see R. v Caley (David)

R. v Bowker (Anthony) [2007] EWCA Crim 1608; [2008] 1 Cr. App. R. (S.) 72; [2007] Crim. L.R. 904, CA (Crim Div) ........ *Digested,* 08/**3423**: *Considered* 14/2680

R. v Bowyer (Barry Francis) see R. v Dawes (Carlos)

R. v Bradley (Kirk Trevor) see R. v Riley (Craig Philip)

R. v Bradshaw (Wayne Martin); *joined case* R. v Waters (Paul Anthony) [2001] R.T.R. 4; Times, December 31, 1994, CA (Crim Div) ........ *Digested,* 95/**1304**: *Considered* 14/2691: *Followed* 00/1126

R. v Bramich (David) see R. v Graham (Hemamali Krishna)

R. v Bravard (Jacques) see R. v May (Raymond George)

R. v Brent LBC Ex p. Baruwa [1997] 3 F.C.R. 97; (1997) 29 H.L.R. 915; [1997] C.O.D. 450; Independent, February 27, 1997, CA (Civ Div); reversing (1996) 28 H.L.R. 361, QBD ........ *Digested,* 97/**2662**: *Considered* 14/1592: *Followed* 98/3010

R. v Brent LBC Ex p. Gunning 84 L.G.R. 168; Times, April 30, 1985, QBD ........ *Digested,* 86/**1127**: *Applied* 08/52, 12/3163, 14/2149: *Considered* 91/94, 93/3679, 95/30, 96/2483, 96/2487, 11/2093, 11/52, 12/2105

R. v Brent LBC Housing Benefit Review Board Ex p. Khadim see R. (on the application of Kadhim) v Brent LBC Housing Benefit Review Board

R. v Briggs-Price (Robert William) [2009] UKHL 19; [2009] 1 A.C. 1026; [2009] 2 W.L.R. 1101; [2009] 4 All E.R. 594; [2009] H.R.L.R. 21; [2009] Lloyd's Rep. F.C. 442; [2010] Crim. L.R. 139; (2009) 153(18) S.J.L.B. 27; Times, April 30, 2009, HL; affirming [2008] EWCA Crim 146, CA (Crim Div) ........ *Digested,* 09/**832**: *Considered* 10/735, 11/260, 12/329, 14/2954

R. v Bright (Michael John) [2008] EWCA Crim 462; [2008] 2 Cr. App. R. (S.) 102; [2008] Lloyd's Rep. F.C. 323; [2008] Crim. L.R. 482, CA (Crim Div) ........ *Digested,* 08/**3274**: *Applied* 08/3304, 11/2820, 13/2723: *Considered* 12/3030, 13/2683, 14/2600

R. v Bristow (Terrence) [2013] EWCA Crim 1540; [2014] Crim. L.R. 457, CA (Crim Div)

R. v Broadway (Gail Julie) see R. v Turbill (Maxine)

R. v Brown (Cory) see R. v Walsh (Anthony)

R. v Brown (Michael) [2013] EWCA Crim 1726; [2014] 1 Cr. App. R. (S.) 84, CA (Crim Div) ........ *Digested,* 14/**2623**

R. v Brown (Richard) [2013] UKSC 43; [2013] 4 All E.R. 860; [2013] N.I. 265, SC; affirming [2011] NICA 47, CA (NI) ........ *Digested,* 14/**674**

R. v Brown (Romeka) [2010] EWCA Crim 1807; [2011] 1 Cr. App. R. (S.) 79, CA (Crim Div) ........ *Digested,* 11/**2990**: *Applied* 13/2732, 14/2664

R. v Bryce (Craig Brian) [2004] EWCA Crim 1231; [2004] 2 Cr. App. R. 35, CA (Crim Div) *Applied* 14/1451: *Considered* 12/1660

R. v Bullen (David Frederick) see R. v Soneji (Kamlesh Kumar)

R. v Bunyan (Peter Mark) [2013] EWCA Crim 1885; [2014] 1 Cr. App. R. (S.) 65, CA (Crim Div) ........ *Digested,* 14/**2652**

R. v Burch (David William) see Attorney General's Reference (Nos 88, 89, 90 and 91 of 2006)

R. v Burinskas (Gintas) see Attorney General's Reference (No.27 of 2013)

R. v Burrows (Ben Peter) see R. v Moore (Mia)

R. v Bush (Liam) [2013] EWCA Crim 1164; [2014] 1 Cr. App. R. (S.) 40, CA (Crim Div) ........ *Digested,* 14/**2621**

R. v BYE see R. v Searle (Terence)

R. v Bygrave (Rosemary) see R. v Morgan (John)
R. v C [2012] EWCA Crim 213, CA (Crim Div) *Distinguished* 14/775
R. v C [2011] EWCA Crim 1872; [2012] 1 Cr. App. R. (S.) 89; [2011] Crim. L.R. 899, CA (Crim Div) ............ *Digested,* 12/**2884**: *Applied* 14/2612
R. v C [2009] UKHL 42; [2009] 1 W.L.R. 1786; [2009] 4 All E.R. 1033; [2010] 1 Cr. App. R. 7; [2009] M.H.L.R. 189; [2010] Crim. L.R. 75; (2009) 153(31) S.J.L.B. 30; Times, August 7, 2009, HL; reversing [2008] EWCA Crim 1155; [2009] 1 Cr. App. R. 15; (2008) 105(23) L.S.G. 26; (2008) 158 N.L.J. 789; (2008) 152(22) S.J.L.B. 31; Times, June 9, 2008, CA (Crim Div) ............ *Digested,* 09/**806**: *Considered* 11/2203, 11/2204, 14/2175
R. v C (James) see R. v R (Amer)
R. v C see Attorney General's Reference (No.27 of 2013)
R. v C see Attorney General's Reference (No.55 of 2008)
R. v C see R. v H
R. v Caceres (Jose) [2013] EWCA Crim 924; [2014] 1 Cr. App. R. (S.) 23, CA (Crim Div) ............ *Digested,* 14/**2643**
R. v Cadman-Smith (David) see R. v Smith (David Cadman)
R. v Cairns (James Philip); *joined cases* R. v Morris (Nigel Leonard); R. v Rafiq (Shahid); R. v Firfire (Asif) [2013] EWCA Crim 467; [2013] 2 Cr. App. R. (S.) 73; [2013] Crim. L.R. 616, CA (Crim Div) ............ *Digested,* 13/**2566**: *Applied* 14/789
R. v Caley (David); *joined cases* R. v McWilliams (Mark); R. v Wain (Darren); R. v Didonga (Kembo); R. v Kamwiziku (Placide); R. v Sanham (Tony Sydney); R. v Bowen (Carl Peter); R. v Perry (Lewis Lawrence); R. v Robertson (Daniel Alexander) [2012] EWCA Crim 2821; [2013] 2 Cr. App. R. (S.) 47; (2013) 177 J.P. 111; [2013] Crim. L.R. 342, CA (Crim Div) ............ *Digested,* 13/**2662**: *Considered* 14/2666, 14/2668
R. v Camden LBC Ex p. Pereira (1999) 31 H.L.R. 317; [1998] N.P.C. 94, CA (Civ Div); reversing [1998] C.O.D. 318, QBD [*Kelvin Rutledge, Barrister, 2 Field Court, Gray's Inn, London*] ............ *Digested,* 99/**3062**: *Applied* 05/1989, 05/1991, 06/2027, 09/1901, 14/1601: *Considered* 05/1990, 05/2006, 14/1600: *Followed* 04/1894, 13/1527, 13/1542
R. v Canns (Jason) [2005] EWCA Crim 2264, CA (Crim Div) *Considered* 14/691
R. v Carrington (Marion) [2014] EWCA Crim 325; [2014] 2 Cr. App. R. (S.) 41, CA (Crim Div) ............ *Digested,* 14/**2608**
R. v Carroll (Robert) [2014] EWCA Crim 1158; [2014] 2 Cr. App. R. (S.) 69, CA (Crim Div)
R. v Carter (Stephen) see R. v Blackshaw (Jordan Philip)
R. v Carter (William Melvin) see R. v Smith (Dean Martin)
R. v Casal (Miguel) see R. v Allpress (Sylvia)
R. v Catchpole (Scott Jamie) [2014] EWCA Crim 1037; [2014] 2 Cr. App. R. (S.) 66, CA (Crim Div) ............ *Digested,* 14/**2699**
R. v Catt (Sarah Louise) [2013] EWCA Crim 1187; [2014] 1 Cr. App. R. (S.) 35, CA (Crim Div) ............ *Digested,* 14/**2589**
R. v CD see Attorney General's Reference (No.55 of 2008)
R. v Central Criminal Court Ex p. W [2001] 1 Cr. App. R. 2; [2000] C.O.D. 442, DC *Applied* 14/46
R. v Chahal (Bhabdeep Singh); *joined case* R. v Chahal (Charanjit Singh) [2014] EWCA Crim 101; [2014] 2 Cr. App. R. (S.) 35, CA (Crim Div) ............ *Digested,* 14/**726**
R. v Chahal (Bhabdeep Singh) see R. v Randhawa (Jagprit)
R. v Chahal (Charanjit Singh) see R. v Chahal (Bhabdeep Singh)
R. v Chahal (Charanjit Singh) see R. v Randhawa (Jagprit)
R. v Chahal (Ranjot) see R. v Dosanjh (Sandeep)
R. v Chapman (Helen) [2013] EWCA Crim 1370; [2014] 1 W.L.R. 1376; [2013] Lloyd's Rep. F.C. 683; [2014] Crim. L.R. 611, CA (Crim Div) ............ *Digested,* 14/**794**
R. v Chargot Ltd (t/a Contract Services) [2008] UKHL 73; [2009] 1 W.L.R. 1; [2009] 2 All E.R. 645; [2009] I.C.R. 263; (2009) 153(1) S.J.L.B. 32; Times, December 16, 2008, HL; affirming [2007] EWCA Crim 3032; [2008] 2 All E.R. 1077; [2008] I.C.R. 517, CA (Crim Div) ............ *Digested,* 09/**1885**: *Considered* 08/1817, 13/3864, 14/772: *Explained* 12/1611: *Followed* 14/2296
R. v Charles (Jerome) (Leave to Appeal); *joined case* R. v Tucker (Lee Nigel) [2001] EWCA Crim 129; [2001] 2 Cr. App. R. 15; [2001] Crim. L.R. 732; Times, February 20, 2001; Daily Telegraph, February 7, 2001, CA (Crim Div) ............ *Digested,* 01/**1096**: *Applied* 14/757
R. v Chawla (Davinder Singh) see R. v Kapoor (Saran Singh)

R. v Chehil 2013 SCC 49; 36 B.H.R.C. 427, Sup Ct (Can)
R. v Cheshire (John) [2014] EWCA Crim 627; [2014] 2 Cr. App. R. (S.) 53, CA (Crim Div) ............ *Digested,* 14/**2601**
R. v Chief Constable of Nottinghamshire Ex p. Sunderland see R. v Chief Constable of the West Midlands Ex p. Wiley
R. v Chief Constable of Thames Valley Ex p. Cotton; *sub nom* R. v Deputy Chief Constable of Thames Valley Ex p. Cotton [1990] I.R.L.R. 344; Times, December 28, 1989; Independent, December 22, 1989, CA (Civ Div); affirming [1989] C.O.D. 318, QBD ............ *Digested,* 91/**95**: *Applied* 06/37, 14/1693: *Considered* 92/955, 94/43, 98/3025, 05/75, 06/4713: *Followed* 99/97
R. v Chief Constable of the Royal Ulster Constabulary Ex p. Begley; *joined case* R. v McWilliams (Thomas) [1997] 1 W.L.R. 1475; [1997] 4 All E.R. 833; [1997] N.I. 275; 3 B.H.R.C. 173; (1997) 94(42) L.S.G. 32; (1997) 147 N.L.J. 1545; (1997) 141 S.J.L.B. 218; Times, October 20, 1997, HL ............ *Digested,* 97/**5188**: *Followed* 14/709
R. v Chief Constable of the West Midlands Ex p. Wiley; *joined case* R. v Chief Constable of Nottinghamshire Ex p. Sunderland [1995] 1 A.C. 274; [1994] 3 W.L.R. 433; [1994] 3 All E.R. 420; [1995] 1 Cr. App. R. 342; [1994] C.O.D. 520; (1994) 91(40) L.S.G. 35; (1994) 144 N.L.J. 1008; (1994) 138 S.J.L.B. 156; Times, July 15, 1994; Independent, July 15, 1994, HL; reversing [1994] 1 W.L.R. 114; [1994] 1 All E.R. 702; [1994] P.I.Q.R. P23; [1993] C.O.D. 431; (1993) 143 N.L.J. 1403; Times, September 30, 1993; Independent, October 8, 1993, CA (Civ Div); affirming (1993) 5 Admin. L.R. 507; (1993) 157 L.G. Rev. 587; (1993) 137 S.J.L.B. 38, QBD ............ *Digested,* 96/**876**: *Applied* 00/5464: *Considered* 95/4123, 95/4124, 10/370, 13/247, 14/294
R. v Chowdhury (Mohamed Jelu) [2013] EWCA Crim 943; [2014] 1 Cr. App. R. (S.) 27, CA (Crim Div) ............ *Digested,* 14/**2596**
R. v Christie (Michael Anthony) see R. v Smith (Dean Martin)
R. v Clark (Lucy) [2014] EWCA Crim 1053; (2014) 178 J.P. 534, CA (Crim Div)
R. v Clarke (Nicholas Henry) see R. v Preston (Stephen)
R. v Clarke (Ronald Augustus); *joined case* R. v McDaid (James Andrew) [2008] UKHL 8; [2008] 1 W.L.R. 338; [2008] 2 All E.R. 665; [2008] 2 Cr. App. R. 2; [2008] Crim. L.R. 551; (2008) 105(7) L.S.G. 31; (2008) 152(6) S.J.L.B. 28; Times, February 7, 2008, HL; reversing [2006] EWCA Crim 1196; [2006] Crim. L.R. 1011, CA (Crim Div) ............ *Digested,* 08/**829**: *Applied* 14/783: *Considered* 08/715, 08/830, 13/736, 14/775: *Followed* 10/766
R. v Clarke (Wayne) see R. v Smith (Steven)
R. v Clayton (Jonathan James); *joined case* R. v Dockerty (Paul Donald) [2014] EWCA Crim 1030; [2014] 1 W.L.R. 3994; [2014] 2 Cr. App. R. 20; [2014] L.L.R. 723, CA (Crim Div) ............ *Digested,* 14/**717**: *Followed* 14/2379
R. v Clifford (Donald) 9702223 X5, CA (Crim Div) *Considered* 14/770
R. v Clipston (Vincent) [2011] EWCA Crim 446; [2011] 2 Cr. App. R. (S.) 101; [2011] Crim. L.R. 488; (2011) 155(10) S.J.L.B. 30, CA (Crim Div) ............ *Digested,* 11/**583**: *Applied* 14/2611: *Considered* 12/2932
R. v Clucas (Joseph) [1949] 2 K.B. 226; [1949] 2 All E.R. 40; 65 T.L.R. 346; (1949) 33 Cr. App. R. 136; (1949) 113 J.P. 355; 47 L.G.R. 563; [1949] L.J.R. 1571; (1949) 93 S.J. 407, CCA ............ *Digested,* 47-51/**2132**: *Distinguished* 93/991, 14/440
R. v Codling (Sadie) see R. v Bezzina (Anthony)
R. v Coleman (George Romero); *joined case* R. v Petch (Thomas) [2007] EWCA Crim 2318, CA (Crim Div) *Considered* 13/503, 14/2646
R. v Collins (Wayne Courtney) see R. v Lewis (Jermaine Nathaniel)
R. v Collins Ex p. S (No.1) see St George's Healthcare NHS Trust v S
R. v Collins-Reed (Kieren) [2012] EWCA Crim 2036; [2013] 1 Cr. App. R. (S.) 95, CA (Crim Div) ............ *Digested,* 13/**2778**: *Applied* 14/2689
R. v Comerford (Thomas Anthony) [1998] 1 W.L.R. 191; [1998] 1 All E.R. 823; [1998] 1 Cr. App. R. 235; [1998] Crim. L.R. 285; (1997) 94(45) L.S.G. 28; (1997) 141 S.J.L.B. 251; Times, November 3, 1997; Independent, October 31, 1997, CA (Crim Div) ............ *Digested,* 97/**1332**: *Applied* 11/793: *Considered* 14/777
R. v Connors (Costs) [2014] 5 Costs L.R. 942, Sen Cts Costs Office
R. v Connors (James) see R. v Underwood (Kevin John)

R. v Cook (David Charles) [2014] EWCA Crim 137; [2014] 2 Cr. App. R. (S.) 31, CA (Crim Div)

R. v Cooke (John); *joined cases* R. v Wildman (John); R. v Beck (James); R. v Cromwell (Jonathan); R. v Swarez (James); R. v McDonald (Paul); R. v Jolly (David) [2014] EWCA Crim 53, CA (Crim Div)
*Considered* 14/2625

R. v Cordingley (Andrew) [2007] EWCA Crim 2174; [2008] Crim. L.R. 299, CA (Crim Div)
*Distinguished* 14/657

R. v Cory (Rodney Phillip) see R. v Norman (Shane Martin)

R. v Cosford (Karen); *joined cases* R. v Flynn (Jacqueline); R. v Falloon (Carolyn) [2013] EWCA Crim 466; [2014] Q.B. 81; [2013] 3 W.L.R. 1064; [2013] 3 All E.R. 649; [2013] 2 Cr. App. R. 8, CA (Crim Div) ........ *Digested,* 13/**649**: *Applied* 14/694

R. v Coulson (Andrew); *sub nom* R. v Edmondson (Ian); R. v Weatherup (James); R. v Kuttner (Stuart) [2013] EWCA Crim 1026; [2014] 1 W.L.R. 1119; [2013] 4 All E.R. 999; [2013] 2 Cr. App. R. 32; (2013) 177 J.P. 513; [2013] 3 C.M.L.R. 51; Times, August 9, 2013, CA (Crim Div) ........ *Digested,* 13/**644**

R. v Cox (Robert Charles) see R. v Bogacki (Steven)

R. v CP see R. v MI

R. v Craven (Stephen) see R. v Blackshaw (Jordan Philip)

R. v Crawley (Scott); *joined cases* R. v Walker (Dale); R. v Forsyth (Daniel); R. v Petrou (Aaron); R. v Daley (Brendan) [2014] EWCA Crim 1028; [2014] 2 Cr. App. R. 16, CA (Crim Div) ........ *Digested,* 14/**809**

R. v Creathorne (Liam Colin) [2014] EWCA Crim 500; [2014] 2 Cr. App. R. (S.) 48, CA (Crim Div)

R. v Criminal Injuries Compensation Board Ex p. Warner; *joined case* R. v Criminal Injuries Compensation Board Ex p. Webb [1987] Q.B. 74; [1986] 3 W.L.R. 251; [1986] 2 All E.R. 478; (1986) 136 N.L.J. 536; (1986) 130 S.J. 468, CA (Civ Div); affirming [1986] Q.B. 184; [1985] 3 W.L.R. 618; [1985] 2 All E.R. 1069; (1985) 81 Cr. App. R. 355; (1985) 135 N.L.J. 412; (1985) 129 S.J. 432; Times, March 28, 1985, QBD ........ *Digested,* 86/**535**: *Applied* 01/1022, 08/821, 11/2369: *Considered* 00/28: *Followed* 92/5537, 93/5068, 98/927, 14/54

R. v Criminal Injuries Compensation Board Ex p. Webb see R. v Criminal Injuries Compensation Board Ex p. Warner

R. v Criminal Injuries Compensation Board Ex p. Williams [2000] P.I.Q.R. Q339, CA (Civ Div); affirming CO/209/1999, QBD ........ *Digested,* 00/**27**: *Considered* 14/2301

R. v Cromwell (Jonathan) see R. v Cooke (John)

R. v Crown Prosecution Service Ex p. Sorani see R. v Uxbridge Magistrates Court Ex p. Adimi

R. v Culpeper (Jason) see Attorney General's Reference (No.37 of 2013)

R. v Curwen (David John) [2014] EWCA Crim 1046; [2014] 2 Cr. App. R. (S.) 52, CA (Crim Div) ........ *Digested,* 14/**2679**

R. v Customs and Excise Commissioners Ex p. Building Societies Ombudsman Co Ltd see R. (on the application of Building Societies Ombudsman Co Ltd) v Customs and Excise Commissioners

R. v Customs and Excise Commissioners Ex p. Daily Mail (81/87) see R. v HM Treasury Ex p. Daily Mail (81/87)

R. v Customs and Excise Commissioners Ex p. Lunn Poly Ltd [1999] S.T.C. 350; [1999] 1 C.M.L.R. 1357; [1999] Eu. L.R. 653; (1999) 96(13) L.S.G. 32; (1999) 143 S.J.L.B. 104; Times, March 11, 1999, CA (Civ Div); affirming [1998] S.T.C. 649; [1998] 2 C.M.L.R. 560; [1998] Eu. L.R. 438; Times, April 8, 1998, DC ........ *Digested,* 99/**4743**: *Applied* 01/5316, 01/5346, 02/4462: *Followed* 01/118, 02/4420, 14/1225: *Referred to* 05/2380

R. v D [2013] EWCA Crim 465; [2014] 1 W.L.R. 525; [2013] 3 All E.R. 242; (2013) 177 J.P. 361; [2014] Crim. L.R. 141, CA (Crim Div) ........ *Digested,* 13/**603**

R. v D [2013] Eq. L.R. 1034, Crown Ct ........ *Digested,* 14/**769**

R. v D see Attorney General's Reference (No.55 of 2008)

R. v D see R. v Gordon (Gavin Stephen)

R. v D see R. v K

R. v D see R. v Reynolds (Michael Edwin)

R. v Daley (Brendan) see R. v Crawley (Scott)

R. v Dallimore (Paul); *joined cases* R. v Miah (Mohammed Suba); R. v Weeks (Alun) [2013] EWCA Crim 1891; [2014] 1 Cr. App. R. (S.) 31, CA (Crim Div) ........ *Digested,* 14/**2668**

R. v Dance (Bryan) [2013] EWCA Crim 1412; [2014] 1 Cr. App. R. (S.) 51, CA (Crim Div) ........ *Digested,* 14/**2599**

R. v Dang (Hung Tuan) see R. v Dang (Manh Toan)

R. v Dang (Manh Toan); *joined cases* R. v Tu (Thuong); R. v Johnson (Freddie Ross); R. v Le (Tuan Van); R. v Dang (Van Quan); R. v Tran (Hai Ban); R. v Ly (Ngoe Tien); R. v Dang (Nhien Van); R. v Dang (Hung Tuan) [2014] EWCA Crim 348; [2014] 1 W.L.R. 3797; [2014] 2 Cr. App. R. 3; [2014] 2 Cr. App. R. (S.) 49; [2014] Crim. L.R. 675, CA (Crim Div) ........ *Digested,* 14/**681**

R. v Dang (Nhien Van) see R. v Dang (Manh Toan)

R. v Dang (Van Quan) see R. v Dang (Manh Toan)

R. v Datsun (Day); *joined case* R. v Razak (Basil) [2013] EWCA Crim 964; [2014] 1 Cr. App. R. (S.) 25, CA (Crim Div) ........ *Digested,* 14/**2610**

R. v Davey (Neil) [2013] EWCA Crim 1662; [2014] 1 Cr. App. R. (S.) 34, CA (Crim Div) ........ *Digested,* 14/**2697**

R. v Davies (Aby) see R. v Birch (Ben)

R. v Davis (Michael George) (No.1); *joined cases* R. v Johnson (Randolph Egbert) (No.1); R. v Rowe (Raphael George) (No.1) [1993] 1 W.L.R. 613; [1993] 2 All E.R. 643; (1993) 97 Cr. App. R. 110; (1993) 137 S.J.L.B. 19; Times, January 19, 1993; Independent, January 22, 1993, CA (Crim Div) ........ *Digested,* 94/**878**: *Applied* 94/876, 97/1342, 00/5464: *Complaint upheld* 00/3219: *Considered* 94/874, 08/1954, 13/247, 14/400: *Followed* 04/872

R. v Davis (Reginald) see R. v Dyer (Richard)

R. v Dawes (Carlos); *joined cases* R. v Bowyer (Barry Francis); R. v Hatter (Mark John) [2013] EWCA Crim 322; [2014] 1 W.L.R. 947; [2013] 3 All E.R. 308; [2013] 2 Cr. App. R. 3; [2013] Crim. L.R. 770, CA (Crim Div) ........ *Digested,* 13/**651**

R. v Dawson (Timothy) see Attorney General's Reference (Nos 4, 5, 6, 7 and 8 of 2014)

R. v Day (Adrian Harold) [2013] EWCA Crim 1648; [2014] 1 Cr. App. R. (S.) 72, CA (Crim Div) ........ *Digested,* 14/**2603**

R. v de Brito (Paulo Aguiar) [2013] EWCA Crim 1134; [2014] 1 Cr. App. R. (S.) 38, CA (Crim Div) ........ *Digested,* 14/**2700**

R. v De Oliveira [1997] Crim. L.R. 600, CA (Crim Div) *Considered* 14/791

R. v De Silva (Charles) (1994) 15 Cr. App. R. (S.) 296, CA (Crim Div) *Considered* 11/2903, 14/2649

R. v Deacon (Nathan) see Attorney General's Reference (Nos 4, 5, 6, 7 and 8 of 2014)

R. v Deacon (Tafari) see Attorney General's Reference (Nos 4, 5, 6, 7 and 8 of 2014)

R. v Deans (Andrew John) see R. v Wiggins (Liam Roy)

R. v Debnath (Anita) [2005] EWCA Crim 3472; [2006] 2 Cr. App. R. (S.) 25; [2006] Crim. L.R. 451, CA (Crim Div) ........ *Digested,* 06/**855**: *Applied* 14/2672

R. v Department of Health Ex p. Source Informatics Ltd (No.1) [2001] Q.B. 424; [2000] 2 W.L.R. 940; [2000] 1 All E.R. 786; [2000] Eu. L.R. 397; [2001] F.S.R. 8; [2000] Lloyd's Rep. Med. 76; (2000) 52 B.M.L.R. 65; [2000] C.O.D. 76; Times, January 18, 2000; Independent, February 21, 2000, CA (Civ Div); reversing [1999] 4 All E.R. 185; [1999] I.T.C.L.R. 374; [1999] Lloyd's Rep. Med. 264; (1999) 49 B.M.L.R. 41; [1999] C.O.D. 413; Times, June 14, 1999, QBD ........ *Digested,* 00/**2909**: *Distinguished* 14/247

R. v Deputy Chief Constable of Thames Valley Ex p. Cotton see R. v Chief Constable of Thames Valley Ex p. Cotton

R. v Derby Crown Court Ex p. Brooks (1985) 80 Cr. App. R. 164; [1985] Crim. L.R. 754; (1984) 148 J.P.N. 573; Times, August 3, 1984, QBD ........ *Digested,* 85/**485**: *Applied* 86/1521, 89/539, 89/596, 89/650, 91/610, 91/612, 92/616, 92/630, 99/2151, 99/5205: *Considered* 90/2267, 91/605, 91/609, 91/849, 92/933, 93/620, 96/1599, 97/1375, 99/5215, 14/810: *Distinguished* 94/939: *Followed* 97/1258

R. v Dettlaff (Stefen) see R. v Hollinshead (Peter Gordon)

R. v Devon CC Ex p. Baker; *joined cases* R. v Devon CC Ex p. Ruxton; R. v Durham CC Ex p. Curtis [1995] 1 All E.R. 73; 91 L.G.R. 479; (1994) 6 Admin. L.R. 113; [1993] C.O.D. 253; Times, January 21, 1993; Independent, February 22, 1993, CA (Civ Div); affirming [1993] C.O.D. 138; Times, October 20, 1992, QBD ........ *Digested,* 95/**88**: *Applied* 95/3252, 96/5526, 03/4083, 08/70, 14/2802: *Considered* 95/68, 01/6790, 07/45, 09/1738: *Followed* 97/4713: *Referred to* 98/3001

R. v Devon CC Ex p. Ruxton see R. v Devon CC Ex p. Baker

R. v Dhabaneey (Ali Ahmed) [2013] EWCA Crim 2184; [2014] L.L.R. 328, CA (Crim Div)

R. v Dhillon (Rajpaul Singh) see R. v Preddy (John Crawford)

R. v Diane (Hammala) [2009] EWCA Crim 1494; [2010] 2 Cr. App. R. 1, CA (Crim Div) ........ *Digested,* 11/**592**: *Applied* 14/665

R. v Dickson (William Ewing); *joined case* R. v Wright (Raymond Eric) [1991] B.C.C. 719; (1992) 94 Cr. App. R. 7; [1991] Crim. L.R. 854, CA (Crim Div) .................. *Digested,* 92/**998**: *Applied* 99/3280: *Considered* 14/1808
R. v Didonga (Kembo) see R. v Caley (David)
R. v Diggin (Richard Joseph) (1981) 72 Cr. App. R. 204; [1981] R.T.R. 83; [1980] Crim. L.R. 656, CA (Crim Div) .................. *Digested,* 81/**540**: *Considered* 14/2554
R. v Dissanayake (Rohan Shivantha) see R. v Nazari (Fazlollah)
R. v Doblys (Dainotas) [2014] EWCA Crim 402; [2014] 2 Cr. App. R. (S.) 44, CA (Crim Div) .................. *Digested,* 14/**2650**
R. v Dobson (Anthony) [2013] EWCA Crim 1416; [2014] 1 Cr. App. R. (S.) 54, CA (Crim Div) .................. *Digested,* 14/**2684**
R. v Docherty (Shaun Kevin) [2014] EWCA Crim 1197; [2014] 2 Cr. App. R. (S.) 76, CA (Crim Div)
R. v Docherty-Puncheon (Christopher) [2013] EWCA Crim 2027; (2014) 178 J.P. 125, CA (Crim Div) .................. *Digested,* 14/**781**
R. v Dockerty (Paul Donald) see R. v Clayton (Jonathan James)
R. v Dodd (Costs) [2014] 6 Costs L.R. 1131, Sen Cts Costs Office
R. v Dodd (Jonathan) see R. v Smith (Steven)
R. v Doherty (Michael Patrick); *joined case* R. v McGregor (Susan) [1997] 2 Cr. App. R. 218; [1997] Crim. L.R. 520, CA (Crim Div) .................. *Digested,* 97/**1265**: *Considered* 14/718
R. v Doncaster MBC Ex p. Boulton (1993) 25 H.L.R. 195; [1993] C.O.D. 261; (1994) 158 L.G. Rev. 61; (1993) 137 S.J.L.B. 23; Times, December 31, 1992, QBD ..... *Digested,* 93/**3678**: *Applied* 95/4612, 14/1689
R. v Donegan (David) see Attorney General's Reference (No.27 of 2013)
R. v Dosanjh (Sandeep); *joined cases* R. v Gill (Navdeep); R. v Chahal (Ranjot) [2013] EWCA Crim 2366; [2014] 1 W.L.R. 1780; [2014] 2 Cr. App. R. (S.) 25, CA (Crim Div) .................. *Digested,* 14/**2600**
R. v Downes (Tony) see R. v Riley (Craig Philip)
R. v Draz (Omar) see R. v Ashton (John)
R. v Dudley Magistrates Court Ex p. Power City Stores Ltd (1990) 154 J.P. 654; (1990) 154 J.P.N. 490; (1990) 140 N.L.J. 361, QBD .................. *Digested,* 90/**892**: *Applied* 14/747: *Considered* 92/747, 97/540, 04/316: *Followed* 98/468: *Referred to* 96/1571
R. v Dunn (Clare) [2010] EWCA Crim 2935; [2011] 1 Cr. App. R. 34; [2010] M.H.L.R. 349, CA (Crim Div) .................. *Digested,* 11/**790**: *Applied* 14/693: *Followed* 12/801
R. v Dunn (Vincent David) see R. v Round (Terence)
R. v Dunne (Costs) [2013] 6 Costs L.R. 1031, Sen Cts Costs Office .................. *Digested,* 14/**2030**
R. v Durham CC Ex p. Curtis see R. v Devon CC Ex p. Baker
R. v Dyer (Richard); *joined cases* R. v Bailey (Pamela Maria); R. v Pecco (Nadia); R. v Thompson (George Weston); R. v McKrieth (Richard); R. v Edwards (Tanya Francene); R. v Reid (Mark); R. v Davis (Reginald) [2013] EWCA Crim 2114; [2014] 2 Cr. App. R. (S.) 11, CA (Crim Div) .................. *Digested,* 14/**2622**
R. v East Berkshire HA Ex p. Walsh [1985] Q.B. 152; [1984] 3 W.L.R. 818; [1984] 3 All E.R. 425; [1984] I.C.R. 743; [1984] I.R.L.R. 278, CA (Civ Div); reversing Times, November 15, 1983, QBD .................. *Digested,* 84/**14**: *Applied* 86/3554, 87/6, 89/18, 11/65, 14/1492: *Considered* 86/1169, 87/10, 94/14, 95/2076: *Distinguished* 84/12, 85/1181: *Followed* 90/4667
R. v Edgington (Nicola Caroline) [2013] EWCA Crim 2185; [2014] 1 Cr. App. R. 24, CA (Crim Div) .................. *Digested,* 14/**647**
R. v Edirin-Etareri (Jamil) [2014] EWCA Crim 1536; [2014] 2 Cr. App. R. (S.) 82, CA (Crim Div)
R. v Edmondson (Ian) see R. v Coulson (Andrew)
R. v Edwards (Christopher James) [2013] EWCA Crim 728; [2014] 1 Cr. App. R. (S.) 9, CA (Crim Div) .................. *Digested,* 14/**2702**
R. v Edwards (Ian Peter) see R. v Saunders (Red)
R. v Edwards (Tanya Francene) see R. v Dyer (Richard)
R. v Egan (Jason) see R. v Norman (Shane Martin)
R. v Ellames (Charles John) [1974] 1 W.L.R. 1391; [1974] 3 All E.R. 130; (1974) 60 Cr. App. R. 7; [1974] Crim. L.R. 554; (1974) 118 S.J. 578, CA (Crim Div) .......... *Digested,* 74/**758**: *Applied* 14/695: *Considered* 88/843, 95/1297
R. v Elliott (Nathan) [2010] EWCA Crim 2378; (2011) 175 J.P. 39, CA (Crim Div) ........ *Digested,* 11/**585**: *Followed* 14/645
R. v Ellis (Johnathon James) [2014] EWCA Crim 593; [2014] 2 Cr. App. R. (S.) 50, CA (Crim Div) .................. *Digested,* 14/**2676**

R. v Elsayed (Shearif Stephen) [2014] EWCA Crim 333; [2014] 1 W.L.R. 3916, CA (Civ Div) ............ *Digested,* 14/**729**

R. v Elvin (Eric Everton) see R. v Bezzina (Anthony)

R. v EM see R. v M

R. v Emmett (Brian); *joined case* R. v Emmett (Michael) [1998] A.C. 773; [1997] 3 W.L.R. 1119; [1997] 4 All E.R. 737; [1998] 1 Cr. App. R. 247; [1998] Crim. L.R. 413; (1997) 94(46) L.S.G. 29; (1997) 147 N.L.J. 1690; (1997) 141 S.J.L.B. 247; Times, November 17, 1997; Independent, November 18, 1997, HL ............ *Digested,* 97/**1470**: *Applied* 14/727: *Considered* 06/337: *Followed* 00/1169

R. v Emmett (Michael) see R. v Emmett (Brian)

R. v Ernest (Sam) [2014] EWCA Crim 1312; [2014] Lloyd's Rep. F.C. 595, CA (Crim Div) ............ *Digested,* 14/**725**

R. v Evans (Ashley) see R. v Wiggins (Liam Roy)

R. v Evans (Dorothy Gertrude) [2004] EWCA Crim 3102; [2005] 1 W.L.R. 1435; [2005] 1 Cr. App. R. 32; (2005) 169 J.P. 129; [2005] Crim. L.R. 654; (2005) 169 J.P.N. 222; (2005) 102(7) L.S.G. 26; Times, December 10, 2004, CA (Crim Div) ............ *Digested,* 05/**796**: *Applied* 09/759, 14/412: *Considered* 06/824

R. v Evans (Eric) [2014] 1 W.L.R. 2817, Crown Ct (Cardiff) ............ *Digested,* 14/**676**

R. v Evans (Peter) [2005] EWCA Crim 1811; [2006] 1 Cr. App. R. (S.) 64; [2005] Crim. L.R. 876, CA (Crim Div) ............ *Digested,* 06/**3714**: *Considered* 14/2638

R. v Evans-Keady (Aaron) [2013] EWCA Crim 1546; [2014] 1 Cr. App. R. (S.) 66, CA (Crim Div) ............ *Digested,* 14/**2661**

R. v Evwierhowa (John) [2011] EWCA Crim 572; [2011] 2 Cr. App. R. (S.) 77; [2011] Crim. L.R. 498, CA (Crim Div) ............ *Digested,* 11/**740**: *Followed* 14/724

R. v Ezechukwu (Nnamdi Chinedu) see R. v Ezeemo (Godwin Chukwnaenya)

R. v Ezeemo (Chika) see R. v Ezeemo (Godwin Chukwnaenya)

R. v Ezeemo (Godwin Chukwnaenya); *joined cases* R. v Ezechukwu (Nnamdi Chinedu); R. v Orient Export Ltd; R. v Benson (Joseph); R. v Ezeemo (Chika); R. v BJ Electronics Ltd; R. v Reliance Export Ltd [2012] EWCA Crim 2064; [2013] 4 All E.R. 1016; [2014] P.T.S.R. 284; [2013] Env. L.R. 15, CA (Crim Div) *Digested,* 13/**1155**

R. v F; *sub nom* R. v JRF [2013] EWCA Crim 424; [2013] 1 W.L.R. 2143; [2013] 2 Cr. App. R. 13; (2013) 177 J.P. 406; [2014] Crim. L.R. 136, CA (Crim Div) ............ *Digested,* 13/**617**

R. v F Howe & Son (Engineers) Ltd [1999] 2 All E.R. 249; [1999] 2 Cr. App. R. (S.) 37; (1999) 163 J.P. 359; [1999] I.R.L.R. 434; [1999] Crim. L.R. 238; (1999) 163 J.P.N. 693; (1998) 95(46) L.S.G. 34; Times, November 27, 1998; Independent, November 13, 1998, CA (Crim Div) ............ *Digested,* 98/**2839**: *Applied* 99/2860, 01/3296, 03/1922, 03/1923, 06/3713, 07/986, 10/2886, 11/2900, 13/2668, 14/2644: *Considered* 00/2968, 01/1348, 01/1350, 02/3968, 03/3715, 05/1945, 05/3630, 06/1971, 06/3712, 07/3655, 11/1631, 11/2899, 12/2925, 13/3981: *Followed* 99/2858

R. v F see Attorney General's Reference (No.55 of 2008)

R. v Falloon (Carolyn) see R. v Cosford (Karen)

R. v Falmouth and Truro Port HA Ex p. South West Water Ltd; *sub nom* Falmouth and Truro Port HA v South West Water Ltd [2001] Q.B. 445; [2000] 3 W.L.R. 1464; [2000] 3 All E.R. 306; [2000] Env. L.R. 658; [2000] E.H.L.R. 306; (2000) 2 L.G.L.R. 1061; [2001] L.L.R. 45; [2000] J.P.L. 1174 (Note); [2000] E.G. 50 (C.S.); (2000) 97(23) L.S.G. 41; [2000] N.P.C. 36; Times, April 24, 2000, CA (Civ Div); affirming (1999) 163 J.P. 589; [1999] Env. L.R. 833; [1999] E.H.L.R. 358; (1999) 1 L.G.L.R. 941; [1999] C.O.D. 305; (1999) 163 J.P.N. 1025; [1999] E.G. 62 (C.S.); (1999) 96(18) L.S.G. 35; [1999] N.P.C. 49; Times, May 6, 1999, QBD ............ *Digested,* 00/**2304**: *Applied* 01/4550, 04/2764, 10/2298: *Considered* 01/2423, 01/2426, 13/1147: *Followed* 14/2226

R. v Farooqi (Munir Ahmed); *joined cases* R. v Newton (Matthew); R. v Malik (Israr Hussain) [2013] EWCA Crim 1649; [2014] 1 Cr. App. R. 8; [2014] Crim. L.R. 239, CA (Crim Div) ............ *Digested,* 14/**812**

R. v Farrell (Joseph) see R. v Riley (Craig Philip)

R. v Fellows (David) see R. v Lewis (Ian)

R. v Feltham Magistrates Court Ex p. DPP see R. (on the application of Ebrahim) v Feltham Magistrates Court

R. v Feltham Magistrates Court Ex p. Ebrahim see R. (on the application of Ebrahim) v Feltham Magistrates Court

R. v Fenton (Steven) [2006] EWCA Crim 2156; [2007] 1 Cr. App. R. (S.) 97, CA (Crim Div) ............ *Digested,* 07/**3738**: *Applied* 12/3018, 14/2685: *Considered* 07/3726, 09/3508, 10/2986

R. v Fenwick (Paul Terrance) see R. v Kenning (David Matthew)

R. v Ferdinand (Sean) [2014] EWCA Crim 1243; [2014] 2 Cr. App. R. 23, CA (Crim Div) ........ *Digested,* 14/**649**

R. v Fernandez (Joseph) see R. v Nazari (Fazlollah)

R. v Fields (Michael); *joined cases* R. v Sanghani (Mitesh); R. v Sagoo (Karamjit); R. v Rajput (Wasim) [2013] EWCA Crim 2042; [2014] 2 W.L.R. 233; [2014] 2 All E.R. 811; [2014] 2 Cr. App. R. (S.) 13; [2014] Lloyd's Rep. F.C. 42; [2014] Crim. L.R. 462, CA (Crim Div) *Reversed in part* 14/728

R. v Fields (Michael) see R. v Ahmad (Shakeel)

R. v Firfire (Asif) see R. v Cairns (James Philip)

R. v Firth (Peter) [2013] EWCA Crim 1201; [2014] 1 Cr. App. R. (S.) 24, CA (Crim Div) ........ *Digested,* 14/**2647**

R. v Fletcher (Alan) [2012] EWCA Crim 2777; [2013] M.H.L.R. 50, CA (Crim Div) ........ *Digested,* 14/**2645**

R. v Fletcher (Michael John) [2011] EWCA Crim 1802; [2012] 1 Cr. App. R. (S.) 62, CA (Crim Div) ........ *Digested,* 12/**2953**: *Considered* 14/2652

R. v Fleury (Alexis Sebastien) [2013] EWCA Crim 2273; [2014] 2 Cr. App. R. (S.) 14, CA (Crim Div)

R. v Flynn (Jacqueline) see R. v Cosford (Karen)

R. v Ford (Kamahl) [2010] EWCA Crim 2250; [2011] Crim. L.R. 475, CA (Crim Div) *Considered* 14/287

R. v Formhals (Allan) [2013] EWCA Crim 2624; [2014] 1 W.L.R. 2219; [2014] 1 Cr. App. R. 35, CA (Crim Div) ........ *Digested,* 14/**770**

R. v Forsyth (Daniel) see R. v Crawley (Scott)

R. v Fort (Jamie Daniel) [2013] EWCA Crim 2332; [2014] 2 Cr. App. R. (S.) 24, CA (Crim Div) ........ *Digested,* 14/**2649**

R. v Fowles (Herbert) see R. v May (Raymond George)

R. v Francis (Nicholas Shaun) see R. v Lewis (Jermaine Nathaniel)

R. v Fraser (Anthony) see R. v Whitnell (Liam)

R. v French (Costs) [2014] 4 Costs L.R. 786, Sen Cts Costs Office ........ *Digested,* 14/**2037**

R. v French (Geraldine) see R. v Rogers (Bradley David)

R. v Fyad (Ahmed Abid) [2011] EWCA Crim 2039, CA (Crim Div) *Followed* 14/2620

R. v G [2008] UKHL 37; [2009] 1 A.C. 92; [2008] 1 W.L.R. 1379; [2008] 3 All E.R. 1071; [2009] 1 Cr. App. R. 8; [2008] H.R.L.R. 36; [2009] U.K.H.R.R. 72; [2008] Crim. L.R. 818; (2008) 152(25) S.J.L.B. 31; Times, June 20, 2008, HL; affirming [2006] EWCA Crim 821; [2006] 1 W.L.R. 2052; [2006] 2 Cr. App. R. 17; [2006] H.R.L.R. 28; [2006] Crim. L.R. 930; Times, May 9, 2006, CA (Crim Div) ........ *Digested,* 08/**722**: *Applied* 08/3294, 14/1646, 14/674: *Considered* 07/258, 09/4824

R. v G; *joined case* R. v R [2003] UKHL 50; [2004] 1 A.C. 1034; [2003] 3 W.L.R. 1060; [2003] 4 All E.R. 765; [2004] 1 Cr. App. R. 21; (2003) 167 J.P. 621; [2004] Crim. L.R. 369; (2003) 167 J.P.N. 955; (2003) 100(43) L.S.G. 31; Times, October 17, 2003, HL; reversing [2002] EWCA Crim 1992; [2003] 3 All E.R. 206; [2003] 1 Cr. App. R. 23; [2002] Crim. L.R. 926; Times, August 1, 2002; Independent, October 21, 2002, CA (Crim Div) ........ *Digested,* 03/**775**: *Applied* 03/1692, 04/753, 05/3787, 06/836, 08/722, 12/521: *Considered* 14/662

R. v G see R. v Saunders (Red)

R. v Gallone (Paulo) [2014] EWCA Crim 1140; [2014] 2 Cr. App. R. (S.) 57, CA (Crim Div)

R. v Gangar (Shinder Singh); *joined case* R. v White (Alan) [2012] EWCA Crim 1378; [2013] 1 W.L.R. 147; [2012] 4 All E.R. 972; [2013] 1 Cr. App. R. (S.) 67; [2012] Lloyd's Rep. F.C. 671; [2012] Crim. L.R. 808; (2012) 109(28) L.S.G. 21, CA (Crim Div) ........ *Digested,* 13/**695**: *Applied* 14/728

R. v Garness (Costs) [2014] 1 Costs L.R. 201, Sen Cts Costs Office ........ *Digested,* 14/**2035**

R. v Gearing (Helen) see DPP v Withers (Ian Douglas)

R. v Gebru [2011] EWCA Crim 3321, CA (Crim Div) *Applied* 14/2630

R. v Geeling (Anthony Charles) see R. v Lewis (Ian)

R. v George (Andrew Harold) [2006] EWCA Crim 1652, CA (Crim Div) *Considered* 11/573, 14/648

R. v Ghafar (Nusrat) [2009] EWCA Crim 2270, CA (Crim Div) *Considered* 14/791

R. v Ghavami (Amir) see R. v Mateta (Koshi Pitshou)

R. v Ghosh (Deb Baran) [1982] Q.B. 1053; [1982] 3 W.L.R. 110; [1982] 2 All E.R. 689; (1982) 75 Cr. App. R. 154; [1982] Crim. L.R. 608; (1982) 126 S.J. 429, CA (Crim Div) .......... *Digested,* 82/**659**: *Applied* 84/677, 88/841, 90/1140, 90/910, 03/4592, 14/2829: *Cited* 93/771, 94/838: *Considered* 86/608, 87/783, 90/909, 90/911, 91/753, 91/762, 92/652, 92/789, 93/780, 97/3828, 01/2343, 11/3495: *Distinguished* 92/806: *Followed* 96/1512

R. v Gill (Navdeep) see R. v Dosanjh (Sandeep)

R. v Gillespie-Doyle (Michael) see R. v Blackshaw (Jordan Philip)

R. v Gilmore (Vincent Martin) see R. v Hanson (Nicky)

R. v Gittins (Marvin); *joined case* R. v Khan (Safdar) [2007] EWCA Crim 806; [2007] 4 Costs L.R. 549, CA (Crim Div) .......... *Digested,* 10/**2128**: *Applied* 14/2033: *Followed* 08/806

R. v Gjoni (Kujtim) [2014] EWCA Crim 691; [2014] Crim. L.R. 765, CA (Crim Div)

R. v Gloucestershire CC Ex p. Barry; *sub nom* R. v Gloucestershire CC Ex p. Mahfood; *joined cases* R. v Gloucestershire CC Ex p. Dartnell; R. v Gloucestershire CC Ex p. Grinham; R. v Islington LBC Ex p. McMillan; R. v Lancashire CC Ex p. Royal Association for Disability and Rehabilitation [1997] A.C. 584; [1997] 2 W.L.R. 459; [1997] 2 All E.R. 1; (1997) 9 Admin. L.R. 209; (1997-98) 1 C.C.L. Rep. 40; (1997) 36 B.M.L.R. 92; [1997] C.O.D. 304; (1997) 94(14) L.S.G. 25; (1997) 147 N.L.J. 453; (1997) 141 S.J.L.B. 91; Times, March 21, 1997; Independent, April 9, 1997, HL; reversing [1996] 4 All E.R. 421; (1997) 9 Admin. L.R. 69; (1997-98) 1 C.C.L. Rep. 19; (1997) 36 B.M.L.R. 69; [1996] C.O.D. 387; (1996) 93(33) L.S.G. 25; (1996) 140 S.J.L.B. 177; Times, July 12, 1996; Independent, July 10, 1996, CA (Civ Div); reversing 94 L.G.R. 593; (1996) 8 Admin. L.R. 181; (1997-98) 1 C.C.L. Rep. 7; (1996) 30 B.M.L.R. 20; [1996] C.O.D. 67; (1996) 160 L.G. Rev. 321; Times, June 21, 1995; Independent, June 20, 1995, DC .......... *Digested,* 97/**4714**: *Applied* 97/2089, 97/4721, 98/2853, 05/3928, 10/3180: *Considered* 96/5528, 99/3052, 99/4623, 11/3207, 12/3164: *Distinguished* 14/949: *Followed* 95/3225, 96/3029, 96/5530, 97/4711, 98/1674, 13/3443

R. v Gloucestershire CC Ex p. Dartnell see R. v Gloucestershire CC Ex p. Barry

R. v Gloucestershire CC Ex p. Grinham see R. v Gloucestershire CC Ex p. Barry

R. v Gloucestershire CC Ex p. Mahfood see R. v Gloucestershire CC Ex p. Barry

R. v Golding (David) [2014] EWCA Crim 889; [2014] Crim. L.R. 686, CA (Crim Div)

R. v Golds (Mark Richard) [2014] EWCA Crim 748; [2014] 4 All E.R. 64; [2014] 2 Cr. App. R. 17; [2014] Crim. L.R. 744, CA (Crim Div) .......... *Digested,* 14/**778**

R. v Goldsmith (Harold Egan) see R. v Avis (Tony)

R. v Goldstein (Harry Chaim) see R. v Rimmington (Anthony)

R. v Gomes Monteiro (Juranir Silvertre) [2014] EWCA Crim 747; [2014] 2 Cr. App. R. (S.) 62; (2014) 178 J.P. 200, CA (Crim Div) .......... *Digested,* 14/**2646**

R. v Goncalves (Christopher) [2011] EWCA Crim 1703; [2014] 1 W.L.R. 775; [2013] 2 Cr. App. R. 14, CA (Crim Div)

R. v Goodale (Gavin) [2013] EWCA Crim 1144; [2014] 1 Cr. App. R. (S.) 37, CA (Crim Div) .......... *Digested,* 14/**2667**

R. v Goodyear (Karl) [2005] EWCA Crim 888; [2005] 1 W.L.R. 2532; [2005] 3 All E.R. 117; [2005] 2 Cr. App. R. 20; [2006] 1 Cr. App. R. (S.) 6; [2005] Crim. L.R. 659; Times, April 21, 2005, CA (Crim Div) .......... *Digested,* 05/**893**: *Applied* 06/1971, 07/3666, 12/2913, 13/738: *Considered* 07/3678, 08/1403, 08/3311, 14/2641, 14/2655: *Explained* 10/2885, 11/2896: *Followed* 06/3867

R. v Gordon (Gavin Stephen); *joined cases* R. v D; R. v McManus (Kevin Peter); R. v Shaukat (Mirza Hamayou); R. v Pusey (Lloyd Aaron); R. v Taylor (Mark William) [2007] EWCA Crim 165; [2007] 1 W.L.R. 2117; [2007] 2 All E.R. 768; [2007] 2 Cr. App. R. (S.) 66; [2007] Crim. L.R. 402; (2007) 151 S.J.L.B. 264; Times, February 13, 2007, CA (Crim Div) .......... *Digested,* 07/**3735**: *Applied* 07/966, 09/3454, 09/852, 11/2831, 11/757, 14/813: *Considered* 09/3495, 12/3029, 14/2612: *Followed* 08/3399, 11/3065

R. v Gore (Raymond); *joined case* R. v Maher (Timothy) [2009] EWCA Crim 1424; [2009] 1 W.L.R. 2454; [2009] 2 Cr. App. R. 27; (2009) 173 J.P. 505; [2009] Crim. L.R. 879; Times, July 17, 2009, CA (Crim Div) .......... *Digested,* 09/**900**: *Applied* 14/792

R. v Governor of Durham Prison Ex p. Singh; *sub nom* R. v Secretary of State for the Home Department Ex p. Singh [1984] 1 W.L.R. 704; [1984] 1 All E.R. 983; [1983] Imm. A.R. 198; (1984) 128 S.J. 349, QBD .......... *Digested,* 84/**1726**: *Applied* 10/1770, 10/1771, 11/1727, 11/1733, 14/1680: *Approved* 03/2236: *Considered* 95/2726, 96/3278, 05/2161, 08/2031, 09/2100, 10/1779, 11/4382, 11/4384, 13/1602: *Distinguished* 00/3347

R. v Graham (Garry Allan) see R. v Graham (Hemamali Krishna)

R. v Graham (Hemamali Krishna); *joined cases* R. v Kansal (Rupe Lal); R. v Ali (Sajid Pasha); R. v Marsh (Terence Colin); R. v Graham (Garry Allan); R. v Price (Paul Graham); R. v Bramich (David) [1997] 1 Cr. App. R. 302; [1997] Crim. L.R. 340; (1996) 93(44) L.S.G. 29; (1996) 140 S.J.L.B. 253; Times, October 28, 1996; Independent, October 30, 1996, CA (Crim Div) ........ *Digested,* 96/**1532**: *Applied* 97/1228, 98/892, 02/809, 11/652, 11/822, 12/795: *Approved* 00/5480: *Considered* 97/1224, 97/1226, 97/1227, 97/1249, 07/971, 13/717, 14/772: *Distinguished* 07/869: *Followed* 97/1126: *Referred to* 97/1225, 97/1229, 97/1230, 97/1231, 97/1304

R. v Grant (Costs) [2006] 1 Costs L.R. 173, Sup Ct Costs Office *Considered* 14/2033

R. v Gray (Robert) (1989) 11 Cr. App. R. (S.) 123, CA (Crim Div) ........ *Digested,* 91/**1062**: *Considered* 14/2661

R. v Gray (Wesley) see R. v Lewis (Jermaine Nathaniel)

R. v Greatorex (Marcus Jonathan) see R. v Wiggins (Liam Roy)

R. v Greaves (Claude Clifford); *joined cases* R. v Botcher (Henrik); R. v Jenkins (Fraser) [2010] EWCA Crim 709; [2011] 1 Cr. App. R. (S.) 8; [2010] Lloyd's Rep. F.C. 423; [2010] Crim. L.R. 650, CA (Crim Div) ........ *Digested,* 10/**2876**: *Applied* 11/2857: *Considered* 14/2655

R. v Green (Colin) [2013] EWCA Crim 873; [2014] 1 Cr. App. R. (S.) 12, CA (Crim Div)

R. v Green (Mark) [2008] UKHL 30; [2008] 1 A.C. 1053; [2008] 2 W.L.R. 1154; [2008] 4 All E.R. 119; [2008] 2 Cr. App. R. 30; [2009] 1 Cr. App. R. (S.) 32; [2008] Lloyd's Rep. F.C. 473; [2008] Crim. L.R. 740; (2008) 152(21) S.J.L.B. 30; Times, May 19, 2008, HL; affirming [2007] EWCA Crim 1248; [2007] 3 All E.R. 751; Times, June 15, 2007, CA (Crim Div) ........ *Digested,* 08/**775**: *Applied* 09/831, 09/841: *Followed* 10/734, 11/723, 12/756, 14/728

R. v Gribbin (Paul) [2014] EWCA Crim 115; [2014] 2 Cr. App. R. (S.) 28, CA (Crim Div)

R. v Griffiths (Kenneth David) see R. v Hollinshead (Peter Gordon)

R. v Gul (Mohammed) [2013] UKSC 64; [2014] A.C. 1260; [2013] 3 W.L.R. 1207; [2014] 1 All E.R. 463; [2014] 1 Cr. App. R. 14; [2014] Crim. L.R. 315; Times, November 5, 2013, SC; affirming [2012] EWCA Crim 280; [2012] 1 W.L.R. 3432; [2012] 3 All E.R. 83; [2012] 1 Cr. App. R. 37; [2012] Crim. L.R. 645; Times, April 9, 2012, CA (Crim Div) ........ *Digested,* 14/**700**

R. v H [2014] EWCA Crim 1555; (2014) 140 B.M.L.R. 59; [2014] Crim. L.R. 905, CA (Crim Div)

R. v H; *joined case* R. v C [2004] UKHL 3; [2004] 2 A.C. 134; [2004] 2 W.L.R. 335; [2004] 1 All E.R. 1269; [2004] 2 Cr. App. R. 10; [2004] H.R.L.R. 20; 16 B.H.R.C. 332; (2004) 101(8) L.S.G. 29; (2004) 148 S.J.L.B. 183; Times, February 6, 2004; Independent, February 10, 2004, HL; affirming [2003] EWCA Crim 2847; [2003] 1 W.L.R. 3006; [2004] 1 Cr. App. R. 17; (2003) 100(43) L.S.G. 31; Times, October 24, 2003; Independent, November 14, 2003, CA (Crim Div) ........ *Digested,* 04/**798**: *Applied* 05/840, 11/793, 14/708: *Considered* 07/1025, 08/408, 09/768, 11/1328, 11/60: *Followed* 05/875, 09/331, 10/1079

R. v Hackney (Paul) [2013] EWCA Crim 1156; [2014] 1 Cr. App. R. (S.) 41, CA (Crim Div) ........ *Digested,* 14/**2673**

R. v Halane (Hassan) [2014] EWCA Crim 477; [2014] 2 Cr. App. R. (S.) 46, CA (Crim Div) ........ *Digested,* 14/**2593**

R. v Hall (Bryan) see R. v Smith (Steven)

R. v Hall (Clifford) [2013] EWCA Crim 2499; [2014] 2 Cr. App. R. (S.) 20, CA (Crim Div) ........ *Digested,* 14/**2617**

R. v Hall (Glyn David) [2004] EWCA Crim 3052, CA (Crim Div) *Considered* 14/2628

R. v Hall (James Stuart) see Attorney General's Reference (No.38 of 2013)

R. v Hall (Robert) see R. v Wynne (Emmet)

R. v Hall (Ronnie) see R. v Perkins (Robert)

R. v Hall (Terence) (1984) 6 Cr. App. R. (S.) 321; [1985] Crim. L.R. 54, CA (Crim Div) *Digested,* 85/**792**: *Applied* 14/789

R. v Halloway (Hassan) see R. v Blackshaw (Jordan Philip)

R. v Hamed (Ossama) see R. v Abdul (Jonathan)

R. v Hammersmith and Fulham LBC Ex p. Burkett see R. (on the application of Burkett) v Hammersmith and Fulham LBC (No.1)

R. v Hammond (Philip); *joined case* R. v Rybak (Andrew) [2013] EWCA Crim 2636; [2014] 1 W.L.R. 4303; [2014] 2 Cr. App. R. 9, CA (Crim Div) ........ *Digested,* 14/**791**

R. v Hampson (Shane Adam) [2012] EWCA Crim 1807; [2014] 1 Cr. App. R. 4, CA (Crim Div) ........ *Digested,* 14/**665**

R. v Hankin (Thomas David) [2013] EWCA Crim 749; [2014] 1 Cr. App. R. (S.) 7, CA (Crim Div) .......... *Digested,* 14/**2624**

R. v Hanson (John) see Attorney General's Reference (No.27 of 2013)

R. v Hanson (Nicky); *joined cases* R. v Gilmore (Vincent Martin); R. v Pickstone (Robert Alan) [2005] EWCA Crim 824; [2005] 1 W.L.R. 3169; [2005] 2 Cr. App. R. 21; (2005) 169 J.P. 250; [2005] Crim. L.R. 787; (2005) 169 J.P.N. 380; (2005) 149 S.J.L.B. 392; Times, March 24, 2005, CA (Crim Div) .......... *Digested,* 05/**736**: *Applied* 06/778, 06/793, 06/811, 06/813, 07/824, 07/839, 08/685, 09/744: *Considered* 05/725, 05/835, 06/780, 07/826, 07/828, 07/836, 07/838, 08/688, 09/742, 11/573: *Distinguished* 07/822, 09/743: *Followed* 05/726, 14/653

R. v Haq (Shakeel Ahmed) [2014] EWCA Crim 2216; (2014) 178 J.P. 528, CA (Crim Div)

R. v Harding (James Benjamin) see R. v Pitts (Aaron)

R. v Hardy (James) [2013] EWCA Crim 2125; [2014] 1 Cr. App. R. (S.) 70, CA (Crim Div) .......... *Digested,* 14/**2683**

R. v Hareem (Khalid); *joined case* R. v Salih (Miqdad) [2013] EWCA Crim 1470; [2014] 1 Cr. App. R. (S.) 50, CA (Crim Div) .......... *Digested,* 14/**2674**

R. v Harmer (Roy Peter) [2005] EWCA Crim 1; [2005] 2 Cr. App. R. 2; [2005] Crim. L.R. 482, CA (Crim Div) .......... *Digested,* 05/**768**: *Applied* 06/834, 14/675

R. v Harries (Michael John); *joined cases* R. v Kai Ho Fan; R. v S; R. v B; R. v S (Robert Michael) [2007] EWCA Crim 1622; [2008] 1 Cr. App. R. (S.) 47; [2007] Crim. L.R. 820; Times, July 9, 2007, CA (Crim Div) .......... *Digested,* 07/**3624**: *Applied* 14/813

R. v Harrod (Martin) [2013] EWCA Crim 1750; [2014] 1 Cr. App. R. (S.) 76, CA (Crim Div) .......... *Digested,* 14/**2626**

R. v Harvey (Jack Frederick) [2013] EWCA Crim 1104; [2014] 1 W.L.R. 124; [2014] 1 Cr. App. R. (S.) 46; [2013] Lloyd's Rep. F.C. 439, CA (Crim Div) .......... *Digested,* 13/**749**

R. v Hatter (Mark John) see R. v Dawes (Carlos)

R. v Heaney (Dawn) [2011] EWCA Crim 2682, CA (Crim Div) *Considered* 14/2688

R. v Hendon Justices Ex p. DPP [1994] Q.B. 167; [1993] 2 W.L.R. 862; [1993] 1 All E.R. 411; (1993) 96 Cr. App. R. 227; (1993) 157 J.P. 181; [1993] Crim. L.R. 215; [1993] C.O.D. 61; (1992) 156 J.P.N. 746; (1992) 142 N.L.J. 1303; Times, July 15, 1992; Independent, July 9, 1992; Guardian, July 15, 1992, QBD .......... *Digested,* 93/**865**: *Applied* 99/4244: *Considered* 14/764, 14/810

R. v Henry (Derek Nicholas) [2013] EWCA Crim 1415; [2014] 1 Cr. App. R. (S.) 55, CA (Crim Div) .......... *Digested,* 14/**2618**

R. v Hercules (Andrew Michael) (1987) 9 Cr. App. R. (S.) 291, CA (Crim Div) .......... *Digested,* 89/**1112**: *Followed* 14/2620

R. v Hertfordshire CC Ex p. Cheung; *joined case* R. v Sefton MBC Ex p. Pau Times, April 4, 1986, CA (Civ Div); affirming Times, July 15, 1985, QBD .......... *Digested,* 86/**1135**: *Applied* 14/787: *Considered* 10/1432

R. v HM Coroner for North Humberside and Scunthorpe Ex p. Jamieson [1995] Q.B. 1; [1994] 3 W.L.R. 82; [1994] 3 All E.R. 972; (1994) 158 J.P. 1011; [1994] 5 Med. L.R. 217; [1994] C.O.D. 455; Times, April 28, 1994; Independent, April 27, 1994, CA (Civ Div); affirming [1994] C.O.D. 173; Times, July 23, 1993; Independent, October 4, 1993; Guardian, July 12, 1993, QBD .......... *Digested,* 94/**631**: *Applied* 00/50, 01/26, 02/26, 03/13, 04/36, 06/16, 07/27, 09/41, 11/30, 13/37, 14/35: *Considered* 95/872, 95/873, 96/42, 96/44, 96/49, 97/39, 00/49, 01/27, 02/25, 04/12, 04/38, 05/17, 06/17, 06/4528, 09/21, 09/2567: *Disapproved* 04/37: *Followed* 11/3599

R. v HM Coroner for Western Somerset Ex p. Middleton see R. (on the application of Middleton) v HM Coroner for Western Somerset

R. v HM Treasury Ex p. Daily Mail (81/87); *joined case* R. v Customs and Excise Commissioners Ex p. Daily Mail (81/87) [1989] Q.B. 446; [1989] 2 W.L.R. 908; [1989] 1 All E.R. 328; [1988] S.T.C. 787; [1988] E.C.R. 5483; [1989] B.C.L.C. 206; [1988] 3 C.M.L.R. 713; (1989) 133 S.J. 693; Times, September 29, 1988, ECJ .......... *Digested,* 89/**1556**: *Applied* 14/514: *Distinguished* 06/1569: *Followed* 01/2499

R. v Hoath (Terence); *joined case* R. v Standage (Terence Edward) [2011] EWCA Crim 274; [2011] 1 W.L.R. 1656; [2011] 4 All E.R. 306, CA (Crim Div) .......... *Digested,* 11/**3062**: *Followed* 14/2686

R. v Hobson (Andrew Craig) [2013] EWCA Crim 819; [2013] 1 W.L.R. 3733; [2013] 2 Cr. App. R. 27; [2014] Crim. L.R. 83; Times, July 17, 2013, CA (Crim Div) .......... *Digested,* 13/**765**

R. v Hodges (Kevin John); *joined case* R. v Walker (John) [2003] EWCA Crim 290; [2003] 2 Cr. App. R. 15; [2003] Crim. L.R. 472, CA (Crim Div) .......... *Digested,* 03/**743**: *Considered* 11/585: *Followed* 14/645

R. v Hoggard (Barrie) [2013] EWCA Crim 1024; [2014] 1 Cr. App. R. (S.) 42; [2013] Crim. L.R. 782, CA (Crim Div) ........ *Digested,* 14/**2611**

R. v Hollinshead (Peter Gordon); *joined cases* R. v Dettlaff (Stefen); R. v Griffiths (Kenneth David) [1985] A.C. 975; [1985] 3 W.L.R. 159; [1985] 2 All E.R. 769; (1985) 81 Cr. App. R. 365; [1985] Crim. L.R. 653; (1985) 82 L.S.G. 2739; (1985) 135 N.L.J. 631; (1985) 129 S.J. 447, HL; reversing [1985] 2 W.L.R. 761; [1985] 1 All E.R. 850; (1985) 80 Cr. App. R. 285; [1985] Crim. L.R. 301; (1985) 82 L.S.G. 1718; (1985) 129 S.J. 219, CA (Crim Div) ........ *Digested,* 85/**524**: *Applied* 08/723: *Considered* 86/513, 08/723, 14/681: *Distinguished* 90/951

R. v Holtom (Colin Charles) [2010] EWCA Crim 934; [2011] 1 Cr. App. R. (S.) 18, CA (Crim Div) ........ *Digested,* 11/**2944**: *Applied* 12/2949, 13/2688: *Considered* 14/2651

R. v Honore (James) see R. v Reynolds (Michael Edwin)

R. v Hopkins (Annette); *joined case* R. v Priest (Margaret) [2011] EWCA Crim 1513; (2012) 123 B.M.L.R. 1; [2011] M.H.L.R. 357, CA (Crim Div) ........ *Digested,* 12/**801**: *Applied* 14/693

R. v Hopkinson (Jessica Marie) [2013] EWCA Crim 795; [2014] 1 Cr. App. R. 3; [2014] Crim. L.R. 310, CA (Crim Div) ........ *Digested,* 14/**721**

R. v Hounsham (Robin Edward) [2005] EWCA Crim 1366; [2005] Crim. L.R. 991; Times, June 16, 2005, CA (Crim Div) ........ *Digested,* 05/**3343**: *Considered* 14/798

R. v Howe (Kevin James) [2014] EWCA Crim 114; [2014] 2 Cr. App. R. (S.) 38; (2014) 137 B.M.L.R. 115; (2014) 158(8) S.J.L.B. 37, CA (Crim Div) ........ *Digested,* 14/**2595**

R. v Hughes (Michael) [2013] UKSC 56; [2013] 1 W.L.R. 2461; [2013] 4 All E.R. 613; [2014] 1 Cr. App. R. 6; [2013] R.T.R. 31; [2014] Crim. L.R. 234; Times, August 20, 2013, SC; reversing [2011] EWCA Crim 1508; [2011] 4 All E.R. 761, CA (Crim Div) ........ *Digested,* 13/**665**: *Considered* 14/679

R. v Hussain (Abad) [2013] EWCA Crim 2243; [2014] 2 Cr. App. R. (S.) 15, CA (Crim Div)

R. v Hussain (Jameed) see R. v Norman (Shane Martin)

R. v Hussain (Zakir) see R. v Sadique (Omar)

R. v Hussain (Zameer Ejaz) see R. v Okedare (Charles)

R. v HVN see R. v L

R. v Ibori (James Onanefe) [2013] EWCA Crim 815; [2014] 1 Cr. App. R. (S.) 15, CA (Crim Div) ........ *Digested,* 14/**2655**

R. v Igbanoi (Ambrose Otsemobor) see R. v Norman (Shane Martin)

R. v Immigration Appeal Tribunal Ex p. Jeyeanthan see R. v Secretary of State for the Home Department Ex p. Jeyeanthan

R. v Immigration Appeal Tribunal Ex p. Rajendrakumar see R. v Secretary of State for the Home Department Ex p. Ravichandran (No.1)

R. v Immigration Appeal Tribunal Ex p. Sandralingam (No.1) see R. v Secretary of State for the Home Department Ex p. Ravichandran (No.1)

R. v Inland Revenue Commissioners Ex p. MFK Underwriting Agencies see R. v Inland Revenue Commissioners Ex p. MFK Underwriting Agents Ltd

R. v Inland Revenue Commissioners Ex p. MFK Underwriting Agents Ltd; *sub nom* R. v Inland Revenue Commissioners Ex p. MFK Underwriting Agencies [1990] 1 W.L.R. 1545; [1990] 1 All E.R. 91; [1990] S.T.C. 873; 62 T.C. 607; [1990] C.O.D. 143; (1989) 139 N.L.J. 1343; Times, July 17, 1989; Independent, August 7, 1989; Financial Times, July 19, 1989; Guardian, July 20, 1989, QBD *Digested,* 90/**2651**: *Applied* 93/32, 94/651, 96/249, 06/3526, 06/4198, 06/4215, 07/4324, 09/1598, 09/3052, 10/3292, 10/3371, 10/3527, 11/63, 14/1611, 14/2912, 14/3084: *Considered* 93/2254, 94/2569, 97/4107, 00/5365, 10/4587, 11/3573: *Followed* 02/1701, 02/46, 09/4130, 12/3277

R. v Inland Revenue Commissioners Ex p. Morgan Grenfell & Co Ltd see R. (on the application of Morgan Grenfell & Co Ltd) v Special Commissioners of Income Tax

R. v Inland Revenue Commissioners Ex p. Rossminster Ltd; *sub nom* Rossminster and Tucker, Re; Inland Revenue Commissioners v Rossminster Ltd [1980] A.C. 952; [1980] 2 W.L.R. 1; [1980] 1 All E.R. 80; [1980] S.T.C. 42; (1980) 70 Cr. App. R. 157; [1979] T.R. 427, HL; reversing [1979] 3 All E.R. 385; [1979] S.T.C. 688; 52 T.C. 160; [1979] T.R. 312; [1980] Crim. L.R. 111; (1979) 123 S.J. 586, CA (Civ Div); reversing [1979] S.T.C. 677; [1979] T.R. 287; (1979) 123 S.J. 554, QBD ........ *Digested,* 80/**2278**: *Applied* 91/2104, 97/1362, 99/4767: *Considered* 82/2572, 89/667, 97/5033, 00/1098: *Followed* 14/1186: *Not applied* 89/3081

R. v Inwood (Roland Joseph) (1974) 60 Cr. App. R. 70, CA (Crim Div) ........................ *Digested,* 75/**699**: *Applied* 91/1052: *Considered* 85/776, 89/964, 97/1715, 10/1071, 14/2608: *Explained* 77/2592
R. v Iqbal (Faisal) [2012] EWCA Crim 766, CA (Crim Div) *Applied* 14/776
R. v Iqbal (Zaffar) see Revenue and Customs Prosecutions Office v Iqbal
R. v Irving (Mark) see R. v Irving (Westley)
R. v Irving (Neil); *joined case* R. v Squires (Mark) [2010] EWCA Crim 189; [2010] 2 Cr. App. R. (S.) 75; [2010] Crim. L.R. 433; Times, February 10, 2010, CA (Crim Div) .................. *Digested,* 11/**2831**: *Considered* 14/2611, 14/2612
R. v Irving (Westley); *joined case* R. v Irving (Mark) [2013] EWCA Crim 1932; [2014] 2 Cr. App. R. (S.) 6, CA (Crim Div)
R. v Islam (Samsul) [2009] UKHL 30; [2009] 1 A.C. 1076; [2009] 3 W.L.R. 1; [2010] 1 All E.R. 493; [2010] 1 Cr. App. R. (S.) 42; [2009] Lloyd's Rep. F.C. 513; [2009] Crim. L.R. 751; (2009) 106(25) L.S.G. 16; Times, June 12, 2009, HL; reversing [2008] EWCA Crim 1740; [2009] 1 Cr. App. R. (S.) 83; [2008] Crim. L.R. 986, CA (Crim Div) .................. *Digested,* 09/**843**: *Applied* 14/729: *Considered* 10/733
R. v Isleworth Crown Court Ex p. King (Murray) see R. (on the application of King) v Isleworth Crown Court
R. v Islington LBC Ex p. McMillan see R. v Gloucestershire CC Ex p. Barry
R. v ITN News; *sub nom* ITN News Ltd, Re [2013] EWCA Crim 773; [2014] 1 W.L.R. 199; [2013] 2 Cr. App. R. 22; [2013] E.M.L.R. 22; [2014] Crim. L.R. 375, CA (Crim Div) .................. *Digested,* 13/**758**
R. v J; *sub nom* R. v JFJ [2013] EWCA Crim 569; [2014] Q.B. 561; [2014] 2 W.L.R. 701; [2013] 2 Cr. App. R. 10; (2013) 177 J.P. 588; [2013] Crim. L.R. 988, CA (Crim Div) .................. *Digested,* 13/**674**: *Considered* 14/764
R. v J; *joined cases* R. v S; R. v V; R. v B [2013] EWCA Crim 2287; [2014] 1 W.L.R. 1857; [2014] 3 All E.R. 301; [2014] 1 Cr. App. R. 21; [2014] Lloyd's Rep. F.C. 87; [2014] Crim. L.R. 534, CA (Crim Div) .................. *Digested,* 14/**678**
R. v J [2014] EWCA Crim 1442; [2014] 2 Cr. App. R. (S.) 77, CA (Crim Div)
R. v Jaddi (Sina) [2012] EWCA Crim 2565, CA (Crim Div) *Followed* 14/696
R. v Jagne (Shireen) see R. v Boakye (Christiana)
R. v Jalibaghodelehzi [2014] 4 Costs L.R. 781, Sen Cts Costs Office .................. *Digested,* 14/**2028**
R. v Japes [1994] Crim. L.R. 605, CA (Crim Div) .................. *Digested,* 95/**1088**: *Applied* 14/779
R. v Jawad (Mohid) [2013] EWCA Crim 644; [2013] 1 W.L.R. 3861; [2014] 1 Cr. App. R. (S.) 16; (2013) 177 J.P. 436; [2013] Crim. L.R. 698, CA (Crim Div) .................. *Digested,* 13/**691**: *Applied* 14/794
R. v Jenkin (John) see Attorney General's Reference (No.34 of 2014)
R. v Jenkins (Edward John) see R. v Wilson (Clarence George)
R. v Jenkins (Fraser) see R. v Greaves (Claude Clifford)
R. v Jenkins (Ronald Patrick) see R. v Wilson (Clarence George)
R. v Jepson (Matthew Joseph) [2013] EWCA Crim 1362; [2014] 1 Cr. App. R. (S.) 43, CA (Crim Div) .................. *Digested,* 14/**2607**
R. v JFJ see R. v J
R. v JK see R. v MI
R. v Johal (Jaswinder Singh) [2013] EWCA Crim 647; [2014] 1 W.L.R. 146, CA (Crim Div) .................. *Digested,* 14/**742**
R. v John (Leon) [2014] EWCA Crim 1240; [2014] 2 Cr. App. R. (S.) 73, CA (Crim Div)
R. v Johnson (Christopher) [2014] EWCA Crim 849; [2014] 2 Cr. App. R. (S.) 47, CA (Crim Div) .................. *Digested,* 14/**2695**
R. v Johnson (Freddie Ross) see R. v Dang (Manh Toan)
R. v Johnson (Randolph Egbert) (No.1) see R. v Davis (Michael George) (No.1)
R. v Johnson (Remmond Theo) see R. v Nnaji (Ogechuku Ferdinand)
R. v Jolleys (Robert) Ex p. Press Association [2013] EWCA Crim 1135; [2014] 1 Cr. App. R. 15; [2014] E.M.L.R. 16, CA (Crim Div) .................. *Digested,* 14/**801**
R. v Jolly (David) see R. v Cooke (John)

R. v Jones (Margaret); *joined cases* R. v Milling (Arthur Paul); R. v Olditch (Toby); R. v Pritchard (Philip); R. v Richards (Josh); Ayliffe v DPP; Swain v DPP [2006] UKHL 16; [2007] 1 A.C. 136; [2006] 2 W.L.R. 772; [2006] 2 All E.R. 741; [2006] 2 Cr. App. R. 9; [2007] Crim. L.R. 66; [2006] A.C.D. 52; (2006) 170 J.P.N. 263; (2006) 103(15) L.S.G. 20; (2006) 156 N.L.J. 600; Times, March 30, 2006, HL; affirming [2004] EWCA Crim 1981; [2005] Q.B. 259; [2004] 3 W.L.R. 1362; [2004] 4 All E.R. 955; [2005] 1 Cr. App. R. 12; [2005] Crim. L.R. 122; [2005] A.C.D. 5; (2004) 148 S.J.L.B. 1149; Times, July 30, 2004, CA (Crim Div); affirming in part (Unreported, May 12, 2004), Crown Ct (Bristol) ........................ *Digested,* 06/**835**: *Applied* 05/754, 06/2622, 07/2234, 12/668: *Followed* 14/667

R. v Jonsyn (Tyron Joseph) [2013] EWCA Crim 1655; [2014] 1 Cr. App. R. (S.) 67, CA (Crim Div) .......... *Digested,* 14/**2642**

R. v Joseph-Bell (Jonathan) see R. v Whitnell (Liam)

R. v Joy (David) [2007] EWCA Crim 3281, CA (Crim Div) *Explained* 14/2601

R. v JRF see R. v F

R. v K; *joined cases* R. v D; R. v M [2013] EWCA Crim 649; [2014] 1 Cr. App. R. (S.) 5, CA (Crim Div) .......... *Digested,* 14/**2605**

R. v Kai Ho Fan see R. v Harries (Michael John)

R. v Kajla (Jaspal) see R. v Khan (Imran)

R. v Kallakis (Achilleas Michalis) see Attorney General's Reference (Nos 7 and 8 of 2013)

R. v Kamwiziku (Placide) see R. v Caley (David)

R. v Kansal (Rupe Lal) see R. v Graham (Hemamali Krishna)

R. v Kapoor (Saran Singh); *joined cases* R. v Sarna (Subir Singh); R. v Chawla (Davinder Singh); R. v Singh (Nermon) [2012] EWCA Crim 435; [2012] 1 W.L.R. 3569; [2012] 2 All E.R. 1205; [2012] 2 Cr. App. R. 11, CA (Crim Div) ..... *Digested,* 12/**1687**: *Distinguished* 14/690

R. v Kasprzak (Marcin) [2013] EWCA Crim 1531; [2014] 1 Cr. App. R. (S.) 20, CA (Crim Div) .......... *Digested,* 14/**2629**

R. v Kayani (Talib Hussein); *joined case* R. v Solliman (Madhat) [2011] EWCA Crim 2871; [2012] 1 W.L.R. 1927; [2012] 2 All E.R. 641; [2012] 1 Cr. App. R. 16; [2012] 2 Cr. App. R. (S.) 38; [2012] 1 F.L.R. 824; [2012] 2 F.C.R. 219; [2012] Crim. L.R. 232; [2012] Fam. Law 259; Times, January 11, 2012, CA (Crim Div) *Digested,* 12/**678**: *Applied* 13/2603: *Considered* 12/2853, 13/2749, 14/1334

R. v KCS Products see R. v Searle (Terence)

R. v Kelham (Damien Anthony) see R. v Mitchell (Billy Richard)

R. v Kelly (Paul Anthony); *joined case* R. v McGirr (Christopher St John) [2014] EWCA Crim 1141; [2014] 2 Cr. App. R. (S.) 70, CA (Crim Div) .......... *Digested,* 14/**2625**

R. v Kenning (David Matthew); *joined cases* R. v Fenwick (Paul Terrance); R. v Blackshaw (Paul James) [2008] EWCA Crim 1534; [2009] Q.B. 221; [2008] 3 W.L.R. 1306; [2008] 2 Cr. App. R. 32; [2009] Crim. L.R. 37; Times, July 10, 2008, CA (Crim Div) .......... *Digested,* 08/**723**: *Considered* 14/681

R. v Kenyon (Lindsay) [2013] EWCA Crim 2123; [2014] 1 Cr. App. R. (S.) 71, CA (Crim Div) .......... *Digested,* 14/**2688**

R. v Kerrigan (David Joseph); *joined case* R. v Walker (Nicholas) [2014] EWCA Crim 2348; (2014) 158(42) S.J.L.B. 37, CA (Crim Div)

R. v Khan (Imran); *joined cases* R. v Kajla (Jaspal); R. v Mahmood (Amjed Khan) [2013] EWCA Crim 2230; [2014] Crim. L.R. 520, CA (Crim Div)

R. v Khan (Kazim Ali); *joined cases* R. v R. v Khan (Mohammed Ahsan); R. v Khan (Mohammed Arfan); R. v Khan (Umar) [2013] EWCA Crim 800; [2014] 1 Cr. App. R. (S.) 10; [2013] Crim. L.R. 704, CA (Crim Div) .......... *Digested,* 14/**2681**: *Considered* 14/2625

R. v Khan (Majid) see R. v Mahmood (Asad)

R. v Khan (Mohammed Arfan) see R. v Khan (Kazim Ali)

R. v Khan (Mohammed Iftiyaz) see R. v Underwood (Kevin John)

R. v Khan (Safdar) see R. v Gittins (Marvin)

R. v Khan (Umar) see R. v Khan (Kazim Ali)

R. v Kimpriktzis (Stelios) [2013] EWCA Crim 734; [2014] 1 Cr. App. R. (S.) 6, CA (Crim Div) .......... *Digested,* 14/**2687**

R. v King (Frederick) [2014] EWCA Crim 971; [2014] 2 Cr. App. R. (S.) 61, CA (Crim Div)

R. v King (Rebecca Mary) [2013] EWCA Crim 1599; [2014] 1 Cr. App. R. (S.) 73, CA (Crim Div) .......... *Digested,* 14/**2653**

R. v King (Scott) [2014] EWCA Crim 621; [2014] 2 Cr. App. R. (S.) 54; [2014] Lloyd's Rep. F.C. 423, CA (Crim Div) .......... *Digested,* 14/**733**

R. v Kirk (Kieran Wesley) see R. v Bailey (Wayne)

R. v Kisieliauskas (Paulius) [2010] EWCA Crim 1553, CA (Crim Div)
*Applied* 14/2654
R. v Kluxen (Patricia); *joined case* R. v Roastas (German) [2010] EWCA Crim 1081; [2011] 1 W.L.R. 218; [2011] 1 Cr. App. R. (S.) 39; [2010] I.N.L.R. 593; [2010] Crim. L.R. 657, CA (Crim Div) ........ *Digested,* 11/**807**:
*Applied* 13/2732: *Considered* 13/2731, 14/2664
R. v Knight (Glenn) see R. v Pitts (Aaron)
R. v Knight (Ian) see R. v Wynne (Emmet)
R. v Kovvali (Bala Subrahmanyam) [2013] EWCA Crim 1056; [2014] 1 Cr. App. R. (S.) 33, CA (Crim Div) ........ *Digested,* 14/**2651**
R. v Koyunco (Hassan) see R. v Blackshaw (Jordan Philip)
R. v Kumar (Durrell) see Attorney General's Reference (Nos 4, 5, 6, 7 and 8 of 2014)
R. v Kunaratnam (Pirunthan) see R. v Rajakumar (Aathavan)
R. v Kuttner (Stuart) see R. v Coulson (Andrew)
R. v Kwaik (Abid Abu) [2013] EWCA Crim 2397; [2014] Crim. L.R. 454, CA (Crim Div)
R. v L; *joined cases* R. v HVN; R. v THN; R. v T [2013] EWCA Crim 991; [2014] 1 All E.R. 113; [2013] 2 Cr. App. R. 23; [2014] Crim. L.R. 150; Times, October 03, 2013, CA (Crim Div) ........ *Digested,* 13/**671**
R. v L (Abraham) see R. v R (Amer)
R. v L see R. v Reynolds (Michael Edwin)
R. v Laidley (Tyrone Martell) see R. v Lewis (Jermaine Nathaniel)
R. v Laing (Beniha) see R. v Lewis (Jermaine Nathaniel)
R. v Lamaletie (Mervyn); *joined case* R. v Royce (Karen) [2008] EWCA Crim 314; (2008) 172 J.P. 249; (2008) 172 J.P.N. 491; (2008) 152(10) S.J.L.B. 28, CA (Crim Div) ........ *Digested,* 08/**717**:
*Considered* 11/573, 14/648
R. v Lancashire CC Ex p. CM (A Minor) [1989] 2 F.L.R. 279; [1989] Fam. Law 395; (1990) 154 L.G. Rev. 112; (1989) 86(17) L.S.G. 37; (1989) 133 S.J. 484, CA (Civ Div); affirming Independent, November 21, 1988, QBD ........ *Digested,* 90/**1797**:
*Applied* 99/1898, 14/942: *Followed* 96/2474
R. v Lancashire CC Ex p. Royal Association for Disability and Rehabilitation see R. v Gloucestershire CC Ex p. Barry
R. v Larsen (John) [2014] EWCA Crim 1514; [2014] 2 Cr. App. R. (S.) 81, CA (Crim Div)
R. v Latchman (Dona Narisa) see R. v Boakye (Christiana)
R. v Lawrence (Nyira) [2013] EWCA Crim 1054; [2014] 1 W.L.R. 106; [2013] 2 Cr. App. R. 24; [2014] Crim. L.R. 237, CA (Crim Div) ........ *Digested,* 13/**717**
R. v Lawrence (Robert) see R. v Whitnell (Liam)
R. v Lawrence (Steven) see R. v May (Raymond George)
R. v Le (Tuan Van) see R. v Dang (Manh Toan)
R. v Leacock (Mark) [2013] EWCA Crim 1994; [2014] 2 Cr. App. R. (S.) 12, CA (Crim Div) ........ *Digested,* 14/**2612**
R. v Leicester Crown Court Ex p. Customs and Excise Commissioners see R. (on the application of Customs and Excise Commissioners) v Leicester Crown Court
R. v Leigh (Kevin) see R. v Bell (David)
R. v Levene (Nicholas David) see Attorney General's Reference (Nos 7 and 8 of 2013)
R. v Levey (Stephen) [2006] EWCA Crim 1902; [2006] 1 W.L.R. 3092; [2007] 1 Cr. App. R. 1; [2007] 1 F.L.R. 462; [2006] 2 F.C.R. 724; [2007] Crim. L.R. 472; [2006] Fam. Law 1021; Times, August 24, 2006, CA (Crim Div) ........ *Digested,* 06/**896**:
*Applied* 07/1022, 09/1520: *Considered* 08/287, 14/1330
R. v Lewes Crown Court Ex p. Hill (1991) 93 Cr. App. R. 60; [1991] Crim. L.R. 376; [1991] C.O.D. 197; Times, November 12, 1990, QBD ........ *Digested,* 92/**981**:
*Applied* 10/787, 14/803: *Considered* 94/1021
R. v Lewis (Ian); *joined cases* R. v Geeling (Anthony Charles); R. v Fellows (David) [2013] EWCA Crim 776, CA (Crim Div)
*Considered* 14/777
R. v Lewis (Jermaine Nathaniel); *joined cases* R. v Francis (Nicholas Shaun); R. v Rehman (Amirul); R. v Laidley (Tyrone Martell); R. v Collins (Wayne Courtney); R. v Laing (Beniha); R. v Gray (Wesley) [2014] EWCA Crim 48; [2014] 2 Cr. App. R. (S.) 27, CA (Crim Div) ........ *Digested,* 14/**645**
R. v Lewis (Kenny Martyn) [2010] EWCA Crim 579; [2010] 2 Cr. App. R. (S.) 104, CA (Crim Div) ........ *Digested,* 10/**2902**:
*Considered* 12/2952, 12/2953, 14/2652
R. v Lewis (Leroy) [2013] EWCA Crim 2596; [2014] 1 W.L.R. 2027; [2014] 1 Cr. App. R. 25, CA (Crim Div) ........ *Digested,* 14/**776**
R. v Lingu (Daniel) [2013] EWCA Crim 825; [2014] 1 Cr. App. R. (S.) 21, CA (Crim Div) ........ *Digested,* 14/**2703**

R. v Lister (Craig) [2009] EWCA Crim 210, CA (Crim Div)
*Considered* 14/2628

R. v Lloyd (Derek William) [1967] 1 Q.B. 175; [1966] 2 W.L.R. 13; [1966] 1 All E.R. 107 (Note); (1966) 50 Cr. App. R. 61; (1966) 130 J.P. 118; (1965) 109 S.J. 955, CCA ........ *Digested,* 66/**2637**:
*Applied* 11/647: *Approved* 92/798: *Considered* 84/653, 14/778

R. v London County Quarter Sessions Appeals Committee Ex p. Rossi; *sub nom* Rossi, Re [1956] 1 Q.B. 682; [1956] 2 W.L.R. 800; [1956] 1 All E.R. 670; (1956) 120 J.P. 239; (1956) 100 S.J. 225, CA ........ *Digested,* 56/**5423**:
*Applied* 70/1975, 74/2128, 89/2125, 90/4586, 96/1174: *Considered* 58/2976, 67/1449, 68/618, 70/2570, 72/2826, 72/2830, 72/3086, 81/2354, 87/1363, 88/1848, 88/1858, 89/2127, 90/2782, 10/771: *Distinguished* 59/2887, 66/11845, 69/576, 97/2227, 99/3667: *Followed* 72/3365, 12/462: *Not applied* 14/2379

R. v London Rent Assessment Committee Ex p. Hanson see Hanson v Church Commissioners for England

R. v London South and South West Region Mental Health Review Tribunal Ex p. M [2000] Lloyd's Rep. Med. 143; [1999] M.H.L.R. 195; Times, February 10, 2000, QBD ........ *Digested,* 00/**4174**:
*Considered* 14/2163

R. v Lopez (Junior Clarke) [2013] EWCA Crim 1744; [2014] Crim. L.R. 384, CA (Crim Div)

R. v Louca (Anastasis) [2013] EWCA Crim 2090; [2014] 2 Cr. App. R. (S.) 9, CA (Crim Div) ........ *Digested,* 14/**738**

R. v Lowndes (David Paul) [2013] EWCA Crim 1747; [2014] 1 Cr. App. R. (S.) 75, CA (Crim Div) ........ *Digested,* 14/**2620**

R. v Lubwama (Abdul Musisi) see R. v Reynolds (Michael Edwin)

R. v Ludlow (Edward Alexander) see Ludlow v Commissioner of Police of the Metropolis

R. v Ly (Ngoe Tien) see R. v Dang (Manh Toan)

R. v M; *sub nom* R. v EM [2014] EWCA Crim 1523; [2014] 2 Cr. App. R. 29; (2014) 178 J.P. 387, CA (Crim Div) ........ *Digested,* 14/**648**

R. v M [2014] EWCA Crim 1457; [2014] Crim. L.R. 823, CA (Crim Div)

R. v M; *sub nom* Revenue and Customs Prosecutions Office v M [2009] EWCA Crim 214; [2009] 2 Cr. App. R. (S.) 66; [2009] Crim. L.R. 469, CA (Crim Div) ........ *Digested,* 09/**960**:
*Applied* 11/731, 11/848: *Considered* 12/755, 14/727

R. v M [2013] EWCA Crim 206, CA (Crim Div)
*Applied* 14/2640

R. v M (Faisal Jamil) see R. v R (Amer)

R. v M see R. v K

R. v Mackle (Benedict) see R. v Mackle (Plunkett Jude)

R. v Mackle (Patrick) see R. v Mackle (Plunkett Jude)

R. v Mackle (Plunkett Jude); *joined cases* R. v Mackle (Benedict); R. v Mackle (Patrick); R. v McLaughlin (Henry) [2014] UKSC 5; [2014] A.C. 678; [2014] 2 W.L.R. 267; [2014] 2 All E.R. 170; [2014] N.I. 292; [2014] 2 Cr. App. R. (S.) 33; [2014] Lloyd's Rep. F.C. 253; Times, February 10, 2014, SC ........ *Digested,* 14/**727**:
*Followed* 14/728

R. v Mahboob (Najamul Saqib); *joined case* R. v Tuohy (Paul) [2014] EWCA Crim 1123; [2014] 2 Cr. App. R. (S.) 67, CA (Crim Div)

R. v Maher (Timothy) see R. v Gore (Raymond)

R. v Mahil (Mundill Kaur); *joined cases* R. v Peters (Darren); R. v Shoker (Harinder) [2013] EWCA Crim 673; [2014] 1 Cr. App. R. (S.) 18, CA (Crim Div) ........ *Digested,* 14/**771**

R. v Mahmood (Amjed Khan) see R. v Khan (Imran)

R. v Mahmood (Asad); *joined case* R. v Khan (Majid) [2013] EWCA Crim 2356; [2014] 1 Cr. App. R. 31; [2014] Crim. L.R. 518, CA (Crim Div) ........ *Digested,* 14/**650**

R. v Maidstone Crown Court Ex p. Harrow LBC [2000] Q.B. 719; [2000] 2 W.L.R. 237; [1999] 3 All E.R. 542; [2000] 1 Cr. App. R. 117; (2000) 53 B.M.L.R. 27; [1999] Crim. L.R. 838; (1999) 96(21) L.S.G. 38; Times, May 14, 1999, QBD ........ *Digested,* 99/**99**:
*Applied* 14/800: *Considered* 02/3228: *Distinguished* 01/1118, 07/21, 08/772

R. v Maitland-Thomas (Kay) [2013] EWCA Crim 1063; [2014] 1 Cr. App. R. (S.) 22, CA (Crim Div) ........ *Digested,* 14/**2591**

R. v Major (Tara) [2010] EWCA Crim 3016; [2011] 1 Cr. App. R. 25; [2011] 2 Cr. App. R. (S.) 26; [2011] Crim. L.R. 328; Times, December 14, 2010, CA (Crim Div) .... *Digested,* 11/**692**:
*Applied* 12/656, 14/2671: *Considered* 12/2987

R. v Makai (Atilla) [2007] EWCA Crim 1652; [2008] 1 Cr. App. R. (S.) 73; (2007) 151 S.J.L.B. 989, CA (Crim Div) ........ *Digested,* 08/**3396**:
*Considered* 14/648

R. v Makuwa (Liliane) [2006] EWCA Crim 175; [2006] 1 W.L.R. 2755; [2006] 2 Cr. App. R. 11; [2006] Crim. L.R. 911; Times, April 28, 2006, CA (Crim Div) ........... *Digested,* 06/**804**: *Applied* 13/656: *Considered* 11/681: *Followed* 14/696

R. v Malik (Israr Hussain) see R. v Farooqi (Munir Ahmed)

R. v Mallourides (Philip) see R. v Randhawa (Jagprit)

R. v Manchester Crown Court Ex p. DPP; *sub nom* Huckfield, Re [1993] 1 W.L.R. 1524; [1993] 4 All E.R. 928; (1994) 98 Cr. App. R. 461; [1994] 1 C.M.L.R. 457; (1993) 143 N.L.J. 1711; Times, November 26, 1993; Independent, December 7, 1993, HL; reversing [1993] 1 W.L.R. 693; [1993] 1 All E.R. 801; (1993) 96 Cr. App. R. 210; [1992] 3 C.M.L.R. 329; [1993] Crim. L.R. 377; [1993] C.O.D. 123; (1992) 136 S.J.L.B. 235; Times, July 29, 1992; Independent, July 3, 1992, QBD .......... *Digested,* 94/**19**: *Applied* 05/71, 07/940: *Considered* 94/35, 95/23, 95/24, 95/969, 09/40, 14/719: *Distinguished* 93/11: *Followed* 96/1550, 98/96

R. v Manchester Crown Court Ex p. M (A Child) see R. (on the application of McCann) v Manchester Crown Court

R. v Mandair (Singh Mandair) [1995] 1 A.C. 208; [1994] 2 W.L.R. 700; [1994] 2 All E.R. 715; (1994) 99 Cr. App. R. 250; (1994) 158 J.P. 685; [1994] Crim. L.R. 666; (1994) 158 J.P.N. 388; (1994) 91(24) L.S.G. 46; (1994) 144 N.L.J. 708; (1994) 138 S.J.L.B. 123; Times, May 20, 1994; Independent, May 20, 1994, HL; reversing (1994) 99 Cr. App. R. 55; [1993] Crim. L.R. 679, CA (Crim Div) ... *Digested,* 94/**1132**: *Considered* 14/772

R. v Mangham (Glen Steven) [2012] EWCA Crim 973; [2013] 1 Cr. App. R. (S.) 11, CA (Crim Div) .......... *Digested,* 13/**2594**: *Considered* 14/2609

R. v Marine A; *joined case* Marine A v Judge Advocate General [2013] EWCA Crim 2367; [2014] 1 W.L.R. 3326; [2014] 1 Cr. App. R. 26; [2014] E.M.L.R. 10; [2014] Crim. L.R. 536, CMAC .......... *Digested,* 14/**664**

R. v Marquez (Shaun) see R. v Avis (Tony)

R. v Marsh (Terence Colin) see R. v Graham (Hemamali Krishna)

R. v Martin (Anthony Edward) [2001] EWCA Crim 2245; [2003] Q.B. 1; [2002] 2 W.L.R. 1; [2002] 1 Cr. App. R. 27; [2002] Crim. L.R. 136; (2001) 98(46) L.S.G. 35; (2001) 145 S.J.L.B. 253; Times, November 1, 2001, CA (Crim Div) ............ *Digested,* 01/**1054**: *Considered* 14/691

R. v Martin (Conner) [2013] EWCA Crim 2565; [2014] 2 Cr. App. R. (S.) 21, CA (Crim Div) .......... *Digested,* 14/**2641**

R. v Martin (Lewys Stephen) [2013] EWCA Crim 1420; [2014] 1 Cr. App. R. (S.) 63, CA (Crim Div) .......... *Digested,* 14/**2609**

R. v Martin (Selina Elizabeth) [2006] EWCA Crim 1035; [2007] 1 Cr. App. R. (S.) 3; Times, June 6, 2006, CA (Crim Div) .......... *Digested,* 06/**3691**: *Considered* 14/2667

R. v Martin (Stephen) see R. v Allpress (Sylvia)

R. v Mason (Craig William) [2013] EWCA Crim 1666; [2014] 1 Cr. App. R. (S.) 78, CA (Crim Div) .......... *Digested,* 14/**2660**

R. v Masterson (Gordon Robert) [2009] EWCA Crim 1059; [2010] 1 Cr. App. R. (S.) 20, CA (Crim Div) .......... *Digested,* 10/**2842**: *Considered* 14/2590

R. v Mateta (Koshi Pitshou); *joined cases* R. v Andukwa (Simon Ebunji); R. v Bashir (Yasin); R. v Afshar (Saeideh); R. v Ghavami (Amir) [2013] EWCA Crim 1372; [2014] 1 W.L.R. 1516; [2014] 1 All E.R. 152; [2013] 2 Cr. App. R. 35; [2014] Crim. L.R. 227, CA (Crim Div) .......... *Digested,* 14/**696**

R. v Mathews (Michael Richard) see Attorney General's Reference (No.27 of 2013)

R. v Mavji (Ramniklal Nathoo) [1987] 1 W.L.R. 1388; [1987] 2 All E.R. 758; [1986] S.T.C. 508; (1987) 84 Cr. App. R. 34; [1987] Crim. L.R. 39; (1987) 131 S.J. 1121, CA (Crim Div) .......... *Digested,* 87/**764**: *Applied* 89/3738: *Considered* 90/1260, 14/2600

R. v Maxwell (Benjamin Joseph) [2014] EWCA Crim 417; [2014] R.T.R. 27, CA (Crim Div) .......... *Digested,* 14/**2560**

R. v Maxwell (James Charles) see DPP of Northern Ireland v Maxwell

R. v May (Andrew) [2013] EWCA Crim 850; [2014] 1 Cr. App. R. (S.) 13, CA (Crim Div) .......... *Digested,* 14/**2696**

R. v May (Raymond George); *joined cases* R. v Lawrence (Steven); R. v Fowles (Herbert); R. v Bravard (Jacques); R. v Stapleton (Vincent John) [2008] UKHL 28; [2008] 1 A.C. 1028; [2008] 2 W.L.R. 1131; [2008] 4 All E.R. 97; [2009] S.T.C. 852; [2008] 2 Cr. App. R. 28; [2009] 1 Cr. App. R. (S.) 31; [2008] Lloyd's Rep. F.C. 453; [2008] Crim. L.R. 737; (2008) 105(21) L.S.G. 21; (2008) 158 N.L.J. 750; (2008) 152(21) S.J.L.B. 29; Times, May 15, 2008, HL; affirming [2005] EWCA Crim 97; [2005] 1 W.L.R. 2902; [2005] 3 All E.R. 523; [2005] 2 Cr. App. R. (S.) 67; (2005) 149 S.J.L.B. 176; Times, February 15, 2005, CA (Crim Div) ........ *Digested,* 08/**776**: *Applied* 05/3901, 05/926, 09/4466, 09/833, 09/840, 10/709, 10/733, 11/724, 11/848, 12/681, 12/755, 12/758, 13/689, 13/749, 14/727, 14/737: *Considered* 07/949, 09/829, 09/835, 11/722, 14/1071, 14/738: *Followed* 08/775, 09/834, 09/836, 09/848, 10/734, 10/735, 11/723, 11/725, 12/756, 13/688, 13/690, 13/695, 14/728

R. v McCalla (Lloyd) see R. v McCalla (Ryan)

R. v McCalla (Ryan); *joined case* R. v McCalla (Lloyd) [2012] EWCA Crim 2252, CA (Crim Div) *Considered* 14/2625, 14/2681

R. v McCallister (Gerard Martin) see Attorney General's Reference (Nos 88, 89, 90 and 91 of 2006)

R. v McCatty (Costs) [2013] 5 Costs L.R. 863, Sen Cts Costs Office ........ *Digested,* 14/**755**

R. v McComb (William Thomas) see R. v Pitts (Aaron)

R. v McDaid (James Andrew) see R. v Clarke (Ronald Augustus)

R. v McDermott (David Steven) [2013] EWCA Crim 1807; [2014] 1 Cr. App. R. (S.) 81, CA (Crim Div) ........ *Digested,* 14/**2670**

R. v McDermott (Scott) see R. v McDermott (Stephen Paul)

R. v McDermott (Stephen Paul); *joined cases* R. v Williams (Stephen David); R. v McDermott (Scott) [2013] EWCA Crim 607; [2014] 1 Cr. App. R. (S.) 1, CA (Crim Div) ........ *Digested,* 14/**2671**

R. v McDonald (Mark Anthony) see R. v Pitts (Aaron)

R. v McDonald (Paul) see R. v Cooke (John)

R. v McDonnell (Michael William) [2009] EWCA Crim 2922; [2010] 2 Cr. App. R. (S.) 49, CA (Crim Div) ........ *Digested,* 10/**2881**: *Considered* 12/3031, 14/2619

R. v McEneaney (John Paul) [2005] EWCA Crim 431; [2005] 2 Cr. App. R. (S.) 86; [2005] Crim. L.R. 579, CA (Crim Div) ........ *Digested,* 05/**3694**: *Considered* 14/2638

R. v McGeary (John) see R. v Povey (Clive Richard)

R. v McGee (Mark Stuart) see Attorney General's Reference (Nos 3, 73 and 75 of 2010)

R. v McGirr (Christopher St John) see R. v Kelly (Paul Anthony)

R. v McGrane (Lorraine) see R. v Blackshaw (Jordan Philip)

R. v McGrath (Henry Paul) [2013] EWCA Crim 1261; [2014] Crim. L.R. 144, CA (Crim Div)

R. v McGregor (Susan) see R. v Doherty (Michael Patrick)

R. v McInerney (Michael) see R. v Rollins (Neil)

R. v McIntosh (Oshane) [2014] EWCA Crim 1003; [2014] 2 Cr. App. R. (S.) 64, CA (Crim Div)

R. v McKenzie (Nikki David) [2013] EWCA Crim 1544; [2014] 1 Cr. App. R. (S.) 68, CA (Crim Div) ........ *Digested,* 14/**2640**

R. v McKrieth (Richard) see R. v Dyer (Richard)

R. v McLaughlin (Gerard Marius) (1983) 76 Cr. App. R. 42, CA (Crim Div) ........ *Digested,* 83/**697**: *Considered* 14/772

R. v McLaughlin (Henry) see R. v Mackle (Plunkett Jude)

R. v McLean (Kurt) see R. v Yusuf (Samir)

R. v McLoughlin (Ian) see Attorney General's Reference (No.69 of 2013)

R. v McManus (Kevin Peter) see R. v Gordon (Gavin Stephen)

R. v McMullen (Martin Anthony) see R. v Baybasin (Mehmet Sirin)

R. v McNally (Justine) [2013] EWCA Crim 1051; [2014] Q.B. 593; [2014] 2 W.L.R. 200; [2013] 2 Cr. App. R. 28, CA (Crim Div) ........ *Digested,* 13/**667**

R. v McQuaid (Daniel) [2014] EWCA Crim 1547; [2014] 2 Cr. App. R. (S.) 78, CA (Crim Div)

R. v McWilliams (Mark) see R. v Caley (David)

R. v McWilliams (Thomas) see R. v Chief Constable of the Royal Ulster Constabulary Ex p. Begley

R. v Medicines Control Agency Ex p. Pharma Nord (UK) Ltd [1998] 3 C.M.L.R. 109; [1999] Eu. L.R. 8; (1998) 10 Admin. L.R. 646; (1998) 44 B.M.L.R. 41; [1998] C.O.D. 315; Times, June 10, 1998, CA (Civ Div); affirming [1997] C.O.D. 439; Times, July 29, 1997, QBD ........ *Digested*, 98/**2655**: *Applied* 14/1528: *Considered* 03/776

R. v Medway (Andrew George) [1976] Q.B. 779; [1976] 2 W.L.R. 528; [1976] 1 All E.R. 527; (1976) 62 Cr. App. R. 85; [1976] Crim. L.R. 118, CA (Crim Div) ........ *Digested*, 76/**399**: *Applied* 82/504, 05/826, 14/707: *Considered* 95/1433, 97/288: *Distinguished* 86/476: *Followed* 97/1260

R. v Meehan (Brian John) see Attorney General's Reference (Nos 88, 89, 90 and 91 of 2006)

R. v Meeking (Caroline) [2012] EWCA Crim 641; [2012] 1 W.L.R. 3349; [2013] R.T.R. 4; [2013] Crim. L.R. 333, CA (Crim Div) ........ *Digested*, 13/**673**: *Considered* 14/2560

R. v Mejia (Johnny Edisson); *joined case* R. v Sneath (Paul Samuel) [2009] EWCA Crim 1940, CA (Crim Div) *Considered* 14/729

R. v Mental Health Review Tribunal Ex p. Hall [2000] 1 W.L.R. 1323; [1999] 4 All E.R. 883; (1999) 2 C.C.L. Rep. 383; [1999] Lloyd's Rep. Med. 417; (2000) 51 B.M.L.R. 117; [1999] C.O.D. 429; (1999) 96(33) L.S.G. 31; (1999) 149 N.L.J. 1368; Times, October 5, 1999, CA (Civ Div); reversing [1999] 3 All E.R. 132; (1999) 2 C.C.L. Rep. 361; [1999] Lloyd's Rep. Med. 274; [1999] C.O.D. 372; (1999) 149 N.L.J. 638; Times, May 20, 1999, QBD ........ *Digested*, 99/**3935**: *Applied* 12/2278, 14/2179: *Considered* 03/2956, 10/3179

R. v Mewaswala (Yusuf) see R. v Patel (Sophia)

R. v MI; *joined cases* R. v RA; R. v JK; R. v CP [2012] EWCA Crim 1792, CA (Crim Div) *Followed* 14/2686

R. v Miah (Abdal); *joined case* R. v Mohammed (Liban) [2014] EWCA Crim 938; (2014) 178 J.P. 297, CA (Crim Div)

R. v Miah (Mohammed Suba) see R. v Dallimore (Paul)

R. v Middlecote (Andrew) see R. v Bell (David)

R. v Milford Haven Port Authority see Environment Agency v Milford Haven Port Authority (The Sea Empress)

R. v Miller [1976] Crim. L.R. 147, CA (Crim Div) ........ *Digested*, 76/**603**: *Considered* 81/540, 14/2554

R. v Miller (Colin Graham) [2013] EWCA Crim 1857; [2014] 1 Cr. App. R. (S.) 82, CA (Crim Div) ........ *Digested*, 14/**2590**

R. v Milling (Arthur Paul) see R. v Jones (Margaret)

R. v Minto (David) [2014] EWCA Crim 297; [2014] 2 Cr. App. R. (S.) 36, CA (Crim Div) ........ *Digested*, 14/**2656**

R. v Mitchell [1995] Crim. L.R. 506, CA (Crim Div) *Considered* 11/647, 14/778

R. v Mitchell (Billy Richard); *joined case* R. v Kelham (Damien Anthony) [2011] EWCA Crim 1652; [2012] 1 Cr. App. R. (S.) 68, CA (Crim Div) ........ *Digested*, 12/**3024**: *Applied* 13/2786, 14/2694

R. v Mitchell (Laura); *joined case* R. v Ballantyne (Henry) [2008] EWCA Crim 2552; [2009] 1 Cr. App. R. 31; [2009] Crim. L.R. 287, CA (Crim Div) ........ *Digested*, 09/**907**: *Applied* 14/692

R. v Mitchell (William Thomas) [2014] EWCA Crim 318; [2014] 2 Cr. App. R. 2, CA (Crim Div) ........ *Digested*, 14/**694**

R. v MN see R. v AM

R. v Moffat (Kevin) [2014] EWCA Crim 332; [2014] 2 Cr. App. R. (S.) 37, CMAC ........ *Digested*, 14/**2635**

R. v Mohammed (Khaleed Abdul); *joined case* R. v Osunnuyi (Emmanuel) [2004] EWCA Crim 678, CA (Crim Div) *Applied* 14/772

R. v Mohammed (Liban) see R. v Miah (Abdal)

R. v Mohamoed (Mohammed Ali) (also known as Ali (Jamal)) see Attorney General's Reference (No.41 of 2013)

R. v Molloy (Andrew) see R. v Baybasin (Mehmet Sirin)

R. v Monopolies and Mergers Commission Ex p. South Yorkshire Passenger Transport Authority see R. v Monopolies and Mergers Commission Ex p. South Yorkshire Transport Ltd

R. v Monopolies and Mergers Commission Ex p. South Yorkshire Transport Ltd; *sub nom* South Yorkshire Transport v Monopolies and Mergers Commission; *joined case* R. v Monopolies and Mergers Commission Ex p. South Yorkshire Passenger Transport Authority [1993] 1 W.L.R. 23; [1993] 1 All E.R. 289; [1993] B.C.C. 111; [1994] E.C.C. 231; (1993) 143 N.L.J. 128; Times, December 17, 1992, HL; reversing [1992] 1 W.L.R. 291; [1992] 1 All E.R. 257; [1992] B.C.C. 340; [1992] E.C.C. 432; (1992) 4 Admin. L.R. 385; [1992] C.O.D. 259; (1992) 156 L.G. Rev. 741; Times, December 9, 1991; Financial Times, December 6, 1991, CA (Civ Div); affirming [1991] B.C.C. 347; [1992] E.C.C. 1; [1991] C.O.D. 432; Times, April 9, 1991; Daily Telegraph, April 25, 1991, QBD . *Digested,* 93/**416**: *Applied* 07/2892: *Considered* 10/72, 11/1581: *Followed* 14/547

R. v Montague (Damian John); *sub nom* R. v Montague (Damien John) [2013] EWCA Crim 1781; [2014] Crim. L.R. 615, CA (Crim Div)

R. v Montague (Damien John) see R. v Montague (Damian John)

R. v Montila (Steven William); *sub nom* R. v Montilla (Steven William) [2004] UKHL 50; [2004] 1 W.L.R. 3141; [2005] 1 All E.R. 113; [2005] 1 Cr. App. R. 26; [2005] Crim. L.R. 479; (2005) 102(3) L.S.G. 30; (2004) 148 S.J.L.B. 1403; Times, November 26, 2004; Independent, November 30, 2004, HL; reversing [2003] EWCA Crim 3082; [2004] 1 W.L.R. 624; [2004] 1 All E.R. 877; [2004] 1 Cr. App. R. 32; (2003) 100(46) L.S.G. 24; (2003) 147 S.J.L.B. 1305; Times, November 12, 2003, CA (Crim Div) .......... *Digested,* 05/**806**: *Applied* 05/768, 06/834, 07/872, 14/675: *Considered* 06/1731

R. v Montilla (Steven William) see R. v Montila (Steven William)

R. v Moore (Mia); *joined case* R. v Burrows (Ben Peter) [2013] EWCA Crim 85; [2014] Crim. L.R. 364, CA (Crim Div)

R. v Morgan (Christopher Lynn) [2013] EWCA Crim 1307; [2014] 1 W.L.R. 3450; [2014] 1 All E.R. 1208; [2014] Env. L.R. 5; [2013] Lloyd's Rep. F.C. 655; [2014] L.L.R. 332, CA (Crim Div) .......... *Digested,* 14/**736**

R. v Morgan (Daniel John) [2013] EWCA Crim 2148; [2014] 2 Cr. App. R. (S.) 10, CA (Crim Div)

R. v Morgan (John); *joined case* R. v Bygrave (Rosemary) [2008] EWCA Crim 1323; [2008] 4 All E.R. 890; [2009] 1 Cr. App. R. (S.) 60; [2008] Lloyd's Rep. F.C. 526; [2008] Crim. L.R. 805, CA (Crim Div) .......... *Digested,* 09/**853**: *Applied* 09/829, 13/749: *Approved* 13/689: *Considered* 09/848, 14/733

R. v Morris (Daryl Howard) [2013] EWCA Crim 436; [2014] 1 W.L.R. 16; [2013] 2 Cr. App. R. 9; [2013] R.T.R. 22; [2013] Crim. L.R. 995, CA (Crim Div) .......... *Digested,* 13/**742**

R. v Morris (Nigel Leonard) see R. v Cairns (James Philip)

R. v Morris (Paul Winter) see R. v Allpress (Sylvia)

R. v Mullen (Nicholas Robert) (No.2) [2000] Q.B. 520; [1999] 3 W.L.R. 777; [1999] 2 Cr. App. R. 143; [1999] Crim. L.R. 561; Times, February 15, 1999, CA (Crim Div) .......... *Digested,* 99/**972**: *Applied* 00/1026, 00/1056, 01/5733, 02/904, 09/816, 11/709, 14/298: *Considered* 00/1025, 05/3343, 05/838: *Distinguished* 05/875, 13/285

R. v Murphy (George Leon) see R. v Pitts (Aaron)

R. v Murray (Costs) [2013] 5 Costs L.R. 867, Sen Cts Costs Office .......... *Digested,* 14/**746**

R. v Mustafa (Imran) see R. v Abdul (Jonathan)

R. v MV see R. v AM

R. v Myrie (Owen Anthony) see Attorney General's Reference (No.68 of 2008)

R. v Napper (Costs) [2014] 5 Costs L.R. 947, Sen Cts Costs Office

R. v Nasri (Sbida) see R. v Boakye (Christiana)

R. v Nazari (Fazlollah); *joined cases* R. v Fernandez (Joseph); R. v Dissanayake (Rohan Shivantha); R. v Anyanwu (Ebenezer Chuwuma); R. v Adamson (Michael Joseph) [1980] 1 W.L.R. 1366; [1980] 3 All E.R. 880; (1980) 71 Cr. App. R. 87; (1980) 2 Cr. App. R. (S.) 84; [1980] Crim. L.R. 447, CA (Crim Div) .. *Digested,* 80/**581**: *Applied* 05/3589, 06/3834, 09/3411, 14/2664: *Cited* 89/1108, 90/1405, 92/1224, 93/1105, 93/1106, 93/1108, 93/1109: *Considered* 80/1422, 87/1996, 91/1206, 92/1228, 94/2481, 97/2907, 99/1129, 03/2232, 05/3768, 06/3723, 08/3355, 10/1776, 11/2991, 13/2731, 13/2732: *Followed* 06/2262, 11/807: *Referred to* 85/1714

R. v Nelson (John Stanley); *sub nom* Crown Prosecution Service v Pathak; Crown Prosecution Service v Nelson; *joined cases* R. v Paulet (Didier); R. v Pathak (Ramesh) [2009] EWCA Crim 1573; [2010] Q.B. 678; [2010] 2 W.L.R. 788; [2010] 4 All E.R. 666; [2010] 1 Cr. App. R. (S.) 82; [2009] Lloyd's Rep. F.C. 663; [2009] Crim. L.R. 811; Times, August 18, 2009, CA (Crim Div) .......... *Digested,* 09/**848**: *Applied* 11/723, 12/756, 13/688: *Complaint upheld* 14/1631: *Considered* 11/739: *Followed* 14/743

R. v Nettleton (Costs) [2014] 2 Costs L.R. 387, Sen Cts Costs Office .......... *Digested,* 14/**753**

R. v Network Rail Infrastructure [2010] EWCA Crim 1225; [2011] 1 Cr. App. R. (S.) 44, CA (Crim Div) .......... *Digested,* 11/**1632**: *Considered* 14/2632
R. v Network Rail Infrastructure Ltd see R. v Sellafield Ltd
R. v Newell (Lee William) see Attorney General's Reference (No.69 of 2013)
R. v Newton (Matthew) see R. v Farooqi (Munir Ahmed)
R. v Nguyen (Khin Quoc) [2010] EWCA Crim 2658, CA (Crim Div) *Considered* 14/681
R. v Nnaji (Ogechuku Ferdinand); *joined case* R. v Johnson (Remmond Theo) [2009] EWCA Crim 468; [2009] 2 Cr. App. R. (S.) 107; [2009] Crim. L.R. 541, CA (Crim Div) .......... *Digested,* 09/**3495**: *Applied* 14/2611: *Considered* 11/2831, 14/2612, 14/813
R. v Noon (Costs) [2013] 4 Costs L.R. 633, Sen Cts Costs Office .......... *Digested,* 14/**748**
R. v Norman (Shane Martin); *joined cases* R. v Hussain (Jameed); R. v Egan (Jason); R. v Walton (Lee Alan); R. v Igbanoi (Ambrose Otsemobor); R. v Cory (Rodney Phillip) [2006] EWCA Crim 1792; [2007] 1 Cr. App. R. (S.) 82; [2006] Crim. L.R. 1072; Times, August 4, 2006, CA (Crim Div) .......... *Digested,* 06/**3833**: *Applied* 14/813: *Considered* 07/3735, 09/852, 14/2612: *Followed* 09/3495
R. v North and East Devon HA Ex p. Coughlan [2001] Q.B. 213; [2000] 2 W.L.R. 622; [2000] 3 All E.R. 850; (2000) 2 L.G.L.R. 1; [1999] B.L.G.R. 703; (1999) 2 C.C.L. Rep. 285; [1999] Lloyd's Rep. Med. 306; (2000) 51 B.M.L.R. 1; [1999] C.O.D. 340; (1999) 96(31) L.S.G. 39; (1999) 143 S.J.L.B. 213; Times, July 20, 1999; Independent, July 20, 1999, CA (Civ Div); affirming (1999) 2 C.C.L. Rep. 27; (1999) 47 B.M.L.R. 27; [1999] C.O.D. 174; Times, December 29, 1998, QBD ... *Digested,* 99/**2643**: *Applied* 00/4526, 01/5879, 02/4293, 02/46, 03/1917, 03/2837, 03/3399, 03/4101, 03/4713, 04/1905, 04/2643, 04/3859, 05/1837, 06/1927, 06/40, 07/3937, 07/716, 08/4302, 08/52, 08/70, 09/1770, 10/2184, 11/2138, 13/2935, 13/2947: *Considered* 03/3399, 05/2154, 06/1163, 06/1436, 06/2224, 07/1946, 07/45, 07/57, 10/2162, 10/3488, 14/2087: *Distinguished* 03/4091, 05/4121: *Followed* 99/3931, 00/1915, 09/4130, 12/2542, 14/2106, 14/2794
R. v Norton (Joseph) [2014] EWCA Crim 1275; [2014] 2 Cr. App. R. (S.) 79, CA (Crim Div)
R. v NS 2012 SCC 72; 34 B.H.R.C. 579, Sup Ct (Can) *Considered* 14/769
R. v Nunn (Adam John) [1996] 2 Cr. App. R. (S.) 136, CA (Crim Div) .......... *Digested,* 96/**1836**: *Applied* 13/2789, 14/2602: *Considered* 99/1321, 00/1155, 03/3799: *Followed* 01/1466: *Not applied* 99/1320
R. v Nurdin (Frank Percival) see R. v Wellburn (Geoffrey Elliott)
R. v Nutting (Costs) [2013] 6 Costs L.R. 1037, Sen Cts Costs Office .......... *Digested,* 14/**2029**
R. v Nwude (Ifeoma Kalistar) see R. v Boakye (Christiana)
R. v O (Claire) see R. v R (Amer)
R. v O see Attorney General's Reference (No.30 of 2013)
R. v O'Brien see Director of the Serious Fraud Office v O'Brien
R. v O'Flaherty (Errol Carlton); *joined cases* R. v Toussaint (Mitchell Paris); R. v Ryan (Phillip Junior) [2004] EWCA Crim 526; [2004] 2 Cr. App. R. 20; [2004] Crim. L.R. 751; (2004) 148 S.J.L.B. 353, CA (Crim Div) .......... *Digested,* 05/**899**: *Applied* 14/692: *Considered* 09/907
R. v O'Reilly (Darren) see R. v Ashton (John)
R. v Odamo (Sunday Adeddayo) [2013] EWCA Crim 1275; [2014] 1 Cr. App. R. (S.) 44, CA (Crim Div) .......... *Digested,* 14/**734**
R. v Okedare (Charles) [2014] EWCA Crim 1173; [2014] 1 W.L.R. 4088; [2014] 2 Cr. App. R. (S.) 68; [2014] Lloyd's Rep. F.C. 585; [2014] Crim. L.R. 916; (2014) 158(20) S.J.L.B. 37, CA (Crim Div) .......... *Digested,* 14/**723**
R. v Okedare (Charles); *joined cases* R. v Hussain (Zameer Ejaz); R. v Anh Kao (Tuan); R. v Ashraf (Mohammed) [2014] EWCA Crim 228; [2014] 1 W.L.R. 4071; [2014] 3 All E.R. 109, CA (Crim Div) .......... *Digested,* 14/**757**
R. v Olditch (Toby) see R. v Jones (Margaret)
R. v Onuigbo (aka Okoronkwo) (Unoamaka) [2014] EWCA Crim 65; [2014] Lloyd's Rep. F.C. 302; [2014] Crim. L.R. 465, CA (Crim Div) .......... *Digested,* 14/**724**
R. v Orient Export Ltd see R. v Ezeemo (Godwin Chukwnaenya)
R. v Osoteko (Costs) [2014] 1 Costs L.R. 190, Sen Cts Costs Office .......... *Digested,* 14/**752**
R. v Osunnuyi (Emmanuel) see R. v Mohammed (Khaleed Abdul)

R. v Oxfordshire CC Ex p. Sunningwell Parish Council [2000] 1 A.C. 335; [1999] 3 W.L.R. 160; [1999] 3 All E.R. 385; [1999] B.L.G.R. 651; (2000) 79 P. & C.R. 199; [1999] 2 E.G.L.R. 94; [1999] 31 E.G. 85; [2000] J.P.L. 384; [1999] E.G. 91 (C.S.); (1999) 96(29) L.S.G. 29; (1999) 149 N.L.J. 1038; (1999) 143 S.J.L.B. 205; [1999] N.P.C. 74; Times, June 25, 1999; Independent, June 29, 1999, HL; reversing FC3 97/6534/D, CA (Civ Div); affirming CO 2744-96, QBD ................ *Digested,* 99/**4393**: *Applied* 04/3205, 08/3116, 09/3191, 13/2469, 14/2526: *Considered* 04/3203, 05/3440, 10/2754, 13/2468: *Followed* 12/2729

R. v Oxfordshire CC Ex p. Wallace; *sub nom* R. v Oxfordshire Education Authority Ex p. W [1987] 2 F.L.R. 193; (1987) 151 L.G. Rev. 590; (1987) 137 N.L.J. 542, DC *Digested,* 87/**2962**: *Applied* 14/942

R. v Oxfordshire Education Authority Ex p. W see R. v Oxfordshire CC Ex p. Wallace

R. v Oye (Seun) [2013] EWCA Crim 1725; [2014] 1 W.L.R. 3354; [2014] 1 All E.R. 902; [2014] 1 Cr. App. R. 11; [2014] Crim. L.R. 544, CA (Crim Div) .................... *Digested,* 14/**691**

R. v Oyebola (Folarin) [2013] EWCA Crim 1052; [2014] 1 Cr. App. R. (S.) 58; [2013] Lloyd's Rep. F.C. 671, CA (Crim Div) .................... *Digested,* 14/**730**

R. v P [2013] EWCA Crim 2331; [2014] 1 W.L.R. 3058; [2014] 1 Cr. App. R. 28; [2014] Crim. L.R. 547, CA (Crim Div) .................... *Digested,* 14/**657**

R. v P (Anthony) see Attorney General's Reference (No.27 of 2013)

R. v P see Attorney General's Reference (No.55 of 2008)

R. v Pace (Martin Edward); *joined case* R. v Rogers (Simon Peter) [2014] EWCA Crim 186; [2014] 1 W.L.R. 2867; [2014] 1 Cr. App. R. 34; (2014) 178 J.P. 133; [2014] Lloyd's Rep. F.C. 319, CA (Crim Div) .................... *Digested,* 14/**675**

R. v Padda (Gurpreet Singh) [2013] EWCA Crim 2330; [2014] 1 W.L.R. 1920; [2014] 2 Cr. App. R. (S.) 22; [2014] Lloyd's Rep. F.C. 223; [2014] Crim. L.R. 469, CA (Crim Div) .................... *Digested,* 14/**741**

R. v Palmer & Harvey McClane Ltd see R. v Palmer & Harvey McLane Ltd

R. v Palmer & Harvey McLane Ltd; *sub nom* R. v Palmer & Harvey McClane Ltd [2012] EWCA Crim 993; [2013] 1 Cr. App. R. (S.) 34, CA (Crim Div) ................ *Digested,* 13/**2668**: *Applied* 14/2644

R. v Palmer (Devana) see R. v Yusuf (Samir)

R. v Parchment (Jamal Sky) see R. v Smith (Dean Martin)

R. v Pash (Ashley James) [2013] EWCA Crim 576; [2014] 1 Cr. App. R. (S.) 4, CA (Crim Div) .................... *Digested,* 14/**2690**

R. v Patel (Hitendra) (Costs); *sub nom* Patel, Re [2012] EWCA Crim 1508; [2012] 5 Costs L.R. 873, CA (Crim Div) .................... *Digested,* 13/**703**: *Considered* 14/2033

R. v Patel (Parulben) [2013] EWCA Crim 965; [2013] Med. L.R. 507; (2013) 133 B.M.L.R. 219, CA (Crim Div) .................... *Digested,* 14/**689**: *Applied* 14/688

R. v Patel (Pravin) see R. v Patel (Sophia)

R. v Patel (Sophia); *joined cases* R. v Bava (Amrit); R. v Patel (Pravin); R. v Mewaswala (Yusuf) [2009] EWCA Crim 67; [2009] 2 Cr. App. R. (S.) 67; [2009] Crim. L.R. 466, CA (Crim Div) .................... *Digested,* 10/**2885**: *Distinguished* 14/690

R. v Pathak (Ramesh) see R. v Nelson (John Stanley)

R. v Pattison (Leslie) [2007] EWCA Crim 1536; [2008] 1 Cr. App. R. (S.) 51; [2008] Crim. L.R. 62, CA (Crim Div) .................... *Digested,* 08/**3270**: *Applied* 14/730: *Approved* 13/689

R. v Paul (Charles Temitope) [2013] EWCA Crim 978; [2013] 2 Cr. App. R. 26; [2014] Crim. L.R. 71, CA (Crim Div) .................... *Digested,* 13/**752**

R. v Paul (Jatinder) [2013] EWCA Crim 2034; [2014] 2 Cr. App. R. (S.) 7, CA (Crim Div)

R. v Paulet (Didier) see R. v Nelson (John Stanley)

R. v PC see Attorney General's Reference (No.55 of 2008)

R. v Pecco (Nadia) see R. v Dyer (Richard)

R. v Pennock (Angela); *joined case* R. v Pennock (Richard John) [2014] EWCA Crim 598; [2014] 2 Cr. App. R. 10, CA (Crim Div) .................... *Digested,* 14/**687**

R. v Pennock (Richard John) see R. v Pennock (Angela)

R. v Perkins (Robert); *joined cases* R. v Hall (Ronnie); R. v Bennett (Billy) [2013] EWCA Crim 323; [2013] 2 Cr. App. R. (S.) 72; [2013] Crim. L.R. 533, CA (Crim Div) .................... *Digested,* 13/**2789**: *Applied* 14/2626

R. v Perry (Lewis Lawrence) see R. v Caley (David)

R. v Petch (Thomas) see R. v Coleman (George Romero)

R. v Peters (Darren) see R. v Mahil (Mundill Kaur)

R. v Petrou (Aaron) see R. v Crawley (Scott)

R. v Pickstone (Robert Alan) see R. v Hanson (Nicky)

R. v Pilling (Craig) [2013] EWCA Crim 1944; [2014] 2 Cr. App. R. (S.) 4, CA (Crim Div) ............ *Digested,* 14/**2685**

R. v Pitchei (Mashain) [2013] EWCA Crim 2108; [2014] L.L.R. 358, CA (Crim Div)

R. v Pitts (Aaron); *joined cases* R. v McComb (William Thomas); R. v Knight (Glenn); R. v Harding (James Benjamin); R. v Murphy (George Leon); R. v Waters (Gordon George); R. v Rooks (Craig); R. v McDonald (Mark Anthony); R. v Booth (Jonathan); R. v Bowden (Peter) [2014] EWCA Crim 1615; [2014] Crim. L.R. 834, CA (Crim Div)

R. v Plant (Ricardo) [2008] EWCA Crim 960; [2008] 2 Cr. App. R. 27; Times, April 21, 2008, CA (Crim Div) ............ *Digested,* 08/**833**: *Applied* 14/776

R. v Poddiapuhamey (Kohulan) see R. v Rajakumar (Aathavan)

R. v Port (Samuel Albert) [2013] EWCA Crim 2668; [2014] 2 Cr. App. R. (S.) 26, CA (Crim Div) ............ *Digested,* 14/**2665**

R. v Povey (Clive Richard); *joined cases* R. v Bleazard (Daniel); R. v Pownall (Clifton Christopher); R. v McGeary (John) [2008] EWCA Crim 1261; [2009] 1 Cr. App. R. (S.) 42; (2009) 173 J.P. 109; [2008] Crim. L.R. 816, CA (Crim Div) ............ *Digested,* 09/**3455**: *Applied* 12/2981, 13/2665, 14/2646: *Considered* 09/3556: *Followed* 11/2959

R. v Powell (Carl Michael) [2014] EWCA Crim 642; [2014] 1 W.L.R. 2757; [2014] 2 Cr. App. R. 31, CA (Crim Div) ............ *Digested,* 14/**774**

R. v Pownall (Clifton Christopher) see R. v Povey (Clive Richard)

R. v Preddy (John Crawford); *joined cases* R. v Slade (Mark); R. v Dhillon (Rajpaul Singh) [1996] A.C. 815; [1996] 3 W.L.R. 255; [1996] 3 All E.R. 481; [1996] 2 Cr. App. R. 524; (1996) 160 J.P. 677; [1996] Crim. L.R. 726; (1996) 160 J.P.N. 936; (1996) 93(31) L.S.G. 29; (1996) 146 N.L.J. 1057; (1996) 140 S.J.L.B. 184; Times, July 11, 1996; Independent, July 17, 1996, HL; reversing [1995] Crim. L.R. 564, CA (Crim Div) ............ *Digested,* 96/**1530**: *Applied* 97/1227, 02/809, 13/689: *Considered* 96/1532, 96/1548, 97/1228, 97/1249, 97/1260, 97/1264, 97/2429, 98/980, 98/981, 99/973, 02/849, 04/756, 11/1819, 11/724: *Distinguished* 00/1013: *Followed* 97/1226, 97/1229, 97/1230, 97/1231, 14/773: *Referred to* 97/1224, 97/1225, 97/1304

R. v Predusca (Gabriel) [2013] EWCA Crim 2433; [2014] 2 Cr. App. R. (S.) 17, CA (Crim Div) ............ *Digested,* 14/**2694**

R. v Preston (Stephen); *joined cases* R. v Preston (Zena); R. v Salter (Jeremy); R. v Austen (Anthony); R. v Clarke (Nicholas Henry) [1994] 2 A.C. 130; [1993] 3 W.L.R. 891; [1993] 4 All E.R. 638; (1994) 98 Cr. App. R. 405; [1994] Crim. L.R. 676; (1993) 137 S.J.L.B. 256; Times, November 8, 1993; Independent, November 9, 1993, HL; affirming (1992) 95 Cr. App. R. 355; [1992] Crim. L.R. 805; (1992) 136 S.J.L.B. 156; Times, May 13, 1992, CA (Crim Div) ............ *Digested,* 94/**864**: *Applied* 00/920: *Cited* 97/1129: *Considered* 00/921, 14/400: *Distinguished* 01/980

R. v Preston (Zena) see R. v Preston (Stephen)

R. v Price (Jamie) [2013] EWCA Crim 1283; [2014] 1 Cr. App. R. (S.) 36, CA (Crim Div) ............ *Digested,* 14/**2592**

R. v Price (Patrick David); *joined case* R. v Bell (Colin James) [2014] EWCA Crim 229; [2014] 1 W.L.R. 3501; [2014] 3 All E.R. 208; [2014] 1 Cr. App. R. 33, CA (Crim Div) ............ *Digested,* 14/**151**

R. v Price (Paul Graham) see R. v Graham (Hemamali Krishna)

R. v Priest (Margaret) see R. v Hopkins (Annette)

R. v Prime (Timothy James) [2013] EWCA Crim 2525; [2014] 2 Cr. App. R. (S.) 19, CA (Crim Div) ............ *Digested,* 14/**2689**

R. v Prince (Henry) (1872-75) L.R. 2 C.C.R. 154, Crown Cases Reserved *Considered* 63/635, 14/674: *Disapproved* 00/1002

R. v Pritchard (Philip) see R. v Jones (Margaret)

R. v Pusey (Lloyd Aaron) see R. v Gordon (Gavin Stephen)

R. v Pyo (Hyung-Woo) see Attorney General's Reference (Nos 3, 73 and 75 of 2010)

R. v Pyranha Mouldings Ltd [2014] EWCA Crim 533; [2014] 2 Cr. App. R. (S.) 43, CA (Crim Div) ............ *Digested,* 14/**2644**

R. v R [2013] EWCA Crim 708; [2014] 1 Cr. App. R. 5; [2014] Crim. L.R. 300, CA (Crim Div) ............ *Digested,* 14/**797**

R. v R (Amer); *joined cases* R. v M (Faisal Jamil); R. v O (Claire); R. v C (James); R. v S (Imran); R. v L (Abraham); R. v V (Abolghasem) [2006] EWCA Crim 1974; [2007] 1 Cr. App. R. 10; [2007] Crim. L.R. 79, CA (Crim Div) ............ *Digested,* 07/**870**: *Applied* 14/773: *Followed* 07/871

R. v R see Attorney General's Reference (No.55 of 2008)

R. v R see R. v G

R. v R. v Khan (Mohammed Ahsan) see R. v Khan (Kazim Ali)

R. v RA see R. v MI

R. v Rafiq (Shahid) see R. v Cairns (James Philip)

R. v Rajakumar (Aathavan); *joined cases* R. v Theivendarampillai (Jeyasuthan); R. v Vivekananthan (Jeyarubin); R. v Selvaratnam (Rubesius); R. v Kunaratnam (Pirunthan); R. v Venayakamoorthy (Kaviloan); R. v Vijasinghe (Juis James); R. v Poddiapuhamey (Kohulan) [2013] EWCA Crim 1512; [2014] 1 Cr. App. R. 12, CA (Crim Div) ........ *Digested,* 14/**692**

R. v Rajput (Wasim) see R. v Fields (Michael)

R. v Ramchurn (Jayant) [2010] EWCA Crim 194; [2010] 2 Cr. App. R. 3; Times, February 22, 2010, CA (Crim Div) ........ *Digested,* 11/**647**: *Considered* 14/778

R. v Randel (David Arthur) see R. v Wellburn (Geoffrey Elliott)

R. v Randhawa (Jagprit); *joined cases* R. v Singh (Jaspal (aka Chahal)); R. v Chahal (Charanjit Singh); R. v Mallourides (Philip); R. v Chahal (Bhabdeep Singh) [2012] EWCA Crim 1; [2012] S.T.C. 901; [2012] 2 Cr. App. R. (S.) 53; [2012] Lloyd's Rep. F.C. 283; [2012] S.T.I. 140, CA (Crim Div) ........ *Digested,* 12/**2852**: *Considered* 14/2600

R. v Raza (Naim) see R. v Bestel (Jean Pierre)

R. v Razak (Basil) see R. v Datsun (Day)

R. v Redmond (Jamie Daryl) [2014] EWCA Crim 1655; [2014] 2 Cr. App. R. (S.) 60, CA (Crim Div)

R. v Rees (Robert) see Attorney General's Reference (No.9 of 2013)

R. v Registrar General Ex p. Segerdal [1970] 2 Q.B. 697; [1970] 3 W.L.R. 479; [1970] 3 All E.R. 886; (1970) 114 S.J. 703, CA (Civ Div); affirming [1970] 1 Q.B. 430; [1970] 2 W.L.R. 140; [1970] 1 All E.R. 1; (1970) 114 S.J. 995; Times, November 15, 1969, DC ........ *Digested,* 70/**838**: *Followed* 13/1393: *Overruled* 14/1480

R. v Rehman (Amirul) see R. v Lewis (Jermaine Nathaniel)

R. v Rehman (Zakir); *joined case* R. v Wood (Gary Dominic) [2005] EWCA Crim 2056; [2006] 1 Cr. App. R. (S.) 77; [2005] Crim. L.R. 878; Times, September 27, 2005, CA (Crim Div) ........ *Digested,* 05/**3693**: *Applied* 06/3717, 08/3292, 09/3544, 10/2879, 10/2880, 11/2867, 11/2869, 12/2901, 14/2634, 14/2637: *Considered* 07/3718, 09/3384, 11/2864, 13/2637, 14/2636: *Distinguished* 07/3791: *Followed* 14/2638: *Referred to* 08/3289

R. v Reid (Mark) see R. v Dyer (Richard)

R. v Reliance Export Ltd see R. v Ezeemo (Godwin Chukwnaenya)

R. v Reynolds (Michael Edwin); *joined cases* R. v Thompson (Amelio); R. v S; R. v D; R. v L; R. v Honore (James); R. v Webb (John Paul); R. v Lubwama (Abdul Musisi) [2007] EWCA Crim 538; [2008] 1 W.L.R. 1075; [2007] 4 All E.R. 369; [2007] 2 Cr. App. R. (S.) 87; [2007] Crim. L.R. 493; Times, March 21, 2007, CA (Crim Div) ........ *Digested,* 07/**966**: *Applied* 11/3061, 14/2699: *Considered* 07/21

R. v Richards (Josh) see R. v Jones (Margaret)

R. v Richardson (Dianne) [2013] EWCA Crim 1905; [2014] 2 Cr. App. R. (S.) 5, CA (Crim Div) ........ *Digested,* 14/**2672**

R. v Riley (Craig Philip); *joined cases* R. v Wilson (Gary); R. v Farrell (Joseph); R. v Bradley (Kirk Trevor); R. v Downes (Tony) [2012] EWCA Crim 2507, CA (Crim Div) *Considered* 14/757

R. v Rimmington (Anthony); *joined case* R. v Goldstein (Harry Chaim) [2005] UKHL 63; [2006] 1 A.C. 459; [2005] 3 W.L.R. 982; [2006] 2 All E.R. 257; [2006] 1 Cr. App. R. 17; [2006] H.R.L.R. 3; [2006] U.K.H.R.R. 1; [2006] L.L.R. 105; [2006] Crim. L.R. 153; (2005) 102(43) L.S.G. 28; (2005) 155 N.L.J. 1685; [2006] Env. L.R. D3; Times, October 28, 2005; Independent, November 1, 2005, HL; reversing [2003] EWCA Crim 3450; [2004] 1 W.L.R. 2878; [2004] 2 All E.R. 589; [2004] 1 Cr. App. R. 27; [2004] U.K.H.R.R. 296; [2004] Crim. L.R. 303; Times, December 17, 2003, CA (Crim Div) ........ *Digested,* 06/**873**: *Applied* 09/2734, 10/710, 13/768, 14/1486, 14/2600: *Considered* 08/2668: *Followed* 08/1399, 14/2065, 14/676

R. v RM see R. v AM

R. v Roastas (German) see R. v Kluxen (Patricia)

R. v Roberts (Stephen John) [2013] EWCA Crim 785; [2013] R.T.R. 32, CA (Crim Div) *Digested,* 14/**2691**

R. v Robertson (Daniel Alexander) see R. v Caley (David)

R. v Robinson-Pierre (Symieon) [2013] EWCA Crim 2396; [2014] 1 W.L.R. 2638; [2014] 1 Cr. App. R. 22; (2014) 178 J.P. 45; (2014) 158(3) S.J.L.B. 37, CA (Crim Div) ........ *Digested,* 14/**679**

R. v Rogers (Bradley David); *joined cases* R. v Samuels (Colin Martin); R. v French (Geraldine); R. v Bell (Mark Julian) [2014] EWCA Crim 1680; [2014] 2 Cr. App. R. 32; [2014] Lloyd's Rep. F.C. 638; [2014] Crim. L.R. 910; (2014) 158(32) S.J.L.B. 41, CA (Crim Div) ........ *Digested,* 14/**788**

R. v Rogers (Simon Peter) see R. v Pace (Martin Edward)
R. v Rollins (Neil); *joined case* R. v McInerney (Michael) [2010] UKSC 39; [2010] 1 W.L.R. 1922; [2010] 4 All E.R. 880; [2010] Bus. L.R. 1529; [2011] 1 Cr. App. R. 4; [2010] Lloyd's Rep. F.C. 585; (2010) 154(30) S.J.L.B. 34; Times, August 2, 2010, SC; affirming [2009] EWCA Crim 1941; [2010] 1 All E.R. 1183; [2010] Bus. L.R. 734; [2010] 1 Cr. App. R. 14; [2010] Lloyd's Rep. F.C. 16; [2010] L.L.R. 340; [2010] Crim. L.R. 772; Times, October 20, 2009, CA (Crim Div) ...... *Digested,* 10/**777**: *Considered* 14/798
R. v Rooks (Craig) see R. v Pitts (Aaron)
R. v Rooney (Jacqueline Mary) [2006] EWCA Crim 1841, CA (Crim Div) *Considered* 14/770
R. v Round (Terence); *joined case* R. v Dunn (Vincent David) [2009] EWCA Crim 2667; [2010] 2 Cr. App. R. (S.) 45; [2010] Crim. L.R. 329; Times, December 22, 2009, CA (Crim Div) ........ *Digested,* 11/**2820**: *Applied* 11/2286, 12/3011, 14/2613: *Considered* 12/3016, 13/2683
R. v Rowe (Raphael George) (No.1) see R. v Davis (Michael George) (No.1)
R. v Royce (Karen) see R. v Lamaletie (Mervyn)
R. v Royle (Mark) [2013] EWCA Crim 1461; [2014] 1 Cr. App. R. (S.) 49, CA (Crim Div)
R. v Ruby (Ian) [2013] EWCA Crim 1653, CA (Crim Div) *Applied* 14/2649
R. v Ryan (Phillip Junior) see R. v O'Flaherty (Errol Carlton)
R. v Rybak (Andrew) see R. v Hammond (Philip)
R. v S [2011] EWCA Crim 1, CA (Crim Div) *Considered* 14/770
R. v S (Graham) [2001] 1 Cr. App. R. 7; [2001] 1 Cr. App. R. (S.) 97; (2000) 97(36) L.S.G. 41; Times, August 29, 2000, CA (Crim Div) ........ *Digested,* 00/**1301**: *Considered* 12/2970: *Disapproved* 14/2682: *Doubted* 05/3640
R. v S (Imran) see R. v R (Amer)
R. v S (Matthew John) [1999] 1 Cr. App. R. (S.) 67, CA (Crim Div) ........ *Digested,* 99/**1095**: *Considered* 14/2660
R. v S (Robert Michael) see R. v Harries (Michael John)
R. v S see R. v Harries (Michael John)
R. v S see R. v J
R. v S see R. v Reynolds (Michael Edwin)
R. v Sadighpour (Ali Reza) [2012] EWCA Crim 2669; [2013] 1 W.L.R. 2725; [2013] 1 Cr. App. R. 20, CA (Crim Div) ........ *Digested,* 13/**656**: *Followed* 14/696
R. v Sadique (Omar) [2013] EWCA Crim 1150; [2014] 1 W.L.R. 986; [2013] 4 All E.R. 924; [2013] 2 Cr. App. R. 31; [2014] Crim. L.R. 61, CA (Crim Div) ........ *Digested,* 14/**683**
R. v Sadique (Omar); *joined case* R. v Hussain (Zakir) [2011] EWCA Crim 2872; [2012] 1 W.L.R. 1700; [2012] 2 All E.R. 793; [2012] 1 Cr. App. R. 19; [2012] Crim. L.R. 449; Times, January 5, 2012, CA (Crim Div) ........ *Digested,* 12/**700**: *Considered* 14/683
R. v Sagoo (Karamjit) see R. v Fields (Michael)
R. v Saik (Abdulrahman) [2006] UKHL 18; [2007] 1 A.C. 18; [2006] 2 W.L.R. 993; [2006] 4 All E.R. 866; [2006] 2 Cr. App. R. 26; [2006] Crim. L.R. 998; (2006) 103(20) L.S.G. 24; (2006) 150 S.J.L.B. 603; Times, May 5, 2006; Independent, May 5, 2006, HL; reversing [2004] EWCA Crim 2936; Times, November 29, 2004, CA (Crim Div) ........ *Digested,* 07/**872**: *Applied* 14/675: *Considered* 07/869, 07/870, 07/871, 07/971, 11/681
R. v Sajid (Mohammed) see R. v Afonso (Americo Practicio)
R. v Sakalauskas (Gytis) [2013] EWCA Crim 2278; [2014] 1 W.L.R. 1204; [2014] 1 All E.R. 1231; [2014] 2 Cr. App. R. 11; (2014) 178 J.P. 30, CA (Crim Div) ........ *Digested,* 14/**695**
R. v Sakyi (Emmanuel Adade) [2014] EWCA Crim 1784; [2014] Crim. L.R. 921, CA (Crim Div)
R. v Sale (Peter John) [2013] EWCA Crim 1306; [2014] 1 W.L.R. 663; [2014] 1 Cr. App. R. (S.) 60; [2013] Lloyd's Rep. F.C. 495, CA (Crim Div) ........ *Digested,* 13/**685**: *Applied* 14/733
R. v Salih (Miqdad) see R. v Hareem (Khalid)
R. v Salter (Jeremy) see R. v Preston (Stephen)
R. v Samuels (Colin Martin) see R. v Rogers (Bradley David)
R. v Samways (Thomas Lewis ) see R. v Wiggins (Liam Roy)
R. v Sana (Costs) [2014] 6 Costs L.R. 1143, Sen Cts Costs Office
R. v Sangha (Bhovinder Singh) see Attorney General's Reference (Nos 88, 89, 90 and 91 of 2006)
R. v Sanghani (Mitesh) see R. v Fields (Michael)
R. v Sanham (Tony Sydney) see R. v Caley (David)

R. v Sarna (Subir Singh) see R. v Kapoor (Saran Singh)

R. v Saunders (Red); *joined cases* R. v G; R. v Edwards (Ian Peter) [2013] EWCA Crim 1027; [2014] 1 Cr. App. R. (S.) 45; [2013] Crim. L.R. 930, CA (Crim Div) .. *Digested,* 14/**2648**

R. v Sayed (George Mohammed) [2014] EWCA Crim 282; [2014] 2 Cr. App. R. (S.) 39, CA (Crim Div)

R. v Schildkamp see DPP v Schildkamp

R. v Scottish and Southern Energy Plc; *sub nom* Surrey Trading Standards v Scottish and Southern Energy Plc [2012] EWCA Crim 539; (2012) 176 J.P. 241; [2012] C.T.L.C. 1; [2014] L.L.R. 780, CA (Crim Div) .......... *Digested,* 12/**3372**

R. v Scunthorpe Justices Ex p. G see R. v Scunthorpe Justices Ex p. M

R. v Scunthorpe Justices Ex p. M; *joined case* R. v Scunthorpe Justices Ex p. G (1998) 162 J.P. 635; Times, March 10, 1998, DC .......... *Digested,* 98/**1038**: *Applied* 00/1047, 05/828, 07/988, 08/765: *Considered* 14/766: *Distinguished* 08/831: *Followed* 98/1037, 00/1048

R. v Searle (Terence); *joined cases* R. v Borjanovic (Barislov); R. v BYE; R. v KCS Products (1995) 16 Cr. App. R. (S.) 944; [1995] 3 C.M.L.R. 196; Times, February 27, 1995; Independent, March 2, 1995, CA (Crim Div) .......... *Digested,* 95/**4920**: *Considered* 14/772

R. v Secretary of State for Social Security Ex p. Sherwin (1996) 32 B.M.L.R. 1, QBD .. *Digested,* 96/**2961**: *Considered* 14/2568

R. v Secretary of State for the Environment Ex p. Powis [1981] 1 W.L.R. 584; [1981] 1 All E.R. 788; 79 L.G.R. 318; (1981) 42 P. & C.R. 73; (1980) 258 E.G. 57; [1981] J.P.L. 270; (1981) 125 S.J. 324, CA (Civ Div); affirming [1980] J.P.L. 673, QBD *Digested,* 81/**1535**: *Applied* 83/3662, 83/3723, 92/2393, 92/2417, 04/1622, 12/547: *Followed* 85/4892, 91/16, 96/3231, 03/65, 14/535

R. v Secretary of State for the Environment, Transport and the Regions Ex p. Holdings & Barnes Plc see R. (on the application of Holding & Barnes Plc) v Secretary of State for the Environment, Transport and the Regions

R. v Secretary of State for the Environment, Transport and the Regions Ex p. Spath Holme Ltd see R. (on the application of Spath Holme Ltd) v Secretary of State for the Environment, Transport and the Regions

R. v Secretary of State for the Home Department Ex p. Abdi (Khalif Mohamed); *joined case* R. v Secretary of State for the Home Department Ex p. Gawe (Abdifatah Abduleh) [1996] 1 W.L.R. 298; [1996] 1 All E.R. 641; [1996] Imm. A.R. 288; (1996) 8 Admin. L.R. 248; (1996) 146 N.L.J. 245; (1996) 140 S.J.L.B. 63; Times, February 17, 1996; Independent, February 21, 1996, HL; affirming [1994] Imm. A.R. 402; [1995] C.O.D. 73; Times, April 25, 1994; Independent, April 21, 1994; Guardian, May 3, 1994, CA (Civ Div); reversing Times, March 10, 1994, QBD .......... *Digested,* 96/**3238**: *Applied* 96/3192: *Considered* 96/3237: *Followed* 14/1664

R. v Secretary of State for the Home Department Ex p. Alexander see R. v Secretary of State for the Home Department Ex p. Oladehinde

R. v Secretary of State for the Home Department Ex p. Ali see R. (on the application of Javed) v Secretary of State for the Home Department

R. v Secretary of State for the Home Department Ex p. Daly see R. (on the application of Daly) v Secretary of State for the Home Department

R. v Secretary of State for the Home Department Ex p. Doody; *joined cases* R. v Secretary of State for the Home Department Ex p. Pegg; R. v Secretary of State for the Home Department Ex p. Smart; R. v Secretary of State for the Home Department Ex p. Pierson [1994] 1 A.C. 531; [1993] 3 W.L.R. 154; [1993] 3 All E.R. 92; (1995) 7 Admin. L.R. 1; (1993) 143 N.L.J. 991; Times, June 29, 1993; Independent, June 25, 1993, HL; affirming [1993] Q.B. 157; [1992] 3 W.L.R. 956; [1993] 1 All E.R. 151; (1993) 5 Admin. L.R. 93; [1992] C.O.D. 458; Times, May 8, 1992; Independent, May 7, 1992; Guardian, May 13, 1992, CA (Civ Div); reversing [1991] C.O.D. 256, QBD .......... *Digested,* 93/**1213**: *Applied* 94/3848, 95/960, 97/1335, 97/3929, 99/5437, 03/2058, 04/2772, 05/1785, 05/4967, 06/4534, 07/2173, 11/1779, 14/2162, 14/70: *Considered* 94/3841, 95/162, 95/2534, 95/2617, 95/42, 96/1954, 96/1975, 96/4579, 96/6855, 97/1595, 97/2443, 98/4079, 00/3334, 00/4326, 02/3234, 04/1904, 11/3204: *Followed* 95/81, 96/1953, 96/3981, 97/1626, 97/2672, 97/2678, 99/5212: *Referred to* 95/1314

R. v Secretary of State for the Home Department Ex p. Draz see R. v Secretary of State for the Home Department Ex p. Yeboah

R. v Secretary of State for the Home Department Ex p. Duggan [1994] 3 All E.R. 277; [1994] C.O.D. 258; Times, December 9, 1993; Independent, January 28, 1994; Guardian, December 13, 1993, DC .......... *Digested,* 94/**3848**: *Applied* 10/2315: *Cited* 00/4329: *Considered* 97/3927, 14/2162: *Followed* 97/3928

R. v Secretary of State for the Home Department Ex p. Gawe (Abdifatah Abduleh) see R. v Secretary of State for the Home Department Ex p. Abdi (Khalif Mohamed)

R. v Secretary of State for the Home Department Ex p. Harry [1998] 1 W.L.R. 1737; [1998] 3 All E.R. 360; (1998) 43 B.M.L.R. 155; (1998) 95(22) L.S.G. 29; Times, May 15, 1998, QBD ........ *Digested,* 98/**3902**: *Considered* 11/2344, 14/2162

R. v Secretary of State for the Home Department Ex p. Javed see R. (on the application of Javed) v Secretary of State for the Home Department

R. v Secretary of State for the Home Department Ex p. Jeyeanthan; *sub nom* Secretary of State for the Home Department v Ravichandran; R. v Immigration Appeal Tribunal Ex p. Jeyeanthan; *joined case* Ravichandran v Secretary of State for the Home Department [2000] 1 W.L.R. 354; [1999] 3 All E.R. 231; [2000] Imm. A.R. 10; [1999] I.N.L.R. 241; (1999) 11 Admin. L.R. 824; [1999] C.O.D. 349; Times, May 26, 1999; Independent, June 8, 1999, CA (Civ Div); affirming [1998] Imm. A.R. 369; [1998] I.N.L.R. 540; Times, April 23, 1998, QBD ........ *Digested,* 99/**3162**: *Applied* 01/4380, 02/858, 04/4156, 06/2699, 06/3291, 06/582, 07/2372, 09/1094, 12/2053, 12/2692, 12/2717, 12/981, 14/2011: *Considered* 04/2012, 05/2826, 07/3059: *Distinguished* 02/4216: *Referred to* 01/4713

R. v Secretary of State for the Home Department Ex p. Kaziu see R. v Uxbridge Magistrates Court Ex p. Adimi

R. v Secretary of State for the Home Department Ex p. Kerrouche (No.1); *sub nom* Kerrouche v Secretary of State for the Home Department (No.1); R. v Special Adjudicator Ex p. Kerrouche (No.1) [1997] Imm. A.R. 610; [1998] I.N.L.R. 88, CA (Civ Div) ........ *Digested,* 98/**3205**: *Considered* 99/3183: *Followed* 14/1664

R. v Secretary of State for the Home Department Ex p. Moon [1997] I.N.L.R. 165; (1996) 8 Admin. L.R. 477; [1996] C.O.D. 54; Times, December 8, 1995; Independent, November 2, 1995, QBD ........ *Digested,* 95/**50**: *Approved* 14/2162

R. v Secretary of State for the Home Department Ex p. Oladehinde; *joined case* R. v Secretary of State for the Home Department Ex p. Alexander [1991] 1 A.C. 254; [1990] 3 W.L.R. 797; [1990] 3 All E.R. 393; (1991) 3 Admin. L.R. 393; (1990) 140 N.L.J. 1498; (1990) 134 S.J. 1264; Independent, October 18, 1990, HL; affirming [1990] 2 W.L.R. 1195; [1990] 2 All E.R. 367; (1991) 3 Admin. L.R. 23; [1990] C.O.D. 254; (1990) 140 N.L.J. 402; Times, March 16, 1990; Independent, March 16, 1990; Guardian, March 16, 1990, CA (Civ Div); reversing Times, March 1, 1990, DC ........ *Digested,* 91/**1981**: *Applied* 95/2691, 98/3222, 02/2593: *Considered* 96/3260, 98/3222, 14/2568: *Followed* 96/2961, 02/5881: *Referred to* 92/2384

R. v Secretary of State for the Home Department Ex p. Pegg see R. v Secretary of State for the Home Department Ex p. Doody

R. v Secretary of State for the Home Department Ex p. Pierson see R. v Secretary of State for the Home Department Ex p. Doody

R. v Secretary of State for the Home Department Ex p. Ravichandran (No.1); *sub nom* R. v Immigration Appeal Tribunal Ex p. Sandralingam (No.1); *joined cases* R. v Secretary of State for the Home Department Ex p. Sandralingham (No.1); R. v Immigration Appeal Tribunal Ex p. Rajendrakumar [1996] Imm. A.R. 97; Times, October 30, 1995, CA (Civ Div) ........ *Digested,* 96/**3216**: *Applied* 98/3174, 03/2234, 07/2277, 13/1579, 14/1657: *Cited* 99/3202: *Considered* 96/3225, 97/2862, 98/3227, 99/3168, 05/2154, 07/2299: *Followed* 97/2863, 00/3322, 05/2215

R. v Secretary of State for the Home Department Ex p. Samaroo see R. (on the application of Samaroo) v Secretary of State for the Home Department

R. v Secretary of State for the Home Department Ex p. Sandralingham (No.1) see R. v Secretary of State for the Home Department Ex p. Ravichandran (No.1)

R. v Secretary of State for the Home Department Ex p. Singh see R. v Governor of Durham Prison Ex p. Singh

R. v Secretary of State for the Home Department Ex p. Smart see R. v Secretary of State for the Home Department Ex p. Doody

R. v Secretary of State for the Home Department Ex p. Sorani see R. v Uxbridge Magistrates Court Ex p. Adimi

R. v Secretary of State for the Home Department Ex p. Turgut; *sub nom* Turgut v Secretary of State for the Home Department [2001] 1 All E.R. 719; [2000] H.R.L.R. 337; [2000] U.K.H.R.R. 403; [2000] Imm. A.R. 306; [2000] I.N.L.R. 292; [2001] A.C.D. 12; (2000) 97(7) L.S.G. 40; (2000) 150 N.L.J. 131; Times, February 15, 2000, CA (Civ Div) ........ *Digested,* 00/**3297**: *Applied* 00/3344, 01/5879: *Considered* 00/3392: *Distinguished* 14/68

R. v Secretary of State for the Home Department Ex p. Yeboah; *joined case* R. v Secretary of State for the Home Department Ex p. Draz [1987] 1 W.L.R. 1586; [1987] 3 All E.R. 999; [1987] Imm. A.R. 414; (1987) 84 L.S.G. 1811; (1987) 131 S.J. 974, CA (Civ Div); affirming [1986] Imm. A.R. 52, QBD .............................. *Digested,* 88/**1848**: *Considered* 96/3309, 97/2227: *Disapproved* 88/1884: *Followed* 14/2379

R. v Secretary of State for Transport Ex p. Factortame Ltd (No.2) [1991] 1 A.C. 603; [1990] 3 W.L.R. 818; [1991] 1 All E.R. 70; [1991] 1 Lloyd's Rep. 10; [1990] 3 C.M.L.R. 375; (1991) 3 Admin. L.R. 333; (1990) 140 N.L.J. 1457; (1990) 134 S.J. 1189, HL .............................. *Digested,* 91/**4032**: *Applied* 91/4030, 94/1981, 95/4734, 02/1510: *Considered* 92/2904, 93/3262, 94/4, 95/4563, 97/4627, 98/2661, 99/5082, 14/323: *Followed* 97/5714, 00/2180, 11/342: *Preliminary ruling given* 96/2803: *Referred to* 95/4937

R. v Secretary of State for Transport Ex p. Factortame Ltd (No.5) [2000] 1 A.C. 524; [1999] 3 W.L.R. 1062; [1999] 4 All E.R. 906; [1999] 3 C.M.L.R. 597; [2000] Eu. L.R. 40; (1999) 96(43) L.S.G. 32; [1999] N.P.C. 126; Times, November 3, 1999, HL; affirming [1999] 2 All E.R. 640 (Note); [1998] 3 C.M.L.R. 192; [1998] Eu. L.R. 456; [1998] C.O.D. 381; [1998] N.P.C. 68; Times, April 28, 1998, CA (Civ Div); affirming [1998] 1 All E.R. 736 (Note); [1998] 1 C.M.L.R. 1353; [1997] Eu. L.R. 475; (1998) 10 Admin. L.R. 107; Times, September 11, 1997, QBD ..... *Digested,* 99/**2259**: *Applied* 01/1092, 10/3278, 14/1853

R. v Sefton MBC Ex p. Pau see R. v Hertfordshire CC Ex p. Cheung

R. v Selby DC Ex p. Oxton Farms [1997] E.G. 60 (C.S.), CA (Civ Div) .............................. *Digested,* 97/**4114**: *Applied* 05/3279, 07/3291, 09/3041, 14/2397

R. v Sellafield Ltd; *joined case* R. v Network Rail Infrastructure Ltd [2014] EWCA Crim 49; [2014] Env. L.R. 19; [2014] L.L.R. 572, CA (Crim Div) .............................. *Digested,* 14/**2632**: *Considered* 14/2627

R. v Selvaratnam (Rubesius) see R. v Rajakumar (Aathavan)

R. v Shabir (Mohammed) [2008] EWCA Crim 1809; [2009] 1 Cr. App. R. (S.) 84; [2009] Lloyd's Rep. F.C. 53; [2008] Crim. L.R. 991, CA (Crim Div) .............................. *Digested,* 09/**835**: *Applied* 09/848, 14/733: *Considered* 09/829, 11/723, 12/756, 14/743

R. v Shaukat (Mirza Hamayou) see R. v Gordon (Gavin Stephen)

R. v Sheidu (Amuda Yousouf) [2014] EWCA Crim 1671; [2014] Crim. L.R. 827, CA (Crim Div)

R. v Sheppard (James Martin); *joined case* R. v Sheppard (Jennifer Christine) [1981] A.C. 394; [1980] 3 W.L.R. 960; [1980] 3 All E.R. 899; (1981) 72 Cr. App. R. 82; [1981] Crim. L.R. 171; (1980) 124 S.J. 864, HL; reversing (1980) 70 Cr. App. R. 210, CA (Crim Div) .............................. *Digested,* 81/**490**: *Applied* 82/638, 93/5089, 14/688: *Considered* 81/1564, 91/988, 04/753, 12/3769, 14/689: *Not applied* 13/3591: *Referred to* 12/801

R. v Sheppard (Jennifer Christine) see R. v Sheppard (James Martin)

R. v Shields (David) [2011] EWCA Crim 2343; [2012] 1 Cr. App. R. 9; [2012] Crim. L.R. 798, CA (Crim Div) .............................. *Digested,* 12/**795**: *Distinguished* 14/775

R. v Shoker (Harinder) see R. v Mahil (Mundill Kaur)

R. v Shropshire CC Ex p. Abdullah see R. v Barnet LBC Ex p. Shah

R. v Simcox [1964] Crim. L.R. 402; Times, February 25, 1964, CCA .............................. *Digested,* 64/**818**: *Considered* 11/647: *Followed* 66/2637, 14/778

R. v Sinclair (Jake Andrew) see R. v Wiggins (Liam Roy)

R. v Singh (James Paul) [2007] EWCA Crim 2140, CA (Crim Div) *Applied* 14/653: *Considered* 11/573

R. v Singh (Jaspal (aka Chahal)) see R. v Randhawa (Jagprit)

R. v Singh (Nermon) see R. v Kapoor (Saran Singh)

R. v Slade (Mark) see R. v Preddy (John Crawford)

R. v Smith (David Cadman); *sub nom* R. v Cadman-Smith (David) [2001] UKHL 68; [2002] 1 W.L.R. 54; [2002] 1 All E.R. 366; [2002] 1 Cr. App. R. 35; [2002] 2 Cr. App. R. (S.) 37; [2002] Crim. L.R. 396; (2002) 99(7) L.S.G. 34; (2002) 146 S.J.L.B. 20; Times, December 17, 2001; Independent, December 18, 2001; Daily Telegraph, December 20, 2001, HL; reversing [2001] 1 Cr. App. R. (S.) 61; (2000) 164 J.P. 575; (2001) 165 J.P.N. 66; Times, July 26, 2000, CA (Crim Div) .............................. *Digested,* 02/**3898**: *Applied* 04/3310, 05/3616, 05/3901, 06/3677, 06/909, 06/910, 08/777, 09/840, 12/758, 13/690, 13/749: *Considered* 06/3672, 14/738: *Distinguished* 03/3659: *Followed* 03/3658, 05/794, 06/3676, 09/848

R. v Smith (Dean Martin); *joined cases* R. v Christie (Michael Anthony); R. v Parchment (Jamal Sky); R. v Wilkins (Leonard James); R. v Carter (William Melvin); R. v Spencer (Carl George) [2008] EWCA Crim 1342; [2009] 1 Cr. App. R. 36; [2009] Crim. L.R. 440, CA (Crim Div) .............................. *Digested,* 09/**767**: *Applied* 10/654, 13/614, 14/692: *Considered* 11/585: *Followed* 14/645

R. v Smith (Kim) [2013] EWCA Crim 502; [2014] 1 W.L.R. 898; [2013] 2 Cr. App. R. (S.) 77; [2013] Crim. L.R. 696, CA (Crim Div) ........ *Digested,* 13/**696**
R. v Smith (Owen) [2014] EWCA Crim 2163; (2014) 158(27) S.J.L.B. 37, CA (Crim Div)
R. v Smith (Paul James) [2013] EWCA Crim 2388; [2014] 2 Cr. App. R. 1; [2014] Crim. L.R. 612, CA (Crim Div) ........ *Digested,* 14/**707**
R. v Smith (Paul Simon) see Attorney General's Reference (No.27 of 2013)
R. v Smith (Paul) see R. v Atkinson (Glynn)
R. v Smith (Steven); *joined cases* R. v Dodd (Jonathan); R. v Hall (Bryan); R. v Clarke (Wayne) [2011] EWCA Crim 1772; [2012] 1 W.L.R. 1316; [2012] 1 All E.R. 451; [2012] 1 Cr. App. R. (S.) 82; [2011] Crim. L.R. 967, CA (Crim Div) ........ *Digested,* 12/**3019**: *Applied* 13/2776, 14/2687: *Considered* 13/2580, 14/2685, 14/2686, 14/3461: *Followed* 13/2125, 14/775
R. v Smith (Wallace Duncan) (No.4) [2004] EWCA Crim 631; [2004] Q.B. 1418; [2004] 3 W.L.R. 229; [2004] 2 Cr. App. R. 17; Times, March 29, 2004, CA (Crim Div) .. *Digested,* 04/**818**: *Applied* 11/688, 14/788
R. v Sneath (Paul Samuel) see R. v Mejia (Johnny Edisson)
R. v Solliman (Madhat) see R. v Kayani (Talib Hussein)
R. v Soneiji (Kamalesh Kumar) see R. v Soneji (Kamlesh Kumar)
R. v Soneji (Kamlesh Kumar); *sub nom* R. v Soneiji (Kamalesh Kumar); *joined case* R. v Bullen (David Frederick) [2005] UKHL 49; [2006] 1 A.C. 340; [2005] 3 W.L.R. 303; [2005] 4 All E.R. 321; [2006] 2 Cr. App. R. 20; [2006] 1 Cr. App. R. (S.) 79; [2006] Crim. L.R. 167; (2005) 102(31) L.S.G. 26; (2005) 155 N.L.J. 1315; (2005) 149 S.J.L.B. 924; Times, July 22, 2005; Independent, July 26, 2005, HL; reversing [2003] EWCA Crim 1765; [2004] 1 Cr. App. R. (S.) 34; [2003] Crim. L.R. 738; (2003) 100(33) L.S.G. 27; (2003) 147 S.J.L.B. 817; Times, July 1, 2003, CA (Crim Div) ........ *Digested,* 05/**842**: *Applied* 04/806, 06/3679, 06/912, 06/950, 08/1394, 09/2685, 09/3578, 09/845, 10/2240, 12/1803, 12/1806, 13/1623, 13/3283, 14/2011, 14/742: *Cited* 10/740: *Complaint upheld* 09/2012: *Considered* 07/3059, 08/3355, 08/589, 09/4031, 11/4480, 12/2334, 12/4196, 13/736: *Followed* 05/841, 10/1774, 11/2747, 11/719, 11/733, 12/981, 13/1672
R. v Southern Water Services Ltd [2014] EWCA Crim 120; [2014] 2 Cr. App. R. (S.) 29, CA (Crim Div) ........ *Digested,* 14/**2627**
R. v Special Adjudicator Ex p. Kerrouche (No.1) see R. v Secretary of State for the Home Department Ex p. Kerrouche (No.1)
R. v Special Commissioners of Income Tax Ex p. Morgan Grenfell & Co Ltd see R. (on the application of Morgan Grenfell & Co Ltd) v Special Commissioners of Income Tax
R. v Speed (Robert James) [2013] EWCA Crim 1650; (2013) 177 J.P. 649, CA (Crim Div) ........ *Digested,* 14/**653**
R. v Spencer (Adam Kenneth) [2013] EWCA Crim 2286; [2014] 2 Cr. App. R. (S.) 18, CA (Crim Div) ........ *Digested,* 14/**2686**
R. v Spencer (Adam) [2014] EWCA Crim 444; [2014] 2 Cr. App. R. (S.) 32, CA (Crim Div)
R. v Spencer (Carl George) see R. v Smith (Dean Martin)
R. v Spencer-Whalley (Nicola Jane) [2014] EWCA Crim 912; [2014] 2 Cr. App. R. (S.) 56, CA (Crim Div)
R. v Squires (Mark) see R. v Irving (Neil)
R. v Standage (Terence Edward) see R. v Hoath (Terence)
R. v Stanton (Adrian Mark); *joined case* R. v Wildman (Lee Paul) [2013] EWCA Crim 1456; [2014] 1 Cr. App. R. (S.) 56, CA (Crim Div) ........ *Digested,* 14/**2598**
R. v Stapleton (Vincent John) see R. v May (Raymond George)
R. v Stewart (James) [2009] EWCA Crim 593; [2009] 1 W.L.R. 2507; [2010] 1 All E.R. 260; [2009] 2 Cr. App. R. 30; [2009] Crim. L.R. 807; Times, July 20, 2009, CA (Crim Div) ........ *Digested,* 09/**786**: *Applied* 14/680
R. v Stocker (Keith Anthony) [2013] EWCA Crim 1993; [2014] 1 Cr. App. R. 18; [2014] Crim. L.R. 319, CA (Crim Div) ........ *Digested,* 14/**775**: *Applied* 14/773
R. v Stoker (Graham) [2013] EWCA Crim 1431; [2014] 1 Cr. App. R. (S.) 47, CA (Crim Div) ........ *Digested,* 14/**2634**
R. v Stone (David) [2013] EWCA Crim 723, CA (Crim Div) *Considered* 14/813
R. v Suleman (Omar Mohammed) [2012] EWCA Crim 1569; [2012] 2 Cr. App. R. 30; [2014] Crim. L.R. 66, CA (Crim Div) ........ *Digested,* 12/**646**
R. v Sunderland City Council Ex p. Beresford see R. (on the application of Beresford) v Sunderland City Council

R. v Supplementary Benefits Commission Ex p. Singer [1973] 1 W.L.R. 713; [1973] 2 All E.R. 931; (1973) 117 S.J. 268, DC ............ *Digested,* 73/**2670**: *Applied* 81/2168, 12/3122: *Considered* 88/1782, 14/1689

R. v Sussex Justices Ex p. McCarthy [1924] 1 K.B. 256, KBD *Applied* 68/3372, 75/741, 85/3432, 08/834, 14/42: *Considered* 47-51/7724, 54/2011, 92/955: *Distinguished* 93/849, 99/3796, 07/248: *Followed* 47-51/6074

R. v Sutcliffe (Perry John) see R. v Blackshaw (Jordan Philip)

R. v Swain (Lee Anthony) see R. v Wiggins (Liam Roy)

R. v Swale BC Ex p. Royal Society for the Protection of Birds (1990) 2 Admin. L.R. 790; [1991] 1 P.L.R. 6; [1991] J.P.L. 39; [1990] C.O.D. 263; Times, April 11, 1990; Independent, April 16, 1990, QBD ............ *Digested,* 92/**4368**: *Applied* 99/4260, 03/3400: *Considered* 14/1187, 14/2425

R. v Swansea Crown Court Ex p. Stacey (1990) 154 J.P. 185; [1990] R.T.R. 183; [1990] Crim. L.R. 260; [1990] C.O.D. 155, DC ............ *Digested,* 90/**861**: *Considered* 14/785

R. v Swarez (James) see R. v Cooke (John)

R. v Swinbourne (Frank Paul) [2013] EWCA Crim 2329; (2014) 178 J.P. 34, CA (Crim Div) ............ *Digested,* 14/**651**

R. v Symeou (Deborah) see R. v Allpress (Sylvia)

R. v T [2010] EWCA Crim 2703, CA (Crim Div) *Considered* 14/742

R. v T see R. v L

R. v Tahir (Mustapha) [2013] EWCA Crim 1866; [2014] 2 Cr. App. R. (S.) 2, CA (Crim Div) ............ *Digested,* 14/**2631**

R. v Tangerine Confectionery Ltd; *joined case* R. v Veolia ES (UK) Ltd [2011] EWCA Crim 2015; (2012) 176 J.P. 349, CA (Crim Div) ............ *Digested,* 12/**1611**: *Followed* 14/2296

R. v Tarcuta (Ionut Alexandra) [2014] EWCA Crim 823; [2014] 2 Cr. App. R. (S.) 63, CA (Crim Div)

R. v Tatham (Philip) [2014] EWCA Crim 226; [2014] Lloyd's Rep. F.C. 354; [2014] Crim. L.R. 672, CA (Crim Div) ............ *Digested,* 14/**739**

R. v Taylor (Liam Karl) [2014] EWCA Crim 1611; [2014] 2 Cr. App. R. (S.) 85, CA (Crim Div)

R. v Taylor (Mark William) see R. v Gordon (Gavin Stephen)

R. v Terrell (Alexander James) [2007] EWCA Crim 3079; [2008] 2 All E.R. 1065; [2008] 2 Cr. App. R. (S.) 49; [2008] Crim. L.R. 320; Times, January 14, 2008, CA (Crim Div) ............ *Digested,* 08/**3314**: *Explained* 14/2601: *Followed* 10/2918, 11/2916

R. v Theivendarampillai (Jeyasuthan) see R. v Rajakumar (Aathavan)

R. v THN see R. v L

R. v Thomas (Richard Bartgerald) see R. v Avis (Tony)

R. v Thompson (Amelio) see R. v Reynolds (Michael Edwin)

R. v Thompson (George Weston) see R. v Dyer (Richard)

R. v Tillwach (Howard John) see R. v Bogacki (Steven)

R. v Tollady (Kim) [2010] EWCA Crim 2614, CA (Crim Div) *Considered* 14/653

R. v Torrington (Richard Edward) see R. v Avis (Tony)

R. v Tote (Cassian Ben) see R. v Bailey (Wayne)

R. v Toussaint (Mitchell Paris) see R. v O'Flaherty (Errol Carlton)

R. v Tran (Hai Ban) see R. v Dang (Manh Toan)

R. v Tu (Thuong) see R. v Dang (Manh Toan)

R. v Tucker (Lee Nigel) see R. v Charles (Jerome) (Leave to Appeal)

R. v Tunwer (Sunil) [2012] EWCA Crim 300, CA (Crim Div) *Considered* 14/2621

R. v Tuohy (Paul) see R. v Mahboob (Najamul Saqib)

R. v Turbill (Maxine); *joined case* R. v Broadway (Gail Julie) [2013] EWCA Crim 1422; [2014] 1 Cr. App. R. 7; (2013) 134 B.M.L.R. 13; [2014] Crim. L.R. 388, CA (Crim Div) ............ *Digested,* 14/**688**

R. v Twaite (Timothy) [2010] EWCA Crim 2973; [2011] 1 W.L.R. 1125; [2011] 1 Cr. App. R. 19; Times, April 6, 2011, CMAC ............ *Digested,* 11/**149**: *Applied* 14/2657

R. v Tyrell (Andrew) see R. v Birch (Ben)

R. v Ul Haq (Mobeen) [2013] EWCA Crim 1478; [2014] 1 Cr. App. R. (S.) 52, CA (Crim Div) ............ *Digested,* 14/**2664**

R. v Underwood (Kevin John); *joined cases* R. v Connors (James); R. v Khan (Mohammed Iftiyaz); R. v Arobieke (Akinwale) [2004] EWCA Crim 2256; [2005] 1 Cr. App. R. 13; [2005] 1 Cr. App. R. (S.) 90; (2004) 148 S.J.L.B. 974; Times, September 1, 2004, CA (Crim Div)
*Applied* 09/3384, 11/2973, 13/2566, 14/789: *Considered* 05/3699

R. v Uxbridge Magistrates Court Ex p. Adimi; *joined cases* R. v Secretary of State for the Home Department Ex p. Kaziu; R. v Secretary of State for the Home Department Ex p. Sorani; R. v Crown Prosecution Service Ex p. Sorani [2001] Q.B. 667; [2000] 3 W.L.R. 434; [1999] 4 All E.R. 520; [1999] Imm. A.R. 560; [1999] I.N.L.R. 490; Times, August 12, 1999, QBD .......... *Digested,* 99/**3164**:
*Approved* 08/735: *Considered* 00/3298, 04/2088, 06/804, 06/857, 14/696

R. v V (Abolghasem) see R. v R (Amer)

R. v V see R. v J

R. v Vanasco (Enrico) see R. v Blackshaw (Jordan Philip)

R. v Vaughan (Georgina) [2014] EWCA Crim 1456; [2014] Crim. L.R. 819, CA (Crim Div)

R. v Venayakamoorthy (Kaviloan) see R. v Rajakumar (Aathavan)

R. v Venclovas (Rimas) [2013] EWCA Crim 2182; [2014] Crim. L.R. 684, CA (Crim Div)

R. v Veolia ES (UK) Ltd see R. v Tangerine Confectionery Ltd

R. v Vernon [1988] Crim. L.R. 445, Crown Ct .......... *Digested,* 89/**552**:
*Considered* 14/646

R. v Vijasinghe (Juis James) see R. v Rajakumar (Aathavan)

R. v Vivekananthan (Jeyarubin) see R. v Rajakumar (Aathavan)

R. v W see Attorney General's Reference (No.55 of 2008)

R. v Wain (Darren) see R. v Caley (David)

R. v Waite (Christopher) [2013] EWCA Crim 761; [2014] 1 Cr. App. R. (S.) 8, CA (Crim Div) .......... *Digested,* 14/**2604**

R. v Walker & Son (Hauliers) Ltd see Walker and Son (Hauliers) Ltd v Environment Agency

R. v Walker (Dale) see R. v Crawley (Scott)

R. v Walker (John) see R. v Hodges (Kevin John)

R. v Walker (Nicholas) see R. v Kerrigan (David Joseph)

R. v Walsh (Anthony); *joined case* R. v Brown (Cory) [2014] EWCA Crim 1155; [2014] 2 Cr. App. R. (S.) 59, CA (Crim Div) .......... *Digested,* 14/**2597**

R. v Waltham Forest LBC Ex p. Vale Times, February 25, 1985, QBD .......... *Digested,* 85/**2165**:
*Applied* 13/2956: *Not applied* 14/2806

R. v Walton (Lee Alan) see R. v Norman (Shane Martin)

R. v Ward (Paul) [2005] EWCA Crim 1926; [2006] 1 Cr. App. R. (S.) 66, CA (Crim Div) .......... *Digested,* 06/**3650**:
*Considered* 07/3598, 14/2600

R. v Ward (Terry) [2013] EWCA Crim 2667; [2014] 1 Cr. App. R. (S.) 74, CA (Crim Div)

R. v Waters (Gordon George) see R. v Pitts (Aaron)

R. v Waters (Matthew Peter); *joined case* R. v Young (Thomas Ronald) [2008] EWCA Crim 2538, CA (Crim Div)
*Followed* 14/2592

R. v Waters (Paul Anthony) see R. v Bradshaw (Wayne Martin)

R. v Watling (Mark) [2012] EWCA Crim 2894; [2013] 2 Cr. App. R. (S.) 37, CA (Crim Div) .......... *Digested,* 13/**2626**:
*Applied* 14/2617: *Considered* 14/2616

R. v Waya (Terry); *sub nom* R. v Waya Solicitors [2012] UKSC 51; [2013] 1 A.C. 294; [2012] 3 W.L.R. 1188; [2013] 1 All E.R. 889; [2013] 2 Cr. App. R. (S.) 20; [2013] H.R.L.R. 5; [2013] Lloyd's Rep. F.C. 187; 35 B.H.R.C. 293; [2013] Crim. L.R. 256; Times, December 10, 2012, SC; reversing [2010] EWCA Crim 412; [2011] 1 Cr. App. R. (S.) 4, CA (Crim Div) .......... *Digested,* 13/**689**:
*Applied* 13/685, 14/736, 14/794: *Considered* 14/1631, 14/730, 14/731, 14/738:
*Doubted* 14/773: *Followed* 13/686, 13/690, 13/691, 13/749, 14/728, 14/729,
14/733, 14/734, 14/741, 14/743, 14/773, 14/798

R. v Waya Solicitors see R. v Waya (Terry)

R. v Weatherup (James) see R. v Coulson (Andrew)

R. v Webb (John Paul) see R. v Reynolds (Michael Edwin)

R. v Weeks (Alun) see R. v Dallimore (Paul)

R. v Wellburn (Geoffrey Elliott); *joined cases* R. v Randel (David Arthur); R. v Nurdin (Frank Percival) (1979) 69 Cr. App. R. 254; (1979) 1 Cr. App. R. (S.) 64, CA (Crim Div) .......... *Digested,* 80/**447**:
*Applied* 86/524, 14/678

R. v Westminster City Council Ex p. Monahan [1990] 1 Q.B. 87; [1989] 3 W.L.R. 408; [1989] 2 All E.R. 74; (1989) 58 P. & C.R. 92; [1989] 1 P.L.R. 36; [1989] J.P.L. 107; [1989] C.O.D. 241; [1988] E.G. 140 (C.S.); (1988) 138 N.L.J. Rep. 311; (1989) 133 S.J. 978; Times, October 29, 1988; Independent, October 20, 1988, CA (Civ Div); affirming [1988] J.P.L. 557; Independent, February 9, 1988, QBD *Digested*, 89/**3613**: *Considered* 94/4435, 95/3099: *Distinguished* 92/4201: *Followed* 94/4462, 14/2431

R. v White (Alan) see R. v Gangar (Shinder Singh)

R. v White (Anthony Alan) [2014] EWCA Crim 714; [2014] 2 Cr. App. R. 14; [2014] Crim. L.R. 747; (2014) 158(17) S.J.L.B. 37, CA (Crim Div) ................................ *Digested*, 14/**773**

R. v White (Daniel Oliver) see R. v Wiggins (Liam Roy)

R. v Whitehouse (Arthur) [1977] Q.B. 868; [1977] 2 W.L.R. 925; [1977] 3 All E.R. 737; (1977) 65 Cr. App. R. 33; [1977] Crim. L.R. 689; (1977) 121 S.J. 171, CA (Crim Div) ........................................................................................................ *Digested*, 77/**577**: *Considered* 95/963, 14/772: *Followed* 06/880

R. v Whitnell (Liam); *joined cases* R. v Lawrence (Robert); R. v Fraser (Anthony); R. v Joseph-Bell (Jonathan) [2013] EWCA Crim 161; [2014] 1 Cr. App. R. 9, CA (Crim Div)

R. v Wicks (Derek John) [2013] EWCA Crim 1414; [2014] 1 Cr. App. R. (S.) 57, CA (Crim Div)

R. v Wicks (Peter Edward) [1998] A.C. 92; [1997] 2 W.L.R. 876; [1997] 2 All E.R. 801; (1997) 161 J.P. 433; (1997) 9 Admin. L.R. 349; [1997] 2 P.L.R. 97; [1997] J.P.L. 1049; (1997) 161 J.P.N. 628; (1997) 94(35) L.S.G. 34; (1997) 147 N.L.J. 883; (1997) 141 S.J.L.B. 127; [1997] N.P.C. 85; Times, May 26, 1997; Independent, June 4, 1997, HL; affirming (1996) 160 J.P. 46; 93 L.G.R. 377; (1996) 8 Admin. L.R. 137; [1996] 1 P.L.R. 12; [1996] J.P.L. 743; (1996) 160 J.P. Rep. 548; (1996) 160 J.P.N. 48; (1995) 92(22) L.S.G. 40; (1995) 139 S.J.L.B. 119; [1995] N.P.C. 72; Times, April 19, 1995; Independent, May 11, 1995, CA (Crim Div) ............................................................................................ *Digested*, 97/**4065**: *Applied* 98/3222, 06/4869, 08/2921: *Considered* 13/2301: *Distinguished* 02/3708, 03/776: *Followed* 98/4203, 01/81, 12/2544, 14/717

R. v Wiggins (Liam Roy); *joined cases* R. v Swain (Lee Anthony); R. v White (Daniel Oliver); R. v Samways (Thomas Lewis ); R. v Evans (Ashley); R. v Atter (Joshua James); R. v Greatorex (Marcus Jonathan); R. v Ashmore (Nathan); R. v Deans (Andrew John); R. v Sinclair (Jake Andrew) [2014] EWCA Crim 1433; [2014] 2 Cr. App. R. (S.) 72, CA (Crim Div)

R. v Wildman (John) see R. v Cooke (John)

R. v Wildman (Lee Paul) see R. v Stanton (Adrian Mark)

R. v Wiles (Alan Ralph) [2004] EWCA Crim 836; [2004] 2 Cr. App. R. (S.) 88; [2004] Crim. L.R. 596, CA (Crim Div) ................................................................................ *Digested*, 05/**3640**: *Applied* 12/2970: *Approved* 14/2682

R. v Wilkins (Leonard James) see R. v Smith (Dean Martin)

R. v Williams (Alexander Martin) see Attorney General's Reference (Nos 7 and 8 of 2013)

R. v Williams (Darren George) [2014] EWCA Crim 1703; [2014] 2 Cr. App. R. (S.) 83, CA (Crim Div)

R. v Williams (Dean) [2013] EWCA Crim 2749; [2014] 1 Cr. App. R. 23, CA (Crim Div) *Digested*, 14/**680**

R. v Williams (John Nicolas) [2012] EWCA Crim 1590, CA (Crim Div) *Applied* 14/2611

R. v Williams (Kevin) [2014] EWCA Crim 765; [2014] 2 Cr. App. R. (S.) 58, CA (Crim Div) ........................................................................................................ *Digested*, 14/**2619**

R. v Williams (Stephen David) see R. v McDermott (Stephen Paul)

R. v Wilson (Clarence George); *joined cases* R. v Jenkins (Edward John); R. v Jenkins (Ronald Patrick) [1984] A.C. 242; [1983] 3 W.L.R. 686; [1983] 3 All E.R. 448; (1983) 77 Cr. App. R. 319; [1984] Crim. L.R. 36; (1983) 133 N.L.J. 1016; (1983) 127 S.J. 712, HL; reversing [1983] 1 W.L.R. 356; [1983] 1 All E.R. 993; (1983) 76 Cr. App. R. 255; [1983] Crim. L.R. 327; (1983) 133 N.L.J. 399, CA (Crim Div) ........................................................................................... *Digested*, 83/**686**: *Applied* 87/763: *Considered* 88/658, 94/1132, 97/1226: *Followed* 92/1131, 92/863, 14/773

R. v Wilson (Gary) see R. v Riley (Craig Philip)

R. v Wilson (Joseph) [2013] EWCA Crim 1745; [2014] 1 Cr. App. R. (S.) 79, CA (Crim Div) ........................................................................................................ *Digested*, 14/**2677**

R. v Wilson (Josiah) see Attorney General's Reference (Nos 4, 5, 6, 7 and 8 of 2014)

R. v Wilson (Lee) [2013] EWCA Crim 830; [2014] 1 Cr. App. R. (S.) 19, CA (Crim Div) *Digested*, 14/**2594**

R. v Wilson (Michael) [2013] EWCA Crim 1780; [2014] Q.B. 704; [2014] 2 W.L.R. 1180; [2014] 1 Cr. App. R. 10; [2014] Crim. L.R. 368, CA (Crim Div) ................. *Digested*, 14/**772**

R. v Wilson (Neil) see Attorney General's Reference (No.53 of 2013)

R. v Wiseman (Anthony Patrick) [2013] EWCA Crim 2492; [2014] 2 Cr. App. R. (S.) 23, CA (Crim Div) ........ *Digested,* 14/**2615**
R. v Withers (Helen) see DPP v Withers (Ian Douglas)
R. v Withers (Ian Douglas) see DPP v Withers (Ian Douglas)
R. v Withers (Phyllis May) see DPP v Withers (Ian Douglas)
R. v Withers (Stuart Robert) see DPP v Withers (Ian Douglas)
R. v Wood (Clive) [2008] EWCA Crim 1305; [2009] 1 W.L.R. 496; [2008] 3 All E.R. 898; [2008] 2 Cr. App. R. 34; [2008] Crim. L.R. 976, CA (Crim Div) ........ *Digested,* 08/**839**: *Applied* 12/695, 14/680: *Followed* 09/786
R. v Wood (Gary Dominic) see R. v Rehman (Zakir)
R. v Woodford (Anthony Graham) [2013] EWCA Crim 1098; [2014] 1 Cr. App. R. (S.) 32, CA (Crim Div) ........ *Digested,* 14/**2616**
R. v Wright (Joseph) see Attorney General's Reference (No.51 of 2013)
R. v Wright (Kevin Wright) [2014] EWCA Crim 376; [2014] 2 Cr. App. R. (S.) 42, CA (Crim Div) ........ *Digested,* 14/**2693**
R. v Wright (Raymond Eric) see R. v Dickson (William Ewing)
R. v Wright (Robert) [2014] EWCA Crim 382; [2014] 1 W.L.R. 2913, CA (Crim Div) ..... *Digested,* 14/**737**
R. v Wynne (Emmet); *joined cases* R. v Hall (Robert); R. v Knight (Ian) [2013] EWCA Crim 945; [2014] 1 Cr. App. R. (S.) 14, CA (Crim Div) ........ *Digested,* 14/**2678**
R. v X (Wasted Costs Order), Re see Joseph Hill & Co Solicitors, Re
R. v X Ltd [2013] EWCA Crim 818; [2014] 1 W.L.R. 591; [2013] 3 All E.R. 995; [2013] 2 Cr. App. R. 15; (2013) 177 J.P. 393; [2013] E.C.C. 32; [2013] C.T.L.C. 145; [2013] L.L.R. 500; [2014] Crim. L.R. 73, CA (Crim Div) ........ *Digested,* 13/**561**
R. v Y [2013] EWCA Crim 1175; [2014] 1 Cr. App. R. (S.) 39, CA (Crim Div) ........ *Digested,* 14/**2680**
R. v Yates (Adam Robert) [2013] EWCA Crim 2252; [2014] 2 Cr. App. R. (S.) 16, CA (Crim Div)
R. v Young (Thomas Ronald) see R. v Waters (Matthew Peter)
R. v Yusuf (Samir); *joined cases* R. v McLean (Kurt); R. v Palmer (Devana) [2014] EWCA Crim 1586; [2014] Crim. L.R. 841, CA (Crim Div)
R. v Zeca (Raul Joao) [2009] EWCA Crim 133; [2009] 2 Cr. App. R. (S.) 65; Times, March 17, 2009, CA (Crim Div) ........ *Digested,* 09/**3551**: *Applied* 11/3068: *Considered* 12/3020, 13/2764, 14/2690
R. v Zhao (Wen) [2013] EWCA Crim 1060; [2014] 1 Cr. App. R. (S.) 17, CA (Crim Div) *Digested,* 14/**2675**
R. v Zhekov (Yordan Marinove) [2013] EWCA Crim 1656; [2014] 1 Cr. App. R. (S.) 69, CA (Crim Div) ........ *Digested,* 14/**2636**
R. v Zinga (Munaf Ahmed); *sub nom* R. (on the application of Virgin Media Ltd) v Zinga [2014] EWCA Crim 52; [2014] 1 W.L.R. 2228; [2014] 3 All E.R. 90; [2014] 1 Cr. App. R. 27; [2014] 2 Cr. App. R. (S.) 30; (2014) 178 J.P. 105, CA (Crim Div) ........ *Digested,* 14/**798**
R. v Zinga (Munaf Ahmed) (Costs) see R. (on the application of Virgin Media Ltd) v Zinga
R. (on the application of A (A Child)) v Leeds Magistrates Court [2004] EWHC 554 (Admin); Times, March 31, 2004, QBD (Admin) ........ *Digested,* 04/**793**: *Applied* 14/2135: *Considered* 05/3357
R. (on the application of A) v Chief Constable of B [2012] EWHC 2141 (Admin); [2012] A.C.D. 125, QBD (Admin) *Considered* 14/2462
R. (on the application of A) v Chief Constable of C [2014] EWHC 216 (Admin); [2014] 1 W.L.R. 2776; [2014] Crim. L.R. 761; [2014] A.C.D. 81, QBD (Admin) ........ *Digested,* 14/**2462**
R. (on the application of A) v Chief Constable of Kent [2013] EWCA Civ 1706; (2014) 135 B.M.L.R. 22, CA (Civ Div); affirming [2013] EWHC 424 (Admin); (2013) 131 B.M.L.R. 231; [2013] A.C.D. 80, QBD (Admin) ........ *Digested,* 14/**2444**
R. (on the application of A) v Lambeth LBC see R. (on the application of G) v Barnet LBC
R. (on the application of A) v Lowestoft Magistrates' Court [2013] EWHC 659 (Admin); [2014] 1 W.L.R. 1489; (2013) 177 J.P. 377; [2013] E.M.L.R. 20; [2013] L.L.R. 407; [2013] Crim. L.R. 763; [2013] A.C.D. 72, QBD (Admin) ........ *Digested,* 13/**1554**
R. (on the application of A) v Secretary of State for Health [2014] EWHC 1364 (Admin); [2014] Med. L.R. 246, QBD (Admin) ........ *Digested,* 14/**1482**
R. (on the application of A) v Secretary of State for the Home Department [2012] EWCA Civ 23; Times, March 5, 2012, CA (Civ Div); affirming [2010] EWHC 3318 (Admin), QBD (Admin) ........ *Digested,* 12/**1699**: *Followed* 14/1700
R. (on the application of AA (Afghanistan)) v Secretary of State for the Home Department [2013] UKSC 49; [2013] 1 W.L.R. 2224; [2013] 4 All E.R. 140; [2013] 3 F.C.R. 515; [2013] H.R.L.R. 34; [2014] I.N.L.R. 51; (2013) 163(7569) N.L.J. 15; Times, August 2, 2013, SC; affirming [2012] EWCA Civ 1383, CA (Civ Div) ........ *Digested,* 13/**1601**

R. (on the application of AA (Nigeria)) v Secretary of State for the Home Department [2010] EWHC 2265 (Admin), QBD (Admin)
*Considered* 14/1681

R. (on the application of AA) v Lambeth LBC [2001] EWHC Admin 741; (2002) 5 C.C.L. Rep. 36, QBD (Admin) ........ *Digested,* 03/**2205**: *Applied* 14/2807

R. (on the application of AB) v Haringey LBC [2013] EWHC 416 (Admin); [2014] 2 F.L.R. 63; [2013] Fam. Law 965, QBD (Admin)

R. (on the application of AB) v Huddersfield Magistrates' Court [2014] EWHC 1089 (Admin); [2014] 4 All E.R. 500; [2014] 2 Cr. App. R. 25; (2014) 178 J.P. 265; [2014] Lloyd's Rep. F.C. 527; [2014] A.C.D. 89, QBD (Admin) ........ *Digested,* 14/**806**

R. (on the application of AB) v Secretary of State for Defence [2013] EWHC 3908 (Admin); [2014] A.C.D. 46, DC

R. (on the application of AB) v Secretary of State for the Home Department [2013] EWHC 3453 (Admin); [2014] 2 C.M.L.R. 22, QBD (Admin) ........ *Digested,* 14/**1672**

R. (on the application of Abbasi) v Secretary of State for the Home Department see R. (on the application of Mirza) v Secretary of State for the Home Department

R. (on the application of Abdulle) v Birmingham City Council see R. (on the application of Aweys) v Birmingham City Council

R. (on the application of Adam) v Birmingham City Council see R. (on the application of Aweys) v Birmingham City Council

R. (on the application of Adam) v Secretary of State for the Home Department see R. (on the application of Limbuela) v Secretary of State for the Home Department

R. (on the application of Adams) v Secretary of State for Justice; *joined cases* McCartney, Re; MacDermott, Re [2011] UKSC 18; [2012] 1 A.C. 48; [2011] 2 W.L.R. 1180; [2011] 3 All E.R. 261; [2011] N.I. 42; 31 B.H.R.C. 71; (2011) 108(21) L.S.G. 16; Times, May 12, 2011, SC; reversing in part [2009] EWCA Civ 1291; [2010] Q.B. 460; [2010] 3 W.L.R. 63; [2010] 1 Cr. App. R. 25, CA (Civ Div); affirming [2009] EWHC 156 (Admin), DC ........ *Digested,* 11/**794**: *Considered* 13/744: *Followed* 14/787

R. (on the application of Adesina) v Nursing and Midwifery Council see Adesina v Nursing and Midwifery Council

R. (on the application of AE (Eritrea)) v Secretary of State for the Home Department see R. (on the application of EM (Eritrea)) v Secretary of State for the Home Department

R. (on the application of Aguilar Quila) v Secretary of State for the Home Department; *sub nom* Bibi v Secretary of State for the Home Department; Aguilar Quila v Secretary of State for the Home Department; Quila v Secretary of State for the Home Department; *joined case* R. (on the application of Bibi) v Secretary of State for the Home Department [2011] UKSC 45; [2012] 1 A.C. 621; [2011] 3 W.L.R. 836; [2012] 1 All E.R. 1011; [2012] 1 F.L.R. 788; [2011] 3 F.C.R. 575; [2012] H.R.L.R. 2; [2011] U.K.H.R.R. 1347; 33 B.H.R.C. 381; [2012] Imm. A.R. 135; [2011] I.N.L.R. 698; [2012] Fam. Law 21; (2011) 108(41) L.S.G. 15; (2011) 155(39) S.J.L.B. 31; Times, October 20, 2011, SC; affirming [2010] EWCA Civ 1482; [2011] 3 All E.R. 81; [2011] 1 F.L.R. 1187; [2011] 2 F.C.R. 462; [2011] H.R.L.R. 11; [2011] U.K.H.R.R. 183; [2011] Imm. A.R. 423; [2011] Fam. Law 232; Times, January 10, 2011, CA (Civ Div) ........ *Digested,* 11/**1762**: *Applied* 12/1720, 14/1703: *Considered* 12/2330: *Followed* 13/1625, 14/1715

R. (on the application of Ahmed) v Secretary of State for the Home Department see R. (on the application of Syed) v Secretary of State for the Home Department

R. (on the application of Akpinar) v Upper Tribunal (Immigration and Asylum Chamber); *sub nom* AV (Democratic Republic of Congo) v Secretary of State for the Home Department; *joined case* Secretary of State for the Home Department v AV (Democratic Republic of Congo) [2014] EWCA Civ 937; Times, July 17, 2014, CA (Civ Div) ........ *Digested,* 14/**1678**

R. (on the application of Al-Rawi) v Secretary of State for Foreign and Commonwealth Affairs [2006] EWCA Civ 1279; [2008] Q.B. 289; [2007] 2 W.L.R. 1219; [2006] H.R.L.R. 42; [2007] U.K.H.R.R. 58; (2006) 103(41) L.S.G. 33; Times, October 18, 2006, CA (Civ Div); affirming [2006] EWHC 972 (Admin); [2006] H.R.L.R. 30; [2006] U.K.H.R.R. 891; [2006] A.C.D. 79; (2006) 156 N.L.J. 797; Times, May 19, 2006, QBD (Admin) ........ *Digested,* 06/**2621**: *Applied* 14/55

R. (on the application of Alansi) v Newham LBC [2013] EWHC 3722 (Admin); [2014] P.T.S.R. 948; [2014] H.L.R. 25; [2014] B.L.G.R. 138, QBD (Admin) ........ *Digested,* 14/**1611**

R. (on the application of Alconbury Developments Ltd) v Secretary of State for the Environment, Transport and the Regions see R. (on the application of Holding & Barnes Plc) v Secretary of State for the Environment, Transport and the Regions

R. (on the application of Ali (Abid)) v Secretary of State for the Home Department see R. (on the application of Javed) v Secretary of State for the Home Department

R. (on the application of Ali (Zulfiqar)) v Secretary of State for the Home Department see R. (on the application of Javed) v Secretary of State for the Home Department

R. (on the application of Ali) v Birmingham City Council see R. (on the application of Aweys) v Birmingham City Council

R. (on the application of Ali) v Secretary of State for Justice; *joined cases* R. (on the application of Lawless) v Secretary of State for Justice; R. (on the application of George) v Secretary of State for Justice; R. (on the application of Dennis) v Secretary of State for Justice; R. (on the application of Tunbridge) v Secretary of State for Justice [2014] EWCA Civ 194; [2014] 1 W.L.R. 3202; [2014] 2 All E.R. 1063; Times, April 22, 2014, CA (Civ Div); affirming in part [2013] EWHC 72 (Admin); [2013] 1 W.L.R. 3536; [2013] 2 All E.R. 1055; [2013] Crim. L.R. 587; [2013] A.C.D. 46, DC ............ *Digested,* 14/**787**

R. (on the application of Allatt) v Chief Constable of Nottinghamshire [2011] EWHC 3908 (Admin), QBD (Admin)
*Followed* 14/2447

R. (on the application of Allen) v Secretary of State for Justice see R. (on the application of Harris) v Secretary of State for the Home Department

R. (on the application of Allensway Recycling Ltd) v Environment Agency [2014] EWHC 1638 (Admin); [2014] 1 W.L.R. 3753; [2014] Env. L.R. 27; [2014] L.L.R. 733, QBD (Admin) ............ *Digested,* 14/**1186**

R. (on the application of Alvi) v Secretary of State for the Home Department [2012] UKSC 33; [2012] 1 W.L.R. 2208; [2012] 4 All E.R. 1041; [2012] Imm. A.R. 998; [2012] I.N.L.R. 504, SC; affirming [2011] EWCA Civ 681, CA (Civ Div); reversing [2010] EWHC 2666 (Admin), QBD (Admin) ............ *Digested,* 12/**1755**:
*Applied* 13/1648, 14/1688, 14/1716: *Considered* 14/1653

R. (on the application of AM (Angola)) v Secretary of State for the Home Department [2012] EWCA Civ 521, CA (Civ Div); reversing [2010] EWHC 684 (Admin), QBD (Admin)
*Considered* 14/1681

R. (on the application of AM (Pakistan)) v Secretary of State for the Home Department see R. (on the application of MM (Lebanon)) v Secretary of State for the Home Department

R. (on the application of AM) v DPP see R. (on the application of Nicklinson) v Ministry of Justice

R. (on the application of Amin (Imtiaz)) v Secretary of State for the Home Department; *sub nom* R. (on the application of Middleton) v HM Coroner for Western Somerset; *joined case* R. (on the application of Middleton) v West Somerset Coroner [2003] UKHL 51; [2004] 1 A.C. 653; [2003] 3 W.L.R. 1169; [1998] 1 W.L.R. 972; [2003] 4 All E.R. 1264; [2004] H.R.L.R. 3; [2004] U.K.H.R.R. 75; 15 B.H.R.C. 362; (2004) 76 B.M.L.R. 143; [2003] Inquest L.R. 1; [2004] Prison L.R. 140; (2003) 100(44) L.S.G. 32; (2003) 153 N.L.J. 1600; Times, October 17, 2003, HL; reversing [2002] EWCA Civ 390; [2003] Q.B. 581; [2002] 3 W.L.R. 505; [2002] 4 All E.R. 336; (2002) 166 J.P. 505; [2002] U.K.H.R.R. 846; [2002] Lloyd's Rep. Med. 187; (2003) 69 B.M.L.R. 35; [2002] Po. L.R. 100; [2002] A.C.D. 74; (2002) 166 J.P.N. 529; (2002) 99(19) L.S.G. 29; (2002) 146 S.J.L.B. 101; Times, April 18, 2002; Independent, April 12, 2002, CA (Civ Div); reversing [2001] EWHC Admin 719; [2001] Inquest L.R. 76; [2002] Po. L.R. 74; [2003] Inquest L.R. 1, QBD (Admin) ............ *Digested,* 03/**2167**:
*Applied* 02/26, 03/12, 03/13, 03/2810, 06/18, 06/2933, 06/2934, 07/28, 09/41, 11/1683: *Considered* 04/12, 04/36, 07/2980, 09/1966, 09/2754, 10/1722, 10/3922, 14/47: *Followed* 10/23: *Reversed in part* 04/37

R. (on the application of An Taisce (National Trust For Ireland)) v Secretary of State for Energy and Climate Change [2014] EWCA Civ 1111; Times, September 1, 2014, CA (Civ Div); affirming [2013] EWHC 4161 (Admin), QBD (Admin) ......... *Digested,* 14/**1188**

R. (on the application of AN) v Secretary of State for the Home Department; *joined case* R. (on the application of FA (A Child)) v Secretary of State for the Home Department [2012] EWCA Civ 1636, CA (Civ Div); reversing [2011] EWHC 2541 (Admin), QBD (Admin)
*Considered* 14/1664

R. (on the application of Anam) v Secretary of State for the Home Department; *sub nom* Anam v Secretary of State for the Home Department [2010] EWCA Civ 1140; [2011] A.C.D. 14, CA (Civ Div); affirming [2009] EWHC 2496 (Admin); [2010] A.C.D. 31, QBD (Admin) ............ *Digested,* 10/**1779**:
*Applied* 10/1815, 14/1681

R. (on the application of Andrews) v Secretary of State for the Environment, Food and Rural Affairs [2014] EWHC 1435 (Admin); [2014] 4 All E.R. 718; [2014] P.T.S.R. 1253; [2014] A.C.D. 128, QBD (Admin)

R. (on the application of Animal Defenders International) v Secretary of State for Culture, Media and Sport [2008] UKHL 15; [2008] 1 A.C. 1312; [2008] 2 W.L.R. 781; [2008] 3 All E.R. 193; [2008] E.M.L.R. 8; [2008] H.R.L.R. 25; [2008] U.K.H.R.R. 477; 24 B.H.R.C. 217; (2008) 152(12) S.J.L.B. 30; Times, March 17, 2008, HL; affirming [2006] EWHC 3069 (Admin); [2007] E.M.L.R. 6; [2007] H.R.L.R. 9; [2007] U.K.H.R.R. 310; [2007] A.C.D. 46, DC ................................ *Digested,* 08/**440**: *Complaint dismissed* 14/1628: *Followed* 12/2243, 13/2779, 14/2152

R. (on the application of Antoniou) v Central and North West London NHS Foundation Trust [2013] EWHC 3055 (Admin); [2013] Med. L.R. 536; (2014) 135 B.M.L.R. 89; [2014] A.C.D. 44, DC ................................ *Digested,* 14/**47**

R. (on the application of Anufrijeva) v Secretary of State for the Home Department [2003] UKHL 36; [2004] 1 A.C. 604; [2003] 3 W.L.R. 252; [2003] 3 All E.R. 827; [2003] H.R.L.R. 31; [2003] Imm. A.R. 570; [2003] I.N.L.R. 521; (2003) 100(33) L.S.G. 29; Times, June 27, 2003; Independent, July 1, 2003, HL; reversing [2002] EWCA Civ 399; Independent, April 18, 2002, CA (Civ Div); affirming [2001] EWHC Admin 895, QBD (Admin) ................................ *Digested,* 03/**2223**: *Considered* 04/4996: *Distinguished* 06/28, 13/65, 14/2403

R. (on the application of AR (Iran)) v Secretary of State for the Home Department [2013] EWCA Civ 778; [2013] 3 C.M.L.R. 40, CA (Civ Div); affirming [2012] EWHC 1207 (Admin), QBD (Admin) ................................ *Digested,* 14/**1654**

R. (on the application of Arogundade) v Secretary of State for Business, Innovation and Skills [2013] EWCA Civ 823; [2013] E.L.R. 466; (2013) 16 C.C.L. Rep. 398, CA (Civ Div); affirming [2012] EWHC 2502 (Admin); [2012] E.L.R. 520; (2012) 109(36) L.S.G. 16, QBD (Admin) ................................ *Digested,* 14/**1729**

R. (on the application of Aroun) v Secretary of State for the Home Department see R. (on the application of Geraldo) v Secretary of State for the Home Department

R. (on the application of Ashworth Hospital Authority) v Mental Health Review Tribunal for West Midlands and North West Region see R. (on the application of H) v Ashworth Hospital Authority

R. (on the application of Assisted Reproduction and Gynaecology Centre) v Human Fertilisation and Embryology Authority; *sub nom* Assisted Reproduction and Gynaecology Centre v Human Fertilisation and Embryology Authority [2013] EWHC 3087 (Admin); [2014] 1 W.L.R. 2540; [2014] A.C.D. 45, QBD (Admin) ... *Digested,* 14/**51**

R. (on the application of Aswat) v Secretary of State for the Home Department [2014] EWHC 1216 (Admin); [2014] A.C.D. 116, DC

R. (on the application of Atamewan) v Secretary of State for the Home Department [2013] EWHC 2727 (Admin); [2014] 1 W.L.R. 1959; [2014] A.C.D. 36, QBD (Admin) ................................ *Digested,* 14/**1655**

R. (on the application of Attfield) v Barnet LBC [2013] EWHC 2089 (Admin); [2014] 1 All E.R. 304; [2013] P.T.S.R. 1559; [2013] R.T.R. 33; [2013] B.L.G.R. 633; [2014] A.C.D. 22, QBD (Admin) ................................ *Digested,* 13/**2525**

R. (on the application of Augustine Housing Trust) v Bolton Magistrates' Court [2013] EWHC 4399 (Admin); [2014] R.V.R. 196, QBD (Admin) ................................ *Digested,* 14/**336**

R. (on the application of AW) v Secretary of State for the Home Department see R. (on the application of T) v Chief Constable of Greater Manchester

R. (on the application of Aweys) v Birmingham City Council; *sub nom* Birmingham City Council v Ali; Birmingham City Council v Aweys; *joined cases* R. (on the application of Omar) v Birmingham City Council; R. (on the application of Ali) v Birmingham City Council; R. (on the application of Abdulle) v Birmingham City Council; R. (on the application of Sharif) v Birmingham City Council; R. (on the application of Mohammed) v Birmingham City Council; R. (on the application of Adam) v Birmingham City Council; Moran v Manchester City Council [2009] UKHL 36; [2009] 1 W.L.R. 1506; [2009] 4 All E.R. 161; [2009] P.T.S.R. 1270; [2009] H.L.R. 41; [2009] B.L.G.R. 749; (2009) 106(28) L.S.G. 16; (2009) 153(26) S.J.L.B. 29; [2009] N.P.C. 88; Times, July 7, 2009, HL; reversing [2008] EWCA Civ 48; [2008] 1 W.L.R. 2305; [2008] 1 F.L.R. 1025; [2008] 2 F.C.R. 474; [2008] H.L.R. 32; [2008] Fam. Law 407; Times, February 27, 2008, CA (Civ Div); affirming [2007] EWHC 52 (Admin); [2007] 1 F.L.R. 2066; [2007] H.L.R. 27; [2007] Fam. Law 493; Times, February 21, 2007, QBD (Admin) ....... *Digested,* 09/**1905**: *Distinguished* 11/1669: *Followed* 14/1603

R. (on the application of Aweys) v Birmingham City Council see Ali v Birmingham City Council

R. (on the application of B (Jamaica)) v Secretary of State for the Home Department see R. (on the application of Brown) v Secretary of State for the Home Department

R. (on the application of B) v Secretary of State for Foreign and Commonwealth Affairs [2004] EWCA Civ 1344; [2005] Q.B. 643; [2005] 2 W.L.R. 618; [2004] H.R.L.R. 41; [2005] Imm. A.R. 32; [2005] I.N.L.R. 36; [2005] A.C.D. 72; (2004) 101(42) L.S.G. 30; (2004) 148 S.J.L.B. 1247; Times, October 25, 2004; Independent, November 10, 2004, CA (Civ Div) .............................................. *Digested,* 04/**2008**:
*Applied* 06/2163, 09/1986: *Followed* 14/1587

R. (on the application of B) v Secretary of State for the Home Department [2014] EWCA Civ 854; [2014] 1 W.L.R. 4188; (2014) 164(7613) N.L.J. 18; Times, July 15, 2014, CA (Civ Div); affirming [2013] EWHC 2281 (Admin); [2014] A.C.D. 12, QBD (Admin) .............................................. *Digested,* 14/**1651**

R. (on the application of B) v Secretary of State for the Home Department see R. (on the application of T) v Chief Constable of Greater Manchester

R. (on the application of B) v Westminster Magistrates' Court; *sub nom* EN v Westminster Magistrates' Court; CM v Westminster Magistrates' Court; CU v Westminster Magistrates' Court; VB v Westminster Magistrates' Court; *joined cases* R. (on the application of N) v Westminster Magistrates' Court; R. (on the application of M) v Westminster Magistrates' Court; R. (on the application of U) v Westminster Magistrates' Court [2014] UKSC 59; [2014] 3 W.L.R. 1336, SC; affirming [2014] EWHC 889 (Admin); [2014] A.C.D. 92, QBD (Admin)

R. (on the application of BA (Nigeria)) v Secretary of State for the Home Department see R. (on the application of PE (Cameroon)) v Secretary of State for the Home Department

R. (on the application of Baiai) v Secretary of State for the Home Department; *joined cases* R. (on the application of Trzcinska) v Secretary of State for the Home Department; R. (on the application of Tilki) v Secretary of State for the Home Department; R. (on the application of Bigoku) v Secretary of State for the Home Department [2008] UKHL 53; [2009] 1 A.C. 287; [2008] 3 W.L.R. 549; [2008] 3 All E.R. 1094; [2008] 2 F.L.R. 1462; [2008] 3 F.C.R. 1; [2008] H.R.L.R. 45; [2008] U.K.H.R.R. 1232; 26 B.H.R.C. 429; [2008] Fam. Law 994; (2008) 158 N.L.J. 1225; (2008) 152(31) S.J.L.B. 29; Times, August 13, 2008, HL; affirming [2007] EWCA Civ 478; [2008] Q.B. 143; [2007] 3 W.L.R. 573; [2007] 4 All E.R. 199; [2007] 2 F.L.R. 627; [2007] 2 F.C.R. 421; [2007] H.R.L.R. 29; [2007] U.K.H.R.R. 771; [2007] Imm. A.R. 730; [2007] Fam. Law 806; (2007) 104(23) L.S.G. 33; (2007) 151 S.J.L.B. 711; Times, June 26, 2007, CA (Civ Div); reversing in part [2006] EWHC 823 (Admin); [2007] 1 W.L.R. 693; [2006] 3 All E.R. 608; [2006] 2 F.L.R. 645; [2006] 2 F.C.R. 131; [2006] Fam. Law 535; (2006) 150 S.J.L.B. 573; Times, April 14, 2006, QBD (Admin) .......................... *Digested,* 08/**2059**:
*Applied* 14/1703: *Considered* 11/1438, 11/1762: *Referred to* 11/1697

R. (on the application of Bailey) v Brent LBC; *sub nom* Bailey v Brent LBC [2011] EWCA Civ 1586; [2012] Eq. L.R. 168; [2012] B.L.G.R. 530, CA (Civ Div); affirming [2011] EWHC 2572 (Admin), QBD (Admin) .......................................... *Digested,* 12/**2211**:
*Applied* 13/2022: *Considered* 14/1509: *Followed* 12/2209, 13/2885

R. (on the application of Baker) v Secretary of State for Communities and Local Government; *sub nom* Baker v Secretary of State for Communities and Local Government [2008] EWCA Civ 141; [2009] P.T.S.R. 809; [2008] B.L.G.R. 239; [2008] 2 P. & C.R. 6; [2008] J.P.L. 1469; [2008] A.C.D. 62; (2008) 105(10) L.S.G. 27; (2008) 152(10) S.J.L.B. 31; [2008] N.P.C. 26, CA (Civ Div); affirming [2007] EWHC 2370 (Admin), QBD (Admin) .......................................... *Digested,* 08/**2934**:
*Applied* 08/920, 10/1548, 12/2611, 12/3156, 13/2356: *Considered* 14/2106:
*Distinguished* 11/2563: *Followed* 12/2209, 12/2586

R. (on the application of Bampton Property Group Ltd) v King; *sub nom* Bampton Property Group Ltd v King (Revenue Officer) [2012] EWCA Civ 1744; [2014] S.T.C. 56; [2013] B.T.C. 24; [2013] S.T.I. 257, CA (Civ Div); affirming [2012] EWHC 361 (Admin); [2012] S.T.C. 1321; [2012] B.T.C. 70; [2012] S.T.I. 543, QBD (Admin) .............................................. *Digested,* 13/**3037**

R. (on the application of Bancoult) v Secretary of State for Foreign and Commonwealth Affairs [2008] UKHL 61; [2009] 1 A.C. 453; [2008] 3 W.L.R. 955; [2008] 4 All E.R. 1055; (2008) 105(42) L.S.G. 20; (2008) 158 N.L.J. 1530; (2008) 152(41) S.J.L.B. 29; Times, October 23, 2008, HL; reversing [2007] EWCA Civ 498; [2008] Q.B. 365; [2007] 3 W.L.R. 768; (2007) 104(23) L.S.G. 31; (2007) 151 S.J.L.B. 707; Times, May 31, 2007, CA (Civ Div); affirming [2006] EWHC 1038 (Admin); [2006] A.C.D. 81; Times, May 23, 2006, DC ........ *Digested,* 09/**645**:
*Applied* 08/2692, 09/1598, 12/3255: *Distinguished* 14/66

R. (on the application of Bancoult) v Secretary of State for Foreign and Commonwealth Affairs [2014] EWCA Civ 708; [2014] 1 W.L.R. 2921; (2014) 158(22) S.J.L.B. 37; [2014] Env. L.R. D4; Times, June 10, 2014, CA (Civ Div); affirming [2013] EWHC 1502 (Admin); [2014] Env. L.R. 2; [2013] A.C.D. 83, QBD (Admin) .............................................. *Digested,* 14/**52**

R. (on the application of Bapio Action Ltd) v Royal College of General Practitioners [2014] EWHC 1416 (Admin); [2014] Eq. L.R. 409; [2014] A.C.D. 119, QBD (Admin) ............ *Digested,* 14/**1509**

R. (on the application of Bar Standards Board) v Disciplinary Tribunal of the Council of the Inns of Court [2014] EWHC 1570 (Admin); [2014] 4 All E.R. 759, QBD (Admin)

R. (on the application of Barclay) v Lord Chancellor see R. (on the application of Barclay) v Secretary of State for Justice

R. (on the application of Barclay) v Secretary of State for Justice; *sub nom* R. (on the application of Barclay) v Lord Chancellor [2014] UKSC 54; [2014] 3 W.L.R. 1142; Times, October 27, 2014, SC; reversing [2013] EWHC 1183 (Admin); [2014] 1 W.L.R. 415, QBD (Admin) ............ *Digested,* 14/**66**

R. (on the application of Barkas) v North Yorkshire CC; *sub nom* Barkas v North Yorkshire CC [2014] UKSC 31; [2014] 2 W.L.R. 1360; [2014] 3 All E.R. 178; [2014] H.L.R. 36; [2014] B.L.G.R. 459; [2014] 2 E.G.L.R. 115; Times, June 3, 2014, SC; affirming [2012] EWCA Civ 1373; [2013] 1 W.L.R. 1521; [2013] B.L.G.R. 32; [2013] 1 P. & C.R. 8; [2013] 1 E.G.L.R. 1; [2013] 2 E.G. 68; [2012] 44 E.G. 95 (C.S.), CA (Civ Div); affirming [2011] EWHC 3653 (Admin), QBD (Admin) ............ *Digested,* 14/**2526**

R. (on the application of Barker) v Brighton and Hove City Council [2014] EWHC 233 (Admin); [2014] J.P.L. 877, QBD (Admin) ............ *Digested,* 14/**2375**

R. (on the application of Barot) v Secretary of State for the Home Department see R. (on the application of Mirza) v Secretary of State for the Home Department

R. (on the application of Bateman) v South Cambridgeshire DC [2011] EWCA Civ 157; [2011] N.P.C. 22, CA (Civ Div); reversing [2010] EWHC 797 (Admin), QBD (Admin)
*Considered* 12/2548, 14/1188, 14/2425: *Followed* 14/2420, 14/2427, 14/2434

R. (on the application of Bavi) v Snaresbrook Crown Court [2013] EWHC 4015 (Admin); [2014] A.C.D. 52, QBD (Admin)

R. (on the application of BB (Algeria)) v Special Immigration Appeals Commission [2012] EWCA Civ 1499; [2013] 1 W.L.R. 1568; [2013] 2 All E.R. 419; [2013] H.R.L.R. 7, CA (Civ Div); affirming [2011] EWHC 2129 (Admin); [2012] 1 All E.R. 229; [2011] H.R.L.R. 39; [2011] U.K.H.R.R. 997; [2012] A.C.D. 12; Times, September 8, 2011, DC ............ *Digested,* 13/**1589**:
*Considered* 14/2237

R. (on the application of Bednash) v Westminster City Council [2014] EWHC 2160 (Admin); [2014] L.L.R. 755, DC

R. (on the application of Begum) v Denbigh High School Governors; *sub nom* R. (on the application of SB) v Denbigh High School Governors [2006] UKHL 15; [2007] 1 A.C. 100; [2006] 2 W.L.R. 719; [2006] 2 All E.R. 487; [2006] 1 F.C.R. 613; [2006] H.R.L.R. 21; [2006] U.K.H.R.R. 708; 23 B.H.R.C. 276; [2006] E.L.R. 273; (2006) 103(14) L.S.G. 29; (2006) 156 N.L.J. 552; Times, March 23, 2006; Independent, March 24, 2006, HL; reversing [2005] EWCA Civ 199; [2005] 1 W.L.R. 3372; [2005] 2 All E.R. 396; [2005] 1 F.C.R. 530; [2005] H.R.L.R. 16; [2005] U.K.H.R.R. 681; 19 B.H.R.C. 126; [2005] E.L.R. 198; (2005) 102(17) L.S.G. 31; (2005) 155 N.L.J. 383; (2005) 149 S.J.L.B. 300; Times, March 4, 2005; Independent, March 8, 2005, CA (Civ Div); reversing [2004] EWHC 1389 (Admin); [2004] E.L.R. 374; [2004] A.C.D. 66; (2004) 101(27) L.S.G. 29; Times, June 18, 2004, QBD (Admin) ............ *Digested,* 06/**1145**:
*Applied* 07/2195, 07/2816, 08/2918, 08/3582, 10/986: *Considered* 07/2193, 07/2194, 09/3007, 14/2444, 14/769: *Disapproved* 09/2089: *Distinguished* 08/1037, 12/2335: *Followed* 09/2089, 09/4361, 12/1301

R. (on the application of Bello) v Salford City Council see R. (on the application of Mensah) v Salford City Council

R. (on the application of Beresford) v Sunderland City Council; *sub nom* R. v Sunderland City Council Ex p. Beresford [2003] UKHL 60; [2004] 1 A.C. 889; [2003] 3 W.L.R. 1306; [2004] 1 All E.R. 160; [2004] 2 P. & C.R. 23; [2004] 1 P.L.R. 85; [2004] 1 E.G.L.R. 94; [2004] J.P.L. 1106; [2003] 47 E.G. 155 (C.S.); (2003) 147 S.J.L.B. 1365; [2003] N.P.C. 139; Times, November 14, 2003, HL; reversing [2001] EWCA Civ 1218; [2002] Q.B. 874; [2002] 2 W.L.R. 693; [2001] 4 All E.R. 565; [2001] B.L.G.R. 469; [2002] 1 P. & C.R. 32; [2001] 3 P.L.R. 120; [2001] J.P.L. 1307; [2001] 32 E.G. 86 (C.S.); (2001) 98(35) L.S.G. 35; (2001) 145 S.J.L.B. 203; [2001] N.P.C. 126; Times, August 29, 2001; Independent, July 31, 2001; Daily Telegraph, September 11, 2001, CA (Civ Div); affirming [2001] 1 W.L.R. 1327; (2001) 82 P. & C.R. 19; [2000] E.G. 134 (C.S.); Times, January 16, 2001; Daily Telegraph, November 28, 2000, QBD (Admin) ............ *Digested,* 04/**3205**:
*Applied* 09/3191: *Considered* 13/2468: *Distinguished* 14/2526: *Followed* 10/2754, 12/2729, 13/2470

R. (on the application of Best) v Chief Land Registrar; *sub nom* Best v Chief Land Registrar [2014] EWHC 1370 (Admin); [2014] 3 All E.R. 637; [2014] 2 E.G.L.R. 133; [2014] A.C.D. 127, QBD (Admin) ........ *Digested,* 14/**2488**

R. (on the application of Bevan & Clarke LLP) v Neath Port Talbot CBC [2012] EWHC 236 (Admin); [2012] B.L.G.R. 728; (2012) 15 C.C.L. Rep. 294; [2012] A.C.D. 62, QBD (Admin) ........ *Digested,* 12/**3176**: *Applied* 12/3157, 13/2934, 14/2797

R. (on the application of BH (A Child)) v Llandudno Youth Court [2014] EWHC 1833 (Admin); (2014) 178 J.P. 305, QBD (Admin) ........ *Digested,* 14/**722**

R. (on the application of Bhagat) v Secretary of State for the Home Department see R. (on the application of Bhgat) v Secretary of State for the Home Department

R. (on the application of Bhatti) v Bury MBC [2013] EWHC 3093 (Admin); (2014) 17 C.C.L. Rep. 64, QBD (Admin) ........ *Digested,* 14/**68**

R. (on the application of Bhgat) v Secretary of State for the Home Department; *sub nom* R. (on the application of Bhagat) v Secretary of State for the Home Department [2014] EWHC 772 (Admin); [2014] 1 W.L.R. 3710, QBD (Admin) ... *Digested,* 14/**1709**

R. (on the application of Bibi) v Secretary of State for the Home Department [2013] EWCA Civ 322; [2014] 1 W.L.R. 208; [2013] 3 All E.R. 778; [2013] H.R.L.R. 28; [2013] Imm. A.R. 1007; [2013] I.N.L.R. 613, CA (Civ Div) ........ *Digested,* 13/**1625**: *Applied* 14/1703

R. (on the application of Bibi) v Secretary of State for the Home Department see R. (on the application of Aguilar Quila) v Secretary of State for the Home Department

R. (on the application of Bigoku) v Secretary of State for the Home Department see R. (on the application of Baiai) v Secretary of State for the Home Department

R. (on the application of Bishop's Stortford Civic Federation) v East Hertfordshire DC; *sub nom* Bishop's Stortford Civic Federation v East Hertfordshire DC [2014] EWHC 348 (Admin); [2014] P.T.S.R. 1035; [2014] B.L.G.R. 161; [2014] J.P.L. 852; [2014] A.C.D. 104, QBD (Admin) ........ *Digested,* 14/**2407**

R. (on the application of Black) v Secretary of State for Justice see R. (on the application of Black) v Secretary of State for the Home Department

R. (on the application of Black) v Secretary of State for the Home Department; *sub nom* R. (on the application of Black) v Secretary of State for Justice [2009] UKHL 1; [2009] 1 A.C. 949; [2009] 2 W.L.R. 282; [2009] 4 All E.R. 1; [2009] H.R.L.R. 15; [2009] U.K.H.R.R. 382; 26 B.H.R.C. 664; [2009] Prison L.R. 395; (2009) 153(4) S.J.L.B. 27; Times, January 30, 2009, HL; reversing [2008] EWCA Civ 359; [2008] 3 W.L.R. 845; [2008] 4 All E.R. 151; [2008] H.R.L.R. 30; [2009] Prison L.R. 63; (2008) 105(17) L.S.G. 26; Times, April 18, 2008, CA (Civ Div); affirming in part [2007] EWHC 1668 (Admin); [2008] Prison L.R. 138, QBD (Admin) ........ *Digested,* 09/**2768**: *Applied* 11/2286: *Considered* 13/2124, 14/2233: *Followed* 10/2874

R. (on the application of Blackside Ltd) v Secretary of State for the Home Department [2013] EWHC 2087 (Admin); [2014] A.C.D. 8, QBD (Admin)

R. (on the application of Blake) v Waltham Forest LBC; *sub nom* Blake v Waltham Forest LBC [2014] EWHC 1027 (Admin); [2014] A.C.D. 102, QBD (Admin)

R. (on the application of Blue Bio Pharmaceuticals Ltd) v Secretary of State for Health [2014] EWHC 1679 (Admin); [2014] Med. L.R. 233; [2014] C.T.L.C. 169, QBD (Admin) ........ *Digested,* 14/**1528**

R. (on the application of Boggis) v Natural England; *sub nom* Boggis v Natural England [2009] EWCA Civ 1061; [2010] 1 All E.R. 159; [2010] P.T.S.R. 725; [2010] Env. L.R. 13; [2010] J.P.L. 571; Times, December 08, 2009, CA (Civ Div); reversing [2008] EWHC 2954 (Admin); [2009] 3 All E.R. 879; [2009] Env. L.R. 20; [2009] 1 P. & C.R. 18; [2009] J.P.L. 729; [2008] N.P.C. 135; Times, February 25, 2009, QBD (Admin) ........ *Digested,* 10/**1227**: *Considered* 14/2427

R. (on the application of Bonhoeffer) v General Medical Council [2011] EWHC 1585 (Admin); [2012] I.R.L.R. 37; [2011] Med. L.R. 519; [2011] A.C.D. 104, DC ........ *Digested,* 12/**304**: *Considered* 14/287

R. (on the application of Booth) v Parole Board see Reilly's Application for Judicial Review, Re

R. (on the application of Boots Management Services Ltd) v Central Arbitration Committee [2014] EWHC 65 (Admin); [2014] I.R.L.R. 278; [2014] A.C.D. 58, QBD (Admin) ........ *Digested,* 14/**1016**

R. (on the application of Boots Management Services Ltd) v Central Arbitration Committee [2014] EWHC 2930 (Admin); [2014] I.R.L.R. 887; (2014) 158(37) S.J.L.B. 37, QBD (Admin) ........ *Digested,* 14/**1017**

R. (on the application of Bourgass) v Secretary of State for Justice see R. (on the application of King) v Secretary of State for Justice

R. (on the application of Bracking) v Secretary of State for Work and Pensions; *joined case* Bracking v Secretary of State for Work and Pensions [2013] EWCA Civ 1345; [2014] Eq. L.R. 60; (2013) 16 C.C.L. Rep. 479, CA (Civ Div); reversing [2013] EWHC 897 (Admin); [2013] Eq. L.R. 621; [2013] A.C.D. 100, QBD (Admin) ........ *Digested,* 14/**2804**

R. (on the application of Bramford Royal British Legion) v Ipswich Magistrates' Court [2014] EWHC 526 (Admin); [2014] L.L.R. 591, QBD (Admin)

R. (on the application of Bredenkamp) v Secretary of State for Foreign and Commonwealth Affairs [2013] EWHC 2480 (Admin); [2013] Lloyd's Rep. F.C. 690, QBD (Admin) ........ *Digested,* 14/**295**

R. (on the application of Bridgerow Ltd) v Cheshire West and Chester BC [2014] EWHC 1187 (Admin); [2014] B.L.G.R. 485, QBD (Admin) ........ *Digested,* 14/**2070**

R. (on the application of Brighton and Hove City Council) v Brighton and Hove Justices [2004] EWHC 1800 (Admin); [2004] R.A. 277; [2005] A.C.D. 38, QBD (Admin) ........ *Digested,* 05/**3357**: *Applied* 05/387, 09/2616, 13/2403, 14/2135, 14/336: *Considered* 13/2036

R. (on the application of Bristol City Council) v Secretary of State for Communities and Local Government [2011] EWHC 4014 (Admin), QBD (Admin) *Considered* 14/2428

R. (on the application of British Sky Broadcasting Ltd) v Central Criminal Court; *sub nom* R. (on the application of British Sky Broadcasting Ltd) v Commissioner of Police of the Metropolis [2014] UKSC 17; [2014] A.C. 885; [2014] 2 W.L.R. 558; [2014] 2 All E.R. 705; [2014] E.M.L.R. 18; [2014] Crim. L.R. 620, SC; affirming [2011] EWHC 3451 (Admin); [2012] Q.B. 785; [2012] 3 W.L.R. 78, QBD (Admin) ........ *Digested,* 14/**441**

R. (on the application of British Sky Broadcasting Ltd) v Commissioner of Police of the Metropolis see R. (on the application of British Sky Broadcasting Ltd) v Central Criminal Court

R. (on the application of Bromley LBC) v Bromley Magistrates' Court [2011] EWHC 432 (Admin); (2011) 175 J.P. 179, DC ........ *Digested,* 11/**768**: *Considered* 14/810

R. (on the application of Brown) v Secretary of State for the Home Department; *sub nom* R. (on the application of B (Jamaica)) v Secretary of State for the Home Department; R. (on the application of JB (Jamaica)) v Secretary of State for the Home Department [2013] EWCA Civ 666; [2014] 1 W.L.R. 836; [2014] 2 All E.R. 91; [2014] Imm. A.R. 105, CA (Civ Div); reversing [2012] EWHC 1660 (Admin), QBD (Admin) ........ *Digested,* 14/**1649**

R. (on the application of Brown) v Secretary of State for Work and Pensions [2008] EWHC 3158 (Admin); [2009] P.T.S.R. 1506, DC *Applied* 10/1537, 10/2199, 13/2356, 13/2947: *Considered* 10/992, 12/914, 14/1509: *Followed* 11/64

R. (on the application of BT (Eritrea)) v Secretary of State for the Home Department (C-648/11) see MA v Secretary of State for the Home Department (C-648/11)

R. (on the application of BT) v Secretary of State for the Home Department; *joined cases* R. (on the application of MA) v Secretary of State for the Home Department; R. (on the application of DA) v Secretary of State for the Home Department [2011] EWCA Civ 1446, CA (Civ Div); no effect [2010] EWHC 3572 (Admin), QBD (Admin) *Preliminary ruling given* 14/1658

R. (on the application of Buck) v Doncaster MBC [2013] EWCA Civ 1190; [2014] P.T.S.R. 111; [2013] B.L.G.R. 847; (2013) 163(7581) N.L.J. 28, CA (Civ Div); affirming [2012] EWHC 2293 (Admin); [2013] P.T.S.R. 316; [2012] B.L.G.R. 663; [2012] A.C.D. 122, QBD (Admin) ........ *Digested,* 14/**2110**: *Followed* 14/2070

R. (on the application of Buckinghamshire CC) v Secretary of State for Transport; *sub nom* R. (on the application of Hillingdon LBC v Secretary of State for Transport); HS2 Action Alliance Ltd v Secretary of State for Transport; *joined cases* R. (on the application of Heathrow Hub Ltd) v Secretary of State for Transport; R. (on the application of HS2 Action Alliance Ltd) v Secretary of State for Transport [2014] UKSC 3; [2014] 1 W.L.R. 324; [2014] 2 All E.R. 109; [2014] P.T.S.R. 182; Times, January 27, 2014, SC; affirming [2013] EWCA Civ 920; [2013] P.T.S.R. 1194; [2014] 1 C.M.L.R. 10, CA (Civ Div); affirming [2013] EWHC 481 (Admin); [2013] P.T.S.R. D25, QBD (Admin) ........ *Digested,* 14/**1201**

R. (on the application of Building Societies Ombudsman Co Ltd) v Customs and Excise Commissioners; *sub nom* R. v Customs and Excise Commissioners Ex p. Building Societies Ombudsman Co Ltd [2000] S.T.C. 892; [2000] B.T.C. 5384; [2001] B.V.C. 3; [2000] S.T.I. 1516; Times, November 8, 2000, CA (Civ Div); reversing [1999] S.T.C. 974; [1999] B.T.C. 5356; [1999] B.V.C. 368; [1999] N.P.C. 90, QBD ........ *Digested,* 00/**5318**:
*Applied* 02/4776: *Considered* 14/3076

R. (on the application of Burke) v General Medical Council [2005] EWCA Civ 1003; [2006] Q.B. 273; [2005] 3 W.L.R. 1132; [2005] 2 F.L.R. 1223; [2005] 3 F.C.R. 169; [2005] H.R.L.R. 35; [2006] U.K.H.R.R. 509; (2005) 8 C.C.L. Rep. 463; [2005] Lloyd's Rep. Med. 403; (2005) 85 B.M.L.R. 1; [2006] A.C.D. 27; [2005] Fam. Law 776; (2005) 155 N.L.J. 1457, CA (Civ Div); reversing [2004] EWHC 1879 (Admin); [2005] Q.B. 424; [2005] 2 W.L.R. 431; [2004] 2 F.L.R. 1121; [2004] 3 F.C.R. 579; (2004) 7 C.C.L. Rep. 609; [2004] Lloyd's Rep. Med. 451; (2004) 79 B.M.L.R. 126; [2004] A.C.D. 84; Times, August 6, 2004, QBD (Admin) ........ *Digested,* 05/**1812**:
*Applied* 14/1569: *Considered* 05/1850, 13/2069: *Doubted* 05/1794

R. (on the application of Burkett) v Hammersmith and Fulham LBC (No.1); *sub nom* R. v Hammersmith and Fulham LBC Ex p. Burkett; Burkett, Re [2002] UKHL 23; [2002] 1 W.L.R. 1593; [2002] 3 All E.R. 97; [2002] C.P. Rep. 66; [2003] Env. L.R. 6; [2003] 1 P. & C.R. 3; [2002] 2 P.L.R. 90; [2002] J.P.L. 1346; [2002] A.C.D. 81; [2002] 22 E.G. 136 (C.S.); (2002) 99(27) L.S.G. 34; (2002) 152 N.L.J. 847; (2002) 146 S.J.L.B. 137; [2002] N.P.C. 75; Times, May 24, 2002; Independent, May 28, 2002, HL; reversing [2001] Env. L.R. 39; [2001] 3 P.L.R. 1; [2001] J.P.L. 775; [2001] A.C.D. 50, CA (Civ Div) ........ *Digested,* 02/**53**:
*Applied* 08/3017, 10/2675, 12/2189: *Considered* 04/793, 12/2581:
*Distinguished* 13/2021, 14/69

R. (on the application of Burridge) v Breckland DC; *sub nom* Burridge v Breckland DC [2013] EWCA Civ 228; [2013] J.P.L. 1308; [2013] 18 E.G. 102 (C.S.); (2013) 157(17) S.J.L.B. 31, CA (Civ Div); affirming [2012] EWHC 1102 (Admin); [2012] Env. L.R. 36; [2012] P.T.S.R. D23, QBD (Admin) ........ *Digested,* 14/**2425**

R. (on the application of Calver) v Adjudication Panel for Wales [2012] EWHC 1172 (Admin); [2013] P.T.S.R. 378; [2012] L.L.R. 684; [2012] A.C.D. 81, QBD (Admin) ........ *Digested,* 13/**2012**:
*Followed* 14/2102

R. (on the application of Campaign for Nuclear Disarmament) v Prime Minister; *sub nom* Campaign for Nuclear Disarmament v Prime Minister of the United Kingdom [2002] EWHC 2777 (Admin); [2003] A.C.D. 36; Times, December 27, 2002, QBD (Admin) ........ *Digested,* 03/**2676**:
*Applied* 06/2396: *Considered* 07/2234, 14/65

R. (on the application of Candlish) v Hastings BC [2005] EWHC 1539 (Admin); [2006] Env. L.R. 13; [2006] 1 P. & C.R. 18; [2005] 4 P.L.R. 60; [2006] J.P.L. 22; [2005] 29 E.G. 98 (C.S.); [2005] N.P.C. 102, QBD (Admin) ........ *Digested,* 06/**3347**:
*Considered* 14/2425

R. (on the application of Cardao-Pito) v Office of the Independent Adjudicator for Higher Education [2012] EWHC 203 (Admin); [2012] E.L.R. 231, QBD (Admin) *Digested,* 12/**969**:
*Applied* 14/916

R. (on the application of Carson) v Secretary of State for Work and Pensions; *sub nom* Carson v Secretary of State for Work and Pensions; *joined case* R. (on the application of Reynolds) v Secretary of State for Work and Pensions [2005] UKHL 37; [2006] 1 A.C. 173; [2005] 2 W.L.R. 1369; [2005] 4 All E.R. 545; [2005] H.R.L.R. 23; [2005] U.K.H.R.R. 1185; 18 B.H.R.C. 677; Times, May 27, 2005, HL; affirming [2003] EWCA Civ 797; [2003] 3 All E.R. 577; [2003] H.R.L.R. 36; [2003] Pens. L.R. 215; [2003] A.C.D. 76; (2003) 100(34) L.S.G. 32; (2003) 147 S.J.L.B. 780; Times, June 28, 2003, CA (Civ Div); affirming [2002] EWHC 978 (Admin); [2002] 3 All E.R. 994; (2002) 99(26) L.S.G. 39; Times, May 24, 2002; Daily Telegraph, May 30, 2002, QBD (Admin) ........ *Digested,* 05/**3835**:
*Applied* 04/2821, 04/3579, 05/1139, 06/2277, 07/2327, 07/3256, 08/2024, 09/2828: *Complaint dismissed* 09/2827: *Considered* 04/1889, 06/3381, 06/4027, 07/2293, 08/3527, 10/4537, 11/3159, 13/240: *Followed* 13/2885, 14/1587

R. (on the application of Cart) v Upper Tribunal; *joined case* R. (on the application of MR (Pakistan)) v Upper Tribunal [2011] UKSC 28; [2012] 1 A.C. 663; [2011] 3 W.L.R. 107; [2011] 4 All E.R. 127; [2011] P.T.S.R. 1053; [2011] S.T.C. 1659; [2012] 1 F.L.R. 997; [2011] Imm. A.R. 704; [2011] M.H.L.R. 196; [2012] Fam. Law 398; [2011] S.T.I. 1943; (2011) 161 N.L.J. 916; (2011) 155(25) S.J.L.B. 35; Times, June 23, 2011, SC; affirming [2010] EWCA Civ 859; [2011] Q.B. 120; [2011] 2 W.L.R. 36; [2010] 4 All E.R. 714; [2011] P.T.S.R. 42; [2010] S.T.C. 2556; [2010] M.H.L.R. 353; [2011] A.C.D. 1; [2010] S.T.I. 2272; (2010) 160 N.L.J. 1115; [2010] N.P.C. 86, CA (Civ Div); affirming [2009] EWHC 3052 (Admin); [2010] 2 W.L.R. 1012; [2010] 1 All E.R. 908; [2010] P.T.S.R. 824; [2010] S.T.C. 493; [2010] 2 F.C.R. 309; [2010] M.H.L.R. 35; [2010] A.C.D. 36; [2009] S.T.I. 3167, DC ........ *Digested,* 11/**48**:
*Applied* 11/1685, 11/59, 12/1770, 12/457: *Considered* 10/3926, 11/3958, 13/350, 14/2939: *Explained* 14/50: *Followed* 13/455: *Referred to* 14/41

R. (on the application of Castle) v Commissioner of Police of the Metropolis see Castle v Commissioner of Police of the Metropolis

R. (on the application of Catt) v Brighton and Hove City Council [2013] EWHC 977 (Admin); [2013] B.L.G.R. 802; [2013] P.T.S.R. D29, QBD (Admin) ........ *Digested,* 14/**2434**

R. (on the application of Cawser) v Secretary of State for the Home Department [2003] EWCA Civ 1522; [2004] U.K.H.R.R. 101; [2004] Prison L.R. 166; (2003) 100(48) L.S.G. 18; Times, November 25, 2003, CA (Civ Div) ........ *Digested,* 04/**2783**:
*Considered* 08/3312, 09/3407: *Followed* 14/2234

R. (on the application of CBRE Lionbrook (General Partners) Ltd) v Rugby BC [2014] EWHC 646 (Admin); [2014] Env. L.R. D3, QBD (Admin)

R. (on the application of Champion) v North Norfolk DC; *sub nom* Champion v North Norfolk DC [2013] EWCA Civ 1657; [2014] Env. L.R. 23, CA (Civ Div); reversing [2013] EWHC 1065 (Admin); [2013] Env. L.R. 38, QBD (Admin) ........ *Digested,* 14/**2426**

R. (on the application of Cherkley Campaign Ltd) v Mole Valley DC [2014] EWCA Civ 567; [2014] 2 E.G.L.R. 98; [2014] P.T.S.R. D14; Times, May 22, 2014, CA (Civ Div); reversing [2013] EWHC 2582 (Admin); [2014] 1 P. & C.R. 12; [2014] A.C.D. 42; (2013) 157(34) S.J.L.B. 40; [2014] P.T.S.R. D1, QBD (Admin) ........ *Digested,* 14/**2392**

R. (on the application of Chester) v Secretary of State for Justice; *sub nom* Chester v Secretary of State for Justice; *joined case* McGeoch v Lord President of the Council [2013] UKSC 63; [2014] A.C. 271; [2013] 3 W.L.R. 1076; [2014] 1 All E.R. 683; 2014 S.C. (U.K.S.C.) 25; 2014 S.L.T. 143; [2014] 1 C.M.L.R. 45; [2014] H.R.L.R. 3; 2013 G.W.D. 34-676, SC; affirming [2010] EWCA Civ 1439; [2011] 1 W.L.R. 1436; [2011] H.R.L.R. 10; [2011] U.K.H.R.R. 53; [2010] 2 Prison L.R. 40; [2011] A.C.D. 30; (2011) 108(1) L.S.G. 15; Times, January 17, 2011, CA (Civ Div); affirming [2009] EWHC 2923 (Admin); [2010] H.R.L.R. 6; [2010] U.K.H.R.R. 317; [2010] 2 Prison L.R. 1; [2010] A.C.D. 28; Times, November 3, 2009, QBD (Admin) ........ *Digested,* 14/**976**:
*Cited* 14/977: *Considered* 11/2294: *Followed* 14/977

R. (on the application of Chief Constable of South Yorkshire) v Sheffield Crown Court; *sub nom* R. (on the application of South Yorkshire Police) v Sheffield Crown Court [2014] EWHC 81 (Admin); [2014] Crim. L.R. 678, QBD (Admin)

R. (on the application of Child Poverty Action Group) v Secretary of State for Work and Pensions [2010] UKSC 54; [2011] 2 A.C. 15; [2011] 2 W.L.R. 1; [2011] 1 All E.R. 729; [2011] P.T.S.R. 185; (2010) 108(2) L.S.G. 19; (2010) 154(47) S.J.L.B. 30; Times, December 13, 2010, SC; affirming [2009] EWCA Civ 1058; [2010] 1 W.L.R. 1886; [2010] 2 All E.R. 113; [2010] P.T.S.R. 958; [2010] A.C.D. 16; Times, October 21, 2009, CA (Civ Div); reversing [2009] EWHC 341 (Admin); [2009] 3 All E.R. 633, QBD (Admin) ........ *Digested,* 11/**3157**:
*Applied* 13/397, 14/1542

R. (on the application of Child Poverty Action Group) v Secretary of State for Work and Pensions; *sub nom* Child Poverty Action Group v Secretary of State for Work and Pensions [2011] EWHC 2616 (Admin); [2011] Eq. L.R. 1233, QBD (Admin) ........ *Digested,* 12/**3112**:
*Considered* 14/2761

R. (on the application of Children's Rights Alliance for England) v Secretary of State for Justice; *sub nom* Children's Rights Alliance for England v Secretary of State for Justice [2013] EWCA Civ 34; [2013] 1 W.L.R. 3667; [2013] H.R.L.R. 17; (2013) 157(7) S.J.L.B. 31, CA (Civ Div); affirming [2012] EWHC 8 (Admin), QBD (Admin) ........ *Digested,* 13/**65**:
*Applied* 14/662

R. (on the application of Chinaka) v Southwark Crown Court [2013] EWHC 3221 (Admin); (2013) 177 J.P. 683; [2014] A.C.D. 30, DC ........ *Digested,* 14/**760**

R. (on the application of Church Commissioners for England) v Hampshire CC see Church Commissioners for England v Hampshire CC

R. (on the application of Cindo) v Immigration Appeal Tribunal [2002] EWHC 246 (Admin), QBD (Admin)
*Applied* 14/1664

R. (on the application of Clays Lane Housing Cooperative Ltd) v Housing Corp [2004] EWCA Civ 1658; [2005] 1 W.L.R. 2229; [2005] H.L.R. 15; [2004] N.P.C. 184; Times, December 27, 2004, CA (Civ Div); affirming [2004] EWHC 1084 (Admin); [2004] H.L.R. 51, QBD (Admin) ........................ *Digested,* 05/**2027**:
*Considered* 08/2917, 08/2918, 14/2102

R. (on the application of Clift) v Secretary of State for the Home Department; *sub nom* Secretary of State for the Home Department v Headley; Secretary of State for the Home Department v Hindawi; Hindawi v Secretary of State for the Home Department; *joined cases* R. (on the application of Hindawi) v Secretary of State for the Home Department; R. (on the application of Headley) v Secretary of State for the Home Department [2006] UKHL 54; [2007] 1 A.C. 484; [2007] 2 W.L.R. 24; [2007] 2 All E.R. 1; [2007] H.R.L.R. 12; [2007] U.K.H.R.R. 348; 21 B.H.R.C. 704; [2007] Prison L.R. 125; [2007] A.C.D. 27; Times, December 21, 2006, HL; affirming [2004] EWCA Civ 514; [2004] 1 W.L.R. 2223; [2004] 3 All E.R. 338; [2005] 1 Prison L.R. 51; (2004) 101(20) L.S.G. 34; (2004) 148 S.J.L.B. 569; Times, May 13, 2004; Independent, May 7, 2004, CA (Civ Div); affirming [2003] EWHC 1337 (Admin); [2003] Prison L.R. 389; [2003] A.C.D. 100; (2003) 100(32) L.S.G. 34; Times, June 25, 2003, QBD (Admin) ................ *Digested,* 07/**2975**:
*Applied* 07/3867, 08/3527, 09/1737, 12/2970: *Considered* 07/2300, 07/2981, 08/2690, 09/2761, 09/2768: *Followed* 14/2234, 14/2682

R. (on the application of CN) v Lewisham LBC see R. (on the application of N) v Lewisham LBC

R. (on the application of Colefax) v First Tier Tribunal (Social Entitlement Chamber); *sub nom* Colefax v First Tier Tribunal (Social Entitlement Chamber) [2014] EWCA Civ 945; [2014] P.I.Q.R. P21, CA (Civ Div) ........................ *Digested,* 14/**2301**

R. (on the application of Commissioner of Police of the Metropolis) v Police Medical Appeal Board; *sub nom* Commissioner of Police of the Metropolis v Police Medical Appeal Board [2013] EWHC 1203 (Admin); [2013] I.C.R. 1245, QBD (Admin) ........................ *Digested,* 14/**2457**

R. (on the application of Condliff) v North Staffordshire Primary Care Trust [2011] EWCA Civ 910; [2012] 1 All E.R. 689; [2012] P.T.S.R. 460; [2011] H.R.L.R. 38; (2011) 14 C.C.L. Rep. 656; [2011] Med. L.R. 572; (2011) 121 B.M.L.R. 192; [2011] A.C.D. 113; (2011) 155(30) S.J.L.B. 31, CA (Civ Div); affirming [2011] EWHC 872 (Admin), QBD (Admin) ........................ *Digested,* 11/**1562**:
*Applied* 14/1516

R. (on the application of Cooke) v DPP; *sub nom* Cooke v DPP [2008] EWHC 2703 (Admin); (2008) 172 J.P. 596; [2008] M.H.L.R. 348, DC ........................ *Digested,* 09/**348**:
*Applied* 14/713

R. (on the application of Cooper) v HM Coroner for North East Kent [2014] EWHC 586 (Admin); (2014) 178 J.P. 505, QBD (Admin)

R. (on the application of Copeland) v Tower Hamlets LBC [2010] EWHC 1845 (Admin); [2010] L.L.R. 654; [2011] J.P.L. 40; Times, June 21, 2010, QBD (Admin) ........................ *Digested,* 10/**2590**:
*Considered* 14/2420

R. (on the application of Corbett) v Cornwall Council [2013] EWHC 3958 (Admin); [2014] P.T.S.R. 727, QBD (Admin) ........................ *Digested,* 14/**2421**

R. (on the application of Core Issues Trust Ltd) v Transport for London [2014] EWHC 2628 (Admin); [2014] P.T.S.R. D26, QBD (Admin)

R. (on the application of Core Issues Trust) v Transport for London; *sub nom* Core Issues Trust v Transport for London [2014] EWCA Civ 34; [2014] P.T.S.R. 785; [2014] Eq. L.R. 164; (2014) 158(5) S.J.L.B. 37, CA (Civ Div); no effect [2013] EWHC 651 (Admin); [2013] P.T.S.R. 1161; [2013] H.R.L.R. 22; [2013] Eq. L.R. 508; [2013] A.C.D. 71, QBD (Admin) ........................ *Digested,* 14/**1629**

R. (on the application of Corner House Research) v Secretary of State for Trade and Industry [2005] EWCA Civ 192; [2005] 1 W.L.R. 2600; [2005] 4 All E.R. 1; [2005] C.P. Rep. 28; [2005] 3 Costs L.R. 455; [2005] A.C.D. 100; (2005) 102(17) L.S.G. 31; (2005) 149 S.J.L.B. 297; Times, March 7, 2005; Independent, March 4, 2005, CA (Civ Div); reversing [2004] EWHC 3011 (Admin), QBD (Admin) ........................ *Digested,* 05/**354**:
*Applied* 06/1706, 08/332, 09/437, 10/322: *Cited* 14/339: *Considered* 05/366, 05/373, 06/5125, 07/402, 07/536, 09/369, 11/2561, 11/2745, 11/342, 14/442: *Followed* 09/381, 10/292, 11/279, 13/376: *Referred to* 09/2559

R. (on the application of Cornwall Council) v Secretary of State for Health [2014] EWCA Civ 12; [2014] 1 W.L.R. 3408; [2014] 3 All E.R. 603; [2014] 2 F.C.R. 606; [2014] H.L.R. 34; [2014] B.L.G.R. 433; (2014) 17 C.C.L. Rep. 78; [2014] A.C.D. 85, CA (Civ Div); reversing [2012] EWHC 3739 (Admin); [2013] 2 F.C.R. 369; [2013] B.L.G.R. 197; (2013) 16 C.C.L. Rep. 82; (2013) 131 B.M.L.R. 1; [2013] A.C.D. 39, QBD (Admin) ........ *Digested,* 14/**2806**

R. (on the application of Coverdale) v Hastings Magistrates' Court [2014] EWHC 2348 (Admin); [2014] R.V.R. 322, QBD (Admin)

R. (on the application of CR) v Independent Review Panel of Lambeth LBC [2014] EWHC 2461 (Admin); [2014] E.L.R. 359, QBD (Admin) ........ *Digested,* 14/**925**

R. (on the application of Crawford) v Legal Ombudsman [2014] EWHC 182 (Admin); [2014] 4 Costs L.O. 560; [2014] A.C.D. 100, QBD (Admin) ........ *Digested,* 14/**2049**

R. (on the application of Crawford) v University of Newcastle Upon Tyne [2014] EWHC 162 (Admin); [2014] E.L.R. 110, QBD (Admin)

R. (on the application of Creed-Miles) v Southwark LBC; *sub nom* Creed-Miles v Southwark LBC [2013] EWHC 853 (Admin); [2013] J.P.L. 1302, QBD (Admin) .. *Digested,* 14/**2418**

R. (on the application of Customs and Excise Commissioners) v Leicester Crown Court; *sub nom* R. v Leicester Crown Court Ex p. Customs and Excise Commissioners [2001] EWHC Admin 33; Times, February 23, 2001; Independent, March 5, 2001, DC ........ *Digested,* 01/**1118**: *Considered* 14/750

R. (on the application of D&D Bar Services Ltd) v Romford Magistrates' Court [2014] EWHC 344 (Admin); [2014] L.L.R. 761, QBD (Admin)

R. (on the application of D) v General Medical Council [2013] EWHC 2839 (Admin); (2013) 134 B.M.L.R. 118, QBD (Admin) ........ *Digested,* 14/**1505**

R. (on the application of D) v Worcestershire CC [2013] EWHC 2490 (Admin); [2013] B.L.G.R. 741; (2013) 16 C.C.L. Rep. 323, QBD (Admin) ........ *Digested,* 14/**2794**

R. (on the application of DA (Iraq)) v Secretary of State for the Home Department (C-648/11) see MA v Secretary of State for the Home Department (C-648/11)

R. (on the application of DA) v Secretary of State for the Home Department see R. (on the application of BT) v Secretary of State for the Home Department

R. (on the application of Daly) v Secretary of State for the Home Department; *sub nom* R. v Secretary of State for the Home Department Ex p. Daly [2001] UKHL 26; [2001] 2 A.C. 532; [2001] 2 W.L.R. 1622; [2001] 3 All E.R. 433; [2001] H.R.L.R. 49; [2001] U.K.H.R.R. 887; [2001] Prison L.R. 322; [2001] A.C.D. 79; (2001) 98(26) L.S.G. 43; (2001) 145 S.J.L.B. 156; Times, May 25, 2001; Daily Telegraph, May 29, 2001, HL; reversing [1999] C.O.D. 388, CA (Civ Div) ........ *Digested,* 01/**4578**: *Applied* 03/3481, 04/2778, 05/2027, 05/2192, 05/2193, 05/2917, 06/2277, 08/1884: *Considered* 01/3660, 01/426, 01/4574, 03/2934, 06/1145, 12/2531, 14/662: *Followed* 09/4361, 11/178

R. (on the application of Das) v Secretary of State for the Home Department [2014] EWCA Civ 45; [2014] 1 W.L.R. 3538; [2014] A.C.D. 78, CA (Civ Div); reversing [2013] EWHC 682 (Admin), QBD (Admin) ........ *Digested,* 14/**1681**

R. (on the application of Davies) v Revenue and Customs Commissioners; *joined case* R. (on the application of Gaines-Cooper) v Revenue and Customs Commissioners [2011] UKSC 47; [2011] 1 W.L.R. 2625; [2012] 1 All E.R. 1048; [2011] S.T.C. 2249; 81 T.C. 134; [2011] B.T.C. 610; [2012] W.T.L.R. 215; [2011] S.T.I. 2847; (2011) 155(40) S.J.L.B. 31; [2011] N.P.C. 107; Times, October 24, 2011, SC; affirming [2010] EWCA Civ 83; [2010] S.T.C. 860; [2010] B.T.C. 198; [2010] W.T.L.R. 681; [2010] S.T.I. 485; (2010) 107(9) L.S.G. 17; Times, February 23, 2010, CA (Civ Div); affirming [2008] EWHC 2642 (Admin), QBD (Admin) ........ *Digested,* 11/**3419**: *Applied* 12/3255: *Considered* 11/3375, 13/435: *Followed* 12/3277, 13/3011

R. (on the application of Daws Hill Neighbourhood Forum) v Wycombe DC; *joined case* Daws Hill Neighbourhood Forum v Wycombe DC [2014] EWCA Civ 228; [2014] 1 W.L.R. 1362; [2014] P.T.S.R. 570; [2014] J.P.L. 866, CA (Civ Div); affirming [2013] EWHC 513 (Admin); [2013] P.T.S.R. 970; [2013] J.P.L. 1113; [2013] 12 E.G. 79 (C.S.), QBD (Admin) ........ *Digested,* 14/**2406**

R. (on the application of DD) v Islington LBC Independent Appeal Panel [2013] EWHC 2262 (Admin); [2013] E.L.R. 483, QBD (Admin) ........ *Digested,* 14/**923**

R. (on the application of de Silva) v Revenue and Customs Commissioners [2014] UKUT 170 (TCC); [2014] S.T.C. 2088; [2014] B.T.C. 514; [2014] S.T.I. 1913, UT (Tax) ........ *Digested,* 14/**2860**

R. (on the application of Dennehy) v Ealing LBC [2013] EWHC 4102 (Admin); [2014] B.L.G.R. 269, QBD (Admin) ........ *Digested,* 14/**2101**

R. (on the application of Dennis) v Secretary of State for Justice see R. (on the application of Ali) v Secretary of State for Justice

R. (on the application of Derrin Brother Properties Ltd) v Revenue and Customs Commissioners [2014] EWHC 1152 (Admin); [2014] S.T.C. 2238; [2014] B.T.C. 21; [2014] A.C.D. 130; [2014] S.T.I. 1835, QBD (Admin) .................................... *Digested,* 14/**2973**

R. (on the application of Derwent Holdings Ltd) v Trafford BC; *sub nom* Derwent Holdings Ltd v Trafford BC [2011] EWCA Civ 832; [2011] N.P.C. 78, CA (Civ Div); affirming [2011] EWHC 491 (Admin); [2011] 11 E.G. 103 (C.S.), QBD (Admin)
*Followed* 13/2350, 14/2431

R. (on the application of Dickie) v Judicial Appointments and Conduct Ombudsman [2013] EWHC 2448 (Admin); [2014] A.C.D. 1, DC

R. (on the application of DK) v Secretary of State for the Home Department [2014] EWHC 3257 (Admin); [2014] Med. L.R. 510, QBD (Admin)

R. (on the application of Donohoe) v Welsh Ministers see R. (on the application of Flatley) v Hywel Dda University Local Health Board

R. (on the application of Donovan) v Burnley Crown Court [2014] EWHC 742 (Admin); (2014) 178 J.P. 511, QBD (Admin)

R. (on the application of DPP) v Sheffield Crown Court [2014] EWHC 2014 (Admin); [2014] 1 W.L.R. 4639; [2014] A.C.D. 112, QBD (Admin)

R. (on the application of DPP) v Stafford Magistrates' Court [2013] EWHC 617 (Admin), DC
*Considered* 14/810

R. (on the application of Drax Power Ltd) v Secretary of State for Energy and Climate Change [2014] EWCA Civ 1153; Times, September 3, 2014, CA (Civ Div); reversing [2014] EWHC 2377 (Admin), QBD (Admin) .................................... *Digested,* 14/**1172**

R. (on the application of Dry) v West Oxfordshire DC [2010] EWCA Civ 1143; [2011] 1 P. & C.R. 16; [2011] J.P.L. 579; [2010] N.P.C. 103, CA (Civ Div); affirming [2010] EWHC 1758 (Admin), QBD (Admin) .................................... *Digested,* 11/**2546**:
*Applied* 14/2399: *Followed* 12/2590, 14/2428

R. (on the application of Duffy) v HM Deputy Coroner for Worcestershire [2013] EWHC 1654 (Admin); (2013) 134 B.M.L.R. 86; [2013] A.C.D. 101, QBD (Admin) .................................... *Digested,* 14/**33**

R. (on the application of Dulai) v Chelmsford Magistrates' Court; *joined case* R. (on the application of Essex CC) v Chelmsford Crown Court [2012] EWHC 1055 (Admin); [2013] 1 W.L.R. 220; [2012] 3 All E.R. 764; [2012] 2 Cr. App. R. 19; [2013] Crim. L.R. 86; [2012] A.C.D. 76, DC .................................... *Digested,* 12/**825**:
*Applied* 14/804: *Considered* 13/770

R. (on the application of E) v Bristol City Council [2005] EWHC 74 (Admin); [2005] M.H.L.R. 83, QBD (Admin)
*Explained* 13/2044: *Not applied* 14/2178

R. (on the application of E) v JFS Governing Body; *joined case* R. (on the application of E) v Office of the Schools Adjudicator [2009] UKSC 15; [2010] 2 A.C. 728; [2010] 2 W.L.R. 153; [2010] 1 All E.R. 319; [2010] P.T.S.R. 147; [2010] I.R.L.R. 136; 27 B.H.R.C. 656; [2010] E.L.R. 26; (2010) 160 N.L.J. 29; (2009) 153(48) S.J.L.B. 32; Times, December 17, 2009, SC; affirming [2009] EWCA Civ 626; [2009] 4 All E.R. 375; [2009] P.T.S.R. 1442; [2009] E.L.R. 407; [2009] A.C.D. 69; (2009) 106(27) L.S.G. 17; (2009) 159 N.L.J. 963; Times, July 8, 2009, CA (Civ Div); reversing [2008] EWHC 1535 (Admin); [2008] E.L.R. 445; [2008] A.C.D. 87; (2008) 152(30) S.J.L.B. 29; Times, July 18, 2008, QBD (Admin) ...... *Digested,* 10/**969**:
*Applied* 08/1037, 14/1639, 14/2444: *Considered* 10/73: *Followed* 11/1063

R. (on the application of E) v Office of the Schools Adjudicator see R. (on the application of E) v JFS Governing Body

R. (on the application of Ealing LBC) v NHS England [2013] EWHC 3255 (Admin); (2014) 135 B.M.L.R. 128, QBD (Admin) .................................... *Digested,* 14/**1572**

R. (on the application of Earl) v Winchester City Council [2014] EWHC 195 (Admin); [2014] E.L.R. 225; [2014] R.V.R. 298, QBD (Admin) .................................... *Digested,* 14/**2090**

R. (on the application of Eastenders Cash & Carry Plc) v Revenue and Customs Commissioners; *sub nom* R. (on the application of First Stop Wholesale Ltd) v Revenue and Customs Commissioners; R. (on the application of Eastenders Cash & Carry Plc) v Revenue and Customs Commissioners [2014] UKSC 34; [2014] 2 W.L.R. 1580; [2014] 4 All E.R. 1; [2014] S.T.C. 1741; [2014] 2 Cr. App. R. 26; (2014) 178 J.P. 314; [2014] B.V.C. 30, SC; reversing [2012] EWCA Civ 15; [2012] 1 W.L.R. 2067; [2012] S.T.C. 817; [2014] B.V.C. 7, CA (Civ Div); reversing [2010] EWHC 2797 (Admin); [2011] 1 W.L.R. 488; [2011] S.T.C. 64; [2010] S.T.I. 2887; Times, December 7, 2010, QBD (Admin) .................................... *Digested,* 14/**820**

R. (on the application of Eastenders Cash & Carry Plc) v Revenue and Customs Commissioners; *sub nom* Eastenders Cash & Carry Plc v Revenue and Customs Commissioners [2012] EWCA Civ 689; [2012] 1 W.L.R. 2912; [2012] S.T.C. 2036; [2012] C.P. Rep. 38; [2012] S.T.I. 2593, CA (Civ Div) .................. *Digested,* 12/**362**: *Affirmed in part* 14/820

R. (on the application of Eastenders Cash & Carry Plc) v Revenue and Customs Commissioners see R. (on the application of Eastenders Cash & Carry Plc) v Revenue and Customs Commissioners

R. (on the application of Eastenders Cash & Carry Plc) v South Western Magistrates' Court; *sub nom* Eastenders Cash & Carry Plc v South Western Magistrates' Court [2011] EWHC 937 (Admin); [2011] 2 Cr. App. R. 11; (2011) 175 J.P. 314, DC .................. *Digested,* 11/**614**: *Applied* 14/663

R. (on the application of Ebrahim) v Feltham Magistrates Court; *sub nom* R. v Feltham Magistrates Court Ex p. Ebrahim; *joined cases* Mouat v DPP; R. v Feltham Magistrates Court Ex p. DPP [2001] EWHC Admin 130; [2001] 1 W.L.R. 1293; [2001] 1 All E.R. 831; [2001] 2 Cr. App. R. 23; [2002] R.T.R. 7; [2001] Crim. L.R. 741; (2001) 151 N.L.J. 304; Times, February 27, 2001; Independent, February 27, 2001, QBD (Admin) .................. *Digested,* 01/**1190**: *Applied* 09/758, 12/3287, 13/3072: *Considered* 04/704, 13/613, 14/810

R. (on the application of Edwards) v Environment Agency; *sub nom* Edwards v Environment Agency [2010] UKSC 57; [2011] 1 W.L.R. 79; [2011] 1 All E.R. 785; [2011] 2 Costs L.R. 151; [2011] Env. L.R. 13; [2011] 1 E.G. 64 (C.S.); (2011) 161 N.L.J. 101; (2010) 154(48) S.J.L.B. 35; [2010] N.P.C. 125; Times, January 6, 2011, SC .................. *Digested,* 11/**278**: *Preliminary ruling given* 14/1183

R. (on the application of Edwards) v Environment Agency [2013] UKSC 78; [2014] 1 W.L.R. 55; [2014] 1 All E.R. 760; [2014] 3 Costs L.O. 319; [2014] 2 C.M.L.R. 25; [2014] Env. L.R. 17, SC .................. *Digested,* 14/**333**

R. (on the application of Edwards) v Environment Agency (C-260/11); *sub nom* Edwards v Environment Agency (C-260/11) [2013] 1 W.L.R. 2914; [2013] 3 C.M.L.R. 18; [2014] All E.R. (EC) 207, ECJ (4th Chamber) .................. *Digested,* 14/**1183**: *Applied* 14/333, 14/339: *Considered* 14/3338: *Followed* 14/442

R. (on the application of EH (Iran)) v Secretary of State for the Home Department see R. (on the application of EM (Eritrea)) v Secretary of State for the Home Department

R. (on the application of El-Baroudy) v General Medical Council [2013] EWHC 2894 (Admin); (2014) 136 B.M.L.R. 184, QBD (Admin) .................. *Digested,* 14/**1495**

R. (on the application of El-Kurd) v Winchester Crown Court [2011] EWHC 1853 (Admin); [2011] Lloyd's Rep. F.C. 469; [2012] Crim. L.R. 138; [2012] A.C.D. 6, QBD (Admin) .................. *Digested,* 11/**818**: *Applied* 14/2467

R. (on the application of Elayathamby) v Secretary of State for the Home Department [2011] EWHC 2182 (Admin); [2011] A.C.D. 117, QBD (Admin) *Applied* 12/1696: *Considered* 14/1652

R. (on the application of Elias) v Secretary of State for Defence; *sub nom* Secretary of State for the Home Department v Elias; Elias v Secretary of State for Defence [2006] EWCA Civ 1293; [2006] 1 W.L.R. 3213; [2006] I.R.L.R. 934; Times, October 17, 2006; Independent, October 18, 2006, CA (Civ Div); affirming [2005] EWHC 1435 (Admin); [2005] I.R.L.R. 788; [2006] A.C.D. 10; (2005) 102(30) L.S.G. 30; Times, August 25, 2005, QBD (Admin) .................. *Digested,* 06/**44**: *Applied* 08/3582, 09/1207, 13/1929, 14/2044: *Considered* 07/1399, 08/920, 09/1163, 11/2095

R. (on the application of Ellaway) v Cardiff CC [2013] EWHC 2907 (Admin); [2014] Env. L.R. 12, QBD (Admin) .................. *Digested,* 14/**2387**

R. (on the application of Elosta) v Commissioner of Police of the Metropolis; *sub nom* Elosta v Commissioner of Police of the Metropolis [2013] EWHC 3397 (Admin); [2014] 1 W.L.R. 239; [2014] Crim. L.R. 378, QBD (Admin) .................. *Digested,* 14/**709**

R. (on the application of EM (Eritrea)) v Secretary of State for the Home Department; *sub nom* EM (Eritrea) v Secretary of State for the Home Department; MA (Eritrea) v Secretary of State for the Home Department; *joined cases* R. (on the application of EH (Iran)) v Secretary of State for the Home Department; R. (on the application of AE (Eritrea)) v Secretary of State for the Home Department; R. (on the application of MA (Eritrea)) v Secretary of State for the Home Department [2014] UKSC 12; [2014] A.C. 1321; [2014] 2 W.L.R. 409; [2014] 2 All E.R. 192; [2014] H.R.L.R. 8; [2014] Imm. A.R. 640; [2014] I.N.L.R. 635; Times, February 27, 2014, SC; reversing [2012] EWCA Civ 1336; [2013] 1 W.L.R. 576; [2013] H.R.L.R. 1; Times, December 6, 2012, CA (Civ Div) ........... *Digested,* 14/**1652**: *Applied* 14/1651

R. (on the application of EM) v Secretary of State for Work and Pensions see R. (on the application of RD) v Secretary of State for Work and Pensions

R. (on the application of Embleton Parish Council) v Northumberland CC [2013] EWHC 3631 (Admin); [2014] Env. L.R. 16, QBD (Admin) .................................. *Digested,* 14/**2414**

R. (on the application of Energy Financing Team Ltd) v Bow Street Magistrates Court; *sub nom* Energy Financing Team Ltd v Director of the Serious Fraud Office [2005] EWHC 1626 (Admin); [2006] 1 W.L.R. 1316; [2005] 4 All E.R. 285; [2006] A.C.D. 8, DC .................................. *Digested,* 05/**930**: *Applied* 10/788, 11/815, 13/694, 13/762, 13/763, 14/1186: *Considered* 07/1931, 11/816

R. (on the application of Essa) v Upper Tribunal (Immigration and Asylum Chamber) [2012] EWCA Civ 1718; [2013] Imm. A.R. 644, CA (Civ Div); reversing [2012] EWHC 1533 (QB); [2012] 3 C.M.L.R. 26, QBD (Admin) .................................. *Digested,* 14/**1675**: *Applied* 14/50

R. (on the application of Essex CC) v Chelmsford Crown Court see R. (on the application of Dulai) v Chelmsford Magistrates' Court

R. (on the application of Evans) v Attorney General [2014] EWCA Civ 254; [2014] Q.B. 855; [2014] 2 W.L.R. 1334; [2014] 3 All E.R. 682; [2014] 3 C.M.L.R. 12; [2014] Env. L.R. 26; [2014] H.R.L.R. 12, CA (Civ Div); reversing [2013] EWHC 1960 (Admin); [2013] 3 W.L.R. 1631; [2014] 1 All E.R. 23; [2014] 1 C.M.L.R. 8; [2014] A.C.D. 2; (2013) 163(7570) N.L.J. 18, DC .................................. *Digested,* 14/**59**

R. (on the application of Evans) v Basingstoke and Deane BC [2013] EWCA Civ 1635; [2014] 1 W.L.R. 2034, CA (Civ Div); affirming [2013] EWHC 899 (Admin), QBD (Admin) .................................. *Digested,* 14/**2377**

R. (on the application of Evans) v Cornwall Council [2013] EWHC 4109 (Admin); [2014] P.T.S.R. 556, QBD (Admin) .................................. *Digested,* 14/**2400**

R. (on the application of Evans) v Secretary of State for Communities and Local Government [2013] EWCA Civ 114; [2013] J.P.L. 1027, CA (Civ Div) ............... *Digested,* 13/**2365**: *Followed* 14/2427

R. (on the application of Extreme Oyster) v Guildford BC; *sub nom* Extreme Oyster v Guildford BC [2013] EWHC 2174 (Admin); [2014] P.T.S.R. 325; (2013) 177 J.P. 481; [2014] L.L.R. 126, QBD (Admin) .................................. *Digested,* 13/**1965**

R. (on the application of F) v DPP [2013] EWHC 945 (Admin); [2014] Q.B. 581; [2014] 2 W.L.R. 190; [2013] 2 Cr. App. R. 21; [2013] A.C.D. 86, DC ........................... *Digested,* 13/**606**: *Applied* 13/667

R. (on the application of F) v Secretary of State for Justice see R. (on the application of F) v Secretary of State for the Home Department

R. (on the application of F) v Secretary of State for the Home Department; *sub nom* R. (on the application of F) v Secretary of State for Justice; *joined case* R. (on the application of Thompson) v Secretary of State for the Home Department [2010] UKSC 17; [2011] 1 A.C. 331; [2010] 2 W.L.R. 992; [2010] 2 All E.R. 707; [2010] H.R.L.R. 23; [2010] U.K.H.R.R. 809; 29 B.H.R.C. 308; (2010) 113 B.M.L.R. 209; 6 A.L.R. Int'l 785; (2010) 154(16) S.J.L.B. 27; Times, April 22, 2010, SC; affirming [2009] EWCA Civ 792; [2010] 1 W.L.R. 76; [2010] 1 All E.R. 1024; [2009] H.R.L.R. 30; [2009] U.K.H.R.R. 1417; (2009) 153(30) S.J.L.B. 29; Times, August 20, 2009, CA (Civ Div); affirming [2008] EWHC 3170 (Admin); [2009] 2 Cr. App. R. (S.) 47; [2009] Crim. L.R. 305; [2009] A.C.D. 24; (2009) 106(4) L.S.G. 15; Times, January 23, 2009, DC .................................. *Digested,* 10/**2970**: *Applied* 12/2970: *Considered* 12/1678, 12/4271, 13/1564, 13/3875, 14/2682: *Distinguished* 13/2779

R. (on the application of F) v Southampton Crown Court [2009] EWHC 2206 (Admin), QBD (Admin)

*Considered* 14/719

R. (on the application of FA (A Child)) v Secretary of State for the Home Department see R. (on the application of AN) v Secretary of State for the Home Department

R. (on the application of Factortame Ltd) v Secretary of State for Transport, Local Government and the Regions (Costs: Champertous Agreement) see Factortame Ltd v Secretary of State for the Environment, Transport and the Regions (Costs) (No.2)

R. (on the application of Fagin) v Southampton Crown Court see R. (on the application of Fergus) v Southampton Crown Court

R. (on the application of Faulkner) v Secretary of State for Justice see R. (on the application of Sturnham) v Parole Board for England and Wales

R. (on the application of Fergus) v Southampton Crown Court; *joined case* R. (on the application of Fagin) v Southampton Crown Court [2008] EWHC 3273 (Admin), QBD (Admin)
*Considered* 14/719

R. (on the application of FI) v Secretary of State for the Home Department; *sub nom* R. (on the application of Z) v Secretary of State for the Home Department [2014] EWCA Civ 1272; [2014] H.R.L.R. 30; (2014) 158(40) S.J.L.B. 37, CA (Civ Div); affirming [2013] EWHC 498 (Admin); [2013] A.C.D. 75, QBD (Admin)

R. (on the application of First Stop Wholesale Ltd) v Revenue and Customs Commissioners see R. (on the application of Eastenders Cash & Carry Plc) v Revenue and Customs Commissioners

R. (on the application of Flatley) v Hywel Dda University Local Health Board; *joined cases* R. (on the application of Donohoe) v Welsh Ministers; R. (on the application of Flatley) v Welsh Ministers [2014] EWHC 2258 (Admin); (2014) 140 B.M.L.R. 1; [2014] P.T.S.R. D22, QBD (Admin)

R. (on the application of Flatley) v Welsh Ministers see R. (on the application of Flatley) v Hywel Dda University Local Health Board

R. (on the application of Flynn) v Secretary of State for Communities and Local Government; *sub nom* Flynn v Secretary of State for Communities and Local Government [2014] EWHC 390 (Admin); [2014] 1 W.L.R. 3270, QBD (Admin) .. *Digested,* 14/**2380**

R. (on the application of Fox Strategic Land and Property Ltd) v Chorley BC [2014] EWHC 1179 (Admin); [2014] J.P.L. 1152, QBD (Admin)

R. (on the application of Francis) v Secretary of State for the Home Department [2014] EWCA Civ 718, CA (Civ Div); reversing in part [2013] EWHC 2115 (Admin); [2014] 1 All E.R. 68, QBD (Admin) .......... *Digested,* 14/**1682**

R. (on the application of Freedman) v Wiltshire Council [2014] EWHC 211 (Admin); [2014] P.T.S.R. 696; [2014] J.P.L. 885, QBD (Admin) .......... *Digested,* 14/**2355**

R. (on the application of G) v Barnet LBC; *joined cases* R. (on the application of W) v Lambeth LBC; R. (on the application of A) v Lambeth LBC [2003] UKHL 57; [2004] 2 A.C. 208; [2003] 3 W.L.R. 1194; [2004] 1 All E.R. 97; [2004] 1 F.L.R. 454; [2003] 3 F.C.R. 419; [2004] H.R.L.R. 4; [2004] H.L.R. 10; [2003] B.L.G.R. 569; (2003) 6 C.C.L. Rep. 500; [2004] Fam. Law 21; (2003) 100(45) L.S.G. 29; [2003] N.P.C. 123; Times, October 24, 2003; Independent, October 29, 2003, HL; affirming [2001] EWCA Civ 540; [2001] 2 F.L.R. 877; [2001] 2 F.C.R. 193; (2001) 33 H.L.R. 59; [2002] B.L.G.R. 34; (2001) 4 C.C.L. Rep. 128; [2001] Fam. Law 662; (2001) 98(24) L.S.G. 43; Times, June 5, 2001; Independent, April 25, 2001, CA (Civ Div); reversing [2001] EWHC Admin 5; [2001] 1 F.C.R. 743; (2001) 4 C.C.L. Rep. 33; [2001] A.C.D. 59, QBD (Admin) .......... *Digested,* 04/**3643**:
*Applied* 05/2004, 07/2165, 07/3941: *Considered* 06/1654, 09/3695:
*Distinguished* 06/2021: *Followed* 04/3636, 14/2148

R. (on the application of G) v Commissioner of Police of the Metropolis [2011] EWHC 3331 (Admin), DC
*Applied* 14/663

R. (on the application of Gaines-Cooper) v Revenue and Customs Commissioners see R. (on the application of Davies) v Revenue and Customs Commissioners

R. (on the application of Gallagher) v Basildon DC [2010] EWHC 2824 (Admin); [2011] P.T.S.R. 731; [2011] B.L.G.R. 227, QBD (Admin) .......... *Digested,* 11/**2170**:
*Applied* 14/70

R. (on the application of Gambrah) v Crown Prosecution Service [2013] EWHC 4126 (Admin); [2014] A.C.D. 61, QBD (Admin)

R. (on the application of Garner) v Elmbridge BC [2010] EWCA Civ 1006; [2011] 3 All E.R. 418; [2012] P.T.S.R. 250; [2011] 1 Costs L.R. 48; [2011] Env. L.R. 10; [2010] 3 E.G.L.R. 137; [2011] J.P.L. 289; [2011] A.C.D. 7, CA (Civ Div); reversing [2010] EWHC 567 (Admin); [2010] A.C.D. 65, QBD (Admin) .......... *Digested,* 11/**279**:
*Cited* 14/339: *Considered* 11/278, 14/1222, 14/333: *Followed* 11/2561, 14/442

R. (on the application of Gate) v Secretary of State for Transport [2013] EWHC 2937 (Admin); [2014] J.P.L. 383; [2014] Env. L.R. D1, QBD (Admin)

R. (on the application of Gavigan) v Enfield Magistrates' Court [2013] EWHC 2805 (Admin); (2013) 177 J.P. 609, DC .......... *Digested,* 14/**792**

R. (on the application of GB) v Oxfordshire CC see Oxfordshire CC v B

R. (on the application of GE (Eritrea)) v Secretary of State for the Home Department [2013] EWHC 2186 (Admin); [2014] P.T.S.R. 124, QBD .................................... *Digested,* 14/**1691**

R. (on the application of George) v Secretary of State for Justice see R. (on the application of Ali) v Secretary of State for Justice

R. (on the application of George) v Secretary of State for the Home Department; *sub nom* George v Secretary of State for the Home Department [2014] UKSC 28; [2014] 1 W.L.R. 1831; [2014] 3 All E.R. 365; [2014] Imm. A.R. 958; [2014] I.N.L.R. 658; (2014) 158(20) S.J.L.B. 37; Times, June 2, 2014, SC; reversing [2012] EWCA Civ 1362; [2013] 1 W.L.R. 1319; [2013] Imm. A.R. 197; [2013] I.N.L.R. 281; [2013] A.C.D. 12; Times, December 17, 2012, CA (Civ Div); reversing [2011] EWHC 3247 (Admin), QBD (Admin) ....................................... *Digested,* 14/**1705**

R. (on the application of Geraldo) v Secretary of State for the Home Department; *joined cases* R. (on the application of Aroun) v Secretary of State for the Home Department; R. (on the application of Iqbal) v Secretary of State for the Home Department [2013] EWHC 2703 (Admin); [2014] Imm. A.R. 400, QBD (Admin) . *Digested,* 14/**1648**

R. (on the application of Gibson) v Secretary of State for Justice [2013] EWHC 2481 (Admin); [2014] 1 W.L.R. 2658; (2013) 157(35) S.J.L.B. 41, QBD (Admin) ........ *Digested,* 14/**732**

R. (on the application of Giles) v Parole Board for England and Wales [2003] UKHL 42; [2004] 1 A.C. 1; [2003] 3 W.L.R. 736; [2003] 4 All E.R. 429; [2003] H.R.L.R. 37; [2003] U.K.H.R.R. 1035; (2003) 153 N.L.J. 1426; (2003) 147 S.J.L.B. 936; Times, August 1, 2003, HL; affirming [2002] EWCA Civ 951; [2003] 2 W.L.R. 196; [2002] 3 All E.R. 1123; [2003] 1 Cr. App. R. (S.) 78; [2004] Prison L.R. 13; [2002] Po. L.R. 11; [2002] Crim. L.R. 743; (2002) 99(35) L.S.G. 38; (2002) 152 N.L.J. 1239; Times, July 23, 2002; Independent, October 14, 2002, CA (Civ Div); reversing [2001] EWHC Admin 834; [2002] 1 W.L.R. 654; [2002] Po. L.R. 1; Independent, December 17, 2001, QBD (Admin) ............................................ *Digested,* 03/**3067**: *Applied* 03/3070, 04/2776, 07/2988, 09/2768, 14/2233: *Considered* 08/2690, 09/2761, 10/2874: *Distinguished* 04/3349

R. (on the application of Gillan) v Commissioner of Police of the Metropolis; *joined case* R. (on the application of Quinton) v Commissioner of Police of the Metropolis [2006] UKHL 12; [2006] 2 A.C. 307; [2006] 2 W.L.R. 537; [2006] 4 All E.R. 1041; [2006] 2 Cr. App. R. 36; [2006] H.R.L.R. 18; [2006] U.K.H.R.R. 740; 21 B.H.R.C. 202; [2006] Po. L.R. 26; [2006] Crim. L.R. 752; (2006) 150 S.J.L.B. 366; Times, March 9, 2006, HL; affirming [2004] EWCA Civ 1067; [2005] Q.B. 388; [2004] 3 W.L.R. 1144; [2005] 1 All E.R. 970; [2004] U.K.H.R.R. 1108; [2005] Crim. L.R. 414; [2004] A.C.D. 94; (2004) 101(35) L.S.G. 35; Times, August 12, 2004; Independent, October 5, 2004, CA (Civ Div); affirming [2003] EWHC 2545 (Admin); [2003] Po. L.R. 397; Times, November 5, 2003, DC ............................................................................ *Digested,* 06/**3409**: *Applied* 08/1999, 10/282: *Cited* 10/1078: *Complaint upheld* 10/1746: *Considered* 06/3407, 13/2125, 14/2461, 14/701

R. (on the application of Gleeson Developments Ltd) v Secretary of State for Communities and Local Government; *sub nom* Gleeson Developments Ltd v Secretary of State for Communities and Local Government [2014] EWCA Civ 1118; [2014] P.T.S.R. 1226; [2014] J.P.L. 1386, CA (Civ Div); reversing [2013] EWHC 3166 (Admin); [2014] P.T.S.R. 135; [2014] J.P.L. 472, QBD (Admin) ..... *Digested,* 14/**2403**

R. (on the application of Global Vision College Ltd) v Secretary of State for the Home Department [2014] EWCA Civ 659; [2014] Imm. A.R. 1109; [2014] E.L.R. 313, CA (Civ Div); affirming [2014] EWHC 205 (Admin), QBD (Admin) ..................... *Digested,* 14/**1688**

R. (on the application of GMGRM North Ltd) v Ritchie [2014] EWCA Civ 844; [2014] B.T.C. 32, CA (Civ Div) ............................................................................ *Digested,* 14/**2879**

R. (on the application of GMGRM North Ltd) v Ritchie [2013] EWHC 4115 (Admin); [2014] B.T.C. 13, QBD (Admin) ............................................................ *Digested,* 14/**2876**

R. (on the application of Godfrey) v Southwark LBC [2012] EWCA Civ 500; [2012] B.L.G.R. 683, CA (Civ Div); affirming [2011] EWHC 2220 (Admin), QBD (Admin) ............................................................................ *Digested,* 12/**2588**: *Applied* 14/2418

R. (on the application of Golfa) v Secretary of State for the Home Department; *sub nom* Golfa v Secretary of State for the Home Department [2005] EWHC 2282 (Admin), QBD (Admin) *Considered* 14/1645

R. (on the application of Golfrate Property Management Ltd) v Southwark Crown Court [2014] EWHC 840 (Admin); [2014] 2 Cr. App. R. 12; [2014] Lloyd's Rep. F.C. 431; [2014] Crim. L.R. 830; [2014] A.C.D. 90, QBD (Admin) ...................... *Digested,* 14/**803**

R. (on the application of Goode) v Nottingham Crown Court [2013] EWHC 1726 (Admin); [2014] A.C.D. 6, QBD (Admin)

R. (on the application of Grace) v Secretary of State for the Home Department [2014] EWCA Civ 1091; [2014] 1 W.L.R. 3432, CA (Civ Div) ....................................... *Digested,* 14/**67**

R. (on the application of Gray) v Aylesbury Crown Court [2013] EWHC 500 (Admin); [2014] 1 W.L.R. 818; [2013] 3 All E.R. 346; (2013) 177 J.P. 329; [2013] C.T.L.C. 157; [2013] A.C.D. 64, QBD (Admin) ........ *Digested,* 13/**90**

R. (on the application of Great Yarmouth Port Co Ltd) v Marine Management Organisation [2013] EWHC 3052 (Admin); [2014] L.L.R. 361; [2014] A.C.D. 23, QBD (Admin)

R. (on the application of Green) v Secretary of State for Justice [2013] EWHC 3491 (Admin); [2014] A.C.D. 63, QBD (Admin)

R. (on the application of Greenwich Community Law Centre) v Greenwich LBC [2012] EWCA Civ 496; [2012] Eq. L.R. 572, CA (Civ Div); affirming [2011] EWHC 3463 (Admin); (2012) 156(1) S.J.L.B. 31, QBD (Admin) ........ *Digested,* 12/**2209**: *Applied* 12/2201: *Considered* 14/2017: *Followed* 13/2885

R. (on the application of Ground Rents (Regisport) Ltd) v Upper Tribunal (Administrative Appeals Chamber) [2013] EWHC 2638 (Admin); [2014] A.C.D. 38, QBD (Admin)

R. (on the application of GSTS Pathology LLP) v Revenue and Customs Commissioners [2013] EWHC 1801 (Admin); [2013] S.T.C. 2017; [2013] S.T.I. 2566, QBD (Admin) ........ *Digested,* 14/**3084**

R. (on the application of Guardian News and Media Ltd) v City of Westminster Magistrates' Court; *sub nom* Guardian News and Media Ltd v City of Westminster Magistrates' Court; *joined case* Guardian News and Media Ltd v United States [2012] EWCA Civ 420; [2013] Q.B. 618; [2012] 3 W.L.R. 1343; [2012] 3 All E.R. 551; [2012] C.P. Rep. 30; [2012] E.M.L.R. 22; (2012) 109(16) L.S.G. 22; (2012) 162 N.L.J. 619; Times, July 12, 2012, CA (Civ Div); reversing [2010] EWHC 3376 (Admin); [2011] 1 W.L.R. 1173; [2011] 3 All E.R. 38; [2011] 1 Cr. App. R. 36; [2011] E.M.L.R. 12; [2011] A.C.D. 27, DC ........ *Digested,* 12/**660**: *Applied* 14/664: *Followed* 14/1791

R. (on the application of Guildhall College) v Secretary of State for Business, Innovation and Skills [2014] EWCA Civ 986, CA (Civ Div); affirming [2013] EWHC 3257 (Admin); [2014] E.L.R. 10, QBD (Admin) ........ *Digested,* 14/**75**

R. (on the application of Gujra) v Crown Prosecution Service [2012] UKSC 52; [2013] 1 A.C. 484; [2012] 3 W.L.R. 1227; [2013] 1 All E.R. 612; [2013] 1 Cr. App. R. 12; [2013] Crim. L.R. 337; Times, November 27, 2012, SC; affirming [2011] EWHC 472 (Admin); [2012] 1 W.L.R. 254; [2011] 2 Cr. App. R. 12; (2011) 175 J.P. 161; [2011] A.C.D. 62, DC ........ *Digested,* 13/**748**: *Considered* 14/798

R. (on the application of Gul) v Secretary of State for Justice [2014] EWHC 373 (Admin); [2014] A.C.D. 106, QBD (Admin)

R. (on the application of H (A Child)) v Newham LBC see R. (on the application of N) v Lewisham LBC

R. (on the application of H) v Ashworth Hospital Authority; *joined case* R. (on the application of Ashworth Hospital Authority) v Mental Health Review Tribunal for West Midlands and North West Region [2002] EWCA Civ 923; [2003] 1 W.L.R. 127; (2002) 5 C.C.L. Rep. 390; (2003) 70 B.M.L.R. 40; [2002] M.H.L.R. 314; [2002] A.C.D. 102; (2002) 99(34) L.S.G. 29; (2002) 146 S.J.L.B. 198; Times, July 10, 2002; Daily Telegraph, July 11, 2002, CA (Civ Div); affirming in part [2001] EWHC Admin 901; (2002) 5 C.C.L. Rep. 78; [2002] M.H.L.R. 13, QBD (Admin) ........ *Digested,* 02/**3230**: *Applied* 03/2953, 05/2822, 07/2910, 09/2711: *Followed* 14/2041

R. (on the application of H) v Kingston upon Hull City Council [2013] EWHC 388 (Admin); [2014] P.T.S.R. 1430; [2014] 1 F.L.R. 1094; [2014] 2 F.C.R. 433; [2014] B.L.G.R. 567; [2013] A.C.D. 91; [2013] Fam. Law 804, QBD (Admin) ..... *Digested,* 14/**1264**

R. (on the application of H) v Secretary of State for the Home Department see R. (on the application of S) v Secretary of State for the Home Office

R. (on the application of H) v Southampton Youth Court [2004] EWHC 2912 (Admin); [2005] 2 Cr. App. R. (S.) 30; (2005) 169 J.P. 37; [2005] Crim. L.R. 395; [2005] A.C.D. 45; (2005) 169 J.P.N. 159, DC ........ *Digested,* 05/**939**: *Applied* 05/940, 06/993, 07/947, 10/730, 14/722

R. (on the application of Hamill) v Chelmsford Magistrates' Court; *sub nom* Hamill v Chelmsford Magistrates' Court [2014] EWHC 2799 (Admin); (2014) 178 J.P. 401; (2014) 158(33) S.J.L.B. 41, QBD (Admin) ........ *Digested,* 14/**808**

R. (on the application of Hampton Bishop PC) v Herefordshire Council [2014] EWCA Civ 878, CA (Civ Div); affirming [2013] EWHC 3947 (Admin); [2014] B.L.G.R. 209, QBD (Admin) ........ *Digested,* 14/**2396**

R. (on the application of Haney) v Secretary of State for Justice; *joined case* R. (on the application of Jarvis) v Secretary of State for Justice [2013] EWHC 803 (Admin); [2013] A.C.D. 78, QBD (Admin) *Affirmed* 14/2234

R. (on the application of Haney) v Secretary of State for Justice see R. (on the application of Kaiyam) v Secretary of State for Justice

R. (on the application of Harris) v Secretary of State for the Home Department; *sub nom* R. (on the application of Allen) v Secretary of State for Justice [2008] EWCA Civ 808; [2009] 2 All E.R. 1; [2009] 1 Cr. App. R. 2; [2008] A.C.D. 85, CA (Civ Div); affirming [2007] EWHC 3218 (Admin), QBD (Admin) .................... *Digested,* 09/**914**: *Complaint dismissed* 14/1630: *Followed* 10/770

R. (on the application of Hashmi) v Secretary of State for the Home Department [2002] EWCA Civ 728; [2002] I.N.L.R. 377, CA (Civ Div); reversing [2001] EWHC Admin 908; [2002] Imm. A.R. 257, QBD (Admin) .................................. *Digested,* 03/**2282**: *Applied* 14/1372

R. (on the application of Hayes) v Visitors to the Inns of Court see R. (on the application of Leathley) v Visitors to the Inns of Court

R. (on the application of HC) v Secretary of State for the Home Department [2013] EWHC 982 (Admin); [2014] 1 W.L.R. 1234; [2013] Crim. L.R. 918; [2013] A.C.D. 94, DC .................................................................................. *Digested,* 14/**662**

R. (on the application of Headley) v Secretary of State for the Home Department see R. (on the application of Clift) v Secretary of State for the Home Department

R. (on the application of Heather Moor & Edgecomb Ltd) v Financial Ombudsman Service [2008] EWCA Civ 642; [2008] Bus. L.R. 1486; (2008) 158 N.L.J. 897, CA (Civ Div) .................................................................................. *Digested,* 09/**73**: *Applied* 11/55, 14/1449: *Considered* 13/2080

R. (on the application of Heathrow Hub Ltd) v Secretary of State for Transport see R. (on the application of Buckinghamshire CC) v Secretary of State for Transport

R. (on the application of Hertfordshire CC) v Hammersmith and Fulham LBC see R. (on the application of M) v Hammersmith and Fulham LBC

R. (on the application of HH) v Westminster City Magistrates' Court; *sub nom* HH v Italy; PH v Italy; *joined case* F-K v Poland [2012] UKSC 25; [2013] 1 A.C. 338; [2012] 3 W.L.R. 90; [2012] 4 All E.R. 539; [2012] H.R.L.R. 25; (2012) 156(25) S.J.L.B. 31; Times, July 2, 2012, SC; affirming [2011] EWHC 1145 (Admin); [2011] A.C.D. 94, DC .................................................................................. *Digested,* 12/**1293**: *Applied* 13/2652, 13/2749, 14/1596, 14/662: *Considered* 12/1289, 14/1650, 14/1668, 14/1704

R. (on the application of Hibbert) v General Medical Council [2013] EWHC 3596 (Admin); [2014] Med. L.R. 84, QBD (Admin) ............................................... *Digested,* 14/**60**

R. (on the application of Hicks) v Commissioner of Police of the Metropolis; *joined cases* R. (on the application of M) v Commissioner of Police of the Metropolis; R. (on the application of Pearce) v Commissioner of Police of the Metropolis; R. (on the application of Middleton) v Bromley Magistrates Court [2014] EWCA Civ 3; [2014] 1 W.L.R. 2152; [2014] 2 Cr. App. R. 4; [2014] H.R.L.R. 11; [2014] Crim. L.R. 681, CA (Civ Div); affirming [2012] EWHC 1947 (Admin); [2012] A.C.D. 102, DC .................................................................................. *Digested,* 14/**2464**

R. (on the application of Hicks) v Snaresbrook Crown Court [2012] EWHC 3348 (Admin), QBD (Admin) *Overruled* 14/2612

R. (on the application of Hill) v Institute of Chartered Accountants in England and Wales [2013] EWCA Civ 555; [2014] 1 W.L.R. 86; Times, July 10, 2013, CA (Civ Div); affirming [2012] EWHC 1731 (QB), QBD (Admin) .............................. *Digested,* 13/**1**

R. (on the application of Hillingdon LBC v Secretary of State for Transport) see R. (on the application of Buckinghamshire CC) v Secretary of State for Transport

R. (on the application of Hindawi) v Secretary of State for the Home Department see R. (on the application of Clift) v Secretary of State for the Home Department

R. (on the application of Hinds) v Blackpool BC [2012] EWCA Civ 466; [2012] J.P.L. 1365, CA (Civ Div); affirming [2011] EWHC 591 (Admin); [2011] N.P.C. 32, QBD (Admin) .................................................................................. *Digested,* 12/**2590**: *Followed* 14/2421

R. (on the application of Hodkin) v Registrar General of Births, Deaths and Marriages [2013] UKSC 77; [2014] A.C. 610; [2014] 2 W.L.R. 23; [2014] 1 All E.R. 737; [2014] P.T.S.R. 1; [2014] 1 F.C.R. 577; (2014) 164(7589) N.L.J. 18; [2014] 1 P. & C.R. DG13, SC; reversing [2012] EWHC 3635 (Admin); [2013] P.T.S.R. 875; [2013] A.C.D. 32; (2013) 157(2) S.J.L.B. 31, QBD (Admin) ............................ *Digested,* 14/**1480**

R. (on the application of Holder) v Gedling BC; *sub nom* Holder v Gedling BC [2014] EWCA Civ 599; [2014] J.P.L. 1087, CA (Civ Div); reversing [2013] EWHC 1611 (Admin); [2013] J.P.L. 1426, QBD (Admin) ......................................................... *Digested,* 14/**2420**

R. (on the application of Holding & Barnes Plc) v Secretary of State for the Environment, Transport and the Regions; *sub nom* R. v Secretary of State for the Environment, Transport and the Regions Ex p. Holdings & Barnes Plc; *joined cases* R. (on the application of Premier Leisure UK Ltd) v Secretary of State for the Environment, Transport and the Regions; R. (on the application of Alconbury Developments Ltd) v Secretary of State for the Environment, Transport and the Regions; Secretary of State for the Environment, Transport and the Regions v Legal & General Assurance Society Ltd [2001] UKHL 23; [2003] 2 A.C. 295; [2001] 2 W.L.R. 1389; [2001] 2 All E.R. 929; [2002] Env. L.R. 12; [2001] H.R.L.R. 45; [2001] U.K.H.R.R. 728; (2001) 3 L.G.L.R. 38; (2001) 82 P. & C.R. 40; [2001] 2 P.L.R. 76; [2001] J.P.L. 920; [2001] 20 E.G. 228 (C.S.); (2001) 98(24) L.S.G. 45; (2001) 151 N.L.J. 727; (2001) 145 S.J.L.B. 140; [2001] N.P.C. 90; Times, May 10, 2001; Independent, June 25, 2001; Daily Telegraph, May 15, 2001, HL; reversing [2001] H.R.L.R. 2; [2001] U.K.H.R.R. 270; (2001) 3 L.G.L.R. 21; [2001] 1 P.L.R. 58; [2001] 1 E.G.L.R. 33; [2001] 05 E.G. 170; [2001] J.P.L. 291; [2001] A.C.D. 65; [2001] 4 E.G. 141 (C.S.); (2001) 151 N.L.J. 135; (2001) 145 S.J.L.B. 84; Times, January 24, 2001; Independent, January 22, 2001, DC ........ *Digested,* 01/**4761**: *Applied* 02/2337, 02/3700, 02/4191, 05/1410, 09/3019, 12/2599, 14/2864: *Cited* 01/6853, 02/1647: *Considered* 02/3696, 02/3699, 03/55, 04/1529, 04/790, 08/2935, 13/350: *Distinguished* 08/1955, 10/1052: *Followed* 02/1526, 03/3446

R. (on the application of Hollis) v Association of Chartered Certified Accountants (ACCA) [2014] EWHC 2572 (Admin); [2014] B.P.I.R. 1317, QBD (Admin) ........ *Digested,* 14/**2472**

R. (on the application of Howard) v Official Receiver [2013] EWHC 1839 (Admin); [2014] Q.B. 930; [2014] 2 W.L.R. 1518; [2014] B.P.I.R. 204; (2013) 163(7568) N.L.J. 20, QBD (Admin) ........ *Digested,* 14/**1815**

R. (on the application of HS) v Upper Tribunal (Immigration and Asylum Chamber) [2012] EWHC 3126 (Admin); [2013] Imm. A.R. 579, QBD (Admin) ........ *Digested,* 14/**50**

R. (on the application of HS2 Action Alliance Ltd) v Secretary of State for Transport [2014] EWCA Civ 1578, CA (Civ Div); affirming [2014] EWHC 2759 (Admin); [2014] P.T.S.R. 1334, QBD (Admin)

R. (on the application of HS2 Action Alliance Ltd) v Secretary of State for Transport see R. (on the application of Buckinghamshire CC) v Secretary of State for Transport

R. (on the application of Huitson) v Revenue and Customs Commissioners [2011] EWCA Civ 893; [2012] Q.B. 489; [2012] 2 W.L.R. 490; [2011] S.T.C. 1860; [2011] B.T.C. 456; 14 I.T.L. Rep. 90; [2011] S.T.I. 2307; [2011] N.P.C. 91, CA (Civ Div); affirming [2010] EWHC 97 (Admin); [2011] Q.B. 174; [2010] 3 W.L.R. 1015; [2010] S.T.C. 715; [2010] U.K.H.R.R. 609; [2010] B.T.C. 175; 12 I.T.L. Rep. 603; [2010] S.T.I. 376; (2010) 160 N.L.J. 180, QBD (Admin) ........ *Digested,* 11/**3384**: *Applied* 11/3437, 14/2964

R. (on the application of Hunt) v North Somerset Council (Costs) see Hunt v North Somerset Council (Costs)

R. (on the application of Hunt) v North Somerset Council see Hunt v North Somerset Council

R. (on the application of Hurley) v Secretary of State for Business, Innovation and Skills [2012] EWHC 201 (Admin); [2012] H.R.L.R. 13; [2012] Eq. L.R. 447; [2012] E.L.R. 297; [2012] A.C.D. 50, DC ........ *Digested,* 12/**1004**: *Considered* 14/1509

R. (on the application of Hussain) v Secretary of State for Justice see R. (on the application of King) v Secretary of State for Justice

R. (on the application of IDT Card Services Ireland Ltd) v Customs and Excise Commissioners; *sub nom* Revenue and Customs Commissioners v IDT Card Services Ireland Ltd [2006] EWCA Civ 29; [2006] S.T.C. 1252; [2006] B.T.C. 5175; [2006] B.V.C. 244; [2006] S.T.I. 239, CA (Civ Div); reversing [2004] EWHC 3188 (Admin); [2005] S.T.C. 314; [2005] B.T.C. 5163; [2005] B.V.C. 194; [2005] S.T.I. 22, QBD (Admin) ........ *Digested,* 06/**4484**: *Applied* 09/4078, 10/1049, 14/823: *Considered* 09/3765, 13/2146: *Distinguished* 11/3519: *Followed* 09/4044, 11/3566

R. (on the application of Ignaoua) v Secretary of State for the Home Department [2013] EWCA Civ 1498; [2014] 1 W.L.R. 651; [2014] 1 All E.R. 649, CA (Civ Div); reversing [2013] EWHC 2512 (Admin); [2014] A.C.D. 37; (2013) 157(34) S.J.L.B. 40, QBD (Admin) ........ *Digested,* 14/**1662**: *Considered* 14/1722

R. (on the application of IM (Nigeria)) v Secretary of State for the Home Department see R. (on the application of Muaza) v Secretary of State for the Home Department

R. (on the application of IM Properties Development Ltd) v Lichfield DC; *sub nom* IM Properties Development Ltd v Lichfield DC [2014] EWHC 2440 (Admin); [2014] P.T.S.R. 1484, QBD (Birmingham)

R. (on the application of Ingenious Media Holdings Plc) v Revenue and Customs Commissioners [2013] EWHC 3258 (Admin); [2014] S.T.C. 673; [2014] B.T.C. 3; [2014] A.C.D. 65; [2013] S.T.I. 3400, QBD (Admin) ........................................ *Digested,* 14/**2971**: *Considered* 14/56

R. (on the application of International Air Transport Association (IATA)) v Department of Transport (C-344/04) [2006] E.C.R. I-403; [2006] 2 C.M.L.R. 20; (2006) 156 N.L.J. 113; Times, January 16, 2006, ECJ ........................................ *Digested,* 06/**1522**: *Applied* 07/1561, 07/3809, 14/165: *Considered* 09/260

R. (on the application of International Association of Independent Tanker Owners (INTERTANKO)) v Secretary of State for Transport [2006] EWHC 1577 (Admin); [2007] Env. L.R. 8; [2006] A.C.D. 89; [2006] N.P.C. 79, QBD (Admin) . *Digested,* 07/**3809**: *Applied* 14/1087: *Preliminary ruling given* 08/1301

R. (on the application of Iqbal) v Secretary of State for the Home Department see R. (on the application of Geraldo) v Secretary of State for the Home Department

R. (on the application of Island Farm Development Ltd) v Bridgend CBC [2006] EWHC 2189 (Admin); [2007] B.L.G.R. 60; [2007] L.L.R. 230; (2006) 103(36) L.S.G. 36; (2006) 150 S.J.L.B. 1153; [2006] N.P.C. 100, QBD (Admin) ........................................ *Digested,* 07/**2867**: *Applied* 14/70

R. (on the application of J) v Worcestershire CC; *sub nom* Worcestershire CC v J [2014] EWCA Civ 1518; (2014) 158(46) S.J.L.B. 37, CA (Civ Div); affirming [2013] EWHC 3845 (Admin); [2014] P.T.S.R. 537; [2014] 1 F.C.R. 395; [2014] B.L.G.R. 81; (2014) 17 C.C.L. Rep. 100; [2014] A.C.D. 62, QBD (Admin) ......... *Digested,* 14/**2148**

R. (on the application of James) v Secretary of State for Justice see R. (on the application of Wells) v Parole Board for England and Wales

R. (on the application of Jan) v Secretary of State for the Home Department [2014] UKUT 265 (IAC); [2014] Imm. A.R. 1004, UT (IAC)

R. (on the application of Jarvis) v Secretary of State for Justice see R. (on the application of Haney) v Secretary of State for Justice

R. (on the application of Jaspers (Treburley) Ltd) v Food Standards Agency [2013] EWHC 1788 (Admin); [2013] P.T.S.R. 1271, QBD (Admin) ........................................ *Digested,* 14/**1473**

R. (on the application of Javed) v Secretary of State for the Home Department; *sub nom* Secretary of State for the Home Department v Javed; R. v Secretary of State for the Home Department Ex p. Ali; R. v Secretary of State for the Home Department Ex p. Javed; *joined cases* R. (on the application of Ali (Zulfiqar)) v Secretary of State for the Home Department; R. (on the application of Ali (Abid)) v Secretary of State for the Home Department [2001] EWCA Civ 789; [2002] Q.B. 129; [2001] 3 W.L.R. 323; [2001] Imm. A.R. 529; [2001] I.N.L.R. 645; (2001) 98(26) L.S.G. 44; (2001) 145 S.J.L.B. 149; Times, May 24, 2001; Independent, July 16, 2001, CA (Civ Div); affirming [2001] EWHC Admin 7; Times, February 9, 2001; Daily Telegraph, February 7, 2001, QBD (Admin) ...... *Digested,* 01/**3651**: *Followed* 14/1649

R. (on the application of Javed) v Secretary of State for the Home Department see R. (on the application of MM (Lebanon)) v Secretary of State for the Home Department

R. (on the application of JB (Jamaica)) v Secretary of State for the Home Department see R. (on the application of Brown) v Secretary of State for the Home Department

R. (on the application of JB) v Secretary of State for the Home Department see R. (on the application of T) v Chief Constable of Greater Manchester

R. (on the application of JC) v Central Criminal Court; *sub nom* JC v Central Criminal Court [2014] EWCA Civ 1777, CA (Civ Div); affirming [2014] EWHC 1041 (Admin); [2014] 1 W.L.R. 3697; [2014] 4 All E.R. 319; [2014] 2 Cr. App. R. 13; (2014) 178 J.P. 188; [2014] E.M.L.R. 20; [2014] 2 F.C.R. 571; [2014] Crim. L.R. 902; [2014] A.C.D. 86; (2014) 164(7603) N.L.J. 21, DC ........................................ *Digested,* 14/**46**

R. (on the application of JF) v Croydon LBC [2006] EWHC 2368 (Admin), QBD (Admin) *Applied* 14/943: *Distinguished* 11/990

R. (on the application of JF) v NHS Sheffield Clinical Commissioning Group [2014] EWHC 1345 (Admin); [2014] A.C.D. 121, QBD (Admin)

R. (on the application of JL) v Secretary of State for Justice see R. (on the application of JL) v Secretary of State for the Home Department

R. (on the application of JL) v Secretary of State for the Home Department; *sub nom* R. (on the application of JL) v Secretary of State for Justice [2008] UKHL 68; [2009] 1 A.C. 588; [2008] 3 W.L.R. 1325; [2009] 2 All E.R. 521; [2009] H.R.L.R. 9; [2009] U.K.H.R.R. 415; 27 B.H.R.C. 24; [2008] Inquest L.R. 88; (2008) 158 N.L.J. 1719; (2008) 152(46) S.J.L.B. 31; Times, December 2, 2008, HL; affirming [2007] EWCA Civ 767; [2008] 1 W.L.R. 158; [2007] H.R.L.R. 39; [2007] Inquest L.R. 202; [2007] A.C.D. 95; Times, October 2, 2007, CA (Civ Div); affirming [2006] EWHC 2558 (Admin); [2006] Inquest L.R. 200; [2007] A.C.D. 31, QBD (Admin) ........ *Digested,* 09/**2754**: *Considered* 14/47: *Explained* 09/2037: *Followed* 09/2037, 10/17, 11/1682

R. (on the application of Jones) v First-tier Tribunal (Social Entitlement Chamber); *sub nom* Jones v First-tier Tribunal (Social Entitlement Chamber) [2013] UKSC 19; [2013] 2 A.C. 48; [2013] 2 W.L.R. 1012; [2013] 2 All E.R. 625; [2013] R.T.R. 28; [2013] P.I.Q.R. P18, SC; reversing [2011] EWCA Civ 400; [2012] Q.B. 345; [2011] 3 W.L.R. 971; [2011] R.T.R. 29, CA (Civ Div); reversing [2010] UKUT 199 (AAC); [2011] R.T.R. 5, UT (AAC) ........ *Digested,* 13/**2194**: *Followed* 14/54

R. (on the application of Jones) v Judicial Appointments Commission [2014] EWHC 1680 (Admin); [2014] A.C.D. 107, DC

R. (on the application of Jones) v Mansfield DC [2003] EWCA Civ 1408; [2004] Env. L.R. 21; [2004] 2 P. & C.R. 14; (2003) 147 S.J.L.B. 1209; [2003] N.P.C. 119; Times, October 31, 2003, CA (Civ Div); affirming [2003] EWHC 7 (Admin); [2003] Env. L.R. 26; [2003] 1 P. & C.R. 31; [2003] J.P.L. 1148; [2003] N.P.C. 5, QBD (Admin) ........ *Digested,* 03/**3421**: *Applied* 05/3270, 05/3298, 08/2967, 10/2601, 11/2530: *Considered* 04/3084: *Followed* 14/2431, 14/2434

R. (on the application of Jorgensen (Listing Officer)) v Gomports see Jorgensen (Listing Officer) v Gomperts

R. (on the application of JS) v Secretary of State for Work and Pensions; *sub nom* R. (on the application of SG) v Secretary of State for Work and Pensions [2014] EWCA Civ 156; [2014] P.T.S.R. 619; [2014] H.R.L.R. 10; [2014] Eq. L.R. 447; [2014] H.L.R. 20, CA (Civ Div); affirming [2013] EWHC 3350 (QB); [2014] P.T.S.R. 23, QBD (Admin) ........ *Digested,* 14/**2744**

R. (on the application of K) v Newcastle City Council see R. (on the application of VC) v Newcastle City Council

R. (on the application of K) v Secretary of State for the Home Department [2014] EWCA Civ 151; [2014] 3 All E.R. 437, CA (Civ Div) ........ *Digested,* 14/**1722**

R. (on the application of K) v Wirral Borough Magistrates Court see R. (on the application of W) v Southampton Youth Court

R. (on the application of Kadhim) v Brent LBC Housing Benefit Review Board; *sub nom* R. (on the application of Khadim) v Brent LBC Housing Benefit Review Board; R. v Brent LBC Housing Benefit Review Board Ex p. Khadim; Kadhim v Brent LBC Housing Benefit Board [2001] Q.B. 955; [2001] 2 W.L.R. 1674; (2001) 33 H.L.R. 79; [2001] A.C.D. 35; (2001) 98(14) L.S.G. 40; [2001] N.P.C. 7; Times, March 27, 2001, CA (Civ Div); reversing [2000] C.O.D. 472, QBD ...... *Digested,* 01/**5021**: *Considered* 14/294

R. (on the application of Kadria) v Secretary of State for the Home Department; *joined case* R. (on the application of Krasniqi) v Secretary of State for the Home Department [2010] EWHC 3405 (Admin), QBD (Admin) *Considered* 14/1723

R. (on the application of Kaiyam) v Secretary of State for Justice [2013] EWHC 1340 (Admin), QBD (Admin) *Affirmed* 14/2234

R. (on the application of Kaiyam) v Secretary of State for Justice; *sub nom* R. (on the application of Massey) v Secretary of State for Justice; R. (on the application of Haney) v Secretary of State for Justice; *joined case* R. (on the application of Robinson) v Governor of Whatton Prison [2014] UKSC 66; Times, December 15, 2014, SC; reversing in part [2013] EWCA Civ 1587; [2014] 1 W.L.R. 1208, CA (Civ Div) ........ *Digested,* 14/**2234**

R. (on the application of Kambadzi) v Secretary of State for the Home Department; *sub nom* Kambadzi v Secretary of State for the Home Department; R. (on the application of SK (Zimbabwe)) v Secretary of State for the Home Department; SK (Zimbabwe) v Secretary of State for the Home Department [2011] UKSC 23; [2011] 1 W.L.R. 1299; [2011] 4 All E.R. 975; (2011) 108(23) L.S.G. 18; Times, June 10, 2011, SC; reversing [2008] EWCA Civ 1204; [2009] 1 W.L.R. 1527; [2009] 2 All E.R. 365; Times, November 21, 2008, CA (Civ Div); reversing [2008] EWHC 98 (Admin); [2008] A.C.D. 37; Times, February 26, 2008, QBD (Admin) ........ *Digested,* 11/**1733**: *Considered* 14/1682: *Followed* 13/1602

R. (on the application of Kay) v Commissioner of Police of the Metropolis see Kay v Commissioner of Police of the Metropolis

R. (on the application of Kaziu) v Secretary of State for the Home Department; *sub nom* Kaziu v Secretary of State for the Home Department [2014] EWHC 832 (Admin); [2014] 4 All E.R. 133; [2014] Imm. A.R. 919; [2014] A.C.D. 98, QBD (Admin) ........ *Digested,* 14/**1723**

R. (on the application of Kebede) v Newcastle City Council [2013] EWCA Civ 960; [2014] P.T.S.R. 82; [2013] 3 F.C.R. 372; [2013] B.L.G.R. 710; [2013] E.L.R. 550; (2013) 16 C.C.L. Rep. 388, CA (Civ Div); affirming [2013] EWHC 355 (Admin), QBD (Admin) ........ *Digested,* 14/**949**

R. (on the application of Kebede) v Secretary of State for Business, Innovation and Skills; *sub nom* Kedebe v Secretary of State for Business, Innovation and Skills [2013] EWHC 2396 (Admin); [2014] P.T.S.R. 92; [2013] Eq. L.R. 961, QBD (Admin) ........ *Digested,* 13/**864**

R. (on the application of Kenneally) v Rampton Hospital Authority see R. (on the application of Kenneally) v Snaresbrook Crown Court

R. (on the application of Kenneally) v Snaresbrook Crown Court; *joined case* R. (on the application of Kenneally) v Rampton Hospital Authority [2001] EWHC Admin 968; [2002] Q.B. 1169; [2002] 2 W.L.R. 1430; [2002] M.H.L.R. 53; [2002] A.C.D. 46; Times, December 17, 2001, DC ........ *Digested,* 02/**3228**: *Applied* 14/800: *Distinguished* 07/21

R. (on the application of Kenya Aid Programme) v Sheffield Magistrates' Court see Kenya Aid Programme v Sheffield City Council

R. (on the application of Keyu) v Secretary of State for Foreign and Commonwealth Affairs; *sub nom* Keyu v Secretary of State for Foreign and Commonwealth Affairs [2014] EWCA Civ 312; [2014] 3 W.L.R. 948; [2014] 4 All E.R. 99, CA (Civ Div); affirming [2012] EWHC 2445 (Admin); (2012) 109(35) L.S.G. 22, DC *Digested,* 14/**62**

R. (on the application of Khadim) v Brent LBC Housing Benefit Review Board see R. (on the application of Kadhim) v Brent LBC Housing Benefit Review Board

R. (on the application of Khaled) v Secretary of State for Foreign and Commonwealth Affairs; *sub nom* Secretary of State for the Foreign Office and Commonwealth Affairs v Maftah; *joined case* R. (on the application of Maftah) v Secretary of State for Foreign and Commonwealth Affairs [2011] EWCA Civ 350; [2012] Q.B. 477; [2012] 2 W.L.R. 251; (2011) 108(17) L.S.G. 14; Times, April 21, 2011, CA (Civ Div); reversing [2010] EWHC 1868 (Admin); [2011] A.C.D. 12, QBD (Admin) ........ *Digested,* 11/**1689**: *Considered* 13/1589, 13/668, 14/2567

R. (on the application of Khan) v Secretary of State for Foreign and Commonwealth Affairs [2014] EWCA Civ 24; [2014] 1 W.L.R. 872, CA (Civ Div); affirming [2012] EWHC 3728 (Admin); [2013] A.C.D. 23, QBD (Admin) ........ *Digested,* 14/**65**

R. (on the application of Khan) v Secretary of State for the Home Department; *joined case* Khan v Secretary of State for the Home Department [2014] EWCA Civ 88; [2014] 1 W.L.R. 3173; [2014] 2 All E.R. 973; [2014] Imm. A.R. 768, CA (Civ Div); affirming [2013] EWHC 601 (Admin); [2013] 3 All E.R. 499, QBD (Admin) . *Digested,* 14/**1679**

R. (on the application of Kides) v South Cambridgeshire DC [2002] EWCA Civ 1370; [2003] 1 P. & C.R. 19; [2002] 4 P.L.R. 66; [2003] J.P.L. 431; [2002] 42 E.G. 160 (C.S.); (2002) 99(43) L.S.G. 35; (2002) 146 S.J.L.B. 230; [2002] N.P.C. 121; Times, October 15, 2002; Independent, October 16, 2002, CA (Civ Div); affirming [2001] EWHC Admin 839; [2003] 1 P. & C.R. 4; [2002] J.P.L. 832; [2001] N.P.C. 153, QBD (Admin) ........ *Digested,* 02/**3662**: *Considered* 07/3264, 10/2602, 11/2546: *Followed* 10/2590, 12/2590, 14/2428

R. (on the application of King) v Isleworth Crown Court; *sub nom* R. v Isleworth Crown Court Ex p. King (Murray) [2001] EWHC Admin 22; [2001] E.H.L.R. 14; [2001] A.C.D. 51; Independent, February 19, 2001; Daily Telegraph, February 13, 2001, DC ........ *Digested,* 01/**3528**: *Applied* 14/1051

R. (on the application of King) v Parole Board for England and Wales [2014] EWHC 564 (Admin); [2014] A.C.D. 103, QBD (Admin)

R. (on the application of King) v Secretary of State for Justice; *sub nom* R. (on the application of Bourgass) v Secretary of State for Justice; R. (on the application of Hussain) v Secretary of State for Justice [2012] EWCA Civ 376; [2012] 1 W.L.R. 3602; [2012] 4 All E.R. 44; [2012] H.R.L.R. 17; Times, June 27, 2012, CA (Civ Div); affirming [2010] EWHC 2522 (Admin); [2011] 1 W.L.R. 2667; [2011] 3 All E.R. 776; [2010] U.K.H.R.R. 1245; [2011] A.C.D. 13; Times, March 8, 2011, QBD (Admin) ........ *Digested,* 12/**2337**: *Considered* 14/2162

R. (on the application of KM (Jamaica)) v Secretary of State for the Home Department see R. (on the application of Lumba) v Secretary of State for the Home Department

R. (on the application of Krasniqi) v Secretary of State for the Home Department see R. (on the application of Kadria) v Secretary of State for the Home Department

R. (on the application of KS) v First-tier Tribunal [2012] UKUT 281 (AAC), UT (AAC) *Applied* 14/944

R. (on the application of Kuteh) v Upper Tribunal (Administrative Appeals Chamber) [2012] EWHC 2196 (Admin), QBD (Admin) *Not followed* 14/50

R. (on the application of Kuteh) v Upper Tribunal Administrative Appeals Chambers [2011] EWHC 2061 (Admin), QBD (Admin) *Not followed* 14/50

R. (on the application of L) v Chief Constable of Cumbria [2013] EWHC 869 (Admin); [2014] 1 W.L.R. 601; [2013] A.C.D. 73, QBD (Admin) ........ *Digested,* 14/**1636**: *Considered* 14/2444

R. (on the application of L) v Commissioner of Police of the Metropolis [2009] UKSC 3; [2010] 1 A.C. 410; [2009] 3 W.L.R. 1056; [2010] 1 All E.R. 113; [2010] P.T.S.R. 245; [2010] 2 F.C.R. 25; [2010] H.R.L.R. 7; [2010] U.K.H.R.R. 115; 28 B.H.R.C. 391; (2009) 12 C.C.L. Rep. 573; [2010] Fam. Law 21; (2009) 159 N.L.J. 1549; (2009) 153(42) S.J.L.B. 30; Times, November 2, 2009, SC; affirming [2007] EWCA Civ 168; [2008] 1 W.L.R. 681; [2007] 4 All E.R. 128; (2008) 11 C.C.L. Rep. 13; [2007] Po. L.R. 115; (2007) 104(11) L.S.G. 32; (2007) 151 S.J.L.B. 336; Times, March 28, 2007, CA (Civ Div); affirming [2006] EWHC 482 (Admin); [2007] Po. L.R. 98, QBD (Admin) ........ *Digested,* 10/**2633**: *Applied* 13/2378: *Considered* 13/1564, 13/2106: *Followed* 11/2588, 12/1678, 13/2379, 14/2445

R. (on the application of L) v West London Mental Health NHS Trust [2014] EWCA Civ 47; [2014] 1 W.L.R. 3103; (2014) 137 B.M.L.R. 76; [2014] A.C.D. 79; (2014) 158(6) S.J.L.B. 37, CA (Civ Div); reversing [2012] EWHC 3200 (Admin); [2013] M.H.L.R. 297; [2013] A.C.D. 15, QBD (Admin) ........ *Digested,* 14/**2162**

R. (on the application of Lamb) v Ministry of Justice see R. (on the application of Nicklinson) v Ministry of Justice

R. (on the application of Lambrou) v Secretary of State for Communities and Local Government [2013] EWHC 325 (Admin); [2014] J.P.L. 538, QBD (Admin) ........ *Digested,* 14/**2376**

R. (on the application of Laporte) v Chief Constable of Gloucestershire [2006] UKHL 55; [2007] 2 A.C. 105; [2007] 2 W.L.R. 46; [2007] 2 All E.R. 529; [2007] H.R.L.R. 13; [2007] U.K.H.R.R. 400; 22 B.H.R.C. 38; [2006] Po. L.R. 309; [2007] Crim. L.R. 576; [2007] A.C.D. 25; (2007) 151 S.J.L.B. 26; Times, December 14, 2006, HL; reversing in part [2004] EWCA Civ 1639; [2005] Q.B. 678; [2005] 2 W.L.R. 789; [2005] 1 All E.R. 473; [2005] H.R.L.R. 6; [2005] Crim. L.R. 467; [2005] A.C.D. 57; (2005) 102(6) L.S.G. 32; Times, December 13, 2004; Independent, December 14, 2004, CA (Civ Div); affirming [2004] EWHC 253 (Admin); [2004] 2 All E.R. 874; [2004] U.K.H.R.R. 484; [2004] Po. L.R. 123; [2004] A.C.D. 34; (2004) 154 N.L.J. 308; Times, February 26, 2004, DC ........ *Digested,* 07/**3317**: *Applied* 07/3316, 14/2444: *Considered* 11/2600, 12/2617

R. (on the application of Lawless) v Secretary of State for Justice see R. (on the application of Ali) v Secretary of State for Justice

R. (on the application of Lawson) v Westminster Magistrates' Court [2013] EWHC 2434 (Admin); [2014] 1 W.L.R. 2085; (2013) 177 J.P. 577, DC ........ *Digested,* 14/**735**

R. (on the application of LE (Jamaica)) v Secretary of State for the Home Department; *sub nom* LE (Jamaica) v Secretary of State for the Home Department [2012] EWCA Civ 597, CA (Civ Div); affirming [2007] EWHC 2980 (Admin), QBD (Admin) *Applied* 14/1681

R. (on the application of Leathley) v Visitors to the Inns of Court; *joined cases* R. (on the application of Mehey) v Visitors to the Inns of Court; R. (on the application of Hayes) v Visitors to the Inns of Court [2014] EWCA Civ 1630, CA (Civ Div); affirming [2013] EWHC 3097 (Admin); [2014] A.C.D. 39, QBD (Admin)

R. (on the application of Lee) v Secretary of State for Justice see R. (on the application of Wells) v Parole Board for England and Wales

R. (on the application of Lee-Hirons) v Secretary of State for Justice [2014] EWCA Civ 553; (2014) 138 B.M.L.R. 44, CA (Civ Div); affirming [2013] EWHC 1784 (Admin); (2013) 134 B.M.L.R. 187; [2014] A.C.D. 16, QBD (Admin) .................. *Digested,* 14/**2192**

R. (on the application of Lewis) v Persimmon Homes Teesside Ltd see R. (on the application of Lewis) v Redcar and Cleveland BC

R. (on the application of Lewis) v Redcar and Cleveland BC; *sub nom* R. (on the application of Lewis) v Persimmon Homes Teesside Ltd; Persimmon Homes Teesside Ltd v Lewis [2008] EWCA Civ 746; [2009] 1 W.L.R. 83; [2008] B.L.G.R. 781; [2008] 2 P. & C.R. 21; [2009] J.P.L. 402; [2008] N.P.C. 78, CA (Civ Div); reversing in part [2007] EWHC 3166 (Admin); [2008] J.P.L. 1156; [2008] A.C.D. 38, QBD (Admin) .................. *Digested,* 08/**2935**:
*Applied* 09/1736, 12/2581: *Considered* 12/4224: *Followed* 09/1015, 10/2572, 12/2575, 14/70

R. (on the application of Lewis) v Redcar and Cleveland BC [2010] UKSC 11; [2010] 2 A.C. 70; [2010] 2 W.L.R. 653; [2010] 2 All E.R. 613; [2010] B.L.G.R. 295; [2010] 2 P. & C.R. 16; [2010] 1 E.G.L.R. 153; [2010] J.P.L. 1135; [2010] 10 E.G. 116 (C.S.); (2010) 160 N.L.J. 390; (2010) 154(9) S.J.L.B. 30; [2010] N.P.C. 27; Times, March 4, 2010, SC; reversing [2009] EWCA Civ 3; [2009] 1 W.L.R. 1461; [2009] 4 All E.R. 1232; [2009] B.L.G.R. 649; [2009] 1 E.G.L.R. 79; [2009] 15 E.G. 100; [2009] J.P.L. 1192; [2009] 3 E.G. 103 (C.S.); [2009] N.P.C. 8, CA (Civ Div); affirming [2008] EWHC 1813 (Admin); [2008] N.P.C. 97, QBD (Admin) .................. *Digested,* 10/**2754**:
*Applied* 14/2526: *Considered* 10/2755, 14/2407: *Followed* 12/2729

R. (on the application of Lewisham LBC) v Secretary of State for Health; *sub nom* Lewisham LBC v South London Healthcare NHS Trust Special Administrator; South London Healthcare NHS Trust Special Administrator v Secretary of State for Health; R. (on the application of Save Lewisham Hospital Campaign Ltd) v Secretary of State for Health [2013] EWCA Civ 1409; [2014] 1 W.L.R. 514; [2014] P.T.S.R. 273; (2014) 135 B.M.L.R. 78, CA (Civ Div); affirming [2013] EWHC 2381 (Admin); [2013] P.T.S.R. 1298; [2013] B.L.G.R. 665; [2014] A.C.D. 11, QBD (Admin) .................. *Digested,* 14/**1564**

R. (on the application of LH) v Shropshire Council [2014] EWCA Civ 404; [2014] P.T.S.R. 1052; (2014) 17 C.C.L. Rep. 216, CA (Civ Div); reversing [2013] EWHC 4222 (Admin), QBD (Admin) .................. *Digested,* 14/**2802**

R. (on the application of Limbuela) v Secretary of State for the Home Department; *joined cases* R. (on the application of Adam) v Secretary of State for the Home Department; R. (on the application of Tesema) v Secretary of State for the Home Department [2005] UKHL 66; [2006] 1 A.C. 396; [2005] 3 W.L.R. 1014; [2007] 1 All E.R. 951; [2006] H.R.L.R. 4; [2006] H.L.R. 10; (2006) 9 C.C.L. Rep. 30; (2005) 102(46) L.S.G. 25; (2005) 149 S.J.L.B. 1354; Times, November 4, 2005, HL; affirming [2004] EWCA Civ 540; [2004] Q.B. 1440; [2004] 3 W.L.R. 561; [2005] 3 All E.R. 29; [2004] H.L.R. 38; (2004) 7 C.C.L. Rep. 267; [2004] A.C.D. 70; (2004) 101(23) L.S.G. 32; Times, May 26, 2004; Independent, May 25, 2004, CA (Civ Div); affirming [2004] EWHC 219 (QB); Times, February 9, 2004, QBD .................. *Digested,* 06/**2217**:
*Applied* 06/2235, 14/1652: *Considered* 05/2157, 07/3908: *Distinguished* 06/844

R. (on the application of Ling (Bridlington) Ltd) v East Riding of Yorkshire Council [2006] EWHC 1604 (Admin); [2007] J.P.L. 396, QBD (Admin) .................. *Digested,* 07/**3273**:
*Applied* 11/2564, 12/2601: *Considered* 07/3284, 14/2397

R. (on the application of Litvinenko) v Secretary of State for the Home Department [2013] EWHC 3135 (Admin); [2014] A.C.D. 25, DC

R. (on the application of Litvinenko) v Secretary of State for the Home Department [2014] EWHC 194 (Admin); [2014] H.R.L.R. 6; [2014] A.C.D. 67, DC .................. *Digested,* 14/**35**

R. (on the application of Liverpool City Council) v Hillingdon LBC [2009] EWCA Civ 43; [2009] P.T.S.R. 1067; [2009] 1 F.L.R. 1536; [2009] 3 F.C.R. 46; [2009] B.L.G.R. 289; (2009) 12 C.C.L. Rep. 286; [2009] Fam. Law 394; Times, February 13, 2009, CA (Civ Div); reversing [2008] EWHC 1702 (Admin); [2009] 1 F.C.R. 252; (2008) 11 C.C.L. Rep. 693; [2009] A.C.D. 11; Times, October 3, 2008, QBD (Admin) .................. *Digested,* 09/**2653**:
*Applied* 14/2148

R. (on the application of Lloyds Pharmacy Ltd) v Leeds City Council [2013] EWHC 4031 (Admin); [2014] J.P.L. 758, QBD (Admin) .................. *Digested,* 14/**2417**

R. (on the application of Loader) v Secretary of State for Communities and Local Government [2012] EWCA Civ 869; [2013] P.T.S.R. 406; [2012] 3 C.M.L.R. 29; [2013] Env. L.R. 7; [2012] B.L.G.R. 862; [2012] J.P.L. 1509, CA (Civ Div); affirming [2011] EWHC 2010 (Admin); [2012] Env. L.R. 8; [2012] J.P.L. 154; [2011] A.C.D. 123, QBD (Admin) ........ *Digested,* 12/**2548**: *Considered* 13/2344, 13/2365: *Followed* 14/2431, 14/2434

R. (on the application of London Capital Group) v Financial Ombudsman Service Ltd [2013] EWHC 2425 (Admin); [2014] A.C.D. 3, QBD (Admin)

R. (on the application of London Christian Radio Ltd) v Radio Advertising Clearance Centre; *sub nom* London Christian Radio Ltd v Radio Advertising Clearance Centre [2013] EWCA Civ 1495; [2014] 1 W.L.R. 307; (2013) 157(45) S.J.L.B. 37, CA (Civ Div); affirming [2012] EWHC 1043 (Admin); [2012] H.R.L.R. 19; [2013] C.T.L.C. 41; [2012] A.C.D. 82, QBD (Admin) ........ *Digested,* 14/**2152**

R. (on the application of Long) v Secretary of State for Defence [2014] EWHC 2391 (Admin); [2014] H.R.L.R. 20, QBD (Admin) ........ *Digested,* 14/**63**

R. (on the application of Lord Carlile of Berriew QC) v Secretary of State for the Home Department; *sub nom* Lord Carlile of Berriew v Secretary of State for the Home Department [2014] UKSC 60; [2014] 3 W.L.R. 1404, SC; affirming [2013] EWCA Civ 199, CA (Civ Div); affirming [2012] EWHC 617 (Admin); [2012] A.C.D. 80, DC

R. (on the application of Lord) v Secretary of State for the Home Department [2003] EWHC 2073 (Admin); [2004] Prison L.R. 65, QBD (Admin) *Considered* 14/2162

R. (on the application of Lumba) v Secretary of State for the Home Department; *sub nom* R. (on the application of KM (Jamaica)) v Secretary of State for the Home Department; R. (on the application of WL (Congo)) v Secretary of State for the Home Department; Lumba v Secretary of State for the Home Department; Mighty v Secretary of State for the Home Department; Madami v Secretary of State for the Home Department; Ashori v Secretary of State for the Home Department; Abdi v Secretary of State for the Home Department; *joined case* R. (on the application of Mighty) v Secretary of State for the Home Department [2011] UKSC 12; [2012] 1 A.C. 245; [2011] 2 W.L.R. 671; [2011] 4 All E.R. 1; [2011] U.K.H.R.R. 437; (2011) 108(14) L.S.G. 20; (2011) 155(12) S.J.L.B. 30; Times, March 24, 2011, SC; reversing in part [2010] EWCA Civ 111; [2010] 1 W.L.R. 2168; [2010] 4 All E.R. 489; [2010] U.K.H.R.R. 366; (2010) 107(9) L.S.G. 18, CA (Civ Div); reversing in part [2008] EWHC 3166 (Admin); [2009] A.C.D. 22, QBD (Admin) ........ *Digested,* 11/**1727**: *Applied* 11/1733, 14/1680, 14/2766: *Considered* 14/1682: *Followed* 12/1712, 13/1601, 13/1602, 14/2234, 14/842

R. (on the application of Lumsdon) v Legal Services Board; *joined case* Lumsdon v Legal Services Board [2014] EWCA Civ 1276; [2014] H.R.L.R. 29; Times, November 27, 2014, CA (Civ Div); affirming [2014] EWHC 28 (Admin), DC

R. (on the application of Lunn) v Governor of Moorland Prison [2006] EWCA Civ 700; [2006] 1 W.L.R. 2870; [2006] 1 Prison L.R. 251; Times, June 27, 2006; Independent, June 7, 2006, CA (Civ Div); reversing [2005] EWHC 2558 (QB); Times, November 2, 2005, QBD ........ *Digested,* 06/**2936**: *Applied* 14/386

R. (on the application of Lunt) v Liverpool City Council [2009] EWHC 2356 (Admin); [2010] R.T.R. 5; [2010] 1 C.M.L.R. 14; [2010] Eu. L.R. 203; [2010] L.L.R. 165; [2010] A.C.D. 17, QBD (Admin) ........ *Digested,* 10/**73**: *Applied* 10/2318: *Considered* 14/2580

R. (on the application of M (A Child)) v Manchester Crown Court see R. (on the application of McCann) v Manchester Crown Court

R. (on the application of M) v Commissioner of Police of the Metropolis see R. (on the application of Hicks) v Commissioner of Police of the Metropolis

R. (on the application of M) v Croydon LBC see M v Croydon LBC

R. (on the application of M) v Hammersmith and Fulham LBC; *joined case* R. (on the application of Hertfordshire CC) v Hammersmith and Fulham LBC [2011] EWCA Civ 77; [2011] P.T.S.R. 1623; [2011] B.L.G.R. 536; (2011) 14 C.C.L. Rep. 224; [2011] Med. L.R. 181; (2011) 119 B.M.L.R. 27; [2011] M.H.L.R. 76; [2011] A.C.D. 60, CA (Civ Div); affirming [2010] EWHC 562 (Admin); [2010] B.L.G.R. 678; (2010) 13 C.C.L. Rep. 217; (2010) 116 B.M.L.R. 46; [2010] M.H.L.R. 110, QBD (Admin) ........ *Digested,* 11/**3205**: *Applied* 12/2278: *Followed* 14/2179

R. (on the application of M) v Hammersmith and Fulham LBC [2008] UKHL 14; [2008] 1 W.L.R. 535; [2008] 4 All E.R. 271; [2008] 1 F.L.R. 1384; [2008] 3 F.C.R. 688; [2008] B.L.G.R. 159; (2008) 11 C.C.L. Rep. 302; [2008] Fam. Law 515; (2008) 158 N.L.J. 370; (2008) 152(9) S.J.L.B. 28; Times, March 3, 2008, HL; affirming [2006] EWCA Civ 917; [2007] 1 F.L.R. 256; [2006] 2 F.C.R. 647; [2007] H.L.R. 6; [2007] B.L.G.R. 127; (2006) 9 C.C.L. Rep. 418; [2006] Fam. Law 1028; Independent, July 7, 2006, CA (Civ Div) ............ *Digested,* 08/**1852**: *Applied* 10/3148, 11/3215, 14/1691: *Considered* 07/3940, 09/3695, 10/3187: *Distinguished* 10/2196: *Followed* 10/1302, 14/2806

R. (on the application of M) v Haringey LBC; *sub nom* R. (on the application of Stirling) v Haringey LBC [2013] EWCA Civ 116; [2013] P.T.S.R. 1285; [2013] B.L.G.R. 251; (2013) 157(9) S.J.L.B. 31, CA (Civ Div); affirming [2013] EWHC 252 (Admin); [2013] A.C.D. 62, QBD (Admin) ............ *Digested,* 13/**2862**: *Reversed* 14/2087

R. (on the application of M) v Hounslow LBC [2013] EWHC 579 (Admin); [2013] P.T.S.R. 942; [2014] E.L.R. 338, QBD (Admin) ............ *Digested,* 13/**897**

R. (on the application of M) v Isleworth Crown Court [2005] EWHC 363 (Admin), DC *Considered* 14/719

R. (on the application of M) v Kingston Crown Court; *joined case* M v Wells Unit West London Mental Health Trust [2014] EWHC 2702 (Admin); (2014) 178 J.P. 438; (2014) 158(31) S.J.L.B. 37, DC ............ *Digested,* 14/**800**

R. (on the application of M) v Waltham Forest Youth Court see R. (on the application of W) v Thetford Youth Court

R. (on the application of M) v West London Youth Court; *joined case* R. (on the application of W) v West London Youth Court [2004] EWHC 1144 (Admin); [2005] A.C.D. 4, QBD (Admin) *Applied* 04/895, 14/722

R. (on the application of M) v Westminster Magistrates' Court see R. (on the application of B) v Westminster Magistrates' Court

R. (on the application of MA (Eritrea)) v Secretary of State for the Home Department (C-648/11) see MA v Secretary of State for the Home Department (C-648/11)

R. (on the application of MA (Eritrea)) v Secretary of State for the Home Department see R. (on the application of EM (Eritrea)) v Secretary of State for the Home Department

R. (on the application of MA) v Secretary of State for the Home Department see R. (on the application of BT) v Secretary of State for the Home Department

R. (on the application of MA) v Secretary of State for Work and Pensions [2014] EWCA Civ 13; [2014] P.T.S.R. 584; [2014] Eq. L.R. 426; [2014] H.L.R. 19, CA (Civ Div); affirming [2013] EWHC 2213 (QB); [2013] P.T.S.R. 1521; [2013] Eq. L.R. 972, DC ............ *Digested,* 14/**2757**

R. (on the application of Maftah) v Secretary of State for Foreign and Commonwealth Affairs see R. (on the application of Khaled) v Secretary of State for Foreign and Commonwealth Affairs

R. (on the application of Majid) v Secretary of State for the Home Department see R. (on the application of MM (Lebanon)) v Secretary of State for the Home Department

R. (on the application of Malik) v Manchester Crown Court; *sub nom* Malik v Manchester Crown Court [2008] EWHC 1362 (Admin); [2008] 4 All E.R. 403; [2008] E.M.L.R. 19; [2008] U.K.H.R.R. 1151, DC ............ *Digested,* 08/**408**: *Applied* 10/418, 10/763, 14/799: *Considered* 09/2489

R. (on the application of Maries) v Merton LBC [2014] EWHC 2689 (Admin); [2014] B.L.G.R. 756, QBD (Admin)

R. (on the application of Marton-cum-Grafton Parish Council) v North Yorkshire CC [2013] EWHC 2406 (Admin); [2014] Env. L.R. 10, QBD (Admin) ............ *Digested,* 14/**2428**

R. (on the application of Masih) v Yousaf see Masih v Yousaf

R. (on the application of Massey) v Secretary of State for Justice see R. (on the application of Kaiyam) v Secretary of State for Justice

R. (on the application of McCann) v Manchester Crown Court; *sub nom* R. v Manchester Crown Court Ex p. M (A Child); R. (on the application of M (A Child)) v Manchester Crown Court; *joined case* Clingham v Kensington and Chelsea RLBC [2002] UKHL 39; [2003] 1 A.C. 787; [2002] 3 W.L.R. 1313; [2002] 4 All E.R. 593; [2003] 1 Cr. App. R. 27; (2002) 166 J.P. 657; [2002] U.K.H.R.R. 1286; 13 B.H.R.C. 482; [2003] H.L.R. 17; [2003] B.L.G.R. 57; [2003] Crim. L.R. 269; (2002) 166 J.P.N. 850; (2002) 146 S.J.L.B. 239; Times, October 21, 2002; Independent, October 23, 2002, HL; affirming [2001] EWCA Civ 281; [2001] 1 W.L.R. 1084; [2001] 4 All E.R. 264; (2001) 165 J.P. 545; [2001] H.R.L.R. 37; (2002) 166 J.P.N. 150; Times, March 9, 2001; Independent, March 20, 2001, CA (Civ Div); affirming [2001] 1 W.L.R. 358; (2001) 165 J.P. 225; (2001) 165 J.P.N. 204; (2001) 98(2) L.S.G. 40; (2000) 144 S.J.L.B. 287; Times, December 22, 2000; Daily Telegraph, December 12, 2000, DC ............ *Digested,* 02/**3**:
*Applied* 01/41, 02/1579, 04/1020, 04/366, 06/902, 07/1949, 07/2171, 09/2008, 09/2649, 10/2324, 10/261, 10/723: *Considered* 03/831, 04/790, 05/1073, 06/304, 06/327, 07/4974, 08/3774, 09/4672, 10/1728, 13/420, 14/2954: *Distinguished* 04/1458, 06/316: *Followed* 05/342

R. (on the application of McDonald) v Kensington and Chelsea RLBC; *sub nom* McDonald v Kensington and Chelsea RLBC [2011] UKSC 33; [2011] 4 All E.R. 881; [2011] P.T.S.R. 1266; [2011] H.R.L.R. 36; [2011] Eq. L.R. 974; [2012] B.L.G.R. 107; (2011) 14 C.C.L. Rep. 341; (2011) 121 B.M.L.R. 164; (2011) 108(29) L.S.G. 17; (2011) 161 N.L.J. 1026; (2011) 155(27) S.J.L.B. 39; Times, July 7, 2011, SC; affirming [2010] EWCA Civ 1109; [2011] B.L.G.R. 246; (2010) 13 C.C.L. Rep. 664; (2011) 118 B.M.L.R. 42; [2011] A.C.D. 40, CA (Civ Div); reversing in part [2009] EWHC 1582 (Admin); (2009) 12 C.C.L. Rep. 421, QBD (Admin) ............ *Digested,* 11/**3207**:
*Applied* 11/2168, 12/1675, 12/3156: *Complaint upheld* 14/1635: *Considered* 11/1562: *Followed* 12/3162, 13/2952

R. (on the application of McIntyre) v Parole Board for England and Wales [2013] EWHC 1969 (Admin); [2014] A.C.D. 17, QBD (Admin)

R. (on the application of MD (Gambia)) v Secretary of State for the Home Department [2011] EWCA Civ 121, CA (Civ Div); reversing in part [2010] EWHC 880 (Admin), QBD (Admin)
*Considered* 14/1649: *Followed* 14/1643

R. (on the application of Mehey) v Visitors to the Inns of Court see R. (on the application of Leathley) v Visitors to the Inns of Court

R. (on the application of Mellor) v Secretary of State for Communities and Local Government (C-75/08); *sub nom* Mellor v Secretary of State for Communities and Local Government (C-75/08) [2010] P.T.S.R. 880; [2009] E.C.R. I-3799; [2010] Env. L.R. 2; [2009] 18 E.G. 84 (C.S.), ECJ (2nd Chamber) ............ *Digested,* 10/**1246**:
*Considered* 12/2570, 14/2425: *Followed* 14/2420

R. (on the application of Members of the Committee of Care North East Northumberland) v Northumberland CC [2013] EWCA Civ 1740; [2014] P.T.S.R. 758; (2014) 17 C.C.L. Rep. 117; (2013) 157(46) S.J.L.B. 37, CA (Civ Div); affirming [2013] EWHC 234 (Admin); [2013] P.T.S.R. 1130; [2013] B.L.G.R. 265; (2013) 16 C.C.L. Rep. 276, QBD (Admin) ............ *Digested,* 14/**2797**

R. (on the application of Mensah) v Salford City Council; *sub nom* Bello v Salford City Council; Mensah v Salford City Council; *joined case* R. (on the application of Bello) v Salford City Council [2014] EWHC 3537 (Admin); (2014) 17 C.C.L. Rep. 492, QBD (Admin)

R. (on the application of Merlot 73 Ltd) v City of Westminster Magistrates' Court [2013] EWHC 3416 (Admin); [2014] L.L.R. 377, QBD (Admin)

R. (on the application of Midcounties Co-operative Ltd) v Forest of Dean DC [2013] EWHC 1908 (Admin); [2013] J.P.L. 1551, QBD (Admin) ............ *Digested,* 14/**2397**

R. (on the application of Midcounties Co-operative Ltd) v Swindon BC [2013] EWHC 3775 (Admin), QBD (Admin)
*Considered* 14/2407

R. (on the application of Middleton) v Bromley Magistrates Court see R. (on the application of Hicks) v Commissioner of Police of the Metropolis

R. (on the application of Middleton) v HM Coroner for Western Somerset; *sub nom* R. (on the application of Middleton) v West Somerset Coroner; R. v HM Coroner for Western Somerset Ex p. Middleton [2004] UKHL 10; [2004] 2 A.C. 182; [2004] 2 W.L.R. 800; [2004] 2 All E.R. 465; (2004) 168 J.P. 329; [2004] H.R.L.R. 29; [2004] U.K.H.R.R. 501; 17 B.H.R.C. 49; [2004] Lloyd's Rep. Med. 288; (2004) 79 B.M.L.R. 51; [2004] Inquest L.R. 17; (2004) 168 J.P.N. 479; (2004) 101(15) L.S.G. 27; (2004) 154 N.L.J. 417; (2004) 148 S.J.L.B. 354; Times, March 12, 2004; Independent, March 16, 2004, HL ................................ *Digested,* 04/**37**: *Applied* 05/34, 06/18, 06/2108, 07/27, 08/17, 08/1975, 09/2041, 09/2754, 09/41, 10/1737, 10/19, 10/20, 10/23, 13/37, 14/47: *Considered* 05/17, 06/17, 07/13, 07/28, 07/2980, 09/21, 10/15, 11/2094, 11/29: *Followed* 04/38, 10/17: *Referred to* 13/36

R. (on the application of Middleton) v HM Coroner for Western Somerset see R. (on the application of Amin (Imtiaz)) v Secretary of State for the Home Department

R. (on the application of Middleton) v West Somerset Coroner see R. (on the application of Amin (Imtiaz)) v Secretary of State for the Home Department

R. (on the application of Middleton) v West Somerset Coroner see R. (on the application of Middleton) v HM Coroner for Western Somerset

R. (on the application of Mighty) v Secretary of State for the Home Department see R. (on the application of Lumba) v Secretary of State for the Home Department

R. (on the application of Mills) v Sussex Police [2014] EWHC 2523 (Admin); [2014] 2 Cr. App. R. 34; [2014] Lloyd's Rep. F.C. 604, QBD (Admin) ................ *Digested,* 14/**804**

R. (on the application of Minter) v Chief Constable of Hampshire [2013] EWCA Civ 697; [2014] 1 W.L.R. 179, CA (Civ Div) ................................ *Digested,* 14/**2682**

R. (on the application of Minter) v Chief Constable of Hampshire [2011] EWHC 1610 (Admin); [2012] 1 W.L.R. 1157; [2012] A.C.D. 19, DC ................ *Digested,* 12/**2970**: *Affirmed* 14/2682

R. (on the application of Miranda) v Secretary of State for the Home Department [2013] EWHC 2609 (Admin); [2014] A.C.D. 27; [2014] A.C.D. 26, DC

R. (on the application of Miranda) v Secretary of State for the Home Department; *sub nom* Miranda v Secretary of State for the Home Department [2014] EWHC 255 (Admin); [2014] 1 W.L.R. 3140; [2014] 3 All E.R. 447; [2014] H.R.L.R. 9; [2014] A.C.D. 88, DC ................................ *Digested,* 14/**703**

R. (on the application of Mirza) v Secretary of State for the Home Department; *sub nom* Mirza v Secretary of State for the Home Department; *joined cases* R. (on the application of Barot) v Secretary of State for the Home Department; R. (on the application of Abbasi) v Secretary of State for the Home Department; R. (on the application of Patel) v Secretary of State for the Home Department [2011] EWCA Civ 159; [2011] Imm. A.R. 484; [2011] I.N.L.R. 464; Times, March 2, 2011, CA (Civ Div); reversing [2010] EWHC 2002 (Admin), QBD (Admin) ......... *Digested,* 11/**1776**: *Applied* 12/1730, 12/1758: *Disapproved* 14/1718: *Followed* 12/1759: *Not followed* 12/1760

R. (on the application of MM (Lebanon)) v Secretary of State for the Home Department; *sub nom* R. (on the application of AM (Pakistan)) v Secretary of State for the Home Department; R. (on the application of SJ (Pakistan)) v Secretary of State for the Home Department; *joined cases* R. (on the application of Majid) v Secretary of State for the Home Department; R. (on the application of Javed) v Secretary of State for the Home Department [2014] EWCA Civ 985; [2014] Imm. A.R. 1207; (2014) 158(29) S.J.L.B. 37; Times, July 18, 2014, CA (Civ Div); reversing [2013] EWHC 1900 (Admin); [2014] 1 W.L.R. 2306; [2014] Imm. A.R. 245, QBD (Admin) ................................ *Digested,* 14/**1703**: *Applied* 14/1710

R. (on the application of MN) v Hackney LBC; *sub nom* MN v Hackney LBC [2013] EWHC 1205 (Admin), QBD (Admin)
*Considered* 14/2805

R. (on the application of Mohamed) v Secretary of State for Foreign and Commonwealth Affairs [2008] EWHC 2048 (Admin); [2009] 1 W.L.R. 2579; (2008) 105(34) L.S.G. 22, DC
*Considered* 14/383

R. (on the application of Mohammed) v Birmingham City Council see R. (on the application of Aweys) v Birmingham City Council

R. (on the application of Mohammed) v Secretary of State for Defence [2012] EWHC 3454 (Admin); [2014] 1 W.L.R. 1071; [2013] 2 All E.R. 897; [2013] A.C.D. 24, QBD (Admin) ................................ *Digested,* 13/**247**: *Doubted* 14/1724

R. (on the application of Mohammed) v Southwark LBC [2009] EWHC 311 (Admin); [2009] B.P.I.R. 882; [2010] R.A. 112, QBD (Admin) ............ *Digested,* 09/**2614**: *Considered* 14/1794

R. (on the application of Morales) v Kettering Magistrates' Court [2013] EWHC 1922 (Admin); (2014) 178 J.P. 22, DC ............ *Digested,* 14/**786**

R. (on the application of Morgan Grenfell & Co Ltd) v Special Commissioners of Income Tax; *sub nom* R. v Special Commissioners of Income Tax Ex p. Morgan Grenfell & Co Ltd; R. v Inland Revenue Commissioners Ex p. Morgan Grenfell & Co Ltd [2002] UKHL 21; [2003] 1 A.C. 563; [2002] 2 W.L.R. 1299; [2002] 3 All E.R. 1; [2002] S.T.C. 786; [2002] H.R.L.R. 42; 74 T.C. 511; [2002] B.T.C. 223; 4 I.T.L. Rep. 809; [2002] S.T.I. 806; (2002) 99(25) L.S.G. 35; (2002) 146 S.J.L.B. 126; [2002] N.P.C. 70; Times, May 20, 2002; Independent, May 21, 2002, HL; reversing [2001] EWCA Civ 329; [2002] 2 W.L.R. 255; [2002] 1 All E.R. 776; [2001] S.T.C. 497; [2001] S.T.I. 281; (2001) 98(18) L.S.G. 45; [2000] N.P.C. 54; Times, April 17, 2001; Independent, March 15, 2001, CA (Civ Div); affirming [2001] 1 All E.R. 535; [2000] S.T.C. 965; [2000] S.T.I. 1609; (2000) 97(48) L.S.G. 37; (2000) 150 N.L.J. 1717; Times, November 22, 2000, QBD (Admin) ............ *Digested,* 02/**4505**: *Applied* 06/4304, 06/839, 08/3863, 11/2172: *Considered* 01/5320, 07/999, 09/4216, 11/2123: *Followed* 14/2973

R. (on the application of Morge) v Hampshire CC; *sub nom* Morge v Hampshire CC [2011] UKSC 2; [2011] 1 W.L.R. 268; [2011] 1 All E.R. 744; [2011] P.T.S.R. 337; [2011] Env. L.R. 19; [2011] B.L.G.R. 271; [2011] J.P.L. 865; [2011] 4 E.G. 101 (C.S.); (2011) 108(5) L.S.G. 20; Times, January 26, 2011, SC; affirming [2010] EWCA Civ 608; [2010] P.T.S.R. 1882; [2011] Env. L.R. 8; [2010] B.L.G.R. 961; [2011] 1 P. & C.R. 13; [2010] J.P.L. 1600; [2010] N.P.C. 67; Times, June 22, 2010, CA (Civ Div); affirming [2009] EWHC 2940 (Admin); [2010] Env. L.R. 26, QBD (Admin) ............ *Digested,* 11/**1233**: *Applied* 13/1158: *Considered* 13/2351, 14/1188, 14/2398, 14/339: *Not applied* 13/1158

R. (on the application of Moseley) v Haringey LBC; *sub nom* R. (on the application of Stirling) v Haringey LBC [2014] UKSC 56; [2014] 1 W.L.R. 3947; [2014] P.T.S.R. 1317; [2014] B.L.G.R. 823; Times, November 5, 2014, SC ............ *Digested,* 14/**2087**

R. (on the application of Mount Cook Land Ltd) v Westminster City Council; *sub nom* Mount Cook Land Ltd v Westminster City Council [2003] EWCA Civ 1346; [2004] C.P. Rep. 12; [2004] 2 Costs L.R. 211; [2004] 2 P. & C.R. 22; [2004] 1 P.L.R. 29; [2004] J.P.L. 470; [2003] 43 E.G. 137 (C.S.); (2003) 147 S.J.L.B. 1272; [2003] N.P.C. 117; Times, October 16, 2003, CA (Civ Div); affirming [2002] EWHC 2125 (Admin), QBD (Admin) ............ *Digested,* 04/**367**: *Applied* 04/1387, 09/3039, 14/366: *Considered* 05/3307, 06/417, 07/402, 07/489, 10/2611: *Distinguished* 08/321

R. (on the application of Mousa) v Secretary of State for Defence [2013] EWHC 1412 (Admin); [2013] H.R.L.R. 32; [2013] A.C.D. 84, DC ............ *Digested,* 14/**147**

R. (on the application of Mousa) v Secretary of State for Defence [2013] EWHC 2941 (Admin); [2014] A.C.D. 35, DC

R. (on the application of MR (Pakistan)) v Upper Tribunal see R. (on the application of Cart) v Upper Tribunal

R. (on the application of Muaza) v Secretary of State for the Home Department; *joined cases* R. (on the application of IM (Nigeria)) v Secretary of State for the Home Department; IM (Nigeria) v Secretary of State for the Home Department [2013] EWCA Civ 1561; [2014] 1 W.L.R. 1870, CA (Civ Div); affirming [2013] EWHC 3764 (Admin), QBD (Admin) ............ *Digested,* 14/**1680**

R. (on the application of Mullen) v Secretary of State for the Home Department [2004] UKHL 18; [2005] 1 A.C. 1; [2004] 2 W.L.R. 1140; [2004] 3 All E.R. 65; [2004] U.K.H.R.R. 745; 16 B.H.R.C. 469; [2004] Po. L.R. 234; (2004) 154 N.L.J. 706; (2004) 148 S.J.L.B. 542; Times, May 3, 2004, HL; reversing [2002] EWCA Civ 1882; [2003] Q.B. 993; [2003] 2 W.L.R. 835; [2003] 1 All E.R. 613; [2002] Po. L.R. 429; (2003) 100(10) L.S.G. 27; Times, December 31, 2002; Independent, January 21, 2003, CA (Civ Div); reversing [2002] EWHC 230 (Admin); [2002] 1 W.L.R. 1857; [2002] 3 All E.R. 293; [2002] Po. L.R. 423; (2002) 99(13) L.S.G. 26; (2002) 146 S.J.L.B. 62; Times, February 27, 2002, DC ............ *Digested,* 04/**869**: *Applied* 05/908, 09/914: *Considered* 02/893, 10/3488, 10/770, 11/794, 14/1630

R. (on the application of Muqtaar) v Secretary of State for the Home Department; *sub nom* Muqtaar v Secretary of State for the Home Department [2012] EWCA Civ 1270; [2013] 1 W.L.R. 649; [2013] A.C.D. 14, CA (Civ Div); affirming [2011] EWHC 2707 (Admin), QBD (Admin) ............ *Digested,* 13/**1602**: *Considered* 14/1682

R. (on the application of Mustafa) v Office for the Independent Adjudicator for Higher Education [2013] EWHC 1379 (Admin); [2013] E.L.R. 446; [2013] A.C.D. 112; (2013) 163(7563) N.L.J. 18, QBD (Admin) ........ *Digested,* 14/**916**

R. (on the application of MV) v Secretary of State for the Home Department [2013] EWHC 1017 (Admin); [2013] Imm. A.R. 1029, QBD (Admin) ........ *Digested,* 14/**1643**

R. (on the application of N) v Lewisham LBC; *sub nom* R. (on the application of ZH) v Newham LBC; R. (on the application of CN) v Lewisham LBC; *joined case* R. (on the application of H (A Child)) v Newham LBC [2014] UKSC 62; [2014] 3 W.L.R. 1548; [2014] B.L.G.R. 842; (2014) 158(45) S.J.L.B. 37; Times, December 1, 2014, SC; affirming [2013] EWCA Civ 804; [2014] 2 W.L.R. 719; [2013] H.L.R. 46; [2013] 30 E.G. 79 (C.S.), CA (Civ Div) ........ *Digested,* 14/**1625**

R. (on the application of N) v Newham LBC; *sub nom* N v Newham LBC [2013] EWHC 2475 (Admin); [2014] 1 F.C.R. 1; [2013] B.L.G.R. 898, QBD (Admin) ........ *Digested,* 14/**2805**

R. (on the application of N) v Secretary of State for the Home Department see N (Kenya) v Secretary of State for the Home Department

R. (on the application of N) v Walsall MBC; *sub nom* R. (on the application of ZYN) v Walsall MBC [2014] EWHC 1918 (Admin); [2014] P.T.S.R. 1356; [2014] C.O.P.L.R. 514; [2014] W.T.L.R. 1649; [2014] A.C.D. 129, QBD (Admin) ........ *Digested,* 14/**2800**

R. (on the application of N) v Westminster Magistrates' Court see R. (on the application of B) v Westminster Magistrates' Court

R. (on the application of Nadarajah) v Secretary of State for the Home Department see R. (on the application of Razgar) v Secretary of State for the Home Department (No.2)

R. (on the application of Nagre) v Secretary of State for the Home Department [2013] EWHC 720 (Admin), QBD (Admin)
*Applied* 14/1710: *Considered* 14/1703

R. (on the application of Naik) v Secretary of State for the Home Department; *sub nom* Naik v Secretary of State for the Home Department [2011] EWCA Civ 1546; [2012] Imm. A.R. 381, CA (Civ Div); affirming [2010] EWHC 2825 (Admin); [2011] H.R.L.R. 5, QBD (Admin) ........ *Digested,* 12/**1720**: *Considered* 14/1724

R. (on the application of Nash) v Barnet LBC [2013] EWCA Civ 1004; [2013] P.T.S.R. 1457, CA (Civ Div) ........ *Digested,* 14/**69**

R. (on the application of Nash) v Chelsea College of Art and Design [2001] EWHC Admin 538; Times, July 25, 2001, QBD (Admin) ........ *Digested,* 01/**95**: *Applied* 05/3281, 09/3038: *Considered* 05/2910, 10/3180, 14/56

R. (on the application of Negassi) v Secretary of State for the Home Department [2013] EWCA Civ 151; [2013] 2 C.M.L.R. 45, CA (Civ Div) ........ *Digested,* 13/**1581**: *Applied* 14/1653

R. (on the application of Nestwood Homes Developments Ltd) v South Holland DC [2014] EWHC 863 (Admin); [2014] B.L.G.R. 354, QBD (Admin) ........ *Digested,* 14/**70**

R. (on the application of New London College Ltd) v Secretary of State for the Home Department; *sub nom* R. (on the application of West London Vocational Training College) v Secretary of State for the Home Department [2013] UKSC 51; [2013] 1 W.L.R. 2358; [2013] 4 All E.R. 195; [2013] P.T.S.R. 995; [2014] Imm. A.R. 151; [2014] I.N.L.R. 66, SC; affirming [2012] EWCA Civ 51; [2012] Imm. A.R. 563; [2012] P.T.S.R. D21, CA (Civ Div); reversing in part [2011] EWHC 856 (Admin), QBD (Admin) ........ *Digested,* 13/**1648**: *Applied* 14/75: *Considered* 12/1755

R. (on the application of Newby Foods Ltd) v Food Standards Agency [2014] EWHC 1340 (Admin); [2014] 1 W.L.R. 4589; [2014] 4 All E.R. 222; [2014] 3 C.M.L.R. 21, QBD (Admin) ........ *Digested,* 14/**323**

R. (on the application of Newhaven Port and Properties Ltd) v East Sussex CC; *sub nom* R. (on the application of Newhaven Port and Properties Ltd) v Secretary of State for the Environment, Food and Rural Affairs [2013] EWCA Civ 276; [2014] Q.B. 186; [2013] 3 W.L.R. 1389; [2013] 3 All E.R. 677; [2013] 2 P. & C.R. 8; [2013] 2 E.G.L.R. 1; [2013] A.C.D. 81; [2013] 15 E.G. 105 (C.S.), CA (Civ Div); reversing [2012] EWHC 647 (Admin); [2012] 3 W.L.R. 709; [2012] 3 All E.R. 1361; [2012] A.C.D. 85; [2012] 14 E.G. 63 (C.S.); (2012) 109(15) L.S.G. 14, QBD (Admin) ........ *Digested,* 13/**2468**: *Affirmed* 13/2469

R. (on the application of Newhaven Port and Properties Ltd) v East Sussex CC see R. (on the application of Newhaven Port and Properties Ltd) v Secretary of State for the Environment, Food and Rural Affairs

R. (on the application of Newhaven Port and Properties Ltd) v Secretary of State for the Environment, Food and Rural Affairs; *sub nom* R. (on the application of Newhaven Port and Properties Ltd) v East Sussex CC [2013] EWCA Civ 673; [2014] Q.B. 282; [2013] 3 W.L.R. 1433; [2013] 3 All E.R. 719; [2013] B.L.G.R. 570; [2013] 2 P. & C.R. 14; [2013] 3 E.G.L.R. 173, CA (Civ Div) ........................ *Digested,* 13/**2469**

R. (on the application of Newhaven Port and Properties Ltd) v Secretary of State for the Environment, Food and Rural Affairs see R. (on the application of Newhaven Port and Properties Ltd) v East Sussex CC

R. (on the application of Nicklinson) v Ministry of Justice; *sub nom* Nicklinson v Ministry of Justice; *joined cases* R. (on the application of AM) v DPP; R. (on the application of Lamb) v Ministry of Justice [2014] UKSC 38; [2014] 3 W.L.R. 200; [2014] 3 All E.R. 843; [2014] 3 F.C.R. 1; [2014] H.R.L.R. 17; 36 B.H.R.C. 465; (2014) 139 B.M.L.R. 1; Times, June 26, 2014, SC; reversing in part [2013] EWCA Civ 961; [2014] 2 All E.R. 32; [2014] 1 F.C.R. 316; [2013] H.R.L.R. 36; (2013) 16 C.C.L. Rep. 413; (2013) 133 B.M.L.R. 46, CA (Civ Div); reversing in part [2012] EWHC 2381 (Admin); [2012] 3 F.C.R. 233; [2012] H.R.L.R. 32; [2012] Med. L.R. 544; (2012) 127 B.M.L.R. 197; [2012] A.C.D. 118; (2012) 109(32) L.S.G. 18; Times, November 13, 2012, DC .......................................... *Digested,* 14/**672**

R. (on the application of Njoroge) v Secretary of State for Foreign and Commonwealth Affairs see R. (on the application of Omar) v Secretary of State for Foreign and Commonwealth Affairs

R. (on the application of Nkromah) v Willesden Magistrates' Court [2014] A.C.D. 72, DC

R. (on the application of North East Lincolnshire DC) v Grimsby and Cleethorpes Magistrates' Court [2013] EWHC 2368 (Admin); [2013] R.V.R. 300, QBD (Admin) ........................................................................................................ *Digested,* 14/**367**

R. (on the application of Nouazli) v Secretary of State for the Home Department [2013] EWCA Civ 1608; [2014] 1 W.L.R. 3313; [2014] 1 All E.R. 1144, CA (Civ Div); affirming [2013] EWHC 567 (Admin); [2013] 2 C.M.L.R. 54, QBD (Admin) *Digested,* 14/**1683**

R. (on the application of NS) v Secretary of State for the Home Department [2014] EWHC 1971 (Admin); [2014] Imm. A.R. 1153, QBD (Admin)

R. (on the application of NS) v Secretary of State for the Home Department (C-411/10); *sub nom* NS v Secretary of State for the Home Department (C-411/10); ME v Refugee Applications Commissioner (C-493/10); *joined case* E v Refugee Applications Commissioner (C-493/10) [2013] Q.B. 102; [2012] 3 W.L.R. 1374; [2012] 2 C.M.L.R. 9; [2012] All E.R. (EC) 1011; (2012) 109(29) L.S.G. 26, ECJ (Grand Chamber) ....................................................................... *Digested,* 12/**1698**:
*Applied* 14/1672: *Considered* 13/1577: *Explained* 14/1652: *Followed* 13/1578

R. (on the application of Nunn) v Chief Constable of Suffolk; *sub nom* Nunn v Chief Constable of Suffolk [2014] UKSC 37; [2014] 3 W.L.R. 77; [2014] 4 All E.R. 21; [2014] 2 Cr. App. R. 22; Times, June 24, 2014, SC; affirming [2012] EWHC 1186 (Admin); [2012] Crim. L.R. 968; [2012] A.C.D. 75, DC .............................. *Digested,* 14/**761**

R. (on the application of O (Kenya)) v Secretary of State for the Home Department [2009] EWHC 827 (Admin); (2009) 159 N.L.J. 631, QBD (Admin)
*Applied* 14/1642: *Followed* 13/1610

R. (on the application of O Twelve Baytree Ltd) v Leasehold Valuation Tribunal; *sub nom* R. (on the application of O Twelve Baytree Ltd) v Rent Assessment Panel [2014] EWHC 1229 (Admin); [2014] 3 All E.R. 732; [2014] 2 E.G.L.R. 185, QBD (Admin) ......................................................................................................... *Digested,* 14/**2010**

R. (on the application of O Twelve Baytree Ltd) v Rent Assessment Panel see R. (on the application of O Twelve Baytree Ltd) v Leasehold Valuation Tribunal

R. (on the application of O) v Secretary of State for Education see O v Secretary of State for Education

R. (on the application of O) v Stratford Youth Court [2004] EWHC 1553 (Admin); (2004) 168 J.P. 469; (2004) 168 J.P.N. 717, DC
*Considered* 14/764

R. (on the application of Oboh) v Secretary of State for the Home Department [2014] EWHC 967 (Admin); [2014] Imm. A.R. 937, QBD (Admin)

R. (on the application of Omar) v Birmingham City Council see R. (on the application of Aweys) v Birmingham City Council

R. (on the application of Omar) v Secretary of State for Foreign and Commonwealth Affairs; *joined case* R. (on the application of Njoroge) v Secretary of State for Foreign and Commonwealth Affairs [2013] EWCA Civ 118; [2014] Q.B. 112; [2013] 3 W.L.R. 439; [2013] 3 All E.R. 95; [2013] A.C.D. 65, CA (Civ Div); affirming [2012] EWHC 1737 (Admin); [2013] 1 All E.R. 161; [2012] A.C.D. 112; (2012) 109(29) L.S.G. 26, QBD (Admin) ........................................................... *Digested,* 13/**397**:
*Considered* 14/383

R. (on the application of OP) v Secretary of State for Justice [2014] EWHC 1944 (Admin); (2014) 178 J.P. 377, DC ........ *Digested,* 14/**658**

R. (on the application of Oriel Support Ltd) v Revenue and Customs Commissioners [2009] EWCA Civ 401; [2009] S.T.C. 1397; [2009] B.T.C. 206; [2009] S.T.I. 1692, CA (Civ Div); affirming [2008] EWHC 1304 (Admin); [2008] S.T.I. 1568, QBD (Admin) ........ *Digested,* 09/**3875**: *Applied* 14/2894

R. (on the application of Osborn) v Parole Board see Reilly's Application for Judicial Review, Re

R. (on the application of P) v Chief Constable of Thames Valley [2014] EWHC 1436 (Admin); (2014) 17 C.C.L. Rep. 250, QBD (Admin) ........ *Digested,* 14/**2445**

R. (on the application of Padden) v Maidstone BC [2014] EWHC 51 (Admin); [2014] Env. L.R. 20, QBD (Admin) ........ *Digested,* 14/**2424**

R. (on the application of Panesar) v Central Criminal Court; *sub nom* Panesar v Revenue and Customs Commissioners; R. (on the application of Panesar) v Revenue and Customs Commissioners [2014] EWCA Civ 1613, CA (Civ Div); affirming [2014] EWHC 2821 (Admin); [2014] Lloyd's Rep. F.C. 662; [2014] B.V.C. 38; (2014) 158(35) S.J.L.B. 37, DC ........ *Digested,* 14/**2467**

R. (on the application of Panesar) v Revenue and Customs Commissioners see R. (on the application of Panesar) v Central Criminal Court

R. (on the application of Patel) v Secretary of State for the Home Department see R. (on the application of Mirza) v Secretary of State for the Home Department

R. (on the application of Patterson) v RSPCA see Patterson v Royal Society for the Prevention of Cruelty to Animals (RSPCA)

R. (on the application of PE (Cameroon)) v Secretary of State for the Home Department; *sub nom* PE (Cameroon) v Secretary of State for the Home Department; *joined case* R. (on the application of BA (Nigeria)) v Secretary of State for the Home Department [2009] UKSC 7; [2010] 1 A.C. 444; [2009] 3 W.L.R. 1253; [2010] 2 All E.R. 95; [2010] Imm. A.R. 363; [2010] I.N.L.R. 307; (2009) 153(46) S.J.L.B. 33; Times, December 1, 2009, SC; affirming [2009] EWCA Civ 119; [2009] Q.B. 686; [2009] 2 W.L.R. 1370; [2009] I.N.L.R. 284; Times, March 23, 2009, CA (Civ Div); reversing [2008] EWHC 1140 (Admin); [2008] 4 All E.R. 798; [2009] Imm. A.R. 61, QBD ........ *Digested,* 10/**1778**: *Considered* 11/1716, 14/1679

R. (on the application of Pearce) v Commissioner of Police of the Metropolis see R. (on the application of Hicks) v Commissioner of Police of the Metropolis

R. (on the application of Perinpanathan) v City of Westminster Magistrates' Court; *sub nom* Perinpanathan v City of Westminster Magistrates' Court [2010] EWCA Civ 40; [2010] 1 W.L.R. 1508; [2010] 4 All E.R. 680; [2010] 4 Costs L.R. 481; [2010] L.L.R. 514; (2010) 160 N.L.J. 217; Times, March 2, 2010, CA (Civ Div); affirming [2009] EWHC 762 (Admin); (2009) 173 J.P. 379; [2009] Po. L.R. 107; [2009] L.L.R. 356, DC ........ *Digested,* 10/**746**: *Applied* 14/2131

R. (on the application of Perry) v Hackney LBC [2014] EWHC 1721 (Admin); [2014] J.P.L. 1329, QBD (Admin)

R. (on the application of Perry) v Hackney LBC [2014] EWHC 3499 (Admin); [2014] P.T.S.R. D30, QBD (Admin)

R. (on the application of Plantagenet Alliance Ltd) v Secretary of State for Justice [2013] EWHC 3164 (Admin); [2014] A.C.D. 26, QBD (Admin)

R. (on the application of PO) v Newham LBC [2014] EWHC 2561 (Admin); (2014) 17 C.C.L. Rep. 325, QBD (Admin)

R. (on the application of Poole) v Secretary of State for Communities and Local Government [2008] EWHC 676 (Admin); [2008] J.P.L. 1774, QBD (Admin) ....... *Digested,* 09/**3004**: *Considered* 14/2411

R. (on the application of Premier Leisure UK Ltd) v Secretary of State for the Environment, Transport and the Regions see R. (on the application of Holding & Barnes Plc) v Secretary of State for the Environment, Transport and the Regions

R. (on the application of Pretty) v DPP (2346/02) see Pretty v United Kingdom (2346/02)

R. (on the application of Privacy International) v Revenue and Customs Commissioners [2014] EWHC 1475 (Admin); [2014] B.T.C. 25; [2014] A.C.D. 108; (2014) 158(22) S.J.L.B. 37, QBD (Admin) ........ *Digested,* 14/**56**

R. (on the application of Prothero) v Secretary of State for the Home Department [2013] EWHC 2830 (Admin); [2014] 1 W.L.R. 1195; [2014] A.C.D. 40; (2013) 157(37) S.J.L.B. 37, DC ........ *Digested,* 14/**2241**

R. (on the application of Prudential Plc) v Special Commissioner of Income Tax [2013] UKSC 1; [2013] 2 A.C. 185; [2013] 2 W.L.R. 325; [2013] 2 All E.R. 247; [2013] S.T.C. 376; [2013] 2 Costs L.R. 275; [2013] 1 F.C.R. 545; 82 T.C. 64; [2013] B.T.C. 45; [2013] C.I.L.L. 3309; [2013] S.T.I. 264; [2013] 5 E.G. 96 (C.S.); (2013) 163 N.L.J. 109; Times, February 5, 2013, SC; affirming [2010] EWCA Civ 1094; [2011] Q.B. 669; [2011] 2 W.L.R. 50; [2011] 1 All E.R. 316; [2010] S.T.C. 2802; [2011] C.P. Rep. 5; [2011] 1 Costs L.R. 92; [2011] 1 F.C.R. 195; [2011] Lloyd's Rep. F.C. 1; [2010] B.T.C. 773; [2011] A.C.D. 19; [2010] S.T.I. 2709; (2010) 107(41) L.S.G. 21; (2010) 160 N.L.J. 1456; [2010] N.P.C. 99, CA (Civ Div); affirming [2009] EWHC 2494 (Admin); [2010] 3 W.L.R. 1042; [2010] 1 All E.R. 1113; [2010] S.T.C. 161; [2009] B.T.C. 680; [2010] A.C.D. 10; [2009] S.T.I. 2770; [2009] N.P.C. 113; Times, November 10, 2009, QBD (Admin) ........ *Digested,* 13/**2390**: *Considered* 12/411: *Followed* 12/305

R. (on the application of Pryor) v Secretary of State for the Home Department [2013] EWHC 2853 (Admin); [2014] Imm. A.R. 341, QBD (Admin) ............................... *Digested,* 14/**1671**

R. (on the application of Public Law Project) v Lord Chancellor see R. (on the application of Public Law Project) v Secretary of State for Justice

R. (on the application of Public Law Project) v Secretary of State for Justice; *sub nom* R. (on the application of Public Law Project) v Lord Chancellor [2014] EWHC 2365 (Admin); [2014] H.R.L.R. 24; [2014] E.L.R. 372, QBD (Admin) .................. *Digested,* 14/**2021**

R. (on the application of Purdy) v DPP [2009] UKHL 45; [2010] 1 A.C. 345; [2009] 3 W.L.R. 403; [2009] 4 All E.R. 1147; [2010] 1 Cr. App. R. 1; [2009] H.R.L.R. 32; [2009] U.K.H.R.R. 1104; 27 B.H.R.C. 126; (2009) 12 C.C.L. Rep. 498; [2009] LS Law Medical 479; (2009) 109 B.M.L.R. 153; (2009) 179 N.L.J. 1175; (2009) 153(31) S.J.L.B. 28; Times, July 31, 2009, HL; reversing [2009] EWCA Civ 92; [2009] 1 Cr. App. R. 32; [2009] U.K.H.R.R. 1005; (2009) 106 B.M.L.R. 170; (2009) 159 N.L.J. 309; (2009) 153(8) S.J.L.B. 27; Times, February 24, 2009, CA (Civ Div); affirming [2008] EWHC 2565 (Admin); [2009] H.R.L.R. 7; [2009] U.K.H.R.R. 94; (2008) 104 B.M.L.R. 231; (2008) 152(43) S.J.L.B. 31; Times, November 17, 2008, DC ........................................................................ *Digested,* 09/**2046**: *Considered* 13/619, 14/672: *Followed* 12/1517, 14/799

R. (on the application of Q) v Secretary of State for the Home Department see R. (on the application of S) v Secretary of State for the Home Office

R. (on the application of Quintavalle) v Secretary of State for Health [2003] UKHL 13; [2003] 2 A.C. 687; [2003] 2 W.L.R. 692; [2003] 2 All E.R. 113; [2003] 1 F.C.R. 577; (2003) 71 B.M.L.R. 209; (2003) 153 N.L.J. 439; Times, March 14, 2003; Independent, March 18, 2003, HL; affirming [2002] EWCA Civ 29; [2002] Q.B. 628; [2002] 2 W.L.R. 550; [2002] 2 All E.R. 625; [2002] 2 F.C.R. 140; (2002) 64 B.M.L.R. 72; (2002) 99(10) L.S.G. 32; (2002) 146 S.J.L.B. 30; Times, January 25, 2002; Independent, January 22, 2002; Daily Telegraph, January 24, 2002, CA (Civ Div); reversing [2001] EWHC Admin 918; [2001] 4 All E.R. 1013; (2002) 63 B.M.L.R. 167; (2001) 151 N.L.J. 1732; Times, December 5, 2001, QBD (Admin) ........................................................................................ *Digested,* 04/**3274**: *Applied* 05/823, 08/3840, 08/3921, 09/2604, 14/814: *Considered* 06/699, 09/1737, 13/2487, 14/3752

R. (on the application of Quinton) v Commissioner of Police of the Metropolis see R. (on the application of Gillan) v Commissioner of Police of the Metropolis

R. (on the application of R) v A Chief Constable [2013] EWHC 2864 (Admin); [2014] 1 Cr. App. R. 16; (2013) 134 B.M.L.R. 98; [2014] Crim. L.R. 524; [2014] A.C.D. 28, DC ........................................................................................................ *Digested,* 14/**659**

R. (on the application of R) v Durham Constabulary; *joined case* R. (on the application of U) v Commissioner of Police of the Metropolis [2005] UKHL 21; [2005] 1 W.L.R. 1184; [2005] 2 All E.R. 369; [2005] H.R.L.R. 18; [2005] U.K.H.R.R. 584; [2005] Po. L.R. 8; [2006] Crim. L.R. 87; (2005) 155 N.L.J. 467; (2005) 149 S.J.L.B. 360; Times, March 18, 2005, HL; reversing [2002] EWHC 2486 (Admin); [2003] 1 W.L.R. 897; [2003] 3 All E.R. 419; [2003] 1 Cr. App. R. 29; [2003] H.R.L.R. 13; [2003] U.K.H.R.R. 287; [2002] Po. L.R. 371; [2003] Crim. L.R. 349; Times, December 10, 2002, DC ......................................................... *Digested,* 05/**925**: *Considered* 14/662

R. (on the application of Rahmani) v Secretary of State for the Home Department see R. (on the application of Salih) v Secretary of State for the Home Department

R. (on the application of Rahmdezfouli) v Wood Green Crown Court [2013] EWHC 2998 (Admin); [2014] 1 W.L.R. 1793; [2014] 1 All E.R. 567; [2014] 1 Cr. App. R. 20; (2013) 177 J.P. 677; [2014] Crim. L.R. 158; [2014] A.C.D. 31, DC ............... *Digested,* 14/**783**

R. (on the application of Rathakrishnan) v Secretary of State for the Home Department [2011] EWHC 1406 (Admin), QBD (Admin) *Applied* 14/68

R. (on the application of Rawlinson and Hunter Trustees) v Central Criminal Court; *joined case* R. (on the application of Tchenguiz) v Director of Serious Fraud Office [2012] EWHC 2254 (Admin); [2013] 1 W.L.R. 1634; [2013] Lloyd's Rep. F.C. 132, DC ........ *Digested,* 13/**211**: *Applied* 13/764, 14/2467, 14/803: *Considered* 14/804

R. (on the application of Razgar) v Secretary of State for the Home Department (No.2); *sub nom* Secretary of State for the Home Department v Razgar; *joined cases* R. (on the application of Nadarajah) v Secretary of State for the Home Department; R. (on the application of Soumahoro) v Secretary of State for the Home Department [2004] UKHL 27; [2004] 2 A.C. 368; [2004] 3 W.L.R. 58; [2004] 3 All E.R. 821; [2004] H.R.L.R. 32; [2004] Imm. A.R. 381; [2004] I.N.L.R. 349; [2004] M.H.L.R. 218; [2004] A.C.D. 83; (2004) 101(28) L.S.G. 33; (2004) 154 N.L.J. 986; (2004) 148 S.J.L.B. 761; Times, June 21, 2004; Independent, June 23, 2004, HL; affirming [2003] EWCA Civ 840; [2003] Imm. A.R. 529; [2003] I.N.L.R. 543; [2003] A.C.D. 81, CA (Civ Div); affirming [2002] EWHC 2554 (Admin); [2003] Imm. A.R. 269, QBD (Admin) ........ *Digested,* 04/**2029**: *Applied* 04/2032, 04/2041, 04/2052, 05/2159, 05/2181, 05/2192, 06/2229, 06/2233, 06/2244, 06/2245, 06/2286, 07/2301, 07/2307, 07/2340, 08/2036, 10/4329, 12/1293, 12/1707: *Cited* 09/2102: *Considered* 04/839, 05/2179, 05/2213, 05/5431, 06/2246, 07/2295, 10/1809, 10/2322, 11/1711, 12/4097: *Explained* 06/2223, 09/2163: *Followed* 07/2313, 09/2075, 10/1790, 11/1789, 14/1715

R. (on the application of RD) v Secretary of State for Work and Pensions; *joined case* R. (on the application of EM) v Secretary of State for Work and Pensions [2010] EWCA Civ 18; [2010] 1 W.L.R. 1782; [2010] H.R.L.R. 19; (2010) 112 B.M.L.R. 140; [2010] M.H.L.R. 72; (2010) 154(4) S.J.L.B. 30; Times, February 1, 2010, CA (Civ Div) ........ *Digested,* 10/**2314**: *Followed* 14/1717

R. (on the application of Redrow Homes Ltd) v Knowsley MBC [2014] EWCA Civ 1433; (2014) 158(43) S.J.L.B. 49, CA (Civ Div); affirming [2013] EWHC 3734 (Admin), QBD (Admin)

R. (on the application of Reed) v Secretary of State for Communities and Local Government see Reed v Secretary of State for Communities and Local Government

R. (on the application of Refugee Action) v Secretary of State for the Home Department [2014] EWHC 1033 (Admin); [2014] A.C.D. 99; [2014] P.T.S.R. D18, QBD (Admin)

R. (on the application of Refugee Legal Centre) v Secretary of State for the Home Department [2004] EWCA Civ 1481; [2005] 1 W.L.R. 2219; [2005] I.N.L.R. 236; [2005] A.C.D. 52; (2005) 102(1) L.S.G. 16; Times, November 24, 2004, CA (Civ Div); affirming [2004] EWHC 684 (Admin); [2004] Imm. A.R. 142, QBD (Admin) *Digested,* 05/**2155**: *Considered* 14/658

R. (on the application of Reilly) v Secretary of State for Work and Pensions [2013] EWCA Civ 66; [2013] 1 W.L.R. 2239; [2013] 3 All E.R. 67; (2013) 163 N.L.J. 236, CA (Civ Div); reversing in part [2012] EWHC 2292 (Admin); (2012) 156(32) S.J.L.B. 31, QBD (Admin) ........ *Digested,* 13/**2890**: *Reversed in part* 14/2766

R. (on the application of Reilly) v Secretary of State for Work and Pensions; *joined case* R. (on the application of Wilson) v Secretary of State for Work and Pensions [2013] UKSC 68; [2014] A.C. 453; [2013] 3 W.L.R. 1276; [2014] 1 All E.R. 505, SC ........ *Digested,* 14/**2766**

R. (on the application of Remedy UK Ltd) v General Medical Council [2010] EWHC 1245 (Admin); [2010] Med. L.R. 330; [2010] A.C.D. 72, DC ........ *Digested,* 11/**1534**: *Applied* 14/1497

R. (on the application of Revenue and Customs Commissioners) v HM Coroner for Liverpool [2014] EWHC 1586 (Admin); [2014] 3 W.L.R. 1660; [2014] B.T.C. 28; [2014] A.C.D. 109, DC ........ *Digested,* 14/**17**

R. (on the application of Reynolds) v Chief Constable of Sussex; *sub nom* R. (on the application of Reynolds) v Independent Police Complaints Commission [2008] EWCA Civ 1160; [2009] 3 All E.R. 237; [2009] P.T.S.R. 1229; [2008] Po. L.R. 339; [2009] A.C.D. 51; (2008) 105(42) L.S.G. 22; Times, November 6, 2008, CA (Civ Div); affirming [2008] EWHC 1240 (Admin); [2008] Po. L.R. 77, QBD (Admin) ........ *Digested,* 09/**3070**: *Applied* 14/2447

R. (on the application of Reynolds) v Independent Police Complaints Commission see R. (on the application of Reynolds) v Chief Constable of Sussex

R. (on the application of Reynolds) v Secretary of State for Work and Pensions see R. (on the application of Carson) v Secretary of State for Work and Pensions

R. (on the application of Richards) v South Bucks DC [2004] EWHC 2145 (Admin), QBD (Admin)
*Applied* 14/2400

R. (on the application of Richardson) v North Yorkshire CC; *sub nom* Richardson v North Yorkshire CC [2003] EWCA Civ 1860; [2004] 1 W.L.R. 1920; [2004] 2 All E.R. 31; [2004] Env. L.R. 34; [2004] B.L.G.R. 351; [2004] 2 P. & C.R. 15; [2004] L.L.R. 542; [2004] J.P.L. 911; [2004] A.C.D. 62; [2004] 2 E.G. 93 (C.S.); (2004) 101(6) L.S.G. 32; (2004) 101(2) L.S.G. 31; (2004) 148 S.J.L.B. 58; Times, January 19, 2004, CA (Civ Div); affirming [2003] EWHC 764 (Admin); [2004] Env. L.R. 13; [2004] 1 P. & C.R. 23; [2003] 18 E.G. 113 (C.S.), QBD (Admin) ........ *Digested,* 04/**3092**:
*Applied* 09/3042, 10/2612: *Considered* 14/2407: *Distinguished* 05/3300:
*Explained* 05/2785: *Followed* 06/3348

R. (on the application of Roberts) v Commissioner of Police of the Metropolis [2014] EWCA Civ 69; [2014] 1 W.L.R. 3299; [2014] 2 Cr. App. R. 6; [2014] H.R.L.R. 5; [2014] A.C.D. 82, CA (Civ Div); affirming [2012] EWHC 1977 (Admin); [2012] H.R.L.R. 28; [2012] A.C.D. 104, QBD (Admin) ........ *Digested,* 14/**2461**

R. (on the application of Robinson) v Governor of Whatton Prison see R. (on the application of Kaiyam) v Secretary of State for Justice

R. (on the application of Robson) v Salford City Council see Robson v Salford City Council

R. (on the application of Romer) v First Secretary of State; *sub nom* Romer v Haringey LBC [2006] EWHC 3480 (Admin); [2007] J.P.L. 1354; [2006] 50 E.G. 84 (C.S.), QBD (Admin) ........ *Digested,* 07/**3232**:
*Considered* 14/2376

R. (on the application of Roomi) v General Medical Council [2009] EWHC 2188 (Admin), QBD (Admin)
*Applied* 14/1495

R. (on the application of Rose) v Thanet Clinical Commissioning Group [2014] EWHC 1182 (Admin); (2014) 138 B.M.L.R. 101; [2014] A.C.D. 120, QBD (Admin)

R. (on the application of Rostami) v Secretary of State for the Home Department [2013] EWHC 1494 (Admin); [2014] Imm. A.R. 56; [2014] I.N.L.R. 497, QBD (Admin) ........ *Digested,* 14/**1653**

R. (on the application of Rotherham MBC) v Secretary of State for Business, Innovation and Skills [2014] EWCA Civ 1080; [2014] P.T.S.R. 1387; [2014] 3 C.M.L.R. 51; [2014] B.L.G.R. 589, CA (Civ Div); affirming [2014] EWHC 232 (Admin); [2014] B.L.G.R. 389; [2014] A.C.D. 75, QBD (Admin) ........ *Digested,* 14/**1481**

R. (on the application of Rouse) v Revenue and Customs Commissioners [2013] UKUT 615 (TCC); [2014] S.T.C. 230; [2014] B.T.C. 501; [2014] S.T.I. 435, UT (Tax) ........ *Digested,* 14/**2958**

R. (on the application of Royal Brompton and Harefield NHS Foundation Trust) v Joint Committee of Primary Care Trusts; *sub nom* Royal Brompton and Harefield NHS Foundation Trust v Joint Committee of Primary Care Trusts [2012] EWCA Civ 472; (2012) 126 B.M.L.R. 134; (2012) 109(18) L.S.G. 20, CA (Civ Div); reversing [2011] EWHC 2986 (Admin); [2012] A.C.D. 31, QBD (Admin) ........ *Digested,* 12/**1557**:
*Applied* 13/2016, 13/2862: *Followed* 14/2794

R. (on the application of Royal London Mutual Insurance Society Ltd) v Secretary of State for Communities and Local Government see Royal London Mutual Insurance Society Ltd v Secretary of State for Communities and Local Government

R. (on the application of S) v Chief Constable of the British Transport Police [2013] EWHC 2189 (Admin); [2014] 1 W.L.R. 1647; [2014] 1 All E.R. 268; (2014) 178 J.P. 221; [2014] A.C.D. 19, QBD (Admin) ........ *Digested,* 14/**2466**

R. (on the application of S) v Northampton Crown Court [2010] EWHC 723 (Admin); [2012] 1 W.L.R. 1; [2010] 2 Cr. App. R. 23; [2010] U.K.H.R.R. 828; [2011] Crim. L.R. 469; [2010] A.C.D. 53, QBD (Admin) ........ *Digested,* 10/**724**:
*Considered* 14/719

R. (on the application of S) v Secretary of State for the Home Department see R. (on the application of S) v Secretary of State for the Home Office

R. (on the application of S) v Secretary of State for the Home Office; *sub nom* R. (on the application of S) v Secretary of State for the Home Department; *joined cases* R. (on the application of Q) v Secretary of State for the Home Department; R. (on the application of H) v Secretary of State for the Home Department [2009] EWCA Civ 142, CA (Civ Div); affirming [2008] EWHC 977 (Admin), QBD (Admin)
*Followed* 14/1648

R. (on the application of S) v Suffolk CC; *sub nom* S v Suffolk CC [2014] EWHC 2780 (Admin); [2014] E.L.R. 413, QBD (Admin) ........ *Digested,* 14/**935**

R. (on the application of S) v Waltham Forest Youth Court [2004] EWHC 715 (Admin); [2004] 2 Cr. App. R. 21; (2004) 168 J.P. 293; (2004) 168 J.P.N. 438, DC .......... *Digested,* 04/**864**: *Considered* 07/856, 10/797, 14/658

R. (on the application of S) v Wandsworth LBC [2001] EWHC Admin 709; [2002] 1 F.L.R. 469; (2001) 4 C.C.L. Rep. 466; [2002] Fam. Law 180; Times, November 15, 2001, QBD (Admin) .......... *Digested,* 01/**4374**: *Applied* 14/2805: *Considered* 08/2577, 14/2148

R. (on the application of SA (A Child)) v A Local Authority; *sub nom* SA (A Child) v A Local Authority [2011] EWCA Civ 1303; [2012] P.T.S.R. 912; [2012] 1 F.L.R. 628; [2012] 1 F.C.R. 355; [2012] Fam. Law 26; Times, December 6, 2011, CA (Civ Div); affirming [2010] EWHC 848 (Admin); [2010] 2 F.L.R. 1721; [2010] 2 F.C.R. 405; [2010] A.C.D. 96; [2010] Fam. Law 925, QBD (Admin) .......... *Digested,* 12/**3172**: *Applied* 14/1308

R. (on the application of Sainsbury's Supermarkets Ltd) v Wolverhampton City Council; *sub nom* Sainsbury's Supermarkets Ltd v Wolverhampton City Council [2010] UKSC 20; [2011] 1 A.C. 437; [2010] 2 W.L.R. 1173; [2010] 4 All E.R. 931; [2010] P.T.S.R. 1103; [2010] B.L.G.R. 727; [2011] 1 P. & C.R. 1; [2010] 2 E.G.L.R. 103; [2010] R.V.R. 237; [2010] J.P.L. 1259; [2010] 20 E.G. 144 (C.S.); (2010) 154(20) S.J.L.B. 36; [2010] N.P.C. 66; Times, May 13, 2010, SC; reversing [2009] EWCA Civ 835; [2009] 3 E.G.L.R. 94; [2009] 44 E.G. 210; [2010] J.P.L. 497; Times, August 21, 2009, CA (Civ Div); affirming [2009] EWHC 134 (Admin); [2009] J.P.L. 1354, QBD (Admin) .......... *Digested,* 10/**2553**: *Followed* 14/2431

R. (on the application of Salih) v Secretary of State for the Home Department; *joined case* R. (on the application of Rahmani) v Secretary of State for the Home Department [2003] EWHC 2273 (QB); Times, October 13, 2003, QBD

*Applied* 14/2766

R. (on the application of Samaroo) v Secretary of State for the Home Department; *sub nom* Samaroo v Secretary of State for the Home Department; R. v Secretary of State for the Home Department Ex p. Samaroo; *joined case* Sezek v Secretary of State for the Home Department [2001] EWCA Civ 1139; [2001] U.K.H.R.R. 1150; [2002] I.N.L.R. 55; (2001) 98(34) L.S.G. 40; (2001) 145 S.J.L.B. 208; Times, September 18, 2001, CA (Civ Div); affirming [2001] Imm. A.R. 324; Daily Telegraph, January 23, 2001, QBD (Admin) .......... *Digested,* 01/**3660**: *Applied* 04/3040, 05/3340, 06/2277, 14/2102: *Considered* 03/2232, 03/3068, 04/3042, 07/2879, 09/3036, 13/372: *Distinguished* 05/2027: *Followed* 04/2051

R. (on the application of San Michael College Ltd) v Secretary of State for the Home Department [2011] EWCA Civ 1336, CA (Civ Div); reversing [2011] EWHC 642 (Admin), QBD (Admin)

*Considered* 14/75

R. (on the application of Sandiford) v Secretary of State for Foreign and Commonwealth Affairs [2014] UKSC 44; [2014] 1 W.L.R. 2697; [2014] 4 All E.R. 843; [2014] H.R.L.R. 21; Times, July 25, 2014, SC; affirming [2013] EWCA Civ 581; [2013] 1 W.L.R. 2938; [2013] 3 All E.R. 757; Times, July 19, 2013, CA (Civ Div); affirming [2013] EWHC 168 (Admin); [2013] A.C.D. 43, QBD (Admin) .......... *Digested,* 14/**2044**

R. (on the application of Save Britain's Heritage) v Secretary of State for Communities and Local Government [2013] EWHC 2268 (Admin); [2014] Env. L.R. 9; [2014] J.P.L. 35; (2013) 157(31) S.J.L.B. 31, QBD (Admin) .......... *Digested,* 14/**1187**

R. (on the application of Save Lewisham Hospital Campaign Ltd) v Secretary of State for Health see R. (on the application of Lewisham LBC) v Secretary of State for Health

R. (on the application of SB) v Denbigh High School Governors see R. (on the application of Begum) v Denbigh High School Governors

R. (on the application of Secretary of State for the Home Department) v Southwark Crown Court [2013] EWHC 4366 (Admin); [2014] 1 W.L.R. 2529; [2014] 3 All E.R. 354; [2014] A.C.D. 51, QBD (Admin) .......... *Digested,* 14/**799**

R. (on the application of Sellars) v Basingstoke and Deane BC [2013] EWHC 3673 (Admin); [2014] J.P.L. 643; [2013] 49 E.G. 76 (C.S.), QBD (Admin) .......... *Digested,* 14/**2354**

R. (on the application of Seroka) v Redhill Magistrates' Court [2012] EWHC 3827 (Admin), DC

*Considered* 14/2566

R. (on the application of SG) v Secretary of State for Work and Pensions see R. (on the application of JS) v Secretary of State for Work and Pensions

R. (on the application of Shah) v Secretary of State for the Home Department [2013] EWHC 2206 (Admin), QBD (Admin)

*Applied* 14/1648

R. (on the application of Sharif) v Birmingham City Council see R. (on the application of Aweys) v Birmingham City Council

R. (on the application of Shergill) v Harrow Crown Court [2005] EWHC 648 (Admin), QBD (Admin) *Considered* 14/719

R. (on the application of Shoesmith) v Ofsted [2011] EWCA Civ 642; [2011] P.T.S.R. 1459; [2011] I.C.R. 1195; [2011] I.R.L.R. 679; [2011] B.L.G.R. 649; (2011) 108(23) L.S.G. 16; (2011) 155(22) S.J.L.B. 35, CA (Civ Div); reversing in part [2010] EWHC 852 (Admin); (2010) 154(17) S.J.L.B. 27; [2011] P.T.S.R. D13, QBD (Admin) ........ *Digested,* 11/**65**: *Considered* 14/60

R. (on the application of Shuai Zhang) v Secretary of State for the Home Department [2013] EWHC 891 (Admin); [2014] 2 All E.R. 560, QBD (Admin) ........ *Digested,* 14/**1715**

R. (on the application of Sienkiewicz) v South Somerset DC [2013] EWHC 4090 (Admin); [2014] J.P.L. 620, QBD (Admin) ........ *Digested,* 14/**2409**

R. (on the application of Sim) v Parole Board for England and Wales; *sub nom* Secretary of State for the Home Department v Sim; R. (on the application of Sim) v Secretary of State for the Home Department [2003] EWCA Civ 1845; [2004] Q.B. 1288; [2004] 2 W.L.R. 1170; [2004] H.R.L.R. 15; [2004] Prison L.R. 44; (2004) 101(5) L.S.G. 29; (2004) 148 S.J.L.B. 60; Times, January 2, 2004, CA (Civ Div); affirming [2003] EWHC 152 (Admin); [2003] 2 W.L.R. 1374; [2003] Prison L.R. 256; [2003] A.C.D. 62; (2003) 100(13) L.S.G. 26; Times, February 21, 2003; Independent, March 17, 2003, QBD (Admin) ........ *Digested,* 04/**3349**: *Considered* 03/831, 10/1544, 12/2970, 14/2682

R. (on the application of Sim) v Secretary of State for the Home Department see R. (on the application of Sim) v Parole Board for England and Wales

R. (on the application of Simpson) v Chief Constable of Greater Manchester [2013] EWHC 1858 (Admin); [2014] A.C.D. 20, QBD (Admin)

R. (on the application of Sinclair Collis Ltd) v Secretary of State for Health; *sub nom* Sinclair Collis Ltd v Secretary of State for Health [2011] EWCA Civ 437; [2012] Q.B. 394; [2012] 2 W.L.R. 304; [2011] 3 C.M.L.R. 37; [2012] Eu. L.R. 50; (2012) 123 B.M.L.R. 36; [2011] L.L.R. 592; [2011] A.C.D. 98; Times, June 28, 2011, CA (Civ Div); affirming [2010] EWHC 3112 (Admin); [2011] Eu. L.R. 344; [2011] U.K.H.R.R. 81; [2011] L.L.R. 125; [2011] A.C.D. 29, QBD (Admin) ........ *Digested,* 11/**1622**: *Applied* 14/1481

R. (on the application of Singh (India)) v Upper Tribunal (Immigration and Asylum Chamber) see Qongwane v Secretary of State for the Home Department

R. (on the application of Singh) v Ealing Magistrates' Court [2014] EWHC 1443 (Admin); (2014) 178 J.P. 253, QBD (Admin) ........ *Digested,* 14/**750**

R. (on the application of SJ (Pakistan)) v Secretary of State for the Home Department see R. (on the application of MM (Lebanon)) v Secretary of State for the Home Department

R. (on the application of SK (Zimbabwe)) v Secretary of State for the Home Department see R. (on the application of Kambadzi) v Secretary of State for the Home Department

R. (on the application of Skillcrown Homes Ltd) v Dartford BC [2014] EWHC 365 (Admin); [2014] J.P.L. 988, QBD (Admin) ........ *Digested,* 14/**2422**

R. (on the application of Sky Blue Sports and Leisure Ltd) v Coventry City Council [2014] EWHC 2089 (Admin); [2014] B.L.G.R. 616, QBD (Admin) ........ *Digested,* 14/**1225**

R. (on the application of SM (Congo)) v Secretary of State for the Home Department see R. (on the application of ZA (Nigeria)) v Secretary of State for the Home Department

R. (on the application of SM) v Secretary of State for the Home Department; *joined case* R. (on the application of SR) v Secretary of State for the Home Department [2013] EWHC 1144 (Admin); [2013] Imm. A.R. 1051, QBD (Admin) ........ *Digested,* 14/**1704**

R. (on the application of Smith) v Land Registry (Peterborough Office) [2010] EWCA Civ 200; [2011] Q.B. 413; [2010] 3 W.L.R. 1223; [2010] 3 All E.R. 113; [2010] 2 P. & C.R. 23; [2010] 2 E.G.L.R. 1; [2010] 21 E.G. 92; [2010] 11 E.G. 121 (C.S.); [2010] N.P.C. 31, CA (Civ Div); affirming [2009] EWHC 328 (Admin), QBD (Admin) ........ *Digested,* 10/**2689**: *Applied* 14/2488

R. (on the application of Smith) v Oxfordshire Assistant Deputy Coroner; *sub nom* R. (on the application of Smith) v Secretary of State for Defence; *joined case* Secretary of State for Defence v Smith [2010] UKSC 29; [2011] 1 A.C. 1; [2010] 3 W.L.R. 223; [2010] 3 All E.R. 1067; [2010] H.R.L.R. 28; [2010] U.K.H.R.R. 1020; 29 B.H.R.C. 497; [2010] Inquest L.R. 119; (2010) 107(28) L.S.G. 17; (2010) 160 N.L.J. 973; (2010) 154(26) S.J.L.B. 28; Times, July 8, 2010, SC; reversing in part [2009] EWCA Civ 441; [2009] 3 W.L.R. 1099; [2009] 4 All E.R. 985; [2009] U.K.H.R.R. 1139; 27 B.H.R.C. 89; [2009] Inquest L.R. 156; [2009] A.C.D. 54; (2009) 159 N.L.J. 790; Times, May 20, 2009, CA (Civ Div); affirming [2008] EWHC 694 (Admin); [2008] 3 W.L.R. 1284; (2008) 103 B.M.L.R. 152; [2008] Inquest L.R. 44; [2008] A.C.D. 45; Times, May 30, 2008, QBD (Admin) .. *Digested,* 10/**1737**: *Applied* 11/1745: *Considered* 09/41, 14/47: *Followed* 10/17, 12/128: *Not followed* 13/121

R. (on the application of Smith) v Parole Board for England and Wales; *sub nom* Smith v Parole Board for England and Wales; *joined case* R. (on the application of West) v Parole Board for England and Wales [2005] UKHL 1; [2005] 1 W.L.R. 350; [2005] 1 All E.R. 755; [2005] H.R.L.R. 8; 18 B.H.R.C. 267; [2005] 2 Prison L.R. 14; (2005) 102(12) L.S.G. 26; (2005) 149 S.J.L.B. 145; Times, January 28, 2005; Independent, February 2, 2005, HL; reversing [2003] EWCA Civ 1269; [2004] 1 W.L.R. 421; [2004] Prison L.R. 31; [2004] Prison L.R. 216; (2003) 100(38) L.S.G. 34; (2003) 153 N.L.J. 1427; Times, September 2, 2003, CA (Civ Div) ........................................................................ *Digested,* 05/**2920**: *Applied* 04/2776, 05/2734, 06/2937, 06/345, 08/2678, 08/2689, 08/4957, 10/2317, 11/2291: *Considered* 05/2907, 07/2981, 09/2761, 09/2768, 13/2124: *Distinguished* 04/3349: *Followed* 04/2782, 11/2286, 11/2290, 13/2115: *Not followed* 14/2233: *Referred to* 08/2680

R. (on the application of Smith) v Secretary of State for Defence see R. (on the application of Smith) v Oxfordshire Assistant Deputy Coroner

R. (on the application of Smoke Club Ltd) v Network Rail Infrastructure Ltd [2013] EWHC 3830 (Admin); [2014] 2 Costs L.O. 123, QBD (Admin) .......................... *Digested,* 14/**366**

R. (on the application of Solomon) v Secretary of State for the Home Department [2011] EWHC 3075 (Admin), QBD (Admin) *Applied* 14/1682

R. (on the application of Soumahoro) v Secretary of State for the Home Department see R. (on the application of Razgar) v Secretary of State for the Home Department (No.2)

R. (on the application of South West Care Homes Ltd) v Devon CC [2012] EWHC 1867 (Admin); [2012] A.C.D. 108, QBD (Admin) ................................................ *Digested,* 12/**3157**: *Applied* 13/2936: *Approved* 14/2797

R. (on the application of South Yorkshire Police) v Sheffield Crown Court see R. (on the application of Chief Constable of South Yorkshire) v Sheffield Crown Court

R. (on the application of Spain) v Bow Street Magistrates' Court see R. (on the application of United States) v Bow Street Magistrates' Court

R. (on the application of Spath Holme Ltd) v Secretary of State for the Environment, Transport and the Regions; *sub nom* R. v Secretary of State for the Environment, Transport and the Regions Ex p. Spath Holme Ltd [2001] 2 A.C. 349; [2001] 2 W.L.R. 15; [2001] 1 All E.R. 195; (2001) 33 H.L.R. 31; [2001] 1 E.G.L.R. 129; [2000] E.G. 152 (C.S.); (2001) 98(8) L.S.G. 44; (2000) 150 N.L.J. 1855; (2001) 145 S.J.L.B. 39; [2000] N.P.C. 139; Times, December 13, 2000, HL; reversing [2000] 3 W.L.R. 141; [2000] 1 All E.R. 884; (2000) 32 H.L.R. 495; [2000] E.G. 10 (C.S.); (2000) 144 S.J.L.B. 100; [2000] N.P.C. 4; Times, February 15, 2000; Independent, March 6, 2000, CA (Civ Div) ......................... *Digested,* 01/**4206**: *Applied* 00/5095, 01/5632, 03/1962, 04/3189: *Considered* 07/3064, 09/3624, 14/2422, 14/3752: *Followed* 11/2338

R. (on the application of SR) v Nottingham Magistrates Court [2001] EWHC Admin 802; (2002) 166 J.P. 132; [2002] Po. L.R. 37; (2002) 166 J.P.N. 209; Independent, December 17, 2001, DC ................................................................ *Digested,* 02/**884**: *Applied* 14/662

R. (on the application of SR) v Secretary of State for the Home Department see R. (on the application of SM) v Secretary of State for the Home Department

R. (on the application of St Matthews (West) Ltd) v HM Treasury; *sub nom* R. (on the application of St Matthews (West) Ltd) v Revenue and Customs Commissioners [2014] EWHC 1848 (Admin); [2014] S.T.C. 2350; [2014] B.T.C. 29; [2014] S.T.I. 2111, QBD (Admin) ................................................................ *Digested,* 14/**2964**

R. (on the application of St Matthews (West) Ltd) v Revenue and Customs Commissioners see R. (on the application of St Matthews (West) Ltd) v HM Treasury

R. (on the application of Star Oyster Ltd) v Guildford Borough Council [2014] EWHC 1412 (Admin); [2014] L.L.R. 768, QBD (Admin)

R. (on the application of Stirling) v Haringey LBC see R. (on the application of M) v Haringey LBC

R. (on the application of Stirling) v Haringey LBC see R. (on the application of Moseley) v Haringey LBC

R. (on the application of Sturnham) v Parole Board for England and Wales; *sub nom* R. (on the application of Sturnham) v Secretary of State for Justice; *joined case* R. (on the application of Faulkner) v Secretary of State for Justice [2013] UKSC 23; [2013] 2 A.C. 254; [2013] 2 W.L.R. 1157; [2013] 2 All E.R. 1013; [2013] H.R.L.R. 24; 35 B.H.R.C. 378; (2013) 157(18) S.J.L.B. 31; Times, June 4, 2013, SC; reversing in part [2012] EWCA Civ 452; [2012] 3 W.L.R. 476, CA (Civ Div); affirming [2011] EWHC 938 (Admin), QBD (Admin) ........................... *Digested,* 13/**2113**: *Affirmed* 13/2112

R. (on the application of Sturnham) v Secretary of State for Justice see R. (on the application of Sturnham) v Parole Board for England and Wales

R. (on the application of Sunderland City Council) v South Tyneside Council [2012] EWCA Civ 1232; [2013] 1 All E.R. 394; [2013] P.T.S.R. 549; [2013] B.L.G.R. 51; (2012) 15 C.C.L. Rep. 701; [2012] M.H.L.R. 404, CA (Civ Div); reversing [2011] EWHC 2355 (Admin); [2011] M.H.L.R. 374, QBD (Admin) ..................... *Digested,* 13/**2058**: *Applied* 14/2179

R. (on the application of Supportways Community Services Ltd) v Hampshire CC; *sub nom* Hampshire CC v Supportways Community Services Ltd; Supportways Community Services Ltd v Hampshire CC [2006] EWCA Civ 1035; [2006] B.L.G.R. 836; (2006) 9 C.C.L. Rep. 484, CA (Civ Div); reversing [2005] EWHC 3101 (Admin); (2006) 9 C.C.L. Rep. 227, QBD (Admin) .................................... *Digested,* 07/**796**: *Applied* 13/2949, 14/1492: *Considered* 12/3158, 13/2934

R. (on the application of Syed) v Secretary of State for the Home Department; *joined case* R. (on the application of Ahmed) v Secretary of State for the Home Department [2013] EWHC 984 (Admin); [2013] Imm. A.R. 1039, QBD (Admin) . *Digested,* 14/**1714**

R. (on the application of T) v Chief Constable of Greater Manchester; *sub nom* R. (on the application of B) v Secretary of State for the Home Department; *joined cases* R. (on the application of T) v Secretary of State for the Home Department; R. (on the application of AW) v Secretary of State for the Home Department; R. (on the application of JB) v Secretary of State for the Home Department [2014] UKSC 35; [2014] 3 W.L.R. 96; [2014] 4 All E.R. 159; [2014] 2 Cr. App. R. 24; Times, June 23, 2014, SC; reversing in part [2013] EWCA Civ 25; [2013] 1 W.L.R. 2515; [2013] 2 All E.R. 813; [2013] 1 Cr. App. R. 27; [2013] H.R.L.R. 14, CA (Civ Div); reversing [2012] EWHC 147 (Admin); [2012] 2 Cr. App. R. 3; [2012] Crim. L.R. 883; [2012] A.C.D. 54, QBD (Admin) ..................... *Digested,* 14/**1637**

R. (on the application of T) v Legal Aid Agency (formerly Legal Services Commission) [2013] EWHC 960 (Admin); [2013] 2 F.L.R. 1315; [2013] Fam. Law 805, QBD (Admin) ........................................................................................................ *Digested,* 14/**2041**

R. (on the application of T) v Secretary of State for the Home Department see R. (on the application of T) v Chief Constable of Greater Manchester

R. (on the application of T) v Sheffield City Council [2013] EWHC 2953 (QB); (2013) 16 C.C.L. Rep. 580, QBD (Admin) ..................................................................... *Digested,* 14/**2106**

R. (on the application of Tabbakh) v Staffordshire and West Midlands Probation Trust [2014] EWCA Civ 827; [2014] 1 W.L.R. 4620, CA (Civ Div); affirming [2013] EWHC 2492 (Admin); [2014] 1 W.L.R. 1022; [2014] A.C.D. 41, QBD (Admin) ... *Digested,* 14/**2237**

R. (on the application of Tapecrown Ltd) v First Secretary of State see Tapecrown Ltd v First Secretary of State

R. (on the application of Tatham Homes Ltd) v First Secretary of State [2005] EWHC 3538 (Admin); [2008] J.P.L. 185, QBD (Admin) ................................................ *Digested,* 08/**2936**: *Considered* 14/2411

R. (on the application of Taylor (t/a David Taylor & Sons)) v Secretary of State for the Environment, Transport and the Regions see Taylor & Sons (Farms) v Secretary of State for the Environment, Transport and the Regions

R. (on the application of Tchenguiz) v Director of Serious Fraud Office see R. (on the application of Rawlinson and Hunter Trustees) v Central Criminal Court

R. (on the application of TD) v Commissioner of Police of the Metropolis [2013] EWHC 2231 (Admin); [2014] A.C.D. 7, QBD (Admin)

R. (on the application of Tekle) v Secretary of State for the Home Department; *sub nom* Tekle v Secretary of State for the Home Department [2008] EWHC 3064 (Admin); [2009] 2 All E.R. 193, QBD (Admin)
*Affirmed* 09/2093: *Considered* 13/1581: *Distinguished* 14/1653: *Doubted* 11/1717

R. (on the application of Teleos Plc) v Customs and Excise Commissioners (C-409/04) [2008] Q.B. 600; [2008] 2 W.L.R. 574; [2008] S.T.C. 706; [2007] E.C.R. I-7797; [2008] 1 C.M.L.R. 6; [2008] C.E.C. 274; [2008] B.T.C. 5585; [2008] B.V.C. 705; [2007] S.T.I. 2216; Times, October 5, 2007, ECJ (3rd Chamber) .... *Digested,* 08/**3990**: *Applied* 08/3991, 09/4045, 09/4064, 09/4132: *Considered* 08/4065, 09/4077, 12/3393, 12/3404: *Followed* 14/3105

R. (on the application of Tesema) v Secretary of State for the Home Department see R. (on the application of Limbuela) v Secretary of State for the Home Department

R. (on the application of Thakeham Village Action Ltd) v Horsham DC [2014] EWHC 67 (Admin); [2014] Env. L.R. 21; [2014] J.P.L. 772, QBD (Admin) .................... *Digested,* 14/**2431**

R. (on the application of Thames Water Utilities Ltd) v Bromley Magistrates' Court; *sub nom* Thames Water Utilities Ltd v Bromley Magistrates' Court [2013] EWHC 472 (Admin); [2013] 1 W.L.R. 3641; [2013] Env. L.R. 25; [2014] L.L.R. 150; [2013] A.C.D. 69; [2013] 13 E.G. 75 (C.S.), QBD (Admin) .............................. *Digested,* 13/**1156**

R. (on the application of Thangarasa) v Secretary of State for the Home Department see R. (on the application of Yogathas) v Secretary of State for the Home Department

R. (on the application of Thapa) v Secretary of State for the Home Department [2014] EWHC 659 (Admin); [2014] 1 W.L.R. 4138, QBD (Admin)

R. (on the application of the Chief Constable of West Yorkshire) v Independent Police Complaints Commission [2014] EWCA Civ 1367, CA (Civ Div); affirming [2013] EWHC 2698 (Admin); [2014] P.T.S.R. 242, QBD (Admin) .............................. *Digested,* 14/**2447**

R. (on the application of the Company of Proprietors of Whitchurch Bridge) v HM Treasury [2012] EWHC 3579 (Admin); [2013] B.V.C. 14; [2013] A.C.D. 40, QBD (Admin) .............................. *Digested,* 13/**3239**: *Considered* 14/2089

R. (on the application of Thompson) v Oxford City Council [2014] EWCA Civ 94; [2014] 1 W.L.R. 1811; [2014] L.L.R. 605, CA (Civ Div); affirming [2013] EWHC 1819 (Admin); [2013] 3 E.G.L.R. 75; [2014] L.L.R. 165, QBD (Admin) ............ *Digested,* 14/**2066**

R. (on the application of Thompson) v Secretary of State for the Home Department see R. (on the application of F) v Secretary of State for the Home Department

R. (on the application of Tigere) v Secretary of State for Business, Innovation and Skills [2014] EWCA Civ 1216; [2014] H.R.L.R. 26, CA (Civ Div); reversing [2014] EWHC 2452 (Admin); [2014] H.R.L.R. 22, QBD (Admin)

R. (on the application of Tilki) v Secretary of State for the Home Department see R. (on the application of Baiai) v Secretary of State for the Home Department

R. (on the application of Tinizaray) v Secretary of State for the Home Department [2011] EWHC 1850 (Admin), QBD (Admin) *Considered* 14/1668

R. (on the application of Tozlukaya) v Secretary of State for the Home Department; *sub nom* Tozlukaya v Secretary of State for the Home Department [2006] EWCA Civ 379; [2006] Imm. A.R. 417; [2006] I.N.L.R. 354, CA (Civ Div); affirming [2005] EWHC 2863 (Admin), QBD (Admin) .............................. *Digested,* 06/**2246**: *Applied* 12/1699: *Considered* 08/2011, 09/2142, 09/2147, 14/1648

R. (on the application of Tracey) v Cambridge University Hospitals NHS Foundation Trust [2014] EWCA Civ 822; [2014] 3 W.L.R. 1054; [2014] Med. L.R. 273; (2014) 138 B.M.L.R. 1, CA (Civ Div) .............................. *Digested,* 14/**1516**

R. (on the application of Trafford) v Blackpool BC [2014] EWHC 85 (Admin); [2014] 2 All E.R. 947; [2014] P.T.S.R. 989; [2014] B.L.G.R. 180; [2014] 1 P. & C.R. DG19, QBD (Admin) .............................. *Digested,* 14/**1975**

R. (on the application of Trail Riders' Fellowship) v Dorset CC [2013] EWCA Civ 553; [2014] 3 All E.R. 429; [2013] P.T.S.R. 987, CA (Civ Div); reversing [2012] EWHC 2634 (Admin); [2013] 1 All E.R. 209; [2013] P.T.S.R. 302, QBD (Admin) *Digested,* 13/**2487**

R. (on the application of Trinity Mirror Plc) v Croydon Crown Court; *sub nom* Trinity Mirror Plc, Re [2008] EWCA Crim 50; [2008] Q.B. 770; [2008] 3 W.L.R. 51; [2008] 2 All E.R. 1159; [2008] 2 Cr. App. R. 1; [2009] E.M.L.R. 3; [2008] Crim. L.R. 554; Times, February 13, 2008, CA (Crim Div) .............................. *Digested,* 08/**14**: *Applied* 14/801: *Followed* 08/855, 13/757

R. (on the application of Trzcinska) v Secretary of State for the Home Department see R. (on the application of Baiai) v Secretary of State for the Home Department

R. (on the application of TUI Travel Plc) v Civil Aviation Authority (C-629/10) see Nelson v Deutsche Lufthansa AG (C-581/10)

R. (on the application of Tunbridge) v Secretary of State for Justice see R. (on the application of Ali) v Secretary of State for Justice

R. (on the application of TWS) v Manchester City Council [2013] EWHC 55 (Admin); [2013] J.P.L. 972, QBD (Admin) .............................. *Digested,* 13/**2334**: *Applied* 14/2434

R. (on the application of U) v Commissioner of Police of the Metropolis see R. (on the application of R) v Durham Constabulary

R. (on the application of U) v Westminster Magistrates' Court see R. (on the application of B) v Westminster Magistrates' Court

R. (on the application of Uddin) v Leeds Crown Court [2013] EWHC 2752 (Admin); [2014] 1 W.L.R. 1742; [2014] 1 Cr. App. R. 13; [2014] Crim. L.R. 305; [2014] A.C.D. 32, QBD (Admin) ........ *Digested,* 14/**719**

R. (on the application of UK Uncut Legal Action Ltd) v Revenue and Customs Commissioners; *sub nom* UK Uncut Legal Action Ltd v Revenue and Customs Commissioners [2013] EWHC 1283 (Admin); [2013] S.T.C. 2357; 81 T.C. 890; [2013] B.T.C. 467; [2013] S.T.I. 1849, QBD (Admin) ........ *Digested,* 13/**3115**

R. (on the application of Ullah (Ahsan)) v Secretary of State for the Home Department see R. (on the application of Ullah) v Special Adjudicator

R. (on the application of Ullah) v Special Adjudicator; *sub nom* Do v Secretary of State for the Home Department; R. (on the application of Ullah (Ahsan)) v Secretary of State for the Home Department; Ullah (Ahsan) v Special Adjudicator; *joined case* Do v Immigration Appeal Tribunal [2004] UKHL 26; [2004] 2 A.C. 323; [2004] 3 W.L.R. 23; [2004] 3 All E.R. 785; [2004] H.R.L.R. 33; [2004] U.K.H.R.R. 995; [2004] Imm. A.R. 419; [2004] I.N.L.R. 381; (2004) 101(28) L.S.G. 33; (2004) 154 N.L.J. 985; (2004) 148 S.J.L.B. 762; Times, June 18, 2004; Independent, June 22, 2004, HL; affirming [2002] EWCA Civ 1856; [2003] 1 W.L.R. 770; [2003] 3 All E.R. 1174; [2003] H.R.L.R. 12; [2003] U.K.H.R.R. 302; [2003] Imm. A.R. 304; [2003] I.N.L.R. 74; [2003] A.C.D. 30; (2003) 100(10) L.S.G. 28; (2003) 147 S.J.L.B. 28; Times, December 18, 2002; Independent, December 20, 2002, CA (Civ Div); affirming [2002] EWHC 1584 (Admin); [2002] Imm. A.R. 601; Times, September 5, 2002; Independent, October 14, 2002, QBD (Admin) ........ *Digested,* 04/**2009**:
*Applied* 04/2052, 05/2195, 05/401, 06/1598, 06/2223, 07/2309, 08/2038, 08/3056, 09/1473: *Considered* 04/2038, 04/839, 05/2140, 05/5431, 06/1605, 07/5169, 07/5432, 10/1265, 10/1266, 13/65: *Followed* 08/1940, 14/1725

R. (on the application of Unison) v Lord Chancellor [2014] EWHC 218 (Admin); [2014] I.C.R. 498; [2014] I.R.L.R. 266; [2014] Eq. L.R. 215, DC ........ *Digested,* 14/**23**

R. (on the application of United Company Rusal Plc) v London Metal Exchange [2014] EWCA Civ 1271, CA (Civ Div); reversing [2014] EWHC 890 (Admin); [2014] A.C.D. 87, QBD (Admin)

R. (on the application of United Road Transport Union) v Secretary of State for Transport [2013] EWCA Civ 962; [2014] R.T.R. 9; [2014] 1 C.M.L.R. 25; [2013] I.R.L.R. 890, CA (Civ Div); affirming [2012] EWHC 1909 (Admin); [2012] 3 C.M.L.R. 40; [2012] I.R.L.R. 941, QBD (Admin) ........ *Digested,* 13/**1083**

R. (on the application of United States) v Bow Street Magistrates' Court; *sub nom* United States v Tollman; Central Examining Court, Madrid v Sander; *joined case* R. (on the application of Spain) v Bow Street Magistrates' Court [2006] EWHC 2256 (Admin); [2007] 1 W.L.R. 1157; [2006] Extradition L.R. 216; (2006) 103(37) L.S.G. 33; (2006) 156 N.L.J. 1440; (2006) 150 S.J.L.B. 1189; Times, September 19, 2006, DC ........ *Digested,* 06/**1608**:
*Cited* 07/1665: *Considered* 14/1228: *Distinguished* 09/1475

R. (on the application of Uplands Junior School Governing Body) v Leicester City Council [2013] EWHC 4128 (Admin); [2014] E.L.R. 143; [2014] A.C.D. 57, QBD (Admin) ........ *Digested,* 14/**907**

R. (on the application of Van der Pijl) v Kingston Crown Court; *sub nom* Van der Pijl v Kingston Crown Court [2012] EWHC 3745 (Admin); [2013] 1 W.L.R. 2706; [2013] Lloyd's Rep. F.C. 287; [2013] A.C.D. 29, DC ........ *Digested,* 13/**763**:
*Applied* 14/2467

R. (on the application of Van der Pijl) v Secretary of State for the Home Department [2014] EWHC 281 (Admin); [2014] Lloyd's Rep. F.C. 362; [2014] A.C.D. 71, QBD (Admin) ........ *Digested,* 14/**656**

R. (on the application of VC) v Newcastle City Council; *joined case* R. (on the application of K) v Newcastle City Council [2011] EWHC 2673 (Admin); [2012] 2 All E.R. 227; [2012] P.T.S.R. 546; [2012] 1 F.L.R. 944; [2012] 1 F.C.R. 206; (2012) 15 C.C.L. Rep. 194; [2012] Fam. Law 280, QBD (Admin) ........ *Digested,* 12/**3155**:
*Applied* 14/2148

R. (on the application of Virgin Media Ltd) v Zinga; *sub nom* R. v Zinga (Munaf Ahmed) (Costs) [2014] EWCA Crim 1823; [2014] 5 Costs L.R. 879; (2014) 178 J.P. 449; [2014] Lloyd's Rep. F.C. 629, CA (Crim Div) ........ *Digested,* 14/**747**

R. (on the application of Virgin Media Ltd) v Zinga see R. v Zinga (Munaf Ahmed)

R. (on the application of W) v Lambeth LBC see R. (on the application of G) v Barnet LBC

R. (on the application of W) v Southampton Youth Court; *sub nom* R. (on the application of K) v Wirral Borough Magistrates Court [2002] EWHC 1640 (Admin); [2003] 1 Cr. App. R. (S.) 87; (2002) 166 J.P. 569; [2002] Crim. L.R. 750; (2002) 166 J.P.N. 709, DC ........ *Digested,* 03/**882**:
*Applied* 03/881, 04/894, 04/895, 12/2865: *Considered* 14/722: *Followed* 05/939

R. (on the application of W) v Thetford Youth Court; *joined case* R. (on the application of M) v Waltham Forest Youth Court [2002] EWHC 1252 (Admin); [2003] 1 Cr. App. R. (S.) 67; (2002) 166 J.P. 453; [2002] Crim. L.R. 681; (2002) 166 J.P.N. 573, DC ........ *Digested,* 03/**3756**:
*Applied* 03/881, 05/940: *Considered* 04/3476, 14/722

R. (on the application of W) v West London Youth Court see R. (on the application of M) v West London Youth Court

R. (on the application of Waghorn) v Staines Magistrates' Court [2013] EWHC 2109 (Admin); [2013] R.V.R. 298, QBD (Admin) ........ *Digested,* 14/**2094**

R. (on the application of Wainwright) v Richmond upon Thames LBC [2001] EWCA Civ 2062; (2002) 99(9) L.S.G. 29; Times, January 16, 2002, CA (Civ Div); reversing [2001] EWHC Admin 310; [2001] 18 E.G. 174 (C.S.), QBD (Admin) ... *Digested,* 02/**2260**:
*Considered* 13/813, 14/2802

R. (on the application of Walford) v Worcestershire CC; *sub nom* Walford v Worcestershire CC [2014] EWHC 234 (Admin); [2014] 3 All E.R. 128; [2014] P.T.S.R. 968; [2014] W.T.L.R. 701; [2014] A.C.D. 84, QBD (Admin) ........ *Digested,* 14/**2745**

R. (on the application of Walker) v Secretary of State for Justice see R. (on the application of Wells) v Parole Board for England and Wales

R. (on the application of Warren Comprehensive School) v Secretary of State for Education [2014] EWHC 2252 (Admin); [2014] E.L.R. 530, QBD (Admin)

R. (on the application of Warren) v Secretary of State for the Home Department [2003] EWHC 1177 (Admin), DC
*Applied* 14/1229

R. (on the application of WB) v Secretary of State for Justice [2014] EWHC 1696 (Admin); [2014] A.C.D. 125, QBD (Admin)

R. (on the application of Weddle) v Secretary of State for Justice [2013] EWHC 2323 (Admin); [2014] A.C.D. 18, QBD (Admin)

R. (on the application of Wells) v Parole Board for England and Wales; *sub nom* Wells v Parole Board for England and Wales; Walker v Secretary of State for the Home Department; Secretary of State for Justice v Walker; Secretary of State for Justice v James (formerly Walker); *joined cases* R. (on the application of Walker) v Secretary of State for Justice; R. (on the application of Lee) v Secretary of State for Justice; R. (on the application of James) v Secretary of State for Justice [2009] UKHL 22; [2010] 1 A.C. 553; [2009] 2 W.L.R. 1149; [2009] 4 All E.R. 255; [2009] H.R.L.R. 23; [2009] U.K.H.R.R. 809; 26 B.H.R.C. 696; [2009] Prison L.R. 371; Times, May 8, 2009, HL; affirming [2008] EWCA Civ 30; [2008] 1 W.L.R. 1977; [2008] 3 All E.R. 104; [2008] H.R.L.R. 22; [2008] U.K.H.R.R. 528; [2008] Prison L.R. 63; (2008) 158 N.L.J. 263; Times, February 6, 2008, CA (Civ Div); reversing in part [2007] EWHC 1835 (Admin); [2008] 1 All E.R. 138; [2008] Prison L.R. 49; [2007] A.C.D. 86; (2007) 157 N.L.J. 1275; Times, October 11, 2007, DC ........ *Digested,* 09/**3407**:
*Applied* 08/2680: *Complaint upheld* 13/1558: *Considered* 11/2289, 11/4588, 12/2935, 13/2112, 14/3702: *Distinguished* 10/2321: *Followed* 11/2913, 14/2234

R. (on the application of Wells) v Secretary of State for Transport, Local Government and the Regions (C-201/02); *sub nom* Wells v Secretary of State for Transport, Local Government and the Regions (C-201/02) [2004] E.C.R. I-723; [2004] 1 C.M.L.R. 31; [2005] All E.R. (EC) 323; [2004] Env. L.R. 27; [2004] N.P.C. 1, ECJ (5th Chamber) ........ *Digested,* 04/**1397**:
*Applied* 07/3269, 07/3271, 07/3272, 08/2729, 14/2372: *Considered* 06/3364, 10/1255, 10/2606, 14/2377

R. (on the application of Welsh Language Commissioner) v National Savings and Investments [2014] EWHC 488 (Admin); [2014] A.C.D. 95; [2014] P.T.S.R. D8, DC

R. (on the application of Welwyn Hatfield BC) v Secretary of State for Communities and Local Government see Welwyn Hatfield Council v Secretary of State for Communities and Local Government

R. (on the application of West London Vocational Training College) v Secretary of State for the Home Department see R. (on the application of New London College Ltd) v Secretary of State for the Home Department

R. (on the application of West) v Parole Board for England and Wales see R. (on the application of Smith) v Parole Board for England and Wales

R. (on the application of West) v Rhondda Cynon Taff CBC [2014] EWHC 2134 (Admin); [2014] E.L.R. 396, QBD (Admin) ........ *Digested,* 14/**915**

R. (on the application of Westminster City Council) v National Asylum Support Service; *sub nom* R. (on the application of Westminster City Council) v Secretary of State for the Home Department; Westminster City Council v National Asylum Support Services [2002] UKHL 38; [2002] 1 W.L.R. 2956; [2002] 4 All E.R. 654; [2002] H.L.R. 58; [2003] B.L.G.R. 23; (2002) 5 C.C.L. Rep. 511; (2002) 146 S.J.L.B. 241; Times, October 18, 2002, HL; affirming [2001] EWCA Civ 512; (2001) 33 H.L.R. 83; (2001) 4 C.C.L. Rep. 143, CA (Civ Div); affirming [2001] EWHC Admin 138, QBD (Admin) .................................... *Digested,* 02/**4288**: *Applied* 03/2237, 04/2020, 07/2312, 11/236, 11/3186: *Considered* 03/4069, 08/2090, 12/3171, 13/2951, 13/3670, 14/2887: *Distinguished* 10/3141: *Followed* 10/3186

R. (on the application of Westminster City Council) v Secretary of State for the Home Department see R. (on the application of Westminster City Council) v National Asylum Support Service

R. (on the application of Whapples) v Birmingham CrossCity Clinical Commissioning Group [2014] EWHC 2647 (Admin); [2014] P.T.S.R. 1413; (2014) 17 C.C.L. Rep. 308; (2014) 140 B.M.L.R. 152, QBD (Admin)

R. (on the application of Whistl UK Ltd (formerly TNT Post UK Ltd)) v Revenue and Customs Commissioners [2014] EWHC 4118 (Admin); [2014] S.T.I. 3706, QBD (Admin)

R. (on the application of Whistl UK Ltd (formerly TNT Post UK Ltd)) v Revenue and Customs Commissioners [2014] EWHC 3480 (Admin); [2014] S.T.I. 3175, QBD (Admin)

R. (on the application of Whiston) v Secretary of State for Justice [2014] UKSC 39; [2014] 3 W.L.R. 436; [2014] 4 All E.R. 251; [2014] H.R.L.R. 19; Times, July 11, 2014, SC; affirming [2012] EWCA Civ 1374; [2014] Q.B. 306; [2013] 2 W.L.R. 1080, CA (Civ Div) .................................... *Digested,* 14/**2233**

R. (on the application of Wilcock) v Lancaster City Council [2013] EWCA Civ 1607; [2014] L.L.R. 388, CA (Civ Div)

R. (on the application of Williamson) v Secretary of State for Education and Employment; *sub nom* Williamson v Secretary of State for Education and Employment [2005] UKHL 15; [2005] 2 A.C. 246; [2005] 2 W.L.R. 590; [2005] 2 All E.R. 1; [2005] 2 F.L.R. 374; [2005] 1 F.C.R. 498; [2005] H.R.L.R. 14; [2005] U.K.H.R.R. 339; 19 B.H.R.C. 99; [2005] E.L.R. 291; [2005] Fam. Law 456; (2005) 102(16) L.S.G. 27; (2005) 155 N.L.J. 324; (2005) 149 S.J.L.B. 266; Times, February 25, 2005; Independent, March 1, 2005, HL; affirming [2002] EWCA Civ 1926; [2003] Q.B. 1300; [2003] 3 W.L.R. 482; [2003] 1 All E.R. 385; [2003] 1 F.L.R. 726; [2003] 1 F.C.R. 1; [2003] H.R.L.R. 10; [2003] U.K.H.R.R. 800; [2003] E.L.R. 176; [2003] Fam. Law 227; (2003) 100(9) L.S.G. 27; Times, December 18, 2002; Independent, December 19, 2002, CA (Civ Div); affirming [2001] EWHC Admin 960; [2002] 1 F.L.R. 493; [2002] H.R.L.R. 14; [2002] E.L.R. 214; [2002] A.C.D. 32; [2002] Fam. Law 257; Times, December 12, 2001, QBD (Admin) .................................... *Digested,* 05/**1019**: *Applied* 04/4349, 08/1037, 09/1234, 09/1955, 10/1025, 12/2335, 14/1112: *Considered* 03/1114, 04/1925, 06/1145, 07/1400, 07/2194, 08/4867, 10/1114, 11/1425

R. (on the application of Wilson) v Office of the Independent Adjudicator for Higher Education [2014] EWHC 558 (Admin); [2014] E.L.R. 273, QBD (Admin)

R. (on the application of Wilson) v Secretary of State for Work and Pensions see R. (on the application of Reilly) v Secretary of State for Work and Pensions

R. (on the application of Wiltshire Council) v Hertfordshire CC [2014] EWCA Civ 712; [2014] P.T.S.R. 1066; [2014] H.L.R. 41; (2014) 17 C.C.L. Rep. 258; (2014) 139 B.M.L.R. 122, CA (Civ Div) .................................... *Digested,* 14/**2179**

R. (on the application of WL (Congo)) v Secretary of State for the Home Department see R. (on the application of Lumba) v Secretary of State for the Home Department

R. (on the application of Wood) v Commissioner of Police of the Metropolis; *sub nom* Wood v Commissioner of Police of the Metropolis [2009] EWCA Civ 414; [2010] 1 W.L.R. 123; [2009] 4 All E.R. 951; [2010] E.M.L.R. 1; [2009] H.R.L.R. 25; [2009] U.K.H.R.R. 1254; [2009] Po. L.R. 203; [2009] A.C.D. 75; (2009) 106(22) L.S.G. 24; (2009) 153(21) S.J.L.B. 30; Times, June 1, 2009, CA (Civ Div); reversing [2008] EWHC 1105 (Admin); [2008] H.R.L.R. 34; [2008] Po. L.R. 93; [2009] Crim. L.R. 376; [2008] A.C.D. 74; Times, June 13, 2008, QBD (Admin) .................................... *Digested,* 09/**2062**: *Applied* 10/1729, 12/1656, 12/782, 14/2237: *Considered* 12/2661

R. (on the application of Wychavon DC) v Secretary of State for Communities and Local Government see Wychavon DC v Secretary of State for Communities and Local Government

R. (on the application of X) v Tower Hamlets LBC [2013] EWCA Civ 904; [2013] 4 All E.R. 237; [2014] 1 F.L.R. 1076; [2013] 3 F.C.R. 192; [2013] B.L.G.R. 721; [2013] Fam. Law 1384, CA (Civ Div); affirming [2013] EWHC 480 (Admin); [2013] 3 All E.R. 157; [2013] 2 F.L.R. 199; [2013] 2 F.C.R. 225; (2013) 16 C.C.L. Rep. 227; [2013] Fam. Law 674, QBD (Admin) ........................................ *Digested,* 13/**2023**

R. (on the application of Y) v Secretary of State for the Home Department [2012] EWHC 1075 (Admin), QBD (Admin)
*Not followed* 14/1655

R. (on the application of Yogathas) v Secretary of State for the Home Department; *joined case* R. (on the application of Thangarasa) v Secretary of State for the Home Department [2002] UKHL 36; [2003] 1 A.C. 920; [2002] 3 W.L.R. 1276; [2002] 4 All E.R. 800; 14 B.H.R.C. 185; [2003] Imm. A.R. 227; [2002] I.N.L.R. 620; (2002) 146 S.J.L.B. 240; Times, October 18, 2002, HL; affirming [2001] EWCA Civ 1611; Times, November 15, 2001, CA (Civ Div); affirming [2001] EWHC Admin 377; Times, July 25, 2001, QBD (Admin) .................................... *Digested,* 02/**2595**:
*Applied* 03/2225, 06/2229, 11/1712, 12/1699: *Considered* 07/2306:
*Followed* 04/2049, 14/1643

R. (on the application of Youssef) v HM Treasury see A v HM Treasury

R. (on the application of Youssef) v Secretary of State for Foreign and Commonwealth Affairs; *sub nom* Youssef v Secretary of State for Foreign and Commonwealth Affairs [2013] EWCA Civ 1302; [2014] Q.B. 728; [2014] 2 W.L.R. 1082, CA (Civ Div); affirming [2012] EWHC 2091 (Admin); [2013] Q.B. 906; [2013] 2 W.L.R. 904; [2012] Lloyd's Rep. F.C. 702; [2012] A.C.D. 110, QBD (Admin) ................ *Digested,* 14/**55**

R. (on the application of YT) v First-tier Tribunal (Social Entitlement Chamber) [2013] UKUT 201 (AAC), UT (AAC)
*Applied* 14/944

R. (on the application of Z) v Secretary of State for the Home Department see R. (on the application of FI) v Secretary of State for the Home Department

R. (on the application of ZA (Nigeria)) v Secretary of State for the Home Department; *sub nom* R. (on the application of SM (Congo)) v Secretary of State for the Home Department [2010] EWCA Civ 926; [2011] Q.B. 722; [2011] 2 W.L.R. 16; [2010] Imm. A.R. 776; [2011] I.N.L.R. 78, CA (Civ Div); affirming [2010] EWHC 718 (Admin), DC
*Applied* 13/1599: *Considered* 14/1679

R. (on the application of Zacchaeus 2000 Trust) v Secretary of State for Work and Pensions [2013] EWCA Civ 1202; [2013] P.T.S.R. 1427, CA (Civ Div); affirming [2013] EWHC 233 (Admin); [2013] P.T.S.R. 785; [2013] Eq. L.R. 609, QBD (Admin) ........................................................................................................ *Digested,* 14/**2761**

R. (on the application of ZH) v Newham LBC see R. (on the application of N) v Lewisham LBC

R. (on the application of ZYN) v Walsall MBC see R. (on the application of N) v Walsall MBC

Raayan Al Iraq Co Ltd v Trans Victory Marine Inc [2013] EWHC 2696 (Comm); [2013] 6 Costs L.R. 911, QBD (Comm) ........................................................................ *Digested,* 14/**394**:
*Considered* 14/393: *Disapproved* 14/445

Racal Group Services Ltd v Ashmore [1995] S.T.C. 1151; 68 T.C. 86, CA (Civ Div); affirming [1994] S.T.C. 416, Ch D .................................................................. *Digested,* 96/**5784**:
*Applied* 04/2530, 08/3616, 11/3502: *Distinguished* 98/3659: *Followed* 14/2831, 14/3029

Rackind v Gross see Gross v Rackind

Radarbeam Ltd v Revenue and Customs Commissioners see Universal Enterprises (EU) Ltd v Revenue and Customs Commissioners

Radmacher v Granatino; *sub nom* G v R (Pre-Nuptial Contract) [2010] UKSC 42; [2011] 1 A.C. 534; [2010] 3 W.L.R. 1367; [2011] 1 All E.R. 373; [2010] 2 F.L.R. 1900; [2010] 3 F.C.R. 583; [2010] Fam. Law 1263; (2010) 107(42) L.S.G. 18; (2010) 160 N.L.J. 1491; (2010) 154(40) S.J.L.B. 37; Times, October 22, 2010, SC; affirming [2009] EWCA Civ 649; [2009] 2 F.L.R. 1181; [2009] 2 F.C.R. 645; [2009] Fam. Law 789; (2009) 159 N.L.J. 996; (2009) 153(27) S.J.L.B. 29; Times, July 13, 2009, CA (Civ Div); reversing [2008] EWHC 1532 (Fam); [2009] 1 F.L.R. 1478; [2009] 1 F.C.R. 35; [2008] Fam. Law 1082, Fam Div ................. *Digested,* 11/**1311**:
*Applied* 12/1437: *Considered* 12/1316: *Distinguished* 10/1295: *Followed* 12/1310, 12/1317, 14/1375

Ragn-Sells AS v Sillamae Linnavalitsus (C-292/12) [2014] P.T.S.R. 709, ECJ (5th Chamber)

Rahman v Secretary of State for the Home Department [2014] EWCA Civ 11; [2014] 1 W.L.R. 3574, CA (Civ Div) ........................................................................................ *Digested,* 14/**1699**

Rahman (t/a Khayam Restaurant) v Customs and Excise Commissioners (No.2) [2002] EWCA Civ 1881; [2003] S.T.C. 150; [2003] B.T.C. 5114; [2003] B.V.C. 170; [2003] S.T.I. 30, CA (Civ Div); affirming [2002] S.T.C. 73; [2002] B.T.C. 5103; [2002] B.V.C. 192; [2001] S.T.I. 1380, Ch D; affirming [2001] B.V.C. 2266, V&DTr ........ *Digested,* 03/**4601**:
*Applied* 04/3971, 10/3469, 14/3037: *Followed* 04/3972

Rai v Ahir [2014] EWHC 2299 (Ch); [2014] P.T.S.R. 1237, Ch D

Raiffeisen Zentralbank Osterreich AG v Royal Bank of Scotland Plc [2010] EWHC 1392 (Comm); [2011] 1 Lloyd's Rep. 123; [2011] Bus. L.R. D65, QBD (Comm) . *Digested,* 11/**566**:
*Applied* 13/2553: *Considered* 14/440

Rainone v Ministero dell'Interno (C-8/12) see Biasci v Ministero dell'Interno (C-660/11)

Rainstorm Pictures Inc v Lombard-Knight; *sub nom* Lombard-Knight v Rainstorm Pictures Inc [2014] EWCA Civ 356; [2014] Bus. L.R. 1196; [2014] 2 Lloyd's Rep. 74; [2014] 1 C.L.C. 406, CA (Civ Div) ........ *Digested,* 14/**122**

Rainy Sky SA v Kookmin Bank; *sub nom* Kookmin Bank v Rainy Sky SA [2011] UKSC 50; [2011] 1 W.L.R. 2900; [2012] 1 All E.R. 1137; [2012] 1 All E.R. (Comm) 1; [2012] Bus. L.R. 313; [2012] 1 Lloyd's Rep. 34; [2011] 2 C.L.C. 923; [2012] B.L.R. 132; 138 Con. L.R. 1; [2011] C.I.L.L. 3105; Times, November 18, 2011, SC; reversing [2010] EWCA Civ 582; [2011] 1 All E.R. (Comm) 18; [2011] 1 Lloyd's Rep. 233; [2010] 1 C.L.C. 829; 130 Con. L.R. 19, CA (Civ Div); reversing [2009] EWHC 2624 (Comm); [2010] 1 All E.R. (Comm) 823, QBD (Comm) ........ *Digested,* 12/**637**:
*Applied* 12/2057, 12/2372, 12/2389, 13/2154, 14/2714, 14/2739, 14/474: *Considered* 12/1053, 13/1893: *Followed* 13/2840, 14/117, 14/1775

Raissi v Commissioner of Police of the Metropolis; *sub nom* Commissioner of Police of the Metropolis v Raissi [2008] EWCA Civ 1237; [2009] Q.B. 564; [2009] 2 W.L.R. 1243; [2009] 3 All E.R. 14; [2009] P.T.S.R. 666; [2008] Po. L.R. 365; (2008) 105(45) L.S.G. 19; (2008) 152(45) S.J.L.B. 26, CA (Civ Div); affirming [2007] EWHC 2842 (QB); [2007] Po. L.R. 226, QBD ........ *Digested,* 09/**772**:
*Considered* 14/2463

Raithatha v Williamson [2012] EWHC 909 (Ch); [2012] 1 W.L.R. 3559; [2012] 3 All E.R. 1028; [2012] B.P.I.R. 621; Times, July 17, 2012, Ch D ........ *Digested,* 12/**1858**:
*Considered* 14/1797

Raju v Secretary of State for the Home Department see Secretary of State for the Home Department v Raju

Ralli Bros v Compania Naviera Sota y Aznar; *sub nom* Compania Naviera Sota y Aznar v Ralli Bros [1920] 2 K.B. 287; (1920) 2 Ll. L. Rep. 550, CA; affirming [1920] 1 K.B. 614; (1919) 1 Ll. L. Rep. 649, KBD (Comm Ct)
*Applied* 57/585, 59/2935, 11/509: *Considered* 08/162, 12/114, 14/238

Ralston v Scottish Ministers see Somerville v Scottish Ministers

Ramac Holdings Ltd v Kent CC [2014] UKUT 109 (LC); [2014] R.V.R. 207; [2014] J.P.L. 897, UT (Lands) ........ *Digested,* 14/**2357**

Ramdeen v Trinidad and Tobago [2014] UKPC 7; [2014] 3 W.L.R. 1523, PC (Trin)

Ramnarine v Ramnarine [2013] UKPC 27; [2014] 1 F.L.R. 594; [2014] Fam. Law 14, PC (Trin)

Ramsahai v Netherlands (52391/99) (2008) 46 E.H.R.R. 43; [2007] Inquest L.R. 103; [2007] Po. L.R. 46, ECHR (Grand Chamber)
*Applied* 08/1970: *Considered* 08/3000, 09/2754, 14/3599, 14/47

Randall v Plumb [1975] 1 W.L.R. 633; [1975] 1 All E.R. 734; [1975] S.T.C. 191; 50 T.C. 392; [1974] T.R. 371; (1975) 119 S.J. 188; Times, December 10, 1974, Ch D ........ *Digested,* 75/**1642**:
*Applied* 97/1070: *Considered* 14/2852: *Distinguished* 00/4922: *Explained* 99/4665

Rank Group Plc v Revenue and Customs Commissioners (C-259/10) see Revenue and Customs Commissioners v Rank Group Plc (C-259/10)

Ranken's Trustees v Ranken 1908 S.C. 3; (1907) 15 S.L.T. 385, IH (2 Div)
*Applied* 14/2982

Ransom (Inspector of Taxes) v Higgs; *sub nom* Dickinson v Kilmorie (Aldridge) Downes; *joined cases* Motley (Inspector of Taxes) v Higgs Settlement Trustees; Dickinson (Inspector of Taxes) v Downes; Grant (Inspector of Taxes) v Downes Settlement Trustees; Kilmorie (Aldridge) Ltd v Dickinson (Inspector of Taxes); Motley v Higgs Trustees; Restorick v Godber, Parry [1974] 1 W.L.R. 1594; [1974] 3 All E.R. 949; [1974] S.T.C. 539; [1974] T.R. 281; (1974) 118 S.J. 849, HL; affirming in part [1973] 1 W.L.R. 1180; [1973] 2 All E.R. 657; [1973] S.T.C. 330; [1973] T.R. 109; (1973) 117 S.J. 467, CA (Civ Div); affirming in part [1972] 2 All E.R. 817; [1971] T.R. 433, Ch D ........ *Digested,* 74/**1873**:
*Applied* 84/463, 91/2116: *Considered* 14/2849: *Followed* 14/2905

Rantsev v Cyprus (25965/04) (2010) 51 E.H.R.R. 1; 28 B.H.R.C. 313, ECHR
*Applied* 11/1684, 13/1543, 14/1728
Rapisarda v Colladon; *sub nom* 180 Irregular Divorces, Re [2014] EWFC 35; [2014] Fam. Law 1667, Fam Ct
Rapisarda v Colladon; *sub nom* 180 Irregular Divorces, Re [2014] EWFC 1406; [2014] E.M.L.R. 26; [2014] Fam. Law 1254, Fam Ct .................................................. *Digested,* 14/**1353**
Rappaz v Switzerland (7317510) (Unreported, March 26, 2013), ECHR
*Considered* 14/1680
Ratcliffe v Eden, et Al. 98 E.R. 1200; (1776) 2 Cowp. 485, KB
*Considered* 14/2448
Rathbone Brothers Plc v Novae Corporate Underwriting Ltd [2014] EWCA Civ 1464, CA (Civ Div); reversing in part [2013] EWHC 3457 (Comm); [2014] Lloyd's Rep. I.R. 203, QBD (Comm) .................................................. *Digested,* 14/**1855**
Ratification of the Treaty on the European Stability Mechanism, Re (2 BvR 1390/12) [2014] 2 C.M.L.R. 42, BverfG (Ger)
Rattan v UBS AG [2014] EWHC 665 (Comm); [2014] 3 Costs L.R. 488, QBD (Comm) *Digested,* 14/**355**
Ravat v Halliburton Manufacturing & Services Ltd; *sub nom* Halliburton Manufacturing & Services Ltd v Ravat [2012] UKSC 1; [2012] 2 All E.R. 905; 2012 S.C. (U.K.S.C.) 265; 2012 S.L.T. 406; [2012] I.C.R. 389; [2012] I.R.L.R. 315; (2012) 156(6) S.J.L.B. 31; 2012 G.W.D. 6-106; Times, February 15, 2012, SC; affirming [2010] CSIH 52; 2010 S.C. 698; 2011 S.L.T. 44; 2010 S.C.L.R. 718; [2010] I.R.L.R. 1053; 2010 G.W.D. 27-536, IH (Ex Div); reversing UKEATS/0012/08/MT, EAT (SC) .................................................. *Digested,* 12/**1176**:
*Applied* 13/1075, 13/945: *Considered* 14/1077: *Distinguished* 12/1181:
*Followed* 13/993
Ravichandran v Secretary of State for the Home Department see R. v Secretary of State for the Home Department Ex p. Jeyeanthan
Rawlinson v Director of the Serious Fraud Office see Tchenguiz v Director of the Serious Fraud Office
Rawlinson & Hunter Trustees SA v Director of the Serious Fraud Office see Tchenguiz v Director of the Serious Fraud Office
Rawlinson and Hunter Trustees SA v Akers see Tchenguiz v Director of the Serious Fraud Office (Non-Party Disclosure)
Rawlinson and Hunter Trustees SA v Director of the Serious Fraud Office see Tchenguiz v Director of the Serious Fraud Office
Rawstron v Freud see Freud (Deceased), Re
Ray v Sekhiri see Sekhri v Ray
Ray v Sekhri see Sekhri v Ray
Raymond v Honey [1983] 1 A.C. 1; [1982] 2 W.L.R. 465; [1982] 1 All E.R. 756; (1982) 75 Cr. App. R. 16, HL; affirming [1981] Q.B. 874; [1981] 3 W.L.R. 218; [1981] 2 All E.R. 1084; (1981) 73 Cr. App. R. 242; Times, April 8, 1981, QBD ................ *Digested,* 82/**2613**:
*Applied* 88/2976, 95/1033: *Considered* 82/2572, 84/2762, 86/2678, 01/4582, 03/2223, 14/13: *Distinguished* 84/2754, 91/5481, 92/3632, 05/2914:
*Followed* 94/3849, 99/4104: *Referred to* 92/6216
Raymond Saul & Co v Holden; *sub nom* Hemming's Estate, Re [2008] EWHC 2731 (Ch); [2009] Ch. 313; [2009] 2 W.L.R. 1257; [2009] B.P.I.R. 50; [2008] W.T.L.R. 1833; [2008] N.P.C. 122; Times, December 9, 2008, Ch D ................................ *Digested,* 09/**3714**:
*Considered* 14/570
Rayner v Lord Chancellor see Murphy v Rayner
Rayner & Keeler Ltd v Courts & Co see Carl Zeiss Stiftung v Rayner & Keeler Ltd
RB v Brighton and Hove City Council [2014] EWCA Civ 561; [2014] C.O.P.L.R. 629; Times, June 12, 2014, CA (Civ Div) .................................................. *Digested,* 14/**2185**
RB (Linguistic evidence: Sprakab: Somalia) see RB (Somalia) v Secretary of State for the Home Department
RB (Male Patient: Sterilisation), Re see A (Mental Patient: Sterilisation), Re
RB (Somalia) v Secretary of State for the Home Department; *sub nom* RB (Linguistic evidence: Sprakab: Somalia) [2012] EWCA Civ 277, CA (Civ Div); affirming [2010] UKUT 329 (IAC), UT (IAC)
*Considered* 14/1641
RBG Resources Plc, Re see Shierson v Rastogi
RBOS Shareholders Action Group Ltd v News Group Newspapers Ltd; *sub nom* RBS Shareholders Action Group Ltd v News Group Newspapers Ltd [2014] EWHC 130 (QB); [2014] E.M.L.R. 15, QBD .................................................. *Digested,* 14/**833**
RBS Shareholders Action Group Ltd v News Group Newspapers Ltd see RBOS Shareholders Action Group Ltd v News Group Newspapers Ltd
RC v CC [2013] EWHC 1424 (COP), CP
*Reversed in part* 14/2184
RC v CC see C v C (Court of Protection: Disclosure)

RC Brewery Ltd v Revenue and Customs Commissioners [2013] EWHC 1184 (Ch); [2013] B.C.C. 718, Ch D (Companies Ct) ........ *Digested,* 14/**1834**

RDF Media Group Plc v Clements [2007] EWHC 2892 (QB); [2008] I.R.L.R. 207, QBD ........ *Digested,* 08/**1120**: *Considered* 10/1034, 11/1068, 14/1022

Reading BC v Holt see Holt v Reading BC

Reagens SpA v European Commission (T-30/10) [2014] 5 C.M.L.R. 7, ECJ (3rd Chamber)

Reagens SpA v European Commission (T-181/10) [2014] 4 C.M.L.R. 28, GC (3rd Chamber)

Realkredit Danmark A/S v York Montague Ltd [1999] C.P.L.R. 272; Times, February 1, 1999; Independent, December 2, 1998, CA (Civ Div) ........ *Digested,* 99/**567**: *Applied* 14/449: *Followed* 14/1034

Realreed Ltd v Cussens see Cussens v Realreed Ltd

Reaney v University Hospital of North Staffordshire NHS Trust [2014] EWHC 3016 (QB); [2014] Med. L.R. 433, QBD

Recall Support Services Ltd v Secretary of State for Culture Media and Sport [2014] EWCA Civ 1370, CA (Civ Div); affirming [2013] EWHC 3091 (Ch); [2014] 2 C.M.L.R. 2, Ch D ........ *Digested,* 14/**2987**

Reckitt & Colman Products Ltd v Borden Inc (No.3); *sub nom* Jif Lemon case [1990] 1 W.L.R. 491; [1990] 1 All E.R. 873; [1990] R.P.C. 341; (1990) 134 S.J. 784; Times, February 9, 1990; Independent, March 13, 1990; Guardian, February 13, 1990, HL; affirming [1988] F.S.R. 601; (1988) 8 Tr. L.R. 97; Times, April 23, 1988; Independent, April 25, 1988; Guardian, April 26, 1988; Daily Telegraph, April 28, 1988, CA (Civ Div); affirming [1987] F.S.R. 505, Ch D ........ *Digested,* 90/**3465**: *Applied* 93/3802, 00/3590, 02/2785, 07/2546, 08/2387, 08/2405, 09/2452, 10/1991, 11/2010: *Considered* 95/4739, 96/5715, 07/2674, 09/2317, 10/1990, 14/1887: *Distinguished* 95/4735: *Followed* 96/6663, 11/1962, 11/2000, 13/1791, 13/1793, 14/1889, 14/1890: *Referred to* 99/3593

Red Discretionary Trustees v Inspector of Taxes see Howell v Trippier (Inspector of Taxes)

Redbridge LBC v Dhinsa; *sub nom* McKinnon v Redbridge LBC [2014] EWCA Civ 178; [2014] I.C.R. 834, CA (Civ Div); affirming [2013] I.C.R. D33, EAT ........ *Digested,* 14/**1135**

Redbridge LBC v G see G (An Adult), Re

Redcar and Cleveland BC v B see B (A Child) (Looked After Child), Re

Reddrock Ltd v Revenue and Customs Commissioners [2014] UKUT 61 (TCC); [2014] S.T.C. 1643; [2014] B.V.C. 508; [2014] S.T.I. 686, UT (Tax) ........ *Digested,* 14/**3059**

Reddrock Ltd v Revenue and Customs Commissioners [2012] UKFTT 46 (TC), FTT (Tax) *Affirmed* 14/3059

Redhill Aerodrome Ltd v Secretary of State for Communities and Local Government; *sub nom* Secretary of State for Communities and Local Government v Redhill Aerodrome Ltd [2014] EWCA Civ 1386, CA (Civ Div); reversing [2014] EWHC 2476 (Admin); (2014) 158(39) S.J.L.B. 37, QBD (Admin)

Redpath v Ministry of Defence see Smith v Ministry of Defence

Redrose Ltd v Thomas (Valuation Officer) [2014] UKUT 311 (LC); [2014] R.A. 538, UT (Lands)

Reed v Secretary of State for Communities and Local Government; *sub nom* R. (on the application of Reed) v Secretary of State for Communities and Local Government [2014] EWCA Civ 241; [2014] J.P.L. 725, CA (Civ Div) ........ *Digested,* 14/**2438**

Reed v Secretary of State for Communities and Local Government [2013] EWHC 787 (Admin), QBD (Admin) *Reversed* 14/2438

Reed Employment Ltd v Revenue and Customs Commissioners [2014] EWCA Civ 32; [2014] S.T.C. 1026; [2014] B.V.C. 6; [2014] S.T.I. 868, CA (Civ Div); affirming [2013] UKUT 109 (TCC); [2013] S.T.C. 1286; [2013] B.V.C. 1593, UT (Tax); affirming [2011] UKFTT 200 (TC); [2011] S.F.T.D. 720; [2011] S.T.I. 1500, FTT (Tax) ........ *Digested,* 14/**3074**: *Considered* 14/3076

Reed Employment Plc v Revenue and Customs Commissioners [2014] UKUT 160 (TCC); [2014] S.T.C. 1982; [2014] B.T.C. 511; [2014] S.T.I. 1769, UT (Tax); affirming [2012] UKFTT 28 (TC); [2012] S.F.T.D. 394; [2012] S.T.I. 550, FTT (Tax) ........ *Digested,* 14/**2912**

Reed Executive Plc v Reed Business Information Ltd [2004] EWCA Civ 159; [2004] E.T.M.R. 56; [2004] Info. T.L.R. 55; [2004] R.P.C. 40; [2004] Masons C.L.R. 29; (2004) 27(6) I.P.D. 27058; (2004) 148 S.J.L.B. 298; Times, March 9, 2004, CA (Civ Div); reversing [2002] EWHC 1015 (Ch); [2003] Info. T.L.R. 7; [2003] R.P.C. 12; [2002] Masons C.L.R. 40; (2002) 99(29) L.S.G. 33; (2002) 146 S.J.L.B. 151; [2003] E.T.M.R. CN7; Times, June 13, 2002, Ch D ........ *Digested,* 04/**2402**: *Applied* 11/1936: *Considered* 04/2394, 08/2397, 12/1969, 14/1926

REEF Trade Mark; *sub nom* South Cone Inc v Bessant (t/a REEF); Bessant v South Cone Inc [2002] EWCA Civ 763; [2003] R.P.C. 5; Times, May 31, 2002, CA (Civ Div); reversing [2002] R.P.C. 19; (2001) 24(11) I.P.D. 24072; (2001) 98(38) L.S.G. 39; [2001] E.T.M.R. CN19; Times, October 9, 2001, Ch D .......... *Digested,* 02/**2897**: *Applied* 02/2859, 05/2568, 07/2684, 12/1981: *Considered* 14/1938: *Followed* 02/2861, 08/2395

Rees v Gateley Wareing (A Firm) [2014] EWCA Civ 1351; [2014] 6 Costs L.O. 953, CA (Civ Div); reversing [2013] EWHC 3708 (Ch); [2014] 2 Costs L.O. 210; [2013] 50 E.G. 103 (C.S.), Ch D ........ *Digested,* 14/**2032**

Rees v John see John v Rees

Rees Will Trusts, Re; *sub nom* Williams v Hopkins [1950] Ch. 204; [1949] 2 All E.R. 1003; 66 T.L.R. (Pt. 1) 23, CA; affirming [1949] Ch. 541; [1949] 1 All E.R. 609, Ch D ........ *Digested,* 47-51/**9766**: *Distinguished* 54/3483, 67/3571: *Followed* 67/4103, 14/2834

Reeves v Capper 132 E.R. 1057; (1838) 5 Bing. N.C. 136, CCP *Considered* 14/273

Reeves v Thrings & Long [1996] P.N.L.R. 265; [1993] E.G. 196 (C.S.); [1993] N.P.C. 159, CA (Civ Div) ........ *Digested,* 96/**4501**: *Considered* 00/1483: *Followed* 98/4018, 14/2214

Reeves (Valuation Officer) v Tunnel Tech Ltd see Tunnel Tech Ltd v Reeves (Valuation Officer)

Refah Partisi (Welfare Party) v Turkey (41340/98) (No.2) (2003) 37 E.H.R.R. 1; 14 B.H.R.C. 1, ECHR (Grand Chamber) ........ *Digested,* 03/**2098**: *Considered* 14/769

Regeneron Pharmaceuticals Inc v Genentech Inc; *joined case* Bayer Pharma AG v Genentech Inc [2013] EWCA Civ 93; [2013] R.P.C. 28, CA (Civ Div); affirming [2012] EWHC 657 (Pat); (2012) 109(25) L.S.G. 19, Ch D (Patents Ct) ........ *Digested,* 13/**1807**: *Applied* 14/1900

Regent International Hotels (UK) v Pageguide Times, May 13, 1985, CA (Civ Div) ...... *Digested,* 85/**404**: *Applied* 05/422: *Considered* 14/409

Regent Lion Properties Ltd v Westminster City Council [1990] 39 E.G. 57; [1990] R.A. 121; [1991] J.P.L. 569; [1990] C.O.D. 472, CA (Civ Div); affirming (1990) 154 J.P. 49; [1990] 04 E.G. 131; [1989] C.O.D. 551; (1989) 153 J.P.N. 757; (1990) 154 L.G. Rev. 36; [1989] E.G. 69 (C.S.); Independent, May 3, 1989, DC .......... *Digested,* 90/**3917**: *Applied* 14/2480

Regent Wealth Ltd v Wiggins see Wiggins v Regent Wealth Ltd

Regional Collection Services Ltd v Heald; *sub nom* H (A Debtor) (No.38-SD of 1997), Re; H (In Bankruptcy), Re [2000] B.P.I.R. 661; Times, May 10, 2000, CA (Civ Div) ........ *Digested,* 00/**3484**: *Followed* 14/1778

Registrar of Companies v Swarbrick [2014] EWHC 1466 (Ch); [2014] Bus. L.R. 625; [2014] 2 B.C.L.C. 695, Ch D ........ *Digested,* 14/**1758**

Rehill v Rider Holdings Ltd [2014] EWCA Civ 42; [2014] 3 Costs L.R. 405, CA (Civ Div) ........ *Digested,* 14/**369**

Rehman v Secretary of State for the Home Department see Secretary of State for the Home Department v Rehman

Reichhold Norway ASA v Goldman Sachs International [2000] 1 W.L.R. 173; [2000] 2 All E.R. 679; [1999] 2 All E.R. (Comm) 174; [1999] 2 Lloyd's Rep. 567; [2000] C.L.C. 11; Times, July 20, 1999, CA (Civ Div); affirming [1999] 1 All E.R. (Comm.) 40; [1999] C.L.C. 486, QBD (Comm) ........ *Digested,* 99/**546**: *Applied* 00/753, 06/514, 06/515, 08/424, 13/1748: *Considered* 06/329, 09/455: *Distinguished* 14/303: *Followed* 13/438

Reilly's Application for Judicial Review, Re; *sub nom* Osborn v Parole Board; Booth v Parole Board; *joined cases* R. (on the application of Osborn) v Parole Board; R. (on the application of Booth) v Parole Board [2013] UKSC 61; [2014] A.C. 1115; [2013] 3 W.L.R. 1020; [2014] 1 All E.R. 369; [2014] N.I. 154; [2014] H.R.L.R. 1; (2013) 157(39) S.J.L.B. 37, SC; reversing [2011] NICA 6; [2012] N.I. 38, CA (NI) ........ *Digested,* 13/**2115**: *Applied* 14/2162, 14/2444: *Considered* 14/2233

Reisen Passagebureau van Ginkel BV v Inspecteur der Omzetbelasting, Utrecht see Beheersmaatschappij Van Ginkel Waddinxveen BV v Inspecteur der Omzetbelasting (C-163/91)

Relational LLC v Hodges [2011] EWCA Civ 774; [2012] I.L.Pr. 4, CA (Civ Div) ............ *Digested,* 12/**392**: *Followed* 14/127

Relaxion Group Plc v Rhys-Harper see Rhys-Harper v Relaxion Group Plc

Relicpride Building Co Ltd v Cordara [2013] EWCA Civ 158; 147 Con. L.R. 92, CA (Civ Div) ............ *Digested,* 13/**596**: *Considered* 14/2278

Repayment of Illegal Taxes, Re (C-104/86) see Commission of the European Communities v Italy (C-104/86)

Rephael v Holon Assessment Officer 16 I.T.L. Rep. 1, District Ct (Tel Aviv)

Resolution Chemicals Ltd v H Lundbeck A/S [2013] EWCA Civ 924; [2014] R.P.C. 5, CA (Civ Div); affirming [2013] EWHC 739 (Pat), Ch D (Patents Ct) ............ *Digested,* 14/**1878**

Resolution Chemicals Ltd v H Lundbeck A/S [2013] EWCA Civ 1515; [2014] 1 W.L.R. 1943, CA (Civ Div); affirming [2013] EWHC 3160 (Pat), Ch D (Patents Ct) ........ *Digested,* 14/**42**

Resource Capital Fund III LP v Commissioner of Taxation; *sub nom* Commissioner of Taxation v Resource Capital Fund III LP [2014] FCAFC 37; 16 I.T.L. Rep. 876, Fed Ct (Aus) (Full Ct); reversing [2013] FCA 363; 15 I.T.L. Rep. 814, Fed Ct (Aus) (Sgl judge)

Restorick v Godber, Parry see Ransom (Inspector of Taxes) v Higgs

Restriction of Competition in Commercial Agency Agreement, Re (VII ZR 56/11) [2014] E.C.C. 18, BGH (Ger)

Resumption of proceedings for grant (J15/13) [2014] E.P.O.R. 44, EPO (Legal Bd App)

Revenue and Customs Commissioners v Airtours Holiday Transport Ltd see Airtours Holiday Transport Ltd (formerly My Travel Group) v Revenue and Customs Commissioners

Revenue and Customs Commissioners v Apollo Fuels Ltd see Apollo Fuels Ltd v Revenue and Customs Commissioners

Revenue and Customs Commissioners v Arkeley Ltd see Arkeley Ltd v Revenue and Customs Commissioners

Revenue and Customs Commissioners v Asda Stores Ltd see Asda Stores Ltd v Revenue and Customs Commissioners

Revenue and Customs Commissioners v Atlantic Electronics Ltd; *sub nom* Atlantic Electronics Ltd v Revenue and Customs Commissioners [2013] EWCA Civ 651; [2013] S.T.C. 1632; [2013] C.P. Rep. 42; [2013] B.V.C. 228; [2013] S.T.I. 2160, CA (Civ Div); affirming [2012] UKUT 423 (TCC); [2013] S.T.C. 856; [2013] B.V.C. 1525, UT (Tax) ............ *Digested,* 13/**3212**: *Distinguished* 14/3095

Revenue and Customs Commissioners v AXA UK Plc see AXA UK Plc v Revenue and Customs Commissioners

Revenue and Customs Commissioners v Bank of Ireland Britain Holdings Ltd [2008] EWCA Civ 58; [2008] S.T.C. 398; [2008] B.T.C. 126; [2008] S.T.I. 252, CA (Civ Div); affirming [2007] EWHC 941 (Ch); [2008] S.T.C. 253; [2007] B.T.C. 389; [2007] S.T.I. 1397, Ch D; affirming [2006] S.T.C. (S.C.D.) 477; [2006] S.T.I. 1793, Sp Comm ............ *Digested,* 08/**3687**: *Considered* 14/2883

Revenue and Customs Commissioners v Baxi Group Ltd (C-55/09) see Revenue and Customs Commissioners v Loyalty Management (UK) Ltd (C-53/09)

Revenue and Customs Commissioners v Ben Nevis (Holdings) Ltd; *sub nom* Ben Nevis (Holdings) Ltd v Revenue and Customs Commissioners [2013] EWCA Civ 578; [2013] S.T.C. 1579; [2013] B.T.C. 485; 15 I.T.L. Rep. 1003; [2014] W.T.L.R. 1; [2013] S.T.I. 1900, CA (Civ Div); affirming [2012] EWHC 1807 (Ch); [2012] S.T.C. 2157; [2012] B.T.C. 240; 15 I.T.L. Rep. 89; [2012] S.T.I. 2465, Ch D ............ *Digested,* 13/**3058**

Revenue and Customs Commissioners v Blue Sphere Global Ltd see Mobilx Ltd (In Administration) v Revenue and Customs Commissioners

Revenue and Customs Commissioners v Bosher [2013] UKUT 579 (TCC); [2014] S.T.C. 617; [2013] B.T.C. 2126; [2013] S.T.I. 3671, UT (Tax); no effect [2012] UKFTT 631 (TC); [2013] S.T.I. 267, FTT (Tax) ............ *Digested,* 14/**2864**

Revenue and Customs Commissioners v BPP Holdings Ltd see BPP University College of Professional Studies v Revenue and Customs Commissioners

Revenue and Customs Commissioners v Bridport and West Dorset Golf Club Ltd (C-495/12); *sub nom* Bridport and West Dorset Golf Club Ltd v Revenue and Customs Commissioners (C-495/12) [2014] S.T.C. 663; [2014] B.V.C. 1; [2014] S.T.I. 257, ECJ (5th Chamber)

Revenue and Customs Commissioners v British Film Institute [2014] UKUT 370 (TCC); [2014] B.V.C. 534, UT (Tax) .................... *Digested,* 14/**3043**

Revenue and Customs Commissioners v British Telecommunications Plc [2014] EWCA Civ 433; [2014] S.T.C. 1926; [2014] B.V.C. 24; [2014] S.T.I. 1760, CA (Civ Div) .................... *Digested,* 14/**3038**

Revenue and Customs Commissioners v Brockenhurst College [2014] UKUT 46 (TCC); [2014] S.T.C. 1332; [2014] B.V.C. 507; [2014] S.T.I. 687, UT (Tax) ....... *Digested,* 14/**3042**

Revenue and Customs Commissioners v Changtel Solutions UK Ltd (formerly Enta Technologies Ltd) see Enta Technologies Ltd, Re

Revenue and Customs Commissioners v Charlton [2012] UKFTT 770 (TCC); [2013] S.T.C. 866; [2013] B.T.C. 1634; [2013] S.T.I. 259, UT (Tax) .................... *Digested,* 13/**3006**: *Applied* 14/2891

Revenue and Customs Commissioners v Colaingrove Ltd see Colaingrove Ltd v Revenue and Customs Commissioners

Revenue and Customs Commissioners v Cotter; *sub nom* Cotter v Revenue and Customs Commissioners [2013] UKSC 69; [2013] 1 W.L.R. 3514; [2014] 1 All E.R. 1; [2013] S.T.C. 2480; [2013] B.T.C. 837; [2013] S.T.I. 3450, SC; reversing [2012] EWCA Civ 81; [2012] S.T.C. 745; [2012] B.T.C. 50; [2012] S.T.I. 352, CA (Civ Div); reversing [2011] EWHC 896 (Ch); [2011] S.T.C. 1646; [2011] B.T.C. 282; [2011] S.T.I. 1522, Ch D (Manchester) .................... *Digested,* 14/**2931**: *Applied* 13/3222: *Considered* 14/2860: *Followed* 14/2958

Revenue and Customs Commissioners v DCC Holdings (UK) Ltd see DCC Holdings (UK) Ltd v Revenue and Customs Commissioners

Revenue and Customs Commissioners v Dhanak [2014] UKUT 68 (TCC); [2014] S.T.C. 1525; [2014] B.T.C. 506; [2014] S.T.I. 745, UT (Tax) .................... *Digested,* 14/**2926**

Revenue and Customs Commissioners v Donaldson [2014] UKUT 536 (TCC); [2014] B.T.C. 531, UT (Tax)

Revenue and Customs Commissioners v DV3 RS Limited Partnership see DV3 RS Limited Partnership v Revenue and Customs Commissioners

Revenue and Customs Commissioners v Earlsferry Thistle Golf Club see Earlsferry Thistle Golf Club v Revenue and Customs Commissioners

Revenue and Customs Commissioners v Eclipse Film Partners No.35 LLP see Eclipse Film Partners No.35 LLP v Revenue and Customs Commissioners

Revenue and Customs Commissioners v Esporta Ltd see Esporta Ltd v Revenue and Customs Commissioners

Revenue and Customs Commissioners v Fairford Group Plc (In Liquidation) see Fairford Group Ltd Plc (In Liquidation) v Revenue and Customs Commissioners

Revenue and Customs Commissioners v Fairford Partnership Ltd (In Liquidation) see Fairford Group Ltd Plc (In Liquidation) v Revenue and Customs Commissioners

Revenue and Customs Commissioners v Finnamore (t/a Hanbidge Storage Services) see Finnamore (t/a Hanbidge Storage Services) v Revenue and Customs Commissioners

Revenue and Customs Commissioners v First Nationwide see First Nationwide v Revenue and Customs Commissioners

Revenue and Customs Commissioners v Forde & McHugh Ltd see Forde & McHugh Ltd v Revenue and Customs Commissioners

Revenue and Customs Commissioners v GB Housley Ltd see GB Housley Ltd v Revenue and Customs Commissioners

Revenue and Customs Commissioners v GMAC UK Plc; *sub nom* GMAC UK Plc v Revenue and Customs Commissioners; *joined case* British Telecommunications Plc v Revenue and Customs Commissioners [2012] UKUT 279 (TCC); [2012] S.T.C. 2349; [2012] B.V.C. 1804; [2012] S.T.I. 2558, UT (Tax) .................... *Digested,* 12/**3381**: *Reversed in part* 14/3038

Revenue and Customs Commissioners v GMAC UK Plc (C-589/12) [2014] S.T.C. 2603; [2014] R.T.R. 33; [2014] B.V.C. 42; [2014] S.T.I. 2791, ECJ (2nd Chamber)

Revenue and Customs Commissioners v Hamilton & Kinneil (Archerfield) Ltd see Hamilton & Kinneil (Archerfield) Ltd v Revenue and Customs Commissioners

Revenue and Customs Commissioners v Healy [2013] UKUT 337 (TCC); [2014] S.T.C. 384; [2013] B.T.C. 1958; [2013] S.T.I. 2861, UT (Tax) .................... *Digested,* 13/**3080**

Revenue and Customs Commissioners v Hok Ltd see Hok Ltd v Revenue and Customs Commissioners

Revenue and Customs Commissioners v Holland; *sub nom* Holland v Revenue and Customs Commissioners; Paycheck Services 3 Ltd, Re [2010] UKSC 51; [2010] 1 W.L.R. 2793; [2011] 1 All E.R. 430; [2011] Bus. L.R. 111; [2011] S.T.C. 269; [2011] B.C.C. 1; [2011] 1 B.C.L.C. 141; [2011] B.P.I.R. 96; [2010] S.T.I. 3074; Times, November 30, 2010, SC; affirming [2009] EWCA Civ 625; [2010] Bus. L.R. 259; [2009] S.T.C. 1639; [2010] B.C.C. 104; [2009] 2 B.C.L.C. 309; [2009] B.P.I.R. 983; [2009] S.T.I. 2026; Times, July 28, 2009, CA (Civ Div); reversing [2008] EWHC 2200 (Ch); [2009] Bus. L.R. 1; [2008] S.T.C. 3142; [2009] B.C.C. 37; [2008] 2 B.C.L.C. 613; [2008] S.T.I. 1642, Ch D (Companies Ct) ........ *Digested,* 11/**412**: *Followed* 11/417, 14/505

Revenue and Customs Commissioners v Honourable Society of Middle Temple see Honourable Society of Middle Temple v Revenue and Customs Commissioners

Revenue and Customs Commissioners v IA Associates Ltd [2013] EWHC 4382 (Ch); [2014] B.V.C. 545, Ch D

Revenue and Customs Commissioners v IDT Card Services Ireland Ltd see R. (on the application of IDT Card Services Ireland Ltd) v Customs and Excise Commissioners

Revenue and Customs Commissioners v IFX Investment Co Ltd; *sub nom* IFX Investment Co Ltd v Revenue and Customs Commissioners; 'Spotting the Ball' Partnership v Revenue and Customs Commissioners; Sportech Plc v Revenue and Customs Commissioners [2014] UKUT 398 (TCC); [2014] B.V.C. 535; [2014] S.T.I. 2976, UT (Tax) ........ *Digested,* 14/**3048**

Revenue and Customs Commissioners v Ingenious Games LLP [2014] UKUT 62 (TCC); [2014] S.T.C. 1416; [2014] B.T.C. 505, UT (Tax) ........ *Digested,* 14/**2889**

Revenue and Customs Commissioners v Jones [2014] I.C.R. D43, EAT

Revenue and Customs Commissioners v Lansdowne Partners LP [2011] EWCA Civ 1578; [2012] S.T.C. 544; 81 T.C. 318; [2012] B.T.C. 12; [2012] S.T.I. 36, CA (Civ Div); affirming [2010] EWHC 2582 (Ch); [2011] S.T.C. 372; [2011] B.T.C. 224; [2010] S.T.I. 2797, Ch D ........ *Digested,* 12/**3295**: *Applied* 13/3006: *Followed* 12/3269

Revenue and Customs Commissioners v Livewire Telecom Ltd see Livewire Telecom Ltd v Revenue and Customs Commissioners

Revenue and Customs Commissioners v Lloyds TSB Equipment Leasing (No.1) Ltd; *sub nom* Revenue and Customs Commissioners v Lloyds TSB Equipment Leasing (No.1) Ltd [2014] EWCA Civ 1062; [2014] S.T.C. 2770; [2014] B.T.C. 37; [2014] S.T.I. 2583, CA (Civ Div); reversing [2013] UKUT 368 (TCC); [2014] S.T.C. 191; [2013] B.T.C. 2016; [2013] S.T.I. 2985, UT (Tax); affirming [2012] UKFTT 47 (TC); [2012] S.F.T.D. 572; [2012] S.T.I. 1203, FTT (Tax) ........ *Digested,* 14/**2867**

Revenue and Customs Commissioners v Lloyds TSB Equipment Leasing (No.1) Ltd see Revenue and Customs Commissioners v Lloyds TSB Equipment Leasing (No.1) Ltd

Revenue and Customs Commissioners v Lok'nstore Group Plc see Lok'nstore Group Plc v Revenue and Customs Commissioners

Revenue and Customs Commissioners v Longridge on the Thames see Longridge on the Thames v Revenue and Customs Commissioners

Revenue and Customs Commissioners v Lord Howard of Henderskelfe's Executors see Lord Howard of Henderskelfe's Executors v Revenue and Customs Commissioners

Revenue and Customs Commissioners v Loyalty Management (UK) Ltd (C-53/09); *joined case* Revenue and Customs Commissioners v Baxi Group Ltd (C-55/09) [2010] S.T.C. 2651; [2011] B.V.C. 1; [2010] S.T.I. 2706, ECJ (2nd Chamber) .... *Digested,* 11/**3543**: *Applied* 12/3397, 14/3061

Revenue and Customs Commissioners v Maco Door & Window Hardware (UK) Ltd see Maco Door & Window Hardware (UK) Ltd v Revenue and Customs Commissioners

Revenue and Customs Commissioners v Marks & Spencer Plc see Marks & Spencer Plc v Revenue and Customs Commissioners

Revenue and Customs Commissioners v Martin see Martin v Revenue and Customs Commissioners

Revenue and Customs Commissioners v Mayes see Mayes v Revenue and Customs Commissioners

Revenue and Customs Commissioners v McCarthy and Stone (Developments) Ltd [2014] UKUT 196 (TCC); [2014] S.T.C. 973; [2014] B.V.C. 504; [2014] S.T.I. 626, UT (Tax) ........ *Digested,* 14/**9**: *Not followed* 14/2983

Revenue and Customs Commissioners v McLaren Racing Ltd see McLaren Racing Ltd v Revenue and Customs Commissioners
Revenue and Customs Commissioners v Morrison; *sub nom* Morrison v Revenue and Customs Commissioners [2014] CSIH 113, IH (1 Div); reversing [2013] UKUT 497 (TCC); [2014] S.T.C. 574; [2013] B.T.C. 2065, UT (Tax) ............................ *Digested,* 14/**2852**
Revenue and Customs Commissioners v Murray Group Holdings Ltd see Murray Group Holdings Ltd v Revenue and Customs Commissioners
Revenue and Customs Commissioners v National Exhibition Centre Ltd see National Exhibition Centre Ltd v Revenue and Customs Commissioners
Revenue and Customs Commissioners v Newey (t/a Ocean Finance) (C-653/11); *sub nom* Newey v Revenue and Customs Commissioners (C-653/11) [2013] S.T.C. 2432; [2013] B.V.C. 259; [2013] S.T.I. 2304, ECJ (3rd Chamber) ........................ *Digested,* 13/**3231**: *Applied* 14/3061, 14/3073
Revenue and Customs Commissioners v Noor see Noor v Revenue and Customs Commissioners
Revenue and Customs Commissioners v Northumbrian Water Ltd see Northumbrian Water Ltd v Revenue and Customs Commissioners
Revenue and Customs Commissioners v O'Rorke see O'Rorke v Revenue and Customs Commissioners
Revenue and Customs Commissioners v Our Communications Ltd see Our Communications Ltd v Revenue and Customs Commissioners
Revenue and Customs Commissioners v PA Holdings Ltd see PA Holdings Ltd v Revenue and Customs Commissioners
Revenue and Customs Commissioners v Patel [2014] UKUT 361 (TCC); [2014] B.V.C. 532, UT (Tax) ........................................................................................ *Digested,* 14/**3062**
Revenue and Customs Commissioners v Patel (Costs) [2014] UKUT 484 (TCC); [2014] B.V.C. 543, UT (Lands)
Revenue and Customs Commissioners v Pendragon Plc see Pendragon Plc v Revenue and Customs Commissioners
Revenue and Customs Commissioners v Pinevale Ltd see Pinevale Ltd v Revenue and Customs Commissioners
Revenue and Customs Commissioners v Procter & Gamble UK see Procter & Gamble UK v Revenue and Customs Commissioners
Revenue and Customs Commissioners v Rank Group Plc [2013] EWCA Civ 1289; [2014] S.T.C. 470; [2013] B.V.C. 526; [2014] L.L.R. 270; [2013] S.T.I. 3396, CA (Civ Div); reversing in part [2009] EWHC 1244 (Ch); [2009] S.T.C. 2304; [2009] B.V.C. 598; [2010] L.L.R. 249; [2009] S.T.I. 1884, Ch D ................................... *Digested,* 14/**3049**
Revenue and Customs Commissioners v Rank Group Plc (C-259/10); *sub nom* Rank Group Plc v Revenue and Customs Commissioners (C-259/10); *joined case* Revenue and Customs Commissioners v Rank Group Plc (C-260/10) [2012] S.T.C. 23; [2011] E.C.R. I-10947; [2012] C.E.C. 884; [2011] B.V.C. 389; [2011] S.T.I. 3045, ECJ (3rd Chamber) ........................................................................ *Digested,* 12/**3388**: *Applied* 13/3245, 14/3098
Revenue and Customs Commissioners v Rank Group Plc (C-260/10) see Revenue and Customs Commissioners v Rank Group Plc (C-259/10)
Revenue and Customs Commissioners v Roger Skinner Ltd see Roger Skinner Ltd v Revenue and Customs Commissioners
Revenue and Customs Commissioners v Secret Hotels2 Ltd (formerly Med Hotels Ltd) see Secret Hotels2 Ltd (formerly Med Hotels Ltd) v Revenue and Customs Commissioners
Revenue and Customs Commissioners v SED Essex Ltd; *sub nom* SED Essex Ltd, Re [2013] EWHC 1583 (Ch); [2014] B.C.C. 628; [2013] B.V.C. 314, Ch D ......... *Digested,* 13/**1708**
Revenue and Customs Commissioners v Shields see Shields v Revenue and Customs Commissioners
Revenue and Customs Commissioners v Southern Cross Employment Agency Ltd see Southern Cross Employment Agency Ltd v Revenue and Customs Commissioners
Revenue and Customs Commissioners v Stolkin see Stolkin v Revenue and Customs Commissioners
Revenue and Customs Commissioners v Sunico ApS (C-49/12) [2014] Q.B. 391; [2014] 2 W.L.R. 335; [2013] 2 All E.R. (Comm) 1117; [2014] S.T.C. 94; [2014] C.E.C. 56; [2013] I.L.Pr. 43; [2013] S.T.I. 3565; (2013) 157(36) S.J.L.B. 37, ECJ (3rd Chamber) ........................................................................................ *Digested,* 14/**443**
Revenue and Customs Commissioners v Thomson see Thomson v Revenue and Customs Commissioners
Revenue and Customs Commissioners v Tower MCashback LLP 1 see Tower MCashback LLP 1 v Revenue and Customs Commissioners

Revenue and Customs Commissioners v UBS AG see UBS AG v Revenue and Customs Commissioners

Revenue and Customs Commissioners v UK Storage Co (SW) Ltd see UK Storage Co (SW) Ltd v Revenue and Customs Commissioners

Revenue and Customs Commissioners v University of Huddersfield Higher Education Corp see University of Huddersfield Higher Education Corp v Revenue and Customs Commissioners

Revenue and Customs Commissioners v Vaccine Research LP see Vaccine Research LP v Revenue and Customs Commissioners

Revenue and Customs Commissioners v Volkswagen Financial Services (UK) Ltd see Volkswagen Financial Services (UK) Ltd v Revenue and Customs Commissioners

Revenue and Customs Commissioners v Waste Recycling Group Ltd see Waste Recycling Group Ltd v Revenue and Customs Commissioners

Revenue and Customs Commissioners v Weald Leasing Ltd (C-103/09) [2011] S.T.C. 596; [2011] C.E.C. 1039; [2011] B.V.C. 118; [2011] S.T.I. 264, ECJ (3rd Chamber) .......... *Digested,* 11/**3535**: *Distinguished* 14/3087: *Followed* 12/3394

Revenue and Customs Commissioners v Winnington Networks Ltd [2014] EWHC 1259 (Ch); [2014] B.C.C. 675, Ch D

Revenue and Customs Prosecutions Office v Hill [2005] EWCA Crim 3271; [2006] S.T.I. 161; Times, December 27, 2005, CA (Crim Div) .......... *Digested,* 06/**976**: *Considered* 14/744

Revenue and Customs Prosecutions Office v Iqbal; *sub nom* R. v Iqbal (Zaffar) [2010] EWCA Crim 376; [2010] 1 W.L.R. 1985; [2010] 2 Cr. App. R. (S.) 72; [2010] Crim. L.R. 511; Times, March 3, 2010, CA (Crim Div) .......... *Digested,* 10/**740**: *Distinguished* 14/742

Revenue and Customs Prosecutions Office v M see R. v M

Revenue and Customs Prosecutions Office v Pigott see Pigott, Re

Reyes v Al-Malki see Al-Malki v Reyes

Reyes v Migrationsverket (C-423/12) [2014] Q.B. 1140; [2014] 3 W.L.R. 1101; [2014] 2 C.M.L.R. 39; [2014] All E.R. (EC) 657; [2014] C.E.C. 1028; [2014] I.N.L.R. 792, ECJ (4th Chamber)

Reynolds v CLFIS (UK) Ltd [2014] I.C.R. 907; [2014] Eq. L.R. 356, EAT .......... *Digested,* 14/**1010**

Reynolds DIY Stores Ltd, Re; *sub nom* Atkinson v Reynolds [2012] EWHC 4370 (Ch); [2014] B.C.C. 601; [2014] B.P.I.R. 296, Ch D

RGB v CWM Taf Health Board [2013] EWHC 23 (COP); [2014] C.O.P.L.R. 83, CP .......... *Digested,* 14/**1569**

RGS Plus Ltd (In Administration), Re see Parmeko Holdings Ltd (In Administration), Re

Rhodes v Rhodes see Rhodes, Re

Rhodes, Re; *sub nom* Rhodes v Rhodes (1890) 44 Ch. D. 94, CA *Applied* 14/2807: *Followed* 12/3113

Rhone v Stephens [1994] 2 A.C. 310; [1994] 2 W.L.R. 429; [1994] 2 All E.R. 65; [1994] 37 E.G. 151; [1994] E.G. 50 (C.S.); (1994) 138 S.J.L.B. 77; [1994] N.P.C. 43; Times, March 18, 1994; Independent, March 23, 1994, HL; affirming (1994) 67 P. & C.R. 9; [1993] E.G. 3 (C.S.); (1993) 137 S.J.L.B. 46; [1993] N.P.C. 11; Times, January 21, 1993, CA (Civ Div) .......... *Digested,* 94/**576**: *Applied* 98/4345, 09/3151, 14/2510: *Considered* 06/2734, 10/2744

Rhys-Harper v Relaxion Group Plc; *sub nom* Relaxion Group Plc v Rhys-Harper; Kirker v British Sugar Plc; *joined cases* Jones v 3M Healthcare Ltd (No.1); Kirker v Ambitions Personnel (Nottinghamshire) Ltd; Angel v New Possibilities NHS Trust; Bond v Hackney Citizens Advice Bureau; D'Souza v Lambeth LBC (No.2) [2003] UKHL 33; [2003] 4 All E.R. 1113; [2003] 2 C.M.L.R. 44; [2003] I.C.R. 867; [2003] I.R.L.R. 484; (2003) 74 B.M.L.R. 109; (2003) 100(30) L.S.G. 30; (2003) 147 S.J.L.B. 782; Times, June 23, 2003; Independent, June 24, 2003, HL; reversing [2001] EWCA Civ 634; [2001] 2 C.M.L.R. 44; [2001] I.C.R. 1176; [2001] I.R.L.R. 460; [2001] Emp. L.R. 646; (2001) 98(24) L.S.G. 43; Times, June 12, 2001; Independent, May 11, 2001; Daily Telegraph, May 15, 2001, CA (Civ Div); affirming [2000] I.R.L.R. 810, EAT .......... *Digested,* 03/**1315**: *Applied* 02/1401, 05/1229, 05/1302: *Considered* 06/1353, 14/1063: *Distinguished* 06/1399, 09/1181, 13/991: *Followed* 06/1398, 13/1027, 13/986

Richards v Bromley LBC [2012] EWCA Civ 1476; [2013] E.L.R. 66, CA (Civ Div) .......... *Digested,* 14/**2997**

Richards v Richards [1984] A.C. 174; [1983] 3 W.L.R. 173; [1983] 2 All E.R. 807; (1984) 12 H.L.R. 68; (1983) 13 Fam. Law 256, HL; reversing [1983] 2 W.L.R. 633; [1983] 1 All E.R. 1017; (1983) 13 Fam. Law 84, CA (Civ Div) .................... *Digested,* 83/**1861**: *Applied* 84/1658, 85/21.u, 86/1667, 88/1668, 95/3562: *Cited* 00/2529: *Considered* 84/1658, 85/1698, 85/20.u, 86/1657, 87/1779, 88/1666, 93/1926, 95/2369, 14/1372: *Distinguished* 83/1863, 83/1869: *Followed* 86/1665, 94/2195: *Referred to* 87/1773

Richards v Secretary of State for Work and Pensions (C-423/04) [2006] E.C.R. I-3585; [2006] 2 C.M.L.R. 49; [2006] All E.R. (EC) 895; [2006] C.E.C. 637; [2006] I.C.R. 1181; [2006] 2 F.L.R. 487; [2006] 3 F.C.R. 229; [2006] Pens. L.R. 123; [2006] Fam. Law 639; Times, May 5, 2006, ECJ (1st Chamber) .................................. *Digested,* 06/**3056**: *Considered* 11/3155, 14/2294: *Followed* 10/2383

Richardson v Chief Constable of the West Midlands [2011] EWHC 773 (QB); [2011] 2 Cr. App. R. 1; [2011] Crim. L.R. 903; Times, April 11, 2011, QBD (Birmingham) *Digested,* 11/**2601**: *Applied* 14/2458: *Considered* 11/2597

Richardson v DPP; *joined case* Nero v DPP [2014] UKSC 8; [2014] A.C. 635; [2014] 2 W.L.R. 288; [2014] 2 All E.R. 20; [2014] 1 Cr. App. R. 29; [2014] Crim. L.R. 817, SC; affirming [2012] EWHC 1238 (Admin); (2012) 176 J.P. 450, QBD (Admin) ........................................................................................ *Digested,* 14/**667**

Richardson v North Yorkshire CC see R. (on the application of Richardson) v North Yorkshire CC

Richardson Ex p. Governors of St Thomas Hospital, Re [1911] 2 K.B. 705, CA *Applied* 67/468: *Considered* 14/1205

Richardson's Estate, Re 17 I.T.E.L.R. 511, Sup Ct (OECS)

Richman v Knowsley MBC [2013] Eq. L.R. 1164, EAT .................................................. *Digested,* 14/**1040**

Richmond Housing Partnership Ltd v Brick Farm Management Ltd see Brick Farm Management Ltd v Richmond Housing Partnership Ltd

Richmond Park Maintenance Ltd v Revenue and Customs Commissioners [2014] UKFTT 743 (TC); [2014] S.T.I. 2734, FTT (Tax)

Richmond Pharmacology Ltd v Chester Overseas Ltd [2014] EWHC 2692 (Ch); [2014] Bus. L.R. 1110, Ch D

Richmond Pharmacology Ltd v Dhaliwal [2009] I.C.R. 724; [2009] I.R.L.R. 336, EAT ... *Digested,* 09/**1229**: *Applied* 11/1107, 13/1045, 14/1108

Richmond upon Thames LBC v Rogers see Hampton Fuel Allotment Charity, Re

Ricotti v Quasar Manufacturing Ltd see Quasar Manufacturing Ltd v Ricotti

Ridehalgh v Horsefield; *joined cases* Allen v Unigate Dairies Ltd; Antonelli v Wade Gery Farr (A Firm); Philex Plc v Golban; Roberts v Coverite (Asphalters) Ltd; Watson v Watson (Wasted Costs Orders) [1994] Ch. 205; [1994] 3 W.L.R. 462; [1994] 3 All E.R. 848; [1994] B.C.C. 390; [1997] Costs L.R. (Core Vol.) 268; [1994] 2 F.L.R. 194; [1955-95] P.N.L.R. 636; [1994] Fam. Law 560; [1994] E.G. 15 (C.S.); (1994) 144 N.L.J. 231; [1994] N.P.C. 7; Times, January 28, 1994; Independent, February 4, 1994, CA (Civ Div) .................................................... *Digested,* 94/**3623**: *Applied* 95/4028, 95/4030, 95/4031, 95/4034, 96/3524, 96/936, 96/939, 97/602, 99/988, 00/4001, 00/470, 00/471, 01/4516, 02/408, 02/409, 03/382, 03/383, 04/323, 04/325, 05/496, 08/1173, 09/2737, 09/385, 09/386, 11/307, 11/311, 11/312, 12/1096, 13/1319, 13/457, 13/771: *Approved* 00/469: *Considered* 94/3620, 95/2273, 95/4673, 96/3899, 96/4508, 97/1387, 97/1388, 97/605, 97/607, 97/610, 98/497, 99/422, 99/989, 00/2466, 01/537, 01/589, 04/324, 10/15, 14/946: *Distinguished* 95/4032: *Followed* 98/496, 98/499, 00/1043, 12/2080

Ridgecrest NZ Ltd v IAG New Zealand Ltd [2014] NZSC 117, SC (NZ); reversing [2013] NZCA 291; [2014] Lloyd's Rep. I.R. 48, CA (NZ); reversing in part [2013] Lloyd's Rep. I.R. 67, HC (NZ)

Ridgewood Properties Group Ltd v Kilpatrick Stockton LLP [2014] EWHC 2502 (Ch); [2014] P.N.L.R. 31, QBD (Admin) ......................................................................... *Digested,* 14/**2209**

Riezniece v Zemkopibas ministrija (C-7/12); *sub nom* Rizniece v Zemkopibas ministrija (C-7/12) [2014] 1 C.M.L.R. 6; [2013] I.C.R. 1096; [2013] I.R.L.R. 828; [2013] Eq. L.R. 826, ECJ (4th Chamber)

Rigby v Chief Constable of Northamptonshire [1985] 1 W.L.R. 1242; [1985] 2 All E.R. 985; (1986) 83 L.S.G. 46, QBD ........................................................................... *Digested,* 85/**3549**: *Considered* 14/2203

Rigcharm Ltd v Revenue and Customs Commissioners see Universal Enterprises (EU) Ltd v Revenue and Customs Commissioners

Rightmatch Ltd v Meisels [2014] B.P.I.R. 733, Ch D .................................................... *Digested,* 14/**1787**

Rigid Containers Group Staff Pension Fund, Re; *sub nom* Sarjeant v Rigid Group Ltd; Rigid Containers Group Works Pension Fund, Re [2013] EWCA Civ 1714; [2014] Pens. L.R. 143, CA (Civ Div) ........................................................................ *Digested,* 14/**2245**

Rigid Containers Group Works Pension Fund, Re see Rigid Containers Group Staff Pension Fund, Re

Rijksdienst voor Pensioenen v Brouwer (C-577/08) (Unreported, July 29, 2010), ECJ *Considered* 14/1120

Riley v Crown Prosecution Service [2013] EWCA Civ 951; [2013] I.R.L.R. 966, CA (Civ Div); affirming UKEAT/0043/12/SM, EAT .......... *Digested,* 14/**1082**

Rimmer v Webster [1902] 2 Ch. 163, Ch D *Applied* 14/2493: *Considered* 84/1324: *Distinguished* 52/3155, 56/7973

Ring v Dansk Almennyttigt Boligselskab DAB (C-335/11) see HK Danmark v Dansk almennyttigt Boligselskab (C-335/11)

Ringtower Holdings, Re; *sub nom* Company (No.005685 of 1988) (No.2), Re (1989) 5 B.C.C. 82, Ch D (Companies Ct) .......... *Digested,* 89/**354**: *Applied* 14/515

Rio Tinto London Ltd v Revenue and Customs Commissioners [2014] UKFTT 1059 (TC); [2014] S.T.I. 3559, FTT (Tax)

Risdal Touring AS v EFTA Surveillance Authority (E-4/12); *joined case* Konkurrenten.no AS v EFTA Surveillance Authority (E-5/12) [2014] 2 C.M.L.R. 8, EFTA

Risk v Rose Bruford College [2013] EWHC 3869 (QB); [2014] E.L.R. 157, QBD .......... *Digested,* 14/**2208**

Risk Management Partners Ltd v Brent LBC see Brent LBC v Risk Management Partners Ltd

Ritz Hotel Casino Ltd v Daher [2014] EWHC 2847 (QB); [2014] C.T.L.C. 265, QBD

Rivella International AG v Office for Harmonisation in the Internal Market (Trade Marks and Designs) (OHIM) (C-445/12 P) [2014] Bus. L.R. 298; [2014] E.T.M.R. 20, ECJ (1st Chamber)

Rizniece v Zemkopibas ministrija (C-7/12) see Riezniece v Zemkopibas ministrija (C-7/12)

RJT Consulting Engineers Ltd v DM Engineering (Northern Ireland) Ltd [2002] EWCA Civ 270; [2002] 1 W.L.R. 2344; [2002] C.L.C. 905; [2002] B.L.R. 217; [2002] T.C.L.R. 21; 83 Con. L.R. 99; (2002) 18 Const. L.J. 425; [2002] C.I.L.L. 1841; (2002) 99(15) L.S.G. 33; (2002) 146 S.J.L.B. 78, CA (Civ Div) *Applied* 03/649, 04/591, 07/433, 07/730, 10/558: *Considered* 14/583: *Distinguished* 08/607: *Followed* 10/553, 11/499

RK v RK (Financial Resources: Trust Assets) [2011] EWHC 3910 (Fam); [2013] 1 F.L.R. 329; [2012] 3 F.C.R. 44; [2012] Fam. Law 1453, Fam Div .......... *Digested,* 12/**1439**: *Applied* 14/1373, 14/1374

RKW Ltd v Revenue and Customs Commissioners [2014] UKFTT 151 (TC); [2014] S.T.I. 1633, FTT (Tax)

RLvS Verlagsgesellschaft mbH v Stuttgarter Wochenblatt GmbH (C-391/12) [2014] 1 All E.R. (Comm) 74; [2014] 2 C.M.L.R. 7; [2014] C.E.C. 865, ECJ (3rd Chamber)

RM (Iraq) v Secretary of State for the Home Department see HF (Iraq) v Secretary of State for the Home Department

RM (Zimbabwe) v Secretary of State for the Home Department [2013] EWCA Civ 775; [2014] 1 W.L.R. 2259; [2013] 3 C.M.L.R. 44; [2014] Imm. A.R. 123, CA (Civ Div) .......... *Digested,* 14/**1738**

RO v A Local Authority [2013] EWHC 31 (Fam); [2014] 2 F.L.R. 998; [2014] Fam. Law 463, Fam Div

RO v A Local Authority [2014] EWHC 97 (Fam); [2014] 2 F.L.R. 1007; [2014] Fam. Law 464, Fam Div .......... *Digested,* 14/**1243**

Roache v News Group Newspapers Ltd [1998] E.M.L.R. 161; Times, November 23, 1992; Independent, December 31, 1992, CA (Civ Div) .......... *Digested,* 92/**3437**: *Applied* 10/1860, 13/339, 14/2297: *Considered* 98/442, 03/3583, 08/390, 13/323

Robb v Green [1895] 2 Q.B. 315, CA; affirming [1895] 2 Q.B. 1, QBD *Applied* 69/3573, 91/408, 03/518, 08/1280: *Considered* 77/958, 86/1167: *Followed* 14/1020

Robbins v Bexley LBC [2013] EWCA Civ 1233; [2014] B.L.R. 11, CA (Civ Div) .......... *Digested,* 14/**2197**

Robbins v Bexley LBC [2012] EWHC 2257 (TCC); [2012] L.L.R. 976, QBD (TCC) *Affirmed* 14/2197

Robeez European Sales Ltd v Ifuago Sarl [2013] EWHC 1356 (Comm); [2013] I.L.Pr. 41, QBD (Merc) .......... *Digested,* 14/**554**

Robert v Momentum Services Ltd [2003] EWCA Civ 299; [2003] 1 W.L.R. 1577; [2003] 2 All E.R. 74; [2003] C.P. Rep. 38; (2003) 100(14) L.S.G. 29; Times, February 13, 2003, CA (Civ Div) .......... *Digested,* 03/**391**: *Applied* 13/365, 14/397: *Followed* 14/398

Robert Sage Ltd (t/a Prestige Nursing Care Ltd) v O'Connell; *joined case* North Somerset Council v O'Connell [2014] I.R.L.R. 428, EAT .......... *Digested,* 14/**1131**

Roberts v Coverite (Asphalters) Ltd see Ridehalgh v Horsefield

Roberts v GB Oils Ltd [2014] I.C.R. 462, EAT .......... *Digested,* 14/**1053**

Roberts v Gill [2008] EWCA Civ 75, CA (Civ Div) *Followed* 14/3026

Roberts v Liverpool Victoria (Unreported, January 17, 2014), CC (Doncaster) [*Robert Skyner, Barrister, 30 Park Square Chambers, Leeds*] .......... *Digested,* 14/**2334**

Roberts (Valuation Officer) v West Coast Marine (Pwllheli) Ltd [2013] UKUT 413 (LC); [2014] R.A. 1, UT (Lands) .......... *Digested,* 14/**2126**

Roberts Petroleum Ltd v Bernard Kenny Ltd (In Liquidation) [1983] 2 A.C. 192; [1983] 2 W.L.R. 305; [1983] 1 All E.R. 564; [1983] Com. L.R. 564; (1983) 127 S.J. 138, HL; reversing [1982] 1 W.L.R. 301; [1982] 1 All E.R. 685, CA (Civ Div) ...... *Digested,* 83/**204**: *Applied* 84/1691, 02/2681, 02/314, 14/490, 14/492: *Considered* 97/3002, 99/3305, 10/1854, 12/323: *Distinguished* 08/3062

Robertson v Department for the Environment, Food and Rural Affairs; *sub nom* Department for the Environment, Food and Rural Affairs v Robertson [2005] EWCA Civ 138; [2005] I.C.R. 750; [2005] I.R.L.R. 363; (2005) 102(15) L.S.G. 33; Times, March 2, 2005; Independent, February 24, 2005, CA (Civ Div); affirming [2004] I.C.R. 1289, EAT .......... *Digested,* 05/**1258**: *Applied* 14/3503: *Considered* 07/1360, 09/1206, 13/1011

Robertson v Swift; *sub nom* Swift (t/a A Swift Move) v Robinson [2014] UKSC 50; [2014] 1 W.L.R. 3438; [2014] 4 All E.R. 869; [2014] 2 All E.R. (Comm) 1083; [2014] Bus. L.R. 1029; [2014] E.C.C. 32, SC; reversing [2012] EWCA Civ 1794; [2013] Bus. L.R. 479; (2013) 177 J.P. 169; [2013] E.C.C. 9; [2013] C.T.L.C. 57; (2013) 157(3) S.J.L.B. 31, CA (Civ Div) .......... *Digested,* 14/**611**: *Applied* 14/610

Robins v Revenue and Customs Commissioners [2013] UKFTT 514 (TC); [2014] S.T.I. 260, FTT (Tax)

Robinson v Bowskill; *joined case* Robinson v Fairhill Medical Practice [2014] I.C.R. D7, EAT

Robinson v Chief Constable of West Yorkshire [2014] EWCA Civ 15; [2014] P.I.Q.R. P14, CA (Civ Div) .......... *Digested,* 14/**2203**

Robinson v Fairhill Medical Practice see Robinson v Bowskill

Robinson v Hall Gregory Recruitment Ltd [2014] I.R.L.R. 761, EAT .......... *Digested,* 14/**1036**

Robinson v Robinson (Practice Note); *sub nom* Practice Note (Fam Div: Final Orders) [1982] 1 W.L.R. 786; [1982] 2 All E.R. 699; (1983) 4 F.L.R. 102; (1982) 12 Fam. Law 175; (1982) 126 S.J. 360, CA (Civ Div) .......... *Digested,* 82/**2483**: *Applied* 85/1049: *Considered* 86/1083, 95/2324, 10/3683, 14/1369: *Followed* 83/1096

Robson v Salford City Council; *sub nom* R. (on the application of Robson) v Salford City Council [2014] EWHC 3481 (Admin); (2014) 17 C.C.L. Rep. 474, QBD (Admin)

Robson (Deceased), Re; *sub nom* White v Matthys [2014] EWHC 295 (Ch); [2014] Ch. 470; [2014] 2 W.L.R. 1435; [2014] W.T.L.R. 725, Ch D .......... *Digested,* 14/**570**

Roche v Roche (Unreported, 1981), CA (Civ Div) .......... *Digested,* 82/**228u**: *Considered* 14/496

Rockall v Revenue and Customs Commissioners [2014] UKFTT 643 (TC); [2014] S.T.I. 2892, FTT (Tax)

Roddy (A Child) (Identification: Restriction on Publication), Re; *sub nom* Torbay BC v News Group Newspapers [2003] EWHC 2927 (Fam); [2004] E.M.L.R. 8; [2004] 2 F.L.R. 949; [2004] 1 F.C.R. 481; [2004] Fam. Law 793, Fam Div .......... *Digested,* 04/**1924**: *Applied* 10/408, 14/1278: *Considered* 06/454, 09/1581: *Followed* 07/1721

Rodenstock GmbH, Re [2011] EWHC 1104 (Ch); [2011] Bus. L.R. 1245; [2012] B.C.C. 459; [2011] I.L.Pr. 34, Ch D (Companies Ct) .......... *Digested,* 11/**1886**: *Applied* 14/1823, 14/500

Rodriguez v Secretary of State for the Home Department see Rodriguez (Flexibility Policy), Re

Rodriguez (Flexibility Policy), Re; *sub nom* Rodriguez v Secretary of State for the Home Department [2013] UKUT 42 (IAC); [2013] Imm. A.R. 509; [2013] I.N.L.R. 467, UT (IAC) .......... *Digested,* 13/**1631**: *Reversed* 14/1711

Roelich v Revenue and Customs Commissioners [2014] UKFTT 579 (TC); [2014] S.T.I. 2891, FTT (Tax)

Rofa Sport Management AG v DHL International (UK) Ltd [1989] 1 W.L.R. 902; [1989] 2 All E.R. 743; (1989) 133 S.J. 1202, CA (Civ Div) .......... *Digested,* 89/**3068**: *Applied* 03/385, 14/565

Rogate Services Ltd v Revenue and Customs Commissioners [2014] UKFTT 312 (TC); [2014] S.T.I. 2092, FTT (Tax)

Roger Skinner Ltd v Revenue and Customs Commissioners; *sub nom* Revenue and Customs Commissioners v Roger Skinner Ltd [2014] UKUT 204 (TCC); [2014] S.T.C. 2335; [2014] B.V.C. 516; [2014] S.T.I. 1980, UT (Tax); affirming [2012] UKFTT 525 (TC); [2012] S.T.I. 2857, FTT (Tax) ............ *Digested,* 14/**3100**

Rogers v Hoyle; *sub nom* Hoyle v Rogers [2014] EWCA Civ 257; [2014] 3 W.L.R. 148; [2014] 3 All E.R. 550; [2014] C.P. Rep. 30; [2014] 1 C.L.C. 316, CA (Civ Div); affirming [2013] EWHC 1409 (QB); (2013) 163(7575) N.L.J. 16, QBD ............ *Digested,* 14/**288**

Rok Building Ltd v Celtic Composting Systems Ltd [2009] EWHC 2664 (TCC); 130 Con. L.R. 61; [2010] C.I.L.L. 2797, QBD (TCC) ............ *Digested,* 10/**844**: *Considered* 14/576

Rolls-Royce Plc v Unite the Union [2009] EWCA Civ 387; [2010] 1 W.L.R. 318; [2010] I.C.R. 1; [2009] I.R.L.R. 576; (2009) 106(21) L.S.G. 15; (2009) 153(20) S.J.L.B. 38; Times, May 27, 2009, CA (Civ Div); affirming [2008] EWHC 2420 (QB); [2009] 1 C.M.L.R. 17; [2009] I.R.L.R. 49; (2008) 152(42) S.J.L.B. 29, QBD ....... *Digested,* 09/**1162**: *Applied* 10/2591, 11/176, 11/1869, 14/2224: *Considered* 12/2612, 13/1730: *Followed* 13/438

Romer v Freie und Hansestadt Hamburg (C-147/08) [2013] 2 C.M.L.R. 11; [2011] Eq. L.R. 921, ECJ (Grand Chamber)
*Applied* 13/2146: *Considered* 14/1120

Romer v Haringey LBC see R. (on the application of Romer) v First Secretary of State

Rondini Ltd v Treasury of the Isle of Man [2014] UKFTT 157 (TC); [2014] S.T.I. 952, FTT (Tax)

Rosenbaum v Burgoyne [1965] A.C. 430; [1964] 3 W.L.R. 277; [1964] 2 All E.R. 988; (1964) 128 J.P. 530; 62 L.G.R. 581; (1964) 108 S.J. 579, HL; reversing [1964] 2 All E.R. 670; 62 L.G.R. 339, DC ............ *Digested,* 64/**1624**: *Applied* 95/2484: *Considered* 14/3048

Rosenbaum's Executor v Revenue and Customs Commissioners [2013] UKFTT 495 (TC); [2014] W.T.L.R. 351, FTT (Tax) ............ *Digested,* 14/**2955**

Rosenzweig v NMC Recordings Ltd [2013] EWHC 3792 (Ch); [2014] P.T.S.R. 261; [2014] W.T.L.R. 1027; [2014] 1 P. & C.R. DG17, Ch D ............ *Digested,* 14/**285**

Ross (Deceased), Re; *sub nom* Petterson v Ross [2013] EWHC 2724 (Ch); [2014] W.T.L.R. 321, Ch D ............ *Digested,* 14/**2837**

Ross River Ltd v Waveley Commercial Ltd [2013] EWCA Civ 910; [2014] 1 B.C.L.C. 545, CA (Civ Div); reversing [2012] EWHC 2487 (Ch), Ch D ............ *Digested,* 14/**2228**

Ross T Smyth & Co Ltd v TD Bailey Son & Co; *sub nom* TD Bailey Son & Co v Ross T Smyth & Co Ltd [1940] 3 All E.R. 60; (1940) 67 Ll. L. Rep. 147, HL; reversing [1939] 3 All E.R. 175; (1939) 64 Ll. L. Rep. 95, CA; reversing [1939] 1 All E.R. 115; (1938) 62 Ll. L. Rep. 242, KBD
*Applied* 77/959, 79/342, 83/1319, 13/2839: *Considered* 14/623

Rosseel NV v Oriental Commercial & Shipping Co (UK) Ltd [1991] E.G. 94 (C.S.); Times, October 11, 1991; Independent, October 9, 1991; Financial Times, October 18, 1991, CA (Civ Div); reversing [1991] 2 Lloyd's Rep. 625; Financial Times, November 23, 1990, QBD (Comm) ............ *Digested,* 91/**548**: *Applied* 14/138: *Considered* 12/117: *Distinguished* 96/360: *Followed* 97/677

Rossetti Marketing Ltd v Diamond Sofa Co Ltd [2012] EWCA Civ 1021; [2013] 1 All E.R. (Comm) 308; [2013] Bus. L.R. 543; [2012] C.P. Rep. 45, CA (Civ Div); reversing in part [2011] EWHC 2482 (QB); [2012] 1 All E.R. (Comm) 18; [2012] Bus. L.R. 571; [2011] E.C.C. 28; [2012] Eu. L.R. 249, QBD ............ *Digested,* 13/**70**: *Applied* 14/310, 14/82

Rossi, Re see R. v London County Quarter Sessions Appeals Committee Ex p. Rossi

Rossminster and Tucker, Re see R. v Inland Revenue Commissioners Ex p. Rossminster Ltd

Rothfarb v Redbridge LBC [2014] P.A.D. 3, Planning Inspector

Rothschild Asset Management Ltd v Ako see Ako v Rothschild Asset Management Ltd

Rouches v Kellogg see Kellogg Estate, Re

Rouner v Wise 16 I.T.E.L.R. 535, US Court

Routier v Revenue and Customs Commissioners [2014] EWHC 3010 (Ch); [2014] B.T.C. 42; [2014] W.T.L.R. 1717; [2014] S.T.I. 2931; (2014) 158(42) S.J.L.B. 37; Times, October 14, 2014, Ch D ............ *Digested,* 14/**2936**

Rowell v Pratt [1938] A.C. 101; [1937] 3 All E.R. 660, HL; reversing [1936] 2 K.B. 226; [1936] 2 All E.R. 576, CA
*Applied* 97/316: *Considered* 82/43.u, 14/762

Rowling v Wilks see William Denby & Sons Ltd Sick and Benevolent Fund, Re

Rowson v Conwy BC [2014] P.A.D. 53, Planning Inspector

Rowstock Ltd v Jessemey; *joined case* Jessemey v Rowstock Ltd [2014] EWCA Civ 185; [2014] 1 W.L.R. 3615; [2014] 3 All E.R. 409; [2014] 3 C.M.L.R. 24; [2014] I.C.R. 550; [2014] I.R.L.R. 368; [2014] Eq. L.R. 230; (2014) 158(9) S.J.L.B. 37; Times, April 15, 2014, CA (Civ Div); reversing [2013] I.C.R. 807; [2013] I.R.L.R. 439; [2013] Eq. L.R. 438, EAT ............ *Digested,* 14/**1063**: *Considered* 14/1104: *Not followed* 13/986

Roy v Prior [1971] A.C. 470; [1970] 3 W.L.R. 202; [1970] 2 All E.R. 729; (1970) 114 S.J. 552, HL; reversing [1970] 1 Q.B. 283; [1969] 3 W.L.R. 365; [1969] 3 All E.R. 1153; (1969) 113 S.J. 609, CA (Civ Div) ............ *Digested,* 70/**1040**: *Applied* 97/4860, 99/528: *Considered* 92/3499, 00/4543, 14/2992: *Distinguished* 71/10220: *Followed* 13/1020

Royal & Sun Alliance Insurance Plc v T&N Ltd (In Administration); *joined case* Smith v T&N Ltd (In Administration) [2002] EWCA Civ 1964; [2003] P.I.Q.R. P26, CA (Civ Div) ............ *Digested,* 03/**312**: *Applied* 13/2187, 14/307: *Followed* 13/3212

Royal and Sun Alliance Insurance Plc v Mayor's Office for Policing and Crime see Mitsui Sumitomo Insurance Co (Europe) Ltd v Mayor's Office for Policing and Crime

Royal Bank of Scotland Plc v Ashton [2011] I.C.R. 632, EAT ............ *Digested,* 11/**1058**: *Applied* 14/1048: *Considered* 13/974

Royal Bank of Scotland Plc v Etridge (No.2); *joined cases* Kenyon-Brown v Desmond Banks & Co (Undue Influence) (No.2); Bank of Scotland v Bennett; UCB Home Loans Corp Ltd v Moore; National Westminster Bank Plc v Gill; Midland Bank Plc v Wallace; Barclays Bank Plc v Harris; Barclays Bank Plc v Coleman [2001] UKHL 44; [2002] 2 A.C. 773; [2001] 3 W.L.R. 1021; [2001] 4 All E.R. 449; [2001] 2 All E.R. (Comm) 1061; [2002] 1 Lloyd's Rep. 343; [2001] 2 F.L.R. 1364; [2001] 3 F.C.R. 481; [2002] H.L.R. 4; [2001] Fam. Law 880; [2001] 43 E.G. 184 (C.S.); (2001) 151 N.L.J. 1538; [2001] N.P.C. 147; [2002] 1 P. & C.R. DG14; Times, October 17, 2001; Daily Telegraph, October 23, 2001, HL; affirming in part [1998] 4 All E.R. 705; [1998] 2 F.L.R. 843; [1998] 3 F.C.R. 675; (1999) 31 H.L.R. 575; [1998] Fam. Law 665; (1998) 95(32) L.S.G. 31; (2001) 151 N.L.J. 1538; (1998) 148 N.L.J. 1390; [1998] N.P.C. 130; (1998) 76 P. & C.R. D39; Times, August 17, 1998, CA (Civ Div) ............ *Digested,* 01/**4880**: *Applied* 00/4664, 01/4879, 03/2379, 03/3556, 03/3587, 03/3588, 03/3612, 03/4118, 03/4122, 03/4124, 04/3671, 05/1423, 05/2673, 05/3402, 05/3438, 05/3442, 05/3968, 06/4094, 07/2415, 08/3096, 08/474, 09/1362, 10/2119, 10/224, 10/2752, 10/3449, 11/204, 11/2711, 12/1824, 12/2301, 13/2467, 13/2979, 14/2836: *Considered* 00/2333, 01/4878, 02/3840, 02/3841, 02/5794, 03/233, 03/5680, 04/1526, 05/4291, 05/4301, 10/2750, 12/3185: *Followed* 00/2334, 00/4273, 04/3246, 10/2753, 11/1895, 11/3498, 12/273, 14/1965, 14/2844: *Referred to* 99/4030

Royal Bank of Scotland Plc v Farley [1996] B.P.I.R. 638, CA (Civ Div) ............ *Digested,* 97/**3009**: *Considered* 13/1709: *Followed* 14/1778

Royal Brompton and Harefield NHS Foundation Trust v Joint Committee of Primary Care Trusts see R. (on the application of Royal Brompton and Harefield NHS Foundation Trust) v Joint Committee of Primary Care Trusts

Royal Brompton Hospital NHS Trust v Hammond (No.3) [2002] UKHL 14; [2002] 1 W.L.R. 1397; [2002] 2 All E.R. 801; [2002] 1 All E.R. (Comm) 897; [2003] 1 C.L.C. 11; [2002] B.L.R. 255; [2002] T.C.L.R. 14; 81 Con. L.R. 1; [2002] P.N.L.R. 37; Times, April 26, 2002, HL; affirming 69 Con. L.R. 145; [2000] Lloyd's Rep. P.N. 643, CA (Civ Div); affirming [1999] B.L.R. 385, QBD (TCC) ... *Digested,* 02/**326**: *Applied* 03/3613, 14/549: *Considered* 07/4248, 08/3953, 09/969, 14/2217: *Distinguished* 09/447: *Followed* 03/4957

Royal Brunei Airlines Sdn Bhd v Philip Tan Kok Ming see Royal Brunei Airlines Sdn Bhd v Tan

Royal Brunei Airlines Sdn Bhd v Tan; *sub nom* Royal Brunei Airlines Sdn Bhd v Philip Tan Kok Ming [1995] 2 A.C. 378; [1995] 3 W.L.R. 64; [1995] 3 All E.R. 97; [1995] B.C.C. 899; (1995) 92(27) L.S.G. 33; (1995) 145 N.L.J. 888; (1995) 139 S.J.L.B. 146; (1995) 70 P. & C.R. D12; Times, May 29, 1995; Independent, June 22, 1995, PC (Bru) ............ *Digested,* 95/**2193**: *Applied* 99/294, 00/3566, 02/249, 13/587: *Considered* 97/3828, 97/692, 01/721, 02/4666, 06/4380, 07/4237, 08/3954, 09/2733, 09/4008, 11/3495, 12/3361, 12/521, 14/2991: *Followed* 95/2191, 98/4871, 99/2217, 00/2316: *Referred to* 00/3713, 00/3768

Royal London Mutual Insurance Society Ltd v Secretary of State for Communities and Local Government; *sub nom* R. (on the application of Royal London Mutual Insurance Society Ltd) v Secretary of State for Communities and Local Government [2013] EWHC 3597 (Admin); [2014] J.P.L. 458, QBD (Admin) ....... *Digested,* 14/**2408**

Royal Society for the Protection of Birds v Secretary of State for Communities and Local Government; *joined case* Lydd Airport Action Group v Secretary of State for Communities and Local Government [2014] EWHC 1523 (Admin); [2014] Env. L.R. 30, QBD (Admin) ........ *Digested,* 14/**2413**

Royscot Commercial Leasing Ltd v Ismail Independent, May 17, 1993, CA (Civ Div) *Considered* 14/256: *Followed* 10/253

Rozanes v Bowen (1928) 32 Ll. L. Rep. 98, CA; affirming (1928) 31 Ll. L. Rep. 231, KBD *Applied* 69/1810, 13/1736: *Followed* 14/1846

Rozanski v Poland see Pomiechowski v Poland

RQ v Bromley LBC [2014] R.V.R. 163, VT ........ *Digested,* 14/**2092**

RR Donnelley Global Document Solutions Group Ltd v Besagni; *joined case* NSL Ltd v Besagni [2014] I.C.R. 1008, EAT ........ *Digested,* 14/**1128**

RS v Criminal Injuries Compensation Authority [2013] EWCA Civ 1040; [2014] 1 W.L.R. 1313, CA (Civ Div) ........ *Digested,* 14/**53**: *Followed* 14/2301

RSPB v Secretary of State for the Environment, Food and Rural Affairs [2014] EWHC 1645 (Admin); [2014] Env. L.R. 29, QBD (Admin) ........ *Digested,* 14/**1197**

RTS Flexible Systems Ltd v Molkerei Alois Muller GmbH & Co KG [2010] UKSC 14; [2010] 1 W.L.R. 753; [2010] 3 All E.R. 1; [2010] 2 All E.R. (Comm) 97; [2010] Bus. L.R. 776; [2010] 1 C.L.C. 388; [2010] B.L.R. 337; 129 Con. L.R. 1; [2010] C.I.L.L. 2868; (2010) 107(12) L.S.G. 20; (2010) 160 N.L.J. 421; (2010) 154(11) S.J.L.B. 28, SC; reversing [2009] EWCA Civ 26; [2009] 2 All E.R. (Comm) 542; [2009] B.L.R. 181; 123 Con. L.R. 130, CA (Civ Div); reversing [2008] EWHC 1087 (TCC), QBD (TCC) ........ *Digested,* 10/**631**: *Applied* 12/1053: *Followed* 12/2102, 12/634, 13/448, 14/636

Rubber Improvement Ltd v Associated Newspapers Ltd see Rubber Improvement Ltd v Daily Telegraph Ltd

Rubber Improvement Ltd v Daily Telegraph Ltd; *joined cases* Rubber Improvement Ltd v Associated Newspapers Ltd; Lewis v Associated Newspapers Ltd; Lewis v Daily Telegraph Ltd [1964] A.C. 234; [1963] 2 W.L.R. 1063; [1963] 2 All E.R. 151; (1963) 107 S.J. 356; Times, July 20, 1961, HL; affirming [1963] 1 Q.B. 340; [1962] 3 W.L.R. 50; [1962] 2 All E.R. 698; (1962) 106 S.J. 307, CA; reversing Times, July 22, 1961, QBD ........ *Digested,* 63/**1998**: *Applied* 63/2002, 99/1623: *Considered* 68/2231, 76/1601, 99/2108, 14/2166: *Distinguished* 06/1040

Rubin v Dweck [2012] B.P.I.R. 854, Ch D (Bankruptcy Ct) ........ *Digested,* 12/**1825**: *Considered* 14/1831

Rubin v Rubin [2014] EWHC 611 (Fam); [2014] 1 W.L.R. 3289; [2014] 2 F.L.R. 1018; [2014] Fam. Law 797, Fam Div ........ *Digested,* 14/**1362**

Ruffer v Pokorna (C-322/13); *sub nom* Grauel Ruffer v Pokorna (C-322/13) [2014] 3 C.M.L.R. 30, ECJ (2nd Chamber)

Rugamer v Sony Music Entertainment UK Ltd see McNicol v Balfour Beatty Rail Maintenance Ltd

Rugby Football Union v Consolidated Information Services (formerly Viagogo Ltd) see Rugby Football Union v Viagogo Ltd

Rugby Football Union v Secretary of State for the Environment, Transport and the Regions see Rugby Football Union v Secretary of State for Transport, Local Government and the Regions

Rugby Football Union v Secretary of State for Transport, Local Government and the Regions; *sub nom* Rugby Football Union v Secretary of State for the Environment, Transport and the Regions [2002] EWCA Civ 1169; [2002] 4 P.L.R. 23; [2003] J.P.L. 96; [2002] 30 E.G. 134 (C.S.); Times, August 13, 2002, CA (Civ Div); affirming [2001] EWHC Admin 927; [2002] J.P.L. 740; Times, November 8, 2001, QBD (Admin) ........ *Digested,* 02/**3691**: *Considered* 14/2408

Rugby Football Union v Viagogo Ltd; *sub nom* Rugby Football Union v Consolidated Information Services (formerly Viagogo Ltd) [2012] UKSC 55; [2012] 1 W.L.R. 3333; [2013] 1 All E.R. 928; [2013] 1 C.M.L.R. 56; [2013] E.M.L.R. 25; [2013] H.R.L.R. 8; [2013] F.S.R. 23; (2012) 162 N.L.J. 1504; (2012) 156(45) S.J.L.B. 31, SC; affirming [2011] EWCA Civ 1585; [2012] 2 C.M.L.R. 3; [2012] F.S.R. 11, CA (Civ Div); affirming [2011] EWHC 764 (QB); [2011] N.P.C. 37, QBD ...... *Digested,* 13/**398**: *Applied* 13/1068: *Considered* 14/383

Ruiz Zambrano v Office National de l'Emploi (ONEm) (C-34/09) [2012] Q.B. 265; [2012] 2 W.L.R. 886; [2011] E.C.R. I-1177; [2011] 2 C.M.L.R. 46; [2011] All E.R. (EC) 491; [2011] 2 F.C.R. 491; [2011] Imm. A.R. 521; [2011] I.N.L.R. 481, ECJ (Grand Chamber)
*Applied* 12/1707, 14/1741: *Considered* 12/1775, 13/1597, 13/3782, 13/3783: *Explained* 13/1533: *Referred to* 13/1636

Ruiz-Picasso v Office for Harmonisation in the Internal Market (Trade Marks and Designs) (OHIM) (C-361/04 P) [2006] E.C.R. I-643; [2006] E.T.M.R. 29, ECJ (1st Chamber) ........ *Digested,* 06/**2555**: *Applied* 08/2372, 09/2417: *Considered* 14/1918

Ruscillo v Council for the Regulation of Health Care Professionals see Council for the Regulation of Health Care Professionals v General Medical Council

Russell v Pal Pak Corrugated Ltd (No.1) see Callery v Gray (No.1)

Rust-Andrews v First-tier Tribunal [2011] EWCA Civ 1548; [2012] P.I.Q.R. P7, CA (Civ Div) ........ *Digested,* 12/**2405**: *Followed* 14/2301

RW v Neath Port Talbot CBC see W (A Child) (Care Proceedings: Welfare Evaluation: Functions of Local Authority), Re

RWE npower Renewables Ltd v JN Bentley Ltd [2014] EWCA Civ 150; [2014] C.I.L.L. 3488, CA (Civ Div); affirming [2013] EWHC 978 (TCC); [2013] C.I.L.L. 3374, QBD (TCC)

Ryabykh v Russia (52854/99) (2005) 40 E.H.R.R. 25, ECHR ........ *Digested,* 05/**2094**: *Applied* 14/59

Ryanair Holdings Plc v Competition and Markets Authority [2014] CAT 6; [2014] Comp. A.R. 312, CAT ........ *Digested,* 14/**537**

Ryanair Holdings Plc v Competition and Markets Authority see Ryanair Holdings Plc v Competition Commission

Ryanair Holdings Plc v Competition Commission; *joined case* Ryanair Holdings Plc v Competition and Markets Authority [2014] CAT 3; [2014] Comp. A.R. 213, CAT *Digested,* 14/**551**

Ryanair Holdings Plc v Competition Commission [2013] CAT 25; [2014] Comp. A.R. 46, CAT

Ryanair Ltd v Esso Italiana Srl [2013] EWCA Civ 1450; [2013] 2 C.L.C. 950; [2014] U.K.C.L.R. 247, CA (Civ Div) ........ *Digested,* 14/**557**

Ryanair Ltd v European Commission (T-512/11) [2014] S.T.I. 3423, GC (9th Chamber)

Ryanair Ltd v Revenue and Customs Commissioners [2014] EWCA Civ 410; [2014] S.T.I. 1725; (2014) 164(7603) N.L.J. 22, CA (Civ Div); affirming [2013] UKUT 176 (TCC); [2013] S.T.C. 1360; [2013] S.T.I. 2046, UT (Tax) ........ *Digested,* 14/**814**

Rye v Rye [1962] A.C. 496; [1962] 2 W.L.R. 361; [1962] 1 All E.R. 146; (1962) 106 S.J. 94, HL; affirming [1961] Ch. 70; [1960] 3 W.L.R. 1052; [1960] 3 All E.R. 810; (1960) 104 S.J. 1076, CA ........ *Digested,* 62/**2590**: *Considered* 88/2047, 89/3186, 11/2668, 14/1995

S v B (Ancillary Relief: Costs) [2004] EWHC 2089 (Fam); [2005] 1 F.L.R. 474, Fam Div ........ *Digested,* 05/**1626**: *Applied* 14/1365

S v Chapman [2008] EWCA Civ 800; [2008] E.L.R. 603; (2008) 152(22) S.J.L.B. 29, CA (Civ Div) ........ *Digested,* 08/**1084**: *Considered* 13/909, 14/916

S v Dundee City Council; *sub nom* BS v Dundee City Council [2013] CSIH 91; 2014 S.C. 254; [2014] I.R.L.R. 131; 2013 G.W.D. 39-751, IH (Ex Div) ........ *Digested,* 14/**3507**

S v GK (t/a T Auktionshaus) [2014] E.C.C. 15, OGH (A)

S v Minister voor Immigratie, Integratie en Asiel (C-457/12); *sub nom* Minister voor Immigratie, Integratie en Asiel v G (C-457/12) [2014] Q.B. 1207; [2014] 3 W.L.R. 843; [2014] 3 C.M.L.R. 18; [2014] All E.R. (EC) 843; [2014] Imm. A.R. 843; [2014] I.N.L.R. 816, ECJ (Grand Chamber)

S v P (Settlement by Collaborative Law Process) [2008] 2 F.L.R. 2040; [2008] Fam. Law 1177, Fam Div ........ *Digested,* 09/**1582**: *Considered* 14/1361

S v S (Abduction: Inherent Jurisdiction) [2014] EWHC 575 (Fam); [2014] Fam. Law 805, Fam Div

S v S (Arbitral Award: Approval); *sub nom* S (Financial Remedies: Arbitral Award) [2014] EWHC 7 (Fam); [2014] 1 W.L.R. 2299; [2014] 1 F.L.R. 1257; [2014] 2 F.C.R. 484; [2014] Fam. Law 448; (2014) 158(3) S.J.L.B. 37, Fam Div ........ *Digested,* 14/**1361**

S v S see Sharland v Sharland

S v Suffolk CC see R. (on the application of S) v Suffolk CC

S v Sweden (5786/08) (2014) 58 E.H.R.R. 36; 36 B.H.R.C. 257, ECHR

S v Teaching Hospital NHS Trust (Unreported, July 10, 2013), QBD [*Stewarts Law LLP, 5, New Street Square, London*] ........ *Digested*, 14/**2325**

S v United Kingdom (30562/04); *joined case* Marper v United Kingdom (30566/04) (2009) 48 E.H.R.R. 50; 25 B.H.R.C. 557; [2008] Po. L.R. 403; [2009] Crim. L.R. 355; (2008) 158 N.L.J. 1755; Times, December 8, 2008, ECHR (Grand Chamber) ........ *Digested*, 09/**2053**: *Applied* 11/1687, 12/2661: *Considered* 09/2062, 14/659

S (A Child) v East Kent Hospitals University NHS Foundation Trust (Unreported, August 24, 2012), CC (Thanet) [*David Juckes, Barrister, Hailsham Chambers, 4 Paper Buildings, Temple, London*] ........ *Digested*, 14/**2324**

S (A Child) v Nottingham City Council; *sub nom* S (A Child) (Care Proceedings: Non-accidental Injuries), Re [2013] EWCA Civ 771; [2014] 1 F.L.R. 739; [2014] 1 F.C.R. 128; [2013] Fam. Law 1249, CA (Civ Div) ........ *Digested*, 14/**1405**

S (A Child) v Stevenage BC (Unreported, November 18, 2013), CC (Worthing) [*Winston Jacob, Barrister, Lamb Chambers, Temple, London*] ........ *Digested*, 14/**2352**

S (A Child) (Adoption Order or Special Guardianship Order), Re; *sub nom* DO v LP [2007] EWCA Civ 54; [2007] 1 F.L.R. 819; [2007] 1 F.C.R. 271; [2007] Fam. Law 390; Times, February 9, 2007, CA (Civ Div) ........ *Digested*, 07/**1799**: *Applied* 07/1681, 08/1575, 14/1269

S (A Child) (Adoption Proceedings: Joinder of Father), Re see R (A Child) (Adoption: Father's Involvement), Re

S (A Child) (Appeal from Sexual Abuse Findings), Re; *sub nom* SS v SA [2013] EWCA Civ 1254; [2014] Fam. Law 153, CA (Civ Div)

S (A Child) (Care Order: Appeal), Re [2013] EWCA Civ 1073; [2014] 2 F.L.R. 775; [2014] 2 F.C.R. 139; [2014] Fam. Law 19, CA (Civ Div) ........ *Digested*, 14/**1250**

S (A Child) (Care Order: Appeal), Re [2013] EWCA Civ 1835; [2014] Fam. Law 424, CA (Civ Div)

S (A Child) (Care Order: Immigration), Re [2014] EWHC 529 (Fam); [2014] Fam. Law 953, Fam Div (Milton Keynes)

S (A Child) (Care Proceedings: Non-accidental Injuries), Re see S (A Child) v Nottingham City Council

S (A Child) (Contact Dispute: Committal), Re [2004] EWCA Civ 1790; [2005] 1 F.L.R. 812; [2005] Fam. Law 206; Times, December 9, 2004, CA (Civ Div) ........ *Digested*, 05/**1571**: *Applied* 14/1323

S (A Child) (Ex Parte Orders), Re see S (A Child) (Family Division: Without Notice Orders), Re

S (A Child) (Family Division: Without Notice Orders), Re; *sub nom* S (A Child) (Ex Parte Orders), Re [2001] 1 W.L.R. 211; [2001] 1 All E.R. 362; [2001] 1 F.L.R. 308; [2001] Fam. Law 21; Times, November 2, 2000, Fam Div ........ *Digested*, 00/**2508**: *Applied* 13/457, 14/1351: *Considered* 12/1410

S (A Child) (Identification: Restriction on Publication), Re see S (A Child) (Identification: Restrictions on Publication), Re

S (A Child) (Identification: Restrictions on Publication), Re; *sub nom* S (A Child) (Identification: Restriction on Publication), Re [2004] UKHL 47; [2005] 1 A.C. 593; [2004] 3 W.L.R. 1129; [2004] 4 All E.R. 683; [2005] E.M.L.R. 2; [2005] 1 F.L.R. 591; [2004] 3 F.C.R. 407; [2005] H.R.L.R. 5; [2005] U.K.H.R.R. 129; 17 B.H.R.C. 646; [2005] Crim. L.R. 310; (2004) 154 N.L.J. 1654; (2004) 148 S.J.L.B. 1285; Times, October 29, 2004; Independent, November 2, 2004, HL; affirming [2003] EWCA Civ 963; [2004] Fam. 43; [2003] 3 W.L.R. 1425; [2003] 2 F.L.R. 1253; [2003] 2 F.C.R. 577; [2003] H.R.L.R. 30; [2003] Fam. Law 818; (2003) 100(34) L.S.G. 29; (2003) 153 N.L.J. 1120; (2003) 147 S.J.L.B. 873; Times, July 21, 2003; Independent, July 15, 2003, CA (Civ Div); affirming [2003] EWHC 254 (Fam), Fam Div ........ *Digested*, 05/**2121**: *Applied* 05/1686, 05/2049, 05/4191, 06/1665, 06/2853, 06/445, 07/1732, 07/1806, 07/2189, 08/1540, 09/1590, 10/1731, 10/1742, 11/599, 11/862, 12/331, 14/1279, 14/664, 14/790: *Considered* 05/923, 06/1711, 08/1514, 08/1886, 09/1603, 10/1743, 11/2199, 12/3920, 13/246, 13/3510, 14/21: *Followed* 08/855, 09/929, 10/408, 11/1331, 12/15, 12/332, 13/2042, 14/801, 14/841

S (A Child) (Interim Care Order: Residential Assessment), Re; *sub nom* S (Parenting Assessment), Re [2014] 2 F.L.R. 575; [2014] Fam. Law 1092, CC (Bournemouth) ........ *Digested*, 14/**1284**

S (A Child) (Jurisdiction: Brussels IIR: Prorogation), Re; *sub nom* PB v SE [2013] EWHC 647 (Fam); [2013] 2 F.L.R. 1584; [2013] Fam. Law 808; (2013) 157(13) S.J.L.B. 31, Fam Div ........ *Digested*, 14/**1349**

S (A Child) (Split Hearing: Fact Finding), Re; *sub nom* Cambridgeshire CC v PS [2014] EWCA Civ 25; [2014] 1 F.L.R. 1421; [2014] 1 F.C.R. 477; [2014] Fam. Law 429; [2014] P.T.S.R. D6, CA (Civ Div) ........ *Digested*, 14/**1283**: *Considered* 14/1347

S (A Child), Re; *sub nom* K v Brent LBC [2013] EWCA Civ 926; [2014] 2 F.C.R. 62; [2013] Fam. Law 1369, CA (Civ Div) ........ *Digested,* 14/**1269**: *Followed* 14/1245

S (A Child), Re see S (Children) (Appeal from Care and Placement Orders), Re

S (A Minor) (Parental Responsibility), Re [1995] 2 F.L.R. 648; [1995] 3 F.C.R. 225; [1995] Fam. Law 596; (1995) 159 J.P.N. 674; Times, February 22, 1995, CA (Civ Div) ........ *Digested,* 96/**596**: *Applied* 96/590: *Considered* 96/592, 96/595, 14/1419

S (A Minor), Re; *sub nom* O v P (Sch.1 Application: Stay: Forum Conveniens) [2014] EWHC 2225 (Fam); [2014] Fam. Law 1525, Fam Div

S (Brussels II: Recognition: Best Interests of Child) (No.1), Re [2003] EWHC 2115 (Fam); [2004] 1 F.L.R. 571; [2004] Fam. Law 19, Fam Div ........ *Digested,* 04/**1486**: *Applied* 14/1432: *Approved* 13/1284: *Considered* 11/1359

S (Children) (Adoption: Changed Circumstances), Re see S (Children) (Appeal from Care and Placement Orders), Re

S (Children) (Appeal from Care and Placement Orders), Re; *sub nom* S (Children) (Adoption: Changed Circumstances), Re; S (A Child), Re [2014] EWCA Civ 135; [2014] 3 F.C.R. 304; [2014] Fam. Law 774, CA (Civ Div) ........ *Digested,* 14/**1254**

S (Children) (Care Order: Implementation of Care Plan), Re; *sub nom* W and B (Children) (Care Plan), Re; W (Children) (Care Plan), Re; *joined case* W (Children) (Care Order: Adequacy of Care Plan), Re [2002] UKHL 10; [2002] 2 A.C. 291; [2002] 2 W.L.R. 720; [2002] 2 All E.R. 192; [2002] 1 F.L.R. 815; [2002] 1 F.C.R. 577; [2002] H.R.L.R. 26; [2002] U.K.H.R.R. 652; [2002] B.L.G.R. 251; [2002] Fam. Law 413; (2002) 99(17) L.S.G. 34; (2002) 146 S.J.L.B. 85; Times, March 15, 2002; Independent, March 20, 2002, HL; reversing in part [2001] EWCA Civ 757; [2001] 2 F.L.R. 582; [2001] 2 F.C.R. 450; [2001] H.R.L.R. 50; [2001] U.K.H.R.R. 928; [2001] Fam. Law 581; Times, June 7, 2001; Independent, June 5, 2001, CA (Civ Div) ........ *Digested,* 02/**1615**: *Applied* 02/1617, 02/856, 04/1461, 11/1686, 12/1301, 14/1256: *Considered* 02/4263, 04/1673, 06/1654, 09/1527, 10/1728: *Followed* 11/1342, 12/1325

S (Children) (Care Proceedings: Fact-finding Hearing), Re; *sub nom* FB v West Sussex CC; S (Children) (Care Proceedings: Split Hearing), Re [2014] EWCA Civ 638; [2014] 3 F.C.R. 218; [2014] Fam. Law 1233; [2014] P.T.S.R. D16, CA (Civ Div) ........ *Digested,* 14/**1347**

S (Children) (Care Proceedings: Split Hearing), Re see S (Children) (Care Proceedings: Fact-finding Hearing), Re

S (Financial Remedies: Arbitral Award) see S v S (Arbitral Award: Approval)

S (Parental Order), Re [2009] EWHC 2977 (Fam); [2010] 1 F.L.R. 1156; [2010] Fam. Law 356, Fam Div ........ *Digested,* 10/**1442**: *Applied* 11/1457, 13/1334, 14/1415

S (Parenting Assessment), Re see S (A Child) (Interim Care Order: Residential Assessment), Re

S (Practice: Muslim Women Giving Evidence), Re [2006] EWHC 3743 (Fam); [2007] 2 F.L.R. 461; [2007] Fam. Law 986, Fam Div ........ *Digested,* 08/**1565**: *Applied* 14/1693

S (Relocation: Parental Responsibility); *sub nom* R v C [2013] EWHC 1295 (Fam); [2013] 2 F.L.R. 1453, Fam Div ........ *Digested,* 14/**1311**

S (Transfer of Residence), Re see TE v SH

S-B (Children) (Care Proceedings: Standard of Proof), Re; *sub nom* S-B (Identification of Perpetrator), Re; S-B (Children) (Non-Accidental Injury), Re [2009] UKSC 17; [2010] 1 A.C. 678; [2010] 2 W.L.R. 238; [2010] 1 All E.R. 705; [2010] P.T.S.R. 456; [2010] 1 F.L.R. 1161; [2010] 1 F.C.R. 321; [2010] Fam. Law 231; (2009) 153(48) S.J.L.B. 33; Times, December 18, 2009, SC; reversing [2009] EWCA Civ 1048; [2009] 3 F.C.R. 663; [2010] Fam. Law 14; (2009) 153(26) S.J.L.B. 29, CA (Civ Div) ........ *Digested,* 10/**1325**: *Considered* 11/1346, 11/1441, 13/1231, 13/1326, 14/3325: *Followed* 12/1352, 13/1216, 13/1227

S-B (Children) (Non-Accidental Injury), Re see S-B (Children) (Care Proceedings: Standard of Proof), Re

S-B (Identification of Perpetrator), Re see S-B (Children) (Care Proceedings: Standard of Proof), Re

S-C (Contempt), Re; *sub nom* SC (Children), Re; SC v HC [2010] EWCA Civ 21; [2010] 1 W.L.R. 1311; [2010] Fam. Law 342; (2010) 107(6) L.S.G. 20, CA (Civ Div) ........ *Digested,* 10/**279**: *Applied* 11/1444: *Considered* 12/336: *Followed* 14/1333

SA v BN see N (Death of a Child in DRC: Fact Finding), Re

SA v BN see N (Death of a Child in DRC: Order for Return: Contempt), Re

SA v Camden LBC Independent Appeal Panel [2013] EWHC 3152 (Admin); [2014] E.L.R. 29, QBD (Admin) ........ *Digested*, 14/**924**
SA v PA (Premarital Agreement: Compensation) [2014] EWHC 392 (Fam); [2014] 2 F.L.R. 1028; [2014] 3 F.C.R. 603; [2014] Fam. Law 799, Fam Div ........ *Digested*, 14/**1367**
SA (A Child) v A Local Authority see R. (on the application of SA (A Child)) v A Local Authority
SA (Afghanistan) v Secretary of State for the Home Department see KA (Afghanistan) v Secretary of State for the Home Department
SA (Pakistan) v Secretary of State for the Home Department; *joined cases* AM (Pakistan) v Secretary of State for the Home Department; DP (India) v Secretary of State for the Home Department; NB (Pakistan) v Secretary of State for the Home Department; PB (India) v Secretary of State for the Home Department [2010] EWCA Civ 210; [2010] I.N.L.R. 523, CA (Civ Div) ........ *Digested*, 11/**1756**: *Considered* 14/1698: *Distinguished* 12/1759
SA (Somalia) v Entry Clearance Officer see Mahad (Ethiopia) v Entry Clearance Officer
SA (Sri Lanka) v Secretary of State for the Home Department [2014] EWCA Civ 683; [2014] Imm. A.R. 1133, CA (Civ Div)
SA des Manufactures de Glaces v Tilghman's Patent Sand Blast Co (1883) 25 Ch. D. 1, CA
*Applied* 94/3435: *Distinguished* 68/2909: *Followed* 14/1901
Sabanchiyeva v Russia (38450/05) (2014) 58 E.H.R.R. 14, ECHR
Sabeh El Leil v France (34869/05) [2011] I.R.L.R. 781; (2012) 54 E.H.R.R. 14, ECHR (Grand Chamber)
*Applied* 14/1123: *Considered* 14/1056
SABIC UK Petrochemicals Ltd (formerly Huntsman Petrochemicals (UK) Ltd) v Punj Lloyd Ltd; *joined case* Punj Lloyd Ltd v SABIC UK Petrochemicals Ltd (formerly Huntsman Petrochemicals (UK) Ltd) [2013] EWHC 2916 (QB); [2014] B.L.R. 43; [2013] Bus. L.R. D81, QBD (TCC) ........ *Digested*, 14/**627**
SAE Education Ltd v Revenue and Customs Commissioners [2014] UKFTT 218 (TC); [2014] S.T.I. 1659, FTT (Tax)
Safetynet Security Ltd v Coppage; *sub nom* Coppage v Safety Net Security Ltd [2013] EWCA Civ 1176; [2013] I.R.L.R. 970, CA (Civ Div); affirming 2BM40032, QBD (Merc) (Birmingham) ........ *Digested*, 14/**1029**
Sagal (t/a Bunz UK) v Atelier Bunz GmbH [2009] EWCA Civ 700; [2009] 4 All E.R. 1253; [2010] 1 All E.R. (Comm) 104; [2009] Bus. L.R. 1527; [2009] 2 Lloyd's Rep. 303; [2009] 2 C.L.C. 1; [2009] E.C.C. 30; (2009) 153(27) S.J.L.B. 28, CA (Civ Div); affirming [2008] EWHC 789 (Comm); [2008] 2 Lloyd's Rep. 158; [2008] 2 C.L.C. 850; [2008] Eu. L.R. 717; (2008) 152(23) S.J.L.B. 28, QBD (Comm) ........ *Digested*, 10/**85**: *Applied* 14/82: *Considered* 10/84, 12/59
Saghinadze v Georgia (18768/05) (2014) 59 E.H.R.R. 24, ECHR
Saigol v Thorney Ltd (t/a Thorney Motorsport) [2014] EWCA Civ 556; [2014] 4 Costs L.O. 592, CA (Civ Div) ........ *Digested*, 14/**372**
Sainsbury's Supermarkets Ltd v Condek Holdings Ltd (formerly Condek Ltd) [2014] EWHC 2016 (TCC); [2014] B.L.R. 574; [2014] T.C.L.R. 5; [2014] C.I.L.L. 3553, QBD (TCC) ........ *Digested*, 14/**2199**
Sainsbury's Supermarkets Ltd v Mastercard Inc [2013] EWHC 4554 (Ch); [2014] U.K.C.L.R. 679, Ch D ........ *Digested*, 14/**531**
Sainsbury's Supermarkets Ltd v Wolverhampton City Council see R. (on the application of Sainsbury's Supermarkets Ltd) v Wolverhampton City Council
Saint Prix v Secretary of State for Work and Pensions (C-507/12); *sub nom* St Prix v Secretary of State for Work and Pensions (C-507/12) [2014] P.T.S.R. 1448; [2014] All E.R. (EC) 987; [2014] Imm. A.R. 1076, ECJ (1st Chamber)
Sakalis v Lithuania see Lithuania v Bucnys
Sakthivel v Entry Clearance Officer see Mahad (Ethiopia) v Entry Clearance Officer
Salabiaku v France (A/141-A) (1991) 13 E.H.R.R. 379, ECHR
*Applied* 00/1169, 00/3229, 02/813, 03/812, 13/634: *Cited* 03/978: *Considered* 00/1004, 01/3504, 03/1938, 06/830, 08/722, 14/2954
Salat v Barutis [2013] EWCA Civ 1499; [2014] E.C.C. 2; [2013] C.T.L.C. 250, CA (Civ Div) ........ *Digested*, 14/**610**
Salekipour v Parmar [2013] EWCA Civ 1376; [2014] 1 Costs L.O. 81, CA (Civ Div) ..... *Digested*, 14/**360**
Salford City Council v BJ (Incapacitated Adult) see BJ (Incapacitated Adult), Re
Salford City Council v Mullen see Hounslow LBC v Powell
Salliss v Hunt; *sub nom* Hunt v Salliss; Salliss, Re [2014] EWHC 229 (Ch); [2014] 1 W.L.R. 2402; [2014] 2 All E.R. 1002; [2014] B.P.I.R. 754, Ch D ........ *Digested*, 14/**1781**
Salliss, Re see Salliss v Hunt

Salmon (Deceased), Re; *sub nom* Coard v National Westminster Bank Ltd [1981] Ch. 167; [1980] 3 W.L.R. 748; [1980] 3 All E.R. 532; (1980) 124 S.J. 813, Ch D ...... *Digested,* 80/**2818**: *Applied* 81/2885, 81/2887, 96/5548, 99/4635, 14/2821, 14/2824: *Considered* 83/594.u, 95/5146, 00/4909

Salomon v Salomon & Co Ltd; *sub nom* Broderip v Salomon; *joined case* Salomon & Co Ltd v Salomon [1897] A.C. 22, HL; reversing [1895] 2 Ch. 323, CA *Applied* 47-51/9135, 62/1718, 66/1369, 77/3268, 80/306, 90/538, 98/618, 01/705, 01/944, 09/1489, 13/1300: *Considered* 60/3342, 69/138, 69/2956, 75/803, 77/174, 78/2678, 84/958, 87/3003, 98/2188, 00/5985, 09/2222, 12/3261, 14/403: *Distinguished* 53/940, 74/1837: *Followed* 97/2379

Salomon & Co Ltd v Salomon see Salomon v Salomon & Co Ltd

Salter v Revenue and Customs Commissioners [2014] UKFTT 427 (TC); [2014] S.T.I. 2046, FTT (Tax)

Saltmarsh v Barrett 45 E.R. 885; (1861) 3 De G.F. & J. 279, Ct of Chancery *Distinguished* 14/2834

Salvesen v Riddell [2013] UKSC 22; 2013 S.C. (U.K.S.C.) 236; 2013 S.L.T. 863; 2014 S.C.L.R. 44; [2013] H.R.L.R. 23; 2013 G.W.D. 14-304, SC; reversing [2012] CSIH 26; 2013 S.C. 69; 2012 S.L.T. 633; 2012 S.C.L.R. 403; 2012 Hous. L.R. 30; 2012 G.W.D. 12-234, IH (2 Div); reversing 2010 S.L.C.R. 107, Land Ct ....... *Digested,* 13/**1865**

Salzgitter Mannesmann Handel GmbH v SC Laminorul SA (C-157/12) [2014] 1 W.L.R. 904; [2014] C.E.C. 500; [2014] I.L.Pr. 6, ECJ (4th Chamber)

Samadian v Revenue and Customs Commissioners [2014] UKUT 13 (TCC); [2014] S.T.C. 763; 82 T.C. 252; [2014] B.T.C. 504; [2014] S.T.I. 586, UT (Tax); affirming [2013] UKFTT 115 (TC), FTT (Tax) ....... *Digested,* 14/**2932**

Samara v MBI Partners UK Ltd [2014] EWHC 563 (QB); [2014] 3 Costs L.R. 457; (2014) 164(7598) N.L.J. 18, QBD ....... *Digested,* 14/**379**: *Applied* 14/447

Samaroo v Secretary of State for the Home Department see R. (on the application of Samaroo) v Secretary of State for the Home Department

Samba Diouf v Ministre du Travail, de l'Emploi et de l'Immigration (C-69/10) [2012] 1 C.M.L.R. 8, ECJ (2nd Chamber) *Applied* 13/1575, 14/1657

Sampson v Croydon Crown Court see Sampson, Re

Sampson's Application, Re see Sampson, Re

Sampson, Re; *sub nom* Sampson v Croydon Crown Court; Sampson's Application, Re [1987] 1 W.L.R. 194; [1987] 1 All E.R. 609; (1987) 84 Cr. App. R. 376; [1987] Crim. L.R. 570; (1987) 84 L.S.G. 825; (1987) 137 N.L.J. 169; (1987) 131 S.J. 225, HL ....... *Digested,* 87/**2282**: *Applied* 93/12, 93/15, 05/71: *Considered* 91/613, 92/39, 93/10, 93/11, 95/23, 07/54, 13/702, 14/719: *Followed* 01/3539

Samsam v Secretary of State for the Home Department; *sub nom* Samsam (EEA: Revocation and Retained Rights: Syria), Re [2011] UKUT 165 (IAC); [2011] Imm. A.R. 563; [2011] I.N.L.R. 745, UT (IAC) ....... *Digested,* 11/**1796**: *Considered* 13/1650: *Doubted* 14/1730

Samsam (EEA: Revocation and Retained Rights: Syria), Re see Samsam v Secretary of State for the Home Department

Samsung Electronics (UK) Ltd v Apple Inc [2012] EWCA Civ 1339; [2013] E.C.D.R. 2; [2013] E.M.L.R. 10; [2013] F.S.R. 9, CA (Civ Div); affirming [2012] EWHC 1882 (Pat); [2013] E.C.D.R. 1, Ch D (Patents Ct) ....... *Digested,* 13/**1813**: *Followed* 14/1884

Samsung Electronics Co Ltd v Apple Retail UK Ltd [2013] EWHC 467 (Pat), Ch D (Patents Ct) *Applied* 14/1897

SAMSUNG/Correction of application documents (J16/13) [2014] E.P.O.R. 45, EPO (Legal Bd App)

Samuda v Secretary of State for Work and Pensions [2014] EWCA Civ 1; [2014] 3 All E.R. 201; [2014] C.P. Rep. 18; [2014] 2 F.C.R. 425, CA (Civ Div) ....... *Digested,* 14/**41**

Samuel v Vale of Glamorgan Council [2014] P.A.D. 15, Planning Inspector

Samways v Burbidge see Hart v Burbidge

San Evans Maritime Inc v Aigaion Insurance Co SA [2014] EWHC 163 (Comm); [2014] 2 Lloyd's Rep. 265; [2014] 1 C.L.C. 883; [2014] Lloyd's Rep. I.R. 462, QBD (Comm) ....... *Digested,* 14/**1843**

San Paulo (Brazilian) Railway Co Ltd v Carter (Surveyor of Taxes) [1896] A.C. 31, HL; affirming [1895] 1 Q.B. 580, CA *Considered* 14/540

San Vicente v Secretary of State for Communities and Local Government [2013] EWHC 2713 (Admin); [2014] J.P.L. 217, QBD (Admin) ....... *Digested,* 14/**2404**

San Vicente v Secretary of State for Communities and Local Government; *sub nom* Secretary of State for Communities and Local Government v Vicente; Secretary of State for Communities and Local Government v San Vicente; Vicente v Secretary of State for Communities and Local Government [2013] EWCA Civ 817; [2014] 1 W.L.R. 966; [2014] 1 P. & C.R. 7; [2013] 3 E.G.L.R. 165; [2013] J.P.L. 1516; [2013] 29 E.G. 104 (C.S.), CA (Civ Div); affirming [2012] EWHC 3585 (Admin); [2013] J.P.L. 642, QBD (Admin) ........................... *Digested,* 14/**2401**

Sanade v Secretary of State for the Home Department see Sanade (British Children: Zambrano: Dereci), Re

Sanade (British Children: Zambrano: Dereci), Re; *sub nom* Harrison v Secretary of State for the Home Department; Walker v Secretary of State for the Home Department; Sanade v Secretary of State for the Home Department [2012] UKUT 48 (IAC); [2012] Imm. A.R. 597; [2012] I.N.L.R. 633, UT (IAC) ............... *Digested,* 12/**1775**: *Considered* 14/1668

Sanatorio Quirurgico Modelo SL's Trade Mark Application [2014] E.T.M.R. 16, Trib Sup (Sp)

Sanctuary Systems Ltd v Orient International Holdings Hong Kong Co Ltd 17 I.T.E.L.R. 49, CFI (HK)

Sanders v Kingston (No.1) [2005] EWHC 1145 (Admin); [2005] B.L.G.R. 719; Times, June 16, 2005, QBD (Admin) ............................................................... *Digested,* 05/**2786**: *Applied* 13/2012, 14/2101: *Considered* 14/2102

Sanderson v Revenue and Customs Commissioners [2013] UKUT 623 (TCC); [2014] S.T.C. 915; [2014] B.T.C. 502; [2014] S.T.I. 433, UT (Tax); affirming [2012] UKFTT 207 (TC); [2012] S.F.T.D. 1033; [2012] S.T.I. 1921, FTT (Tax) ............. *Digested,* 14/**2891**

Sandwell and West Birmingham Hospitals NHS Trust v CD [2014] EWCOP 23; [2014] C.O.P.L.R. 650; (2014) 17 C.C.L. Rep. 395; [2014] Med. L.R. 424, CP ............. *Digested,* 14/**494**

Sanger v Newham LBC [2014] EWHC 1922 (Admin); [2014] 2 Cr. App. R. 27; [2014] 2 P. & C.R. 16; [2014] J.P.L. 1218; [2014] A.C.D. 126, DC .................................. *Digested,* 14/**2379**

Sanitec Europe Oy v European Commission (T-381/10) see Keramag Keramische Werke AG v European Commission (T-379/10)

Sankar v Secretary of State for the Home Department see Secretary of State for the Home Department v Pankina

Sannie v Secretary of State for the Home Department [2013] EWCA Civ 1638; [2014] Imm. A.R. 703, CA (Civ Div) ........................................................................ *Digested,* 14/**1730**

Santander UK v RA Legal Solicitors [2014] EWCA Civ 183; [2014] Lloyd's Rep. F.C. 282; [2014] P.N.L.R. 20; [2014] 2 E.G.L.R. 73; [2014] W.T.L.R. 813; [2014] 2 P. & C.R. DG6, CA (Civ Div); reversing [2013] EWHC 1380 (QB); [2013] P.N.L.R. 24; [2014] W.T.L.R. 495, QBD ............................................................................ *Digested,* 14/**2058**: *Considered* 14/2059

Sapkota v Secretary of State for the Home Department; *joined case* KA (Pakistan) v Secretary of State for the Home Department [2011] EWCA Civ 1320; [2012] Imm. A.R. 254; [2012] I.N.L.R. 218, CA (Civ Div) .............................................. *Digested,* 12/**1759**: *Applied* 12/1730: *Considered* 14/1698: *Disapproved* 14/1718: *Not followed* 12/1760

Sapporo Breweries Ltd v Lupofresh Ltd; *sub nom* Lupofresh Ltd v Sapporo Breweries Ltd [2013] EWCA Civ 948; [2014] 1 All E.R. (Comm) 484; [2013] 2 Lloyd's Rep. 444, CA (Civ Div); affirming [2012] EWHC 2013 (QB), QBD ............................. *Digested,* 13/**582**

Saramati v France (Admissibility) (78166/01) see Behrami v France (Admissibility) (71412/01)

Sardar v NHS Commissioning Board [2014] EWHC 38 (QB); [2014] Med. L.R. 12, QBD ...................................................................................................... *Digested,* 14/**2196**

Sargespace Ltd v Eustace [2013] EWHC 2944 (QB); [2014] 1 P. & C.R. DG8, QBD

Sarjantson v Chief Constable of Humberside [2013] EWCA Civ 1252; [2014] Q.B. 411; [2013] 3 W.L.R. 1540; [2014] 1 All E.R. 960; [2014] Med. L.R. 63, CA (Civ Div) . *Digested,* 14/**2460**

Sarjeant v Rigid Group Ltd see Rigid Containers Group Staff Pension Fund, Re

Sarkar v Secretary of State for the Home Department; *sub nom* BS (Bangladesh) v Secretary of State for the Home Department [2014] EWCA Civ 195; [2014] Imm. A.R. 911, CA (Civ Div)

Sarrio SA v Kuwait Investment Authority [1999] 1 A.C. 32; [1997] 3 W.L.R. 1143; [1997] 4 All E.R. 929; [1998] 1 Lloyd's Rep. 129; [1998] Lloyd's Rep. Bank. 57; [1997] C.L.C. 1640; [1998] I.L.Pr. 319; (1997) 141 S.J.L.B. 248; Times, November 17, 1997; Independent, November 19, 1997, HL; reversing [1997] 1 Lloyd's Rep. 113; [1997] C.L.C. 280; [1997] I.L.Pr. 481; Independent, October 3, 1996, CA (Civ Div); reversing [1996] 1 Lloyd's Rep. 650; [1996] C.L.C. 211, QBD (Comm) ............................................................................................. *Digested,* 97/**900**: *Applied* 01/809, 07/501, 14/416: *Considered* 00/738

SAS v France (43835/11) 36 B.H.R.C. 617; [2014] Eq. L.R. 590, ECHR (Grand Chamber)

SAS Institute Inc v World Programming Ltd [2013] EWCA Civ 1482; [2014] R.P.C. 8, CA (Civ Div); affirming [2013] EWHC 69 (Ch); [2013] R.P.C. 17, Ch D .............. *Digested,* 14/**1870**
Sasol v European Commission (T-541/08) [2014] 5 C.M.L.R. 16, GC (3rd Chamber)
Satelscoop BV, Re see Brown v City of London Corp
Satnam Investments Ltd v Dunlop Heywood & Co Ltd [1999] 3 All E.R. 652; [1999] 1 B.C.L.C 385; [1999] F.S.R. 722; [1999] Lloyd's Rep. P.N. 201; [1998] E.G. 190 (C.S.); (1999) 96(6) L.S.G. 33; (1999) 96(2) L.S.G. 30; [1998] N.P.C. 169; Times, December 31, 1998, CA (Civ Div); reversing (1999) 96(2) L.S.G. 30; [1998] N.P.C. 169, Ch D .............. *Digested,* 99/**585**: *Considered* 14/2991
Saunders v Anglia Building Society (formerly Northampton Town and County Building Society); *sub nom* Gallie v Lee [1971] A.C. 1004; [1970] 3 W.L.R. 1078; [1970] 3 All E.R. 961; (1971) 22 P. & C.R. 300; (1970) 114 S.J. 885; Times, November 10, 1970, HL; affirming [1969] 2 Ch. 17; [1969] 2 W.L.R. 901; [1969] 1 All E.R. 1062; (1969) 20 P. & C.R. 310, CA (Civ Div); reversing [1968] 1 W.L.R. 1190; [1968] 2 All E.R. 322; (1968) 19 P. & C.R. 493, Ch D .............. *Digested,* 71/**1805**: *Applied* 76/161, 76/339, 76/340, 90/653, 92/2638: *Considered* 71/9364, 85/1289, 96/1173, 14/628: *Not followed* 80/364
Saunders v United Kingdom (19187/91); *sub nom* Saunders v United Kingdom (43/1994/490/572) [1997] B.C.C. 872; [1998] 1 B.C.L.C. 362; (1997) 23 E.H.R.R. 313; 2 B.H.R.C. 358; Times, December 18, 1996; Independent, January 14, 1997, ECHR; affirming (1994) 18 E.H.R.R. CD23; Independent, September 30, 1994, Eur Comm HR .............. *Digested,* 97/**2816**: *Applied* 01/1047, 05/2092, 09/2226, 14/701: *Considered* 97/2818, 98/3150, 00/5473, 00/6043, 01/6319, 01/974, 02/2664, 02/849, 07/855, 09/2227, 09/764: *Distinguished* 00/2300, 00/667, 04/1951, 05/765: *Followed* 97/817, 00/3234: *Not applied* 98/682
Saunders v United Kingdom (43/1994/490/572) see Saunders v United Kingdom (19187/91)
Savash v CIS General Insurance Ltd [2014] EWHC 375 (TCC); [2014] Lloyd's Rep. I.R. 471, QBD (TCC) .............. *Digested,* 14/**1838**
Savile's Estate, Re see National Westminster Bank Plc v Lucas
Saville v Central Capital Ltd [2014] EWCA Civ 337; [2014] C.T.L.C. 97, CA (Civ Div) .. *Digested,* 14/**1854**
Savings & Investment Bank Ltd (In Liquidation) v Fincken [2003] EWCA Civ 1630; [2004] 1 W.L.R. 667; [2004] 1 All E.R. 1125; [2004] C.P. Rep. 16; (2004) 101(2) L.S.G. 30; Times, November 25, 2003, CA (Civ Div); reversing [2003] EWHC 719 (Ch); [2003] 3 All E.R. 1091, Ch D .............. *Digested,* 04/**261**: *Applied* 12/2295, 14/1008, 14/462: *Considered* 10/1054
Sawiris v Benedetti see Benedetti v Sawiris
Saxton v Bayliss [2013] EWHC 3136 (Ch); [2014] 2 Costs L.O. 111, Ch D
Sayers v Clarke Walker [2002] EWCA Civ 645; [2002] 1 W.L.R. 3095; [2002] 3 All E.R. 490; [2002] C.P. Rep. 61; Times, June 3, 2002; Independent, May 22, 2002, CA (Civ Div) .............. *Digested,* 02/**304**: *Applied* 10/3229, 11/1899, 14/455: *Considered* 07/3368, 08/1473: *Followed* 09/3738, 11/328
SB (Minors), Re see Bristol City Council v A Mother
SC v BH (Passport Order) see C v H
SC v East Riding of Yorkshire Council; *joined case* CW v East Riding of Yorkshire Council [2014] R.A. 279, VT .............. *Digested,* 14/**2097**
SC v HC see S-C (Contempt), Re
SC (Children), Re see S-C (Contempt), Re
SC BCR Leasing IFN SA v Agentia Nationala de Administrare Fiscala - Directia generala de administrare a marilor contribuabili (C-438/13) [2014] B.V.C. 35, ECJ (7th Chamber)
SC DG Petrol Srl v Vitol Broking Ltd [2013] EWHC 3920 (Comm); [2014] 2 Costs L.R. 205, QBD (Comm) .............. *Digested,* 14/**455**
SC Fatorie SRL v Directia Generala a Finantelor Publice Bihor (C-424/12) [2014] B.V.C. 19, ECJ (2nd Chamber)
SCA Packaging Ltd v Boyle; *sub nom* Boyle v SCA Packaging Ltd [2009] UKHL 37; [2009] 4 All E.R. 1181; [2009] N.I. 317; [2009] I.C.R. 1056; [2009] I.R.L.R. 746; (2009) 109 B.M.L.R. 53; (2009) 153(26) S.J.L.B. 27; Times, July 6, 2009, HL (NI); affirming [2008] NICA 48; [2009] I.R.L.R. 54, CA (NI) .............. *Digested,* 09/**4260**: *Applied* 14/2890
Scally v McCammon see Gillingham Football Club Ltd v McCammon
Scandic Distilleries SA v Directia Generala de Administrare a Marilor Contribuabili (C-663/11) [2014] S.T.C. 1, ECJ (5th Chamber)
Scarborough RUFC v Scarborough BC [2014] P.A.D. 21, Planning Inspector

Schering Agrochemicals Ltd v Resibel NV SA (Unreported, November 26, 1992), CA (Civ Div)
*Considered* 14/617: *Distinguished* 98/4384: *Referred to* 96/1248

Schini v Land Berlin (C-506/12) see Specht v Land Berlin (C-501/12)

Schlecker (t/a Firma Anton Schlecker) v Boedeker (C-64/12); *sub nom* Boedeker v Schlecker (t/a Firma Anton Schlecker) (C-64/12) [2014] Q.B. 320; [2014] 2 W.L.R. 45; [2014] All E.R. (EC) 682; [2014] C.E.C. 415; [2014] I.L.Pr. 2; [2013] I.C.R. 1274; [2014] I.R.L.R. 151; (2013) 157(36) S.J.L.B. 37, ECJ (3rd Chamber)

Schmeel v Germany (C-540/12) see Specht v Land Berlin (C-501/12)

Schmid v Hertel (C-328/12) [2014] 1 W.L.R. 633; [2014] C.E.C. 846; [2014] I.L.Pr. 11; [2014] B.P.I.R. 504; (2014) 164(7593) N.L.J. 19, ECJ (1st Chamber)

Schmitt v Deichmann; *sub nom* Phoenix Kapitaldienst GmbH, Re [2012] EWHC 62 (Ch); [2013] Ch. 61; [2012] 3 W.L.R. 681; [2012] 2 All E.R. 1217; [2012] B.C.C. 561; [2014] 1 B.C.L.C. 663; [2012] I.L.Pr. 18; [2012] B.P.I.R. 392; (2012) 162 N.L.J. 214; Times, January 31, 2012, Ch D ........ *Digested,* 12/**1810**

Schneider, Re (C-386/12) see Proceedings Brought by Schneider (C-386/12)

Schombera v Land Berlin (C-502/12) see Specht v Land Berlin (C-501/12)

Schonefeld v Land Berlin (C-504/12) see Specht v Land Berlin (C-501/12)

School of Finance and Management (London) Ltd v Customs and Excise Commissioners; *sub nom* Customs and Excise Commissioners v School of Finance and Management (London) Ltd [2001] S.T.C. 1690; [2002] B.T.C. 5030; [2002] B.V.C. 158; [2001] S.T.I. 1663, Ch D; affirming [2001] B.V.C. 2284; [2001] V. & D.R. 402; [2001] S.T.I. 1145, V&DTr ........ *Digested,* 02/**4740**:
*Considered* 14/3041, 14/3045

Schrade v Sparkasse Ludencheid [2014] EWHC 1049 (Ch); [2014] B.P.I.R. 1058, Ch D ........ *Digested,* 14/**1785**

Schrade v Sparkasse Ludenscheid [2013] B.P.I.R. 911, Ch D ........ *Digested,* 14/**1786**

Schrems v Data Protection Commissioner [2014] IEHC 351; [2014] 3 C.M.L.R. 38, HC (Irl)

Schrems v Data Protection Commissioner [2014] IEHC 310; [2014] 3 C.M.L.R. 37, HC (Irl)

Schroder Exempt Property Unit Trust v Birmingham City Council [2014] EWHC 2207 (Admin); [2014] B.C.C. 690; [2014] B.P.I.R. 1338; [2014] 2 P. & C.R. 15; [2014] 3 E.G.L.R. 91, QBD (Admin) ........ *Digested,* 14/**1972**

Schuh Ltd v Assessor for Glasgow [2013] CSIH 93; 2014 S.L.T. 184; [2014] R.V.R. 62; 2013 G.W.D. 39-754, LVAC ........ *Digested,* 14/**3678**:
*Cited* 14/3676

Schuitemaker v Netherlands (15906/08) (Unreported, May 4, 2010), ECHR
*Considered* 14/2766

Schulke & Mayr UK Ltd v Alkapharm UK Ltd [1999] F.S.R. 161; (1997) 20(11) I.P.D. 20106, Ch D ........ *Digested,* 99/**4853**:
*Considered* 14/2995

Schulte v Deutsche Bausparkasse Badenia AG (C350/03) [2005] E.C.R. I-9215; [2006] 1 C.M.L.R. 11; [2006] All E.R. (EC) 420; [2006] C.E.C. 115, ECJ ........ *Digested,* 06/**697**:
*Applied* 14/611

Schumann v Veale Wasbrough; *joined case* Chinnock v Rea [2013] EWHC 3730 (QB); (2014) 136 B.M.L.R. 214; [2014] P.N.L.R. 14, QBD ........ *Digested,* 14/**2212**

Schuster v Germany (C-541/12) see Specht v Land Berlin (C-501/12)

Schutz (UK) Ltd v Werit (UK) Ltd see Schutz (UK) Ltd v Werit UK Ltd

Schutz (UK) Ltd v Werit UK Ltd; *sub nom* Schutz (UK) Ltd v Werit (UK) Ltd [2013] UKSC 16; [2013] 2 All E.R. 177; [2013] Bus. L.R. 565; [2013] 3 Costs L.O. 500; [2013] R.P.C. 16, SC; reversing [2011] EWCA Civ 303; [2011] Bus. L.R. 1510; [2011] F.S.R. 19, CA (Civ Div); reversing in part [2010] EWHC 660 (Pat); [2010] Bus. L.R. 1244; [2010] F.S.R. 22, Ch D (Patents Ct) ........ *Digested,* 13/**1779**:
*Considered* 14/1877

Schwabe v Germany (8080/08); *joined case* MG v Germany (8577/08) (2014) 59 E.H.R.R. 28; 32 B.H.R.C. 141, ECHR ........ *Digested,* 12/**1668**

Schwarz v Stadt Bochum (C-291/12) [2014] 2 C.M.L.R. 5, ECJ (4th Chamber)

Science & Media LLP, Re; *sub nom* Williams v Bennett [2014] B.P.I.R. 774, Ch D (Companies Ct) ........ *Digested,* 14/**1829**

Scoppola v Italy (126/05) [2013] 1 Costs L.O. 62; (2013) 56 E.H.R.R. 19; 33 B.H.R.C. 126; Times, June 12, 2012, ECHR (Grand Chamber)
*Applied* 14/976

Scotland v British Credit Trust Ltd [2014] EWCA Civ 790; [2014] Bus. L.R. 1079, CA (Civ Div)

Scott v Duncan [2012] EWHC 1792 (QB); [2012] 4 Costs L.R. 787, QBD ........ *Digested,* 12/**377**:
*Considered* 14/343

Scott v Russell [2013] EWCA Civ 1432; [2014] 1 Costs L.O. 95, CA (Civ Div) .............. *Digested,* 14/**1074**

Scott v Scott; *sub nom* Morgan v Scott [1913] A.C. 417, HL; reversing [1912] P. 241, CA; affirming [1912] P. 4, PDAD
*Applied* 52/494, 57/2759, 63/1807, 93/3033, 94/5047, 01/2622, 01/564, 06/353, 07/940, 11/373, 11/4, 13/374, 14/2184: *Considered* 53/1034, 53/2752, 63/1092, 65/203, 75/955, 77/1965, 79/2120, 81/2144, 84/2250, 84/866, 88/692, 89/784, 92/693, 92/969, 93/2835, 95/3545, 95/3959, 01/2622, 02/1695, 09/1590: *Distinguished* 47-51/7548, 04/185, 04/809: *Followed* 58/2473, 96/2980, 10/276, 14/1693: *Not applied* 08/714: *Referred to* 53/1034

Scott v Southern Pacific Mortgages Ltd see North East Property Buyers Litigation, Re

Scottbridge Construction Ltd v Wright; *sub nom* Wright v Scottbridge Construction Ltd 2003 S.C. 520; 2002 S.L.T. 1356; [2003] I.R.L.R. 21; 2002 G.W.D. 34-1150, IH (1 Div); affirming [2001] I.R.L.R. 589, EAT .............. *Digested,* 02/**5575**:
*Applied* 08/1177, 14/1091: *Considered* 11/1100, 12/1112: *Distinguished* 03/1286

Scottish & Newcastle Plc v GD Construction (St Albans) Ltd; *sub nom* GD Construction (St Albans) Ltd v Scottish & Newcastle Plc [2003] EWCA Civ 16; [2003] B.L.R. 131; 86 Con. L.R. 1; [2003] Lloyd's Rep. I.R. 809; [2003] 6 E.G. 144 (C.S.); (2003) 100(11) L.S.G. 31; [2003] N.P.C. 8; Times, January 28, 2003, CA (Civ Div); reversing (2001) 3 T.C.L.R. 24; 80 Con. L.R. 75; [2002] Lloyd's Rep. I.R. 77; (2002) 18 Const. L.J. 246, QBD (TCC) .............. *Digested,* 03/**669**:
*Considered* 07/739, 14/1855: *Distinguished* 08/596

Scottish Exhibition Centre Ltd v Customs and Excise Commissioners see Scottish Exhibition Centre Ltd v Revenue and Customs Commissioners

Scottish Exhibition Centre Ltd v Revenue and Customs Commissioners; *sub nom* Scottish Exhibition Centre Ltd v Customs and Excise Commissioners [2006] CSIH 42; [2008] S.T.C. 967; 2006 S.C. 702; 2006 S.C.L.R. 849; [2007] B.T.C. 5769; [2007] B.V.C. 716; [2006] S.T.I. 1918, IH (Ex Div); reversing [2005] B.V.C. 2529; [2005] S.T.I. 896, V&DTr (Edinburgh) .............. *Digested,* 07/**5568**:
*Applied* 14/3046

Scottish Ministers v Ellis [2014] CSOH 10; 2014 S.C.L.R. 434; [2014] Lloyd's Rep. F.C. 268; 2014 G.W.D. 4-78, OH .............. *Digested,* 14/**3453**

Scottish Ministers v Stirton [2013] CSIH 81; 2014 S.C. 218; 2013 S.L.T. 1141; [2014] Lloyd's Rep. F.C. 18; 2013 G.W.D. 34-666, IH (2 Div); affirming [2012] CSOH 15; 2012 G.W.D. 6-100, OH .............. *Digested,* 14/**3325**

Scottish Ministers v Stirton 2006 S.L.T. 306; 2006 G.W.D. 4-68, OH .............. *Digested,* 06/**5227**:
*Disapproved* 14/3325

Scottish Premier League Ltd v Lisini Pub Management Co Ltd; *sub nom* Scottish Professional Football League Ltd v Lisini Pub Management Co Ltd [2013] CSIH 97; 2014 S.C. 300; 2014 S.L.T. 99; [2014] U.K.C.L.R. 366; [2014] L.L.R. 794; 2013 G.W.D. 40-757, IH (Ex Div); affirming [2013] CSOH 48; 2013 S.L.T. 629; [2013] U.K.C.L.R. 166; 2013 G.W.D. 13-272, OH .............. *Digested,* 14/**3354**

Scottish Professional Football League Ltd v Lisini Pub Management Co Ltd [2014] CSIH 6; [2014] U.K.C.L.R. 389; 2014 G.W.D. 6-117, IH (Ex Div) .............. *Digested,* 14/**3349**

Scottish Professional Football League Ltd v Lisini Pub Management Co Ltd see Scottish Premier League Ltd v Lisini Pub Management Co Ltd

Scotto v Clarke see Scotto v Petch

Scotto v Petch; *sub nom* Sedgefield Steeplechase Co (1927) Ltd, Re; *joined case* Scotto v Clarke [2001] B.C.C. 889; Times, February 8, 2001, CA (Civ Div); affirming [2000] 2 B.C.L.C. 211; (2000) 97(6) L.S.G. 33; (2000) 144 S.J.L.B. 107; Times, February 16, 2000, Ch D .............. *Digested,* 01/**744**:
*Applied* 14/515

Scotts Atlantic Management Ltd (In Liquidation) v Revenue and Customs Commissioners [2013] UKFTT 299 (TC); [2014] S.F.T.D. 210; [2013] S.T.I. 2574, FTT (Tax) .............. *Digested,* 14/**2872**

SCRABBLE Trade Mark see JW Spear & Sons Ltd v Zynga Inc

Scrimsign (Micro-Electronics) Ltd v Revenue and Customs Commissioners [2014] UKFTT 866 (TC); [2014] S.T.I. 2909, FTT (Tax)

Scrivens v Secretary of State for Communities and Local Government [2013] EWHC 3549 (Admin); [2014] J.P.L. 521, QBD (Admin) .............. *Digested,* 14/**2436**

SE (Zimbabwe) v Secretary of State for the Home Department [2014] EWCA Civ 256; [2014] Imm. A.R. 855, CA (Civ Div) .............. *Digested,* 14/**1670**

Sea Glory Maritime Co v Al Sagr National Insurance Co (The Nancy) [2013] EWHC 2116 (Comm); [2013] 2 All E.R. (Comm) 913; [2014] 1 Lloyd's Rep. 14; [2013] 2 C.L.C. 114; [2014] Lloyd's Rep. I.R. 112; [2013] Bus. L.R. D51, QBD (Comm) *Digested,* 14/**1850**

Sea-Cargo Skips AS v State Bank of India [2013] EWHC 177 (Comm); [2013] 2 Lloyd's Rep. 477, QBD (Comm) .............. *Digested,* 14/**265**

Seabrook v Alexander (Valuation Officer) [2014] R.A. 382, VT .............. *Digested,* 14/**2133**

Seagrain LLC v Glencore Grain BV [2013] EWCA Civ 1627; [2014] 1 All E.R. (Comm) 540; [2014] 1 Lloyd's Rep. 598; [2014] 1 C.L.C. 14, CA (Civ Div); affirming [2013] EWHC 1189 (Comm); [2013] 2 All E.R. (Comm) 640; [2013] 2 Lloyd's Rep. 590; [2013] 1 C.L.C. 919, QBD (Comm) .......... *Digested,* 14/**1964**

Seakom Ltd v Knowledgepool Group Ltd [2014] EWCA Civ 1164; [2014] 5 Costs L.R. 820, CA (Civ Div) .......... *Digested,* 14/**469**

Seawind Tankers Corp v Bayoil SA see Bayoil SA, Re

Secondus v Atkinson [2013] B.P.I.R. 632, Ch D (NI) .......... *Digested,* 14/**3198**

Secret Hotels2 Ltd (formerly Med Hotels Ltd) v Revenue and Customs Commissioners; *sub nom* Revenue and Customs Commissioners v Secret Hotels2 Ltd (formerly Med Hotels Ltd) [2014] UKSC 16; [2014] 2 All E.R. 685; [2014] S.T.C. 937; [2014] B.V.C. 9; [2014] S.T.I. 864, SC; reversing [2012] EWCA Civ 1571; [2013] S.T.C. 452; [2013] B.V.C. 26; [2012] S.T.I. 3404, CA (Civ Div); reversing [2011] UKUT 308 (TCC); [2011] S.T.C. 1750; [2011] B.V.C. 1700; [2012] L.L.R. 253; [2011] S.T.I. 2496, UT (Tax); reversing [2010] UKFTT 120 (TC); [2010] B.V.C. 2234; [2010] S.F.T.D. 807, FTT (Tax) .......... *Digested,* 14/**3073**

Secretary of State for Business, Enterprise and Regulatory Reform v Neufeld; *sub nom* Neufeld v Secretary of State for Business, Enterprise and Regulatory Reform; *joined case* Howe v Secretary of State for Business, Enterprise and Regulatory Reform [2009] EWCA Civ 280; [2009] 3 All E.R. 790; [2009] B.C.C. 687; [2009] 2 B.C.L.C. 273; [2009] I.C.R. 1183; [2009] I.R.L.R. 475; [2009] B.P.I.R. 909; (2009) 106(15) L.S.G. 15; Times, April 10, 2009, CA (Civ Div) ...... *Digested,* 09/**1199**: *Followed* 14/1110

Secretary of State for Business, Innovation and Skills v Feld; *sub nom* Feld v Secretary of State for Business, Innovation and Skills [2014] EWHC 1383 (Ch); [2014] 1 W.L.R. 3396, Ch D (Companies Ct) .......... *Digested,* 14/**412**

Secretary of State for Business, Innovation and Skills v Knight [2014] I.R.L.R. 605, EAT .......... *Digested,* 14/**1110**

Secretary of State for Business, Innovation and Skills v Melaris see Waterfall Media (In Administration), Re

Secretary of State for Business, Innovation and Skills v Sky Land Consultants Plc see Sky Land Consultants Plc, Re

Secretary of State for Business, Innovation and Skills v Weston [2014] EWHC 2933 (Ch); [2014] B.C.C. 581; [2014] Lloyd's Rep. F.C. 648, Ch D (Birmingham)

Secretary of State for Communities and Local Government v Hopkins Development Ltd see Hopkins Developments Ltd v Secretary of State for Communities and Local Government

Secretary of State for Communities and Local Government v Ioannou see Ioannou v Secretary of State for Communities and Local Government

Secretary of State for Communities and Local Government v Redhill Aerodrome Ltd see Redhill Aerodrome Ltd v Secretary of State for Communities and Local Government

Secretary of State for Communities and Local Government v San Vicente see San Vicente v Secretary of State for Communities and Local Government

Secretary of State for Communities and Local Government v Venn see Venn v Secretary of State for Communities and Local Government

Secretary of State for Communities and Local Government v Vicente see San Vicente v Secretary of State for Communities and Local Government

Secretary of State for Communities and Local Government v Welwyn Hatfield BC see Welwyn Hatfield Council v Secretary of State for Communities and Local Government

Secretary of State for Culture, Media and Sport v BT Pension Scheme Trustees Ltd see BT Pension Scheme Trustees Ltd v British Telecommunications Plc

Secretary of State for Defence v San Miguel Alvarado 35 B.H.R.C. 428, CA (Gib)

Secretary of State for Defence v Smith see R. (on the application of Smith) v Oxfordshire Assistant Deputy Coroner

Secretary of State for Defence v Turner Estate Solutions Ltd [2014] EWHC 244 (TCC); [2014] C.I.L.L. 3492, QBD (TCC)

Secretary of State for Education and Science v Tameside MBC [1977] A.C. 1014; [1976] 3 W.L.R. 641; [1976] 3 All E.R. 665; (1976) 120 S.J. 735, HL; affirming (1976) 120 S.J. 539, CA (Civ Div) .......... *Digested,* 76/**829**: *Applied* 78/861, 82/1453, 83/359, 83/3723, 94/4593, 98/1901, 00/3115, 00/5397, 07/1485, 10/2618, 10/491: *Considered* 79/198, 79/810, 81/1535, 87/31, 89/3586, 95/1911, 12/2105, 14/2744: *Distinguished* 91/67, 99/4248: *Followed* 80/1378

Secretary of State for Energy and Climate Change v Jones see Jones v Secretary of State for Energy and Climate Change

Secretary of State for Foreign and Commonwealth Affairs v Assistant Deputy Coroner for Inner North London [2013] EWHC 1786 (Admin); [2014] A.C.D. 24, QBD (Admin)

Secretary of State for Foreign and Commonwealth Affairs v Assistant Deputy Coroner for Inner North London [2013] EWHC 3724 (Admin); [2014] A.C.D. 43, DC

Secretary of State for Health v Servier Laboratories Ltd [2012] EWHC 2761 (Ch), Ch D
*Affirmed* 14/539: *Applied* 14/529

Secretary of State for Health v Servier Laboratories Ltd; *joined case* National Grid Electricity Transmission Plc v ABB Ltd [2013] EWCA Civ 1234; [2014] 1 W.L.R. 4383; [2014] U.K.C.L.R. 263; [2014] Lloyd's Rep. F.C. 175, CA (Civ Div) .......... *Digested,* 14/**539**

Secretary of State For Health v Servier Laboratories Ltd [2012] EWHC 3663 (Ch), Ch D
*Affirmed* 14/539

Secretary of State for Justice v James (formerly Walker) see R. (on the application of Wells) v Parole Board for England and Wales

Secretary of State for Justice v MP [2013] UKUT 25 (AAC); [2013] M.H.L.R. 154, UT (AAC) .......... *Digested,* 14/**2177**

Secretary of State for Justice v RB [2011] EWCA Civ 1608; [2012] 1 W.L.R. 2043; (2012) 124 B.M.L.R. 13; [2012] M.H.L.R. 131; Times, January 19, 2012, CA (Civ Div); reversing [2010] UKUT 454 (AAC); [2011] M.H.L.R. 37, UT (AAC) ..... *Digested,* 12/**2280**: *Applied* 14/2939

Secretary of State for Justice v Walker see R. (on the application of Wells) v Parole Board for England and Wales

Secretary of State for the Environment, Transport and the Regions v Legal & General Assurance Society Ltd see R. (on the application of Holding & Barnes Plc) v Secretary of State for the Environment, Transport and the Regions

Secretary of State for the Foreign Office and Commonwealth Affairs v Maftah see R. (on the application of Khaled) v Secretary of State for Foreign and Commonwealth Affairs

Secretary of State for the Home Department v Abdi (Dhudi Saleban) [1996] Imm. A.R. 148, CA (Civ Div) .......... *Digested,* 96/**3181**: *Applied* 09/2099, 14/1700: *Considered* 97/2912

Secretary of State for the Home Department v Adamally see Adamally (Section 47 Removal Decisions: Tribunal Procedures), Re

Secretary of State for the Home Department v Adhikari see Secretary of State for the Home Department v Raju

Secretary of State for the Home Department v Ahmadi see Ahmadi (S.47 Decision: Validity: Sapkota: Afghanistan), Re

Secretary of State for the Home Department v Al Islam see Secretary of State for the Home Department v Raju

Secretary of State for the Home Department v Al-Jedda see Al-Jedda v Secretary of State for the Home Department

Secretary of State for the Home Department v Aladeselu see Aladeselu v Secretary of State for the Home Department

Secretary of State for the Home Department v AP [2010] UKSC 26; [2010] 1 W.L.R. 1652; [2010] 4 All E.R. 259; [2010] H.R.L.R. 26; [2010] U.K.H.R.R. 1014; (2010) 160 N.L.J. 941; Times, June 28, 2010, SC .......... *Digested,* 10/**1716**: *Applied* 14/664

Secretary of State for the Home Department v AR (Afghanistan) see WM (Democratic Republic of Congo) v Secretary of State for the Home Department

Secretary of State for the Home Department v AV (Democratic Republic of Congo) see R. (on the application of Akpinar) v Upper Tribunal (Immigration and Asylum Chamber)

Secretary of State for the Home Department v CC; *sub nom* CF v Secretary of State for the Home Department; Mohamed v Secretary of State for the Home Department; *joined case* Secretary of State for the Home Department v CF [2014] EWCA Civ 559; [2014] 1 W.L.R. 4240; [2014] 3 All E.R. 760; Times, May 9, 2014, CA (Civ Div); reversing in part [2012] EWHC 2837 (Admin); [2013] 1 W.L.R. 2171; Times, January 1, 2013, QBD (Admin) .......... *Digested,* 14/**298**

Secretary of State for the Home Department v CF see Secretary of State for the Home Department v CC

Secretary of State for the Home Department v Elias see R. (on the application of Elias) v Secretary of State for Defence

Secretary of State for the Home Department v F; *joined cases* Secretary of State for the Home Department v N; E v Secretary of State for the Home Department [2009] UKHL 28; [2010] 2 A.C. 269; [2009] 3 W.L.R. 74; [2009] 3 All E.R. 643; [2009] H.R.L.R. 26; [2009] U.K.H.R.R. 1177; 26 B.H.R.C. 738; (2009) 106(25) L.S.G. 14; Times, June 11, 2009, HL; reversing [2008] EWCA Civ 1148; [2009] 2 W.L.R. 423; [2009] 2 All E.R. 602; [2009] H.R.L.R. 4; [2009] U.K.H.R.R. 176; [2009] A.C.D. 7; Times, October 29, 2008, CA (Civ Div) .................................... *Digested,* 09/**428**: *Applied* 10/1728, 10/348, 10/383, 10/384, 11/1685, 11/2230, 12/342, 13/668, 14/2162: *Considered* 10/382, 10/724, 11/1798, 11/60: *Followed* 10/1079, 10/70, 14/298: *Not applied* 11/793

Secretary of State for the Home Department v FV (Italy); *sub nom* FV (Italy) v Secretary of State for the Home Department [2012] EWCA Civ 1199; [2013] 1 W.L.R. 3339; [2013] 1 All E.R. 1180; [2012] 3 C.M.L.R. 56; [2013] Imm. A.R. 114; [2013] I.N.L.R. 293; (2012) 109(37) L.S.G. 20, CA (Civ Div) ....................... *Digested,* 13/**1595**: *Followed* 14/1676

Secretary of State for the Home Department v Greenwood see Greenwood (Automatic Deportation: Order of Events), Re

Secretary of State for the Home Department v Gulshan see Gulshan (Article 8: New Rules: Correct Approach)

Secretary of State for the Home Department v Hayat see Hayat v Secretary of State for the Home Department

Secretary of State for the Home Department v Headley see R. (on the application of Clift) v Secretary of State for the Home Department

Secretary of State for the Home Department v Hindawi see R. (on the application of Clift) v Secretary of State for the Home Department

Secretary of State for the Home Department v Javed see R. (on the application of Javed) v Secretary of State for the Home Department

Secretary of State for the Home Department v Khatel see Secretary of State for the Home Department v Raju

Secretary of State for the Home Department v KK (Congo) [2005] UKIAT 54, IAT *Considered* 11/1720, 14/1659

Secretary of State for the Home Department v KY see N v Advocate General for Scotland

Secretary of State for the Home Department v Marghia see Marghia (Procedural Fairness)

Secretary of State for the Home Department v MG (Portugal) (C-400/12) [2014] 1 W.L.R. 2441; [2014] 2 C.M.L.R. 40; [2014] Imm. A.R. 561; [2014] I.N.L.R. 670, ECJ (2nd Chamber) .............................................................................................. *Digested,* 14/**1666**

Secretary of State for the Home Department v MG (Portugal) see MG (EU deportation: Article 28(3): Imprisonment: Portugal), Re

Secretary of State for the Home Department v MK (India) see MK (Best Interests of Child: India), Re

Secretary of State for the Home Department v MN see N v Advocate General for Scotland

Secretary of State for the Home Department v N see Secretary of State for the Home Department v F

Secretary of State for the Home Department v Pankina; *sub nom* Pankina v Secretary of State for the Home Department; *joined cases* Sankar v Secretary of State for the Home Department; Ali v Secretary of State for the Home Department; Junaideen v Secretary of State for the Home Department; Ahmed v Secretary of State for the Home Department; Malekia v Secretary of State for the Home Department [2010] EWCA Civ 719; [2011] Q.B. 376; [2010] 3 W.L.R. 1526; [2011] 1 All E.R. 1043; [2010] Imm. A.R. 689; [2010] I.N.L.R. 529; [2010] A.C.D. 93; Times, July 20, 2010, CA (Civ Div) .................................................. *Digested,* 10/**1796**: *Applied* 11/1782, 11/1783, 12/1741, 12/1757, 12/1763: *Considered* 12/1755, 12/1756, 12/4102, 14/1703: *Explained* 11/1778, 12/1764: *Followed* 12/1740: *Not applied* 12/1767

Secretary of State for the Home Department v Rahman (C-83/11) [2013] Q.B. 249; [2013] 2 W.L.R. 230; [2012] 3 C.M.L.R. 55; [2014] All E.R. (EC) 340; [2013] Imm. A.R. 73; [2013] I.N.L.R. 334, ECJ (Grand Chamber) ................................ *Digested,* 13/**1646**: *Applied* 14/1732: *Distinguished* 14/1740

Secretary of State for the Home Department v Raju; *sub nom* Raju v Secretary of State for the Home Department; Khatel (S.85A: Effect of Continuing Application), Re; Khatel v Secretary of State for the Home Department; *joined cases* Secretary of State for the Home Department v Khatel; Secretary of State for the Home Department v Adhikari; Secretary of State for the Home Department v Al Islam [2013] EWCA Civ 754; [2014] 1 W.L.R. 1768; [2013] 4 All E.R. 1043; [2013] Imm. A.R. 969; [2013] I.N.L.R. 654, CA (Civ Div); reversing [2013] UKUT 44 (IAC); [2013] I.N.L.R. 439, UT (IAC) ........................ *Digested,* 14/**1713**: *Followed* 14/1711

Secretary of State for the Home Department v Ravichandran see R. v Secretary of State for the Home Department Ex p. Jeyeanthan

Secretary of State for the Home Department v Razgar see R. (on the application of Razgar) v Secretary of State for the Home Department (No.2)

Secretary of State for the Home Department v Rehman; *sub nom* Rehman v Secretary of State for the Home Department [2001] UKHL 47; [2003] 1 A.C. 153; [2001] 3 W.L.R. 877; [2002] 1 All E.R. 122; 11 B.H.R.C. 413; [2002] Imm. A.R. 98; [2002] I.N.L.R. 92; [2002] A.C.D. 6; (2001) 98(42) L.S.G. 37; (2001) 145 S.J.L.B. 238; Times, October 15, 2001; Independent, October 17, 2001, HL; affirming [2000] 3 W.L.R. 1240; [2000] 3 All E.R. 778; [2001] Imm. A.R. 30; [2000] I.N.L.R. 531; (2000) 97(24) L.S.G. 40; Times, May 31, 2000; Independent, May 26, 2000, CA (Civ Div); reversing [1999] I.N.L.R. 517, Sp Imm App Comm ........................ *Digested,* 01/**3662**: *Applied* 06/2859, 08/4142, 13/64: *Considered* 04/2004, 14/1724: *Followed* 05/2825

Secretary of State for the Home Department v Robb [1995] Fam. 127; [1995] 2 W.L.R. 722; [1995] 1 All E.R. 677; [1995] 1 F.L.R. 412; [1995] 1 F.C.R. 557; [1995] Fam. Law 185; (1994) 144 N.L.J. 1695; Times, October 21, 1994; Independent, October 10, 1994, Fam Div ........................ *Digested,* 95/**4266**: *Applied* 14/1525

Secretary of State for the Home Department v Rodriguez; *joined case* Mandalia v Secretary of State for the Home Department [2014] EWCA Civ 2; [2014] Imm. A.R. 588; [2014] I.N.L.R. 307, CA (Civ Div) ........................ *Digested,* 14/**1711**

Secretary of State for the Home Department v Seye see Seye (Chen Children: Employment), Re

Secretary of State for the Home Department v Shahzad see Shahzad (Art 8: Legitimate Aim)

Secretary of State for the Home Department v Sim see R. (on the application of Sim) v Parole Board for England and Wales

Secretary of State for Trade and Industry v Bairstow; *sub nom* Queens Moat Houses Plc, Re [2003] EWCA Civ 321; [2004] Ch. 1; [2003] 3 W.L.R. 841; [2004] 4 All E.R. 325; [2003] C.P. Rep. 46; [2003] B.C.C. 682; [2003] 1 B.C.L.C. 696; (2003) 100(18) L.S.G. 36; (2003) 153 N.L.J. 440; Times, March 31, 2003; Independent, March 20, 2003, CA (Civ Div); reversing 751 of 2000, Ch D ......... *Digested,* 03/**509**: *Applied* 07/339, 07/345, 11/240, 14/297: *Considered* 07/571, 08/266, 10/258: *Distinguished* 08/2125, 09/336: *Followed* 14/2209

Secretary of State for Trade and Industry v Gray see Grayan Building Services Ltd (In Liquidation), Re

Secretary of State for Trade and Industry v Jones [1999] B.C.C. 336, Ch D ................ *Digested,* 99/**610**: *Applied* 14/505

Secretary of State for Work and Pensions v Alam [2010] I.C.R. 665; [2010] I.R.L.R. 283, EAT ........................ *Digested,* 10/**1047**: *Cited* 14/1049: *Explained* 12/1063

Secretary of State for Work and Pensions v Dias [2009] EWCA Civ 807; [2010] 1 C.M.L.R. 4, CA (Civ Div) ........................ *Digested,* 10/**3087**: *Applied* 11/1768: *Followed* 12/3117, 14/1733: *Preliminary ruling given* 12/1275

Secretary of State for Work and Pensions v Dias (C-325/09) [2011] 3 C.M.L.R. 40; [2012] All E.R. (EC) 199; [2012] C.E.C. 344; [2011] Imm. A.R. 855; [2011] I.N.L.R. 772, ECJ (3rd Chamber) ........................ *Digested,* 12/**1275**: *Applied* 14/1735

Secretary of State for Work and Pensions v Higgins [2014] I.C.R. 341; [2013] Eq. L.R. 1180, EAT ........................ *Digested,* 14/**1045**

Secretary of State for Work and Pensions v Lassal (C-162/09) [2011] 1 C.M.L.R. 31; [2011] All E.R. (EC) 1169; [2011] Imm. A.R. 134, ECJ (3rd Chamber) *Applied* 14/1738: *Considered* 11/1767

Secretary of State for Work and Pensions v R. (on the application of MM) see MM v Secretary of State for Work and Pensions

SED Essex Ltd, Re see Revenue and Customs Commissioners v SED Essex Ltd

Seddon Homes Ltd v Cheshire East Council [2014] P.A.D. 12, Planning Inspector

Sedgefield Steeplechase Co (1927) Ltd, Re see Scotto v Petch
Seeberger v Studentenwerk Heidelberg (C-585/11) see Prinz v Region Hannover (C-523/11)
Seele Middle East FZE v Drake and Scull Int SA Co [2013] EWHC 4350 (TCC); [2014] C.I.L.L. 3472, QBD (TCC)
Seesurrun v Revenue and Customs Commissioners [2014] UKFTT 783 (TC); [2014] S.T.I. 3196, FTT (Tax)
Segelman (Deceased), Re [1996] Ch. 171; [1996] 2 W.L.R. 173; [1995] 3 All E.R. 676, Ch D ........ *Digested,* 96/**5557**: *Applied* 07/3966, 09/3731, 13/2976, 13/2977, 14/2833: *Considered* 11/3264, 12/3196, 12/3197
Sekhri v Ray; *sub nom* Ray v Sekhiri; *joined case* Ray v Sekhri [2014] EWCA Civ 119; [2014] 2 F.L.R. 1168; [2014] 2 F.C.R. 167; [2014] Fam. Law 784, CA (Civ Div); affirming [2013] EWHC 2290 (Fam); [2014] 1 F.L.R. 612; [2013] Fam. Law 1522, Fam Div ........ *Digested,* 14/**1325**
Seldon v Clarkson Wright & Jakes [2014] I.C.R. 1275; [2014] I.R.L.R. 748; [2014] Eq. L.R. 517, EAT ........ *Digested,* 14/**1012**
Seldon v Clarkson Wright & Jakes [2012] UKSC 16; [2012] 3 All E.R. 1301; [2012] 2 C.M.L.R. 50; [2012] I.C.R. 716; [2012] I.R.L.R. 590; [2012] Eq. L.R. 579; [2012] Pens. L.R. 239; (2012) 109(19) L.S.G. 18; (2012) 162 N.L.J. 653; (2012) 156(17) S.J.L.B. 31; Times, May 2, 2012, SC; affirming [2010] EWCA Civ 899; [2011] 1 All E.R. 770; [2011] 1 C.M.L.R. 5; [2011] I.C.R. 60; [2010] I.R.L.R. 865; [2010] Eq. L.R. 89, CA (Civ Div); affirming [2009] 3 All E.R. 435; [2009] I.R.L.R. 267, EAT ........ *Digested,* 12/**1037**: *Followed* 14/1012
SELEXYS/Anyi-p-selectin antibodies (T2317/13) [2014] E.P.O.R. 33, EPO (Technical Bd App)
Selkent Bus Co Ltd v Moore [1996] I.C.R. 836; [1996] I.R.L.R. 661, EAT ........ *Digested,* 96/**2661**: *Applied* 00/2207, 09/4869, 13/1016, 14/1070: *Considered* 05/1278, 12/1120: *Distinguished* 07/1339: *Explained* 14/1090
Selkirk v McIntyre 16 I.T.E.L.R. 245, HC (NZ)
Sembcorp Marine Ltd v PPL Holdings Pte Ltd [2013] SGCA 43; 151 Con. L.R. 170, CA (Sing)
Sempra Metals Ltd (formerly Metallgesellschaft Ltd) v Inland Revenue Commissioners [2007] UKHL 34; [2008] 1 A.C. 561; [2007] 3 W.L.R. 354; [2007] 4 All E.R. 657; [2008] Bus. L.R. 49; [2007] S.T.C. 1559; [2008] Eu. L.R. 1; [2007] B.T.C. 509; [2007] S.T.I. 1865; (2007) 104(31) L.S.G. 25; (2007) 157 N.L.J. 1082; (2007) 151 S.J.L.B. 985; Times, July 25, 2007, HL; affirming in part [2005] EWCA Civ 389; [2006] Q.B. 37; [2005] 3 W.L.R. 521; [2005] S.T.C. 687; [2005] 2 C.M.L.R. 30; [2005] Eu. L.R. 773; [2005] B.T.C. 202; [2005] S.T.I. 831; [2005] N.P.C. 52; Times, April 26, 2005; Independent, April 22, 2005, CA (Civ Div); affirming [2004] EWHC 2387 (Ch); [2004] S.T.C. 1178; [2004] Eu. L.R. 939; [2004] B.T.C. 358; [2004] S.T.I. 1495; Times, June 25, 2004, Ch D ........ *Digested,* 07/**1052**: *Applied* 07/4311, 07/4359, 09/4081, 10/3506, 14/3079: *Cited* 09/458: *Considered* 10/3507, 10/3512, 11/857, 12/2812: *Followed* 10/3268, 14/1892, 14/2874: *Referred to* 11/2267
Sen v Steelform Engineering Co Ltd see Lagden v O'Connor
Sengupta v Holmes [2002] EWCA Civ 1104; (2002) 99(39) L.S.G. 39; Times, August 19, 2002; Independent, October 3, 2002, CA (Civ Div) ........ *Digested,* 02/**452**: *Applied* 02/1347, 10/1274: *Considered* 05/2170, 13/48, 14/67
Senturk v Turkey (13423/09) 35 B.H.R.C. 685, ECHR
Serco Ltd v Lawson see Lawson v Serco Ltd
Serebryannay vek EOOD v Direktor na Direktsia 'Obzhalvane i upravlenie na izpalnenieto' - Varna pri Tsentralno upravlenie na Natsionalna agentsia za prihodite (C-283/12) [2014] S.T.C. 427; [2013] B.V.C. 487; [2013] S.T.I. 3262, ECJ (8th Chamber)
Serious Fraud Office v Wastell see Stanford International Bank Ltd (In Receivership), Re
Serious Organised Crime Agency v Azam [2013] EWCA Civ 970; [2013] 1 W.L.R. 3800; [2014] 1 All E.R. 206; [2013] C.P. Rep. 47; [2013] Lloyd's Rep. F.C. 513, CA (Civ Div); reversing [2013] EWHC 1480 (QB), QBD ........ *Digested,* 13/**415**

Serious Organised Crime Agency v Gale; *sub nom* Gale v Serious Organised Crime Agency [2011] UKSC 49; [2011] 1 W.L.R. 2760; [2012] 2 All E.R. 1; [2012] 1 Costs L.R. 21; [2012] H.R.L.R. 5; [2012] Lloyd's Rep. F.C. 1; (2011) 155(41) S.J.L.B. 31; Times, November 17, 2011, SC; affirming [2010] EWCA Civ 759; [2010] 1 W.L.R. 2881; [2010] Lloyd's Rep. F.C. 557; Times, November 22, 2010, CA (Civ Div); reversing in part [2009] EWHC 1015 (QB); [2010] Lloyd's Rep. F.C. 39, QBD ........ *Digested,* 12/**329**:
*Applied* 13/728: *Considered* 14/2954: *Followed* 12/467

Serious Organised Crime Agency v Gibbons see Serious Organised Crime Agency v O'Docherty

Serious Organised Crime Agency v Namli; *sub nom* National Crime Agency (formerly Serious Organised Crime Agency) v Namli [2014] EWCA Civ 411; [2014] Lloyd's Rep. F.C. 409, CA (Civ Div); reversing in part [2013] EWHC 1200 (QB), QBD ........ *Digested,* 14/**440**

Serious Organised Crime Agency v O'Docherty; *sub nom* Serious Organised Crime Agency v Gibbons [2013] EWCA Civ 518; [2013] C.P. Rep. 35, CA (Civ Div) .... *Digested,* 13/**276**:
*Applied* 14/731

Serious Organised Crime Agency v Szepietowski; *sub nom* Szepietowski v National Crime Agency; Szepietowski v Serious Organised Crime Agency; National Crime Agency v Szepietowski [2013] UKSC 65; [2014] A.C. 338; [2013] 3 W.L.R. 1250; [2014] 1 All E.R. 225; [2014] 1 B.C.L.C. 143; [2014] Lloyd's Rep. F.C. 1; [2014] 1 P. & C.R. 14; [2014] 1 E.G.L.R. 55, SC; reversing [2011] EWCA Civ 856; [2011] 3 Costs L.O. 408; [2011] Lloyd's Rep. F.C. 537; [2011] W.T.L.R. 1435; Times, August 25, 2011, CA (Civ Div); affirming [2010] EWHC 2570 (Ch); [2011] 1 B.C.L.C. 458; [2011] Lloyd's Rep. F.C. 81; [2010] N.P.C. 101; [2011] 1 P. & C.R. DG12, Ch D ........ *Digested,* 14/**1206**:
*Considered* 13/1160

Serpentine Trust Ltd v Revenue and Customs Commissioners [2014] UKFTT 876 (TC); [2014] S.T.I. 2949, FTT (Tax)

SET Select Energy GmbH v F&M Bunkering Ltd [2014] EWHC 192 (Comm); [2014] 1 Lloyd's Rep. 652, QBD (Comm) ........ *Digested,* 14/**558**

Setchim v Secretary of State for Foreign and Commonwealth Affairs see Commonwealth Institute (In Members' Voluntary Liquidation), Re

Sevy v Sevy 2013 BCSC 2255; 16 I.T.E.L.R. 829, Sup Ct (BC)

Seye (Chen Children: Employment), Re; *sub nom* Secretary of State for the Home Department v Seye [2013] UKUT 178 (IAC); [2013] Imm. A.R. 704, UT (IAC) .... *Digested,* 14/**1734**

Sezek v Secretary of State for the Home Department see R. (on the application of Samaroo) v Secretary of State for the Home Department

SG v Bromley LBC [2013] UKUT 619 (AAC); [2014] E.L.R. 190, UT (AAC) ........ *Digested,* 14/**942**

SG South Ltd v Swan Yard (Cirencester) Ltd [2010] EWHC 376 (TCC); [2010] 2 E.G.L.R. 7; [2010] 19 E.G. 110, QBD (TCC) ........ *Digested,* 10/**558**:
*Applied* 14/583

SGW Ltd v Secretary of State for Social Security see Tullett & Tokyo Forex International Ltd v Secretary of State for Social Security

Shabani v Secretary of State for the Home Department see Shabani (EEA: Jobseekers: Nursery Education), Re

Shabani (EEA: Jobseekers: Nursery Education), Re; *sub nom* Shabani v Secretary of State for the Home Department [2013] UKUT 315 (IAC); [2013] Imm. A.R. 934; [2014] I.N.L.R. 229, UT (IAC) ........ *Digested,* 14/**1733**

Shabpar v Barnet LBC see R. v Barnet LBC Ex p. Shah

Shackell & Co v Chorlton & Sons [1895] 1 Ch. 378, Ch D
*Approved* 14/1756: *Not followed* 10/1835

Shah v Shah [2001] EWCA Civ 527; [2002] Q.B. 35; [2001] 3 W.L.R. 31; [2001] 4 All E.R. 138; Times, May 15, 2001; Daily Telegraph, April 24, 2001, CA (Civ Div) .. *Digested,* 01/**2433**:
*Considered* 14/2262: *Distinguished* 03/1422

Shah (Jitendra) v Barnet LBC see R. v Barnet LBC Ex p. Shah

Shahzad (Art 8: Legitimate Aim); *sub nom* Secretary of State for the Home Department v Shahzad [2014] UKUT 85 (IAC); [2014] Imm. A.R. 788, UT (IAC)

Shamoon v Chief Constable of the Royal Ulster Constabulary [2003] UKHL 11; [2003] 2 All E.R. 26; [2003] N.I. 174; [2003] I.C.R. 337; [2003] I.R.L.R. 285; (2003) 147 S.J.L.B. 268; Times, March 4, 2003, HL (NI); affirming [2001] I.R.L.R. 520, CA (NI) ........ *Digested,* 03/**4767**:
*Applied* 03/1297, 05/1337, 06/1303, 07/1388, 07/1402, 09/1172, 10/1137, 11/1055, 12/1126, 12/1153, 12/3527: *Considered* 04/1275, 05/1291, 06/1349, 06/1365, 07/1401, 09/1180, 10/1021, 12/1121, 14/1024: *Followed* 12/1060

Shanks v Unilever Plc [2014] EWHC 1647 (Pat); [2014] R.P.C. 29; (2014) 158(23) S.J.L.B. 41, Ch D (Patents Ct)

Shanks & McEwan (Teesside) Ltd v Environment Agency [1999] Q.B. 333; [1998] 2 W.L.R. 452; [1997] 2 All E.R. 332; [1997] Env. L.R. 305; [1997] J.P.L. 824; [1997] Crim. L.R. 684; Times, January 28, 1997, QBD ...... *Digested,* 97/**2353**: *Considered* 13/1156, 14/684

Sharbatly v Shagroon; *sub nom* W v H [2013] EWHC 3756 (Fam); [2014] 2 F.L.R. 209; [2014] Fam. Law 437, Fam Div ...... *Digested,* 14/**1393**

Sharland v Sharland; *sub nom* S v S [2014] EWCA Civ 95; [2014] 2 F.L.R. 89; [2014] 2 F.C.R. 189; [2014] Fam. Law 449, CA (Civ Div); affirming [2013] EWHC 991 (Fam); [2013] 2 F.L.R. 1598; [2013] Fam. Law 960, Fam Div ...... *Digested,* 14/**1366**

Sharma v Sharma [2013] EWCA Civ 1287; [2014] B.C.C. 73; [2014] W.T.L.R. 111, CA (Civ Div) ...... *Digested,* 14/**512**

Sharp v Chelmsford City Council [2013] EWHC 4180 (Admin); [2014] A.C.D. 64, QBD (Admin)

Sharpe v Worcester Diocesan Board of Finance Ltd [2014] I.C.R. D9, EAT *Applied* 14/1068

Shaw v Doleman; *sub nom* Doleman v Shaw [2009] EWCA Civ 279; [2009] Bus. L.R. 1175; [2009] B.C.C. 730; [2009] 2 B.C.L.C. 123; [2009] B.P.I.R. 945; [2009] 2 P. & C.R. 12; [2009] L. & T.R. 27; [2009] 2 E.G.L.R. 35; [2009] 27 E.G. 92; [2009] 14 E.G. 86 (C.S.); (2009) 106(15) L.S.G. 16; [2009] 2 P. & C.R. DG9; Times, April 22, 2009, CA (Civ Div) ...... *Digested,* 09/**2514**: *Followed* 14/1972

Shaw v Logue [2014] EWHC 5 (Admin); (2014) 164(7591) N.L.J. 17, QBD (Admin)

Shearman (t/a Charles Shearman Agencies) v Hunter Boot Ltd [2014] EWHC 47 (QB); [2014] 1 All E.R. (Comm) 689; [2014] 1 C.L.C. 240; [2014] E.C.C. 12, QBD (Merc) (London) ...... *Digested,* 14/**81**

Shearson Lehman Brothers Inc v Maclaine Watson & Co Ltd [1988] 1 W.L.R. 16; [1988] 1 All E.R. 116; (1988) 85(2) L.S.G. 35; (1987) 131 S.J. 1658, HL; reversing Independent, August 12, 1987; Financial Times, August 5, 1987, CA (Civ Div) ...... *Digested,* 88/**1586**: *Applied* 90/3804: *Considered* 88/2890, 90/3707, 91/2892, 14/52

Shebelle Enterprises Ltd v Hampstead Garden Suburb Trust Ltd [2014] EWCA Civ 305; [2014] 2 P. & C.R. 6; [2014] 2 E.G.L.R. 35, CA (Civ Div); affirming [2013] EWHC 948 (Ch); [2013] 2 E.G.L.R. 76; [2013] 18 E.G. 103 (C.S.), Ch D ...... *Digested,* 14/**2508**

Sheffield v Sheffield [2013] EWHC 3927 (Ch); [2014] W.T.L.R. 1039, Ch D ...... *Digested,* 14/**3024**

Sheffield City Council v E; *sub nom* E (Alleged Patient), Re [2004] EWHC 2808 (Fam); [2005] Fam. 326; [2005] 2 W.L.R. 953; [2005] 1 F.L.R. 965; [2005] Lloyd's Rep. Med. 223; [2005] Fam. Law 279; (2005) 102(9) L.S.G. 30; Times, January 20, 2005, Fam Div *Applied* 05/1673, 08/3568, 13/2055, 14/2172: *Considered* 08/3583, 11/2203

Sheffield City Council v Kenya Aid Programme see Kenya Aid Programme v Sheffield City Council

Shelfer v City of London Electric Lighting Co (No.1); *joined case* Meux's Brewery Co v City of London Electric Lighting Co [1895] 1 Ch. 287, CA *Applied* 57/3609, 61/6344, 65/3985, 67/3170, 80/2251, 84/1150, 93/4040, 94/622, 95/4142, 07/3425, 09/2744: *Considered* 70/2290, 80/2007, 91/2676, 91/2976, 92/3602, 96/1267, 00/5127, 07/2962, 09/2318, 10/1937, 14/2223: *Distinguished* 69/2866, 70/2882, 82/2671: *Followed* 95/3766, 11/2682, 14/1895

Shell Tankers UK Ltd v Dawson see Shell Tankers UK Ltd v Jeromson

Shell Tankers UK Ltd v Jeromson; *sub nom* Dawson v Cherry Tree Machine Co Ltd; Jeromson v Shell Tankers UK Ltd; *joined cases* Shell Tankers UK Ltd v Dawson; Cherry Tree Machine Co Ltd v Dawson [2001] EWCA Civ 101; [2001] I.C.R. 1223; [2001] P.I.Q.R. P19; Times, March 2, 2001; Daily Telegraph, February 27, 2001, CA (Civ Div) ...... *Digested,* 01/**4492**: *Applied* 14/2998: *Considered* 05/2864

Shelley v United Kingdom (Admissibility) (23800/06) [2009] Prison L.R. 5; (2008) 46 E.H.R.R. SE16, ECHR *Considered* 14/1635

Shen v Secretary of State for the Home Department see Shen (Paper Appeals: Proving Dishonesty)

Shen (Paper Appeals: Proving Dishonesty); *sub nom* Shen v Secretary of State for the Home Department [2014] UKUT 236 (IAC); [2014] Imm. A.R. 971, UT (IAC)

Sheppard v McKnight (Inspector of Taxes) see McKnight (Inspector of Taxes) v Sheppard

Shepway DC v Unknown Owner see Unknown Owner v Shepway DC

Shergill v Khaira see Khaira v Shergill

Sheridan v Basildon BC (formerly Basildon DC) [2012] EWCA Civ 335; [2012] H.L.R. 29; [2012] B.L.G.R. 702; [2013] P.T.S.R. D9, CA (Civ Div) ...... *Digested,* 12/**1626**: *Followed* 14/1605

Shield v Shield [2014] EWHC 23 (Fam); [2014] 2 F.L.R. 1422; [2014] Fam. Law 801, Fam Div

Shields v Crossroads (Orkney) [2013] CSOH 144; 2014 S.L.T. 190; 2013 S.C.L.R. 730; [2014] P.N.L.R. 5; 2013 Rep. L.R. 116; 2013 G.W.D. 29-573, OH ............. *Digested,* 13/**3901**

Shields v Revenue and Customs Commissioners; *sub nom* Revenue and Customs Commissioners v Shields [2014] UKUT 453 (TCC); [2014] B.V.C. 541; [2014] S.T.I. 3237, UT (Tax); reversing [2013] UKFTT 424 (TC); [2013] S.T.I. 3143, FTT (Tax)

Shields & Sons Partnership v Revenue and Customs Commissioners [2014] UKFTT 944 (TC); [2014] S.T.I. 3178, FTT (Tax)

Shiels' Application for Judicial Review, Re see Fitzpatrick's Application for Judicial Review, Re

Shierson v Rastogi; *sub nom* RBG Resources Plc, Re [2002] EWCA Civ 1624; [2003] 1 W.L.R. 586; [2002] B.C.C. 1005; [2003] B.P.I.R. 148; (2003) 100(2) L.S.G. 31; Times, November 20, 2002; Independent, November 13, 2002, CA (Civ Div); affirming [2002] EWHC 1612 (Ch), Ch D ............ *Digested,* 02/**2687**: *Applied* 05/2302, 14/1802

Shierson v Rastogi (A Bankrupt) [2007] EWHC 1266 (Ch); [2007] B.P.I.R. 891; (2007) 104(25) L.S.G. 39, Ch D (Bankruptcy Ct) ............ *Digested,* 08/**2125**: *Applied* 14/1787, 14/1796: *Considered* 13/1700

SHIMANO/Petition for review (R18/12) [2014] E.P.O.R. 30, EPO (Enlarged Bd App)

SHIMANO/Shift control device (T2500/10) [2014] E.P.O.R. 49, EPO (Technical Bd App)

Shimizu Europe Ltd v Automajor Ltd [2002] B.L.R. 113; (2002) 18 Const. L.J. 259, QBD (TCC) ............ *Digested,* 02/**659**: *Applied* 10/558: *Considered* 04/592, 14/130

Shimovolos v Russia (30194/09) (2014) 58 E.H.R.R. 26; 31 B.H.R.C. 506, ECHR

Shindler v United Kingdom (19840/09) (2014) 58 E.H.R.R. 5; 35 B.H.R.C. 455; Times, June 17, 2013, ECHR ............ *Digested,* 14/**1633**

Shinorvic Trust, Re; *sub nom* Bastrust Corp Ltd v MF [2013] W.T.L.R. 337; 16 I.T.E.L.R. 171, Royal Ct (Jer)

Shipman v Shipman [1991] 1 F.L.R. 250; [1991] F.C.R. 628; [1991] Fam. Law 145, Fam Div ............ *Digested,* 91/**1813**: *Doubted* 14/496

SHL v Secretary of State for the Home Department see SHL (Tracing Obligation/Trafficking: Afghanistan), Re

SHL (Tracing Obligation/Trafficking: Afghanistan), Re; *sub nom* SHL v Secretary of State for the Home Department [2013] UKUT 312 (IAC); [2013] Imm. A.R. 875, UT (IAC) ............ *Digested,* 14/**1656**: *Disapproved* 14/1700

Shop Direct Group v Revenue and Customs Commissioners [2014] EWCA Civ 255; [2014] S.T.C. 1383; [2014] B.T.C. 11; [2014] S.T.I. 866, CA (Civ Div); affirming [2013] EWHC 942 (Ch); [2013] S.T.C. 1709; [2013] B.T.C. 1824, Ch D; affirming [2012] UKFTT 128 (TC); [2012] S.F.T.D. 723; [2012] S.T.I. 1517, FTT (Tax) ............ *Digested,* 14/**2886**

Shore v Airbus Operations Ltd 1IQ61280, CC (Stoke on Trent) [*Marc Willems, Barrister, Cobden House Chambers, 19 Quay Street, Manchester*] ............ *Digested,* 14/**2338**

Shri Lal Mahal Ltd v Progetto Grano SpA 152 Con. L.R. 87, Sup Ct (Ind)

Shumba v Park Cakes Ltd; *joined case* Park Cakes Ltd v Shumba [2013] EWCA Civ 974; [2013] I.R.L.R. 800, CA (Civ Div); affirming UKEAT/0219/11/RN, EAT ....... *Digested,* 13/**1043**: *Applied* 14/1098

Shuttleworth v South African Reserve Bank 17 I.T.L. Rep. 309, Sup Ct (SA)

SIAC Construction Ltd v Mayo CC (C-19/00) [2001] E.C.R. I-7725; [2002] T.C.L.R. 16; [2001] 3 C.M.L.R. 59; [2002] All E.R. (EC) 272, ECJ (5th Chamber) ............ *Digested,* 02/**3784**: *Applied* 04/3162, 09/4438, 10/3792, 14/2475

Sidabras v Lithuania (55480/2000) (2006) 42 E.H.R.R. 6, ECHR *Considered* 05/190, 11/1717: *Distinguished* 14/1653

Sidaway v Board of Governors of the Bethlem Royal Hospital [1985] A.C. 871; [1985] 2 W.L.R. 480; [1985] 1 All E.R. 643; (1985) 82 L.S.G. 1256; (1985) 135 N.L.J. 203; (1985) 129 S.J. 154, HL; affirming [1984] Q.B. 493; [1984] 2 W.L.R. 778; [1984] 1 All E.R. 1018; (1984) 81 L.S.G. 899; (1984) 128 S.J. 301, CA (Civ Div) ............ *Digested,* 85/**2318**: *Applied* 84/3570, 00/4194: *Considered* 85/2651, 88/2453, 90/5498, 95/3622, 00/4247, 09/2842, 13/3892, 14/2198: *Followed* 98/3986: *Not followed* 87/2603

Sidhu v British Airways Plc see Abnett v British Airways Plc

Sidwick v Revenue and Customs Commissioners see Matthews v Revenue and Customs Commissioners

Siemens AG v European Commission (C-239/11 P); *joined cases* Toshiba Corp v European Commission (C-498/11 P); Mitsubishi Electric Corp v European Commission (C-489/11 P) [2014] 4 C.M.L.R. 18, ECJ (4th Chamber)
Siemens Hearing Instruments Ltd v Friends Life Ltd; *sub nom* Friends Life Ltd v Siemens Hearing Instruments Ltd [2014] EWCA Civ 382; [2014] 2 P. & C.R. 5; [2014] L. & T.R. 27; [2014] 2 E.G.L.R. 41, CA (Civ Div); reversing [2014] L. & T.R. 8, Ch D ........ *Digested,* 14/**1970**
Sig Bergesen DY & Co v Mobil Shipping and Transportation Co (The Berge Sund) [1993] 2 Lloyd's Rep. 453; Times, May 5, 1993, CA (Civ Div); reversing [1992] 1 Lloyd's Rep. 460; Financial Times, January 31, 1992, QBD (Comm) ........ *Digested,* 94/**4064**: *Applied* 13/2836: *Followed* 14/2740
Sigma Tau Pharmaceutical Ltd, Re [2013] EWHC 3279 (Ch); [2014] B.C.C. 70, Ch D . *Digested,* 14/**501**
Silberquelle GmbH v Maselli-Strickmode GmbH (C-495/07) [2009] E.C.R. I-137; [2009] E.T.M.R. 28; [2009] Bus. L.R. D45, ECJ (1st Chamber) ........ *Digested,* 09/**2447**: *Followed* 14/1931
Silih v Slovenia (71463/01) (2009) 49 E.H.R.R. 37; [2009] Inquest L.R. 117, ECHR *Applied* 11/1695: *Considered* 14/47
Silkstone v Tatnall; *sub nom* Chief Land Registrar v Silkstone [2011] EWCA Civ 801; [2012] 1 W.L.R. 400; [2011] 2 P. & C.R. 16; [2011] 3 E.G.L.R. 47; [2011] 41 E.G. 116; [2011] 29 E.G. 88 (C.S.); [2011] N.P.C. 76, CA (Civ Div); affirming [2010] EWHC 1627 (Ch); [2010] 3 E.G.L.R. 25; [2010] 39 E.G. 110; [2010] 28 E.G. 84 (C.S.); [2010] N.P.C. 76, Ch D ........ *Digested,* 11/**2657**: *Applied* 14/2010
Silva v Spain (69966/01) (2014) 58 E.H.R.R. 6, ECHR
Simmons v Castle [2012] EWCA Civ 1039; [2013] 1 W.L.R. 1239; [2013] 1 All E.R. 334; [2012] C.P. Rep. 43; [2012] 5 Costs L.R. 931; [2013] E.M.L.R. 3; [2012] P.I.Q.R. P22; [2013] Med. L.R. 1, CA (Civ Div) ........ *Digested,* 12/**852**: *Applied* 14/2333: *Considered* 14/2311, 14/2326
Simmons v Castle [2012] EWCA Civ 1288; [2013] 1 W.L.R. 1239; [2013] 1 All E.R. 334; [2013] C.P. Rep. 3; [2012] 6 Costs L.R. 1150; [2013] E.M.L.R. 4; [2013] P.I.Q.R. P2; [2013] Med. L.R. 4; (2012) 162 N.L.J. 1324; (2012) 156(39) S.J.L.B. 31, CA (Civ Div) ........ *Digested,* 13/**782**: *Considered* 13/2241, 13/2260, 14/2320, 14/2331, 14/2351
Simmons v Castle [2012] EWCA Civ 242, CA (Civ Div) *Applied* 14/2312, 14/2325
Simmons and Simmons LLP v Hickox [2013] EWHC 2141 (QB); [2014] 3 Costs L.O. 311, QBD
Simms v Conlon see Conlon v Simms
Simon v Byford; *sub nom* Simon (Deceased), Re [2014] EWCA Civ 280; [2014] W.T.L.R. 1097; 17 I.T.E.L.R. 536, CA (Civ Div); affirming [2013] EWHC 1490 (Ch); [2013] W.T.L.R. 1615; (2013) 157(23) S.J.L.B. 31, Ch D ........ *Digested,* 14/**2838**
Simon v Denbighshire CC [2010] UKUT 488 (LC); [2014] J.P.L. 268, UT (Lands) ........ *Digested,* 14/**1617**
Simon (Deceased), Re see Simon v Byford
Simon Carves Ltd v Ensus UK Ltd [2011] EWHC 657 (TCC); [2011] B.L.R. 340; 135 Con. L.R. 96, QBD (TCC) ........ *Digested,* 11/**510**: *Applied* 14/411
Simpson (Davidson's Trustees) v Ogilvie; *sub nom* Davidson's Trustees v Ogilvie 1910 S.C. 294; 1910 1 S.L.T. 45, IH (2 Div) *Applied* 14/2982
Simpson (t/a Harrow Solicitors and Advocates) v Godson [2013] EWCA Civ 1339; [2014] 1 Costs L.O. 77, CA (Civ Div) ........ *Digested,* 14/**350**
Sims v Dacorum BC; *sub nom* Dacorum BC v Sims [2014] UKSC 63; [2014] 3 W.L.R. 1600; [2014] B.L.G.R. 898; (2014) 158(45) S.J.L.B. 37; Times, December 2, 2014, SC; affirming [2013] EWCA Civ 12; [2013] C.P. Rep. 19; [2013] H.L.R. 14; [2013] 2 P. & C.R. 1; [2013] L. & T.R. 22; [2013] 1 E.G.L.R. 52; [2013] 15 E.G. 106; (2013) 157(4) S.J.L.B. 43; [2013] 1 P. & C.R. DG17, CA (Civ Div) ........ *Digested,* 13/**1561**
Sims v Foster Wheeler [1966] 1 W.L.R. 769; [1966] 2 All E.R. 313; 1 K.I.R. 1; (1966) 110 S.J. 189, CA ........ *Digested,* 66/**3451**: *Applied* 67/365, 69/2409, 14/599
Sinclair Collis Ltd v Secretary of State for Health see R. (on the application of Sinclair Collis Ltd) v Secretary of State for Health
Sinclair Gardens Investments (Kensington) Ltd v Oak Investments RTM Co Ltd [2005] R.V.R. 426, Lands Tr ........ *Digested,* 06/**2699**: *Considered* 14/2011

Sinclair Gardens Investments (Kensington) Ltd v Poets Chase Freehold Co Ltd [2007] EWHC 1776 (Ch); [2008] 1 W.L.R. 768; [2008] 2 All E.R. 187; [2008] L. & T.R. 8; [2007] 3 E.G.L.R. 29; [2007] 49 E.G. 104; [2007] 32 E.G. 89 (C.S.); (2007) 157 S.J.L.B. 1427; [2007] N.P.C. 96, Ch D .......... *Digested,* 08/**2445**: *Considered* 14/2011

Sinclair Gardens Investments (Kensington) Ltd, Re [2014] UKUT 79 (LC); [2014] 3 E.G.L.R. 147, UT (Lands)

Sinclair Investments (UK) Ltd v Versailles Trade Finance Ltd (In Administration) [2011] EWCA Civ 347; [2012] Ch. 453; [2011] 3 W.L.R. 1153; [2011] 4 All E.R. 335; [2011] Bus. L.R. 1126; [2011] 2 B.C.L.C. 501; [2011] W.T.L.R. 1043; [2011] 2 P. & C.R. DG6, CA (Civ Div); affirming [2010] EWHC 1614 (Ch); [2011] 1 B.C.L.C. 202; [2011] W.T.L.R. 839, Ch D .......... *Digested,* 11/**3499**: *Applied* 14/2588: *Distinguished* 13/71: *Followed* 13/345

Sindicatul Pastorul cel Bun v Romania (2330/09) [2014] I.R.L.R. 49; (2014) 58 E.H.R.R. 10, ECHR (Grand Chamber)

Singh v Belgium (33210/11) (Unreported, October 2, 2012), ECHR *Considered* 14/1726

Singh v Moorlands Primary School Governing Body see Singh v Reading BC

Singh v Reading BC; *sub nom* Singh v Moorlands Primary School Governing Body [2013] EWCA Civ 909; [2013] 1 W.L.R. 3052; [2013] C.P. Rep. 46; [2013] I.C.R. 1158; [2013] I.R.L.R. 820, CA (Civ Div); reversing [2013] I.C.R. 738; [2013] I.R.L.R. 444, EAT .......... *Digested,* 13/**1020**: *Applied* 14/2992

Singh v Secretary of State for the Home Department [2014] EWCA Civ 932; [2014] Imm. A.R. 1141, CA (Civ Div)

Singh v Secretary of State for the Home Department [2014] EWCA Civ 438; [2014] 1 W.L.R. 3585, CA (Civ Div) .......... *Digested,* 14/**1743**

Singh v Singh [2013] EWHC 4783 (Ch); [2014] B.P.I.R. 1555, Ch D

Singh v Singh see Singh Brothers Contractors (North West) Ltd, Re

Singh Brothers Contractors (North West) Ltd, Re; *sub nom* Singh v Singh [2013] EWHC 2138 (Ch); [2014] 1 B.C.L.C. 649, Ch D (Manchester)

Singularis Holdings Ltd v PricewaterhouseCoopers [2014] UKPC 36; [2014] 2 B.C.L.C. 597; (2014) 158(44) S.J.L.B. 37, PC (Ber)

Sintax Trading Ou v Maksu- ja Tolliamet (C-583/12) [2014] E.C.D.R. 11, ECJ (2nd Chamber)

Siporex Trade SA v Banque Indosuez [1986] 2 Lloyd's Rep. 146, QBD (Comm) .......... *Digested,* 86/**168**: *Applied* 01/379, 14/265: *Considered* 91/256: *Distinguished* 05/703

Sir Robert McAlpine Ltd v Alfred McAlpine Plc [2004] EWHC 630 (Ch); [2004] R.P.C. 36; (2004) 27(7) I.P.D. 27071, Ch D .......... *Digested,* 04/**2271**: *Considered* 10/1990, 14/1926

Siragusa v Regione Sicilia - Soprintendenza Beni Culturali e Ambientali di Palermo (C-206/13) [2014] 3 C.M.L.R. 13, ECJ (10th Chamber)

Sita UK Ltd v Greater Manchester Waste Disposal Authority [2011] EWCA Civ 156; [2012] P.T.S.R. 645; [2011] T.C.L.R. 3; 134 Con. L.R. 1; [2011] 2 C.M.L.R. 32; [2011] Eu. L.R. 719; [2011] B.L.G.R. 419; (2011) 108(10) L.S.G. 22, CA (Civ Div); affirming [2010] EWHC 680 (Ch); [2010] 2 C.M.L.R. 48, Ch D .......... *Digested,* 11/**2633**: *Applied* 11/2629, 12/3686: *Followed* 14/418, 14/430

Situ Ventures Ltd v Bonham-Carter see Bonham-Carter v Situ Ventures Ltd

SJ (A Child) (Habitual Residence: Application to Set Aside), Re [2014] EWHC 58 (Fam); [2014] Fam. Law 964, Fam Div

SJ&J Monk (A Firm) v Newbigin (Valuation Officer); *sub nom* Newbigin (Valuation Officer) v SJ&J Monk (A Firm) [2014] UKUT 14 (LC); [2014] R.A. 195, UT (Lands)

SK v HD see K v D (Committal: Application to Strike Out)

SK (Zimbabwe) v Secretary of State for the Home Department see R. (on the application of Kambadzi) v Secretary of State for the Home Department

SK, Re [2012] EWHC 1990 (COP); [2013] P.I.Q.R. P4, CP .......... *Digested,* 13/**386**: *Applied* 14/436

Skandia America Corp (USA) v Skatteverket (C-7/13) [2014] B.V.C. 43, ECJ (2nd Chamber)

Skatteverket v AB SKF (C-29/08) [2010] S.T.C. 419; [2009] E.C.R. I-10413; [2011] B.V.C. 359; [2009] S.T.I. 2835, ECJ (3rd Chamber) *Applied* 14/3056: *Considered* 11/3546, 12/3396

Skatteverket v PFC Clinic AB (C-91/12) [2013] S.T.C. 1253; [2013] B.V.C. 117; [2013] S.T.I. 1717, ECJ (3rd Chamber) *Considered* 14/3051

Skrytek v Secretary of State for Communities and Local Government [2013] EWCA Civ 1231; [2014] Env. L.R. 15, CA (Civ Div) .......... *Digested,* 14/**2439**

Skuse v Granada Television Ltd [1996] E.M.L.R. 278; Independent, April 2, 1993, CA (Civ Div) ........ *Digested,* 93/**2584**: *Applied* 01/1830, 05/982, 07/1070: *Considered* 02/953, 02/955, 14/837: *Followed* 95/3131

Sky Blue Sports & Leisure Ltd v Coventry City Council [2013] EWHC 3366 (Admin); [2014] B.L.G.R. 34; [2014] A.C.D. 48, QBD (Admin) ........ *Digested,* 14/**483**

Sky Italia srl v Autorita per le Garanzie nelle Comunicazioni (C-234/12) [2014] 1 C.M.L.R. 22; [2014] C.E.C. 287, ECJ (2nd Chamber)

Sky Land Consultants Plc, Re; *sub nom* Secretary of State for Business, Innovation and Skills v Sky Land Consultants Plc [2010] EWHC 399 (Ch), DR (Manchester) *Applied* 13/476, 14/1439, 14/1459

Skyview Ballooning Ltd v Revenue and Customs Commissioners [2014] UKFTT 32 (TC); [2014] S.T.I. 541, FTT (Tax)

Skyward Aviation 2008 Ltd v Tower Insurance Ltd [2014] NZCA 76; [2014] Lloyd's Rep. I.R. 565, CA (NZ)

Slade v Slade [2009] EWCA Civ 748; [2010] 1 W.L.R. 1262; [2010] 1 All E.R. 1231; [2010] C.P. Rep. 3; [2010] 1 F.L.R. 160; [2010] 1 F.C.R. 227; [2009] Fam. Law 925; (2009) 159 N.L.J. 1065; Times, August 20, 2009, CA (Civ Div) ........ *Digested,* 09/**356**: *Applied* 11/1460: *Followed* 14/13

Slattery v Basildon BC [2014] EWCA Civ 30; [2014] H.L.R. 16, CA (Civ Div) ........ *Digested,* 14/**1605**

Slide & Seek Ltd v Revenue and Customs Commissioners [2014] UKFTT 512 (TC); [2014] S.T.I. 2160, FTT (Tax)

Slough BC v C [2004] EWHC 1759 (Admin); [2005] B.L.G.R. 368; [2004] E.L.R. 546; [2005] A.C.D. 9; (2004) 101(34) L.S.G. 30; Times, August 27, 2004, QBD (Admin) ........ *Digested,* 04/**1085**: *Considered* 14/945

Slough Estates v Slough BC (No.1); *sub nom* Slough Estates v Slough Corp (No.2) [1971] A.C. 958; [1970] 2 W.L.R. 1187; [1970] 2 All E.R. 216; 68 L.G.R. 669; (1970) 21 P. & C.R. 573; (1970) 114 S.J. 435, HL; affirming [1969] 2 Ch. 305; [1969] 2 W.L.R. 1157; [1969] 2 All E.R. 988; (1969) 133 J.P. 479; (1969) 20 P. & C.R. 363; (1969) 113 S.J. 307, CA (Civ Div); affirming [1968] Ch. 299; [1967] 2 W.L.R. 1511; [1967] 2 All E.R. 270; (1967) 18 P. & C.R. 459; (1967) 111 S.J. 374, Ch D ........ *Digested,* 70/**2775**: *Considered* 72/3363, 79/2634, 80/2679, 82/721.u, 84/3465, 90/4372, 91/3520, 06/3350: *Followed* 14/2378

Slough Estates v Slough Corp (No.2) see Slough Estates v Slough BC (No.1)

Slough Heat and Power Ltd v Thomson (Valuation Officer) [2009] R.A. 1, Lands Tr ..... *Digested,* 09/**2683**: *Considered* 11/2646, 14/2137

Slovakia v Katrencik; *sub nom* District Court Bratislava Iii Slovakia v Katrencik [2014] EWHC 2062 (Admin); [2014] A.C.D. 117, DC

Slutsker v Haron Investments Ltd [2013] EWCA Civ 430; [2014] 1 F.L.R. 1114; 16 I.T.E.L.R. 257; [2013] Fam. Law 967, CA (Civ Div); affirming [2012] EWHC 2539 (Ch); (2012) 156(36) S.J.L.B. 31, Ch D ........ *Digested,* 14/**2491**

SM v Entry Clearance Officer, Bangkok see MA (Zambrano: EU Children outside EU: Iran), Re

SM v Hackney Learning Trust [2013] UKUT 78 (AAC); [2013] E.L.R. 321, UT (AAC) ... *Digested,* 13/**902**: *Reversed* 14/945

SM v Hackney Learning Trust [2014] EWCA Civ 397; [2014] P.T.S.R. 826; [2014] E.L.R. 350, CA (Civ Div) ........ *Digested,* 14/**945**

SM v HM see HM (A Child), Re

SM (Pakistan) v Secretary of State for the Home Department see SM (Withdrawal of Appealed Decision: Effect: Pakistan)

SM (Withdrawal of Appealed Decision: Effect: Pakistan); *sub nom* SM (Pakistan) v Secretary of State for the Home Department [2014] UKUT 64 (IAC); [2014] Imm. A.R. 662; [2014] I.N.L.R. 681, UT (IAC)

Smallwood v United Kingdom (29779/96) (1999) 27 E.H.R.R. CD155, ECHR *Applied* 13/1337, 14/1424

Smart v Lambeth LBC [2013] EWCA Civ 1375; [2014] H.L.R. 7; [2013] 46 E.G. 108 (C.S.), CA (Civ Div) ........ *Digested,* 14/**1588**

Smith v Bailey [2014] EWHC 2569 (QB); [2014] Med. L.R. 408, QBD ........ *Digested,* 14/**2305**

Smith v Bottomley [2013] EWCA Civ 953; [2014] 1 F.L.R. 626; [2014] Fam. Law 35; [2013] 2 P. & C.R. DG25, CA (Civ Div) ........ *Digested,* 14/**2495**

Smith v Carillion (JM) Ltd [2014] I.R.L.R. 344, EAT ........ *Digested,* 14/**1064**

Smith v Chief Constable of Sussex see Van Colle v Chief Constable of Hertfordshire

Smith v Henniker-Major & Co [2002] EWCA Civ 762; [2003] Ch. 182; [2002] 3 W.L.R. 1848; [2002] B.C.C. 768; [2002] 2 B.C.L.C. 655; (2002) 99(37) L.S.G. 36; Times, August 29, 2002; Independent, October 21, 2002, CA (Civ Div); affirming [2002] B.C.C. 544, Ch D ............ *Digested,* 02/**559**: *Applied* 04/472, 07/2920, 09/430: *Followed* 14/1784

Smith v Hughes see Cranfield v Bridgegrove Ltd

Smith v Information Officer see Oakley Smith v Information Officer

Smith v Jafton Properties Ltd [2013] 2 E.G.L.R. 104, CC (Central London) ............ *Digested,* 14/**1982**

Smith v Ministry of Defence; *sub nom* Ministry of Defence v Allbutt; Ministry of Defence v Ellis; *joined cases* Redpath v Ministry of Defence; Ellis v Ministry of Defence; Allbutt v Ministry of Defence [2013] UKSC 41; [2014] A.C. 52; [2013] 3 W.L.R. 69; [2013] 4 All E.R. 794; [2013] H.R.L.R. 27; 35 B.H.R.C. 711; [2014] P.I.Q.R. P2; Times, July 24, 2013, SC; reversing in part [2012] EWCA Civ 1365; [2013] 2 W.L.R. 27; [2013] 1 All E.R. 778; [2013] H.R.L.R. 2; [2013] P.I.Q.R. P3; Times, November 20, 2012, CA (Civ Div); affirming [2011] EWHC 1676 (QB); [2011] H.R.L.R. 35, QBD ............ *Digested,* 13/**121**: *Considered* 14/63

Smith v Parole Board for England and Wales see R. (on the application of Smith) v Parole Board for England and Wales

Smith v Scott [2007] CSIH 9; 2007 S.C. 345; 2007 S.L.T. 137; 2007 S.C.L.R. 268; [2008] Prison L.R. 177; 2007 G.W.D. 3-46; Times, February 5, 2007, Registration App Ct (SC) ............ *Digested,* 07/**5431**: *Considered* 10/1730: *Referred to* 14/976

Smith v Secretary of State for Energy and Climate Change [2013] EWCA Civ 1585; [2014] 1 W.L.R. 2283, CA (Civ Div) ............ *Digested,* 14/**438**

Smith v Smith (Contempt: Committal) [1991] 2 F.L.R. 55; [1991] F.C.R. 233; [1991] Fam. Law 412; (1991) 155 J.P.N. 138; Times, October 8, 1990, CA (Civ Div) .... *Digested,* 92/**1211**: *Applied* 09/356: *Followed* 96/1811, 14/13

Smith v T&N Ltd (In Administration) see Royal & Sun Alliance Insurance Plc v T&N Ltd (In Administration)

Smith & Nephew Plc v Convatec Technologies Inc [2013] EWHC 3955 (Pat); [2014] R.P.C. 22, Ch D (Patents Ct) ............ *Digested,* 14/**1879**

Smith New Court Securities Ltd v Citibank NA; *sub nom* Smith New Court Securities Ltd v Scrimgeour Vickers (Asset Management) Ltd [1997] A.C. 254; [1996] 3 W.L.R. 1051; [1996] 4 All E.R. 769; [1997] 1 B.C.L.C. 350; [1996] C.L.C. 1958; (1996) 93(46) L.S.G. 28; (1996) 146 N.L.J. 1722; (1997) 141 S.J.L.B. 5; Times, November 22, 1996; Independent, November 27, 1996, HL; reversing [1994] 1 W.L.R. 1271; [1994] 4 All E.R. 225; [1994] 2 B.C.L.C. 212; [1994] C.L.C. 203; (1994) 91(22) L.S.G. 32; (1994) 91(15) L.S.G. 35; (1994) 138 S.J.L.B. 77; Times, March 8, 1994, CA (Civ Div); reversing [1992] B.C.L.C. 1104; Times, April 7, 1992, Ch D ............ *Digested,* 96/**996**: *Applied* 00/1452, 01/965, 03/535, 04/920, 07/2918, 08/893, 10/828, 11/537: *Considered* 11/857, 14/3215: *Followed* 97/3370, 09/407

Smith New Court Securities Ltd v Scrimgeour Vickers (Asset Management) Ltd see Smith New Court Securities Ltd v Citibank NA

Smith-Evans v Smailes [2013] EWHC 3199 (Ch); [2014] 1 W.L.R. 1548; [2014] B.P.I.R. 306, Ch D ............ *Digested,* 14/**1784**: *Considered* 14/1799

Smith-Twigger v Abbey Protection Group Ltd [2014] I.C.R. D33, EAT ............ *Digested,* 14/**1116**

SmithKline Beecham Plc v Apotex Europe Ltd [2003] EWCA Civ 137; [2003] F.S.R. 31; (2003) 26(4) I.P.D. 26020, CA (Civ Div); affirming [2002] EWHC 2556 (Pat); [2003] F.S.R. 30; (2003) 26(1) I.P.D. 26005, Ch D (Patents Ct) ............ *Digested,* 03/**2573**: *Considered* 14/409

SmithKline Beecham Plc's Paroxetine Methanesulfonate Patent (No.2) see Synthon BV v SmithKline Beecham Plc (No.2)

Smithton Ltd (formerly Hobart Capital Markets Ltd) v Naggar [2014] EWCA Civ 939; [2014] B.C.C. 482; (2014) 158(29) S.J.L.B. 37; Times, August 19, 2014, CA (Civ Div); affirming [2013] EWHC 1961 (Ch); [2014] 1 B.C.L.C. 602, Ch D ......... *Digested,* 14/**505**

Smoker v London Fire and Civil Defence Authority; *joined case* Wood v British Coal Corp [1991] 2 A.C. 502; [1991] 2 W.L.R. 1052; [1991] 2 All E.R. 449; [1991] I.C.R. 449; [1991] F.C.R. 449; [1992] P.I.Q.R. Q39; [1991] Pens. L.R. 63; (1991) 135 S.J. 507; Times, April 18, 1991; Independent, April 12, 1991; Financial Times, April 15, 1991; Guardian, May 16, 1991; Daily Telegraph, April 19, 1991, HL; affirming [1991] I.R.L.R. 22; Times, October 10, 1990; Independent, October 18, 1990; Daily Telegraph, December 21, 1990, CA (Civ Div); reversing [1991] 2 W.L.R. 422; [1990] I.R.L.R. 271; [1990] Pens. L.R. 67; Times, January 19, 1990; Independent, February 13, 1990, QBD ............ *Digested,* 91/**1327**: *Applied* 06/1385, 14/827: *Considered* 96/6896

SN v Nottinghamshire CC [2014] UKUT 2 (AAC); [2014] E.L.R. 286, UT (AAC) .......... *Digested,* 14/**876**

SNAPNAMES.COM INC/Domain name acquisition and management system and method (T2017/12) [2014] E.P.O.R. 35, EPO (Technical Bd App)

Sneller v DAS Nederlandse Rechtsbijstand Verzekeringsmaatschappij NV (C-442/12) [2014] Bus. L.R. 180; [2014] Lloyd's Rep. I.R. 238, ECJ (8th Chamber)

Snelling v Burstow Parish Council [2013] EWCA Civ 1411; [2014] 1 W.L.R. 2388; [2013] 47 E.G. 129 (C.S.); (2013) 157(44) S.J.L.B. 37, CA (Civ Div); affirming [2013] EWHC 46 (Ch); [2013] 1 W.L.R. 2271; [2013] 5 E.G. 97 (C.S.); Times, February 21, 2013, Ch D .......... *Digested,* 14/**2146**

Snickers Workwear AB v Administrative Regional Court, Latvia 16 I.T.L. Rep. 916, AT (LA)

Snook v London and West Riding Investments Ltd [1967] 2 Q.B. 786; [1967] 2 W.L.R. 1020; [1967] 1 All E.R. 518; (1967) 111 S.J. 71, CA (Civ Div) .......... *Digested,* 67/**1836**: *Applied* 99/4764, 00/3879, 01/5319, 04/3954, 07/3396, 09/1199, 09/2205, 12/2049: *Considered* 84/1915, 88/2043, 89/2112, 89/2145, 09/1194, 11/1074, 14/2494: *Followed* 99/2485, 02/5841, 05/4313, 13/2420, 13/478

Sobam BV, Re see Brown v City of London Corp

Societe Anonyme des Bains de Mer et du Cercle des Etrangers a Monaco v Anglofile International Ltd (t/a Monte Carlo Casino Entertainment) [2013] EWPCC 38; [2014] E.T.M.R. 9, PCC .......... *Digested,* 14/**1917**

Societe Cooperative de Production Sea France SA v Competition Commission see Groupe Eurotunnel SA v Competition Commission

Societe des Produits Nestle SA v Cadbury UK Ltd [2014] EWHC 16 (Ch); [2014] E.T.M.R. 17; [2014] F.S.R. 28, Ch D .......... *Digested,* 14/**1932**: *Considered* 14/1935

Societe des Produits Nestle SA v Cadbury UK Ltd; *sub nom* Cadbury UK Ltd v Societe des Produits Nestle SA [2013] EWCA Civ 1174; [2014] 1 All E.R. 1079; [2014] Bus. L.R. 134; [2014] E.T.M.R. 3; [2014] R.P.C. 7, CA (Civ Div); reversing [2012] EWHC 2637 (Ch); [2013] E.C.C. 5; [2013] E.T.M.R. 2; [2013] R.P.C. 14, Ch D .......... *Digested,* 14/**1933**: *Considered* 13/1758, 14/1934

Societe des Produits Nestle SA v Mars UK Ltd (C-353/03) [2005] E.C.R. I-6135; [2005] 3 C.M.L.R. 12; [2006] All E.R. (EC) 348; [2006] C.E.C. 3; [2005] E.T.M.R. 96; [2006] F.S.R. 2; (2005) 28(10) I.P.D. 28071; Times, July 20, 2005, ECJ (2nd Chamber) .......... *Digested,* 06/**2587**: *Applied* 09/2424: *Followed* 14/1937

Societe Generale (London Branch) v Geys see Geys v Societe Generale

Societe Nationale Industrielle Aerospatiale (SNIA) v Lee Kui Jak [1987] A.C. 871; [1987] 3 W.L.R. 59; [1987] 3 All E.R. 510; (1987) 84 L.S.G. 2048, PC (Bru) ...... *Digested,* 87/**3024**: *Applied* 97/4597, 97/879, 98/757, 02/643, 04/573: *Considered* 89/1729, 94/3708, 96/5344, 00/747, 02/641, 05/1623, 14/302: *Distinguished* 95/4149: *Followed* 89/381, 91/5405, 95/6052, 97/885

Societe pour la Recherche, la Production, le Transport, la Transformation et la Commercialisation des Hydrocarbures SpA (Sonatrach) v Statoil Natural Gas LLC (Statoil) [2014] EWHC 875 (Comm); [2014] 2 All E.R. (Comm) 857; [2014] 2 Lloyd's Rep. 252; [2014] 1 C.L.C. 473, QBD (Comm) .......... *Digested,* 14/**128**

Socimer International Bank Ltd (In Liquidation) v Standard Bank London Ltd (No.2) [2008] EWCA Civ 116; [2008] Bus. L.R. 1304; [2008] 1 Lloyd's Rep. 558, CA (Civ Div); reversing [2006] EWHC 718 (Comm), QBD (Comm) .......... *Digested,* 08/**669**: *Applied* 13/217, 14/242

Sodirep Textiles SA-NV, Re 17 I.T.L. Rep. 355, C d'A (Douai)

Soering v United Kingdom (A/161) (1989) 11 E.H.R.R. 439; Times, July 8, 1989; Independent, July 11, 1989; Guardian, July 13, 1989; Daily Telegraph, October 2, 1989, ECHR .......... *Digested,* 89/**1712**: *Applied* 97/2764, 02/2577, 05/2167, 09/1473, 14/1652: *Considered* 03/2162, 03/2256, 04/2009, 04/839, 05/2058, 05/2076, 08/1940, 09/2033, 10/1265, 10/1266, 10/1736, 12/128, 13/1184, 13/1593, 14/564: *Explained* 06/2244: *Followed* 02/2514

Sofaer v Anglo Irish Asset Finance Plc [2011] EWHC 1480 (Ch); [2011] B.P.I.R. 1736, Ch D .......... *Digested,* 12/**1861**: *Applied* 14/1827

Sofra Bakery Ltd (In Liquidation), Re; *sub nom* Kubrik v Ucar [2013] EWHC 1499 (Ch); [2014] B.P.I.R. 435, Ch D (Leeds) .......... *Digested,* 14/**1810**

Softhouse Consulting Ltd v Revenue and Customs Commissioners [2014] UKUT 197 (TCC); [2014] B.V.C. 511; [2014] S.T.I. 748, UT (Tax) .......... *Digested,* 14/**3091**

Sokratis Rokopoulos v Esperia SpA (The Aros) [1978] 1 Lloyd's Rep. 456, QBD (Comm) ........ *Digested*, 78/**93**: *Applied* 14/586

Soleh Boneh International v Uganda and National Housing Corp [1993] 2 Lloyd's Rep. 208; Times, March 18, 1993, CA (Civ Div) ........ *Digested*, 94/**3758**: *Applied* 01/342: *Considered* 05/213, 09/187, 14/137: *Distinguished* 03/196: *Followed* 02/219, 12/117

Solicitor General v Dodd [2014] EWHC 240 (QB); [2014] F.S.R. 27, QBD ........ *Digested*, 14/**319**

Solicitor General v Jones; *sub nom* Jones (Alleged Contempt of Court), Re [2013] EWHC 2579 (Fam); [2014] 1 F.L.R. 852; [2014] 2 F.C.R. 354; [2013] Fam. Law 1521, Fam Div ........ *Digested*, 14/**1333**

Solicitor, Re see Taxation of Costs, Re

Solihull MBC v Gallagher Homes Ltd see Gallagher Homes Ltd v Solihull MBC

Solihull MBC v Khan [2014] EWCA Civ 41; [2014] H.L.R. 33, CA (Civ Div) ........ *Digested*, 14/**1593**

Soliver NV v European Commission (T-68/09) [2014] 5 C.M.L.R. 24, GC (2nd Chamber)

Solon South West Housing Association Ltd v James [2004] EWCA Civ 1847; [2005] H.L.R. 24, CA (Civ Div) ........ *Digested*, 05/**298**: *Applied* 14/1999

Solovyev v Solovyeva [2014] EWFC 1546; [2014] Fam. Law 1240, Fam Ct

Solvay v Region Wallonne (C-182/10) [2012] 2 C.M.L.R. 19; [2012] Env. L.R. 27, ECJ (4th Chamber) *Considered* 13/2351, 14/1201

Solvay SA v European Commission (C-455/11 P) [2014] 4 C.M.L.R. 17, ECJ (3rd Chamber)

Somak Travel Ltd v Secretary of State for the Environment (1988) 55 P. & C.R. 250; [1987] J.P.L. 630, QBD ........ *Digested*, 88/**3439**: *Applied* 13/2303: *Considered* 14/2385

Somerfield Stores Ltd v Office of Fair Trading; *joined case* Gallaher Group Ltd v Office of Fair Trading [2013] CAT 12; [2013] Comp. A.R. 321, CAT ........ *Digested*, 14/**536**

Somerfield Stores Ltd v Office of Fair Trading; *sub nom* Office of Fair Trading v Gallaher Group Ltd; Office of Fair Trading v Somerfield Stores Ltd; *joined case* Gallaher Group Ltd v Office of Fair Trading [2014] EWCA Civ 400; [2014] U.K.C.L.R. 1215, CA (Civ Div); reversing [2013] CAT 5; [2013] Comp. A.R. 165, CAT ........ *Digested*, 13/**492**

Somerville v Scottish Ministers; *joined cases* Blanco v Scottish Ministers; Henderson v Scottish Ministers; Ralston v Scottish Ministers [2007] UKHL 44; [2007] 1 W.L.R. 2734; 2008 S.C. (H.L.) 45; 2007 S.L.T. 1113; 2007 S.C.L.R. 830; [2008] H.R.L.R. 3; [2008] U.K.H.R.R. 570; (2007) 151 S.J.L.B. 1398; 2007 G.W.D. 37-656, HL; reversing in part [2006] CSIH 52; 2007 S.C. 140; 2007 S.L.T. 96; 2007 G.W.D. 4-67, IH (1 Div) ........ *Digested*, 08/**4963**: *Considered* 08/18, 12/771, 13/247, 14/400: *Followed* 14/3300

Sompo Japan Insurance Inc v Transfercom Ltd [2007] EWHC 146 (Ch), Ch D (Companies Ct) *Applied* 14/500

Sood Enterprises Ltd v Healey see Sood Enterprises Ltd v Healy

Sood Enterprises Ltd v Healy; *sub nom* Sood Enterprises Ltd v Healey [2014] 2 C.M.L.R. 15; [2013] I.C.R. 1361; [2013] I.R.L.R. 865, EAT (SC) ........ *Digested*, 13/**3680**

Soor v Redbridge LBC [2013] EWHC 1239 (Admin); [2014] R.V.R. 129, QBD (Admin)

Soufflet Negoce SA v Fedcominvest Europe Sarl [2014] EWHC 2405 (Comm); [2014] 2 Lloyd's Rep. 537, QBD (Comm)

Sourdais (Societe) v Bouchonnerie Jocondienne (Societe) [2014] I.L.Pr. 3, Cass (F)

South Africa v Dewani [2012] EWHC 842 (Admin); [2013] 1 W.L.R. 82; (2012) 109(15) L.S.G. 13, DC ........ *Digested*, 13/**1183**: *Considered* 14/1229

South Africa v Dewani [2014] EWHC 153 (Admin); [2014] 1 W.L.R. 3220; [2014] 3 All E.R. 266; [2014] A.C.D. 74, DC ........ *Digested*, 14/**1230**

South African Tourist Board v Revenue and Customs Commissioners [2014] UKUT 280 (TCC); [2014] S.T.C. 2650; [2014] B.V.C. 524; [2014] S.T.I. 2412, UT (Tax); reversing in part [2013] UKFTT 780 (TC); [2013] S.F.T.D. 508; [2013] S.T.I. 232, FTT (Tax) ........ *Digested*, 14/**3085**

South African Transport and Allied Workers Union v Garvas 35 B.H.R.C. 49, Const Ct (SA)

South Australia Asset Management Corp v York Montague Ltd; *joined cases* United Bank of Kuwait Plc v Prudential Property Services Ltd; Nykredit Mortgage Bank Plc v Edward Erdman Group Ltd [1997] A.C. 191; [1996] 3 W.L.R. 87; [1996] 3 All E.R. 365; [1996] 5 Bank. L.R. 211; [1996] C.L.C. 1179; 80 B.L.R. 1; 50 Con. L.R. 153; [1996] P.N.L.R. 455; [1996] 2 E.G.L.R. 93; [1996] 27 E.G. 125; [1996] E.G. 107 (C.S.); (1996) 93(32) L.S.G. 33; (1996) 146 N.L.J. 956; (1996) 140 S.J.L.B. 156; [1996] N.P.C. 100; Times, June 24, 1996; Independent, July 2, 1996, HL; affirming [1995] E.G. 71 (C.S.); [1995] N.P.C. 66, QBD (Comm) ....... *Digested,* 96/**4519**: *Applied* 97/3846, 98/4005, 98/4027, 98/4031, 98/4384, 99/1389, 99/4053, 00/1486, 00/4249, 00/4280, 01/4504, 01/4532, 03/2994, 03/3014, 06/2897, 06/2901, 07/2480, 09/2725, 10/827, 13/487: *Considered* 97/3827, 97/3839, 98/3999, 98/4032, 98/5724, 00/4009, 00/4247, 00/4275, 00/4279, 01/2511, 01/4263, 06/2451, 10/626, 11/536, 12/263: *Distinguished* 02/3292: *Explained* 08/160: *Followed* 98/3959, 98/3987, 99/4018, 99/4057, 99/804, 01/4529, 11/2259, 11/3472, 12/2305, 14/2195, 14/2217: *Referred to* 97/4871

South Buckinghamshire DC v Porter (No.2); *sub nom* South Buckinghamshire DC v Secretary of State for Transport, Local Government and the Regions [2004] UKHL 33; [2004] 1 W.L.R. 1953; [2004] 4 All E.R. 775; [2005] 1 P. & C.R. 6; [2004] 4 P.L.R. 50; [2004] 28 E.G. 177 (C.S.); (2004) 101(31) L.S.G. 25; (2004) 148 S.J.L.B. 825; [2004] N.P.C. 108; Times, July 2, 2004; Independent, July 6, 2004, HL; reversing [2003] EWCA Civ 687; [2004] 1 P. & C.R. 8; [2004] J.P.L. 207; (2003) 147 S.J.L.B. 628; [2003] N.P.C. 68; Times, May 23, 2003; Independent, May 23, 2003, CA (Civ Div); reversing [2002] EWHC 2136 (Admin), QBD (Admin) ....... *Digested,* 04/**3087**: *Applied* 05/3296, 07/1157, 07/3277, 08/2930, 08/4956, 09/3059, 10/3180, 12/1459, 13/112, 13/2351, 14/70: *Considered* 09/4974, 12/51: *Followed* 05/3304, 11/2508, 11/2511, 13/2348, 14/2066, 14/2439

South Buckinghamshire DC v Secretary of State for Transport, Local Government and the Regions see South Buckinghamshire DC v Porter (No.2)

South Cone Inc v Bessant (t/a REEF) see REEF Trade Mark

South Lakeland DC v Carlisle Diocesan Parsonages Board see South Lakeland DC v Secretary of State for the Environment

South Lakeland DC v Secretary of State for the Environment; *joined case* South Lakeland DC v Carlisle Diocesan Parsonages Board [1992] 2 A.C. 141; [1992] 2 W.L.R. 204; [1992] 1 All E.R. 573; 90 L.G.R. 201; (1992) 64 P. & C.R. 128; [1992] 1 P.L.R. 143; (1992) 156 L.G. Rev. 602; (1992) 142 N.L.J. 159; (1992) 136 S.J.L.B. 61; [1992] N.P.C. 16; Times, February 3, 1992; Independent, February 13, 1992; Guardian, February 5, 1992, HL; affirming [1991] 1 W.L.R. 1322; [1992] 1 All E.R. 45; 89 L.G.R. 857; (1991) 62 P. & C.R. 617; [1991] 2 P.L.R. 97; [1991] J.P.L. 654; (1992) 156 L.G. Rev. 143; [1991] E.G. 41 (C.S.); Times, March 21, 1991; Daily Telegraph, April 12, 1991, CA (Civ Div); reversing [1991] J.P.L. 149, QBD ....... *Digested,* 92/**4186**: *Applied* 03/3434, 07/3266: *Considered* 10/4470: *Followed* 92/6514, 93/3925, 12/2587, 14/2388

South Lanarkshire Council v Scottish Information Commissioner [2013] UKSC 55; [2013] 1 W.L.R. 2421; [2013] 4 All E.R. 629; 2014 S.C. (U.K.S.C.) 1; 2013 S.L.T. 799; [2014] 1 C.M.L.R. 17; [2013] I.R.L.R. 899; [2013] Eq. L.R. 1006; 2013 G.W.D. 25-508, SC; affirming [2012] CSIH 30; 2012 S.L.T. 691; 2012 G.W.D. 13-264, IH (Ex Div) ....... *Digested,* 13/**61**

South London Healthcare NHS Trust Special Administrator v Secretary of State for Health see R. (on the application of Lewisham LBC) v Secretary of State for Health

South Manchester Abbeyfield Society Ltd v Hopkins [2011] I.C.R. 254; [2011] I.R.L.R. 300, EAT ....... *Digested,* 11/**1100**: *Considered* 12/1112, 14/1091: *Doubted* 14/1092

South Northamptonshire Council v Secretary of State for Communities and Local Government [2014] EWHC 570 (Admin); [2014] J.P.L. 1026, QBD (Admin) ....... *Digested,* 14/**2430**

South Wales Fire and Rescue Service v Smith [2011] EWHC 1749 (Admin), DC *Applied* 12/338: *Approved* 12/458: *Considered* 14/319

South Yorkshire Transport v Monopolies and Mergers Commission see R. v Monopolies and Mergers Commission Ex p. South Yorkshire Transport Ltd

Southampton City Council v A Mother see B (A Child), Re

Southend United Football Club Ltd v Revenue and Customs Commissioners [2013] UKFTT 715 (TC); [2014] S.T.I. 390, FTT (Tax)

Southend-on-Sea BC v Armour [2014] EWCA Civ 231; [2014] H.L.R. 23; [2014] 2 P. & C.R. DG7, CA (Civ Div); affirming [2012] EWHC 3361 (QB), QBD ....... *Digested,* 14/**2000**

Southend-on-Sea BC v Odeniran see Odeniran v Southend on Sea BC

Southern Cross Employment Agency Ltd v Revenue and Customs Commissioners; *sub nom* Revenue and Customs Commissioners v Southern Cross Employment Agency Ltd [2014] UKFTT 88 (TC); [2014] S.T.I. 545, FTT (Tax)

Southern Pacific Mortgages Ltd v Scott see North East Property Buyers Litigation, Re

Southern Pacific Personal Loans Ltd, Re see Oakley Smith v Information Officer

Southgate v Sutton see Sutton v England

Southwark LBC v Mills; *sub nom* Southwark LBC v Tanner; *joined case* Baxter v Camden LBC (No.2) [2001] 1 A.C. 1; [1999] 3 W.L.R. 939; [1999] 4 All E.R. 449; [2000] Env. L.R. 112; (2000) 32 H.L.R. 148; [2000] B.L.G.R. 138; [2000] L. & T.R. 159; [1999] 3 E.G.L.R. 35; [1999] 45 E.G. 179; [1999] E.G. 122 (C.S.); (1999) 96(42) L.S.G. 41; (1999) 96(42) L.S.G. 45; (1999) 149 N.L.J. 1618; (1999) 143 S.J.L.B. 249; [1999] N.P.C. 123; (2000) 79 P. & C.R. D13; Times, October 22, 1999, HL; affirming [2001] Ch. 1; [1999] 2 W.L.R. 409; (1999) 31 H.L.R. 187; [1999] B.L.G.R. 71; (1998) 10 Admin. L.R. 621; [1998] L. & T.R. 251; [1998] 3 E.G.L.R. 46; [1998] 45 E.G. 151; (1998) 162 J.P.N. 945; [1998] E.G. 132 (C.S.); (1998) 95(34) L.S.G. 31; (1998) 142 S.J.L.B. 221; [1998] N.P.C. 126; Times, August 20, 1998; Independent, October 2, 1998, CA (Civ Div); reversing [1998] 3 W.L.R. 49; (1998) 10 Admin. L.R. 353; [1998] 2 E.G.L.R. 30; [1998] 22 E.G. 151; (1998) 162 J.P.N. 722; [1998] E.G. 39 (C.S.); (1998) 95(16) L.S.G. 25; (1998) 142 S.J.L.B. 119; [1998] N.P.C. 34; Times, March 11, 1998, Ch D ........ *Digested,* 99/**3672**:
*Applied* 08/2461, 11/2070: *Considered* 06/2918, 11/3220: *Followed* 02/3058, 14/2221, 14/2508

Southwark LBC v Tanner see Southwark LBC v Mills

Southwark LBC v Woelke [2013] UKUT 349 (LC); [2014] L. & T.R. 9, UT (Lands) ........ *Digested,* 14/**2007**

Southwell v Blackburn [2014] EWCA Civ 1347; [2014] H.L.R. 47, CA (Civ Div)

Spaceright Europe Ltd v Baillavoine [2011] EWCA Civ 1565; [2012] 2 All E.R. 812; [2012] I.C.R. 520; [2012] I.R.L.R. 111, CA (Civ Div); affirming UKEAT/0339/10/SM, EAT ........ *Digested,* 12/**1164**:
*Considered* 13/1060: *Distinguished* 14/1130

Spain v United Kingdom (C-145/04); *sub nom* Gibraltar European Elections, Re (C-145/04) [2006] E.C.R. I-7917; [2007] 1 C.M.L.R. 3; [2007] All E.R. (EC) 486; Times, November 6, 2006, ECJ ........ *Digested,* 07/**1553**:
*Considered* 14/976

Spanish Raw Tabacco Cartel, Re see Alliance One International Inc. v European Commission (C-679/11)

Sparekassernes Datacenter (SDC) v Skatteministeriet (C-2/95) [1997] S.T.C. 932; [1997] E.C.R. I-3017; [1997] 3 C.M.L.R. 999; [1997] All E.R. (EC) 610; [1997] B.T.C. 5395; [1997] B.V.C. 509, ECJ (5th Chamber) ........ *Digested,* 97/**4987**:
*Applied* 98/4900, 02/4755, 03/4538, 06/4435, 08/3993, 08/4041, 09/4105, 11/3526, 14/3046: *Considered* 00/5294, 07/5568: *Followed* 98/4921, 12/3387

Sparkasse Bremen AG v Armutcu [2012] EWHC 4026 (Ch); [2013] B.P.I.R. 210, Ch D *Digested,* 13/**1680**:
*Applied* 14/1783

Sparkasse Hilden Ratingen Velbert v Benk [2012] EWHC 2432 (Ch); [2012] B.P.I.R. 1258, Ch D (Birmingham) ........ *Digested,* 13/**1688**:
*Applied* 14/1786

Specht v Land Berlin (C-501/12); *joined cases* Schombera v Land Berlin (C-502/12); Wieland v Land Berlin (C-503/12); Schonefeld v Land Berlin (C-504/12); Wilke v Land Berlin (C-505/12); Schini v Land Berlin (C-506/12); Schmeel v Germany (C-540/12); Schuster v Germany (C-541/12) [2014] All E.R. (EC) 1116; [2014] I.C.R. 966; [2014] Eq. L.R. 573, ECJ (2nd Chamber)

Special Effects Ltd v L'Oreal SA [2007] EWCA Civ 1; [2007] Bus. L.R. 759; [2007] E.T.M.R. 51; [2007] R.P.C. 15; (2007) 151 S.J.L.B. 126; Times, January 24, 2007, CA (Civ Div); reversing [2006] EWHC 481 (Ch); [2006] R.P.C. 33; (2006) 29(5) I.P.D. 29041; Times, May 1, 2006, Ch D ........ *Digested,* 07/**2677**:
*Considered* 14/1878

Speciality European Pharma Ltd v Doncaster Pharmaceuticals Group Ltd [2013] EWHC 3624 (Ch); [2014] E.T.M.R. 11; [2014] R.P.C. 11; (2014) 136 B.M.L.R. 161, Ch D ........ *Digested,* 14/**1925**

Speciality Produce Ltd v Secretary of State for the Environment, Food and Rural Affairs [2014] EWCA Civ 225; [2014] C.P. Rep. 29, CA (Civ Div); affirming [2013] EWHC 2196 (Ch), Ch D ........ *Digested,* 14/**64**

Specsavers International Healthcare Ltd v Asda Stores Ltd [2012] EWCA Civ 24; [2012] E.T.M.R. 17; [2012] F.S.R. 19, CA (Civ Div); reversing in part [2010] EWHC 2035 (Ch); [2011] F.S.R. 1, Ch D ........ *Digested,* 12/**1915**:
*Applied* 13/1761, 14/1930: *Considered* 14/1926: *Followed* 14/1915, 14/1917, 14/1928: *Preliminary ruling given* 14/1912

Specsavers International Healthcare Ltd v Asda Stores Ltd (C-252/12) [2013] Bus. L.R. 1277; [2013] E.T.M.R. 46; [2014] F.S.R. 4; Times, October 1, 2013, ECJ (3rd Chamber) ........ *Digested,* 14/**1912**

Spedition Welter GmbH v Avanssur SA (C-306/12) [2014] R.T.R. 5; [2014] Lloyd's Rep. I.R. 360, ECJ (2nd Chamber)

Speechley v Allott [2014] EWCA Civ 230; [2014] L.L.R. 817, CA (Civ Div)

Spence v British Railways Board [2001] I.C.R. 232; [2000] Po. L.R. 341, EAT ........ *Digested,* 01/**2346**: *Considered* 14/1135

Spencer v Onceriu (Unreported, November 12, 2013), CC (Nottingham) [*Mark Anderson, Medical Protection Society, 1 Victoria House, 2 Victoria Place, Leeds*] ........ *Digested,* 14/**2326**

Spencer v Paragon Wallpapers [1977] I.C.R. 301; (1976) 11 I.T.R. 294, EAT ........ *Digested,* 77/**1151**: *Applied* 77/1142, 78/1129: *Considered* 14/3507: *Distinguished* 77/1144, 80/1026

Spencer v Spencer [2009] EWHC 1529 (Fam); [2009] E.M.L.R. 25; [2009] 2 F.L.R. 1416; [2009] Fam. Law 790, Fam Div ........ *Digested,* 09/**1590**: *Applied* 14/1279: *Considered* 10/1392, 11/1286

Spencer v Spencer [2013] NZCA 449; 16 I.T.E.L.R. 459, CA (NZ)

Spencer v Taylor see Taylor v Spencer

Spiliada Maritime Corp v Cansulex Ltd (The Spiliada) [1987] A.C. 460; [1986] 3 W.L.R. 972; [1986] 3 All E.R. 843; [1987] 1 Lloyd's Rep. 1; [1987] E.C.C. 168; [1987] 1 F.T.L.R. 103; (1987) 84 L.S.G. 113; (1986) 136 N.L.J. 1137; (1986) 130 S.J. 925; Financial Times, November 25, 1986, HL; reversing [1985] 2 Lloyd's Rep. 116; (1985) 82 L.S.G. 1416, CA (Civ Div) ........ *Digested,* 87/**3135**: *Applied* 86/2705, 89/1722, 89/3095, 90/3768, 91/475, 91/476, 92/475, 93/3571, 93/5876, 94/4040, 94/483, 95/696, 96/846, 97/908, 98/4398, 99/2405, 99/717, 99/719, 99/750, 00/775, 01/815, 03/599, 04/1493, 05/622, 06/634, 07/683, 09/448, 09/449, 09/603, 11/1088, 11/3256, 12/474, 14/2186: *Considered* 87/3095, 87/399, 89/2725, 89/3042, 90/3709, 94/3256, 95/3484, 96/1089, 96/1091, 98/764, 02/2756, 02/477, 05/611, 06/24, 09/1497, 10/503, 13/472: *Distinguished* 87/3024, 03/2215, 08/2271: *Explained* 00/769: *Followed* 91/5142, 95/6052, 95/690, 97/2453, 98/748, 98/749, 05/978, 11/325, 11/469, 11/470, 13/1777, 14/477, 14/567

Sportech Plc v Revenue and Customs Commissioners see Revenue and Customs Commissioners v IFX Investment Co Ltd

Sportech Plc, Petitioner [2012] CSOH 58; 2012 S.L.T. 895; 2012 G.W.D. 14-271, OH . *Digested,* 12/**3861**: *Applied* 14/517

Sports Direct International Plc v Competition Commission [2009] CAT 32; [2010] Comp. A.R. 175; [2010] A.C.D. 32, CAT ........ *Digested,* 10/**492**: *Considered* 14/545

Spotting the Ball Partnership v Revenue and Customs Commissioners [2013] UKFTT 210 (TC); [2013] S.F.T.D. 1004; [2013] L.L.R. 845; [2013] S.T.I. 1746, FTT (Tax) ........ *Digested,* 13/**3189**: *Reversed* 14/3048

Spring Radio Cars Ltd v Glasgow City Council [2014] CSIH 21; 2014 S.C. 529; 2014 S.L.T. 393; 2014 S.C.L.R. 381; [2014] L.L.R. 837; 2014 G.W.D. 8-164, IH (Ex Div); affirming [2013] CSOH 15; 2013 S.L.T. 491; [2014] L.L.R. 191; 2013 G.W.D. 6-151, OH ........ *Digested,* 14/**3647**

Spring Salmon & Seafood Ltd v Revenue and Customs Commissioners [2014] UKFTT 887 (TC); [2014] S.T.I. 3522, FTT (Tax)

Spring Salmon & Seafood Ltd v Revenue and Customs Commissioners [2014] UKUT 488 (TCC); [2014] B.T.C. 529, UT (Tax); affirming [2013] UKFTT 320 (TC); [2013] S.T.I. 2750, FTT (Tax)

Springwell Navigation Corp v JP Morgan Chase Bank (formerly Chase Manhattan Bank) [2010] EWCA Civ 1221; [2010] 2 C.L.C. 705, CA (Civ Div) ........ *Digested,* 11/**193**: *Applied* 11/212, 13/2553: *Considered* 13/595: *Distinguished* 14/1034: *Followed* 11/186

Spritebeam Ltd v Revenue and Customs Commissioners see Versteegh Ltd v Revenue and Customs Commissioners

Squibb Group Ltd v Vertase FLI Ltd [2012] EWHC 1958 (TCC); [2012] B.L.R. 408; [2013] B.L.R. 11; [2012] C.I.L.L. 3220, QBD (TCC) ........ *Digested,* 13/**519**: *Considered* 14/576

SR (A Child), Re see Poole BC v W

SRI International v Revenue and Customs Commissioners [2014] B.V.C. 526, UT (Tax)

SS v SA see S (A Child) (Appeal from Sexual Abuse Findings), Re

SS v United Kingdom (Admissibility) (9909/10) (2014) 59 E.H.R.R. SE11, ECHR

SS (Bangladesh) v Secretary of State for the Home Department see PR (Sri Lanka) v Secretary of State for the Home Department

SS (Malaysia) v Secretary of State for the Home Department [2013] EWCA Civ 888; [2014] Imm. A.R. 170, CA (Civ Div) .................... *Digested,* 14/**1692**

SS (Nepal) v Entry Clearance Officer [2013] EWCA Civ 1206; [2014] Imm. A.R. 321; [2014] I.N.L.R. 537, CA (Civ Div) .................... *Digested,* 14/**1686**

SS (Nigeria) v Secretary of State for the Home Department [2013] EWCA Civ 550; [2014] 1 W.L.R. 998; [2013] Imm. A.R. 1106, CA (Civ Div) .................... *Digested,* 14/**1668**: *Followed* 14/1670

St Mary the Virgin, Burton, Latimer, Re (Unreported, October 26, 1995), Arches Ct *Considered* 14/849

ST (Child Asylum Seekers: Sri Lanka), Re; *sub nom* ST (Sri Lanka) v Secretary of State for the Home Department [2013] UKUT 292 (IAC); [2013] Imm. A.R. 813; [2014] I.N.L.R. 332, UT (IAC) .................... *Digested,* 14/**1644**

ST (Sri Lanka) v Secretary of State for the Home Department see ST (Child Asylum Seekers: Sri Lanka), Re

St Albans City and District Council v Hunston Properties Ltd see Hunston Properties Ltd v Secretary of State for Communities and Local Government

St Anselm Development Co Ltd v Bolton see Bolton v Godwin-Austen

St Chad's Churchyard, Bishop's Tachbrook, Re [2014] Fam. 118; [2014] 3 W.L.R. 47, Cons Ct (Coventry) .................... *Digested,* 14/**854**

St George's Healthcare NHS Trust v S; *joined case* R. v Collins Ex p. S (No.1) [1999] Fam. 26; [1998] 3 W.L.R. 936; [1998] 3 All E.R. 673; [1998] 2 F.L.R. 728; [1998] 2 F.C.R. 685; (1997-98) 1 C.C.L. Rep. 410; (1998) 44 B.M.L.R. 160; [1998] C.O.D. 396; [1998] Fam. Law 526; (1998) 95(22) L.S.G. 29; (1998) 148 N.L.J. 693; (1998) 142 S.J.L.B. 164; Times, May 8, 1998; Independent, May 12, 1998, CA (Civ Div) .................... *Digested,* 98/**2648**: *Applied* 01/2934, 13/2045, 14/1525: *Considered* 04/1690, 09/415, 09/4392

St Gregory Tredington, Re see St Gregory's, Tredington, Re

St Gregory's, Tredington, Re; *sub nom* St Gregory Tredington, Re [1972] Fam. 236; [1971] 2 W.L.R. 796; [1971] 3 All E.R. 269; (1971) 115 S.J. 284, Arches Ct .................... *Digested,* 71/**3773**: *Applied* 76/822, 85/1094, 87/1241, 07/1086, 09/998: *Considered* 95/1868, 05/990, 14/849

St John's, Chelsea, Re [1962] 1 W.L.R. 706; [1962] 2 All E.R. 850; (1962) 106 S.J. 314, Cons Ct (London) .................... *Digested,* 62/**1094**: *Applied* 69/1165, 71/3775, 89/1305: *Considered* 14/854

St Lawrence, Oakley with Wootton St Lawrence, Re see St Lawrence, Wootton, Re

St Lawrence, Wootton, Re; *sub nom* St Lawrence, Oakley with Wootton St Lawrence, Re [2014] 3 W.L.R. 984, Arches Ct .................... *Digested,* 14/**849**

St Maximus Shipping Co Ltd v AP Moller-Maersk A/S [2014] EWHC 1643 (Comm); [2014] 2 Lloyd's Rep. 377, QBD (Comm) .................... *Digested,* 14/**2741**

St Paul Fire & Marine Insurance Co (UK) Ltd v McConnell Dowell Constructors Ltd; *sub nom* St Paul Fire & Marine Insurance Co (UK) Ltd v McDonnell Dowell Constructors Ltd [1996] 1 All E.R. 96; [1995] 2 Lloyd's Rep. 116; [1995] C.L.C. 818; 74 B.L.R. 112; 45 Con. L.R. 89; [1995] 4 Re. L.R. 293; Lloyd's List, June 8, 1995, CA (Civ Div); affirming [1993] 2 Lloyd's Rep. 503; 67 B.L.R. 72; 37 Con. L.R. 96, QBD (Comm) .................... *Digested,* 95/**2895**: *Considered* 01/3840, 08/2219, 14/1836

St Paul Fire & Marine Insurance Co (UK) Ltd v McDonnell Dowell Constructors Ltd see St Paul Fire & Marine Insurance Co (UK) Ltd v McConnell Dowell Constructors Ltd

St Peter's, Draycott, Re [2009] Fam. 93; [2009] 3 W.L.R. 248; [2009] P.T.S.R. 1251, Arches Ct .................... *Digested,* 09/**998**: *Considered* 12/876, 14/849

St Prix v Secretary of State for Work and Pensions [2012] UKSC 49; [2013] 1 All E.R. 752; [2013] 1 C.M.L.R. 38, SC .................... *Digested,* 13/**1167**: *Considered* 14/1733

St Prix v Secretary of State for Work and Pensions [2011] EWCA Civ 806; [2011] 3 C.M.L.R. 48; (2011) 155(28) S.J.L.B. 31; [2011] P.T.S.R. D51, CA (Civ Div) ...... *Digested,* 12/**3117**: *Followed* 14/1733

St Prix v Secretary of State for Work and Pensions (C-507/12) see Saint Prix v Secretary of State for Work and Pensions (C-507/12)

Staatssecretaris van Financien v X BV (C-651/11) [2013] S.T.C. 1893; [2013] B.V.C. 209; [2013] S.T.I. 2072, ECJ (9th Chamber) *Followed* 14/3056

Stacey (t/a Lazydays Motorhomes) v Revenue and Customs Commissioners [2014] UKFTT 1026 (TC); [2014] S.T.I. 3442, FTT (Tax)

Stack v Dowden; *sub nom* Dowden v Stack [2007] UKHL 17; [2007] 2 A.C. 432; [2007] 2 W.L.R. 831; [2007] 2 All E.R. 929; [2007] 1 F.L.R. 1858; [2007] 2 F.C.R. 280; [2007] B.P.I.R. 913; [2008] 2 P. & C.R. 4; [2007] W.T.L.R. 1053; (2006-07) 9 I.T.E.L.R. 815; [2007] Fam. Law 593; [2007] 18 E.G. 153 (C.S.); (2007) 157 N.L.J. 634; (2007) 151 S.J.L.B. 575; [2007] N.P.C. 47; [2007] 2 P. & C.R. DG11; Times, April 26, 2007, HL; affirming [2005] EWCA Civ 857; [2006] 1 F.L.R. 254; [2005] 2 F.C.R. 739; [2006] 1 P. & C.R. 15; [2006] W.T.L.R. 511; (2005-06) 8 I.T.E.L.R. 174; [2005] Fam. Law 864; [2005] N.P.C. 93; [2006] 1 P. & C.R. DG3, CA (Civ Div) .......... *Digested,* 07/**3367**:
*Applied* 07/3362, 07/3366, 08/2145, 08/3060, 08/3102, 08/3122, 08/3615, 09/3119, 09/3719, 10/2692, 13/2421, 13/693: *Considered* 07/2408, 08/3064, 09/1363, 10/3442, 11/1292, 12/2024, 13/2422, 14/2492: *Distinguished* 08/3104: *Followed* 10/2691, 12/1319, 12/1457, 12/1825, 12/2705, 12/752, 13/2420, 14/3196

Stadium Capital Holdings No.2 Ltd v Secretary of State for Communities and Local Government [2013] EWHC 3548 (Admin); [2014] J.P.L. 533, QBD (Admin) .......... *Digested,* 14/**2374**

Stadnik-Borowiec v Southern Health and Social Care Trust [2014] NICA 53; [2014] I.R.L.R. 723, CA (NI) .......... *Digested,* 14/**3144**

Stafford v Lee (1993) 65 P. & C.R. 172; [1992] E.G. 136 (C.S.); [1992] N.P.C. 142; Times, November 16, 1992, CA (Civ Div) .......... *Digested,* 93/**1615**:
*Applied* 02/3821: *Followed* 14/2520

Stag Line Ltd v Foscolo Mango & Co Ltd; *sub nom* Foscolo, Mango & Co Ltd, v Stag Line Ltd; Foscolo, Mango & Co Ltd, and HC Vivian Ltd v Stag Line Ltd; Foscolo, Mango & Co Ltd, and HC Vivian Ltd v Stag Line Ltd; Foscolo Mango & Co Ltd v Stag Line Ltd [1932] A.C. 328; (1931) 41 Ll. L. Rep. 165, HL; affirming [1931] 2 K.B. 48; (1931) 39 Ll. L. Rep. 101, CA; affirming (1930) 38 Ll. L. Rep. 271, KBD
*Applied* 77/248, 80/128, 14/2309: *Considered* 59/3034, 91/3223

Stagecoach South Western Trains Ltd v Hind [2014] EWHC 1891 (TCC); [2014] 3 E.G.L.R. 59; [2014] C.I.L.L. 3540, QBD (TCC)

Standard Bank Plc v EFAD Real Estate Co WLL [2014] EWHC 1834 (Comm); [2014] 2 All E.R. (Comm) 208, QBD (Comm) .......... *Digested,* 14/**562**

Standard Chartered Bank Ltd v Walker [1982] 1 W.L.R. 1410; [1982] 3 All E.R. 938; [1982] Com. L.R. 233; (1982) 264 E.G. 345; (1982) 79 L.S.G. 1137; 264 S.J. 479, CA (Civ Div) .......... *Digested,* 82/**2098**:
*Applied* 14/278: *Considered* 91/2655, 06/2387: *Referred to* 04/3240

Standard Chartered Plc v Revenue and Customs Commissioners; *joined case* Lloyds Banking Group Plc v Revenue and Customs Commissioners [2014] UKFTT 316 (TC); [2014] S.F.T.D. 1270, FTT (Tax)

Standard Life Assurance Ltd v Topland Col Ltd [2010] EWHC 1781 (Ch); [2011] 1 W.L.R. 2162, Ch D
*Considered* 14/762

Standfast Corporate Underwriters Ltd v Revenue and Customs Commissioners [2014] UKFTT 182 (TC); [2014] S.F.T.D. 957, FTT (Tax)

Stanford International Bank Ltd v Director of the Serious Fraud Office see Stanford International Bank Ltd (In Receivership), Re

Stanford International Bank Ltd (In Receivership), Re; *sub nom* Stanford International Bank Ltd v Director of the Serious Fraud Office; Janvey v Wastell; Serious Fraud Office v Wastell [2010] EWCA Civ 137; [2011] Ch. 33; [2010] 3 W.L.R. 941; [2010] Bus. L.R. 1270; [2011] B.C.C. 211; [2010] Lloyd's Rep. F.C. 357; [2010] B.P.I.R. 679, CA (Civ Div); affirming [2009] EWHC 1441 (Ch); [2009] B.P.I.R. 1157, Ch D (Companies Ct) .......... *Digested,* 10/**1873**:
*Applied* 11/1873, 13/764: *Approved* 14/802: *Followed* 14/1817, 14/803

Stannard (t/a Wyvern Tyres) v Gore see Gore v Stannard (t/a Wyvern Tyres)

Stansbury v Datapulse Plc Troy Holdings International Plc [2003] EWCA Civ 1335, CA (Civ Div)
*Applied* 14/1080

Starbucks (HK) Ltd v British Sky Broadcasting Group Plc [2013] EWCA Civ 1465; [2014] E.C.C. 4; [2014] F.S.R. 20, CA (Civ Div); affirming [2012] EWHC 3074 (Ch); [2013] F.S.R. 29, Ch D .......... *Digested,* 14/**1914**:
*Applied* 13/1838

Starbucks (UK) Ltd v British Sky Broadcasting Group Plc; *joined case* EMI (IP) Ltd v British Sky Broadcasting Group Plc [2012] EWCA Civ 1201; [2013] Bus. L.R. 633; [2012] E.T.M.R. 59; [2013] F.S.R. 16, CA (Civ Div) .......... *Digested,* 13/**1759**:
*Followed* 14/1863, 14/1920

Starglade Properties Ltd v Nash [2010] EWCA Civ 1314; [2011] Lloyd's Rep. F.C. 102; [2011] 1 P. & C.R. DG17, CA (Civ Div); reversing [2010] EWHC 148 (Ch); [2010] W.T.L.R. 1267, Ch D ............ *Digested,* 11/**3495**: *Considered* 11/1924, 14/511

Starks v Chief Constable of Hertfordshire [2013] EWCA Civ 782; [2014] R.T.R. 4, CA (Civ Div) ............ *Digested,* 14/**2329**

Starlight Shipping Co v Allianz Marine & Aviation Versicherungs AG; *joined cases* Brit UW Ltd v Imperial Marine Co; Brit UW Ltd v Starlight Shipping Co [2013] UKSC 70; [2014] 1 All E.R. 590; [2014] 1 All E.R. (Comm) 337; [2014] Bus. L.R. 873; [2014] 1 Lloyd's Rep. 223; [2013] 2 C.L.C. 713; [2014] Lloyd's Rep. I.R. 327, SC; reversing in part [2012] EWCA Civ 1714; [2013] 1 All E.R. (Comm) 1297; [2013] 1 Lloyd's Rep. 217; [2013] 1 C.L.C. 123; [2013] I.L.Pr. 15, CA (Civ Div); reversing in part [2011] EWHC 3381 (Comm); [2012] 2 All E.R. (Comm) 608; [2012] 1 Lloyd's Rep. 162; [2012] 1 C.L.C. 100, QBD (Comm) ............ *Digested,* 14/**565**: *Considered* 14/558: *Followed* 14/1920

Starlight Shipping Co v Allianz Marine & Aviation Versicherungs AG; *sub nom* Brit UW Ltd v Imperial Marine Co; Brit UW Ltd v Starlight Shipping Co; *joined case* Alexandros T, The [2014] EWCA Civ 1010; [2014] 2 Lloyd's Rep. 544, CA (Civ Div)

Starlight Shipping Co v Allianz Marine & Aviation Versicherungs AG; *joined cases* Brit UW Ltd v Starlight Shipping Co; Hellenic Hull Mutual Association Plc v Starlight Shipping Co; Allanz Marine and Aviation Vericherungs AG v Imperial Marine Co [2014] EWHC 3068 (Comm); [2014] 2 Lloyd's Rep. 579, QBD (Comm)

State Trading Corp of India Ltd v Doyle Carriers Inc (The Jute Express) [1991] 2 Lloyd's Rep. 55, QBD (Admlty) ............ *Digested,* 92/**3952**: *Considered* 14/2741

Steamship Mutual Underwriting Association Ltd v Trollope & Colls (City) Ltd 33 B.L.R. 77; 6 Con. L.R. 11; (1986) 2 Const. L.J. 224, CA (Civ Div); affirming 11 Con. L.R. 91; (1986) 2 Const. L.J. 75, DC ............ *Digested,* 86/**2699**: *Applied* 90/3795, 97/3592, 13/403, 14/427: *Considered* 93/3300, 07/492, 08/422, 10/391: *Distinguished* 97/734, 99/3944, 11/362

Stedman's Executors v Inland Revenue Commissioners see Inland Revenue Commissioners v George

Steel v Joy see Halsey v Milton Keynes General NHS Trust

Steel v United Kingdom (24838/94) (1999) 28 E.H.R.R. 603; 5 B.H.R.C. 339; [1998] Crim. L.R. 893; [1998] H.R.C.D. 872; Times, October 1, 1998, ECHR ............ *Digested,* 98/**3068**: *Considered* 02/3768, 06/5238, 07/3317, 12/668, 14/2464: *Distinguished* 00/3185, 01/10

Steen v ASP Packaging Ltd [2014] I.C.R. 56, EAT ............ *Digested,* 14/**1133**

Steliou v Compton see Woodhouse v Consignia Plc

Stemcor (SEA) Pte Ltd, Re [2014] EWHC 1096 (Ch); [2014] 2 B.C.L.C. 373, Ch D (Companies Ct) ............ *Digested,* 14/**1822**

Stephen, Petitioner [2011] CSOH 119; [2012] B.C.C. 537; 2011 G.W.D. 24-546, OH *Considered* 14/1760

Stephens v Calderdale MBC [2014] P.A.D. 19, Planning Inspector

Stevens v Bell; *sub nom* Airways Pension Scheme, Re; British Airways Pension Trustees Ltd v British Airways Plc [2002] EWCA Civ 672; [2002] O.P.L.R. 207; [2002] Pens. L.R. 247, CA (Civ Div); affirming in part [2001] O.P.L.R. 135; [2001] Pens. L.R. 99, Ch D ............ *Digested,* 02/**3390**: *Applied* 05/2944, 10/2337, 14/2245: *Considered* 10/2338, 12/2384

Stevens v Equity Syndicate Management Ltd [2014] EWHC 689 (QB); [2014] R.T.R. 34, QBD (Bristol) ............ *Digested,* 14/**830**

Stevens v Secretary of State for Communities and Local Government [2013] EWHC 792 (Admin); [2013] 2 E.G.L.R. 145; [2013] J.P.L. 1383; [2013] A.C.D. 97, QBD (Admin) ............ *Digested,* 13/**2367**: *Applied* 14/1596: *Approved* 14/2437

Stevenson v Patonpond Ltd (t/a British Button Industries) (Unreported), IT *Considered* 14/1090

Stichting Ostade Blade v Netherlands (8406/06) (2014) 59 E.H.R.R. SE9, ECHR

Stichting Regionaal Opleidingen Centrum Noord-Kennemerland/West-Friesland (Horizon College) v Staatssecretaris van Financien (C-434/05) [2008] S.T.C. 2145; [2007] E.C.R. I-4793; [2007] 3 C.M.L.R. 18; [2007] C.E.C. 855; [2010] B.V.C. 281; [2007] S.T.I. 1735, ECJ (3rd Chamber) ............ *Digested,* 08/**4003**: *Applied* 14/3042, 14/3044: *Considered* 08/5102: *Referred to* 09/4108

Stirling v Maitland 122 E.R. 1043; (1864) 5 B. & S. 840, QB *Considered* 14/638: *Followed* 60/418, 80/357

Stockport MBC v British Gas Plc see Transco Plc v Stockport MBC

Stockport MBC v Reddish Vale Golf Club see Transco Plc v Stockport MBC

Stocznia Gdanska SA v Latreefers Inc; *sub nom* Latreefers Inc, Re; *joined case* Stocznia Gdanska SA v Latvian Shipping Co (Abuse of Process) [2000] C.P.L.R. 65; [2001] B.C.C. 174; [2001] 2 B.C.L.C. 116; [2001] C.L.C. 1267; Times, March 15, 2000; Independent, February 15, 2000, CA (Civ Div); affirming [1999] 1 B.C.L.C. 271; Times, January 18, 1999, Ch D ........................ *Digested,* 00/**3472**: *Applied* 01/716, 14/1783, 14/1823: *Considered* 10/1905

Stocznia Gdanska SA v Latvian Shipping Co (Abuse of Process) see Stocznia Gdanska SA v Latreefers Inc

Stokes v Oxfordshire CC [2014] EWHC 2177 (Ch); [2014] Pens. L.R. 631, Ch D ......... *Digested,* 14/**2284**

Stokes Pension Fund Trustees v Western Power Distribution (South West) Plc; *sub nom* Trustees of the Stokes Pension Fund v Western Power Distribution (South West) Plc [2005] EWCA Civ 854; [2005] 1 W.L.R. 3595; [2005] 3 All E.R. 775; [2005] C.P. Rep. 40; [2005] B.L.R. 497; [2006] 2 Costs L.R. 226; (2005) 102(30) L.S.G. 28; Times, July 28, 2005; Independent, July 15, 2005, CA (Civ Div) ........................ *Digested,* 05/**374**: *Applied* 06/358, 06/382, 10/388: *Considered* 12/352, 12/387, 14/369: *Followed* 12/3050

Stolkin v Revenue and Customs Commissioners; *sub nom* Revenue and Customs Commissioners v Stolkin [2014] UKUT 165 (TCC); [2014] S.T.C. 2672; [2014] B.T.C. 512; [2014] S.T.I. 1764, UT (Tax); reversing [2011] UKFTT 831 (TC); [2012] S.F.T.D. 541; [2012] S.T.I. 223, FTT (Tax) ........................ *Digested,* 14/**2857**

Stolkin (Deceased), Re see Greaves v Stolkin

Stone & Rolls Ltd (In Liquidation) v Moore Stephens (A Firm); *sub nom* Moore Stephens (A Firm) v Stone & Rolls Ltd (In Liquidation) [2009] UKHL 39; [2009] 1 A.C. 1391; [2009] 3 W.L.R. 455; [2009] 4 All E.R. 431; [2010] 1 All E.R. (Comm) 125; [2009] Bus. L.R. 1356; [2009] 2 Lloyd's Rep. 537; [2009] 2 B.C.L.C. 563; [2009] 2 C.L.C. 121; [2009] Lloyd's Rep. F.C. 557; [2009] B.P.I.R. 1191; [2009] P.N.L.R. 36; (2009) 159 N.L.J. 1218; (2009) 153(31) S.J.L.B. 28; Times, August 11, 2009, HL; affirming [2008] EWCA Civ 644; [2008] 3 W.L.R. 1146; [2008] Bus. L.R. 1579; [2008] 2 Lloyd's Rep. 319; [2008] 2 B.C.L.C. 461; [2008] Lloyd's Rep. F.C. 426; [2008] P.N.L.R. 36; (2008) 105(25) L.S.G. 26, CA (Civ Div); reversing [2007] EWHC 1826 (Comm); [2008] Bus. L.R. 304; [2008] 1 B.C.L.C. 697; [2008] Lloyd's Rep. F.C. 47; [2008] P.N.L.R. 4; (2007) 157 N.L.J. 1154, QBD (Comm) ........................ *Digested,* 09/**2733**: *Applied* 14/1809: *Considered* 10/2293, 11/338, 14/2994: *Distinguished* 12/1869, 14/1807: *Followed* 10/446, 12/3401, 14/510

Stone Rowe Brewer LLP v Just Costs Ltd [2014] EWHC 219 (QB); [2014] 3 All E.R. 723; [2014] 2 Costs L.R. 266, QBD ........................ *Digested,* 14/**329**

Stonehouse Coaches Ltd v Smith [2014] I.C.R. D14, EAT (SC)

Storm Funding Ltd (In Administration), Re [2013] EWHC 4019 (Ch); [2014] Bus. L.R. 454; [2014] Pens. L.R. 73, Ch D (Companies Ct) ........................ *Digested,* 14/**2280**

Stott v Thomas Cook Tour Operators Ltd see Hook v British Airways Plc

Stoute v LTA Operations Ltd (t/a Lawn Tennis Association) [2014] EWCA Civ 657; (2014) 158(21) S.J.L.B. 37, CA (Civ Div)

Stoyanovi v Bulgaria (42980/04) (Unreported, November 9, 2010), ECHR *Applied* 13/121: *Considered* 14/63

Strabag Benelux NV v Council of the European Union (T183/00) [2003] E.C.R. II-135, CFI *Considered* 14/2475

Strack v European Commission (C-127/13 P) (2014) 158(39) S.J.L.B. 37, ECJ

Strain (Deceased), Re see Allnutt v Wilding

Stran Greek Refineries v Greece (A/301-B) (1995) 19 E.H.R.R. 293, ECHR ................ *Digested,* 95/**2620**: *Applied* 02/2444, 07/2209: *Considered* 14/59: *Followed* 01/3544, 02/2497

Strategic Technologies (Societe) v Procurement Bureau of the Republic of China - Ministry of National Defence - Taiwan [2014] I.L.Pr. 43, Cass (F)

Stratford on Avon DC v Secretary of State for Communities and Local Government [2013] EWHC 2074 (Admin); [2014] J.P.L. 104, QBD (Admin) ........................ *Digested,* 14/**2433**

Stretch v United Kingdom (44277/98) (2004) 38 E.H.R.R. 12; [2004] B.L.G.R. 401; [2004] 1 E.G.L.R. 11; [2004] 03 E.G. 100; [2003] 29 E.G. 118 (C.S.); [2003] N.P.C. 125; Times, July 3, 2003, ECHR ........................ *Digested,* 04/**2513**: *Considered* 06/4613, 14/610

Stribog Ltd v FKI Engineering Ltd see FKI Engineering Ltd v Stribog Ltd

Strojirny Prostejov as v Odvolaci financni reditelstvi (C-53/13); *joined case* ACO Industries Tabor sro v Odvolaci financni reditelstvi (C-80/13) [2014] B.T.C. 35; [2014] S.T.I. 2291, ECJ (1st Chamber)

Strong & Co Ltd v Woodifield (Surveyor of Taxes) see Strong & Co of Romsey Ltd v Woodifield (Surveyor of Taxes)

Strong & Co of Romsey Ltd v Woodifield (Surveyor of Taxes); *sub nom* Strong & Co Ltd v Woodifield (Surveyor of Taxes) [1906] A.C. 448, HL; affirming [1905] 2 K.B. 350, CA
*Applied* 47-51/4608, 47-51/4729, 54/1561, 62/1510: *Considered* 96/1294: *Distinguished* 52/1654, 53/1699: *Followed* 47-51/4728, 14/2975

Strouthos v London Underground Ltd see London Underground Ltd v Strouthos

Sturgeon v Condor Flugdienst GmbH (C-402/07); *joined case* Bock v Air France SA (C-432/07) [2010] 2 All E.R. (Comm) 983; [2010] Bus. L.R. 1206; [2010] 1 Lloyd's Rep. 522; [2009] E.C.R. I-10923; [2010] 2 C.M.L.R. 12; [2010] All E.R. (EC) 660; [2010] C.E.C. 692, ECJ (4th Chamber)
*Applied* 14/165: *Considered* 14/166

Stynes v Western Power (East Midlands) Plc [2013] UKUT 214 (LC); [2014] R.V.R. 15, UT (Lands) ........ *Digested,* 14/**2522**

SU (Afghanistan) v Secretary of State for the Home Department see KA (Afghanistan) v Secretary of State for the Home Department

Sub One Ltd (t/a Subway) v Revenue and Customs Commissioners [2014] EWCA Civ 773; [2014] S.T.C. 2508; [2014] B.V.C. 29; [2014] S.T.I. 2111, CA (Civ Div); affirming [2012] UKUT 34 (TCC); [2013] S.T.C. 318; [2012] B.V.C. 1871; [2012] S.T.I. 3275, UT (Tax); affirming [2010] UKFTT 487 (TC); [2010] S.T.I. 3137, FTT (Tax) ........ *Digested,* 14/**3098**

Subesh v Secretary of State for the Home Department; *joined cases* Vanniyasingam v Secretary of State for the Home Department; Nagulananthan v Secretary of State for the Home Department; Suthan v Secretary of State for the Home Department [2004] EWCA Civ 56; [2004] Imm. A.R. 112; [2004] I.N.L.R. 417, CA (Civ Div) ........ *Digested,* 04/**2079**:
*Applied* 05/2184, 11/3484, 14/2102: *Followed* 04/2044, 05/2150

Sud v Ealing LBC [2013] EWCA Civ 949; [2013] 5 Costs L.R. 777; [2013] Eq. L.R. 993; [2013] I.C.R. D39; Times, October 23, 2013, CA (Civ Div); affirming UKEAT/0482/11/LA; UKEAT/0483/11/LA, EAT ........ *Digested,* 13/**969**:
*Followed* 14/1074

Sudarshan Chemical Industries Ltd v Clariant Produkte (Deutschland) GmbH [2013] EWCA Civ 919; [2013] Bus. L.R. 1188; [2014] R.P.C. 6, CA (Civ Div); affirming in part [2012] EWHC 1569 (Ch); (2012) 109(27) L.S.G. 18, Ch D (Patents Ct) ... *Digested,* 13/**1798**

Sudbrook Trading Estate Ltd v Eggleton [1983] 1 A.C. 444; [1982] 3 W.L.R. 315; [1982] 3 All E.R. 1; (1982) 44 P. & C.R. 153; (1983) 265 E.G. 215; (1982) 79 L.S.G. 1175; (1982) 126 S.J. 512, HL; reversing [1981] 3 W.L.R. 361; [1981] 3 All E.R. 105; (1981) 260 E.G. 1033; (1981) 125 S.J. 513, CA (Civ Div) ........ *Digested,* 82/**1776**:
*Applied* 83/2100, 84/3673, 88/2089, 95/3059, 96/3805, 97/3320, 01/5164: *Considered* 84/117, 85/1858, 89/2192, 01/956, 06/748: *Distinguished* 83/2671, 00/901: *Followed* 14/2006

Suffolk Constabulary v Revenue and Customs Commissioners [2014] UKFTT 517 (TC); [2014] S.T.I. 2162, FTT (Tax)

Sufi v United Kingdom (8319/07); *joined case* Elmi v United Kingdom (11449/07) (2012) 54 E.H.R.R. 9; [2011] Crim. L.R. 882; (2011) 108(28) L.S.G. 20, ECHR . *Digested,* 12/**1659**:
*Considered* 12/1689, 14/1664: *Referred to* 13/1602

Sugarman v CJS Investments LLP [2014] EWCA Civ 1239; [2014] 3 E.G.L.R. 127, CA (Civ Div)

Sul America Cia Nacional de Seguros SA v Enesa Engenharia SA see Sulamerica Cia Nacional de Seguros SA v Enesa Engenharia SA

Sulamerica Cia Nacional de Seguros SA v Enesa Engenharia SA; *sub nom* Sul America Cia Nacional de Seguros SA v Enesa Engenharia SA [2012] EWCA Civ 638; [2013] 1 W.L.R. 102; [2012] 2 All E.R. (Comm) 795; [2012] 1 Lloyd's Rep. 671; [2012] 2 C.L.C. 216; [2012] Lloyd's Rep. I.R. 405; Times, August 24, 2012, CA (Civ Div); affirming [2012] EWHC 42 (Comm); [2012] 1 Lloyd's Rep. 275; [2012] Lloyd's Rep. I.R. 198, QBD (Comm) ........ *Digested,* 12/**104**:
*Applied* 13/801: *Distinguished* 14/629: *Followed* 13/98

Sullivan v United States [2012] EWHC 1680 (Admin); (2012) 156(25) S.J.L.B. 31, QBD (Admin)
*Applied* 14/1230

Summit Navigation Ltd v Generali Romania Asigurare Reasigurare SA [2014] EWHC 398 (Comm); [2014] 1 W.L.R. 3472; [2014] 2 Costs L.R. 367, QBD (Comm) ..... *Digested,* 14/**456**:
*Applied* 14/355, 14/462

Sumner v Davies see Davies v Sumner

Sun Microsystems Inc v M-Tech Data Ltd; *sub nom* Oracle America Inc v M-Tech Data Ltd [2012] UKSC 27; [2012] 1 W.L.R. 2026; [2012] 4 All E.R. 338; [2012] Bus. L.R. 1631; [2012] 3 C.M.L.R. 28; [2012] E.C.C. 27; [2012] Eu. L.R. 727; [2012] E.T.M.R. 43; [2012] Info. T.L.R. 173; [2013] F.S.R. 14; Times, July 16, 2012, SC; reversing [2010] EWCA Civ 997; [2011] 1 C.M.L.R. 43; [2011] E.C.C. 4; [2011] Eu. L.R. 117; [2010] E.T.M.R. 64; [2010] Info. T.L.R. 315; [2011] F.S.R. 2, CA (Civ Div); reversing [2009] EWHC 2992 (Pat); [2010] 2 C.M.L.R. 7; [2010] E.T.M.R. 13; [2010] F.S.R. 9; (2010) 33(2) I.P.D. 33010, Ch D (Patents Ct) ........ *Digested,* 12/**1970**: *Applied* 14/1860

Sun United Maritime Ltd v Kasteli Marine Inc [2014] EWHC 1476 (Comm); [2014] 2 Lloyd's Rep. 386, QBD (Comm) ........ *Digested,* 14/**120**

Sunday Times v United Kingdom (A/30) (1979-80) 2 E.H.R.R. 245; (1979) 76 L.S.G. 328, ECHR ........ *Digested,* 80/**1385**: *Applied* 98/3090, 01/3472, 09/1940, 13/2125, 14/1629: *Considered* 04/1615, 10/765, 13/619, 14/906

Sunderland City Council v P; *sub nom* PS (Incapacitated or Vulnerable Adult), Re; Sunderland City Council v PS [2007] EWHC 623 (Fam); [2007] 2 F.L.R. 1083; (2007) 10 C.C.L. Rep. 295; [2007] LS Law Medical 507; [2007] Fam. Law 695, Fam Div ........ *Digested,* 07/**3911**: *Applied* 09/1801, 09/2701, 14/2187: *Followed* 11/2237

Sunderland City Council v PS see Sunderland City Council v P

Sunderland City Council v Stirling Investment Properties LLP [2013] EWHC 1413 (Admin); [2013] R.A. 411; [2013] 23 E.G. 77 (C.S.), QBD (Admin) ........ *Digested,* 14/**2141**

Sunico A/S v Revenue and Customs Commissioners [2014] EWCA Civ 1108; [2014] B.V.C. 34, CA (Civ Div) ........ *Digested,* 14/**432**

Sunlife Europe Properties Ltd v Tiger Aspect Holdings Ltd [2013] EWCA Civ 1656; [2014] 1 E.G.L.R. 30; [2014] Bus. L.R. D1; [2014] 1 P. & C.R. DG14, CA (Civ Div); affirming [2013] EWHC 463 (TCC); 147 Con. L.R. 105; [2013] 2 P. & C.R. 4; [2013] 2 E.G.L.R. 55; [2013] Bus. L.R. D56, QBD (TCC) ........ *Digested,* 13/**1873**

Sunningdale Golf Club v Customs and Excise Commissioners [1997] V. & D.R. 79, V&DTr
*Applied* 14/3057

Sunrider Corp v Office for Harmonisation in the Internal Market (Trade Marks and Designs) (OHIM) (C416/04) [2006] E.C.R. I-4237, ECJ
*Applied* 08/1318: *Followed* 14/1931

Sunrise Brokers LLP v Rodgers [2014] EWCA Civ 1373, CA (Civ Div); affirming [2014] EWHC 2633 (QB); [2014] I.R.L.R. 780, QBD ........ *Digested,* 14/**1114**

Sunrise Radio Ltd, Re; *sub nom* Kohli v Lit [2012] EWHC 1337 (Ch), Ch D (Companies Ct)
*Reversed in part* 14/525

Sunrise Radio Ltd, Re; *sub nom* Kohli v Avtar Lit [2011] EWHC 3821 (Ch), Ch D
*Reversed in part* 14/525

Sunrise Radio Ltd, Re; *sub nom* Kohli v Lit [2013] EWCA Civ 667; [2014] 1 B.C.L.C. 427, CA (Civ Div); affirming [2009] EWHC 2893 (Ch); [2010] 1 B.C.L.C. 367, Ch D (Companies Ct) ........ *Digested,* 14/**525**

Superstrike Ltd v Rodrigues [2013] EWCA Civ 669; [2013] 1 W.L.R. 3848; [2013] H.L.R. 42; [2013] L. & T.R. 33; [2013] 2 E.G.L.R. 91; [2013] 2 P. & C.R. DG19, CA (Civ Div) ........ *Digested,* 14/**2016**

Supperstone v Hurst [2005] EWHC 2808 (Ch); [2006] B.P.I.R. 517, Ch D ........ *Digested,* 06/**2340**: *Applied* 14/343

Supportways Community Services Ltd v Hampshire CC see R. (on the application of Supportways Community Services Ltd) v Hampshire CC

Surdonja v Ealing LBC see Mohamed v Hammersmith and Fulham LBC

Surrey CC v Al-Hilli [2013] EWHC 3404 (Fam); [2014] 2 F.L.R. 217; [2014] Fam. Law 298, Fam Div ........ *Digested,* 14/**1423**

Surrey CC v Al-Hilli see Al-Hilli (Reporting Restrictions), Re

Surrey CC v Al-Hilli see Al-Hilli (Summary of Final Judgment), Re

Surrey CC v Associated Newspapers Ltd see Surrey CC v ME

Surrey CC v CA; *sub nom* P v Surrey CC; MIG, Re [2011] EWCA Civ 190; [2012] Fam. 170; [2012] 2 W.L.R. 1056; [2012] P.T.S.R. 727; [2011] 2 F.L.R. 583; [2011] 1 F.C.R. 559; [2011] H.R.L.R. 19; [2011] U.K.H.R.R. 584; (2011) 14 C.C.L. Rep. 209; [2011] M.H.L.R. 125; [2011] Fam. Law 475, CA (Civ Div); affirming [2010] EWHC 785 (Fam); [2011] M.H.L.R. 108; [2011] Fam. Law 29, CP ........ *Digested,* 11/**3225**: *Applied* 12/2279, 12/2288: *Approved* 12/2288: *Reversed* 14/2189

Surrey CC v M [2013] EWHC 2400 (Fam); [2014] 1 F.C.R. 429; (2013) 157(32) S.J.L.B. 31, Fam Div ........ *Digested,* 14/**1292**

Surrey CC v ME; *sub nom* Surrey CC v Associated Newspapers Ltd [2014] EWHC 489 (Fam); [2014] 2 F.L.R. 1267; [2014] Fam. Law 815, Fam Div
Surrey CC v P see Cheshire West and Chester Council v P
Surrey CC v S [2014] EWCA Civ 601; [2014] 3 F.C.R. 453; [2014] Fam. Law 1093, CA (Civ Div)
Surrey Trading Standards v Scottish and Southern Energy Plc see R. v Scottish and Southern Energy Plc
Surzur Overseas Ltd v Ocean Reliance Shipping Co Ltd 1997 F-No.83, QBD (Comm) *Digested*, 97/**906**: *Considered* 14/2711
Sussex Pharmaceutical Ltd, Re see Nygate v E-Squared Ltd
Sussex University v Customs and Excise Commissioners see Marks & Spencer Plc v Customs and Excise Commissioners (No.5)
Suthan v Secretary of State for the Home Department see Subesh v Secretary of State for the Home Department
Sutherland Professional Funding Ltd v Bakewells [2013] EWHC 2685 (QB); [2014] C.T.L.C. 1, QBD (Merc) ........ *Digested*, 14/**274**
Sutton v England; *sub nom* Southgate v Sutton [2011] EWCA Civ 637; [2012] 1 W.L.R. 326; [2011] W.T.L.R. 1235; [2011] N.P.C. 59; [2011] 2 P. & C.R. DG15, CA (Civ Div); reversing [2009] EWHC 3270 (Ch); [2010] W.T.L.R. 335, Ch D .... *Digested*, 11/**3496**: *Followed* 14/3030
Sutton, Re [2014] B.P.I.R. 1349, Ch D (Bankruptcy Ct)
Svensson v Retriever Sverige AB (C-466/12) [2014] Bus. L.R. 259; [2014] 3 C.M.L.R. 4; [2014] All E.R. (EC) 609; [2014] E.C.D.R. 9, ECJ (4th Chamber)
Svinarenko v Russia (32541/08) 37 B.H.R.C. 628, ECHR (Grand Chamber)
SW v RC see W v C
Swain v DPP see Ayliffe v DPP
Swain v DPP see R. v Jones (Margaret)
Swain Mason v Mills & Reeve; *sub nom* Swaine (Deceased), Re [2011] EWCA Civ 14; [2011] 1 W.L.R. 2735; [2011] C.P. Rep. 19; Times, February 15, 2011, CA (Civ Div); reversing in part [2010] EWHC 3198 (Ch), Ch D ........ *Digested*, 11/**389**: *Applied* 12/2295, 14/462: *Considered* 12/303: *Distinguished* 12/1841: *Followed* 13/1768
Swaine (Deceased), Re see Swain Mason v Mills & Reeve
Swallowfalls Ltd v Monaco Yachting and Technologies SAM [2014] EWCA Civ 186; [2014] 2 All E.R. (Comm) 185; [2014] 2 Lloyd's Rep. 50, CA (Civ Div); affirming [2013] EWHC 236 (Comm), QBD (Comm) ........ *Digested*, 14/**638**
Swan Housing Association Ltd v Gill [2013] EWCA Civ 1566; [2014] H.L.R. 18; [2014] 1 P. & C.R. DG12, CA (Civ Div) ........ *Digested*, 14/**2017**
Sweeney v Assessor for Ayrshire Valuation Joint Board; *sub nom* Sweeney v Ayrshire Valuation Joint Board Assessor [2013] CSIH 107; [2014] R.V.R. 126; 2014 G.W.D. 1-26, LVAC ........ *Digested*, 14/**3662**
Sweeney v Ayrshire Valuation Joint Board Assessor see Sweeney v Assessor for Ayrshire Valuation Joint Board
Sweeney v Westminster Magistrates' Court [2014] EWHC 2068 (Admin); (2014) 178 J.P. 336; [2014] Env. L.R. 31; [2014] Lloyd's Rep. F.C. 685, DC ........ *Digested*, 14/**807**
Sweet v Parsley [1970] A.C. 132; [1969] 2 W.L.R. 470; [1969] 1 All E.R. 347; (1969) 53 Cr. App. R. 221; (1969) 133 J.P. 188; (1969) 113 S.J. 86, HL; reversing [1968] 2 Q.B. 418; [1968] 2 W.L.R. 1360; [1968] 2 All E.R. 337; (1968) 112 S.J. 330, DC ........ *Digested*, 69/**2210**: *Applied* 70/1680, 70/1681, 75/496, 80/2684, 81/1739, 82/296, 84/951, 86/664, 94/1092, 00/1002, 04/751, 10/679: *Considered* 69/112, 69/3135, 69/845, 71/2186, 74/3419, 76/2369, 77/1417, 77/487, 77/506, 82/3206, 82/641, 83/612, 84/959, 85/656, 87/117, 87/3735, 88/3111, 91/203, 91/972, 94/3860, 95/4802, 06/832, 12/3906, 14/674, 14/679: *Distinguished* 74/710, 91/1289: *Followed* 70/1684, 01/1014, 12/731
Sweetman v An Bord Pleanala (C-258/11) [2014] P.T.S.R. 1092; [2013] 3 C.M.L.R. 16, ECJ (3rd Chamber)
Swetenham v Walkley [2014] W.T.L.R. 845, CC (Central London) ........ *Digested*, 14/**2822**
SWIATEK & COWLES/Vehicle accessory power connector (T1862/09) [2014] E.P.O.R. 5, EPO (Technical Bd App)
Swift v Secretary of State for Justice [2013] EWCA Civ 193; [2014] Q.B. 373; [2013] 3 W.L.R. 1151; [2013] 2 F.C.R. 1; [2013] H.R.L.R. 21; [2013] P.I.Q.R. P14; (2013) 163(7555) N.L.J. 17, CA (Civ Div); affirming [2012] EWHC 2000 (QB); [2012] P.I.Q.R. P21, QBD ........ *Digested*, 13/**2196**: *Applied* 13/1582, 14/3226
Swift (t/a A Swift Move) v Robinson see Robertson v Swift
Swift Advances Plc v Dalrimple see Swift Advances Plc v McKay

Swift Advances Plc v McKay; *joined case* Swift Advances Plc v Dalrimple [2013] NICh 3; [2014] E.C.C. 9, Ch D (NI)
Swiggs v Nagarajan (No.2) see Nagarajan v London Regional Transport
SWJJ Ltd v Revenue and Customs Commissioners [2014] UKFTT 448 (TC); [2014] S.T.I. 2049, FTT (Tax)
Swynson Ltd v Lowick Rose LLP (In Liquidation) (formerly Hurst Morrison Thomson LLP) [2014] EWHC 2085 (Ch); [2014] P.N.L.R. 27, Ch D .................................. *Digested,* 14/**2210**
SXH v Crown Prosecution Service [2014] EWCA Civ 90; [2014] 1 W.L.R. 3238, CA (Civ Div); affirming [2013] EWHC 71 (QB), QBD .................................. *Digested,* 14/**1646**
Syarikat Takaful Malaysia Bhd v Global Process Systems Inc see Global Process Systems Inc v Syarikat Takaful Malaysia Bhd (The Cendor Mopu)
Sycamore Bidco Ltd v Breslin [2013] EWHC 174 (Ch), Ch D
*Applied* 14/408
Syed v Secretary of State for the Home Department see Syed (Curtailment of Leave: Notice), Re
Syed (Curtailment of Leave: Notice), Re; *sub nom* Syed v Secretary of State for the Home Department [2013] UKUT 144 (IAC); [2013] Imm. A.R. 685, UT (IAC) ..... *Digested,* 14/**1712**
Sykes v Crown Prosecution Service see Crown Prosecution Service v Sykes
Sykes v Midland Bank Executor & Trustee Co Ltd [1971] 1 Q.B. 113; [1970] 3 W.L.R. 273; [1970] 2 All E.R. 471; (1970) 114 S.J. 225, CA (Civ Div); reversing [1969] 2 Q.B. 518; [1969] 2 W.L.R. 1173; [1969] 2 All E.R. 1238; (1969) 113 S.J. 243, QBD .................................. *Digested,* 70/**2710**:
*Applied* 94/2687: *Considered* 82/1849, 84/3362, 85/2319, 86/2285, 91/2657, 14/2214: *Distinguished* 84/3361, 98/4018
Sylvester v Sylvester [2014] W.T.L.R. 127, Ch D
Symes v St George's Healthcare NHS Trust [2014] EWHC 2505 (QB); [2014] Med. L.R. 449; (2014) 140 B.M.L.R. 171, QBD
Symonds (t/a Symonds Solicitors) v Redmond-Ord [2014] I.C.R. D6, EAT
Symphony Group Plc v Hodgson [1994] Q.B. 179; [1993] 3 W.L.R. 830; [1993] 4 All E.R. 143; [1997] Costs L.R. (Core Vol.) 319; (1993) 143 N.L.J. 725; (1993) 137 S.J.L.B. 134; Times, May 4, 1993; Independent, May 14, 1993, CA (Civ Div) .... *Digested,* 93/**3153**:
*Applied* 95/3994, 95/3995, 96/710, 99/389, 00/416, 00/423, 00/455, 01/474, 05/363, 06/369, 08/328, 14/368: *Approved* 99/749: *Considered* 94/3623, 96/701, 97/3113, 97/3343, 99/390, 99/391, 02/393, 02/394, 07/428, 09/384, 11/292: *Followed* 96/3464, 99/387, 99/392, 12/376
Synthon BV v SmithKline Beecham Plc (No.2); *sub nom* SmithKline Beecham Plc's Paroxetine Methanesulfonate Patent (No.2) [2005] UKHL 59; [2006] 1 All E.R. 685; [2006] R.P.C. 10; (2005) 86 B.M.L.R. 130, HL; reversing [2003] EWCA Civ 861; [2003] R.P.C. 43; (2003) 147 S.J.L.B. 814, CA (Civ Div); reversing [2002] EWHC 2573 (Pat); [2003] E.N.P.R. 10; [2003] R.P.C. 33; (2003) 26(1) I.P.D. 26004, Ch D (Patents Ct) .................................. *Digested,* 06/**2525**:
*Applied* 07/2614, 09/2362, 09/2394, 09/2406, 09/2407, 10/1960, 10/1966, 10/1981, 10/2014: *Followed* 11/1956, 14/1897
Szeja v Land Berlin (C-425/10) see Ziolkowski v Land Berlin (C-424/10)
Szepietowski v National Crime Agency see Serious Organised Crime Agency v Szepietowski
Szepietowski v Serious Organised Crime Agency see Serious Organised Crime Agency v Szepietowski

T v Belgium 17 I.T.L. Rep. 328, RB (B)
T v DPP [2003] EWHC 2408 (Admin); (2004) 168 J.P. 194; [2005] Crim. L.R. 739; (2004) 168 J.P.N. 186; Times, October 13, 2003, DC .................................. *Digested,* 03/**884**:
*Applied* 14/46
T v Hackney LBC see Temur v Hackney LBC
T v M (Appeal against Strike Out of Application to Vary) [2013] EWHC 1585 (Fam); [2014] 1 F.L.R. 380; [2013] Fam. Law 1254, Fam Div .................................. *Digested,* 14/**1370**
T v R [2013] EWHC 1829 (Fam); [2014] Fam. Law 27, Fam Div
T v S [2013] EWHC 2521 (Fam); [2014] Fam. Law 1664, Fam Div
T v T (Ancillary Relief: Need: Departure from Equality), Re see Tattersall v Tattersall
T v T (Brussels II Revised: Article 15) [2010] EWHC 3928 (Fam); [2013] 2 F.L.R. 1326; [2013] Fam. Law 809, Fam Div .................................. *Digested,* 14/**1329**
T v T (Hemain Injunction) [2012] EWHC 3462 (Fam); [2014] 1 F.L.R. 96; [2013] Fam. Law 540, Fam Div
T v T (Jurisdiction) [2012] EWHC 2877 (Fam); [2013] 1 F.L.R. 1419; [2013] 2 F.C.R. 265; [2014] Fam. Law 1391, Fam Div

T v United Kingdom (24724/94); *joined case* V v United Kingdom (24888/94) [2000] 2 All E.R. 1024 (Note); (2000) 30 E.H.R.R. 121; 7 B.H.R.C. 659; [1999] Prison L.R. 189; 12 Fed. Sent. R. 266; [2000] Crim. L.R. 187; Times, December 17, 1999, ECHR; no effect [1999] Crim. L.R. 579, Eur Comm HR ............ *Digested,* 00/**3198**: *Applied* 03/882: *Cited* 00/1078, 00/1331: *Considered* 01/1410, 05/2082, 05/2923: *Distinguished* 03/3781: *Followed* 14/43: *Referred to* 00/1090, 00/1095

T (A Child) v Eryildiz (Unreported, July 31, 2012), CC (Basildon) [*Stephen Garner, Barrister, Old Square Chambers, 10-11 Bedford Row, London*] ............ *Digested,* 14/**2318**

T (A Child) (Care Proceedings: Request to Assume Jurisdiction), Re; *sub nom* K (A Child) (Care Proceedings: Jurisdiction), Re; A Local Authority v A Mother; T (A Child: Article 15 of Brussels II Revised), Re; K (A Child) (Brussels II Revised: Art.15), Re [2013] EWCA Civ 895; [2014] Fam. 130; [2014] 2 W.L.R. 1204; [2014] 1 F.L.R. 749; [2014] 2 F.C.R. 369; [2013] Fam. Law 1381; [2014] Fam. Law 281, CA (Civ Div); affirming in part [2013] EWHC 521 (Fam); [2013] Fam. 253; [2013] 2 W.L.R. 1263; [2013] 2 F.L.R. 909; [2013] Fam. Law 788, Fam Div *Digested,* 14/**1355**: *Applied* 14/1287: *Considered* 14/1285

T (A Child: Article 15 of Brussels II Revised), Re see T (A Child) (Care Proceedings: Request to Assume Jurisdiction), Re

T (Care Proceedings: Costs: Serious Allegations Not Proved), Re [2012] UKSC 36; [2012] 1 W.L.R. 2281; [2012] 4 All E.R. 1137; [2012] P.T.S.R. 1379; [2012] 5 Costs L.R. 914; [2013] 1 F.L.R. 133; [2012] 3 F.C.R. 137; [2012] Fam. Law 1325; Times, August 14, 2012, SC; reversing [2010] EWCA Civ 1585; [2011] 2 F.L.R. 264; [2011] 1 F.C.R. 1585; [2011] Fam. Law 579, CA (Civ Div) ............ *Digested,* 12/**1340**: *Applied* 12/1399: *Considered* 14/1254: *Followed* 13/396

T (Children) (Abduction: Child's Objections to Return), Re; *sub nom* T (Children) (Abduction: Custody Rights), Re [2000] 2 F.L.R. 192; [2000] 2 F.C.R. 159; [2000] Fam. Law 594; Times, April 24, 2000, CA (Civ Div) ............ *Digested,* 00/**2443**: *Applied* 04/1465, 08/1461, 10/1340: *Considered* 14/1379: *Followed* 09/4295, 11/1348

T (Children) (Abduction: Custody Rights), Re see T (Children) (Abduction: Child's Objections to Return), Re

T (Children) (Placement Order), Re [2008] EWCA Civ 248; [2008] 1 F.L.R. 1721; [2008] 1 F.C.R. 633; [2008] Fam. Law 608; (2008) 152(13) S.J.L.B. 31, CA (Civ Div) ............ *Digested,* 08/**1573**: *Applied* 08/1415: *Distinguished* 08/1575: *Followed* 14/1253

T Clarke (Scotland) Ltd v Mmaxx Underfloor Heating Ltd [2014] CSIH 83; 2014 G.W.D. 33-633, IH (Ex Div); affirming [2014] CSOH 62; [2014] B.L.R. 341; 2014 G.W.D. 13-226, OH ............ *Digested,* 14/**3360**

T&N Ltd, Re [2006] EWHC 1447 (Ch); [2007] 1 All E.R. 851; [2007] Bus. L.R. 1411; [2007] 1 B.C.L.C. 563; [2006] B.P.I.R. 1283; [2006] Lloyd's Rep. I.R. 817, Ch D (Companies Ct) ............ *Digested,* 07/**2450**: *Considered* 10/1893, 14/1820

TA v AA see A (A Patient) (Court of Protection: Appeal), Re

Tachie v Welwyn Hatfield BC [2013] EWHC 3972 (QB); [2014] P.T.S.R. 662; [2014] B.L.G.R. 100, QBD ............ *Digested,* 14/**1619**

Tadros v Barratt see Tadros (Deceased), Re

Tadros (Deceased), Re; *joined case* Tadros v Barratt [2014] EWHC 2860 (Ch); [2014] W.T.L.R. 1753, Ch D

TAEL One Partners Ltd v Morgan Stanley & Co International Plc; *sub nom* Morgan Stanley & Co International Plc v TAEL One Partners Ltd [2013] EWCA Civ 473; [2013] 1 C.L.C. 879, CA (Civ Div); reversing [2012] EWHC 1858 (Comm), QBD (Comm) ............ *Digested,* 14/**276**

Tahery v United Kingdom (22228/06) see Al-Khawaja v United Kingdom (26766/05)

Taiga v Taiga see Moses-Taiga v Taiga

Taittinger SA v Allbev Ltd [1994] 4 All E.R. 75; [1993] 2 C.M.L.R. 741; [1993] F.S.R. 641; (1993) 12 Tr. L.R. 165; Times, June 28, 1993; Independent, June 30, 1993; Guardian, June 28, 1993, CA (Civ Div); reversing [1993] 1 C.M.L.R. 597; Times, February 11, 1993; Independent, February 11, 1993; Guardian, February 12, 1993, Ch D ............ *Digested,* 94/**4491**: *Applied* 08/2389: *Considered* 95/4734, 96/5717, 02/2783, 10/1990: *Followed* 14/1889: *Referred to* 97/4905

Taiwo v Olaigbe; *joined case* Onu v Akwiwu [2014] EWCA Civ 279; [2014] 1 W.L.R. 3636; [2014] I.C.R. 571; [2014] I.R.L.R. 448; [2014] Eq. L.R. 243, CA (Civ Div); affirming [2013] I.C.R. 770; [2013] Eq. L.R. 446, EAT ............ *Digested,* 14/**1104**: *Not followed* 13/986

Talacre Beach Caravan Sales Ltd v Customs and Excise Commissioners (C-251/05) [2006] S.T.C. 1671; [2006] E.C.R. I-6269; [2006] 3 C.M.L.R. 31; [2006] C.E.C. 1000; [2007] B.T.C. 5455; [2007] B.V.C. 366; [2006] S.T.I. 1855; [2006] N.P.C. 80, ECJ (1st Chamber); no effect [2006] E.C.R. I-6269; [2006] S.T.I. 1484, AGO ........ *Digested,* 07/**4362**:
*Applied* 14/3102: *Considered* 12/3431, 14/3058: *Distinguished* 14/3050: *Explained* 13/3227: *Followed* 13/3221

Tallington Lakes Ltd v Ancasta International Boat Sales Ltd [2012] EWCA Civ 1712; [2013] C.P. Rep. 18; [2014] B.C.C. 327, CA (Civ Div) ........ *Digested,* 13/**1717**

Talmon v Netherlands (30300/96) (Unreported, February 26, 2007), ECHR
*Considered* 14/2766

Tambrook Jersey Ltd, Re; *sub nom* HSBC Bank Plc v Tambrook Jersey Ltd [2013] EWCA Civ 576; [2014] Ch. 252; [2014] 2 W.L.R. 71; [2013] 3 All E.R. 850; [2013] B.C.C. 472; [2013] 2 B.C.L.C. 186; [2013] B.P.I.R. 484; Times, July 2, 2013, CA (Civ Div); reversing [2013] EWHC 866 (Ch); [2013] 2 W.L.R. 1249; (2013) 163(7560) N.L.J. 15, Ch D ........ *Digested,* 13/**1665**

Tan v Choy [2014] EWCA Civ 251; [2014] Fam. Law 807, CA (Civ Div)

Tanfern Ltd v Cameron-MacDonald [2000] 1 W.L.R. 1311; [2000] 2 All E.R. 801; [2001] C.P. Rep. 8; [2000] 2 Costs L.R. 260; (2000) 97(24) L.S.G. 41; Times, May 17, 2000; Independent, May 16, 2000, CA (Civ Div) ........ *Digested,* 00/**358**:
*Applied* 04/2186, 11/254, 12/336, 13/452, 14/1814: *Considered* 02/302, 03/2480: *Explained* 03/298, 04/3844: *Followed* 02/290, 04/276, 09/1640, 12/1412

Tanner v Millar [2013] EWHC 750 (Ch); [2014] B.P.I.R. 512, Ch D

Tapecrown Ltd v First Secretary of State; *sub nom* R. (on the application of Tapecrown Ltd) v First Secretary of State [2006] EWCA Civ 1744; [2007] 2 P. & C.R. 7; (2007) 151 S.J.L.B. 64; [2007] N.P.C. 4, CA (Civ Div); affirming [2006] EWHC 1012 (Admin); [2006] J.P.L. 1816, QBD (Admin) ........ *Digested,* 07/**3262**:
*Applied* 13/2314: *Considered* 14/2423

Tappenden (t/a English & American Autos) v Artus [1964] 2 Q.B. 185; [1963] 3 W.L.R. 685; [1963] 3 All E.R. 213; (1963) 107 S.J. 572, CA ........ *Digested,* 63/**176**:
*Applied* 14/2528: *Considered* 06/2433

Tarafdar (t/a Shah Indian Cuisine) v Revenue and Customs Commissioners [2014] UKUT 362 (TCC); [2014] B.V.C. 533, UT (Tax); affirming [2013] UKFTT 398 (TC); [2013] S.T.I. 2869, FTT (Tax) ........ *Digested,* 14/**3037**

Taranenko v Russia (19554/05) 37 B.H.R.C. 285, ECHR

Target Holdings Ltd v Redferns [1996] A.C. 421; [1995] 3 W.L.R. 352; [1995] 3 All E.R. 785; [1995] C.L.C. 1052; (1995) 139 S.J.L.B. 195; [1995] N.P.C. 136; Times, July 21, 1995; Independent, August 10, 1995, HL; reversing [1994] 1 W.L.R. 1089; [1994] 2 All E.R. 337; Times, November 24, 1993; Independent, December 3, 1993, CA (Civ Div) ........ *Digested,* 95/**2195**:
*Applied* 00/2332, 03/4472, 13/689: *Considered* 96/3909, 97/3979, 99/1401, 01/729, 03/4475, 11/2707, 12/275, 13/3172: *Followed* 13/227, 14/2055

Task Technology Pty Ltd v Commissioner of Taxation [2014] FCAFC 113; 17 I.T.L. Rep. 191, Fed Ct (Aus) (Full Ct); affirming [2014] FCA 38; 16 I.T.L. Rep. 749, Fed Ct (Aus) (Sgl judge)

Tasleem v Beverley; *joined case* Bartkauskaite v Bartkauskiene [2013] EWCA Civ 1805; [2014] 1 W.L.R. 3567; [2014] C.P. Rep. 25; [2014] 4 Costs L.O. 551, CA (Civ Div) ........ *Digested,* 14/**328**

Tatar v Hungary (26005/08) (2014) 59 E.H.R.R. 8, ECHR

Tate Building Services Ltd v B&M McHugh Ltd [2014] EWHC 2971 (TCC); [2014] B.P.I.R. 1560, QBD (TCC)

Tate Gallery Board of Trustees v Duffy Construction Ltd [2007] EWHC 361 (TCC); [2007] 1 All E.R. (Comm) 1004; [2007] B.L.R. 216; [2007] Lloyd's Rep. I.R. 758, QBD (TCC) ........ *Digested,* 07/**740**:
*Considered* 14/1855

Tattersall v Tattersall; *sub nom* T v T (Ancillary Relief: Need: Departure from Equality), Re; Tattershall v Tattershall [2013] EWCA Civ 774; [2014] 1 F.L.R. 997; [2013] 3 F.C.R. 453; [2013] Fam. Law 1375, CA (Civ Div) ........ *Digested,* 14/**1365**

Tattershall v Tattershall see Tattersall v Tattersall

Taurus Petroleum Ltd v State Oil Marketing Co (Costs) [2013] EWHC 4495 (Comm); [2014] 1 Lloyd's Rep. 432, QBD (Comm)

Taurus Petroleum Ltd v State Oil Marketing Co of the Ministry of Oil, Iraq [2013] EWHC 3494 (Comm); [2014] 1 All E.R. (Comm) 942; [2014] 1 Lloyd's Rep. 432; [2013] 2 C.L.C. 835, QBD (Comm) ........ *Digested,* 14/**563**

Tavoulareas v Alexander G Tsavliris & Sons see Tavoulareas v Tsavliris (The Atlas Pride)

Tavoulareas v Tsavliris (The Atlas Pride); *joined case* Tavoulareas v Alexander G Tsavliris & Sons [2006] EWCA Civ 1772; [2007] 1 W.L.R. 1573; [2007] 2 All E.R. (Comm) 356; [2007] C.P. Rep. 16; [2006] 2 C.L.C. 1034; Times, January 5, 2007, CA (Civ Div); affirming [2006] EWHC 414 (Comm); [2006] 1 C.L.C. 466; [2006] I.L.Pr. 33, QBD (Comm) ........ *Digested,* 07/**507**: *Applied* 14/1289

Taxation of Costs, Re; *sub nom* Solicitor, Re [1936] 1 K.B. 523; [1936] 1 All E.R. 491, CA
*Considered* 47-51/9784: *Followed* 14/332

Taylor v A Novo (UK) Ltd [2013] EWCA Civ 194; [2014] Q.B. 150; [2013] 3 W.L.R. 989; [2013] P.I.Q.R. P15; [2013] Med. L.R. 100, CA (Civ Div) ........ *Digested,* 13/**2204**: *Applied* 14/53

Taylor v Betterment Properties (Weymouth) Ltd see Betterment Properties (Weymouth) Ltd v Dorset CC

Taylor v Betterment Properties (Weymouth) Ltd see Paddico (267) Ltd v Kirklees Metropolitan Council

Taylor v Bowers (1876) 1 Q.B.D. 291, CA
*Applied* 53/3754, 14/264: *Distinguished* 47-51/1751

Taylor v British Legal Life Assurance Co Ltd [1925] Ch. 395; (1925) 94 L.J. Ch. 284, Ch D
*Applied* 14/2509: *Considered* 07/3400

Taylor v Burton [2014] EWCA Civ 21; [2014] 3 Costs L.O. 337, CA (Civ Div) ........ *Digested,* 14/**365**

Taylor v Chief Constable of Thames Valley [2004] EWCA Civ 858; [2004] 1 W.L.R. 3155; [2004] 3 All E.R. 503; (2004) 101(32) L.S.G. 36; (2004) 148 S.J.L.B. 877; Times, July 13, 2004, CA (Civ Div) ........ *Digested,* 04/**891**: *Applied* 07/2292: *Followed* 14/2468

Taylor v Director of the Serious Fraud Office; *sub nom* Taylor v Serious Fraud Office [1999] 2 A.C. 177; [1998] 3 W.L.R. 1040; [1998] 4 All E.R. 801; [1999] E.M.L.R. 1; Times, November 4, 1998; Independent, November 3, 1998, HL; affirming [1997] 4 All E.R. 887; [1998] E.M.L.R. 463; (1997) 94(36) L.S.G. 44; (1997) 147 N.L.J. 1309; (1997) 141 S.J.L.B. 216; Times, August 27, 1997; Independent, July 24, 1997, CA (Civ Div) ........ *Digested,* 98/**1768**: *Applied* 07/1073, 07/438, 08/905, 14/2992: *Considered* 99/4296, 00/2627, 00/934, 14/762: *Distinguished* 99/878: *Followed* 13/1020

Taylor v Herefordshire DC [2014] R.A. 188, VT ........ *Digested,* 14/**2089**

Taylor v Lawrence [2002] EWCA Civ 90; [2003] Q.B. 528; [2002] 3 W.L.R. 640; [2002] 2 All E.R. 353; [2002] C.P. Rep. 29; (2002) 99(12) L.S.G. 35; (2002) 152 N.L.J. 221; (2002) 146 S.J.L.B. 50; Times, February 8, 2002; Independent, February 14, 2002; Daily Telegraph, February 14, 2002, CA (Civ Div) ........ *Digested,* 02/**294**: *Applied* 02/296, 03/443, 04/255, 05/464, 06/30, 11/372, 11/762: *Considered* 03/453, 06/518, 07/3387, 07/510, 14/1604: *Distinguished* 08/1937: *Explained* 04/870: *Followed* 03/842, 11/493

Taylor v Maguire [2013] EWHC 3804 (IPEC); [2014] E.C.D.R. 4, IPEC ........ *Digested,* 14/**1866**

Taylor v Manchester City Council [2012] EWHC 3467 (Admin); [2013] 2 All E.R. 490; [2014] P.T.S.R. 57; (2013) 177 J.P. 1; [2013] L.L.R. 179; [2013] A.C.D. 36, QBD (Admin) ........ *Digested,* 13/**1966**

Taylor v Motability Finance Ltd [2004] EWHC 2619 (Comm), QBD (Comm)
*Applied* 14/622

Taylor v OCS Group Ltd; *sub nom* OCS Group Ltd v Taylor [2006] EWCA Civ 702; [2006] I.C.R. 1602; [2006] I.R.L.R. 613; (2006) 103(24) L.S.G. 28; (2006) 150 S.J.L.B. 810; Times, July 12, 2006, CA (Civ Div); reversing UKEAT/0803/04/MAA, EAT ........ *Digested,* 06/**1301**: *Applied* 08/2466, 14/1115

Taylor v Salmon 41 E.R. 53; (1838) 4 My. & C. 134, Ct of Chancery
*Applied* 14/2588

Taylor v Serious Fraud Office see Taylor v Director of the Serious Fraud Office

Taylor v Southern Pacific Mortgages Ltd see North East Property Buyers Litigation, Re

Taylor v Spencer; *sub nom* Spencer v Taylor [2013] EWCA Civ 1600; [2014] H.L.R. 9; [2014] L. & T.R. 21; [2014] 1 E.G.L.R. 27, CA (Civ Div) ........ *Digested,* 14/**1996**

Taylor & Sons (Farms) v Secretary of State for the Environment, Transport and the Regions; *sub nom* R. (on the application of Taylor (t/a David Taylor & Sons)) v Secretary of State for the Environment, Transport and the Regions [2001] EWCA Civ 1254; [2002] 1 P.L.R. 16; [2002] P.L.C.R. 11; (2001) 98(38) L.S.G. 40; [2001] N.P.C. 134; Times, October 16, 2001, CA (Civ Div); reversing [2001] P.L.C.R. 25; [2001] J.P.L. 996 (Note); (2001) 98(8) L.S.G. 45; Times, January 30, 2001, QBD (Admin) ........ *Digested,* 01/**4721**: *Considered* 14/2423

Taylor (Deceased) v Revenue and Customs Commissioners [2013] UKFTT 483 (TC); [2014] W.T.L.R. 357, FTT (Tax) ........ *Digested,* 14/**2901**

Taylor (Inspector of Taxes) v MEPC Holdings Ltd; *sub nom* MEPC Holdings Ltd v Taylor (Inspector of Taxes) [2003] UKHL 70; [2004] 1 W.L.R. 82; [2004] 1 All E.R. 536; [2004] S.T.C. 123; 75 T.C. 632; [2004] B.T.C. 20; [2004] S.T.I. 50; (2004) 101(4) L.S.G. 31; (2004) 148 S.J.L.B. 29; Times, January 9, 2004, HL; reversing [2002] EWCA Civ 883; [2002] S.T.C. 997; [2002] B.T.C. 276; [2002] S.T.I. 934; (2002) 99(31) L.S.G. 34; Times, July 3, 2002, CA (Civ Div); affirming [2002] S.T.C. 430; [2002] B.T.C. 162; [2001] S.T.I. 834; Times, June 12, 2001; Independent, June 25, 2001, Ch D; reversing [2000] S.T.C. (S.C.D.) 504; [2000] S.T.I. 1468, Sp Comm ........ *Digested,* 04/**3725**: *Applied* 07/4023, 14/2977: *Considered* 09/3760

Taylor Clark Leisure Plc v Revenue and Customs Commissioners [2014] UKUT 396 (TCC); [2014] B.V.C. 536; [2014] S.T.I. 2977, UT (Tax); affirming [2013] UKFTT 792 (TC); [2013] S.F.T.D. 381; [2013] S.T.I. 233, FTT (Tax) ........ *Digested,* 14/**3097**

Taylor Walton (A Firm) v Laing see Laing v Taylor Walton (A Firm)

Taylor Woodrow Property Co Ltd v Strathclyde RC 1996 G.W.D. 7-397, OH *Approved* 14/1978: *Considered* 97/6179

Tayside Valuation Joint Board Assessor v Hutchison 3G (UK) Ltd see Assessor for Tayside Valuation Joint Board v Hutchison 3G (UK) Ltd

TB v Essex CC [2013] UKUT 534 (AAC); [2014] E.L.R. 46, UT (AAC) ........ *Digested,* 14/**947**

TB v JB (formerly JH) (Abduction: Grave Risk of Harm) [2001] 2 F.L.R. 515; [2001] 2 F.C.R. 497; [2001] Fam. Law 576, CA (Civ Div) ........ *Digested,* 01/**2546**: *Applied* 03/1503, 05/1545, 10/1331, 14/1383: *Considered* 02/1632

TBG Ltd v Staatssecretaris van Financien (C-27/12) see X BV v Staatssecretaris van Financien (C-24/12)

TC (Zimbabwe) v Secretary of State for the Home Department see PR (Sri Lanka) v Secretary of State for the Home Department

Tchenguiz v Director of the Serious Fraud Office [2014] EWHC 1315 (Comm); [2014] Lloyd's Rep. F.C. 539; (2014) 164(7605) N.L.J. 20, QBD (Comm) ........ *Digested,* 14/**382**

Tchenguiz v Director of the Serious Fraud Office; *joined case* Rawlinson v Director of the Serious Fraud Office [2013] EWHC 2128 (QB); [2014] 1 W.L.R. 1476, QBD *Digested,* 14/**762**

Tchenguiz v Director of the Serious Fraud Office; *sub nom* Rawlinson & Hunter Trustees SA v Director of the Serious Fraud Office [2014] EWCA Civ 1129; [2014] C.P. Rep. 45, CA (Civ Div); reversing in part [2014] EWHC 1102 (Comm), QBD (Comm) ........ *Digested,* 14/**294**

Tchenguiz v Director of the Serious Fraud Office [2014] EWCA Civ 1333; Times, November 11, 2014, CA (Civ Div) ........ *Digested,* 14/**482**

Tchenguiz v Director of the Serious Fraud Office; *joined case* Rawlinson and Hunter Trustees SA v Director of the Serious Fraud Office [2014] EWCA Civ 472; [2014] C.P. Rep. 35; [2014] Lloyd's Rep. F.C. 519, CA (Civ Div); affirming [2013] EWHC 1578 (QB); [2013] Lloyd's Rep. F.C. 535, QBD ........ *Digested,* 14/**386**

Tchenguiz v Director of the Serious Fraud Office (Non-Party Disclosure); *sub nom* Rawlinson and Hunter Trustees SA v Akers [2014] EWCA Civ 136; [2014] 4 All E.R. 627; [2014] 2 All E.R. (Comm) 571; [2014] 2 B.C.L.C. 1; [2014] Lloyd's Rep. F.C. 502, CA (Civ Div); affirming [2013] EWHC 2297 (QB), QBD ........ *Digested,* 14/**293**

Tchenguiz v Imerman; *sub nom* Imerman v Tchenguiz; *joined case* Imerman v Imerman [2010] EWCA Civ 908; [2011] Fam. 116; [2011] 2 W.L.R. 592; [2011] 1 All E.R. 555; [2010] 2 F.L.R. 814; [2010] 3 F.C.R. 371; [2010] Fam. Law 1177; (2010) 154(30) S.J.L.B. 32; Times, September 2, 2010, CA (Civ Div) ...... *Digested,* 10/**1280**: *Applied* 14/496: *Followed* 11/369

Tchenguiz-Imerman v Imerman [2012] EWHC 4047 (Fam); [2014] 1 F.L.R. 232; [2013] Fam. Law 966, Fam Div ........ *Digested,* 14/**1339**

Tchenguiz-Imerman v Imerman [2013] EWHC 3627 (Fam); [2014] 2 F.L.R. 939; [2014] W.T.L.R. 145; [2014] Fam. Law 451, Fam Div ........ *Digested,* 14/**1373**

Tchenguiz-Imerman v Imerman (Application for Joinder) [2012] EWHC 4277 (Fam); [2014] 1 F.L.R. 865; [2013] Fam. Law 1376, Fam Div ........ *Digested,* 14/**1371**

TCI Trans Commodities AG v Islamic Solidarity Shipping Co Jordan Inc see Jindal Iron & Steel Co Ltd v Islamic Solidarity Shipping Co Jordan Inc

TD v Minister for Justice, Equality and Law Reform [2014] IESC 29; [2014] 3 C.M.L.R. 19, Sup Ct (Irl); reversing [2011] IEHC 37; [2012] Eu. L.R. 1, HC (Irl)

TD Bailey Son & Co v Ross T Smyth & Co Ltd see Ross T Smyth & Co Ltd v TD Bailey Son & Co

TE v SH; *sub nom* S (Transfer of Residence), Re [2010] EWHC 192 (Fam); [2010] 1 F.L.R. 1785; [2010] Fam. Law 355, Fam Div ........ *Digested,* 10/**1434**: *Approved* 14/1323

Teal Assurance Co Ltd v WR Berkley Insurance (Europe) Ltd [2013] UKSC 57; [2013] 4 All E.R. 643; [2013] 2 All E.R. (Comm) 1009; [2013] Bus. L.R. 1091; [2013] 2 C.L.C. 390; [2014] Lloyd's Rep. I.R. 56, SC; affirming [2011] EWCA Civ 1570; [2012] 1 All E.R. (Comm) 969; [2012] Lloyd's Rep. I.R. 315, CA (Civ Div); affirming [2011] EWHC 91 (Comm); [2011] Lloyd's Rep. I.R. 285, QBD (Comm) ............ *Digested,* 13/**1732**

TECHNION/Culturing stem cells (T2221/10) [2014] E.P.O.R. 23, EPO (Technical Bd App)

Technische Universitat Darmstadt v Eugen Ulmer KG (C-117/13) [2014] E.C.D.R. 23; (2014) 158(37) S.J.L.B. 37; (2014) 158(36) S.J.L.B. 37, ECJ (4th Chamber)

Technische Universitat Hamburg-Harburg v Datenlotsen Informationssysteme GmbH (C-15/13) [2014] P.T.S.R. 1293, ECJ (5th Chamber)

Teckal Srl v Comune di Viano (Reggio Emilia) (C-107/98) [1999] E.C.R. I-8121, ECJ (5th Chamber)
*Applied* 07/1642, 07/3328, 08/3018, 11/2635, 14/1619: *Considered* 08/3017, 10/2204, 14/3503: *Distinguished* 06/3419

Teddy Bear Clinic for Abused Children v Minister of Justice and Constitutional Development 36 B.H.R.C. 228, Const Ct (SA)

Tekle v Secretary of State for the Home Department see R. (on the application of Tekle) v Secretary of State for the Home Department

Telaustria Verlags GmbH v Telekom Austria AG (C-324/98) [2000] E.C.R. I-10745, ECJ (6th Chamber)
*Applied* 08/1356, 10/3791, 14/2149: *Considered* 06/3421, 08/3020: *Followed* 09/1281

Telchadder v Wickland (Holdings) Ltd; *sub nom* Wickland (Holdings) Ltd v Telchadder [2014] UKSC 57; [2014] 1 W.L.R. 4004; Times, November 19, 2014, SC; reversing [2012] EWCA Civ 635; [2012] H.L.R. 35, CA (Civ Div) ............ *Digested,* 12/**1643**

Telefonica O2 UK Ltd v British Telecommunications Plc; *sub nom* British Telecommunications Plc v Telefonica O2 UK Ltd [2014] UKSC 42; [2014] 4 All E.R. 907; [2014] 2 All E.R. (Comm) 877; [2014] Bus. L.R. 765; Times, July 24, 2014, SC; reversing [2012] EWCA Civ 1002, CA (Civ Div) ............ *Digested,* 14/**2986**

Telefonica SA v European Commission (C-295/12 P) [2014] 5 C.M.L.R. 18, ECJ (5th Chamber)

TeleTech Canada Inc v Minister of National Revenue 16 I.T.L. Rep. 248, Fed Ct (Can)

Telfer v Sakellarios [2013] EWHC 1556 (Comm); [2013] S.T.C. 2413; [2013] S.T.I. 2216, QBD (Comm) ............ *Digested,* 14/**2894**

Telford and Wrekin Council v Secretary of State for Communities and Local Government [2013] EWHC 79 (Admin); [2013] 1 E.G.L.R. 87; [2013] 17 E.G. 100; [2013] J.P.L. 865, QBD (Admin) ............ *Digested,* 13/**2333**: *Applied* 14/2408

Telford Homes (Creekside) Ltd v Ampurius Nu Homes Holdings Ltd see Ampurius Nu Homes Holdings Ltd v Telford Homes (Creekside) Ltd

Temple Retail Ltd v Revenue and Customs Commissioners [2014] UKFTT 702 (TC); [2014] S.T.I. 2733, FTT (Tax)

Temporal v Temporal [1990] 2 F.L.R. 98, CA (Civ Div) ............ *Digested,* 91/**2803**: *Followed* 14/1333

Temur v Hackney LBC; *sub nom* T v Hackney LBC [2014] EWCA Civ 877; [2014] H.L.R. 39; [2014] B.L.G.R. 689, CA (Civ Div) ............ *Digested,* 14/**1603**

Ten Oever v Stichting Bedrijfspensioenfonds voor het Glazenwassers- en Schoonmaakbedrijf (C-109/91); *joined cases* Moroni v Collo GmbH (C-110/91); Neath v Hugh Steeper Ltd (C-152/91); Coloroll Pension Trustees Ltd v Russell (C-200/91) [1993] E.C.R. I-4879; [1995] 2 C.M.L.R. 357; [1995] I.C.R. 74; [1993] I.R.L.R. 601; [1993] Pens. L.R. 317; Times, October 12, 1993; Financial Times, October 5, 1993, ECJ; no effect [1993] E.C.R. I-4879; [1993] Pens. L.R. 89, AGO ............ *Digested,* 94/**4814**: *Applied* 08/2732, 14/1120: *Followed* 14/1087

Terna Bahrain Holding Co WLL v Al Shamsi; *joined case* Al Shamsi v Terna Bahrain Holding Co WLL [2012] EWHC 3283 (Comm); [2013] 1 All E.R. (Comm) 580; [2013] 1 Lloyd's Rep. 86; [2013] 2 C.L.C. 1; 145 Con. L.R. 114, QBD (Comm) .. *Digested,* 13/**113**: *Considered* 14/133

Terre Wallonne ASBL v Region Wallonne (C-105/09) [2011] Env. L.R. D8, ECJ (4th Chamber)
*Followed* 14/1201

Terveys- ja sosiaalialan neuvottelujarjesto TSN ry v Terveyspalvelualan Liitto ry (C-512/11) [2014] I.C.R. D15, ECJ (3rd Chamber)

Tesco Plc v Customs and Excise Commissioners [2003] EWCA Civ 1367; [2003] S.T.C. 1561; [2003] B.T.C. 5608; [2003] S.T.I. 1820; (2003) 100(42) L.S.G. 32; Times, October 16, 2003; Independent, October 17, 2003, CA (Civ Div); affirming [2002] EWHC 2131 (Ch); [2002] S.T.C. 1332; [2003] 1 C.M.L.R. 5; [2002] B.T.C. 5613; [2003] B.V.C. 39; [2002] S.T.I. 1393, Ch D; reversing in part [2001] B.V.C. 2416; [2001] V. & D.R. 366; [2002] S.T.I. 363, V&DTr .......... *Digested,* 04/**4015**: *Applied* 05/4394, 08/4028, 11/3567, 14/3086: *Considered* 09/4114: *Followed* 11/3572

Tesco Stores Ltd v Constable [2008] EWCA Civ 362; [2008] 1 C.L.C. 727; [2008] Lloyd's Rep. I.R. 636; [2008] C.I.L.L. 2593; (2008) 105(17) L.S.G. 28, CA (Civ Div); affirming [2007] EWHC 2088 (Comm); [2007] 2 C.L.C. 493; [2008] Lloyd's Rep. I.R. 302; [2007] C.I.L.L. 2522; (2007) 104(38) L.S.G. 32, QBD (Comm) .... *Digested,* 08/**2218**: *Applied* 13/1733: *Considered* 14/1856

Tesco Stores Ltd v Dundee City Council [2012] UKSC 13; [2012] P.T.S.R. 983; 2012 S.C. (U.K.S.C.) 278; 2012 S.L.T. 739; [2012] 2 P. & C.R. 9; [2012] J.P.L. 1078; [2012] 13 E.G. 91 (C.S.); 2012 G.W.D. 12-235, SC; affirming [2011] CSIH 9; 2011 S.C. 457; 2011 G.W.D. 7-191, IH (2 Div); affirming [2010] CSOH 128; 2010 G.W.D. 33-688, OH .......... *Digested,* 12/**2595**: *Applied* 12/2542, 13/2290: *Followed* 14/2384, 14/2395, 14/2397

Tesco Stores Ltd v Secretary of State for the Environment; *joined cases* Tesco Stores Ltd v West Oxfordshire DC; Tesco Stores Ltd v Tarmac Provincial Properties Ltd [1995] 1 W.L.R. 759; [1995] 2 All E.R. 636; 93 L.G.R. 403; (1995) 70 P. & C.R. 184; [1995] 2 P.L.R. 72; [1995] 2 E.G.L.R. 147; [1995] 27 E.G. 154; [1995] E.G. 82 (C.S.); (1995) 92(24) L.S.G. 39; (1995) 145 N.L.J. 724; (1995) 139 S.J.L.B. 145; Times, May 13, 1995, HL; affirming (1994) 68 P. & C.R. 219; [1994] 1 P.L.R. 97; [1994] E.G. 103 (C.S.); [1994] N.P.C. 80, CA (Civ Div); reversing (1994) 67 P. & C.R. 216; [1993] 2 P.L.R. 108; [1994] J.P.L. 227; [1993] E.G. 133 (C.S.), QBD .......... *Digested,* 95/**4784**: *Applied* 96/4779, 99/4215, 01/4682, 01/4731, 03/2057, 11/2551, 12/2324, 13/2358: *Considered* 99/3049, 07/2988, 07/3291, 09/1736, 09/2981, 12/2577, 13/2349, 14/2354: *Followed* 03/3438, 13/2348, 14/2399, 14/2422

Tesco Stores Ltd v Tarmac Provincial Properties Ltd see Tesco Stores Ltd v Secretary of State for the Environment

Tesco Stores Ltd v West Oxfordshire DC see Tesco Stores Ltd v Secretary of State for the Environment

Teshome v Lord President of the Council [2014] EWHC 1468 (Admin); [2014] 3 C.M.L.R. 28, QBD (Admin) .......... *Digested,* 14/**977**

Tesla Motors Ltd v BBC [2013] EWCA Civ 152; (2013) 163 N.L.J. 290, CA (Civ Div); affirming [2012] EWHC 310 (QB), QBD *Followed* 14/2995

Tessenderlo Chemie v Belgium [2014] 4 C.M.L.R. 29, Cour Const (B)

Test Claimants in the FII Group Litigation v Inland Revenue Commissioners; *sub nom* Inland Revenue Commissioners v Test Claimants in the Franked Investment Income Group Litigation; Test Claimants in the Franked Investment Income Group Litigation v Inland Revenue Commissioners [2014] EWCA Civ 1214; [2014] B.T.C. 41; [2014] S.T.I. 2927, CA (Civ Div); affirming [2013] EWHC 3757 (Ch); [2013] B.T.C. 826; [2013] S.T.I. 3669, Ch D .......... *Digested,* 14/**2865**

Test Claimants in the FII Group Litigation v Inland Revenue Commissioners (C-35/11); *sub nom* Test Claimants in the FII Group Litigation v Revenue and Customs Commissioners (C-35/11) [2013] Ch. 431; [2013] 2 W.L.R. 1416; [2013] S.T.C. 612; [2013] 1 C.M.L.R. 50; [2013] B.T.C. 424; [2012] S.T.I. 3271, ECJ (Grand Chamber) *Followed* 14/2874

Test Claimants in the FII Group Litigation v Inland Revenue Commissioners (C-362/12); *sub nom* Test Claimants in the Franked Investment Income Group Litigation v Revenue and Customs Commissioners (C-362/12) [2014] A.C. 1161; [2014] 3 W.L.R. 743; [2014] S.T.C. 638; [2014] 2 C.M.L.R. 33; [2014] All E.R. (EC) 375; [2014] C.E.C. 930; [2014] B.T.C. 27; [2014] S.T.I. 246, ECJ (3rd Chamber) .......... *Digested,* 14/**2885**

Test Claimants in the FII Group Litigation v Revenue and Customs Commissioners; *sub nom* Test Claimants in the Franked Investment Group Litigation v Inland Revenue Commissioners; Test Claimants in the Franked Investment Income Group Litigation v Revenue and Customs Commissioners [2012] UKSC 19; [2012] 2 A.C. 337; [2012] 2 W.L.R. 1149; [2012] 3 All E.R. 909; [2012] Bus. L.R. 1033; [2012] S.T.C. 1362; [2012] B.T.C. 312; [2012] S.T.I. 1707, SC; reversing in part [2010] EWCA Civ 103; [2010] S.T.C. 1251; [2010] B.T.C. 265; [2010] S.T.I. 562, CA (Civ Div); reversing in part [2008] EWHC 2893 (Ch); [2009] S.T.C. 254; [2009] Eu. L.R. 413; [2009] B.T.C. 443; [2008] S.T.I. 2726, Ch D ........ *Digested,* 12/**3251**: *Applied* 13/3219: *Cited* 12/3430: *Considered* 10/3512, 11/3303: *Followed* 10/3507: *Preliminary ruling given* 14/2885: *Referred to* 10/367

Test Claimants in the FII Group Litigation v Revenue and Customs Commissioners (C-35/11) see Test Claimants in the FII Group Litigation v Inland Revenue Commissioners (C-35/11)

Test Claimants in the Franked Investment Group Litigation v Inland Revenue Commissioners see Test Claimants in the FII Group Litigation v Revenue and Customs Commissioners

Test Claimants in the Franked Investment Income Group Litigation v Inland Revenue Commissioners see Test Claimants in the FII Group Litigation v Inland Revenue Commissioners

Test Claimants in the Franked Investment Income Group Litigation v Revenue and Customs Commissioners (C-362/12) see Test Claimants in the FII Group Litigation v Inland Revenue Commissioners (C-362/12)

Test Claimants in the Franked Investment Income Group Litigation v Revenue and Customs Commissioners see Test Claimants in the FII Group Litigation v Revenue and Customs Commissioners

Tetra Pak Ltd v Biddle & Co see Biddle & Co v Tetra Pak Ltd

Texan Management Ltd v Pacific Electric Wire and Cable Co Ltd [2009] UKPC 46, PC (BVI) *Considered* 14/558

Texdata Software GmbH (C-418/11) [2014] 1 C.M.L.R. 52, ECJ (4th Chamber)

Texuna International Ltd v Cairn Energy Plc [2004] EWHC 1102 (Comm); [2005] 1 B.C.L.C. 579, QBD (Comm) *Disapproved* 14/433

TF v PJ (Reversal of Judgment) see F (A Child) (Return Order: Power to Revoke), Re

TFL Management Ltd v Lloyds TSB Bank Plc; *joined case* TFL Management Services Ltd v Lloyds Bank Plc (formerly Lloyds TSB Bank Plc) [2013] EWCA Civ 1415; [2014] 1 W.L.R. 2006; [2013] 2 C.L.C. 810, CA (Civ Div); reversing [2013] EWHC 772 (Ch), Ch D ........ *Digested,* 14/**2529**

TFL Management Services Ltd v Lloyds Bank Plc (formerly Lloyds TSB Bank Plc) see TFL Management Ltd v Lloyds TSB Bank Plc

TG (A Child) (Care Proceedings: Biomechanical Engineering Evidence), Re; *sub nom* TG (Children) (Care Proceedings: Case Management: Expert Evidence), Re [2013] EWCA Civ 5; [2013] 1 F.L.R. 1250; [2013] 1 F.C.R. 229; (2013) 130 B.M.L.R. 169; [2013] Fam. Law 264, CA (Civ Div) ........ *Digested,* 13/**1224**: *Applied* 14/1322

TG (Children) (Care Proceedings: Case Management: Expert Evidence), Re see TG (A Child) (Care Proceedings: Biomechanical Engineering Evidence), Re

TGA Chapman Ltd v Christopher [1998] 1 W.L.R. 12; [1998] 2 All E.R. 873; [1997] C.L.C. 1306; [1998] Lloyd's Rep. I.R. 1; Times, July 21, 1997, CA (Civ Div) ...... *Digested,* 97/**3111**: *Applied* 99/3422, 08/326, 14/1835: *Considered* 00/413, 01/474, 11/302: *Followed* 99/388

TGH (Construction) Ltd v Revenue and Customs Commissioners [2014] UKFTT 1039 (TC); [2014] S.T.I. 3554, FTT (Tax)

TH Goldschmidt AG v EOC Belgium NV (Validity of Patents) CH 1997 T. No. 6275, CH 1998 T. No. 360, Ch D (Patents Ct) *Considered* 14/1879

Thames Water Utilities Ltd v Bromley Magistrates' Court see R. (on the application of Thames Water Utilities Ltd) v Bromley Magistrates' Court

Thameside Construction Co Ltd v Stevens [2013] EWHC 2071 (TCC); [2013] B.L.R. 543; 149 Con. L.R. 195; [2013] C.I.L.L. 3392; [2013] Bus. L.R. D59, QBD (TCC) ........ *Digested,* 14/**576**

Thamesmead Town Ltd v Allotey (1998) 30 H.L.R. 1052; (2000) 79 P. & C.R. 557; [1998] 3 E.G.L.R. 97; [1998] 37 E.G. 161; (1998) 95(3) L.S.G. 26; (1998) 76 P. & C.R. D20, CA (Civ Div) ........ *Digested,* 98/**4345**: *Applied* 14/2510

Themeline Ltd v Vowden Investments [2011] UKUT 168 (LC), UT (Lands)
*Considered* 14/1985

Themis Holdings Pty Ltd v Canehire Pty Ltd [2014] QSC 38; 17 I.T.E.L.R. 75, Sup Ct (Qld)

Thevarajah v Riordan [2014] EWCA Civ 14; [2014] C.P. Rep. 19; [2014] 1 Costs L.R. 163, CA (Civ Div); reversing [2013] EWHC 3179 (Ch), Ch D ............................ *Digested,* 14/**457**

Thinc Group Ltd v Kingdom [2013] EWCA Civ 1306; [2014] C.P. Rep. 8, CA (Civ Div) . *Digested,* 14/**349**

Thlimmenos v Greece (34369/97) (2001) 31 E.H.R.R. 15; 9 B.H.R.C. 12, ECHR (Grand Chamber) ............................ *Digested,* 01/**3485**:
*Applied* 08/2529: *Considered* 04/3579, 04/4349, 10/1781, 14/2757

Thomas v Edmondson; *sub nom* Edmondson, Re [2014] EWHC 1494 (Ch); [2014] 3 All E.R. 976; [2014] B.P.I.R. 1070, Ch D ............................ *Digested,* 14/**1770**

Thomas v Merthyr Tydfil Car Auction Ltd; *joined case* Merthyr Tydfil Car Auction Ltd v Thomas [2013] EWCA Civ 815; 149 Con. L.R. 105; [2014] Env. L.R. 4; [2014] L.L.R. 550, CA (Civ Div); affirming [2012] EWHC 2654 (QB); [2013] Env. L.R. 12, QBD ............................ *Digested,* 14/**2222**

Thomas v Pearce [2000] F.S.R. 718, CA (Civ Div) ............................ *Digested,* 00/**3566**:
*Distinguished* 14/247

Thomas v Thomas [1995] 2 F.L.R. 668; [1996] 2 F.C.R. 544; [1995] Fam. Law 672; Independent, May 4, 1995, CA (Civ Div) ............................ *Digested,* 95/**2357**:
*Applied* 02/1676, 02/1680, 08/1433, 09/1494, 11/1307, 12/1439, 14/1373:
*Considered* 04/1518, 06/1631, 12/1431: *Referred to* 11/1315

Thomas v Thomas [1947] A.C. 484; [1947] 1 All E.R. 582; 1947 S.C. (H.L.) 45; 1948 S.L.T. 2; 1947 S.L.T. (Notes) 53; 63 T.L.R. 314; [1948] L.J.R. 515; 176 L.T. 498, HL; reversing 1946 S.C. 81; 1946 S.L.T. 63, IH (2 Div) ............................ *Digested,* 47-51/**7496**:
*Applied* 47-51/10957, 47-51/2723, 47-51/9902, 52/987, 55/2078, 59/431, 70/3157, 76/338, 98/5439, 98/6102, 01/6217, 03/3539, 13/3902, 13/3956:
*Considered* 74/1069, 91/5082, 94/3280, 94/3439, 03/5285, 05/10:
*Distinguished* 90/4099: *Followed* 86/4416, 88/4930, 08/5003, 13/6, 14/1579: *Not applied* 51/3869

Thomas & Agnes Carvel Foundation v Carvel [2007] EWHC 1314 (Ch); [2008] Ch. 395; [2008] 2 W.L.R. 1234; [2007] 4 All E.R. 81; [2007] W.T.L.R. 1297; (2007-08) 10 I.T.E.L.R. 455, Ch D ............................ *Digested,* 07/**3956**:
*Applied* 10/3205, 14/3276

Thomas & Davies (Merthyr Tydfil) Ltd v Denly (Valuation Officer) [2014] UKUT 146 (LC); [2014] R.A. 515, UT (Lands)

Thomas Estates Ltd (t/a Beacon Bingo) v Revenue and Customs Commissioners [2013] UKFTT 662 (TC); [2014] S.F.T.D. 651; [2014] L.L.R. 392, FTT (Tax) ...... *Digested,* 14/**2847**

Thomas Newall Ltd v Lancaster City Council; *sub nom* Lancaster City Council v Thomas Newell Ltd [2013] EWCA Civ 802; [2013] R.V.R. 309; [2013] J.P.L. 1531, CA (Civ Div); reversing in part [2011] UKUT 437 (LC); [2012] R.V.R. 65; [2013] R.V.R. 304, UT (Lands) ............................ *Digested,* 14/**2359**

Thomas Pink Ltd v Victoria's Secret UK Ltd [2014] EWHC 2631 (Ch); [2014] E.T.M.R. 57; [2014] F.S.R. 40; [2014] Bus. L.R. D23, Ch D ............................ *Digested,* 14/**1919**

Thomas Wilson Sons & Co v Owners of Cargo of the Xantho (The Xantho) (1887) 12 App.Cas. 503, HL; reversing (1886) 11 P.D. 170, CA
*Considered* 90/4065: *Followed* 14/1851

Thompson v Bee [2009] EWCA Civ 1212; [2010] Ch. 412; [2010] 2 W.L.R. 1355; [2010] W.T.L.R. 357; (2009) 153(45) S.J.L.B. 30; [2009] N.P.C. 134; Times, December 4, 2009, CA (Civ Div) ............................ *Digested,* 10/**2743**:
*Followed* 14/2521

Thompson v Hurst; *sub nom* Thompson v Hurst [2012] EWCA Civ 1752; [2014] 1 F.L.R. 238; [2013] 1 F.C.R. 522; [2013] Fam. Law 396, CA (Civ Div) ................ *Digested,* 13/**2422**

Thompson v Hurst see Thompson v Hurst

Thompson v James [2014] EWCA Civ 600; [2014] B.L.G.R. 664, CA (Civ Div); affirming [2013] EWHC 515 (QB), QBD ............................ *Digested,* 14/**836**:
*Applied* 14/2995

Thompson v Renwick Group Plc [2014] EWCA Civ 635; [2014] 2 B.C.L.C. 97; [2014] P.I.Q.R. P18, CA (Civ Div) ............................ *Digested,* 14/**2202**

Thompson v Revenue and Customs Commissioners [2014] UKFTT 826 (TC); [2014] S.T.I. 3085, FTT (Tax)

Thomson v Alloa Motor Co [1983] I.R.L.R. 403, EAT ............................ *Digested,* 83/**1315**:
*Followed* 14/3505

Thomson v Revenue and Customs Commissioners; *joined case* Revenue and Customs Commissioners v Thomson [2014] UKUT 360 (TCC); [2014] B.T.C. 524, UT (Tax) ............................ *Digested,* 14/**2849**

Thomson v Revenue and Customs Commissioners [2013] UKFTT 468 (TC); [2013] S.T.I. 3576, FTT (Tax)
*Affirmed* 14/2849

Thomson (Inspector of Taxes) v Gurneville Securities Ltd; *joined case* Gurneville Securities Ltd v Thomson (Inspector of Taxes) [1972] A.C. 661; [1971] 3 W.L.R. 692; [1971] 3 All E.R. 1071; 47 T.C. 633; [1971] T.R. 299; (1971) 115 S.J. 851, HL; reversing [1970] 1 W.L.R. 477; Times, December 19, 1969, CA (Civ Div); reversing [1969] 2 All E.R. 1195; (1969) 48 A.T.C. 130; [1969] T.R. 139, Ch D ........ *Digested,* 71/**1920**:
*Applied* 14/2981

Thomson Ecology Ltd v Apem Ltd [2013] EWHC 2875 (Ch); [2014] I.R.L.R. 184, Ch D *Digested,* 14/**1025**

Thorn EMI Electronics Ltd v Coldicott (Inspector of Taxes) see EMI Group Electronics Ltd v Coldicott (Inspector of Taxes)

Thorne v House of Commons Commission [2014] EWHC 93 (QB); [2014] I.R.L.R. 260, QBD ........ *Digested,* 14/**1098**

Thorne v Revenue and Customs Commissioners [2014] UKFTT 730 (TC); [2014] S.T.I. 3025, FTT (Tax)

Thornhill (Trustee in Bankruptcy) v Atherton [2004] EWCA Civ 1858; [2005] B.P.I.R. 437, CA (Civ Div) ........ *Digested,* 05/**2270**:
*Applied* 13/1714: *Considered* 14/1780: *Followed* 11/1852

Thorold v Martell Press Ltd EAT/0343/01, EAT
*Applied* 14/1089

Three Rivers DC v Bank of England (Disclosure) (No.4) [2004] UKHL 48; [2005] 1 A.C. 610; [2004] 3 W.L.R. 1274; [2005] 4 All E.R. 948; (2004) 101(46) L.S.G. 34; (2004) 154 N.L.J. 1727; (2004) 148 S.J.L.B. 1369; Times, November 12, 2004; Independent, November 16, 2004, HL; reversing [2004] EWCA Civ 218; [2004] Q.B. 916; [2004] 2 W.L.R. 1065; [2004] 3 All E.R. 168; (2004) 101(11) L.S.G. 36; (2004) 154 N.L.J. 382; (2004) 148 S.J.L.B. 297; Times, March 3, 2004; Independent, March 10, 2004, CA (Civ Div); affirming [2003] EWHC 2565 (Comm), QBD (Comm) ........ *Digested,* 05/**299**:
*Applied* 07/470, 08/3863, 14/2934: *Considered* 04/257, 07/999, 09/4206:
*Followed* 12/548

Threlfall v ECD Insight Ltd (Costs) [2013] EWCA Civ 1444; [2014] 2 Costs L.O. 129; (2013) 163(7586) N.L.J. 18, CA (Civ Div) ........ *Digested,* 14/**337**

Through Transport Mutual Insurance Association (Eurasia) Ltd v New India Assurance Co Ltd (The Hari Bhum) (No.1) [2004] EWCA Civ 1598; [2005] 1 All E.R. (Comm) 715; [2005] 1 Lloyd's Rep. 67; [2004] 2 C.L.C. 1189; [2005] I.L.Pr. 30; (2004) 148 S.J.L.B. 1435, CA (Civ Div); reversing in part [2003] EWHC 3158 (Comm); [2004] 1 Lloyd's Rep. 206; [2004] 1 C.L.C. 794, QBD (Comm) ........ *Digested,* 05/**599**:
*Applied* 05/2357, 08/278, 09/602: *Considered* 09/611, 14/129:
*Distinguished* 12/312

Thurrock BC v West [2012] EWCA Civ 1435; [2013] H.L.R. 5; [2013] 1 P. & C.R. 12; [2013] L. & T.R. 11; [2013] 1 P. & C.R. DG9, CA (Civ Div) ........ *Digested,* 13/**1890**:
*Applied* 14/2000

Thursfield v Thursfield [2013] EWCA Civ 840; [2013] C.P. Rep. 44; [2014] 1 F.L.R. 389; [2013] 3 F.C.R. 469; [2013] Fam. Law 1251, CA (Civ Div) ........ *Digested,* 14/**12**

Tibbles v SIG Plc (t/a Asphaltic Roofing Supplies) [2012] EWCA Civ 518; [2012] 1 W.L.R. 2591; [2012] 4 All E.R. 259; [2012] C.P. Rep. 32; [2013] 1 Costs L.O. 41, CA (Civ Div) ........ *Digested,* 12/**443**:
*Followed* 13/451, 14/457

Tidal Energy Ltd v Bank of Scotland Plc [2014] EWCA Civ 1107; [2014] Bus. L.R. 1167; [2014] 2 Lloyd's Rep. 549; Times, August 28, 2014, CA (Civ Div); affirming [2013] EWHC 2780 (QB); [2013] Bus. L.R. 1379; [2013] 2 Lloyd's Rep. 605; [2013] 2 C.L.C. 407, QBD (Merc) (Bristol) ........ *Digested,* 14/**244**

Tiensia v Vision Enterprises Ltd (t/a Universal Estates); *sub nom* Vision Enterprises Ltd (t/a Universal Estates) v Tiensia; *joined case* Honeysuckle Properties v Fletcher [2010] EWCA Civ 1224; [2012] 1 W.L.R. 94; [2011] 1 All E.R. 1059; [2011] H.L.R. 10; [2011] L. & T.R. 10; [2010] 3 E.G.L.R. 53; [2010] 49 E.G. 80; [2010] 46 E.G. 117 (C.S.); (2010) 160 N.L.J. 1614; [2010] N.P.C. 112; [2011] 1 P. & C.R. DG14, CA (Civ Div) ........ *Digested,* 11/**2076**:
*Considered* 11/2074: *Followed* 11/2075, 12/2067: *Superseded* 14/2016

Tigana Ltd v Decoro Ltd [2003] EWHC 23 (QB); [2003] E.C.C. 23; [2003] Eu. L.R. 189, QBD ........ *Digested,* 03/**79**:
*Applied* 06/59, 14/82: *Approved* 04/89: *Considered* 06/58, 06/61, 07/68

Tigray v Chubb see Mengiste v Endowment Fund for the Rehabilitation of Tigray

Timbrell v Secretary of State for Work and Pensions [2010] EWCA Civ 701; [2010] 3 C.M.L.R. 42; [2010] Eu. L.R. 739; [2010] I.C.R. 1369; [2011] 1 F.L.R. 332; [2010] Pens. L.R. 245; [2010] Fam. Law 921; (2010) 107(27) L.S.G. 15, CA (Civ Div) ........ *Digested,* 10/**2383**:
*Applied* 11/3155: *Considered* 14/2294

Times Newspapers Ltd v McNamara [2013] B.P.I.R. 1092, Ch D (Bankruptcy Ct) ........ *Digested,* 14/**1791**

Timmel v Aviso Zeta AG (C-359/12) [2014] Bus. L.R. 922, ECJ (2nd Chamber)

Tindale v Revenue and Customs Commissioners [2014] UKUT 324 (TCC); [2014] B.T.C. 522, UT (Tax); affirming [2013] UKFTT 346 (TC), FTT (Tax) ........ *Digested,* 14/**2914**

Tindall Cobham 1 Ltd v Adda Hotels [2014] EWCA Civ 1215; [2014] 3 E.G.L.R. 36, CA (Civ Div); affirming in part [2014] EWHC 2637 (Ch), Ch D

Tinsley v Milligan [1994] 1 A.C. 340; [1993] 3 W.L.R. 126; [1993] 3 All E.R. 65; [1993] 2 F.L.R. 963; (1994) 68 P. & C.R. 412; [1993] E.G. 118 (C.S.); [1993] N.P.C. 97; Times, June 28, 1993; Independent, July 6, 1993, HL; affirming [1992] Ch. 310; [1992] 2 W.L.R. 508; [1992] 2 All E.R. 391; (1992) 63 P. & C.R. 152; (1991) 88(33) L.S.G. 32; (1991) 135 S.J.L.B. 108; [1991] N.P.C. 100; Times, August 22, 1991, CA (Civ Div) ........ *Digested,* 93/**1839**:
*Applied* 97/4730, 99/4368, 99/680, 02/3835, 03/4504, 04/3264, 08/2648, 09/1363, 09/2150, 10/2000, 13/216: *Considered* 95/3660, 96/1489, 96/5554, 00/3879, 06/4377, 08/3058, 08/3943, 14/2994: *Distinguished* 93/1840, 03/1421: *Followed* 96/5000, 01/5349, 07/3358, 11/2684, 13/590: *Not applied* 08/2649: *Referred to* 94/5488

TIP-Europe, Re (1987) 3 B.C.C. 647; [1988] B.C.L.C. 231; [1988] P.C.C. 28, Ch D (Companies Ct) ........ *Digested,* 88/**346**:
*Considered* 14/502

Tiverton Estates Ltd v Wearwell Ltd [1975] Ch. 146; [1974] 2 W.L.R. 176; [1974] 1 All E.R. 209; (1974) 27 P. & C.R. 24; (1978) 117 S.J. 913, CA (Civ Div) ........ *Digested,* 74/**3952**:
*Applied* 85/389, 07/3955, 14/2512: *Considered* 75/1842, 75/3540, 78/2501, 79/2780, 83/3052, 83/3894, 87/2111, 88/2065, 90/3701: *Explained* 77/2374

Tivg Ltd, Re see Harris v Secretary of State for Business, Innovation and Skills

TJ Charters LLP v Revenue and Customs Commissioners [2014] UKFTT 896 (TC); [2014] S.T.I. 2954, FTT (Tax)

TL v Coventry City Council see A (A Child) (Adoption), Re

TL v ML (Ancillary Relief: Claim against Assets of Extended Family) [2005] EWHC 2860 (Fam); [2006] 1 F.L.R. 1263; [2006] 1 F.C.R. 465; [2006] Fam. Law 183, Fam Div ........ *Digested,* 06/**1631**:
*Applied* 08/1425, 11/1314, 12/1314, 14/1362: *Approved* 07/1707: *Considered* 07/1704, 09/360, 10/1408, 11/1412, 12/1319

TLLC Ltd v Revenue and Customs Commissioners [2013] UKFTT 467 (TC); [2014] S.F.T.D. 438; [2013] S.T.I. 3282, FTT (Tax) ........ *Digested,* 14/**3056**

TM (Medical Treatment), Re [2013] EWHC 4103 (Fam); (2014) 136 B.M.L.R. 153; [2014] Fam. Law 296, Fam Div ........ *Digested,* 14/**1305**

TN (Afghanistan) v Secretary of State for the Home Department; *joined case* MA (Afghanistan) v Secretary of State for the Home Department [2013] EWCA Civ 1609; [2014] 1 W.L.R. 2095; [2014] 2 C.M.L.R. 31; [2014] I.N.L.R. 542, CA (Civ Div); affirming [2011] EWHC 3296 (Admin), QBD (Admin) ........ *Digested,* 14/**1657**

Toal v GB Oils Ltd [2013] I.R.L.R. 696, EAT ........ *Digested,* 13/**1017**:
*Applied* 14/1053

Tociapski v Tociapski; *sub nom* Tociapski (Deceased), Re [2013] EWHC 1770 (Ch); [2013] W.T.L.R. 1821, Ch D ........ *Digested,* 14/**2836**

Tociapski (Deceased), Re see Tociapski v Tociapski

Tod-Heatly v Benham (1888) 40 Ch. D. 80, CA
*Applied* 53/3099: *Considered* 13/2455: *Distinguished* 14/2514: *Followed* 68/3139

Toftgaard v Indenrigs- og Sundhedsministeriet (C-546/11) see Dansk Jurist- og Okonomforbund v Indenrigs- og Sundhedsministeriet (C-546/11)

Tokio Marine Europe Insurance Ltd v Novae Corporate Underwriting Ltd [2014] EWHC 2105 (Comm); [2014] Lloyd's Rep. I.R. 638, QBD (Comm)

Tokio Marine Europe Insurance Ltd v Novae Corporate Underwriting Ltd [2013] EWHC 3362 (Comm); [2013] 2 C.L.C. 769; [2014] Lloyd's Rep. I.R. 490, QBD (Comm) ........ *Digested,* 14/**1844**

Tolsma v Inspecteur der Omzetbelasting, Leeuwarden (C-16/93) [1994] S.T.C. 509; [1994] E.C.R. I-743; [1994] 2 C.M.L.R. 908; [1994] B.V.C. 117; [1994] S.T.I. 424; Times, March 29, 1994, ECJ (6th Chamber) ........ *Digested,* 94/**4962**:
*Applied* 00/5347, 06/4469, 06/4488, 07/4284, 11/3568, 14/3085: *Considered* 98/4891, 02/4790, 08/4029

Tom Tom Sales BV (UK Branch) v Revenue and Customs Commissioners [2014] UKFTT 141 (TC); [2014] S.T.I. 950, FTT (Tax)

Tomlinson v Birmingham City Council see Ali v Birmingham City Council

Tomlinson v Congleton BC [2003] UKHL 47; [2004] 1 A.C. 46; [2003] 3 W.L.R. 705; [2003] 3 All E.R. 1122; [2004] P.I.Q.R. P8; [2003] 32 E.G. 68 (C.S.); (2003) 100(34) L.S.G. 33; (2003) 153 N.L.J. 1238; (2003) 147 S.J.L.B. 937; [2003] N.P.C. 102; Times, August 1, 2003; Independent, October 7, 2003, HL; reversing [2002] EWCA Civ 309; [2003] 2 W.L.R. 1120; [2002] P.I.Q.R. P30; [2002] 12 E.G. 136 (C.S.); (2002) 99(18) L.S.G. 38; (2002) 146 S.J.L.B. 92; [2002] N.P.C. 42; Times, March 22, 2002; Independent, March 21, 2002, CA (Civ Div) ........ *Digested,* 03/**4360**:
*Applied* 03/2980, 05/1955, 06/4334, 06/4338, 08/2761, 13/2084: *Considered* 03/4361, 05/4194, 05/4196, 06/4333: *Followed* 11/3474, 14/2208

Toni & Guys (St Paul's) Ltd v Georgiou [2013] I.C.R. 1356, EAT ........ *Digested,* 14/**1132**

Topcic-Rosenberg v Croatia (19391/11) (2014) 58 E.H.R.R. 39, ECHR

Topland Portfolio No.1 Ltd v Smiths News Trading Ltd [2014] EWCA Civ 18; [2014] 1 P. & C.R. 17; [2014] L. & T.R. 22; [2014] 1 E.G.L.R. 38, CA (Civ Div); affirming [2013] EWHC 1445 (Ch); [2014] 1 P. & C.R. 2; [2013] L. & T.R. 34; [2013] 2 E.G.L.R. 86; [2013] 25 E.G. 109 (C.S.), Ch D ........ *Digested,* 14/**1980**

Torbay BC v News Group Newspapers see Roddy (A Child) (Identification: Restriction on Publication), Re

Torralbo Marcos v Korota SA (C-265/13) [2014] 3 C.M.L.R. 27, ECJ (2nd Chamber)

Toshiba Corp v European Commission (C-498/11 P) see Siemens AG v European Commission (C-239/11 P)

Toshiba Corp v European Commission (T-519/09) [2014] 5 C.M.L.R. 8, GC (3rd Chamber)

Toshoku Finance UK Plc (In Liquidation), Re; *sub nom* Inland Revenue Commissioners v Kahn; Kahn v Inland Revenue Commissioners; Khan v Inland Revenue Commissioners [2002] UKHL 6; [2002] 1 W.L.R. 671; [2002] 3 All E.R. 961; [2002] S.T.C. 368; [2002] B.C.C. 110; [2002] 1 B.C.L.C. 598; [2002] B.P.I.R. 790; [2003] R.V.R. 106; [2002] B.T.C. 69; [2002] S.T.I. 237; (2002) 99(12) L.S.G. 33; (2002) 146 S.J.L.B. 55; Times, February 25, 2002, HL; affirming [2000] 1 W.L.R. 2478; [2000] 3 All E.R. 938; [2000] S.T.C. 301; [2001] B.C.C. 373; [2000] 1 B.C.L.C. 683; [2000] B.T.C. 96; [2000] S.T.I. 503; (2000) 97(15) L.S.G. 39; (2000) 144 S.J.L.B. 165; Times, March 29, 2000, CA (Civ Div); reversing [1999] S.T.C. 922; [1999] 2 B.C.L.C. 777; [1999] B.T.C. 367, Ch D ........ *Digested,* 02/**2718**:
*Applied* 07/2393, 12/1794, 13/287: *Considered* 10/1835, 11/1818, 11/4392, 13/1662, 13/2138: *Distinguished* 05/2260: *Followed* 10/1837, 11/1820, 12/1791, 14/1756

Total Fulfilment Logistics Ltd v May (Valuation Officer); *sub nom* Fulfilment Logistics Ltd v May (Valuation Officer) [2014] UKUT 354 (LC); [2014] R.V.R. 300; [2014] J.P.L. 1395, UT (Lands)

Totel Distribution Ltd v Revenue and Customs Commissioners [2014] UKUT 307 (TCC); [2014] B.V.C. 525; [2014] S.T.I. 2411, UT (Tax); affirming [2011] UKFTT 217 (TC), FTT (Tax) ........ *Digested,* 14/**3071**

ToTel Ltd v Revenue and Customs Commissioners [2014] UKUT 485 (TCC); [2014] B.V.C. 542, UT (Tax)

Toth v Nemzeti Ado-es Vamhivatal Eszak-magyarorszagi Regionalis Ado Foigazgatosaga (C-324/11) [2013] S.T.C. 185; [2012] S.T.I. 2833, ECJ (3rd Chamber)
*Applied* 14/3070: *Considered* 14/3069

Touch Solar Ltd v Department of Energy and Climate Change see Breyer Group Plc v Department of Energy and Climate Change

Touch Worldwide Oy v Revenue and Customs Commissioners [2014] UKFTT 868 (TC); [2014] S.T.I. 2910, FTT (Tax)

Tower Hamlets LBC v Ali [2014] EWHC 845 (Fam); [2014] Fam. Law 1097, Fam Div

Tower Hamlets LBC v Begum (Nipa) see Begum (Nipa) v Tower Hamlets LBC

Tower Hamlets LBC v Begum (Runa) see Begum v Tower Hamlets LBC

Tower Hamlets LBC v Deugi; *sub nom* Deugi v Tower Hamlets LBC [2006] EWCA Civ 159; [2006] H.L.R. 28, CA (Civ Div) ........ *Digested,* 06/**2026**:
*Applied* 06/2028: *Followed* 14/1598

Tower Hamlets LBC v St Katherine by the Tower 80 L.G.R. 843; 264 E.G. 529, Unknown court ........ *Digested,* 83/**3136**:
*Applied* 14/2480: *Considered* 90/3917

Tower MCashback LLP 1 v Revenue and Customs Commissioners; *sub nom* Revenue and Customs Commissioners v Tower MCashback LLP 1 [2011] UKSC 19; [2011] 2 A.C. 457; [2011] 2 W.L.R. 1131; [2011] 3 All E.R. 171; [2011] S.T.C. 1143; 80 T.C. 641; [2011] B.T.C. 294; [2011] S.T.I. 1620; (2011) 108(21) L.S.G. 19; Times, May 16, 2011, SC; reversing in part [2010] EWCA Civ 32; [2010] S.T.C. 809; [2010] B.T.C. 154; [2010] S.T.I. 435, CA (Civ Div); reversing in part [2008] EWHC 2387 (Ch); [2008] S.T.C. 3366; [2008] B.T.C. 805; [2008] S.T.I. 2249, Ch D; reversing [2008] S.T.C. (S.C.D.) 1, Sp Comm .... *Digested,* 11/**3277**: *Applied* 12/3255, 13/3086, 14/2905, 14/2926: *Considered* 09/3917, 10/3368, 11/3285, 11/3308, 11/3411, 14/2975: *Distinguished* 09/3781, 09/3885

Tower Radio Ltd v Revenue and Customs Commissioners [2013] UKFTT 387 (TC); [2014] S.F.T.D. 377; [2013] S.T.I. 3135; [2013] S.T.I. 3243, FTT (Tax) ............. *Digested,* 14/**2921**

Tozlukaya v Secretary of State for the Home Department see R. (on the application of Tozlukaya) v Secretary of State for the Home Department

TP v United Kingdom (28945/95) [2001] 2 F.L.R. 549; [2001] 2 F.C.R. 289; (2002) 34 E.H.R.R. 2; (2001) 3 L.G.L.R. 52; (2001) 4 C.C.L. Rep. 398; [2001] Fam. Law 590; Times, May 31, 2001, ECHR; no effect (2000) 2 L.G.L.R. 181, Eur Comm HR ............ *Digested,* 01/**2571**: *Applied* 03/3004, 08/1947: *Considered* 03/1522, 03/2198, 07/2934, 14/2181

TR Technology Investment Trust, Re (1988) 4 B.C.C. 244; [1988] B.C.L.C. 256; [1988] P.C.C. 462; [1988] 1 F.T.L.R. 483, Ch D (Companies Ct) ........................ *Digested,* 88/**350**: *Considered* 14/520

Tracey v United Kingdom see Brogan v United Kingdom (A/145-B)

Trade Marks with VOLKS- Prefix, Re (I ZR 214/11) [2014] E.T.M.R. 47, BGH (Ger)

Traders' North Staffordshire Carrying Co, Re; *sub nom* North Staffordshire Railway Co, Ex p. (1874-75) L.R. 19 Eq. 60, Ct of Chancery *Doubted* 14/1756

Tradigrain SA v King Diamond Marine Ltd (The Spiros C); *sub nom* Tradigrain SA v King Diamond Shipping SA (The Spiros C) [2000] 2 All E.R. (Comm) 542; [2000] 2 Lloyd's Rep. 319; [2000] C.L.C. 1503; Independent, October 9, 2000, CA (Civ Div); reversing [1999] 1 All E.R. 837; [1999] 2 Lloyd's Rep. 91; [1999] C.L.C. 1136, QBD (Comm) ............ *Digested,* 00/**4699**: *Applied* 09/709, 14/2705: *Considered* 13/2835: *Followed* 14/116

Tradigrain SA v King Diamond Shipping SA (The Spiros C) see Tradigrain SA v King Diamond Marine Ltd (The Spiros C)

Trafford Housing Trust Ltd v Rubinstein [2013] UKUT 581 (LC); [2014] 1 E.G.L.R. 34, UT (Lands)

Trafigura Beheer BV v Navigazione Montanari SpA [2014] EWHC 129 (Comm); [2014] 1 Lloyd's Rep. 550; [2014] 1 C.L.C. 70, QBD (Comm) ............ *Digested,* 14/**2714**

Trailfinders v Razuki [1988] 30 E.G. 59, Unknown court ............ *Digested,* 88/**2040**: *Approved* 14/2509: *Considered* 07/3400

Train v Secretary of State for Defence [2014] EWHC 1928 (QB); [2014] R.T.R. 28, QBD ............ *Digested,* 14/**2332**

Transco Plc v Stockport MBC; *sub nom* British Gas Plc v Stockport MBC; Stockport MBC v British Gas Plc; *joined case* Stockport MBC v Reddish Vale Golf Club [2003] UKHL 61; [2004] 2 A.C. 1; [2003] 3 W.L.R. 1467; [2004] 1 All E.R. 589; 91 Con. L.R. 28; [2004] Env. L.R. 24; [2003] 48 E.G. 127 (C.S.); (2003) 153 N.L.J. 1791; (2003) 147 S.J.L.B. 1367; [2003] N.P.C. 143; [2004] 1 P. & C.R. DG12; Times, November 20, 2003; Independent, November 25, 2003, HL; affirming [2001] EWCA Civ 212; [2001] Env. L.R. 44; (2001) 3 L.G.L.R. 33; [2001] 9 E.G. 228 (C.S.); (2001) 98(9) L.S.G. 42; [2001] Env. L.R. D11; Daily Telegraph, March 6, 2001, CA (Civ Div) ............ *Digested,* 04/**3848**: *Applied* 11/2275: *Considered* 13/3143: *Distinguished* 06/4340, 08/2668: *Followed* 14/2219

Transition Feeds LLP (formerly known as Advanced Liquid Feeds LLP) v Itochu Europe Plc; *sub nom* Advanced Liquid Feeds LLP v Itochu Europe Plc [2013] EWHC 3629 (Comm); [2013] 2 C.L.C. 920, QBD (Comm) ............ *Digested,* 14/**135**

Transpetrol Maritime Services Ltd v SJB (Marine Energy) BV [2012] EWCA Civ 198; [2012] 1 Lloyd's Rep. 564; [2012] 1 C.L.C. 415, CA (Civ Div); reversing [2011] EWHC 3374 (Comm); [2011] 2 Lloyd's Rep. 331, QBD (Comm) ............ *Digested,* 12/**3077**: *Considered* 14/1850

Transposition of Directive 85/337, Re (C-427/07) see Commission of the European Communities v Ireland (C-427/07)

Tranter (t/a Dynamic Yoga) v Revenue and Customs Commissioners [2014] UKFTT 959 (TC); [2014] S.T.I. 3180, FTT (Tax)

Traum EOOD v Direktor na Direktsia 'Obzhalvane i danachno-osiguritelna praktika' Varna pri Tsentralno upravlenie na Natsionalnata agentsia za prihodite (C-492/13) [2014] B.V.C. 46; [2014] S.T.I. 3081, ECJ (5th Chamber)

Travelers Insurance Co Ltd v Countrywide Surveyors Ltd [2010] EWHC 2455 (TCC); [2011] 1 All E.R. (Comm) 631; [2011] Lloyd's Rep. I.R. 213; [2010] C.I.L.L. 2947, QBD (TCC) ........ *Digested,* 11/**368**: *Applied* 14/437

Travis Coal Restructured Holdings LLC v Essar Global Fund Ltd [2014] EWHC 2510 (Comm); [2014] 2 Lloyd's Rep. 494; 155 Con. L.R. 61, QBD (Comm) ........ *Digested,* 14/**121**

Travis Perkins Trading Co Ltd v Caerphilly CBC [2014] EWHC 1498 (TCC); [2014] B.L.R. 465; 154 Con. L.R. 61, QBD (TCC) ........ *Digested,* 14/**418**

Treebhowan v Secretary of State for the Home Department see Hayat v Secretary of State for the Home Department

Treharne v Brabon see Brabon, Re

Trengove v Walsall MBC see Burnip v Birmingham City Council

Trento Sviluppo srl v Autorita Garante della Concorrenza e del Mercato (C-281/12) [2014] 1 W.L.R. 890; [2014] 1 All E.R. (Comm) 113; [2014] C.T.L.C. 326, ECJ (6th Chamber)

Trevivian v Revenue and Customs Commissioners [2014] UKFTT 1011 (TC); [2014] S.T.I. 3378, FTT (Tax)

Triangular Conflicts of Multiple Residence of Employees, Re (I R 19/13) 17 I.T.L. Rep. 421, BFH (Ger)

Tribe v Tribe [1996] Ch. 107; [1995] 3 W.L.R. 913; [1995] 4 All E.R. 236; [1995] C.L.C. 1474; [1995] 2 F.L.R. 966; [1996] 1 F.C.R. 338; (1996) 71 P. & C.R. 503; [1996] Fam. Law 29; (1995) 92(28) L.S.G. 30; (1995) 145 N.L.J. 1445; (1995) 139 S.J.L.B. 203; [1995] N.P.C. 151; (1995) 70 P. & C.R. D38; Times, August 14, 1995, CA (Civ Div) ........ *Digested,* 96/**5554**: *Applied* 03/4504, 08/3943, 14/264: *Considered* 08/165

Triffit Nurseries v Salads Etcetera Ltd [2000] 1 All E.R. (Comm) 737; [2000] 2 Lloyd's Rep. 74; [2001] B.C.C. 457; [2000] 1 B.C.L.C. 761; Times, April 26, 2000; Independent, May 12, 2000, CA (Civ Div); affirming [1999] 1 All E.R. (Comm.) 110; [1999] 1 Lloyd's Rep. 697; [2000] B.C.C. 98; [2000] 1 B.C.L.C. 262, Ch D . *Digested,* 00/**114**: *Followed* 14/78

Trimble Trust, Re 16 I.T.E.L.R. 222, US Court

Trinder Anderson & Co v North Queensland Insurance Co see Trinder Anderson & Co v Thames and Mersey Marine Insurance Co

Trinder Anderson & Co v Thames and Mersey Marine Insurance Co; *joined cases* Trinder Anderson & Co v Weston Crocker & Co; Trinder Anderson & Co v North Queensland Insurance Co [1898] 2 Q.B. 114, CA *Followed* 14/1851

Trinder Anderson & Co v Weston Crocker & Co see Trinder Anderson & Co v Thames and Mersey Marine Insurance Co

Trinity Mirror Plc v Revenue and Customs Commissioners [2014] UKFTT 355 (TC); [2014] S.T.I. 1922, FTT (Tax)

Trinity Mirror Plc, Re see R. (on the application of Trinity Mirror Plc) v Croydon Crown Court

Trollope & Colls Ltd (t/a Nuclear Civil Constructions) v Atomic Power Constructions Ltd [1963] 1 W.L.R. 333; [1962] 3 All E.R. 1035; (1963) 107 S.J. 254, QBD ....... *Digested,* 63/**552**: *Applied* 79/338, 93/294, 04/621, 14/592

Troutbeck SA v White see White v Troutbeck SA

Trowbridge v Trowbridge [2002] EWHC 3114 (Ch); [2003] 2 F.L.R. 231; [2004] 2 F.C.R. 79; [2003] B.P.I.R. 258; [2003] Fam. Law 476, Ch D ........ *Digested,* 03/**2421**: *Applied* 14/1372

Truslove v Scottish Ambulance Service [2014] I.C.R. 1232, EAT (SC)

Trust Inns Ltd v City of Glasgow Licensing Board [2015] CSIH 5, IH; affirming [2014] L.L.R. 861; 2014 G.W.D. 4-92, Sh Ct (Glasgow)

Trustees of Abdul Gaffoor Trust v Income Tax Commissioner, Colombo see Caffoor (Trustees of the Abdul Gaffoor Trust) v Income Tax Commissioner (Colombo)

Trustees of Olympic Airlines SA Pension and Life Assurance Scheme v Olympic Airlines SA see Olympic Airlines SA, Re

Trustees of the BT Pension Scheme v Revenue and Customs Commissioners [2014] EWCA Civ 23; [2014] S.T.C. 1156; [2014] B.T.C. 4; [2014] S.T.I. 472, CA (Civ Div); affirming [2013] UKUT 105 (TCC); [2013] S.T.C. 1781; [2013] 2 C.M.L.R. 38; [2013] B.T.C. 1656; [2013] S.T.I. 594, UT (Tax); affirming [2011] UKFTT 392 (TC); [2012] S.F.T.D. 107; [2011] S.T.I. 2406, FTT (Tax) ........ *Digested,* 14/**2977**

Trustees of the Duke of Westminster's Estate v United Kingdom (8793/79) see James v United Kingdom (A/98)

Trustees of the Lehman Brothers Pension Scheme v Pensions Regulator; *sub nom* LB RE Financing No.1 Ltd v Trustees of the Lehman Brothers Pension Scheme [2013] EWCA Civ 751; [2013] 4 All E.R. 744; [2013] Pens. L.R. 255, CA (Civ Div); affirming [2012] Pens. L.R. 435, UT (Tax) ........ *Digested,* 13/**2162**: *Considered* 14/2247, 14/3219

Trustees of the Stokes Pension Fund v Western Power Distribution (South West) Plc see Stokes Pension Fund Trustees v Western Power Distribution (South West) Plc

Trustees of the Travers Will Trust v Revenue and Customs Commissioners [2013] UKFTT 436 (TC); [2014] S.F.T.D. 265; [2013] W.T.L.R. 1831; [2013] S.T.I. 3402, FTT (Tax) ........ *Digested,* 14/**2982**

TSB Nuclear Energy Investment UK Ltd, Re [2014] EWHC 1272 (Ch); [2014] B.C.C. 531, Ch D

Tse Kwong Lam v Wong Chit Sen [1983] 1 W.L.R. 1349; [1983] 3 All E.R. 54; (1983) 80 L.S.G. 2368; (1983) 127 S.J. 632, PC (HK) ........ *Digested,* 83/**2484**: *Applied* 14/278: *Considered* 03/3584, 13/230: *Followed* 96/4988

TUBITAK-UZAY/Induction cooktop (T2411/09) [2014] E.P.O.R. 25, EPO (Technical Bd App)

Tucker v Atkins [2013] EWHC 4469 (Ch); [2014] B.P.I.R. 1359, Ch D ........ *Digested,* 14/**1795**

Tuckers Solicitors v Lord Chancellor [2013] EWHC 3817 (QB); [2014] 1 Costs L.R. 29, QBD ........ *Digested,* 14/**2046**

Tulane Education Fund v Comptroller General of Patents see Tulane Education Fund's Supplementary Protection Certificate, Re

Tulane Education Fund's Supplementary Protection Certificate, Re; *sub nom* Tulane Education Fund v Comptroller General of Patents [2013] EWCA Civ 890; [2013] Bus. L.R. 1225; [2014] R.P.C. 10, CA (Civ Div); affirming [2012] EWHC 932 (Pat); [2013] Bus. L.R. 53, Ch D ........ *Digested,* 14/**1911**

Tulip Diamonds FZE v Minister for Justice and Constitutional Development 35 B.H.R.C. 261, Const Ct (SA)

Tull Properties Ltd v South Gloucestershire Council [2014] R.A. 180, VT ........ *Digested,* 14/**2478**

Tullett & Tokyo Forex International Ltd v Secretary of State for Social Security; *joined cases* SGW Ltd v Secretary of State for Social Security; Barclays De Zoete Wedd Services Ltd v Secretary of State for Social Security Independent, July 10, 2000, QBD *Approved* 14/2950: *Disapproved* 12/3321: *Distinguished* 08/3828: *Followed* 11/3415

Tullett Prebon Plc v BGC Brokers LP; *joined case* BGC Brokers LP v Tullett Prebon Plc [2011] EWCA Civ 131; [2011] I.R.L.R. 420, CA (Civ Div); affirming [2010] EWHC 484 (QB); [2010] I.R.L.R. 648; (2010) 154(12) S.J.L.B. 37, QBD ........ *Digested,* 11/**1049**: *Considered* 11/1068, 14/1022, 14/1023

Tullow Tanzania BV v Commissioner General, TRA 16 I.T.L. Rep. 675, HC (Tan)

Tullow Uganda Ltd v Heritage Oil and Gas Ltd; *sub nom* Heritage Oil and Gas Ltd v Tullow Uganda Ltd [2014] EWCA Civ 1048, CA (Civ Div); affirming in part [2013] EWHC 1656 (Comm); [2014] 1 All E.R. (Comm) 22, QBD (Comm) ........ *Digested,* 14/**633**

Tunnel Tech Ltd v Reeves (Valuation Officer); *sub nom* Reeves (Valuation Officer) v Tunnel Tech Ltd [2014] UKUT 159 (LC); [2014] R.A. 293, UT (Lands); reversing [2013] R.A. 37, VT ........ *Digested,* 13/**2402**

Turcan, Re (1888) 40 Ch. D. 5, CA *Considered* 61/4038, 06/268, 14/591

Turek v Slovakia (57986/00) (2007) 44 E.H.R.R. 43, ECHR ........ *Digested,* 07/**2249**: *Applied* 14/2237

Turgut v Secretary of State for the Home Department see R. v Secretary of State for the Home Department Ex p. Turgut

Turkey v Awadh [2005] EWCA Civ 382; [2005] 2 F.C.R. 7; [2005] 2 P. & C.R. 29; [2006] W.T.L.R. 553, CA (Civ Div) ........ *Digested,* 05/**3402**: *Considered* 14/1207

Turner v Royal Bank of Scotland Plc (Relitigation) [2000] B.P.I.R. 683, CA (Civ Div) .... *Digested,* 00/**3434**: *Applied* 01/374, 03/2350, 05/2336, 10/1858, 14/1787: *Considered* 05/2279, 06/2333: *Distinguished* 03/2347: *Followed* 10/1857, 14/1788

Turner & Bell (Trading as Avroluxury Coaches) v Searles (Stanford-le-Hope) (1977) 33 P. & C.R. 208; (1977) 244 E.G. 1023, CA (Civ Div) ........ *Digested,* 77/**1709**: *Followed* 14/1976

Turullols v Revenue and Customs Commissioners [2014] UKFTT 672 (TC); [2014] S.F.T.D. 1099; [2014] S.T.I. 2933, FTT (Tax) ........ *Digested,* 14/**2908**

TVI - Televisao Independente SA v Fazenda Publica (C-618/11) [2014] B.V.C. 5; [2014] S.T.I. 251, ECJ (3rd Chamber)

TW v Enfield LBC [2014] EWCA Civ 362; [2014] 1 W.L.R. 3665; (2014) 17 C.C.L. Rep. 264; (2014) 138 B.M.L.R. 66; (2014) 164(7602) N.L.J. 20; (2014) 158(14) S.J.L.B. 37, CA (Civ Div); reversing [2013] EWHC 1180 (QB); (2013) 132 B.M.L.R. 227; [2013] M.H.L.R. 214, QBD ........ *Digested,* 14/**2178**

TW v PL (Agreement) see W v L

Tweddle v Southern Pacific Mortgages Ltd see North East Property Buyers Litigation, Re

Tweed v Parades Commission for Northern Ireland [2006] UKHL 53; [2007] 1 A.C. 650; [2007] 2 W.L.R. 1; [2007] 2 All E.R. 273; [2007] N.I. 66; [2007] H.R.L.R. 11; [2007] U.K.H.R.R. 456; 22 B.H.R.C. 92; (2007) 151 S.J.L.B. 24; Times, December 15, 2006, HL (NI) ........ *Digested,* 07/**4434**: *Applied* 14/483: *Considered* 08/355, 10/72: *Followed* 08/542, 12/1466, 14/295

Twentieth Century Fox Film Corp v British Telecommunications Plc [2011] EWHC 1981 (Ch); [2012] 1 All E.R. 806; [2012] Bus. L.R. 1461; [2011] R.P.C. 28; (2011) 155(31) S.J.L.B. 31, Ch D ........ *Digested,* 12/**1922**: *Applied* 13/1752, 14/1868

Twentieth Century Fox Film Corp v Harris [2013] EWHC 159 (Ch); [2014] Ch. 41; [2013] 2 W.L.R. 1454; [2013] E.M.L.R. 16; [2014] F.S.R. 7; Times, March 15, 2013, Ch D ........ *Digested,* 13/**1764**

Twinsectra Ltd v Yardley [2002] UKHL 12; [2002] 2 A.C. 164; [2002] 2 W.L.R. 802; [2002] 2 All E.R. 377; [2002] P.N.L.R. 30; [2002] W.T.L.R. 423; [2002] 38 E.G. 204 (C.S.); (2002) 99(19) L.S.G. 32; (2002) 152 N.L.J. 469; (2002) 146 S.J.L.B. 84; [2002] N.P.C. 47; Times, March 25, 2002, HL; reversing [1999] Lloyd's Rep. Bank. 438; [2000] Lloyd's Rep. P.N. 239; [2000] W.T.L.R. 527, CA (Civ Div) ..... *Digested,* 02/**249**: *Applied* 04/3940, 05/2731, 05/2732, 06/4381, 07/4251, 08/2169, 08/3944, 09/2586, 10/1876, 10/1930, 13/1952: *Considered* 04/2408, 05/2325, 06/4380, 07/4237, 10/3441, 11/3470, 13/1950: *Distinguished* 03/1421: *Followed* 99/278, 11/1896, 11/3495, 14/286, 14/3028

Twintec Ltd v Volkerfitzpatrick Ltd [2014] EWHC 10 (TCC); [2014] B.L.R. 150; [2014] C.I.L.L. 3476, QBD (TCC) ........ *Digested,* 14/**592**

Twyford v Puntschart [1947] 1 All E.R. 773; 63 T.L.R. 329; (1947) 111 J.P. 315; 177 L.T. 30; (1947) 91 S.J. 264, KBD ........ *Digested,* 47-51/**6180**: *Considered* 14/1486

Tyco Fire & Integrated Solutions (UK) Ltd (formerly Wormald Ansul (UK) Ltd) v Rolls Royce Motor Cars Ltd (formerly Hireus Ltd) [2008] EWCA Civ 286; [2008] 2 All E.R. (Comm) 584; [2008] 1 C.L.C. 625; [2008] B.L.R. 285; 118 Con. L.R. 25; [2008] Lloyd's Rep. I.R. 617; [2008] 2 E.G.L.R. 113; [2008] 14 E.G. 100 (C.S.); (2008) 105(15) L.S.G. 25; (2008) 152(14) S.J.L.B. 31, CA (Civ Div); reversing [2007] EWHC 3159 (TCC); [2007] B.L.R. 419; (2008) 24 Const. L.J. 60, QBD (TCC) ........ *Digested,* 08/**596**: *Considered* 14/1855

Tymoshenko v Ukraine (49872/11) (2014) 58 E.H.R.R. 3; 34 B.H.R.C. 671, ECHR

Tyne Valley Motorhomes v Revenue and Customs Commissioners [2014] UKFTT 969 (TC); [2014] S.T.I. 3218, FTT (Tax)

Tyrrell v Bank of London 11 E.R. 934; (1862) 10 H.L. Cas. 26, HL *Applied* 13/71: *Disapproved* 94/2083: *Not followed* 14/79

Tysiac v Poland (5410/03) [2007] 1 F.C.R. 666; (2007) 45 E.H.R.R. 42; 22 B.H.R.C. 155, ECHR ........ *Digested,* 07/**2244**: *Applied* 14/1516: *Considered* 11/1562, 14/1482

U (A Child) v Liverpool City Council; *sub nom* KU (A Child) v Liverpool City Council [2005] EWCA Civ 475; [2005] 1 W.L.R. 2657; [2005] 4 Costs L.R. 600; Times, May 16, 2005, CA (Civ Div) ........ *Digested,* 06/**2741**: *Applied* 10/2117, 10/350: *Considered* 06/400, 12/2079, 14/2047

U (A Child) (Serious Injury: Standard of Proof) (Permission to Reopen Appeal), Re; *sub nom* U (Re-Opening of Appeal), Re [2005] EWCA Civ 52; [2005] 1 W.L.R. 2398; [2005] 3 All E.R. 550; [2005] 2 F.L.R. 444; [2005] 1 F.C.R. 583; [2005] Fam. Law 449; (2005) 102(16) L.S.G. 30; (2005) 155 N.L.J. 325; (2005) 149 S.J.L.B. 266; Times, March 31, 2005, CA (Civ Div) ........ *Digested,* 05/**464**: *Applied* 11/372, 14/2000

U (A Minor) (Specific Issue Orders: Muslim Upbringing and Circumcision), Re see J (A Minor) (Prohibited Steps Order: Circumcision), Re

U (Re-Opening of Appeal), Re see U (A Child) (Serious Injury: Standard of Proof) (Permission to Reopen Appeal), Re

UAB Juvelta v VI Lietuvos prabavimo rumai (C-481/12) [2014] 2 C.M.L.R. 43, ECJ (2nd Chamber)

UBS AG v Revenue and Customs Commissioners; *sub nom* USB AG v Revenue and Customs Commissioners; Revenue and Customs Commissioners v UBS AG [2007] EWCA Civ 119; [2007] S.T.C. 588; [2007] B.T.C. 285; 9 I.T.L. Rep. 767; [2007] S.T.I. 411, CA (Civ Div); reversing in part [2006] EWHC 117 (Ch); [2006] S.T.C. 716; [2006] B.T.C. 232; 8 I.T.L. Rep. 595; [2006] S.T.I. 379; Times, February 21, 2006, Ch D; reversing [2005] S.T.C. (S.C.D.) 589; 7 I.T.L. Rep. 893, Sp Comm ........ *Digested,* 07/**4023**: *Considered* 13/3055, 14/2977

UBS AG v Revenue and Customs Commissioners; *sub nom* Deutsche Bank Group Services (UK) Ltd v Revenue and Customs Commissioners; *joined case* DB Group Services (UK) Ltd v Revenue and Customs Commissioners [2014] EWCA Civ 452; [2014] S.T.C. 2278; [2014] B.T.C. 20; [2014] S.T.I. 1833, CA (Civ Div); reversing in part [2012] UKUT 320 (TCC); [2013] S.T.C. 68; [2013] B.T.C. 1525; [2012] S.T.I. 2883, UT (Tax) ........ *Digested,* 14/**2969**: *Applied* 14/2921

UBS AG New York v Fairfield Sentry Ltd (In Liquidation) see Fairfield Sentry Ltd (In Liquidation) v Migani

UBS Wealth Management (UK) Ltd v Vestra Wealth LLP [2008] EWHC 1974 (QB); [2008] I.R.L.R. 965; (2008) 105(37) L.S.G. 21, QBD ........ *Digested,* 09/**1237**: *Applied* 14/1025

UCB Home Loans Corp Ltd v Moore see Royal Bank of Scotland Plc v Etridge (No.2)

Uddin v Associated Portland Cement Manufacturers Ltd [1965] 2 Q.B. 582; [1965] 2 W.L.R. 1183; [1965] 2 All E.R. 213; 63 L.G.R. 241; (1965) 109 S.J. 313, CA; affirming [1965] 2 Q.B. 15; [1965] 2 W.L.R. 327; [1965] 1 All E.R. 347; (1965) 109 S.J. 151, QBD ........ *Digested,* 65/**1636**: *Applied* 65/1631, 14/2998: *Considered* 72/2394, 73/2324

Uddin v Islington LBC [2014] P.A.D. 38, Planning Inspector

UDL Construction Plc v Customs and Excise Commissioners [1995] V. & D.R. 396, V&DTr *Considered* 14/3060

UDL Holdings Ltd, Re [2002] 1 H.K. Cases 172, CFI (HK) *Considered* 14/1820

UF v X County Council [2014] EWCOP 18; (2014) 17 C.C.L. Rep. 445, CP

UF, Re [2013] EWHC 4289 (COP); [2014] C.O.P.L.R. 93, CP ........ *Digested,* 14/**2159**

UK Coal Mine Holdings Ltd, Re see UK Coal Operations Ltd, Re

UK Coal Mining Ltd v Secretary of State for Communities and Local Government [2013] EWHC 2142 (Admin); [2014] J.P.L. 14, QBD (Admin) ........ *Digested,* 14/**2395**

UK Coal Operations Ltd, Re; *sub nom* Mining Services Ltd, Re; UK Coal Surface Mining Ltd, Re; UK Coal Mine Holdings Ltd, Re [2013] EWHC 2581 (Ch); [2014] 1 B.C.L.C. 471, Ch D ........ *Digested,* 14/**1764**

UK Coal Surface Mining Ltd, Re see UK Coal Operations Ltd, Re

UK Housing Alliance (North West) Ltd (In Administration), Re; *sub nom* Mackay v Kaupthing Singer & Friedlander Ltd (In Administration) [2013] EWHC 2553 (Ch); [2013] B.C.C. 752, Ch D (Companies Ct) ........ *Digested,* 14/**1755**

UK Storage Co (SW) Ltd v Revenue and Customs Commissioners; *sub nom* Revenue and Customs Commissioners v UK Storage Co (SW) Ltd [2012] UKUT 359 (TCC); [2013] S.T.C. 361; [2012] B.V.C. 1955; [2012] S.T.I. 3233, UT (Tax); reversing [2011] UKFTT 549 (TC); [2011] S.F.T.D. 1233, FTT (Tax) ........ *Digested,* 13/**3194**: *Applied* 14/3052

UK Uncut Legal Action Ltd v Revenue and Customs Commissioners see R. (on the application of UK Uncut Legal Action Ltd) v Revenue and Customs Commissioners

UKI (Kingsway) Ltd v Westminster City Council [2014] R.A. 367, VT ........ *Digested,* 14/**2083**

UL v BK (Freezing Orders: Safeguards: Standard Examples) [2013] EWHC 1735 (Fam); [2014] Fam. 35; [2014] 2 W.L.R. 914; [2013] Fam. Law 1379, Fam Div .. *Digested,* 14/**496**

Ullah v Ullah [2013] EWHC 2296 (Ch); [2013] B.P.I.R. 928, Ch D ........ *Digested,* 14/**2489**

Ullah (Ahsan) v Special Adjudicator see R. (on the application of Ullah) v Special Adjudicator

Ullusow v Secretary of State for Work and Pensions see Abdirahman v Secretary of State for Work and Pensions

Ultimate Products Ltd v Woolley [2014] EWHC 2706 (Ch); [2014] 5 Costs L.O. 787, Ch D ........ *Digested,* 14/**453**

Ultraframe (UK) Ltd v Fielding; *joined cases* Northstar Systems Ltd (In Liquidation) v Fielding; Burnden Group Plc v Northstar Systems Ltd (In Liquidation) [2005] EWHC 1638 (Ch); [2006] F.S.R. 17; [2007] W.T.L.R. 835; (2005) 28(9) I.P.D. 28069, Ch D ........ *Digested,* 06/**543**: *Considered* 10/1990: *Doubted* 14/511

Ultraframe (UK) Ltd v Fielding (Costs); *sub nom* Ultraframe (UK) Ltd v Fielding (No.2); *joined case* Northstar Systems Ltd v Fielding (Costs) [2006] EWCA Civ 1660; [2007] 2 All E.R. 983; [2007] C.P. Rep. 12; [2007] 2 Costs L.R. 264; Times, January 8, 2007, CA (Civ Div); affirming [2005] EWHC 2506 (Ch), Ch D ........... *Digested,* 07/**391**: *Applied* 10/319, 14/369: *Distinguished* 08/1423

Ultraframe (UK) Ltd v Fielding (No.2) see Ultraframe (UK) Ltd v Fielding (Costs)

Umerji v Khan see Zurich Insurance Plc v Umerji

UMICORE/LiCoM oxides (T2367/10) [2014] E.P.O.R. 12, EPO (Technical Bd App)

Unaoil Ltd v Leighton Offshore Pte Ltd [2014] EWHC 2965 (Comm); 156 Con. L.R. 24, QBD (Comm)

Uner v Netherlands (46410/99) [2006] 3 F.C.R. 340; (2007) 45 E.H.R.R. 14; [2007] Imm. A.R. 303; [2007] I.N.L.R. 273, ECHR (Grand Chamber) ........................... *Digested,* 07/**2252**: *Applied* 07/2259, 07/2262, 08/1993, 09/2067, 10/1745, 10/1773, 11/1734, 11/1770, 11/1790, 12/1677: *Considered* 09/2070, 10/1266, 10/1777, 14/1678

Ungureanu v Poland see Pomiechowski v Poland

Unilever Plc v Procter & Gamble Co [2000] 1 W.L.R. 2436; [2001] 1 All E.R. 783; [2000] F.S.R. 344; (2000) 23(1) I.P.D. 23001; (1999) 96(44) L.S.G. 40; (1999) 143 S.J.L.B. 268; Times, November 4, 1999; Independent, November 5, 1999, CA (Civ Div); affirming [1999] 1 W.L.R. 1630; [1999] 2 All E.R. 691; [1999] F.S.R. 849; (1999) 22(5) I.P.D. 22042; (1999) 149 N.L.J. 370; Times, March 18, 1999, Ch D (Patents Ct) ........................................................................ *Digested,* 99/**349**: *Applied* 00/334, 02/276, 03/277, 03/293, 04/251, 04/261, 05/289, 07/1078, 09/764, 10/1054, 10/1994, 10/254, 12/485: *Considered* 01/3966, 01/397, 03/288, 07/2555, 08/3056, 09/329, 11/2001: *Followed* 00/337, 14/1008

Union des associations europeennes de football (UEFA) v European Commission (C-201/11 P) [2014] 1 C.M.L.R. 18, ECJ (3rd Chamber)

Unipac (Scotland) Ltd v Aegon Insurance Co (UK) Ltd 1996 S.L.T. 1197; [1996] C.L.C. 918, IH (2 Div); affirming [1995] C.L.C. 694, OH ..................................... *Digested,* 96/**7091**: *Considered* 14/1846

Uniserve Ltd v Croxen [2012] EWHC 1190 (Ch); [2013] B.C.C. 825, Ch D .................. *Digested,* 14/**1762**

Unisoft Group (No.2), Re [1993] B.C.L.C. 532, Ch D (Companies Ct) .......................... *Digested,* 93/**3165**: *Applied* 05/465, 14/127: *Explained* 08/415

Unisoft Group Ltd (No.2), Re see Unisoft Group Ltd (No.3), Re

Unisoft Group Ltd (No.3), Re; *sub nom* Unisoft Group Ltd (No.2), Re [1994] B.C.C. 766; [1994] 1 B.C.L.C. 609, Ch D (Companies Ct) ............................................ *Digested,* 95/**4194**: *Considered* 14/523

Unison v Glasgow City Council see Glasgow City Council v Fox Cross Claimants

Unister GmbH v Office for Harmonisation in the Internal Market (Trade Marks and Designs) (OHIM) (T-244/12) [2014] E.T.M.R. 23, GC (2nd Chamber)

Unite Group Plc v Unite the Union; *sub nom* Unite the Union's Trade Mark Applications [2014] R.P.C. 14, App Person

Unite the Union's Trade Mark Applications see Unite Group Plc v Unite the Union

United Antwerp Maritime Agencies (Unamar) NV v Navigation Maritime Bulgare (C-184/12) [2014] 1 All E.R. (Comm) 625; [2014] 1 Lloyd's Rep. 161, ECJ (3rd Chamber)

United Bank of Kuwait Plc v Prudential Property Services Ltd see South Australia Asset Management Corp v York Montague Ltd

United Dominions Trust (Commercial) v Eagle Aircraft Services; *sub nom* United Dominions Trust (Commercial) v Eagle Aviation [1968] 1 W.L.R. 74; [1968] 1 All E.R. 104; (1967) 111 S.J. 849, CA (Civ Div); reversing (1967) 117 N.L.J. 324, HC .................................................................................................... *Digested,* 68/**1777**: *Applied* 14/1970

United Dominions Trust (Commercial) v Eagle Aviation see United Dominions Trust (Commercial) v Eagle Aircraft Services

United Grand Lodge of England v Revenue and Customs Commissioners [2014] UKFTT 164 (TC); [2014] S.T.I. 953, FTT (Tax)

United Group Rail Services Ltd v Rail Corp New South Wales 127 Con. L.R. 202, CA (NSW) *Applied* 14/629

United Guarding Services Ltd v Hermoza see United Guarding Services Ltd v St James Security Group Ltd

United Guarding Services Ltd v St James Security Group Ltd; *joined case* United Guarding Services Ltd v Hermoza UKEAT/0770/03/RN, EAT *Applied* 14/1131

United International Pictures v Cine Bes Filmcilik ve Yapimcilik AS; *sub nom* Cine Bes Filmcheck ve Yapimcilik AS v United International Pictures [2003] EWCA Civ 1669; [2004] 1 C.L.C. 401; (2003) 147 S.J.L.B. 1396, CA (Civ Div); reversing in part [2003] EWHC 798 (Comm), QBD (Comm)
*Applied* 06/768: *Considered* 14/642

United Kingdom v Council of the European Union (C-209/13) [2014] S.T.C. 1228; [2014] 3 C.M.L.R. 48; [2014] All E.R. (EC) 951; [2014] B.T.C. 23; [2014] S.T.I. 1911, ECJ (2nd Chamber) ........ *Digested,* 14/**1213**

United Kingdom v Council of the European Union (C-270/12) see United Kingdom v European Parliament (C-270/12)

United Kingdom v Council of the European Union (C-431/11) [2014] 1 C.M.L.R. 49, ECJ (1st Chamber)

United Kingdom v Council of the European Union (C-656/11 R) [2014] 3 C.M.L.R. 11, ECJ

United Kingdom v Council of the European Union (C-656/11) [2014] 1 W.L.R. 2970; [2014] 3 C.M.L.R. 10; [2014] All E.R. (EC) 829, ECJ (3rd Chamber)

United Kingdom v European Parliament (C-270/12); *sub nom* United Kingdom v Council of the European Union (C-270/12) [2014] 2 C.M.L.R. 44; [2014] All E.R. (EC) 251, ECJ (Grand Chamber)

United Lincolnshire Hospitals NHS Trust v N [2014] EWCOP 16; [2014] C.O.P.L.R. 660; (2014) 140 B.M.L.R. 204, CP

United Scientific Holdings Ltd v Burnley BC; *joined case* Cheapside Land Development Co Ltd v Messels Service Co [1978] A.C. 904; [1977] 2 W.L.R. 806; [1977] 2 All E.R. 62; 75 L.G.R. 407; (1977) 33 P. & C.R. 220; (1977) 243 E.G. 43; (1977) 121 S.J. 223, HL; reversing [1976] Ch. 128; [1976] 2 W.L.R. 686; [1976] 2 All E.R. 220; 74 L.G.R. 316; (1976) 32 P. & C.R. 183; (1976) 238 E.G. 487; (1976) 120 S.J. 183, CA (Civ Div); affirming (1974) 231 E.G. 1543, Ch D ........ *Digested,* 77/**1758**:
*Applied* 79/1638, 80/1637, 81/1573, 83/2080, 83/2126, 83/2138, 83/2139, 84/1947, 84/1951, 84/1952, 84/1956, 85/1935, 85/1937, 87/2202, 87/4626, 88/2075, 92/2743, 96/3814, 01/4208, 05/2679, 08/2471, 12/2723, 14/1970: *Considered* 76/1566, 77/1757, 78/101, 80/1635, 81/1582, 81/2433, 82/1801, 82/27, 83/2128, 83/2130, 83/2132, 83/2135, 83/2137, 84/1939, 84/1947, 84/1949, 85/1918, 85/1920, 86/1913, 87/2200, 87/2206, 87/2212, 89/2153, 89/2155, 90/2855, 90/2857, 90/2859, 90/2861, 91/2271, 91/557, 92/2726, 92/2746, 93/182, 93/2462, 93/2536, 95/2965, 95/3068, 00/3914, 05/2667, 06/2704: *Distinguished* 77/1726, 86/405, 97/3320: *Followed* 77/1759, 78/1810, 81/1585, 81/1588, 83/2140, 91/5178, 01/4207, 13/2839

United States v Abacha [2014] EWHC 993 (Comm); [2014] Lloyd's Rep. F.C. 392, QBD (Comm)
*Reversed* 14/406

United States v Abacha see Blue Holding (1) Pte Ltd v United States

United States v Nolan [2014] EWCA Civ 71; [2014] I.C.R. 685; [2014] I.R.L.R. 302, CA (Civ Div) ........ *Digested,* 14/**1109**

United States v Nolan [2010] EWCA Civ 1223; [2011] I.R.L.R. 40, CA (Civ Div); no effect [2009] I.R.L.R. 923; (2009) 153(22) S.J.L.B. 32, EAT ........ *Digested,* 11/**1045**:
*Affirmed* 14/1109

United States v Philip Morris Inc (No.1) [2004] EWCA Civ 330; [2004] 1 C.L.C. 811; (2004) 148 S.J.L.B. 388; Times, April 16, 2004, CA (Civ Div); affirming [2003] EWHC 3028 (Comm), QBD (Comm) ........ *Digested,* 04/**257**:
*Considered* 11/1930: *Followed* 14/293

United States v Tollman see R. (on the application of United States) v Bow Street Magistrates' Court

United States v Wood [2013] EWHC 1971 (Admin); [2014] A.C.D. 10, QBD (Admin)

United Wire Ltd v Screen Repair Services (Scotland) Ltd [2000] 4 All E.R. 353; [2000] E.N.P.R. 324; [2001] F.S.R. 24; [2001] R.P.C. 24; (2000) 23(12) I.P.D. 23099; Times, July 21, 2000; Independent, October 23, 2000, HL; affirming [2000] F.S.R. 204; (1999) 22(11) I.P.D. 22106; Times, August 18, 1999, CA (Civ Div); reversing (1997) 20(12) I.P.D. 20121; Times, August 20, 1997, Ch D ........ *Digested,* 00/**3674**:
*Applied* 02/2910: *Considered* 13/1779, 14/1877: *Followed* 10/1961, 11/1968

Universal Cargo Carriers Corp v Citati (No.1) [1957] 1 W.L.R. 979; [1957] 3 All E.R. 234; [1957] 2 Lloyd's Rep. 191; (1957) 101 S.J. 762, CA; affirming [1957] 2 Q.B. 401; [1957] 2 W.L.R. 713; [1957] 2 All E.R. 70; [1957] 1 Lloyd's Rep. 174; (1957) 101 S.J. 320, QBD ........ *Digested,* 57/**130**:
*Applied* 62/2838, 79/2449, 81/2403: *Considered* 73/3109, 86/1259, 00/870, 04/3490, 14/2738: *Followed* 99/5791

Universal Enterprises (EU) Ltd v Revenue and Customs Commissioners; *joined cases* Excel RTI Solutions Ltd v Revenue and Customs Commissioners; Masstech Corp Ltd v Revenue and Customs Commissioners; Radarbeam Ltd v Revenue and Customs Commissioners; Rigcharm Ltd v Revenue and Customs Commissioners; Lifeline Europe Ltd v Revenue and Customs Commissioners; Pelix Ltd (in administration) v Revenue and Customs Commissioners [2014] S.T.C. 1515; [2014] B.V.C. 510, UT (Tax) ........ *Digested,* 14/**3092**

Universal Permanent Building Society v Cooke [1952] Ch. 95; [1951] 2 All E.R. 893; [1951] 2 T.L.R. 962, CA ........ *Digested,* 47-51/**6348**: *Applied* 54/2109: *Considered* 88/2047, 14/2505: *Followed* 96/4956

Universal succession (T2357/12) [2014] E.P.O.R. 31, EPO (Technical Bd App)

University College Union v University of Stirling; *sub nom* University of Stirling v University and College Union [2014] CSIH 5; 2014 S.C. 414; 2014 S.L.T. 352; [2014] I.R.L.R. 287; 2014 G.W.D. 5-106, IH (Ex Div) ........ *Digested,* 14/**3502**

University of Brighton v Dovehouse Interiors Ltd see Brighton University v Dovehouse Interiors Ltd

University of Cambridge v Revenue and Customs Commissioners [2009] EWHC 434 (Ch); [2009] S.T.C. 1288; [2009] B.T.C. 5278; [2009] B.V.C. 277; [2009] S.T.I. 684; [2009] N.P.C. 39, Ch D; affirming [2008] B.V.C. 2274; [2008] V. & D.R. 579, V&DTr (London) ........ *Digested,* 09/**4121**: *Applied* 14/3044

University of Huddersfield Higher Education Corp v Revenue and Customs Commissioners; *sub nom* Revenue and Customs Commissioners v University of Huddersfield Higher Education Corp [2014] UKUT 438 (TCC); [2014] B.V.C. 537; [2014] S.T.I. 3076, UT (Tax); reversing [2013] UKFTT 429 (TC); [2014] S.F.T.D. 78; [2013] S.T.I. 2892; [2013] S.T.I. 3144, FTT (Tax) ........ *Digested,* 14/**3087**

University of Kent v Customs and Excise Commissioners [2004] B.V.C. 2215; [2004] V. & D.R. 372; [2004] S.T.I. 1948, V&DTr (London) ........ *Digested,* 05/**4421**: *Applied* 14/3101

University of Stirling v University and College Union [2012] I.C.R. 803; [2012] I.R.L.R. 266; [2012] E.L.R. 398, EAT (SC) ........ *Digested,* 12/**3984**: *Affirmed* 14/3502

University of Stirling v University and College Union see University College Union v University of Stirling

Unknown Owner v Shepway DC; *sub nom* Shepway DC v Unknown Owner [2013] UKUT 190 (LC); [2014] R.V.R. 333, UT (Lands)

UPC Telekabel Wien GmbH v Constantin Film Verleih GmbH (C-314/12) [2014] Bus. L.R. 541; [2014] E.C.D.R. 12, ECJ (4th Chamber)

Uphill v BRB (Residuary) Ltd [2005] EWCA Civ 60; [2005] 1 W.L.R. 2070; [2005] 3 All E.R. 264; [2005] C.P. Rep. 20; (2005) 102(15) L.S.G. 35; (2005) 149 S.J.L.B. 181; Times, February 8, 2005; Independent, February 17, 2005, CA (Civ Div) ... *Digested,* 05/**403**: *Applied* 07/538, 12/1770: *Considered* 06/2022, 12/457, 14/50

Upjohn SA Danmark v Paranova A/S (C-379/97) see Pharmacia & Upjohn SA (formerly Upjohn SA) v Paranova A/S (C-379/97)

Uprichard v Fife Council see Uprichard v Scottish Ministers

Uprichard v Scottish Ministers; *sub nom* Uprichard v Fife Council [2013] UKSC 21; 2013 S.C. (U.K.S.C.) 219; 2013 S.L.T. 1218; 2013 G.W.D. 14-307; [2013] P.T.S.R. D37, SC; affirming [2011] CSIH 59; 2012 S.C. 172; 2011 G.W.D. 30-655, IH (2 Div); affirming [2010] CSOH 105; 2010 G.W.D. 30-628, OH ........ *Digested,* 14/**2373**

Urban Edge Group Ltd v London Underground Ltd [2009] UKUT 103 (LC); [2009] R.V.R. 361, UT (Lands) ........ *Digested,* 10/**2543**: *Applied* 10/2547, 10/2551: *Considered* 14/2361

Urban I (Blonk Street) Ltd v Ayres [2013] EWCA Civ 816; [2014] 1 W.L.R. 756; [2013] B.L.R. 505; [2014] 1 P. & C.R. 1; [2013] 3 E.G.L.R. 91; [2013] 29 E.G. 105 (C.S.), CA (Civ Div) ........ *Digested,* 14/**596**

Urban Ventures Ltd v Thomas see Black Ant Co Ltd (In Administration), Re

US v SR [2014] EWFC 24; [2014] Fam. Law 1673, Fam Div

US S Corp's German Withholding Tax Status, Re (I R 48/12) 16 I.T.L. Rep. 428, BFH (Ger)

USB AG v Revenue and Customs Commissioners see UBS AG v Revenue and Customs Commissioners

USDAW v Ethel Austin Ltd (In Administration); *sub nom* USDAW v WW Realisation I Ltd; *joined case* USDAW v Unite the Union [2014] EWCA Civ 142; [2014] 2 C.M.L.R. 45, CA (Civ Div); no effect [2014] 1 C.M.L.R. 23; [2013] I.C.R. 1300; [2013] I.R.L.R. 686, EAT ........ *Digested,* 14/**1018**

USDAW v Unite the Union see USDAW v Ethel Austin Ltd (In Administration)

USDAW v WW Realisation I Ltd see USDAW v Ethel Austin Ltd (In Administration)

Ust-Kamenogorsk Hydropower Plant JSC v AES Ust-Kamenogorsk Hydropower Plant LLP see AES Ust-Kamenogorsk Hydropower Plant LLP v Ust-Kamenogorsk Hydropower Plant JSC

Utilise TDS Ltd v Cranstoun Davies [2014] EWHC 834 (Ch); [2014] 3 Costs L.O. 417, Ch D (Manchester) *Reversed* 14/454

Utilise TDS Ltd v Cranstoun Davies see Denton v TH White Ltd

Utopia Tableware Ltd v BBP Marketing Ltd [2013] EWHC 3483 (IPEC); [2014] E.C.C. 34, IPEC

Utopia Tableware Ltd v BBP Marketing Ltd [2013] EWPCC 28; [2013] F.S.R. 43, PCC *Digested,* 14/**322**

V v Addet & Stanhope School see Vakante v Addey and Stanhope School Governing Body

V v UBS Companies [2014] I.L.Pr. 36, Cass (F)

V v United Kingdom (24888/94) see T v United Kingdom (24724/94)

V (A Child) (Care Proceedings: Human Rights Claims), Re [2004] EWCA Civ 54; [2004] 1 W.L.R. 1433; [2004] 1 All E.R. 997; [2004] 1 F.L.R. 944; [2004] 1 F.C.R. 338; [2004] Fam. Law 328; (2004) 101(11) L.S.G. 33; Times, February 17, 2004; Independent, February 12, 2004, CA (Civ Div) .................................. *Digested,* 04/**1461**: *Applied* 14/2182

V (A Child) (Contact: Domestic Violence), Re see L (A Child) (Contact: Domestic Violence), Re

V (Children) (Long-term Fostering versus Adoption), Re [2013] EWCA Civ 913; [2014] 1 F.L.R. 1009; [2013] 3 F.C.R. 407; [2013] Fam. Law 1362, CA (Civ Div) .......... *Digested,* 14/**1249**

V8680 Ltd v Revenue and Customs Commissioners [2014] UKFTT 934 (TC); [2014] S.T.I. 3094, FTT (Tax)

VA v Hertfordshire Partnership NHS Foundation Trust [2011] EWHC 3524 (Fam), CP *Applied* 14/346

Vaccine Research LP v Revenue and Customs Commissioners [2013] UKFTT 73 (TC), FTT (Tax) *Affirmed* 14/2905

Vaccine Research LP v Revenue and Customs Commissioners; *sub nom* Revenue and Customs Commissioners v Vaccine Research LP [2014] UKUT 389 (TCC); [2014] B.T.C. 525, UT (Tax) .................................................................................. *Digested,* 14/**2905**

Vaitkus v Dresser-Rand UK Ltd [2014] EWHC 170 (Ch); [2014] Pens. L.R. 153, Ch D . *Digested,* 14/**2258**

Vakante v Addey and Stanhope School Governing Body; *sub nom* V v Addet & Stanhope School; Addey and Stanhope School v Vakante [2004] EWCA Civ 1065; [2004] 4 All E.R. 1056; [2005] 1 C.M.L.R. 3; [2005] I.C.R. 231; (2004) 101(36) L.S.G. 33; Times, September 28, 2004, CA (Civ Div); affirming [2004] I.C.R. 279, EAT .................................................................................................. *Digested,* 04/**1278**: *Applied* 09/1171, 12/1055: *Considered* 14/2994: *Distinguished* 14/1119: *Followed* 12/1173

Valchev v Bulgaria (Admissibility) (47450/11) (2014) 58 E.H.R.R. SE16, ECHR

Valentine v Valentine see Valentine's Settlement, Re

Valentine's Settlement, Re; *sub nom* Valentine v Valentine [1965] Ch. 831; [1965] 2 W.L.R. 1015; [1965] 2 All E.R. 226; (1965) 109 S.J. 237, CA; affirming [1965] Ch. 226; [1964] 3 W.L.R. 768; [1964] 3 All E.R. 174; (1964) 108 S.J. 582, Ch D *Digested,* 65/**3556**: *Applied* 67/1991, 00/2436, 10/1275: *Followed* 96/467, 13/1194, 14/1242

Valilas v Januzaj [2014] EWCA Civ 436; 154 Con. L.R. 38, CA (Civ Div) ...................... *Digested,* 14/**623**

Vallee v Birchwood; *sub nom* Bogusz (Deceased), Re [2013] EWHC 1449 (Ch); [2014] Ch. 271; [2014] 2 W.L.R. 543; [2013] W.T.L.R. 1095; 16 I.T.E.L.R. 305; [2013] 2 P. & C.R. DG15, Ch D ........................................................................ *Digested,* 13/**2970**: *Applied* 14/2817

Vallianatos v Greece (29381/09) (2014) 59 E.H.R.R. 12; 36 B.H.R.C. 149, ECHR (Grand Chamber)

VALSPAR/Core-shell powder particle (T1834/11) [2014] E.P.O.R. 26, EPO (Technical Bd App)

Valuer-General of New South Wales v Pyntoe Pty Ltd [2013] NSWCA 346; [2014] R.V.R. 65, CA (NSW)

Van Buggenhout v Banque Internationale a Luxembourg SA (C-251/12) [2013] Bus. L.R. 1322; [2014] I.L.Pr. 28; (2013) 163(7579) N.L.J. 18, ECJ (3rd Chamber)

van Caster v Finanzamt Essen-Sud (C-326/12); *sub nom* Caster v Finanzamt Essen-Sud (C-326/12) [2014] B.T.C. 48; [2014] S.T.I. 3078, ECJ (1st Chamber)

Van Colle v Chief Constable of Hertfordshire; *sub nom* Chief Constable of Hertfordshire v Van Colle; *joined case* Smith v Chief Constable of Sussex [2008] UKHL 50; [2009] 1 A.C. 225; [2008] 3 W.L.R. 593; [2008] 3 All E.R. 977; [2009] 1 Cr. App. R. 12; [2008] H.R.L.R. 44; [2008] U.K.H.R.R. 967; [2009] P.I.Q.R. P2; [2009] LS Law Medical 1; [2008] Po. L.R. 151; [2008] Inquest L.R. 176; (2008) 152(32) S.J.L.B. 31; Times, August 4, 2008, HL; reversing [2007] EWCA Civ 325; [2007] 1 W.L.R. 1821; [2007] 3 All E.R. 122; [2007] 2 Cr. App. R. 32; [2007] 2 F.C.R. 469; [2007] H.R.L.R. 25; [2007] U.K.H.R.R. 869; [2007] P.I.Q.R. Q7; [2007] Po. L.R. 7; [2007] Inquest L.R. 69; (2007) 151 S.J.L.B. 576; Times, May 10, 2007, CA (Civ Div); reversing in part [2006] EWHC 360 (QB); [2006] 3 All E.R. 963; [2006] 1 F.C.R. 755; [2006] H.R.L.R. 25; [2006] Inquest L.R. 68; [2006] Po. L.R. 47; Times, March 28, 2006; Independent, March 22, 2006, QBD ........ *Digested*, 08/**2646**:
*Applied* 10/1738, 14/2203: *Complaint dismissed* 13/1559: *Considered* 07/2238, 09/22, 10/3420, 11/2256, 11/868, 12/2294, 12/2629: *Followed* 11/2255, 13/2387

van der Helder v College voor zorgverzekeringen (C-321/12) [2014] 2 C.M.L.R. 4; [2014] I.C.R. 108, ECJ (3rd Chamber)

Van der Mussele v Belgium (8919/80) (1984) 6 E.H.R.R. 163, ECHR
*Applied* 07/2265, 08/1903, 13/2890: *Considered* 06/4044, 14/2766

Van der Pijl v Kingston Crown Court see R. (on the application of Van der Pijl) v Kingston Crown Court

Van Gulck v Wasabi Frog Ltd see Wasabi Frog Ltd v Gulck

Van Leuven v Belgium (A/43) see Le Compte v Belgium (A/43)

Vanniyasingam v Secretary of State for the Home Department see Subesh v Secretary of State for the Home Department

Vapenik v Thurner (C-508/12) [2014] 1 W.L.R. 2486; [2014] C.E.C. 963; [2014] I.L.Pr. 19, ECJ (9th Chamber)

Various Claimants v Catholic Child Welfare Society see Various Claimants v Institute of the Brothers of the Christian Schools

Various Claimants v Institute of the Brothers of the Christian Schools; *sub nom* Various Claimants v Catholic Child Welfare Society; Catholic Child Welfare Society v Various Claimants [2012] UKSC 56; [2013] 2 A.C. 1; [2012] 3 W.L.R. 1319; [2013] 1 All E.R. 670; [2013] I.R.L.R. 219; [2013] E.L.R. 1; [2013] P.I.Q.R. P6; (2012) 162 N.L.J. 1505; (2012) 156(45) S.J.L.B. 31; Times, December 18, 2012, SC; reversing [2010] EWCA Civ 1106, CA (Civ Div); affirming 5dw01675 6dw00102 6dw20001 7dw90002 8dw00116, QBD DR ........ *Digested*, 13/**2099**:
*Followed* 14/2343

Various Claimants v News Group Newspapers Ltd [2013] EWHC 2119 (Ch); [2014] Ch. 400; [2014] 2 W.L.R. 756; [2014] E.M.L.R. 6, Ch D ........ *Digested*, 14/**383**

Vasey v Surrey Free Inns Plc [1996] P.I.Q.R. P373, CA (Civ Div) ........ *Digested*, 95/**3735**:
*Considered* 02/4555, 14/3000

Vasiliou v Hajigeorgiou; *sub nom* Hajigeorgiou v Vasiliou [2005] EWCA Civ 236; [2005] 1 W.L.R. 2195; [2005] 3 All E.R. 17; [2005] C.P. Rep. 27; (2005) 102(18) L.S.G. 22; [2005] N.P.C. 39; Times, March 22, 2005, CA (Civ Div) ........ *Digested*, 05/**296**:
*Applied* 14/291: *Considered* 11/327

VB v Westminster Magistrates' Court see R. (on the application of B) v Westminster Magistrates' Court

VC v Slovakia (18968/07) (2014) 59 E.H.R.R. 29, ECHR

Ved v Secretary of State for the Home Department see Ved (Appealable Decisions: Permission Applications: Basnet)

Ved (Appealable Decisions: Permission Applications: Basnet); *sub nom* Ved v Secretary of State for the Home Department [2014] UKUT 150 (IAC); [2014] Imm. A.R. 868, UT (IAC)

Vee Networks Ltd v Econet Wireless International Ltd [2004] EWHC 2909 (Comm); [2005] 1 All E.R. (Comm) 303; [2005] 1 Lloyd's Rep. 192, QBD (Comm) ........ *Digested*, 05/**202**:
*Applied* 09/185, 14/131: *Considered* 10/173

Vegetarian Society v Scott; *sub nom* Viva! Campaigns Ltd v Scott [2013] EWHC 4097 (Ch); [2014] W.T.L.R. 525, Ch D (Birmingham) ........ *Digested*, 14/**2842**

Vehicle Inspectorate v Cantabrica Coach Holdings Ltd; *sub nom* Cantabrica Coach Holdings Ltd v Vehicle Inspectorate [2001] UKHL 60; [2001] 1 W.L.R. 2288; [2002] 1 All E.R. 595; (2002) 166 J.P. 423; [2002] R.T.R. 8; (2002) 166 J.P.N. 550; (2002) 99(4) L.S.G. 31; (2001) 145 S.J.L.B. 275; Times, November 28, 2001, HL; affirming (2000) 164 J.P. 593; [2000] R.T.R. 286; (2000) 97(18) L.S.G. 37; Times, April 13, 2000, DC ........ *Digested*, 01/**5489**:
*Considered* 14/1186

Veiss v Latvia (15152/12) [2014] Fam. Law 452, ECHR

Veitch v Red Sky Group Ltd [2010] NICA 39; [2011] Eq. L.R. 181, CA (NI)
*Considered* 14/3144
Vejdeland v Sweden (1813/07) (2014) 58 E.H.R.R. 15; 32 B.H.R.C. 474; [2012] Eq. L.R. 369, ECHR
Velev v Bulgaria (16032/07) 37 B.H.R.C. 406; [2014] E.L.R. 424, ECHR
Venetico Marine SA v International General Insurance Co Ltd [2013] EWHC 3644 (Comm); [2014] 1 Lloyd's Rep. 349; [2014] Lloyd's Rep. I.R. 243, QBD (Comm) *Digested,* 14/**1851**
Venn v Secretary of State for Communities and Local Government; *sub nom* Secretary of State for Communities and Local Government v Venn [2014] EWCA Civ 1539, CA (Civ Div); reversing [2013] EWHC 3546 (Admin); [2014] J.P.L. 447, QBD (Admin) .......... *Digested,* 14/**442**
Vento v Chief Constable of West Yorkshire; *sub nom* Chief Constable of West Yorkshire v Vento (No.2) [2002] EWCA Civ 1871; [2003] I.C.R. 318; [2003] I.R.L.R. 102; [2003] Po. L.R. 171; (2003) 100(10) L.S.G. 28; (2003) 147 S.J.L.B. 181; Times, December 27, 2002, CA (Civ Div); affirming [2002] I.R.L.R. 177; [2002] Emp. L.R. 111, EAT .......... *Digested,* 03/**1306**:
*Applied* 06/1363, 07/1413, 09/3815, 10/1116, 10/1125, 13/1038:
*Considered* 04/1276, 04/917, 06/1371, 08/1136, 08/891, 10/1042, 11/1064, 11/1071, 12/1116, 13/794, 14/1099, 14/3476: *Followed* 04/1306, 05/1318, 13/786
Venulum Property Investments Ltd v Space Architects Ltd [2013] EWHC 3948 (TCC); [2014] B.L.R. 127, QBD (TCC) .......... *Digested,* 14/**2523**
Veolia Environmental Services UK v Gumbs [2014] Eq. L.R. 364, EAT .......... *Digested,* 14/**1100**
Verest v Belgium (C-489/13) [2014] B.T.C. 43, ECJ (7th Chamber)
Verizon Communications Singapore Pte Ltd v Income Tax Officer 16 I.T.L. Rep. 463, HC (Ind)
Vernon v Bosley (No.1) [1997] 1 All E.R. 577; [1997] R.T.R. 1; [1998] 1 F.L.R. 297; [1997] P.I.Q.R. P255; (1997) 35 B.M.L.R. 135; [1997] Fam. Law 476; (1996) 146 N.L.J. 589; Times, April 4, 1996, CA (Civ Div) .......... *Digested,* 96/**2156**:
*Considered* 14/1672
Vernon Knight Associates v Cornwall Council [2013] EWCA Civ 950; [2013] B.L.R. 519; [2014] Env. L.R. 6; [2013] 3 E.G.L.R. 69, CA (Civ Div) .......... *Digested,* 14/**2220**
Verrechia (t/a Freightmaster Commercials) v Commissioner of Police of the Metropolis see English v Emery Reimbold & Strick Ltd
Versalis SpA v European Commission (C-511/11 P) [2013] 5 C.M.L.R. 24; [2014] C.E.C. 158, ECJ (1st Chamber)
Versteegh Ltd v Revenue and Customs Commissioners; *sub nom* Spritebeam Ltd v Revenue and Customs Commissioners [2013] UKFTT 642 (TC); [2014] S.F.T.D. 547; [2014] S.T.I. 475, FTT (Tax) .......... *Digested,* 14/**2972**
Viackiene v Tower Hamlets LBC [2013] EWCA Civ 1764; [2014] H.L.R. 13, CA (Civ Div) .......... *Digested,* 14/**1595**
Vibe Technologies Ltd's Trade Mark Application (No.2390030) [2009] E.T.M.R. 12, App Person
*Considered* 13/1825, 14/1932
Vibroplant Ltd v Holland (Inspector of Taxes) [1982] 1 All E.R. 792; [1982] S.T.C. 164; 54 T.C. 658; [1981] T.R. 485; (1982) 126 S.J. 82, CA (Civ Div); affirming [1981] 1 All E.R. 526; [1980] S.T.C. 671; [1980] T.R. 313; (1980) 124 S.J. 561, Ch D .. *Digested,* 82/**472**:
*Considered* 96/5565, 08/3647, 14/2882
Vicente v Secretary of State for Communities and Local Government see San Vicente v Secretary of State for Communities and Local Government
Vicomtesse Montmort v Broers see Letterstedt v Broers
Victorangle Ltd v Revenue and Customs Commissioners [2013] UKFTT 607 (TC); [2014] L.L.R. 402; [2013] S.T.I. 3510, FTT (Tax)
Vidal-Hall v Google Inc; *sub nom* Google Inc v Vidal-Hall [2014] EWHC 13 (QB); [2014] 1 W.L.R. 4155; [2014] 1 C.L.C. 201; [2014] E.M.L.R. 14; [2014] F.S.R. 30, QBD .......... *Digested,* 14/**415**
Vietnam Shipbuilding Industry Group, Re [2013] EWHC 2476 (Ch); [2014] B.C.C. 433; [2014] 1 B.C.L.C. 400, Ch D .......... *Digested,* 14/**1821**
Vigon v DPP (1998) 162 J.P. 115; [1998] Crim. L.R. 289; (1998) 162 J.P.N. 88; Times, December 9, 1997, DC .......... *Digested,* 98/**970**:
*Considered* 14/673
Vilnes v Norway (52806/09); *joined case* Muledal v Norway (22703/10) 36 B.H.R.C. 297; (2014) 139 B.M.L.R. 199, ECHR
Vilvarajah v United Kingdom (13163/87) (1992) 14 E.H.R.R. 248; Times, November 12, 1991; Independent, November 5, 1991; Guardian, November 6, 1991, ECHR .......... *Digested,* 92/**2333**:
*Applied* 97/2764, 97/2787, 02/2511, 08/1911, 14/1672: *Considered* 14/1657:
*Followed* 02/2514

Vince v Wyatt; *sub nom* Wyatt v Vince [2013] EWCA Civ 495; [2013] 1 W.L.R. 3525; [2014] 1 F.L.R. 246; [2013] 3 F.C.R. 1; [2013] Fam. Law 1126; (2013) 163(7561) N.L.J. 20, CA (Civ Div) ............ *Digested,* 13/**1306**

Vince v Wyatt [2013] EWCA Civ 934; [2014] 1 F.L.R. 399, CA (Civ Div) ............ *Digested,* 14/**1364**

Vine Products Ltd v Mackenzie & Co Ltd (No.3) [1967] F.S.R. 402; [1969] R.P.C. 1, Ch D ............ *Digested,* 67/**3943**: *Applied* 11/1961, 14/1889: *Considered* 72/3429, 93/3799: *Followed* 70/2854

Vintage Tea House Ltd v Revenue and Customs Commissioners [2014] UKFTT 19 (TC); [2014] S.T.I. 541, FTT (Tax)

Vinter v United Kingdom (66069/09); *joined cases* Moore v United Kingdom (3896/10); Bamber v United Kingdom (130/10) 34 B.H.R.C. 605; [2014] Crim. L.R. 81; Times, July 11, 2013, ECHR ............ *Digested,* 13/**1550**: *Considered* 14/2701

Virgin Atlantic Airways Ltd v Air Canada see Virgin Atlantic Airways Ltd v Jet Airways (India) Ltd

Virgin Atlantic Airways Ltd v Delta Air Lines Inc see Virgin Atlantic Airways Ltd v Jet Airways (India) Ltd

Virgin Atlantic Airways Ltd v Jet Airways (India) Ltd; *sub nom* Virgin Atlantic Airways Ltd v Jet Airways (India) Ltd; *joined cases* Virgin Atlantic Airways Ltd v Delta Air Lines Inc; Virgin Atlantic Airways Ltd v Air Canada; Contour Aerospace Ltd v Virgin Atlantic Airways Ltd; Premium Aircraft Interiors Ltd v Comptroller General of Patents [2013] EWCA Civ 1713; [2014] Bus. L.R. 491; [2014] R.P.C. 18, CA (Civ Div); affirming [2012] EWHC 2153 (Pat); [2013] R.P.C. 10, Ch D (Patents Ct) ............ *Digested,* 14/**1893**

Virgin Atlantic Airways Ltd v Jet Airways (India) Ltd see Virgin Atlantic Airways Ltd v Jet Airways (India) Ltd

Virgin Atlantic Airways Ltd v Premium Aircraft Interiors UK Ltd; *sub nom* Virgin Atlantic Airways Ltd v Zodiac Seats UK Ltd (formerly Contour Aerospace Ltd) [2013] UKSC 46; [2014] A.C. 160; [2013] 3 W.L.R. 299; [2013] 4 All E.R. 715; [2013] R.P.C. 29, SC; reversing [2011] EWCA Civ 163; [2011] F.S.R. 27, CA (Civ Div) *Digested,* 13/**1806**: *Followed* 14/1903

Virgin Atlantic Airways Ltd v Zodiac Seats UK Ltd (formerly Contour Aerospace Ltd) see Virgin Atlantic Airways Ltd v Premium Aircraft Interiors UK Ltd

Virgin Enterprises Ltd v One in a Million Ltd see British Telecommunications Plc v One in a Million Ltd

Virk v Secretary of State for the Home Department [2013] EWCA Civ 652; [2014] Imm. A.R. 95; [2014] I.N.L.R. 358, CA (Civ Div) ............ *Digested,* 14/**1698**: *Followed* 14/1642

Viscous Global Investment Ltd v Palladium Navigation Corp [2014] EWHC 2654 (Comm); [2014] 2 Lloyd's Rep. 600, QBD (Comm)

Vision Enterprises Ltd (t/a Universal Estates) v Tiensia see Tiensia v Vision Enterprises Ltd (t/a Universal Estates)

Vistins v Latvia (71243/01) (2014) 59 E.H.R.R. 21, ECHR

Vistins v Latvia (71243/01) (2014) 58 E.H.R.R. 4, ECHR (Grand Chamber)

Visvaratnam v Brent Magistrates' Court [2009] EWHC 3017 (Admin); (2010) 174 J.P. 61; [2010] A.C.D. 22, DC ............ *Digested,* 10/**793**: *Applied* 10/794: *Distinguished* 14/710

Vitol SA v Norelf Ltd (The Santa Clara) [1996] A.C. 800; [1996] 3 W.L.R. 105; [1996] 3 All E.R. 193; [1996] 2 Lloyd's Rep. 225; [1996] C.L.C. 1159; (1996) 15 Tr. L.R. 347; (1996) 93(26) L.S.G. 19; (1996) 146 N.L.J. 957; (1996) 140 S.J.L.B. 147; Times, July 1, 1996; Independent, June 28, 1996, HL; reversing [1996] Q.B. 108; [1995] 3 W.L.R. 549; [1995] 3 All E.R. 971; [1995] 2 Lloyd's Rep. 128; [1995] C.L.C. 1018; (1995) 14 Tr. L.R. 451; Times, June 2, 1995; Independent, June 12, 1995, CA (Civ Div); reversing [1994] 1 W.L.R. 1390; [1994] 4 All E.R. 109; [1993] 2 Lloyd's Rep. 301; (1993) 90(30) L.S.G. 36; (1993) 137 S.J.L.B. 146; Times, May 20, 1993; Lloyd's List, July 16, 1993, QBD (Comm) ............ *Digested,* 96/**1242**: *Applied* 09/991: *Considered* 08/160: *Followed* 14/624

Viva! Campaigns Ltd v Scott (Costs); *sub nom* McKeen (Deceased), Re (Costs) [2013] EWHC 3639 (Ch); [2014] W.T.L.R. 461, Ch D (Birmingham) ............ *Digested,* 14/**363**

Viva! Campaigns Ltd v Scott see Vegetarian Society v Scott

Vivendi SA v Richards [2013] EWHC 3006 (Ch); [2013] B.C.C. 771; [2013] Bus. L.R. D63, Ch D ............ *Digested,* 14/**511**: *Applied* 14/1402

Vivendi SA, Re 17 I.T.L. Rep. 246, Trib Ad (F)

VK v CC see K (A Child) (Abduction: Rights of Custody), Re

Vlaamse Oliemaatschappij NV v FOD Financien (C-499/10) (Unreported, December 21, 2011), ECJ *Applied* 14/823

Vlad v Romania (40756/06) (2014) 59 E.H.R.R. 13, ECHR
Vlassopoulou v Ministerium fur Justiz, Bundes- und Europaangelegenheiten Baden-Wurttemberg (C-340/89) [1991] E.C.R. I-2357; [1993] 2 C.M.L.R. 221; (1991) 135 S.J.L.B. 92; Times, June 3, 1991; Independent, June 24, 1991, ECJ .......... *Digested,* 91/**3989**: *Applied* 04/1416, 09/1430, 14/1498: *Considered* 92/4783, 02/1573
Vlieland-Boddy v Dexter Ltd [2003] EWHC 2592 (Ch); [2004] B.P.I.R. 235, Ch D ......... *Digested,* 04/**2157**: *Considered* 14/1799
VLM Holdings Ltd v Ravensworth Digital Services Ltd [2013] EWHC 228 (Ch); [2014] F.S.R. 9, Ch D .......... *Digested,* 14/**1886**
Vocalspruce Ltd v Revenue and Customs Commissioners [2014] EWCA Civ 1302; [2014] B.T.C. 50; [2014] S.T.I. 3235, CA (Civ Div); affirming [2013] UKUT 276 (TCC); [2013] S.T.C. 2261; [2013] B.T.C. 1889; [2013] S.T.I. 2421, UT (Tax); affirming [2012] UKFTT 36 (TC); [2012] S.F.T.D. 659; [2012] S.T.I. 553, FTT (Tax) .......... *Digested,* 13/**3040**
Vodafone v Office of Communications [2008] CAT 39, CAT *Considered* 14/537: *Distinguished* 10/471
Vodafone 2 v Revenue and Customs Commissioners [2009] EWCA Civ 446; [2010] Ch. 77; [2010] 2 W.L.R. 288; [2010] Bus. L.R. 96; [2009] S.T.C. 1480; [2010] Eu. L.R. 110; [2009] B.T.C. 273; [2009] S.T.I. 1795; Times, June 26, 2009, CA (Civ Div); reversing [2008] EWHC 1569 (Ch); [2009] Ch. 123; [2009] 2 W.L.R. 210; [2009] Bus. L.R. 96; [2008] S.T.C. 2391; [2009] 3 C.M.L.R. 30; [2008] 3 C.M.L.R. 21; [2008] B.T.C. 526; 10 I.T.L. Rep. 1052; [2008] S.T.I. 1675, Ch D; reversing [2008] S.T.C. (S.C.D.) 55; 10 I.T.L. Rep. 110, Sp Comm .......... *Digested,* 09/**3765**: *Applied* 10/3495: *Considered* 14/1063
Vodafone Group Plc, Re [2014] EWHC 1357 (Ch); [2014] B.C.C. 554; [2014] 2 B.C.L.C. 422, Ch D (Companies Ct) .......... *Digested,* 14/**517**
Vodafone Group Services Ltd v Revenue and Customs Commissioners [2014] UKFTT 701 (TC); [2014] S.T.I. 2670, FTT (Tax)
Vodafone India Service Pvt Ltd v India 16 I.T.L. Rep. 134, HC (Ind)
Vodafone India Services Pvt Ltd v India 17 I.T.L. Rep. 209, HC (Ind)
Volaw Trust & Corporate Services Ltd v Office of the Comptroller of Taxes 17 I.T.L. Rep. 1, CA (Jer); affirming 16 I.T.L. Rep. 758, Royal Ct (Jer) .......... *Digested,* 14/**2893**
Volkov v Ukraine (21722/11) [2013] I.R.L.R. 480; (2013) 57 E.H.R.R. 1; 35 B.H.R.C. 487, ECHR
Volkswagen AG v Garcia [2013] EWHC 1832 (Ch); [2014] F.S.R. 12, Ch D .......... *Digested,* 14/**1864**
Volkswagen Financial Services (UK) Ltd v Revenue and Customs Commissioners; *sub nom* Revenue and Customs Commissioners v Volkswagen Financial Services (UK) Ltd [2012] UKUT 394 (TCC); [2013] S.T.C. 716; [2013] B.V.C. 1501; [2012] S.T.I. 3277, UT (Tax); reversing [2011] UKFTT 556 (TC); [2012] S.F.T.D. 190, FTT (Tax) .......... *Digested,* 13/**3206**: *Considered* 14/3089
Von Hannover v Germany (59320/00) [2004] E.M.L.R. 21; (2005) 40 E.H.R.R. 1; 16 B.H.R.C. 545, ECHR *Applied* 07/1072: *Considered* 06/2853, 07/2247, 07/2250, 08/1984, 09/929, 10/4, 11/1680, 11/339, 11/341, 11/862, 14/842
Vona v Hungary (35943/10) 37 B.H.R.C. 239, ECHR
Voyazides v Eyre; *sub nom* Voyazides v Lomas [2013] UKUT 13 (LC); [2014] R.V.R. 38, UT (Lands) .......... *Digested,* 14/**2504**
Voyazides v Lomas see Voyazides v Eyre
Voyvoda v Grosvenor West End Properties [2013] UKUT 334 (LC); [2014] L. & T.R. 10; [2013] 3 E.G.L.R. 55, UT (Lands) .......... *Digested,* 14/**1981**
VRCC Ltd v French (Valuation Officer) [2013] UKUT 627 (LC); [2014] R.A. 261, UT (Lands)
Vroege v NCIV Instituut voor Volkshuisvesting BV (C-57/93); *joined case* Fisscher v Voorhuis Hengelo BV (C-128/93) [1994] E.C.R. I-4541; [1995] 1 C.M.L.R. 881; [1995] All E.R. (E.C.) 193; [1995] I.C.R. 635; [1994] I.R.L.R. 651; Times, December 7, 1994; Financial Times, October 4, 1994, ECJ; no effect [1994] E.C.R. I-4541; [1994] Pens. L.R. 123, AGO .......... *Digested,* 95/**2000**: *Applied* 04/2799: *Considered* 98/4134, 14/1120: *Referred to* 97/2214, 97/3983
VS (Sri Lanka) v Entry Clearance Officer see Mahad (Ethiopia) v Entry Clearance Officer

VTB Capital Plc v Nutritek International Corp [2013] UKSC 5; [2013] 2 A.C. 337; [2013] 2 W.L.R. 398; [2013] 1 All E.R. 1296; [2013] 1 All E.R. (Comm) 1009; [2013] 1 Lloyd's Rep. 466; [2013] B.C.C. 514; [2013] 1 B.C.L.C. 179; [2013] 1 C.L.C. 153, SC; affirming [2012] EWCA Civ 808; [2012] 2 Lloyd's Rep. 313; [2012] 2 B.C.L.C. 437; [2012] 2 C.L.C. 431, CA (Civ Div); affirming [2011] EWHC 3107 (Ch), Ch D ........ *Digested,* 13/**472**: *Applied* 13/1300, 13/362, 13/427, 13/428: *Considered* 13/1304: *Followed* 12/473, 14/479

Vuckovic v Serbia (Nos17153/11) (2014) 59 E.H.R.R. 19, ECHR

VW (Uganda) v Secretary of State for the Home Department; *joined case* AB (Somalia) v Secretary of State for the Home Department [2009] EWCA Civ 5; [2009] Imm. A.R. 436; [2009] I.N.L.R. 295, CA (Civ Div) ........ *Digested,* 09/**2163**: *Considered* 14/1715: *Followed* 11/1728, 13/1618, 14/1725

Vyerentsov v Ukraine (20372/11) (2014) 58 E.H.R.R. 9; 35 B.H.R.C. 12, ECHR

W v A City Council see W (Children) (Care Order: Sexual Abuse), Re

W v C; *sub nom* SW v RC [2008] EWHC 73 (Fam); [2008] 1 F.L.R. 1703; [2008] 2 F.C.R. 663; [2008] Fam. Law 400, Fam Div ........ *Digested,* 08/**1561**: *Considered* 14/1360

W v H see Sharbatly v Shagroon

W v L; *sub nom* TW v PL (Agreement) [2013] EWHC 3078 (Fam); [2014] 2 F.L.R. 106; [2014] Fam. Law 155, Fam Div ........ *Digested,* 14/**1387**

W v M see M (Adult Patient) (Minimally Conscious State: Withdrawal of Treatment), Re

W v Veolia Environmental Services (UK) Plc [2011] EWHC 2020 (QB); [2012] 1 All E.R. (Comm) 667; [2012] Lloyd's Rep. I.R. 419; [2011] C.T.L.C. 193, QBD (Merc) (London) ........ *Digested,* 12/**1898**: *Considered* 12/1902, 14/610

W v W (A Minor) (Mirror Order); *sub nom* W (Jurisdiction: Mirror Order), Re [2011] EWCA Civ 703; [2014] 1 F.L.R. 1530; [2011] 3 F.C.R. 151; [2011] Fam. Law 937; (2011) 108(27) L.S.G. 22, CA (Civ Div) ........ *Digested,* 11/**1393**: *Followed* 13/1234

W v W (Residence: Enforcement of Order) [2005] EWHC 1881 (Fam), Fam Div *Applied* 14/1432

W (A Child) v Groupama Insurance Ltd (Unreported, September 10, 2013), CC (Leeds) [*Spencers Solicitors, Millennium Way, Chesterfield, Derbyshire*] ........ *Digested,* 14/**2322**

W (A Child) (Abduction: Committal), Re; *sub nom* Wilkinson v Anjum [2011] EWCA Civ 1196; [2012] 1 W.L.R. 1036; [2012] 2 F.L.R. 133; [2012] Fam. Law 389; Times, September 15, 2011, CA (Civ Div) ........ *Digested,* 12/**1367**: *Considered* 14/1334: *Followed* 14/1332, 14/1333

W (A Child) (Adoption Order: Leave to Oppose), Re; *joined case* H (Children) (Adoption Order: Application for Permission for Leave to Oppose), Re [2013] EWCA Civ 1177; [2014] 1 W.L.R. 1993; [2014] 1 F.L.R. 1266; [2014] 1 F.C.R. 191; [2014] Fam. Law 12, CA (Civ Div) ........ *Digested,* 14/**1246**: *Considered* 14/1330: *Followed* 14/1247, 14/1248, 14/1254

W (A Child) (Adoption Order: Set Aside and Leave to Oppose), Re [2010] EWCA Civ 1535; [2011] 1 F.L.R. 2153; [2011] 1 F.C.R. 342; [2011] Fam. Law 221, CA (Civ Div) ........ *Digested,* 11/**1282**: *Not followed* 14/1245

W (A Child) (Care Proceedings: ABE Interviews), Re; *sub nom* W (A Child) (Placement Order), Re; Lancashire CC v SB [2013] EWHC 653 (Fam); [2013] 2 F.L.R. 1344; [2013] Fam. Law 791, Fam Div ........ *Digested,* 14/**1433**

W (A Child) (Care Proceedings: Welfare Evaluation: Functions of Local Authority), Re; *sub nom* RW v Neath Port Talbot CBC [2013] EWCA Civ 1227; [2014] 1 W.L.R. 1611; [2014] 2 F.L.R. 431; [2014] 1 F.C.R. 260; [2014] B.L.G.R. 313; [2014] Fam. Law 430; (2013) 157(40) S.J.L.B. 37, CA (Civ Div) ........ *Digested,* 14/**1266**

W (A Child) (Change of Name), Re see W (A Child) (Illegitimate Child: Change of Surname), Re

W (A Child) (Illegitimate Child: Change of Surname), Re; *sub nom* W (A Child) (Change of Name), Re; *joined cases* A (A Child) (Change of Name), Re; B (Children) (Change of Name), Re [2001] Fam. 1; [2000] 2 W.L.R. 258; [1999] 2 F.L.R. 930; [1999] 3 F.C.R. 337; [1999] Fam. Law 688; (1999) 96(33) L.S.G. 29; Times, August 5, 1999, CA (Civ Div) ........ *Digested,* 99/**2375**: *Considered* 02/1652, 08/1465, 14/1425: *Followed* 14/1303

W (A Child) (Inherent Jurisdiction: Permission Application: Revocation and Adoption Order), Re; *sub nom* W (A Child) (Revocation of Adoption: Inherent Jurisdiction), Re [2013] EWHC 1957 (Fam); [2013] 2 F.L.R. 1609; [2013] 3 F.C.R. 336; [2013] Fam. Law 1127, Fam Div ........ *Digested,* 14/**1231**

W (A Child) (Interim Care Order: Threshold), Re see W (A Child) (Proportionality of Interim Care Order), Re

W (A Child) (Parental Responsibility Order: Inter-Relationship with Direct Contact), Re [2013] EWCA Civ 335; [2013] 2 F.L.R. 1337; [2013] Fam. Law 810, CA (Civ Div) ........ *Digested,* 14/**1421**

W (A Child) (Placement Order), Re see W (A Child) (Care Proceedings: ABE Interviews), Re

W (A Child) (Proportionality of Interim Care Order), Re; *sub nom* W (A Child) (Interim Care Order: Threshold), Re [2014] EWCA Civ 772; [2014] 3 F.C.R. 339; [2014] Fam. Law 1235, CA (Civ Div)

W (A Child) (Revocation of Adoption: Inherent Jurisdiction), Re see W (A Child) (Inherent Jurisdiction: Permission Application: Revocation and Adoption Order), Re

W (Adoption Order), Re see Poole BC v W

W (Children) (Abuse: Oral Evidence), Re see W (Children) (Family Proceedings: Evidence), Re

W (Children) (Care Order: Adequacy of Care Plan), Re see S (Children) (Care Order: Implementation of Care Plan), Re

W (Children) (Care Order: Sexual Abuse), Re; *sub nom* W v A City Council; W (Children) (Concurrent Care and Criminal Proceedings), Re [2009] EWCA Civ 644; [2009] 2 Cr. App. R. 23; [2009] 2 F.L.R. 1106; [2009] 3 F.C.R. 1; [2009] Fam. Law 795, CA (Civ Div) ........ *Digested,* 09/**1520**: *Considered* 10/1327, 14/1330: *Overruled* 10/1398

W (Children) (Care Plan), Re see S (Children) (Care Order: Implementation of Care Plan), Re

W (Children) (Change of Name), Re [2013] EWCA Civ 1488; [2014] 2 F.L.R. 221; [2014] 3 F.C.R. 175; [2014] Fam. Law 147, CA (Civ Div) ........ *Digested,* 14/**1303**

W (Children) (Concurrent Care and Criminal Proceedings), Re see W (Children) (Care Order: Sexual Abuse), Re

W (Children) (Contact Dispute), Re [2014] EWCA Civ 401; [2014] Fam. Law 958, CA (Civ Div)

W (Children) (Direct Contact), Re [2012] EWCA Civ 999; [2013] 1 F.L.R. 494; [2012] 3 F.C.R. 277; [2012] Fam. Law 1322, CA (Civ Div) ........ *Digested,* 12/**1450**: *Considered* 13/1332: *Followed* 14/1421

W (Children) (Domestic Violence), Re [2012] EWCA Civ 528; [2014] 1 F.L.R. 260; [2012] Fam. Law 797, CA (Civ Div) ........ *Digested,* 14/**1321**

W (Children) (Fact-finding: Hearsay Evidence), Re [2013] EWCA Civ 1374; [2014] 2 F.L.R. 703; [2014] 1 F.C.R. 303; [2014] Fam. Law 154, CA (Civ Div) ........ *Digested,* 14/**1275**

W (Children) (Family Proceedings: Evidence), Re; *sub nom* W (Children) (Abuse: Oral Evidence), Re [2010] UKSC 12; [2010] 1 W.L.R. 701; [2010] 2 All E.R. 418; [2010] P.T.S.R. 775; [2010] 1 F.L.R. 1485; [2010] 1 F.C.R. 615; [2010] H.R.L.R. 22; [2010] Fam. Law 449; (2010) 107(11) L.S.G. 15; (2010) 160 N.L.J. 389; (2010) 154(9) S.J.L.B. 28; Times, March 8, 2010, SC; reversing [2010] EWCA Civ 57; [2010] 2 F.L.R. 256; [2010] 1 F.C.R. 365; [2010] Fam. Law 447; (2010) 154(7) S.J.L.B. 37, CA (Civ Div) ........ *Digested,* 10/**1398**: *Applied* 12/1334, 12/1335, 14/1412: *Considered* 12/1336, 14/1309: *Followed* 11/1370, 12/1338

W (Children) (Identification: Restrictions on Publication), Re; *sub nom* A Local Authority v W [2005] EWHC 1564 (Fam); [2006] 1 F.L.R. 1; [2007] 3 F.C.R. 69; [2005] Fam. Law 868; Times, July 21, 2005, Fam Div ........ *Digested,* 05/**1686**: *Applied* 07/1806, 07/2189, 14/1279

W (Children) (Parental Agreement with Local Authority), Re [2014] EWCA Civ 1065; [2014] Fam. Law 1394, CA (Civ Div)

W (Children) (Strict Compliance with Court Orders), Re [2014] EWFC 22; [2014] Fam. Law 1383; (2014) 164(7619) N.L.J. 16, Fam Ct

W (Children), Re [2010] EWCA Civ 520; [2010] 2 F.L.R. 1165; [2010] Fam. Law 787, CA (Civ Div) ........ *Digested,* 11/**1349**: *Considered* 14/1379: *Followed* 11/1358

W (Children), Re; *sub nom* Webster v Norfolk CC [2009] EWCA Civ 59; [2009] 2 All E.R. 1156; [2009] 1 F.L.R. 1378; [2009] 1 F.C.R. 673; [2009] Fam. Law 381; (2009) 159 N.L.J. 280; (2009) 153(7) S.J.L.B. 31, CA (Civ Div) ........ *Digested,* 09/**1484**: *Considered* 14/1231

W (China) v Secretary of State for the Home Department [2006] EWCA Civ 1494; [2007] 1 W.L.R. 1514; [2007] 1 C.M.L.R. 17; [2007] Eu. L.R. 293; [2007] Imm. A.R. 326; [2007] I.N.L.R. 115; (2006) 103(45) L.S.G. 27; Times, December 13, 2006; Independent, November 17, 2006, CA (Civ Div) ........ *Digested,* 07/**2367**: *Applied* 08/2095, 14/1734: *Followed* 14/1739

W (Jurisdiction: Mirror Order), Re see W v W (A Minor) (Mirror Order)

W (Wardship: Discharge: Publicity), Re [1995] 2 F.L.R. 466; [1995] Fam. Law 612, CA (Civ Div) .......... *Digested,* 96/**646**: *Applied* 04/1924, 14/1278

W and B (Children) (Care Plan), Re see S (Children) (Care Order: Implementation of Care Plan), Re

W-B (A Child), Re [2012] EWCA Civ 592; [2013] 1 F.L.R. 394; [2012] Fam. Law 1203, CA (Civ Div) .......... *Digested,* 13/**1268**: *Followed* 14/1285

Wabco Europe v European Commission (T-380/10) [2014] 4 C.M.L.R. 4, GC (4th Chamber)

Wagenaar v Weekend Travel Ltd (t/a Ski Weekend) [2014] EWCA Civ 1105; [2014] C.P. Rep. 46; [2014] 5 Costs L.O. 803; [2014] P.I.Q.R. P23, CA (Civ Div) .......... *Digested,* 14/**340**

Wagstaff v Revenue and Customs Commissioners [2014] UKFTT 43 (TC); [2014] W.T.L.R. 547; [2014] S.T.I. 883, FTT (Tax) .......... *Digested,* 14/**2957**

Wah v Grant Thornton International Ltd; *sub nom* Wah (also known as Tang) v Grant Thornton International Ltd [2012] EWHC 3198 (Ch); [2013] 1 All E.R. (Comm) 1226; [2013] 1 Lloyd's Rep. 11, Ch D .......... *Digested,* 13/**801**: *Considered* 14/1403

Wah (also known as Tang) v Grant Thornton International Ltd see Wah v Grant Thornton International Ltd

Wahl v Iceland (E-15/12) [2014] 1 C.M.L.R. 29, EFTA

Wain v Glos CC see Wain v Gloucestershire CC

Wain v Gloucestershire CC; *sub nom* Wain v Glos CC [2014] EWHC 1274 (TCC); [2014] 4 Costs L.O. 585, QBD (TCC) .......... *Digested,* 14/**446**

Wainhomes (Northwest) Ltd v Cheshire East Council [2014] P.A.D. 46, Planning Inspector

Wakefield City MDC v Media see B (Children), Re

Wakefield College v Revenue and Customs Commissioners [2013] UKFTT 731 (TC); [2014] S.T.I. 449, FTT (Tax)

Wakil (t/a Orya Textiles) v Hammersmith and Fulham LBC [2013] EWHC 2833 (Admin); [2014] Env. L.R. 14, QBD (Admin) .......... *Digested,* 14/**2399**

Wald v Revenue and Customs Commissioners [2011] UKFTT 183 (TC), FTT (Tax) *Not followed* 14/2979

Wales and West Utilities Ltd v PPS Pipeline Systems GmbH [2014] EWHC 54 (TCC); [2014] B.L.R. 163, QBD (TCC) .......... *Digested,* 14/**130**

Walford v Miles [1992] 2 A.C. 128; [1992] 2 W.L.R. 174; [1992] 1 All E.R. 453; (1992) 64 P. & C.R. 166; [1992] 1 E.G.L.R. 207; [1992] 11 E.G. 115; [1992] N.P.C. 4; Times, January 27, 1992; Independent, January 29, 1992, HL; affirming (1991) 62 P. & C.R. 410; [1991] 2 E.G.L.R. 185; [1991] 28 E.G. 81; [1991] 27 E.G. 114; [1990] E.G. 158 (C.S.); Independent, January 15, 1991, CA (Civ Div); reversing [1990] 1 E.G.L.R. 212; [1990] 12 E.G. 107, QBD .......... *Digested,* 92/**514**: *Applied* 05/309, 13/587: *Considered* 94/2734, 94/570, 06/757, 11/530, 12/639: *Distinguished* 97/4535, 14/629: *Followed* 12/635, 13/585

Walford v Worcestershire CC see R. (on the application of Walford) v Worcestershire CC

Walker v Burton [2013] EWCA Civ 1228; [2014] 1 P. & C.R. 9; [2013] 3 E.G.L.R. 129; [2013] 43 E.G. 126 (C.S.), CA (Civ Div); affirming [2012] EWHC 978 (Ch), Ch D .......... *Digested,* 14/**2506**

Walker v Commissioner of Police of the Metropolis [2014] EWCA Civ 897; Times, July 16, 2014, CA (Civ Div) .......... *Digested,* 14/**2468**

Walker v Rome; *sub nom* Walker v Rowe [1999] 2 All E.R. (Comm) 961; [2000] 1 Lloyd's Rep. 116; [2000] C.L.C. 265; Independent, January 24, 2000, QBD (Comm) .......... *Digested,* 00/**231**: *Considered* 14/128: *Distinguished* 08/171

Walker v Rowe see Walker v Rome

Walker v Secretary of State for the Home Department see R. (on the application of Wells) v Parole Board for England and Wales

Walker v Secretary of State for the Home Department see Sanade (British Children: Zambrano: Dereci), Re

Walker and Son (Hauliers) Ltd v Environment Agency; *sub nom* R. v Walker & Son (Hauliers) Ltd [2014] EWCA Crim 100; [2014] 4 All E.R. 825; [2014] P.T.S.R. 929; [2014] 1 Cr. App. R. 30; [2014] Env. L.R. 22; [2014] L.L.R. 625, CA (Crim Div) .......... *Digested,* 14/**684**

Walker Construction (UK) Ltd v Quayside Homes Ltd [2014] EWCA Civ 93; [2014] 1 C.L.C. 121; [2014] B.L.R. 215; 153 Con. L.R. 26; [2014] 3 Costs L.O. 362; [2014] 1 E.G.L.R. 97, CA (Civ Div) .......... *Digested,* 14/**358**

Walker-Smith v General Medical Council [2012] EWHC 503 (Admin); [2013] Med. L.R. 462; (2012) 126 B.M.L.R. 1; (2012) 109(12) L.S.G. 20, QBD (Admin) .......... *Digested,* 14/**1496**

Wall v Mutuelle de Poitiers Assurances [2014] EWCA Civ 138; [2014] 1 W.L.R. 4263; [2014] 3 All E.R. 340; [2014] C.P. Rep. 23; [2014] 1 C.L.C. 253; [2014] R.T.R. 17; [2014] I.L.Pr. 18; [2014] P.I.Q.R. P15; Times, March 10, 2014, CA (Civ Div); affirming [2013] EWHC 53 (QB); [2013] 1 W.L.R. 3890; [2013] 2 All E.R. 709; [2013] R.T.R. 18; [2013] I.L.Pr. 20; [2013] P.I.Q.R. P9, QBD ............................ *Digested,* 14/**828**

Wallace v Shoa Leasing (Singapore) PTE Ltd; *sub nom* Japan Leasing (Europe) Plc, Re [1999] B.P.I.R. 911; [2000] W.T.L.R. 301, Ch D .......................................... *Digested,* 00/**3433**: *Considered* 14/1755: *Doubted* 14/78

Wallbank v Wallbank Fox Designs Ltd see Weddall v Barchester Healthcare Ltd

Wallentin-Hermann v Alitalia - Linee Aeree Italiane SpA (C-549/07) [2009] Bus. L.R. 1016; [2009] 1 Lloyd's Rep. 406; [2008] E.C.R. I-11061; [2009] 2 C.M.L.R. 9; Times, February 16, 2009, ECJ (4th Chamber) ................................................. *Digested,* 09/**260**: *Considered* 14/166

Wallingford v Mutual Society (1880) 5 App. Cas. 685, HL *Considered* 71/640, 73/9.u: *Followed* 14/277

Walsall MBC v K [2013] EWHC 3192 (Fam); [2014] 2 F.L.R. 227, Fam Div (Birmingham)

Walsh v Misseldine [2000] C.P. Rep. 74; [2000] C.P.L.R. 201, CA (Civ Div) ................ *Digested,* 00/**618**: *Applied* 14/487

Walters v Shell Refining Co Ltd see Walters v Whessoe Ltd

Walters v Whessoe Ltd; *joined case* Walters v Shell Refining Co Ltd [1968] 2 All E.R. 816 (Note); 6 B.L.R. 23, CA *Considered* 14/599: *Followed* 68/2647

Waltham Forest LBC v AD [2014] EWHC 1985 (Fam); [2014] Fam. Law 1253, Fam Div

Waltham Forest LBC v F [2014] EWFC 14; [2014] Fam. Law 1382, Fam Ct

Waltham Forest LBC v F [2014] EWFC 13; [2014] Fam. Law 1381, Fam Ct

Waltham Forest LBC v Omilaju (No.2) see Omilaju v Waltham Forest LBC (No.2)

Waltham Forest LBC v Zafar [2014] EWHC 791 (Ch); [2014] B.P.I.R. 1012, Ch D ....... *Digested,* 14/**1828**

Walton v Scottish Ministers [2012] UKSC 44; [2013] P.T.S.R. 51; 2013 S.C. (U.K.S.C.) 67; 2012 S.L.T. 1211; [2013] 1 C.M.L.R. 28; [2013] Env. L.R. 16; [2013] J.P.L. 323; 2012 G.W.D. 34-689, SC; affirming [2012] CSIH 19; 2012 G.W.D. 14-269, IH (Ex Div); affirming [2011] CSOH 131; 2011 S.C.L.R. 686; 2011 G.W.D. 34-703, OH ........................................................................................................ *Digested,* 13/**3703**: *Applied* 13/2358, 14/3730: *Considered* 13/3409, 14/2419

Walton Homes Ltd v Staffordshire CC [2013] EWHC 2554 (Ch); [2014] 1 P. & C.R. 10; [2013] 42 E.G. 125 (C.S.), Ch D ........................................................................ *Digested,* 14/**2503**

Wandsworth Clinical Commissioning Group v IA [2014] EWHC 990 (COP); (2014) 139 B.M.L.R. 180, CP

Wang v Secretary of State for the Home Department see Liu v Secretary of State for the Home Department

WAP Fyfe v Assessor for Fife Council; *sub nom* Fyfe (WAP) v Fife Assessor 2014 S.L.T. (Lands Tr) 10; [2014] R.V.R. 98; 2014 G.W.D. 1-29, Lands Tr (Scot) ...... *Digested,* 14/**3666**

Ward (A Child), Re; *sub nom* A v VW [2010] EWHC 16 (Fam); [2010] 1 F.L.R. 1497; (2010) 114 B.M.L.R. 48; [2010] Fam. Law 353, Fam Div ................................. *Digested,* 10/**1299**: *Applied* 11/1331, 14/1278: *Considered* 14/1268, 14/1436

Warm Zones v Thurley [2014] EWHC 988 (QB); [2014] I.R.L.R. 791, QBD .................. *Digested,* 14/**1020**

Warner v Armfield Retail & Leisure Ltd [2014] I.C.R. 239; [2014] Eq. L.R. 122, EAT .... *Digested,* 14/**1089**

Warrant Finance Co's Case (No.1) see Humber Ironworks & Shipbuilding Co, Re

Warren v Attorney General of Jersey [2011] UKPC 10; [2012] 1 A.C. 22; [2011] 3 W.L.R. 464; [2011] 2 All E.R. 513; [2011] 2 Cr. App. R. 29; Times, March 29, 2011, PC (Jer) ........................................................................................................ *Digested,* 11/**709**: *Applied* 14/298: *Considered* 12/1290

Warren v Care Fertility (Northampton) Ltd; *sub nom* Warren, Re [2014] EWHC 602 (Fam); [2014] 3 W.L.R. 1310; [2014] 2 F.L.R. 1284; [2014] 2 F.C.R. 311; [2014] Med. L.R. 217; [2014] Fam. Law 803; (2014) 158(12) S.J.L.B. 41, Fam Div ....... *Digested,* 14/**1262**

Warren v Henlys Ltd [1948] 2 All E.R. 935; [1948] W.N. 449; (1948) 92 S.J. 706, KBD *Digested,* 47-51/**3604**: *Considered* 14/3000

Warren, Re see Warren v Care Fertility (Northampton) Ltd

Warwickshire CC v M; *sub nom* M v Warwickshire CC; M (Children) (Placement Order), Re [2007] EWCA Civ 1084; [2008] 1 W.L.R. 991; [2008] 1 F.L.R. 1093; [2007] 3 F.C.R. 681; [2008] Fam. Law 10; (2007) 104(44) L.S.G. 30; (2007) 151 S.J.L.B. 1435; Times, December 21, 2007, CA (Civ Div) ............................ *Digested,* 07/**1679**: *Applied* 08/1554, 08/1576, 10/1440: *Considered* 14/1251

Wasabi Frog Ltd v Gulck; *sub nom* Van Gulck v Wasabi Frog Ltd [2014] R.P.C. 33, App Person

Waste Recycling Group Ltd v Revenue and Customs Commissioners; *sub nom* Revenue and Customs Commissioners v Waste Recycling Group Ltd [2008] EWCA Civ 849; [2009] S.T.C. 200; [2009] Env. L.R. 5; [2008] B.T.C. 8076; [2008] S.T.I. 1871, CA (Civ Div); affirming [2007] EWHC 3014 (Ch); [2008] S.T.C. 1037; [2008] Env. L.R. 19; [2008] B.T.C. 8003; [2008] S.T.I. 25, Ch D .... *Digested,* 08/**3818**: *Applied* 14/2946
Waterdance Ltd v Kingston Marine Services Ltd [2014] EWHC 224 (TCC); [2014] B.L.R. 141, QBD (TCC) .... *Digested,* 14/**829**
Waterfall Media (In Administration), Re; *sub nom* Secretary of State for Business, Innovation and Skills v Melaris [2013] B.P.I.R. 1109, Ch D .... *Digested,* 14/**508**
Waterworks Trust v Cheshire EBC [2014] P.A.D. 33, Planning Inspector
Watkins v Woolas [2010] EWHC 2702 (QB); (2010) 107(45) L.S.G. 20; Times, November 16, 2010, DC .... *Digested,* 11/**1014**: *Considered* 14/2102
Watson v Progressive Financial Services [2009] C.C.L.R. 10, CC (Liverpool) *Doubted* 14/608
Watson v Watson (Wasted Costs Orders) see Ridehalgh v Horsefield
Watson (Deceased), Re [1999] 1 F.L.R. 878; [1999] 3 F.C.R. 595; [1999] Fam. Law 211; (1999) 96(2) L.S.G. 28; (1999) 143 S.J.L.B. 51; Times, December 31, 1998, Ch D .... *Digested,* 99/**4636**: *Applied* 08/3618, 14/2822: *Considered* 10/3208
Watson (t/a Kirkwood Coaches) v Revenue and Customs Commissioners [2013] UKFTT 553 (TC); [2014] S.T.I. 535, FTT (Tax)
Watt (formerly Carter) v Ahsan see Carter v Ahsan
Watts v Watts [2014] W.T.L.R. 1781, Ch D
Watts v Watts see Fyfe v Watts
Way Ahead Group Ltd v Revenue and Customs Commissioners [2014] UKFTT 178 (TC); [2014] S.T.I. 1607, FTT (Tax)
We R Your IT Ltd v Revenue and Customs Commissioners [2013] UKFTT 738 (TC); [2014] S.T.I. 450, FTT (Tax)
Webb v Stenton (1883) 11 Q.B.D. 518, CA *Applied* 14/491
Webb Resolutions Ltd v E-Surv Ltd [2014] EWHC 49 (QB); [2014] 1 Costs L.R. 182, QBD .... *Digested,* 14/**395**: *Considered* 14/391
Weber v Weber (C-438/12) EU:C:2014:212; [2014] I.L.Pr. 29, ECJ (3rd Chamber)
Weber's Wine World Handels GmbH v Abgabenberufungskommission Wien (C147/01) [2003] E.C.R. I-11365; [2004] 1 C.M.L.R. 7; [2005] All E.R. (EC) 224; [2003] C.E.C. 501; [2004] B.T.C. 8019, ECJ (5th Chamber) .... *Digested,* 04/**908**: *Applied* 03/4569: *Considered* 10/3278, 13/3220: *Followed* 14/3074
Webley v St George's Hospital NHS Trust [2014] EWHC 299 (QB); (2014) 138 B.M.L.R. 190, QBD
Websense International Technology Ltd v Itway SpA [2012] IEHC 446; [2014] I.L.Pr. 14, HC (Irl)
Websons (8) Ltd v Revenue and Customs Commissioners [2013] UKFTT 229 (TC); [2013] S.T.I. 1786, FTT (Tax) *Considered* 14/3076
Webster v Brunel University see Wong v Igen Ltd (formerly Leeds Careers Guidance)
Webster v Liddington [2014] EWCA Civ 560; (2014) 138 B.M.L.R. 135; [2014] P.N.L.R. 26, CA (Civ Div) .... *Digested,* 14/**640**
Webster v Mackay [2014] EWCA Civ 525, CA (Civ Div); affirming [2013] EWHC 2571 (Ch); [2013] B.P.I.R. 1136, Ch D .... *Digested,* 14/**1779**
Webster v Norfolk CC see W (Children), Re
Webster v Official Receiver see Migration Services International Ltd, Re
Weddall v Barchester Healthcare Ltd; *joined case* Wallbank v Wallbank Fox Designs Ltd [2012] EWCA Civ 25; [2012] I.R.L.R. 307, CA (Civ Div) .... *Digested,* 12/**3344**: *Considered* 14/3000
Weeks v Magill see Porter v Magill
Wegrzynowski v Poland (33846/07) 36 B.H.R.C. 573, ECHR
Welford v Transport for London [2011] EWCA Civ 129; [2011] R.V.R. 172, CA (Civ Div); affirming [2010] UKUT 99 (LC); [2010] R.V.R. 200, UT (Lands) .... *Digested,* 11/**2675**: *Considered* 14/2359
Weller v Associated Newspapers Ltd [2014] EWHC 1163 (QB); [2014] E.M.L.R. 24, QBD .... *Digested,* 14/**842**
Wellesley Partners LLP v Withers LLP [2014] EWHC 556 (Ch); [2014] P.N.L.R. 22, Ch D .... *Digested,* 14/**2214**

Wells v Parole Board for England and Wales see R. (on the application of Wells) v Parole Board for England and Wales

Wells v Secretary of State for Transport, Local Government and the Regions (C-201/02) see R. (on the application of Wells) v Secretary of State for Transport, Local Government and the Regions (C-201/02)

Wells v United Kingdom (57715/09) see James v United Kingdom (25119/09)

Welmory sp z oo v Dyrektor Izby Skarbowej w Gdansku (C-605/12) [2014] B.V.C. 47, ECJ (3rd Chamber)

Welsh Development Agency v Redpath Dorman Long Ltd [1994] 1 W.L.R. 1409; [1994] 4 All E.R. 10; 67 B.L.R. 1; 38 Con. L.R. 106; (1994) 10 Const. L.J. 325; (1994) 91(21) L.S.G. 42; (1994) 138 S.J.L.B. 87; Times, April 4, 1994; Independent, May 2, 1994, CA (Civ Div) ........ *Digested,* 95/**4191**: *Applied* 97/1047, 07/491, 14/426, 14/427: *Considered* 96/859, 97/2719, 99/481, 05/479, 10/394: *Distinguished* 96/820, 99/542: *Followed* 12/308

Welte v Finanzamt Velbert (C-181/12) [2014] 2 C.M.L.R. 11; [2013] B.T.C. 707, ECJ (3rd Chamber)

Welwyn Hatfield Council v Secretary of State for Communities and Local Government; *sub nom* Secretary of State for Communities and Local Government v Welwyn Hatfield BC; R. (on the application of Welwyn Hatfield BC) v Secretary of State for Communities and Local Government [2011] UKSC 15; [2011] 2 A.C. 304; [2011] 2 W.L.R. 905; [2011] 4 All E.R. 851; [2011] P.T.S.R. 825; [2011] B.L.G.R. 459; [2011] 2 P. & C.R. 10; [2011] 2 E.G.L.R. 151; [2011] J.P.L. 1183; [2011] 15 E.G. 93 (C.S.); (2011) 108(16) L.S.G. 16; (2011) 161 N.L.J. 550; (2011) 155(14) S.J.L.B. 30; [2011] N.P.C. 40; Times, April 8, 2011, SC; reversing [2010] EWCA Civ 26; [2010] P.T.S.R. 1296; [2010] 2 P. & C.R. 10; [2010] 1 E.G.L.R. 98; [2010] 13 E.G. 84; [2010] J.P.L. 1095; [2010] 5 E.G. 113 (C.S.); (2010) 107(7) L.S.G. 19; (2010) 154(5) S.J.L.B. 28; [2010] N.P.C. 10; Times, February 9, 2010, CA (Civ Div); reversing [2009] EWHC 966 (Admin); [2010] J.P.L. 352, QBD (Admin) ........ *Digested,* 11/**2510**: *Considered* 10/2538, 14/1729

Wermuth v Wermuth [2003] EWCA Civ 50; [2003] 1 W.L.R. 942; [2003] 4 All E.R. 531; [2003] 1 F.C.R. 289; [2003] Fam. Law 308; Times, February 7, 2003, CA (Civ Div) ........ *Digested,* 03/**1585**: *Applied* 07/1772, 14/1326

Werner v Finanzamt Aachen-Innenstadt (C-112/91) [1996] S.T.C. 961; [1993] E.C.R. I-429; Financial Times, February 1, 1993, ECJ ........ *Digested,* 93/**4356**: *Applied* 12/3335: *Considered* 14/2916

West v Ian Finlay and Associates [2014] EWCA Civ 316; [2014] B.L.R. 324; 153 Con. L.R. 1; [2014] 2 E.G.L.R. 63; [2014] C.I.L.L. 3507, CA (Civ Div); reversing [2013] EWHC 868 (TCC), QBD (TCC) ........ *Digested,* 14/**595**

West v Sharp (2000) 79 P. & C.R. 327; (1999) 96(19) L.S.G. 29; (1999) 78 P. & C.R. D31, CA (Civ Div) ........ *Digested,* 00/**4638**: *Followed* 14/2519

West Bowers Farm Products v Essex CC (1985) 50 P. & C.R. 368; [1985] 1 E.G.L.R. 271; [1985] R.V.R. 176; [1985] J.P.L. 857; Times, June 25, 1985, CA (Civ Div) . *Digested,* 86/**3326**: *Applied* 06/5633, 14/2378: *Considered* 01/4659

West Bromwich Building Society v Crammer (Application for Permission to Appeal) [2002] EWCA Civ 1924, CA (Civ Div) *Applied* 03/2347, 14/1787: *Considered* 05/2279

West Faulkner Associates v Newham LBC 71 B.L.R. 1; (1995) 11 Const. L.J. 157; [1994] E.G. 179 (C.S.); [1994] N.P.C. 142; Times, November 16, 1994; Independent, December 19, 1994, CA (Civ Div); affirming 61 B.L.R. 81; (1993) 9 Const. L.J. 232; [1992] E.G. 139 (C.S.), QBD ........ *Digested,* 95/**490**: *Applied* 14/627

West London Mental Health NHS Trust v Chhabra see Chhabra v West London Mental Health NHS Trust

West London Pipeline & Storage Ltd v Total UK Ltd [2008] EWHC 1296 (Comm); [2008] C.P. Rep. 35; [2008] 1 C.L.C. 935; [2008] Lloyd's Rep. I.R. 688, QBD (Comm) ........ *Digested,* 08/**352**: *Applied* 14/465

West Mercia Safetywear Ltd (In Liquidation) v Dodd see Liquidator of West Mercia Safetywear Ltd v Dodd

West Midlands Cooperative Society v Tipton [1986] A.C. 536; [1986] 2 W.L.R. 306; [1986] 1 All E.R. 513; [1986] I.C.R. 192; [1986] I.R.L.R. 112; (1986) 83 L.S.G. 780; (1986) 136 N.L.J. 163; (1986) 130 S.J. 143, HL; reversing [1985] I.C.R. 444; [1985] I.R.L.R. 116; (1985) 82 L.S.G. 2009, CA (Civ Div); reversing [1983] I.R.L.R. 276, EAT ........ *Digested,* 86/**1285**: *Applied* 86/1283, 87/1407, 89/1500, 06/1383, 14/1115, 14/1140: *Approved* 94/2017: *Considered* 87/1319, 91/1696, 04/1310, 11/3700: *Distinguished* 98/2232

West Midlands Passenger Transport Executive v AJS Pressings (Unreported, November 11, 1988), QBD *Considered* 14/826

West Midlands Travel Ltd v Aviva Insurance UK Ltd [2013] EWCA Civ 887; [2014] R.T.R. 10; [2014] Lloyd's Rep. I.R. 66, CA (Civ Div) ........ *Digested,* 14/**826**

West of England Ship Owners Insurance Services Ltd Retirement Benefits Scheme, Re; *sub nom* Board of the Pension Protection Fund v Trustees of the West of England Ship Owners Insurance Services Ltd Retirement Benefits Scheme [2014] EWHC 20 (Ch); [2014] Pens. L.R. 167, Ch D (Companies Ct) ........ *Digested,* 14/**2276**

West Reading Social Club, Re see Baker v West Reading Social Club

West Sussex CC v Pierce [2013] EWCA Civ 1230; [2014] E.L.R. 62; [2014] P.I.Q.R. P5, CA (Civ Div) ........ *Digested,* 14/**2999**

West, Re [2014] EWCA Crim 1480; [2014] 2 Cr. App. R. 28, CA (Crim Div) ........ *Digested,* 14/**745**

West-Link Toll Bridge Ltd v Commissioner of Valuation see Celtic Roads Group (Dundalk) Ltd v Commissioner of Valuation

Westbrook Dolphin Square Ltd v Friends Life Ltd [2014] EWHC 2433 (Ch); [2014] L. & T.R. 28, Ch D

Westcott v Westcott [2008] EWCA Civ 818; [2009] Q.B. 407; [2009] 2 W.L.R. 838; [2009] 1 All E.R. 727; [2009] E.M.L.R. 2; [2008] Po. L.R. 132; (2008) 105(30) L.S.G. 17; Times, August 27, 2008, CA (Civ Div); affirming [2007] EWHC 2501 (QB), QBD ........ *Digested,* 08/**905**: *Applied* 14/2992

Western Excavating (ECC) Ltd v Sharp [1978] Q.B. 761; [1978] 2 W.L.R. 344; [1978] 1 All E.R. 713; [1978] I.C.R. 221; [1978] I.R.L.R. 27; (1978) 13 I.T.R. 132; (1987) 121 S.J. 814; Times, November 16, 1977, CA (Civ Div); reversing [1977] I.R.L.R. 25, EAT ........ *Digested,* 78/**900**: *Applied* 78/891, 78/893, 78/904, 79/838, 80/892, 81/981, 82/1097, 84/1194, 88/1247, 90/1929, 01/2234, 02/1427, 03/1214, 03/1221, 09/1255, 10/1032: *Considered* 78/897, 78/905, 80/1008, 80/883, 81/103u, 81/808, 86/1261, 89/1458, 99/2030, 14/3506: *Distinguished* 79/846: *Explained* 80/893

Western Sealanes Corp v Unimarine SA (The Pythia) [1982] 2 Lloyd's Rep. 160; [1982] Com. L.R. 78, QBD (Comm) ........ *Digested,* 82/**2941**: *Applied* 13/2836: *Approved* 14/2740

Westinsure Group Ltd v Revenue and Customs Commissioners [2014] UKUT 452 (TCC); [2014] B.V.C. 540; [2014] S.T.I. 3194, UT (Tax); affirming [2013] UKFTT 114 (TC); [2013] S.F.T.D. 873; [2013] S.T.I. 1437, FTT (Tax) ........ *Digested,* 13/**3191**

Westlink Toll Bridge Ltd v Commissioner of Valuation see Celtic Roads Group (Dundalk) Ltd v Commissioner of Valuation

Westminster City Council v Croyalgrange Ltd [1986] 1 W.L.R. 674; [1986] 2 All E.R. 353; (1986) 83 Cr. App. R. 155; (1986) 150 J.P. 449; 84 L.G.R. 801; [1986] Crim. L.R. 693; (1986) 83 L.S.G. 2089; (1986) 136 N.L.J. 491; (1986) 130 S.J. 409, HL; affirming [1985] 1 All E.R. 740; (1985) 149 J.P. 161; 84 L.G.R. 68; (1985) 149 J.P.N. 149, QBD ........ *Digested,* 86/**909**: *Applied* 97/3424: *Considered* 93/3933: *Not applied* 14/684

Westminster City Council v Dwyer see Dwyer v Westminster City Council

Westminster City Council v Great Portland Estates Plc; *sub nom* Great Portland Estates Plc v Westminster City Council [1985] A.C. 661; [1984] 3 W.L.R. 1035; [1984] 3 All E.R. 744; (1985) 50 P. & C.R. 34; [1985] J.P.L. 108; (1984) 81 L.S.G. 3501; (1984) 128 S.J. 784, HL; reversing (1985) 50 P. & C.R. 20; [1984] J.P.L. 510, CA (Civ Div) ........ *Digested,* 84/**3413**: *Applied* 92/450, 95/4767, 01/4683, 01/4762: *Considered* 85/3437, 90/4428, 91/3561, 92/4277, 93/3938, 97/4090, 98/4213, 00/5658, 01/4708, 02/3733, 14/2373: *Distinguished* 92/4264: *Followed* 97/2357, 97/4070, 01/4733, 10/2590: *Referred to* 84/3442, 93/3947

Westminster City Council v McDonald [2003] EWHC 2698 (Admin); [2005] Env. L.R. 1; [2014] L.L.R. 632, DC ........ *Digested,* 05/**2894**

Westminster City Council v National Asylum Support Services see R. (on the application of Westminster City Council) v National Asylum Support Service

Westminster City Council v Sykes (2014) 17 C.C.L. Rep. 139, CP ........ *Digested,* 14/**2191**

Westshield Civil Engineering Ltd v Buckingham Group Contracting Ltd [2013] EWHC 1825 (TCC); 150 Con. L.R. 225; [2013] C.I.L.L. 3395; [2013] 28 E.G. 85 (C.S.); (2013) 163(7568) N.L.J. 21, QBD (TCC) ............ *Digested,* 14/**580**

Westshield Ltd v Whitehouse [2013] EWHC 3576 (TCC); [2014] Bus. L.R. 268; [2014] B.P.I.R. 317; [2014] 1 E.G.L.R. 1; [2014] C.I.L.L. 3457, QBD (TCC) ............ *Digested,* 14/**578**

Westwood v Knight [2011] EWPCC 11; [2011] 4 Costs L.R. 654; [2011] F.S.R. 37, PCC ............ *Digested,* 11/**1984**: *Considered* 12/482: *Followed* 14/356

WH v Warrington BC; *sub nom* H v Warrington BC [2014] EWCA Civ 398; [2014] 3 All E.R. 747; [2014] P.T.S.R. 811; [2014] B.L.G.R. 374; [2014] E.L.R. 212, CA (Civ Div); reversing [2013] UKUT 391 (AAC); [2013] E.L.R. 569, UT (AAC) ............ *Digested,* 14/**937**

WH Newson Holding Ltd v IMI Plc [2013] EWCA Civ 1377; [2014] 1 All E.R. 1132; [2014] Bus. L.R. 156; [2014] E.C.C. 8; (2013) 163(7585) N.L.J. 16, CA (Civ Div); reversing in part [2012] EWHC 3680 (Ch); [2013] Bus. L.R. 599; [2013] U.K.C.L.R. 122, Ch D ............ *Digested,* 14/**541**: *Followed* 14/549

WH Newson Holding Ltd v IMI Plc [2013] EWHC 3788 (Ch); [2014] U.K.C.L.R. 306, Ch D ............ *Digested,* 14/**549**

WHA Ltd v Revenue and Customs Commissioners [2013] UKSC 24; [2013] 2 All E.R. 907; [2013] S.T.C. 943; [2013] B.V.C. 155; [2013] S.T.I. 1769, SC; affirming [2007] EWCA Civ 728; [2007] S.T.C. 1695; [2008] 1 C.M.L.R. 21; [2007] B.T.C. 5748; [2007] B.V.C. 695; [2007] S.T.I. 1869, CA (Civ Div) ............ *Digested,* 13/**3209**: *Applied* 10/3486, 14/3087: *Considered* 08/4007, 10/3522: *Followed* 11/3561

Whaley v Whaley [2011] EWCA Civ 617; [2012] 1 F.L.R. 735; [2011] 2 F.C.R. 323; [2011] W.T.L.R. 1267; 14 I.T.E.L.R. 1; [2011] Fam. Law 804; [2011] N.P.C. 53, CA (Civ Div) ............ *Digested,* 11/**1301**: *Applied* 14/1374: *Considered* 12/1439

Wharton v Bancroft [2011] EWHC 3250 (Ch); [2012] W.T.L.R. 693, Ch D ............ *Digested,* 12/**3200**: *Applied* 14/2836, 14/2845

Wheeldon v Burrows (1879) 12 Ch. D. 31; [1874-90] All E.R. Rep. 669; (1879) 48 L.J. Ch. 853; (1879) 41 L.T. 327, CA
*Applied* 69/1158, 00/4631, 05/3403: *Considered* 70/823, 72/1109, 77/333, 80/93.u, 81/743, 83/224, 87/1231, 88/1181, 88/2088, 95/3740, 96/5016, 00/4640, 07/3429, 08/3114, 09/3183: *Distinguished* 68/1313: *Followed* 47-51/3227, 93/3007, 14/2509: *Not followed* 66/4176

Wheels Common Investment Fund Trustees Ltd v Revenue and Customs Commissioners (C-424/11) [2014] S.T.C. 495; [2013] Pens. L.R. 149; [2013] S.T.I. 589, ECJ (1st Chamber)

Whishaw v Stephens see Gulbenkian's Settlement Trusts (No.1), Re

White v Jones [1995] 2 A.C. 207; [1995] 2 W.L.R. 187; [1995] 1 All E.R. 691; [1995] 3 F.C.R. 51; (1995) 145 N.L.J. 251; (1995) 139 S.J.L.B. 83; [1995] N.P.C. 31; Times, February 17, 1995; Independent, February 17, 1995, HL; affirming [1993] 3 W.L.R. 730; [1993] 3 All E.R. 481; (1993) 90(23) L.S.G. 43; (1993) 143 N.L.J. 473; [1993] N.P.C. 37; Times, March 9, 1993; Independent, March 5, 1993, CA (Civ Div) ............ *Digested,* 95/**3701**: *Applied* 98/4593, 98/4595, 01/4507, 01/4524, 01/4538, 02/3297, 10/2290: *Considered* 96/4484, 97/331, 97/3830, 97/692, 98/3921, 98/3927, 98/3931, 98/3951, 98/4019, 00/4219, 00/4225, 01/4487, 01/4525, 04/2725, 04/2740, 08/2658, 10/2267, 11/4485, 13/2094, 13/4023, 13/4024: *Distinguished* 97/3833, 98/4584, 99/3400, 99/4050, 04/2733, 04/3673, 09/5081, 11/4493: *Followed* 97/3834, 98/4021, 00/4253, 00/4259, 01/4534, 01/4537, 02/6000, 14/511: *Referred to* 95/5841

White v Matthys see Robson (Deceased), Re

White v Mellin; *sub nom* Mellin v White [1895] A.C. 154, HL; reversing [1894] 3 Ch. 276, CA
*Cited* 94/4290: *Considered* 14/2995

White v Nursing and Midwifery Council [2014] EWHC 520 (Admin); [2014] Med. L.R. 205, QBD (Admin) ............ *Digested,* 14/**287**

White v Revenue and Customs Commissioners [2014] UKFTT 214 (TC); [2014] S.T.I. 1877, FTT (Tax)

White v Troutbeck SA; *sub nom* Troutbeck SA v White [2013] EWCA Civ 1171; [2013] I.R.L.R. 949; [2014] I.C.R. D5, CA (Civ Div); affirming [2013] I.R.L.R. 286, EAT *Digested,* 14/**1066**

White (Pamela) v White (Martin) [2001] 1 A.C. 596; [2000] 3 W.L.R. 1571; [2001] 1 All E.R. 1; [2000] 2 F.L.R. 981; [2000] 3 F.C.R. 555; [2001] Fam. Law 12; (2000) 97(43) L.S.G. 38; (2000) 150 N.L.J. 1716; (2000) 144 S.J.L.B. 266; [2000] N.P.C. 111; Times, October 31, 2000; Independent, November 1, 2000; Daily Telegraph, November 7, 2000, HL; affirming [1999] Fam. 304; [1999] 2 W.L.R. 1213; [1998] 4 All E.R. 659; [1998] 2 F.L.R. 310; [1998] 3 F.C.R. 45; [1998] Fam. Law 522; Times, July 13, 1998; Independent, June 29, 1998, CA (Civ Div) ........ *Digested,* 00/**2530**: *Applied* 01/2634, 01/5156, 02/1678, 02/1679, 02/1682, 02/1687, 02/1690, 03/1581, 03/1589, 05/1656, 06/1623, 06/1626, 07/1695, 07/1700, 12/1423: *Considered* 01/2632, 01/2635, 01/2639, 03/1579, 04/1515, 04/4216, 05/1688, 06/1633, 06/4090, 07/1691, 07/1706, 08/1422, 09/2739, 10/1288, 10/1292, 10/3212, 11/1311, 12/1427, 12/1440, 14/1361: *Followed* 01/2633, 09/1491, 09/1504, 11/1296, 11/1302, 13/1309: *Referred to* 12/1421

White Horse Distillers Ltd v Gregson Associates Ltd [1984] R.P.C. 61, Ch D *Considered* 14/289: *Not applied* 85/3389

White Rosebay Shipping SA v Hong Kong Chain Glory Shipping Ltd [2013] EWHC 1355 (Comm); [2013] 2 All E.R. (Comm) 449; [2013] 2 Lloyd's Rep. 618; [2013] 2 C.L.C. 884, QBD (Comm) ........ *Digested,* 13/**2838**: *Applied* 14/118

Whitefields Golf Club Ltd v Revenue and Customs Commissioners [2014] UKFTT 458 (TC); [2014] S.T.I. 2051, FTT (Tax)

Whitefields Golf Club Ltd v Revenue and Customs Commissioners [2014] UKFTT 495 (TC); [2014] S.T.I. 2099, FTT (Tax)

Whitehead v Searle; *sub nom* Hibbert Pownall & Newton (A Firm) v Whitehead; McLeish (Deceased), Re [2008] EWCA Civ 285; [2009] 1 W.L.R. 549; (2008) 102 B.M.L.R. 57; [2008] P.N.L.R. 25; (2008) 152(16) S.J.L.B. 32; Times, May 14, 2008, CA (Civ Div); reversing in part [2007] EWHC 1060 (QB); (2007) 151 S.J.L.B. 810, QBD ........ *Digested,* 08/**2653**: *Considered* 14/2212, 14/2281

Whitfield v Al Jaber see Hotel Company 42 The Calls Ltd, Re

Whiting, Re [2014] C.O.P.L.R. 107, Fam Div ........ *Digested,* 14/**320**

Whittlestone v BJP Home Support Ltd [2014] I.C.R. 275; [2014] I.R.L.R. 176, EAT ...... *Digested,* 14/**1092**

Wickland (Holdings) Ltd v Telchadder see Telchadder v Wickland (Holdings) Ltd

Wieland v Land Berlin (C-503/12) see Specht v Land Berlin (C-501/12)

Wiggin Alloys v Jenkins [1981] I.R.L.R. 275, EAT ........ *Digested,* 81/**958**: *Considered* 00/2148: *Followed* 14/1073

Wiggins v Regent Wealth Ltd; *sub nom* Regent Wealth Ltd v Wiggins [2014] EWCA Civ 1078; [2014] H.L.R. 45; [2014] L. & T.R. 29; [2014] 3 E.G.L.R. 157, CA (Civ Div)

Wigginton v Broxtowe BC [2014] P.A.D. 9, Planning Inspector

Wijesundera v Heathrow 3PL Logistics Ltd [2014] I.C.R. 523, EAT ........ *Digested,* 14/**1119**

Wildfowl and Wetland Trust v Revenue and Customs Commissioners [2013] UKFTT 423 (TC); [2014] L.L.R. 216; [2013] S.T.I. 3141, FTT (Tax)

Wildin v Revenue and Customs Commissioners [2014] UKFTT 459 (TC); [2014] S.T.I. 2727, FTT (Tax)

Wilke v Land Berlin (C-505/12) see Specht v Land Berlin (C-501/12)

Wilkin v Goldthorpe [1998] E.L.R. 345, QBD ........ *Digested,* 98/**1980**: *Considered* 14/906: *Followed* 13/900

Wilkinson v Anjum see W (A Child) (Abduction: Committal), Re

Wilkinson v Kerdene Ltd [2013] EWCA Civ 44; [2013] 2 E.G.L.R. 163; [2013] 7 E.G. 98 (C.S.); [2013] 1 P. & C.R. DG19, CA (Civ Div) ........ *Digested,* 14/**2510**

Wilkinson v London SHA (Costs) [2012] EWPCC 55, PCC *Applied* 14/364

William Denby & Sons Ltd Sick and Benevolent Fund, Re; *sub nom* Rowling v Wilks [1971] 1 W.L.R. 973; [1971] 2 All E.R. 1196; (1971) 115 S.J. 290, Ch D ........ *Digested,* 71/**1229**: *Considered* 94/3626, 14/526

William Tomkinson & Sons Ltd v Parochial Church Council of St Michael (1990) 6 Const. L.J. 319, Unknown court ........ *Digested,* 91/**337**: *Applied* 05/654: *Considered* 99/792, 14/597: *Followed* 96/1153

Williams v Arkle (1874-75) L.R. 7 H.L. 606, HL *Distinguished* 14/2834

Williams v Bennett see Science & Media LLP, Re

Williams v Central Bank of Nigeria; *sub nom* Central Bank of Nigeria v Williams [2014] UKSC 10; [2014] A.C. 1189; [2014] 2 W.L.R. 355; [2014] 2 All E.R. 489; [2014] W.T.L.R. 873; 16 I.T.E.L.R. 740; (2014) 164(7596) N.L.J. 16; Times, March 5, 2014, SC; reversing [2012] EWCA Civ 415; [2013] Q.B. 499; [2012] 3 W.L.R. 1501; [2012] 3 All E.R. 579; [2012] C.P. Rep. 28; [2012] W.T.L.R. 745; (2012) 162 N.L.J. 576; [2012] 2 P. & C.R. DG6; Times, July 23, 2012, CA (Civ Div); affirming [2011] EWHC 876 (QB), QBD ........ *Digested,* 14/**3023**: *Applied* 14/2991: *Followed* 14/511

Williams v City and Council of Swansea [2014] P.A.D. 51, Planning Inspector

Williams v Glover see GP Aviation Group International Ltd, Re

Williams v Hopkins see Rees Will Trusts, Re

Williams v Kiley (t/a CK Supermarkets Ltd) (No.1) [2002] EWCA Civ 1645; [2003] L. & T.R. 20; [2003] 1 E.G.L.R. 46; [2003] 06 E.G. 147; [2002] 49 E.G. 122 (C.S.); (2003) 100(4) L.S.G. 32; (2002) 152 N.L.J. 1809; (2002) 146 S.J.L.B. 270; [2002] N.P.C. 149; [2003] 1 P. & C.R. DG20; Times, December 5, 2002, CA (Civ Div) ........ *Digested,* 03/**2765**: *Followed* 14/1979

Williams v Mohammed [2012] B.P.I.R. 238, Ch D ........ *Digested,* 12/**1814**: *Applied* 14/1776

Williams v Secretary of State for Communities and Local Government [2013] EWCA Civ 958; [2014] J.P.L. 124, CA (Civ Div); reversing [2012] EWHC 3466 (Admin); [2013] J.P.L. 692, QBD (Admin) ........ *Digested,* 14/**2378**

Williams v Watson Luxury Coaches [1990] I.C.R. 536; [1990] I.R.L.R. 164, EAT ........ *Digested,* 91/**1695**: *Considered* 14/1089

Williams v Westminster City Council [2014] P.A.D. 40, Planning Inspector

Williamson v Secretary of State for Education and Employment see R. (on the application of Williamson) v Secretary of State for Education and Employment

Willingale (Inspector of Taxes) v International Commercial Bank Ltd [1978] A.C. 834; [1978] 2 W.L.R. 452; [1978] 1 All E.R. 754; [1978] S.T.C. 75; 52 T.C. 242; [1978] T.R. 5; (1978) 122 S.J. 129, HL; affirming [1977] Ch. 78; [1977] 3 W.L.R. 109; [1977] 2 All E.R. 618; [1977] S.T.C. 183; [1977] T.R. 33; (1977) 121 S.J. 337, CA (Civ Div); affirming [1976] 1 W.L.R. 657; [1976] 2 All E.R. 468; [1976] S.T.C. 188; [1976] T.R. 77; (1976) 120 S.J. 317, Ch D ........ *Digested,* 78/**365**: *Applied* 14/2920: *Considered* 83/1945: *Followed* 11/3367

Willis v MRJ Rundell & Associates Ltd [2013] EWHC 2923 (TCC); [2013] 6 Costs L.R. 924; [2013] 3 E.G.L.R. 13; [2013] C.I.L.L. 3428, QBD (TCC) ........ *Digested,* 14/**354**

Willmott Growers Group Inc v Willmott Forests Ltd [2013] HCA 51; [2014] B.P.I.R. 785, HC (Aus)

Willowtech Ltd v Neath Port Talbot CBC [2010] UKUT 44 (LC); [2010] R.V.R. 314, UT (Lands) ........ *Digested,* 11/**2519**: *Considered* 14/2359

Wilson v De Keyser Ltd see De Keyser Ltd v Wilson

Wilson v First County Trust Ltd (No.2); *sub nom* Wilson v Secretary of State for Trade and Industry [2003] UKHL 40; [2004] 1 A.C. 816; [2003] 3 W.L.R. 568; [2003] 4 All E.R. 97; [2003] 2 All E.R. (Comm) 491; [2003] H.R.L.R. 33; [2003] U.K.H.R.R. 1085; (2003) 100(35) L.S.G. 39; (2003) 147 S.J.L.B. 872; Times, July 11, 2003; Independent, November 3, 2003, HL; reversing [2001] EWCA Civ 633; [2002] Q.B. 74; [2001] 3 W.L.R. 42; [2001] 3 All E.R. 229; [2001] 2 All E.R. (Comm) 134; [2001] E.C.C. 37; [2001] H.R.L.R. 44; [2001] U.K.H.R.R. 1175; (2001) 98(24) L.S.G. 44; (2001) 145 S.J.L.B. 125; Times, May 16, 2001; Independent, May 8, 2001; Daily Telegraph, May 8, 2001, CA (Civ Div) ........ *Digested,* 04/**628**: *Applied* 01/2315, 04/2222, 05/1410, 05/190, 05/3376, 05/672, 06/2735, 08/3105, 08/860, 10/3523, 12/3366, 13/3058, 13/3182, 13/409, 14/610: *Considered* 01/100, 01/3504, 04/1312, 04/3581, 05/17, 09/2137, 10/3925, 10/4537, 10/594, 12/1205, 12/1654: *Followed* 07/3293, 14/2241

Wilson v Howard Pawnbrokers; *sub nom* Wilson v Howard [2005] EWCA Civ 147, CA (Civ Div) *Distinguished* 14/608

Wilson v Howard see Wilson v Howard Pawnbrokers

Wilson v Jaymarke Estates Ltd [2007] UKHL 29; 2007 S.C. (H.L.) 135; 2007 S.L.T. 958; 2007 S.C.L.R. 712; [2007] B.C.C. 883; (2007) 151 S.J.L.B. 854; 2007 G.W.D. 26-450; Times, June 28, 2007, HL; affirming 2006 S.C.L.R. 510, IH (1 Div); affirming 2002 G.W.D. 28-962, Sh Ct (Grampian) ........ *Digested,* 07/**4976**: *Referred to* 14/2373

Wilson v Monaghan see Colour Trusts, Re

Wilson v Secretary of State for Trade and Industry see Wilson v First County Trust Ltd (No.2)

Wilson v United Kingdom (Admissibility) (10601/09) (2014) 58 E.H.R.R. SE10, ECHR

Wilson (D) (Birmingham) v Metropolitan Property Developments [1975] 2 All E.R. 814, CA (Civ Div) ........ *Digested,* 75/**318**: *Applied* 14/492: *Considered* 14/1814

Wilson (Inspector of Taxes) v Clayton [2004] EWCA Civ 1657; [2005] S.T.C. 157; [2005] I.R.L.R. 108; 77 T.C. 1; [2004] B.T.C. 477; [2004] S.T.I. 2543; (2005) 102(2) L.S.G. 30; (2005) 149 S.J.L.B. 24; Times, January 12, 2005, CA (Civ Div); affirming [2004] EWHC 898 (Ch); [2004] S.T.C. 1022; [2004] I.R.L.R. 611; [2004] S.T.I. 1121; (2004) 101(19) L.S.G. 29; Times, June 7, 2004, Ch D ........ *Digested,* 05/**4071**: *Applied* 14/2911

Wiltonpark Ltd v Revenue and Customs Commissioners [2014] UKFTT 115 (TC); [2014] L.L.R. 641; [2014] S.T.I. 947, FTT (Tax)

Wiltshire CC v F see BB (A Child), Re

Wiltshire Council v N see A (Care Proceedings: Learning Disabled Parent), Re

Wimbledon Construction Co 2000 Ltd v Vago [2005] EWHC 1086 (TCC); [2005] B.L.R. 374; 101 Con. L.R. 99, QBD (TCC) ........ *Digested,* 06/**664**: *Applied* 07/526, 08/607, 10/559, 10/560, 11/495, 12/600, 14/579, 14/580, 14/581: *Considered* 09/652, 09/656

Winchester City Council v Handcock (Valuation Officer) [2006] R.A. 265, Lands Tr ...... *Digested,* 07/**3345**: *Applied* 14/2129

Windermere Marina Village Ltd v Wild [2014] UKUT 163 (LC); [2014] L. & T.R. 30; [2014] 3 E.G.L.R. 12, UT (Lands)

Windle v Secretary of State for Justice; *joined case* Arada v Windle [2014] I.R.L.R. 914; [2014] Eq. L.R. 662, EAT

Windsurfing Chiemsee Produktions und Vertriebs GmbH v Attenberger (C-109/97) see Windsurfing Chiemsee Produktions- und Vertriebs GmbH v Boots- und Segelzubehor Walter Huber (C-108/97)

Windsurfing Chiemsee Produktions- und Vertriebs GmbH v Boots- und Segelzubehor Walter Huber (C-108/97); *joined case* Windsurfing Chiemsee Produktions und Vertriebs GmbH v Attenberger (C-109/97) [2000] Ch. 523; [2000] 2 W.L.R. 205; [1999] E.C.R. I-2779; [1999] E.T.M.R. 585; Times, May 18, 1999, ECJ ........ *Digested,* 99/**3530**: *Applied* 00/3705, 00/3718, 04/2372, 08/2405: *Considered* 00/3724, 00/3758, 02/2885, 03/2651, 04/2398, 08/2397, 13/1825, 14/1872: *Followed* 05/2557, 14/1917

Winslet v Associated Newspapers Ltd [2009] EWHC 2735 (QB); [2010] E.M.L.R. 11, QBD ........ *Digested,* 10/**842**: *Considered* 14/840

Wintershall (E&P) Ltd v Revenue and Customs Commissioners [2014] UKFTT 318 (TC); [2014] S.T.I. 2183, FTT (Tax)

Winterwerp v Netherlands (A/33) (1979-80) 2 E.H.R.R. 387, ECHR ........ *Digested,* 81/**1089**: *Applied* 04/2686, 06/2160, 06/5461, 07/2197, 14/2164: *Considered* 02/3239, 09/2024, 09/2698, 10/2263, 12/2280: *Distinguished* 00/3171

Wise v Jimenez [2014] W.T.L.R. 163; [2014] 1 P. & C.R. DG9, Ch D ........ *Digested,* 14/**3028**

WM (Democratic Republic of Congo) v Secretary of State for the Home Department; *joined case* Secretary of State for the Home Department v AR (Afghanistan) [2006] EWCA Civ 1495; [2007] Imm. A.R. 337; [2007] I.N.L.R. 126; (2006) 103(45) L.S.G. 27; Times, December 1, 2006, CA (Civ Div) ........ *Digested,* 07/**2295**: *Considered* 09/2075, 11/1716: *Followed* 11/1715, 14/1671

Wm Morrison Supermarkets Plc v MasterCard Inc [2013] EWHC 1071 (Comm); [2013] U.K.C.L.R. 197, QBD (Comm) ........ *Digested,* 13/**436**: *Applied* 14/529

Wm Morrison Supermarkets Plc v MasterCard Inc [2013] EWHC 3082 (Comm); [2014] U.K.C.L.R. 49, QBD (Comm) ........ *Digested,* 14/**486**

Wm Morrison Supermarkets Plc v MasterCard Inc [2013] EWHC 3271 (Comm); [2014] U.K.C.L.R. 56, QBD (Comm) ........ *Digested,* 14/**429**

WN v Secretary of State for the Home Department; *sub nom* WN (Surendran: Credibility: New Evidence: Democratic Republic of Congo), Re [2004] UKIAT 213; [2005] I.N.L.R. 340, IAT ........ *Digested,* 05/**2153**: *Applied* 14/1644

WN (Gambia) v Secretary of State for the Home Department see JD (Congo) v Secretary of State for the Home Department

WN (Surendran: Credibility: New Evidence: Democratic Republic of Congo), Re see WN v Secretary of State for the Home Department

Wnek v Director of Border Revenue [2013] UKFTT 575 (TC); [2014] 1 C.M.L.R. 48, FTT (Tax) ........ *Digested,* 14/**821**

Woking Museum and Arts and Crafts Centre v Revenue and Customs Commissioners [2014] UKFTT 176 (TC); [2014] S.T.I. 1606, FTT (Tax)

Wokingham BC v Oxford Diocesan Board of Finance see Oxford Diocesan Board of Finance v Secretary of State for Communities and Local Government

Wokuri v Kassam [2012] EWHC 105 (Ch); [2013] Ch. 80; [2012] 3 W.L.R. 427; [2012] 2 All E.R. 1195; [2012] I.C.R. 1283; (2012) 109(20) L.S.G. 26; Times, February 7, 2012, Ch D ........ *Digested,* 12/**1076**: *Applied* 13/1019: *Considered* 14/1056

Wong v Igen Ltd (formerly Leeds Careers Guidance); *sub nom* Igen Ltd (formerly Leeds Careers Guidance) v Wong; Brunel University v Webster; Chambelin Solicitors v Emokpae; *joined cases* Emokpae v Chamberlin Solicitors; Webster v Brunel University [2005] EWCA Civ 142; [2005] 3 All E.R. 812; [2005] I.C.R. 931; [2005] I.R.L.R. 258; (2005) 102(13) L.S.G. 28; (2005) 149 S.J.L.B. 264; Times, March 3, 2005, CA (Civ Div); affirming UKEAT/0944/03/RN, EAT .......... *Digested,* 05/**1221**: *Applied* 06/1349, 06/1354, 06/1368, 07/1184, 07/1401, 08/4301, 09/4267: *Approved* 12/1072: *Considered* 07/1388, 07/1433, 08/1181, 11/4223, 12/1033, 12/1117, 13/1032, 13/1033: *Followed* 10/1123, 11/1103, 14/1010: *Referred to* 13/986

Wong v Manchester City Council [2013] UKUT 431 (LC); [2014] R.V.R. 134, UT (Lands) ........ *Digested,* 14/**2501**

Wong Liu Sheung v Burt [2004] NZCA 174; [2005] W.T.L.R. 291; (2004-05) 7 I.T.E.L.R. 263, CA (NZ) ........ *Digested,* 05/**4317**: *Considered* 14/3027

Wood v British Coal Corp see Smoker v London Fire and Civil Defence Authority

Wood v Commissioner of Police of the Metropolis see R. (on the application of Wood) v Commissioner of Police of the Metropolis

Wood v Gorbunova; *sub nom* Berezovsky (Deceased), Re [2013] EWHC 1935 (Ch); [2014] 1 B.C.L.C. 487; [2013] 5 Costs L.R. 713, Ch D ........ *Digested,* 13/**346**

Wood v Revenue and Customs Commissioners [2014] UKFTT 532 (TC); [2014] S.T.I. 2163, FTT (Tax)

Wood v Waddington [2014] EWHC 1358 (Ch); [2014] 2 E.G.L.R. 151; [2014] 2 P. & C.R. DG11, Ch D

Wood Preservation v Prior [1969] 1 W.L.R. 1077; [1969] 1 All E.R. 364; 45 T.C. 112; [1968] T.R. 353; (1968) 112 S.J. 927, CA; affirming [1968] 2 All E.R. 849; [1968] T.R. 37; (1968) 112 S.J. 275, Ch D ........ *Digested,* 69/**1676**: *Applied* 70/2715, 77/2890, 14/2878: *Distinguished* 92/605

Wood's Estate, Re 17 I.T.E.L.R. 166, Sup Ct (NT) (Sgl judge)

Wood-Luxford v Wood [2013] NZSC 153; 16 I.T.E.L.R. 848, Sup Ct (NZ)

Woodcock Holdings Ltd v Mid-Sussex DC [2014] P.A.D. 54, Planning Inspector

Woodhouse v Consignia Plc; *joined case* Steliou v Compton [2002] EWCA Civ 275; [2002] 1 W.L.R. 2558; [2002] 2 All E.R. 737; [2002] C.P. Rep. 42; (2002) 99(16) L.S.G. 38; (2002) 152 N.L.J. 517; (2002) 146 S.J.L.B. 76; Times, April 5, 2002; Independent, March 13, 2002, CA (Civ Div) ........ *Digested,* 02/**307**: *Applied* 02/455, 05/413: *Considered* 12/484: *Distinguished* 14/457

Woodhouse v Nigerian Produce Marketing Co Ltd see Woodhouse AC Israel Cocoa SA v Nigerian Produce Marketing Co Ltd

Woodhouse v West North West Homes Leeds Ltd [2013] I.R.L.R. 773; [2013] Eq. L.R. 796, EAT ........ *Digested,* 14/**1107**: *Doubted* 14/1093

Woodhouse AC Israel Cocoa SA v Nigerian Produce Marketing Co Ltd; *sub nom* Woodhouse v Nigerian Produce Marketing Co Ltd [1972] A.C. 741; [1972] 2 W.L.R. 1090; [1972] 2 All E.R. 271; [1972] 1 Lloyd's Rep. 439; (1972) 116 S.J. 329, HL; affirming [1971] 2 Q.B. 23; [1971] 2 W.L.R. 272; [1971] 1 All E.R. 665; [1971] 1 Lloyd's Rep. 25; (1970) 115 S.J. 56; Times, November 25, 1970, CA (Civ Div); reversing [1970] 2 All E.R. 124; [1970] 1 Lloyd's Rep. 295, QBD (Comm) ........ *Digested,* 72/**495**: *Applied* 77/2669, 04/2209: *Considered* 80/2791, 82/421, 92/3611, 95/1264, 14/1760: *Followed* 01/931, 02/2734, 13/1161

Woodland v Essex CC see Woodland v Swimming Teachers Association

Woodland v Swimming Teachers Association; *sub nom* Woodland v Essex CC [2013] UKSC 66; [2014] A.C. 537; [2013] 3 W.L.R. 1227; [2014] 1 All E.R. 482; [2014] E.L.R. 67; (2013) 16 C.C.L. Rep. 532; [2014] P.I.Q.R. P6; (2013) 163(7582) N.L.J. 15; (2013) 157(41) S.J.L.B. 39; Times, November 1, 2013, SC; reversing [2012] EWCA Civ 239; [2014] A.C. 537; [2013] 3 W.L.R. 853; [2012] B.L.G.R. 879; [2012] E.L.R. 327; [2012] P.I.Q.R. P12; [2012] Med. L.R. 419, CA (Civ Div); affirming [2011] EWHC 2631 (QB); [2012] E.L.R. 76; [2012] P.I.Q.R. P3; (2011) 155(41) S.J.L.B. 31, QBD (Manchester) ........ *Digested,* 14/**2200**

Woodland Trust v Loring see Loring v Woodland Trust

Woodlands Oak Ltd v Conwell [2011] EWCA Civ 254; [2011] B.L.R. 365, CA (Civ Div) *Digested,* 11/**531**: *Considered* 14/597

Woods v Legal Complaints Review Officer 16 I.T.E.L.R. 154, HC (NZ)

Woods v WM Car Services (Peterborough) Ltd [1982] Com. L.R. 208; [1982] I.C.R. 693; [1982] I.R.L.R. 413, CA (Civ Div); affirming [1981] I.C.R. 666; [1981] I.R.L.R. 347; Times, June 24, 1981, EAT ........ *Digested,* 83/**1204**: *Applied* 91/1612, 91/2725, 04/1196, 07/1320: *Cited* 14/1023: *Considered* 84/1194, 99/838, 03/1221: *Followed* 11/1049

Woodward v Smith 17 I.T.E.L.R. 517, HC (NZ)

Woolley v UP Global Sourcing UK Ltd [2014] EWHC 493 (Ch); [2014] F.S.R. 37, Ch D ........ *Digested,* 14/**1887**

Woolway (Valuation Officer) v Mazars LLP [2013] EWCA Civ 368; [2013] 2 E.G.L.R. 129; [2013] R.A. 263; [2013] 17 E.G. 99 (C.S.), CA (Civ Div); affirming [2012] UKUT 165 (LC); [2012] 3 E.G.L.R. 73; [2012] 37 E.G. 128; [2012] R.V.R. 203, UT (Lands) ........ *Digested,* 13/**2410**: *Considered* 14/2137

Woolwich Equitable Building Society v Inland Revenue Commissioners [1993] A.C. 70; [1992] 3 W.L.R. 366; [1992] 3 All E.R. 737; [1992] S.T.C. 657; (1993) 5 Admin. L.R. 265; 65 T.C. 265; (1992) 142 N.L.J. 1196; (1992) 136 S.J.L.B. 230; Times, July 22, 1992; Independent, August 13, 1992; Guardian, August 19, 1992, HL; affirming [1991] 3 W.L.R. 790; [1991] 4 All E.R. 577; [1991] S.T.C. 364; (1991) 135 S.J.L.B. 46; Times, May 27, 1991, CA (Civ Div); reversing [1989] 1 W.L.R. 137; [1989] S.T.C. 111; (1989) 133 S.J. 291, QBD ........ *Digested,* 92/**2508**: *Applied* 94/4567, 07/3438: *Cited* 12/3430, 14/2874: *Considered* 94/3900, 94/6018, 05/4129, 06/4141, 07/3973, 08/3841, 10/3268, 10/3512, 12/3251, 13/1963, 13/3219: *Distinguished* 96/5578, 01/5024: *Followed* 97/1735

Woolwich Equitable Building Society v Marshall [1952] Ch. 1; [1951] 2 All E.R. 769; [1951] 2 T.L.R. 783, Ch D ........ *Digested,* 47-51/**6347**: *Applied* 53/2309, 54/2109: *Considered* 14/2505

Worcestershire CC v J see R. (on the application of J) v Worcestershire CC

Worcestershire CC v JJ [2014] UKUT 406 (AAC); [2014] E.L.R. 553, UT (AAC)

World Marine & General Insurances Pty Ltd, Re see HIH Casualty & General Insurance Ltd, Re

Worldwide Corp Ltd v GPT Ltd LTA 98/7526/3, CA (Civ Div) ........ *Digested,* 99/**499**: *Applied* 12/2295, 14/462: *Considered* 99/3517, 12/303: *Followed* 11/389: *Referred to* 99/497

Wotherspoon (John Maxwell) v HM Advocate 1978 J.C. 74, HCJ ........ *Digested,* 80/**3180**: *Applied* 07/2075: *Considered* 14/772

Wray v JW Lees & Co (Brewers) Ltd [2012] I.C.R. 43, EAT ........ *Digested,* 12/**1112**: *Considered* 14/1091

Wright v North Ayrshire Council [2014] I.C.R. 77; [2014] I.R.L.R. 4, EAT (SC) ........ *Digested,* 14/**3500**

Wright v Revenue and Customs Commissioners [2013] UKUT 481 (TCC); [2013] B.T.C. 2048; [2014] S.T.I. 249, UT (Tax); reversing [2011] UKFTT 824 (TC); [2012] S.T.I. 222, FTT (Tax) ........ *Digested,* 14/**399**

Wright v Scottbridge Construction Ltd see Scottbridge Construction Ltd v Wright

Wright v Thompson (Unreported, May 15, 2014), CC (Gateshead) [*Morgan Brien, Barrister, Trinity Chambers, The Custom House, Quayside, Newcastle-Upon-Tyne*] ........ *Digested,* 14/**2344**

Wright-Gordon v Legister; *sub nom* Gordon v Legister [2014] EWHC 2041 (Ch); [2014] W.T.L.R. 1675, Ch D

WT (Foreign Surrogacy), Re [2014] EWHC 1303 (Fam); [2014] Fam. Law 1117, Fam Div

WT Ramsay Ltd v Inland Revenue Commissioners; *joined case* Eilbeck (Inspector of Taxes) v Rawling [1982] A.C. 300; [1981] 2 W.L.R. 449; [1981] 1 All E.R. 865; [1981] S.T.C. 174; 54 T.C. 101; [1982] T.R. 123; (1981) 11 A.T.R. 752; (1981) 125 S.J. 220, HL; affirming [1979] 1 W.L.R. 974; [1979] 3 All E.R. 213; [1979] S.T.C. 582; (1979) 123 S.J. 456, CA (Civ Div); affirming [1978] 1 W.L.R. 1313; [1978] 2 All E.R. 321; 8 B.L.R. 169; [1978] T.R. 113; (1978) 122 S.J. 249, Ch D *Digested,* 81/**1385**: *Applied* 82/1576, 83/1980, 84/270, 85/3407, 86/2203, 86/258, 86/3204, 88/257, 91/2090, 92/2518, 93/2296, 95/876, 96/1310, 97/2975, 97/2979, 00/4942, 00/5043, 01/5237, 03/4233, 05/4037, 05/4084, 05/4158, 08/3661, 09/3741, 09/3755, 10/3290, 13/3010, 13/3044, 13/3096: *Cited* 97/1073: *Considered* 82/476, 85/1909, 85/243, 86/262, 87/2036, 87/274, 90/2685, 92/2505, 92/611, 96/3958, 96/428, 98/4627, 00/4916, 01/5199, 02/4457, 08/3765, 09/3781, 09/3876, 10/3344, 12/3332, 14/2851, 14/2975, 14/3807: *Distinguished* 82/1582, 83/1955, 87/282, 92/2519, 93/337, 95/2750, 98/4631, 99/4709: *Followed* 03/4145, 10/3249, 11/3285, 11/3366, 11/3383, 12/3233, 13/3095: *Referred to* 82/485, 85/456, 95/527

Wuhan Guoyu Logistics Group Co Ltd v Emporiki Bank of Greece SA [2012] EWCA Civ 1629; [2013] 1 All E.R. (Comm) 1191; [2014] 1 Lloyd's Rep. 266; [2012] 2 C.L.C. 986; [2013] B.L.R. 74; [2013] C.I.L.L. 3300; [2013] Bus. L.R. D76, CA (Civ Div); reversing [2012] EWHC 1715 (Comm); [2012] 2 All E.R. (Comm) 685; [2013] 1 Lloyd's Rep. 161; [2012] C.I.L.L. 3236, QBD (Comm) .................. *Digested,* 13/**2832**

Wuhan Guoyu Logistics Group Co Ltd v Emporiki Bank of Greece SA [2013] EWCA Civ 1679; [2014] 1 All E.R. (Comm) 870; [2014] 1 Lloyd's Rep. 273; [2014] 1 C.L.C. 40; [2014] B.L.R. 119; [2014] C.I.L.L. 3460, CA (Civ Div) ....................... *Digested,* 14/**2734**

Wyatt v Vince see Vince v Wyatt

Wychavon DC v Secretary of State for Communities and Local Government; *sub nom* R. (on the application of Wychavon DC) v Secretary of State for Communities and Local Government [2008] EWCA Civ 692; [2009] P.T.S.R. 19; [2009] 1 P. & C.R. 15; [2009] J.P.L. 197; Times, July 1, 2008, CA (Civ Div); reversing [2007] EWHC 3209 (Admin); [2008] J.P.L. 1193, QBD (Admin) ......................... *Digested,* 08/**2969**: *Applied* 10/2626, 13/2311, 14/2407: *Considered* 10/2572

Wyche v Careforce Group Plc [2013] EWHC 3282 (Comm); [2014] 1 Costs L.R. 1, QBD (Comm) ........................................................................................ *Digested,* 14/**459**: *Approved* 14/445: *Considered* 14/452

Wynn Realisations Ltd v Vogue Holdings Inc [1999] S.T.C. 524; [1999] B.T.C. 5224; [1999] B.V.C. 245, CA (Civ Div) ........................................................................ *Digested,* 99/**4968**: *Considered* 14/632

X v Austria (19010/07) [2013] 1 F.C.R. 387; (2013) 57 E.H.R.R. 14; 35 B.H.R.C. 85; [2013] Eq. L.R. 396, ECHR (Grand Chamber)

X v Federal Tax Administration 17 I.T.L. Rep. 64, BG (Swi)

X v Latvia (27853/09) [2014] 1 F.L.R. 1135; (2014) 59 E.H.R.R. 3; [2014] Fam. Law 269, ECHR (Grand Chamber)

X v Liverpool City Council [2005] EWCA Civ 1173; [2006] 1 W.L.R. 375; [2006] 2 All E.R. 202; [2006] 1 F.L.R. 342; [2005] 3 F.C.R. 303; [2006] B.L.G.R. 453; [2006] Fam. Law 94; Times, October 19, 2005; Independent, October 25, 2005, CA (Civ Div) ........................................................................................................ *Digested,* 05/**1567**: *Followed* 11/1362, 14/2463

X v Minister van Financien (C-302/12) [2014] R.T.R. 11; [2013] S.T.I. 3572, ECJ (2nd Chamber)

X v Netherlands (7602/1976) (1976) 7 D. & R. 161, ECHR *Considered* 14/2766

X v Nova Electro International (Societe) (In Liquidation) [2014] I.L.Pr. 23, Cass (F)

X v Royal Bank of Scotland [2014] I.L.Pr. 22, Cass (F)

X v Service Navigation de Plaisance Boat Service (Societe) [2014] I.L.Pr. 24, Cass (F)

X v United Kingdom (7566/76) (Unreported, December 11, 1976), ECHR *Considered* 14/1633

X v Y [2014] I.L.Pr. 4, Cass (F)

X v Y [2014] I.L.Pr. 30, Cass (F)

X v Y (Employment: Sex Offender); *sub nom* X v Y (Unfair Dismissal) [2004] EWCA Civ 662; [2004] I.C.R. 1634; [2004] I.R.L.R. 625; [2004] U.K.H.R.R. 1172; (2004) 148 S.J.L.B. 697; Times, June 16, 2004; Independent, June 9, 2004, CA (Civ Div); affirming [2003] I.C.R. 1138; [2003] I.R.L.R. 561, EAT ....................... *Digested,* 04/**1312**: *Applied* 13/1065: *Considered* 09/2056, 14/1022

X v Y (Unfair Dismissal) see X v Y (Employment: Sex Offender)

X v Y see Z (A Child), Re

X v Z (Children) see Z (Children) (Application for Release of DNA Profiles), Re

X (A Child) (Capacity to Consent to Termination), Re [2014] EWHC 1871 (Fam); (2014) 139 B.M.L.R. 143; [2014] Fam. Law 1227, Fam Div

X (A Child) (Parental Order: Time Limit), Re; *sub nom* X (A Child) (Surrogacy: Time Limit), Re [2014] EWHC 3135 (Fam); [2014] Fam. Law 1681, Fam Div (Birmingham)

X (A Child) (Residence and Contact: Rights of Media Attendance), Re [2009] EWHC 1728 (Fam); [2009] E.M.L.R. 26; [2009] 2 F.L.R. 1467; [2009] 3 F.C.R. 370; [2009] Fam. Law 930; Times, July 27, 2009, Fam Div ....................................... *Digested,* 09/**1603**: *Applied* 14/1279: *Considered* 11/1331

X (A Child) (Surrogacy: Time Limit), Re see X (A Child) (Parental Order: Time Limit), Re

X (A Child), Re; *sub nom* X (Emergency Protection Orders), Re [2006] EWHC 510 (Fam); [2006] 2 F.L.R. 701; [2007] 1 F.C.R. 551; [2006] Fam. Law 627; Times, April 21, 2006, Fam Div .......................................................................................... *Digested,* 06/**1676**: *Applied* 13/396, 14/1292

X (Adopted Child: Access to Court File), Re [2014] EWFC 33; [2014] Fam. Law 1514, Fam Ct
X (Adoption Application: Gateway Requirements), Re see AB v BC (Adoption Application: Gateway Requirements)
X (aka Y) v Culture Press (Societe) [2013] E.C.C. 27; [2014] E.C.D.R. 8, Cass (F)
X (Application for Income Payments Order), Re [2014] B.P.I.R. 1081, Ch D ................ *Digested,* 14/**1797**
X (Application to Open Insolvency Proceedings), Re [2014] I.L.Pr. 35, Cass (F)
X (C-318/13) [2014] I.R.L.R. 975, ECJ (2nd Chamber)
X (Children) (Disclosure for Purposes of Criminal Proceedings), Re [2008] EWHC 242 (Fam); [2008] 3 All E.R. 958; [2008] 2 F.L.R. 944; [2008] 3 F.C.R. 23; [2008] Fam. Law 725, Fam Div ................ *Digested,* 08/**1450**: *Applied* 09/1616: *Considered* 14/1330
X (Children) (Disclosure of Judgment to Police), Re; *sub nom* A Local Authority v A Mother [2014] EWHC 278 (Fam); [2014] Fam. Law 961, Fam Div
X (Children) (Parental Order: Foreign Surrogacy), Re [2008] EWHC 3030 (Fam); [2009] Fam. 71; [2009] 2 W.L.R. 1274; [2009] 1 F.L.R. 733; [2009] 2 F.C.R. 312; (2011) 118 B.M.L.R. 1; [2009] Fam. Law 115, Fam Div ................ *Digested,* 09/**1646**: *Applied* 10/1442, 11/1457, 12/1454, 13/1334, 14/1414, 14/1415
X (Children) (Payments from Patient's Estate for Children's Maintenance), Re see A Local Authority v P
X (Children), Re [2007] EWHC 1719 (Fam); [2008] 1 F.L.R. 589; [2008] Fam. Law 23, Fam Div ................ *Digested,* 08/**1540**: *Applied* 08/1450, 09/1616: *Considered* 11/1325, 14/1330
X (Deprivation of Liberty), Re [2014] EWCOP 37; (2014) 17 C.C.L. Rep. 464; [2014] Med. L.R. 545, CP
X (Deprivation of Liberty), Re [2014] EWCOP 25; [2014] C.O.P.L.R. 674; (2014) 17 C.C.L. Rep. 297; (2014) 158(34) S.J.L.B. 37, CP
X (Emergency Protection Orders), Re see X (A Child), Re
X (Minors) v Bedfordshire CC; *joined cases* Keating v Bromley LBC (No.2); Christmas v Hampshire CC (Duty of Care); E (A Minor) v Dorset CC (Appeal); M (A Minor) v Newham LBC [1995] 2 A.C. 633; [1995] 3 W.L.R. 152; [1995] 3 All E.R. 353; [1995] 2 F.L.R. 276; [1995] 3 F.C.R. 337; 94 L.G.R. 313; (1995) 7 Admin. L.R. 705; [1995] E.L.R. 404; [1995] Fam. Law 537; (1996) 160 L.G. Rev. 103; (1996) 160 L.G. Rev. 123; (1995) 145 N.L.J. 993; Times, June 30, 1995; Independent, June 30, 1995, HL; affirming [1994] 2 W.L.R. 554; [1994] 4 All E.R. 602; [1994] 1 F.L.R. 431; 92 L.G.R. 427; [1994] Fam. Law 434; (1994) 144 N.L.J. 357; Times, March 3, 1994; Independent, February 24, 1994; Guardian, February 28, 1994, CA (Civ Div); affirming [1993] 2 F.L.R. 575; [1994] P.I.Q.R. P515; [1993] Fam. Law 575; (1993) 143 N.L.J. 1783; Times, November 24, 1993; Independent, December 23, 1993, QBD ................ *Digested,* 95/**3452**: *Applied* 98/2570, 98/3935, 98/3944, 98/3945, 99/1765, 99/3968, 99/5435, 00/5662, 01/4470, 03/364, 05/976, 10/3406: *Complaint upheld* 01/2571: *Considered* 96/4140, 96/4441, 97/2692, 97/2879, 97/3775, 98/3931, 98/3937, 98/3942, 99/1889, 99/5434, 03/1118, 03/3004, 07/2937, 08/2644, 09/2850, 10/2279, 13/3251, 14/241: *Distinguished* 95/1927, 99/3966, 05/2858: *Doubted* 00/1947: *Followed* 96/3913, 97/2142, 97/4087, 97/424, 97/4860, 98/1965, 99/3967, 10/2757, 10/81
X (Societe) v CNH France (Societe) [2014] E.C.C. 5, Cass (F)
X AG v Inspecteur van de Belastingdienst Amsterdam (C-40/13) see Inspecteur van de Belastingdienst/Noord/kantoor Groningen v SCA Group Holding BV (C-39/13)
X AG v Inspecteur van de Belastingdienst Amsterdam (C-40/13) see Inspecteur van de Belastingdienst/Noord/kantoor Groningen v SCA Group Holding BV (C-39/13)
X BV v Staatssecretaris van Financien (C-24/12); *joined case* TBG Ltd v Staatssecretaris van Financien (C-27/12) [2014] S.T.C. 2394; [2014] 3 C.M.L.R. 54; [2014] B.T.C. 31; [2014] S.T.I. 2225, ECJ (3rd Chamber)
X City Council v MB [2006] EWHC 168 (Fam); [2006] 2 F.L.R. 968; [2007] 3 F.C.R. 371; [2006] Fam. Law 637, Fam Div ................ *Digested,* 07/**1833**: *Applied* 08/1437, 08/3568, 08/756, 11/2204, 14/2175: *Approved* 08/1567: *Considered* 09/806
X Council v B; *sub nom* B (Children), Re [2008] EWHC 270 (Fam); [2008] 1 F.L.R. 1460; [2008] Fam. Law 522, Fam Div (Liverpool) ................ *Digested,* 08/**1443**: *Applied* 10/1299, 14/1436
X Local Authority v Trimega Laboratories Ltd; *sub nom* A Local Authority v Trimega Laboratories Ltd [2014] 2 F.L.R. 232; [2014] P.N.L.R. 7; [2014] Fam. Law 152, Fam Div ................ *Digested,* 14/**1288**

X Trust Co Ltd v RW; *sub nom* H Trust, Re [2007] W.T.L.R. 677; (2006-07) 9 I.T.E.L.R. 133; 2006 Jer. L.R. 280, Royal Ct (Jer) ............ *Digested,* 07/**4262**: *Considered* 14/1371

X, Re see A (A Child) (Disclosure of Third Party Information), Re

X-Scape Milton Keynes Ltd v Luminar Oceana Ltd see Leisure (Norwich) II Ltd v Luminar Lava Ignite Ltd (In Administration)

XCC v AA [2012] EWHC 2183 (COP); [2013] 2 All E.R. 988; [2013] 2 F.C.R. 401; (2012) 15 C.C.L. Rep. 447; [2012] W.T.L.R. 1645, CP ............ *Digested,* 13/**2067**: *Applied* 14/2190

Xena Systems Ltd v Cantideck [2013] EWPCC 1; [2013] F.S.R. 41, PCC ............ *Digested,* 14/**1892**

Xenakis v Birkett Long LLP [2014] EWHC 171 (QB); [2014] P.N.L.R. 16, QBD ............ *Digested,* 14/**2213**

XL (Maidstone) Ltd v Luminar Gems Ltd see Leisure (Norwich) II Ltd v Luminar Lava Ignite Ltd (In Administration)

XL (Maidstone) Ltd v Luminar Liquid Ltd see Leisure (Norwich) II Ltd v Luminar Lava Ignite Ltd (In Administration)

Xydhias v Xydhias [1999] 2 All E.R. 386; [1999] 1 F.L.R. 683; [1999] 1 F.C.R. 289; [1999] Fam. Law 301; (1999) 96(6) L.S.G. 34; (1999) 149 N.L.J. 52; Times, January 13, 1999; Independent, January 21, 1999, CA (Civ Div) ............ *Digested,* 99/**2416**: *Applied* 07/1709: *Considered* 08/1427, 11/1292, 14/1361

XYZ v Various Companies; *sub nom* PIP Breast Implant Litigation, Re [2013] EWHC 3643 (QB); [2014] 2 Costs L.O. 197; [2014] Lloyd's Rep. I.R. 431, QBD ............ *Digested,* 14/**465**

Y v Advocate General for Scotland see N v Advocate General for Scotland

Y v General Medical Council [2013] EWHC 860 (Admin); [2013] Med. L.R. 227; (2013) 163(7560) N.L.J. 16, QBD (Admin) ............ *Digested,* 14/**1494**

Y v I see I (A Child) (Contact Application: Jurisdiction), Re

Y v X [2014] E.C.C. 21, Cass (F)

Y v Z (Publicity: Sch I Proceedings) [2014] EWHC 650 (Fam); [2014] 2 F.L.R. 1311; [2014] Fam. Law 973, Fam Div

Y (Children) (Care Proceedings: Transfer of Proceedings within UK Jurisdiction), Re see PC (A Child) (Brussels II Revised: Jurisdiction within United Kingdom), Re

Y (Children) (Removal from Jurisdiction: Failure to Consider Family Segmentation), Re see Y (Children) (Removal from Jurisdiction: Interests of Non-subject Child), Re

Y (Children) (Removal from Jurisdiction: Interests of Non-subject Child), Re; *sub nom* Y (Children) (Removal from Jurisdiction: Failure to Consider Family Segmentation), Re [2014] EWCA Civ 1287; [2014] 3 F.C.R. 483; [2014] Fam. Law 1680, CA (Civ Div)

Y (Sri Lanka) v Secretary of State for the Home Department; *joined case* Z (Sri Lanka) v Secretary of State for the Home Department [2009] EWCA Civ 362; [2009] H.R.L.R. 22; [2010] I.N.L.R. 178; Times, May 5, 2009, CA (Civ Div) ............ *Digested,* 09/**2082**: *Considered* 13/1576: *Followed* 14/1647

Yagiz v Turkey (27473/02) (2014) 59 E.H.R.R. 4, ECHR

Yang v Official Receiver [2013] EWHC 3577 (Ch); [2014] B.P.I.R. 826, Ch D (Manchester) ............ *Digested,* 14/**1778**

Yanko-Weiss Holdings (1996) Ltd v Holon Assessing Office 16 I.T.L. Rep. 536, District Ct (Tel Aviv)

Yarce (Adequate Maintenance: Benefits: Spain), Re; *sub nom* Entry Clearance Officer, Madrid v Yarce [2012] UKUT 425 (IAC); [2013] Imm. A.R. 177, UT (IAC) ............ *Digested,* 14/**1689**

Yarl's Wood Immigration Ltd v Bedfordshire Police Authority [2009] EWCA Civ 1110; [2010] Q.B. 698; [2010] 2 W.L.R. 1322; [2010] 2 All E.R. 221; [2009] Po. L.R. 362, CA (Civ Div); reversing [2008] EWHC 2207 (Comm); [2009] 1 All E.R. 886; [2008] Po. L.R. 281; (2008) 158 N.L.J. 1415, QBD (Comm) ............ *Digested,* 10/**2648**: *Considered* 14/2448

Yarmouth v France (1887) 19 Q.B.D. 647, QBD
*Applied* 74/2612, 79/1441: *Considered* 62/1464, 63/1705, 69/1662, 69/3998, 74/1272: *Explained* 14/2854

Yassin v Secretary of State for the Home Department see Kharug v Upper Tribunal (Immigration and Asylum Chamber)

Yates v National Trust [2014] EWHC 222 (QB); [2014] P.I.Q.R. P16, QBD ............ *Digested,* 14/**2996**

Yates v Revenue and Customs Commissioners; *sub nom* Dalton (Deceased), Re [2014] EWHC 2311 (QB); [2014] P.I.Q.R. P24; [2014] B.T.C. 39, QBD ............ *Digested,* 14/**2310**

Yates Building Co Ltd v RJ Pulleyn & Sons (York) Ltd (1975) 237 E.G. 183; (1975) 119 S.J. 370, CA (Civ Div); reversing (1973) 229 E.G. 1597, Ch D ............ *Digested,* 75/**388**: *Applied* 98/3440: *Considered* 13/575, 14/1970: *Distinguished* 96/7107, 09/2515: *Followed* 95/6071

YC v United Kingdom (4547/10) [2012] 2 F.L.R. 332; [2013] 2 F.C.R. 36; (2012) 55 E.H.R.R. 33; [2012] Fam. Law 932, ECHR ........ *Digested,* 12/**1330**: *Applied* 12/1297, 14/1234

Yearwood v Commissioner of Police of the Metropolis; *joined cases* Commissioner of Police of the Metropolis v Miller; Chief Constable of Merseyside v Husain; Kochar v Commissioner of Police of the Metropolis; Jeffrey v Commissioner of Police of the Metropolis [2004] I.C.R. 1660, EAT ........ *Digested,* 05/**3333**: *Applied* 12/1136: *Considered* 14/1099

Yellon v NHS Commissioning Board (NHS England) see NHS Commissioning Board (NHS England) v Bargain Dentist.Com

Yemgas FZCO v Superior Pescadores SA Panama (The Superior Pescadores) [2014] EWHC 971 (comm); [2014] 1 Lloyd's Rep. 660; [2014] 1 C.L.C. 496, QBD (Comm) ........ *Digested,* 14/**2706**

Yeo v Times Newspapers Ltd [2014] EWHC 2853 (QB); [2014] 5 Costs L.O. 823; [2014] E.M.L.R. 32; (2014) 158(35) S.J.L.B. 37; Times, September 4, 2014, QBD ........ *Digested,* 14/**838**

Yerrakalva v Barnsley MBC; *sub nom* Barnsley MBC v Yerrakalva [2011] EWCA Civ 1255; [2012] 2 All E.R. 215; [2012] I.C.R. 420; [2012] I.R.L.R. 78; (2011) 161 N.L.J. 1595, CA (Civ Div); reversing in part [2011] 1 Costs L.O. 74; [2011] I.C.R. D6, EAT ........ *Digested,* 12/**1091**: *Applied* 12/1090, 12/1092, 13/969, 14/1073: *Considered* 13/3518: *Followed* 14/1074

Yeung v Potel; *sub nom* Potel v Yeung [2014] EWCA Civ 481; [2014] H.L.R. 35; [2014] 2 E.G.L.R. 125; [2014] 2 P. & C.R. DG9, CA (Civ Div) ........ *Digested,* 14/**2509**

Yiacoub v Queen, The [2014] UKPC 22; [2014] 1 W.L.R. 2996; Times, July 23, 2014, PC (Cy)

YKK Corp v European Commission (C-408/12 P) [2014] Bus. L.R. 1376; [2014] 5 C.M.L.R. 26, ECJ (2nd Chamber)

YLA v PM see A v M

YM Mars Tankers Ltd v Shield Petroleum Co (Nigeria) Ltd [2012] EWHC 2652 (Comm), QBD (Comm) *Applied* 14/2707

YOKOHAMA RUBBER/Searches (T2473/12) [2014] E.P.O.R. 9, EPO (Technical Bd App)

Yonge v Toynbee [1910] 1 K.B. 215, CA *Applied* 13/308: *Considered* 05/489: *Followed* 14/2053

York City Council v C; *sub nom* CYC v PC; PC v City of York Council [2013] EWCA Civ 478; [2014] Fam. 10; [2014] 2 W.L.R. 1; (2013) 16 C.C.L. Rep. 298; [2013] Med. L.R. 213; Times, June 25, 2013, CA (Civ Div); reversing in part [2013] Med. L.R. 26, CP ........ *Digested,* 14/**2172**: *Applied* 14/2175

Yorkshire Building Society v United Kingdom (21675/93) see National & Provincial Building Society v United Kingdom (21319/93)

Young v Anglo American South Africa Ltd [2014] EWCA Civ 1130; [2014] Bus. L.R. 1434; [2014] 2 Lloyd's Rep. 606; [2014] C.P. Rep. 47; [2014] I.L.Pr. 40, CA (Civ Div) ........ *Digested,* 14/**514**

Young v Hamilton [2014] NICA 48; [2014] P.N.L.R. 30, CA (NI); reversing [2012] NICh 4, Ch D (NI) ........ *Digested,* 14/**3215**

Young v Hamilton [2011] NICh 19, Ch D (NI) *Reversed in part* 14/3215

Young v Murphy [1996] V.R. 279, CA (Vic) *Applied* 14/3026: *Considered* 08/3961, 13/2158

Young v Oxfordshire CC [2014] P.A.D. 45, Planning Inspector

Young v Young [2013] EWHC 3637 (Fam); [2014] 2 Costs L.O. 136; [2014] 2 F.L.R. 786; [2014] 2 F.C.R. 495; [2014] Fam. Law 291, Fam Div ........ *Digested,* 14/**1363**

Young v Young [2013] EWHC 34 (Fam); [2014] 1 F.L.R. 269; [2013] Fam. Law 382, Fam Div

Your Response Ltd v Datateam Business Media Ltd [2014] EWCA Civ 281; [2014] 3 W.L.R. 887; [2014] 4 All E.R. 928; [2014] 2 All E.R. (Comm) 899; [2014] C.P. Rep. 31; [2014] 1 C.L.C. 915, CA (Civ Div) ........ *Digested,* 14/**2528**

Youssef v Secretary of State for Foreign and Commonwealth Affairs see R. (on the application of Youssef) v Secretary of State for Foreign and Commonwealth Affairs

Youssefi v Mussellwhite; *sub nom* Mussellwhite v Youssefi [2014] EWCA Civ 885; [2014] 2 P. & C.R. 14; [2014] 3 E.G.L.R. 22, CA (Civ Div) ........ *Digested,* 14/**1994**

Youth Inititative for Human Rights v Serbia (48135/06) 36 B.H.R.C. 687, ECHR

YS (Degree Level Study: Mauritius), Re [2006] UKAIT 94, AIT *Applied* 14/1714

Yu, Re [2013] QSC 322; 16 I.T.E.L.R. 563, Sup Ct (Qld)
Yukos Capital Sarl v OJSC Oil Co Rosneft [2014] EWHC 2188 (Comm); [2014] 2 Lloyd's Rep. 435; 155 Con. L.R. 221, QBD (Comm) ............ *Digested,* 14/**124**
Yukos Capital Sarl v OJSC Rosneft Oil Co [2012] EWCA Civ 855; [2014] Q.B. 458; [2013] 3 W.L.R. 1329; [2013] 1 All E.R. 223; [2013] 1 All E.R. (Comm) 327; [2012] 2 Lloyd's Rep. 208; [2012] 2 C.L.C. 549; 143 Con. L.R. 1, CA (Civ Div); reversing [2011] EWHC 1461 (Comm); [2012] 1 All E.R. (Comm) 479; [2011] 2 Lloyd's Rep. 443; [2011] 2 C.L.C. 129; [2011] Arb. L.R. 39; (2011) 108(26) L.S.G. 17, QBD (Comm) ............ *Digested,* 12/**120**: *Considered* 14/65
Yukos Capital Sarl v OJSC Rosneft Oil Co [2010] EWHC 784 (Comm); [2011] 1 All E.R. (Comm) 172, QBD (Comm) ............ *Digested,* 11/**332**: *Considered* 14/125
Yukos Oil Co v Dardana Ltd see Dardana Ltd v Yukos Oil Co (No.1)
Yuzhny Zavod Metall Profil LLC v EEMS Beheerder BV [2013] 2 Lloyd's Rep. 487, QBD (Admlty) ............ *Digested,* 14/**2705**

Z v A; *joined case* A v Z [2014] I.R.L.R. 244, EAT ............ *Digested,* 14/**1137**
Z v A (Financial Remedy after Overseas Divorce) [2012] EWHC 1434 (Fam); [2014] 2 F.L.R. 109; [2013] Fam. Law 393, Fam Div
Z v A Government Department (C-363/12) [2014] 3 C.M.L.R. 20; [2014] I.R.L.R. 563; [2014] Eq. L.R. 316, ECJ (Grand Chamber)
Z v Minister voor Immigratie en Asiel (C-201/12) see Minister voor Immigratie en Asiel v X (C-199/12)
Z v Y see A (Abduction: Child's Objections to Return), Re
Z v Z (Recognition of Brazilian Adoption Order) [2013] EWHC 747 (Fam); [2014] 1 F.L.R. 1295; [2013] Fam. Law 937, Fam Div
Z (A Child) v Burrows (Unreported, April 9, 2014), CC (Croydon) [*Robert Golin, Barrister, Farrar's Building, Temple, London*] ............ *Digested,* 14/**2346**
Z (A Child) (Independent Social Work Assessment), Re [2014] EWHC 729 (Fam); [2014] Fam. Law 779, Fam Div
Z (A Child), Re; *sub nom* X v Y [2014] EWHC 2147 (Fam); [2014] Fam. Law 1392, Fam Div
Z (Children) (Application for Release of DNA Profiles), Re; *sub nom* X v Z (Children) [2014] EWHC 1999 (Fam); [2014] Fam. Law 1235, Fam Div
Z (Children) (Care Proceedings: Review of Findings), Re; *sub nom* ZZ (Children) (Care Proceedings: Retraction of Testimony), Re [2014] EWFC 9; [2014] Fam. Law 1237; (2014) 158(25) S.J.L.B. 45, Fam Ct
Z (Sri Lanka) v Secretary of State for the Home Department see Y (Sri Lanka) v Secretary of State for the Home Department
ZA v NA (Abduction: Habitual Residence) see A v A (Children) (Habitual Residence)
Zakharkin v Russia (2014) 59 E.H.R.R. 17, ECHR
Zalco Marine Services v Humboldt Shipping (Unreported, 1998), CA (Sing) *Considered* 14/2735
ZAM v CFW [2013] EWHC 662 (QB); [2013] E.M.L.R. 27, QBD ............ *Digested,* 14/**832**
Zambarda v Shipbreaking (Queenborough) Ltd [2013] EWHC 2263 (QB), QBD [*Achas Burin, Barrister, 12 King's Bench Walk, London*] ............ *Digested,* 14/**2315**
Zamberk v Financni reditelstvi v Hradci Kralove (C-18/12) [2014] S.T.C. 1703, ECJ (5th Chamber) *Considered* 14/3043
Zarbafi v Zarbafi [2014] EWCA Civ 1267; [2014] 1 W.L.R. 4122; Times, November 3, 2014, CA (Civ Div); reversing [2014] EWHC 1787 (Ch), Ch D
Zarrinkhat v Kamal [2013] W.T.L.R. 1477, Ch D ............ *Digested,* 14/**2821**
Zee Entertainment Enterprises Ltd v Zeebox Ltd [2014] EWCA Civ 82; [2014] F.S.R. 26, CA (Civ Div); affirming [2013] EWHC 1644 (Ch); [2014] F.S.R. 10, Ch D ..... *Digested,* 14/**289**: *Applied* 14/1935
Zehentner v Austria (20082/02) (2011) 52 E.H.R.R. 22, ECHR *Applied* 11/2066: *Considered* 14/1968
Zenios v Hampstead Garden Suburb Trust Ltd see Zenios, Re
Zenios, Re; *sub nom* Zenios v Hampstead Garden Suburb Trust Ltd [2011] EWCA Civ 1645, CA (Civ Div); affirming [2010] UKUT 260 (LC), UT (Lands) *Considered* 14/2508
ZENON/Correction of identity of applicant (G1/12) [2014] E.P.O.R. 41, EPO (Enlarged Bd App)
Zentralbetriebsrat der gemeinnutzigen Salzburger Landeskliniken Betriebs GmbH v Land Salzburg (C-514/12) [2014] 2 C.M.L.R. 26, ECJ (2nd Chamber)
Zeus Estates Ltd v Islington LBC [2014] P.A.D. 25, Planning Inspector

ZH (Tanzania) v Secretary of State for the Home Department [2011] UKSC 4; [2011] 2 A.C. 166; [2011] 2 W.L.R. 148; [2011] 2 All E.R. 783; [2011] 1 F.L.R. 2170; [2011] 1 F.C.R. 221; [2011] H.R.L.R. 15; [2011] U.K.H.R.R. 371; [2011] Imm. A.R. 395; [2011] I.N.L.R. 369; [2011] Fam. Law 468; (2011) 108(7) L.S.G. 17; (2011) 155(5) S.J.L.B. 30; Times, February 8, 2011, SC ........ *Digested,* 11/**1790**:
*Applied* 11/1711, 12/1289, 12/1707, 12/1751, 14/1596, 14/1668, 14/662: *Considered* 12/1293, 12/1663, 12/1738, 12/1750, 12/1775, 12/4099, 13/1605, 13/2366, 13/3776, 13/3778, 14/1650, 14/1704: *Followed* 11/1736, 12/1718, 13/1578, 14/1673, 14/1725

Zhu v Secretary of State for the Home Department (C-200/02) see Chen v Secretary of State for the Home Department (C-200/02)

Zim Integrated Shipping Services Ltd v European Container KS [2013] EWHC 3581 (Comm); [2013] 2 C.L.C. 800, QBD (Comm) ........ *Digested,* 14/**139**

Ziolkowski v Land Berlin (C-424/10); *joined case* Szeja v Land Berlin (C-425/10) [2013] 3 C.M.L.R. 37; [2014] All E.R. (EC) 314; [2012] Imm. A.R. 421; [2012] I.N.L.R. 467, ECJ (Grand Chamber)
*Applied* 13/1170: *Considered* 13/1526: *Followed* 14/1739

Zipvit Ltd v Revenue and Customs Commissioners [2014] UKFTT 649 (TC); [2014] S.F.T.D. 1309; [2014] S.T.I. 2601, FTT (Tax)

Zlomrex International Finance SA, Re [2013] EWHC 3866 (Ch); [2014] B.C.C. 440, Ch D (Companies Ct) ........ *Digested,* 14/**1823**

ZM v AM (Stranded Spouse) [2014] EWHC 2110 (Fam); [2014] Fam. Law 1402, Fam Div

Zodiac Pool Solutions North America Inc, Re see Zodiac Pool Solutions SAS, Re

Zodiac Pool Solutions SAS, Re; *sub nom* Zodiac Pool Solutions North America Inc, Re; Marine Investment Finland Oy, Re [2014] EWHC 2365 (Ch); [2014] B.C.C. 569, Ch D (Companies Ct)

Zolotas v Greece (66610/09) 35 B.H.R.C. 443, ECHR

Zoumbas v Secretary of State for the Home Department see FZ (Democratic Republic of Congo) v Secretary of State for the Home Department

Zrilic v Croatia (46726/11) (Unreported, October 3, 2013), ECHR
*Considered* 14/1968

Zubair v Secretary of State for the Home Department see Zubair (EEA Regs: Self-Employed Persons), Re

Zubair (EEA Regs: Self-Employed Persons), Re; *sub nom* Zubair v Secretary of State for the Home Department [2013] UKUT 196 (IAC); [2013] Imm. A.R. 740; [2014] I.N.L.R. 105, UT (IAC) ........ *Digested,* 14/**1706**

Zuckerfabrik Soest GmbH v Hauptzollamt Paderborn (C-92/89) see Zuckerfabrik Suderdithmarschen AG v Hauptzollamt Itzehoe (C-143/88)

Zuckerfabrik Suderdithmarschen AG v Hauptzollamt Itzehoe (C-143/88); *joined case* Zuckerfabrik Soest GmbH v Hauptzollamt Paderborn (C-92/89) [1991] E.C.R. I-415; [1993] 3 C.M.L.R. 1; (1991) 135 S.J.L.B. 6; Times, March 27, 1991, ECJ .. *Digested,* 91/**4051**:
*Applied* 04/647, 06/1538, 14/323: *Considered* 96/222, 01/2462: *Referred to* 00/2356

Zuckerman v Calthorpe Estates Trustees [2009] UKUT 235 (LC); [2011] L. & T.R. 12; [2010] 1 E.G.L.R. 187, UT (Lands) ........ *Digested,* 10/**2062**:
*Applied* 10/2056, 12/2032, 13/1884: *Considered* 14/1981

Zuk v Zuk [2012] EWCA Civ 1871; [2013] 2 F.L.R. 1466; [2013] 3 F.C.R. 633; [2013] Fam. Law 536, CA (Civ Div) ........ *Digested,* 14/**321**

Zulhayir v JJ Food Services Ltd; *joined case* JJ Food Service Ltd v Zulhayir [2013] EWCA Civ 1226; [2014] I.C.R. D3, CA (Civ Div); reversing UKEAT/0275/12/RN, EAT

Zurich Insurance Plc v Umerji; *sub nom* Umerji v Khan [2014] EWCA Civ 357; [2014] R.T.R. 23, CA (Civ Div) ........ *Digested,* 14/**831**

ZZ v Secretary of State for the Home Department [2011] EWCA Civ 440, CA (Civ Div)
*Preliminary ruling given* 14/1223

ZZ (Children) (Care Proceedings: Retraction of Testimony), Re see Z (Children) (Care Proceedings: Review of Findings), Re

ZZ (France) v Secretary of State for the Home Department [2014] EWCA Civ 7; [2014] Q.B. 820; [2014] 2 W.L.R. 791; [2014] 3 All E.R. 587; [2014] 2 C.M.L.R. 49; [2014] I.N.L.R. 858, CA (Civ Div) ........ *Digested,* 14/**1708**

ZZ (France) v Secretary of State for the Home Department (C-300/11) [2013] Q.B. 1136; [2013] 3 W.L.R. 813; [2013] 3 C.M.L.R. 46; [2014] All E.R. (EC) 56; [2014] C.E.C. 109; [2014] Imm. A.R. 1; [2014] I.N.L.R. 368, ECJ (Grand Chamber) ........ *Digested,* 14/**1223**

## PART II

## SCOTTISH CASE CITATOR 2014

**This section contains:**
**(i) Details of cases decided or judicially considered in the Scottish courts during 2014**
**(ii) References to English cases judicially considered in Scotland during2014**
**Scottish cases published in English Law Reports are included in both the English and Scottish sections**
**Figures appearing in bold type indicate the main substantive paragraph**

@SIPP (Pension Trustees) Ltd v Insight Travel Services Ltd [2014] CSOH 137; 2014 Hous. L.R. 54; 2014 G.W.D. 29-579, OH

A v B (1895) 22 R. 402, IH (1 Div) — *Considered* 14/3371

A v B 2014 G.W.D. 2-37, Sh Ct (South Strathclyde) (Kirkcudbright)

A v BBC see BBC, Re

A v Chief Constable, Police Service of Scotland 2014 G.W.D. 27-546, Sh Ct (Tayside) (Falkirk)

A v HM Advocate; *sub nom* HMCA v HM Advocate [2014] HCJAC 41; 2014 G.W.D. 16-291, HCJ

A v HM Advocate [2012] HCJAC 29; 2012 J.C. 343; 2012 S.L.T. 511; 2012 S.C.L. 568; 2012 S.C.C.R. 384; 2012 G.W.D. 9-165, HCJ ........ *Digested,* 12/**3939**: *Distinguished* 14/3400

A v Murphy [2014] HCJAC 96; 2014 S.C.L. 784; 2014 G.W.D. 28-565, HCJ ........ *Digested,* 14/**3784**

A v N; *sub nom* EA v GN [2013] CSOH 161; 2014 S.C.L.R. 225; 2013 G.W.D. 33-661, OH ........ *Digested,* 14/**3719**

A v S 2014 G.W.D. 14-257, Sh Ct (Glasgow)

A v Secretary of State for the Home Department see BBC, Re

A v Secretary of State for the Home Department see IA (Iran) v Secretary of State for the Home Department

A v Secretary of State for the Home Department see SA (Nigeria) v Secretary of State for the Home Department

A J Allan (Blairnyle) Ltd v Strathclyde Fire Board [2014] CSOH 135; 2014 G.W.D. 29-568, OH

A Ltd v F [2014] CSOH 169; 2014 G.W.D. 40-721, OH

A, Petitioner [2014] CSOH 27; 2014 G.W.D. 8-152, OH

A, Petitioner [2014] CSIH 25; 2014 G.W.D. 11-200, IH (Ex Div)

AA (Pakistan) v Secretary of State for the Home Department [2014] CSIH 35; 2014 G.W.D. 14-260, IH (Ex Div)

AA (Turkey) v Secretary of State for the Home Department [2014] CSIH 9; 2014 G.W.D. 3-68, IH (Ex Div); affirming [2013] CSOH 58; 2013 G.W.D. 15-321, OH

AAA (Pakistan) v Secretary of State for the Home Department [2014] CSOH 81; 2014 G.W.D. 18-345, OH

AAN (Malawi) v Secretary of State for the Home Department [2013] CSIH 111; 2014 G.W.D. 14-258, IH (Ex Div); reversing [2012] CSOH 151; 2012 G.W.D. 32-650, OH

Abbycars (West Horndon) Ltd v Ford UKEAT/0472/07/DA, EAT — *Applied* 14/3500

Abdel-Rahman v University of Edinburgh [2013] CSOH 201; 2014 G.W.D. 4-76, OH

Abdi (Rahim Abuka) v HM Advocate see Haashi (Shirwa Abdisayed) v HM Advocate

Aberdeen Asset Management Plc v Revenue and Customs Commissioners [2012] UKUT 43 (TCC); [2012] S.T.C. 650; [2012] B.T.C. 1514; [2012] S.T.I. 1376, UT (Tax); affirming [2010] UKFTT 524 (TC), FTT (Tax) ........ *Digested,* 12/**3301**: *Applied* 13/3095: *Distinguished* 14/2921: *Followed* 14/2872: *Reversed in part* 14/3807

Aberdeen Asset Management Plc v Revenue and Customs Commissioners [2013] CSIH 84; [2014] S.T.C. 438; 2014 S.C. 271; 2014 S.L.T. 54; [2013] B.T.C. 726; 2013 G.W.D. 40-773, IH (1 Div) ........ *Digested,* 14/**3807**

Aberdeen City Council v McNeill; *sub nom* McNeill v Aberdeen City Council [2013] CSIH 102; 2014 S.C. 335; 2014 S.L.T. 312; [2014] I.R.L.R. 113; 2014 G.W.D. 1-15, IH (Ex Div); reversing [2010] I.R.L.R. 374, EAT (SC) ............ *Digested,* 14/**3506**: *Followed* 14/1022

Aberdeen City Council v Morrison 2014 S.L.T. (Lands Tr) 113; [2014] R.V.R. 334; 2014 G.W.D. 25-502, Lands Tr (Scot)

Aberdeenshire Council v Evans 2013 Hous. L.R. 59; 2013 G.W.D. 26-534, Sh Ct (Grampian) (Banff) ............ *Digested,* 14/**3596**

Aberdeenshire Council, Petitioners see W v Aberdeenshire Council

Abrahm v British International Helicopters Ltd [2014] CSIH 53; 2014 G.W.D. 22-412, IH (2 Div); affirming [2013] CSOH 69; 2013 G.W.D. 17-347, OH

Abu Qatada v United Kingdom (8139/09) see Othman v United Kingdom (8139/09)

Accord Mortgages Ltd v Dickson 2013 Hous. L.R. 2, Sh Ct (South Strathclyde) (Hamilton) ............ *Digested,* 14/**3351**

Addison (Kevin Colin) v HM Advocate [2014] HCJAC 110; 2014 S.L.T. 995; 2014 S.C.L. 835; 2014 S.C.C.R. 608; 2014 G.W.D. 32-626, HCJ ............ *Digested,* 14/**3459**

ADM, Petitioner see M, Petitioner

Advice Centre for Mortgages Ltd v McNicoll 2006 S.L.T. 591; 2006 S.C.L.R. 602; 2006 Hous. L.R. 22; 2006 G.W.D. 19-413, OH ............ *Digested,* 06/**5548**: *Followed* 14/3631

Afzal (Sajjad) v HM Advocate [2013] HCJAC 103; 2013 S.C.L. 954; 2013 G.W.D. 30-596, HCJ ............ *Digested,* 14/**3443**

AG v Principal Reporter; *sub nom* X, Appellants 2013 S.L.T. (Sh Ct) 125; 2013 Fam. L.R. 100; 2013 G.W.D. 30-600, Sh Ct (Tayside) (Kirkcaldy) ............ *Digested,* 14/**3525**

Agri Energy v McCallion [2014] CSOH 13; 2014 G.W.D. 5-101, OH

Agri Energy v McCallion [2014] CSOH 14; 2014 G.W.D. 5-102, OH

Ahmed v Iqbal 2014 Fam. L.R. 93; 2014 G.W.D. 21-390, Sh Ct (Glasgow) ............ *Digested,* 14/**3533**

Akdeniz v Cameron; *sub nom* Akdeniz (Durmus) v HM Advocate [2012] HCJAC 26; 2014 J.C. 13; 2012 S.L.T. 585; 2012 S.C.L. 513; 2012 G.W.D. 8-143, HCJ ...... *Digested,* 12/**4272**

Akdeniz (Durmus) v HM Advocate see Akdeniz v Cameron

Akhtar v Murphy; *joined cases* Ali v Murphy; Kuwar v Murphy; Mahmood v Murphy [2014] HCJAC 80; 2014 S.L.T. 923; 2014 S.C.L. 651; 2014 S.C.C.R. 475; 2014 G.W.D. 25-491, HCJ ............ *Digested,* 14/**3464**

Albacroft Ltd v Thomson 2014 G.W.D. 14-254, Sh Ct (Glasgow)

Alcock v Chief Constable of South Yorkshire; *sub nom* Jones v Wright; *joined cases* Copoc v Chief Constable of South Yorkshire; Jones v Chief Constable of South Yorkshire; Penk v Wright [1992] 1 A.C. 310; [1991] 3 W.L.R. 1057; [1991] 4 All E.R. 907; [1992] P.I.Q.R. P1; (1992) 89(3) L.S.G. 34; (1991) 141 N.L.J. 166; (1992) 136 S.J.L.B. 9; Times, November 29, 1991; Independent, November 29, 1991; Guardian, December 11, 1991, HL; affirming [1991] 3 All E.R. 88; Times, May 6, 1991; Independent, May 10, 1991; Guardian, May 9, 1991, CA (Civ Div); affirming [1991] 2 W.L.R. 814; [1991] 1 All E.R. 353; (1990) 140 N.L.J. 1717; Independent, December 7, 1990, QBD ............ *Digested,* 92/**3250**: *Applied* 92/3253, 93/2972, 95/6157, 98/3938, 00/531, 01/5352, 01/6665, 02/948, 03/5828: *Considered* 95/3682, 97/2615, 98/4035, 99/4059, 00/4213, 00/4220, 00/6598, 03/3132, 03/5844, 05/2834, 07/4654, 14/3469: *Distinguished* 03/3028: *Followed* 13/2185, 13/2204

Alcohol Focus Scotland, Applicants [2014] CSIH 64; 2014 G.W.D. 24-444, IH (Ex Div)

Ali v Murphy see Akhtar v Murphy

Allan v Amlin UK Ltd [2013] CSOH 156; 2014 S.L.T. 75; 2014 S.C.L.R. 189; 2014 Rep. L.R. 30; 2013 G.W.D. 31-623, OH ............ *Digested,* 14/**3474**

Allan (Jack) v HM Advocate [2014] HCJAC 60; 2014 S.C.L. 639; 2014 G.W.D. 23-433, HCJ ............ *Digested,* 14/**3374**

Allied Vehicles Ltd v Glasgow City Council [2013] CSOH 192; 2014 G.W.D. 4-79, OH

AM (Algeria), Applicant [2014] CSIH 1; 2014 G.W.D. 4-88, IH

AMN Group Ltd v Gilcomston North Ltd see ANM Group Ltd v Gilcomston North Ltd

AMT, Petitioners see T, Petitioner

AN v Secretary of State for the Home Department [2014] CSOH 37; 2014 G.W.D. 10-187, OH

Anderson v Crofters Commission 2014 S.L.C.R. 1; 2014 G.W.D. 13-225, Land Ct

Anderson (James McAulay) v HM Advocate 1996 J.C. 29; 1996 S.L.T. 155, HCJ Appeal ............ *Digested,* 96/**6764**: *Applied* 04/4679, 06/5173, 08/4663: *Cited* 09/4820: *Considered* 06/5192, 07/5078, 09/4815, 14/3459: *Distinguished* 00/6091, 08/4677: *Followed* 03/5379: *Referred to* 97/5804

Anderson's Executor v Shetland Islands Council [2014] CSOH 25; 2014 G.W.D. 9-175, OH

Anderson's Executor Dative v Nicholson Bros 2014 G.W.D. 18-333, Sh Ct (Grampian) (Lerwick)
Angiolini v Green [2013] CSOH 196; 2014 G.W.D. 5-104, OH
ANM Group Ltd v Gilcomston North Ltd; *sub nom* AMN Group Ltd v Gilcomston North Ltd [2008] CSOH 90; 2008 S.L.T. 835; 2009 S.C.L.R. 1; [2008] B.L.R. 481; 2008 Rep. L.R. 130; 2008 G.W.D. 27-429, OH .......... *Digested,* 09/**5157**: *Doubted* 14/2470
Anwar v Cassidy [2013] HCJAC 134; 2013 S.C.C.R. 575, HCJ .......... *Digested,* 14/**3452**
AOL (Nigeria) v Secretary of State for the Home Department [2014] CSIH 37; 2014 G.W.D. 15-276, IH
Apollo Engineering Ltd v James Scott Ltd [2013] UKSC 37; 2013 S.C. (U.K.S.C.) 286; 2014 S.L.T. 32; 2013 G.W.D. 21-409; Times, August 6, 2013, SC; no effect [2012] CSIH 88; 2012 G.W.D. 40-777, IH (Ex Div) .......... *Digested,* 13/**3540**
Application for directions by West Lothian Council in respect of Y 2014 S.L.T. (Sh Ct) 93; 2014 G.W.D. 22-425, Sh Ct (Lothian) (Livingston) .......... *Digested,* 14/**3799**
Application for Guardianship in respect of NW see Application for Guardianship in respect of W
Application for Guardianship in respect of W; *sub nom* Application for Guardianship in respect of NW 2014 S.L.T. (Sh Ct) 83; 2014 G.W.D. 18-357, Sh Ct (Glasgow) .. *Digested,* 14/**3685**
Application in respect of A and B 2014 Fam. L.R. 137; 2014 G.W.D. 38-698, Sh Ct (Lothian) (Haddington)
AR (Iran) v Secretary of State for the Home Department [2013] CSOH 195; 2014 G.W.D. 3-67, OH
AR Communications & Electronics Ltd, Petitioners [2014] CSOH 125; 2014 S.L.T. 949; 2014 G.W.D. 29-583, OH .......... *Digested,* 14/**3810**
Arbitration Application No.1 of 2013 [2014] CSOH 83; 2014 G.W.D. 16-284, OH
Archer (Paul Graham) v HM Advocate [2013] HCJAC 162; 2014 S.L.T. 133; 2014 S.C.L. 150; 2014 G.W.D. 1-34, HCJ .......... *Digested,* 14/**3772**
Archid Architecture and Interior Design v Dundee City Council [2013] CSOH 137; 2014 S.L.T. 81; [2014] J.P.L. 336; 2013 G.W.D. 28-569, OH .......... *Digested,* 14/**3736**
Ardagh Glass Ltd v Assesor for Ayrshire Valuation Joint Board 2014 S.L.T. (Lands Tr) 32; [2014] R.V.R. 103; 2014 G.W.D. 1-31, Lands Tr (Scot) .......... *Digested,* 14/**3669**
Arlington Business Parks GP Ltd v Scottish & Newcastle Ltd [2014] CSOH 77; 2014 G.W.D. 14-261, OH
Arthur v Murphy [2014] HCJAC 4; 2014 S.C.L. 218; 2014 G.W.D. 3-72, HCJ .......... *Digested,* 14/**3770**
Arveladze v MacFarlane 2014 Hous. L.R. 61, Sh Ct (North Strathclyde) (Paisley)
Assessor for Dunbartonshire, Argyll and Bute v Akram; *sub nom* Dunbartonshire, Argyll and Bute Assessor v Akram [2011] CSIH 79; 2012 S.C. 235; [2012] R.A. 137; 2012 G.W.D. 1-6, LVAC .......... *Digested,* 12/**4241**: *Followed* 13/3943, 14/3678
Assessor for Glasgow v Schuh Ltd [2012] CSIH 40; 2012 S.L.T. 903; [2012] R.A. 245; 2012 G.W.D. 17-355, LVAC .......... *Digested,* 12/**4244**: *Cited* 14/3676
Assessor for Lanarkshire Valuation Joint Board v Jane Norman Ltd; *sub nom* Lanarkshire Valuation Joint Board Assessor v Jane Norman Ltd [2012] CSIH 50; [2012] R.A. 387; 2012 G.W.D. 22-449, LVAC .......... *Digested,* 13/**3948**: *Considered* 14/3670
Assessor for Lothian Valuation Joint Board v Over The Counter Ltd; *sub nom* Lothian Valuation Joint Board Assessor v Over The Counter Ltd [2014] CSIH 28; [2014] R.V.R. 231; 2014 G.W.D. 12-223, LVAC .......... *Digested,* 14/**3665**
Assessor for Tayside Valuation Joint Board v Hutchison 3G (UK) Ltd; *sub nom* Tayside Valuation Joint Board Assessor v Hutchison 3G (UK) Ltd [2014] CSIH 40; 2014 S.L.T. 699; [2014] R.A. 356; 2014 G.W.D. 16-302, LVAC .......... *Digested,* 14/**3664**
Assets Co Ltd v Bain's Trustees see Watt v Assets Co Ltd
Assets Co Ltd v Phillip's Trustees see Watt v Assets Co Ltd
Auchnie v Auchnie 2014 G.W.D. 27-552, Sh Ct (Grampian) (Banff)
Austin (David) v HM Advocate [2014] HCJAC 58; 2014 G.W.D. 19-373, HCJ
Aviva Investors Pensions Ltd v McDonald's Restaurants Ltd 2014 G.W.D. 7-146, OH
AXA General Insurance Ltd v HM Advocate see AXA General Insurance Ltd, Petitioners
AXA General Insurance Ltd v Lord Advocate see AXA General Insurance Ltd, Petitioners

AXA General Insurance Ltd, Petitioners; *sub nom* AXA General Insurance Ltd v HM Advocate; AXA General Insurance Ltd v Lord Advocate [2011] UKSC 46; [2012] 1 A.C. 868; [2011] 3 W.L.R. 871; 2012 S.C. (U.K.S.C.) 122; 2011 S.L.T. 1061; [2012] H.R.L.R. 3; [2011] U.K.H.R.R. 1221; (2011) 122 B.M.L.R. 149; (2011) 108(41) L.S.G. 22; Times, October 19, 2011, SC; reversing in part [2011] CSIH 31; 2011 S.C. 662; 2011 S.L.T. 439; 2011 S.C.L.R. 305; 2011 G.W.D. 14-325; Times, May 3, 2011, IH (1 Div); reversing in part [2010] CSOH 2; 2010 S.L.T. 179; 2010 G.W.D. 7-118; Times, January 19, 2010, OH ............ *Digested,* 11/**473**: *Applied* 14/2444, 14/2964: *Cited* 14/3730: *Considered* 12/4206, 13/3703

AY (Iran), Petitioner [2014] CSOH 91; 2014 G.W.D. 18-347, OH

B v Authority Reporter 2014 G.W.D. 16-285, Sh Ct (Lothian) (Edinburgh)

B v Authority Reporter 2014 G.W.D. 16-286, Sh Ct (Lothian) (Edinburgh)

B v B [2012] CSOH 21; 2012 Fam. L.R. 65; 2012 G.W.D. 9-169, OH .......................... *Digested,* 12/**4016**: *Followed* 14/3534

B v B 2014 G.W.D. 30-593, Sh Ct (Lothian) (Edinburgh)

B v General Medical Council 2014 G.W.D. 7-134, Sh Ct (South Strathclyde) (Ayr)

B v General Teaching Council for Scotland [2013] CSIH 114; 2014 G.W.D. 4-83, IH (Ex Div)

B v Glasgow City Council; *sub nom* JB v Glasgow City Council [2013] CSIH 77; 2014 S.C. 209; 2013 S.L.T. 1050; 2014 S.C.L.R. 309; 2013 G.W.D. 30-597, IH (Ex Div) .......................... *Digested,* 14/**3477**

B v H 2014 S.L.T. (Sh Ct) 160; 2014 G.W.D. 34-652, Sh Ct (Tayside) (Forfar)

B v Harrower 2011 S.C.C.R. 393, HCJ .......................... *Digested,* 14/**3384**

B v Murphy [2014] HCJAC 56; 2014 S.C.L. 563; 2014 G.W.D. 20-378, HCJ .............. *Digested,* 14/**3430**

B (A Child) (Care Order: Proportionality: Criterion for Review), Re see B (A Child) (Care Proceedings: Appeal), Re

B (A Child) (Care Proceedings: Appeal), Re; *sub nom* B (A Child) (Care Proceedings: Threshold Criteria), Re; B (A Child) (Care Order: Proportionality: Criterion for Review), Re [2013] UKSC 33; [2013] 1 W.L.R. 1911; [2013] 3 All E.R. 929; [2013] 2 F.L.R. 1075; [2013] 2 F.C.R. 525; [2013] H.R.L.R. 29; [2013] Fam. Law 946; (2013) 157(24) S.J.L.B. 37, SC; affirming [2012] EWCA Civ 1475; [2013] 2 F.L.R. 388; [2013] Fam. Law 139, CA (Civ Div) .......................... *Digested,* 13/**1213**: *Applied* 14/1238, 14/1247, 14/1250, 14/1283, 14/1323, 14/1346, 14/1672, 14/2444: *Considered* 14/1243, 14/1404: *Followed* 13/1221, 14/1232, 14/1245, 14/1579

B (A Child) (Care Proceedings: Threshold Criteria), Re see B (A Child) (Care Proceedings: Appeal), Re

B, Minuter 2014 S.L.T. (Sh Ct) 5; 2013 G.W.D. 34-684, Sh Ct (Glasgow) .................. *Digested,* 14/**3683**

B, Petitioner [2013] CSOH 187; 2014 Fam. L.R. 41; 2014 G.W.D. 2-43, OH

B, Petitioner [2014] CSOH 66; 2014 G.W.D. 13-238, OH

B, Petitioner [2013] CSOH 91; 2013 S.L.T. 990; 2013 G.W.D. 20-391, OH .................. *Digested,* 13/**3478**: *Approved* 14/3600

BAE Systems Surface Ships Ltd v Assessor for Glasgow; *sub nom* BAE Systems Surface Ships Ltd v Glasgow Assessor 2014 S.L.T. (Lands Tr) 2; [2014] R.V.R. 12; 2013 G.W.D. 35-700, Lands Tr (Scot) .......................... *Digested,* 14/**3675**

BAE Systems Surface Ships Ltd v Glasgow Assessor see BAE Systems Surface Ships Ltd v Assessor for Glasgow

Bain v Assets Co Ltd (No.2) see Watt v Assets Co Ltd

Balfour & Manson LLP v Fleming & Reid 2014 G.W.D. 19-359, Sh Ct (Lothian) (Edinburgh)

Balfour (Bruce James) v HM Advocate see Ferguson (James Douglas) v HM Advocate

BAM Buchanan Ltd v Arcadia Group Ltd 2013 Hous. L.R. 42; 2013 G.W.D. 25-506, OH .......................... *Digested,* 14/**3636**

Bambrick (Scott) v HM Advocate [2014] HCJAC 86; 2014 S.C.L. 667; 2014 G.W.D. 25-492, HCJ .......................... *Digested,* 14/**3444**

Bank of Credit and Commerce International SA (In Liquidation) v Ali (No.1) [2001] UKHL 8; [2002] 1 A.C. 251; [2001] 2 W.L.R. 735; [2001] 1 All E.R. 961; [2001] I.C.R. 337; [2001] I.R.L.R. 292; [2001] Emp. L.R. 359; (2001) 98(15) L.S.G. 32; (2001) 151 N.L.J. 351; (2001) 145 S.J.L.B. 67; (2001) 145 S.J.L.B. 70; Times, March 6, 2001, HL; affirming [2000] 3 All E.R. 51; [2000] I.C.R. 1410; [2000] I.R.L.R. 398; Times, May 10, 2000, CA (Civ Div); reversing [1999] 2 All E.R. 1005; [1999] I.C.R. 1068; [1999] I.R.L.R. 226; (1999) 96(7) L.S.G. 35; (1999) 149 N.L.J. 53; Times, January 25, 1999, Ch D .......................... *Digested,* 01/**2228**: *Applied* 02/207, 02/217, 03/2723, 06/203, 06/2411, 07/2760, 08/663, 12/2023, 14/381: *Considered* 07/2500, 08/2178, 08/2195, 08/648, 09/722, 10/613, 12/2389, 13/578, 14/3354: *Distinguished* 02/703

Bank of Scotland v Seitz 1990 S.L.T. 584; 1990 S.C.L.R. 418; [1991] I.L.Pr. 426, IH; affirming 1989 S.L.T. 641; 1989 S.C.L.R. 270, OH ............................................ *Digested,* 90/**5353**: *Applied* 10/506, 14/3364: *Followed* 92/5933, 94/5960, 00/5927
Bank of Scotland Plc v Gallacher 2013 Hous. L.R. 36, Sh Ct (Glasgow) ....................... *Digested,* 14/**3753**
Barnett v Lambeth LBC see Kay v Lambeth LBC
Baron of Bachuil v Paine [2013] CSIH 110; 2014 G.W.D. 2-40, IH (Ex Div); reversing in part [2012] CSOH 161; 2012 G.W.D. 35-707, OH
Barr v East Renfrewshire Council [2013] CSIH 113; 2014 G.W.D. 3-71, IH (Ex Div)
Bavaird v Sir Robert McAlpine Ltd [2013] CSIH 98; 2014 S.C. 322; 2014 S.L.T. 39; 2013 G.W.D. 39-752, IH (Ex Div); reversing [2012] CSOH 157; 2013 S.C.L.R. 263; 2012 G.W.D. 33-680, OH ............................................................................ *Digested,* 14/**3696**
BBC, Re; *sub nom* A v BBC; A v Secretary of State for the Home Department [2014] UKSC 25; [2014] 2 W.L.R. 1243; [2014] 2 All E.R. 1037; 2014 S.C. (U.K.S.C.) 151; 2014 S.L.T. 613; 2014 S.C.L.R. 593; [2014] E.M.L.R. 25; 37 B.H.R.C. 664; 2014 G.W.D. 15-266; Times, May 15, 2014, SC; affirming [2013] CSIH 43; 2013 S.C. 533; 2013 S.L.T. 749; 2013 G.W.D. 19-377, IH (1 Div) ..................... *Digested,* 14/**43**: *Applied* 14/3433: *Considered* 14/790
BBM Solicitors v Younger 2014 G.W.D. 34-644, Sh Ct (Grampian) (Lerwick)
BC (Zimbabwe), Petitioner [2014] CSOH 149; 2014 G.W.D. 33-638, OH
Beggs v Scottish Information Commissioner [2014] CSIH 10; 2014 G.W.D. 5-113, IH (Ex Div)
Belgium v Recolta Recycling SPRL (C-440/04) see Kittel v Belgium (C-439/04)
Belhaven Brewery Co Ltd v Assessor for Ayrshire Valuation Joint Board [2014] CSIH 89; 2014 G.W.D. 36-676, LVAC
Bell v Inkersall Investments Ltd [2007] CSIH 60; 2007 S.C. 823; 2007 S.L.T. 737; 2007 G.W.D. 23-382, IH (2 Div) ........................................................................ *Digested,* 07/**5351**: *Considered* 14/3639
Bell (Graeme) v HM Advocate [2014] HCJAC 127; 2014 G.W.D. 38-696, HCJ
Bellingham v Todd [2011] CSOH 74; 2011 S.L.T. 1124; 2012 S.C.L.R. 491; 2011 Rep. L.R. 68; 2011 G.W.D. 17-419, OH ........................................................................ *Digested,* 11/**4507**: *Considered* 12/4206, 12/4207, 14/3469
Bent v Highways and Utilities Construction see Pattni v First Leicester Buses Ltd
Beurskens (Gordon) v HM Advocate [2014] HCJAC 99; 2014 S.L.T. 965; 2014 S.C.L. 708; 2014 S.C.C.R. 447; 2014 G.W.D. 30-588, HCJ
BH v Lord Advocate see H v Lord Advocate
Bialas-Krug v EUI Ltd 2014 G.W.D. 28-553, Sh Ct (Lothian) (Edinburgh)
Birch v Paulson [2012] EWCA Civ 487, CA (Civ Div); affirming [2011] EWHC 1614 (QB), QBD (Manchester) *Distinguished* 14/3699
Birmingham City Council v Frisby see Hounslow LBC v Powell
Bishop v 3i Investments Plc [2014] CSOH 152; 2014 G.W.D. 33-634, OH
BJ v HG [2014] CSOH 2; 2014 G.W.D. 5-114, OH
BK (India), Petitioner [2014] CSOH 109; 2014 G.W.D. 24-462, OH
Blance (Andrew) v HM Advocate; *joined cases* Walker (Leon William) v HM Advocate; Raynes (Charles David) v HM Advocate; Low (Ryan David) v HM Advocate; Easton (Warner King) v HM Advocate; Cockburn (Alexander George) v HM Advocate [2013] HCJAC 131; 2014 S.C.L. 13; 2013 S.C.C.R. 557; 2013 G.W.D. 34-670, HCJ ........................................................................ *Digested,* 14/**3451**
Blanco v Scottish Ministers see Somerville v Scottish Ministers
BM (Uganda), Petitioner [2012] CSOH 142; 2012 G.W.D. 30-617, OH *Disapproved* 14/3600
Board of Managers of St Mary's Kenmure v East Dunbartonshire Council; *joined case* Cora Foundation v East Dunbartonshire Council [2014] CSIH 46; 2014 S.C. 665; 2014 S.L.T. 731; 2014 G.W.D. 18-356, IH (Ex Div); affirming [2012] CSOH 198; 2013 S.L.T. 285; 2013 S.C.L.R. 335; 2013 G.W.D. 3-107, OH .................. *Digested,* 14/**3752**
Boatland Properties v Abdul 2014 S.C.L.R. 792, Sh Ct (Tayside) (Perth)
Bonik EOOD v Direktor na Direktsia Obzhalvane i upravlenie na izpalnenieto - Varna pri Tsentralno upravlenie na Natsionalnata agentsia za prihodite (C-285/11) [2013] S.T.C. 773; [2013] S.T.I. 64, ECJ (3rd Chamber) *Applied* 14/3070: *Cited* 14/3810
Bournemouth University Higher Education Corp v Buckland; *sub nom* Buckland v Bournemouth University Higher Education Corp [2010] EWCA Civ 121; [2011] Q.B. 323; [2010] 3 W.L.R. 1664; [2010] 4 All E.R. 186; [2010] I.C.R. 908; [2010] I.R.L.R. 445; (2010) 154(8) S.J.L.B. 28; Times, May 3, 2010, CA (Civ Div); reversing in part [2009] I.C.R. 1042; [2009] I.R.L.R. 606, EAT ........................... *Digested,* 10/**1032**: *Applied* 14/3500: *Considered* 12/1063, 14/1021: *Followed* 14/1024
Bouygues E&S Contracting UK Ltd v Vital Energi Utilities Ltd [2014] CSOH 115; 2014 G.W.D. 25-476, OH

Bova v Highland Council [2013] CSIH 41; 2013 S.C. 510; 2013 G.W.D. 17-363, IH (Ex Div); affirming [2011] CSOH 140; 2011 S.C.L.R. 751; 2011 G.W.D. 28-610, OH Digested, 14/**3738**
Bow v Harvie see Paterson v Harvie
Bowes v Harvie [2014] HCJAC 83; 2014 S.C.L. 674; 2014 G.W.D. 25-482, HCJ .......... *Digested,* 14/**3382**
Bowie v Harvey see Bowie v Harvie
Bowie v Harvie; *sub nom* Bowie v Harvey [2014] HCJAC 65; 2014 S.C.L. 546; 2014 G.W.D. 21-396, HCJ .......... *Digested,* 14/**3428**
Boyd v Fortune [2014] CSIH 93; 2014 G.W.D. 37-680, IH
Bradley (Dawn) v Donaldson [2010] HCJAC 136; 2011 G.W.D. 1-60, HCJ *Considered* 14/3785
Branney (Leslie McPherson) v HM Advocate [2014] HCJAC 78; 2014 S.C.L. 728; 2014 S.C.C.R. 620; 2014 G.W.D. 31-606, HCJ .......... *Digested,* 14/**3380**
Bremner v Martin (t/a George Martin Engineering) 2006 S.L.T. 169; 2006 G.W.D. 4-73, OH .......... *Digested,* 06/**5089**: *Followed* 14/3322
Briess v Rosher see Briess v Woolley
Briess v Woolley; *sub nom* Briess v Rosher [1954] A.C. 333; [1954] 2 W.L.R. 832; [1954] 1 All E.R. 909; (1954) 98 S.J. 286, HL; reversing [1953] 2 Q.B. 218; [1953] 2 W.L.R. 608; [1953] 1 All E.R. 717; (1953) 97 S.J. 209, CA .......... *Digested,* 54/**468**: *Applied* 14/2201: *Approved* 66/9912
British Railways Board v Glasgow Corp 1976 S.C. 224, IH (2 Div); affirming 1974 S.C. 261; 1975 S.L.T. 45, OH .......... *Digested,* 79/**3297**: *Considered* 92/5891: *Followed* 14/3301
British Sky Broadcasting Group Plc v Avalonbar Ltd [2014] CSOH 39; 2014 G.W.D. 9-177, OH
British Telecommunications Plc v Common Services Agency [2014] CSOH 44; 2014 G.W.D. 10-193, OH
Brodie (George) v HM Advocate [2012] HCJAC 147; 2013 J.C. 142; 2013 S.C.L. 116; 2013 S.C.C.R. 23; 2012 G.W.D. 38-755, HCJ .......... *Digested,* 13/**3631**: *Followed* 14/3442
Brown v Crofters Commission 2014 S.L.C.R. 12; 2014 G.W.D. 13-243, Land Ct
Brown v Parole Board for Scotland [2013] CSOH 200; 2014 G.W.D. 2-36, OH
Brown v Sabre Insurance Co Ltd [2014] CSOH 51; 2014 G.W.D. 18-342, OH
Brown (Jason) v HM Advocate [2014] HCJAC 120; 2014 G.W.D. 35-653, HCJ
Bryceland (George Mackie) v HM Advocate see Bryceland, Petitioner
Bryceland, Petitioner; *sub nom* Lynch (Rosemary Burns) v HM Advocate; Bryceland (George Mackie) v HM Advocate; *joined case* Lynch, Petitioner 2003 S.L.T. 54; 2002 S.C.C.R. 995; 2002 G.W.D. 33-1104, HCJ .......... *Digested,* 03/**5395**: *Followed* 14/3764
BS v Dundee City Council see S v Dundee City Council
Buckland v Bournemouth University Higher Education Corp see Bournemouth University Higher Education Corp v Buckland
Burdis v Livsey see Lagden v O'Connor
BurgerKing Ltd v Castlebrook Holdings Ltd [2014] CSOH 36; 2014 G.W.D. 9-178, OH
Burns v Royal Mail Group Ltd 2014 S.L.T. (Sh Ct) 73; 2014 G.W.D. 13-234, Sh Ct (Lothian) (Edinburgh) .......... *Digested,* 14/**3336**
Burns (John) v Wilson (Sentencing) 1993 S.L.T. 809; 1993 S.C.C.R. 418, HCJ Appeal *Digested,* 93/**4976**: *Considered* 93/4977, 14/3421
Burton v Keeper of the Registers of Scotland 2014 S.L.T. (Lands Tr) 69; 2014 G.W.D. 25-499, Lands Tr (Scot) .......... *Digested,* 14/**3589**

C v Authority Reporter 2014 Fam. L.R. 72; 2014 G.W.D. 20-384, Sh Ct (Glasgow) ...... *Digested,* 14/**3528**
C v HM Advocate [2014] HCJAC 12; 2014 G.W.D. 6-119, HCJ
C v M 2014 S.L.T. (Sh Ct) 109; 2014 G.W.D. 23-440, Sh Ct (Tayside) (Forfar) .......... *Digested,* 14/**3800**
Caduceus Investments Ltd v Border Property Development Ltd 2014 G.W.D. 20-375, Sh Ct (Lothian) (Edinburgh)
Caglayan v Turkey (30461/02) (Unreported, October 21, 2008), ECHR *Considered* 14/3599
Cairney v Glasgow City Council 2014 G.W.D. 25-473, Sh Ct (Glasgow)
Cairngorms Campaign v Cairngorms National Park Authority [2013] CSIH 65; 2014 S.C. 37; 2013 G.W.D. 25-516, IH (Ex Div); affirming [2012] CSOH 153; 2012 G.W.D. 36-732, OH .......... *Digested,* 14/**3729**
Calltel Telecom Ltd v Revenue and Customs Commissioners see Mobilx Ltd (In Administration) v Revenue and Customs Commissioners
CalMac Ferries Ltd v Wallace [2014] I.C.R. 453; [2014] Eq. L.R. 115, EAT (SC) .......... *Digested,* 14/**3504**
Cameron v Lukes 2014 G.W.D. 7-144, Sh Ct (Glasgow)

Cameron (Alan) v HM Advocate [2011] HCJAC 29; 2011 S.C.L. 633; 2011 G.W.D. 14-328, HCJ ........ *Digested,* 11/**4084**: *Considered* 12/4266: *Overruled* 14/3775
Cameron (Stuart) v HM Advocate see Ferguson (James Douglas) v HM Advocate
Campbell v Peter Gordon Joiners Ltd [2013] CSOH 181; 2014 S.L.T. 178; 2014 G.W.D. 1-5, OH ........ *Digested,* 14/**3356**
Campbell (Thomas) v HM Advocate [2013] HCJAC 104; 2013 S.C.L. 927; 2013 G.W.D. 29-575, HCJ ........ *Digested,* 14/**3368**
Cannell (Paul) v HM Advocate [2009] HCJAC 6; 2009 S.C.L. 484; 2009 S.C.C.R. 207; 2009 G.W.D. 5-77, HCJ ........ *Digested,* 09/**4744**: *Doubted* 11/4165: *Followed* 14/3381
Capital Investment Corp of Montreal Ltd v Elliot 2014 S.L.C.R. 19; 2014 G.W.D. 23-427, Land Ct
Capitol Investments (Scotland) Ltd v BAA Ltd see Riva v BAA Ltd
Capitol Investments (Scotland) Ltd v Edinburgh Airport Ltd see Riva v Edinburgh Airport Ltd
Carberry (Frank) v HM Advocate [2013] HCJAC 101; 2014 J.C. 56; 2013 S.C.L. 934; 2013 S.C.C.R. 587; 2013 G.W.D. 30-593, HCJ ........ *Digested,* 14/**3422**
Carberry (Frank) v HM Advocate [2013] HCJAC 136; 2013 S.C.C.R. 587; 2013 G.W.D. 34-672, HCJ ........ *Digested,* 14/**3460**
Carlin (John) v HM Advocate; *joined case* McLuckie (James) v HM Advocate [2014] HCJAC 122; 2014 G.W.D. 38-695, HCJ
Carlyle v Royal Bank of Scotland Plc see Royal Bank of Scotland Plc v Carlyle
Caroll v Scottish Borders Council [2014] CSOH 6; 2014 S.C.L.R. 532; 2014 G.W.D. 4-94, OH ........ *Digested,* 14/**3737**
Carr (Daniel Kimet Thomas) v HM Advocate; *joined case* MacNeill (Grant) v HM Advocate [2012] HCJAC 130; 2013 S.C.L. 918; 2013 G.W.D. 30-595, HCJ *Distinguished* 14/3441
Carr Berman Crichton Ltd v Jones 2014 G.W.D. 6-124, Sh Ct (Glasgow)
Carroll v Scottish Borders Council [2014] CSOH 30; 2014 S.L.T. 659; 2014 G.W.D. 8-160, OH ........ *Digested,* 14/**3338**
Cathcart v Law Society of Scotland [2013] CSIH 104; 2014 G.W.D. 1-23, IH (Ex Div)
Centre for Maritime and Industrial Safety Technology Ltd v Ineos Manufacturing Scotland Ltd [2014] CSOH 5; 2014 G.W.D. 5-100, OH
Chalmers v Chalmers [2014] CSOH 161; 2014 G.W.D. 38-699, OH
Chalmers (Robert Davidson) v HM Advocate [2014] HCJAC 24; 2014 J.C. 220; 2014 S.L.T. 688; 2014 S.C.L. 442; 2014 S.C.C.R. 291; 2014 G.W.D. 13-249, HCJ .... *Digested,* 14/**3775**
Chalmers (Robert) v HM Advocate [2014] HCJAC 59; 2014 J.C. 229, HCJ
Charles Henshaw & Sons Ltd v Stewart & Shields Ltd [2014] CSIH 55; 2014 G.W.D. 22-415, IH (Ex Div)
Charles Henshaw and Sons Ltd v Stewart & Shields Ltd 2014 G.W.D. 10-183, Sh Ct (Lothian) (Edinburgh)
Charlton v Secretary of State for Work and Pensions [2009] EWCA Civ 42, CA (Civ Div) *Considered* 14/3792
Chen (Xin) v HM Advocate see Lin (Jie) v HM Advocate
Chester v Secretary of State for Justice see R. (on the application of Chester) v Secretary of State for Justice
Chief Constable of the Police Service of Scotland v D 2014 G.W.D. 22-414, Sh Ct (Tayside) (Falkirk)
Chief Constable of the Police Service of Scotland v DJR see Chief Constable of the Police Service of Scotland v R
Chief Constable of the Police Service of Scotland v R 2013 G.W.D. 33-657, Sh Ct (Lothian) (Edinburgh) *Affirmed* 14/3353
Chief Constable of the Police Service of Scotland v R; *sub nom* Chief Constable of the Police Service of Scotland v DJR [2014] CSIH 8; 2014 S.C. 448; 2014 S.L.T. 209; 2014 G.W.D. 3-60, IH (2 Div) ........ *Digested,* 14/**3353**
Chief Constable of West Yorkshire v Vento (No.2) see Vento v Chief Constable of West Yorkshire
Child Maintenance and Enforcement Commission v Wilson [2013] CSIH 95; 2014 S.L.T. 46; 2013 G.W.D. 39-744, IH (Ex Div) ........ *Digested,* 14/**3347**
Child Maintenance and Enforcement Commission Child Support Agency v Roy [2013] CSIH 105; 2014 G.W.D. 1-4, IH (Ex Div)
Childs v McLeod 1981 S.L.T. (Notes) 27, HCJ Appeal ........ *Digested,* 81/**3019**: *Distinguished* 14/3428
Citifinancial Europe Plc v Rice; *sub nom* Cititfinancial Europe Plc v Rice 2013 Hous. L.R. 23, Sh Ct (Glasgow) ........ *Digested,* 14/**3361**

Cititfinancial Europe Plc v Rice see Citifinancial Europe Plc v Rice
City Assessor, Glasgow City Council v HMV UK Ltd [2013] CSIH 94; 2014 S.L.T. 188; 2013 G.W.D. 39-753, LVAC ........ *Digested,* 14/**3676**
City of Edinburgh Council v B [2014] CSOH 128; 2014 G.W.D. 27-545, OH
City of Edinburgh Council v Lothian Valuation Appeal Committee; *sub nom* Edinburgh City Council's Appeal, Re [2014] CSIH 32; [2014] R.A. 410; 2014 G.W.D. 14-262, IH (Ex Div) ........ *Digested,* 14/**3651**
City of Edinburgh Council v X 2014 G.W.D. 19-365, Sh Ct (Lothian) (Livingston)
City of Edinburgh Council v X 2014 G.W.D. 19-366, Sh Ct (Lothian) (Livingston)
CJD v Royal Bank of Scotland see D v Royal Bank of Scotland
CJM v HM Advocate see M v HM Advocate (No.2)
Clark v Ardington Electrical Services see Lagden v O'Connor
Clark v TripAdvisor LLC [2014] CSIH 110, IH (Ex Div); affirming [2014] CSOH 20; 2014 S.L.T. 418; 2014 S.C.L.R. 563; 2014 G.W.D. 7-138, OH ........ *Digested,* 14/**3345**
Clark v Tull (t/a Ardington Electrical Services) see Lagden v O'Connor
Clark (David) v HM Advocate [2014] HCJAC 108; 2014 S.C.L. 873; 2014 G.W.D. 31-620, HCJ
Clarke v Edinburgh & District Tramways Co Ltd 1919 S.C. (H.L.) 35; (1919) 1 S.L.T. 247, HL
*Applied* 01/6217, 03/5252: *Followed* 13/6, 14/1579
Cloburn Quarry Co Ltd v Revenue and Customs Commissioners [2013] CSOH 203; [2014] S.T.C. 1073; 2014 S.L.T. 303; 2014 G.W.D. 2-35, OH ........ *Digested,* 14/**3803**
CM v State Hospitals Board for Scotland see M v State Hospitals Board for Scotland
CM, Petitioner see M v State Hospitals Board for Scotland
Co-operative Group (CWS) Ltd v Pritchard; *sub nom* Pritchard v Co-operative Group (CWS) Ltd [2011] EWCA Civ 329; [2012] Q.B. 320; [2011] 3 W.L.R. 1272; [2012] 1 All E.R. 205, CA (Civ Div) ........ *Digested,* 12/**3346**: *Considered* 14/3720
Coalter (Adrian Robert) v HM Advocate; *joined case* Ferns (William James) v HM Advocate [2013] HCJAC 115; 2013 S.C.L. 1024; 2013 S.C.C.R. 668; 2013 G.W.D. 32-635, HCJ ........ *Digested,* 14/**3378**
Coats (Colin) v HM Advocate see Wade (Philip) v HM Advocate
Cockburn (Alexander George) v HM Advocate see Blance (Andrew) v HM Advocate
Cole v Lambeth LBC see Kay v Lambeth LBC
Collins v Sweeney 2013 G.W.D. 11-230, Sh Ct (Glasgow); no effect 2014 G.W.D. 12-214, Sh Ct (Glasgow)
Collins (Kenneth) v HM Advocate [2013] HCJAC 167; 2014 S.L.T. 704; 2014 S.C.L. 465; 2014 S.C.C.R. 466; 2014 G.W.D. 17-318, HCJ ........ *Digested,* 14/**3420**
Color Drack GmbH v Lexx International Vertriebs GmbH (C-386/05) [2010] 1 W.L.R. 1909; [2008] 1 All E.R. (Comm) 168; [2010] Bus. L.R. 1044; [2007] E.C.R. I-3699; [2008] All E.R. (EC) 1044; [2007] I.L.Pr. 35, ECJ (4th Chamber) ........ *Digested,* 07/**1576**: *Considered* 08/556, 14/3346
Comhairle Nan Eilean Siar v Scottish Ministers [2013] CSIH 45; 2013 S.C. 548; 2013 S.L.T. 687; 2014 S.C.L.R. 90; 2013 G.W.D. 19-383, IH (Ex Div) ........ *Digested,* 13/**3670**
Company (No.000709 of 1992), Re see O'Neill v Phillips
Connal v Dunn [2014] HCJAC 57; 2014 S.L.T. 786; 2014 S.C.L. 630; 2014 S.C.C.R. 513; 2014 G.W.D. 24-450, HCJ ........ *Digested,* 14/**3461**
Connal v Dunn [2014] HCJAC 77; 2014 G.W.D. 25-489, HCJ
Conquer v Lothian Health Board [2014] CSOH 132; 2014 G.W.D. 28-564, OH
Constantine v Lambeth LBC see Kay v Lambeth LBC
Construction Centre Group Ltd v Highland Council 2003 S.C. 464; 2003 S.L.T. 623; 2003 G.W.D. 13-399, IH (Ex Div); affirming 2002 S.L.T. 1274; [2002] B.L.R. 476; 2002 G.W.D. 27-932, OH ........ *Digested,* 03/**5321**: *Distinguished* 11/4059, 14/3618
Contempt of court proceedings in respect of M and L 2014 S.L.T. (Sh Ct) 21; 2014 G.W.D. 3-58, Sh Ct (Lothian) (Edinburgh) ........ *Digested,* 14/**3549**
Cook v Cadman 2014 S.L.T. (Lands Tr) 13; 2014 G.W.D. 3-66, Lands Tr (Scot) ........ *Digested,* 14/**3587**
Cooper v Bank of Scotland Plc [2014] CSOH 16; 2014 G.W.D. 6-126, OH
Copoc v Chief Constable of South Yorkshire see Alcock v Chief Constable of South Yorkshire
Cora Foundation v East Dunbartonshire Council see Board of Managers of St Mary's Kenmure v East Dunbartonshire Council
Coubrough's Executrix v HM Advocate [2010] HCJAC 32; 2010 S.L.T. 577; 2010 S.C.L. 689; 2010 S.C.C.R. 473; 2010 G.W.D. 15-287, HCJ ........ *Digested,* 10/**4107**: *Doubted* 11/4167: *Followed* 14/3442
Courage v Richardson [2013] HCJAC 97; 2013 S.C.C.R. 476, HCJ ........ *Digested,* 14/**3771**
Cowan v Hardey [2014] CSIH 11; 2014 G.W.D. 5-111, IH (Ex Div)
Cox v Dundee City Council [2014] CSOH 3; 2014 G.W.D. 4-93, OH

Cox v Dunn [2013] HCJAC 176; 2014 S.C.L. 185; 2014 G.W.D. 2-41, HCJ .................. *Digested*, 14/**3447**

Coyle v Lanarkshire Health Board [2014] CSIH 78; 2014 G.W.D. 31-617, IH (Ex Div); affirming [2013] CSOH 167; 2013 G.W.D. 37-722, OH

Crabbe v Reid 2014 G.W.D. 12-208, Sh Ct (Glasgow)

Craig v Thomson see Gill v Thomson

Cramaso LLP v Earl of Seafield see Cramaso LLP v Viscount Reidhaven's Trustees

Cramaso LLP v Ogilvie-Grant see Cramaso LLP v Viscount Reidhaven's Trustees

Cramaso LLP v Viscount Reidhaven's Trustees; *sub nom* Cramaso LLP v Earl of Seafield; Cramaso LLP v Ogilvie-Grant [2014] UKSC 9; [2014] A.C. 1093; [2014] 2 W.L.R. 317; [2014] 2 All E.R. 270; [2014] 1 All E.R. (Comm) 830; 2014 S.C. (U.K.S.C.) 121; 2014 S.L.T. 521; 2014 S.C.L.R. 484; (2014) 158(7) S.J.L.B. 37; Times, February 20, 2014, SC; reversing [2011] CSIH 81; 2012 S.C. 240; 2012 G.W.D. 1-11, IH (2 Div); affirming [2010] CSOH 62; 2010 G.W.D. 20-403, OH .......... *Digested*, 14/**2201**

Credit Suisse v Beegas Nominees Ltd [1994] 4 All E.R. 803; (1995) 69 P. & C.R. 177; [1994] 12 E.G. 189; [1994] 11 E.G. 151; [1993] E.G. 157 (C.S.); [1993] N.P.C. 123; Independent, September 15, 1993, Ch D .......... *Digested*, 95/**2982**: *Applied* 99/3738: *Approved* 14/1978: *Considered* 99/3695

Criminal Proceedings against Keck (C-267/91); *joined case* Criminal Proceedings against Mithouard (C-268/91) [1993] E.C.R. I-6097; [1995] 1 C.M.L.R. 101; Times, November 25, 1993; Financial Times, November 30, 1993, ECJ .......... *Digested*, 94/**4885**: *Applied* 05/500, 06/1557, 06/1559, 06/1561, 08/1331, 09/1404: *Considered* 95/4907, 95/642, 96/2801, 01/2486, 03/1455, 12/4151, 14/3647: *Distinguished* 05/1449: *Followed* 98/3855, 00/4165, 04/636

Criminal Proceedings against Mithouard (C-268/91) see Criminal Proceedings against Keck (C-267/91)

Croal (Brian) v HM Advocate [2014] HCJAC 34; 2014 S.C.L. 423; 2014 G.W.D. 15-271, HCJ .......... *Digested*, 14/**3400**

Crofters Commission's Reference, Re 2012 S.L.C.R. 159, Land Ct .......... *Digested*, 14/**3627**

Crombie (Michael George) v HM Advocate [2014] HCJAC 118; 2014 G.W.D. 36-669, HCJ

Cross v Aberdeen Property Leasing 2014 S.L.T. (Sh Ct) 46; 2014 Hous. L.R. 14; 2014 G.W.D. 8-163, Sh Ct (Grampian) (Aberdeen) .......... *Digested*, 14/**3633**

Cuadrench More v Koninklijke Luchtvaart Maatschappij NV (C-139/11) [2013] 2 All E.R. (Comm) 1152; [2013] 1 Lloyd's Rep. 341; [2013] 2 C.M.L.R. 4, ECJ (3rd Chamber) *Applied* 14/165: *Cited* 14/3319

Cunningham v Cameron [2013] CSOH 193; 2014 G.W.D. 3-69, OH

Cunningham (David James) v HM Advocate [2012] HCJAC 90; 2012 S.C.L. 884; 2012 S.C.C.R. 605; 2012 G.W.D. 25-520, HCJ .......... *Digested*, 13/**3598**: *Followed* 14/3405

Curran v Angus Estates Tealing Ltd [2013] CSIH 92; 2014 S.L.T. 49; 2013 G.W.D. 38-727, IH (1 Div) .......... *Digested*, 14/**3323**

Currie v Esure Services Ltd [2014] CSIH 112, IH (2 Div); affirming [2014] CSOH 34; 2014 S.L.T. 631; 2014 Rep. L.R. 57; 2014 G.W.D. 10-185, OH .......... *Digested*, 14/**3471**: *Considered* 14/3468

Cusick v Harvie; *sub nom* Cusick v McPherson [2014] HCJAC 39; 2014 G.W.D. 17-314, HCJ .......... *Digested*, 14/**3762**

Cusick v McPherson see Cusick v Harvie

D v HM Advocate; *sub nom* TD v HM Advocate [2013] HCJAC 130; 2013 S.C.L. 1047; 2013 S.C.C.R. 696; 2013 G.W.D. 34-673, HCJ .......... *Digested*, 14/**3416**

D v Mental Health Tribunal for Scotland 2014 S.L.T. (Sh Ct) 39; 2014 G.W.D. 13-246, Sh Ct (Lothian) (Edinburgh) .......... *Digested*, 14/**3686**

D v Nursing and Midwifery Council [2014] CSIH 90; 2014 S.L.T. 1069; 2014 G.W.D. 36-674, IH (Ex Div)

D v Royal Bank of Scotland; *sub nom* CJD v Royal Bank of Scotland [2013] CSIH 86; [2014] I.R.L.R. 25; 2013 G.W.D. 35-691, IH (Ex Div) .......... *Digested*, 14/**3505**

D (S) v HM Advocate [2014] HCJAC 17; 2014 S.C.L. 352; 2014 G.W.D. 8-158, HCJ ... *Digested*, 14/**3455**

D'Arcy (Ernest) v HM Advocate [2013] HCJAC 173; 2014 G.W.D. 1-12, HCJ

D, Appellant 2014 Fam. L.R. 66; 2014 G.W.D. 21-405, Sh Ct (Tayside) (Falkirk) .......... *Digested*, 14/**3523**

Danzan 2003 Trust v Assessor for Lothian 2014 S.L.T. (Lands Tr) 4; [2014] R.V.R. 36; 2013 G.W.D. 35-699, Lands Tr (Scot) .......... *Digested*, 14/**3677**: *Cited* 14/3666

David v Nemzeti Ado- es Vamhivatal Eszak-alfoldi Regionalis Ado Foigazgatosaga (C-142/11) see Mahageben kft v Nemzeti Ado- es Vamhivatal Del-dunantuli Regionalis Ado Foigazgatosaga (C-80/11)

David T Morrison & Co Ltd (t/a Gael Home Interiors) v ICL Plastics Ltd [2014] UKSC 48; 2014 S.C. (U.K.S.C.) 222; 2014 S.L.T. 791; 2014 S.C.L.R. 711; [2014] C.I.L.L. 3561; 2014 G.W.D. 25-504, SC; reversing [2013] CSIH 19; 2013 S.C. 391; 2013 S.L.T. 413; 2013 S.C.L.R. 674; 2013 G.W.D. 11-237, IH (Ex Div); reversing [2012] CSOH 44; 2012 S.L.T. 813; 2012 Rep. L.R. 118; 2012 G.W.D. 12-236, OH ............ *Digested,* 14/**2470**

Dawson v Page [2013] CSIH 24; 2013 S.C. 432; 2013 G.W.D. 13-289, IH (Ex Div); affirming [2012] CSOH 33; 2012 Rep. L.R. 56; 2012 G.W.D. 11-217, OH .......... *Digested,* 14/**3698**

De Fazio v De Fazio [2014] CSOH 56; 2014 G.W.D. 13-251, OH

Deeney (Paul) v HM Advocate [2014] HCJAC 104; 2014 S.C.L. 858; 2014 G.W.D. 32-629, HCJ

Dem-Master Demolition Ltd v Alba Plastics Ltd [2014] CSIH 58; 2014 G.W.D. 24-446, IH (Ex Div); no effect [2014] CSOH 84; 2014 Hous. L.R. 32; 2014 G.W.D. 16-288, OH

Dennard v Plant see Lagden v O'Connor

Department for the Environment, Food and Rural Affairs v Robertson see Robertson v Department for the Environment, Food and Rural Affairs

Deutsche Lufthansa AG v Flughafen Frankfurt-Hahn GmbH (C-284/12) [2014] 2 C.M.L.R. 20, ECJ (2nd Chamber)
*Considered* 14/3803

Dickson v Brown [2013] HCJAC 157; 2014 S.L.T. 126; 2014 S.C.L. 73; 2013 G.W.D. 40-761, HCJ ............ *Digested,* 14/**3404**

Dickson v President of the Mental Health Tribunal for Scotland [2014] CSOH 58; 2014 S.L.T. 581; 2014 G.W.D. 12-207, OH ............ *Digested,* 14/**3682**

Dimond v Lovell [2002] 1 A.C. 384; [2000] 2 W.L.R. 1121; [2000] 2 All E.R. 897; [2000] R.T.R. 243; [2000] C.C.L.R. 57; 2000 Rep. L.R. 62; (2000) 97(22) L.S.G. 47; (2000) 150 N.L.J. 740; Times, May 12, 2000; Independent, May 17, 2000, HL; affirming [2000] Q.B. 216; [1999] 3 W.L.R. 561; [1999] 3 All E.R. 1; [1999] R.T.R. 297; [1999] C.C.L.R. 46; (1999) 96(21) L.S.G. 40; (1999) 149 N.L.J. 681; (1999) 143 S.J.L.B. 181; Times, May 3, 1999, CA (Civ Div); reversing (Unreported, May 1, 1998), CC (Sheffield) [*Cottrill Stone Lawless Solicitors, 18 Lloyd Street, Albert Square, Manchester*] ............ *Digested,* 00/**2566**:
*Applied* 99/2470, 99/2471, 99/2475, 99/2478, 00/2570, 00/2587, 01/1527, 01/881, 01/900, 07/2497, 12/1898, 13/3033, 14/1852, 14/829: *Cited* 99/2458, 99/2461, 99/2476, 99/2499, 00/2574, 00/2580, 00/2592, 00/2593, 01/3830, 01/896, 01/899, 02/685: *Considered* 99/2453, 99/2454, 99/2459, 99/2460, 99/2465, 99/2466, 99/2467, 99/2468, 99/2477, 99/2479, 99/2481, 99/2496, 99/532, 00/2589, 00/311, 00/425, 01/885, 01/888, 01/890, 01/898, 06/702, 09/683, 09/970, 11/2258, 14/3473: *Distinguished* 99/2452, 99/2482, 99/2491, 99/2504, 99/535, 00/2578, 00/2585, 00/2597, 01/893, 01/894, 02/932, 04/630: *Followed* 99/2463, 99/2489, 00/2565, 00/2577, 00/2579, 01/657, 01/887, 01/901, 04/628, 12/1902, 12/2812, 14/610: *Referred to* 99/2451, 99/2464, 99/2472, 99/2473, 99/2474, 99/2483, 99/2485, 99/2487, 99/2490, 00/2562, 01/1542

Din v Bridging Loans Ltd [2014] CSIH 49; 2014 G.W.D. 18-332, IH (2 Div)

Dinnell v Scottish Ministers [2013] CSOH 204; 2014 G.W.D. 4-82, OH

DM (Algeria) v Secretary of State for the Home Department; *sub nom* M v Secretary of State for the Home Department [2014] CSIH 29; 2014 S.C. 635; 2014 S.L.T. 650; 2014 G.W.D. 13-241, IH (Ex Div) ............ *Digested,* 14/**3607**

DN (Rwanda), Petitioner [2014] CSOH 142; 2014 G.W.D. 30-598, OH

Docherty v SW Global Resourcing Ltd [2013] CSIH 72; 2014 S.C. 180; [2013] I.R.L.R. 874; 2013 G.W.D. 28-559, IH (1 Div) ............ *Digested,* 13/**3677**

Docherty (Martin) v HM Advocate [2014] HCJAC 71; 2014 S.C.C.R. 495; 2014 G.W.D. 25-479, HCJ

Docherty (Patrick) v HM Advocate [2014] HCJAC 115; 2014 G.W.D. 34-645, HCJ

Docherty (Patrick) v HM Advocate [2014] HCJAC 94; 2014 S.C.L. 758; 2014 G.W.D. 29-572, HCJ ............ *Digested,* 14/**3390**

Donaldson v Donaldson [2014] CSIH 88; 2014 Fam. L.R. 126; 2014 G.W.D. 36-665, IH (Ex Div)

Donaldson v Donaldson 2014 G.W.D. 12-209, Sh Ct (Glasgow)

Donaldson v Scottish Legal Aid Board [2014] CSIH 31; 2014 S.C. 689; 2014 S.L.T. 459; 2014 G.W.D. 12-218, IH (Ex Div); affirming [2012] CSOH 176; 2013 S.L.T. 35; 2012 G.W.D. 39-760, OH ............ *Digested,* 14/**3642**

Donoghue v Stevenson; *sub nom* McAlister v Stevenson [1932] A.C. 562; 1932 S.C. (H.L.) 31; 1932 S.L.T. 317; [1932] W.N. 139, HL
*Applied* 47-51/6681, 47-51/6693, 47-51/6761, 47-51/6881, 47-51/6897, 52/1563, 52/2362, 53/2422, 53/639, 56/904, 57/1415, 57/2371, 61/825, 62/2028, 62/2188, 63/2362, 64/1670, 65/2669, 65/416, 68/4511, 69/2403, 70/1493, 70/1850, 72/1104, 72/2350, 72/2352, 72/2408, 72/2409, 74/2579, 75/3994, 75/933, 77/2025, 78/2065, 78/3538, 81/1849, 82/2135, 85/2301, 87/2579, 88/3410, 89/1286, 01/4509, 04/2747, 07/5426, 14/3697: *Considered* 47-51/351, 47-51/6734, 47-51/9691, 54/2200, 55/1839, 57/2369, 62/2083, 62/3080, 63/2416, 65/2663, 65/2671, 69/1157, 70/1849, 72/2528, 74/363, 74/3638, 75/2343, 76/228, 78/2088, 87/2580, 88/2418, 88/2433, 88/3376, 88/3409, 91/2657, 91/2661, 93/2983, 93/2997, 94/5335, 95/3698, 95/4519, 98/3995, 99/3960, 00/4227: *Distinguished* 47-51/6584, 47-51/6705, 47-51/7886, 51/3988, 52/4290, 57/2366, 57/2639, 63/2360, 63/330, 64/2516, 66/6884, 72/2361, 83/2746: *Followed* 76/3296, 85/4437, 11/2270, 11/4487: *Referred to* 79/1866

Doonin Plant Ltd v HM Advocate [2014] HCJAC 26; 2014 J.C. 207; 2014 S.C.C.R. 234; 2014 G.W.D. 13-232, HCJ ........ *Digested,* 14/**3405**

Douglas v Bell 2014 Fam. L.R. 2, Sh Ct (South Strathclyde) (Hamilton)

Downie v Christie & Son (Metal Merchants) Ltd [2014] CSOH 108; 2014 G.W.D. 23-428, OH

Drimsynie Estate Ltd v Ramsay [2014] CSOH 93; 2014 G.W.D. 19-361, OH

Dryburgh v Scots Media Tax Ltd see Dryburgh v Scotts Media Tax Ltd

Dryburgh v Scotts Media Tax Ltd; *sub nom* Dryburgh v Scots Media Tax Ltd [2014] CSIH 45; 2014 S.C. 651; 2014 S.C.L.R. 749; 2014 G.W.D. 19-371, IH (Ex Div); reversing [2011] CSOH 147; 2011 G.W.D. 31-658, OH ........ *Digested,* 14/**3743**

DS v HM Advocate; *sub nom* HM Advocate v DS [2007] UKPC D1; 2007 S.C. (P.C.) 1; 2007 S.L.T. 1026; 2007 S.C.C.R. 222; [2007] H.R.L.R. 28; 24 B.H.R.C. 412; Times, June 12, 2007, PC (Sc) ........ *Digested,* 07/**5019**:
*Considered* 13/3558: *Followed* 14/3425

DSM Nutritional Products v Assessor for Ayrshire Valuation Joint Board 2014 S.L.T. (Lands Tr) 7; [2014] R.V.R. 100; 2014 G.W.D. 1-30, Lands Tr (Scot) ........ *Digested,* 14/**3673**

DTE Financial Services Ltd v Wilson (Inspector of Taxes) [2001] EWCA Civ 455; [2001] S.T.C. 777; 74 T.C. 14; [2001] B.T.C. 159; [2001] S.T.I. 670; (2001) 98(21) L.S.G. 40; Times, May 3, 2001; Daily Telegraph, April 10, 2001, CA (Civ Div); affirming [1999] S.T.C. 1061; [1999] B.T.C. 415; (1999) 96(44) L.S.G. 41; (1999) 143 S.J.L.B. 270; Times, November 9, 1999, Ch D; affirming [1999] S.T.C. (S.C.D.) 121, Sp Comm ........ *Digested,* 01/**5237**:
*Applied* 07/4085, 08/3671, 13/3094: *Considered* 14/3807: *Distinguished* 03/4233

Duff v Chief Constable of Dumfries and Galloway 2014 G.W.D. 26-513, Sh Ct (South Strathclyde) (Dumfries)

Duff v Shearer [2014] CSIH 20; 2014 G.W.D. 7-135, IH (Ex Div)

Duff, Petitioner [2013] CSIH 112; 2014 G.W.D. 3-57, IH

Duffus v McWhirter 2014 G.W.D. 34-647, Lands Tr (Scot)

Duffy v Harvie [2014] HCJAC 81; 2014 G.W.D. 25-484, HCJ

Dunbartonshire, Argyll and Bute Assessor v Akram see Assessor for Dunbartonshire, Argyll and Bute v Akram

Duncan v Scottish Ministers [2014] CSOH 24; 2014 S.L.T. 531; 2014 G.W.D. 9-167, OH ........ *Digested,* 14/**3702**

Dundee City Council v D Geddes (Contractors) Ltd [2014] CSOH 164; 2014 G.W.D. 38-694, OH

Durkin v DSG Retail Ltd [2014] UKSC 21; [2014] 1 W.L.R. 1148; [2014] 2 All E.R. 715; [2014] 1 All E.R. (Comm) 929; 2014 S.C. (U.K.S.C.) 139; 2014 S.L.T. 468; 2014 S.C.L.R. 403; [2014] E.C.C. 20; 2014 G.W.D. 12-211; Times, April 4, 2014, SC; reversing [2010] CSIH 49; 2010 S.C. 662; 2011 S.L.T. 114; 2010 S.C.L.R. 692; [2010] C.T.L.C. 252; 2010 G.W.D. 28-574, IH (1 Div) ........ *Digested,* 14/**613**

Dutch v Parole Board for Scotland [2013] CSOH 172; 2014 S.L.T. 285; 2013 G.W.D. 38-726, OH ........ *Digested,* 14/**3701**

Dymny v Lambeth LBC see Kay v Lambeth LBC

Dzhaksybergenov v Ukraine (12343/10) (Unreported, January 11, 2011), ECHR
*Considered* 14/3521

Dzhurayev v Russia (71386/10) (2013) 57 E.H.R.R. 22, ECHR
*Considered* 14/3521

E v W 2014 G.W.D. 26-514, Sh Ct (South Strathclyde) (Dumfries)

EA v GN see A v N

Eadie Cairns Ltd v Fife Council [2013] CSIH 109; 2014 G.W.D. 15-279, IH (2 Div)

East Ayrshire Council v Zurich Insurance Plc [2014] CSOH 102; 2014 G.W.D. 23-432, OH

East Lothian Council v Martin 2014 G.W.D. 27-537, Sh Ct (Lothian) (Edinburgh)
East of Scotland Water Authority v Livingstone; *sub nom* Livingstone v East of Scotland Water Authority 1999 S.C. 65; 1999 S.L.T. 869; 1998 S.C.L.R. 1049; 1998 Hous. L.R. 124; 1998 G.W.D. 36-1881, IH (1 Div); affirming 1997 S.L.T. (Lands Tr) 28; 1998 Hous. L.R. 58, Lands Tr (Scot) .......................................... *Digested,* 99/**6272**: *Considered* 00/6466: *Distinguished* 09/5051, 14/3634: *Followed* 00/6467, 01/6698
East Renfrewshire Council, Petitioner [2014] CSOH 129; 2014 G.W.D. 27-549, OH
Eastmoor LLP v Bulman 2014 G.W.D. 26-529, Sh Ct (South Strathclyde) (Dumfries)
Easton (Warner King) v HM Advocate see Blance (Andrew) v HM Advocate
EB (Kosovo) v Secretary of State for the Home Department; *joined cases* FI (Nigeria) v Secretary of State for the Home Department; HB (Ethiopia) v Secretary of State for the Home Department; JL (Sierra Leone) v Secretary of State for the Home Department [2008] UKHL 41; [2009] 1 A.C. 1159; [2008] 3 W.L.R. 178; [2008] 4 All E.R. 28; [2008] H.R.L.R. 40; [2008] U.K.H.R.R. 1087; 25 B.H.R.C. 228; [2008] Imm. A.R. 713; [2008] I.N.L.R. 516; (2008) 105(26) L.S.G. 21; (2008) 158 N.L.J. 968; (2008) 152(26) S.J.L.B. 30; Times, June 30, 2008, HL; reversing in part [2006] EWCA Civ 1713; [2007] Imm. A.R. 396; [2007] I.N.L.R. 150; (2007) 104(1) L.S.G. 12, CA (Civ Div) .......................................... *Digested,* 08/**2037**: *Applied* 08/2075, 09/2141, 11/1770, 14/1671: *Considered* 10/1777, 10/1806, 11/1790, 13/3776, 14/1650: *Followed* 09/2163, 10/1761, 10/1790, 11/1735, 11/1789, 13/1618
Eba v Advocate General for Scotland [2011] UKSC 29; [2012] 1 A.C. 710; [2011] 3 W.L.R. 149; [2011] P.T.S.R. 1095; [2011] S.T.C. 1705; 2012 S.C. (U.K.S.C.) 1; 2011 S.L.T. 768; [2011] Imm. A.R. 745; [2011] S.T.I. 1941; (2011) 108(27) L.S.G. 24; (2011) 161 N.L.J. 917, SC; affirming [2010] CSIH 78; [2010] S.T.C. 2689; 2011 S.C. 70; 2010 S.L.T. 1047; 2010 S.C.L.R. 759; [2010] S.T.I. 2617; 2010 G.W.D. 31-634; Times, October 20, 2010, IH (1 Div); reversing [2010] CSOH 45; 2010 S.L.T. 547; 2010 S.C.L.R. 345; 2010 G.W.D. 14-253, OH ........ *Digested,* 11/**3958**: *Applied* 12/1770, 13/3478, 14/3810: *Cited* 14/3606: *Considered* 13/3778, 14/3600
Edgar v Edgar [2014] CSOH 60; 2014 G.W.D. 13-236, OH
Edinburgh City Council v Additional Support Needs Tribunal for Scotland see Edinburgh City Council v K
Edinburgh City Council v K; *sub nom* Edinburgh City Council v Additional Support Needs Tribunal for Scotland [2009] CSIH 46; 2009 S.C. 625; 2009 G.W.D. 22-358, IH (Ex Div) .......................................... *Digested,* 10/**4145**: *Followed* 14/3477
Edinburgh City Council's Appeal, Re see City of Edinburgh Council v Lothian Valuation Appeal Committee
Edinburgh Woollen Mill Ltd v Singh 2013 S.L.T. (Sh Ct) 141; 2013 Hous. L.R. 54; 2013 G.W.D. 30-607, Sh Ct (Lothian) (Edinburgh) .......................................... *Digested,* 14/**3625**
Educational Institute of Scotland v Glasgow City Council [2014] CSIH 13; 2014 S.C. 457; 2014 S.L.T. 291; 2014 G.W.D. 5-96, IH (Ex Div) .......................................... *Digested,* 14/**3493**
Edwards v Environment Agency (C-260/11) see R. (on the application of Edwards) v Environment Agency (C-260/11)
Eilbeck (Inspector of Taxes) v Rawling see WT Ramsay Ltd v Inland Revenue Commissioners
ELB Securities Ltd v Love 2014 G.W.D. 28-562, Sh Ct (Glasgow)
Elida Gibbs Ltd v Customs and Excise Commissioners (C-317/94) [1997] Q.B. 499; [1996] S.T.C. 1387; [1996] E.C.R. I-5339; [1996] C.E.C. 1022; [1997] B.V.C. 80; Times, November 12, 1996, ECJ (6th Chamber) .......................................... *Digested,* 96/**5908**: *Applied* 07/4323, 09/4074, 12/3382, 13/3217: *Considered* 01/5556, 03/4569, 04/3983, 04/4024, 08/4026, 08/4029, 09/4081, 11/1261, 11/3572, 12/3408: *Distinguished* 01/5614, 04/3981, 08/4028, 14/3809: *Followed* 09/4092
Eman v College van Burgemeester en Wethouders van den Haag (C-300/04) [2006] E.C.R. I-8055; [2007] 1 C.M.L.R. 4; [2007] All E.R. (EC) 486, ECJ .................... *Digested,* 07/**1582**: *Applied* 12/1030: *Considered* 14/976
Emslie v Scottish Ministers 2014 S.L.T. (Lands Tr) 39; [2014] R.V.R. 302; 2014 G.W.D. 6-132, Lands Tr (Scot) .......................................... *Digested,* 14/**3725**
EN (Zimbabwe) v Secretary of State for the Home Department [2014] CSIH 47; 2014 G.W.D. 19-368, IH
Environment Agency v Stout see Mineral Resources Ltd, Re
EP (Zimbabwe) v Secretary of State for the Home Department [2014] CSIH 30; 2014 S.C. 706; 2014 G.W.D. 13-239, IH (Ex Div)
Epic Group Scotland Ltd v Shanks [2014] HCJAC 20; 2014 S.C.L. 348; 2014 S.C.C.R. 230; 2014 G.W.D. 10-184, HCJ .......................................... *Digested,* 14/**3407**
Evans (Murray Taylor) v HM Advocate; *sub nom* Evans, Petitioner 1992 S.L.T. 401; 1991 S.C.C.R. 160, HCJ Appeal .......................................... *Digested,* 91/**4655**: *Considered* 14/3437

Evans, Petitioner see Evans (Murray Taylor) v HM Advocate
Evn AG v Austria (C-448/01) [2003] E.C.R. I-14527; [2004] 1 C.M.L.R. 22, ECJ (6th Chamber) ........ *Digested,* 04/**3163**: *Applied* 11/2109, 14/2475

F v H 2014 G.W.D. 26-515, Sh Ct (South Strathclyde) (Dumfries)
F v Principal Reporter 2014 Fam. L.R. 57; 2014 G.W.D. 13-235, Sh Ct (Glasgow) ....... *Digested,* 14/**3526**
F-K v Poland see R. (on the application of HH) v Westminster City Magistrates' Court
Falkirk Council, Applicant 2014 G.W.D. 22-424, Sh Ct (Tayside) (Falkirk)
Farrell v Harvie [2014] HCJAC 55; 2014 S.C.L. 664; 2014 G.W.D. 25-483, HCJ ......... *Digested,* 14/**3399**
Fee v Child Maintenance and Enforcement Commission [2014] CSOH 32; 2014 G.W.D. 16-290, OH
Feeney v Harvie [2014] HCJAC 84; 2014 S.C.L. 677; 2014 S.C.C.R. 504; [2014] L.L.R. 701; 2014 G.W.D. 25-485, HCJ ........ *Digested,* 14/**3406**
Fenton (William) v HM Advocate [2014] HCJAC 70; 2014 S.C.C.R. 489, HCJ
Ferguson v J & A Lawson (Joiners) Ltd [2014] CSIH 82; 2014 G.W.D. 33-640, IH (Ex Div); affirming [2013] CSOH 146; 2013 G.W.D. 29-583, OH
Ferguson (James Douglas) v HM Advocate; *joined cases* Cameron (Stuart) v HM Advocate; Balfour (Bruce James) v HM Advocate; Nolan (Thomas) v HM Advocate [2014] HCJAC 19; 2014 S.L.T. 431; 2014 S.C.C.R. 244; 2014 G.W.D. 10-194, HCJ ........ *Digested,* 14/**3778**
Ferns (William James) v HM Advocate see Coalter (Adrian Robert) v HM Advocate
FH (Afghanistan) v Secretary of State for the Home Department [2014] CSOH 18; 2014 G.W.D. 7-145, OH
FI (Nigeria) v Secretary of State for the Home Department see EB (Kosovo) v Secretary of State for the Home Department
Findlay v Findlay 2014 G.W.D. 12-213, Sh Ct (Glasgow)
Firm A v Council of the Law Society for Scotland [2013] CSIH 30; 2013 S.C. 475; 2013 G.W.D. 15-323, IH (Ex Div) ........ *Digested,* 14/**3645**
Fishers Services Ltd v All Thai'd Up Ltd (t/a Richmond House Hotel) 2013 S.L.T. (Sh Ct) 121; 2013 G.W.D. 13-273, Sh Ct (Tayside) (Cupar) ........ *Digested,* 14/**3346**
Fitzpatrick v Harvie; *joined cases* Philips v Harvie; McFeeley v Harvie [2014] HCJAC 69; 2014 S.L.T. 844; 2014 S.C.L. 616; 2014 G.W.D. 24-448, HCJ ........ *Digested,* 14/**3372**
Fleming's Trustee v Fleming; *sub nom* Jackson v Fleming 2000 S.C. 206; 2000 S.L.T. 406; 2000 G.W.D. 2-61, IH (Ex Div); affirming 1998 S.C.L.R. 1070; 1998 G.W.D. 38-1972, Sh Ct ........ *Digested,* 00/**6508**: *Considered* 14/3802
Flynn (Edward) v HM Advocate [2014] HCJAC 64; 2014 S.C.L. 538; 2014 G.W.D. 21-394, HCJ ........ *Digested,* 14/**3387**
Football Association Premier League Ltd v QC Leisure (C-403/08); *joined case* Murphy v Media Protection Services Ltd (C-429/08) [2012] Bus. L.R. 1321; [2011] E.C.R. I-9083; [2012] 1 C.M.L.R. 29; [2012] All E.R. (EC) 629; [2012] C.E.C. 242; [2012] E.C.D.R. 8; [2012] F.S.R. 1; (2011) 108(40) L.S.G. 22; (2011) 161 N.L.J. 1415; Times, November 23, 2011, ECJ (Grand Chamber); no effect [2011] E.C.D.R. 11, AGO ........ *Digested,* 12/**1924**: *Applied* 12/1920, 12/1925, 13/1769: *Considered* 13/1762, 13/3542, 14/1860, 14/3349, 14/3354: *Followed* 12/1928
Forbes v Strathclyde Partnership for Transport [2014] CSIH 33; 2014 S.C. 717; 2014 G.W.D. 15-265, IH (Ex Div)
Fordell Estates Ltd v Deloitte LLP [2014] CSOH 55; 2014 G.W.D. 12-212, OH
Forest Bio Products Ltd v Forever Fuels Ltd [2013] CSIH 103; 2014 G.W.D. 1-7, IH (Ex Div) ........ *Digested,* 14/**3363**
Forrest v Fleming Buildings Ltd [2014] CSOH 158; 2014 G.W.D. 36-667, OH
Fowler (Danielle) v HM Advocate; *joined case* Scobbie (Mark) v HM Advocate [2013] HCJAC 166; 2014 G.W.D. 2-42, HCJ
Fox v United Biscuits (UK) Ltd 2014 G.W.D. 22-413, Sh Ct (Glasgow)
Foye (Robert) v HM Advocate see Petch (Morris) v HM Advocate
Frank Houlgate Investment Co Ltd v Biggart Baillie LLP [2014] CSIH 79; 2014 S.L.T. 1001; 2014 G.W.D. 31-618, IH (Ex Div) ........ *Digested,* 14/**3646**
Franklin v Lawson 2013 S.L.T. (Lands Tr) 81; 2013 G.W.D. 21-414, Lands Tr (Scot) ... *Digested,* 14/**3588**
Fraser v Deveney [2014] HCJAC 3; 2014 S.C.L. 242; 2014 S.C.C.R. 147; 2014 G.W.D. 3-63, HCJ ........ *Digested,* 14/**3435**
Fraser v Fraser 2014 Hous. L.R. 66; 2014 G.W.D. 38-700, Sh Ct (Grampian) (Banff)
Fraser v Meehan 2013 S.L.T. (Sh Ct) 119; 2013 Hous. L.R. 78; 2013 G.W.D. 30-606, Sh Ct (Lothian) (Edinburgh) ........ *Digested,* 14/**3637**
Fraser (Nat Gordon) v HM Advocate [2013] HCJAC 117; 2014 J.C. 115; 2013 S.C.L. 1031; 2013 S.C.C.R. 674; 2013 G.W.D. 33-652, HCJ ........ *Digested,* 14/**3448**

Friend v Lord Advocate; *sub nom* Whaley v Lord Advocate [2007] UKHL 53; 2008 S.C. (H.L.) 107; 2007 S.L.T. 1209; 2008 S.C.L.R. 128; [2008] H.R.L.R. 11; [2008] U.K.H.R.R. 157; (2007) 151 S.J.L.B. 1565; 2007 G.W.D. 39-680, HL; affirming 2006 S.C. 121; 2005 G.W.D. 30-577, IH (Ex Div); affirming 2004 S.C. 78; 2004 S.L.T. 425; 2003 G.W.D. 22-651, OH ............ *Digested,* 08/**4867**: *Applied* 14/3703

Friends of Loch Etive, Petitioner [2014] CSOH 116; 2014 G.W.D. 25-471, OH

Friends Provident Life Assurance Ltd v Sir Robert McAlpine Ltd [2014] CSOH 74; 2014 G.W.D. 16-289, OH

Frisby v Birmingham City Council see Hounslow LBC v Powell

Fulwood v O'Halloran 2014 G.W.D. 11-196, Sh Ct (Glasgow)

Fyfe (WAP) v Fife Assessor see WAP Fyfe v Assessor for Fife Council

FZ (Democratic Republic of Congo) v Secretary of State for the Home Department; *sub nom* Zoumbas v Secretary of State for the Home Department [2013] UKSC 74; [2013] 1 W.L.R. 3690; [2014] 1 All E.R. 638; 2014 S.C. (U.K.S.C.) 75; [2014] 1 F.C.R. 141; [2014] Imm. A.R. 479; [2014] I.N.L.R. 262, SC; affirming [2012] CSIH 87; 2012 G.W.D. 40-785, IH (Ex Div); affirming [2012] CSOH 47; 2012 G.W.D. 13-259, OH ............ *Digested,* 14/**1650**: *Applied* 14/1651

G v G [2014] CSOH 88; 2014 G.W.D. 17-323, OH ............ *Digested,* 14/**3548**

G v Mental Health Tribunal for Scotland; *sub nom* G v Scottish Ministers [2013] UKSC 79; 2014 S.C. (U.K.S.C.) 84; 2014 S.L.T. 247; 2014 S.C.L.R. 415, SC; affirming [2011] CSIH 55; 2012 S.C. 138; 2011 S.C.L.R. 770; [2011] M.H.L.R. 387; 2011 G.W.D. 29-638, IH (2 Div) ............ *Digested,* 14/**2180**

G v Scottish Ministers see G v Mental Health Tribunal for Scotland

G v Secretary of State for the Home Department see HHG (Iraq) v Secretary of State for the Home Department

G v Watson [2014] CSIH 81; 2014 S.L.T. 1030; 2014 G.W.D. 32-621, IH (Ex Div); reversing [2013] CSOH 88; 2013 S.L.T. 934; 2013 G.W.D. 20-397, OH ............ *Digested,* 14/**3501**

G v West Lothian Council 2014 G.W.D. 40-730, Sh Ct (Lothian) (Edinburgh)

G1 Venues Ltd, Petitioners [2013] CSOH 202; 2014 G.W.D. 4-75, OH

Gage (William Lewis) v HM Advocate [2011] HCJAC 40; 2011 S.C.L. 645; 2012 S.C.C.R. 161; 2011 G.W.D. 15-362, HCJ ............ *Digested,* 11/**4092**: *Applied* 12/3876: *Followed* 14/3389

Galbraith (Kim) v HM Advocate (No.2) 2002 J.C. 1; 2001 S.L.T. 953; 2001 S.C.C.R. 551; 2001 G.W.D. 25-924, HCJ Appeal ............ *Digested,* 01/**6335**: *Considered* 11/4083, 11/4177, 14/3424

Gallagher v SC Cheadle Hume Ltd [2014] CSOH 103; 2014 G.W.D. 23-435, OH

Gardiner v Merton LBC see Merton LBC v Gardiner

Garrad v Inglis 2014 G.W.D. 1-17, Sh Ct (Lothian) (Edinburgh)

Gemmell (James Kelly) v HM Advocate; *joined cases* Nisbet v Ogilvie; Hart v Brown; Ross v Richardson; McCourt (Peter Stephen) v HM Advocate; Gibson (David Alexander) v HM Advocate; Robertson (Paul) v HM Advocate [2011] HCJAC 129; 2012 J.C. 223; 2012 S.L.T. 484; 2012 S.C.L. 385; 2012 S.C.C.R. 176; 2012 G.W.D. 4-78, HCJ ............ *Digested,* 12/**4277**: *Cited* 12/3912: *Considered* 13/3972, 13/3990, 14/3771

GFR v HM Advocate see R v HM Advocate

Gibraltar European Elections, Re (C-145/04) see Spain v United Kingdom (C-145/04)

Gibson v Gow 2014 G.W.D. 13-228, Sh Ct (Tayside) (Dundee)

Gibson (David Alexander) v HM Advocate see Gemmell (James Kelly) v HM Advocate

Gill v Thomson; *joined cases* Montgomery v Thomson; Craig v Thomson [2010] HCJAC 99; 2012 J.C. 137; 2011 S.C.L. 164; 2010 S.C.C.R. 922; 2010 G.W.D. 33-678, HCJ ............ *Digested,* 11/**4101**: *Considered* 14/3785

Gilmour (John) v HM Advocate [2014] HCJAC 2; 2014 S.C.L. 162; 2014 G.W.D. 3-61, HCJ ............ *Digested,* 14/**3379**

Gilmour (Robert) v HM Advocate [2014] HCJAC 49; 2014 G.W.D. 17-312, HCJ ............ *Digested,* 14/**3393**

Gisda Cyf v Barratt [2010] UKSC 41; [2010] 4 All E.R. 851; [2010] I.C.R. 1475; [2010] I.R.L.R. 1073; (2010) 160 N.L.J. 1457; (2010) 154(39) S.J.L.B. 30; Times, October 19, 2010, SC; affirming [2009] EWCA Civ 648; [2009] I.C.R. 1408; [2009] I.R.L.R. 934, CA (Civ Div); affirming UKEAT/0173/08/ZT, EAT ............ *Digested,* 10/**1142**: *Applied* 13/987: *Considered* 11/1122, 14/3506

Glasgow Airport Ltd v Assessor for Renfrewshire Valuation Joint Board 2014 S.L.T. (Lands Tr) 46; [2014] R.V.R. 34; 2013 G.W.D. 36-710, Lands Tr (Scot) ............ *Digested,* 14/**3672**

Glasgow City Council v Board of Managers of Springboig St John's School [2014] CSOH 76; 2014 G.W.D. 16-287, OH

Glasgow City Council v Fox Cross Claimants; *sub nom* Glasgow City Council v Unison; *joined cases* Unison v Glasgow City Council; GMB v Glasgow City Council [2014] CSIH 27; 2014 S.C. 610; 2014 S.L.T. 716; [2014] I.R.L.R. 532; [2014] Eq. L.R. 271; 2014 G.W.D. 18-341, IH (Ex Div); affirming [2013] I.C.R. 954; [2013] Eq. L.R. 460, EAT (SC) ........ *Digested,* 14/**3503**

Glasgow City Council v Marshall [2000] 1 W.L.R. 333; [2000] 1 All E.R. 641; 2000 S.C. (H.L.) 67; 2000 S.L.T. 429; 2000 S.C.L.R. 889; [2000] I.C.R. 196; [2000] I.R.L.R. 272; (2000) 2 L.G.L.R. 679; [2000] B.L.G.R. 229; (2000) 97(7) L.S.G. 39; (2000) 144 S.J.L.B. 101; Times, February 8, 2000; Independent, March 27, 2000, HL; affirming 1998 S.C. 274; 1998 S.L.T. 799; 1998 S.C.L.R. 33; 1997 G.W.D. 40-2089, IH (1 Div) ........ *Digested,* 00/**6214**: *Applied* 06/1368, 10/1083, 11/1116, 14/3504: *Considered* 10/1084: *Followed* 04/1255, 12/1100

Glasgow City Council v Unison see Glasgow City Council v Fox Cross Claimants

Glover (Alan) v HM Advocate; *joined case* Vanbeck (Fiona) v HM Advocate [2013] HCJAC 143; 2014 S.C.L. 86; 2014 S.C.C.R. 68; 2013 G.W.D. 38-732, HCJ ...... *Digested,* 14/**3438**

GMB v Glasgow City Council see Glasgow City Council v Fox Cross Claimants

Gordon v S & B Removals t/a Aztec Removals 2014 G.W.D. 34-648, Sh Ct (North Strathclyde) (Campbeltown)

Gordon (Taylor John David) v HM Advocate; *joined case* Paterson (Drew Russell) v HM Advocate [2014] HCJAC 92; 2014 S.C.L. 725; 2014 G.W.D. 28-560, HCJ .. *Digested,* 14/**3450**

Gorman v Lambeth LBC see Kay v Lambeth LBC

Gorrie v MacLeod [2014] HCJAC 10; 2014 S.C.L. 293; 2014 S.C.C.R. 187; 2014 G.W.D. 7-151, HCJ ........ *Digested,* 14/**3767**

Gough v McFadyen see Robertson (Stewart) v HM Advocate

Gough (Stephen Peter) v HM Advocate see Robertson (Stewart) v HM Advocate

Gow v Grant [2012] UKSC 29; 2013 S.C. (U.K.S.C.) 1; 2012 S.L.T. 829; [2012] 3 F.C.R. 73; 2012 Fam. L.R. 80; (2012) 156(27) S.J.L.B. 31; 2012 G.W.D. 23-461; Times, August 31, 2012, SC; reversing [2011] CSIH 25; 2011 S.C. 618; 2011 Fam. L.R. 50; 2011 G.W.D. 12-280, IH (2 Div); reversing 2010 Fam. L.R. 21; 2010 G.W.D. 7-125, Sh Ct (Lothian) (Edinburgh) ........ *Digested,* 12/**1441**: *Considered* 11/4288, 13/3725: *Explained* 14/3536: *Followed* 12/4022, 13/3724

Graham (Wendy Patricia) v HM Advocate [2013] HCJAC 149; 2014 S.C.L. 24; 2013 G.W.D. 38-729, HCJ ........ *Digested,* 14/**3423**

Graham (Wendy) v HM Advocate [2013] HCJAC 140; 2014 S.C.L. 18; 2013 G.W.D. 36-704, HCJ ........ *Digested,* 14/**3424**

Graham's Executors v Deanston Partnership 2014 S.L.C.R. 67; 2014 G.W.D. 13-245, Land Ct

Grant (William Gavin) v HM Advocate [2006] HCJAC 42; 2006 J.C. 205; 2006 S.L.T. 563; 2006 S.C.C.R. 365; 2006 G.W.D. 18-368, HCJ ........ *Digested,* 06/**5192**: *Applied* 14/3459: *Considered* 14/3424

Gray v Keeper of the Registers of Scotland 2014 S.L.T. (Lands Tr) 117; 2014 G.W.D. 35-659, Lands Tr (Scot)

Gray v Thames Trains Ltd [2009] UKHL 33; [2009] 1 A.C. 1339; [2009] 3 W.L.R. 167; [2009] 4 All E.R. 81; [2009] P.I.Q.R. P22; [2009] LS Law Medical 409; (2009) 108 B.M.L.R. 205; [2009] M.H.L.R. 73; [2009] Po. L.R. 229; (2009) 159 N.L.J. 925; (2009) 153(24) S.J.L.B. 33; Times, June 19, 2009, HL; reversing in part [2008] EWCA Civ 713; [2009] 2 W.L.R. 351; [2008] P.I.Q.R. P20; [2008] M.H.L.R. 180; (2008) 105(26) L.S.G. 22; Times, July 9, 2008, CA (Civ Div); reversing [2007] EWHC 1558 (QB), QBD ........ *Digested,* 09/**2836**: *Applied* 12/2415, 13/2195: *Considered* 10/2293, 10/3411, 13/1797, 14/2994, 14/3718: *Followed* 10/2285, 12/2417

Greater Glasgow Health Board v Baxter Clark & Paul 1990 S.C. 237; 1992 S.L.T. 35, OH ........ *Digested,* 92/**6209**: *Approved* 96/6667: *Cited* 97/5682: *Considered* 96/6666: *Distinguished* 00/6638: *Overruled* 14/2470

Greens v United Kingdom (60041/08) (2011) 53 E.H.R.R. 21; [2010] 2 Prison L.R. 22; (2010) 160 N.L.J. 1685; Times, November 24, 2010, ECHR ........ *Digested,* 11/**1703**: *Applied* 11/1687, 14/976: *Considered* 11/1702

Greig (Paul William) v HM Advocate [2012] HCJAC 127; 2013 J.C. 115; 2012 S.C.L. 1095; 2012 S.C.C.R. 757; 2012 G.W.D. 33-684, HCJ ........ *Digested,* 13/**3993**: *Distinguished* 14/3780

Griffith (Javaughn) v HM Advocate [2013] HCJAC 84; 2014 J.C. 141; 2013 S.L.T. 944; 2013 S.C.L. 804; 2013 S.C.C.R. 448; 2013 G.W.D. 25-482, HCJ ........ *Digested,* 13/**3572**

Griffith (Javaughn) v HM Advocate [2013] HCJAC 138; 2014 S.C.L. 39; 2013 G.W.D. 35-688, HCJ ........ *Digested,* 14/**3425**

Griffiths v R; *sub nom* Nisbet v JR 2014 S.C.L. 61; 2014 S.C.C.R. 18; 2013 G.W.D. 38-733, Sh Ct (Tayside) (Dundee) ........ *Digested,* 14/**3467**

Grove Investments Ltd v Cape Building Products Ltd [2014] CSIH 43; 2014 Hous. L.R. 35; 2014 G.W.D. 17-327, IH (Ex Div) .......... *Digested,* 14/**3630**
Gul (Saima) v HM Advocate; *joined case* Rahim (Fazli) v HM Advocate [2013] HCJAC 177; 2014 S.C.L. 211; 2014 G.W.D. 2-52, HCJ .......... *Digested,* 14/**3776**
Gutcher v Butcher 2014 G.W.D. 31-610, Sh Ct (Grampian) (Kirkwall)
Gyle Shopping Centre General Partners Ltd v Marks & Spencer Plc [2014] CSOH 122; 2014 G.W.D. 26-527, OH .......... *Digested,* 14/**3631**
Gyle Shopping Centre General Partners Ltd v Marks and Spencer Plc [2014] CSOH 59; 2014 G.W.D. 18-352, OH

H v H see Harris v Harris
H v HM Advocate see HJL v HM Advocate
H v Lord Advocate; *sub nom* Howes, Re; BH v Lord Advocate; *joined case* KAS v Lord Advocate [2012] UKSC 24; [2013] 1 A.C. 413; [2012] 3 W.L.R. 151; [2012] 4 All E.R. 600; 2012 S.C. (U.K.S.C.) 308; 2012 S.L.T. 799; 2012 S.C.L. 635; 2012 S.C.C.R. 562; [2012] H.R.L.R. 24; (2012) 109(27) L.S.G. 19; 2012 G.W.D. 21-432; Times, July 3, 2012, SC; affirming [2011] HCJAC 77; 2011 S.C.L. 978; 2012 S.C.C.R. 1; 2011 G.W.D. 26-587, HCJ; reversing in part 2008 G.W.D. 14-263, Sh Ct (Lothian) .......... *Digested,* 12/**1289**: *Applied* 13/1187: *Considered* 14/1650
H v Scottish Children's Reporter 2014 Fam. L.R. 63; 2014 G.W.D. 15-273, Sh Ct (Lothian) (Haddington) .......... *Digested,* 14/**3524**
H, Petitioner [2014] CSOH 79; 2014 G.W.D. 15-274, OH
Haashi (Shirwa Abdisayed) v HM Advocate; *joined case* Abdi (Rahim Abuka) v HM Advocate [2014] HCJAC 48; 2014 G.W.D. 17-313, HCJ .......... *Digested,* 14/**3392**
HAH (Iraq) v Secretary of State for the Home Department [2014] CSOH 110; 2014 G.W.D. 24-455, OH
Hainey (Kimberley Mary) v HM Advocate [2013] HCJAC 47; 2014 J.C. 33; 2013 S.L.T. 525; 2013 S.C.L. 499; 2013 S.C.C.R. 309; 2013 G.W.D. 14-297, HCJ .......... *Digested,* 13/**3632**: *Followed* 14/3370
Halcrow v Shanks [2012] HCJAC 23; 2014 J.C. 1; 2012 S.L.T. 579; 2012 S.C.L. 517; 2012 G.W.D. 8-144, HCJ .......... *Digested,* 12/**4273**
Halistra Common Grazings, Trustees for the Proprietors v Lambert 1997 S.L.T. (Land Ct) 7; 1996 S.L.C.R. 80, Land Ct .......... *Digested,* 97/**6427**: *Not followed* 14/3627
Hall v Hall 2014 G.W.D. 26-521, Sh Ct (Grampian) (Aberdeen)
Hall v Leeds City Council see Hounslow LBC v Powell
Hamilton v Ferguson Transport (Spean Bridge) Ltd; *joined case* Thomson v Dennis Thomson Builders Ltd [2012] CSIH 52; 2012 S.C. 486; 2012 S.L.T. 715; 2012 S.C.L.R. 707; 2012 Rep. L.R. 79; 2012 G.W.D. 21-430, IH (1 Div) .......... *Digested,* 12/**4206**: *Considered* 14/3468, 14/3469, 14/3471
Happy Feet Nursery and Out of School Club Ltd v Assessor for Lanarkshire [2014] CSIH 87; 2014 S.L.T. 1066; 2014 G.W.D. 35-663, LVAC
Harbro Group Ltd v MHA Auchlochan [2014] CSIH 14; 2014 S.C.L.R. 555; 2014 G.W.D. 29-569, IH (Ex Div); reversing [2013] CSOH 8; 2013 G.W.D. 4-114, OH
Harley v Thompson 2014 G.W.D. 36-673, Sh Ct (Lothian) (Livingston)
Harris v Harris; *sub nom* H v H 2013 Fam. L.R. 122; 2013 G.W.D. 16-337, Sh Ct (Lothian) (Edinburgh) .......... *Digested,* 14/**3535**
Harrison v Nisbet see McGill (James) v HM Advocate
Hart v Brown see Gemmell (James Kelly) v HM Advocate
Harvie v C (H) [2014] HCJAC 68; 2014 G.W.D. 23-434, HCJ
Havlin v Hailes 2014 G.W.D. 27-544, Sh Ct (Glasgow)
Hawthorne v Anderson [2014] CSOH 65; 2014 G.W.D. 13-247, OH
Hay v Advanced Stairlifts (Scotland) Ltd [2014] CSOH 118; 2014 Rep. L.R. 102; 2014 G.W.D. 26-532, OH .......... *Digested,* 14/**3694**
Hay v Richardson see Hay (Ian Morris) v HM Advocate
Hay (Ian Morris) v HM Advocate; *joined case* Hay v Richardson [2012] HCJAC 28; 2014 J.C. 19; 2012 S.L.T. 569; 2012 S.C.L. 492; 2012 S.C.C.R. 281; 2012 G.W.D. 8-142, HCJ .......... *Digested,* 12/**4271**
Hayburn (Deborah) v HM Advocate see O'Neill (William) v HM Advocate
HB (Ethiopia) v Secretary of State for the Home Department see EB (Kosovo) v Secretary of State for the Home Department
He (Qing Guang) v HM Advocate see Lin (Jie) v HM Advocate

Healthcare at Home Ltd v Common Services Agency [2014] UKSC 49; [2014] 4 All E.R. 210; [2014] P.T.S.R. 1081; 2014 S.C. (U.K.S.C.) 247; 2014 S.L.T. 769; 2014 G.W.D. 25-505; Times, August 7, 2014, SC; affirming [2013] CSIH 22; 2013 S.C. 411; 2013 G.W.D. 13-291, IH (2 Div); affirming [2012] CSOH 75; [2012] Eu. L.R. 684; 2012 G.W.D. 18-359, OH ........ *Digested,* 14/**2475**

Healy (Elizabeth Kirwan) v HM Advocate 1990 S.C.C.R. 110, HCJ Appeal ........ *Digested,* 90/**4908**: *Applied* 93/5003, 96/6774, 97/5822, 98/5624, 14/3437: *Followed* 12/3925

Heary v Phinn (t/a Phinn Parts) 2013 S.L.T. (Sh Ct) 145; 2013 G.W.D. 29-585, Sh Ct (Tayside) (Dundee) ........ *Digested,* 14/**3697**

Heatherall v McGowan [2012] HCJAC 25; 2014 J.C. 8; 2012 S.L.T. 583; 2012 S.C.L. 521; 2012 G.W.D. 8-141, HCJ ........ *Digested,* 12/**4270**

Henderson v Foxworth Investments Ltd; *sub nom* Liquidator of Letham Grange Development Co Ltd v Foxworth Investments Ltd [2014] UKSC 41; [2014] 1 W.L.R. 2600; 2014 S.C. (U.K.S.C.) 203; 2014 S.L.T. 775; 2014 S.C.L.R. 692; (2014) 158(27) S.J.L.B. 37; 2014 G.W.D. 23-437, SC; reversing [2013] CSIH 13; 2013 S.L.T. 445; 2013 G.W.D. 10-218, IH (Ex Div); reversing [2011] CSOH 66; 2011 S.L.T. 1152; 2011 G.W.D. 14-341, OH ........ *Digested,* 14/**1579**

Henderson v Greater Glasgow Health Board [2014] CSIH 41; 2014 S.C. 681; 2014 G.W.D. 17-307, IH (Ex Div) ........ *Digested,* 14/**3322**

Henderson v Scottish Ministers see Somerville v Scottish Ministers

Hendrick v Chief Constable of Strathclyde [2014] CSIH 22; 2014 S.C. 551; 2014 S.L.T. 382; 2014 G.W.D. 7-136, IH (Ex Div); affirming [2013] CSOH 66; 2013 G.W.D. 15-312, OH ........ *Digested,* 14/**3300**

Hendrick v Chief Constable of Strathclyde [2014] CSIH 75; 2014 S.L.T. 955; 2014 G.W.D. 30-591, IH (Ex Div) ........ *Digested,* 14/**3337**

HF (Pakistan), Petitioner [2013] CSOH 198; 2014 G.W.D. 2-46, OH

HH v Italy see R. (on the application of HH) v Westminster City Magistrates' Court

HHG (Iraq) v Secretary of State for the Home Department; *sub nom* G v Secretary of State for the Home Department [2014] CSOH 48; 2014 S.L.T. 693; 2014 G.W.D. 11-201, OH ........ *Digested,* 14/**3605**

Highland Council v Scottish Ministers [2014] CSIH 74; 2014 G.W.D. 29-582, IH (1 Div)

Highlands and Islands Airports Ltd v Shetland Islands Council [2014] CSOH 17; 2014 S.L.T. 424; 2014 G.W.D. 7-150, OH ........ *Digested,* 14/**3745**

Hill (Brian) v HM Advocate [2014] HCJAC 117; 2014 S.L.T. 1061; 2014 S.C.C.R. 659; 2014 G.W.D. 35-655, HCJ

Hill of Rubislaw (Q Seven) Ltd v Rubislaw Quarry Aberdeen Ltd [2014] CSIH 105; 2014 G.W.D. 40-723, IH (Ex Div); affirming [2013] CSOH 131; 2013 G.W.D. 27-545, OH

Hirst v United Kingdom (74025/01) (2006) 42 E.H.R.R. 41; 19 B.H.R.C. 546; [2006] 1 Prison L.R. 220; (2005) 155 N.L.J. 1551; Times, October 10, 2005, ECHR (Grand Chamber) ........ *Digested,* 06/**2150**: *Applied* 11/1702, 11/1703, 14/976: *Considered* 07/5431, 10/1730, 11/2294, 14/3703: *Distinguished* 13/1544

Historic Scotland Executive Agency v Highland and Western Isles Valuation Joint Board Assessor 2014 S.L.T. (Lands Tr) 50; [2014] R.V.R. 14; 2013 G.W.D. 37-723, Lands Tr (Scot) ........ *Digested,* 14/**3674**

HJL v HM Advocate; *sub nom* H v HM Advocate 2003 S.C.C.R. 120; 2003 G.W.D. 2-44, HCJ ........ *Digested,* 03/**5401**: *Considered* 14/3780

HM Advocate v AJV see HM Advocate v V

HM Advocate v Al-Megrahi (Abdelbaset Ali) (No.4); *sub nom* Megrahi (Abdelbaset Ali) v HM Advocate (No.4); HM Advocate v Megrahi (Abdelbaset Ali) (No.4) 2002 J.C. 99; 2002 S.L.T. 1433; 2002 S.C.C.R. 509; 2002 G.W.D. 11-335, HCJ Appeal; affirming 2001 G.W.D. 5-177, HCJ ........ *Digested,* 03/**5384**: *Applied* 08/4627, 08/4632, 09/4732, 09/4740, 09/4768, 14/3389: *Considered* 06/5236

HM Advocate v B; *sub nom* HM Advocate v PB; *joined case* HM Advocate v W [2013] HCJ 71; 2013 S.L.T. 810; 2013 S.C.L. 592; 2013 S.C.C.R. 361; 2013 G.W.D. 20-398, HCJ ........ *Digested,* 13/**3559**: *Distinguished* 14/3378

HM Advocate v Boyle (Brian Robert); *joined cases* HM Advocate v Maddock (Greig); HM Advocate v Kelly (Robert) [2009] HCJAC 89; 2010 J.C. 66; 2010 S.L.T. 29; 2010 S.C.L. 198; 2010 S.C.C.R. 103; 2009 G.W.D. 39-674, HCJ ........ *Digested,* 10/**4531**: *Applied* 13/3986: *Cited* 14/3439: *Considered* 11/4586, 12/4266, 12/4267, 14/3777: *Followed* 11/4584, 12/4264

HM Advocate v Callandar (Darrin Alexander) see HM Advocate v Callander (Darrin Alexander)

HM Advocate v Callander (Darrin Alexander); *sub nom* HM Advocate v Callandar (Darrin Alexander) [2013] HCJAC 159; 2014 S.C.L. 206; 2014 S.C.C.R. 135; 2014 G.W.D. 1-32, HCJ ........ *Digested,* 14/**3777**

HM Advocate v Collins (Craig) [2014] HCJAC 11; 2014 S.L.T. 372; 2014 S.C.L. 225; 2014 S.C.C.R. 105; 2014 G.W.D. 6-120, HCJ ........ *Digested,* 14/**3462**

HM Advocate v DS see DS v HM Advocate

HM Advocate v Graham (David William) [2010] HCJAC 50; 2011 J.C. 1; 2010 S.L.T. 715; 2010 S.C.L. 789; 2010 S.C.C.R. 641; 2010 G.W.D. 19-384, HCJ ........ *Digested,* 10/**4523**: *Followed* 14/3772

HM Advocate v H; *sub nom* HM Advocate v KH [2014] HCJAC 36; 2014 J.C. 195; 2014 S.C.L. 525; 2014 S.C.C.R. 485; 2014 G.W.D. 15-280, HCJ ........ *Digested,* 14/**3783**

HM Advocate v Hutchison (James David) [2013] HCJAC 91; 2013 S.C.C.R. 479; 2013 G.W.D. 26-528, HCJ ........ *Digested,* 14/**3396**

HM Advocate v Kelly (Robert) see HM Advocate v Boyle (Brian Robert)

HM Advocate v KH see HM Advocate v H

HM Advocate v Maddock (Greig) see HM Advocate v Boyle (Brian Robert)

HM Advocate v Mair (Gareth James) [2013] HCJAC 89; 2014 J.C. 137; 2013 S.C.L. 759; 2013 G.W.D. 25-486, HCJ ........ *Digested,* 13/**3640**

HM Advocate v McAllister (Jason) [2014] HCJ 111; 2014 S.L.T. 1023; 2014 S.C.L. 799; 2014 G.W.D. 32-627, HCJ ........ *Digested,* 14/**3433**

HM Advocate v McAllister (Jason) [2014] HCJ 112; 2014 S.C.L. 807; 2014 G.W.D. 32-622, HCJ

HM Advocate v McCourt (Gary Andrew) [2013] HCJAC 114; 2014 J.C. 94; 2013 S.L.T. 1081; 2013 S.C.L. 991; 2013 S.C.C.R. 646; 2013 G.W.D. 32-646, HCJ .. *Digested,* 14/**3766**

HM Advocate v McCrossan (Darryl); *joined case* HM Advocate v Wilson (Keith) [2013] HCJAC 95; 2014 J.C. 161; 2013 S.L.T. 1026; 2013 S.C.L. 820; 2013 S.C.C.R. 524; 2013 G.W.D. 27-551, HCJ ........ *Digested,* 13/**3810**

HM Advocate v Megrahi (Abdelbaset Ali) (No.4) see HM Advocate v Al-Megrahi (Abdelbaset Ali) (No.4)

HM Advocate v PB see HM Advocate v B

HM Advocate v Pyne (David) [2014] HCJAC 129; 2014 G.W.D. 37-684, HCJ

HM Advocate v Sinclair (Angus Robertson); *sub nom* Sinclair (Angus Robertson) v HM Advocate [2014] HCJAC 131; 2014 S.L.T. 1092; 2014 S.C.C.R. 554; 2014 G.W.D. 39-713, HCJ

HM Advocate v Sinclair (Angus Robertson); *sub nom* Sinclair (Angus Robertson) v HM Advocate [2014] HCJAC 130; 2014 S.L.T. 1087; 2014 S.C.C.R. 545; 2014 G.W.D. 39-712, HCJ

HM Advocate v Small (Darren) 2014 S.L.T. (Sh Ct) 49; 2014 S.C.L. 367; 2014 G.W.D. 9-172, Sh Ct (Tayside) (Dundee) ........ *Digested,* 14/**3367**

HM Advocate v Smith (Gary) [2013] HCJAC 137; 2014 S.C.L. 45; 2014 S.C.C.R. 39; 2013 G.W.D. 36-712, HCJ ........ *Digested,* 14/**3782**

HM Advocate v Swift (James Aloysius) 1984 J.C. 83; 1985 S.L.T. 26; 1984 S.C.C.R. 216, HCJ ........ *Digested,* 84/**3906**: *Applied* 88/3921, 97/5801, 98/5594, 09/4798, 10/4078, 13/3622, 14/3415, 14/3416, 14/3420: *Considered* 97/5861, 97/5862, 06/5205, 07/5068, 08/4646, 13/3621, 14/3417: *Followed* 97/5803, 01/6344, 03/5378: *Referred to* 92/5423, 93/4935

HM Advocate v Thomson (Stuart Rae) [2014] HCJ 107; 2014 S.C.L. 825; 2014 S.C.C.R. 598; 2014 G.W.D. 31-607, HCJ

HM Advocate v V; *sub nom* HM Advocate v AJV [2014] HCJAC 126; 2014 G.W.D. 38-703, HCJ

HM Advocate v W [2014] HCJAC 47; 2014 S.C.C.R. 361; 2014 G.W.D. 17-319, HCJ .. *Digested,* 14/**3417**

HM Advocate v W see HM Advocate v B

HM Advocate v Wilson (Keith) see HM Advocate v McCrossan (Darryl)

HM Advocate v Younas (Mohammed) [2014] HCJ 123; 2014 G.W.D. 37-685, HCJ

HMcA v HM Advocate see A v HM Advocate

HMR (Iraq) v Secretary of State for the Home Department [2014] CSOH 63; 2014 G.W.D. 13-242, OH

Hoblyn v Barclays Bank Plc [2014] CSIH 52; 2014 Hous. L.R. 26; 2014 G.W.D. 20-376, IH (Ex Div)

Holdich v Lothian Health Board [2013] CSOH 197; 2014 S.L.T. 495; 2014 G.W.D. 10-182, OH ........ *Digested,* 14/**3695**

Hood (Owen) v HM Advocate [2014] HCJAC 85; 2014 S.C.L. 699; 2014 G.W.D. 25-487, HCJ ........ *Digested,* 14/**3429**

Hounslow LBC v Powell; *sub nom* Powell v Hounslow LBC; Hall v Leeds City Council; Frisby v Birmingham City Council; Mushin v Manchester City Council; Mullen v Salford City Council; *joined cases* Salford City Council v Mullen; Leeds City Council v Hall; Birmingham City Council v Frisby [2011] UKSC 8; [2011] 2 A.C. 186; [2011] 2 W.L.R. 287; [2011] 2 All E.R. 129; [2011] P.T.S.R. 512; [2011] H.R.L.R. 18; [2011] U.K.H.R.R. 548; [2011] H.L.R. 23; [2011] B.L.G.R. 363; [2011] 1 P. & C.R. 20; [2011] 9 E.G. 164 (C.S.); (2011) 155(8) S.J.L.B. 31; [2011] N.P.C. 24; Times, March 1, 2011, SC; reversing in part [2010] EWCA Civ 336; [2011] 1 All E.R. 119; [2010] H.L.R. 35; [2010] B.L.G.R. 559; [2010] 15 E.G. 95 (C.S.); [2010] N.P.C. 43, CA (Civ Div) .......... *Digested,* 11/**2069**: *Applied* 14/1997, 14/3635: *Considered* 13/1892, 14/1625: *Followed* 12/1645, 12/2055, 13/1562, 13/1890, 13/3806, 14/2524

Howard v Lawson 2012 S.L.C.R. 121, Land Ct (Div Ct) .......... *Digested,* 14/**3626**

Howden (John) v HM Advocate 1994 S.C.C.R. 19, HCJ Appeal .......... *Digested,* 94/**5531**: *Considered* 96/6722, 02/5440, 10/4103: *Distinguished* 14/3371

Howes, Re see H v Lord Advocate

HSBC Bank Plc v Collinge 2014 Hous. L.R. 78; 2014 G.W.D. 29-566, Sh Ct (South Strathclyde) (Dumfries)

Hughes (Barry) v HM Advocate [2014] HCJAC 74; 2014 S.C.C.R. 506; 2014 G.W.D. 25-507, HCJ

Hughes (Christopher) v HM Advocate [2014] HCJAC 18; 2014 S.C.L. 363; 2014 G.W.D. 9-180, HCJ .......... *Digested,* 14/**3786**

Hunter v Hanley 1955 S.C. 200; 1955 S.L.T. 213; [1955-95] P.N.L.R. 1, IH (1 Div); reversing 1954 S.L.T. 303, OH .......... *Digested,* 55/**3451**: *Applied* 83/2548, 83/3962, 84/2322, 90/3264, 97/6302, 00/6588, 03/5826, 04/5055, 13/3857, 14/3688: *Considered* 86/3608, 89/2558, 03/5825: *Distinguished* 00/6585: *Followed* 90/5498: *Not applied* 88/4930, 89/4195: *Referred to* 00/6603

Hunter (David Ronald Shanks) v HM Advocate [2014] HCJAC 28; 2014 G.W.D. 13-233, HCJ

Hutchinson 3G (UK) Ltd v Renfrewshire Valuation Joint Board Assessor [2013] R.A. 454, Lands Tr (Scot) .......... *Digested,* 14/**3663**

HY (Iran) v Secretary of State for the Home Department [2014] CSOH 72; 2014 G.W.D. 14-259, OH

I v Dunn [2014] HCJAC 9; 2014 S.C.L. 281; 2014 G.W.D. 6-121, HCJ .......... *Digested,* 14/**3463**

I v HM Advocate see L v HM Advocate

IA (Iran) v Secretary of State for the Home Department; *sub nom* A v Secretary of State for the Home Department [2014] UKSC 6; [2014] 1 W.L.R. 384; [2014] 1 All E.R. 1015; 2014 S.C. (U.K.S.C.) 105; 2014 S.L.T. 598; 2014 S.C.L.R. 366; [2014] Imm. A.R. 613; [2014] I.N.L.R. 559; 2014 G.W.D. 4-86; Times, February 4, 2014, SC; affirming [2011] CSIH 28; 2011 S.C. 625; 2011 S.L.T. 706; 2011 G.W.D. 14-344, IH (Ex Div) .......... *Digested,* 14/**1659**

ICL Tech Ltd v Johnston Oils Ltd [2013] CSOH 159; 2013 S.L.T. 1090; 2013 G.W.D. 32-643, OH .......... *Digested,* 14/**3689**

IGL Ltd (In Liquidation) v Malcolm Insulation Supplies Ltd [2014] CSOH 170; 2014 G.W.D. 40-726, OH

Ingham (David) v HM Advocate [2014] HCJAC 21; 2014 G.W.D. 11-199, HCJ

Ishaq (Adel) v HM Advocate see Rehman (Asif) v HM Advocate

IU (Pakistan), Applicant [2014] CSIH 85; 2014 G.W.D. 33-639, IH (Ex Div)

J v S 2014 G.W.D. 21-408, Sh Ct (Tayside) (Perth)

Jackson v Fleming see Fleming's Trustee v Fleming

Jakovlev (Vladimir) v HM Advocate; *joined case* Podgornoi (Aleksandr) v HM Advocate [2011] HCJAC 90; 2012 J.C. 120; 2012 S.L.T. 87; 2012 S.C.L. 59; 2011 S.C.C.R. 608; 2011 G.W.D. 32-687, HCJ .......... *Digested,* 12/**4266**: *Followed* 14/3776

James v United Kingdom (25119/09); *joined cases* Wells v United Kingdom (57715/09); Lee v United Kingdom (57877/09) (2013) 56 E.H.R.R. 12; 33 B.H.R.C. 617; (2012) 109(37) L.S.G. 20, ECHR .......... *Digested,* 13/**1558**: *Considered* 13/2112, 13/2113, 13/3878, 14/2234: *Followed* 14/3702

Jamieson v Jamieson [1952] A.C. 525; [1952] 1 All E.R. 875; 1952 S.C. (H.L.) 44; 1952 S.L.T. 257; [1952] 1 T.L.R. 833; (1952) 116 J.P. 226, HL; reversing 1951 S.C. 286; 1951 S.L.T. 174, IH (1 Div) .......... *Digested,* 52/**985**: *Applied* 52/984, 54/950, 54/951, 55/782, 55/788, 56/2542, 60/951, 62/911, 62/921, 94/6150, 95/6163, 00/6599, 06/5122, 06/5150, 06/5156, 08/4861, 08/4976, 09/5081, 10/3997, 11/4481: *Considered* 73/886, 12/3821, 12/3842, 14/3354: *Distinguished* 54/943: *Followed* 57/1025, 01/6252, 03/5278

Jamieson v O'Neill [2014] CSOH 117; 2014 Rep. L.R. 98; 2014 G.W.D. 25-503, OH ... *Digested,* 14/**3744**
Jamieson (Brian) v HM Advocate (No.2) 1994 J.C. 251; 1995 S.L.T. 666; 1994 S.C.C.R. 610, HCJ ........ *Digested,* 94/**5513**: *Considered* 09/4836, 12/3939, 14/3400
JB v Glasgow City Council see B v Glasgow City Council
JB (Nigeria) v Secretary of State for the Home Department [2014] CSOH 126; 2014 G.W.D. 27-548, OH
Jennings (Robert Michael) v HM Advocate see Snowden (Scott Leslie) v HM Advocate
JL v HM Advocate see L v HM Advocate
JL (Sierra Leone) v Secretary of State for the Home Department see EB (Kosovo) v Secretary of State for the Home Department
JN (India) v Secretary of State for the Home Department [2014] CSOH 49; 2014 G.W.D. 11-202, OH
John G Sibbald & Son Ltd v Johnston [2014] CSOH 94; 2014 G.W.D. 19-372, OH
John Pollock and Sons Ltd v Robert Rennie (A Firm) 2014 S.L.T. (Land Ct) 86; 2014 S.L.C.R. 76; 2014 G.W.D. 19-358, Land Ct ........ *Digested,* 14/**3310**
John W Raeside & Son's Trustees v Chalmers 2014 G.W.D. 35-660, Lands Tr (Scot)
Johnston (James) v HM Advocate [2014] HCJAC 27; 2014 G.W.D. 13-231, HCJ
Johnstone (John Stewart) v HM Advocate [2013] HCJAC 92; 2013 S.L.T. 1115; 2013 S.C.L. 868; 2013 S.C.C.R. 487; 2013 G.W.D. 26-539, HCJ ........ *Digested,* 13/**3978**: *Followed* 14/3387
Joint Administrators of Connaught Partnerships Ltd v Perth and Kinross Council [2013] CSOH 149; 2014 S.L.T. 608; 2014 G.W.D. 13-229, OH ........ *Digested,* 14/**3618**
Joint Administrators of Oceancrown Ltd v Stonegale Ltd [2013] CSOH 189; 2014 G.W.D. 2-47, OH
Joint Liquidators of the Scottish Coal Co Ltd v Scottish Environment Protection Agency see Joint Liquidators of the Scottish Coal Co Ltd, Noters
Joint Liquidators of the Scottish Coal Co Ltd, Noters; *sub nom* Joint Liquidators of the Scottish Coal Co Ltd v Scottish Environment Protection Agency; Scottish Environment Protection Agency v Joint Liquidators of the Scottish Coal Co Ltd [2013] CSIH 108; 2014 S.C. 372; 2014 S.L.T. 259; 2014 G.W.D. 2-48, IH (2 Div); reversing [2013] CSOH 124; 2013 S.L.T. 1055; 2013 G.W.D. 25-505, OH. *Digested,* 14/**3622**
Jollie v Lennie [2014] CSOH 45; 2014 G.W.D. 10-195, OH
Jolly (Andrew) v HM Advocate [2013] HCJAC 96; 2014 J.C. 171; 2013 S.L.T. 1100; 2013 S.C.L. 832; 2013 S.C.C.R. 511; 2013 G.W.D. 29-576, HCJ ........ *Digested,* 13/**3564**: *Overruled* 14/3410
Jones v Chief Constable of South Yorkshire see Alcock v Chief Constable of South Yorkshire
Jones v F Sirl & Son (Furnishers) Ltd [1997] I.R.L.R. 493, EAT ........ *Digested,* 97/**2206**: *Doubted* 14/3500
Jones v Wright see Alcock v Chief Constable of South Yorkshire
Jones (Craig) v HM Advocate [2013] HCJAC 175; 2014 G.W.D. 2-51, HCJ
JP v FM see P v M

K v General Pharmaceutical Council [2014] CSIH 61; 2014 G.W.D. 24-454, IH (Ex Div)
K v Secretary of State for the Home Department see SK (Namibia) v Secretary of State for the Home Department
KA (Afghanistan) v Secretary of State for the Home Department [2013] CSOH 184; 2014 G.W.D. 1-2, OH
Kalyanjee (Ashok) v HM Advocate [2014] HCJAC 44; 2014 J.C. 233; 2014 S.L.T. 740; 2014 S.C.L. 488; 2014 S.C.C.R. 397; 2014 G.W.D. 18-339, HCJ ........ *Digested,* 14/**3437**
Kapri v Lord Advocate see Kapri (Fatjon) v HM Advocate
Kapri (Fatjon) v HM Advocate; *sub nom* Kapri v Lord Advocate [2014] HCJAC 33; 2014 S.L.T. 557; 2014 S.C.L. 377; 2014 S.C.C.R. 310; 2014 G.W.D. 16-293, HCJ ........ *Digested,* 14/**3521**
Kapri (Fatjon) v Lord Advocate [2014] HCJAC 63; 2014 G.W.D. 21-395, HCJ
Karus v Scottish Legal Complaints Commission [2014] CSIH 59; 2014 S.C. 754; 2014 G.W.D. 24-463, IH (Ex Div)
KAS v Lord Advocate see H v Lord Advocate
KASY v Advocate General for Scotland see N v Advocate General for Scotland

Kay v Lambeth LBC; *sub nom* Leeds City Council v Price; Lambeth LBC v Kay; *joined cases* Gorman v Lambeth LBC; Constantine v Lambeth LBC; Barnett v Lambeth LBC; Cole v Lambeth LBC; Dymny v Lambeth LBC; Price v Leeds City Council [2006] UKHL 10; [2006] 2 A.C. 465; [2006] 2 W.L.R. 570; [2006] 4 All E.R. 128; [2006] 2 F.C.R. 20; [2006] H.R.L.R. 17; [2006] U.K.H.R.R. 640; 20 B.H.R.C. 33; [2006] H.L.R. 22; [2006] B.L.G.R. 323; [2006] 2 P. & C.R. 25; [2006] L. & T.R. 8; [2006] 11 E.G. 194 (C.S.); (2006) 150 S.J.L.B. 365; [2006] N.P.C. 29; Times, March 10, 2006; Independent, March 14, 2006, HL; affirming [2004] EWCA Civ 926; [2005] Q.B. 352; [2004] 3 W.L.R. 1396; [2004] H.L.R. 56; Times, July 26, 2004, CA (Civ Div) ........ *Digested,* 06/**2173**: *Applied* 06/2708, 06/499, 07/2247, 07/2403, 08/1978, 08/2467, 09/1560, 09/2534, 09/2544, 10/2063, 10/2080: *Complaint upheld* 11/1699: *Considered* 05/3424, 07/2242, 07/3867, 07/543, 07/855, 08/2449, 10/2059, 10/2076, 13/66: *Distinguished* 07/2816: *Followed* 09/2533, 09/3173, 10/1705, 10/2061, 13/1562, 14/2234, 14/3702: *Not followed* 11/2066, 13/412

Kaye v Hunter 1958 S.C. 208, IH (1 Div) ........ *Digested,* 59/**3914**: *Considered* 14/3331: *Distinguished* 78/3353: *Followed* 76/3149, 80/3183: *Overruled* 92/5785

Kelly v Riverside Inverclyde (Property Holdings) Ltd [2014] CSOH 86; 2014 G.W.D. 18-355, OH

Kennedy v Cordia (Services) LLP [2014] CSIH 76; 2014 S.L.T. 984; 2014 Rep. L.R. 127; 2014 G.W.D. 31-616, IH (Ex Div); reversing [2013] CSOH 130; 2013 Rep. L.R. 126; 2013 G.W.D. 28-568, OH ........ *Digested,* 14/**3693**

Kennedy (Brian Jack) v HM Advocate [2014] HCJAC 14; 2014 S.C.L. 305; 2014 G.W.D. 6-122, HCJ ........ *Digested,* 14/**3398**

Kerr v Mangan [2014] CSIH 69; 2014 S.L.T. 866; 2014 Fam. L.R. 78; 2014 G.W.D. 25-509, IH (Ex Div); affirming 2013 S.L.T. (Sh Ct) 102; 2013 Fam. L.R. 38; 2013 G.W.D. 8-185, Sh Ct (Tayside) (Perth) ........ *Digested,* 14/**3801**

KH (Afghanistan) v Secretary of State for the Home Department [2014] CSOH 97; 2014 G.W.D. 20-388, OH

Kilpatrick (William James) v HM Advocate [2014] HCJAC 73; 2014 S.C.C.R. 509; 2014 G.W.D. 25-486, HCJ

Kindness (Steven) v HM Advocate [2014] HCJAC 5; 2014 S.C.L. 289; 2014 G.W.D. 3-73, HCJ ........ *Digested,* 14/**3765**

Kinley v Devine [2014] CSOH 67; 2014 G.W.D. 14-255, OH

Kippax Ltd v Glasgow Harbour Development Ltd [2014] CSOH 29; 2014 G.W.D. 8-157, OH

Kirk Care Housing Association Ltd v Crerar and Partners 1996 S.L.T. 150, OH ........ *Digested,* 96/**6666**: *Overruled* 14/2470

Kittel v Belgium (C-439/04); *joined case* Belgium v Recolta Recycling SPRL (C-440/04) [2008] S.T.C. 1537; [2006] E.C.R. I-6161; [2008] B.T.C. 5439; [2008] B.V.C. 559; [2006] S.T.I. 1851, ECJ (3rd Chamber) ........ *Digested,* 08/**4052**: *Applied* 07/4317, 07/4318, 09/4061, 09/4063, 09/4064, 09/4078, 10/3495, 11/3533, 11/3556, 12/3402, 12/3405, 14/3066, 14/3070: *Considered* 07/4312, 09/4077, 09/4126, 09/4131, 10/3497, 12/3404, 14/3810: *Followed* 10/3502, 12/3401, 14/3065, 14/3067, 14/3069, 14/3071, 14/3092: *Referred to* 09/4079

KM (Pakistan) v Secretary of State for the Home Department [2014] CSOH 70; 2014 G.W.D. 16-296, OH

Knockman Community Co v McCort 2014 S.L.T. (Lands Tr) 30; 2014 G.W.D. 6-125, Lands Tr (Scot) ........ *Digested,* 14/**3334**

Krajciova v Feroz 2014 G.W.D. 27-536, Sh Ct (Grampian) (Aberdeen)

Kroupa v Donnelly [2013] HCJAC 113; 2013 S.C.L. 1009; 2013 S.C.C.R. 662; 2013 G.W.D. 33-653, HCJ ........ *Digested,* 14/**3466**

Kupka v HM Advocate [2014] HCJAC 37; 2014 S.C.C.R. 383; 2014 G.W.D. 19-364, HCJ ........ *Digested,* 14/**3376**

Kuwar v Murphy see Akhtar v Murphy

KY (Nigeria) v Secretary of State for the Home Department [2014] CSIH 63; 2014 G.W.D. 24-442, IH (Ex Div)

KY (Somalia) v Secretary of State for the Home Department see N v Advocate General for Scotland

L v Board of State Hospital [2011] CSOH 21; 2011 S.L.T. 233; (2011) 121 B.M.L.R. 1; [2011] M.H.L.R. 290; 2011 G.W.D. 4-120, OH ........ *Digested,* 11/**4479**: *Considered* 14/3573

L v HM Advocate; *sub nom* JL v HM Advocate; *joined case* I v HM Advocate [2014] HCJAC 35; 2014 J.C. 199; 2014 S.C.L. 475; 2014 S.C.C.R. 353; 2014 G.W.D. 15-269, HCJ ........ *Digested,* 14/**3369**

L (China), Petitioner [2014] CSOH 147; 2014 G.W.D. 32-631, OH

L Batley Pet Products Ltd v North Lanarkshire Council [2014] UKSC 27; [2014] 3 All E.R. 64; [2014] Bus. L.R. 615; 2014 S.C. (U.K.S.C.) 174; 2014 S.L.T. 593; 2014 S.C.L.R. 501; [2014] 2 P. & C.R. 9; Times, May 12, 2014, SC; reversing [2012] CSIH 83; 2012 G.W.D. 37-745, IH (Ex Div); reversing [2012] CSOH 209; 2012 G.W.D. 4-73, OH ........ *Digested,* 14/**1978**

L'Office Cherifien des Phosphates Unitramp SA v Yamashita-Shinnihon Steamship Co Ltd (The Boucraa) [1994] 1 A.C. 486; [1994] 2 W.L.R. 39; [1994] 1 All E.R. 20; [1994] 1 Lloyd's Rep. 251; (1994) 138 S.J.L.B. 19; Times, December 20, 1993; Independent, January 19, 1994, HL; reversing [1993] 3 W.L.R. 266; [1993] 3 All E.R. 686; [1993] 2 Lloyd's Rep. 149; [1993] N.P.C. 64; Times, April 16, 1993, CA (Civ Div) ........ *Digested,* 94/**221**: *Applied* 95/2038, 96/3566, 13/1619: *Considered* 94/1211, 97/1075, 97/82, 09/2137, 14/3344: *Followed* 99/5471, 00/105

L, Petitioner [2014] CSOH 168; 2014 G.W.D. 39-715, OH

Laboratoires Boiron SA v Agence Centrale des Organismes de Securite Sociale (ACOSS) (C-526/04) see Laboratoires Boiron SA v Union de Recouvrement des Cotisations de Securite Sociale et d'Allocations Familiales (URSSAF) de Lyon (C-526/04)

Laboratoires Boiron SA v Union de Recouvrement des Cotisations de Securite Sociale et d'Allocations Familiales (URSSAF) de Lyon (C-526/04); *sub nom* Laboratoires Boiron SA v Agence Centrale des Organismes de Securite Sociale (ACOSS) (C-526/04) [2006] E.C.R. I-7529; [2006] 3 C.M.L.R. 50; [2007] C.E.C. 77, ECJ (2nd Chamber) ........ *Digested,* 07/**649**: *Considered* 14/3803

Lagden v O'Connor; *sub nom* Clark v Tull (t/a Ardington Electrical Services); *joined cases* Clark v Ardington Electrical Services; Dennard v Plant; Sen v Steelform Engineering Co Ltd; Burdis v Livsey [2003] UKHL 64; [2004] 1 A.C. 1067; [2003] 3 W.L.R. 1571; [2004] 1 All E.R. 277; [2004] R.T.R. 24; [2004] Lloyd's Rep. I.R. 315; (2003) 153 N.L.J. 1869; (2003) 147 S.J.L.B. 1430; Times, December 5, 2003, HL; affirming [2002] EWCA Civ 510; [2003] Q.B. 36; [2002] 3 W.L.R. 762; [2003] R.T.R. 3; [2002] Lloyd's Rep. I.R. 524, CA (Civ Div); reversing in part [2002] Lloyd's Rep. I.R. 138, CC (Oxford) ........ *Digested,* 04/**630**: *Applied* 06/5246, 06/703, 07/1066, 08/896, 14/829: *Cited* 02/687, 11/4036: *Considered* 07/2497, 07/767, 14/3473, 14/830: *Distinguished* 11/4192, 11/858: *Followed* 06/1033, 11/858, 12/1898, 12/1902, 12/2812, 14/2302

Lamb v Wray 2014 S.L.T. (Sh Ct) 2; 2014 S.C.L.R. 303; 2013 G.W.D. 40-765, Sh Ct (Lothian) (Edinburgh) ........ *Digested,* 14/**3688**

Lambeth LBC v Kay see Kay v Lambeth LBC

Lammerzahl GmbH v Freie Hansestadt Bremen (C-241/06) [2007] E.C.R. I-8415; [2008] 1 C.M.L.R. 19, ECJ (3rd Chamber) ........ *Digested,* 08/**3019**: *Applied* 11/2634: *Considered* 14/2475

Lanark CC v East Kilbride Burgh; *sub nom* Lanarkshire CC v East Kilbride Town Council 1967 S.C. 235; 1967 S.L.T. 305, IH (1 Div) ........ *Digested,* 67/**4481**: *Considered* 14/3301

Lanarkshire CC v East Kilbride Town Council see Lanark CC v East Kilbride Burgh

Lanarkshire Valuation Joint Board Assessor v Jane Norman Ltd see Assessor for Lanarkshire Valuation Joint Board v Jane Norman Ltd

Lands Improvement Holdings Landmatch Sarl v Cole 2014 S.L.C.R. 85, Land Ct

Lauchlan (William Hugh) v HM Advocate; *joined case* O'Neill (Charles Bernard) v HM Advocate [2014] HCJAC 62; 2014 S.L.T. 813; 2014 S.C.L. 570; 2014 G.W.D. 22-416, HCJ ........ *Digested,* 14/**3381**

Lauchlan (William Hugh) v HM Advocate; *joined case* O'Neill (Charles Bernard) v HM Advocate [2014] HCJAC 22; 2014 G.W.D. 21-393, HCJ

Law Society of Scotland v O'Donnell [2014] CSOH 167; 2014 G.W.D. 39-709, OH

Law Society of Scotland v O'Donnell [2014] CSOH 166; 2014 G.W.D. 39-706, OH

Lawrence v Regent Office Care Ltd (C-320/00) [2002] E.C.R. I-7325; [2002] 3 C.M.L.R. 27; [2003] I.C.R. 1092; [2002] I.R.L.R. 822; [2002] Emp. L.R. 1248; Times, October 10, 2002, ECJ ........ *Digested,* 02/**1363**: *Applied* 05/1258, 13/1011: *Considered* 04/1253, 04/1258, 09/1206, 14/3503

Lawson v Lawson 1996 S.L.T. (Sh Ct) 83, Sh Pr ........ *Digested,* 96/**6913**: *Considered* 04/4750: *Distinguished* 00/6276, 14/3536

Lawson v Sabre Insurance Co 2014 S.L.T. (Sh Ct) 10; 2013 G.W.D. 30-599, Sh Ct (Grampian) (Peterhead) ........ *Digested,* 14/**3335**

Lee v United Kingdom (57877/09) see James v United Kingdom (25119/09)

Leeds City Council v Hall see Hounslow LBC v Powell

Leeds City Council v Price see Kay v Lambeth LBC

Lennie (Ross) v HM Advocate [2014] HCJAC 103; 2014 S.C.L. 848; 2014 G.W.D. 31-605, HCJ

Leonard v Loch Lomond and the Trossachs National Park Authority [2014] CSOH 38; 2014 Rep. L.R. 46; 2014 G.W.D. 12-220, OH ........ *Digested,* 14/**3700**
Liddell (Ryan Thomas) v HM Advocate [2013] HCJAC 86; 2013 S.C.L. 846; 2013 G.W.D. 26-538, HCJ ........ *Digested,* 13/**3987**: *Followed* 14/3778
Lidl UK GmbH v Glasgow Licensing Board [2013] CSIH 25; 2013 S.C. 442; [2013] L.L.R. 474; 2013 G.W.D. 14-306, IH (Ex Div) ........ *Digested,* 14/**3648**
Lin (Jie) v HM Advocate; *joined cases* Lu (Sheng) v HM Advocate; He (Qing Guang) v HM Advocate; Chen (Xin) v HM Advocate [2012] HCJAC 151; 2014 S.L.T. 173; 2014 S.C.L. 120; 2014 S.C.C.R. 109; 2013 G.W.D. 40-762, HCJ
Liquidator of Letham Grange Development Co Ltd v Foxworth Investments Ltd see Henderson v Foxworth Investments Ltd
Little v Glen [2014] CSIH 99; 2014 G.W.D. 38-702, IH (Ex Div); affirming [2013] CSOH 153; 2013 G.W.D. 31-630, OH
Little Cumbrae Estate Ltd v Rolyat1 Ltd [2014] CSOH 163; 2014 S.L.T. 1118; 2014 G.W.D. 37-682, OH
Livingstone v East of Scotland Water Authority see East of Scotland Water Authority v Livingstone
Livingstone (Gavin) v HM Advocate [2014] HCJAC 102; 2014 S.C.L. 868; 2014 G.W.D. 32-625, HCJ
London & Clydeside Estates Ltd v Aberdeen DC [1980] 1 W.L.R. 182; [1979] 3 All E.R. 876; 1980 S.C. (H.L.) 1; 1980 S.L.T. 81; (1980) 39 P. & C.R. 549; (1979) 253 E.G. 1011; (1980) 124 S.J. 100, HL; reversing 1979 S.L.T. 221, IH (2 Div); affirming in part 1977 S.L.T. 162, OH ........ *Digested,* 80/**315**: *Applied* 85/3463, 92/6121, 95/4375, 02/1829, 12/2053: *Considered* 85/2919, 85/3415, 86/2159, 86/3258, 87/2319, 96/2689, 96/4652, 08/4571, 14/3686: *Followed* 83/3648, 00/6438, 12/981
Lorimer v Griffiths 2013 Hous. L.R. 63; 2013 G.W.D. 34-667, Sh Ct (Lothian) (Edinburgh) ........ *Digested,* 14/**3628**
Lormor Ltd v Glasgow City Council [2014] CSIH 80; 2014 S.L.T. 1055; 2014 G.W.D. 31-612, IH (Ex Div)
Lothian Valuation Joint Board Assessor v Over The Counter Ltd see Assessor for Lothian Valuation Joint Board v Over The Counter Ltd
Louden v Chief Constable of Police Scotland 2014 S.L.T. (Sh Ct) 97; 2014 G.W.D. 20-381, Sh Ct (Tayside) (Forfar) ........ *Digested,* 14/**3808**
Love v Dunn see Paterson v Harvie
Low (Ryan David) v HM Advocate see Blance (Andrew) v HM Advocate
Lowe v Quayle Munro Ltd 1997 S.C. 346; 1997 S.L.T. 1168; 1997 S.C.L.R. 701; 1997 G.W.D. 10-438, OH ........ *Digested,* 97/**6179**: *Approved* 14/1978
Lu (Sheng) v HM Advocate see Lin (Jie) v HM Advocate
Lundin Homes Ltd v Keeper of the Registers of Scotland 2013 S.L.T. (Lands Tr) 73; 2013 G.W.D. 26-532, Lands Tr (Scot) ........ *Digested,* 14/**3582**
LWF (China) v Secretary of State for the Home Department [2014] CSIH 77; 2014 G.W.D. 31-611, IH (Ex Div)
Lynch (Rosemary Burns) v HM Advocate see Bryceland, Petitioner
Lynch, Petitioner see Bryceland, Petitioner
Lyons v Chief Constable of Strathclyde; *sub nom* Lyons v House [2013] CSIH 46; 2014 S.C.L.R. 281; [2013] L.L.R. 748; 2013 G.W.D. 20-401, IH (Ex Div); affirming [2012] CSOH 45; 2012 Rep. L.R. 108; 2012 G.W.D. 13-240, OH ........ *Digested,* 12/**3953**
Lyons v House see Lyons v Chief Constable of Strathclyde

M v Advocate General for Scotland [2013] CSOH 169; 2014 S.L.T. 475; 2013 G.W.D. 36-702, OH ........ *Digested,* 14/**3299**
M v Authority Reporter 2014 S.L.T. (Sh Ct) 57; 2011 G.W.D. 2-94, Sh Ct (Glasgow)
M v Fife Council 2014 S.L.T. (Sh Ct) 147; 2014 G.W.D. 32-630, Sh Ct (Tayside) (Kirkcaldy) ........ *Digested,* 14/**3476**
M v HM Advocate [2014] HCJAC 91; 2014 S.C.L. 695; 2014 G.W.D. 28-559, HCJ ........ *Digested,* 14/**3418**
M v HM Advocate; *sub nom* RM v HM Advocate [2012] HCJAC 66; 2012 S.C.L. 890; 2012 S.C.C.R. 611; 2012 G.W.D. 20-415, HCJ ........ *Digested,* 13/**3630**: *Followed* 14/3443
M v HM Advocate (No.2); *sub nom* CJM v HM Advocate [2013] HCJAC 22; 2013 S.L.T. 380; 2013 S.C.L. 361; 2013 S.C.C.R. 215; 2013 G.W.D. 8-170, HCJ ........ *Digested,* 13/**3558**: *Considered* 13/3561, 14/3371
M v K 2014 G.W.D. 25-496, Sh Ct (Lothian) (Edinburgh)
M v Locality Reporter Manager [2014] CSIH 62; 2014 Fam. L.R. 102; 2014 G.W.D. 24-453, IH (Ex Div)
M v M 2014 S.L.T. (Sh Ct) 37; 2014 G.W.D. 8-166, Sh Ct (Lothian) (Edinburgh)

M v M [2014] CSOH 136; 2014 Fam. L.R. 116; 2014 G.W.D. 29-576, OH
M v Secretary of State for the Home Department see DM (Algeria) v Secretary of State for the Home Department
M v State Hospitals Board for Scotland; *sub nom* CM v State Hospitals Board for Scotland; CM, Petitioner [2014] CSIH 71; 2014 S.L.T. 905; 2014 S.C.L.R. 817; 2014 G.W.D. 27-534, IH (2 Div); reversing [2013] CSOH 143; 2013 S.L.T. 1001; 2013 S.C.L.R. 745; 2013 G.W.D. 29-570, OH .......... *Digested,* 14/**3573**
M (Iraq) v Secretary of State for the Home Department [2013] CSOH 182; 2014 G.W.D. 1-19, OH
M (Pakistan) v Secretary of State for the Home Department [2013] CSOH 186; 2014 G.W.D. 1-20, OH
M, Appellant 2014 Fam. L.R. 55; 2014 G.W.D. 4-84, Sh Ct (Tayside) (Kirkcaldy) .......... *Digested,* 14/**3527**
M, Applicant [2014] CSIH 104; 2014 G.W.D. 39-717, IH (Ex Div)
M, Petitioner; *sub nom* ADM, Petitioner [2013] CSIH 69; 2014 S.C. 165; 2013 S.L.T. 951; 2013 Fam. L.R. 84; 2013 G.W.D. 25-473, IH (2 Div) .......... *Digested,* 13/**3511**
M, Petitioner [2013] CSOH 160; 2013 S.L.T. 1043; 2013 G.W.D. 32-641, OH .......... *Digested,* 14/**3639**
M, Petitioner; *sub nom* TJM, Petitioner [2014] CSOH 28; 2014 S.L.T. 483; 2014 G.W.D. 8-153, OH
*Reversed* 14/3606
M, Petitioner [2014] CSIH 68; 2014 S.L.T. 851; 2014 G.W.D. 25-467, IH (Ex Div) .......... *Digested,* 14/**3606**
MABN v Advocate General for Scotland see N v Advocate General for Scotland
MacDonald v Aberdeenshire Council [2013] CSIH 83; 2014 S.C. 114; 2014 S.L.T. 2; 2014 S.C.L.R. 111; 2014 Rep. L.R. 2; 2013 G.W.D. 36-709, IH (Ex Div); reversing in part [2012] CSOH 101; 2012 S.L.T. 863; 2012 S.C.L.R. 620; 2012 Rep. L.R. 143; 2012 G.W.D. 22-447, OH .......... *Digested,* 14/**3690**
Macdonald v Munro 1997 S.L.T. 446; 1996 S.C.C.R. 595, HCJ Appeal .......... *Digested,* 96/**6789**: *Considered* 14/3373
MacGillivray v Crofters Commission 2014 G.W.D. 13-224, Land Ct
MacGillivray v Crofting Commission 2014 S.L.C.R. 102, Land Ct
MacInnes v Forth Ports Ltd [2014] CSOH 92; 2014 G.W.D. 20-374, OH
Mackay v Gaylor 2014 S.L.T. (Sh Ct) 131; 2001 G.W.D. 1-59, Sh Ct (Lothian) (Jedburgh)
MacKay v McGowan 2014 G.W.D. 37-687, Lands Tr (Scot)
Mackinnon v Hadfield (t/a Ben Nevis Inn) 2014 S.C.L.R. 510; 2014 G.W.D. 7-141, OH
Macklin (Paul Alexander) v HM Advocate [2013] HCJAC 80; 2013 S.C.C.R. 616; 2013 G.W.D. 31-619, HCJ .......... *Digested,* 14/**3442**
MacLachlan v Bruce 2014 S.L.C.R. 133, Land Ct
Maclay Murray & Spens v Orr [2014] CSIH 107, IH (Ex Div); affirming 2014 G.W.D. 18-330, Sh Ct (Glasgow)
Maclehose v Wilson [2014] CSOH 50; 2014 G.W.D. 11-204, OH
Maclennan v Dunedin Canmore Housing Association Ltd 2014 S.L.T. (Lands Tr) 25; 2014 G.W.D. 7-147, Lands Tr (Scot) .......... *Digested,* 14/**3634**
Macnab v Castle Leod Maintenance Fund Trustees 2014 S.L.C.R. 169; 2014 G.W.D. 40-727, Land Ct
Macnabs LLP v Fordlane Ltd 2014 S.L.T. (Sh Ct) 80; 2014 G.W.D. 11-198, Sh Ct (Tayside) (Dundee) .......... *Digested,* 14/**3355**
MacNeill (Grant) v HM Advocate see Carr (Daniel Kimet Thomas) v HM Advocate
MacRoberts LLP v McCrindle Group Ltd [2014] CSOH 99; 2014 G.W.D. 21-409, OH
Maguire v 5 PM Ltd 2014 G.W.D. 28-557, Sh Ct (Glasgow)
Mahageben kft v Nemzeti Ado- es Vamhivatal Del-dunantuli Regionalis Ado Foigazgatosaga (C-80/11); *joined case* David v Nemzeti Ado- es Vamhivatal Eszak-alfoldi Regionalis Ado Foigazgatosaga (C-142/11) [2012] S.T.C. 1934; [2013] C.E.C. 306; [2012] S.T.I. 2733, ECJ (3rd Chamber)
*Applied* 14/3070: *Cited* 14/3810: *Considered* 14/3069
Mahmood v Murphy see Akhtar v Murphy
Mahony v East Holyford Mining Co Ltd (1874-75) L.R. 7 H.L. 869, HL (UK-Irl)
*Considered* 14/3355: *Distinguished* 52/464

Manchester City Council v Pinnock; *sub nom* Pinnock v Manchester City Council [2010] UKSC 45; [2011] 2 A.C. 104; [2010] 3 W.L.R. 1441; [2011] 1 All E.R. 285; [2011] P.T.S.R. 61; [2011] H.R.L.R. 3; [2010] U.K.H.R.R. 1213; 31 B.H.R.C. 670; [2011] H.L.R. 7; [2010] B.L.G.R. 909; [2011] L. & T.R. 2; [2010] 3 E.G.L.R. 113; [2010] 45 E.G. 93 (C.S.); (2010) 107(44) L.S.G. 16; (2011) 108(8) L.S.G. 20; (2010) 154(42) S.J.L.B. 30; [2010] N.P.C. 109; Times, November 4, 2010, SC; affirming in part [2009] EWCA Civ 852; [2010] 1 W.L.R. 713; [2010] 3 All E.R. 201; [2010] P.T.S.R. 423; [2010] H.L.R. 7; [2009] B.L.G.R. 869; [2009] 32 E.G. 68 (C.S.), CA (Civ Div) ........................................ *Digested,* 11/**2066**: *Applied* 11/2069, 14/1997, 14/3635: *Considered* 13/1892, 14/1625: *Distinguished* 12/2599: *Followed* 10/1705, 12/1301, 12/1645, 12/2055, 13/1562, 13/1890, 14/2000

Manorgate Ltd v First Scottish Property Services Ltd [2013] CSOH 108; [2014] P.N.L.R. 1; 2013 G.W.D. 25-491, OH ........................................ *Digested,* 14/**3687**

Marks & Spencer Plc v Assessor for Highland and Western Isles Valuation Joint Board [2013] CSIH 96; 2014 S.L.T. 241; [2014] R.A. 171; 2013 G.W.D. 40-768, LVAC ........................................ *Digested,* 14/**3670**

Marshall v Fife Health Board [2013] CSOH 140; 2013 S.L.T. 1129; 2013 G.W.D. 28-561, OH ........................................ *Digested,* 14/**3339**

Martin v Martin (Husband & Wife: Evidence) (1954) 70 Sh. Ct. Rep. 306, Sh Ct (Lothian) ........................................ *Digested,* 54/**3791**: *Considered* 14/3367

Martin (Leanne) v HM Advocate; *sub nom* Martin, Petitioner [2014] HCJAC 15; 2014 S.C.L. 249; 2014 S.C.C.R. 160; 2014 G.W.D. 7-140, HCJ ........................................ *Digested,* 14/**3427**

Martin and Co (UK) Ltd, Petitioner [2014] CSOH 33; 2014 G.W.D. 9-168, OH

Martin and Co (UK) Ltd, Petitioners [2013] CSIH 99; 2014 S.L.T. 71; 2013 G.W.D. 40-759, IH (Ex Div) ........................................ *Digested,* 14/**3352**

Martin, Petitioner see Martin (Leanne) v HM Advocate

Masri v Consolidated Contractors International Co SAL [2009] UKHL 43; [2010] 1 A.C. 90; [2009] 3 W.L.R. 385; [2009] 4 All E.R. 847; [2010] 1 All E.R. (Comm) 220; [2009] Bus. L.R. 1269; [2009] 2 Lloyd's Rep. 473; [2009] C.P. Rep. 47; [2010] B.C.C. 25; [2009] 2 B.C.L.C. 382; [2009] 2 C.L.C. 366; [2009] B.P.I.R. 1029; (2009) 159 N.L.J. 1137; (2009) 159 N.L.J. 1250; Times, August 13, 2009, HL; reversing [2008] EWCA Civ 876; [2009] 2 W.L.R. 699; [2009] Bus. L.R. 246; [2009] 1 Lloyd's Rep. 42; [2008] C.P. Rep. 42; [2008] 2 C.L.C. 126; [2009] I.L.Pr. 9; [2008] B.P.I.R. 1524, CA (Civ Div) ........................................ *Digested,* 09/**408**: *Considered* 10/268, 10/404, 13/248, 14/3345, 14/539: *Distinguished* 14/305

Matulewicz v Brown [2014] HCJAC 7; 2014 S.C.C.R. 154; 2014 G.W.D. 3-62, HCJ ..... *Digested,* 14/**3385**

MBK (Democratic Republic of Congo) v Secretary of State for the Home Department [2014] CSOH 31; 2014 G.W.D. 9-176, OH

MBR (Iran) v Secretary of State for the Home Department; *sub nom* R v Secretary of State for the Home Department [2013] CSIH 66; 2013 S.L.T. 1108; 2013 G.W.D. 24-448, IH (2 Div) ........................................ *Digested,* 14/**3348**

McAlister v Stevenson see Donoghue v Stevenson

McAteer v Glasgow City Council [2014] CSOH 42; 2014 Rep. L.R. 54; 2014 G.W.D. 9-174, OH ........................................ *Digested,* 14/**3340**

McAughey (Charles Gray) v HM Advocate [2013] HCJAC 163; 2014 S.C.L. 165; 2014 S.C.C.R. 11; 2014 G.W.D. 1-9, HCJ ........................................ *Digested,* 14/**3391**

McCabe v Greater Glasgow Health Board [2014] I.C.R. D41, EAT (SC)

McCadden (Patrick) v HM Advocate 1985 J.C. 98; 1986 S.L.T. 138; 1985 S.C.C.R. 282, HCJ Appeal ........................................ *Digested,* 86/**3832**: *Applied* 97/5818, 99/5875, 14/3422: *Considered* 87/4185, 88/4018, 99/5832: *Followed* 94/5639

McCann v Waddell & McIntosh Solicitors [2014] CSOH 15; 2014 G.W.D. 7-149, OH

McCarn v Secretary of State for Business, Innovation and Skills [2014] CSOH 121; 2014 Rep. L.R. 138; 2014 G.W.D. 26-519, OH ........................................ *Digested,* 14/**3468**

McCormack (Alexander) v Cottam [2014] HCJAC 6; 2014 G.W.D. 4-95, HCJ

McCourt (Peter Stephen) v HM Advocate see Gemmell (James Kelly) v HM Advocate

McCowan v Dunn [2013] HCJAC 119; 2013 S.C.C.R. 623; 2013 G.W.D. 32-638, HCJ *Digested,* 14/**3465**

McCue v Glasgow City Council [2014] CSOH 124; 2014 S.L.T. 891; 2014 G.W.D. 26-510, OH ........................................ *Digested,* 14/**3301**

McDermott v Guthrie 2014 G.W.D. 1-3, Sh Ct (Glasgow)

McEntee v Westminster Motor Insurance Association Ltd [2014] CSIH 57; 2014 G.W.D. 24-443, IH (Ex Div)

McEwan v Lothian Buses Plc [2014] CSIH 12; 2014 G.W.D. 5-97, IH (Ex Div)

McFadyen v McGhee 2014 G.W.D. 17-308, Sh Ct (South Strathclyde) (Airdrie) ........... *Digested,* 14/**3343**

McFeeley v Harvie see Fitzpatrick v Harvie

McGeadie v ATOS Healthcare [2013] CSIH 106; 2014 G.W.D. 2-39, IH (Ex Div); affirming [2013] CSOH 19; 2013 G.W.D. 6-144, OH

McGeoch v Lord President of the Council [2011] CSIH 67; 2012 S.C. 410; 2012 S.L.T. 224; [2012] Eu. L.R. 345; 2011 G.W.D. 38-773, IH (Ex Div); affirming [2011] CSOH 65; 2011 S.L.T. 633; 2011 G.W.D. 14-320, OH .......... *Digested,* 12/**3970**: *Affirmed* 14/976

McGeoch v Lord President of the Council see R. (on the application of Chester) v Secretary of State for Justice

McGill v McGill 2014 G.W.D. 25-498, Sh Ct (Glasgow)

McGill (James) v HM Advocate; *joined case* Harrison v Nisbet [2013] HCJAC 150; 2014 S.L.T. 238; 2014 S.C.L. 143; 2014 S.C.C.R. 46; 2013 G.W.D. 40-770, HCJ .......... *Digested,* 14/**3768**

McGinty v Scottish Ministers [2013] CSIH 78; 2014 S.C. 81; 2014 S.C.L.R. 318; 2013 G.W.D. 31-631, IH (Ex Div); affirming [2011] CSOH 163; 2011 G.W.D. 37-752, OH .......... *Digested,* 14/**3730**

McGovern v Scottish Ministers [2014] CSOH 134; 2014 G.W.D. 29-567, OH

McGowan v B [2011] UKSC 54; [2011] 1 W.L.R. 3121; 2012 S.C. (U.K.S.C.) 182; 2012 S.L.T. 37; 2012 S.C.L. 85; 2012 S.C.C.R. 109; [2012] H.R.L.R. 7; (2011) 155(45) S.J.L.B. 31; Times, November 25, 2011, SC .......... *Digested,* 12/**3909**: *Considered* 12/771, 14/662: *Followed* 12/3875, 12/743, 14/3458

McGraddie v McGraddie [2013] UKSC 58; [2013] 1 W.L.R. 2477; 2014 S.C. (U.K.S.C.) 12; 2013 S.L.T. 1212; 2013 G.W.D. 25-471, SC; reversing [2012] CSIH 23; 2012 G.W.D. 15-310, IH (Ex Div); reversing [2010] CSOH 60; 2010 G.W.D. 21-404, OH .......... *Digested,* 13/**6**: *Followed* 14/1579

McGregor Glazing Ltd v McGregor 2014 G.W.D. 27-540, Sh Ct (Grampian) (Aberdeen); reversing 2013 G.W.D. 19-379, Sh Ct (Grampian) (Aberdeen)

McGrory (Barry John) v HM Advocate [2013] HCJAC 165; 2014 S.C.L. 178; 2014 S.C.C.R. 140; 2014 G.W.D. 1-14, HCJ .......... *Digested,* 14/**3439**

McGuiness v Brown [2013] HCJAC 82; 2014 J.C. 131; 2013 S.C.L. 798; 2013 S.C.C.R. 442; 2013 G.W.D. 25-484, HCJ .......... *Digested,* 13/**3588**

McGuire v Higson 2003 S.L.T. 890; 2003 S.C.C.R. 440; 2003 G.W.D. 21-624, HCJ .... *Digested,* 03/**5367**: *Considered* 14/3414

McInally v Arcus FM Ltd [2014] CSOH 146; 2014 G.W.D. 32-632, OH

McIntosh v Castle Rock Edinvar Housing Association Ltd 2014 S.L.T. (Lands Tr) 35; 2013 Hous. L.R. 74; 2013 G.W.D. 38-739, Lands Tr (Scot) .......... *Digested,* 14/**3638**

McIntyre v Stewart 2014 Fam. L.R. 7, Sh Ct (Lothian) (Haddington)

McKay v McNabb 2014 G.W.D. 30-599, Sh Ct (Lothian) (Edinburgh)

McKechnie v Murphy see Strawbridge v Murphy

McKenzie v Murphy; *sub nom* McKenzie v Procurator Fiscal [2014] HCJAC 132; 2014 G.W.D. 40-724, HCJ

McKenzie v Procurator Fiscal see McKenzie v Murphy

McLaughlin v Harvie [2014] HCJAC 98; 2014 S.L.T. 961; 2014 S.C.L. 776; 2014 G.W.D. 30-589, HCJ .......... *Digested,* 14/**3402**

McLaughlin v Morrison [2013] CSOH 163; 2014 S.L.T. 111; 2013 G.W.D. 35-686, OH *Digested,* 14/**3718**

McLaughlin v Morrison [2014] CSOH 123; 2014 S.L.T. 862; 2014 G.W.D. 26-531, OH *Digested,* 14/**3720**

McLeod v Tayside Health Board [2014] CSOH 141; 2014 G.W.D. 30-602, OH

McLuckie (James) v HM Advocate see Carlin (John) v HM Advocate

McMahon v Dear [2014] CSOH 100; 2014 S.L.T. 823; 2014 S.C.L.R. 616; 2014 Rep. L.R. 71; 2014 G.W.D. 22-421, OH .......... *Digested,* 14/**3691**

McNeil (Denise) v HM Advocate see O'Neill (William) v HM Advocate

McNeill v Aberdeen City Council see Aberdeen City Council v McNeill

McPake v SRCL Ltd [2013] CSOH 157; 2014 S.C.L.R. 199; 2014 Rep. L.R. 41; 2013 G.W.D. 32-644, OH .......... *Digested,* 14/**3692**

McVicar v D [2014] CSOH 61; 2014 G.W.D. 13-227, OH

McWatters v Inverclyde Council 2014 S.L.T. (Sh Ct) 155; 2014 Hous. L.R. 70; 2014 G.W.D. 35-661, Sh Ct (North Strathclyde) (Greenock)

Medicina Ltd v Midlothian Council [2013] CSOH 106; 2014 Rep. L.R. 36; 2013 G.W.D. 25-479, OH .......... *Digested,* 14/**3473**

Megrahi (Abdelbaset Ali) v HM Advocate (No.4) see HM Advocate v Al-Megrahi (Abdelbaset Ali) (No.4)

Meikle v Nottinghamshire CC; *sub nom* Nottinghamshire CC v Meikle [2004] EWCA Civ 859; [2004] 4 All E.R. 97; [2005] I.C.R. 1; [2004] I.R.L.R. 703; (2004) 80 B.M.L.R. 129; (2004) 148 S.J.L.B. 908; Times, July 15, 2004; Independent, July 14, 2004, CA (Civ Div); affirming EAT/0033/03 RN, EAT .......... *Digested,* 04/**1193**: *Applied* 05/1227, 06/1282, 08/1122, 10/1034, 14/3500: *Considered* 06/1300: *Followed* 14/1023

Meikle (Tracy) v HM Advocate [2014] HCJAC 116; 2014 S.L.T. 1062; 2014 G.W.D. 35-654, HCJ

Menni (Nasserdine) v HM Advocate [2014] HCJAC 54; 2014 J.C. 258; 2014 S.C.L. 552; 2014 S.C.C.R. 430; 2014 G.W.D. 20-380, HCJ ........ *Digested,* 14/**3394**

Menni (Nasserdine) v HM Advocate [2013] HCJAC 158; 2014 S.C.L. 191; 2014 G.W.D. 1-10, HCJ ........ *Digested,* 14/**3409**

Mentmore Towers Ltd v Packman Lucas Ltd [2010] EWHC 457 (TCC); [2010] C.P. Rep. 34; [2010] B.L.R. 393; [2010] C.I.L.L. 2846; [2010] Bus. L.R. D114, QBD (TCC) ........ *Digested,* 10/**849**: *Considered* 14/3360

Merton LBC v Gardiner; *sub nom* Gardiner v Merton LBC [1981] Q.B. 269; [1981] 2 W.L.R. 232; [1981] I.C.R. 186; [1980] I.R.L.R. 472; 79 L.G.R. 374; (1981) 125 S.J. 97; Times, November 26, 1980, CA (Civ Div); affirming [1980] I.R.L.R. 302, EAT ........ *Digested,* 81/**815**: *Considered* 90/1957, 13/3679, 14/3503

MGW (Iraq) v Secretary of State for the Home Department [2014] CSOH 104; 2014 G.W.D. 24-457, OH

MH (Bangladesh) v Secretary of State for the Home Department [2014] CSOH 143; 2014 G.W.D. 30-597, OH

MH (China) v Secretary of State for the Home Department [2014] CSOH 112; 2014 G.W.D. 24-459, OH

MH (Palestine) v Secretary of State for the Home Department [2014] CSOH 130; 2014 G.W.D. 29-578, OH

Middlemiss v Fraser [2013] HCJAC 132; 2014 J.C. 111; 2014 S.C.L. 53; 2013 G.W.D. 35-701, HCJ ........ *Digested,* 14/**3769**

Midlothian Council v CMP see Midlothian Council v M

Midlothian Council v M; *sub nom* Midlothian Council v CMP [2013] CSIH 71; 2014 S.C. 168; 2013 Fam. L.R. 104; 2013 G.W.D. 37-720, IH (Ex Div); affirming [2012] CSOH 63; 2012 G.W.D. 16-330, OH ........ *Digested,* 14/**3550**

Mikiashvili v Georgia (18996/06) (Unreported, October 9, 2012), ECHR *Considered* 14/3599

Miller v Chivas Brothers Ltd [2014] CSIH 65; 2014 G.W.D. 24-452, IH (Ex Div)

Miller v Miller 2014 G.W.D. 22-420, Sh Ct (Lothian) (Edinburgh)

Miller Construction (UK) Ltd v Building Design Partnership Ltd [2014] CSOH 80; 2014 G.W.D. 15-268, OH

Miller Homes Ltd v Keeper of the Registers of Scotland 2014 S.L.T. (Lands Tr) 79; 2014 G.W.D. 21-406, Lands Tr (Scot) ........ *Digested,* 14/**3583**

Mineral Resources Ltd, Re; *sub nom* Environment Agency v Stout [1999] 1 All E.R. 746; [1999] B.C.C. 422; [1999] 2 B.C.L.C. 516; [1999] Env. L.R. 407; [1998] B.P.I.R. 576; [1998] 4 P.L.R. 56; [1998] E.G. 78 (C.S.); [1998] N.P.C. 78, Ch D (Companies Ct) ........ *Digested,* 99/**3309**: *Applied* 99/3279: *Considered* 14/3622: *Followed* 99/3263: *Not followed* 99/3308

Ministry of Defence v Assessor for Fife Council; *sub nom* Ministry of Defence v Fife Assessor 2014 S.L.T. (Lands Tr) 34; [2014] R.V.R. 128; 2014 G.W.D. 1-28, Lands Tr (Scot) ........ *Digested,* 14/**3668**

Ministry of Defence v Fife Assessor see Ministry of Defence v Assessor for Fife Council

Ministry of Defence v Grampian Assessor 2014 S.L.T. (Lands Tr) 44; [2014] R.V.R. 102; 2014 G.W.D. 1-27, Lands Tr (Scot) ........ *Digested,* 14/**3667**

Mirza v Aslam see Mirza v Salim

Mirza v Salim; *sub nom* Mirza v Aslam [2014] CSIH 51; 2014 S.L.T. 875; 2014 S.C.L.R. 764; 2014 G.W.D. 24-445, IH (Ex Div); reversing [2013] CSOH 73; 2013 G.W.D. 17-348, OH ........ *Digested,* 14/**3344**

MJ (Gambia) v Advocate General for Scotland [2014] CSOH 107; 2014 G.W.D. 23-438, OH

ML (China) v Secretary of State for the Home Department [2014] CSOH 54; 2014 G.W.D. 12-216, OH

MM (Iran) v Secretary of State for the Home Department [2010] EWCA Civ 1457; [2011] I.N.L.R. 206, CA (Civ Div) ........ *Digested,* 11/**1720**: *Considered* 11/4380, 14/1659

MMM (Zimbabwe) v Secretary of State for the Home Department [2014] CSOH 43; 2014 G.W.D. 10-186, OH

MN (Somalia) v Secretary of State for the Home Department see N v Advocate General for Scotland

Mobilx Ltd (In Administration) v Revenue and Customs Commissioners; *joined cases* Revenue and Customs Commissioners v Blue Sphere Global Ltd; Calltel Telecom Ltd v Revenue and Customs Commissioners [2010] EWCA Civ 517; [2010] S.T.C. 1436; [2010] Lloyd's Rep. F.C. 445; [2010] B.V.C. 638; [2010] S.T.I. 1589; Times, June 2, 2010, CA (Civ Div) ........ *Digested,* 10/**3502**: *Applied* 11/3533, 14/3066, 14/3070: *Considered* 11/3538, 11/3556, 12/3398, 14/3071, 14/3810: *Followed* 11/3554, 12/3401, 12/3402, 12/3404, 12/3405, 14/3065, 14/3067, 14/3069, 14/3092

Moir v Hunter (1832) 11 S. 32, IH (1 Div) *Considered* 14/3344

Moness Country Club v First National Trustee Co Ltd [2013] CSOH 188; 2014 G.W.D. 15-283, OH

Montgomery v Thomson see Gill v Thomson

Moohan v Lord Advocate see Moohan, Petitioner

Moohan, Petitioner; *sub nom* Moohan v Lord Advocate [2014] UKSC 67, SC; affirming [2014] CSIH 56; 2014 S.L.T. 755; 2014 S.C.L.R. 801; 2014 G.W.D. 23-426, IH (1 Div); affirming [2013] CSOH 199; 2014 S.L.T. 213; 2014 G.W.D. 3-55, OH ... *Digested,* 14/**3703**

Morrison (Adam Edward) v HM Advocate [2013] HCJAC 108; 2014 J.C. 74; 2013 S.C.L. 965; 2013 S.C.C.R. 626; 2013 G.W.D. 31-622, HCJ ........ *Digested,* 14/**3454**

Mortgages 1 Ltd v Chaudhary 2014 S.L.T. (Sh Ct) 35; 2013 G.W.D. 39-745, Sh Ct (South Strathclyde) (Airdrie) ........ *Digested,* 14/**3329**

Morton v William Dixon Ltd 1909 S.C. 807; (1909) 1 S.L.T. 346, IH (Ct of 5 judges) *Applied* 47-51/6857, 57/1405, 14/3693: *Considered* 52/3987, 52/4309, 60/2183: *Explained* 59/2251: *Followed* 71/7944

Morton (Henry) v HM Advocate 1938 J.C. 50; 1937 S.N. 108; 1938 S.L.T. 27, HCJ Appeal *Considered* 57/4331: *Explained* 14/3367: *Followed* 76/3405

Mowbray v Scottish Ministers [2014] CSIH 100; 2014 Hous. L.R. 64; 2014 G.W.D. 39-718, IH (Ex Div)

Muirhead (Warren) v HM Advocate [2014] HCJAC 90; 2014 S.C.L. 702; 2014 G.W.D. 27-551, HCJ ........ *Digested,* 14/**3763**

Mullen v Salford City Council see Hounslow LBC v Powell

Munjaz v United Kingdom (2913/06) [2012] M.H.L.R. 351; Times, October 9, 2012, ECHR *Applied* 14/3573

Munro (John Roberts) v HM Advocate [2014] HCJAC 40; 2014 S.C.L. 461; 2014 G.W.D. 16-292, HCJ ........ *Digested,* 14/**3397**

Murdoch v Airtours Holidays Ltd 2014 G.W.D. 27-539, Sh Ct (Grampian) (Aberdeen)

Murphy v B; *sub nom* Murphy v SB [2014] HCJAC 82; 2014 S.C.L. 648; 2014 S.C.C.R. 501; 2014 G.W.D. 25-490, HCJ ........ *Digested,* 14/**3421**

Murphy v Cameron 2014 S.L.T. (Sh Ct) 90; 2014 S.C.L. 590; 2014 G.W.D. 21-397, Sh Ct (Grampian) (Peterhead) ........ *Digested,* 14/**3457**

Murphy v Martin [2014] HCJAC 97; 2014 S.C.L. 770; 2014 G.W.D. 29-573, HCJ ........ *Digested,* 14/**3408**

Murphy v Media Protection Services Ltd (C-429/08) see Football Association Premier League Ltd v QC Leisure (C-403/08)

Murphy v SB see Murphy v B

Murray (Iain Alexander) v HM Advocate see Wilson (Brian) v HM Advocate

Murray (Stephen) v HM Advocate [2013] HCJAC 3; 2013 S.C.L. 243; 2013 S.C.C.R. 88; 2013 G.W.D. 2-86, HCJ ........ *Digested,* 13/**3972**: *Cited* 14/3765

Mushin v Manchester City Council see Hounslow LBC v Powell

Mutebi (Rogers) v HM Advocate [2013] HCJAC 142; 2014 S.C.L. 5; 2014 S.C.C.R. 52; 2013 G.W.D. 37-716, HCJ ........ *Digested,* 14/**3395**

N v Advocate General for Scotland; *sub nom* KASY v Advocate General for Scotland; MABN v Advocate General for Scotland; Secretary of State for the Home Department v MN; Secretary of State for the Home Department v KY; MN (Somalia) v Secretary of State for the Home Department; KY (Somalia) v Secretary of State for the Home Department; *joined case* Y v Advocate General for Scotland [2014] UKSC 30; [2014] 1 W.L.R. 2064; [2014] 4 All E.R. 443; 2014 S.C. (U.K.S.C.) 183; 2014 S.L.T. 669; [2014] Imm. A.R. 981; [2014] I.N.L.R. 590; 2014 G.W.D. 17-325; Times, June 6, 2014, SC; affirming [2013] CSIH 68; 2013 S.L.T. 1143; 2013 G.W.D. 37-721, IH (Ex Div) ........ *Digested,* 14/**1641**

Najafli v Azerbaijan (2594/07) (Unreported, October 2, 2012), ECHR *Considered* 14/3599

National House Building Council v Penman [2014] CSOH 120; 2014 G.W.D. 25-474, OH

Nationwide Gritting Services Ltd v Scottish Ministers [2014] CSOH 41; 2014 G.W.D. 8-156, OH

Nationwide Gritting Services Ltd v Scottish Ministers [2014] CSOH 151; 2014 G.W.D. 34-650, OH

Neill (James) v HM Advocate [2014] HCJAC 67; 2014 G.W.D. 24-466, HCJ

Network Rail Infrastructure Ltd v Scottish Ministers [2013] CSIH 64; 2014 S.C. 15; [2014] R.V.R. 200; 2013 G.W.D. 24-463, IH (2 Div) .......... *Digested,* 14/**3724**

Newlands (John) v HM Advocate [2013] HCJAC 148; 2014 J.C. 183; 2014 S.C.L. 135; 2014 S.C.C.R. 25; 2013 G.W.D. 38-730, HCJ .......... *Digested,* 14/**3764**

NHS Greater Glasgow & Clyde v Assessor for Renfrewshire Valuation Joint Board 2014 S.L.T. (Lands Tr) 97; 2014 G.W.D. 30-603, Lands Tr (Scot)

NHS Greater Glasgow and Clyde v Assessor for Renfrewshire 2014 S.L.T. (Lands Tr) 52; [2014] R.V.R. 32; 2013 G.W.D. 36-711, Lands Tr (Scot) .......... *Digested,* 14/**3671**

Nicholson Bros v Anderson's Executor [2014] CSOH 114; 2014 G.W.D. 24-447, OH

Nisbet v Humphries 2014 S.L.T. (Sh Ct) 71; 2014 S.C.L. 596; 2014 G.W.D. 19-363, Sh Ct (Tayside) (Dundee) .......... *Digested,* 14/**3366**

Nisbet v JR see Griffiths v R

Nisbet v Ogilvie see Gemmell (James Kelly) v HM Advocate

Nolan v Advance Construction (Scotland) Ltd [2014] CSOH 4; 2014 S.C.L.R. 351; 2014 G.W.D. 5-107, OH .......... *Digested,* 14/**3515**

Nolan (Thomas) v HM Advocate see Ferguson (James Douglas) v HM Advocate

North Lanarkshire Council v McMeekin 2014 G.W.D. 3-56, Sh Ct (South Strathclyde) (Airdrie)

Northern Rock (Asset Management) Plc v Steel [2014] CSOH 40; 2014 G.W.D. 10-191, OH

Nottinghamshire CC v Meikle see Meikle v Nottinghamshire CC

NS v Secretary of State for the Home Department see S v Secretary of State for the Home Department

O'Donnell (Kevin) v HM Advocate [2014] HCJAC 43; 2014 G.W.D. 18-340, HCJ

O'Leary (Thomas) v HM Advocate [2014] HCJAC 45; 2014 S.L.T. 711; 2014 S.C.L. 515; 2014 S.C.C.R. 421; 2014 G.W.D. 18-343, HCJ .......... *Digested,* 14/**3708**

O'Neill v Phillips; *sub nom* Pectel Ltd, Re; Company (No.000709 of 1992), Re [1999] 1 W.L.R. 1092; [1999] 2 All E.R. 961; [1999] B.C.C. 600; [1999] 2 B.C.L.C. 1; (1999) 96(23) L.S.G. 33; (1999) 149 N.L.J. 805; Times, May 21, 1999, HL; affirming [1998] B.C.C. 405; [1997] 2 B.C.L.C. 739, CA (Civ Div) .......... *Digested,* 99/**634**: *Applied* 00/691, 01/747, 02/5375, 05/39, 06/565, 07/563, 07/586, 09/539, 13/3679, 14/3503, 14/521: *Considered* 04/477, 04/478, 06/553, 06/567, 11/428, 12/517, 14/523: *Distinguished* 03/545, 13/486: *Followed* 14/522

O'Neill (Charles Bernard) v HM Advocate see Lauchlan (William Hugh) v HM Advocate

O'Neill (Charles Bernard) v HM Advocate see Lauchlan (William Hugh) v HM Advocate

O'Neill (William) v HM Advocate; *joined cases* McNeil (Denise) v HM Advocate; Hayburn (Deborah) v HM Advocate [2014] HCJAC 124; 2014 G.W.D. 39-714, HCJ

Oliphant v Scottish Legal Complaints Commission [2014] CSIH 94; 2014 G.W.D. 37-681, IH (Ex Div)

Opal Glen Properties Ltd v Central Scotland Valuation Joint Board Assessor 2014 S.L.T. (Lands Tr) 22; [2014] R.V.R. 69; 2013 G.W.D. 38-741, Lands Tr (Scot) .. *Digested,* 14/**3679**

Orr v D S Orr & Sons (Holdings) Ltd [2014] CSOH 96; 2014 G.W.D. 21-398, OH

Othman v United Kingdom (8139/09); *sub nom* Abu Qatada v United Kingdom (8139/09) (2012) 55 E.H.R.R. 1; 32 B.H.R.C. 62; Times, January 25, 2012, ECHR .......... *Digested,* 12/**1664**: *Applied* 14/3521: *Considered* 13/1187

P v Locality Reporter Manager [2014] CSIH 66; 2014 G.W.D. 25-470, IH (Ex Div)

P v M; *sub nom* JP v FM [2014] CSIH 19; 2014 S.C. 518; 2014 Fam. L.R. 35; 2014 G.W.D. 7-143, IH (Ex Div) .......... *Digested,* 14/**3540**

P v O 2014 Hous. L.R. 44; 2014 G.W.D. 26-528, Sh Ct (South Strathclyde) (Dumfries)

P v P; *sub nom* P, Petitioner; TLMP, Petitioner [2013] CSOH 40; 2013 S.C.L.R. 646; 2013 G.W.D. 12-253, OH .......... *Digested,* 14/**3539**

P, Petitioner see P v P

Paragon Housing Association Ltd v Manclark 2013 Hous. L.R. 28; 2013 G.W.D. 7-161, Sh Ct (Tayside) (Alloa) .......... *Digested,* 14/**3595**

Parfinowski (Andrew) v HM Advocate [2013] HCJAC 123; 2014 S.C.L. 29; 2014 S.C.C.R. 30; 2013 G.W.D. 38-731, HCJ .......... *Digested,* 14/**3449**

Park's of Hamilton (Holdings) Ltd v Campbell; *sub nom* Parks of Hamilton (Holdings) Ltd v Campbell [2014] CSIH 36; 2014 S.C. 726; 2014 G.W.D. 18-338, IH (Ex Div); affirming [2013] CSOH 67; 2013 G.W.D. 17-361, OH
Parker v Parker [2014] CSOH 159; 2014 G.W.D. 35-657, OH
Parks of Hamilton (Holdings) Ltd v Campbell see Park's of Hamilton (Holdings) Ltd v Campbell
Pate's Curator ad Litem v Stewart Homes (Scotland) Ltd see Wallace v Stewart Homes (Scotland) Ltd
Paterson v Harvie; *joined cases* Love v Dunn; Bow v Harvie [2014] HCJAC 87; 2014 S.L.T. 857; 2014 S.C.L. 606; 2014 S.C.C.R. 521; 2014 G.W.D. 26-517, HCJ .... *Digested,* 14/**3410**
Paterson (Archibald) v HM Advocate [2013] HCJAC 156; 2014 S.C.C.R. 217; 2013 G.W.D. 40-763, HCJ .... *Digested,* 14/**3441**
Paterson (Drew Russell) v HM Advocate see Gordon (Taylor John David) v HM Advocate
Paterson (Scott) v McPherson [2012] HCJAC 61; 2012 G.W.D. 19-384, HCJ
*Followed* 14/3465
Patersons of Greenoakhill Ltd v Scottish Ministers [2014] CSIH 24; 2014 G.W.D. 10-192, IH (Ex Div)
Patersons of Greenoakhill Ltd v South Lanarkshire Council [2014] CSOH 21; 2014 S.C.L.R. 583; 2014 G.W.D. 8-165, OH .... *Digested,* 14/**3747**
Pattie v Keeper of the Registers of Scotland 2014 S.L.T. (Lands Tr) 28; 2014 G.W.D. 6-123, Lands Tr (Scot) .... *Digested,* 14/**3333**
Pattni v First Leicester Buses Ltd; *sub nom* Bent v Highways and Utilities Construction [2011] EWCA Civ 1384; [2012] R.T.R. 17; [2012] Lloyd's Rep. I.R. 577; [2012] P.I.Q.R. Q1, CA (Civ Div) .... *Digested,* 12/**2812**:
*Considered* 14/3474: *Followed* 13/2528
Paul (Ross Duncan) v HM Advocate [2013] HCJAC 13; 2014 S.C.L. 230; 2014 S.C.C.R. 119; 2014 G.W.D. 6-118, HCJ .... *Digested,* 14/**3375**
Peat's Executors v Assembly Theatre Ltd [2014] CSOH 144; 2014 S.L.T. 1017; 2014 G.W.D. 31-615, OH .... *Digested,* 14/**3350**
Pectel Ltd, Re see O'Neill v Phillips
Pelagic Freezing Ltd v Lovie Construction Ltd [2010] CSOH 145; 2010 G.W.D. 37-763, OH
*Doubted* 14/2470: *Followed* 11/4545
Pelosi v O'Donnell [2014] CSOH 46; 2014 G.W.D. 11-206, OH
Penk v Wright see Alcock v Chief Constable of South Yorkshire
Percy v Hall [1997] Q.B. 924; [1997] 3 W.L.R. 573; [1996] 4 All E.R. 523; (1996) 160 J.P. Rep. 788; (1996) 93(23) L.S.G. 36; (1996) 140 S.J.L.B. 130; [1996] N.P.C. 74; Times, May 31, 1996, CA (Civ Div) .... *Digested,* 96/**5688**:
*Applied* 97/4856, 13/253, 14/386: *Considered* 14/3344
Petch (Morris) v HM Advocate; *joined case* Foye (Robert) v HM Advocate [2011] HCJAC 20; 2011 J.C. 210; 2011 S.L.T. 391; 2011 S.C.L. 372; 2011 S.C.C.R. 199; 2011 G.W.D. 8-207, HCJ .... *Digested,* 11/**4595**:
*Applied* 12/4274, 14/3774: *Followed* 11/4582, 11/4594, 11/4597, 13/3988
PH v Italy see R. (on the application of HH) v Westminster City Magistrates' Court
Phee v Gordon [2014] CSIH 50; 2014 G.W.D. 20-383, IH (Ex Div)
Philips v Harvie see Fitzpatrick v Harvie
Phillips (Raymond) v HM Advocate [2014] HCJAC 51; 2014 G.W.D. 17-315, HCJ .... *Digested,* 14/**3419**
Pinnacle Cloud Solutions Ltd v Maclellan Property Ltd [2014] CSOH 155; 2014 G.W.D. 37-679, OH
Pinnock v Manchester City Council see Manchester City Council v Pinnock
Platt (Gordon) v HM Advocate 2004 J.C. 113; 2004 S.L.T. 333; 2004 S.C.C.R. 209; 2004 G.W.D. 8-169, HCJ .... *Digested,* 04/**4621**:
*Followed* 14/3374
PMP Plus Ltd v Keeper of the Registers of Scotland 2009 S.L.T. (Lands Tr) 2; 2009 G.W.D. 5-83, Lands Tr (Scot) .... *Digested,* 09/**4994**:
*Cited* 14/3582: *Followed* 14/3583
Podgornoi (Aleksandr) v HM Advocate see Jakovlev (Vladimir) v HM Advocate
Pollacchi v Campbell 2014 S.L.T. (Lands Tr) 55; 2014 G.W.D. 15-275, Lands Tr (Scot) .... *Digested,* 14/**3586**
Polley v West Lothian Council [2014] CSOH 98; 2014 G.W.D. 21-391, OH
Povey v Povey's Executor Nominate [2014] CSOH 68; 2014 S.L.T. 643; 2014 G.W.D. 14-264, OH .... *Digested,* 14/**3802**
Powell v Hounslow LBC see Hounslow LBC v Powell
Price v Leeds City Council see Kay v Lambeth LBC
Principal Reporter v N 2014 G.W.D. 30-592, Sh Ct (South Strathclyde) (Dumfries)
Pritchard v Co-operative Group (CWS) Ltd see Co-operative Group (CWS) Ltd v Pritchard

R. (on the application of Chester) v Secretary of State for Justice; *sub nom* Chester v Secretary of State for Justice; *joined case* McGeoch v Lord President of the Council [2013] UKSC 63; [2014] A.C. 271; [2013] 3 W.L.R. 1076; [2014] 1 All E.R. 683; 2014 S.C. (U.K.S.C.) 25; 2014 S.L.T. 143; [2014] 1 C.M.L.R. 45; [2014] H.R.L.R. 3; 2013 G.W.D. 34-676, SC; affirming [2010] EWCA Civ 1439; [2011] 1 W.L.R. 1436; [2011] H.R.L.R. 10; [2011] U.K.H.R.R. 53; [2010] 2 Prison L.R. 40; [2011] A.C.D. 30; (2011) 108(1) L.S.G. 15; Times, January 17, 2011, CA (Civ Div); affirming [2009] EWHC 2923 (Admin); [2010] H.R.L.R. 6; [2010] U.K.H.R.R. 317; [2010] 2 Prison L.R. 1; [2010] A.C.D. 28; Times, November 3, 2009, QBD (Admin) ........ *Digested,* 14/**976**: *Cited* 14/977: *Considered* 11/2294: *Followed* 14/977

R. (on the application of Edwards) v Environment Agency (C-260/11); *sub nom* Edwards v Environment Agency (C-260/11) [2013] 1 W.L.R. 2914; [2013] 3 C.M.L.R. 18; [2014] All E.R. (EC) 207, ECJ (4th Chamber) ........ *Digested,* 14/**1183**: *Applied* 14/333, 14/339: *Considered* 14/3338: *Followed* 14/442

R. (on the application of HH) v Westminster City Magistrates' Court; *sub nom* HH v Italy; PH v Italy; *joined case* F-K v Poland [2012] UKSC 25; [2013] 1 A.C. 338; [2012] 3 W.L.R. 90; [2012] 4 All E.R. 539; [2012] H.R.L.R. 25; (2012) 156(25) S.J.L.B. 31; Times, July 2, 2012, SC; affirming [2011] EWHC 1145 (Admin); [2011] A.C.D. 94, DC ........ *Digested,* 12/**1293**: *Applied* 13/2652, 13/2749, 14/1596, 14/662: *Considered* 12/1289, 14/1650, 14/1668, 14/1704

R. (on the application of J) v Secretary of State for the Home Department [2009] EWHC 705 (Admin), QBD (Admin) *Considered* 13/1599, 14/3602

R. (on the application of James) v Secretary of State for Justice see R. (on the application of Wells) v Parole Board for England and Wales

R. (on the application of Lee) v Secretary of State for Justice see R. (on the application of Wells) v Parole Board for England and Wales

R. (on the application of Quintavalle) v Secretary of State for Health [2003] UKHL 13; [2003] 2 A.C. 687; [2003] 2 W.L.R. 692; [2003] 2 All E.R. 113; [2003] 1 F.C.R. 577; (2003) 71 B.M.L.R. 209; (2003) 153 N.L.J. 439; Times, March 14, 2003; Independent, March 18, 2003, HL; affirming [2002] EWCA Civ 29; [2002] Q.B. 628; [2002] 2 W.L.R. 550; [2002] 2 All E.R. 625; [2002] 2 F.C.R. 140; (2002) 64 B.M.L.R. 72; (2002) 99(10) L.S.G. 32; (2002) 146 S.J.L.B. 30; Times, January 25, 2002; Independent, January 22, 2002; Daily Telegraph, January 24, 2002, CA (Civ Div); reversing [2001] EWHC Admin 918; [2001] 4 All E.R. 1013; (2002) 63 B.M.L.R. 167; (2001) 151 N.L.J. 1732; Times, December 5, 2001, QBD (Admin) ........ *Digested,* 04/**3274**: *Applied* 05/823, 08/3840, 08/3921, 09/2604, 14/814: *Considered* 06/699, 09/1737, 13/2487, 14/3752

R. (on the application of Spath Holme Ltd) v Secretary of State for the Environment, Transport and the Regions; *sub nom* R. v Secretary of State for the Environment, Transport and the Regions Ex p. Spath Holme Ltd [2001] 2 A.C. 349; [2001] 2 W.L.R. 15; [2001] 1 All E.R. 195; (2001) 33 H.L.R. 31; [2001] 1 E.G.L.R. 129; [2000] E.G. 152 (C.S.); (2001) 98(8) L.S.G. 44; (2000) 150 N.L.J. 1855; (2001) 145 S.J.L.B. 39; [2000] N.P.C. 139; Times, December 13, 2000, HL; reversing [2000] 3 W.L.R. 141; [2000] 1 All E.R. 884; (2000) 32 H.L.R. 495; [2000] E.G. 10 (C.S.); (2000) 144 S.J.L.B. 100; [2000] N.P.C. 4; Times, February 15, 2000; Independent, March 6, 2000, CA (Civ Div) ........ *Digested,* 01/**4206**: *Applied* 00/5095, 01/5632, 03/1962, 04/3189: *Considered* 07/3064, 09/3624, 14/2422, 14/3752: *Followed* 11/2338

R. (on the application of Walker) v Secretary of State for Justice see R. (on the application of Wells) v Parole Board for England and Wales

R. (on the application of Wells) v Parole Board for England and Wales; *sub nom* Wells v Parole Board for England and Wales; Walker v Secretary of State for the Home Department; Secretary of State for Justice v Walker; Secretary of State for Justice v James (formerly Walker); *joined cases* R. (on the application of Walker) v Secretary of State for Justice; R. (on the application of Lee) v Secretary of State for Justice; R. (on the application of James) v Secretary of State for Justice [2009] UKHL 22; [2010] 1 A.C. 553; [2009] 2 W.L.R. 1149; [2009] 4 All E.R. 255; [2009] H.R.L.R. 23; [2009] U.K.H.R.R. 809; 26 B.H.R.C. 696; [2009] Prison L.R. 371; Times, May 8, 2009, HL; affirming [2008] EWCA Civ 30; [2008] 1 W.L.R. 1977; [2008] 3 All E.R. 104; [2008] H.R.L.R. 22; [2008] U.K.H.R.R. 528; [2008] Prison L.R. 63; (2008) 158 N.L.J. 263; Times, February 6, 2008, CA (Civ Div); reversing in part [2007] EWHC 1835 (Admin); [2008] 1 All E.R. 138; [2008] Prison L.R. 49; [2007] A.C.D. 86; (2007) 157 N.L.J. 1275; Times, October 11, 2007, DC ........ *Digested,* 09/**3407**: *Applied* 08/2680: *Complaint upheld* 13/1558: *Considered* 11/2289, 11/4588, 12/2935, 13/2112, 14/3702: *Distinguished* 10/2321: *Followed* 11/2913, 14/2234

RAA (Iran) v Secretary of State for the Home Department [2014] CSOH 7; 2014 G.W.D. 5-108, OH

Radic (Ernest) v HM Advocate [2014] HCJAC 76; 2014 G.W.D. 25-480, HCJ

Rahim (Fazli) v HM Advocate see Gul (Saima) v HM Advocate

Ralston v Scottish Ministers see Somerville v Scottish Ministers

Ramirez Sanchez v France (59450/00) (2007) 45 E.H.R.R. 49; [2007] Prison L.R. 169, ECHR (Grand Chamber) ........ *Digested,* 08/**1916**: *Considered* 12/2281, 14/3704

Ramsahai v Netherlands (52391/99) (2008) 46 E.H.R.R. 43; [2007] Inquest L.R. 103; [2007] Po. L.R. 46, ECHR (Grand Chamber) *Applied* 08/1970: *Considered* 08/3000, 09/2754, 14/3599, 14/47

Raynes (Charles David) v HM Advocate see Blance (Andrew) v HM Advocate

RB (Linguistic evidence: Sprakab: Somalia) see RB (Somalia) v Secretary of State for the Home Department

RB (Somalia) v Secretary of State for the Home Department; *sub nom* RB (Linguistic evidence: Sprakab: Somalia) [2012] EWCA Civ 277, CA (Civ Div); affirming [2010] UKUT 329 (IAC), UT (IAC) *Considered* 14/1641

RBS Invoice Finance Ltd v ASC Anglo Scottish Concrete Ltd 2014 G.W.D. 14-253, Sh Ct (Glasgow)

Ready (Gary) v HM Advocate [2009] HCJAC 21; 2009 S.C.L. 710; 2009 S.C.C.R. 380; 2009 G.W.D. 11-169, HCJ ........ *Digested,* 09/**4741**: *Considered* 14/3382

Reedie (Graham John) v HM Advocate [2005] HCJAC 55; 2005 S.L.T. 742; 2005 S.C.C.R. 407; 2005 G.W.D. 25-475, HCJ ........ *Digested,* 05/**5132**: *Applied* 14/3437

Reeves v Yates [2014] CSOH 47; 2014 G.W.D. 11-197, OH

Regus (Maxim) Ltd v Bank of Scotland Plc [2013] CSIH 12; 2013 S.C. 331; 2013 S.L.T. 477; 2014 S.C.L.R. 33; 2013 G.W.D. 9-191, IH (1 Div); affirming [2011] CSOH 129; 2011 G.W.D. 27-600, OH ........ *Digested,* 13/**3554**

Rehman (Asif) v HM Advocate; *joined case* Ishaq (Adel) v HM Advocate [2013] HCJAC 172; 2014 S.C.C.R. 166; 2014 G.W.D. 3-64, HCJ ........ *Digested,* 14/**3445**

Reid (Alan) v Watson [2014] HCJAC 16; 2014 G.W.D. 8-159, HCJ

Revenue and Customs Commissioners v Blue Sphere Global Ltd see Mobilx Ltd (In Administration) v Revenue and Customs Commissioners

Revenue and Customs Commissioners v Simpson & Marwick see Simpson & Marwick v Revenue and Customs Commissioners

Rezac's Executors v Rezac's Executrix Nominate 2014 G.W.D. 15-281, Sh Ct (Lothian) (Edinburgh)

Richardson v Pitt-Stanley [1995] Q.B. 123; [1995] 2 W.L.R. 26; [1995] 1 All E.R. 460; [1995] I.C.R. 303; [1994] P.I.Q.R. P496; Times, August 11, 1994; Independent, September 6, 1994, CA (Civ Div) ........ *Digested,* 95/**2901**: *Considered* 14/3356: *Not followed* 98/5805

Riva v BAA Ltd; *joined case* Capitol Investments (Scotland) Ltd v BAA Ltd 2013 S.L.T. (Lands Tr) 67; [2013] R.V.R. 338; 2013 G.W.D. 29-580, Lands Tr (Scot) ........ *Digested,* 14/**3722**

Riva v Edinburgh Airport Ltd; *joined case* Capitol Investments (Scotland) Ltd v Edinburgh Airport Ltd 2013 S.L.T. (Lands Tr) 61; [2013] R.V.R. 342; 2013 G.W.D. 29-571, Lands Tr (Scot) ........ *Digested,* 14/**3723**

RK (Democratic Republic of Congo), Applicant [2014] CSIH 2; 2014 G.W.D. 4-89, IH

RM v HM Advocate see M v HM Advocate

Robertson v Anderson 2003 S.L.T. 235; [2003] L.L.R. 177; 2002 G.W.D. 40-1330; Times, January 2, 2003, IH (Ex Div); affirming 2014 S.L.T. 709; 2001 G.W.D. 17-669, OH ........ *Digested,* 03/**5331**

Robertson v Department for the Environment, Food and Rural Affairs; *sub nom* Department for the Environment, Food and Rural Affairs v Robertson [2005] EWCA Civ 138; [2005] I.C.R. 750; [2005] I.R.L.R. 363; (2005) 102(15) L.S.G. 33; Times, March 2, 2005; Independent, February 24, 2005, CA (Civ Div); affirming [2004] I.C.R. 1289, EAT ........ *Digested,* 05/**1258**: *Applied* 14/3503: *Considered* 07/1360, 09/1206, 13/1011

Robertson (Paul) v HM Advocate see Gemmell (James Kelly) v HM Advocate

Robertson (Stewart) v HM Advocate; *sub nom* Gough v McFadyen; Robertson, Petitioner; *joined case* Gough (Stephen Peter) v HM Advocate [2007] HCJAC 63; 2008 J.C. 146; 2007 S.L.T. 1153; 2008 S.C.L. 80; 2008 S.C.C.R. 20; 2007 G.W.D. 37-643, HCJ ........ *Digested,* 08/**4650**: *Followed* 14/3427

Robertson, Petitioner (No.1) [2009] CSIH 58; 2010 S.L.T. 143; 2009 G.W.D. 26-414, IH (1 Div); affirming [2009] CSOH 23; 2009 G.W.D. 16-249, OH ........ *Digested,* 10/**4000**: *Doubted* 14/3352

Robertson, Petitioner see Robertson (Stewart) v HM Advocate

Robson (Greg) v HM Advocate [2014] HCJAC 53; 2014 G.W.D. 20-379, HCJ

Robson (Greg) v HM Advocate [2014] HCJAC 109; 2014 S.C.L. 856, HCJ

Robson (Timothy) v HM Advocate [2014] HCJAC 8; 2014 G.W.D. 9-173, HCJ

Ronald v Duke of Buccleuch [2014] CSOH 101; 2014 G.W.D. 21-392, OH

Rondos (Michal) v HM Advocate [2014] HCJAC 119; 2014 G.W.D. 36-668, HCJ

Rose's Trustee, Applicant [2013] B.P.I.R. 955; 2013 G.W.D. 22-424, Sh Ct (Grampian) (Banff) ........ *Digested,* 14/**3612**

Ross v Richardson see Gemmell (James Kelly) v HM Advocate

Ross (Colin) v HM Advocate [2013] HCJAC 111; 2013 S.C.L. 1054; 2013 G.W.D. 33-663, HCJ ........ *Digested,* 14/**3774**

Royal Bank of Scotland v O'Donnell [2014] CSIH 84; 2014 G.W.D. 33-641, IH (Ex Div); affirming [2013] CSOH 78; 2013 G.W.D. 19-388, OH

Royal Bank of Scotland Plc v Carlyle; *sub nom* Carlyle v Royal Bank of Scotland Plc [2013] CSIH 75; 2014 S.C. 188; 2014 S.C.L.R. 167; 2013 G.W.D. 31-617, IH (2 Div) ........ *Digested,* 14/**3365**

Royal British Bank v Turquand [1843-60] All E.R. Rep. 435; 119 E.R. 886; (1856) 6 El. & Bl. 327, Ex Chamber
*Applied* 58/14: *Considered* 85/306, 04/87, 14/3355: *Distinguished* 61/1065

RT v Thomson see T v Thomson

Ruddy v Chief Constable of Strathclyde [2013] CSIH 73; 2014 S.C. 58; 2013 S.L.T. 1199; 2014 S.C.L.R. 145; 2013 G.W.D. 30-588, IH (Ex Div) ........ *Digested,* 14/**3599**

Russell v National Farmers' Union Mutual Insurance Society Ltd [2014] CSOH 157; 2014 G.W.D. 35-662, OH

Ryan v Murphy [2014] HCJAC 106; 2014 S.L.T. 1027; 2014 G.W.D. 34-651, HCJ ........ *Digested,* 14/**3785**

Ryder v Highland Council [2013] CSOH 95; 2013 S.L.T. 847; 2014 Rep. L.R. 17; 2013 G.W.D. 23-446, OH ........ *Digested,* 13/**3903**

S v Dundee City Council; *sub nom* BS v Dundee City Council [2013] CSIH 91; 2014 S.C. 254; [2014] I.R.L.R. 131; 2013 G.W.D. 39-751, IH (Ex Div) ........ *Digested,* 14/**3507**

S v Edinburgh City Council; *sub nom* SM, Appellant; S, Petitioner 2007 Fam. L.R. 2; 2007 G.W.D. 2-28, OH ........ *Digested,* 07/**5121**: *Distinguished* 08/4726: *Followed* 14/3477

S v Locality Reporter Manager [2014] CSIH 70; 2014 Fam. L.R. 109; 2014 G.W.D. 26-525, IH (Ex Div)

S v S [2014] CSOH 95; 2014 G.W.D. 20-385, OH

S v S 2014 S.L.T. (Sh Ct) 165; 2014 G.W.D. 36-671, Sh Ct (Lothian) (Livingston)

S v Secretary of State for the Home Department; *sub nom* NS v Secretary of State for the Home Department [2014] CSIH 91; 2014 S.L.T. 1120; 2014 G.W.D. 37-688, IH (Ex Div)

S v Secretary of State for the Home Department see Shehadeh v Secretary of State for the Home Department

S (Palestine), Applicant [2014] CSIH 4; 2014 G.W.D. 4-87, IH

S, Petitioner [2014] CSIH 42; 2014 Fam. L.R. 23; 2014 G.W.D. 21-403, IH (Ex Div)

S, Petitioner see S v Edinburgh City Council

S-B (Children) (Care Proceedings: Standard of Proof), Re; *sub nom* S-B (Identification of Perpetrator), Re; S-B (Children) (Non-Accidental Injury), Re [2009] UKSC 17; [2010] 1 A.C. 678; [2010] 2 W.L.R. 238; [2010] 1 All E.R. 705; [2010] P.T.S.R. 456; [2010] 1 F.L.R. 1161; [2010] 1 F.C.R. 321; [2010] Fam. Law 231; (2009) 153(48) S.J.L.B. 33; Times, December 18, 2009, SC; reversing [2009] EWCA Civ 1048; [2009] 3 F.C.R. 663; [2010] Fam. Law 14; (2009) 153(26) S.J.L.B. 29, CA (Civ Div) ........ *Digested,* 10/**1325**:
*Considered* 11/1346, 11/1441, 13/1231, 13/1326, 14/3325: *Followed* 12/1352, 13/1216, 13/1227

S-B (Children) (Non-Accidental Injury), Re see S-B (Children) (Care Proceedings: Standard of Proof), Re

S-B (Identification of Perpetrator), Re see S-B (Children) (Care Proceedings: Standard of Proof), Re

SA (Nigeria) v Secretary of State for the Home Department; *sub nom* A v Secretary of State for the Home Department [2013] CSIH 62; 2014 S.C. 1; 2013 S.L.T. 1132; 2013 G.W.D. 26-535, IH (2 Div) ........ *Digested,* 14/**3600**

Sabiu v Wyllie [2013] HCJAC 160; 2014 S.C.C.R. 59; 2014 G.W.D. 1-18, HCJ ........ *Digested,* 14/**3458**

SAC (Bangladesh) v Secretary of State for the Home Department [2014] CSOH 8; 2014 G.W.D. 5-110, OH

Safdar and A&N Brothers (A Partnership) v Falkirk Council 2013 S.L.T. (Sh Ct) 127; 2013 G.W.D. 16-335, Sh Ct (Tayside) (Falkirk) ........ *Digested,* 14/**3331**

Salford City Council v Mullen see Hounslow LBC v Powell

Salvesen v Riddell [2013] UKSC 22; 2013 S.C. (U.K.S.C.) 236; 2013 S.L.T. 863; 2014 S.C.L.R. 44; [2013] H.R.L.R. 23; 2013 G.W.D. 14-304, SC; reversing [2012] CSIH 26; 2013 S.C. 69; 2012 S.L.T. 633; 2012 S.C.L.R. 403; 2012 Hous. L.R. 30; 2012 G.W.D. 12-234, IH (2 Div); reversing 2010 S.L.C.R. 107, Land Ct ........ *Digested,* 13/**1865**

SAN v KJN 2014 G.W.D. 4-85, Sh Ct (Grampian) (Lerwick)

Saunders v Martin 2014 Fam. L.R. 86; 2014 G.W.D. 23-436, Sh Ct (Tayside) (Kirkcaldy) ........ *Digested,* 14/**3536**

Sayers v Harlow Urban DC [1958] 1 W.L.R. 623; [1958] 2 All E.R. 342; (1958) 122 J.P. 351; (1958) 102 S.J. 419, CA ........ *Digested,* 58/**2220**:
*Applied* 74/427, 86/366, 88/413: *Considered* 75/2324, 84/368, 14/3697

Schuh Ltd v Assessor for Glasgow [2013] CSIH 93; 2014 S.L.T. 184; [2014] R.V.R. 62; 2013 G.W.D. 39-754, LVAC ........ *Digested,* 14/**3678**:
*Cited* 14/3676

Scobbie (Mark) v HM Advocate see Fowler (Danielle) v HM Advocate

Scoppola v Italy (126/05) [2013] 1 Costs L.O. 62; (2013) 56 E.H.R.R. 19; 33 B.H.R.C. 126; Times, June 12, 2012, ECHR (Grand Chamber)
*Applied* 14/976

Scotbeef Ltd v Dunn [2014] HCJAC 61; 2014 G.W.D. 21-411, HCJ

Scotch Whisky Association v Lord Advocate [2014] CSIH 38; 2014 G.W.D. 17-309, IH (Ex Div) ........ *Digested,* 14/**3555**

Scottish Borders Council v Johnstone 2014 G.W.D. 40-720, Sh Ct (Lothian) (Edinburgh)

Scottish Borders Council, Petitioners 2014 S.L.T. (Sh Ct) 140; 2014 G.W.D. 29-574, Sh Ct (Lothian) (Edinburgh) ........ *Digested,* 14/**3532**

Scottish Environment Protection Agency v Joint Liquidators of the Scottish Coal Co Ltd see Joint Liquidators of the Scottish Coal Co Ltd, Noters

Scottish Ministers v Ellis [2014] CSOH 10; 2014 S.C.L.R. 434; [2014] Lloyd's Rep. F.C. 268; 2014 G.W.D. 4-78, OH ........ *Digested,* 14/**3453**

Scottish Ministers v M [2014] CSOH 131; 2014 S.L.T. 929; 2014 G.W.D. 27-541, OH . *Digested,* 14/**3330**

Scottish Ministers v Mirza [2014] CSIH 103; 2014 G.W.D. 39-710, IH (Ex Div)

Scottish Ministers v Stirton [2013] CSIH 81; 2014 S.C. 218; 2013 S.L.T. 1141; [2014] Lloyd's Rep. F.C. 18; 2013 G.W.D. 34-666, IH (2 Div); affirming [2012] CSOH 15; 2012 G.W.D. 6-100, OH ........ *Digested,* 14/**3325**

Scottish Ministers v Stirton 2014 G.W.D. 5-99, Sh Ct (North Strathclyde) (Dumbarton)

Scottish Ministers v Stirton 2006 S.L.T. 306; 2006 G.W.D. 4-68, OH ........ *Digested,* 06/**5227**:
*Disapproved* 14/3325

Scottish Ministers v Stirton [2014] CSIH 92; 2014 G.W.D. 37-683, IH (2 Div)

Scottish Premier League Ltd v Lisini Pub Management Co Ltd; *sub nom* Scottish Professional Football League Ltd v Lisini Pub Management Co Ltd [2013] CSIH 97; 2014 S.C. 300; 2014 S.L.T. 99; [2014] U.K.C.L.R. 366; [2014] L.L.R. 794; 2013 G.W.D. 40-757, IH (Ex Div); affirming [2013] CSOH 48; 2013 S.L.T. 629; [2013] U.K.C.L.R. 166; 2013 G.W.D. 13-272, OH ........ *Digested,* 14/**3354**

Scottish Professional Football League Ltd v Lisini Pub Management Co Ltd [2014] CSIH 6; [2014] U.K.C.L.R. 389; 2014 G.W.D. 6-117, IH (Ex Div) ........ *Digested,* 14/**3349**

Scottish Professional Football League Ltd v Lisini Pub Management Co Ltd see Scottish Premier League Ltd v Lisini Pub Management Co Ltd

Scottish Water Business Stream Ltd v Automatic Retailing (Scotland) Ltd [2014] CSOH 57; 2014 G.W.D. 12-219, OH
Scotts Atlantic Investments Ltd v Dryburgh [2014] CSOH 165; 2014 G.W.D. 40-722, OH
Secretary of State for Business, Innovation and Skills v Hamilton [2014] CSOH 89; 2014 G.W.D. 18-334, OH
Secretary of State for Business, Innovation and Skills v Millar [2014] CSOH 127; 2014 G.W.D. 28-556, OH
Secretary of State for Business, Innovation and Skills v Whyte [2014] CSOH 148; 2014 G.W.D. 32-624, OH
Secretary of State for Justice v James (formerly Walker) see R. (on the application of Wells) v Parole Board for England and Wales
Secretary of State for Justice v Walker see R. (on the application of Wells) v Parole Board for England and Wales
Secretary of State for the Home Department v KK (Congo) [2005] UKIAT 54, IAT
*Considered* 11/1720, 14/1659
Secretary of State for the Home Department v KY see N v Advocate General for Scotland
Secretary of State for the Home Department v MN see N v Advocate General for Scotland
Secretary of State for Work & Pensions, The Child Support Agency v Anderson 2014 G.W.D. 17-306, Sh Ct (Lothian) (Edinburgh) ........ *Digested,* 14/**3541**
Secretary of State for Work and Pensions v Brade [2014] CSIH 39; 2014 S.C. 742; 2014 S.L.T. 680; 2014 S.C.L.R. 737; 2014 G.W.D. 16-303, IH (Ex Div) ........ *Digested,* 14/**3792**
Sekanina v Austria (A/266-A) (1994) 17 E.H.R.R. 221, ECHR ........ *Digested,* 94/**2388**:
*Applied* 02/2453, 07/2227: *Considered* 12/329, 14/3381: *Followed* 03/2143
Sen v Steelform Engineering Co Ltd see Lagden v O'Connor
Service Temps Inc v MacLeod [2013] CSOH 162; 2014 S.L.T. 375; 2013 G.W.D. 35-687, OH ........ *Digested,* 14/**3342**
Shad v Irfan 2014 S.L.T. (Sh Ct) 125; 2014 G.W.D. 25-495, Sh Ct (South Strathclyde) (Airdrie) ........ *Digested,* 14/**3332**
Shaher v British Aerospace Flying College Ltd 2003 S.C. 540; 2003 S.L.T. 791; 2003 Rep. L.R. 78; 2003 G.W.D. 19-585, IH (Ex Div); reversing 2002 S.L.T. 833 (Note); 2002 Rep. L.R. 96; 2002 G.W.D. 19-630, OH ........ *Digested,* 03/**5444**:
*Considered* 14/3471
Shahid v Scottish Ministers 2014 S.C. 490; 2014 S.L.T. 335; 2014 G.W.D. 6-131, IH (Ex Div); affirming [2011] CSOH 192; 2012 S.L.T. 178; 2012 Rep. L.R. 2; 2011 G.W.D. 40-816, OH ........ *Digested,* 14/**3704**
Shanks v Masterson 2014 G.W.D. 4-81, Sh Ct (Grampian) (Elgin)
Shanks v Scottish Ministers 2014 G.W.D. 3-65, Sh Ct (South Strathclyde) (Dumfries)
Sharpe v Murphy see Strawbridge v Murphy
Shehadeh v Secretary of State for the Home Department; *sub nom* S v Secretary of State for the Home Department [2013] CSOH 139; 2014 S.L.T. 199; 2013 G.W.D. 28-564, OH ........ *Digested,* 14/**3604**
Shepherd v Elliot (Expenses) (1896) 23 R. 695; (1896) 3 S.L.T. 330, IH (1 Div); affirming (1896) 3 S.L.T. 259, OH
*Considered* 14/3336
Shepherd v Travelodge Hotels Ltd [2014] CSOH 162; 2014 G.W.D. 37-691, OH
Shetland Islands Council v Anderson's Executor [2014] CSIH 73; 2014 G.W.D. 28-555, IH (Ex Div); affirming [2014] CSOH 23; 2014 G.W.D. 9-171, OH
Shetland Islands Council v Fisher 2014 S.L.T. (Sh Ct) 107; 2014 Hous. L.R. 24; 2014 G.W.D. 20-386, Sh Ct (Grampian) (Lerwick) ........ *Digested,* 14/**3598**
Shetland Leasing & Property Developments Ltd v Younger 2014 Hous. L.R. 9; 2014 G.W.D. 4-77, Sh Ct (Grampian) (Lerwick) ........ *Digested,* 14/**3624**
Shetland Line (1984) Ltd v Scottish Ministers [2014] CSOH 12; 2014 S.C.L.R. 549; 2014 G.W.D. 5-116, OH ........ *Digested,* 14/**3748**
Shields v Crossroads (Orkney) [2013] CSOH 144; 2014 S.L.T. 190; 2013 S.C.L.R. 730; [2014] P.N.L.R. 5; 2013 Rep. L.R. 116; 2013 G.W.D. 29-573, OH ........ *Digested,* 13/**3901**
SIAC Construction Ltd v Mayo CC (C-19/00) [2001] E.C.R. I-7725; [2002] T.C.L.R. 16; [2001] 3 C.M.L.R. 59; [2002] All E.R. (EC) 272, ECJ (5th Chamber) ........ *Digested,* 02/**3784**:
*Applied* 04/3162, 09/4438, 10/3792, 14/2475
Sidebottom v Green 2014 G.W.D. 19-367, Sh Ct (Grampian) (Banff)
Simpson & Marwick v Revenue and Customs Commissioners; *sub nom* Revenue and Customs Commissioners v Simpson & Marwick [2013] CSIH 29; [2013] S.T.C. 2275; [2013] B.V.C. 393, IH (Ex Div); reversing [2011] UKUT 498 (TCC); [2012] S.T.C. 611; [2012] B.V.C. 1533; [2012] S.T.I. 142; (2012) 109(5) L.S.G. 19, UT (Tax); reversing [2010] UKFTT 380 (TC); [2011] S.F.T.D. 1, FTT (Tax) ........ *Digested,* 14/**3809**

Sinclair (Angus Robertson) v HM Advocate see HM Advocate v Sinclair (Angus Robertson)
Sinclair (Angus Robertson) v HM Advocate see HM Advocate v Sinclair (Angus Robertson)
Singh v Napier [2014] CSIH 54; 2014 G.W.D. 21-400, IH (Ex Div)
SK (Namibia) v Secretary of State for the Home Department; *sub nom* K v Secretary of State for the Home Department [2014] CSOH 52; 2014 S.L.T. 587; 2014 G.W.D. 12-215, OH .......... *Digested,* 14/**3602**
SK (Pakistan), Petitioner [2014] CSOH 35; 2014 G.W.D. 11-203, OH
Skipton Financial Services Ltd v Allan [2014] CSOH 106; 2014 G.W.D. 23-429, OH
SM (Pakistan) v Secretary of State for the Home Department [2014] CSIH 98; 2014 G.W.D. 38-701, IH (Ex Div)
SM, Appellant see S v Edinburgh City Council
SMB (Pakistan) v Secretary of State for the Home Department [2014] CSOH 139; 2014 G.W.D. 30-595, OH
Smith v Bluebird Buses Ltd [2014] CSOH 75; 2014 Rep. L.R. 91; 2014 G.W.D. 16-298, OH .......... *Digested,* 14/**3699**
Smith v Coogans 2014 G.W.D. 14-252, Sh Ct (South Strathclyde) (Ayr)
Smith v Greater Glasgow & Clyde NHS Health Board [2013] CSOH 178; 2014 S.L.T. 137; 2013 G.W.D. 40-756, OH .......... *Digested,* 14/**3341**
Smith v Lees 1997 J.C. 73; 1997 S.L.T. 690; 1997 S.C.C.R. 139; 1997 G.W.D. 6-225, HCJ .......... *Digested,* 97/**5761**:
*Applied* 04/4624: *Considered* 08/4629, 11/4089, 14/3380: *Distinguished* 05/5092: *Followed* 09/4753
Smith v Muir Construction Ltd [2014] CSOH 171; 2014 G.W.D. 40-728, OH
Smith v Scott [2007] CSIH 9; 2007 S.C. 345; 2007 S.L.T. 137; 2007 S.C.L.R. 268; [2008] Prison L.R. 177; 2007 G.W.D. 3-46; Times, February 5, 2007, Registration App Ct (SC) .......... *Digested,* 07/**5431**:
*Considered* 10/1730: *Referred to* 14/976
Smith v Scottish Water [2014] CSOH 140; 2014 G.W.D. 30-600, OH
Smith v Shanks [2014] HCJAC 25; 2014 S.L.T. 626; 2014 S.C.L. 427; 2014 S.C.C.R. 300; 2014 G.W.D. 13-230, HCJ .......... *Digested,* 14/**3414**
Smyth v Romanes's Executors [2014] CSOH 150; 2014 G.W.D. 33-642, OH
SN (South Africa) v Secretary of State for the Home Department [2014] CSIH 7; 2014 G.W.D. 5-109, IH (Ex Div)
Snowden (Scott Leslie) v HM Advocate; *joined case* Jennings (Robert Michael) v HM Advocate [2014] HCJAC 100; 2014 S.C.L. 736; 2014 G.W.D. 31-609, HCJ .......... *Digested,* 14/**3389**
Somerville v Scottish Ministers; *joined cases* Blanco v Scottish Ministers; Henderson v Scottish Ministers; Ralston v Scottish Ministers [2007] UKHL 44; [2007] 1 W.L.R. 2734; 2008 S.C. (H.L.) 45; 2007 S.L.T. 1113; 2007 S.C.L.R. 830; [2008] H.R.L.R. 3; [2008] U.K.H.R.R. 570; (2007) 151 S.J.L.B. 1398; 2007 G.W.D. 37-656, HL; reversing in part [2006] CSIH 52; 2007 S.C. 140; 2007 S.L.T. 96; 2007 G.W.D. 4-67, IH (1 Div) .......... *Digested,* 08/**4963**:
*Considered* 08/18, 12/771, 13/247, 14/400: *Followed* 14/3300
Sood v Aberdeen City Council Licensing Committee 2014 G.W.D. 28-563, Sh Ct (Grampian) (Aberdeen)
Sood Enterprises Ltd v Healey see Sood Enterprises Ltd v Healy
Sood Enterprises Ltd v Healy; *sub nom* Sood Enterprises Ltd v Healey [2014] 2 C.M.L.R. 15; [2013] I.C.R. 1361; [2013] I.R.L.R. 865, EAT (SC) .......... *Digested,* 13/**3680**
Sorbie v Kennedy 2014 S.L.C.R. 193; 2014 G.W.D. 38-692, Land Ct
South Lanarkshire Council v George 2013 Hous. L.R. 49; 2013 G.W.D. 30-587, Sh Ct (South Strathclyde) (Hamilton) .......... *Digested,* 14/**3328**
South Lanarkshire Council v McKenna 2010 Hous. L.R. 82; 2010 G.W.D. 40-808, Sh Ct (Glasgow) .......... *Digested,* 11/**4372**:
*Affirmed* 14/3635
South Lanarkshire Council v McKenna 2014 S.L.T. (Sh Ct) 51; 2014 Hous. L.R. 2, Sh Ct (Glasgow and Strathkelvin) .......... *Digested,* 14/**3635**
South Lanarkshire Council v McKenna 2010 Hous. L.R. 36; 2010 G.W.D. 20-401, Sh Ct (Glasgow) .......... *Digested,* 10/**4363**:
*Affirmed* 14/3635
South Lanarkshire Council v Scottish Information Commissioner [2013] UKSC 55; [2013] 1 W.L.R. 2421; [2013] 4 All E.R. 629; 2014 S.C. (U.K.S.C.) 1; 2013 S.L.T. 799; [2014] 1 C.M.L.R. 17; [2013] I.R.L.R. 899; [2013] Eq. L.R. 1006; 2013 G.W.D. 25-508, SC; affirming [2012] CSIH 30; 2012 S.L.T. 691; 2012 G.W.D. 13-264, IH (Ex Div) .......... *Digested,* 13/**61**

Spain v United Kingdom (C-145/04); *sub nom* Gibraltar European Elections, Re (C-145/04) [2006] E.C.R. I-7917; [2007] 1 C.M.L.R. 3; [2007] All E.R. (EC) 486; Times, November 6, 2006, ECJ ........ *Digested,* 07/**1553**: *Considered* 14/976

Speirs (Allan) v HM Advocate [2013] HCJAC 151; 2014 S.C.L. 58; 2013 G.W.D. 38-743, HCJ ........ *Digested,* 14/**3773**

Spencer v Paragon Wallpapers [1977] I.C.R. 301; (1976) 11 I.T.R. 294, EAT ........ *Digested,* 77/**1151**: *Applied* 77/1142, 78/1129: *Considered* 14/3507: *Distinguished* 77/1144, 80/1026

Spring Radio Cars Ltd v Glasgow City Council [2014] CSIH 21; 2014 S.C. 529; 2014 S.L.T. 393; 2014 S.C.L.R. 381; [2014] L.L.R. 837; 2014 G.W.D. 8-164, IH (Ex Div); affirming [2013] CSOH 15; 2013 S.L.T. 491; [2014] L.L.R. 191; 2013 G.W.D. 6-151, OH ........ *Digested,* 14/**3647**

SS (Democratic Republic of Congo) v Secretary of State for the Home Department [2014] CSIH 101; 2014 G.W.D. 39-716, IH (Ex Div)

Stalker v Greater Glasgow & Clyde Health Board [2013] CSOH 194; 2014 G.W.D. 2-49, OH

Steel v Scottish Ministers 2014 G.W.D. 40-729, Lands Tr (Scot)

Stephen v Milne 1960 J.C. 119; 1960 S.L.T. 276, HCJ ........ *Digested,* 60/**89**: *Considered* 14/3404

Stevenson v Glasgow Corp 1908 S.C. 1034; (1908) 16 S.L.T. 302, IH (1 Div); reversing (1908) 16 S.L.T. 43, OH
*Applied* 14/3700: *Distinguished* 06/5600

Stewart v Glaze [2009] EWHC 704 (QB); (2009) 153(16) S.J.L.B. 28, QBD (Liverpool)
*Distinguished* 14/3699

Stewart & Mcisaac v Scottish Legal Complaints Commission [2014] CSIH 23; 2014 S.C. 569; 2014 S.L.T. 454; 2014 G.W.D. 10-188, IH (Ex Div) ........ *Digested,* 14/**3644**

Stewart (David) v HM Advocate [2014] HCJAC 93; 2014 G.W.D. 28-558, HCJ

Stewart (Derek David McClymont) v HM Advocate [2013] HCJAC 152; 2014 S.C.C.R. 1; 2013 G.W.D. 39-749, HCJ

Stirling Council v Harrower 2013 Hous. L.R. 32; 2013 G.W.D. 8-180, Sh Ct (Tayside) (Stirling) ........ *Digested,* 14/**3632**

Stirton v Ladybank Tyres Ltd [2014] CSOH 71; 2014 G.W.D. 15-278, OH

Stonehouse Coaches Ltd v Smith [2014] I.C.R. D14, EAT (SC)

Strabag Benelux NV v Council of the European Union (T183/00) [2003] E.C.R. II-135, CFI
*Considered* 14/2475

Strawbridge v Murphy; *sub nom* Strawbridge (Andrew) v HM Advocate; *joined cases* Sharpe v Murphy; McKechnie v Murphy [2014] HCJAC 32; 2014 S.C.L. 437; 2014 S.C.C.R. 286; 2014 G.W.D. 15-272, HCJ ........ *Digested,* 14/**3426**

Strawbridge (Andrew) v HM Advocate see Strawbridge v Murphy

Street Lighting Supplies & Co Ltd v Scotland Excel [2014] CSOH 145; 2014 G.W.D. 31-619, OH

Strickland v Blemain Finance Ltd 2014 Hous. L.R. 75; 2014 G.W.D. 33-637, Sh Ct (Glasgow)

Stuart v Reid 2014 Rep. L.R. 107; 2014 G.W.D. 25-493, OH ........ *Digested,* 14/**3470**

Sturridge v General Teaching Council for Scotland [2014] CSIH 16; 2014 S.C. 478; 2014 S.L.T. 489; 2014 G.W.D. 7-142, IH (Ex Div) ........ *Digested,* 14/**3499**

STV Central Ltd v Semple Fraser LLP [2014] CSOH 82; 2014 G.W.D. 16-299, OH

Suburban Taverns Ltd v Glasgow Assessor [2014] CSIH 86; 2014 G.W.D. 35-664, LVAC

Sustainable Shetland v Scottish Ministers [2013] CSIH 116; 2014 G.W.D. 2-38, IH (2 Div)

Sustainable Shetland v Scottish Ministers [2013] CSOH 158; 2013 S.L.T. 1173; 2013 G.W.D. 34-664, OH ........ *Digested,* 14/**3512**: *Not followed* 14/3508

Sustainable Shetland v Scottish Ministers [2014] CSIH 60; 2014 S.L.T. 806; 2014 G.W.D. 24-464, IH (1 Div) ........ *Digested,* 14/**3509**

Sutherland v Bank of Scotland Plc [2014] CSOH 113; 2014 G.W.D. 25-477, OH

Sutherland Estates v Sutherland 1998 S.L.T. (Land Ct) 37; 1997 S.L.C.R. 144; 1998 G.W.D. 12-630, Land Ct ........ *Digested,* 98/**6029**: *Applied* 09/4615, 14/3626

SW v TW see W v W

Sweeney v Assessor for Ayrshire Valuation Joint Board; *sub nom* Sweeney v Ayrshire Valuation Joint Board Assessor [2013] CSIH 107; [2014] R.V.R. 126; 2014 G.W.D. 1-26, LVAC ........ *Digested,* 14/**3662**

Sweeney v Ayrshire Valuation Joint Board Assessor see Sweeney v Assessor for Ayrshire Valuation Joint Board

T v HM Advocate [2014] HCJAC 31; 2014 S.C.L. 452; 2014 G.W.D. 13-250, HCJ ....... *Digested,* 14/**3780**
T v K 2014 G.W.D. 26-523, Sh Ct (South Strathclyde) (Dumfries)
T v K 2014 G.W.D. 26-524, Sh Ct (South Strathclyde) (Dumfries)
T v K 2014 G.W.D. 26-522, Sh Ct (South Strathclyde) (Dumfries)
T v Thomson; *sub nom* RT v Thomson [2013] CSOH 123; 2014 S.C.L.R. 847; 2013 G.W.D. 26-529, OH
T v United Kingdom (24724/94); *joined case* V v United Kingdom (24888/94) [2000] 2 All E.R. 1024 (Note); (2000) 30 E.H.R.R. 121; 7 B.H.R.C. 659; [1999] Prison L.R. 189; 12 Fed. Sent. R. 266; [2000] Crim. L.R. 187; Times, December 17, 1999, ECHR; no effect [1999] Crim. L.R. 579, Eur Comm HR ........................... *Digested,* 00/**3198**: *Applied* 03/882: *Cited* 00/1078, 00/1331: *Considered* 01/1410, 05/2082, 05/2923: *Distinguished* 03/3781: *Followed* 14/43: *Referred to* 00/1090, 00/1095
T Clarke (Scotland) Ltd v Mmaxx Underfloor Heating Ltd [2014] CSIH 83; 2014 G.W.D. 33-633, IH (Ex Div); affirming [2014] CSOH 62; [2014] B.L.R. 341; 2014 G.W.D. 13-226, OH ........................................................................ *Digested,* 14/**3360**
T, Petitioner; *sub nom* AMT, Petitioners 1997 S.L.T. 724; 1996 S.C.L.R. 897; [1997] Fam. Law 225; [1997] Fam. Law 8; Times, August 20, 1996, IH (1 Div) ............. *Digested,* 96/**6596**: *Applied* 00/6485, 05/5250: *Considered* 14/3642
Talbot v Babcock International Ltd [2014] CSOH 160; 2014 S.L.T. 1077; 2014 G.W.D. 36-666, OH
Tarmac Econowaste Ltd v Assessor for Lothian Region 1991 S.L.T. 77, OH ................ *Digested,* 91/**5502**: *Applied* 01/6096: *Considered* 14/3301: *Referred to* 92/6511
Tarves Health Ltd v Grampian Health Board [2014] CSOH 138; 2014 S.L.T. 974; 2014 G.W.D. 30-585, OH ........................................................................................ *Digested,* 14/**3576**
Taylor v Magistrates of Saltcoats see Taylor v Saltcoats Town Council
Taylor v Saltcoats Town Council; *sub nom* Taylor v Magistrates of Saltcoats 1912 S.C. 880; 1912 1 S.L.T. 363, IH (1 Div) *Applied* 14/3700
Taylor Woodrow Property Co Ltd v Strathclyde RC 1996 G.W.D. 7-397, OH *Approved* 14/1978: *Considered* 97/6179
Tayside Contracts v D Geddes (Contractors) Ltd [2014] CSOH 105; 2014 S.L.T. 764; 2014 G.W.D. 23-430, OH ........................................................................ *Digested,* 14/**3324**
Tayside Valuation Joint Board Assessor v Hutchison 3G (UK) Ltd see Assessor for Tayside Valuation Joint Board v Hutchison 3G (UK) Ltd
TCM v AFMM 2014 Fam. L.R. 11, Sh Ct (Lothian) (Edinburgh) .................................... *Digested,* 14/**3538**
TD v HM Advocate see D v HM Advocate
Teckal Srl v Comune di Viano (Reggio Emilia) (C-107/98) [1999] E.C.R. I-8121, ECJ (5th Chamber) *Applied* 07/1642, 07/3328, 08/3018, 11/2635, 14/1619: *Considered* 08/3017, 10/2204, 14/3503: *Distinguished* 06/3419
Ted Jacob Engineering Group Inc v RMJM; *sub nom* Ted Jacob Engineering Group Inc v Robert Matthew, Johnson-Marshall and Partners [2014] CSIH 18; 2014 S.C. 579; 2014 S.C.L.R. 454; 2014 G.W.D. 29-570, IH (Ex Div) ........................ *Digested,* 14/**3326**
Ted Jacob Engineering Group Inc v Robert Matthew, Johnson-Marshall and Partners see Ted Jacob Engineering Group Inc v RMJM
Telfer v Buccleuch Estates Ltd 2012 S.L.C.R. 207, Land Ct ......................................... *Digested,* 14/**3623**
Telford (Derek) v HM Advocate [2014] HCJAC 128; 2014 G.W.D. 38-697, HCJ
Tenzin v Russell 2014 Hous. L.R. 17; 2014 G.W.D. 4-90, Sh Ct (Lothian) (Edinburgh) *Digested,* 14/**3629**
Tesco Stores Ltd v Perth and Kinross Council [2014] CSOH 153; 2014 G.W.D. 34-649, OH
Thomas v Thomas [1947] A.C. 484; [1947] 1 All E.R. 582; 1947 S.C. (H.L.) 45; 1948 S.L.T. 2; 1947 S.L.T. (Notes) 53; 63 T.L.R. 314; [1948] L.J.R. 515; 176 L.T. 498, HL; reversing 1946 S.C. 81; 1946 S.L.T. 63, IH (2 Div) .............................*Digested,* 47-51/**7496**: *Applied* 47-51/10957, 47-51/2723, 47-51/9902, 52/987, 55/2078, 59/431, 70/3157, 76/338, 98/5439, 98/6102, 01/6217, 03/3539, 13/3902, 13/3956: *Considered* 74/1069, 91/5082, 94/3280, 94/3439, 03/5285, 05/10: *Distinguished* 90/4099: *Followed* 86/4416, 88/4930, 08/5003, 13/6, 14/1579: *Not applied* 51/3869
Thomas (Rio Shakilah) v HM Advocate [2014] HCJAC 66; 2014 G.W.D. 22-417, HCJ
Thompson v Dunn [2012] HCJAC 27; 2014 J.C. 16; 2012 S.L.T. 577; 2012 S.C.L. 508; 2012 S.C.C.R. 298; 2012 G.W.D. 8-140, HCJ ............................................ *Digested,* 12/**3944**
Thomson v Alloa Motor Co [1983] I.R.L.R. 403, EAT ..................................................... *Digested,* 83/**1315**: *Followed* 14/3505
Thomson v Dennis Thomson Builders Ltd see Hamilton v Ferguson Transport (Spean Bridge) Ltd
Thomson v Mooney [2013] CSIH 115; 2014 Fam. L.R. 15; 2014 G.W.D. 14-263, IH (Ex Div); reversing [2012] CSOH 177; 2012 G.W.D. 39-769, OH
Thomson (Craig) v HM Advocate [2014] HCJAC 1; 2014 G.W.D. 2-53, HCJ

TJM, Petitioner see M, Petitioner
TLMP, Petitioner see P v P
TN (Zimbabwe) v Secretary of State for the Home Department [2014] CSOH 85; 2014 G.W.D. 18-344, OH
Tods Murray WS v Arakin Ltd [2014] CSIH 106; 2014 G.W.D. 40-725, IH (Ex Div)
Tods Murray WS v Arakin Ltd [2014] CSIH 67; 2014 G.W.D. 25-472, IH (Ex Div); affirming [2013] CSOH 134; 2013 G.W.D. 28-560, OH
Tole (Callum Stephen) v HM Advocate [2013] HCJAC 109; 2013 S.L.T. 1227; 2013 S.C.L. 912; 2014 S.C.C.R. 5; 2013 G.W.D. 30-590, HCJ ........ *Digested,* 14/**3373**
Trump International Golf Club Scotland Ltd v Scottish Ministers [2014] CSOH 22; 2014 S.L.T. 406; 2014 G.W.D. 8-154, OH ........ *Digested,* 14/**3508**: *Applied* 14/3509
Truslove v Scottish Ambulance Service [2014] I.C.R. 1232, EAT (SC)
Trust Inns Ltd v City of Glasgow Licensing Board [2015] CSIH 5, IH; affirming [2014] L.L.R. 861; 2014 G.W.D. 4-92, Sh Ct (Glasgow)
Trustees for S & A Kilcoyne v Sadiq's Judicial Factor [2014] CSIH 34; 2014 G.W.D. 17-310, IH (Ex Div) ........ *Digested,* 14/**3472**
Trustees of the Dyglen Engineering Ltd Pension Scheme No.2 v Russell 2014 G.W.D. 1-6, Sh Ct (Tayside) (Kirkcaldy)
Trustees of the Scottish Solicitors Staff Pension Fund v Pattison & Sim [2014] CSOH 119; 2014 G.W.D. 26-533, OH
Tummel Valley Leisure Ltd v Scottish Natural Heritage 2014 S.L.C.R. 201, Land Ct
TW v Aberdeenshire Council see W v Aberdeenshire Council

UK Acorn Finance Ltd v Smith 2014 Hous. L.R. 50; 2014 G.W.D. 25-475, Sh Ct (Grampian) (Banff)
Unison v Glasgow City Council see Glasgow City Council v Fox Cross Claimants
University College Union v University of Stirling; *sub nom* University of Stirling v University and College Union [2014] CSIH 5; 2014 S.C. 414; 2014 S.L.T. 352; [2014] I.R.L.R. 287; 2014 G.W.D. 5-106, IH (Ex Div) ........ *Digested,* 14/**3502**
University of Stirling v University and College Union [2012] I.C.R. 803; [2012] I.R.L.R. 266; [2012] E.L.R. 398, EAT (SC) ........ *Digested,* 12/**3984**: *Affirmed* 14/3502
University of Stirling v University and College Union see University College Union v University of Stirling
Urras Oighreachd Ghabhsainn v Crofters of South Dell 2014 S.L.T. (Land Ct) 49; 2014 S.L.C.R. 222; 2014 G.W.D. 17-329, Land Ct ........ *Digested,* 14/**3306**
Uruk (Bilal) v HM Advocate [2014] HCJAC 46; 2014 S.C.C.R. 369; 2014 G.W.D. 17-320, HCJ ........ *Digested,* 14/**3415**

V v United Kingdom (24888/94) see T v United Kingdom (24724/94)
Vaickuviene v J Sainsbury Plc [2013] CSIH 67; 2014 S.C. 147; 2013 S.L.T. 1032; [2013] I.R.L.R. 792; 2013 Rep. L.R. 106; 2013 G.W.D. 25-512, IH (2 Div); reversing [2012] CSOH 69; 2012 S.L.T. 849; 2012 G.W.D. 16-337, OH ........ *Digested,* 13/**3862**
Van Eck v Keeper of the Registers of Scotland 2014 S.L.T. (Lands Tr) 92; 2014 G.W.D. 25-500, Lands Tr (Scot) ........ *Digested,* 14/**3584**
Vanbeck (Fiona) v HM Advocate see Glover (Alan) v HM Advocate
Vento v Chief Constable of West Yorkshire; *sub nom* Chief Constable of West Yorkshire v Vento (No.2) [2002] EWCA Civ 1871; [2003] I.C.R. 318; [2003] I.R.L.R. 102; [2003] Po. L.R. 171; (2003) 100(10) L.S.G. 28; (2003) 147 S.J.L.B. 181; Times, December 27, 2002, CA (Civ Div); affirming [2002] I.R.L.R. 177; [2002] Emp. L.R. 111, EAT ........ *Digested,* 03/**1306**: *Applied* 06/1363, 07/1413, 09/3815, 10/1116, 10/1125, 13/1038: *Considered* 04/1276, 04/917, 06/1371, 08/1136, 08/891, 10/1042, 11/1064, 11/1071, 12/1116, 13/794, 14/1099, 14/3476: *Followed* 04/1306, 05/1318, 13/786
Vergara v Ryanair Ltd 2014 S.L.T. (Sh Ct) 119; 2014 G.W.D. 26-511, Sh Ct (South Strathclyde) (Ayr) ........ *Digested,* 14/**3319**

W v Aberdeenshire Council; *sub nom* TW v Aberdeenshire Council; Aberdeenshire Council, Petitioners [2012] CSIH 37; 2013 S.C. 108; 2012 Fam. L.R. 91; 2012 G.W.D. 14-284, IH (Ex Div); affirming 2011 S.L.T. (Sh Ct) 186; 2011 G.W.D. 19-456, Sh Pr; reversing 2011 S.L.T. (Sh Ct) 104; 2011 G.W.D. 5-147, Sh Ct (Grampian) (Banff) ........ *Digested,* 13/**3710**: *Applied* 14/3550
W v Trustees of the Roman Catholic Archdiocese of St Andrews and Edinburgh [2013] CSOH 185; 2014 G.W.D. 1-25, OH
W v W; *sub nom* SW v TW [2013] CSOH 136; 2014 S.C.L.R. 63; 2013 Fam. L.R. 85; 2013 G.W.D. 31-627, OH ........ *Digested,* 14/**3537**

W v W see Wilson v Wilson
W J Henderson & Sons v Scottish Ministers 2012 S.L.C.R. 92, Land Ct ....................... *Digested,* 14/**3308**
Wade (Philip) v HM Advocate; *joined case* Coats (Colin) v HM Advocate [2014] HCJAC 88; 2014 S.C.L. 680; 2014 G.W.D. 25-481, HCJ .................................. *Digested,* 14/**3377**
Walker v Secretary of State for the Home Department see R. (on the application of Wells) v Parole Board for England and Wales
Walker (Leon William) v HM Advocate see Blance (Andrew) v HM Advocate
Walker (Ross) v HM Advocate [2013] HCJAC 83; 2014 J.C. 154; 2013 S.C.C.R. 483; 2013 G.W.D. 25-488, HCJ
Wallace v Stewart Homes (Scotland) Ltd; *sub nom* Pate's Curator ad Litem v Stewart Homes (Scotland) Ltd [2013] CSOH 30; 2014 S.C.L.R. 1; 2013 G.W.D. 9-204, OH
Walters v Babergh DC 82 L.G.R. 235; (1983) 127 S.J. 595; Times, June 21, 1983, QBD ........................................ *Digested,* 84/**2072**:
*Applied* 06/1439: *Considered* 94/3900: *Followed* 14/3696
Walton v Scottish Ministers [2012] UKSC 44; [2013] P.T.S.R. 51; 2013 S.C. (U.K.S.C.) 67; 2012 S.L.T. 1211; [2013] 1 C.M.L.R. 28; [2013] Env. L.R. 16; [2013] J.P.L. 323; 2012 G.W.D. 34-689, SC; affirming [2012] CSIH 19; 2012 G.W.D. 14-269, IH (Ex Div); affirming [2011] CSOH 131; 2011 S.C.L.R. 686; 2011 G.W.D. 34-703, OH ........................................ *Digested,* 13/**3703**:
*Applied* 13/2358, 14/3730: *Considered* 13/3409, 14/2419
Wanchoo v Aberdeen City Council 2014 G.W.D. 27-543, Sh Ct (Grampian) (Aberdeen)
WAP Fyfe v Assessor for Fife Council; *sub nom* Fyfe (WAP) v Fife Assessor 2014 S.L.T. (Lands Tr) 10; [2014] R.V.R. 98; 2014 G.W.D. 1-29, Lands Tr (Scot) ...... *Digested,* 14/**3666**
Ward, Appellant 2014 S.L.T. (Sh Ct) 15; 2014 G.W.D. 3-59, Sh Ct (North Strathclyde) (Paisley) ........................................ *Digested,* 14/**3684**
Watt v Assets Co Ltd; *sub nom* Assets Co Ltd v Bain's Trustees; Assets Co Ltd v Phillip's Trustees; *joined case* Bain v Assets Co Ltd (No.2) [1905] A.C. 317; (1905) 7 F. (H.L.) 104; (1905) 13 S.L.T. 147, HL; reversing (1904) 6 F. 692; (1904) 6 F. 754; (1904) 12 S.L.T. 48, IH (Ct of 7 judges); affirming (Unreported, June 13, 1903), IH (2 Div); reversing (1903) 11 S.L.T. 131, OH
*Considered* 10/3993: *Distinguished* 14/3300
WB v HM Advocate [2014] HCJAC 52; 2014 S.C.C.R. 376; 2014 G.W.D. 17-317, HCJ *Digested,* 14/**3388**
Webster (Malcolm John) v HM Advocate [2013] HCJAC 161; 2014 S.C.L. 256; 2014 G.W.D. 4-80, HCJ ........................................ *Digested,* 14/**3383**
Wells v Parole Board for England and Wales see R. (on the application of Wells) v Parole Board for England and Wales
Wells v United Kingdom (57715/09) see James v United Kingdom (25119/09)
West v Scottish Prison Service see West v Secretary of State for Scotland
West v Secretary of State for Scotland; *sub nom* West v Scottish Prison Service 1992 S.C. 385; 1992 S.L.T. 636; 1992 S.C.L.R. 504; Times, June 11, 1992; Scotsman, May 5, 1992, IH (1 Div); affirming 1991 S.C.L.R. 795, OH ................ *Digested,* 92/**5191**:
*Applied* 95/5443, 97/5714, 97/6043, 97/6359, 03/5265: *Considered* 95/5441, 00/6205, 03/5192, 04/4478, 04/4543: *Explained* 93/4730: *Followed* 00/5832, 10/3995, 11/4329, 12/3822, 14/3301
West Lothian Council, Petitioner [2014] CSOH 73; 2014 G.W.D. 14-256, OH
Western Excavating (ECC) Ltd v Sharp [1978] Q.B. 761; [1978] 2 W.L.R. 344; [1978] 1 All E.R. 713; [1978] I.C.R. 221; [1978] I.R.L.R. 27; (1978) 13 I.T.R. 132; (1987) 121 S.J. 814; Times, November 16, 1977, CA (Civ Div); reversing [1977] I.R.L.R. 25, EAT ........................................ *Digested,* 78/**900**:
*Applied* 78/891, 78/893, 78/904, 79/838, 80/892, 81/981, 82/1097, 84/1194, 88/1247, 90/1929, 01/2234, 02/1427, 03/1214, 03/1221, 09/1255, 10/1032: *Considered* 78/897, 78/905, 80/1008, 80/883, 81/103u, 81/808, 86/1261, 89/1458, 99/2030, 14/3506: *Distinguished* 79/846: *Explained* 80/893
WH Smith Plc v Assessor for Lanarkshire Valuation Joint Board [2014] CSIH 72; 2014 G.W.D. 27-550, LVAC
Whaley v Lord Advocate see Friend v Lord Advocate
Wheeldon's Executor Nominate v Spence's Executrix Nominate [2014] CSOH 69; 2014 G.W.D. 15-267, OH
Whitham (James) v HM Advocate [2013] HCJAC 154; 2014 S.L.T. 51; 2014 S.C.L. 130; 2013 S.C.C.R. 612; 2013 G.W.D. 40-772, HCJ .......................................... *Digested,* 14/**3781**
Willox v Auchnie [2014] CSIH 102; 2014 G.W.D. 39-708, IH (2 Div)
Wilson v North Lanarkshire Council [2014] CSIH 26; 2014 G.W.D. 12-222, IH (Ex Div); affirming [2011] CSOH 178; 2011 G.W.D. 38-789, OH
Wilson v North Star Shipping (Aberdeen) Ltd [2014] CSOH 156; 2014 G.W.D. 36-675, OH

Wilson v Wilson; *sub nom* W v W 2013 Fam. L.R. 113; 2013 G.W.D. 34-678, Sh Ct (Lothian) (Edinburgh) ........ *Digested,* 14/**3534**

Wilson (Brian) v HM Advocate; *joined case* Murray (Iain Alexander) v HM Advocate [2009] HCJAC 58; 2009 J.C. 336; 2009 S.C.L. 1047; 2009 S.C.C.R. 666; 2009 G.W.D. 24-385, HCJ ........ *Digested,* 09/**4773**: *Applied* 14/3693

Wilson (Hazel) v Wilson (Stewart James) 1999 S.L.T. 249; 1998 S.C.L.R. 1103; 1998 G.W.D. 23-1177, OH ........ *Digested,* 99/**6074**: *Distinguished* 14/3537

Wishart (Michael) v HM Advocate [2013] HCJAC 168; 2014 J.C. 190; 2014 S.C.L. 173; 2014 S.C.C.R. 130; 2014 G.W.D. 1-13, HCJ ........ *Digested,* 14/**3440**

Wolff v John Moulds (Kilmarnock) Ltd [2011] CSOH 159; 2012 S.L.T. 231; 2011 G.W.D. 32-683, OH ........ *Digested,* 12/**4207**: *Cited* 14/3468: *Considered* 12/4206, 14/3469

Worbey v Elliott [2014] CSOH 19; 2014 S.C.L.R. 573; 2014 G.W.D. 7-137, OH ........ *Digested,* 14/**3364**

Wright v North Ayrshire Council [2014] I.C.R. 77; [2014] I.R.L.R. 4, EAT (SC) ........ *Digested,* 14/**3500**

WT Ramsay Ltd v Inland Revenue Commissioners; *joined case* Eilbeck (Inspector of Taxes) v Rawling [1982] A.C. 300; [1981] 2 W.L.R. 449; [1981] 1 All E.R. 865; [1981] S.T.C. 174; 54 T.C. 101; [1982] T.R. 123; (1981) 11 A.T.R. 752; (1981) 125 S.J. 220, HL; affirming [1979] 1 W.L.R. 974; [1979] 3 All E.R. 213; [1979] S.T.C. 582; (1979) 123 S.J. 456, CA (Civ Div); affirming [1978] 1 W.L.R. 1313; [1978] 2 All E.R. 321; 8 B.L.R. 169; [1978] T.R. 113; (1978) 122 S.J. 249, Ch D *Digested,* 81/**1385**: *Applied* 82/1576, 83/1980, 84/270, 85/3407, 86/2203, 86/258, 86/3204, 88/257, 91/2090, 92/2518, 93/2296, 95/876, 96/1310, 97/2975, 97/2979, 00/4942, 00/5043, 01/5237, 03/4233, 05/4037, 05/4084, 05/4158, 08/3661, 09/3741, 09/3755, 10/3290, 13/3010, 13/3044, 13/3096: *Cited* 97/1073: *Considered* 82/476, 85/1909, 85/243, 86/262, 87/2036, 87/274, 90/2685, 92/2505, 92/611, 96/3958, 96/428, 98/4627, 00/4916, 01/5199, 02/4457, 08/3765, 09/3781, 09/3876, 10/3344, 12/3332, 14/2851, 14/2975, 14/3807: *Distinguished* 82/1582, 83/1955, 87/282, 92/2519, 93/337, 95/2750, 98/4631, 99/4709: *Followed* 03/4145, 10/3249, 11/3285, 11/3366, 11/3383, 12/3233, 13/3095: *Referred to* 82/485, 85/456, 95/527

Wylie v Avon Insurance Co Ltd 1988 S.C.L.R. 570, OH ........ *Digested,* 89/**4813**: *Distinguished* 14/3745

X, Appellants see AG v Principal Reporter

Y v Advocate General for Scotland see N v Advocate General for Scotland

YAN (Angola) v Secretary of State for the Home Department [2014] CSOH 90; 2014 G.W.D. 18-351, OH

YHY (China), Petitioner [2014] CSOH 11; 2014 G.W.D. 6-128, OH

YMCA Glasgow v Hamad 2013 Hous. L.R. 81, Sh Ct (Glasgow) ........ *Digested,* 14/**3603**

Younas (Faisal) v HM Advocate [2014] HCJAC 114; 2014 S.L.T. 1043; 2014 S.C.C.R. 628; 2014 G.W.D. 34-646, HCJ

Young v Brown [2012] HCJAC 24; 2014 J.C. 4; 2012 S.L.T. 581; 2012 S.C.L. 526; 2012 G.W.D. 8-139, HCJ ........ *Digested,* 12/**4269**

Young v MacVean [2014] CSOH 133; 2014 S.L.T. 934; 2014 Rep. L.R. 113; 2014 G.W.D. 28-561, OH ........ *Digested,* 14/**3469**

Young v Markey 2014 S.L.T. (Lands Tr) 61; 2014 G.W.D. 13-237, Lands Tr (Scot) ........ *Digested,* 14/**3585**

Young v Scottish Criminal Cases Review Commission [2013] CSOH 183; 2014 G.W.D. 1-1, OH

Young (Adam Clark) v MacDonald [2014] HCJAC 42; 2014 G.W.D. 17-316, HCJ ........ *Digested,* 14/**3446**

Young (Thomas Ross) v HM Advocate [2013] HCJAC 145; 2014 S.L.T. 21; 2014 S.C.L. 98; 2014 S.C.C.R. 78; 2013 G.W.D. 39-748, HCJ ........ *Digested,* 14/**3370**

Young (Thomas Ross) v HM Advocate [2014] HCJAC 113; 2014 S.L.T. 1037; 2014 S.C.C.R. 649; 2014 G.W.D. 33-635, HCJ ........ *Digested,* 14/**3371**

YZ (China) v Secretary of State for the Home Department [2014] CSOH 87; 2014 G.W.D. 18-348, OH

Z (China), Applicant [2014] CSIH 48; 2014 G.W.D. 19-370, IH

Z (China), Petitioner [2014] CSOH 111; 2014 G.W.D. 24-461, OH

Zelilof v Greece (17060/03) (Unreported, May 24, 2007), ECHR *Considered* 14/3599

ZH (Tanzania) v Secretary of State for the Home Department [2011] UKSC 4; [2011] 2 A.C. 166; [2011] 2 W.L.R. 148; [2011] 2 All E.R. 783; [2011] 1 F.L.R. 2170; [2011] 1 F.C.R. 221; [2011] H.R.L.R. 15; [2011] U.K.H.R.R. 371; [2011] Imm. A.R. 395; [2011] I.N.L.R. 369; [2011] Fam. Law 468; (2011) 108(7) L.S.G. 17; (2011) 155(5) S.J.L.B. 30; Times, February 8, 2011, SC .................................... *Digested,* 11/**1790**:
*Applied* 11/1711, 12/1289, 12/1707, 12/1751, 14/1596, 14/1668, 14/662:
*Considered* 12/1293, 12/1663, 12/1738, 12/1750, 12/1775, 12/4099, 13/1605, 13/2366, 13/3776, 13/3778, 14/1650, 14/1704: *Followed* 11/1736, 12/1718, 13/1578, 14/1673, 14/1725

Zoumbas v Secretary of State for the Home Department see FZ (Democratic Republic of Congo) v Secretary of State for the Home Department

# PART III

## SHIPS' NAME INDEX 2014